PORTFOLIO MANAGEMENT IN PRACTICE

Volume I

CFA Institute is the premier association for investment professionals around the world, with over 170,000 members more than 160 countries. Since 1963 the organization has developed and administered the renowned Chartered Financial Analyst Program. With a rich history of leading the investment profession, CFA Institute has set the highest standards in ethics, education, and professional excellence within the global investment community, and is the foremost authority on investment profession conduct and practice.

Each book in the CFA Institute Investment Series is geared toward industry practitioners along with graduate-level finance students and covers the most important topics in the industry. The authors of these cutting-edge books are themselves industry professionals and academics and bring their wealth of knowledge and expertise to this series.

PORTFOLIO MANAGEMENT IN PRACTICE

Volume I

Investment Management

WILEY

For general information on our other products and services or for technical support, please contact our Customer Care Department within the United States at (800) 762-2974, outside the United States at (317) 572-3993, or fax (317) 572-4002.

Wiley publishes in a variety of print and electronic formats and by print-on-demand. Some material included with standard print versions of this book may not be included in e-books or in print-on-demand. If this book refers to media such as a CD or DVD that is not included in the version you purchased, you may download this material at http://booksupport.wiley.com. For more information about Wiley products, visit www.wiley.com.

ISBN 978-1-119-74369-9 (Hardcover)
ISBN 978-1-119-74371-2 (ePDF)
ISBN 978-1-119-74372-9 (ePub)

Printed in the United States of America.
SKY10071031_032624

CONTENTS

CHAPTER 3

Capital Market Expectations, Part 1: Framework and Macro Considerations   37

CHAPTER 4

Capital Market Expectations, Part 2: Forecasting Asset Class Returns   93

CHAPTER 6
Principles of Asset Allocation   211

CHAPTER 7
Asset Allocation with Real-World Constraints   307

CHAPTER 8
Currency Management: An Introduction   369

CHAPTER 9
Overview of Fixed-Income Portfolio Management   453

CHAPTER 13
Active Equity Investing: Strategies   647

CHAPTER 14
Hedge Fund Strategies

CHAPTER 15
Overview of Private Wealth Management

CHAPTER 16
Topics in Private Wealth Management

CHAPTER 17
Portfolio Management for Institutional Investors   949

PREFACE

We are pleased to bring you Portfolio Management in Practice. This book serves as a particularly important resource for investment professionals who recognize that portfolio management is an integrated set of activities. The text's topic coverage is organized according to a well-articulated portfolio management decision-making process. This organizing principle—in addition to the breadth of coverage, the currency and quality of content, and its meticulous pedagogy—distinguishes this book from other investment texts that deal with portfolio management.

The content was developed in partnership by a team of distinguished academics and practitioners, chosen for their acknowledged expertise in the field, and guided by CFA Institute. It is written specifically with the investment practitioner in mind and is replete with examples and practice problems that reinforce the learning outcomes and demonstrate real-world applicability.

The CFA Program curriculum, from which the content of this book was drawn, is subjected to a rigorous review process to assure that it is:

- faithful to the findings of our ongoing industry practice analysis
- Valuable to members, employers, and investors
- Globally relevant
- Generalist (as opposed to specialist) in nature
- replete with sufficient examples and practice opportunities
- Pedagogically sound

The accompanying workbook is a useful reference that provides Learning Outcome Statements, which describe exactly what readers will learn and be able to demonstrate after mastering the accompanying material. additionally, the workbook has summary overviews and practice problems for each chapter.

We hope you will find this and other books in the CFA Institute Investment Series helpful in your efforts to grow your investment knowledge, whether you are a relatively new entrant or an experienced veteran striving to keep up to date in the ever-changing market environment. CFA Institute, as a long-term committed participant in the investment profession and a not- for-profit global membership association, is pleased to provide you with this opportunity.

ACKNOWLEDGMENTS

Special thanks to all the reviewers, advisors, and question writers who helped to ensure high practical relevance, technical correctness, and understandability of the material presented here.

We would like to thank the many others who played a role in the conception and production of this book: the Curriculum and Learning Experience team at CFA Institute with special thanks to the curriculum directors, past and present, who worked with the authors and reviewers to produce the chapters in this book, the Practice Analysis team at CFA Institute, and the Publishing and Technology team for bringing this book to production.

ABOUT THE CFA INSTITUTE INVESTMENT SERIES

CFA Institute is pleased to provide the CFA Institute Investment Series, which covers major areas in the field of investments. We provide this best-in-class series for the same reason we have been chartering investment professionals for more than 45 years: to lead the investment profession globally by setting the highest standards of ethics, education, and professional excellence.

The books in the CFA Institute Investment Series contain practical, globally relevant material. They are intended both for those contemplating entry into the extremely competitive field of investment management as well as for those seeking a means of keeping their knowledge fresh and up to date. This series was designed to be user friendly and highly relevant.

We hope you find this series helpful in your efforts to grow your investment knowledge, whether you are a relatively new entrant or an experienced veteran ethically bound to keep up to date in the ever-changing market environment. As a long-term, committed participant in the investment profession and a not-for-profit global membership association, CFA Institute is pleased to provide you with this opportunity.

THE TEXTS

Corporate Finance: A Practical Approach is a solid foundation for those looking to achieve lasting business growth. In today's competitive business environment, companies must find innovative ways to enable rapid and sustainable growth. This text equips readers with the foundational knowledge and tools for making smart business decisions and formulating strategies to maximize company value. It covers everything from managing relationships between stakeholders to evaluating merger and acquisition bids, as well as the companies behind them. Through extensive use of real-world examples, readers will gain critical perspective into interpreting corporate financial data, evaluating projects, and allocating funds in ways that increase corporate value. Readers will gain insights into the tools and strategies used in modern corporate financial management.

Equity Asset Valuation is a particularly cogent and important resource for anyone involved in estimating the value of securities and understanding security pricing. A well-informed professional knows that the common forms of equity valuation—dividend discount modeling, free cash flow modeling, price/earnings modeling, and residual income modeling—can all be reconciled with one another under certain assumptions. With a deep understanding of the underlying assumptions, the professional investor can better understand what other investors assume when calculating their valuation estimates. This text has a global orientation, including emerging markets.

Fixed Income Analysis has been at the forefront of new concepts in recent years, and this particular text offers some of the most recent material for the seasoned professional who is not a fixed-income specialist. The application of option and derivative technology to the once staid province of fixed income has helped contribute to an explosion of thought in this area. Professionals have been challenged to stay up to speed with credit derivatives, swaptions, collateralized mortgage securities, mortgage-backed securities, and other vehicles, and this explosion of products has strained the world's financial markets and tested central banks to provide sufficient oversight. Armed with a thorough grasp of the new exposures, the professional investor is much better able to anticipate and understand the challenges our central bankers and markets face.

International Financial Statement Analysis is designed to address the ever-increasing need for investment professionals and students to think about financial statement analysis from a global perspective. The text is a practically oriented introduction to financial statement analysis that is distinguished by its combination of a true international orientation, a structured presentation style, and abundant illustrations and tools covering concepts as they are introduced in the text. The authors cover this discipline comprehensively and with an eye to ensuring the reader's success at all levels in the complex world of financial statement analysis.

Investments: Principles of Portfolio and Equity Analysis provides an accessible yet rigorous introduction to portfolio and equity analysis. Portfolio planning and portfolio management are presented within a context of up-to-date, global coverage of security markets, trading, and market-related concepts and products. The essentials of equity analysis and valuation are explained in detail and profusely illustrated. The book includes coverage of practitioner-important but often neglected topics, such as industry analysis. Throughout, the focus is on the practical application of key concepts with examples drawn from both emerging and developed markets. Each chapter affords the reader many opportunities to self-check his or her understanding of topics.

All books in the CFA Institute Investment Series are available through all major booksellers. And, all titles are available on the Wiley Custom Select platform at http://customselect.wiley.com/ where individual chapters for all the books may be mixed and matched to create custom textbooks for the classroom.

CHAPTER 1

PROFESSIONALISM IN THE INVESTMENT INDUSTRY

Bidhan L. Parmar, PhD
Dorothy C. Kelly, CFA
Colin McLean, MBA, FIA, FSIP
Nitin M. Mehta, CFA
David B. Stevens, CIMC, CFA

LEARNING OUTCOMES

The candidate should be able to:

- describe how professions establish trust;
- explain professionalism in investment management;
- describe expectations of investment professionals;
- describe a framework for ethical decision-making.

1. INTRODUCTION

The sections covering ethics and professional standards demonstrate that ethical behavior is central to creating trust. Professional behavior is equally important. Professions help maintain trust by establishing codes and setting standards that establish a framework for ethical behavior and technical competence. Professions also set wider goals of gaining and maintaining the trust of society as a whole. In this regard, professions have a sense of purpose that society values.

This chapter explains attributes of professions and establishes what is expected of an investment professional. Professions are growing in size and number, partly as a result of government and regulator encouragement and requirement, but also owing to demand from

Portfolio Management, Second Edition, by Bidhan L. Parmar, PhD, Dorothy C. Kelly, CFA, Colin McLean, MBA, FIA, FSIP, Nitin M. Mehta, CFA, and David B. Stevens, CIMC, CFA . Copyright © 2019 by CFA Institute.

clients. Practitioners in some new areas of expertise are also choosing to serve clients within the framework of a profession to protect standards and gain public trust. The concept of professionalism is based on cultural norms, and interpretation of these norms varies by region and country. Such variation is a challenge to defining professionalism globally, but some universal aspects are common to most professions.

Section 2 of this chapter describes professions in general and how they establish trust. Section 3 describes professionalism in investment management. Section 4 addresses expectations of investment professionals, and Section 5 provides a high-level review of the framework for ethical decision-making. The chapter concludes with Section 6, a summary of challenges for investment professionals. A listing of key points in Section 7 concludes the chapter.

2. PROFESSIONS

A **profession** is an occupational group that has specific education, expert knowledge, and a framework of practice and behavior that underpins community trust, respect, and recognition. Most professions emphasize an ethical approach, the importance of good service, and empathy with the client.

Professions have grown in size and number over the last century: the rise of new specialist areas of expertise has created new professions. Driving forces of a new profession include governments and regulators, which encourage the formation of an ethical relationship between professionals and society at large. There is also demand for professions from individuals who see an advantage in working as a professional and from clients who desire to work with professionals.

Professions have not developed in every country. But in most countries, those who work in specialized areas—such as doctors, lawyers, actuaries, accountants, architects, and engineers—are subject to some combination of licensed status and technical standards. These standards distinguish professions from the craft guilds and trade bodies that were established in many countries. One clear difference is the requirement for members of professions to uphold high ethical standards. Another difference is that trade bodies do not normally have a mission to serve society or to set and enforce professional conduct rules for practitioners.

2.1. How Professions Establish Trust

For a profession to be credible, a primary goal is to establish trust among clients and among society in general. In doing so, professions have a number of common characteristics that, when combined, greatly increase confidence and credibility in professionals and their organizations.

2.1.1. Professions normalize practitioner behavior
Professionalism is underpinned by a **code of ethics** and **standards of conduct** developed by professional bodies. Regulators typically support professional ethics and recognize the framework for ethics that professions can provide. Many regulators around the world have engaged closely with professional bodies to understand their codes of ethics (codes) and standards of conduct (standards), as well as how they are enforced. Codes and standards developed by practitioners can be complementary to regulations, codifying many more individual practices than the high-level principles set by regulation.

Many governments have recognized that a profession can develop a more sophisticated system of standards than a regulator can, via continuous practitioner input and a strong mutual interest within the profession to maintain good standards and adopt best practices. Government support of professions is attributable to the role of professions in helping the public and ensuring expert and principled performance of complex services.

2.1.2. Professions provide a service to society

There is an obligation for professionals to go beyond codes and standards. Professionals should advocate for higher educational and ethical standards in the industry, individually and through their companies. Professions can widen access to services and support economic activity by encouraging trust in the industries they serve. Professions have realized that earning community trust not only creates professional pride and acceptance but also delivers commercial benefits. A profession that earns trust may ultimately have greater flexibility and independence from government and regulators to manage its own affairs, which allows members of the profession to develop service models that are both useful to clients and beneficial to members.

2.1.3. Professions are client focused

An integral part of a profession's mission is to develop and administer codes, best practice guidelines, and standards that guide an industry. These codes, standards, and guidelines help ensure that all professionals place the integrity of their profession and the interests of clients above their own personal interests. At a minimum, professionals must act in the best interest of the client, exercising a reasonable level of care, skill, and diligence. The obligation to deliver a high standard of care when acting for the benefit of another party is called **fiduciary duty**. Other entities, including employers, regulators, trade associations, and not-for-profit organizations, may also support an industry but are not the same as professional bodies. Unlike professions, these other entities generally do not exist to set and maintain professional standards. Most employers encourage employees to be members of relevant professions, and many give financial support for this membership to ideally improve the quality of client service and reinforce ethical awareness.

2.1.4. Professions have high entry standards

Membership in a profession is a signal to the market that the professional will deliver high-quality service of a promised standard, going beyond simply academic credentials. Professions develop curricula that equip future professionals with competence, including knowledge, technical skills, and ethics.

2.1.5. Professions possess a body of expert knowledge

A repository of knowledge, developed by experienced and skilled practitioners, is made available to all members of a profession. This knowledge helps members work effectively and ethically and is based on best practice.

2.1.6. Professions encourage and facilitate professional development

Entry into a profession does not, on its own, guarantee that an individual will maintain competency and continue to uphold professional standards. After qualification and throughout the working life of a professional, there will be changes in knowledge and technical skills to perform certain jobs, in technology and standards of ethical behavior, in services that can be offered, and in the legal and business environment in which professional services are delivered. These all require the development of competence and ethical awareness. Most professional bodies make it a condition of membership that a specific amount of new learning is undertaken each year. Typically, such conditions specify a time commitment, which may be separated into different competencies and types of learning activity. This is often referred to as continuing professional development and is seen as an important part of maintaining professional standards. The training and education that professionals undertake increase the value of human capital, which can contribute to economic growth and social mobility.

2.1.7. Professions monitor professional conduct

Members of a profession must be held accountable for their conduct to maintain the integrity and reputation of an industry. Doing so often involves self-regulation by professional bodies through monitoring and imposition of sanctions on members.

2.1.8. Professions are collegial

Professionals should be respectful to each other, even when they are competing. At the very least, they must respect the rights, dignity, and autonomy of others.

2.1.9. Professions are recognized oversight bodies

Many professional bodies are not-for-profit organizations with a mission emphasizing excellence, integrity, and public service. Although it is the responsibility of individual professionals to remain competent, an oversight body typically monitors this responsibility. Such bodies provide individuals with ongoing educational resources and access to information about changes in standards and imposes a framework of discipline. Continuing membership indicates sustained competence in (and updating of) practical skills while maintaining ongoing compliance with a code of ethics and standards of conduct.

2.1.10. Professions encourage the engagement of members

Participation by members as volunteers is part of the essence of a profession. Professionals are more likely to refer to, use, and adhere to values that they have helped develop, and they typically have the power as members to revise these values. A good professional will want to mentor and inspire others who recently entered or wish to enter the profession. Professionals should be willing to volunteer to advance the profession and engage with peers to develop expertise and ethics. Professionals should volunteer to help educate new generations in ethical knowledge and ethical decision-making and to foster a productive debate about new areas of ethics. Most professionals find that the experience of volunteering within the profession enhances their skills and widens their contacts within the industry. Membership in a professional body fosters engagement with other professionals.

2.2. Professions Are Evolving

No profession stands still. Trends such as greater transparency and public accountability force professions to adapt to change. Meanwhile, technology opens up possibilities for new services and different ways of working. In addition, key processes of a profession's responsibilities may need to be reviewed by a government agency or independent public body. In general, professions often engage with non-member individuals. This can help a profession evaluate the viewpoints of the public, clients, or other stakeholders when determining policy and practice and can encourage public trust for a profession's conduct and disciplinary process.

Effective professions continue to develop their role to account for changing best practices. Some medical professional bodies, for instance, have been established for more than 500 years but may now have the same need to adapt as the much younger investment profession. This means that at any point in time, society may recognize an area of work as a profession even if it has not fully or universally implemented all the expectations. As the requirements for a profession evolve, gaps open up that may take time to remedy. Effective professions also actively learn from other professions, particularly in the area of ethics. For example, new standards of conduct in the accounting profession may influence standards considered in the investment profession.

3. PROFESSIONALISM IN INVESTMENT MANAGEMENT

> Successful investing professionals are disciplined and consistent and they think a
> great deal about what they do and how they do it.
> —Benjamin Graham,[1] *The Intelligent Investor* (1949)

Investment management is a relatively young profession, which means that public understanding of its practice, codes, and standards is still developing. Recognition by regulators and employers also lags established professions. Not everyone engaged in investment management is a professional; some practitioners have not undertaken specific investment training or are not members of a professional body. This creates a challenge for the investment profession to gain trust, because not all practitioners need to be committed to high ethical standards. However, key elements of the profession have been steadily established over several decades. For example, the publication of Graham and Dodd's *Security Analysis* in 1934 was an important step in establishing a body of knowledge for investment.

The investment profession meets most, but currently not all, of the expectations of a profession. In most countries, some form of certification or licensing is needed to practice, but there may not be a requirement to join a professional body. Globally, the trend is to require examined entry to practice investment management and to maintain competence. But few professions have perfect implementation of all the expected attributes. The investment profession, similar to other professions, is on a journey to improve implementation and keep up with changing demands.

The investment profession has become increasingly global as capital markets have opened up around the world. Investment professionals may seek cross-border opportunities or may need to relocate between offices within multinational asset management firms. Regulatory coordination across borders and the emergence of technology are contributing factors to this globalization of investment management. Various investment professional bodies have developed in individual countries, and several of these bodies have expanded internationally. In addition, several other professional bodies, including those focused on actuarial and accountancy services, have investment professionals as members.

---

[1]In the 1940s, Benjamin Graham recognized the need for a professional certification for financial analysts.

3.1. Trust in the Investment Industry

The investment professional today has similarities with professionals in longer-established professions, such as medicine and law. Like doctors and lawyers, investment professionals are trusted to draw on a body of formal knowledge and apply that knowledge with care and judgment. In comparison to clients, investment professionals are also expected to have superior financial expertise, technical knowledge, and knowledge of the applicable laws and regulations. There is a risk that clients may not be fully aware of the conflicts, risks, and fees involved, so investment professionals must always handle and fully disclose these issues in a way that serves the best interests of clients. Compliance with codes of ethics and professional standards is essential, and practice must be guided by care, transparency, and integrity.

The investment profession and investment firms must be interdependent to foster trust. Employers and regulators have their own standards and practices that may differ from regulations and standards set by professional bodies. The investment professional bodies typically direct professionals in how to resolve these differences.

In many countries, the investment profession affects many key aspects of the economy, including savings, retirement planning, and the pricing and allocation of capital. In most countries, skilled evaluation of securities leads to more efficient capital allocation and, combined with ethical corporate governance, can assist in attracting investment from international investors. The investment profession can deliver more value to society when higher levels of trust and better capital allocation reduce transaction costs and help meet client objectives. These reasons explain why practitioners, clients, regulators, and governments have supported the development of an investment management profession.

3.2. CFA Institute as an Investment Professional Body

CFA Institute is the largest global association of investment professionals. Created in the early 1960s, it moved beyond North America in the 1980s, reflecting the globalization of investment management. CFA Institute initiated a number of other changes in line with the growth of investment management. One significant change occurred in 2015, when CFA Institute decided to implement the highest standards of governance in the US not-for-profit sector. The Board of Governors resolved "to implement US Public Company Standards and US not-for-profit leading practices, unless the Board determines that it is not in the best interest of the membership or organization to do so."

The mission of CFA Institute is "to lead the investment profession globally, by promoting the highest standards of ethics, education, and professional excellence for the ultimate benefit of society." The CFA Institute Code of Ethics and Standards of Professional Conduct (Code and Standards) promote the integrity of members[2] and establish a model for ethical behavior. CFA Institute candidates and members must meet the highest standards among those established by CFA Institute, regulators, or the employer. Where client interests and market interests conflict, the Code and Standards set an investment professional's duty to market integrity as the overriding obligation. The advocacy efforts of CFA Institute aim to build market integrity by calling for regulations that align the interests of firms and clients.

As a professional body, CFA Institute gathers knowledge from practicing investment professionals, develops high-quality curricula, conducts rigorous examinations, and ensures

---

[2]Eligibility and requirements for becoming a member of CFA Institute vary by jurisdiction. Please consult https://www.cfainstitute.org for further details.

practitioner involvement in developing its codes and values. Through interactions with practicing investment professionals, CFA Institute has developed a body of knowledge for the investment profession. This body of knowledge is updated on an ongoing basis through a process known as practice analysis. Practice analysis helps ensure that the CFA Institute Global Body of Investment Knowledge (GBIK) and the CFA Program Candidates Body of Knowledge (CBOK) remain current and globally relevant. The CFA Program CBOK focuses on the core knowledge, skills, and abilities (competencies) that are generally accepted and applied by investment professionals. These competencies are used in practice in a generalist context and are expected to be demonstrated by a recently qualified CFA charterholder.

CFA Institute also contributes to the dissemination of new research and ideas in finance with the publication of the *Financial Analysts Journal* and CFA Institute Research Foundation monographs, research briefs, and literature reviews. In addition, Future of Finance develops CFA Institute thought leadership to help shape a more trustworthy, forward-thinking investment profession that better serves society

CFA Institute encourages members to engage in their professional communities and involves members in its initiatives, including through their local societies. CFA Institute assists local societies with providing continuing professional development that facilitate member engagement. In many jurisdictions, membership in a local society is an important route to maintaining professionalism, particularly for continuing professional development.

CFA charterholders and CFA Program candidates are required to adhere to the Code and Standards and to sign annually a statement attesting to that continued adherence. Charterholders and candidates must maintain and improve their professional competence and strive to maintain and improve the competence of other investment professionals.

4. EXPECTATIONS OF INVESTMENT PROFESSIONALS

> Thus, the issue faced by CFA charterholders and other financial industry participants is not choosing between professional values and business values. Rather, it is balancing that ever-competing pair in a way that places the best interests of consumers and clients above our own corporate and personal interests.
>
> All investment professionals . . . would do well to . . . develop a keener awareness of the "big picture" of our financial system, a profound introspection into how we can make it better, a knowledge of the long history of finance, and a deep involvement in fostering in our profession the highest character it requires if we are to serve investors effectively, honestly, and prudently in the years ahead.
>
> —John C. Bogle, "Balancing Professional Values and Business Values" (2017)

Characteristics and behavior expected of all professionals include honesty, integrity, altruism, continuous improvement, excellence, loyalty, and respect for colleagues, employers, and clients. Extremely high standards, but not perfection, are expected, including behavior in public. Professionals should, through their actions, uphold the reputation of their profession and be responsible, accountable, and reliable in their work. Professionals should reflect regularly about the cycle of self-improvement, starting with a self-assessment, identification of knowledge gaps, compiling a program of continuing professional development to fill those gaps, putting the new learning into practice, and then evaluating the results in order to inform the next cycle. Key duties of professionals are to provide independent advice, avoid or disclose conflicts of interest, and respect client information, objectivity, transparency, and confidentiality.

The behaviors expected will vary by profession, but some attributes are shared by most professions. These include the duty to be honest and open in dealings, which covers all aspects of professional practice, ranging from writing resumes, presenting advice, record keeping, and achieving—to the greatest extent possible—informed consent from clients. This means ensuring that clients understand the consequences of decisions, the range of outcomes, and risks. A client will not have the level of knowledge that the expert professional does, but the professional should not abuse this more specialized knowledge. There will at times be adverse outcomes for clients arising from errors in judgment and practice. Professionals should be prepared to acknowledge mistakes promptly, learn from them, and correct them, including making clients whole, where appropriate. Some professional codes state that professionals must disassociate themselves from any violation of laws or regulations. This means that individuals may need to act themselves in response to a concern even if they are unable to alter the conduct of others.

During their careers, investment professionals may encounter dilemmas, including those with ethical implications. How they choose to handle these can have important implications for clients, trust in their profession, their employer, and even their own career. The right balance between an employer's practice, codes, and standards may be unclear or nuanced. During these situations, investment professionals should not avoid responsibility for acting, but they do need to consider carefully how to determine the facts of the issue and assess the implications for clients, their employer, and their own career.

Investment professionals should understand how to apply judgment in relating the codes and standards of their professional body to their loyalty to their employer. Ethical behavior means that an investment professional must be able to balance competing interests and motivations even if that appears to create a personal disadvantage. At times, professionals may need courage to uphold the highest ethical standards. Utilizing a framework for ethical decision-making can help investment professionals analyze conduct in the case of conflicting interests. To prepare for dilemmas they may face, investment professionals should maintain and improve their ethical decision-making skills.

Professionals in general may opt to raise a concern with various parties, including the following:

- Colleagues or contemporaries
- Supervisors
- A firm's compliance or ethics officer
- A mentor outside the firm
- A professional body hotline
- Senior individuals in the firm
- A firm's whistleblowing (or "speak-up") line
- A regulator or law enforcement agency

When a dilemma occurs, raising an issue internally is often a good starting place and creates an opportunity for independent internal review. In seeking the advice of others, a professional should carefully consider confidentiality. An employer's compliance function may focus on protecting the firm from the risk or consequences of regulatory breaches. Protecting the client and the firm may take priority over the position of an individual professional raising a concern. It should be clear, however, that client interests supersede firm or individual interests in areas where there are regulatory consequences.

5. FRAMEWORK FOR ETHICAL DECISION-MAKING

Laws, regulations, codes of ethics, and professional standards of conduct can guide ethical behavior, but individual judgment is a critical ingredient in making principled choices and engaging in appropriate conduct. One strategy to increase trust in the investment profession is to increase the ability and motivation of market participants to act ethically and help them minimize the likelihood of unethical actions. Firms can enhance the ability and the motivation of their employees to act ethically by integrating ethics into all decision-making activities. An investment professional's natural desire to "do the right thing" can be reinforced by building a culture of integrity and accountability in the workplace. Development, maintenance, and demonstration of a strong culture of integrity within the firm by senior management may be the single most important factor in promoting ethical behavior among the firm's employees.

Adopting a code that clearly lays out the **ethical principles** that guide the thought processes and conduct the firm expects from its employees is a critical first step. But a code of ethics, although necessary, is insufficient. We need to exercise ethical decision-making skills to develop the ability necessary for fundamentally ethical people to make good decisions despite the reality of conflicts. A strong ethical culture built on a defined set of ethical principles that helps honest people engage in ethical behavior will foster the trust of investors, lead to robust global financial markets, and ultimately benefit society. That is why ethics matter.

5.1. Description of the Framework

When faced with decisions that can affect multiple stakeholders, investment professionals must have a well-developed set of principles. Otherwise, their thought processes can lead to, at best, indecision and, at worst, fraudulent conduct and destruction of the public trust. Establishing an ethical framework to guide an investment professional's internal thought process regarding how to act is a crucial step to engaging in ethical conduct.

Investment professionals are generally comfortable analyzing and making decisions from an economic (profit/loss) perspective. Given the importance of ethical behavior in carrying out professional responsibilities, it is also important to analyze decisions and their potential consequences from an ethical perspective. Using a framework for ethical decision-making will help investment professionals to effectively examine their choices in the context of conflicting interests common to their professional obligations (e.g., researching and gathering information, developing investment recommendations, and managing money for others). Such a framework provides investment professionals with a tool to help them adhere to a code of ethics and allows them to analyze and choose options to meet high standards of ethical behavior. By applying the framework and analyzing the particular circumstances of each available alternative, investment professionals are able to determine the best course of action to fulfill their responsibilities in an ethical manner.

An ethical decision-making framework helps a decision maker see the situation from multiple perspectives and pay attention to aspects of the situation that may be less evident with a short-term, self-focused perspective. The goal of getting a broader picture of a situation is to be able to create a plan of action that is less likely to harm stakeholders and more likely to benefit them. If a decision maker does not know or understand the effects of her or his actions on stakeholders, the likelihood of making a decision and taking action that harms stakeholders is more likely to occur, even if unintentionally. Finally, an ethical decision-making framework helps decision makers explain and justify their actions to a broader audience of stakeholders.

An ethical decision-making framework is designed to facilitate the decision-making process for all decisions. It helps people look at and evaluate a decision from multiple perspectives to identify important issues they might not otherwise consider. Using an ethical decision-making framework consistently helps develop sound judgment and decision-making skills and avoid making decisions that have unanticipated ethical consequences. Ethical decision-making frameworks come in many forms with varying degrees of detail. A general ethical decision-making framework is shown in **Exhibit 1**.

EXHIBIT 1   Ethical Decision-Making Framework

- Identify: Relevant facts, stakeholders and duties owed, relevant ethical principles and/or legal requirements, conflicts of interest
- Consider: Situational influences and behavioral biases, additional guidance, alternative actions
- Decide and act
- Reflect: Was the outcome as anticipated? Why or why not?

An ethical decision-making process includes multiple phases, each of which has multiple components. The process is often iterative, and the decision maker may move between phases in an order different from what is presented. For simplicity, we will discuss the phases sequentially.

In the first phase, you will want to identify the important facts that you have available to you, as well as information that you may not have but would like to have to give yourself a more complete understanding of the situation. It is helpful to distinguish between facts and personal opinions, judgments, and biases. You will also want to identify the stakeholders and the duties you have to each of them. You will then identify relevant ethical principles and/or legal requirements that might apply to the situation. You should also identify any potential conflicts of interest inherent in the situation or conflicts in the duties you hold to others. For example, your duty to your client may conflict with your duty to your employer.

In the second phase of ethical decision-making, you will take time to consider the **situational influences** as well as **behavioral biases** that could affect your thinking and thus decision-making. During this phase, you may seek additional guidance from trusted sources and you may turn to your compliance department for assistance or you may even consult outside legal counsel. Seeking additional guidance is a critical step in viewing the situation from different perspectives. You should seek guidance from someone, possibly external to the firm, who is not affected by the same situational influences and behavioral biases as you are and can, therefore, provide a fresh perspective. You should also seek guidance from your firm's policies and procedures and the CFA Institute Code and Standards. A helpful technique can be to imagine how an ethical peer or role model might act in the situation.

The third phase of ethical decision-making is to decide and act.

After you have acted on your decision, the fourth phase is to reflect on and assess your decision and its outcome. Was the outcome what you anticipated? Why or why not? Had you properly identified all the relevant facts, stakeholders and duties owed, relevant ethical principles and/or legal requirements, and conflicts of interest? Had you considered the situational influences? Did you identify behavioral biases that might affect your thinking? Had you sought additional guidance? Had you considered and properly evaluated a variety of alternative actions? You may want to reflect on the decision multiple times as the immediate and longer-term consequences of your decision and actions become apparent.

The ethical decision-making process is often iterative. After identifying the relevant facts and considering situational influences, you may, for example, decide that you cannot decide without more information. You may seek additional guidance on how to obtain the information you need. You may also begin considering alternative actions regarding how to proceed based on expectations of what the additional information will reveal, or you may wait until you have more information, reflect on what you have done and learned so far, and start the process over again. Sometimes cases can be complicated and multiple iterations may reveal that no totally acceptable solution can be created. Applying an ethical decision-making framework can help you evaluate the situation so you can make the best possible decision.

Using an ethical decision-making framework will help you evaluate situations from multiple perspectives, avoid poor decision-making, and avoid the consequences that can result from taking an ill-conceived course of action. Using an ethical decision-making framework is no guarantee of a positive outcome but may help you avoid making unethical decisions.

6. CHALLENGES FOR INVESTMENT PROFESSIONALS

New trends are reshaping the investment industry and the expectations of investment professionals. Such change is not new; the contracts between professions and society are constantly redefined. The erosion of trust in financial markets and institutions is shown in the "2017 Edelman Trust Barometer" (Edelman Intelligence 2017), which found "the largest-ever drop in trust across the institutions of government, business, media and NGOs [non-governmental organizations]." More specifically, the broad area of financial services ranked as the sector least trusted in both 2016 and 2017 when compared with the energy, consumer packaged goods, food and beverage, and technology sectors. The financial services industry is increasingly viewed as not managing conflicts of interest well.

Regulation has become increasingly commonplace across the world, in large part following the 2007–2008 global financial crisis, because of serious ethical breaches that occurred in financial markets and institutions. Some regulators now require investment advisers to belong to a professional body, adhere to an acceptable code of conduct, achieve a minimum level of relevant education, commit to continuing professional development, and comply with sanctions for any wrongdoing. Regulation has helped raise professional standards by making them a requirement for practice, although sometimes at the expense of the autonomy and flexibility required for professions to adapt and evolve.

Globalization has resulted in more common practice around the world and greater international harmonization of investment practices and regulation. This has, in turn, allowed global professional organizations, such as CFA Institute, to develop and expand their reach. Globalization may bring challenges, however, if large global investment firms seek to establish their own standards and practices that conflict with the codes of individual professional bodies.

Perhaps the greatest challenge for the investment profession comes from technology. Rapid advances in computing power, data storage, and internet connectivity threaten to alter the definition of professional expertise and how it is applied to serve investors. Already index replication, risk management, trade execution, asset allocation, algorithmic trading, and quantitative investment management are being automated, replacing or enhancing many of the functions of an investment professional. Developments in artificial intelligence are likely to accelerate this trend. The effects are many, from the need for evolved continuing education programs to new codes of practice and standards that recognize the growing intersection between human and artificial skill.

Making ethical decisions in an environment filled with challenges can be daunting. Practice with applying a framework for ethical decision-making can help prepare you for that.

7. SUMMARY

- A profession is an occupational group that has specific education, expert knowledge, and a framework of practice and behavior that underpins community trust, respect, and recognition.
- The requirement to uphold high ethical standards is one clear difference between professions and craft guilds or trade bodies.
- A primary goal of professions is to establish trust among clients and among society in general.
- Common characteristics of professions include normalization of practitioner behavior, service to society, client focus, high entry standards, a body of expert knowledge, encouragement and facilitation of continuing education, monitoring of professional conduct, collegiality, recognized overseeing bodies, and encouragement of member engagement.
- The investment profession has become increasingly global, driven by the opening of capital markets, coordination of regulation across borders, and the emergence of technology.
- Investment professionals are trusted to draw on a body of formal knowledge and apply that knowledge with care and judgment. In comparison to clients, investment professionals are also expected to have superior financial expertise, technical knowledge, and knowledge of the applicable laws and regulations.
- As a professional body, CFA Institute gathers knowledge from practicing investment professionals, develops high-quality curricula, conducts rigorous examinations, contributes to new research in finance, and ensures practitioner involvement in developing its codes and values.
- Legal standards are often rule based. Ethical conduct goes beyond legal standards, balancing self-interest with the direct and indirect consequences of behavior on others.
- Investment professionals are likely to encounter dilemmas, including those with ethical implications. Professionals should consider carefully how to determine the facts of the issue and assess the implications.
- A framework for ethical decision-making can help people look at and evaluate a decision from different perspectives, enabling them to identify important issues, make wise decisions, and limit unintended consequences.

- Regulation has helped raise professional standards by making them a requirement for practice, although sometimes at the expense of autonomy and flexibility.
- Perhaps the greatest challenge for the investment management profession comes from technology. Rapid advances in computing power, data storage, and internet connectivity are changing the definition of professional expertise and how it is applied to serve investors.

REFERENCES

Beaton, George Ramsay. 2010. "Why Professionalism is Still Relevant." University of Melbourne Legal Studies Research Paper No. 445. Available at SSRN: https://ssrn.com/abstract=1545509.

Bellis, C. S. 2000. "Professions in Society." *British Actuarial Journal* 6 (2): 317–64.

Bogle, John C. 2017. "Balancing Professional Values and Business Values." *Financial Analysts Journal* 73 (2): 14–23.

CFA Institute. 2017. "Future State of the Investment Profession." www.cfainstitute.org/learning/future/ Documents/future_state_of_investment_profession.pdf

CFA Society UK. April 2016. "The Value of the Investment Profession: A Report on Stakeholders' Views." www.cfauk.org/-/media/files/pdf/professionalism/value-of-the-investment-profession-report.pdf

Edelman Intelligence. 2017. "2017 Edelman Trust Barometer" (17 January). https://www.edelman.com/ trust2017/.

Graham, Benjamin. 1949. *The Intelligent Investor.* New York: HarperCollins.

Graham, Benjamin, and Dodd. 1934. *Security Analysis.* New York: McGraw-Hill.

Sanders, Deen, and Roberts. 2015. "Professionalisation of Financial Services." White Paper. https:// www.psc.gov.au/sites/default/files/NEW-PSC%20Whitepaper_final.pdf.

PRACTICE PROBLEMS

1. High ethical standards are distinguishing features of which of the following bodies?
   A. Craft guilds
   B. Trade bodies
   C. Professional bodies

2. Fiduciary duty is a standard *most likely* to be upheld by members of a(n):
   A. employer.
   B. profession.
   C. not-for-profit body.

3. To maintain trust, the investment management profession must be interdependent with:
   A. regulators.
   B. employers.
   C. investment firms.

4. When an ethical dilemma occurs, an investment professional should *most likely* first raise the issue with a:
   A. mentor outside the firm.
   B. professional body's hotline.
   C. senior individual in the firm.

CHAPTER 2

FINTECH IN INVESTMENT MANAGEMENT

Robert Kissell, PhD
Barbara J. Mack

LEARNING OUTCOMES

The candidate should be able to:

- describe "fintech;"
- describe Big Data, artificial intelligence, and machine learning;
- describe fintech applications to investment management;
- describe financial applications of distributed ledger technology.

1. INTRODUCTION

The meeting of finance and technology, commonly known as *fintech*, is changing the landscape of investment management. Advancements include the use of Big Data, artificial intelligence, and machine learning to evaluate investment opportunities, optimize portfolios, and mitigate risks. These developments are affecting not only quantitative asset managers but also fundamental asset managers who make use of these tools and technologies to engage in hybrid forms of investment decision-making.

Investment advisory services are undergoing changes with the growth of automated wealth advisers or "robo-advisers." Robo-advisers may assist investors without the intervention of a human adviser, or they may be used in combination with a human adviser. The desired outcome is the ability to provide tailored, actionable advice to investors with greater ease of access and at lower cost.

In the area of financial record keeping, blockchain and distributed ledger technology (DLT) are creating new ways to record, track, and store transactions for financial assets. An early example of this trend is the cryptocurrency bitcoin, but the technology is being considered in a broader set of applications.

This chapter is divided into seven main sections, which together define fintech and outline some of its key areas of impact in the field of investment management. Section 2 explains the concept and areas of fintech. Sections 3 and 4 discuss Big Data, artificial intelligence, and machine learning. Section 5 discusses data science, and Section 6 provides applications of fintech to investment management. Section 7 examines DLT. A summary of key points completes the chapter.

2. WHAT IS FINTECH?

In its broadest sense, the term "fintech" generally refers to technology-driven innovation occurring in the financial services industry. For the purposes of this chapter, **fintech** refers to technological innovation in the design and delivery of financial services and products. Note, however, that in common usage, fintech can also refer to companies (often new, startup companies) involved in developing the new technologies and their applications, as well as the business sector that comprises such companies. Many of these innovations are challenging the traditional business models of incumbent financial services providers.

Early forms of fintech included data processing and the automation of routine tasks. Then followed systems that provided execution of decisions according to specified rules and instructions. Fintech has since advanced into decision-making applications based on complex machine-learning logic, where computer programs are able to "learn" how to complete tasks over time. In some applications, advanced computer systems are performing tasks at levels far surpassing human capabilities. Fintech has changed the financial services industry in many ways, giving rise to new systems for investment advice, financial planning, business lending, and payments.

Whereas fintech covers a broad range of services and applications, areas of fintech development that are more directly relevant to the investment industry include the following:

- **Analysis of large datasets.** In addition to growing amounts of traditional data, such as security prices, corporate financial statements, and economic indicators, massive amounts of alternative data generated from non-traditional data sources, such as social media and sensor networks, can now be integrated into a portfolio manager's investment decision-making process and used to help generate alpha and reduce losses.
- **Analytical tools.** For extremely large datasets, techniques involving **artificial intelligence** (AI)—computer systems capable of performing tasks that previously required human intelligence—may be better suited to identify complex, non-linear relationships than traditional quantitative methods and statistical analysis. Advances in AI-based techniques are enabling different data analysis approaches. For example, analysts are turning to artificial intelligence to sort through the enormous amounts of data from company filings, annual reports, and earnings calls to determine which data are most important and to help uncover trends and generate insights relating to human sentiment and behavior.
- **Automated trading.** Executing investment decisions through computer algorithms or automated trading applications may provide a number of benefits to investors, including more efficient trading, lower transaction costs, anonymity, and greater access to market liquidity.

- **Automated advice. Robo-advisers** or automated personal wealth management services provide investment services to a larger number of retail investors at lower cost than traditional adviser models can provide.
- **Financial record keeping.** New technology, such as DLT, may provide secure ways to track ownership of financial assets on a peer-to-peer (P2P) basis. By allowing P2P interactions—in which individuals or firms transact directly with each other without mediation by a third party—DLT reduces the need for financial intermediaries.

Drivers underlying fintech development in these areas include extremely rapid growth in data—including their quantity, types, sources, and quality—and technological advances that enable the capture and extraction of information from them. The data explosion is addressed in Section 3, and selected technological advances and data science are addressed in Sections 4 and 5, respectively.

3. BIG DATA

As noted, datasets are growing rapidly in terms of the size and diversity of data types that are available for analysis. The term **Big Data** has been in use since the late 1990s and refers to the vast amount of data being generated by industry, governments, individuals, and electronic devices. Big Data includes data generated from traditional sources—such as stock exchanges, companies, and governments—as well as non-traditional data types, also known as **alternative data**, arising from the use of electronic devices, social media, sensor networks, and company exhaust (data generated in the normal course of doing business).

Traditional data sources include corporate data in the form of annual reports, regulatory filings, sales and earnings figures, and conference calls with analysts. Traditional data also include data that are generated in the financial markets, including trade prices and volumes. Because the world has become increasingly connected, we can now obtain data from a wide range of devices, including smart phones, cameras, microphones, radio-frequency identification (RFID) readers, wireless sensors, and satellites that are now in use all over the world. As the internet and the presence of such networked devices have grown, the use of non-traditional data sources, or alternative data sources—including social media (posts, tweets, and blogs), email and text communications, web traffic, online news sites, and other electronic information sources—has risen.

The term *Big Data* typically refers to datasets having the following characteristics:

- **Volume:** The amount of data collected in files, records, and tables is very large, representing many millions, or even billions, of data points.
- **Velocity:** The speed with which the data are communicated is extremely great. Real-time or near-real-time data have become the norm in many areas.
- **Variety:** The data are collected from many different sources and in a variety of formats, including structured data (e.g., SQL tables or CSV files), semi-structured data (e.g., HTML code), and unstructured data (e.g., video messages).

Features relating to Big Data's volume, velocity, and variety are shown in Exhibit 1.

Exhibit 1 shows that data volumes are growing from megabytes (MB) and gigabytes (GB) to far larger sizes, such as terabytes (TB) and petabytes (PB), as more data are being generated, captured, and stored. At the same time, more data, traditional and non-traditional,

EXHIBIT 1   Big Data Characteristics: Volume, Velocity, and Variety

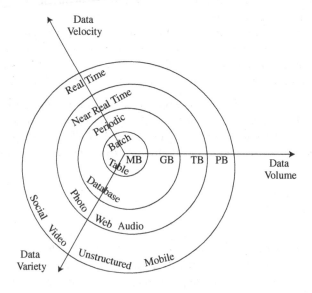

Data	Volume Key	Bytes of Information
MB	Megabyte	One Million
GB	Gigabyte	One Billion
TB	Terabyte	One Trillion
PB	Petabyte	One Quadrillion

Source: http://whatis.techtarget.com/definition/3Vs.

are available on a real-time or near-real-time basis with far greater variety in data types than ever before.

Big Data may be structured, semi-structured, or unstructured data. Structured data items can be organized in tables and are commonly stored in a database where each field represents the same type of information. Unstructured data may be disparate, unorganized data that cannot be represented in tabular form. Unstructured data, such as those generated by social media, email, text messages, voice recordings, pictures, blogs, scanners, and sensors, often require different, specialized applications or custom programs before they can be useful to investment professionals. For example, in order to analyze data contained in emails or texts, specially developed or customized computer code may be required to first process these files. Semi-structured data may have attributes of both structured and unstructured data.

3.1. Sources of Big Data

Big Data, therefore, encompasses data generated by:

- financial markets (e.g., equity, fixed income, futures, options, and other derivatives),
- businesses (e.g., corporate financials, commercial transactions, and credit card purchases),
- governments (e.g., trade, economic, employment, and payroll data),

- individuals (e.g., credit card purchases, product reviews, internet search logs, and social media posts),
- sensors (e.g., satellite imagery, shipping cargo information, and traffic patterns), and, in particular,
- the Internet of Things, or IoT (e.g., data generated by "smart" buildings, where the building is providing a steady stream of information about climate control, energy consumption, security, and other operational details).

In gathering business intelligence, historically, analysts have tended to draw on traditional data sources, employing statistical methods to measure performance, predict future growth, and analyze sector and market trends. In contrast, the analysis of Big Data incorporates the use of alternative data sources.

From retail sales data to social media sentiment to satellite imagery that may reveal information about agriculture, shipping, and oil rigs, alternative datasets may provide additional insights about consumer behavior, firm performance, trends, and other factors important for investment-related activities. Such information is having a significant effect on the way that professional investors, particularly quantitative investors, approach financial analysis and decision-making processes.

There are three main sources of alternative data:

- data generated by individuals,
- data generated by business processes, and
- data generated by sensors.

Data generated by individuals are often produced in text, video, photo, and audio formats and may also be generated through such means as website clicks or time spent on a webpage. This type of data tends to be unstructured. The volume of this type of data is growing dramatically as people participate in greater numbers and more frequently in online activities, such as social media and e-commerce, including online reviews of products, services, and entire companies, and as they make personal data available through web searches, email, and other electronic trails.

Business process data include information flows from corporations and other public entities. These data tend to be structured data and include direct sales information, such as credit card data, as well as corporate exhaust. Corporate exhaust includes corporate supply chain information, banking records, and retail point-of-sale scanner data. Business process data can be leading or real-time indicators of business performance, whereas traditional corporate metrics may be reported only on a quarterly or even yearly basis and are typically lagging indicators of performance.

Sensor data are collected from such devices as smart phones, cameras, RFID chips, and satellites that are usually connected to computers via wireless networks. Sensor data can be unstructured, and the volume of data is many orders of magnitude greater than that of individual or business process datastreams. This form of data is growing exponentially because microprocessors and networking technology are increasingly present in a wide array of personal and commercial electronic devices. Extended to office buildings, homes, vehicles, and many other physical forms, this culminates in a network arrangement, known as the **Internet of Things**, that is formed by the vast array of physical devices, home appliances, smart buildings, vehicles, and other items that are embedded with electronics, sensors, software, and network connections that enable the objects in the system to interact and share information.

Exhibit 2 shows a classification of alternative data sources and includes examples for each.

EXHIBIT 2   Classification of Alternative Data Sources

Individuals	Business Processes	Sensors
Social media	Transaction data	Satellites
News, reviews	Corporate data	Geolocation
Web searches, personal data		Internet of Things
		Other sensors

In the search to identify new factors that may affect security prices, enhance asset selection, improve trade execution, and uncover trends, alternative data are being used to support data-driven investment models and decisions. As interest in alternative data has risen, there has been a growth in the number of specialized firms that collect, aggregate, and sell alternative datasets.

While the marketplace for alternative data is expanding, investment professionals should understand potential legal and ethical issues related to information that is not in the public domain. For example, the scraping of web data could potentially capture personal information that is protected by regulations or that may have been published or provided without the explicit knowledge and consent of the individuals involved. Best practices are still in development in many jurisdictions, and because of varying approaches taken by national regulators, there may be conflicting forms of guidance.

3.2. Big Data Challenges

Big Data poses several challenges when it is used in investment analysis, including the quality, volume, and appropriateness of the data. Key issues revolve around the following questions, among others: Does the dataset have selection bias, missing data, or data outliers? Is the volume of collected data sufficient? Is the dataset well suited for the type of analysis? In most instances, the data must be sourced, cleansed, and organized before analysis can occur. This process can be extremely difficult with alternative data owing to the unstructured characteristics of the data involved, which are more often qualitative (e.g., texts, photos, and videos) than quantitative in nature.

Given the size and complexity of alternative datasets, traditional analytical methods cannot always be used to interpret and evaluate these datasets. To address this challenge, artificial intelligence and machine learning techniques have emerged that support work on such large and complex sources of information.

4. ADVANCED ANALYTICAL TOOLS: ARTIFICIAL INTELLIGENCE AND MACHINE LEARNING

Artificial intelligence computer systems are capable of performing tasks that have traditionally required human intelligence. AI technology has enabled the development of computer systems that exhibit cognitive and decision-making ability comparable or superior to that of human beings.

An early example of AI was the "expert system," a type of computer programming that attempted to simulate the knowledge base and analytical abilities of human experts in specific problem-solving contexts. This was often accomplished through the use of "if-then" rules. By the late 1990s, faster networks and more powerful processors enabled AI to be deployed in logistics, data mining, financial analysis, medical diagnosis, and other areas. Since the 1980s, financial institutions have made use of AI—particularly, **neural networks**, programming based on how our brain learns and processes information—to detect abnormal charges or claims in credit card fraud detection systems.

Machine learning (ML) involves computer-based techniques that seek to extract knowledge from large amounts of data without making any assumptions on the data's underlying probability distribution. The goal of ML algorithms is to automate decision-making processes by generalizing, or "learning," from known examples to determine an underlying structure in the data. The emphasis is on the ability of the algorithm to generate structure or predictions without any help from a human. Simply put, ML algorithms aim to "find the pattern, apply the pattern."

As it is currently used in the investing context, ML requires massive amounts of data for "training," so although some ML techniques have existed for years, insufficient data have historically limited broader application. Previously, these algorithms lacked access to the large amounts of data needed to model relationships successfully. The growth in Big Data has provided ML algorithms, such as neural networks, with sufficient data to improve modeling and predictive accuracy, and greater use of ML techniques is now possible.

In ML, the computer algorithm is given "inputs" (a set of variables or datasets) and may be given "outputs" (the target data). The algorithm "learns" from the data provided how best to model inputs to outputs (if provided) or how to identify or describe underlying data structure if no outputs are given. Training occurs as the algorithm identifies relationships in the data and uses that information to refine its learning process.

ML involves splitting the dataset into three distinct subsets: a training dataset, a validation dataset, and a test dataset. The training dataset allows the algorithm to identify relationships between inputs and outputs based on historical patterns in the data. These relationships are then validated, and the model tuned, using the validation dataset. The test dataset is used to test the model's ability to predict well on new data. Once an algorithm has been trained, validated, and tested, the ML model can be used to predict outcomes based on other datasets.

ML still requires human judgment in understanding the underlying data and selecting the appropriate techniques for data analysis. Before they can be used, the data must be clean and free of biases and spurious data. As noted, ML models also require sufficiently large amounts of data and may not perform well where there may not be enough available data to train and validate the model.

Analysts must also be cognizant of errors that may arise from **overfitting** the data, because models that overfit the data may discover "false" relationships or "unsubstantiated" patterns that will lead to prediction errors and incorrect output forecasts. Overfitting occurs when the ML model learns the input and target dataset too precisely. In such cases, the model has been "over-trained" on the data and treats noise in the data as true parameters. An ML model that has been overfitted is not able to accurately predict outcomes using a different dataset and may be too complex. When a model has been underfitted, the ML model treats true parameters as if they are noise and is not able to recognize relationships within the training data. In such cases, the model may be too simplistic. Underfitted models will typically fail to fully discover patterns that underlie the data.

In addition, since they are not explicitly programmed, ML techniques can appear to be opaque or "black box" approaches, which arrive at outcomes that may not be entirely understood or explainable.

4.1. Types of Machine Learning

ML approaches can help identify relationships between variables, detect patterns or trends, and create structure from data, including data classification. Machine learning can be broadly divided into three distinct classes of techniques: supervised learning, unsupervised learning, and deep learning.

In **supervised learning**, computers learn to model relationships based on labeled training data. In supervised learning, inputs and outputs are labeled, or identified, for the algorithm. After learning how best to model relationships for the labeled data, the trained algorithms are used to model or predict outcomes for new datasets. Trying to identify the best signal, or variable, to forecast future returns on a stock or trying to predict whether local stock market performance will be up, down, or flat during the next business day are problems that may be approached using supervised learning techniques.

In **unsupervised learning**, computers are not given labeled data but instead are given only data from which the algorithm seeks to describe the data and their structure. Trying to group companies into peer groups based on their characteristics rather than using standard sector or country groupings is a problem that may be approached using unsupervised learning techniques.

Underlying AI advances have been key developments relating to neural networks. In **deep learning**, (or **deep learning nets**), computers use neural networks, often with many hidden layers, to perform multistage, non-linear data processing to identify patterns. Deep learning may use supervised or unsupervised machine learning approaches. By taking a layered or multistage approach to data analysis, deep learning develops an understanding of simple concepts that informs analysis of more complex concepts. Neural networks have existed since 1958 and have been used for many applications, such as forecasting and pattern recognition, since the early 1990s. Improvements in the algorithms underlying neural networks are providing more accurate models that better incorporate and learn from data. As a result, these algorithms are now far better at such activities as image, pattern, and speech recognition. In many cases, the advanced algorithms require less computing power than the earlier neural networks, and their improved solution enables analysts to discover insights and identify relationships that were previously too difficult or too time consuming to uncover.

Advances in Artificial Intelligence outside Finance

Non-finance-related AI breakthroughs include victories in the general knowledge game show *Jeopardy!* (by IBM's Watson in 2011) and in the ancient Chinese board game Go (by Google's DeepMind in 2016). Not only is AI providing solutions where there is perfect information (all players have equal access to the same information), such as checkers, chess, and Go, but AI is also providing insight in cases where information may be imperfect and players have hidden information; AI successes at the game of poker (by DeepStack) are an example. AI has also been behind the rise of virtual assistants, such as Siri (from Apple), Google's Translate app, and Amazon's product recommendation engine.

The ability to analyze Big Data using ML techniques, alongside more traditional statistical methods, represents a significant development in investment research, supported by the presence of greater data availability and advances in the algorithms themselves. Improvements in computing power and software processing speeds and falling storage costs have further supported this evolution.

ML techniques are being used for Big Data analysis to help predict trends or market events, such as the likelihood of a successful merger or an outcome to a political election. Image recognition algorithms can now analyze data from satellite-imaging systems to provide intelligence on the number of consumers in retail store parking lots, shipping activity and manufacturing facilities, and yields on agricultural crops, to name just a few examples.

Such information may provide insights into individual firms or at national or global levels and may be used as inputs into valuation or economic models.

5. DATA SCIENCE: EXTRACTING INFORMATION FROM BIG DATA

Data science can be defined as an interdisciplinary field that harnesses advances in computer science (including machine learning), statistics, and other disciplines for the purpose of extracting information from Big Data (or data in general). Companies rely on the expertise of data scientists/analysts to extract information and insights from Big Data for a wide variety of business and investment purposes.

An important consideration for the data scientist is the structure of the data. As noted in the discussion on Big Data, because of their unstructured nature, alternative data often require specialized treatment before they can be used for analysis.

5.1. Data Processing Methods

To help determine the best data management technique needed for Big Data analysis, data scientists use various data processing methods, including capture, curation, storage, search, and transfer.

- Capture—Data capture refers to how the data are collected and transformed into a format that can be used by the analytical process. Low-latency systems—systems that operate on networks that communicate high volumes of data with minimal delay (latency)—are essential for automated trading applications that make decisions based on real-time prices and market events. In contrast, high-latency systems do not require access to real-time data and calculations.
- Curation—Data curation refers to the process of ensuring data quality and accuracy through a data cleaning exercise. This process consists of reviewing all data to detect and uncover data errors—bad or inaccurate data—and making adjustments for missing data when appropriate.
- Storage—Data storage refers to how the data will be recorded, archived, and accessed and the underlying database design. An important consideration for data storage is whether the data are structured or unstructured and whether analytical needs require low-latency solutions.
- Search—Search refers to how to query data. Big Data has created the need for advanced applications capable of examining and reviewing large quantities of data to locate requested data content.
- Transfer—Transfer refers to how the data will move from the underlying data source or storage location to the underlying analytical tool. This could be through a direct data feed, such as a stock exchange's price feed.

5.2. Data Visualization

Data visualization is an important tool for understanding Big Data. Visualization refers to how the data will be formatted, displayed, and summarized in graphical form. Traditional structured data can be visualized using tables, charts, and trends, whereas non-traditional unstructured data require new techniques of data visualization. These visualization tools include, for example, interactive three-dimensional (3D) graphics, where users can focus in on specified data ranges and rotate the data across 3D axes to help identify trends and uncover relationships. Multidimensional data analysis consisting of more than three variables requires additional data visualization techniques—for example, adding color, shapes, and sizes to the 3D charts. Further, a wide variety of solutions exists to reflect the structure of the data through the geometry of the visualization, with interactive graphics allowing for especially rich possibilities. Examples include heat maps, tree diagrams, and network graphs.

Another valuable Big Data visualization technique that is applicable to textual data is a "tag cloud," where words are sized and displayed on the basis of the frequency of the word in the data file. For example, words that appear more often are shown with a larger font, and words that appear less often are shown with a smaller font. A "mind map" is another data visualization technique; it is a variation of the tag cloud, but rather than displaying the frequency of words, a mind map shows how different concepts are related to each other.

Exhibit 3 shows an example of a "tag cloud" based on a section of this chapter. The more frequently a word is found within the text, the larger it becomes in the tag cloud. As shown in the tag cloud, the words appearing most frequently in Section 4 include "data," "ML," "learning," "AI," "techniques," "model," and "relationships."

EXHIBIT 3   Data Visualization Tag Cloud: Section 4, Advanced Analytical Tools

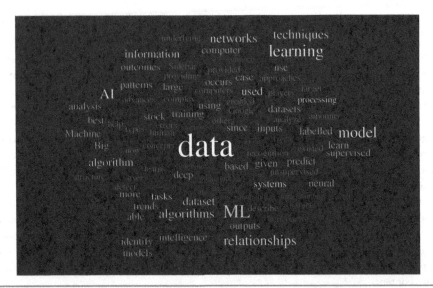

Source: https://worditout.com/word-cloud/create.

Programming Languages and Databases

Some of the more common programming languages used in data science include the following:

- **Python:** Python is an open source, free programming language that does not require an in-depth understanding of computer programming. Python allows individuals with little or no programming experience to develop computer applications for advanced analytical use and is the basis for many fintech applications.
- **R:** R is an open source, free programming language traditionally used for statistical analysis. R has mathematical packages for statistical analysis, machine learning, optimization, econometrics, and financial analysis.
- **Java:** Java is a programming language that can run on different computers, servers, and operating systems. Java is the underlying program language used in many internet applications.
- **C/C++:** C/C++ is a specialized programming language that provides the ability to optimize source code to achieve superior calculation speed and processing performance. C/C++ is used in applications for algorithmic and high-frequency trading.
- **Excel VBA:** Excel VBA helps bridge the gap between programming and manual data processing by allowing users to run macros to automate tasks, such as updating data tables and formulas, running data queries and collecting data from different web locations, and performing calculations. Excel VBA allows users to develop customized reports and analyses that rely on data that are updated from different applications and databases.

Some of the more common databases in use include the following:

- **SQL:** SQL is a database for structured data where the data can be stored in tables with rows and columns. SQL databases need to be run on a server that is accessed by users.
- **SQLite:** SQLite is a database for structured data. SQLite databases are embedded into the program and do not need to be run on a server. It is the most common database for mobile apps that require access to data.
- **NoSQL:** NoSQL is a database used for unstructured data where the data cannot be summarized in traditional tables with rows and columns.

6. SELECTED APPLICATIONS OF FINTECH TO INVESTMENT MANAGEMENT

Fintech is being used in numerous areas of investment management. Applications for investment management include text analytics and natural language processing, robo-advisory services, risk analysis, and algorithmic trading.

6.1. Text Analytics and Natural Language Processing

Text analytics involves the use of computer programs to analyze and derive meaning typically from large, unstructured text- or voice-based datasets, such as company filings, written reports, quarterly earnings calls, social media, email, internet postings, and surveys. Text analytics includes using computer programs to perform automated information retrieval from different, unrelated sources in order to aid the decision-making process. More analytical usage includes lexical analysis, or the analysis of word frequency in a document and pattern recognition based on key words and phrases. Text analytics may be used in predictive analysis to help identify indicators of future performance, such as consumer sentiment.

Natural language processing (NLP) is a field of research at the intersection of computer science, artificial intelligence, and linguistics that focuses on developing computer programs to analyze and interpret human language. Within the larger field of text analytics, NLP is an important application. Automated tasks using NLP include translation, speech recognition, text mining, sentiment analysis, and topic analysis. NLP may also be employed in compliance functions to review employee voice and electronic communications for adherence to company or regulatory policy, inappropriate conduct, or fraud or for ensuring private or customer information is kept confidential.

Consider that all the public corporations worldwide generate millions of pages of annual reports and tens of thousands of hours of earnings calls each year. This is more information than any individual analyst or team of researchers can assess. NLP, especially when aided by ML algorithms, can analyze annual reports, call transcripts, news articles, social media posts, and other text- and audio-based data to identify trends in shorter timespans and with greater scale and accuracy than is humanly possible.

For example, NLP may be used to monitor analyst commentary to aid investment decision-making. Financial analysts may generate earnings-per-share (EPS) forecasts reflecting their views on a company's near-term prospects. Focusing on forecasted EPS numbers could mean investors miss subtleties contained in an analyst's written research report. Since analysts tend not to change their buy, hold, and sell recommendations for a company frequently, they may instead offer nuanced commentary without making a change in their investment recommendation. After analyzing analyst commentary, NLP can assign sentiment ratings ranging from very negative to very positive for each. NLP can, therefore, be used to detect, monitor, and tag shifts in sentiment, potentially ahead of an analyst's recommendation change. Machine capabilities enable this analysis to scale across thousands of companies worldwide, performing work previously done by humans.

Similarly, communications and transcripts from policymakers, such as the European Central Bank or the US Federal Reserve, offer an opportunity for NLP-based analysis, because officials at these institutions may send subtle messages through their choice of topics, words, and inferred tone. NLP can help analyze nuances within text to provide insights around trending or waning topics of interest, such as interest rate policy, aggregate output, or inflation expectations.

Models using NLP analysis may incorporate non-traditional information to evaluate what people are saying—via their preferences, opinions, likes, or dislikes—in an attempt to identify trends and short-term indicators about a company, a stock, or an economic event that might have a bearing on future performance. Past research has evaluated the predictive power of Twitter sentiment regarding IPO performance, for example.[1] The effect of positive and negative news sentiment on stock returns has also been researched.[2]

6.2. Robo-Advisory Services

Since their emergence in 2008, a number of startup firms, as well as large asset managers, have introduced robo-advisory services, which provide investment solutions through online platforms, reducing the need for direct interaction with financial advisers.

As robo-advisers have been incorporated into the investment landscape, they have drawn the attention of regulatory authorities. In the United States, robo-advisers must be established as registered investment advisers, and they are regulated by the Securities and Exchange Commission. In the United Kingdom, they are regulated by the Financial Conduct Authority. In Australia, all financial advisers must obtain an Australian Financial Services license, with guidance on digital advisers coming from the Australian Securities and Investments Commission. Robo-advisers are also on the rise in parts of Asia and the rest of the world. Although regulatory conditions vary, robo-advisers are likely to be held to a similar level of scrutiny and code of conduct as other investment professionals in the given region.

Robo-advice tends to start with an investor questionnaire, which may include many of the categories and subcategories shown in Exhibit 4. Exhibit 4 is a synthesis of questionnaires created by the researchers attributed in the source below. Once assets, liabilities, risk preferences, and target investment returns have been digitally entered by a client, the robo-adviser software produces recommendations, based on algorithmic rules and historical market data, that incorporate the client's stated investment parameters. According to research by Michael Tertilt and Peter Scholz, robo-advisers do not seem to incorporate the full range of available information into their recommendations;[3] further research will be necessary over time to see how this may affect performance and the evolution of digital advisory services. Nevertheless, current robo-advisory services include automated asset allocation, trade execution, portfolio optimization, tax-loss harvesting, and rebalancing for investor portfolios.

Although their analyses and recommendations can cover both active and passive management styles, most robo-advisers follow a passive investment approach. These robo-advisers typically have low fees and low account minimums, implementing their recommendations with low-cost, diversified index mutual funds or exchange-traded funds (ETFs). A diverse range of asset classes can be managed in this manner, including stocks, bonds, commodities, futures, and real estate. Because of their low-cost structure, robo-advisers can reach underserved populations, such as the mass affluent or mass market segments, which are less able to afford a traditional financial adviser.

Two types of wealth management services dominate the robo-advice sector: fully automated digital wealth managers and adviser-assisted digital wealth managers.

---

[1]Jim Kyung-Soo Liew and Garrett Zhengyuan Wang, "Twitter Sentiment and IPO Performance: A Cross-Sectional Examination," *Journal of Portfolio Management*, vol. 42, no. 4 (Summer 2016): 129–135.

[2]Steven L. Heston and Nitish Ranjan Sinha, "News vs. Sentiment: Predicting Stock Returns from News Stories," *Financial Analysts Journal*, vol. 73, no. 3 (Third Quarter 2017): 67–83. (https://www.cfapubs.-org/doi/abs/10.2469/faj.v73.n3.3).

[3]Michael Tertilt and Peter Scholz, "To Advise, or Not to Advise — How Robo-Advisors Evaluate the Risk Preferences of Private Investors" (June 12, 2017). Available at SSRN: https://ssrn.com/abstract=2913178 or http://dx.doi.org/10.2139/ssrn.2913178.

EXHIBIT 4   Categories and Subcategories for Investor Questionnaires

General Information	Risk Tolerance
Income	Age
Investment Amount	Association with Investing
Job Description	Association with Risk
Other	Choose Portfolio Risk Level
Source of Income	Comfort Investing in Stock
Spendings	Credit Based Investments
Time to Retirement	Dealing with Financial Decisions
Type of Account	Degree of Financial Risk Taken
Working Status	Education
Risk Capacity	Ever Interested in Risky Asset for Thrill
Dependence on Withdrawal of Investment Amount	Experience of Drop/Reaction on Drop/Max Drop before Selling
Income Prediction	Family and Household Status
Investment Amount/Savings Rate Ratio	Financial Knowledge
Investment Amount/Total Capital Ratio	Gender
Investment Horizon	Investment Experience
Liabilities	Investment Goal
Savings Rate	Investor Type/Self-Assessment Risk Tolerance
Total Capital	Preference Return vs. Risk

Source: Michael Tertilt and Peter Scholz, 2017 "To Advise, or Not to Advise—How Robo-Advisors Evaluate the Risk Preferences of Private Investors," working paper (13 June): Table 1: Categories and Subcategories for Questionnaires.

- **Fully Automated Digital Wealth Managers**
  The fully automated model does not rely on assistance from a human financial adviser. These services seek to offer a low-cost solution to investing and recommend an investment portfolio, which is often composed of ETFs. The service package may include direct deposits, periodic rebalancing, and dividend reinvestment options.
- **Adviser-Assisted Digital Wealth Managers**
  Adviser-assisted digital wealth managers provide automated investment services along with a virtual financial adviser, who is available to offer basic financial planning advice and periodic reviews by phone. Adviser-assisted digital wealth managers are capable of providing additional services that may involve a more holistic analysis of a client's assets and liabilities.

Wealthy and ultra-wealthy individuals typically have had access to human advisory teams, but there has been a gap in the availability and quality of advisers to serve investors with less wealth. The advent of robo-advisers offers a cost-effective and easily accessible form of financial guidance. In following a typically passive investment approach, research suggests that robo-advisers tend to offer fairly conservative advice.

However, critics of robo-advisers have wondered what would happen in a time of crisis, when people most often look to human expertise for guidance. It may not always be completely transparent why a robo-adviser chooses to make a recommendation or take a trading action that it did, unlike a human adviser who can provide his or her rationale. And finally, there may be trust issues in allowing computers to make these decisions, including worries of instances where robo-advisers might recommend inappropriate investments.

As the complexity and size of an investor's portfolio grows, robo-advisers may not be able to sufficiently address the particular preferences and needs of the investor. In the case of extremely affluent investors who may own a greater number of asset types—including alternative investments (e.g., venture capital, private equity, hedge funds, and real estate)—in addition to global stocks and bonds and have greater demands for customization, the need for a team of human advisers, each with particular areas of investment or wealth-management expertise, is likely to endure.

6.3. Risk Analysis

As mandated by regulators worldwide, the global investment industry has undertaken major steps in stress testing and risk assessment that involve the analysis of vast amounts of quantitative and qualitative risk data. Required data include information on the liquidity of the firm and its trading partners, balance sheet positions, credit exposures, risk-weighted assets, and risk parameters. Stress tests may also take qualitative information into consideration, such as capital planning procedures, expected business plan changes, business model sustainability, and operational risk.

There is increasing interest in monitoring risk in real time. To do so, relevant data must be taken by a firm, mapped to known risks, and identified as it moves within the firm. Data may be aggregated for reporting purposes or used as inputs to risk models. Big Data may provide insights into real-time and changing market circumstances to help identify weakening market conditions and adverse trends in advance, allowing managers to employ risk management techniques and hedging practices sooner to help preserve asset value. For example, evaluation of alternative data using ML techniques may help foreshadow declining company earnings and future stock performance. Furthermore, analysis of real-time market data and trading patterns may help analysts detect buying or selling pressure in the stock.

ML techniques may be used to help assess data quality. To help ensure accurate and reliable data that may originate from numerous alternative data sources, ML techniques can help validate data quality by identifying questionable data, potential errors, and data outliers before integration with traditional data for use in risk models and in risk management applications.

Portfolio risk management often makes use of scenario analysis—analyzing the likely performance of the portfolio and liquidation costs under a hypothetical stress scenario or the repeat of a historical stress event. For example, to understand the implications of holding or liquidating positions during adverse or extreme market periods, such as the financial crisis, fund managers may perform "what-if" scenario analysis and portfolio backtesting using point-in-time data to understand liquidation costs and portfolio consequences under differing market conditions. These backtesting simulations are often computationally intense and may be facilitated through the use of advanced AI-based techniques.

6.4. Algorithmic Trading

Algorithmic trading is the computerized buying and selling of financial instruments, in accordance with pre-specified rules and guidelines. Algorithmic trading is often used to execute large institutional orders, slicing orders into smaller pieces and executing across different exchanges and trading venues. Algorithmic trading provides investors with many benefits, including speed of execution, anonymity, and lower transaction costs. Over the course of a day, algorithms may continuously update and revise their execution strategy on the basis of changing prices, volumes, and market volatility. Algorithms may also determine the best way to price the order (e.g., limit or market order) and the most appropriate trading venue (e.g., exchange or dark pool) to route for execution.

High-frequency trading (HFT) is a form of algorithmic trading that makes use of vast quantities of granular financial data (tick data, for example) to automatically place trades when certain conditions are met. Trades are executed on ultra-high-speed, low-latency networks in fractions of a second. HFT algorithms decide what to buy or sell and where to execute on the basis of real-time prices and market conditions, seeking to earn a profit from intraday market mispricings.

Global financial markets have undergone substantial change as markets have fragmented into multiple trading destinations consisting of electronic exchanges, alternative trading systems, and so-called dark pools, and average trade sizes have fallen. In this environment, and with markets continuously reflecting real-time information, algorithmic trading has been viewed as an important tool.

7. DISTRIBUTED LEDGER TECHNOLOGY

Distributed ledger technology—technology based on a distributed ledger (defined below)— represents a fintech development that offers potential improvements in the area of financial record keeping. DLT networks are being considered as an efficient means to create, exchange, and track ownership of financial assets on a peer-to-peer basis. Potential benefits include greater accuracy, transparency, and security in record keeping; faster transfer of ownership; and peer-to-peer interactions. However, the technology is not fully secure, and breaches in privacy and data protection are possible. In addition, the processes underlying DLT generally require massive amounts of energy to verify transaction activity.

A **distributed ledger** is a type of database that may be shared among entities in a network. In a distributed ledger, entries are recorded, stored, and distributed across a network of participants so that each participant has a matching copy of the digital database. Basic elements of a DLT network include a digital ledger, a consensus mechanism used to confirm new entries, and a participant network.

The consensus mechanism is the process by which the computer entities (or nodes) in a network agree on a common state of the ledger. Consensus generally involves two steps: transaction validation and agreement on ledger update by network parties. These features enable the creation of records that are, for the most part, considered immutable, or unchangeable, yet they are transparent and accessible to network participants on a near-real-time basis.

Features of DLT include the use of **cryptography**—an algorithmic process to encrypt data, making the data unusable if received by unauthorized parties—which enables a high level of network security and database integrity. For example, DLT uses cryptographic methods of proof to verify network participant identity and for data encryption.

DLT has the potential to accommodate "**smart contracts**," which are computer programs that self-execute on the basis of pre-specified terms and conditions agreed to by the parties to a contract. Examples of smart contract use are the automatic execution of contingent claims for derivatives and the instantaneous transfer of collateral in the event of default.

Exhibit 5 illustrates a distributed ledger network in which all nodes are connected to one another, each having a copy of the distributed ledger. The term "Consensus" is shown in the center of the network and represents the consensus mechanism in which the nodes agree on new transactions and ledger updates.

Blockchain is a type of digital ledger in which information, such as changes in ownership, is recorded sequentially within blocks that are then linked or "chained" together and secured using cryptographic methods. Each block contains a grouping of transactions (or entries) and a secure link (known as a hash) to the previous block. New transactions are inserted into the chain only after validation via a consensus mechanism in which authorized members agree on the transaction and the preceding order, or history, in which previous transactions have occurred.

The consensus mechanism used to verify a transaction includes a cryptographic problem

EXHIBIT 5 Distributed Ledger Network Setup

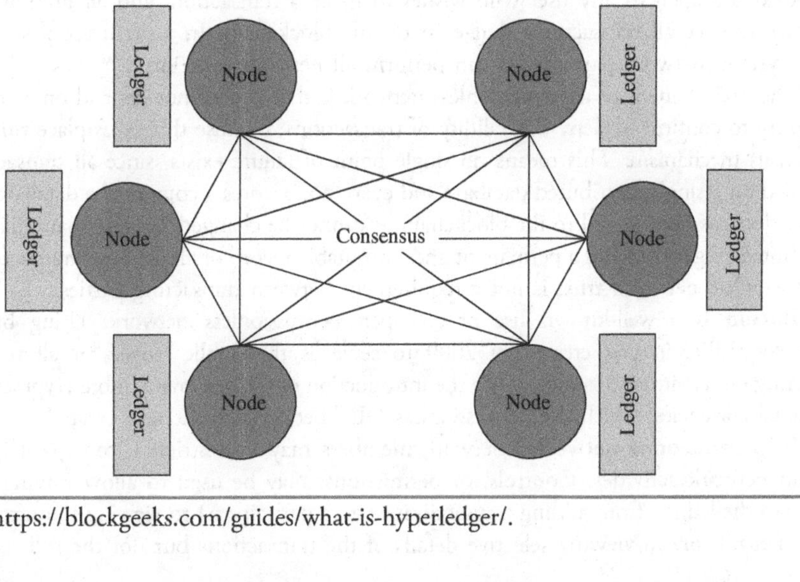

Source: https://blockgeeks.com/guides/what-is-hyperledger/.

that must be solved by some computers on the network (known as miners) each time a transaction takes place. The process to update the blockchain can require substantial amounts of computing power, making it very difficult and extremely expensive for an individual third party to manipulate historical data. To manipulate historical data, an individual or entity would have to control the majority of nodes in the network. The success of the network, therefore, relies on broad network participation.

Blockchain (Distributed Ledger) Network—How Do Transactions Get Added?

Outlined below are the steps involved in adding a transaction to a blockchain distributed ledger.

1. Transaction takes place between buyer and seller
2. Transaction is broadcast to the network of computers (nodes)
3. Nodes validate the transaction details and parties to the transaction
4. Once verified, the transaction is combined with other transactions to form a new block (of predetermined size) of data for the ledger
5. This block of data is then added or linked (using a cryptographic process) to the previous block(s) containing data
6. Transaction is considered complete and ledger has been updated

7.1. Permissioned and Permissionless Networks

DLT can take the form of permissionless or permissioned networks. **Permissionless networks** are open to any user who wishes to make a transaction, and all users within the network can see all transactions that exist on the blockchain. In a permissionless, or open, DLT system, network participants can perform all network functions.

The main benefit of a permissionless network is that it does not depend on a centralized authority to confirm or deny the validity of transactions, because this takes place through the consensus mechanism. This means no single point of failure exists, since all transactions are recorded on a single distributed database and every node stores a copy of the database. Once a transaction has been added to the blockchain, it cannot be changed, barring manipulation; the distributed ledger becomes a permanent and immutable record of all previous transactions. In a permissionless network, trust is not a requirement between transacting parties.

Bitcoin is a well-known use of an open permissionless network. Using blockchain technology, Bitcoin was created in 2009 to serve as the public ledger for all transactions occurring on its virtual currency. Since the introduction of bitcoin, many more cryptocurrencies, or digital currencies, which use permissionless DLT networks, have been created.

In **permissioned networks**, network members may be restricted from participating in certain network activities. Controls, or permissions, may be used to allow varying levels of access to the ledger, from adding transactions (e.g., a participant) to viewing transactions only (e.g., a regulator) to viewing selective details of the transactions but not the full record.

7.2. Applications of Distributed Ledger Technology to Investment Management

Potential applications of DLT to investment management include cryptocurrencies, tokenization, post-trade clearing and settlement, and compliance.

7.2.1. Cryptocurrencies

A **cryptocurrency**, also known as a digital currency, operates as electronic currency and allows near-real-time transactions between parties without the need for an intermediary, such as a bank. As electronic mediums of exchange, cryptocurrencies lack physical form and are issued privately by individuals, companies, and other organizations. Most issued cryptocurrencies utilize open DLT systems in which a decentralized distributed ledger is used to record and verify all digital currency transactions. Cryptocurrencies have not traditionally been government backed or regulated. Central banks around the world, however, are recognizing potential benefits and examining use cases for their own cryptocurrency versions.

Many cryptocurrencies have a self-imposed limit on the total amount of currency they may issue. Although such limits could help maintain their store of value, it is important to note that many cryptocurrencies have experienced high levels of price volatility. A lack of clear fundamentals underlying these currencies has contributed to their volatility.

Cryptocurrencies have proven to be an attractive means for companies looking to raise capital. An **initial coin offering** (ICO) is an unregulated process whereby companies sell their crypto tokens to investors in exchange for fiat money or for another agreed upon cryptocurrency. An ICO is typically structured to issue digital tokens to investors that can be used to purchase future products or services being developed by the issuer. ICOs provide an alternative to traditional, regulated capital-raising processes, such as initial public offerings (IPOs). Compared to the regulated IPO market, ICOs may have lower associated issuance costs and shorter capital raising time frames. However, most ICOs do not typically have attached voting rights. Regulation for ICOs is under consideration in a number of jurisdictions, and there have been numerous instances of investor loss resulting from fraudulent schemes.

7.2.2. Tokenization

Transactions involving physical assets, such as real estate, luxury goods, and commodities, often require substantial efforts in ownership verification and examination each time a transfer in ownership takes place. Through **tokenization**, the process of representing ownership rights to physical assets on a blockchain or distributed ledger, DLT has the potential to streamline this process by creating a single, digital record of ownership with which to verify ownership title and authenticity, including all historical activity. Real estate transactions that require ownership and identify verification may be one area to benefit from tokenization, because these transactions are typically labor intensive and costly, involving decentralized, paper-based records and multiple parties.

7.2.3. Post-Trade Clearing and Settlement

In the financial securities markets, post-trade processes to confirm, clear, and settle transactions are often complex and labor intensive, requiring multiple interactions between counterparties and financial intermediaries. DLT has the ability to streamline existing post-trade processes by providing near-real-time trade verification, reconciliation, and settlement, thereby reducing the complexity, time, and costs associated with processing transactions. A single distributed record of ownership between network peers would eliminate the need for independent and duplicative reconciliation efforts between parties and reduce the need for third-party facilitation. A shortened settlement time frame could lessen the time exposed to counterparty risk and associated collateral requirements while increasing the potential liquidity of assets and funds. Additionally, the use of automated contracts may also help to reduce post-trade time frames, lowering exposure to counterparty credit risk and trade fails.

7.2.4. Compliance

Regulators worldwide have imposed more stringent reporting requirements and demand greater transparency and access to data. To meet these requirements, many firms have added staff to their post-trade and compliance groups. But these functions remain predominantly manual. To comply with regulations, firms need to maintain and process large amounts of risk-related data. DLT may allow regulators and firms to maintain near-real-time review over transactions and other compliance-related processes. Improved post-trade reconciliation and automation through DLT could lead to more accurate record keeping and create operational efficiencies for a firm's compliance and regulatory reporting processes, while providing greater transparency and auditability for external authorities and regulators.

DLT-based compliance may better support shared information, communications, and transparency within and between firms, exchanges, custodians, and regulators. Closed or permissioned networks could offer advantages in security and privacy. These platforms could store highly sensitive information in a way that is secure but easily accessible to internal and external authorities. DLT could help uncover fraudulent activity and reduce compliance costs associated with know-your-customer and anti-money-laundering regulations, which entail verifying the identity of clients and business partners.

DLT Challenges

A number of challenges exist before DLT may be successfully adopted by the investment industry. These include the following:

- There is a lack of DLT network standardization, as well as difficulty integrating with legacy systems.
- DLT processing capabilities may not be financially competitive with existing solutions.
- Increasing the scale of DLT systems requires substantial (storage) resources.
- Immutability of transactions means accidental or "canceled" trades can be undone only by submitting an equal and offsetting trade.
- DLT requires huge amounts of computer power normally associated with high electricity usage.
- Regulatory approaches may differ by jurisdiction.

SUMMARY

- The term "fintech" refers to technological innovation in the design and delivery of financial services and products.

- Areas of fintech development include the analysis of large datasets, analytical techniques, automated trading, automated advice, and financial record keeping.
- Big Data is characterized by the three Vs—volume, velocity, and variety—and includes both traditional and non-traditional (or alternative) datasets.
- Among the main sources of alternative data are data generated by individuals, business processes, and sensors.
- Artificial intelligence computer systems are capable of performing tasks that traditionally required human intelligence at levels comparable (or superior) to those of human beings.
- Machine learning seeks to extract knowledge from large amounts of data by "learning" from known examples and then generating structure or predictions. Simply put, ML algorithms aim to "find the pattern, apply the pattern." Main types of ML include supervised learning, unsupervised learning, and deep learning.
- Natural language processing is an application of text analytics that uses insight into the structure of human language to analyze and interpret text- and voice-based data.
- Robo-advisory services are providing automated advisory services to increasing numbers of retail investors. Services include asset allocation, portfolio optimization, trade execution, rebalancing, and tax strategies.
- Big Data and ML techniques may provide insights into real-time and changing market circumstances to help identify weakening or adverse trends in advance, allowing for improved risk management and investment decision-making.
- Algorithmic traders use automated trading programs to determine when, where, and how to trade an order on the basis of pre-specified rules and market conditions. Benefits include speed of executions, lower trading costs, and anonymity.
- Blockchain and distributed ledger technology (DLT) may offer a new way to store, record, and track financial assets on a secure, distributed basis. Applications include cryptocurrencies and tokenization. Additionally, DLT may bring efficiencies to post-trade and compliance processes through automation, smart contracts, and identity verification.

PRACTICE PROBLEMS

1. A correct description of fintech is that it:
    A. is driven by rapid growth in data and related technological advances.
    B. increases the need for intermediaries.
    C. is at its most advanced state using systems that follow specified rules and instructions.

2. A characteristic of Big Data is that:
    A. one of its traditional sources is business processes.
    B. it involves formats with diverse types of structures.
    C. real-time communication of it is uncommon due to vast content.

3. In the use of machine learning (ML):
    A. some techniques are termed "black box" due to data biases.
    B. human judgment is not needed because algorithms continuously learn from data.
    C. training data can be learned too precisely, resulting in inaccurate predictions when used with different datasets.

4. Text Analytics is appropriate for application to:
   A. economic trend analysis.
   B. large, structured datasets.
   C. public but not private information.

5. In providing investment services, robo-advisers are *most likely* to:
   A. rely on their cost effectiveness to pursue active strategies.
   B. offer fairly conservative advice as easily accessible guidance.
   C. be free from regulation when acting as fully-automated wealth managers.

6. Which of the following statements on fintech's use of data as part of risk analysis is correct?
   A. Stress testing requires precise inputs and excludes qualitative data.
   B. Machine learning ensures that traditional and alternative data are fully segregated.
   C. For real-time risk monitoring, data may be aggregated for reporting and used as model inputs.

7. A factor associated with the widespread adoption of algorithmic trading is increased:
   A. market efficiency.
   B. average trade sizes.
   C. trading destinations.

8. A benefit of distributed ledger technology (DLT) favoring its use by the investment industry is its:
   A. scalability of underlying systems.
   B. ease of integration with existing systems.
   C. streamlining of current post-trade processes.

9. What is a distributed ledger technology (DLT) application suited for physical assets?
   A. Tokenization
   B. Cryptocurrencies
   C. Permissioned networks

CHAPTER 3

CAPITAL MARKET EXPECTATIONS, PART 1: FRAMEWORK AND MACRO CONSIDERATIONS

Christopher D. Piros, PhD, CFA

Parts of this chapter have been adapted from a former Capital Market Expectations chapter authored by John P. Calverley; Alan M. Meder, CPA, CFA; Brian D. Singer, CFA; and Renato Staub, PhD

LEARNING OUTCOMES

The candidate should be able to:

- discuss the role of, and a framework for, capital market expectations in the portfolio management process;
- discuss challenges in developing capital market forecasts;
- explain how exogenous shocks may affect economic growth trends;
- discuss the application of economic growth trend analysis to the formulation of capital market expectations;
- compare major approaches to economic forecasting;
- discuss how business cycles affect short- and long-term expectations;
- explain the relationship of inflation to the business cycle and the implications of inflation for cash, bonds, equity, and real estate returns;
- discuss the effects of monetary and fiscal policy on business cycles;
- interpret the shape of the yield curve as an economic predictor and discuss the relationship between the yield curve and fiscal and monetary policy;
- identify and interpret macroeconomic, interest rate, and exchange rate linkages between economies.

Portfolio Management, Second Edition, by Christopher D. Piros, PhD, CFA. Copyright © 2019 by CFA Institute.

1. INTRODUCTION

A noted investment authority has written that the "fundamental law of investing is the uncertainty of the future."[1] Investors have no choice but to forecast elements of the future because nearly all investment decisions look toward it. Specifically, investment decisions incorporate the decision maker's expectations concerning factors and events believed to affect investment values. The decision maker integrates these views into expectations about the risk and return prospects of individual assets and groups of assets.

This chapter's focus is **capital market expectations** (CME): expectations concerning the risk and return prospects of asset classes, however broadly or narrowly the investor defines those asset classes. Capital market expectations are an essential input to formulating a strategic asset allocation. For example, if an investor's investment policy statement specifies and defines eight permissible asset classes, the investor will need to have formulated long-term expectations concerning each of those asset classes. The investor may also act on short-term expectations. Insights into capital markets gleaned during CME setting should also help in formulating the expectations concerning individual assets that are needed in security selection and valuation.

This is the first of two chapters on capital market expectations. A central theme of both chapters is that a disciplined approach to setting expectations will be rewarded. With that in mind, Section 2 of this chapter presents a general framework for developing capital market expectations and alerts the reader to the range of problems and pitfalls that await investors and analysts in this arena. Section 3 focuses on the use of macroeconomic analysis in setting expectations. The second of the two CME chapters builds on this foundation to address setting expectations for specific asset classes: equities, fixed income, real estate, and currencies. Various analytical tools are reviewed as needed throughout both chapters.

2. FRAMEWORK AND CHALLENGES

In this section, we provide a guide to collecting, organizing, combining, and interpreting investment information. After outlining the process, we turn to a discussion of typical problems and challenges to formulating the most informed judgments possible.

Before laying out the framework, we must be clear about what it needs to accomplish. The ultimate objective is to develop a set of projections with which to make informed investment decisions, specifically asset allocation decisions. As obvious as this goal may seem, it has important implications.

Asset allocation is the primary determinant of long-run portfolio performance.[2] The projections underlying these decisions are among the most important determinants of whether investors achieve their long-term goals. It thus follows that it is vital to get the long-run *level* of returns (approximately) right. Until the late 1990s, it was standard practice for institutional investors to extrapolate historical return data into forecasts. At the height of the

---

[1]Peter L. Bernstein in the foreword to Rapaport and Mauboussin (2001), p. xiii.
[2]See Brinson, Hood, and Beebower (1986) and Ibbotson and Kaplan (2000).

technology bubble,[3] this practice led many to project double-digit portfolio returns into the indefinite future. Such inflated projections allowed institutions to underfund their obligations and/or set unrealistic goals, many of which have had to be scaled back. Since that time, most institutions have adopted explicitly forward-looking methods of the type(s) discussed in our two CME chapters, and return projections have declined sharply. Indeed, as of the beginning of 2018, consensus rate of return projections seemed to imply that US private foundations, which must distribute at least 5% of assets annually, could struggle to prudently generate long-run returns sufficient to cover their required distributions, their expenses, and inflation. To reiterate, projecting a realistic overall level of returns has to be a top priority.

As appealing as it is to think we could project asset returns with precision, that idea is unrealistic. Even the most sophisticated methods are likely to be subject to frustratingly large forecast errors over relevant horizons. We should, of course, seek to limit our forecast errors. We should not, however, put undue emphasis on the precision of projections for individual asset classes. Far more important objectives are to ensure internal consistency across asset classes (**cross-sectional consistency**) and over various time horizons (**intertemporal consistency**). This emphasis stems once again from the primary use of the projections—asset allocation decisions. Inconsistency across asset classes is likely to result in portfolios with poor risk–return characteristics over any horizon, whereas intertemporal inconsistency is likely to distort the connection between portfolio decisions and investment horizon.

Our discussion adopts the perspective of an analyst or team responsible for developing projections to be used by the firm's investment professionals in advising and/or managing portfolios for its clients. As the setting of explicit capital market expectations has become both more common and more sophisticated, many asset managers have adopted this centralized approach, enabling them to leverage the requisite expertise and deliver more consistent advice to all their clients.

2.1. A Framework for Developing Capital Market Expectations

The following is a framework for a disciplined approach to setting CME.

1. *Specify the set of expectations needed, including the time horizon(s) to which they apply.* This step requires the analyst to formulate an explicit list of the asset classes and investment horizon(s) for which projections are needed.
2. *Research the historical record.* Most forecasts have some connection to the past. For many markets, the historical record contains useful information on the asset's investment characteristics, suggesting at least some possible ranges for future results. Beyond the raw historical facts, the analyst should seek to identify and understand the factors that affect asset class returns.
3. *Specify the method(s) and/or model(s) to be used and their information requirements.* The analyst or team responsible for developing CME should be explicit about the method(s) and/or model(s) that will be used and should be able to justify the selection.
4. *Determine the best sources for information needs.* The analyst or team must identify those sources that provide the most accurate and timely information tailored to their needs.

---

[3]Explosive growth of the internet in the late 1990s was accompanied by soaring valuations for virtually any internet-related investment. The NASDAQ composite index, which was very heavily weighted in technology stocks, nearly quintupled from 1997 to early 2000, then gave up all of those gains by mid-2002. A variety of names have been given to this episode including the tech or technology bubble.

5. *Interpret the current investment environment using the selected data and methods, applying experience and judgment.* Care should be taken to apply a common set of assumptions, compatible methodologies, and consistent judgments in order to ensure mutually consistent projections across asset classes and over time horizons.
6. *Provide the set of expectations needed, documenting conclusions.* The projections should be accompanied by the reasoning and assumptions behind them.
7. *Monitor actual outcomes and compare them with expectations, providing feedback to improve the expectations-setting process.* The most effective practice is likely to synchronize this step with the expectations-setting process, monitoring and reviewing outcomes on the same cycle as the projections are updated, although several cycles may be required to validate conclusions.

The first step in the CME framework requires the analyst to define the universe of asset classes for which she will develop expectations. The universe should include all of the asset classes that will typically be accorded a distinct allocation in client portfolios. To put it another way, the universe needs to reflect the key dimensions of decision-making in the firm's investment process. On the other hand, the universe should be as small as possible because even pared down to minimum needs, the expectations-setting process can be quite challenging.

Steps 2 and 3 in the process involve understanding the historical performance of the asset classes and researching their return drivers. The information that needs to be collected mirrors considerations that defined the universe of assets in step 1. The more granular the classification of assets, the more granular the breakdown of information will need to be to support the investment process. Except in the simplest of cases, the analyst will need to slice the data in multiple dimensions. Among these are the following:

- Geography: global, regional, domestic versus non-domestic, economic blocs (e.g., the European Union), individual countries;
- Major asset classes: equity, fixed-income, real assets;
- Sub-asset classes:
  o Equities: styles, sizes, sectors, industries;
  o Fixed income: maturities, credit quality, securitization, fixed versus floating, nominal or inflation-protected;
  o Real assets: real estate, commodities, timber.

How each analyst approaches this task depends on the hierarchy of decisions in their investment process. One firm may prioritize segmenting the global equity market by Global Industry Classification Standard (GIC) sector, with geographic distinctions accorded secondary consideration, while another firm prioritizes decisions with respect to geography considering sector breakdowns as secondary.[4]

In Step 3, the analyst needs to be sensitive to the fact that both the effectiveness of forecasting approaches and relationships among variables are related to the investor's time horizon. As an example, a discounted cash flow approach to setting equity market expectations is usually considered to be most appropriate to long-range forecasting. If forecasts are also to be made for shorter, finite horizons, intertemporal consistency dictates that the method used for those projections must be calibrated so that its projections converge to the long-range forecast as the horizon extends.

---

[4]There is extensive literature on the relative importance of country versus industry factors in global equity markets. Marcelo, Quiros, and Martins (2013) summarized the evidence as "vast and contradictory."

Executing the fourth step—determining the best information sources—requires researching the quality of alternative data sources and striving to fully understand the data. Using flawed or misunderstood data is a recipe for faulty analysis. Furthermore, analysts should be alert to new, superior data sources. Large, commercially available databases and reputable financial publications are likely the best avenue for obtaining widely disseminated information covering the broad spectrum of asset classes and geographies. Trade publications, academic studies, government and central bank reports, corporate filings, and broker/dealer and third-party research often provide more specialized information. Appropriate data frequencies must be selected. Daily series are of more use for setting shorter-term expectations. Monthly, quarterly, or annual data series are useful for setting longer-term CME.

The first four steps lay the foundation for the heart of the process: the fifth and sixth steps. Monitoring and interpreting the economic and market environment and assessing the implications for relevant investments are activities the analyst should be doing every day. In essence, step five could be labeled "implement your investment/research process" and step six could be labeled "at designated times, synthesize, document, and defend your views." Perhaps what most distinguishes these steps from the day-to-day investment process is that the analyst must make simultaneous projections for all asset classes and all designated, concrete horizons.

Finally, in step 7 we use experience to improve the expectations-setting process. We measure our previously formed expectations against actual results to assess the level of accuracy the process is delivering. Generally, good forecasts are:

- unbiased, objective, and well researched;
- efficient, in the sense of minimizing the size of forecast errors; and
- internally consistent, both cross-sectionally and intertemporally.

Although it is important to monitor outcomes for ways in which our forecasting process can be improved, our ability to assess the accuracy of our forecasts may be severely limited. A standard rule of thumb in statistics is that we need at least 30 observations to meaningfully test a hypothesis. Quantitative evaluation of forecast errors in real time may be of limited value in refining a process that is already reasonably well constructed (i.e., not subject to obvious gross errors). Hence, the most valuable part of the feedback loop will often be qualitative and judgmental.

EXAMPLE 1   Capital Market Expectations Setting: Information Requirements

Consider two investment strategists charged with developing capital market expectations for their firms, John Pearson and Michael Wu. Pearson works for a bank trust department that runs US balanced separately managed accounts (SMAs) for high-net-worth individuals. These accounts' mandates restrict investments to US equities, US investment-grade fixed-income instruments, and prime US money market instruments. The investment objective is long-term capital growth and income. In contrast, Wu works for a large Hong Kong SAR–based, internationally focused asset manager that uses the following types of assets within its investment process:

Equities	Fixed Income	Alternative Investments
Asian equities	Eurozone sovereign	Eastern European
Eurozone	US government	venture capital
US large-cap		New Zealand timber
US small-cap		US commercial real
Canadian large-cap		estate

Wu's firm runs SMAs with generally long-term time horizons and global tactical asset allocation (GTAA) programs. Compare and contrast the information and knowledge requirements of Pearson and Wu.

Guideline answer:
Pearson's in-depth information requirements relate to US equity and fixed-income markets. By contrast, Wu's information requirements relate not only to US and non-US equity and fixed-income markets but also to three alternative investment types with non-public markets, located on three different continents. Wu has a more urgent need to be current on political, social, economic, and trading-oriented operational details worldwide than Pearson. Given their respective investment time horizons, Pearson's focus is on the long term whereas Wu needs to focus not only on the long term but also on near-term disequilibria among markets (for GTAA decisions). One challenge that Pearson has in US fixed-income markets that Wu does not face is the need to cover corporate and municipal as well as government debt securities. Nevertheless, Wu's overall information and knowledge requirements are clearly more demanding than Pearson's.

2.2. Challenges in Forecasting

A range of problems can frustrate analysts' expectations-setting efforts. Expectations reflecting faulty analysis or assumptions may cause a portfolio manager to construct a portfolio that is inappropriate for the client. At the least, the portfolio manager may incur the costs of changing portfolio composition without any offsetting benefits. The following sections provide guidance on points that warrant special caution. The discussion focuses on problems in the use of data and on analyst mistakes and biases.

2.2.1. Limitations of Economic Data
The analyst needs to understand the definition, construction, timeliness, and accuracy of any data used, including any biases. The time lag with which economic data are collected, processed, and disseminated can impede their use because data that are not timely may be of little value in assessing current conditions. Some economic data may be reported with a lag as short as one week, whereas other important data may be reported with a lag of more than a quarter. The International Monetary Fund sometimes reports data for developing economies with a lag of two years or more. Older data increase the uncertainty concerning the current state of the economy with respect to that variable.

Furthermore, one or more official revisions to initial data values are common. Sometimes these revisions are substantial, which may give rise to significantly different inferences. Often only the most recent data point is revised. Other series are subject to periodic "benchmark revisions" that simultaneously revise all or a portion of the historical data series. In either case— routine updating of the most recent release or benchmark revision—the analyst must be aware that using revised data as if it were known at the time to which it applies often suggests strong historical relationships that are unreliable for forecasting.

Definitions and calculation methods change too. For example, the US Bureau of Labor Statistics (BLS) made significant changes to the Consumer Price Index for All Urban Consumers (CPI-U) in 1983 (treatment of owner-occupied housing) and again in 1991 (regression-based product quality adjustments). Analysts should also be aware that suppliers of economic and financial indexes periodically **re-base** these indexes, meaning that the specific period used as the base of the index is changed. Analysts should take care to avoid inadvertently mixing data relating to different base periods.

2.2.2. Data Measurement Errors and Biases

Analysts need to be aware of possible biases and/or errors in data series, including the following:

- **Transcription errors**. These are errors in gathering and recording data.
- **Survivorship bias**. This bias arises when a data series reflects only entities that survived to the end of the period. Without correction, statistics from such data can be misleading. Data on alternative assets such as hedge funds are notorious for survivorship bias.
- **Appraisal (smoothed) data**. For certain assets without liquid public markets, notably but not only real estate, appraisal data are used in lieu of transaction data. Appraised values tend to be less volatile than market-determined values. As a result, measured volatilities are biased downward and correlations with other assets tend to be understated.

2.2.3. The Limitations of Historical Estimates

Although history is often a helpful guide, the past should not be extrapolated uncritically. There are two primary issues with respect to using historical data. First, the data may not be representative of the future period for which an analyst needs to forecast. Second, even if the data are representative of the future, statistics calculated from that data may be poor estimates of the desired metrics. Both of these issues can be addressed to some extent by imposing structure (that is, a model) on how data is presumed to have been generated in the past and how it is expected to be generated in the future.

Changes in technological, political, legal, and regulatory environments; disruptions such as wars and other calamities; and changes in policy stances can all alter risk–return relationships. Such shifts are known as changes in **regime** (the governing set of relationships) and give rise to the statistical problem of **nonstationarity** (meaning, informally, that different parts of a data series reflect different underlying statistical properties). Statistical tools are available to help identify and model such changes or turning points.

A practical approach for an analyst to decide whether to use the whole of a long data series or only part of it involves answering two questions.

1. Is there any reason to believe that the entirety of the sample period is no longer relevant? In other words, has there been a fundamental regime change (such as political, economic, market, or asset class structure) during the sample period?
2. Do the data support the hypothesis that such a change has occurred?

If the answer to both questions is yes, the analyst should use only that part of the time series that appears relevant to the present. Alternatively, he may apply statistical techniques that account for regime changes in the past data as well as the possibility of subsequent regime changes. Exhibit 1 illustrates examples of changes in regime.

EXHIBIT 1   Regimes and the Relevance of Historical Bond Returns

In the 1970s, oil price shocks combined with accommodative monetary policy by the US Federal Reserve fueled sharply rising inflation. In 1980, the Fed abruptly shifted to an aggressively tight stance. After the initial shock of sharply higher interest rates, US bond yields trended downward for roughly 35 years as the Fed kept downward pressure on inflation. Throughout the 1980s and 1990s, the Fed eased monetary policy in the aftermath of the technology bubble. Then, switching to an extraordinarily expansionary policy in the midst of the 2008–2009 global financial crisis, the Fed reduced its policy rate to 0% in December 2008. Subsequently, it aggressively bought Treasury bonds and mortgage-backed securities. The Fed finally raised its policy rate target in December 2015. In October 2017, it stopped rolling over maturing bonds, allowing its balance sheet to shrink, albeit very slowly. It can be argued that bond returns from the 1970s through 2015 reflect at least three distinct regimes: the inflationary 1970s with accommodative Fed policy, the 1980–2008 period of disinflationary policy and secularly falling yields, and the unprecedented 2009–2015 period of zero interest rates and explosive liquidity provision. As of mid-2018, nominal interest rates were still negative in some developed markets, and major central banks including the Fed were aiming to "normalize" policy over the next few years. There is ample reason to believe that future bond returns will reflect a regime like none before.

In general, the analyst should use the longest data history for which there is reasonable assurance of stationarity. This guideline follows from the fact that sample statistics from a longer history are more precise than those with fewer observations. Although it is tempting to assume that using higher-frequency data (e.g., monthly rather than annual observations) will also provide more precise estimates, this assumption is not necessarily true. Although higher-frequency data improve the precision of sample variances, covariances, and correlations, they do *not* improve the precision of the sample mean.

When many variables are considered, a large number of observations may be a statistical necessity. For example, to calculate a sample covariance matrix, the number of observations must exceed the number of variables (assets). Otherwise, some asset combinations (i.e., portfolios) will spuriously appear to have zero volatility. This problem arises frequently in investment analysis, and a remedy is available. Covariance matrices are routinely estimated even for huge numbers of assets by assuming that returns are driven by a smaller set of common factors plus uncorrelated asset-specific components.

As the frequency of observations increases, the likelihood increases that data may be asynchronous (i.e., not simultaneous or concurrent in time) across variables. This means that data points for different variables may not reflect exactly the same period even though they are labeled as if they do. For example, daily data from different countries are typically asynchronous because of time zone differences. Asynchronicity can be a significant problem for daily, and perhaps even weekly data, because it distorts measured correlations and induces lead–lag relationships that might not exist if the data were measured synchronously. Lower-frequency data (e.g., monthly or quarterly) are less susceptible to asynchrony, although it can still arise. For example, two series that are released and labeled as monthly could reflect data collected at different times of the month.

As a final note on historical data, some care should be taken with respect to whether data are normally distributed. Historical asset returns, in particular, routinely exhibit skewness and "fat tails," which cause them to fail formal tests of normality. The cost in terms of analytical complexity of accounting for non-normality, however, can be quite high. As a practical matter, the added complexity is often not worth the cost.[5]

2.2.4. *Ex Post* Risk Can Be a Biased Measure of *Ex Ante* Risk

In interpreting historical prices and returns over a given sample period, the analyst needs to evaluate whether asset prices reflected the possibility of a very negative event that did not materialize during the period. This phenomenon is often referred to as the "peso problem." Looking backward, we are likely to underestimate *ex ante* risk and overestimate *ex ante* anticipated returns. The key point is that high *ex post* returns that reflect fears of adverse events that did not materialize provide a poor estimate of *ex ante* expected returns.

The 1970s Peso Devaluation

In the mid-1970s, the Mexican peso was pegged to the US dollar, but peso-denominated interest rates were persistently well above corresponding dollar rates because investors feared the Mexican government would devalue the peso. In 1976, the peso was indeed devalued by nearly 50%, but data from before that event would suggest that holding the peso was a high expected return, low risk strategy.

The opposite situation is also a problem, especially for risk measures that consider only the subset of worst-case outcomes (e.g., value at risk, or VaR). If our data series includes even one observation of a rare event, we may substantially overstate the likelihood of such events happening in the future. Within a finite sample, the observed frequency of this bad outcome will far exceed its true probability. As a simple example, there were 21 trading days in July 2018. On 26 July, the price of Facebook stock closed down 19%. Based on this sample, the (interpolated) daily 5% VaR on Facebook stock is 17.3%. That is, an investor in Facebook shares would expect to lose at least 17.3% once every 20 days.

---

[5]See Chapter 5 of Stewart, Piros, and Heisler (forthcoming 2019) for discussion of the effect of alternative probability distributions on asset allocation decisions.

2.2.5. Biases in Analysts' Methods

Analysts naturally search for relationships that will help in developing better capital market expectations. Among the preventable biases that the analyst may introduce are the following:

- **Data-mining bias** arises from repeatedly searching a dataset until a statistically significant pattern emerges. It is almost inevitable that some relationship will appear. Such patterns cannot be expected to have predictive value. Lack of an explicit economic rationale for a variable's usefulness is a warning sign of a data-mining problem: no story, no future.[6] Of course, the analyst must be wary of inventing the story after discovering the relationship and bear in mind that correlation does not imply causation.
- **Time-period bias** relates to results that are period specific. Research findings often turn out to be sensitive to the selection of specific starting and/or ending dates.

Small Cap Outperformance and Time-Period Bias

Evidence suggesting that small-cap stocks outperform large-cap stocks over time (the so-called small firm effect) is very sensitive to the choice of sample period. From 1926 through 1974, US small-cap stocks outperformed large caps by 0.43% per year, but if we skip the Great Depression and start in 1932, the differential becomes 3.49% per year. Similarly, small caps outperformed by 3.46% per year from 1975 through 2016 but by only 0.09% per year from 1984 through 2016. In the nine years from 1975 through 1983, small caps outperformed by 16.85% per year![7]

How might analysts avoid using an irrelevant variable in a forecasting model? The analyst should scrutinize the variable selection process for data-mining bias and be able to provide an economic rationale for the variable's usefulness in a forecasting model. A further practical check is to examine the forecasting relationship out of sample (i.e., on data that was not used to estimate the relationship).

2.2.6. The Failure to Account for Conditioning Information

The discussion of regimes introduced the notion that assets' risk and return characteristics vary with the economic and market environment. That fact explains why economic analysis is important in expectation setting. The analyst should not ignore relevant information or analysis in formulating expectations. Unconditional forecasts, which dilute this information by averaging over environments, can lead to misperception of prospective risk and return. Exhibit 2 illustrates how an analyst may use conditioning information.

---

[6]See McQueen and Thorley (1999).
[7]Source: Ibbotson Associates database (Morningstar). Returns calculated by the author.

EXHIBIT 2   Incorporating Conditioning Information

Noah Sota uses the CAPM to set capital market expectations. He estimates that one asset class has a beta of 0.8 in economic expansions and 1.2 in recessions. The expected return on the market is 12% in an expansion and 4% in a recession. The risk-free rate is assumed to be constant at 2%. Expansion and recession are equally likely. Sota aims to calculate the unconditional expected return for the asset class.

The conditional expected returns on the asset are 10% = 2% + 0.8 × (12% − 2%) in an expansion and 4.4% = 2% + 1.2 × (4% − 2%) in a recession. Weighting by the probabilities of expansion and recession, the unconditional expected return is 7.2% = [(0.5 × 10%) + (0.5 × 4.4%)].

EXAMPLE 2   Ignoring Conditioning Information

Following on from the scenario in Exhibit 2, one of Noah Sota's colleagues suggests an alternative approach to calculate the unconditional expected return for the asset class. His method is to calculate the unconditional beta to be used in the CAPM formula, 1.0 = (0.5 × 0.8) + (0.5 × 1.2). He then works out the unconditional expected return on the market portfolio, 8% = (0.5 × 12%) + (0.5 × 4%). Finally, using the unconditional beta and the unconditional market return, he calculates the unconditional expected return on the asset class as 8.0% = 2.0% + 1.0 × (8% − 2%).

Explain why the alternative approach is right or wrong.

Guideline answer:
The approach suggested by Sota's colleague is wrong. It ignores the fact that the market excess return and the asset's beta vary with the business cycle. The expected return of 8% calculated this way would overestimate the (unconditional) expected return on this asset class. Such a return forecast would ignore the fact that the beta differs for expansion (0.8) and recession (1.2).

2.2.7. Misinterpretation of Correlations

When a variable *A* is found to be significantly correlated with another variable *B*, there are at least four possible explanations: (1) A predicts B, (2) B predicts A, (3) a third variable C predicts both A and B, or (4) the relationship is spurious. The observed correlation alone does not allow us to distinguish among these situations. Consequently, correlation relationships should not be used in a predictive model without investigating the underlying linkages.

Although apparently significant correlations can be spurious, it is also true that lack of a strong correlation can be misleading. A negligible measured correlation may reflect a strong but *nonlinear* relationship. Analysts should explore this possibility if they have a solid reason for believing a relationship exists.

2.2.8. Psychological Biases

The behavioral finance literature documents a long and growing list of psychological biases that can affect investment decisions. Only a few of the more prominent ones that could undermine the analyst's ability to make accurate and unbiased forecasts are outlined here. Furthermore, note that the literature contains various names and definitions of behavioral biases, which are not necessarily mutually exclusive.

- **Anchoring bias** is the tendency to give disproportionate weight to the first information received or first number envisioned, which is then adjusted. Such adjustment is often insufficient, and approximations are consequently biased. Analysts can try to avoid anchoring bias by consciously attempting to avoid premature conclusions.
- **Status quo bias** reflects the tendency for forecasts to perpetuate recent observations—that is, to avoid making changes and preserve the status quo, and/or to accept a default option. This bias may reflect greater pain from errors of commission (making a change) than from errors of omission (doing nothing). Status quo bias can be mitigated by disciplined effort to avoid "anchoring" on the status quo.
- **Confirmation bias** is the tendency to seek and overweight evidence or information that confirms one's existing or preferred beliefs and to discount evidence that contradicts those beliefs. This bias can be mitigated by examining all evidence with equal rigor and/or debating with a knowledgeable person capable of arguing against one's own views.
- **Overconfidence bias** is unwarranted confidence in one's own intuitive reasoning, judgment, knowledge, and/or ability. This bias may lead an analyst to overestimate the accuracy of her forecasts and/or fail to consider a sufficiently broad range of possible outcomes or scenarios. Analysts may not only fail to fully account for uncertainty about which they are aware (sometimes described as "known unknowns") but they also are very likely to ignore the possibility of uncertainties about which they are not even aware (sometimes described as "unknown unknowns").
- **Prudence bias** reflects the tendency to temper forecasts so that they do not appear extreme or the tendency to be overly cautious in forecasting. In decision-making contexts, one may be too cautious when making decisions that could damage one's career or reputation. This bias can be mitigated by conscious effort to identify plausible scenarios that would give rise to more extreme outcomes and to give greater weight to such scenarios in the forecast.
- **Availability bias** is the tendency to be overly influenced by events that have left a strong impression and/or for which it is easy to recall an example. Recent events may likewise be overemphasized. The effect of this bias can be mitigated by attempting to base conclusions on objective evidence and analytical procedures.

EXAMPLE 3   Biases in Forecasting and Decision-Making

Cynthia Casey is a London-based investment adviser with a clientele of ultra-high-net-worth individuals in the UK, the US, and the EU. Within the equity portion of her portfolios, she rarely deviates significantly from the country weightings of the MSCI World Index, even though more often than not she tilts the allocation in the right direction. Hence, she can claim a good tactical track record despite having added little value in terms of return through tactical allocation. Because most investors have an implicit "home bias," her European clients tend to view their portfolios as significantly overweight the US (nearly 50% of the World index) and are happy because the US market outperformed the MSCI World ex-US Index by about 4% per year over the 10 years ending September 2018. Conversely, her US clients are unhappy because Casey persistently projected US outperformance but maintained what they instinctively perceive as a significant underweight in the United States. Citing year-to-date performance as of 28 September 2018—US up 9%, World ex-US down 1%, with 10 of 15 European markets down in local currencies—Casey's US clients are pressuring her to aggressively increase allocations to US equities. Although experience has taught her to be wary of chasing a strong market, Casey vividly remembers losing clients in the late 1990s because she doubted that the explosive rally in technology stocks would be sustained. With that in mind, she has looked for and found a rationale for a bullish view on US stocks—very robust year-to-date earnings growth.

What psychological biases are Casey and her clients exhibiting?

Guideline answer:

Casey's clients are implicitly anchoring their expectations on the performance of their respective domestic markets. In pressing Casey to increase the allocation to US stocks based on recent outperformance, her US clients are clearly projecting continuation of the trend, a status quo bias. Casey herself is exhibiting several biases. Prudence bias is apparent in the fact that she has a good record of projecting the correct direction of relative performance among markets but has not translated that into reallocations large enough to add meaningful value. We cannot assess whether that bias affects the magnitude of her forecasts, the extent to which she responds to the opportunities, or both. Losing clients when she doubted the sustainability of the late 1990s technology rally made a very strong impression on Casey, so much so that she has apparently convinced herself to look for a reason to believe the recent relative performance trends will persist. This is indicative of availability bias. Searching for evidence to support a favored view (continued strength of the US market) is a clear sign of confirmation bias, whereas finding support for that view in the recent strength of earnings growth reflects status quo bias.

2.2.9. Model Uncertainty

The analyst usually encounters at least three kinds of uncertainty in conducting an analysis. **Model uncertainty** pertains to whether a selected model is structurally and/or conceptually correct. **Parameter uncertainty** arises because a quantitative model's parameters are invariably estimated with error. **Input uncertainty** concerns whether the inputs are correct. Any or all of these may give rise to erroneous forecasts and/or cause the unwary analyst to overestimate the accuracy and reliability of his forecasts.

The effects of parameter uncertainty can be mitigated through due attention to estimation errors. Input uncertainty arises primarily from the need to proxy for an unobservable variable such as "the market portfolio" in the CAPM. Whether or not this is a serious issue depends on the context. It is a problem if the analyst wants to test the validity of the underlying theory or identify "anomalies" relative to the model. It is less of an issue if the analyst is merely focused on useful empirical relationships rather than proof of concept/ theory. Model uncertainty is potentially the most serious issue because the wrong model may lead an analyst to fundamentally flawed conclusions.

Our discussion of the limitations of historical data touched on a model that led many investors far astray in the late 1990s. Up to that point, the implicit model used by many, if not most, institutional investors for setting long-term equity expectations was, "The *ex ante* expected return is, was, and always will be a constant number μ, and the best estimate of that number is the mean over the longest sample available." As the market soared in the late 1990s, the historical estimate of μ rose steadily, leading investors to shift more heavily into equities, which fueled further price appreciation and more reallocation toward equities, and so on, until the technology bubble burst. Ironically, belief in the sanctity of historical estimates coincided with the diametrically opposed notion that the "new economy" made historical economic and market relationships obsolete. There seemed to be no limits to growth or to valuations, at least in some segments of the market. But, of course, there were. This description of the technology bubble illustrates the breakdown of a particular forecasting model. It is not a literal description of anyone's thought process. For various reasons, however —competitive pressures, status quo/availability/prudence biases—many investors acted *as if* they were following the model.

Another flawed model unraveled during the global financial crisis of 2007–2009. One component of that model was the notion that housing price declines are geographically isolated events: There was no risk of a nationwide housing slump. A second component involved "originate to sell" loan pipelines: businesses that made loans with the intention of immediately selling them to investors and therefore had very little incentive to vet loan quality. A third component was the notion that the macro risk of an ever-growing supply of increasingly poor-quality mortgages could be diversified away by progressive layers of securitization. End investors were implicitly sold the notion that the securities were low risk because numerous computer simulations showed that the "micro" risk of individual loans was well diversified. The macro risk of a housing crisis, however, was not reflected in prices and yields—until, of course, the model proved to be flawed. The scenario highlighted here provides another illustration of a particular model breaking down. In this case, it was a flawed model of risk and diversification, and its breakdown was one of many aspects of the financial crisis.

3. ECONOMIC AND MARKET ANALYSIS

The previous section outlined various pitfalls in forecasting. Each of these is important. Yet they pale in comparison to a fundamental mistake: losing sight of the fact that investment outcomes are inherently linked to the economy. The technology bubble and the global financial crisis offer two extreme illustrations of the consequences of falling into this trap. Less dramatic, but still consequential, instances of this mistake regularly contribute to the differential investment performance that separates "winners" and "losers." The remainder of this chapter is dedicated to effective incorporation of economic and market analysis into capital market expectations.

3.1. The Role of Economic Analysis

History has shown that there is a direct yet variable relationship among actual realized asset returns, expectations for future asset returns, and economic activity. Analysts need to be familiar with the historical relationships that empirical research has uncovered concerning the direction, strength, and lead–lag relationships between economic variables and capital market returns.

The analyst who understands which economic variables may be most relevant to the current economic environment has a competitive advantage, as does the analyst who can discern or forecast changes in acceleration and deceleration of a trend.

Economic output has both cyclical and trend growth components. Trend growth is of obvious relevance for setting long-term return expectations for asset classes such as equities. Cyclical variation affects variables such as corporate profits and interest rates, which are directly related to asset class returns and risk. In the following sections, we address trend growth, business cycles, the role of monetary and fiscal policies, and international interactions.

3.2. Analysis of Economic Growth

The economic growth trend is the long-term average growth path of GDP around which the economy experiences semi-regular business cycles. The analyst needs to understand and analyze both the trend and the cycles. Though each could exist without the other, they are related.

It might seem that trends are inherently easier to forecast than cycles. After all, trends are about long-term averages, whereas cycles are about shorter-term movements and turning points. The assumption that trends are easier to forecast would be true if trend growth rates were constant. But trend growth rates do change, which is what makes forecasting them relevant for investment analysis. Some changes are fairly easy to forecast because they are driven by slowly evolving and easily observable factors such as demographics. Trend changes that arise from significant "exogenous shocks" to underlying economic and/or market relationships are not only impossible to foresee but also difficult to identify, assess, and quantify until the change is well-established and retrospectively revealed in the data. Virtually by definition, the effect of truly exogenous shocks on the level and/or growth rate of the economy will not have been built into asset prices in advance—although the risk of such events will likely have been reflected in prices to some degree.

3.2.1. Exogenous Shocks to Growth

Shocks arise from various sources. Some are purely domestic. Others are transmitted from other parts of the globe. Some are negative for potential growth, while others enhance it. Significant shocks typically arise from the following:

- **Policy changes.** Elements of pro-growth government policies include sound fiscal policy, minimal intrusion on the private sector, encouraging competition within the private sector, support for infrastructure and human capital development, and sound tax policies. Any significant, unexpected change in these policies that is likely to persist will change the expected trend rate of growth. The overhaul of US business taxes at the end of 2017, although not entirely unexpected, was intended to be a pro-growth change in policy. On the other hand, standard economic arguments indicate that erecting trade barriers will diminish trend growth.

- **New products and technologies.** Creation and assimilation of new products, markets, and technologies enhances potential growth. Consider the printing press, steam engine, telegraph and telephone, railroad, automobile, airplane, transistor, random-access memory (RAM), integrated circuits, internet, wireless communication (radio, TV, smartphone), rockets, and satellites, to name just a few.
- **Geopolitics.** Geopolitical conflict has the potential to reduce growth by diverting resources to less economically productive uses (e.g., accumulating and maintaining weapons, discouraging beneficial trade). The fall of the Berlin wall, which triggered German reunification and a "peace dividend" for governments as they cut defense spending, was a growth-enhancing geopolitical shock. Interestingly, geopolitical tensions (e.g., the space race) can also spur innovation that results in growth-enhancing technologies.
- **Natural disasters.** Natural disasters destroy productive capacity. In the short run, a disaster is likely to reduce growth, but it may actually enhance long-run growth if old capacity is replaced with more efficient facilities.
- **Natural resources/critical inputs.** Discovery of new natural resources or of new ways to recover them (e.g., fracking) can be expected to enhance potential growth, directly via production of those resources and indirectly by reducing the cost of production for other products. Conversely, sustained reduction in the supply of important resources diminishes growth (e.g., the OPEC oil shock in 1973).
- **Financial crises.** The financial system allows the economy to channel resources to their most efficient use. Financial crises arise when market participants lose confidence in others' ability (or willingness) to meet their obligations and cease to provide funding—first to specific counterparties and then more broadly as potential losses cascade through the system. As discussed in Exhibit 3, a financial crisis may affect both the level of output and the trend growth rate.

EXHIBIT 3   Trend Growth after a Financial Crisis

An extensive study of growth and debt dynamics in the wake of the 2007–2009 global financial crisis identified three types of crises:

- Type 1: A persistent (permanent, one-time) decline in the level of output, but the subsequent trend rate of growth is unchanged.
- Type 2: No persistent decline in the level of output, but the subsequent trend rate of growth is reduced.
- Type 3: Both a persistent decline in the level of output and a reduction in the subsequent trend rate of growth.

The Eurozone experienced a sharp, apparently permanent drop in output after the global financial crisis, and subsequent growth was markedly lower than before the crisis, suggesting a Type 3 crisis.

The Eurozone's stagnant growth may be traced to structural problems in conjunction with policy missteps. Structural issues included rigid labor markets, a relatively rapid aging of the population, legal and regulatory barriers, cultural differences among countries, use of a common currency in dissimilar economies, and lack of a unified fiscal policy. In terms of policy response, the European Central Bank was slow to cut rates, was slow to expand its balance sheet, and failed to sustain that expansion. Insolvent banks were allowed to remain operational, thwarting deleveraging of the financial system. In part as the result of a lack of fiscal integration that would have facilitated cross-country transfers, several countries were forced to adopt drastic budget cuts that magnified the impact on their particular economies, the differential impact across countries, and the consequences of structural impediments.

Note: See Luigi Buttiglione, Philip R. Lane, Lucrezia Reichlin, and Vincent Reinhart, "Deleveraging? What Deleveraging?", September 2014, International Center for Monetary and Banking Studies.

It should be clear that any of the shocks listed would likely constitute a "regime change" as discussed earlier.

EXAMPLE 4   Impact of Exogenous Shocks on Trend Growth

Philippe Leblanc, an analyst focusing on economic forecasting, recently read about a discovery by scientists at a major university that may allow the efficiency of solar panels to double every two to three years, a result similar to Moore's Law with respect to computer chips. In further reading, he found new research at Tsinghua University that may rapidly increase the distance over which electricity can be transmitted.

What implications should Leblanc draw with regard to growth trends if either, or both, of these developments come to fruition? What government policy changes might offset the impact?

Guideline answer:
Either of these developments would be expected to increase trend growth. They would be especially powerful together. Rapid increases in solar panel efficiency would drive down the cost of energy over time, especially in areas with long days and intense sunlight. The closer to the equator, the larger the potential effect. The developments would also make it increasingly possible to bring large-scale power production to remote areas, thereby expanding the range and scale of economically viable businesses in those areas. Extending the range of electrical transmission would allow moving lower-cost energy (regardless of how it is generated) to where it is most efficiently used. A variety of government actions could undermine the pro-growth nature of these developments; for example, tariffs on solar panels, restrictions on electrical transmission lines, subsidies to support less efficient energy sources, failure to protect intellectual property rights, or prohibition on transfer of technology.

3.2.2. Application of Growth Analysis to Capital Market Expectations

The expected trend rate of economic growth is a key consideration in a variety of contexts. First, it is an important input to discounted cash flow models of expected return. The trend growth rate imposes discipline on forecasts of fundamental metrics such as earnings because these must be kept consistent with aggregate long-run growth at the trend rate. Second, a country with a higher trend rate of growth may offer equity investors a particularly good return if that growth has not already been priced into the market. Third, a higher trend rate of growth in the economy allows actual growth to be faster before accelerating inflation becomes a significant concern. This fact is especially important in projecting the likely path of monetary policy and bond yields. Fourth, theory implies, and empirical evidence confirms, that the average level of real government bond yields is linked to the trend growth rate. Faster trend growth implies higher average real yields.

Most countries have had periods of faster and slower trend growth during their development. Emerging countries often experience rapid growth as they catch up with the leading industrial countries, but the more developed they become, the more likely it is that their growth will slow.

3.2.2.1. A Decomposition of GDP Growth and Its Use in Forecasting

The simplest way to analyze an economy's aggregate trend growth is to split it into the following components:

- growth from labor inputs, consisting of
  o growth in potential labor force size and
  o growth in actual labor force participation, plus

- growth from labor productivity, consisting of
  o growth from increasing capital inputs and
  o growth in total factor productivity.

Labor input encompasses both the number of workers and the average number of hours they work. Growth in the potential labor force size is driven by demographics such as the population's age distribution, net migration, and workplace norms such as the length of the work week. All of these factors tend to change slowly, making growth in the potential labor force relatively predictable. Trends in net migration and workplace norms, however, may change abruptly in response to sudden structural changes, such as changes in government policies.

Labor force participation primarily reflects labor versus leisure decisions by workers. All else the same, we should expect labor force participation to decline (or at least grow more slowly) as a country becomes more affluent. On the other hand, rising real wages tend to attract workers back into the labor force. Social norms and government policies also play a large role.

Growth in labor productivity comes from investment in additional capital per worker ("capital deepening") and from increases in **total factor productivity** (TFP), which is often taken to be synonymous with technological improvement.[8] Government policy (e.g.,

---

[8]Total factor productivity captures a variety of effects, such as the impact of adding not just *more* physical capital (i.e., "capital deepening") but *better* capital, as well as the impact of increasingly skilled labor (i.e., increases in "human capital"). Earlier chapters provide a more granular breakdown of the drivers/ components of growth.

regulations) can also influence TFP. In historical analyses, TFP is often measured as a "residual"—that is, output growth that is not accounted for by the other factors.

The trend rate of growth in mature, developed markets is generally fairly stable. As a result, extrapolating past trends in the components outlined in the foregoing can be expected to provide a reasonable initial estimate of the future growth trend. This forecast should then be adjusted to reflect observable information indicating how future patterns are likely to differ from past patterns. This same approach can be applied to less developed markets. It must be recognized, however, that these economies are likely to be undergoing rapid structural changes that may require the analyst to make more significant adjustments relative to past trends.

3.2.2.2. Anchoring Asset Returns to Trend Growth

Both theory and empirical evidence indicate that the average level of real (nominal) default-free bond yields is linked to the trend rate of real (nominal) growth.[9] To put it another way, bond yields will be pulled toward this level over time. Thus, the trend rate of growth provides an important anchor for estimating bond returns over horizons long enough for this reversion to prevail over cyclical and short-term forces. Intertemporal consistency demands that this anchor be factored into forecasts even for shorter horizons.

The trend growth rate also provides an anchor for long-run equity appreciation.[10] We can express the aggregate market value of equity, V^e, as the product of three factors: the level of nominal GDP, the share of profits in the economy, S^k (earnings/GDP), and the P/E ratio (PE).

$$V_t^e = \text{GDP}_t \times S_t^k \times PE_t$$

It is clear that over long periods, capital's share of income cannot continually increase or decrease. The same is true for the P/E multiple applied to earnings. As a result, in the long run, the growth rate of the total value of equity in an economy is linked to the growth rate of GDP. Over finite horizons, the way in which the share of capital and the P/E multiple are expected to change will also affect the forecast of the total value of equity, as well as its corresponding growth rate over that period.

This argument applies to the capital appreciation component of equity returns. It does not supply a way to estimate the other component: the dividend yield. An estimate for the dividend yield (annual dividends/market value) can be obtained by noting that the dividend yield equals the dividend payout ratio (dividends/profit) divided by the profit multiple (market value/profit). The analyst may set any two of these three ratios and infer the third.

EXAMPLE 5   Long-Run Equity Returns and Economic Growth

In January 2000, Alena Bjornsdottir, CFA, was updating her firm's projections for US equity returns. The firm had always used the historical average return with little adjustment. Bjornsdottir was aware that historical averages are subject to large sampling errors and was especially concerned about this fact because of the sequence of very high returns in the late 1990s. She decided to examine whether US equity returns since

---

[9]With regard to nominal yields and growth, it is assumed that inflation is sufficiently well behaved.

[10]See Stewart, Piros, and Heisler (forthcoming 2019) for more thorough development of these arguments.

World War II had been consistent with economic growth. For the period 1946–1999, the continuously compounded (i.e., logarithmic) return was 12.18% per annum, which reflected the following components:

Real GDP Growth	Inflation	EPS/GDP (Chg)	P/E (Chg)	Dividend Yield
3.14%	4.12%	0.00%	0.95%	3.97%

Questions
1. What conclusion was Bjornsdottir likely to have drawn from this analysis?
2. If she believed that in the long run the US labor input would grow by 0.9% per annum and labor productivity by 1.5%, inflation would be 2.1%, the dividend yield would be 2.25%, and there would be no further growth in P/E, what is likely to have been her baseline projection for continuously compounded long-term US equity returns?
3. In light of her analysis, how might she have adjusted her baseline projection?

Guideline answers:
1. Bjornsdottir is likely have concluded that the post-war stock return exceeded what would have been consistent with growth of the economy. In particular, the rising P/E added 0.95% of "extra" return per year for 54 years, adding 51.3% (= 54 × 0.95%) to the cumulative, continuously compounded return and leaving the market 67% (exp[51.3%] = 1.67) above "fair value."
2. Her baseline projection is likely to have been 6.75% = 0.9% + 1.5% + 2.1% + 2.25%.
3. She is likely to have adjusted her projection downward to some degree to reflect the likelihood that the effect of the P/E would decline toward zero over time. Assuming, for example, that this would occur over 30 years would imply reducing the baseline projection by 1.71% = (51.3%/30) per year.

Note: The P/E impact was actually eliminated by the end of 2005. Had Bjornsdottir anticipated such a rapid correction, she would have needed to reduce her projection by 10.26% = 51.3%/5 per year to −3.51% = 6.75% − 10.26%.

Studies have shown that countries with higher economic growth rates do not reliably generate higher equity market returns.[11] A partial explanation is likely to be that the higher growth rate was already reflected in market prices. The sources of growth may be a second factor. Stock market returns ultimately reflect the rate of return on invested capital. If the capital stock is growing rapidly, the rate of return on invested capital may be driven down. Both of these explanations are consistent with the arguments outlined earlier. High growth need not translate one-for-one into higher return unless it can be expected to continue forever. Declining return on investment essentially means that either

[11]Joachim Klement, "What's Growth Got to Do With It? Equity Returns and Economic Growth," *Journal of Investing* (Summer 2015) is one such study covering 44 countries.

GDP growth slows or profits decline as a share of GDP, or both. And, of course, valuation multiples do matter.

3.3. Approaches to Economic Forecasting

Whereas the trend growth rate is a long-term average and reflects only the supply side of the economy, most macroeconomic forecasting focuses on short- to intermediate-term fluctuations around the trend—that is, the business cycle. These fluctuations are usually ascribed primarily to shifts in aggregate demand, although shifts in the short-term aggregate supply curve also play a role.

Before discussing the business cycle, we outline the main approaches available for tracking and projecting these movements. There are at least three distinct approaches:

- Econometric models: the most formal and mathematical.
- Indicators: variables that lead, lag, or coincide with turns in the economy.
- Checklists: subjective integration of the answers to relevant questions.

These approaches are not mutually exclusive. Indeed, thorough analysis is likely to incorporate elements of all three.

3.3.1. Econometric Modeling

Econometrics is the application of statistical methods to model relationships among economic variables. **Structural models** specify functional relationships among variables based on economic theory. The functional form and parameters of these models are derived from the underlying theory. **Reduced-form models** have a looser connection to theory. As the name suggests, some such models are simply more compact representations of underlying structural models. At the other end of the spectrum are models that are essentially data driven, with only a heuristic rationale for selection of variables and/or functional forms.

Econometric models vary from small models with a handful of equations to large, complex models with hundreds of equations. They are all used in essentially the same way, however. The estimated system of equations is used to forecast the future values of economic variables, with the forecaster supplying values for the exogenous variables. For example, such a model may require the forecaster to enter exchange rates, interest rates, commodity prices, and/or policy variables. The model then uses the estimated past relationships to forecast the future. It is important to consider that the forecaster's future values for the exogenous variables are themselves subject to estimation error. This fact will increase the variability of potential forecast errors of the endogenous variables beyond what results from errors in the estimated parameter values. The analyst should examine a realistic range of values for the exogenous variables to assess the forecast's sensitivity to these inputs.

Econometric models are widely regarded as very useful for simulating the effects of changes in key variables. The great merit of the econometric approach is that it constrains the forecaster to a certain degree of consistency and also challenges the modeler to reassess prior views based on what the model concludes. It does have important limitations, however. Econometric models require the user to find adequate measures for the real-world activities and relationships to be modeled. These measures may be unavailable. Variables may also be measured with error. Relationships among the variables may change over time because of changes in economic structure and/or because the model may have been based on faulty assumptions as to how the world works. As a result, the econometric model may be mis-specified. In practice, therefore, skillful econometric modelers monitor the model's recent forecasts for signs of systematic errors. Persistent forecast errors should ideally lead to a complete overhaul of the model. In practice, however, a more pragmatic approach is often adopted: Past forecast errors are incorporated into the model as an additional explanatory variable.

3.3.2. Economic Indicators

Economic indicators are economic statistics published by official agencies and/or private organizations. These indicators contain information on an economy's recent past activity or its current or future position in the business cycle. Lagging economic indicators and coincident indicators reflect recent past and current economic activity, respectively. A **leading economic indicator** (LEI) moves ahead of the business cycle by a fairly consistent time interval. Most analysts focus primarily on leading indicators because they purport to provide information about upcoming changes in economic activity, inflation, interest rates, and security prices.

Leading indicator–based analysis is the simplest forecasting approach to use because it requires following only a limited number of statistics. It also has the advantage of not requiring the analyst to make assumptions about the path of exogenous variables. Analysts use both individual LEIs and composite LEIs, reflecting a collection of economic data releases combined to give an overall reading. The OECD composite LEI for each country or region is based on five to nine variables such as share prices, manufacturing metrics, inflation, interest rates, and monetary data that exhibit cyclical fluctuations similar to GDP, with peaks and troughs occurring six to nine months earlier with reasonable consistency. Individual LEIs can also be combined into a so-called **diffusion index**, which measures how many indicators are pointing up and how many down. For example, if 7 out of 10 are pointing upward, then the odds are that the economy is accelerating.

One of the drawbacks of the (composite) leading indicator methodology is that the entire history may be revised each month. As a result, the most recently published historical indicator series will almost certainly appear to have fit past business cycles (i.e., GDP) better than it actually did in real time. This distortion is known as "look ahead" bias. Correspondingly, the LEI may be less reliable in predicting the current/next cycle than history suggests.

Business cycle indicators have been published for decades. A new methodology for tracking the business cycle, known generically as "nowcasting," emerged in the United States in the wake of the global financial crisis. The best-known of these forecasts, the Federal Reserve Bank of Atlanta's "GDPNow," was first published on 1 May 2014 for the second quarter of that year. The objective is to forecast GDP for the current quarter (which will not be released until after quarter-end) based on data as it is released throughout the quarter. To do this, the Atlanta Fed attempts to use the same methodology and data as will be used by the Bureau of Economic Analysis (BEA) to estimate GDP, replacing data that has not yet been released with forecasts based on the data already observed. As the quarter progresses, more of the actual data will have been observed, and GDPNow should, at least on average, converge to what will be released by the BEA.

BEA releases of estimates

The BEA releases a sequence of three GDP estimates for each quarter. The first, labeled the "advance" estimate, is released four weeks after the end of the quarter and tends to have the greatest market impact. The "preliminary" estimate is released a month later, and the "final" estimate comes at the end of the following quarter. The Atlanta Fed's GDPNow is actually a forecast of the BEA's advance estimate, not of the final GDP release.

It remains to be seen how useful nowcasting will be for investment analysts. It has a couple of clear advantages: It is updated in real time, and it is focused directly on a variable of primary interest (GDP and its components). Nowcasting is not designed to be predictive of anything beyond the end of the current quarter, however. In addition, it tends to be very volatile until a significant portion of the data for the quarter has been observed, at which point it may have lost some of its usefulness as a guide for investment decisions.

3.3.3. Checklist Approach

Formally or informally, many forecasters consider a whole range of economic data to assess the economy's future position. Checklist assessments are straightforward but time-consuming because they require continually monitoring the widest possible range of data. The data may then be extrapolated into forecasts via objective statistical methods, such as time-series analysis, or via more subjective or judgmental means. An analyst may then assess whether the measures are in an equilibrium state or nearer to an extreme reading.

The subjectivity of the checklist approach is perhaps its main weakness. The checklist's strength is its flexibility. It allows the forecaster to quickly take into account changes in economic structure by changing the variables or the weights assigned to variables within the analysis.

3.3.4. Economic Forecasting Approaches: Summary of Strengths and Weaknesses

Exhibit 4 summarizes the advantages and disadvantages of forecasting using econometric models, leading indicators, and checklists.

EXHIBIT 4   Economic Forecasting Approaches: Strengths and Weaknesses

Strengths	Weaknesses
Econometric Models Approach	
• Models can be quite robust, with many factors included to approximate reality.	• Complex and time-consuming to formulate.
• New data may be collected and consistently used within models to quickly generate output.	• Data inputs not easy to forecast.
• Delivers quantitative estimates of impact of changes in exogenous variables.	• Relationships not static. Model may be mis-specified.
• Imposes discipline/consistency on analysis.	• May give false sense of precision.
	• Rarely forecasts turning points well.
Leading Indicator–Based Approach	
• Usually intuitive and simple in construction.	• History subject to frequent revision.
• Focuses primarily on identifying turning points.	• "Current" data not reliable as input for historical analysis.
• May be available from third parties. Easy to track.	• Overfitted in-sample. Likely overstates forecast accuracy.
	• Can provide false signals.
	• May provide little more than binary (no/yes) directional guidance.
Checklist Approach	
• Limited complexity.	• Subjective. Arbitrary. Judgmental.
• Flexible.	• Time-consuming.
• Structural changes easily incorporated.	• Manual process limits depth of analysis. No clear mechanism for combining disparate information.
• Items easily added/dropped.	
• Can draw on any information, from any source, as desired.	• Imposes no consistency of analysis across items or at different points in time. May allow use of biased and/or inconsistent views, theories, assumptions.
• Breadth: Can include virtually any topics, perspectives, theories, and assumptions.	

EXAMPLE 6   Approaches to Forecasting

Sara Izek and Adam Berke are members of the asset allocation committee at Cycle Point Advisors, which emphasizes the business cycle within its tactical asset allocation process. Berke has developed a time series model of the business cycle that uses a published LEI series as a key input. He presents forecasts based on the model at each asset allocation meeting. Izek is eclectic in her approach, preferring to sample research from a wide variety of sources each month and then focus on whatever perspectives and results seem most interesting. She usually brings a stack of charts she has copied to the asset allocation meeting.

Questions:
1. Which of the main forecasting approaches (or combination of approaches) best describe(s) each analyst's own practice?
2. What strength(s) are likely to have appealed to each analyst?
3. What weaknesses might each analyst be overlooking?

Guideline answers:
1. Berke uses the econometric modeling approach in conjunction with the LEI approach. Izek's practice is essentially a checklist approach.
2. Berke is probably attracted to the quantitative output provided by a model, the consistency and discipline it imposes on the process, and the ability to generate explicit forecasts. He may have included the LEI in the model because it is designed to capture cyclical turning points or simply because doing so improves the model's statistical fit of the model.

   Izek is probably drawn to the flexibility of the checklist approach with respect to what is included/excluded and how to evaluate the information.
3. Berke may be overlooking potential mis-specification of his model, which is apt to make his forecasts systematically inaccurate (i.e., biased). He may also be failing to recognize the likely magnitude of the forecast errors that will be present even if the model is unbiased (i.e., overestimating the precision of the forecasts). By using the historical LEI series as an input to the model, he may be incorporating look-ahead bias into the model.

   Izek is likely overlooking the subjective, judgmental, and idiosyncratic nature of her approach. Her practice of basing her "checklist" on what seems most interesting in other analysts' current research makes her process especially vulnerable to inconsistency and cognitive biases.

3.4. Business Cycle Analysis

The trend rate of economic growth provides a vital anchor for setting very long-run investment expectations, which in turn provide a starting point for developing projections over short- to intermediate-term horizons. Virtually by definition, deviations from trend wash out in the long run, making information about the current economic and market environment of limited value over very long horizons. Over short to intermediate horizons, however, such information can be very important. From a macroeconomic perspective, the most useful such information typically pertains to fluctuations associated with the **business cycle**.

It is useful to think of fluctuations in economic activity as a superposition of many cycles varying in frequency from very short (days) to very long (decades), each with stochastic amplitude. The business cycle is not a specific, well-defined cycle. It is the result of many intermediate frequency cycles that jointly generate most of the variation in aggregate economic activity (i.e., GDP) around the trend. This fact explains why historical business cycles have varied in both duration and intensity—each was a different realization of a range of underlying stochastic cycles. It also helps to explain why it is difficult to project turning points in real time.

Business cycle peaks and troughs

The best-known record of business cycle peaks and troughs is published for the United States by the National Bureau of Economic research (NBER). According to NBER, the United States has experienced 66 complete business cycles since 1854, averaging 56 months from peak to peak. The longest cycle was 128 months, the shortest only 17 months. Fifty percent of the cycles lasted between 38 and 69 months. On average, the cycle's contraction phase (peak to trough) lasted 17 months, whereas the expansion phase (trough to peak) lasted 39 months.

At a fundamental level, the business cycle arises in response to the interaction of uncertainty, expectational errors, and rigidities that prevent instantaneous adjustment to unexpected events. It reflects decisions that

a. are made based on imperfect information and/or analysis with the expectation of future benefits,
b. require significant current resources and/or time to implement, and
c. are difficult and/or costly to reverse.

Such decisions are, broadly defined, investment decisions. Much of the uncertainty that sustains the cycle is endogenous to the system. Competitors, suppliers, employers, creditors, customers, and policymakers do not behave as expected. Prices and quantities adjust more or less than expected. Other sources of uncertainty are more exogenous. Technological breakthroughs threaten to disrupt whole industries and/or create new ones. Fracking, gene sequencing, e-commerce, "big data," digital advertising, cybersecurity, 3-D printing, the internet of things, and driverless cars are among those now playing out. Weather patterns affect agriculture, construction, and transportation. Natural disasters devastate local economies. Political and geopolitical shifts favor some entities and disadvantage others. And, of course, shocks in one part of the global economy are often transmitted to other parts of the world through trade relations, financial markets, and the prices of goods and services.

Numerous variables can be used to monitor the business cycle. Among them are GDP growth, industrial production (IP), employment/unemployment, purchasing managers' indexes, orders for durable goods, the output gap (the difference between GDP estimated as if the economy were on its trend growth path and the actual value of GDP), and the leading indicator indexes discussed earlier.

3.4.1. Phases of the Business Cycle

There are various ways to delineate phases of the business cycle. The most obvious is to divide it into two primary segments (the expansion and the contraction) with two key turning points at which growth changes sign (the peak and the trough). These two periods are fairly easy to identify, at least in retrospect. Subdividing the cycle more finely is more ambiguous, even in retrospect, because it requires identifying more nuanced changes such as acceleration or deceleration of growth without a change in direction. Nonetheless, it is useful to divide the cycle into several phases distinguished through both economic and financial market characteristics. For the purpose of setting expectations for capital markets, we use five phases of the business cycle here: initial recovery, early expansion, late expansion, slowdown, and contraction. The first four occur within the overall expansion.

1. **Initial recovery.** This period is usually a short phase of a few months beginning at the trough of the cycle in which the economy picks up, business confidence rises, stimulative policies are still in place, the output gap is large, and inflation is typically decelerating. Recovery is often supported by an upturn in spending on housing and consumer durables.

    Capital market effects: Short-term rates and government bond yields are low. Bond yields may continue to decline in anticipation of further disinflation but are likely to be bottoming. Stock markets may rise briskly as fears of a longer recession (or even a depression) dissipate. Cyclical assets—and riskier assets, such as small stocks, higher-yield corporate bonds, and emerging market equities and bonds—attract investors and typically perform well.

2. **Early expansion.** The economy is gaining some momentum, unemployment starts to fall but the output gap remains negative, consumers borrow and spend, and businesses step up production and investment. Profits typically rise rapidly. Demand for housing and consumer durables is strong.

    Capital market effects: Short rates are moving up as the central bank starts to withdraw stimulus put in place during the recession. Longer-maturity bond yields are likely to be stable or rising slightly. The yield curve is flattening. Stocks trend upward.

3. **Late expansion.** The output gap has closed, and the economy is increasingly in danger of overheating. A boom mentality prevails. Unemployment is low, profits are strong, both wages and inflation are rising, and capacity pressures boost investment spending. Debt coverage ratios may deteriorate as balance sheets expand and interest rates rise. The central bank may aim for a "soft landing" while fiscal balances improve.

    Capital market effects: Interest rates are typically rising as monetary policy becomes restrictive. Bond yields are usually rising, more slowly than short rates, so the yield curve continues to flatten. Private sector borrowing puts pressure on credit markets. Stock markets often rise but may be volatile as nervous investors endeavor to detect signs of looming deceleration. Cyclical assets may underperform while inflation hedges such as commodities outperform.

4. **Slowdown.** The economy is slowing and approaching the eventual peak, usually in response to rising interest rates, fewer viable investment projects, and accumulated debt. It is especially vulnerable to a shock at this juncture. Business confidence wavers. Inflation often continues to rise as firms raise prices in an attempt to stay ahead of rising costs imposed by other firms doing the same.

    Capital market effects: Short-term interest rates are high, perhaps still rising, but likely to peak. Government bond yields top out at the first clear sign of a slowing economy and may then decline sharply. The yield curve may invert, especially if the central bank continues to exert upward pressure on short rates. Credit spreads, especially for weaker credits generally widen. The stock market may fall, with interest-sensitive stocks such as utilities and "quality" stocks with stable earnings performing best.

5. **Contraction.** Recessions typically last 12 to 18 months. Investment spending, broadly defined, typically leads the contraction. Firms cut production sharply. Once the recession is confirmed, the central bank eases monetary policy. Profits drop sharply. Tightening credit magnifies downward pressure on the economy. Recessions are often punctuated by major bankruptcies, incidents of uncovered fraud, exposure of aggressive accounting practices, or a financial crisis. Unemployment can rise quickly, impairing household financial positions.

   Capital market effects: Short-term interest rates drop during this phase, as do bond yields. The yield curve steepens substantially. The stock market declines in the earlier stages of the contraction but usually starts to rise in the later stages, well before the recovery emerges. Credit spreads typically widen and remain elevated until signs of a trough emerge and it becomes apparent that firms will be able to roll over near-term debt maturities.

3.4.2. Market Expectations and the Business Cycle

This description of a typical business cycle may suggest that forming capital market expectations for short and intermediate horizons should be relatively straightforward. If an investor can identify the current phase of the cycle and correctly predict when the next phase will begin, is it not easy to make money? Unfortunately, it is not that simple.

First, the phases of the business cycle vary in length and amplitude. Recessions can be steep, and downturns (such as in the 1930s and in 2007–2009) can be frightening. On the other hand, recessions also can be short lived, with only a small decline in output and only a modest rise in unemployment. Sometimes, the weakest phase of the cycle does not even involve a recession but merely a period of slower economic growth or a "growth recession." Similarly, expansions vary in length and intensity.

Second, it is not always easy to distinguish between cyclical forces and secular forces acting on the economy and the markets. The prolonged recovery following the 2007–2009 global financial crisis is a prime example. Interest rates and inflation went far lower and remained extraordinarily low far longer than virtually anyone would have predicted based on a purely cyclical view.

Third, although the connection between the real economy and capital market returns is strong, it is subject to substantial uncertainty. Capital market prices reflect a composite of investors' expectations and attitudes toward risk with respect to all future horizons. How, when, and by how much the markets respond to the business cycle are as uncertain as the cycle itself—perhaps more so.

What does all of this variation and uncertainty imply for setting capital market projections? First, as with virtually any investment information, business cycle analysis generates a noisy signal with respect to prospective opportunities. Second, the signal is likely to be most reliable (a higher "signal-to-noise" ratio), and hence most valuable, over horizons within the range of likely expansion and contraction phases—perhaps one to three years. Returns over substantially shorter horizons are likely to be driven primarily by market reactions to more transitory developments, undermining the cycle's predictive value. On the other hand, as the forecast horizon extends beyond this range, it becomes increasingly likely that one or more turning points will occur within the horizon, implying returns that increasingly reflect averaging over the cycle.

EXAMPLE 7   Cycles, Horizons, and Expectations

Lee Kim uses a statistical model that divides the business cycle into two "regimes": expansion and contraction. The expected (continuously compounded) return on equities is +2% per month during expansions and −2% per month during contractions. Consistent with NBER's historical record (see earlier sidebar), the probabilities of transitioning between regimes imply that expansions last 39 months on average, whereas contractions average 20 months. Correspondingly, over the long run, the economy expands roughly two-thirds of the time and contracts one-third of the time. Hence, the long-term expected equity return is 0.67% = [(2% × 2/3) + (−2% × 1/3)] per month, or 8% per year. Kim's model indicates that the economy recently transitioned into contraction. For the upcoming asset allocation committee meeting, he will prepare equity return forecasts for horizons of 3 months, 1 year, 5 years, and 10 years.

Explain how you would expect the choice of time horizon to affect Kim's projections.

Guideline answer:
The longer the horizon, the more likely that one or more transitions will occur between contraction and expansion; more generally, the more likely it is that the horizon spans more than one business cycle phase or even more than one full cycle. As a result, the longer the horizon, the more Kim's forecast should reflect averaging over periods of expansion and contraction and the closer it will be to the "information-less" average of 8% per year.

Over the next three months, it is highly likely that the economy will remain in contraction, so Kim's forecast for that period should be very close to −2% per month [cumulatively −6%]. Because contractions last 20 months on average in the model, Kim's forecast for a one-year horizon should reflect only a modestly higher probability of having transitioned to expansion at some point within the period. So, his forecast might be −18% (an average of −1.5% per month) instead of −24% (−2% per month). Over a five-year horizon, it is very likely that the economy will have spent time in both contraction and expansion. As a result, Kim's forecast will put significant weight on each phase. Because the economy starts in contraction (i.e., the starting point is not random), the weight on that phase will probably be somewhat higher than its long-term frequency of 1/3, say 0.40. This assumption implies a forecast of 4.8% per year [= 12 × (0.6 × 2%) + (0.4 × −2%)]. Over a 10-year horizon, the frequency of expansion and contraction months is likely to be very close to the 2-to-1 long-run ratio. So, Kim's forecast should be very close to 8% per year.

3.4.3. Inflation and Deflation: Trends and Relation to the Business Cycle

Until the early 20th century, the money supply was largely dictated by the supply of specie—gold and/or silver used in coins and to back bank deposits. Periods of both inflation and deflation were common. Today, currencies are backed by the credibility of governments and central banks rather than specie, and people expect the prices of goods and services to trend upward. Persistent deflation is rare. Expectation of an upward trend in prices reflects recognition of an asymmetry in a central bank's so-called "reaction function." It is generally accepted that a central bank's policy tools are more effective in slowing economic activity than in accelerating sluggish activity. Hence, central banks may tend to be more aggressive in combating downward pressure on demand than in reining in strong demand. In addition, it is widely believed that outright deflation damages the economy because it undermines:

- debt-financed investments. Servicing and repayment of nominally fixed debt becomes more onerous as nominal income flows and the nominal value of real assets both decline; and
- the power of central banks. In a deflationary environment, interest rates fall to levels close to (or even below) zero. When interest rates are already very low, the central bank has less leeway to stimulate the economy by lowering interest rates.

In contrast, moderate inflation is generally considered to impose only modest costs on the economy. Both the differential effectiveness of policy and the differential costs of inflation versus deflation suggest that central banks will, implicitly or explicitly, target positive inflation, and investors set their expectations accordingly. The result is that asset prices in general and bond yields in particular generally build in compensation for a positive average inflation rate.

Inflation is procyclical, accelerating in the later stages of the business cycle when the output gap has closed and decelerating when, during a recession or the early years afterward, there is a large output gap, which puts downward pressure on wages and prices. If the central bank's target is credible, the average rate of inflation over the cycle should be near the target.

Because the cyclical pattern of inflation is well known, inflation expectations will also be procyclical. It is important, however, to differentiate inflation expectations by horizon. Very long-term inflation expectations should be virtually unaffected by cyclical fluctuations provided investors maintain confidence in the central bank's target. Short horizon expectations will tend to have about the same amplitude as actual inflation. Inflation, and therefore inflation expectations, over intermediate horizons will be a blend of the different phases of the current and subsequent cycles. Hence, the amplitude of expectations will decline with horizon—again, provided investors do not lose confidence in the central bank's target.

The pattern just described implies a "horizon structure" of inflation expectations that is countercyclical—upward sloping at the trough of the business cycle and inverted at the peak. Because inflation expectations are an important component of bond yields, this countercyclical pattern is one of the reasons that the yield curve's slope is countercyclical.[12]

To assess the effect of inflation on asset classes, we must consider both the cash flows and the discount rates. We consider "cash," nominal bonds, stocks, and real estate.

- *Cash:* In this context, cash is taken to mean short-term interest-bearing instruments, not currency or zero-interest deposits. As long as short-term interest rates adjust with expected

---

[12]As will be discussed later, compensation for taking duration risk (the "term premium") is procyclical. As a result, an inverted "horizon structure" of expected inflation does not necessarily imply an inverted yield curve.

inflation, cash is essentially a zero-duration, inflation-protected asset that earns a floating real rate. Inflation above or below expectation contributes to temporary fluctuations in the realized real return. Because central banks aim to stabilize actual and expected inflation, they tend to make the real rate on cash procyclical around a long-term level consistent with their target inflation rate. Hence, cash is relatively attractive (unattractive) in a rising (declining) rate environment. Deflation may make cash particularly attractive if a zero-lower-bound is binding on the nominal interest rate. Otherwise deflation is simply a component of the required short-term real rate.

- *Bonds:* Because the cash flows are fixed in nominal terms, the effect of inflation is transmitted solely through the discount rates (i.e., the yield curve). Rising (falling) inflation induces capital losses (gains) as the expected inflation component of yields rises (falls). If inflation remains within the expected cyclical range, shorter-term yields rise/fall more than longer yields but have less price impact as a result of shorter duration. If, however, inflation moves out of the expected range, longer-term yields may rise/fall more sharply as investors reassess the likelihood of a change in the long-run average level of inflation. Persistent deflation benefits the highest-quality bonds because it increases the purchasing power of the cash flows, but it is likely to impair the creditworthiness of lower-quality debt.

- *Stocks:* As long as inflation stays within the expected cyclical range, there should be little effect on stocks because both expected future cash flows (earnings and dividends) and associated discount rates rise/fall in line with the horizon structure of inflation expectations. Signs that inflation is moving out of the expected range, however, indicate a potential threat. Unexpectedly high and/or rapidly rising inflation could mean that the central bank needs to act to slow the economy, whereas very low and/or falling inflation (possibly deflation) threatens a recession and a decline in asset prices. Within the stock market, higher inflation benefits firms that are able to pass along rising costs, whereas deflation is especially detrimental for asset-intensive, commodity-producing, and/or highly leveraged firms.

- *Real estate:* Short- to intermediate-term nominal cash flows are generally dictated by existing leases, with the speed of adjustment depending on the type of real estate asset held. As long as inflation remains within the expected range, renewal of leases will likely generate rental income rising with expected inflation, accompanied by stable asset values. Higher-than-expected inflation is likely to coincide with high demand for real estate, expectations that rental income will rise even faster than general inflation, and rising property values. The impact may be quite idiosyncratic, however, depending on the length of leases, the existing supply of similar properties, and the likelihood of new supply hitting the market when leases come up for renewal. On the other hand, unexpectedly low inflation (or deflation) will put downward pressure on expected rental income and property values, especially for less-than-prime properties, which may have to cut rents sharply to avoid rising vacancies.

EXAMPLE 8   Inflation

Kesia Jabari believes the quantitative easing undertaken by major central banks in the wake of the global financial crisis is finally about to induce a surge in inflation. She believes that without extraordinary policy actions from the central banks, the inflation rate will ultimately rise to the upper end of central banks' tolerance ranges at the peak of the current business cycle.

Assuming Jabari is correct, discuss the likely implications for floating-rate instruments ("cash"), bonds, stocks, and real estate if:

a. the market shares Jabari's view, or
b. once inflation begins to rise, the market doubts that the central banks will be able to contain it.

Guideline answers:
a. If the market agrees with Jabari, then the relationship of inflation and the asset classes to the business cycle should be fairly normal. Short-term rates and bond yields will rise with inflation expectations. The yield curve should flatten because long-term inflation expectations should remain well anchored. Floating-rate instruments (cash) will be relatively attractive, and intermediate maturities ("the belly of the curve") will be the most vulnerable. In general, the rise in inflation should not have much independent impact on stocks or real estate because both cash flows and discount rates will be expected to rise. Firms with pricing power and real estate with relatively short lease-renewal cycles are set to perform best.
b. If the market doubts that central banks can contain inflation within previously perceived tolerances, then long-run inflation expectations will rise and the yield curve may steepen rather than flatten, at least initially. Floating-rate instruments will still be relatively attractive, but now it is the longest maturities that will be the most vulnerable. Stocks are likely to suffer because the market expects central banks to be aggressive in fighting inflation. Real estate with long-term leases and little long-term, fixed-rate debt will suffer. Real estate with substantial long-term, fixed-rate debt should do relatively well, especially high-quality properties with little new supply nearby, which are likely to avoid significant vacancies even in a recession.

In the interest of completeness, we should note a caveat before leaving the topic of inflation. The preceding discussion implicitly assumes that the short-run aggregate supply curve is upward sloping and that the business cycle is primarily driven by fluctuations in aggregate demand. Together, these assumptions imply that inflation is pro-cyclical. Although globalization may have reduced the sensitivity of domestic prices to domestic output, it seems unlikely that domestic output/growth no longer matters. Thus, the aggregate supply curve may be *flatter* but is unlikely to be *flat*. With regard to what drives the cycle, if aggregate supply shocks predominate, then inflation will tend to be *counter*cyclical, reflecting alternating periods of "stagflation" and disinflationary boom. The 1970s oil crisis is a prime example. This pattern is more likely to be the exception rather than the rule, however.

3.5. Analysis of Monetary and Fiscal Policy

Actual and anticipated actions by monetary and fiscal authorities affect the decisions and actions of all other participants in the economy and the markets. As a result, it is somewhat difficult to isolate their role(s) from our broader discussion. Indeed, the foregoing sections have made numerous references to these policies. Nonetheless it is worthwhile to focus directly on these policies from the perspective of setting capital market expectations.

Monetary policy is often used as a mechanism for intervention in the business cycle. Indeed, this use is inherent in the mandates of most central banks to maintain price stability and/or growth consistent with the economy's potential. Each central bank interprets its mandate somewhat differently, sets its own operational objectives and guidelines, and selects its own mix of the tools (e.g., policy rates and liquidity provision) at its disposal. The common theme is that central banks virtually always aim to moderate the cyclical behavior of growth and inflation, in both directions. Thus, monetary policy aims to be countercyclical. The impact of monetary policy, however, is famously subject to "long and variable lags," as well as substantial uncertainty. As a result, a central bank's ability to fine-tune the economy is limited, and there is always risk that policy measures will exacerbate rather than moderate the business cycle. This risk is greatest at the top of the cycle, when the central bank may overestimate the economy's momentum and/or underestimate the effects of restrictive policies. In such situations, monetary policy may trigger a contraction that it cannot immediately counteract. In contrast, expansionary monetary policy rarely, if ever, suffices to turn a contraction into a strong recovery. This asymmetry is captured in a classic analogy: Expansionary policy is like "pushing" on a string, whereas restrictive policy is like "pulling" on a string.

Fiscal policy (government spending and taxation) can also be used to counteract cyclical fluctuations in the economy. Aside from extreme situations, however—such as the Great Depression of the 1930s and recovery from the 2007–2009 global financial crisis—fiscal policy typically addresses objectives other than regulating short-term growth, for at least two main reasons. First, in all but the most authoritarian regimes, the fiscal decision-making process is too lengthy to make timely adjustments to aggregate spending and taxation aimed at short-term objectives. Second, frequent changes of a meaningful magnitude would be disruptive to the ongoing process of providing and funding government services.

Notwithstanding these considerations, fiscal policy often does play a role in mitigating cyclical fluctuations. Progressive tax regimes imply that the effective tax rate on the private sector is pro-cyclical—rising as the economy expands and falling as the economy contracts. Similarly, means-based transfer payments vary inversely with the economy, helping to mitigate fluctuations in disposable income for the most vulnerable households. The effect of these so-called automatic stabilizers should not be overlooked in setting expectations for the economy and the markets.

From the perspective of an investment analyst focused on establishing expectations for broad asset classes, having a handle on monetary policy is mission-critical with respect to cyclical patterns. Under normal conditions, fiscal adjustments are important but likely to be secondary considerations. The reverse is likely with respect to assessing the long run. Of course, if a major change in fiscal stance is contemplated or has been implemented, the impact warrants significant attention with respect to all horizons. The major overhaul of the US tax code at the end of 2017 is a good example of these points. It almost certainly provided a short-term stimulus, especially with respect to capital expenditures. But it was not a short-term policy adjustment. It was the most significant change to the tax code in decades, a major structural change that may affect the path of both the economy and the markets for many years.

3.5.1. Monetary Policy

Central banks can, and do, carry out their mandates somewhat differently. In general, they seek to mitigate extremes in inflation and/or growth via countercyclical policy measures. As a generic illustration of how this might work, we briefly review the **Taylor rule**. In the current context, it can be viewed as a tool for assessing a central bank's stance and a guide to predicting how that stance is likely to evolve.

In essence, the Taylor rule links a central bank's target short-term nominal interest rate to the expected growth rate of the economy and inflation, relative to trend growth and the central bank's inflation target.

$$i^* = r_{\text{neutral}} + \pi_e + 0.5(\widehat{Y}_e - \widehat{Y}_{\text{trend}}) + 0.5(\pi_e - \pi_{\text{target}})$$

where

$$i^* = \text{target nominal policy rate}$$
$$r_{\text{neutral}} = \text{real policy rate that would be targeted if growth is expected to be at trend and inflation on target}$$
$$\pi_e, \pi_{\text{target}} = \text{respectively, the expected and target inflation rates}$$
$$\widehat{Y}_e, \widehat{Y}_{\text{trend}} = \text{respectively, the expected and trend real GDP growth rates}$$

The rule can be re-expressed in terms of the real, inflation-adjusted target rate by moving the expected inflation rate to the left-hand side of the equation.

$$i^* - \pi_e = r_{\text{neutral}} + 0.5(\widehat{Y}_e - \widehat{Y}_{\text{trend}}) + 0.5(\pi_e - \pi_{\text{target}})$$

From this rearrangement, we see that the real, inflation-adjusted policy rate deviates from neutral by one-half the amount by which growth and inflation deviate from their respective targets. As an example, suppose the neutral real policy rate is 2.25%, the target inflation rate is 2%, and trend growth is estimated to be 2.5%. If growth is expected to be 3.5% and inflation is expected to be 3%, the Taylor rule would call for a 6.25% nominal policy rate:

$$2.25\% + 3\% + 0.5\ (3.5\% - 2.5\%) + 0.5\ (3.0\% - 2.0\%) = 6.25\%$$

With expected inflation at 3%, this calculation corresponds to a 3.25% real policy rate.

Even if a central bank were to set its policy rate according to the Taylor rule, there could still be substantial judgment left in the process. None of the inputs to the rule are objectively observable. To make the rule operational, policymakers and their staffs have to specify how the requisite expectations will be generated, and by whom. Whose estimate of trend growth is to be used? What is the appropriate neutral real policy rate? Over what horizon(s) do the expectations apply? Models could be developed to answer all these questions, but there would be judgments to be made in doing so. The upshot for the investment analyst is that monetary policy cannot be reduced to a simple equation. The Taylor rule, or some customized variant, provides a good framework for analyzing the thrust and likely evolution of monetary policy, but the analyst must pay careful attention to situational signals from the central bank. This is why, for example, the investment community literally scrutinizes every word in the Federal Reserve's post-meeting statements and speeches by officials, looking for any hint of a change in the Fed's own interpretation of the environment.

EXAMPLE 9   Policies and the Business Cycle

Albert Grant, CFA, is an institutional portfolio strategist at Camford Advisors. After a period of trend growth, inflation at the central bank's target, and neutral monetary policy, the economy has been hit by a substantial deflationary shock.

Questions
1.   How are monetary and fiscal policies likely to respond to the shock?

Camford's economics department estimates that growth is now 1% below trend and inflation is 2% below the central bank's target. Camford's chief investment officer (CIO) has asked Grant to put together a projection of the likely path of policy rates for the next five years.

2.   If Grant believes the central bank will respond in accordance with the Taylor rule, what other information will he need in order to project the path of policy rates?
3.   What pattern should Grant expect for growth, inflation, and market interest rates if the central bank does *not* respond to the shock?
4.   Assuming the central bank does respond and that its reaction function is well approximated by the Taylor rule, how will this alter Grant's expectations regarding the paths of growth, inflation, and short-term rates over the next five years?

Guideline answers:
1.   A countercyclical response can be expected from both monetary and fiscal policy. Assuming the central bank uses a policy rate target as its primary tool, it will cut that rate. On the fiscal side, there may be no explicit expansionary policy action (tax cut or spending increase), but automatic stabilizers built into tax and transfer programs can be expected to cushion the shock's impact on private sector disposable incomes.
2.   Grant will need to know what values the central bank uses for the neutral real rate, trend growth rate, and inflation target. He will also need to know how the central bank forms its expectations of growth and inflation. Finally, he will need to know how growth and inflation are likely to evolve, including how they will be affected by the path of policy rates.
3.   The deflationary shock is very likely to induce a contractionary phase of the business cycle, putting additional downward pressure on growth and inflation. Short-term market interest rates will be dragged downward by weak demand and inflation. Risky asset prices are likely to fall sharply. A deep and/or protracted recession may be required before conditions conducive to recovery are in place. Grant should therefore expect a deep "U-shaped" path for growth, inflation, and short-term rates.
4.   If the central bank responds as expected, it will push short-term rates down farther and faster than they would otherwise fall in an effort to mitigate the downward momentum of growth and inflation. If the central bank correctly calibrates its policy, growth and inflation should decline less, bottom out sooner, and recover more quickly toward trend growth and the target inflation level, respectively, than in the absence of a policy response. Whereas the central bank is virtually certain to

drive short rates down farther and faster, it may be inclined to let the market dictate the pace at which rates eventually rise. That is, it may simply "accommodate" the need for higher rates rather than risk unduly restraining the recovery once it is established.

3.5.2. What Happens When Interest Rates Are Zero or Negative?

Prior to the 2007–2009 global financial crisis, it was generally accepted that central banks could not successfully implement negative interest rate policies. Belief in a "zero lower bound" on policy rates assumed that individuals would choose to hold currency (coins and notes) if faced with earning a negative interest rate on short-term instruments, including deposits. The move toward holding currency would drain deposits and reserves from the banking system, causing bank balance sheets to shrink. The resulting credit contraction would put upward pressure on interest rates, thwarting the central bank's attempt to maintain negative rates. The contraction of credit would likely also put additional downward pressure on economic growth, thereby reinforcing the need for stimulative policies.

This line of reasoning raised questions about the effectiveness of traditional monetary policy when the economy is so weak that economic growth fails to respond to (nominal) interest rates approaching zero. Following the global financial crisis, central banks faced with this situation pursued less conventional measures.

One important measure was quantitative easing (QE), in which central banks committed to large-scale, ongoing purchases of high-quality domestic fixed-income securities. These purchases were funded by creating an equally large quantity of bank reserves in the form of central bank deposits. As a result of QE, central bank balance sheets and bank reserves grew significantly and sovereign bond yields fell. QE was pursued by (among others) the US Federal Reserve, the European Central Bank, the Bank of Japan, and the Bank of England.

Conventional reasoning suggests that QE should have resulted in the desired growth in nominal spending. In theory, banks could use the increased reserves to extend loans, and low interest rates would stimulate businesses and households to borrow. The borrowing was expected to fund capital expenditure by businesses as well as current consumption and purchases of durables (e.g., houses and cars) by households, thereby stimulating the economy. With interest rates low, investors were expected to bid up the prices of stocks and real estate. Although asset prices did increase and businesses that could issue bonds borrowed heavily, proceeds were more often used to fund dividends and stock buybacks rather than capital expenditures. At the same time, household spending ability was significantly curtailed by the legacy of the global financial crisis.

Whether or not QE was effective remains subject to debate. To achieve desired levels of economic growth, central banks tried the previously unthinkable: targeting negative interest rates. The central banks of Denmark, Sweden, Japan, Switzerland, and the euro area were among those that adopted negative policy rates. Contrary to the notion of a "zero lower bound," negative policy rates proved to be sustainable.

The move into currency did not occur as expected because the scale and speed of transactions inherent in modern economies cannot be supported using physical cash as the primary method of exchange.[13] Trillions of dollars change hands daily to facilitate trade in goods, services, and financial instruments, and these transactions cannot be accomplished using physical cash. Bank deposits and bank reserves held at the central bank, rather than as vault cash, have an implicit yield or convenience value that cash does not. As long as this value exceeds the explicit cost of holding those deposits—in the form of a negative interest rate—there is no incentive to convert deposits into cash. In such circumstances, negative policy rates may be achievable and sustainable.

In theory, using negative nominal rates to stimulate an economy should work similarly to using low but still positive rates. Businesses and consumers are encouraged to hold fewer deposits for transaction purposes; investors are encouraged to seek higher expected returns on other assets; consumers are encouraged to save less and/or borrow more against future income; businesses are encouraged to invest in profitable projects; and banks are encouraged to use their reserves in support of larger loan books. All of this is expected to stimulate economic growth.

For consumers, investors, businesses, and banks to behave as described, however, each must believe they will be adequately rewarded for taking the inherent risks. In a negative interest rate environment, these entities are likely to have greater levels of uncertainty as to whether they will be adequately compensated for risks taken, and therefore they may not act as desired by monetary policy makers. As a result, the effectiveness of expansionary monetary policy is more tenuous at low and negative interest rate levels than at higher interest rate levels.

3.5.3. Implications of Negative Interest Rates for Capital Market Expectations

Long-run capital market expectations typically take the level of the "risk-free rate" as a baseline to which various risk premiums are added to arrive at long-run expected returns for risky assets such as long-term bonds and equities. The implicit assumption is that the risk-free rate is at its long-term equilibrium level. When short-term rates are negative, the long-run equilibrium short-term rate can be used as the baseline rate in these models instead of the observed negative rate. This rate can be estimated using the neutral policy rate ($r_{neutral}$) in the Taylor rule (or more generally in the central bank's presumed reaction function), adjusted for a modest spread between policy rates and default-free rates available to investors.

In forming capital market expectations for shorter time horizons, analysts and investors must consider the expected path of interest rates. Paths should be considered that, on average, converge to the long-run equilibrium rate estimate. With negative policy rates in place, this approach means a negative starting point. In theory, many possible scenarios, each appropriately weighted by its likelihood, should be considered. In practice, it may suffice to consider only a few scenarios. Because shorter horizons provide less opportunity for the impact of events to average out, the shorter the forecast horizon, the more important it is to consider deviations from the most likely path.

Negative policy rates are expected to produce asset class returns similar to those occurring in the contraction and early recovery phrases of a "more normal" business/policy cycle.

---

[13]It should also be noted that banks were reluctant to directly impose negative rates on their retail and commercial deposit customers. In general, rates on these accounts remained non-negative. Thus, the aggregate incentive to move into cash was mitigated somewhat. Various fees (e.g., for overdraft protection) and conditions imposed on the accounts (e.g., compensating balance requirements), however, may still have resulted in a net cost for deposit customers.

Although such historical periods may provide a reasonable starting point in formulating appropriate scenarios, it is important to note that negative rate periods may indicate severe distress in the economy and thus involve greater uncertainty regarding the timing and strength of recovery.

Key considerations when forming capital market expectations in a negative interest rate environment include the following:

- Historical data are less likely to be reliable.
  - o Useful data may exist on only a few historical business cycles, which may not include instances of negative rates. In addition, fundamental structural/institutional changes in markets and the economy may have occurred since this data was generated.
  - o Quantitative models, especially statistical models, tend to break down in situations that differ from those on which they were estimated/calibrated.
  - o Forecasting must account for differences between the current environment and historical averages. Historical averages, which average out differences across phases of the cycle, will be even less reliable than usual.

- The effects of other monetary policy measures occurring simultaneously (e.g., quantitative easing) may distort market relationships, such as the shape of the yield curve or the performance of specific sectors.

Incorporating uncertain dynamics, including negative interest rates, into capital market expectations over finite horizons is much more difficult than projecting long-term average levels. The challenge arises from the fact that asset prices depend not only on investor expectations regarding longer term "equilibrium" levels but also on the path taken to get there.

3.5.4. The Monetary and Fiscal Policy Mix

Fiscal policy is inherently political. Central banks ultimately derive their powers from governments, but most strive to be, or at least appear to be, independent of the political process in order to maintain credibility. As a result, to the extent that monetary and fiscal policy are coordinated, it is usually the case that the central bank takes the expected fiscal stance as given in formulating its own policy and disdains guidance from politicians regarding its policy.

The mix of monetary and fiscal policies has its most apparent impact on the level of interest rates and the shape of the yield curve. We first consider the effect of persistently loose or tight policies on the average level of rates. All else the same, loose fiscal policies (large deficits) increase the level of *real* interest rates because the domestic private sector must be induced to save more/investing less and/or additional capital must be attracted from abroad. Conversely, tight fiscal policies reduce real rates. Persistently loose monetary policy generally results in higher actual and expected inflation. Attempts by the central bank to hold down nominal rates will prove self-defeating, ultimately resulting in higher rather than lower nominal interest rates.[14] Conversely, persistently tight monetary policy ultimately reduces actual and expected inflation resulting in lower, rather than higher, nominal rates. Exhibit 5 summarizes the impact of persistent policy mixes on the level of real and nominal rates. In each case, the impact on real rates and on expected inflation is clear. Two cases involve a mix of loose and tight policy. In these cases, the combined impact could be higher or lower nominal rates. Nominal rates are labeled as "mid" level for these cases.

---

[14]This was one of the crucial insights presented in Friedman (1968).

EXHIBIT 5   Effect of Persistent Policy Mix on the Average Level of Rates

		Fiscal Policy	
		Loose	**Tight**
	Loose	High Real Rates	Low Real Rates
		+	+
		High Expected Inflation	High Expected Inflation
		=	=
		High Nominal Rates	Mid Nominal Rates
Monetary Policy	**Tight**	High Real Rates	Low Real Rates
		+	+
		Low Expected Inflation	Low Expected Inflation
		=	=
		Mid Nominal Rates	Low Nominal Rates

The second impact of policy is on the slope of the yield curve. The slope of the term structure of (default-free) interest rates depends primarily on (1) the expected future path of short-term rates and (2) a risk premium required to compensate for the greater price volatility inherent in longer-maturity bonds. The maturity premium explains why the term structure is normally upward sloping. Changes in the curve's slope—flattening and steepening—are primarily driven by the evolution of short rate expectations, which are mainly driven by the business cycle and policies. This dynamic was described in an earlier discussion on business cycles. Exhibit 6 summarizes the main points regarding the evolution of rates, policy, and the yield curve.

EXHIBIT 6   Rates, Policy, and the Yield Curve over the Business Cycle

Cycle Phase	Monetary Policy & Automatic Stabilizers	Money Market Rates	Bond Yields and the Yield Curve
Initial Recovery	Stimulative stance. Transitioning to tightening mode.	Low/bottoming. Increases expected over progressively shorter horizons.	Long rates bottoming. Shortest yields begin to rise first. Curve is steep.
Early expansion	Withdrawing stimulus	Moving up. Pace may be expected to accelerate.	Yields rising. Possibly stable at longest maturities. Front section of yield curve steepening, back half likely flattening.
Late expansion	Becoming restrictive	Above average and rising. Expectations tempered by eventual peak/decline.	Rising. Pace slows. Curve flattening from longest maturities inward.
Slowdown	Tight. Tax revenues may surge as accumulated capital gains are realized.	Approaching/reaching peak.	Peak. May then decline sharply. Curve flat to inverted.
Contraction	Progressively more stimulative. Aiming to counteract downward momentum.	Declining.	Declining. Curve steepening. Likely steepest on cusp of Initial Recovery phase.

There is a third factor related to monetary and fiscal policy that may, or may not, be significant with respect to the shape of the yield curve and the effectiveness of policy: the relative supply of (government) bonds at various maturities. Does it matter what maturities the government issues in order to fund deficits? Does it matter what maturities the central bank chooses to buy/sell in its open market operations or its quantitative easing? There is no clear answer. The issue became important, however, in the wake of the global financial crisis for at least two reasons.

First, although it is now apparent that there is no clear lower bound on nominal interest rates, the effectiveness of conventional interest rate policies at very low rate levels remains in question. In particular, the central bank's ability to influence long-term rates may be even more tenuous than usual. Second, governments have run, and continue to run, large deficits while quantitative easing by major central banks has caused them to accumulate massive holdings of government debt (and other securities), which they may ultimately need or want to sell. If relative supply of debt along the yield curve really matters, then how governments fund their deficits in the future and how the central banks manage the maturity of their holdings could have significant implications for the yield curve and the broader financial markets.

It is difficult to draw firm conclusions with respect to maturity management. The existing evidence in conjunction with broader observation of markets, however, suggests the following: Sufficiently large purchases/sales at different maturities are likely to have a meaningful effect on the curve while they are occurring, but the effect is unlikely to be sustained for long once the buy/sell operation ends. To put it another way, a sufficiently large *flow* of supply may have a noticeable impact on relative yields, but discrete changes in the quantity of each maturity outstanding are much less likely to have a lasting impact. Government bonds are very liquid, and investors can and do move up and down the yield curve to exploit even very small yield differentials. Having said that, an important caveat pertaining to very long maturities is appropriate. Pension funds and other entities with very long-dated liabilities need correspondingly very long-maturity assets. Severely limiting the available supply of those assets would undoubtedly drive down their yield. Low yields at the very long end of the UK yield curve have been attributed to this effect at various times.

As a final comment on the interaction of monetary and fiscal policy, we acknowledge the potential for politicization of the central bank. If the level of government debt is high relative to the economy (GDP), and especially if it is also rising because of large fiscal deficits, there is a risk that the central bank may be coerced into inflating away the real value of the debt with very accommodative monetary policy. The risk that this dynamic *may* subsequently occur is almost certain to steepen the yield curve. If it *does* occur, such an event is likely to lead to an inflationary spiral, as higher inflation leads to higher nominal rates, which lead to faster accumulation of debt, which call forth even more accommodative monetary policy, and so on.

3.5.5. The Shape of the Yield Curve and the Business Cycle

The shape of the yield curve is frequently cited as a predictor of economic growth and as an indicator of where the economy is in the business cycle. Both casual observation and formal econometric analysis support its usefulness (an extensive bibliography is available at www.newyorkfed.org). The underlying rationale was summarized earlier in Exhibit 6. In simplest terms, the curve tends to be steep at the bottom of the cycle, flatten during the expansion until it is very flat or even inverted at the peak, and re-steepen during the subsequent contraction. Because expectations with respect to the path of short-term rates are the primary determinant of the curve's shape, the shape of the curve contains information about how market participants perceive the state and likely evolution of the economy as well as the impact they expect policymakers to have on that path. Thus, the empirical link between the shape of the yield curve and subsequent growth passes the test set out earlier for a good model—there is a solid rationale for believing it should be predictive. One must, of course, be aware that very few macroeconomic variables are truly exogenous and very few endogenous variables are completely unaffected by the past. "A" (shape of the yield curve) may predict "B" (growth next period), but it may also be the case that "B" predicts "A" in the period after that. The point is that the analyst should be aware of the fact that both the shape of the yield curve and economic growth (i.e., the business cycle) are endogenous within the economy. This is not to suggest throwing out a useful relationship but merely a reminder to interpret results with care.

EXAMPLE 10   The Business Cycle and the Yield Curve

Camford's quantitative analysis team helped Albert Grant incorporate the central bank's reaction function into a reduced-form model of growth and inflation. With this model, he will be able to project the path of short-term rates in the wake of the deflationary shock described in Example 9. Camford's CIO has now asked him to extend the analysis to project the path of bond yields as well.

Questions
1. What will Grant need in order to project the path of bond yields?
2. Even before he can undertake the formal analysis, a large client asks Grant to explain the likely implications for the yield curve. What can he say?

Guideline answers:
1. Grant will need a model linking bond yields to the policy rate. In essence, he needs a model of the yield curve.
2. Following the deflationary shock, the economy is very likely to enter into the contraction phase of the business cycle. The central bank will be cutting the policy rate, perhaps sharply. Long-term yields could drop even faster initially as the market anticipates that policy, but then the curve will steepen as the central bank cuts rates because long-maturity yields will incorporate the expectation of short-term rates rising again once the economy gains sufficient traction. The curve will likely reach its steepest point near the trough of the policy cycle and then gradually flatten as the economy gains strength and the central bank begins to tighten policy.

3.6. International Interactions

In general, the dependence of any particular country on international interactions is a function of its relative size and its degree of specialization. Large countries with diverse economies, such as the so-called G–7 (the United States, United Kingdom, Germany, France, Italy, Japan, and Canada), tend to be less influenced by developments elsewhere than smaller economies, such as Chile, whose output depends significantly on a few commodities like copper. Nonetheless, increasing globalization of trade, capital flows, and direct investment in recent decades has increased the importance of international interactions for nearly all countries.

3.6.1. Macroeconomic Linkages

Macroeconomic linkages between countries are expressed through their respective current and capital accounts. The current account reflects net exports of goods and services, net investment income flows, and unilateral transfers. The capital account, which for the purposes of this discussion also includes what is known as the financial account, reflects net investment flows for Foreign Direct Investment (FDI)—purchase and sale of productive assets across borders—and Portfolio Investment (PI) flows involving transactions in financial assets. By construction, if a country has a surplus on current account, it must have a matching deficit on capital account, or vice versa. Anything that affects one account must induce an equal and opposite change in the other account.

A nation's current and capital accounts are linked to the broader economy by the fact that net exports, virtually always the most significant component of the current account, contributes directly to aggregate demand for the nation's output. National income accounting also implies the following important relationship among net exports $(X - M)$, saving (S), investment (I), and the government surplus $(T - G)$:

$$(X - M) = (S - I) + (T - G)$$

Net exports always equal net private saving (the excess of domestic private saving over investment spending) plus the government surplus. Anything that changes net exports must also change net private saving, the government surplus, or both. Conversely, changes in either of these will be transmitted to the rest of the world through the current account. Of course, because the current account and capital accounts are mirror images, we can reverse all the signs in the foregoing equation and make corresponding statements about the capital account. A surplus on capital account is how a nation funds an excess of investment and government spending over domestic saving plus taxes.

There are four primary mechanisms by which the current and capital accounts are kept in balance: changes in income (GDP), relative prices, interest rates and asset prices, and exchange rates. Strictly speaking, all of these tools can play a role in both the real economy (the current account and FDI) and the financial markets, and they are determined simultaneously. However, markets do not all move at the same pace. In particular, investment markets adjust much more quickly than the real economy. In the short run, interest rates, exchange rates, and financial asset prices must adjust to keep the capital account in balance with the more slowly evolving current account. Meanwhile, the current account, in conjunction with real output and the relative prices of goods and services, tends to reflect secular trends and the pace of the business cycle.

EXAMPLE 11   International Macroeconomic Linkages

A large, diversified economy recently instituted a substantial tax cut, primarily aimed at reducing business taxes. Some provisions of the new law were designed to stem the tide of domestic firms moving production facilities abroad and encourage an increase in corporate investment in the domestic economy. There was no reduction in government spending. Prior to the tax cut, the country had both a current account deficit and a government deficit.

Questions:

1. What impact is this tax cut likely to have on
   a. the country's current account balance?
   b. the country's capital account balance?
   c. growth in other countries?
   d. the current and capital accounts of other countries?

2. What adjustments is the tax cut likely to induce in the financial markets?

Guideline answers:

1. a. The deficit on current account will almost certainly increase. The government deficit will increase which, all else the same, will result in a one-for-one increase in the current account deficit. If the tax cut works as intended, domestic investment will increase, reducing net private saving and further increasing the current account deficit. Private saving will increase as a result of rising income (GDP), which will diminish the impact on the current account somewhat. Unless saving increases by the full amount of the tax cut plus the increase in investment spending, however, the net effect will be an increase in the current account deficit. In principle, this increase could be thwarted by movements in the financial markets that make it impossible to fund it, but this is unlikely.

   b. Because the current account deficit will increase, the country's capital account surplus must increase by the same amount. In effect, the tax cut will be funded primarily by borrowing from abroad and/or selling assets to non-domestic investors. Part of the adjustment is likely to come from a reduction in FDI by domestic firms (i.e., purchases of productive assets abroad) provided the new tax provisions work as intended.

   c. Growth in other countries is likely to increase as the tax cut stimulates demand for their exports and that increase in turn generates additional demand within their domestic economies.

   d. In the aggregate, other countries must already be running current account surpluses and capital account deficits matching the balances of the country that has cut taxes. Their aggregate current account surplus and capital account deficit will increase by the same amount as the increase in current account deficit and capital account surplus of the tax-cutting country.

2. The country must attract additional capital flows from abroad. This endeavor is likely to be facilitated, at least in part, by the expectation of rising after-tax profits resulting from the business taxes. Equity values should therefore rise. The adjustment may also require interest rates and bond yields to rise relative to the rest of the world. The impact on the exchange rate is less clear. Because the current account and the capital account represent exactly offsetting flows, there is no *a priori* change in demand for the currency. The net impact will be determined by what investors *expect* to happen. (See the following section for a discussion of exchange rate linkages.)

3.6.2. Interest Rate/Exchange Rate Linkages

One of the linkages of greatest concern to investors involves interest rates and exchange rates. The two are inextricably linked. This fact is perhaps most evident in the proposition that a country cannot simultaneously

- allow unrestricted capital flows;
- maintain a fixed exchange rate; and
- pursue an independent monetary policy.

The essence of this proposition is that if the central bank attempts to push interest rates down (up), capital will flow out (in), putting downward (upward) pressure on the exchange rate, forcing the bank to buy (sell) its own currency, and thereby reversing the expansionary (contractionary) policy. Carrying this argument to its logical conclusion suggests that, with perfect capital mobility and a fixed exchange rate, "the" interest rate must be the same in countries whose currencies are pegged to each other.

Can we extend this proposition to encompass the whole (default-free) yield curve? Yes, but in doing so, we have to be somewhat more precise. Under what conditions would two markets share a yield curve? First, there must be unrestricted capital mobility between the markets ensuring that risk-adjusted expected returns will be equalized. The second condition is more difficult: The exchange rate between the currencies must be credibly fixed *forever*.[15] That is, investors must believe there is no risk that the currencies will exchange at a different rate in the future. Otherwise, yield differentials will emerge, giving rise to differential risk and return expectations in the two markets and allowing each market to trade on its own fundamentals. Thus, it is the lack of credibly fixed exchange rates that allows (default-free) yield curves, and hence bond returns, to be less than perfectly correlated across markets.

If a currency is linked to another without full credibility, then bond yields in the weaker currency are nearly always higher. This has been true even in the eurozone where, technically, separate currencies no longer exist—Greece, Italy, and Spain have always traded at meaningful, but varying, spreads over Germany and France. As long as there is no imminent risk of a devaluation, spreads at the very shortest maturities should be comparatively narrow. As demonstrated by the Greek exit ("Grexit") crisis, however, the situation changes sharply when the market perceives an imminent threat of devaluation (or a withdrawal from the common currency). Spreads then widen throughout the curve, but especially at the shortest maturities, and the curve will almost certainly invert. Why? Because in the event of a devaluation, yields in the devaluing currency will decline sharply (as the currency-risk premium collapses), generating much larger capital gains on longer-term bonds and thereby mitigating more of the currency loss.

When the exchange rate is allowed to float, the link between interest rates and exchange rates is primarily expectational. To equalize risk-adjusted expected returns across markets, interest rates must generally be higher (lower) in a currency that is expected to depreciate (appreciate). Ironically, this dynamic can lead to seemingly perverse situations in which the exchange rate "overshoots" in one direction to generate the expectation of movement in the opposite direction. The expectational linkage among exchange rates, interest rates, and asset prices is covered in detail at a later stage.

Capital mobility alone is clearly insufficient to eliminate differences in *nominal* interest rates and bond yields across countries. To a greater or lesser extent, each market responds to

---

[15]These conditions are necessary and sufficient for permanent convergence. See Chapter 10 of Stewart, Piros, and Heisler (forthcoming 2019) for a full exposition.

its own fundamentals, including policies. But what about *real* yields? We need to look at this question from two perspectives: the financial markets and the real economy.

An investor cares about the real return that she expects to earn *in her own currency*. In terms of a non-domestic asset, what matters is the *nominal* return and the change in the exchange rate. Even if non-domestic interest rates remain unchanged, the real return earned by the investor will not equal the non-domestic real interest rate unless purchasing power parity (PPP) holds over the investor's horizon. The empirical evidence overwhelmingly indicates that PPP does not hold over relevant investment horizons. Hence, we cannot rely on the simplistic notion that real interest rate differentials represent exploitable opportunities and should be eliminated by portfolio investment flows.

The preceding point is somewhat subtle and should not be construed to mean that real interest rate differentials are irrelevant for cross-market investment decisions. On the contrary, they can, but do not always, point to the likelihood of favorable *nominal* yield and exchange rate movements. The investor needs to assess non-domestic real rates from that perspective.

Ultimately, real interest rates must be consistent with the real saving and investment decisions that drive economic growth and the productivity of capital. As discussed earlier, saving and investment decisions are linked across countries through their current accounts. "Excess" saving in one country funds "excess" investment in another. In essence, there is a global market in which capital flows to where it is expected to be most productive. Although real rates around the world need not be equal, they are linked through the requirement that global savings must always equal global investment. Hence, they will tend to move together. As an example, the widespread low level of real interest rates that persisted in the aftermath of the global financial crisis was widely attributed to a very high level of global saving—primarily in Asia—and an unusually low level of capital investment in many developed markets, notably the United States.

4. SUMMARY

This is the first of two chapters on how investment professionals should address the setting of capital market expectations. The chapter began with a general framework for developing capital market expectations followed by a review of various challenges and pitfalls that analysts may encounter in the forecasting process. The remainder of the chapter focused on the use of macroeconomic analysis in setting expectations. The following are the main points covered in the chapter:

- Capital market expectations are essential inputs for strategic as well as tactical asset allocation.
- The ultimate objective is a set of projections with which to make informed investment decisions, specifically asset allocation decisions.
- Undue emphasis should not be placed on the accuracy of projections for individual asset classes. Internal consistency across asset classes (cross-sectional consistency) and over various time horizons (intertemporal consistency) are far more important objectives.
- The process of capital market expectations setting involves the following steps:
  1. Specify the set of expectations that are needed, including the time horizon(s) to which they apply.
  2. Research the historical record.

3. Specify the method(s) and/or model(s) that will be used and their information requirements.
4. Determine the best sources for information needs.
5. Interpret the current investment environment using the selected data and methods, applying experience and judgment.
6. Provide the set of expectations and document the conclusions.
7. Monitor outcomes, compare to forecasts, and provide feedback.

- Among the challenges in setting capital market expectations are:
  o *limitations of economic data* including lack of timeliness as well as changing definitions and calculations;
  o *data measurement errors and biases* including transcription errors, survivorship bias, and appraisal (smoothed) data;
  o *limitations of historical estimates* including lack of precision, nonstationarity, asynchronous observations, and distributional considerations such as fat tails and skewness;
  o ex post *risk as a biased risk measure* such as when historical returns reflect expectations of a low-probability catastrophe that did not occur or capture a low-probability event that did happen to occur;
  o *bias in methods* including data-mining and time-period biases;
  o *failure to account for conditioning information*;
  o *misinterpretation of correlations*;
  o *psychological biases* including anchoring, status quo, confirmation, overconfidence, prudence, and availability biases; and
  o *model uncertainty*.

- Losing sight of the connection between investment outcomes and the economy is a fundamental, and potentially costly, mistake in setting capital market expectations.
- Some growth trend changes are driven by slowly evolving and easily observable factors that are easy to forecast. Trend changes arising from exogenous shocks are impossible to forecast and difficult to identify, assess, and quantify until the change is well established.
- Among the most important sources of shocks are policy changes, new products and technologies, geopolitics, natural disasters, natural resources/critical inputs, and financial crises.
- An economy's aggregate trend growth rate reflects growth in labor inputs and growth in labor productivity. Extrapolating past trends in these components can provide a reasonable initial estimate of the future growth trend, which can be adjusted based on observable information. Less developed economies may require more significant adjustments because they are likely to be undergoing more rapid structural changes.
- The average level of real (nominal) default-free bond yields is linked to the trend rate of real (nominal) growth. The trend rate of growth provides an important anchor for estimating bond returns over horizons long enough for this reversion to prevail over cyclical and short-term forces.
- The trend growth rate provides an anchor for long-run equity appreciation. In the very long run, the aggregate value of equity must grow at a rate very close to the rate of GDP growth.
- There are three main approaches to economic forecasting:
  o *Econometric models*: structural and reduced-form statistical models of key variables generate quantitative estimates, impose discipline on forecasts, may be robust enough to

approximate reality, and can readily forecast the impact of exogenous variables or shocks. However, they tend to be complex, time-consuming to formulate, and potentially mis-specified, and they rarely forecast turning points well.

o *Indicators*: variables that lead, lag, or coincide with turns in the economy. This approach is the simplest, requiring only a limited number of published statistics. It can generate false signals, however, and is vulnerable to revisions that may overfit past data at the expense of the reliability of out-of-sample forecasts.

o *Checklist(s)*: subjective integration of information deemed relevant by the analyst. This approach is the most flexible but also the most subjective. It readily adapts to a changing environment, but ongoing collection and assessment of information make it time-consuming and also limit the depth and consistency of the analysis.

• The business cycle is the result of many intermediate frequency cycles that jointly generate most of the variation in aggregate economic activity. This explains why historical business cycles have varied in both duration and intensity and why it is difficult to project turning points in real time.

• The business cycle reflects decisions that (a) are made based on imperfect information and/or analysis with the expectation of future benefits, (b) require significant current resources and/or time to implement, and (c) are difficult and/or costly to reverse. Such decisions are, broadly defined, investment decisions.

• A typical business cycle has a number of phases. We split the cycle into five phases with the following capital market implications:

o **Initial Recovery.** Short-term interest rates and bond yields are low. Bond yields are likely to bottom. Stock markets may rise strongly. Cyclical/riskier assets such as small stocks, high-yield bonds, and emerging market securities perform well.

o **Early Expansion.** Short rates are moving up. Longer-maturity bond yields are stable or rising slightly. Stocks are trending up.

o **Late Expansion.** Interest rates rise, and the yield curve flattens. Stock markets often rise but may be volatile. Cyclical assets may underperform while inflation hedges outperform.

o **Slowdown.** Short-term interest rates are at or nearing a peak. Government bond yields peak and may then decline sharply. The yield curve may invert. Credit spreads widen, especially for weaker credits. Stocks may fall. Interest-sensitive stocks and "quality" stocks with stable earnings perform best.

o **Contraction.** Interest rates and bond yields drop. The yield curve steepens. The stock market drops initially but usually starts to rise well before the recovery emerges. Credit spreads widen and remain elevated until clear signs of a cycle trough emerge.

• At least three factors complicate translation of business cycle information into capital market expectations and profitable investment decisions. First, the phases of the cycle vary in length and amplitude. Second, it is not always easy to distinguish between cyclical forces and secular forces acting on the economy and the markets. Third, how, when, and by how much the markets respond to the business cycle is as uncertain as the cycle itself—perhaps more so.

• Business cycle information is likely to be most reliable/valuable in setting capital market expectations over horizons within the range of likely expansion and contraction phases. Transitory developments cloud shorter-term forecasts, whereas significantly longer horizons likely cover portions of multiple cycle phases. Information about the current cyclical state of the economy has no predictive value over very long horizons.

- Monetary policy is often used as a mechanism for intervention in the business cycle. This mechanism is inherent in the mandates of most central banks to maintain price stability and/or growth consistent with potential.

- Monetary policy aims to be countercyclical, but the ability to fine-tune the economy is limited and policy measures may exacerbate rather than moderate the business cycle. This risk is greatest at the top of the cycle when the central bank may overestimate the economy's momentum and/or underestimate the potency of restrictive policies.

- Fiscal policy—government spending and taxation—can be used to counteract cyclical fluctuations in the economy. Aside from extreme situations, however, fiscal policy typically addresses objectives other than regulating short-term growth. So-called automatic stabilizers do play an important role in mitigating cyclical fluctuations.

- The Taylor rule is a useful tool for assessing a central bank's stance and for predicting how that stance is likely to evolve.

- The expectation that central banks could not implement negative policy rates proved to be unfounded in the aftermath of the 2007–2009 global financial crisis. Because major central banks combined negative policy rates with other extraordinary measures (notably quantitative easing), however, the effectiveness of the negative rate policy is unclear. The effectiveness of quantitative easing is also unclear.

- Negative interest rates, and the environment that gives rise to them, make the task of setting capital market expectations even more complex. Among the issues that arise are the following:
  o It is difficult to justify negative rates as a "risk-free rate" to which risk premiums can be added to establish long-term "equilibrium" asset class returns.
  o Historical data and quantitative models are even less likely to be reliable.
  o Market relationships (e.g., the yield curve) are likely to be distorted by other concurrent policy measures.

- The mix of monetary and fiscal policies has its most apparent effect on the average level of interest rates and inflation. Persistently loose (tight) fiscal policy increases (reduces) the average level of real interest rates. Persistently loose (tight) monetary policy increases (reduces) the average levels of actual and expected inflation. The impact on nominal rates is ambiguous if one policy is persistently tight and the other persistently loose.

- Changes in the slope of the yield curve are driven primarily by the evolution of short rate expectations, which are driven mainly by the business cycle and policies. The slope of the curve may also be affected by debt management.

- The slope of the yield curve is useful as a predictor of economic growth and as an indicator of where the economy is in the business cycle.

- Macroeconomic linkages between countries are expressed through their respective current and capital accounts.

- There are four primary mechanisms by which the current and capital accounts are kept in balance: changes in income (GDP), relative prices, interest rates and asset prices, and exchange rates.

- In the short run, interest rates, exchange rates, and financial asset prices must adjust to keep the capital account in balance with the more slowly evolving current account. The current account, in conjunction with real output and the relative prices of goods and services, tends to reflect secular trends and the pace of the business cycle.

- Interest rates and currency exchange rates are inextricably linked. This relationship is evident in the fact that a country cannot simultaneously allow unfettered capital flows, maintain a fixed exchange rate, and pursue an independent monetary policy.
- Two countries will share a default-free yield curve if (and only if) there is perfect capital mobility and the exchange rate is credibly fixed *forever*. It is the lack of credibly fixed exchange rates that allows (default-free) yield curves, and hence bond returns, to be less than perfectly correlated across markets.
- With floating exchange rates, the link between interest rates and exchange rates is primarily expectational. To equalize risk-adjusted expected returns across markets, interest rates must be higher (lower) in a currency that is expected to depreciate (appreciate). This dynamic can lead to the exchange rate "overshooting" in one direction to generate the expectation of movement in the opposite direction.
- An investor cares about the real return that he or she expects to earn *in his or her own currency*. In terms of a foreign asset, what matters is the *nominal* return and the change in the exchange rate.
- Although real interest rates around the world need not be equal, they are linked through the requirement that global savings must always equal global investment. Hence, they will tend to move together.

REFERENCES

Brinson, Gary, Randolph Hood, and Gilbert Beebower. 1986. "Determinants of Portfolio Performance." *Financial Analysts Journal* 42 (4): 39–44.

Buttiglione, Luigi, Philip R. Lane, Lucrezia Reichlin, and Vincent Reinhart. 2014. *Deleveraging? What Deleveraging?* International Center for Monetary and Banking Studies.

Friedman, Milton. 1968. "The Role of Monetary Policy." *American Economic Review* 58 (1): 1–17.

Ibbotson, Roger, and Paul Kaplan. 2000. "Does Asset Allocation Policy Explain 40, 90, or 100 Percent of Performance?" *Financial Analysts Journal* 56 (1): 26–33.

Klement, Joachim. 2015. "What's Growth Got to Do With It? Equity Returns and Economic Growth." *Journal of Investing* 24 (2): 74–78.

Marcelo, Jose Luis Miralles, Luis Miralles Quiros Jose, and Jose Luis Martins. 2013. "The Role of Country and Industry Factors During Volatile Times." *Journal of International Financial Markets, Institutions and Money* 26:273–90.

McQueen, Grant, and Steven Thorley. 1999. "Mining Fools Gold." *Financial Analysts Journal* 55 (2): 61–72.

Rapaport, Alfred, and Michael Mauboussin. 2001. *Expectations Investing: Reading Stock Prices for Better Returns.* Boston: Harvard Business School Press.

Stewart, Scott D., Christopher D. Piros, and Jeffrey C. Heisler. 2019, Forthcoming. *Portfolio Management: Theory and Practice.* Hoboken, NJ: John Wiley & Sons.

PRACTICE PROBLEMS

The following information relates to Questions 1–8

Neshie Wakuluk is an investment strategist who develops capital market expectations for an investment firm that invests across asset classes and global markets. Wakuluk started her career when the global markets were experiencing significant volatility and poor returns; as a result, she is now careful to base her conclusions on objective evidence and analytical procedures to mitigate any potential biases.

Wakuluk's approach to economic forecasting utilizes a structural model in conjunction with a diffusion index to determine the current phase of a country's business cycle. This approach has produced successful predictions in the past, thus Wakuluk has high confidence in the predictions. Wakuluk also determines whether any adjustments need to be made to her initial estimates of the respective aggregate economic growth trends based on historical rates of growth for Countries X and Y (both developed markets) and Country Z (a developing market). Exhibit 1 summarizes Wakuluk's predictions:

EXHIBIT 1   Prediction for Current Phase of the Business Cycle

Country X	Country Y	Country Z
Initial Recovery	Contraction	Late Upswing

Wakuluk assumes short-term interest rates adjust with expected inflation and are procyclical. Wakuluk reviews the historical short-term interest rate trends for each country, which further confirms her predictions shown in Exhibit 1.

Wakuluk decides to focus on Country Y to determine the path of nominal interest rates, the potential economic response of Country Y's economy to this path, and the timing for when Country Y's economy may move into the next business cycle. Wakuluk makes the following observations:

Observation 1:   Monetary policy has been persistently loose for Country Y, while fiscal policies have been persistently tight.

Observation 2:   Country Y is expected to significantly increase transfer payments and introduce a more progressive tax regime.

Observation 3:   The current yield curve for Country Y suggests that the business cycle is in the slowdown phase, with bond yields starting to reflect contractionary conditions.

1. Wakuluk *most likely* seeks to mitigate which of the following biases in developing capital market forecasts?
   A. Availability
   B. Time period
   C. Survivorship

2. Wakuluk's approach to economic forecasting:
   A. is flexible and limited in complexity.
   B. can give a false sense of precision and provide false signals.
   C. imposes no consistency of analysis across items or at different points in time.

3. Wakuluk is *most likely* to make significant adjustments to her estimate of the future growth trend for which of the following countries?
   A. Country Y only
   B. Country Z only
   C. Countries Y and Z

4. Based on Exhibit 1 and Wakuluk's assumptions about short-term rates and expected inflation, short-term rates in Country X are *most likely* to be:
   A. low and bottoming.
   B. approaching a peak.
   C. above average and rising.

5. Based on Exhibit 1, what capital market effect is Country Z *most likely* to experience in the short-term?
   A. Cyclical assets attract investors.
   B. Monetary policy becomes restrictive.
   C. The yield curve steepens substantially.

6. Based on Observation 1, fiscal and monetary policies in Country Y will *most likely* lead to:
   A. low nominal rates.
   B. high nominal rates.
   C. either high or low nominal rates.

7. Based on Observation 2, what impact will the policy changes have on the trend rate of growth for Country Y?
   A. Negative
   B. Neutral
   C. Positive

8. Based on Observation 3, Wakuluk *most likely* expects Country Y's yield curve in the near term to:
   A. invert.
   B. flatten.
   C. steepen.

The following information relates to Questions 9–10

Jennifer Wuyan is an investment strategist responsible for developing long-term capital market expectations for an investment firm that invests in domestic equities. She presents a report to the firm's investment committee describing the statistical model used to formulate capital market expectations, which is based on a dividend discount method. In the report, she notes that in developing the model, she researched the historical data seeking to identify the relevant variables and determined the best source of data for the model. She also notes her interpretation of the current economic and market environment.

9. **Explain** what additional step(s) Wuyan should have taken in the process of setting capital market expectations.

Wuyan reports that after repeatedly searching the most recent 10 years of data, she eventually identified variables that had a statistically significant relationship with equity returns. Wuyan used these variables to forecast equity returns. She documented, in a separate section of the report, a high correlation between nominal GDP and equity returns. Based on this noted high correlation, Wuyan concludes that nominal GDP predicts equity returns. Based on her statistical results, Wuyan expects equities to underperform over the next 12 months and recommends that the firm underweight equities.

Commenting on the report, John Tommanson, an investment adviser for the firm, suggests extending the starting point of the historical data back another 20 years to obtain more robust statistical results. Doing so would enable the analysis to include different economic and central bank policy environments. Tommanson is reluctant to underweight equities for his clients, citing the strong performance of equities over the last quarter, and believes the most recent quarterly data should be weighted more heavily in setting capital market expectations.

10. **Discuss** how *each* of the following forecasting challenges evident in Wuyan's report and in Tommanson's comments affects the setting of capital market expectations:
    i.   Status quo bias
    ii. Data-mining bias
    iii. Risk of regime change
    iv. Misinterpretation of correlation

Discuss how *each* of the following forecasting challenges evident in Wuyan's report and in Tommanson's comments affects the setting of capital market expectations:

Status quo bias	
Data-mining bias	
Risk of regime change	
Misinterpretation of correlation	

The following information relates to Questions 11–13

Jan Cambo is chief market strategist at a US asset management firm. While preparing a report for the upcoming investment committee meeting, Cambo updates her long-term forecast for US equity returns. As an input into her forecasting model, she uses the following long-term annualized forecasts from the firm's chief economist:

- Labor input will grow 0.5%.
- Labor productivity will grow 1.3%.
- Inflation will be 2.2%.
- Dividend yield will be 2.8%.

Based on these forecasts, Cambo predicts a long-term 9.0% annual equity return in the US market. Her forecast assumes no change in the share of profits in the economy, and she expects some contribution to equity returns from a change in the price-to-earnings ratio (P/E).

11. **Calculate** the implied contribution to Cambo's US equity return forecast from the expected change in the P/E.

At the investment committee meeting, the firm's chief economist predicts that the economy will enter the late expansion phase of the business cycle in the next 12 months.

12. **Discuss**, based on the chief economist's prediction, the implications for the following:
    i.   Bond yields
    ii. Equity returns
    iii. Short-term interest rates

Discuss, based on the chief economist's prediction, the implications for the following:

Bond yields	
Equity returns	
Short-term interest rates	

Cambo compares her business cycle forecasting approach to the approach used by the chief economist. Cambo bases her equity market forecast on a time-series model using a composite index of leading indicators as the key input, whereas the chief economist uses a detailed econometric model to generate his economic forecasts.

13. **Discuss** strengths and weaknesses of the economic forecasting approaches used by Cambo and the chief economist.

Discuss strengths and weaknesses of the economic forecasting approaches used by Cambo and the chief economist.

	Cambo's Forecasting Approach	Chief Economist's Forecasting Approach
Strengths		
Weaknesses		

The following information relates to Questions 14–16

Robert Hadpret is the chief economist at Agree Partners, an asset management firm located in the developed country of Eastland. He has prepared an economic report on Eastland for the firm's asset allocation committee. Hadpret notes that the composite index of leading economic indicators has declined for three consecutive months and that the yield curve has inverted. Private sector borrowing is also projected to decline. Based on these recent events, Hadpret predicts an economic contraction and forecasts lower inflation and possibly deflation over the next 12 months.

Helen Smitherman, a portfolio manager at Agree, considers Hadpret's economic forecast when determining the tactical allocation for the firm's Balanced Fund (the fund). Smitherman notes that the fund has considerable exposure to real estate, shares of asset-intensive and commodity-producing firms, and high-quality debt. The fund's cash holdings are at cyclical lows.

14. **Discuss** the implications of Hadpret's inflation forecast on the expected returns of the fund's holdings of:
    i.   cash.
    ii. bonds.
    iii. equities.
    iv. real estate.

Discuss the implications of Hadpret's inflation forecast on the expected returns of the fund's holdings of:

Cash	
Bonds	
Equities	
Real Estate	

In response to the projected cyclical decline in the Eastland economy and in private sector borrowing over the next year, Hadpret expects a change in the monetary and fiscal policy mix. He forecasts that the Eastland central bank will ease monetary policy. On the fiscal side, Hadpret expects the Eastland government to enact a substantial tax cut. As a result, Hadpret forecasts large government deficits that will be financed by the issuance of long-term government securities.

15. **Discuss** the relationship between the shape of the yield curve and the monetary and fiscal policy mix projected by Hadpret.

Currently, Eastland's currency is fixed relative to the currency of the country of Northland, and Eastland maintains policies that allow unrestricted capital flows. Hadpret examines the relationship between interest rates and exchange rates. He considers three possible scenarios for the Eastland economy:

Scenario 1.   Shift in policy restricting capital flows
Scenario 2.   Shift in policy allowing the currency to float
Scenario 3.   Shift in investor belief toward a lack of full credibility that the exchange rate will
be fixed forever

16.   **Discuss** how interest rate and exchange rate linkages between Eastland and Northland
might change under *each* scenario.
Note: Consider *each* scenario independently.

Discuss how interest rate and exchange rate linkages between Eastland and Northland might change
under *each* scenario. (Note: Consider *each* scenario independently.)

Scenario 1	
Scenario 2	
Scenario 3	

CHAPTER 4

CAPITAL MARKET EXPECTATIONS, PART 2: FORECASTING ASSET CLASS RETURNS

Christopher D. Piros, PhD, CFA

Parts of this chapter have been adapted from a former Capital Market Expectations chapter authored by John P. Calverley, Alan M. Meder, CPA, CFA, Brian D. Singer, CFA, and Renato Staub, PhD.

LEARNING OUTCOMES

The candidate should be able to:

- discuss approaches to setting expectations for fixed-income returns;
- discuss risks faced by investors in emerging market fixed-income securities and the country risk analysis techniques used to evaluate emerging market economies;
- discuss approaches to setting expectations for equity investment market returns;
- discuss risks faced by investors in emerging market equity securities;
- explain how economic and competitive factors can affect expectations for real estate investment markets and sector returns;
- discuss major approaches to forecasting exchange rates;
- discuss methods of forecasting volatility;
- recommend and justify changes in the component weights of a global investment portfolio based on trends and expected changes in macroeconomic factors.

1. INTRODUCTION

This is the second of two chapters focusing on capital market expectations. A central theme of both chapters is that a disciplined approach to setting expectations will be rewarded. After outlining a framework for developing expectations and reviewing potential pitfalls, the first chapter focused on the use of macroeconomic analysis in setting expectations. This chapter builds on that foundation and examines setting expectations for specific asset classes—fixed income, equities, real estate, and currencies. Estimation of variance–covariance matrices is covered as well.

The chapter begins with an overview of the techniques frequently used to develop capital market expectations. The discussion of specific asset classes begins with fixed income in Section 3, followed by equities, real estate, and currencies in Sections 4–6. Estimation of variance–covariance structures is addressed in Section 7. Section 8 illustrates the use of macroeconomic analysis to develop and justify adjustments to a global portfolio.

2. OVERVIEW OF TOOLS AND APPROACHES

This section provides a brief overview of the main concepts, approaches, and tools used in professional forecasting of capital market returns. Whereas subsequent sections focus on specific asset classes, the emphasis here is on the commonality of techniques.

2.1. The Nature of the Problem

Few investment practitioners are likely to question the notion that investment opportunities change in systematic, but imperfectly predictable ways over time. Yet the ramifications of that fact are often not explicitly recognized. Forecasting returns is not simply a matter of estimating constant, but unknown, parameters—for example, expected returns, variances, and correlations. Time horizons matter. The previous chapter highlighted two aspects of this issue: the need to ensure intertemporal consistency and the relative usefulness of specific information (e.g., the business cycle) over short, intermediate, and long horizons. The choice among forecasting techniques is effectively a choice of the information on which forecasts will be based (in statistical terms, the information on which the forecast is "conditioned") and how that information will be incorporated into the forecasts. The fact that opportunities change over time should, at least in principle, affect strategic investment decisions and how positions respond to changing forecasts.[1]

Although investment opportunities are not constant, virtually all forecasting techniques rely on notions of central tendency, toward which opportunities tend to revert over time. This fact means that although asset prices, risk premiums, volatilities, valuation ratios, and other metrics may exhibit momentum, persistence, and clustering in the short run, over sufficiently long horizons, they tend to converge to levels consistent with economic and financial fundamentals.

---

[1]For example, in general, it is not optimal to choose a portfolio on the mean–variance-efficient frontier based on forecasts for the coming period. In addition, the distinction between "strategic" and "tactical" asset allocation is less clear cut since, in general, the optimal allocation evolves with the investor's remaining investment horizon. See Piros (2015) for a non-technical exposition of these issues.

What are we trying to forecast? In principle, we are interested in the whole probability distribution of future returns. In practice, however, forecasting expected return is by far the most important consideration, both because it is the dominant driver of most investment decisions and because it is generally more difficult to forecast within practical tolerances than such risk metrics as volatility. Hence, the primary focus here is on expected return. In terms of risk metrics, we limit our attention to variances and covariances.

2.2. Approaches to Forecasting

At a very high level, there are essentially three approaches to forecasting: (1) formal tools, (2) surveys, and (3) judgment. Formal tools are established research methods amenable to precise definition and independent replication of results. Surveys involve asking a group of experts for their opinions. Judgment can be described as a qualitative synthesis of information derived from various sources and filtered through the lens of experience.

Surveys are probably most useful as a way to gauge consensus views, which can serve as inputs into formal tools and the analyst's own judgment. Judgment is always important. There is ample scope for applying judgment—in particular, economic and psychological insight—to improve forecasts and numbers, including those produced by elaborate quantitative models. In using survey results and applying their own judgment, analysts must be wary of the psychological traps discussed in the Capital Market Expectations Part 1 chapter. Beyond these brief observations, however, there is not much new to be said about surveys and judgment.

The formal forecasting tools most commonly used in forecasting capital market returns fall into three broad categories: statistical methods, discounted cash flow models, and risk premium models. The distinctions among these methods will become clear as they are discussed and applied throughout the chapter.

2.2.1. Statistical Methods

All the formal tools involve data and statistical analysis to some degree. Methods that are primarily, if not exclusively, statistical impose relatively little structure on the data. As a result, the forecasts inherit the statistical properties of the data with limited, if any, regard for economic or financial reasoning. Three types of statistical methods will be covered in this chapter. The first approach is to use well-known sample statistics, such as sample means, variances, and correlations, to describe the distribution of future returns. This is undoubtedly the clearest example of simply taking the data at face value. Unfortunately, sampling error makes some of these statistics—in particular, the sample mean—very imprecise. The second approach, **shrinkage estimation**, involves taking a weighted average of two estimates of the same parameter—one based on historical sample data and the other based on some other source or information, such as the analyst's "prior" knowledge. This "two-estimates-are-better-than-one" approach has the desirable property of reducing forecast errors relative to simple sample statistics. The third method, **time-series estimation**, involves forecasting a variable on the basis of lagged values of the variable being forecast and often lagged values of other selected variables. These models have the benefit of explicitly incorporating dynamics into the forecasting process. However, since they are reduced-form models, they may summarize the historical data well without providing much insight into the underlying drivers of the forecasts.

2.2.2. Discounted Cash Flow

Discounted cash flow (DCF) models express the idea that an asset's value is the present value of its expected cash flows. They are a basic method for establishing the intrinsic value of an asset on the basis of fundamentals and its fair required rate of return. Conversely, they are used to estimate the required rate of return implied by the asset's current price.

2.2.3. Risk Premium Models

The risk premium approach expresses the expected return on a risky asset as the sum of the risk-free rate of interest and one or more risk premiums that compensate investors for the asset's exposure to sources of *priced risk* (risk for which investors demand compensation). There are three main methods for modeling risk premiums: (1) an equilibrium model, such as the CAPM, (2) a factor model, and (3) building blocks. Each of these methods was discussed in earlier chapters. Equilibrium models and factor models both impose a structure on how returns are assumed to be generated. Hence, they can be used to generate estimates of (1) expected returns and (2) variances and covariances.

3. FORECASTING FIXED-INCOME RETURNS

There are three main ways to approach forecasting fixed-income returns. The first is discounted cash flow. This method is really the only one that is precise enough to use in support of trades involving individual fixed-income securities. This type of "micro" analysis will not be discussed in detail here since it is covered extensively elsewhere in CFA Program curriculum chapters that focus on fixed income. DCF concepts are also useful in forecasting the more aggregated performance needed to support asset allocation decisions. The second approach is the risk premium approach, which is often applied to fixed income, in part because fixed-income premiums are among the building blocks used to estimate expected returns on riskier asset classes, such as equities. The third approach is to include fixed-income asset classes in an equilibrium model. Doing so has the advantage of imposing consistency across asset classes and is especially useful as a first step in applying the Black–Litterman framework, which will be discussed in a later chapter.

3.1. Applying DCF to Fixed Income

Fixed income is really all about discounted cash flow. This stems from the facts that almost all fixed-income securities have finite maturities and that the (promised) cash flows are known, governed by explicit rules, or can be modeled with a reasonably high degree of accuracy (e.g., mortgage-backed security prepayments). Using modern arbitrage-free models, we can value virtually any fixed-income instrument. The most straightforward and, undoubtedly, most precise way to forecast fixed-income returns is to explicitly value the securities on the basis of the assumed evolution of the critical inputs to the valuation model—for example, the spot yield curve, the term structure of volatilities, and prepayment speeds. A whole distribution of returns can be generated by doing this for a variety of scenarios. As noted previously, this is essentially the only option if we need the "micro" precision of accounting for rolling down the yield curve, changes in the shape of the yield curve, changes in rate volatilities, or changes in the sensitivity of contingent cash flows. But for many purposes—for example, asset allocation— we usually do not need such granularity.

Yield to maturity (YTM)—the single discount rate that equates the present value of a bond's cash flows to its market price—is by far the most commonly quoted metric of valuation and, implicitly, of expected return for bonds. For bond portfolios, the YTM is usually calculated as if it were simply an average of the individual bonds' YTM, which is not exactly accurate but is a reasonable approximation.[2] Forecasting bond returns would be very easy if we could simply equate yield to maturity with expected return. It is not that simple, but YTM does provide a reasonable and readily available first approximation.

Assuming cash flows are received in full and on time, there are two main reasons why realized return may not equal the initial yield to maturity. First, if the investment horizon is shorter than the amount of time until the bond's maturity, any change in interest rate (i.e., the bond's YTM) will generate a capital gain or loss at the horizon. Second, the cash flows may be reinvested at rates above or below the initial YTM. The longer the horizon, the more sensitive the realized return will be to reinvestment rates. These two issues work in opposite directions: Rising (falling) rates induce capital losses (gains) but increase (decrease) reinvestment income. If the investment horizon equals the (Macaulay) duration of the bond or portfolio, the capital gain/loss and reinvestment effects will roughly offset, leaving the realized return close to the original YTM. This relationship is exact if (a) the yield curve is flat and (b) the change in rates occurs immediately in a single step. In practice, the relationship is only an approximation. Nonetheless, it provides an important insight: *Over horizons shorter than the duration, the capital gain/loss impact will tend to dominate such that rising (declining) rates imply lower (higher) return, whereas over horizons longer than the duration, the reinvestment impact will tend to dominate such that rising (declining) rates imply higher (lower) return.*

Note that the timing of rate changes matters. It will not have much effect, if any, on the capital gain/loss component because that ultimately depends on the beginning and ending values of the bond or portfolio. But it does affect the reinvestment return. The longer the horizon, the more it matters. Hence, for long-term forecasts, we should break the forecast horizon into subperiods corresponding to when we expect the largest rate changes to occur.

EXAMPLE 1   Forecasting Return Based on Yield to Maturity

Jesper Bloch works for Discrete Asset Management (DAM) in Zurich. Many of the firm's more risk-averse clients invest in a currency-hedged global government bond strategy that uses cash flows to purchase new issues and seasoned bonds all along the yield curve to maintain a roughly constant maturity and duration profile. The yield to maturity of the portfolio is 3.25% (compounded annually), and the modified duration is 4.84. DAM's chief investment officer believes global government yields are likely to rise by 200 bps over the next two years as central banks remove extraordinarily accommodative policies and inflation surges. Bloch has been asked to project approximate returns for this strategy over horizons of two, five, and seven years. What conclusions is Bloch likely to draw?

---

[2]Bear in mind that yield to maturity does not account for optionality. However, various yield measures derived from option-adjusted valuation can be viewed as conveying similar information. To keep the present discussion as simple as possible, we ignore the distinction here. If optionality is critical to the forecast, it may be necessary to apply the more granular DCF framework discussed previously.

Solution: If yields were not expected to change, the return would be very close to the yield to maturity (3.25%) over each horizon. The Macaulay duration is 5.0 (= 4.84 × 1.0325), so if the yield change occurred immediately, the capital gain/loss and reinvestment impacts on return would roughly balance over five years. Ignoring convexity (which is not given), the capital loss at the end of two years will be approximately 9.68% (= 4.84 × 2%). Assuming yields rise linearly over the initial two-year period, the higher reinvestment rates will boost the cumulative return by approximately 1.0% over two years, so the annual return over two years will be approximately −1.09% [= 3.25 + (−9.68 + 1.0)/2]. Reinvesting for three more years at the 2.0% higher rate adds another 6.0% to the cumulative return, so the five-year annual return would be approximately 2.71% [= 3.25 + (−9.68 + 1.0 + 6.0)/5]. With an additional two years of reinvestment income, the seven-year annual return would be about 3.44% [= 3.25 + (−9.68 + 1.0 + 6.0 + 4.0)/7]. As expected, the capital loss dominated the return over two years, and higher reinvestment rates dominated over seven years. The gradual nature of the yield increase extended the horizon over which the capital gain/loss and reinvestment effects would balance beyond the initial five-year Macaulay duration.

We have extended the DCF approach beyond simply finding the discount rates implied by current market prices (e.g., YTMs), which might be considered the "pure" DCF approach. For other asset classes (e.g., equities), the connection between discount rates and valuations/ returns is vague because there is so much uncertainty with respect to the cash flows. For these asset classes, discounted cash flow is essentially a conceptual framework rather than a precise valuation model. In contrast, in fixed income there is a tight connection between discount rates, valuations, and returns. We are, therefore, able to refine the "pure" DCF forecast by incorporating projections of how rates will evolve over the investment horizon. Doing so is particularly useful in formulating short-term forecasts.

3.2. The Building Block Approach to Fixed-Income Returns

The building block approach forms an estimate of expected return in terms of required compensation for specific types of risk. The required return for fixed-income asset classes has four components: the one-period default-free rate, the term premium, the credit premium, and the liquidity premium. As the names indicate, the premiums reflect compensation for interest rate risk, duration risk, credit risk, and illiquidity, respectively. Only one of the four components—the short-term default-free rate—is (potentially) observable. For example, the term premium and the credit premium are implicitly embedded in yield spreads, but they are not *equal* to observed yield spreads. Next, we will consider each of these components and summarize applicable empirical regularities.

3.2.1. The Short-Term Default-Free Rate

In principle, the short-term default-free rate is the rate on the highest-quality, most liquid instrument with a maturity that matches the forecast horizon. In practice, it is usually taken to be a government zero-coupon bill at a maturity that is issued frequently—say, every three months. This rate is virtually always tied closely to the central bank's policy rate and, therefore, mirrors the cyclical dynamics of monetary policy. Secular movements are closely tied to expected inflation levels.

Under normal circumstances, the observed rate is a reasonable base on which to build expected returns for risky assets. In extreme circumstances, however, it may be necessary to adopt a normalized rate. For example, when policy rates or short-term government rates are negative, using the observed rate without adjustment may unduly reduce the required/expected return estimate for risky instruments. An alternative to normalizing the short rate in this circumstance would be to raise the estimate of one or more of the risk premiums on the basis of the notion that the observed negative short rate reflects an elevated willingness to pay for safety or, conversely, elevated required compensation for risk.

Forecast horizons substantially longer than the maturity of the standard short-term instrument call for a different type of adjustment. There are essentially two approaches. The first is to use the yield on a longer zero-coupon bond with a maturity that matches the horizon. In theory, that is the right thing to do. It does, however, call into question the role of the term premium since the longer-term rate will already incorporate the term premium. The second approach is to replace today's observed short-term rate with an estimate of the return that would be generated by rolling the short-term instrument over the forecast horizon; that is, take account of the likely path of short-term rates. This approach does not change the interpretation of the term premium. In addition to helping establish the baseline return to which risk premiums will be added, explicitly projecting the path of short-term rates may help in estimating the term premium.

In many markets, there are futures contracts for short-term instruments. The rates implied by these contracts are frequently interpreted as the market's expected path of short-term rates. As such, they provide an excellent starting point for analysts in formulating their own projections. Some central banks—for example, the US Federal Reserve Board—publish projections of future policy rates that can also serve as a guide for analysts. Quantitative models, such as the Taylor rule, provide another tool.[3]

3.2.2. The Term Premium

The default-free spot rate curve reflects the expected path of short-term rates and the required term premiums for each maturity. It is tempting to think that given a projected path of short-term rates, we can easily deduce the term premiums from the spot curve. We can, of course, derive a set of forward rates in the usual way and subtract the projected short-term rate for each future period. Doing so would give an implied sequence of period-by-period premiums. This may be a useful exercise, but it will not give us what we really want—the expected returns for bonds of different maturities over our forecast horizon. The implication is that although the yield curve contains the information we want and may be useful in forecasting returns, we cannot derive the term premium directly from the curve itself.

A vast amount of academic research has been devoted over many decades to addressing three fundamental questions: Do term premiums exist? If so, are they constant? And if they exist, how are they related to maturity? The evidence indicates that term premiums are positive and increase with maturity, are roughly proportional to duration, and vary over time. The first of these properties implies that term premiums are important. The second allows the analyst to be pragmatic, focusing on a single term premium, which is then scaled by duration. The third property implies that basing estimates on current information is essential.

---

[3]See the Capital Market Expectations Part 1 chapter for discussion of the Taylor rule.

Ilmanen (2012) argued that there are four main drivers of the term premium for nominal bonds.

- *Level-dependent inflation uncertainty:* Inflation is arguably the main driver of long-run variation in both nominal yields and the term premium. Higher (lower) levels of inflation tend to coincide with greater (less) inflation uncertainty. Hence, nominal yields rise (fall) with inflation because of changes in both expected inflation and the inflation risk component of the term premium.
- *Ability to hedge recession risk:* In theory, assets earn a low (or negative) risk premium if they tend to perform well when the economy is weak. When growth and inflation are primarily driven by aggregate demand, nominal bond returns tend to be negatively correlated with growth and a relatively low term premium is warranted. Conversely, when growth and inflation are primarily driven by aggregate supply, nominal bond returns tend to be positively correlated with growth, necessitating a higher term premium.
- *Supply and demand:* The relative outstanding supply of short-maturity and long-maturity default-free bonds influences the slope of the yield curve.[4] This phenomenon is largely attributable to the term premium since the maturity structure of outstanding debt should have little impact on the expected future path of short-term rates.[5]
- *Cyclical effects:* The slope of the yield curve varies substantially over the business cycle: It is steep around the trough of the cycle and flat or even inverted around the peak. Much of this movement reflects changes in the expected path of short-term rates. However, it also reflects countercyclical changes in the term premium.

Although the slope of the yield curve is useful information on which to base forecasts of the term premium, other indicators work as well or better. Exhibit 1 shows correlations with subsequent excess bond returns (7- to 10-year Treasury bond return minus 3-month Treasury bill return) over 1-quarter, 1-year, and 5-year horizons for eight indicators. The indicators are listed in descending order of the (absolute value of the) correlation with one-year returns. The first four are derived from the bond market. The *ex ante* real yield has the strongest relationship over each horizon. Next on the list are the two most complex indicators. The Cochrane and Piazzesi curve factor is a composite measure capturing both the slope and the curvature of the yield curve.[6] The Kim and Wright premium is derived from a three-factor term structure model.[7] The slope of the yield curve is next on the list. Note that it has the weakest relationship over the five-year horizon. The supply indicator—the share of debt with maturity greater than 10 years—has a particularly strong relationship over the longest horizon. Since this variable tends to change gradually over time, it is not surprising that it is more closely related to long-run average returns than it is to shorter-term returns. The three

---

[4]As discussed in the Capital Market Expectations Part 1 chapter, temporary changes in the relative *flow* of bonds to the market may not have a lasting impact on the curve unless they result in a significant, permanent change in the amounts outstanding.

[5]Supply/demand effects will be more pronounced if there are reasons for certain investors to prefer or require bonds of specific maturities. This is most likely to occur at the very long end of the curve because the supply of very long-term bonds is typically limited and some institutions must fund very long-term liabilities. As an example, the long end of the UK curve was severely squeezed in the 1990s.

[6]See Cochrane and Piazzesi (2005).

[7]See Kim and Wright (2005). The three factors in the theoretical model do not correspond directly with observable variables but may be thought of as proxies for the level, slope, and curvature of the term structure.

EXHIBIT 1   Correlations with Future Excess Bond Returns, 1962–2009

Current Indicator	Return Horizon		
	1 Quarter	1 Year	5 Years
Ex ante real yield	0.28	0.48	0.69
Cochrane and Piazzesi curve factor	0.24	0.44	0.32
Kim and Wright model premium*	0.25	0.43	0.34
Yield curve slope (10 year − 3 month)	0.21	0.34	0.06
Share of debt > 10 years	0.13	0.28	0.66
Corporate profit/GDP	−0.13	−0.25	−0.52
ISM business confidence	−0.10	−0.20	−0.30
Unemployment rate	0.11	0.18	0.24

* Kim and Wright model results are for 1990–2009.
Source: Ilmanen (2012, Exhibit 3.14).

cyclical proxies—the corporate profit-to-GDP ratio, business confidence, and the unemployment rate—are at the bottom of the list since they had the weakest correlation with return over the next year.

3.2.3. The Credit Premium

The credit premium is the additional expected return demanded for bearing the risk of default losses—importantly, in addition to compensation for the *expected* level of losses. Both expected default losses and the credit premium are embedded in credit spreads. They cannot be recovered from those spreads unless we impose some structure (i.e., a model) on default-free rates, default probabilities, and recovery rates. The two main types of models—structural credit models and reduced-form credit models—are described in detail in other chapters.[8] In the following discussion, we will focus on the empirical behavior of the credit premium.

An analysis of 150 years of defaults among US non-financial corporate bonds showed that the severity of default losses accounted for only about half of the 1.53% average yield spread.[9] Hence, holders of corporate bonds did, on average, earn a credit premium to bear the risk of default. However, the pattern of actual defaults suggests the premium was earned very unevenly over time. In particular, high and low default rates tended to persist, causing clusters of high and low annual default rates and resultant losses. The study found that the previous year's default rate, stock market return, stock market volatility, and GDP growth rate were predictive of the subsequent year's default rate. However, the aggregate credit spread was not predictive of subsequent defaults. Contemporaneous financial market variables—stock returns, stock volatility, and the riskless rate—were significant in explaining the credit spread, but neither GDP growth nor changes in the default rate helped explain the credit spread. This

---

[8]See the CFA Program curriculum chapter "Credit Analysis Models." More in-depth coverage can be found in Jarrow and van Deventer (2015).
[9]See Giesecke, Longstaff, Schaefer, and Strebulaev (2011). Default rates were measured as a fraction of the par value of outstanding bonds. The authors did not document actual recovery rates, instead assuming 50% recovery. Hence, the true level of losses could have been somewhat higher or lower.

EXHIBIT 2   Correlations with US Investment-Grade Corporate Excess Returns, 1990–2009

	Return Horizon	
Current Indicator	**1 Quarter**	**1 Year**
Corporate option-adjusted spread	0.25	0.46
VIX implied equity volatility	0.28	0.39
Yield curve slope (10 year − 2 year)	0.20	0.27

Source: Ilmanen (2012, Exhibit 4.15).

finding suggests that credit spreads were driven primarily by the credit risk premium and financial market conditions and only secondarily by fundamental changes in the expected level of default losses. Thus, credit spreads do contain information relevant to predicting the credit premium.

Ilmanen (2012) hypothesized that credit spreads and the credit premiums embedded in them are driven by different factors, depending on credit quality. Default rates on top-quality (AAA and AA) bonds are extremely low, so very little of the spread/premium is due to the likelihood of actual default in the absence of a change in credit quality. Instead, the main driver is "downgrade bias"—the fact that a deterioration in credit quality (resulting in a rating downgrade) is much more likely than an improvement in credit quality (leading to an upgrade) and that downgrades induce larger spread changes than upgrades do.[10] Bonds rated A and BBB have moderate default rates. They still do not have a high likelihood of actual default losses, but their prospects are more sensitive to cyclical forces and their spreads/ premiums vary more (countercyclically) over the cycle. Default losses are of utmost concern for below-investment-grade bonds. Defaults tend to cluster in times when the economy is in recession. In addition, the default rate and the severity of losses in default tend to rise and fall together. These characteristics imply big losses at the worst times, necessitating substantial compensation for this risk. Not too surprisingly, high-yield spreads/premiums tend to rise ahead of realized default rates.

Exhibit 2 shows three variables that have tended to predict excess returns (over T-bills) for an index of US investment-grade corporate bonds over the next quarter and the next year. Not surprisingly, a high corporate option-adjusted spread is bullish for corporate bond performance because it indicates a large cushion against credit losses—that is, a higher credit premium. A steep Treasury curve is also bullish because, as mentioned earlier, it tends to correspond to the trough of the business cycle when default rates begin to decline. Combining these insights with those from Exhibit 1, the implication is that a steep yield curve predicts both a high term premium and a high credit premium. Higher implied volatility in the equity market was also bullish for corporates, most likely reflecting risk-averse pricing—that is, high risk premiums—across all markets.

How are credit premiums related to maturity? Aside from situations of imminent default, there is greater risk of default losses the longer one must wait for payment. We might, therefore, expect that longer-maturity corporate bonds would offer higher credit risk

---

[10]Liquidity relative to government bonds is also an important contributor to yield spreads on very high-quality private sector bonds. By definition, of course, this is really the liquidity premium, rather than part of the credit premium.

premiums. The historical evidence suggests that this has not been the case. Credit premiums tend to be especially generous at the short end of the curve. This may be due to "event risk," in the sense that a default, no matter how unlikely, could still cause a huge proportional loss but there is no way that the bond will pay more than the issuer promised. It may also be due, in part, to illiquidity since many short-maturity bonds are old issues that rarely trade as they gradually approach maturity. As a result, many portfolio managers use a strategy known as a "credit barbell" in which they concentrate credit exposure at short maturities and take interest rate/duration risk via long-maturity government bonds.

3.2.4. The Liquidity Premium

Relatively few bond issues trade actively for more than a few weeks after issuance. Secondary market trading occurs primarily in the most recently issued sovereign bonds, current coupon mortgage-backed securities, and a few of the largest high-quality corporate bonds. The liquidity of other bonds largely depends on the willingness of dealers to hold them in inventory long enough to find a buyer. In general, liquidity tends to be better for bonds that are (a) priced near par/reflective of current market levels, (b) relatively new, (c) from a relatively large issue, (d) from a well-known/frequent issuer, (e) standard/simple in structure, and (f) high quality. These factors tend to reduce the dealer's risk in holding the bond and increase the likelihood of finding a buyer quickly.

As a baseline estimate of the "pure" liquidity premium in a particular market, the analyst can look to the yield spread between fixed-rate, option-free bonds from the highest-quality issuer (virtually always the sovereign) and the next highest-quality large issuer of similar bonds (often a government agency or quasi-agency). Adjustments should then be made for the factors listed previously. In general, the impact of each factor is likely to increase disproportionately as one moves away from baseline attributes. For example, each step lower in credit quality is likely to have a bigger impact on liquidity than that of the preceding step.

EXAMPLE 2   Fixed-Income Building Blocks

Salimah Rahman works for SMECo, a Middle Eastern sovereign wealth fund. Each year, the fund's staff updates its projected returns for the following year on the basis of developments in the preceding year. The fund uses the building block approach in making its fixed-income projections. Rahman has been assigned the task of revising the key building block components for a major European bond market. The following table shows last year's values:

	Description	Value
Risk-free rate	3-month government bill	3.50%
Term premium	5-year duration	0.50%
Credit premium	Baa/BBB corporate	0.90%
Liquidity premium	Government-guaranteed agency	0.15%

Although inflation rose modestly, the central bank cut its policy rate by 50 bps in response to weakening growth. Aggregate corporate profits have remained solid, and after a modest correction, the stock market finished higher for the year. However, defaults on leveraged loans were unexpectedly high this year, and confidence surveys weakened again recently. Equity option volatility spiked mid-year but ended the year somewhat lower. The interest rate futures curve has flattened but remains upward sloping. The 10-year government yield declined only a few basis points, while the yield on comparable government agency bonds remained unchanged and corporate spreads—both nominal and option adjusted—widened.

Indicate the developments that are likely to cause Rahman to increase/decrease each of the key building blocks relative to last year.

Guideline answer:

Based on the reduction in policy rates and the flattening of the interest rate futures curve, Rahman is virtually certain to reduce the short-term rate component. Steepening of the yield curve (10-year yield barely responded to the 50 bp rate cut) indicates an increase in both the term premium and the credit premium. Declining confidence also suggests a higher term premium. Widening of credit spreads is also indicative of a higher credit premium. However, the increase in loan defaults suggests that credit losses are likely to be higher next year as well, since defaults tend to cluster. All else the same, this reduces the expected return on corporate bonds/loans. Hence, the credit premium should increase less than would otherwise be implied by the steeper yield curve and wider credit spreads. Modest widening of the government agency spread indicates an increase in the liquidity premium. The resilience of the equity market and the decline in equity option volatility suggest that investors are not demanding a general increase in risk premiums.

3.3. Risks in Emerging Market Bonds

Emerging market debt was once nearly synonymous with crisis. The Latin American debt crisis of the 1980s involved bank loans but essentially triggered development of a market for emerging market bonds. In the early 1990s, the Mexican crisis occurred. In the late 1990s, there was the Asian crisis, followed by the Russian crisis, which contributed to the turmoil that sank the giant hedge fund Long-Term Capital Management. There have been other, more isolated events, such as Argentina's forced restructuring of its debt, but the emerging market bond market has grown, deepened, and matured. What started with only a few government issuers borrowing in hard currencies (from their perspective foreign, but widely used, currencies) has grown into a market in which corporations as well as governments issue in their local currencies and in hard currencies. The discussion here applies not just to emerging markets but also to what are known as "frontier" markets (when they are treated separately or as a subset of emerging markets).

Investing in emerging market debt involves all the same risks as investing in developed country debt, such as interest rate movements, currency movements, and potential defaults. In addition, it poses risks that are, although not entirely absent, less significant in developed markets. These risks fall roughly into two categories: (1) economic and (2) political and legal. A slightly different breakdown would be "ability to pay" and "willingness to pay."

Before discussing these country risks, note that some countries that are labeled as emerging markets may in fact be healthy, prosperous economies with strong fundamentals. Likewise, the political and legal issues discussed in this section may or may not apply to any particular country. Furthermore, these risks will, in general, apply in varying degrees across countries. Emerging markets are widely recognized as a very heterogeneous group. It is up to the analyst to assess which considerations are relevant to a particular investment decision.

3.3.1. Economic Risks/Ability to Pay

Emerging market economies as a whole have characteristics that make them potentially more vulnerable to distress and hence less likely to be able to pay their debts on time or in full, such as the following:

- Greater concentration of wealth and income; less diverse tax base
- Greater dependence on specific industries, especially cyclical industries, such as commodities and agriculture; low potential for pricing power in world markets
- Restrictions on trade, capital flows, and currency conversion
- Poor fiscal controls and monetary discipline
- Less educated and less skilled work force; poor or limited physical infrastructure; lower level of industrialization and technological sophistication
- Reliance on foreign borrowing, often in hard currencies not their own
- Small/less sophisticated financial markets and institutions
- Susceptibility to capital flight; perceived vulnerability contributing to actual vulnerability

Although history is at best an imperfect guide to the future, the analyst should examine a country's track record on critical issues. Have there been crises in the past? If so, how were they handled/resolved? Has the sovereign defaulted? Is there restructured debt? How have authorities responded to fiscal challenges? Is there inflation or currency instability?

The analyst should, of course, examine the health of the macroeconomy in some detail. A few indicative guidelines can be helpful. If there is one ratio that is most closely watched, it is the ratio of the fiscal deficit to GDP. Most emerging countries have deficits and perpetually struggle to reduce them. A persistent ratio above 4% is likely a cause for concern. A debt-to-GDP ratio exceeding 70%–80%, perhaps of only mild concern for a developed market, is a sign of vulnerability for an emerging market. A persistent annual real growth rate less than 4% suggests that an emerging market is catching up with more advanced economies only slowly, if at all, and per capita income might even be falling—a potential source of political stress. Persistent current account deficits greater than 4% of GDP probably indicate lack of competitiveness. Foreign debt greater than 50% of GDP or greater than 200% of current account receipts is also a sign of danger. Finally, foreign exchange reserves less than 100% of short-term debt is risky, whereas a ratio greater than 200% is ample. It must be emphasized that the numbers given here are merely suggestive of levels that may indicate a need for further scrutiny.

When all else fails, a country may need to call on external support mechanisms. Hence, the analyst should consider whether the country has access to support from the International Monetary Fund (IMF), the World Bank, or other international agencies.

3.3.2. Political and Legal Risks/Willingness to Pay

Investors in emerging market debt may be unable to enforce their claims or recover their investments. Weak property rights laws and weak enforcement of contract laws are clearly of concern in this regard. Inability to enforce seniority structures within private sector claims is one important example. The principle of sovereign immunity makes it very difficult to force a sovereign borrower to pay its debts. Confiscation of property, nationalization of companies, and corruption are also relevant hazards. Coalition governments may also pose political instability problems. Meanwhile, the imposition of capital controls or restrictions on currency conversion may make it difficult, or even impossible, to repatriate capital.

As with economic risks, history may provide some guidance with respect to the severity of political and legal risks. The following are some pertinent questions: Is there a history of nationalization, expropriation, or other violations of property rights? How have international disputes been resolved and under which legal jurisdiction? Has the integrity of the judicial system and process been questioned? Are political institutions stable? Are they recognized as legitimate and subject to reasonable checks and balances? Has the transfer of power been peaceful, orderly, and lawful? Does the political process give rise to fragile coalitions that collapse whenever events strain the initial compromises with respect to policy?

EXAMPLE 3   Emerging Market Bonds

Belvia has big aspirations. Although still a poor country, it has been growing rapidly, averaging 6% real and 10% nominal growth for the last five years. At the beginning of this period of growth, a centrist coalition gained a narrow majority over the authoritarian, fiscally irresponsible, anti-investor, anti-business party that had been in power for decades. The government has removed the old barriers to trade, including the signing of a regional free-trade agreement, and removed capital controls. Much of its growth has been fueled by investment in its dominant industry—natural resources—financed by debt and foreign direct investment flows. These policies have been popular with the business community, as has the relaxation of regulations affecting key constituencies. Meanwhile, to ensure that prosperity flows rapidly to the people, the government has allowed redistributive social payments to grow even faster than GDP, resulting in a large and rising fiscal deficit (5% of GDP this year, projected to be 7% in two years). The current account deficit is 8% of GDP. Despite the large current account deficit, the local currency has appreciated significantly since it was allowed to float two years ago. The government has just announced that it will issue a large 10-year local currency bond under Belvian law— the first issue of its kind in many years.

Despite a very strong relationship with the bank marketing the bond, Peter Valt has decided not to invest in it. When pressed for his reasoning, what risks is he likely to identify?

Solution: There are several significant risks and warning signs. Coalition governments are often unstable, and the most likely alternative would appear to be a return to the previously dominant party that lacks fiscal discipline. That regime is likely to undo the recent pro-growth policies and might even disavow the debt, including this new bond. The bond will be governed by Belvian law, which, combined with the principle of sovereign immunity, will make it very difficult for foreigners to enforce their claims. In addition, the relaxation of regulations affecting key constituencies hints strongly at corruption and possibly at payoffs within the current regime. With respect to the economy, fiscal discipline remains poor, there is heavy reliance on a single industry, and the current account deficit is almost certainly unsustainable (e.g., over the 10-year life of this bond). In addition, the currency is very likely to be overvalued, which will both make it very difficult to broaden global competitiveness beyond natural resources and increase the investor's risk of substantial currency losses.

4. FORECASTING EQUITY RETURNS

The task of forecasting equity market returns is often the central focus of setting capital market expectations. In this section, we discuss applying each of the major methodologies to equities.

4.1. Historical Statistics Approach to Equity Returns

The *Credit Suisse Global Investment Returns Yearbook 2018*[11] updated the seminal work of Dimson, Marsh, and Staunton (2002) to include asset returns in 21 countries for the 118-year period of 1900–2017. Exhibit 3 shows the mean real return for each market portfolio centered within a 95% confidence interval. Results are also shown for a world portfolio, a world ex-US portfolio, and Europe. The portfolios are ordered from left to right on the basis of the mean return.

The means range from a low of 5.0% for Austria to a high of 9.4% in South Africa. Note that both of these values lie within the confidence interval for every country. From a statistical perspective, there is really no difference among these markets in terms of mean real return. This illustrates the fact that sample averages, even derived from seemingly long histories, are very imprecise estimates unless the volatility of the data is small relative to the mean. Clearly that is not the case for equity returns. Nonetheless, sample means are frequently cited without regard to the quality of information they convey.

As indicated in Section 2, shrinkage estimators can often provide more reliable estimates by combining the sample mean with a second estimate of the mean return. However, the application of a common shrinkage estimator confirms that there is no basis for believing that the true expected returns for the countries in Exhibit 3 are different.

4.2. DCF Approach to Equity Returns

Analysts have frequently used the Gordon (constant) growth model form of the dividend discount model, solved for the required rate of return, to formulate the long-term expected return of equity markets. Although this model is quite simple, it has a big advantage over using historical stock returns to project future returns. The vast majority of the "noise" in historical stock returns comes from fluctuations in the price-to-earnings ratio (P/E) and the ratio of earnings to GDP. Since the amount of earnings appears in the numerator of one ratio and the denominator of the other, the impact of these ratios tends to cancel out over time, leaving the relationship between equity market appreciation and GDP growth much more stable. And GDP growth itself, especially the real growth component, is much less volatile and hence

---

[11]Dimson, Marsh, and Staunton (2018).

EXHIBIT 3   Historical Mean Returns with Confidence Intervals by Country, 1900–2017

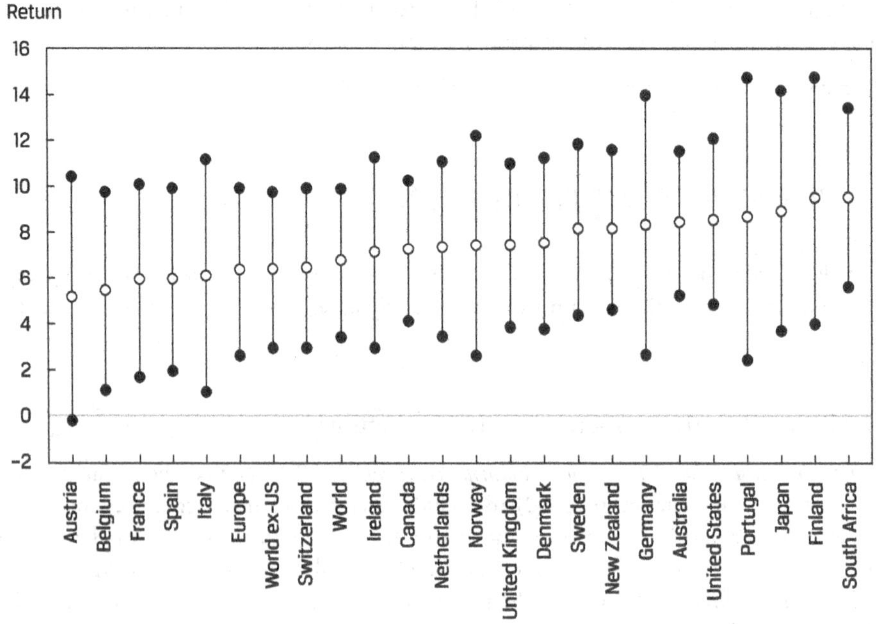

Source: Dimson, Marsh, and Staunton (2018, Chapter 1, Table 1. Real, local currency percent returns).

EXHIBIT 4   Historical Comparison of Standard Deviations in the United States, 1946–2016

S&P 500	P/E	Earnings/GDP	Real GDP Growth	Inflation
16.1	28.5	28.9	3.0	3.2

Note: Standard deviation of % changes.

relatively predictable.[12] As an illustration, Exhibit 4 shows historical volatilities (defined as the standard deviation of percentage changes) for the S&P 500 Index return, P/E, the earnings-to-GDP ratio, real US GDP growth, and inflation for 1946–2016. The Gordon growth model allows us to take advantage of this relative stability by linking long-term equity appreciation to a more stable foundation—economic growth.

In the United States and other major markets, share repurchases have become an important way for companies to distribute cash to shareholders. Grinold and Kroner (2002) provided a restatement of the Gordon growth model that takes explicit account of repurchases. Their model also provides a means for analysts to incorporate expectations of valuation levels through the familiar price-to-earnings ratio. The Grinold–Kroner model[13] is

---

[12]See the previous chapter for a discussion of projecting trend growth.

[13]See Grinold and Kroner (2002) for a derivation. The model is shown here in a slightly modified form.

$$E(R_e) \approx \frac{D}{P} + (\%\Delta E - \%\Delta S) + \%\Delta P/E \qquad (1)$$

where $E(R_e)$ is the expected equity return, D/P is the dividend yield, $\%\Delta E$ is the expected percentage change in total earnings, $\%\Delta S$ is the expected percentage change in shares outstanding, and $\%\Delta P/E$ is the expected percentage change in the price-to-earnings ratio. The term in parentheses, $(\%\Delta E - \%\Delta S)$, is the growth rate of earnings per share. Net share repurchases ($\%\Delta S < 0$) imply that earnings per share grows faster than total earnings.

With a minor rearrangement of the equation, the expected return can be divided into three components:

- Expected cash flow ("income") return: $D/P - \%\Delta S$
- Expected nominal earnings growth return: $\%\Delta E$
- Expected repricing return: $\%\Delta P/E$

The expected nominal earnings growth return and the expected repricing return constitute the expected capital gains.

In principle, the Grinold–Kroner model assumes an infinite horizon. In practice, the analyst typically needs to make projections for finite horizons, perhaps several horizons. In applying the model, the analyst needs to be aware of the implications of constant growth rate assumptions over different horizons. Failure to tailor growth rates to the horizon can easily lead to implausible results. As an example, suppose the P/E is currently 16.0 and the analyst believes that it will revert to a level of 20 and be stable thereafter. The P/E growth rates for various horizons that are consistent with this view are 4.56% for 5 years, 2.26% for 10 years, 0.75% for 30 years, and an arbitrarily small positive number for a truly long-term horizon. Treating, say, the 2.26% 10-year number as if it is appropriate for the "long run" would imply an ever-rising P/E rather than convergence to a plausible long-run valuation. The only very long-run assumptions that are consistent with economically plausible relationships are $\%\Delta E$ = Nominal GDP growth, $\%\Delta S = 0$, and $\%\Delta P/E = 0$. The longer the (finite) horizon, the less the analyst's projection should deviate from these values.

EXAMPLE 4   Forecasting the Equity Return Using the Grinold–Kroner Model

---

Cynthia Casey uses the Grinold–Kroner model in forecasting developed market equity returns. Casey makes the following forecasts:

- a 2.25% dividend yield on Canadian equities, based on the S&P/TSE Composite Index;
- a 1% rate of net share repurchases for Canadian equities;
- a long-term corporate earnings growth rate of 6% per year, based on a 1 percentage point (pp) premium for corporate earnings growth over her expected Canadian (nominal) GDP growth rate of 5%; and
- an expansion rate for P/E multiples of 0.25% per year.

1. Based on the information given, what expected rate of return on Canadian equities is implied by Casey's assumptions?
2. Are Casey's assumptions plausible for the long run and for a 10-year horizon?

Solution to 1: The expected rate of return on Canadian equities based on Casey's assumptions would be 9.5%, calculated as

$$E(R_e) \approx 2.25\% + [6.0\% - (-1.0\%)] + 0.25\% = 9.5\%$$

Solution to 2: Casey's assumptions are not plausible for the very long run. The assumption that earnings will grow 1% faster than GDP implies one of two things: either an ever-rising ratio of economy-wide earnings to GDP or the earnings accruing to businesses not included in the index (e.g., private firms) continually shrinking relative to GDP. Neither is likely to persist indefinitely. Similarly, perpetual share repurchases would eventually eliminate all shares, whereas a perpetually rising P/E would lead to an arbitrarily high price per Canadian dollar of earnings per share. Based on Casey's economic growth forecast, a more reasonable long-run expected return would be 7.25% = 2.25% + 5.0%.

Casey's assumptions are plausible for a 10-year horizon. Over 10 years, the ratio of earnings to GDP would rise by roughly $10.5\% = (1.01)^{10} - 1$, shares outstanding would shrink by roughly $9.6\% = 1 - (0.99)^{10}$, and the P/E would rise by about $2.5\% = (1.0025)^{10} - 1$.

Most of the inputs to the Grinold–Kroner model are fairly readily available. Economic growth forecasts can easily be found in investment research publications, reports from such agencies as the IMF, the World Bank, and the OECD, and likely from the analyst firm's own economists. Data on the rate of share repurchases are less straightforward but are likely to be tracked by sell-side firms and occasionally mentioned in research publications. The big question is how to gauge valuation of the market in order to project changes in the P/E.

The fundamental valuation metrics used in practice typically take the form of a ratio of price to some fundamental flow variable—such as earnings, cash flow, or sales—with seemingly endless variations in how the measures are defined and calculated. Whatever the metric, the implicit assumption is that it has a well-defined long-run mean value to which it will revert. In statistical terms, it is a stationary random variable. Extensive empirical evidence indicates that these valuation measures are poor predictors of short-term performance. Over multi-year horizons, however, there is a reasonably strong tendency for extreme values to be corrected. Thus, these metrics do provide guidance for projecting intermediate-term movements in valuation.

Gauging what is or is not an extreme value is complicated by the fact that all the fundamental flow variables as well as stock prices are heavily influenced by the business cycle. One method of dealing with this issue is to "cyclically adjust" the valuation measure. The most widely known metric is the cyclically adjusted P/E (CAPE). For this measure, the current price level is divided by the average level of earnings for the last 10 years (adjusted for inflation), rather than by the most current earnings. The idea is to average away cyclical variation in earnings and provide a more reliable base against which to assess the current market price.

4.3. Risk Premium Approaches to Equity Returns

The Grinold–Kroner model and similar models are sometimes said to reflect the "supply" of equity returns since they outline the sources of return. In contrast, risk premiums reflect "demand" for returns.

4.3.1. Defining and Forecasting the Equity Premium

The term "equity premium" is most frequently used to describe the amount by which the expected return on equities exceeds the riskless rate ("equity versus bills"). However, the same term is sometimes used to refer to the amount by which the expected return on equities exceeds the expected return on default-free bonds ("equity versus bonds"). From the discussion of fixed-income building blocks in Section 3, we know that the difference between these two definitions is the term premium built into the expected return on default-free bonds. The equity-versus-bonds premium reflects an incremental/building block approach to developing expected equity returns, whereas the equity-versus-bills premium reflects a single composite premium for the risk of equity investment.

Exhibit 5 shows historical averages for both of these equity premium concepts by country for the period 1900–2017.[14] For each country, the bottom portion of the column is the realized term premium (i.e., bonds minus bills) and the top segment is the realized equity-versus-bonds premium. The whole column represents the equity-versus-bills premium. The equity-versus-bills premiums range from 3.0% to 6.3%, the equity-versus-bonds premiums range from 1.8% to 5.2%, and the term premiums range from −0.6% to 2.9%.

As with the mean equity returns in Exhibit 3, these historical premiums are subject to substantial estimation error. Statistically, there is no meaningful difference among them. Thus, the long-run cross section of returns/premiums provides virtually no reliable information with which to differentiate among countries.

Since equity returns are much more volatile than returns on either bills or bonds, forecasting either definition of the equity premium is just as difficult as projecting the absolute level of equity returns. That is, simply shifting to focus on risk premiums provides little, if any, specific insight with which to improve forecasts. The analyst must, therefore, use the other modes of analysis discussed here to forecast equity returns/premiums.

4.3.2. An Equilibrium Approach

There are various global/international extensions of the familiar capital asset pricing model (CAPM). We will discuss a version proposed by Singer and Terhaar (1997) that is intended to capture the impact of incomplete integration of global markets.

The Singer–Terhaar model is actually a combination of two underlying CAPM models. The first assumes that all global markets and asset classes are fully integrated. The full integration assumption allows the use of a single global market portfolio to determine equity-versus-bills risk premiums for all assets. The second underlying CAPM assumes complete segmentation of markets such that each asset class in each country is priced without regard to any other country/asset class. For example, the markets for German equities and German bonds are completely segmented. Clearly, this is a very extreme assumption.

---

[14]These premiums reflect geometric returns. Therefore, the equity-vs-bills premium is the sum of the term premium and the equity-vs-bonds premium. Premiums using arithmetic returns are systematically higher and are not additive.

EXHIBIT 5   Historical Equity Premiums by Country, 1900–2017

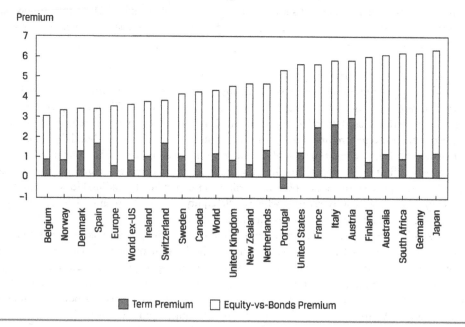

Source: Dimson et al. (2018, Chapter 2, Tables 8 and 9).
Notes: Germany excludes 1922–1923. Austria excludes 1921–1922. Returns are shown in percentages.

Recall the basic CAPM pricing relationship:

$$RP_i = \beta_{i,M} RP_M \qquad (2)$$

where $RP_i = [E(R_i) - R_F]$ is the risk premium on the ith asset, RP_M is the risk premium on the market portfolio, R_F is the risk-free rate, and $\beta_{i,M}$—asset i's sensitivity to the market portfolio—is given by

$$\beta_{i,M} = \frac{\text{Cov}(R_i, R_M)}{\text{Var}(R_M)} = \rho_{i,M}\left(\frac{\sigma_i}{\sigma_M}\right) \qquad (3)$$

Standard deviations are denoted by σ, and ρ denotes correlation.

Under the assumption of full integration, every asset is priced relative to the global capitalization-weighted market portfolio. Using Equations 2 and 3 and denoting the global market portfolio by "GM," the first component of the Singer–Terhaar model is

$$RP_i^G = \beta_{i,GM} RP_{GM} = \rho_{i,GM}\sigma_i\left(\frac{RP_{GM}}{\sigma_{GM}}\right) \qquad (4)$$

A superscript "G" has been added on the asset's risk premium to indicate that it reflects the global equilibrium. The term in parentheses on the far right is the Sharpe ratio for the global market portfolio, the risk premium per unit of global market risk.

Now consider the case of completely segmented markets. In this case, the risk premium for each asset will be determined in isolation without regard to other markets or opportunities for diversification. The risk premium will be whatever is required to induce investors with access to that market/asset to hold the existing supply. In terms of the CAPM framework, this implies treating each asset as its own "market portfolio." Formally, we can simply set β equal to 1 and ρ equal to 1 in the previous equations since each asset is perfectly correlated with itself. Using a superscript "S" to denote the segmented market equilibrium and replacing the global market portfolio with asset i itself in Equation 4, the segmented market equilibrium risk premium for asset i is

$$RP_i^S = 1 \times RP_i^S = 1 \times \sigma_i \left(\frac{RP_i^S}{\sigma_i} \right) \tag{5}$$

This is the second component of the Singer–Terhaar model. Note that the first equality in Equation 5 is an identity; it conveys no information. It reflects the fact that in a completely segmented market, the required risk premium could take any value. The second equality is more useful because it breaks the risk premium into two parts: the risk of the asset (σ_i) and the Sharpe ratio (i.e., compensation per unit of risk) in the segmented market.[15]

The final Singer–Terhaar risk premium estimate for asset i is a weighted average of the two component estimates

$$RP_i = \varphi RP_i^G + (1 - \varphi)RP_i^S \tag{6}$$

To implement the model, the analyst must supply values for the Sharpe ratios in the globally integrated market and the asset's segmented market; the degree to which the asset is globally integrated, denoted by φ; the asset's volatility; and the asset's β with respect to the global market portfolio. A pragmatic approach to specifying the Sharpe ratios for each asset under complete segmentation is to assume that compensation for non-diversifiable risk (i.e., "market risk") is the same in every market. That is, assume all the Sharpe ratios equal the global Sharpe ratio.

In practice, the analyst must make a judgment about the degree of integration/ segmentation—that is, the value of φ in the Singer–Terhaar model. With that in mind, some representative values that can serve as starting points for refinement can be helpful. Developed market equities and bonds are highly integrated, so a range of 0.75–0.90 would be reasonable for φ. Emerging markets are noticeably less integrated, especially during stressful periods, and there are likely to be greater differences among these markets, so a range of 0.50–0.75 would be reasonable for emerging market equities and bonds. Real estate market integration is increasing but remains far behind developed market financial assets, perhaps on par with emerging market stocks and bonds overall. In general, relative real estate market integration is likely to reflect the relative integration of the associated financial markets. Commodities for which there are actively traded, high-volume futures contracts should be on the higher end of the integration scale.?A3B2 re 2?>

To illustrate the Singer–Terhaar model, suppose that an investor has developed the following projections for German shares and bonds.

---

[15]A somewhat more complex model would allow for integration of asset classes within each country. Doing so would entail incorporating local market portfolios and allowing assets to be less than perfectly correlated with those portfolios. Equation (5) would then look exactly like equation (4) with the local segmented market portfolio replacing the global market portfolio ("GM").

	German Shares	German Bonds
Volatility (σ_i)	17.0%	7.0%
Correlation with global market ($\rho_{i,M}$)	0.70	0.50
Degree of integration (φ)	0.85	0.85
Segmented market Sharpe ratio (RP_i^S/σ_i)	0.35	0.25

The risk-free rate is 3.0%, and the investor's estimate of the global Sharpe ratio is 0.30. Note that the investor expects compensation for undiversifiable risk to be higher in the German stock market and lower in the German bond market under full segmentation. The following are the fully integrated risk premiums for each of the assets (from Equation 4):

$$\text{Equities: } 0.70 \times 17.0\% \times 0.30 = 3.57\%$$

$$\text{Bonds: } 0.50 \times 7.0\% \times 0.30 = 1.05\%$$

The following are the fully segmented risk premiums (from Equation 5):

$$\text{Equities: } 17.0\% \times 0.35 = 5.95\%$$

$$\text{Bonds: } 7.0\% \times 0.25 = 1.75\%$$

Based on 85% integration ($\varphi = 0.85$), the final risk estimates (from Equation 6) would be as follows:

$$\text{Equities: } (0.85 \times 3.57\%) + (1 - 0.85) \times 5.95\% = 3.93\%$$

$$\text{Bonds: } (0.85 \times 1.05\%) + (1 - 0.85) \times 1.75\% = 1.16\%$$

Adding in the risk-free rate, the expected returns for German shares and bonds would be 6.93% and 4.16%, respectively.

Virtually all equilibrium models implicitly assume perfectly liquid markets. Thus, the analyst should assess the actual liquidity of each asset class and add appropriate liquidity premiums. Although market segmentation and market liquidity are conceptually distinct, in practice they are likely to be related. Highly integrated markets are likely to be relatively liquid, and illiquidity is one reason that a market may remain segmented.

EXAMPLE 5   Using the Singer–Terhaar Model

Stacy Adkins believes the equity market in one of the emerging markets that she models has become more fully integrated with the global market. As a result, she expects it to be more highly correlated with the global market. However, she thinks its overall volatility will decline. Her old and new estimates are as follows:

If she uses the Singer–Terhaar model, what will the net impact of these changes be on her risk premium estimate for this market?

	Previous Data	New Data
Volatility (σ_i)	22.0%	18.0%
Correlation with global market $(\rho_{i,M})$	0.50	0.70
Degree of integration (φ)	0.55	0.75
Sharpe ratio (global and segmented markets)	0.30	0.30

Solution: The segmented market risk premium will decline from 6.6% (calculated as 22.0% × 0.30 = 6.6%) to 5.4% (= 18% × 0.30). The fully integrated risk premium will increase from 3.30% (= 0.50 × 22.0% × 0.30) to 3.78% (= 0.70 × 18.0% × 0.30). The weighted average premium will decline from 4.79% [= (0.55 × 3.30%) + (0.45 × 6.60%)] to 4.19% [= (0.75 × 3.78%) + (0.25 × 5.40%)], so the net effect is a decline of 60 bps.

4.4. Risks in Emerging Market Equities

Most of the issues underlying the risks of emerging market (and "frontier market" if they are classified as such) bonds also present risks for emerging market equities: more fragile economies, less stable political and policy frameworks, and weaker legal protections. However, the risks take somewhat different forms because of the different nature of equity and debt claims. Again, note that emerging markets are a very heterogeneous group. The political, legal, and economic issues that are often associated with emerging markets may not, in fact, apply to a particular market or country being analyzed.

There has been a debate about the relative importance of "country" versus "industry" risk factors in global equity markets for over 40 years. The empirical evidence has been summarized quite accurately as "vast and contradictory."[16] Both matter, but on the whole, country effects still tend to be more important than (global) industry effects. This is particularly true for emerging markets. Emerging markets are generally less fully integrated into the global economy and the global markets. Hence, local economic and market factors exert greater influence on risk and return in these markets than in developed markets.

Political, legal, and regulatory weaknesses—in the form of weak standards and/or weak enforcement—affect emerging market equity investors in various ways. The standards of corporate governance may allow interested parties to manipulate the capital structure of companies and to misuse business assets. Accounting standards may allow management and other insiders to hide or misstate important information. Weak disclosure rules may also impede transparency and favor insiders. Inadequate property rights laws, lack of enforcement,

---

[16]Marcelo, Quirós, and Martins (2013).

and weak checks and balances on governmental actions may permit seizure of property, nationalization of companies, and prejudicial and unpredictable regulatory actions.

Whereas the emerging market debt investor needs to focus on ability and willingness to pay specific obligations, emerging market equity investors need to focus on the many ways that the value of their ownership claims might be expropriated by the government, corporate insiders, or dominant shareholders.

EXAMPLE 6   Emerging Market Equity Risks

Bill Dwight has been discussing investment opportunities in Belvia with his colleague, Peter Valt (see **Example 3**). He is aware that Valt declined to buy the recently issued government bond, but he believes the country's equities may be attractive. He notes the rapid growth, substantial investment spending, free trade agreement, deregulation, and strong capital inflows as factors favoring a strong equity market. In addition, solid global growth has been boosting demand for Belvia's natural resources. Roughly half of the public equity market is represented by companies in the natural resources sector. The other half is a reasonably diversified mix of other industries. Many of these firms remain closely held, having floated a minority stake on the local exchange in the last few years. Listed firms are required to have published two years of financial statements conforming to standards set by the Belvia Public Accounting Board, which is made up of the heads of the three largest domestic accounting firms. With the help of a local broker, Dwight has identified a diversified basket of stocks that he intends to buy.

Discuss the risks Dwight might be overlooking.

Guideline answer:
Dwight might be overlooking several risks. He is almost certainly underestimating the vulnerability of the local economy and the vulnerability of the equity market to local developments. The economy's rapid growth is being driven by a large and growing fiscal deficit, in particular, rapidly rising redistributive social payments, and investment spending financed by foreign capital. Appreciation of the currency has made industries other than natural resources less competitive, so the free trade agreement provides little support for the economy. When the government is forced to tighten fiscal policy or capital flows shrink, the domestic economy is likely to be hit hard. Political risk is also a concern. A return to the prior regime is likely to result in a less pro-growth, less business-friendly environment, which would most likely result in attempts by foreign investors to repatriate their capital. Dwight should also have serious concerns about corporate governance, given that most listed companies are closely held, with dominant shareholders posing expropriation risk. He should also be concerned about transparency (e.g., limited history available) and accounting standards (local standards set by the auditing firms themselves).

5. FORECASTING REAL ESTATE RETURNS

Real estate is inherently quite different from equities, bonds, and cash. It is a physical asset rather than a financial asset. It is heterogeneous, indivisible, and immobile. It is a factor of production, like capital equipment and labor, and as such, it directly produces a return in the form of services. Its services can be sold but can be used/consumed only in one location. Owning and operating real estate involves operating and maintenance costs. All these factors contribute to making real estate illiquid and costly to transfer. The characteristics just described apply to direct investment in real estate (raw land, which does not produce income, is an exception). We will address the investment characteristics of equity REITs versus direct real estate, but unless otherwise stated, the focus is on directly held, unlevered, income-producing real estate.

5.1. Historical Real Estate Returns

The heterogeneity, indivisibility, immobility, and illiquidity of real estate pose a severe problem for historical analysis. Properties trade infrequently, so there is virtually no chance of getting a sequence of simultaneous, periodic (say, quarterly) transaction prices for a cross section of properties. Real estate owners/investors must rely heavily on appraisals, rather than transactions, in valuing properties. Owing to infrequent transactions and the heterogeneity of properties, these appraisals tend to reflect slowly moving averages of past market conditions. As a result, returns calculated from appraisals represent weighted averages of (unobservable) "true" returns—returns that would have been observed if there had been transaction prices—in previous periods. This averaging does not, in general, bias the mean return. It does, however, significantly distort estimates of volatility and correlations. The published return series is too smooth; that is, the usual sample volatility substantially understates the true volatility of returns. Meanwhile, by disguising the timing of response to market information, the smoothing tends to understate the strength of contemporaneous correlation with other market variables and spuriously induce a lead/lag structure of correlations.

In order to undertake any meaningful analysis of real estate as an asset class, the analyst must first deal with this data issue. It has become standard to "unsmooth" appraisal-based returns using a time-series model. Such techniques, which also apply to private equity funds, private debt funds, and hedge funds, are briefly described in a later section.

5.2. Real Estate Cycles

Real estate is subject to cycles that both drive and are driven by the business cycle. Real estate is a major factor of production in the economy. Virtually every business requires it. Every household consumes "housing services." Demand for the services provided by real estate rises and falls with the pace of economic activity. The supply of real estate is vast but essentially fixed at any point in time.[17] As a result, there is a strong cyclical pattern to property values, rents, and occupancy rates. The extent to which this pattern is observable depends on the type of real estate. As emphasized previously, changes in property values are obscured by the appraisal process, although indications can be gleaned from transactions as they occur. The

---

[17]Yau, Schneeweis, Szado, Robinson, and Weiss (2018) found that real estate represents from one-third to as much as two-thirds of global wealth.

extent to which actual rents and occupancy rates fully reflect the balance of supply and demand depends primarily on the type of property and the quality of the property. High-quality properties with long leases will tend to have little turnover, so fluctuations in actual rents and occupancy rates are likely to be relatively small. In contrast, demand for low-quality properties is likely to be more sensitive to the economy, leading to more substantial swings in occupancy and possibly rents as well. Properties with short leases will see rents adjust more completely to current supply/demand imbalances. Room rates and occupancy at low-quality hotels will tend to be the most volatile.

Fluctuations in the balance of supply and demand set up a classic boom–bust cycle in real estate. First, the boom: Perceptions of rising demand, property values, lease rates, and occupancy induce development of new properties. This investment spending helps drive and/or sustain economic activity, which, in turn, reinforces the perceived profitability of building new capacity. Then, the bust: Inevitably, optimistic projections lead to overbuilding and declining property values, lease rates, and occupancy. Since property has a very long life and is immobile, leases are typically for multiple years and staggered across tenants. In addition, since moving is costly for tenants, it may take many months or years for the excess supply to be absorbed.

A study by Clayton, Fabozzi, Gilberto, Gordon, Hudson-Wilson, Hughes, Liang, MacKinnon, and Mansour (2011) suggested that the US commercial real estate crash following the global financial crisis was the first to have been driven by the capital markets rather than by a boom–bust cycle in real estate fundamentals.[18] The catalyst was not overbuilding, Clayton et al. argued, but rather excess leverage and investment in more speculative types of properties. Consistent with that hypothesis, both the collapse in property prices and the subsequent recovery were unusually rapid. The authors attributed the accelerated response to underlying conditions to appraisers responding more vigorously to signals from the REIT and commercial mortgage-backed security markets. It remains to be seen whether this phenomenon will persist in less extreme circumstances.

5.3. Capitalization Rates

The capitalization (cap) rate, defined as net operating income (NOI) in the current period divided by the property value, is the standard valuation metric for commercial real estate. It is analogous to the earnings yield (E/P) for equities. It is not, strictly speaking, a cash flow yield because a portion of operating income may be reinvested in the property.[19] As with equities, an estimate of the long-run expected/required rate of return can be derived from this ratio by assuming a constant growth rate for NOI—that is, by applying the Gordon growth model.

$$E(R_{re}) = \text{Cap rate} + \text{NOI growth rate} \tag{7}$$

The long-run, steady-state NOI growth rate for commercial real estate as a whole should be reasonably close to the growth rate of GDP. The observation that over a 30-year period

---

[18]Data from the Investment Property Databank indicate that commercial property values dropped by 21.8% globally and US property values decreased by 33.2% in 2008–2009. Other countries suffered steep losses as well, notably Ireland (55.5%) and Spain (20.1%).

[19]Ilmanen (2012) indicated that the difference between cap rates and cash flow yields may be on the order of 3 percentage points. Although significant reinvestment of NOI reduces the cash flow yield, it should increase the growth rate of NOI if the investment is productive.

UK nominal rental income grew about 6.5% per annum, roughly 2.5% in real terms,[20] is consistent with this relationship.

Over finite horizons, it is appropriate to adjust this equation to reflect the anticipated rate of change in the cap rate.

$$E(R_{re}) = \text{Cap rate} + \text{NOI growth rate} - \%\Delta\text{Cap rate} \tag{8}$$

This equation is analogous to the Grinold–Kroner model for equities, except there is no term for share buybacks. The growth rate of NOI could, of course, be split into a real component and inflation.

Exhibit 6 shows private market cap rates as of March 2018 for US commercial properties differentiated by type, location, and quality. The rates range from 4.7% for offices in gateway cities, such as New York City, to 9.5% for skilled nursing (i.e., 24-hour old-age care) properties. There is a clear pattern of high cap rates for riskier property types (hotels versus apartments, skilled nursing facilities versus medical offices), lower-quality properties (low-productivity versus high-productivity malls), and less attractive locations (offices in secondary versus gateway cities).

EXHIBIT 6   Cap Rates (%) as of March 2018

Property Type	Average	Higher Risk	Lower Risk
Hotels	7.2	Limited Service 7.7	Full Service 7.1
Health Care	6.6	Skilled Nursing 9.5	Medical Office 5.7
Retail Malls	5.6	Low Productivity 8.8	High Productivity 5.0
Industrial	5.4		
Office	5.2	Secondary Cities 6.6	Gateway Cities 4.7
Apartments	4.8		

Source: CenterSquare Investment Management (2018). Gateway cities include Boston, Chicago, Los Angeles, New York City, San Francisco, and Washington, DC.

Retail properties provide a good example of the impact of competition on real estate. Brick-and-mortar stores have been under increasing competitive pressure from online retailers, such as Amazon. The pressure is especially intense for lower-productivity (less profitable) locations. As a result, cap rates for high- and low-productivity malls began to diverge even before the global financial crisis. In 2006, the difference in cap rates was 1.2 percentage points; by 2018, it was 3.2 percentage points.[21]

Cap rates reflect long-term discount rates. As such, we should expect them to rise and fall with the general level of long-term interest rates, which tends to make them pro-cyclical. However, they are also sensitive to credit spreads and the availability of credit. Peyton (2009) found that the spread between cap rates and the 10-year Treasury yield is positively related to the option-adjusted spread on three- to five-year B-rated corporate bonds and negatively related to ratios of household and non-financial-sector debt to GDP. The countercyclical

---

[20]Based on data from Investment Property Databank Limited.

[21]CenterSquare Investment Management (2018). These are cap rates implied by REIT pricing, which is why the 2018 differential does not exactly match the private market figures given in Exhibit 6.

nature of credit spreads mitigates the cyclicality of cap rates. The debt ratios are effectively proxies for the availability of debt financing for leveraged investment in real estate. Since real estate transactions typically involve substantial leverage, greater availability of debt financing is likely to translate into a lower required liquidity premium component of expected real estate returns. Not surprisingly, higher vacancy rates induce higher cap rates.

5.4. The Risk Premium Perspective on Real Estate Expected Return

As a very long-lived asset, real estate is quite sensitive to the level of long-term rates; that is, it has a high effective duration. Indeed, this is often the one and only characteristic mentioned in broad assessments of the likely performance of real estate as an asset class. Hence, real estate must earn a significant term premium. Income-earning properties are exposed to the credit risk of the tenants. In essence, a fixed-term lease with a stable stream of payments is like a corporate bond issued by the tenant secured with physical assets. The landlord must, therefore, demand a credit premium commensurate with what his or her average tenant would have to pay to issue such debt. Real estate must also earn a significant equity risk premium (relative to corporate debt) since the owner bears the full brunt of fluctuations in property values as well as uncertainty with respect to rent growth, lease rollover/termination, and vacancies. The most volatile component of return arises, of course, from changes in property values. As noted previously, these values are strongly pro-cyclical, which implies the need for a significant equity risk premium. Combining the bond-like components (term premium plus credit premium) with a stock-like component implies a risk premium somewhere between those of corporate bonds and equities.

Liquidity is an especially important risk for direct real estate ownership. There are two main ways to view illiquidity. For publicly traded equities and bonds, the question is not whether one can sell the security quickly but, rather, at what price. For real estate, however, it may be better to think of illiquidity as a total inability to sell the asset except at randomly spaced points in time. From this perspective, the degree of liquidity depends on the average frequency of these trading opportunities. By adopting this perspective, one can ask how large the liquidity premium must be to induce investors to hold an asset with a given level of liquidity. Ang, Papanikolaou, and Westerfield (2014) analyzed this question. Their results suggest liquidity premiums on the order of 0.60% for quarterly average liquidity, 0.90% for annual liquidity, and 2%, 4%, and 6% for liquidity on average every 2, 5, and 10 years, respectively.[22] All things considered, a liquidity premium of 2%–4% would seem reasonable for commercial real estate.

5.5. Real Estate in Equilibrium

Real estate can be incorporated into an equilibrium framework (such as the Singer–Terhaar model). Indeed, doing so might be deemed a necessity given the importance of real estate in global wealth. There are, however, a few important considerations. First, the impact of smoothing must have been removed from the risk/return data and metrics used for real estate. Otherwise, inclusion of real estate will distort the results for all asset classes. Second, it is important to recognize the implicit assumption of fully liquid assets in equilibrium models.

---

[22]See Table 3 in Ang et al. (2014). The numbers cited here reflect an assumption of zero correlation between the investor's liquid and illiquid assets.

Adjusting the equilibrium for illiquidity—that is, adding a liquidity premium—is especially important for real estate and other private assets. Third, although real estate investors increasingly venture outside their home markets, real estate is still location specific and may, therefore, be more closely related to local, as opposed to global, economic/market factors than are financial claims.

5.6. Public vs. Private Real Estate

Many institutional investors and some ultra-wealthy individuals are able to assemble diversified portfolios of direct real estate holdings. Investors with smaller portfolios must typically choose between limited, undiversified direct real estate holdings or obtaining real estate exposure through financial instruments, such as REIT shares. Assessing whether these alternatives—direct real estate and REITs—have similar investment characteristics is difficult because of return smoothing, heterogeneity of properties, and variations in leverage.

A careful analysis of this issue requires (1) transaction-based returns for unlevered direct real estate holdings, (2) firm-by-firm deleveraging of REIT returns based on their individual balance sheets over time, and (3) carefully constructing direct real estate and REIT portfolios with matching property characteristics. Exhibit 7 shows the results of such an analysis.

Deleveraging the REITs substantially reduces both their mean returns and their volatilities. The volatilities are roughly cut in half. Clearly, the deleveraged REIT returns are much more similar to the direct real estate returns than are the levered REIT returns. In the aggregate, REITs outperformed direct real estate by 49 bps per year with lower volatility. Looking at specific property types, REITs had higher returns and lower volatility in two categories—office and retail. Industrial REITs had essentially the same return as directly owned industrial properties but with higher volatility. Apartment REITs lagged the direct market but with significantly lower volatility.

Exhibit 7 certainly shows some interesting differences. The pattern of unlevered REIT returns by property type is not the same as for direct real estate. Retail REITs had the highest return, and industrial REITs had the lowest. Among directly owned properties, apartments had the highest return and offices the lowest. A similar mismatch appears with respect to volatilities.

EXHIBIT 7   Direct Real Estate vs. REITs: Four Property Types, 1994–2012

	Mean Return (%)			Standard Deviation (%)		
		REITs			REITs	
	Direct Real Estate	Unlevered	Levered	Direct Real Estate	Unlevered	Levered
Aggregate	8.80	9.29		11.09	9.71	
Apartment	9.49	9.08	11.77	11.42	9.50	20.69
Office	8.43	9.37	10.49	10.97	10.58	23.78
Industrial	9.00	9.02	9.57	11.14	11.65	23.46
Retail	8.96	9.90	12.04	11.54	10.03	23.73

Source: Ling and Naranjo (2015, Table 1).

Overall, this study tends to support the general conclusion reached by most comparisons: Public and private commercial real estate are different. The extent of the difference is less clear. It does appear that once we account for differences in leverage, REIT investors are not sacrificing performance to obtain the liquidity afforded by publicly traded shares. Perhaps REIT investors are able to capture a significant portion of the liquidity risk premium garnered by direct investors (because the REIT is a direct investor) as well as benefit from professional management.

What about the diversification benefits of real estate as an asset class? REITs are traded securities, and that fact shows up in their much higher short-term correlation with equities. In contrast, direct real estate is often touted as a good diversifier based on the notion that it is not very highly correlated with equities. As noted previously, the smoothed nature of most published real estate returns is a major contributor to the appearance of low correlation with financial assets, including with REITs. Once that is corrected, however, the correlation is higher, even over reasonably short horizons, such as a quarter or a year. Importantly, REITs are more highly correlated with direct real estate and less highly correlated with equities over multi-year horizons.[23] Thus, although REITs tend to act like "stocks" in the short run, they act like "real estate" in the longer run. From a strategic asset allocation perspective, REITs and direct real estate are more comparable than conventional metrics suggest.

5.7. Long-Term Housing Returns

Savills World Research (2016) estimated that residential real estate accounts for 75% of the total value of developed properties globally. Most individuals' homes are their primary, perhaps only, real estate investment. A relatively new database provides a global perspective on the long-term performance of residential real estate (housing), equities, and bonds.[24] The database covers 145 years (1870–2015) and 16 countries.

Jordà, Knoll, Kuvshinov, Schularick, and Taylor (2017) found that residential real estate was the best performing asset class over the entire sample period, with a higher real return and much lower volatility than equities. However, performance characteristics differed before and after World War II:

- Residential real estate had a higher (lower) real return than equities before (after) World War II.
- Residential real estate had a higher real return than equities in every country except Switzerland, the United Kingdom, and the United States over 1950–1980 but a lower return than equities in every country for 1980–2015.
- Residential real estate and equities had similar patterns—that is, a strong correlation—prior to the war but a low correlation after the war.
- Equity returns became increasingly correlated across countries after the war, but residential real estate returns are essentially uncorrelated across countries.

Exhibit 8 shows the real returns for equities and residential real estate in each country since 1950.

---

[23]Stefek and Suryanarayanan (2012).
[24]The database was developed for and is described in Jordà, Knoll, Kuvshinov, Schularick, and Taylor (2017).

EXHIBIT 8   Real Equity and Housing Returns by Country, 1950–2015

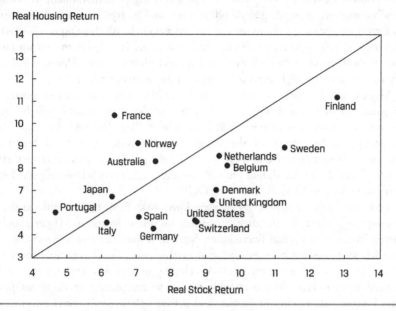

Source: Jordà et al. (2017).
Note: Annual percentage returns are shown.

EXAMPLE 7   Assessing Real Estate Investments

Tammi Sinclair, an analyst at a large retirement fund, recently attended investor presentations by three private real estate firms looking to fund new projects. Office Growth Partners specializes in building and owning low-cost, standardized office space for firms seeking to place sales representatives in the most rapidly growing small population areas across the region. Mega-Box Properties builds and owns large, custom-designed distribution facilities for multinational makers of brand-name products. The facilities are strategically located near major global transportation hubs. Exclusive Elegance Inc. develops and then manages some of the world's most luxurious, sought-after residential buildings in prime locations. It never breaks ground on a new property until at least 85% of the units have been sold and, to date, has never failed to sell out before construction is complete.

Identify important characteristics of each business that Sinclair will need to consider in establishing a required rate of return for each potential investment.

Guideline answer:

Office Growth Partners (OGP) is likely to be a very high-risk investment. It essentially chases hot markets, it builds generic office space, and its typical tenants (opportunistic sales forces) are apt to opt out as soon as the market cools. All these aspects suggest that its business is very exposed to a boom-and-bust cycle. It is likely to end up owning properties with persistently high vacancy rates and high turnover. Hence, Sinclair will likely require a rather high expected return on an investment in OGP.

Mega-Box's business should be fairly stable. The distribution centers are strategically located and designed to meet the needs of the tenant, which suggests long-term leases and low turnover will benefit both Mega-Box and the tenant firms. The average credit quality of the tenants—multinational makers of brand-name products—is likely to be solid and disciplined by the public bond and loan markets. All things considered, Sinclair should probably require a significantly lower expected return on an investment in Mega-Box than in OGP.

Exclusive Elegance appears to be even lower risk. First, it deals only in the very highest-quality, most sought-after properties in prime locations. These should be relatively immune to cyclical fluctuations. Second, it does not retain ownership of the properties, so it does not bear the equity/ownership risks. Third, it is fairly conservative in the riskiest portion of its business—developing new properties. However, Sinclair will need to investigate its record with respect to completing development projects within budget, maintaining properties, and delivering top-quality service to residents.

6. FORECASTING EXCHANGE RATES

Forecasting exchange rates is generally acknowledged to be especially difficult—so difficult that many asset managers either passively accept the impact of currency movements on their portfolio returns or routinely hedge out the currency exposure even if doing so is costly.

To get a sense for why exchange rates are so difficult to forecast, it is useful to distinguish between "money" and the currency in which it is denominated. Like equities and bonds, money is an asset denominated in a currency. Currencies are the units of account in which the prices of everything else—goods, services, real assets, financial assets, liabilities, flows, and balances—are quoted. An exchange rate movement changes the values of everything denominated in one currency relative to everything denominated in every other currency. That is a very powerful force. It works in the other direction as well. Anything that affects quantities, prices, or values within one currency relative to those in another will exert some degree of pressure on exchange rates. Perhaps even more importantly, anything that changes *expectations* of prices, quantities, or values within any currency can change expectations about the future path of currencies, causing an immediate reaction in exchange rates as people adjust their exposures.

Of course, currencies are not abstract accounting ledgers. They are inherently tied to governments, financial systems, legal systems, and geographies. The laws, regulations, customs, and conventions within and between these systems also influence exchange rates, especially when exchange rates are used as instruments or targets of policy. The consequence of all these aspects is that there is very little firm ground on which to stand for analysts trying to forecast exchange rates. The best we can hope to do is to identify the forces that are likely to be exerting the most powerful influences and assess their relative strength. On a related note, it is not possible to identify mutually exclusive approaches to exchange rate forecasting that are each complete enough to stand alone. Hence, the perspectives discussed in this section should be viewed as complementary rather than as alternatives.

6.1. Focus on Goods and Services, Trade, and the Current Account

There are three primary ways in which trade in goods and services can influence the exchange rate. The first is directly through flows. The second is through quasi-arbitrage of prices. The third is through competitiveness and sustainability.

6.1.1. Trade Flows

Trade flows do not, in general, exert a significant impact on contemporaneous exchange rate movements, provided they can be financed. Although gross trade flows may be large, net flows (exports minus imports) are typically much smaller relative to the economy and relative to actual and potential financial flows. If trade-related flows through the foreign exchange market become large relative to financing/investment flows, it is likely that a crisis is emerging.

6.1.2. Purchasing Power Parity

Purchasing power parity (PPP) is based on the notion that the prices of goods and services should change at the same rate regardless of currency denomination.[25] Thus, *the expected percentage change in the exchange rate should be equal to the difference in expected inflation rates.* If we define the *real exchange rate* as the ratio of price levels converted to a common currency, then PPP says that *the expected change in the real exchange rate should be zero.*

The mechanism underlying PPP is a quasi-arbitrage. Free and competitive trade should force alignment of the prices of similar products after conversion to a common currency. This is a very powerful force. It works, but it is slow and incomplete. As a result, the evidence indicates that PPP is a poor predictor of exchange rates over short to intermediate horizons but is a better guide to currency movements over progressively longer multi-year horizons.[26]

There are numerous reasons for deviations from PPP. The starting point matters. Relative PPP implicitly assumes that prices and exchange rates are already well aligned. If not, it will take time before the PPP relationship re-emerges. Not all goods are traded, and virtually every country imposes some trade barriers. PPP completely ignores the impact of capital flows, which often exert much more acute pressure on exchange rates over significant periods of time. Finally, economic developments may necessitate changes in the country's terms of trade; that is, contrary to PPP, the real exchange rate may need to change over time.

The impact of relative purchasing power on exchange rates tends to be most evident when inflation differentials are large, persistent, and driven primarily by monetary conditions. Under these conditions, PPP may describe exchange rate movements reasonably well over all but the shortest horizons. Indeed, the well-known "monetary approach" to exchange rates

---

[25]This version of PPP is usually referred to as "relative PPP" to distinguish it from a stricter notion called "absolute PPP." Absolute PPP is an important concept but is not useful for practical forecasting. See previous CFA Program currency chapters for a broader discussion of PPP concepts.

[26]See, for example, Abuaf and Jorion (1990); Exhibit 2 in "Currency Exchange Rates: Understanding Equilibrium Value" provides a useful visual illustration of PPP over different horizons.

essentially boils down to two assumptions: (1) PPP holds, and (2) inflation is determined by the money supply.

6.1.3. Competitiveness and Sustainability of the Current Account

It is axiomatic that in the absence of capital flows, prices, quantities, and exchange rates would have to adjust so that trade is always balanced. Since the prices of goods and services, production levels, and spending decisions tend to adjust only gradually, the onus of adjustment would fall primarily on exchange rates. Allowing for capital flows mitigates this pressure on exchange rates. The fact remains, however, that imposition of restrictions on capital flows will increase the sensitivity of exchange rates to the trade balance or, more generally, the current account balance.[27] This is not usually a major consideration for large, developed economies with sophisticated financial markets but can be important in small or developing economies.

Aside from the issue of restrictions on capital mobility, the extent to which the current account balance influences the exchange rate depends primarily on whether it is likely to be persistent and, if so, whether it can be sustained. These issues, in turn, depend mainly on the size of the imbalance and its source. Small current account balances—say, less than 2% of GDP—are likely to be sustainable for many years and hence would exert little influence on exchange rates. Similarly, larger imbalances that are expected to be transitory may not generate a significant, lasting impact on currencies.

The current account balance equals the difference between national saving and investment.[28] A current account surplus indicates that household saving plus business profits and the government surplus/deficit exceeds domestic investment spending. A current account deficit reflects the opposite. A current account deficit that reflects strong, profitable investment spending is more likely to be sustainable than a deficit reflecting high household spending (low saving), low business profits, or substantial government deficits because it is likely to attract the required capital inflow for as long as attractive investment opportunities persist. A large current account surplus may not be very sustainable either because it poses a sustainability problem for deficit countries or because the surplus country becomes unwilling to maintain such a high level of aggregate saving.

Whether an imbalance is likely to persist in the absence of terms-of-trade adjustments largely depends on whether the imbalance is structural. Structural imbalances arise from (1) persistent fiscal imbalances; (2) preferences, demographics, and institutional characteristics affecting saving decisions; (3) abundance or lack of important resources; (4) availability/absence of profitable investment opportunities associated with growth, capital deepening, and innovation; and, of course, (5) the prevailing terms of trade. Temporary imbalances mainly arise from business cycles (at home and abroad) and associated policy actions.

If a change in the (nominal) exchange rate is to bring about a necessary change in the current account balance, it will have to induce changes in spending patterns, consumption/saving decisions, and production/investment decisions. These adjustments typically occur slowly and are often resisted by decision makers who hope they can be avoided. Rapid adjustment of the exchange rate may also be resisted because people only gradually adjust

---

[27]The Mundell–Fleming model of monetary and fiscal policy effects on the exchange rate with high/low capital mobility provides an important illustration of this point. See the CFA Program chapter "Currency Exchange Rates: Understanding Equilibrium Value."

[28]See Chapter 4 of Piros and Pinto (2013) for discussion of balance of payments accounting.

their expectations of its ultimate level. Hence, both the exchange rate and current account adjustments are likely to be gradual.

6.2. Focus on Capital Flows

Since the current account and the capital account must always balance and the drivers of the current account tend to adjust only gradually, virtually all of the short-term adjustment and much of the intermediate-term adjustment must occur in the capital account. Asset prices, interest rates, and exchange rates are all part of the equilibrating mechanism. Since a change in the exchange rate simultaneously affects the relative values of all assets denominated in different currencies, we should expect significant pressure to be exerted on the exchange rate whenever an adjustment of capital flows is required.

6.2.1. Implications of Capital Mobility

Capital seeks the highest risk-adjusted expected return. The investments available in each currency can be viewed as a portfolio. Designating one as domestic (*d*) and one as foreign (*f*), in a world of perfect capital mobility the exchange rate (expressed as domestic currency per foreign currency unit) will be driven to the point at which the expected percentage change in the exchange rate equals the "excess" risk-adjusted expected return on the domestic portfolio over the foreign portfolio. This idea can be expressed concretely using a building block approach to expected returns.

$$E(\%\Delta S_{d/f}) = (r^d - r^f) + (\text{Term}^d - \text{Term}^f) + (\text{Credit}^d - \text{Credit}^f) \\ + (\text{Equity}^d - \text{Equity}^f) + (\text{Liquid}^d - \text{Liquid}^f) \tag{9}$$

The expected change in the exchange rate ($\%\Delta S_{d/f}$) will reflect the differences in the nominal short-term interest rates (*r*), term premiums (Term), credit premiums (Credit), equity premiums (Equity), and liquidity premiums (Liquid) in the two markets. The components of this equation can be associated with the expected return on various segments of the portfolio: the money market (first term), government bonds (first and second), corporate bonds (first–third), publicly traded equities (first–fourth), and private assets (all terms), including direct investment in plant and equipment.

As an example, suppose the domestic market has a 1% higher short-term rate, a 0.25% lower term premium, a 0.50% higher credit premium, and the same equity and liquidity premiums as the foreign market. Equation 9 implies that the domestic currency must be expected to depreciate by 1.25% (= 1% − 0.25% + 0.5%)—that is, $E(\%\Delta S_{d/f}) = 1.25\%$— to equalize risk-adjusted expected returns.

It may seem counterintuitive that the domestic currency should be expected to depreciate if its portfolio offers a higher risk-adjusted expected return. The puzzle is resolved by the key phrase "driven to the point . . ." in this subsection's opening paragraph. In theory, the exchange rate will instantly move ("jump") to a level where the currency with higher (lower) risk-adjusted expected return will be so strong (weak) that it will be expected to depreciate (appreciate) going forward. This is known as the *overshooting* mechanism, introduced by Dornbusch (1976). In reality, the move will not be instantaneous, but it may occur very quickly if there is a consensus about the relative attractiveness of assets denominated in each currency. Of course, asset prices will also be adjusting.

The overshooting mechanism suggests that there are likely to be three phases in response to relative improvement in investment opportunities. First, the exchange rate will appreciate ($S_{d/f}$ will decline) as capital flows toward the more attractive market. The more vigorous the flow, the faster and greater the appreciation of the domestic currency and the more the flow will also drive up asset prices in that market. Second, in the intermediate term, there will be a period of consolidation as investors begin to question the extended level of the exchange rate and to form expectations of a reversal. Third, in the longer run, there will be a retracement of some or all of the exchange rate move depending on the extent to which underlying opportunities have been equalized by asset price adjustments. This is the phase that is reflected in Equation 9.

Importantly, these three phases imply that the relationship between currency appreciation/depreciation and apparent investment incentives will not always be in the same direction. This fact is especially important with respect to interest rate differentials since they are directly observable. At some times, higher–interest rate currencies appreciate; at other times, they depreciate.

6.2.2. Uncovered Interest Rate Parity and Hot Money Flows

Uncovered interest rate parity (UIP) asserts that the expected percentage change in the exchange rate should be equal to the nominal interest rate differential. That is, only the first term in Equation 9 matters. The implicit assumption is that the response to short-term interest rate differentials will be so strong that it overwhelms all other considerations.

Contrary to UIP, the empirical evidence consistently shows that *carry trades*—borrowing in low-rate currencies and lending in high-rate currencies—earn meaningful profits on average. For example, Burnside, Eichenbaum, Kleshchelski, and Rebelo (2011) found that from February 1976 to July 2009, a strategy of rolling carry trades involving portfolios of high- and low-rate currencies returned 4.31% per annum after transaction costs versus the US dollar and 2.88% per annum versus the British pound.

The profitability of carry trades is usually ascribed to a risk premium, which is clearly consistent with the idea that the risk premiums in Equation 9 matter. The empirical results may also be capturing primarily the overshooting phase of the response to interest rate differentials. In any case, carry trades tend to be profitable on average, and UIP does not hold up well as a predictor of exchange rates.

Vigorous flows of capital in response to interest rate differentials are often referred to as *hot money flows*. Hot money flows are problematic for central banks. First, they limit the central bank's ability to run an effective monetary policy. This is the key message of the Mundell–Fleming model with respect to monetary policy in economies characterized by the free flow of capital. Second, a flood of readily available short-term financing may encourage firms to fund longer-term needs with short-term money, setting the stage for a crisis when the financing dries up. Third, the nearly inevitable overshooting of the exchange rate is likely to disrupt non-financial businesses. These issues are generally most acute for emerging markets since their economies and financial markets tend to be more fragile. Central banks often try to combat hot money flows by intervening in the currency market to offset the exchange rate impact of the flows. They may also attempt to *sterilize* the impact on domestic liquidity by selling government securities to limit the growth of bank reserves or maintain a target level of interest rates. If the hot money is flowing *out* rather than *in*, the central bank would do the opposite: sell foreign currency (thereby draining domestic liquidity) to limit/avoid depreciation of the domestic currency and buy government securities (thereby providing liquidity) to sterilize the impact on bank reserves and interest rates. In either case, if intervention is not effective or sufficient, capital controls may be imposed.

6.2.3. Portfolio Balance, Portfolio Composition, and Sustainability Issues

The earlier discussion on the implications of capital mobility implicitly introduced a portfolio balance perspective. Each country/currency has a unique portfolio of assets that makes up part of the global "market portfolio." Exchange rates provide an across-the-board mechanism for adjusting the relative sizes of these portfolios to match investors' desire to hold them. We will look at this from three angles: tactical allocations, strategic/secular allocations, and the implications of wealth transfer.

The relative sizes of different currency portfolios within the global market portfolio do not, in general, change significantly over short to intermediate horizons. Hence, investors do not need to be induced to make changes in their long-term allocations. However, they are likely to want to make tactical allocation changes in response to evolving opportunities—notably, those related to the relative strength of various economies and related policy measures. Overall, capital is likely to flow into the currencies of countries in the strongest phases of the business cycle. The attraction should be especially strong if the economic expansion is led by robust investment in real, productive assets (e.g., plant and equipment) since that can be expected to generate a new stream of long-run profits.

In the long run, the relative size of each currency portfolio depends primarily on relative trend growth rates and current account balances. Rapid economic growth is almost certain to be accompanied by an expanding share of the global market portfolio being denominated in the associated currency. Thus, investors will have to be induced to increase their strategic allocations to assets in that country/currency. All else the same, this would tend to weaken that currency—partially offsetting the increase in the currency's share of the global portfolio—and upward pressure on risk premiums in that market. However, there are several mitigating factors.

- *With growth comes wealth accumulation:* The share of global wealth owned by domestic investors will be rising along with the supply of assets denominated in their currency. Since investors generally exhibit a strong *home country bias* for domestic assets, domestic investors are likely to willingly absorb a large portion of the newly created assets.
- *Productivity-driven growth:* If high growth reflects strong productivity gains, both foreign and domestic investors are likely to willingly fund it with both financial flows and foreign direct investment.
- *Small initial weight in global portfolios:* Countries with exceptionally high trend growth rates are typically relatively small, have previously restricted foreign access to their local-currency financial markets, and/or have previously funded external deficits in major currencies (not their own). Almost by definition, these are emerging and frontier markets. Any of these factors would suggest greater capacity to increase the share of local-currency-denominated assets in global portfolios without undermining the currency.

Large, persistent current account deficits funded in local currency will also put downward pressure on the exchange rate over time as investors are required to shift strategic allocations toward that currency. Again, there are mitigating considerations.

- *The source of the deficit matters:* As discussed previously, current account deficits arising from strong investment spending are relatively easy to finance as long as they are expected to be sufficiently profitable. Deficits due to a low saving rate or weak fiscal discipline are much more problematic.

- *Special status of reserve currencies:* A few currencies—notably, the US dollar—have a special status because the bulk of official reserves are held in these currencies, the associated sovereign debt issuer is viewed as a safe haven, major commodities (e.g., oil) are priced in these currencies, and international trade transactions are often settled in them. A small current account deficit in a reserve-currency country is welcome because it helps provide liquidity to the global financial system. Historically, however, reserve currency status has not proven to be permanent.

Current account surpluses/deficits reflect a transfer of wealth from the deficit country to the surplus country. In an ideal world of fully integrated markets, perfect capital mobility, homogeneous expectations, and identical preferences,[29] a transfer of wealth would have virtually no impact on asset prices or exchange rates because everyone would be happy with the same portfolio composition. This is not the case in practice. To pick just one example, as long as investors have a home country bias, the transfer of wealth will increase the demand for the current-account-surplus country's assets and currency and decrease demand for those of the deficit country.

Does the composition of a particular currency's portfolio matter? A look back at Equation 9 suggests that it should matter to some degree. For the most part, however, we would expect asset price adjustments (changes in interest rates and risk premiums) to eliminate most of the pressure that might otherwise be exerted on the exchange rate. Nonetheless, some types of flows and holdings are often considered to be more or less supportive of the currency. Foreign direct investment flows are generally considered to be the most favorable because they indicate a long-term commitment and they contribute directly to the productivity/profitability of the economy. Similarly, investments in private real estate and private equity represent long-term capital committed to the market, although they may or may not represent the creation of new real assets. Public equity would likely be considered the next most supportive of the currency. Although it is less permanent than private investments, it is still a residual claim on the profitability of the economy that does not have to be repaid. Debt has to be serviced and must either be repaid or refinanced, potentially triggering a crisis. Hence, a high and rising ratio of debt to GDP gives rise to *debt sustainability* concerns with respect to the economy. This issue could apply to private sector debt. But it is usually associated with fiscal deficits because the government is typically the largest single borrower; typically borrows to fund consumption and transfers, rather than productive investment; and may be borrowing in excess of what can be serviced without a significant increase in taxes. Finally, as noted previously with respect to hot money flows, large or rapid accumulation of short-term borrowing is usually viewed as a clear warning sign for the currency.

EXAMPLE 8   Currency Forecasts

After many years of running moderately high current account deficits (2%–4% of GDP) but doing little infrastructure investment, Atlandia plans to increase the yearly government deficit by 3% of GDP and maintain that level of deficit for the next 20 years, devoting the increase to infrastructure spending. The deficits will be financed with local-currency government debt. Pete Stevens, CFA, is faced with the task of

---

[29]Note that these are essentially the assumptions underlying the standard CAPM.

assessing the impact of this announcement on the Atlandian currency. After talking with members of the economics department at his firm, he has established the following baseline assumptions:

- All else the same, current account deficits will persistently exceed 6% of GDP while the program is in place. Setting aside any lasting impact of the policy/spending, the current account deficit will then fall back to 3% of GDP, provided the economy has remained competitive.
- Pressure on wages will boost inflation to 1.5% above the global inflation rate. Because of limitations on factor substitutability, costs in the traded good sector will rise disproportionately.
- Expectations of faster growth will raise the equity premium.
- The central bank will likely tighten policy—that is, raise rates.

Questions:

1. What would purchasing power parity imply about the exchange rate?
2. What are the implications for competitiveness for the currency?
3. What is the likely short-term impact of capital flows on the exchange rate?
4. What does the overshooting mechanism imply about the path of the exchange rate over time? How does this fit with the answers to Questions 1–3?
5. What does a sustainability perspective imply?

Solutions:

1. Purchasing power parity would imply that the Atlandian currency will depreciate by 1.5% per year. The exchange rate, quoted in domestic (Atlandian) units per foreign unit as in Equation 9, will rise by a factor of $1.015^{10} = 1.1605$, corresponding to a 13.83% ($= 1 - 1/1.1605$) decline in the value of the domestic currency.[30]
2. Since costs in the traded sector will rise faster than inflation, the exchange rate would need to depreciate faster than PPP implies in order to maintain competitiveness. Thus, to remain competitive and re-establish a 3% current account deficit after 10 years, the *real* exchange rate needs to depreciate.
3. Both the increase in short-term rates and the increase in the equity premium are likely to induce strong short-term capital inflows even before the current account deficit actually increases. This should put significant pressure on the Atlandian currency to appreciate (i.e., the $S_{d/f}$ exchange rate will decline if the Atlandian currency is defined as the domestic currency). The initial impact may be offset to some extent by flows out of government bonds as investors push yields up in anticipation of increasing supply, but as bonds are repriced to offer a higher expected return (a higher term premium), it will reinforce the upward pressure on the exchange rate.
4. The overshooting mechanism would imply that the initial appreciation of the Atlandian currency discussed previously will extend to a level from which the currency is then expected to depreciate at a pace that equalizes risk-adjusted expected returns across markets and maintains equality between the current and

---

[30]Note that a slightly different number is obtained if the 1.5% rate is applied directly to the foreign currency value of the Atlandian currency (i.e., the exchange rate expressed as foreign units per domestic unit). That calculation would give a cumulative depreciation of 14.03% ($= 1 - 0.985^{10}$). The difference arises because $(1/1.015)$ is not exactly equal to 0.985.

capital accounts. The initial appreciation of the currency in this scenario is clearly inconsistent with PPP, but the subsequent longer-term depreciation phase (from a stronger level) is likely to bring the exchange rate into reasonable alignment with PPP and competitiveness considerations in the long run.

5. It is highly unlikely that a current account deficit in excess of 6% of GDP is sustainable for 10 years. It would entail an increase in net foreign liabilities equaling 60% (= 6% × 10) of GDP. Servicing that additional obligation would add, say, 2%–3% of GDP to the current account deficit forever. Adding that to the baseline projection of 3% would mean that the current account deficit would remain in the 5%–6% range even after the infrastructure spending ended, so net foreign liabilities would still be accumulating rapidly. Closing that gap will require a very large increase in net national saving: 5%–6% of annual GDP *in addition to* the 3% reduction in infrastructure spending when the program ends. Standard macroeconomic analysis implies that such an adjustment would require some combination of a very deep recession and a very large depreciation in the real value of the Atlandian currency (i.e., the real $S_{d/f}$ exchange rate must increase sharply). As soon as investors recognize this, a crisis is almost certain to occur. Bond yields would increase sharply, and equity prices and the currency will fall substantially.

7. FORECASTING VOLATILITY

In some applications, the analyst is concerned with forecasting the variance for only a single asset. More often, however, the analyst needs to forecast the variance–covariance matrix for several, perhaps many, assets in order to analyze the risk of portfolios. Estimating a single variance that is believed to be constant is straightforward: The familiar sample variance is unbiased and its precision can be enhanced by using higher-frequency data. The analyst's task becomes more complicated if the variance is not believed to be constant or the analyst needs to forecast a variance–covariance (VCV) matrix. These issues are addressed in this section. In addition, we elaborate on de-smoothing real estate and other returns.

7.1. Estimating a Constant VCV Matrix with Sample Statistics

The simplest and most heavily used method for estimating constant variances and covariances is to use the corresponding sample statistic—variance or covariance—computed from historical return data. These elements are then assembled into a VCV matrix. There are two main problems with this method, both related to sample size. First, given the short to intermediate sample periods typical in finance, the method cannot be used to estimate the VCV matrix for large numbers of assets. If the number of assets exceeds the number of historical observations, then some portfolios will erroneously appear to be riskless. Second, given typical sample sizes, this method is subject to substantial sampling error. A useful rule of thumb that addresses both of these issues is that the number of observations should be at least 10 times the number of assets in order for the sample VCV matrix to be deemed reliable. In addition, since each element is estimated without regard to any of the others, this method does not address the issue of imposing cross-sectional consistency.

7.2. VCV Matrices from Multi-Factor Models

Factor models have become the standard method of imposing structure on the VCV matrix of asset returns. From this perspective, their main advantage is that the number of assets can be very large relative to the number of observations. The key to making this work is that the covariances are fully determined by exposures to a small number of common factors whereas each variance includes an asset-specific component.

In a model with K common factors, the return on the ith asset is given by

$$r_i = \alpha_i + \sum_{k=1}^{K} \beta_{ik} F_k + \varepsilon_i \tag{10}$$

where α_i is a constant intercept, β_{ik} is the asset's sensitivity to the kth factor, F_k is the kth common factor return, and ε_i is a stochastic term with a mean of zero that is unique to the ith asset. In general, the factors will be correlated. Given the model, the variance of the ith asset is

$$\sigma_i^2 = \sum_{m=1}^{K} \sum_{n=1}^{K} \beta_{im} \beta_{in} \rho_{mn} + \nu_i^2 \tag{11}$$

where ρ_{mn} is the covariance between the mth and nth factors and ν_i^2 is the variance of the unique component of the ith asset's return. The covariance between the ith and jth assets is

$$\sigma_{ij} = \sum_{m=1}^{K} \sum_{n=1}^{K} \beta_{im} \beta_{jn} \rho_{mn} \tag{12}$$

As long as none of the factors are redundant and none of the asset returns are completely determined by the factors (so $\nu_i^2 \neq 0$), there will not be any portfolios that erroneously appear to be riskless. That is, we will not encounter the first problem mentioned in Section 7.1, with respect to using sample statistics.

Imposing structure with a factor model makes the VCV matrix much simpler. With N assets, there are $[N(N-1)/2]$ distinct covariance elements in the VCV matrix. For example, if $N = 100$, there are 4,950 distinct covariances to be estimated. The factor model reduces this problem to estimating $[N \times K]$ factor sensitivities plus $[K(K+1)/2]$ elements of the factor VCV matrix, Ω. With $N = 100$ and $K = 5$, this would mean "only" 500 sensitivities and 15 elements of the factor VCV matrix—almost a 90% reduction in items to estimate. (Of course, we also need to estimate the asset-specific variance terms, ν_i^2, in order to get the N variances, σ_i^2.) If the factors are chosen well, the factor-based VCV matrix will contain substantially less estimation error than the sample VCV matrix does.

A well-specified factor model can also improve cross-sectional consistency. To illustrate, suppose we somehow know that the true covariance of any asset i with any asset j is proportional to asset i's covariance with any third asset, k, so

$$\frac{\sigma_{ij}}{\sigma_{ik}} = \text{Constant} \tag{13}$$

for any assets i, j, and k. We would want our estimates to come as close as possible to satisfying this relationship. Sample covariances computed from any given sample of returns will not, in general, do so. However, using Equation 12 with only one factor (i.e., $K = 1$) shows that the covariances from a single-factor model will satisfy

$$\frac{\sigma_{ij}}{\sigma_{ik}} = \frac{\beta_j}{\beta_k} \tag{14}$$

for all assets i, j, and k. Thus, in this simple example, a single-factor model imposes exactly the right cross-sectional structure.

The benefits obtained by imposing a factor structure—handling large numbers of assets, a reduced number of parameters to be estimated, imposition of cross-sectional structure, and a potentially substantial reduction of estimation error—come at a cost. In contrast to the simple example just discussed, in general, the factor model will almost certainly be mis-specified. The structure it imposes will not be exactly right. As a result, the factor-based VCV matrix is *biased*; that is, the expected value is not equal to the true (unobservable) VCV matrix of the returns. To put it differently, the matrix is not correct even "on average." The matrix is also *inconsistent*; that is, it does not converge to the true matrix as the sample size gets arbitrarily large. In contrast, the sample VCV matrix is unbiased and consistent. Thus, when we use a factor-based matrix instead of the sample VCV matrix, we are choosing to estimate something that is "not quite right" with relative precision rather than the "right thing" with a lot of noise. The point is that although factor models are very useful, they are not a panacea.

7.3. Shrinkage Estimation of VCV Matrices

As with shrinkage estimation in general, the idea here is to combine the information in the sample data, the sample VCV matrix, with an alternative estimate, the target VCV matrix—which reflects assumed "prior" knowledge of the structure of the true VCV matrix—and thereby mitigate the impact of estimation error on the final matrix. Each element (variance or covariance) of the final shrinkage estimate of the VCV matrix is simply a weighted average of the corresponding elements of the sample VCV matrix and the target VCV matrix. The same weights are used for all elements of the matrix. The analyst must determine how much weight to put on the target matrix (the "prior" knowledge) and how much weight to put on the sample data (the sample VCV matrix).

Aside from a technical condition that rules out the appearance of riskless portfolios, virtually any choice of target VCV matrix will increase (or at least not decrease) the efficiency of the estimates versus the sample VCV matrix. "Efficiency" in this context means a smaller mean-squared error (MSE), which is equal to an estimator's variance plus the square of its bias. Although the shrinkage estimator is biased, its MSE will in general be smaller than the MSE of the (unbiased) sample VCV matrix. The more plausible (and presumably less biased) the selected target matrix, the greater the improvement will be. A factor-model-based VCV matrix would be a reasonable candidate for the target.

EXAMPLE 9   Estimating the VCV Matrix

Isa Berkitz is an analyst at Barnsby & Culp (B&C), a recently formed multi-family office. Berkitz has been asked to propose the method for estimating the variance–covariance matrix to be used in B&C's asset allocation process for all clients. After examining the existing client portfolios and talking with the clients and portfolio managers, Berkitz concludes that in order to support B&C's strategic and tactical allocation needs, the VCV matrix will need to include 25 asset classes. For many of these classes, she will be able to obtain less than 10 years of monthly return data. Berkitz has decided to incorporate both the sample statistics and factor-model approaches using shrinkage estimation.

Explain the strengths and weaknesses of the two basic approaches and why Berkitz would choose to combine them using the shrinkage framework.

Solution: The VCV matrix based on sample statistics is correct on average (it is unbiased) and convergences to the true VCV matrix as the sample size gets arbitrarily large (it is "consistent"). The sample VCV method cannot be used if the number of assets exceeds the number of observations, which is not an issue in this case. However, it is subject to large sampling errors unless the number of observations is large relative to the number of assets. A 10-to-1 rule of thumb would suggest that Berkitz needs more than 250 observations (20+ years of monthly data) in order for the sample VCV matrix to give her reliable estimates, but she has at most 120 observations. In addition, the sample VCV matrix does not impose any cross-sectional consistency on the estimates. A factor-model-based VCV matrix can be used even if the number of assets exceeds the number of observations. It can substantially reduce the number of unique parameters to be estimated, it imposes cross-sectional structure, and it can substantially reduce estimation errors. However, unless the structure imposed by the factor model is exactly correct, the VCV matrix will not be correct on average (it will be biased). Shrinkage estimation—a weighted average of the sample VCV and factor-based VCV matrices—will increase (or at least not decrease) the efficiency of the estimates. In effect, the shrinkage estimator captures the benefits of each underlying methodology and mitigates their respective limitations.

7.4. Estimating Volatility from Smoothed Returns

The available return data for such asset classes as private real estate, private equity, and hedge funds generally reflect smoothing of unobservable underlying "true" returns. The smoothing dampens the volatility of the observed data and distorts correlations with other assets. Thus, the raw data tend to understate the risk and overstate the diversification benefits of these asset classes. Failure to adjust for the impact of smoothing will almost certainly lead to distorted portfolio analysis and hence poor asset allocation decisions.

The basic idea is that the observed returns are a weighted average of current and past true, unobservable returns. One of the simplest and most widely used models implies that the current observed return, R_t, is a weighted average of the current true return, r_t, and the previous observed return:

$$R_t = (1-\lambda)r_t + \lambda R_{t-1} \tag{15}$$

where $0 < \lambda < 1$. From this equation, it can be shown that

$$\text{var}(r) = \left(\frac{1+\lambda}{1-\lambda}\right)\text{var}(R) > \text{var}(R) \tag{16}$$

As an example, if $\lambda = 0.8$, then the true variance, $\text{var}(r)$, of the asset is 9 times the variance of the observed data. Equivalently, the standard deviation is 3 times larger.

This model cannot be estimated directly because the true return, r_t, is not observable. To get around this problem, the analyst assumes a relationship between the unobservable return and one or more observable variables. For private real estate, a natural choice might be a REIT index, whereas for private equity, an index of similar publicly traded equities could be used.

EXAMPLE 10   Estimating Volatility from Smoothed Data

While developing the VCV matrix for B&C, Isa Berkitz noted that the volatilities for several asset classes—notably, real estate and private equity categories—calculated directly from available return data appear to be very low. The data are from reputable sources, but Berkitz is skeptical because similar publicly traded classes—for example, REITs and small-cap equities—exhibit much higher volatilities. What is the likely cause of the issue?

Guideline answer:
The very low volatilities are very likely due to smoothing within the reported private asset returns. That is, the observed data reflect a weighted average of current and past true returns. For real estate, this smoothing arises primarily because the underlying property values used to calculate "current" returns are based primarily on backward-looking appraisals rather than concurrent transactions.

7.5. Time-Varying Volatility: ARCH Models

The discussion up to this point has focused on estimating variances and covariances under the assumption that their true values do not change over time. It is well known, however, that financial asset returns tend to exhibit **volatility clustering**, evidenced by periods of high and low volatility. A class of models known collectively as autoregressive conditional heteroskedasticity (ARCH) models has been developed to address these time-varying volatilities.[31]

One of the simplest and most heavily used forms of this broad class of models specifies that the variance in period t is given by

$$\sigma_t^2 = \gamma + \alpha\sigma_{t-1}^2 + \beta\eta_t^2 = \gamma + (\alpha + \beta)\sigma_{t-1}^2 + \beta(\eta_t^2 - \sigma_{t-1}^2) \qquad (17)$$

where α, β, and γ are non-negative parameters such that $(\alpha + \beta) < 1$. The term η_t is the unexpected component of return in period t; that is, it is a random variable with a mean of zero conditional on information at time $(t - 1)$. Rearranging the equation as in the second line shows that $(\eta_t^2 - \sigma_{t-1}^2)$ can be interpreted as the "shock" to the variance in period t. Thus, the variance in period t depends on the variance in period $(t - 1)$ plus a shock. The parameter β controls how much of the current "shock" feeds into the variance. In the extreme, if $\beta = 0$, then variance would be deterministic. The quantity $(\alpha + \beta)$ determines the extent to which the variance in future periods is influenced by the current level of volatility. The higher $(\alpha + \beta)$ is, the more the variance "remembers" what happened in the past and the more it "clusters" at high or low levels. The unconditional expected value of the variance is $[\gamma/(1 - \alpha - \beta)]$.

As an example, assume that $\gamma = 0.000002$, $\alpha = 0.9$, and $\beta = 0.08$ and that we are estimating daily equity volatility. Given these parameters, the unconditional expected value of the variance is 0.0001, implying that the daily standard deviation is 1% (0.01). Suppose the estimated variance at time $(t - 1)$ was 0.0004 $(= 0.02^2)$ and the return in period t was 3% above expectations $(\eta_t = 0.03)$. Then the variance in period t would be

---

[31]Chapter 12 of Campbell, Lo, and MacKinlay (1997) provides an excellent, detailed explanation of these models. The present discussion draws on that book.

$$\sigma_t^2 = 0.000002 + (0.9 \times 0.0004) + (0.08 \times 0.032) = 0.000434$$

which is equivalent to a standard deviation of 2.0833%. Without the shock to the variance (i.e., with $\eta_t^2 = \sigma_{t-1}^2 = 0.0004$), the standard deviation would have been 1.9849%. Even without the shock, the volatility would have remained well above its long-run mean of 1.0%. Including the shock, the volatility actually increased. Note that the impact on volatility would have been the same if the return had been 3% *below* expectations rather than above expectations.

The ARCH methodology can be extended to multiple assets—that is, to estimation of a VCV matrix. The most straightforward extensions tend to be limited to only a few assets since the number of parameters rises very rapidly. However, Engle (2002) developed a class of models with the potential to handle large matrices with relatively few parameters.

EXAMPLE 11   ARCH

Sam Akai has noticed that daily returns for a variety of asset classes tend to exhibit periods of high and low volatility but the volatility does seem to revert toward a fairly stable average level over time. Many market participants capture this tendency by estimating volatilities using a 60-day moving window. Akai notes that this method implicitly assumes volatility is constant within each 60-day window but somehow not constant from one day to the next. He has heard that ARCH models can explicitly incorporate time variation and capture the observed clustering pattern.

Explain the models to him.

Guideline answer:

The key idea is to model variance as a linear time-series process in which the current volatility depends on its own recent history or recent shocks. The shocks to volatility arise from unexpectedly large or small returns. In one of the simplest ARCH models, the current variance depends only on the variance in the previous period and the unexpected component of the current return (squared). Provided the coefficients are positive and not "too large," the variance will exhibit the properties Akai has observed: periods of time at high/low levels relative to a well-defined average level.

---

8. ADJUSTING A GLOBAL PORTFOLIO

The coverage of capital market expectations has provided an intensive examination of topics with which analysts need to be familiar in order to establish capital market expectations for client portfolios. This section brings some of this material together to illustrate how analysts can develop and justify recommendations for adjusting a portfolio. The discussion that follows is selective in the range of assets and scenarios it considers. It focuses on connecting expectations to the portfolio and is about "direction of change" rather than the details of specific forecasts.

8.1. Macro-Based Recommendations

Suppose we start with a fairly generic portfolio of global equities and bonds (we assume no other asset classes are included or considered) and we are asked to recommend changes based primarily on macroeconomic considerations. Further assume that the portfolio reflects a reasonable strategic allocation for our clients. Hence, we do not need to make any wholesale changes and can focus on incremental improvements based on assessment of current opportunities. To be specific, we limit our potential recommendations to the following:

- Change the overall allocations to equities and bonds.
- Reallocate equities/bonds between countries.
- Adjust the average credit quality of our bond portfolios.
- Adjust duration and positioning on the yield curves.
- Adjust our exposures to currencies.

To approach the task systematically, we begin with a checklist of questions.

1. Have there been significant changes in the drivers of trend growth, globally or in particular countries?
2. Are any of the markets becoming more/less globally integrated?
3. Where does each country stand within its business cycle? Are they synchronized?
4. Are monetary and fiscal policies consistent with long-term stability and the phases of the business cycle?
5. Are current account balances trending and sustainable?
6. Are any currencies under pressure to adjust or trending? Have capital flows driven any currencies to extended levels? Have any of the economies become uncompetitive/super-competitive because of currency movements?

There are certainly many more questions we could ask. In practice, the analyst will need to look into the details. But these questions suffice for our illustration. We will examine each in turn. It must be noted, however, that they are inherently interrelated.

8.1.1. Trend Growth

All else the same, an increase in trend growth favors equities because it implies more rapid long-run earnings growth. Faster growth due to productivity is especially beneficial. In contrast, higher trend growth generally results in somewhat higher real interest rates, a negative for currently outstanding bonds. Identifiable changes in trend growth that have not already been fully factored into asset prices are most likely to have arisen from a shock (e.g., new technology). A global change would provide a basis for adjusting the overall equity/bond allocation. Country-specific or regional changes provide a basis for reallocation within equities toward the markets experiencing enhanced growth prospects that have not already been reflected in market prices.

8.1.2. Global Integration

All else the same, the Singer–Terhaar model implies that when a market becomes more globally integrated, its required return should decline. As prices adjust to a lower required return, the market should deliver an even higher return than was previously expected or required by the market. Therefore, expected increases in integration provide a rationale for adjusting allocations toward those markets and reductions in markets that are already highly integrated. Doing so will typically entail a shift from developed markets to emerging markets.

8.1.3. Phases of the Business Cycle

The best time to buy equities is generally when the economy is approaching the trough of the business cycle. Valuation multiples and expected earnings growth rates are low and set to rise. The Grinold–Kroner model could be used to formalize a recommendation to buy equities. At this stage of the cycle, the term premium is high (the yield curve is steep) and the credit premium is high (credit spreads are wide). However, (short-term) interest rates are likely to start rising soon and the yield curve can be expected to flatten again as the economy gains strength. All else the same, the overall allocation to bonds will need to be reduced to facilitate the increased allocation to equities. Within the bond portfolio, overall duration should be reduced, positions with intermediate maturities should be reduced in favor of shorter maturities (and perhaps a small amount of longer maturities) to establish a "barbell" posture with the desired duration, and exposure to credit should be increased (a "down in quality" trade). The opposite recommendations would apply when the analyst judges that the economy is at or near the peak of the cycle.

To the extent that business cycles are synchronized across markets, this same prescription would apply to the overall portfolio. It is likely, however, that some markets will be out of phase—leading or lagging other markets—by enough to warrant reallocations between markets. In this case, the recommendation would be to reallocate equities from (to) markets nearest the peak (trough) of their respective cycles and to do the opposite within the bond portfolio with corresponding adjustments to duration, yield curve positioning, and credit exposure within each market.

8.1.4. Monetary and Fiscal Policies

Investors devote substantial energy dissecting every nuance of monetary and fiscal policy. If policymakers are doing what we would expect them to be doing at any particular stage of the business cycle—for example, moderate countercyclical actions and attending to longer-term objectives, such as controlling inflation and maintaining fiscal discipline—their activities may already be reflected in asset prices. In addition, the analyst should have factored expected policy actions into the assessment of trend growth and business cycles.

Significant opportunities to add value by reallocating the portfolio are more likely to arise from structural policy changes (e.g., a shift from interest rate targeting to money growth targeting, quantitative easing, and restructuring of the tax code) or evidence that the response to policy measures is not within the range of outcomes that policymakers would have expected (e.g., if massive quantitative easing induced little inflation response). Structural policy changes are clearly intentional and the impact on the economy and the markets is likely to be consistent with standard macroeconomic analysis, so the investment recommendations will follow from the implications for growth trends and business cycles. Almost by definition, standard modes of analysis may be ineffective if policy measures have not induced the expected responses. In this case, the analyst's challenge is to determine what, why, and how underlying linkages have changed and identify the value-added opportunities.

8.1.5. Current Account Balances

Current account balances ultimately reflect national saving and investment decisions, including the fiscal budget. Current accounts must, of course, net out across countries. In the short run, this is brought about in large measure by the fact that household saving and corporate profits (business saving) are effectively residuals whereas consumption and capital expenditures are more explicitly planned. Hence, purely cyclical fluctuations in the current account are just part of the business cycle. Longer-term trends in the current account require adjustments to induce deliberate changes in saving/investment decisions. A rising current account deficit will tend to put upward pressure on real required returns (downward pressure on asset prices) in order to induce a higher saving rate in the deficit country (to mitigate the widening deficit) and to attract the increased flow of capital from abroad required to fund the deficit. An expanding current account surplus will, in general, require the opposite in order to reduce "excess" saving. This suggests that the analyst should consider reallocation of portfolio assets from countries with secularly rising current account deficits to those with secularly rising current account surpluses (or narrowing deficits).

8.1.6. Capital Accounts and Currencies

Setting aside very high inflation situations in which purchasing power parity may be important even in the short term, currencies are primarily influenced by capital flows. When investors perceive that the portfolio of assets denominated in a particular currency offers a higher risk-adjusted expected return than is available in other currencies, the initial surge of capital tends to drive the exchange rate higher, often to a level from which it is more likely to depreciate rather than continue to appreciate. At that point, the underlying assets may remain attractive in their native currency but not in conjunction with the currency exposure. An analyst recommending reallocation of a portfolio toward assets denominated in a particular currency must, therefore, assess whether the attractiveness of the assets has already caused an "overshoot" in the currency or whether a case can be made that there is meaningful appreciation yet to come. In the former case, the analyst needs to consider whether the assets remain attractive after taking account of the cost of currency hedging.

There is one final question that needs to be addressed for all asset classes and currencies. The previous discussion alluded to it, but it is important enough to be asked directly: *What is already reflected in asset prices?* There is no avoiding the fact that valuations matter.

8.2. Quantifying the Views

Although the analyst may not be required to quantify the views underlying his or her recommendations, we can very briefly sketch a process that may be used for doing so using some of the tools discussed in earlier sections.

Step 1. Use appropriate techniques to estimate the VCV matrix for all asset classes.

Step 2. Use the Singer–Terhaar model and the estimated VCV matrix to determine equilibrium expected returns for all asset classes.

Step 3. Use the Grinold–Kroner model to estimate returns for equity markets based on assessments of economic growth, earnings growth, valuation multiples, dividends, and net share repurchases.

Step 4. Use the building block approach to estimate expected returns for bond classes based primarily on cyclical and policy considerations.

Step 5. Establish directional views on currencies relative to the portfolio's base currency based on the perceived attractiveness of assets and the likelihood of having overshot sustainable levels. Set modest rates of expected appreciation/depreciation.

Step 6. Incorporate a currency component into expected returns for equities and bonds.

Step 7. Use the Black–Litterman framework (described in a later chapter) to combine equilibrium expected returns from Step 2 with the expected returns determined in Steps 3–6.

SUMMARY

The following are the main points covered in the chapter.

- The choice among forecasting techniques is effectively a choice of the information on which forecasts will be conditioned and how that information will be incorporated into the forecasts.
- The formal forecasting tools most commonly used in forecasting capital market returns fall into three broad categories: statistical methods, discounted cash flow models, and risk premium models.
- Sample statistics, especially the sample mean, are subject to substantial estimation error.
- Shrinkage estimation combines two estimates (or sets of estimates) into a more precise estimate.
- Time-series estimators, which explicitly incorporate dynamics, may summarize historical data well without providing insight into the underlying drivers of forecasts.
- Discounted cash flow models are used to estimate the required return implied by an asset's current price.
- The risk premium approach expresses expected return as the sum of the risk-free rate of interest and one or more risk premiums.
- There are three methods for modeling risk premiums: equilibrium models, such as the CAPM; factor models; and building blocks.
- The DCF method is the only one that is precise enough to use in support of trades involving individual fixed-income securities.
- There are three main methods for developing expected returns for fixed-income asset classes: DCF, building blocks, and inclusion in an equilibrium model.
- As a forecast of bond return, YTM, the most commonly quoted metric, can be improved by incorporating the impact of yield changes on reinvestment of cash flows and valuation at the investment horizon.
- The building blocks for fixed-income expected returns are the short-term default-free rate, the term premium, the credit premium, and the liquidity premium.
- Term premiums are roughly proportional to duration, whereas credit premiums tend to be larger at the short end of the curve.
- Both term premiums and credit premiums are positively related to the slope of the yield curve.
- Credit spreads reflect both the credit premium (i.e., additional expected return) and expected losses due to default.
- A baseline estimate of the liquidity premium can be based on the yield spread between the highest-quality issuer in a market (usually the sovereign) and the next highest-quality large issuer (often a government agency).
- Emerging market debt exposes investors to heightened risk with respect to both ability to pay and willingness to pay, which can be associated with the economy and political/legal weaknesses, respectively.
- The Grinold–Kroner model decomposes the expected return on equities into three components: (1) expected cash flow return, composed of the dividend yield minus the rate of change in shares outstanding; (2) expected return due to nominal earnings growth; and (3) expected repricing return, reflecting the rate of change in the P/E.

- Forecasting the equity premium directly is just as difficult as projecting the absolute level of equity returns, so the building block approach provides little, if any, specific insight with which to improve equity return forecasts.
- The Singer–Terhaar version of the international capital asset pricing model combines a global CAPM equilibrium that assumes full market integration with expected returns for each asset class based on complete segmentation.
- Emerging market equities expose investors to the same underlying risks as emerging market debt does: more fragile economies, less stable political and policy frameworks, and weaker legal protections.
- Emerging market investors need to pay particular attention to the ways in which the value of their ownership claims might be expropriated. Among the areas of concern are standards of corporate governance, accounting and disclosure standards, property rights laws, and checks and balances on governmental actions.
- Historical return data for real estate is subject to substantial smoothing, which biases standard volatility estimates downward and distorts correlations with other asset classes. Meaningful analysis of real estate as an asset class requires explicit handling of this data issue.
- Real estate is subject to boom–bust cycles that both drive and are driven by the business cycle.
- The cap rate, defined as net operating income in the current period divided by the property value, is the standard valuation metric for commercial real estate.
- A model similar to the Grinold–Kroner model can be applied to estimate the expected return on real estate:

$$E(R_{re}) = \text{Cap rate} + \text{NOI growth rate} - \%\Delta\text{Cap rate}$$

- There is a clear pattern of higher cap rates for riskier property types, lower-quality properties, and less attractive locations.
- Real estate expected returns contain all the standard building block risk premiums:
  o Term premium: As a very long-lived asset with relatively stable cash flows, income-producing real estate has a high duration.
  o Credit premium: A fixed-term lease is like a corporate bond issued by the leaseholder and secured by the property.
  o Equity premium: Owners bear the risk of property value fluctuations, as well as risk associated with rent growth, lease renewal, and vacancies.
  o Liquidity premium: Real estate trades infrequently and is costly to transact.

- Currency exchange rates are especially difficult to forecast because they are tied to governments, financial systems, legal systems, and geographies. Forecasting exchange rates requires identification and assessment of the forces that are likely to exert the most influence.
- Provided they can be financed, trade flows do not usually exert a significant impact on exchange rates. International capital flows are typically larger and more volatile than trade-financing flows.
- PPP is a poor predictor of exchange rate movements over short to intermediate horizons but is a better guide to currency movements over progressively longer multi-year horizons.
- The extent to which the current account balance influences the exchange rate depends primarily on whether it is likely to be persistent and, if so, whether it can be sustained.

- Capital seeks the highest risk-adjusted expected return. In a world of perfect capital mobility, in the long run, the exchange rate will be driven to the point at which the expected percentage change equals the "excess" risk-adjusted expected return on the portfolio of assets denominated in the domestic currency over that of the portfolio of assets denominated in the foreign currency. However, in the short run, there can be an exchange rate overshoot in the opposite direction as hot money chases higher returns.
- Carry trades are profitable on average, which is contrary to the predictions of uncovered interest rate parity.
- Each country/currency has a unique portfolio of assets that makes up part of the global "market portfolio." Exchange rates provide an across-the-board mechanism for adjusting the relative sizes of these portfolios to match investors' desire to hold them.
- The portfolio balance perspective implies that exchange rates adjust in response to changes in the relative sizes and compositions of the aggregate portfolios denominated in each currency.
- The sample variance–covariance matrix is an unbiased estimate of the true VCV structure; that is, it will be correct on average.
- There are two main problems with using the sample VCV matrix as an estimate/forecast of the true VCV matrix: It cannot be used for large numbers of asset classes, and it is subject to substantial sampling error.
- Linear factor models impose structure on the VCV matrix that allows them to handle very large numbers of asset classes. The drawback is that the VCV matrix is biased and inconsistent unless the assumed structure is true.
- Shrinkage estimation of the VCV matrix is a weighted average of the sample VCV matrix and a target VCV matrix that reflects assumed "prior" knowledge of the true VCV structure.
- Failure to adjust for the impact of smoothing in observed return data for real estate and other private assets will almost certainly lead to distorted portfolio analysis and hence poor asset allocation decisions.
- Financial asset returns exhibit volatility clustering, evidenced by periods of high and low volatilities. ARCH models were developed to address these time-varying volatilities.
- One of the simplest and most used ARCH models represents today's variance as a linear combination of yesterday's variance and a new "shock" to volatility. With appropriate parameter values, the model exhibits the volatility clustering characteristic of financial asset returns.

REFERENCES

Abuaf, Niso, and Philippe Jorion. 1990. "Purchasing Power Parity in the Long Run." *Journal of Finance* (March): 157–74.

Ang, Andrew, Dimitris Papanikolaou, and Mark M. Westerfield. 2014. "Portfolio Choice with Illiquid Assets." *Management Science* 6 (11). 10.1287/mnsc.2014.1986.

Burnside, Craig, Martin Eichenbaum, Isaac Kleshchelski, and Sergio Rebelo. 2011. "Do Peso Problems Explain the Returns to the Carry Trade?" *Review of Financial Studies* 24 (3): 853–91.

Campbell, John Y., Andrew W. Lo, and A. Craig MacKinlay. 1997. *The Econometrics of Financial Markets.* Princeton, NJ: Princeton University Press.

CenterSquare Investment Management Plc. 2018. "The REIT Cap Rate Perspective" (March). www.centersquare.com/documents/20182/32181/March+2018_CenterSquare+REIT+Cap+ Rate+Perspective/0f802c79-00bd-4e18-8655-98ca90a87e63. Accessed January 2019.

Clayton, Jim, Frank J. Fabozzi, S. Michael Gilberto, Jacques N. Gordon, Susan Hudson-Wilson, William Hughes, Youguo Liang, Greg MacKinnon, and Asieh Mansour. 2011. "The Changing Face of Real Estate Investment Management." Special Real Estate Issue *Journal of Portfolio Management*: 12–23.

Cochrane, John H, and Monika Piazzesi. 2005. "Bond Risk Premia." *American Economic Review* (March): 138–60.

Dimson, Elroy, Paul Marsh, and Mike Staunton. 2002. *Triumph of the Optimists*. Princeton, NJ: Princeton University Press.

Dimson, Elroy, Paul Marsh, and Mike Staunton. 2018. *Credit Suisse Global Investment Returns Yearbook 2018*. Zurich: Credit Suisse Research Institute.

Dornbusch, R. December 1976. "Expectations and Exchange Rate Dynamics." *Journal of Political Economy* 84 (6): 1161–76.

Engle, Robert. 2002. "Dynamic Conditional Correlation: A Simple Class of Multivariate Generalized Autoregressive Conditional Heteroskedasticity Models." *Journal of Business & Economic Statistics* (July): 339–50.

Giesecke, Kay, Francis A. Longstaff, Stephen Schaefer, and Ilya Strebulaev. 2011. "Corporate Bond Default Risk: A 150-Year Perspective." *Journal of Financial Economics* 102 (2): 233–50.

Grinold, Richard, and Ken Kroner. 2002. "The Equity Risk Premium: Analyzing the Long-Run Prospects for the Stock Market." *InvestmentInsights* 5 (3).

Ilmanen, Antti. 2012. *Expected Returns on Major Asset Classes*. Charlottesville, VA: Research Foundation of CFA Institute.

Jarrow, Robert A., and Donald R. van Deventer. 2015. "Credit Analysis Models." In *Fixed Income Analysis*, 3rd ed. CFA Institute Investment Series/Wiley.

Jordà, Òscar, Katharina Knoll, Dmitry Kuvshinov, Moritz Schularick, and Alan M. Taylor. 2017. "The Rate of Return on Everything, 1870–2015." NBER Working Paper No. 24112 (December).

Kim, Don H., and Jonathan H. Wright. 2005. "An Arbitrage-Free Three-Factor Term Structure Model and the Recent Behavior of Long-Term Yields and Distant-Horizon Forward Rates." Federal Reserve Board Working Paper 2005-33 (August).

Ling, David C., and Andy Naranjo. 2015. "Returns and Information Transmission Dynamics in Public and Private Real Estate Markets." *Real Estate Economics* 43 (1): 163–208.

Marcelo, José Luis Miralles, Luis Miralles Quirós José, and José Luís Martins. 2013. "The Role of Country and Industry Factors during Volatile Times." *Journal of International Financial Markets, Institutions and Money* 26 (October): 273–90.

Peyton, Martha S. 2009. "Capital Markets Impact on Commercial Real Estate Cap Rates: A Practitioner's View." Special Real Estate Issue *Journal of Portfolio Management* 38–49.

Piros, Christopher D. 2015. "Strategic Asset Allocation: Plus ça change, plus c'est la meme chose" *Investments & Wealth Monitor* (March/April): 5–8.

Piros, Christopher D., and Jerald E. Pinto. 2013. *Economics for Investment Decision Makers Workbook: Micro, Macro, and International Economics*. Hoboken, NJ: John Wiley & Sons, Inc.

Savills World Research. 2016. *Around the World in Dollars and Cents*. London: Savills.

Singer, Brian D., and Kevin Terhaar. 1997. *Economic Foundations of Capital Market Returns*. Charlottesville, VA: Research Foundation of the Institute of Chartered Financial Analysts.

Stefek, Daniel, and Raghu Suryanarayanan. 2012. "Private and Public Real Estate: What Is the Link?" *Journal of Alternative Investments* (Winter): 66–75.

Yau, Jot K., Thomas Schneeweis, Edward A. Szado, Thomas R. Robinson, and Lisa R. Weiss. 2018. "*Alternative Investments Portfolio Management*." CFA Program Level III Curriculum Chapter 26.

PRACTICE PROBLEMS

1. An investor is considering adding three new securities to her internationally focused, fixed-income portfolio. She considers the following non-callable securities:
   * 1-year government bond
   * 10-year government bond
   * 10-year BBB rated corporate bond

   She plans to invest equally in all three securities being analyzed or will invest in none of them at this time. She will only make the added investment provided that the expected spread/premium of the equally weighted investment is at least 1.5 percent (150bp) over the 1-year government bond. She has gathered the following information:

Risk-free interest rate (1-year, incorporating 2.6% inflation expectation)	3.8%
Term premium (10-year vs. 1-year government bond)	1%
10-year BBB credit premium (over 10-year government bond)	75bp
Estimated liquidity premium on 10-year corporate bonds	55bp

   Using only the information given, address the following problems using the risk premium approach:
   A. Calculate the expected return that an equal-weighted investment in the three securities could provide.
   B. Calculate the expected total risk premium of the three securities and determine the investor's probable course of action.

2. Jo Akumba's portfolio is invested in a range of developed markets fixed-income securities. She asks her adviser about the possibility of diversifying her investments to include emerging and frontier markets government and corporate fixed-income securities. Her adviser makes the following comment regarding risk:
   "All emerging and frontier fixed-income securities pose economic, political, and legal risk. Economic risks arise from the fact that emerging market countries have poor fiscal discipline, rely on foreign borrowing, have less diverse tax base, and significant dependence on specific industries. They are susceptible to capital flight. Their ability to pay is limited. In addition, weak property rights, weak enforcement of contract laws, and political instability pose hazards for emerging markets debt investors."
   Discuss the statement made.

3. An Australian investor currently holds an A$240 million equity portfolio. He is considering rebalancing the portfolio based on an assessment of the risk and return prospects facing the Australian economy. Information relating to the Australian investment markets and the economy has been collected in the following table:

10-Year Historical	Current	Capital Market Expectations
Average government bond yield: 2.8%	10-year government bond yield: 2.3%	
Average annual equity return: 4.6%	Year-over-year equity return: −9.4%	
Average annual inflation rate: 2.3%	Year-over-year inflation rate: 2.1%	Expected annual inflation: 2.3%
Equity market P/E (beginning of period): 15×	Current equity market P/E: 14.5×	Expected equity market P/E: 14.0×
Average annual dividend income return: 2.6%		Expected annual income return: 2.4%
Average annual real earnings growth: 6.0%		Expected annual real earnings growth: 5.0%

Using the information in the table, address the following problems:

A. Calculate the historical Australian equity risk premium using the "equity-vs-bonds" premium method.

B. Calculate the expected annual equity return using the Grinold–Kroner model (assume no change in the number of shares outstanding).

C. Using your answer to Part B, calculate the expected annual equity risk premium.

4. An analyst is reviewing various asset alternatives and is presented with the following information relating to the broad equity market of Switzerland and various industries within the Swiss market that are of particular investment interest.

Expected risk premium for overall global investable market (GIM) portfolio	3.5%
Expected standard deviation for the GIM portfolio	8.5%
Expected standard deviation for Swiss Healthcare Industry equity investments	12.0%
Expected standard deviation for Swiss Watch Industry equity investments	6.0%
Expected standard deviation for Swiss Consumer Products Industry equity investments	7.5%

Assume that the Swiss market is perfectly integrated with the world markets.
Swiss Healthcare has a correlation of 0.7 with the GIM portfolio.
Swiss Watch has a correlation of 0.8 with the GIM portfolio.
Swiss Consumer Products has a correlation of 0.8 with the GIM portfolio.

A. Basing your answers only upon the data presented in the table above and using the international capital asset pricing model—in particular, the Singer–Terhaar approach—estimate the expected risk premium for the following:
   i.   Swiss Healthcare Industry
   ii. Swiss Watch Industry
   iii. Swiss Consumer Products Industry

B. Judge which industry is most attractive from a valuation perspective.

5. Identify risks faced by investors in emerging market equities over and above those that are faced by fixed-income investors in such markets.
6. Describe the main issues that arise when conducting historical analysis of real estate returns.
7. An analyst at a real estate investment management firm seeks to establish expectations for rate of return for properties in the industrial sector over the next year. She has obtained the following information:

Current industrial sector capitalization rate ("cap" rate)	5.7%
Expected cap rate at the end of the period	5.5%
NOI growth rate (real)	1%
Inflation expectation	1.5%

Estimate the expected return from the industrial sector properties based on the data provided.

8. A client has asked his adviser to explain the key considerations in forecasting exchange rates. The adviser's firm uses two broad complementary approaches when setting expectations for exchange rate movements, namely focus on trade in goods and services and, secondly, focus on capital flows. Identify the main considerations that the adviser should explain to the client under the two approaches.
9. Looking independently at each of the economic observations below, indicate the country where an analyst would expect to see a strengthening currency for each observation.

	Country X	Country Y
Expected inflation over next year	2.0%	3.0%
Short-term (1-month) government rate	Decrease	Increase
Expected (forward-looking) GDP growth over next year	2.0%	3.3%
New national laws have been passed that enable foreign direct investment in real estate/financial companies	Yes	No
Current account surplus (deficit)	8%	−1%

10. Fap is a small country whose currency is the Fip. Three years ago, the exchange rate was considered to be reflecting purchasing power parity (PPP). Since then, the country's inflation has exceeded inflation in the other countries by about 5% per annum. The Fip exchange rate, however, remained broadly unchanged.

What would you have expected the Fip exchange rate to show if PPP prevailed? Are Fips over-or undervalued, according to PPP?

The following information relates to Questions 11–18

Richard Martin is chief investment officer for the Trunch Foundation (the foundation), which has a large, globally diversified investment portfolio. Martin meets with the foundation's fixed-income and real estate portfolio managers to review expected return forecasts and potential investments, as well as to consider short-term modifications to asset weights within the total fund strategic asset allocation.

Martin asks the real estate portfolio manager to discuss the performance characteristics of real estate. The real estate portfolio manager makes the following statements:

Statement 1: Adding traded REIT securities to an equity portfolio should substantially improve the portfolio's diversification over the next year.

Statement 2: Traded REIT securities are more highly correlated with direct real estate and less highly correlated with equities over multi-year horizons.

Martin looks over the long-run valuation metrics the manager is using for commercial real estate, shown in Exhibit 1.

EXHIBIT 1   Commercial Real Estate Valuation Metrics

Cap Rate	GDP Growth Rate
4.70%	4.60%

The real estate team uses an in-house model for private real estate to estimate the true volatility of returns over time. The model assumes that the current observed return equals the weighted average of the current true return and the previous observed return. Because the true return is not observable, the model assumes a relationship between true returns and observable REIT index returns; therefore, it uses REIT index returns as proxies for both the unobservable current true return and the previous observed return.

Martin asks the fixed-income portfolio manager to review the foundation's bond portfolios. The existing aggregate bond portfolio is broadly diversified in domestic and international developed markets. The first segment of the portfolio to be reviewed is the domestic sovereign portfolio. The bond manager notes that there is a market consensus that the domestic yield curve will likely experience a single 20 bp increase in the near term as a result of monetary tightening and then remain relatively flat and stable for the next three years. Martin then reviews duration and yield measures for the short-term domestic sovereign bond portfolio in Exhibit 2.

EXHIBIT 2   Short-Term Domestic Sovereign Bond Portfolio

Macaulay Duration	Modified Duration	Yield to Maturity
3.00	2.94	2.00%

The discussion turns to the international developed fixed-income market. The foundation invested in bonds issued by Country XYZ, a foreign developed country. XYZ's sovereign yield curve is currently upward sloping, and the yield spread between 2-year and 10-year XYZ bonds is 100 bps.

The fixed-income portfolio manager tells Martin that he is interested in a domestic market corporate bond issued by Zeus Manufacturing Corporation (ZMC). ZMC has just been downgraded two steps by a major credit rating agency. In addition to expected monetary actions that will raise short-term rates, the yield spread between three-year sovereign bonds and the next highest-quality government agency bond widened by 10 bps.

Although the foundation's fixed-income portfolios have focused primarily on developed markets, the portfolio manager presents data in Exhibit 3 on two emerging markets for Martin to consider. Both economies increased exports of their mineral resources over the last decade.

EXHIBIT 3   Emerging Market Data

Factor	Emerging Republic A	Emerging Republic B
Fiscal deficit/GDP	6.50%	8.20%
Debt/GDP	90.10%	104.20%
Current account deficit	5.20% of GDP	7.10% of GDP
Foreign exchange reserves	90.30% of short-term debt	70.10% of short-term debt

The fixed-income portfolio manager also presents information on a new investment opportunity in an international developed market. The team is considering the bonds of Xdelp, a large energy exploration and production company. Both the domestic and international markets are experiencing synchronized growth in GDP midway between the trough and the peak of the business cycle. The foreign country's government has displayed a disciplined approach to maintaining stable monetary and fiscal policies and has experienced a rising current account surplus and an appreciating currency. It is expected that with the improvements in free cash flow and earnings, the credit rating of the Xdelp bonds will be upgraded. Martin refers to the foundation's asset allocation policy in Exhibit 4 before making any changes to either the fixed-income or real estate portfolios.

EXHIBIT 4   Trunch Foundation Strategic Asset Allocation—Select Data

Asset Class	Minimum Weight	Maximum Weight	Actual Weight
Fixed income—Domestic	40.00%	80.00%	43.22%
Fixed income—International	5.00%	10.00%	6.17%
Fixed income—Emerging markets	0.00%	2.00%	0.00%
Alternatives—Real estate	2.00%	6.00%	3.34%

11. Which of the real estate portfolio manager's statements is correct?
    A. Only Statement 1
    B. Only Statement 2
    C. Both Statement 1 and Statement 2

12. Based only on Exhibit 1, the long-run expected return for commercial real estate:
    A. is approximately double the cap rate.
    B. incorporates a cap rate greater than the discount rate.
    C. needs to include the cap rate's anticipated rate of change.

13. Based on the private real estate model developed to estimate return volatility, the true variance is *most likely*:
    A. lower than the variance of the observed data.
    B. approximately equal to the variance of the observed data.
    C. greater than the variance of the observed data.

14. Based on Exhibit 2 and the anticipated effects of the monetary policy change, the expected annual return over a three-year investment horizon will *most likely* be:
    A. lower than 2.00%.
    B. approximately equal to 2.00%.
    C. greater than 2.00%.

15. Based on the building block approach to fixed-income returns, the dominant source of the yield spread for Country XYZ is *most likely* the:
    A. term premium.
    B. credit premium.
    C. liquidity premium.

16. Using the building block approach, the required rate of return for the ZMC bond will *most likely*:
    A. increase based on the change in the credit premium.
    B. decrease based on the change in the default-free rate.
    C. decrease based on the change in the liquidity premium.

17. Based only on Exhibit #3, the foundation would *most likely* consider buying bonds issued by:
    A. only Emerging Republic A.
    B. only Emerging Republic B.
    C. neither Emerging Republic A nor Emerging Republic B.

18. Based only on Exhibits 3 and 4 and the information provided by the portfolio managers, the action *most likely* to enhance returns is to:
    A. decrease existing investments in real estate by 2.00%.
    B. initiate a commitment to emerging market debt of 1.00%.
    C. increase the investments in international market bonds by 1.00%.

The following information relates to Questions 19–26

Judith Bader is a senior analyst for a company that specializes in managing international developed and emerging markets equities. Next week, Bader must present proposed changes to client portfolios to the Investment Committee, and she is preparing a presentation to support the views underlying her recommendations.

Bader begins by analyzing portfolio risk. She decides to forecast a variance–covariance matrix (VCV) for 20 asset classes, using 10 years of monthly returns and incorporating both the sample statistics and the factor-model methods. To mitigate the impact of estimation error, Bader is considering combining the results of the two methods in an alternative target VCV matrix, using shrinkage estimation.

Bader asks her research assistant to comment on the two approaches and the benefits of applying shrinkage estimation. The assistant makes the following statements:

Statement 1.   Shrinkage estimation of VCV matrices will decrease the efficiency of the estimates versus the sample VCV matrix.

Statement 2.   Your proposed approach for estimating the VCV matrix will not be reliable because a sample VCV matrix is biased and inconsistent.

Statement 3.   A factor-based VCV matrix approach may result in some portfolios that erroneously appear to be riskless if any asset returns can be completely determined by the common factors or some of the factors are redundant.

Bader then uses the Singer–Terhaar model and the final shrinkage-estimated VCV matrix to determine the equilibrium expected equity returns for all international asset classes by country. Three of the markets under consideration are located in Country A (developed market), Country B (emerging market), and Country C (emerging market). Bader projects that in relation to the global market, the equity market in Country A will remain highly integrated, the equity market in Country B will become more segmented, and the equity market in Country C will become more fully integrated.

Next, Bader applies the Grinold–Kroner model to estimate the expected equity returns for the various markets under consideration. For Country A, Bader assumes a very long-term corporate earnings growth rate of 4% per year (equal to the expected nominal GDP growth rate), a 2% rate of net share repurchases for Country A's equities, and an expansion rate for P/E multiples of 0.5% per year.

In reviewing Countries B and C, Bader's research assistant comments that emerging markets are especially risky owing to issues related to politics, competition, and accounting standards. As an example, Bader and her assistant discuss the risk implications of the following information related to Country B:

• Experiencing declining per capita income
• Expected to continue its persistent current account deficit below 2% of GDP
• Transitioning to International Financial Reporting Standards, with full convergence scheduled to be completed within two years

Bader shifts her focus to currency expectations relative to clients' base currency and summarizes her assumptions in Exhibit 1.

During a conversation about Exhibit 1, Bader and her research assistant discuss the composition of each country's currency portfolio and the potential for triggering a crisis. Bader notes that some flows and holdings are more or less supportive of the currency, stating that investments in private equity make up the majority of Country A's currency portfolio, investments in public equity make up the majority of Country B's currency portfolio, and investments in public debt make up the majority of Country C's currency portfolio.

EXHIBIT 1   Baseline Assumptions for Currency Forecasts

	Country A	Country B	Country C
Historical current account	Persistent current account deficit of 5% of GDP	Persistent current account deficit of 2% of GDP	Persistent current account surplus of 2% of GDP
Expectation for secular trend in current account	Rising current account deficit	Narrowing current account deficit	Rising current account surplus
Long-term inflation expectation relative to global inflation	Expected to rise	Expected to keep pace	Expected to fall
Capital flows	Steady inflows	Hot money flowing out	Hot money flowing in

19. Which of the following statements made by Bader's research assistant is correct?
    A. Statement 1
    B. Statement 2
    C. Statement 3

20. Based on expectations for changes in integration with the global market, all else being equal, the Singer–Terhaar model implies that Bader should shift capital from Country A to:
    A. only Country B.
    B. only Country C.
    C. both Countries B and C.

21. Using the Grinold–Kroner model, which of the following assumptions for forecasting Country A's expected equity returns is plausible for the very long run?
    A. Rate of net share repurchases
    B. Corporate earnings growth rate
    C. Expansion rate for P/E multiples

22. Based only on the emerging markets discussion, developments in which of the following areas *most likely* signal increasing risk for Country B's equity market?
    A. Politics
    B. Competitiveness
    C. Accounting standards

23. Based on Bader's expectations for current account secular trends as shown in Exhibit 1, Bader should reallocate capital, all else being equal, from:
    A. Country A to Country C.
    B. Country B to Country A.
    C. Country C to Country A.

24. Based on Bader's inflation expectations as shown in Exhibit 1, purchasing power parity implies that which of the following countries' currencies should depreciate, all else being equal?
    A. Country A
    B. Country B
    C. Country C

25. Based on Exhibit 1, which country's central bank is *most likely* to buy domestic bonds near term to sterilize the impact of money flows on domestic liquidity?
    A. Country A
    B. Country B
    C. Country C

26. Based on the composition of each country's currency portfolio, which country is most vulnerable to a potential crisis?
    A. Country A
    B. Country B
    C. Country C

CHAPTER 5

OVERVIEW OF ASSET ALLOCATION

William W. Jennings, PhD, CFA
Eugene L. Podkaminer, CFA

LEARNING OUTCOMES

The candidate should be able to:

- describe elements of effective investment governance and investment governance considerations in asset allocation;
- prepare an economic balance sheet for a client and interpret its implications for asset allocation;
- compare the investment objectives of asset-only, liability-relative, and goals-based asset allocation approaches;
- contrast concepts of risk relevant to asset-only, liability-relative, and goals-based asset allocation approaches;
- explain how asset classes are used to represent exposures to systematic risk and discuss criteria for asset class specification;
- explain the use of risk factors in asset allocation and their relation to traditional asset class–based approaches;
- select and justify an asset allocation based on an investor's objectives and constraints;
- describe the use of the global market portfolio as a baseline portfolio in asset allocation;
- discuss strategic implementation choices in asset allocation, including passive/active choices and vehicles for implementing passive and active mandates;
- discuss strategic considerations in rebalancing asset allocations.

1. INTRODUCTION

Asset owners are concerned with accumulating and maintaining the wealth needed to meet their needs and aspirations. In that endeavor, investment portfolios—including individuals'

Portfolio Management, Second Edition, by William W. Jennings, PhD, CFA, and Eugene L. Podkaminer, CFA. Copyright © 2019 by CFA Institute.

portfolios and institutional funds—play important roles. Asset allocation is a strategic—and often a first or early—decision in portfolio construction. Because it holds that position, it is widely accepted as important and meriting careful attention. Among the questions addressed in this chapter are the following:

- What is a sound governance context for making asset allocation decisions?
- How broad a picture should an adviser have of an asset owner's assets and liabilities in recommending an asset allocation?
- How can an asset owner's objectives and sensitivities to risk be represented in asset allocation?
- What are the broad approaches available in developing an asset allocation recommendation, and when might one approach be more or less appropriate than another?
- What are the top-level decisions that need to be made in implementing a chosen asset allocation?
- How may asset allocations be rebalanced as asset prices change?

The strategic asset allocation decision determines return levels[1] in which allocations are invested, irrespective of the degree of active management. Because of its strategic importance, the investment committee, at the highest level of the governance hierarchy, typically retains approval of the strategic asset allocation decision. Often a proposal is developed only after a formal asset allocation study that incorporates obligations, objectives, and constraints; simulates possible investment outcomes over an agreed-on investment horizon; and evaluates the risk and return characteristics of the possible allocation strategies.

In providing an overview of asset allocation, this chapter's focus is the alignment of asset allocation with the asset owner's investment objectives, constraints, and overall financial condition. This is the first chapter in several sequences of chapters that address, respectively, asset allocation and portfolio management of equities, fixed income, and alternative investments. Asset allocation is also linked to other facets of portfolio management, including risk management and behavioral finance. As coverage of asset allocation progresses in the sequence of chapters, various connections to these topics, covered in detail in other areas of the curriculum, will be made.[2]

In the asset allocation sequence, the role of this chapter is the "big picture." It also offers definitions that will provide a coordinated treatment of many later topics in portfolio management. The second chapter provides the basic "how" of developing an asset allocation, and the third chapter explores various common, real-world complexities in developing an asset allocation.

This chapter is organized as follows: Section 2 explains the importance of asset allocation in investment management. Section 3 addresses the investment governance context in which asset allocation decisions are made. Section 4 considers asset allocation from the comprehensive perspective offered by the asset owner's economic balance sheet. Section 5 distinguishes three broad approaches to asset allocation and explains how they differ in investment objective and risk. In Section 6, these three approaches are discussed at a high level in relation to three cases. Section 7 provides a top-level orientation to how a chosen asset

---

[1]See Ibbotson and Kaplan (2000, p. 30) and Xiong, Ibbotson, and Chen (2010). The conclusion for the aggregate follows from the premise that active management is a zero-sum game overall (Sharpe 1991).
[2]Among these chapters, see Blanchett, Cordell, Finke, and Idzorek (2016) concerning human capital and longevity and other risks and Pompian (2011a and 2011b) and Pompian, McLean, and Byrne (2011) concerning behavioral finance.

allocation may be implemented, providing a set of definitions that underlie subsequent chapters. Section 8 discusses rebalancing considerations, and Section 9 provides a summary of the chapter.

2. ASSET ALLOCATION: IMPORTANCE IN INVESTMENT MANAGEMENT

Exhibit 1 places asset allocation in a stylized model of the investment management process viewed as an integrated set of activities aimed at attaining investor objectives.

Exhibit 1 shows that an investment process that is in the asset owner's best interest rests on a foundation of good investment governance, which includes the assignment of decision-making responsibilities to qualified individuals and oversight of processes. The balance at the top of the chart suggests that the portfolio management process must reconcile (balance) investor objectives (on the left) with the possibilities offered by the investment opportunity set (on the right).

EXHIBIT 1   The Portfolio Management Process

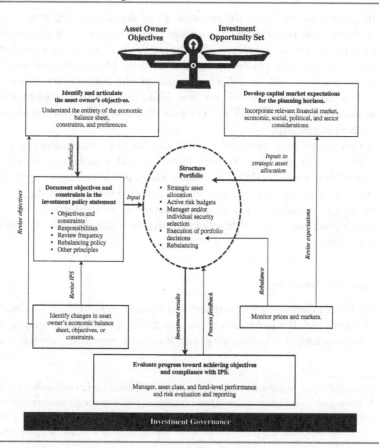

The investment process shows a sequence of activities that begins with understanding the asset owner's entire circumstance; objectives, including any constraints; and preferences. These factors, in conjunction with capital market inputs,[3] form the basis for asset allocation as a first step in portfolio construction and give a structure within which other decisions—such as the decision to invest passively or actively—take place. In the flow chart, thick lines show initial flows (or relations of logic) and thin lines show feedback flows.

Asset allocation is widely considered to be the most important decision in the investment process. The strategic asset allocation decision completely determines return levels[4] in which allocations are invested passively and also in the aggregate of all investors, irrespective of the degree of active management.

In providing an overview of asset allocation, this chapter's focus is the alignment of asset allocation with the asset owner's investment objectives, constraints, and overall financial condition. The presentation begins with an introduction to the investment governance context of asset allocation. It then moves to present the economic balance sheet as the financial context for asset allocation itself.

3. THE INVESTMENT GOVERNANCE BACKGROUND TO ASSET ALLOCATION

Investment governance represents the organization of decision-making responsibilities and oversight activities. Effective investment governance ensures that assets are invested to achieve the asset owner's investment objectives within the asset owner's risk tolerance and constraints, and in compliance with all applicable laws and regulations. In addition, effective governance ensures that decisions are made by individuals or groups with the necessary skills and capacity.

Investment performance depends on asset allocation *and* its implementation. Sound investment governance practices seek to align asset allocation and implementation to achieve the asset owner's stated goals.

Investment governance structures are relevant to both institutional and individual investors. Because such structures are often formalized and articulated in detail for defined benefit pension plans, we will build our discussion using a pension plan governance framework. Elements of pension plan governance that are not directly related to the management of plan assets—plan design, funding policy, and communications to participants—are not discussed in this chapter. Instead, we focus on those aspects of governance that directly affect the asset allocation decision.

3.1. Governance Structures

Governance and management are two separate but related functions. Both are directed toward achieving the same end. But governance focuses on clarifying the mission, creating a plan, and reviewing progress toward achieving long- and short-term objectives, whereas management

---

[3]The set of potential inputs to portfolio construction shown in Exhibit 1 is not exhaustive. For example, for investors delegating asset management, investment managers' performance records are relevant.
[4]See Ibbotson and Kaplan (2000, p.30) and Xiong, Ibbotson, Idzorek, and Chen (2010). The conclusion for the aggregate follows from the premise that active management is a zero-sum game overall (Sharpe 1991).

efforts are geared to outcomes—the execution of the plan to achieve the agreed-on goals and objectives. A common governance structure in an institutional investor context will have three levels within the governance hierarchy:

- governing investment committee
- investment staff
- third-party resources

The investment committee may be a committee of the board of directors, or the board of directors may have delegated its oversight responsibilities to an internal investment committee made up of staff. Investment staff may be large, with full in-house asset management capabilities, or small—for example, two to five investment staff responsible for overseeing external investment managers and consultants. It may even be part time—a treasurer or chief financial officer with many other, competing responsibilities. The term "third-party resources" is used to describe a range of professional resources—investment managers, investment consultants, custodians, and actuaries, for example.

Although there are many governance models in use, most effective models share six common elements. Effective governance models perform the following tasks:

1. Articulate the long- and short-term objectives of the investment program.
2. Allocate decision rights and responsibilities among the functional units in the governance hierarchy effectively, taking account of their knowledge, capacity, time, and position in the governance hierarchy.
3. Specify processes for developing and approving the investment policy statement that will govern the day-to-day operations of the investment program.
4. Specify processes for developing and approving the program's strategic asset allocation.
5. Establish a reporting framework to monitor the program's progress toward the agreed-on goals and objectives.
6. Periodically undertake a governance audit.

In the sections that follow, we will discuss selected elements from this list.

3.2. Articulating Investment Objectives

Articulating long- and short-term objectives for an investor first requires an understanding of purpose—that is, what the investor is trying to achieve. Below are examples of simple investment objective statements that can be clearly tied to purposes:

- *Defined benefit pension fund.* The investment objective of the fund is to ensure that plan assets are sufficient to meet current and future pension liabilities.
- *Endowment fund.* The investment objective of the endowment is to earn a rate of return in excess of the return required to fund, after accounting for inflation, ongoing distributions consistent with the endowment's mission.
- *Individual investor.* The investment objective is to provide for retirement at the investor's desired retirement age, family needs, and bequests, subject to stated risk tolerance and investment constraints.

A return requirement is often considered the essence of an investment objective statement, but for that portion of the objective statement to be properly understood requires additional context, including the obligations the assets are expected to fund, the nature of cash flows into and out of the fund, and the asset owner's willingness and ability to withstand interim changes in portfolio value. The ultimate goal is to find the best risk/return trade-off consistent with the asset owner's resource constraints and risk tolerance.

As an example of how the overall context can affect decision-making, the pension fund may be an active plan, with new participants added as they are hired, or it may be "frozen" (no additional benefits are being accrued by participants in the plan). The status of the plan, considered in conjunction with its funded ratio (the ratio of pension assets to pension liabilities), has a bearing on future contributions and benefit payments. The company offering the pension benefit may operate in a highly cyclical industry, where revenues ebb and flow over the course of the economic cycle. In this case, the plan sponsor may prefer a more conservative asset allocation to minimize the year-to-year fluctuations in its pension contribution.

The nature of inflows and outflows for an endowment fund can be quite different from those of a pension fund. An endowment fund may be used to support scholarships, capital improvements, or university operating expenses. The fund sponsor has some degree of control over the outflows from the fund but very little control over the timing and amounts of contributions to the fund because the contributions are typically coming from external donors.

These cash inflow and outflow characteristics must be considered when establishing the goals and objectives of the fund.

A third, inter-related aspect of defining the sponsor's goals and objectives is determining and communicating risk tolerance. There are multiple dimensions of risk to be considered: liquidity risk, volatility, risk of loss, and risk of abandoning a chosen course of action at the wrong time.

Effective investment governance requires consideration of the liquidity needs of the fund and the liquidity characteristics of the fund's investments. For example, too large an allocation to relatively illiquid assets, such as real estate or private equity, might impair the ability to make payouts in times of market stress.

A high risk/high expected return asset allocation is likely to lead to wider swings in interim valuations. Any minimum thresholds for funded status that, if breached, would trigger an adverse event, such as higher pension insurance premiums, must be considered in the asset allocation decision.

For individual investors, the risk of substantial losses may be unacceptable for a variety of financial and psychological reasons. When such losses occur after retirement, lost capital cannot be replaced with future earnings.

Asset owners have their own unique return requirements and risk sensitivities. Managing an investment program without a clear understanding of long- and short-term objectives is similar to navigating without a map: Arriving at the correct destination on time and intact is not compatible with leaving much to chance.

3.3. Allocation of Rights and Responsibilities

The rights and responsibilities necessary to execute the investment program are generally determined at the highest level of investment governance. The allocation of those rights and responsibilities among the governance units is likely to vary depending on the size of the investment program; the knowledge, skills, and abilities of the internal staff; and the amount of time staff can devote to the investment program if they have other, competing responsibilities. Above all, good governance requires that decisions be delegated to those best qualified to make an informed decision.

The resources available to an organization will affect the scope and complexity of the investment program and the allocation of rights and responsibilities. A small investment program may result in having a narrower opportunity set because of either asset size (too small to diversify across the range of asset classes and investment managers) or staffing constraints (insufficient asset size to justify a dedicated internal staff). Complex strategies may be beyond the reach of entities that have chosen not to develop investment expertise internally or whose oversight committee lacks individuals with sufficient investment understanding. Organizations willing to invest in attracting, developing, and retaining staff resources and in developing strong internal control processes, including risk management systems, are better able to adopt more complex investment programs. The largest investors, however, may find their size creates governance issues: Manager capacity constraints might lead to so many managers that it challenges the investor's oversight capacity.

Allocation of rights and responsibilities across the governance hierarchy is a key element in the success of an investment program. Effective governance requires that the individuals charged with any given decision have the required *knowledge* and expertise to thoroughly evaluate the alternative courses of action and the *capacity* to take on the ongoing responsibility of those decisions, and they must be able to execute those decisions in a timely fashion. (Individual investors engaging a private wealth manager are delegating these expertise, capacity, and execution responsibilities.)

Exhibit 2 presents a systematic way of allocating among governance units the primary duties and responsibilities of running an investment program.

EXHIBIT 2   Allocation of Rights and Responsibilities

Investment Activity	Investment Committee	Investment Staff	Third-Party Resource
Mission	Craft and approve	n/a	n/a
Investment policy statement	Approve	Draft	Consultants provide input
Asset allocation policy	Approve with input from staff and consultants	Draft with input from consultants	Consultants provide input
Investment manager and other service provider selection	Delegate to investment staff; approval authority retained for certain service providers	Research, evaluation, and selection of investment managers and service providers	Consultants provide input
Portfolio construction (individual asset selection)	Delegate to outside managers, or to staff if sufficient internal resources	Execution if assets are managed in-house	Execution by independent investment manager
Monitoring asset prices & portfolio rebalancing	Delegate to staff within confines of the investment policy statement	Assure that the sum of all sub-portfolios equals the desired overall portfolio positioning; approve and execute rebalancing	Consultants and custodian provide input

Investment Activity	Investment Committee	Investment Staff	Third-Party Resource
Risk management	Approve principles and conduct oversight	Create risk management infrastructure and design reporting	Investment manager manages portfolio within established risk guidelines; consultants may provide input and support
Investment manager monitoring	Oversight	Ongoing assessment of managers	Consultants and custodian provide input
Performance evaluation and reporting	Oversight	Evaluate manager's continued suitability for assigned role; analyze sources of portfolio return	Consultants and custodian provide input
Governance audit	Commission and assess	Responds and corrects	Investment Committee contracts with an independent third party for the audit

The available knowledge and expertise at each level of the hierarchy, the resource capacity of the decision makers, and the ability to act on a timely basis all influence the allocation of these rights and responsibilities.

3.4. Investment Policy Statement

The investment policy statement (IPS) is the foundation of an effective investment program. A well-crafted IPS can serve as a blueprint for ongoing fund management and assures stakeholders that program assets are managed with the appropriate care and diligence.

Often, the IPS itself will be a foundation document that is revised slowly over time, whereas information relating to more variable aspects of the program—the asset allocation policy and guidelines for individual investment managers—will be contained in a more easily modified appendix.

3.5. Asset Allocation and Rebalancing Policy

Because of its strategic importance, the investment committee, at the highest level of the governance hierarchy, typically retains approval of the strategic asset allocation decision. A proposal is often developed only after a formal asset allocation study that incorporates obligations, objectives, and constraints; simulates possible investment outcomes over an agreed-on investment horizon; and evaluates the risk and return characteristics of the possible allocation strategies.

Governance considerations inform not only the overall strategic asset allocation decision but also rebalancing decisions. The IPS should contain at least general orienting information relevant to rebalancing. In an institutional setting, rebalancing policy might be the responsibility of the investment committee, organizational staff, or the external consultant. Likewise, individual investors might specify that they have delegated rebalancing authority to their investment adviser. Specification of rebalancing responsibilities is good governance.

3.6. Reporting Framework

The reporting framework in a well-run investment program should be designed in a manner that enables the overseers to evaluate quickly and clearly how well the investment program is progressing toward the agreed-on goals and objectives. The reporting should be clear and concise, accurately answering the following three questions:

- Where are we now?
- Where are we relative to the goals and objectives?
- What value has been added or subtracted by management decisions?

Key elements of a reporting framework should address performance evaluation, compliance with investment guidelines, and progress toward achieving the stated goals and objectives.

- Benchmarking is necessary for performance measurement, attribution, and evaluation. Effective benchmarking allows the investment committee to evaluate staff and external managers. Two separate levels of benchmarks are appropriate: one that measures the success of the investment managers relative to the purpose for which they were hired and another to measure the gap between the policy portfolio and the portfolio as actually implemented.
- Management reporting, typically prepared by staff with input from consultants and custodians, provides responsible parties with the information necessary to understand which parts of the portfolio are performing ahead of or behind the plan and why, as well as whether assets are being managed in accordance with investment guidelines.
- Governance reporting, which addresses strengths and weaknesses in program execution, should be structured in such a way that regular committee meetings can efficiently address any concerns. Although a crisis might necessitate calling an extraordinary meeting, good governance structures minimize this need.

3.7. The Governance Audit

The purpose of the governance audit is to ensure that the established policies, procedures, and governance structures are effective. The audit should be performed by an independent third party. The governance auditor examines the fund's governing documents, assesses the capacity of the organization to execute effectively within the confines of those governing documents, and evaluates the existing portfolio for its "efficiency" given the governance constraints.

Effective investment governance ensures the durability or survivability of the investment program. An investment program must be able to survive unexpected market turmoil, and good investment governance makes certain that the consequences of such turmoil are considered before it is experienced. Good governance seeks to avoid **decision-reversal risk**— the risk of reversing a chosen course of action at exactly the wrong time, the point of maximum loss. Good investment governance also considers the effect of investment committee member and staff turnover on the durability of the investment program. Orientation sessions for new committee members and proper documentation of investment beliefs, policies, and decisions enhance the likelihood that the chosen course of action will be given sufficient time to succeed. New staff or investment committee members should be able to perceive easily the design and intent of the investment program and be able to continue to execute it. Similarly, good investment governance prevents key person risk—overreliance on any one staff member or long-term, illiquid investments dependent on a staff member.

Good governance works to assure accountability. O'Barr and Conley (1992, p.21), who studied investment management organizations using anthropological techniques, found that blame avoidance (not accepting personal responsibility when appropriate to do so) is a common feature of institutional investors. Good governance works to prevent such behavior.

EXAMPLE 1   Investment Governance: Hypothetical Case 1

In January 2016, the Caflandia Office Workers Union Pension (COWUP) made the following announcement:

"COWUP will fully exit all hedge funds and funds of funds. Assets currently amounting to 15% of its investment program are involved. Although hedge funds are a viable strategy for some, when judged against their complexity and cost, hedge fund investment is no longer warranted for COWUP."

One week later, a financial news service reported the following:
"The COWUP decision on hedge funds was precipitated by an allegation of wrongdoing by a senior executive with hedge fund selection responsibilities in COWUP's alternative investments strategy group."

1. Considering only the first statement, state what facts would be relevant in evaluating whether the decision to exit hedge funds was consistent with effective investment governance.
2. Considering both statements, identify deficiencies in COWUP's investment governance.

Solution to 1: The knowledge, capacity, and time available within COWUP to have an effective hedge fund investment program would need to be assessed against the stated concern for complexity and cost. The investment purpose served by hedge funds in COWUP's investment program before it exited them needs to be analyzed.

Solution to 2: The second statement raises these concerns about the decision described in the first statement:

- Hiring and oversight of COWUP executives may have been inadequate.
- The initial COWUP information release was incomplete and possibly misleading. Public communications appear not to have received adequate oversight.
- Divesting hedge funds may be a reaction to the personnel issue rather than being based on investment considerations.

EXAMPLE 2   Investment Governance: Hypothetical Case 2

The imaginary country of Caflandia has a sovereign wealth fund with assets of CAF$40 billion. A governance audit includes the following:

"The professional chief investment officer (CIO) reports to a nine-member appointed investment committee board of directors headed by an executive director. Investment staff members draft asset allocation policy in conjunction with consultants and make recommendation to the investment committee; the investment committee reviews and approves policy and any changes in policy, including the strategic asset allocation. The investment committee makes manager structure, conducts manager analysis, and makes manager selection decisions. The CIO has built a staff organization, which includes heads for each major asset class. In examining decisions over the last five years, we have noted several instances in which political or non-economic considerations appear to have influenced the investment program, including the selection of local private equity investments. Generally, the board spends much of its time debating individual manager strategies for inclusion in the portfolio and in evaluating investment managers' performance with comparatively little time devoted to asset allocation or risk management."

Based on this information and that in Exhibit 2, identify sound and questionable governance practices in the management of the Caflandia sovereign wealth fund.

Solution:

Sound practices: The allocation of responsibilities for asset allocation between investment staff and the investment committee is sound practice. Staff investment expertise should be reflected in the process of asset allocation policy and analysis. The investment committee assumes final responsibility for choices and decisions, which is appropriate given its position in receiving information from all parts of the organization and from all interested parties.

Questionable practices: The investment committee's level of involvement in individual manager selection and evaluation is probably too deep. Exhibit 2 indicates that these functions more effectively reside with staff. Individual manager selection is an implementation and execution decision designed to achieve strategic decisions made by the investment committee and is typically not a strategic decision itself. Manager evaluation has substantial data analysis and technical elements that can be efficiently provided by staff experts and consultants. The finding about political/non-economic influences indicates multiple problems. It confirms that the investment manager analysis and selection processes were misplaced. It also suggests that the investment committee has an inadequate set of governance principles or checks and balances as relates to the investment committee itself.

---

4. THE ECONOMIC BALANCE SHEET AND ASSET ALLOCATION

An accounting balance sheet reflects a point-in-time snapshot of an organization's financial condition and shows the assets, liabilities, and owners' equity recognized by accountants. An **economic balance sheet** includes conventional assets and liabilities (called "financial assets" and "financial liabilities" in this chapter) as well as additional assets and liabilities—known as **extended portfolio assets and liabilities**—that are relevant in making asset allocation decisions but do not appear on conventional balance sheets.

For individual investors, extended portfolio assets include human capital (the present value of future earnings), the present value of pension income, and the present value of expected inheritances. Likewise, the present value of future consumption is an extended portfolio liability.

For an institutional investor, extended portfolio assets might include underground mineral resources or the present value of future intellectual property royalties. Extended portfolio liabilities might include the present value of prospective payouts for foundations, whereas grants payable would appear as conventional liabilities.

Theory and, increasingly, practice suggest that asset allocation should consider the full range of assets and liabilities—both the financial portfolio and extended portfolio assets and liabilities—to arrive at an appropriate asset allocation choice. For example, an asset allocation process that considers the extended balance sheet, including the sensitivity of an individual investor's earnings to equity market risk (and that of the industry in which the individual is working), may result in a more appropriate allocation to equities than one that does not.

Life-cycle balanced funds (also known as target date funds) are examples of investments that seek to coordinate asset allocation with human capital. A 2040 life-cycle balanced fund seeks to provide a retirement investment vehicle appropriate for many individuals retiring in 2040. Exhibit 3 illustrates a typical path for the composition of an individual's economic balance sheet from age 25 through age 65.

At age 25, with most of the individual's working life ahead of him, human capital dominates the economic balance sheet. As the individual progresses through life, the present value of human capital declines as human capital is transformed into earnings. Earnings saved

EXHIBIT 3   Human Capital (HC) and Financial Capital (FC) Relative to Total Wealth

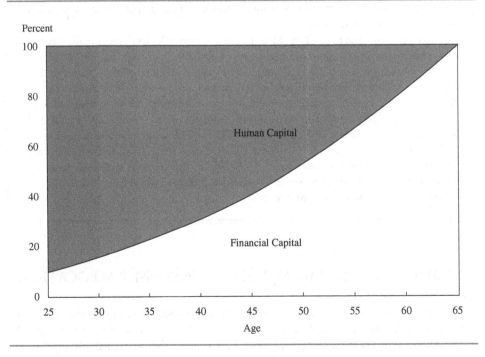

and invested build financial capital balances. By a retirement age of 65, the conversion of human capital to earnings and financial capital is assumed to be complete.

Life-cycle balanced funds reflect these extended portfolio assets. Research indicates that, on average, human capital is roughly 30% equity-like and 70% bond-like, with significant variation among industries.[5] Making the simplifying assumption that investors have approximately constant risk tolerance through life, their asset allocation for total overall wealth (including human capital and financial capital) should be, in theory, constant over time. In this case, the asset allocation chosen for financial capital should reflect an increasing allocation to bonds as human capital declines to age 65, holding all else constant. Exhibit 4 shows the glide path for the equity/bond allocation chosen by one US mutual fund family. The increasing allocation to bonds is consistent with the view that human capital has preponderant bond-like characteristics.

EXHIBIT 4   Glide Path of Target Date Investment Funds in One Family

Assumed Age	Equity Allocation	Bond Allocation
25	85%	15%
35	82	18
45	77	23
55	63	37
65	49	51

Note: Allocations as of 31 December 2009.
Source: Based on data in Idzorek, Stempien, and Voris (2013).

Although estimating human capital is quite complex, including human capital and other extended portfolio assets and economic liabilities in asset allocation decisions is good practice.[6]

EXAMPLE 3   The Economic Balance Sheet of Auldberg University Endowment

- *Name*: Auldberg University Endowment (AUE)
- *Narrative*: AUE was established in 1852 in Caflandia and largely serves the tiny province of Auldberg. AUE supports about one-sixth of Auldberg University's CAF$60 million operating budget; real estate income and provincial subsidies provide the remainder and

---

[5]See Blanchett and Straehl (2015) and Blanchett and Straehl (2017).
[6]Human capital is non-tradable, cannot be hedged, is subject to unspecified future taxes, and is a function of an individual's mortality. Human capital is technically defined as the net present value of an investor's future expected labor income weighted by the probability of surviving to each future age (see Ibbotson, Milevsky, Chen, and Zhu 2007). Thus, the present value of future earnings and pensions should be valued with mortality-weighted probabilities of receiving future cash flows, not the present value over life expectancy. There is meaningful extra value from the low-odds event of extreme longevity, which has an important portfolio implication in that individual investors can outlive their financial portfolios but not lifetime annuity payments.

have been relatively stable. The endowment has historically had a portfolio limited to domestic equities, bonds, and real estate holdings; that policy is under current review. Auldberg University itself (not the endowment) has a CAF$350 million investment in domestic commercial real estate assets, including office buildings and industrial parks, much of it near the campus. AUE employs a well-qualified staff with substantial diverse experience in equities, fixed income, and real estate.

- *Assets*: Endowment assets include CAF$100 million in domestic equities, CAF $60 million in domestic government debt, and CAF$40 million in Class B office real estate. The present value of expected future contributions (from real estate and provincial subsidies) is estimated to be CAF$400 million.
- *Liabilities*: These include CAF$10 million in short-term borrowings and CAF $35 million in mortgage debt related to real estate investments. Although it has no specific legal requirement, AUE has a policy to distribute to the university 5% of 36-month moving average net assets. In effect, the endowment supports $10 million of Auldberg University's annual operating budget. The present value of expected future support is CAF$450 million.

1. Prepare an economic balance sheet for AUE.
2. Describe elements in Auldberg University's investments that might affect AUE's asset allocation choices.

Solution to 1: The economic balance sheet for the endowment (given in the following table) does not include the real estate owned by Auldberg University. The economic net worth is found as a plug item (600 − 10 − 35 − 450 = 105).

AUE Economic Balance Sheet (in CAF$ millions) 31 December 20x6

Assets		Liabilities and Economic Net Worth	
Financial Assets		*Financial Liabilities*	
Domestic equities	100	Short-term borrowing	10
Domestic fixed income	60	Mortgage debt	35
Class B office real estate	40		
Extended Assets		*Extended Liabilities*	
Present value of expected future contributions to AUE	400	Present value of expected future support	450
		Economic Net Worth	
		Economic net worth (Economic assets − Economic liabilities)	105
Total	600		600

Solution to 2: AUE's Class B real estate investments' value and income are likely to be stressed during the same economic circumstances as the university's own real estate investments. In such periods, the university may look to the endowment for increased operating support and AUE may not be well positioned to meet that need. Thus, the AUE's real estate investment is actually less diversifying than it may appear and the allocation to it may need to be re-examined. Similar considerations apply to AUE's holdings in equities in relation to Auldberg University's.

5. APPROACHES TO ASSET ALLOCATION

We can identify three broad approaches to asset allocation: (1) **asset-only**, (2) **liability-relative**, and (3) **goals-based**. These are decision-making frameworks that take account of or emphasize different aspects of the investment problem.

Asset-only approaches to asset allocation focus solely on the asset side of the investor's balance sheet. Liabilities are not explicitly modeled. Mean–variance optimization (MVO) is the most familiar and deeply studied asset-only approach. MVO considers only the expected returns, risks, and correlations of the asset classes in the opportunity set. In contrast, liability-relative and goals-based approaches explicitly account for the liabilities side of the economic balance sheet, dedicating assets to meet, respectively, legal liabilities and quasi-liabilities (other needs that are not strictly liabilities but are treated as such) or goals.

Liability-relative approaches to asset allocation choose an asset allocation in relation to the objective of funding liabilities. The phrase "funding of liabilities" means to provide for the money to pay liabilities when they come due. An example is surplus optimization: mean–variance optimization applied to surplus (defined as the value of the investor's assets minus the present value of the investor's liabilities). In modeling, liabilities might be represented by a short position in a bond or series of bonds matched to the present value and duration of the liabilities. Another approach involves constructing a liability-hedging portfolio focused on funding liabilities and, for any remaining balance of assets, a risky-asset portfolio (so called because it is risky or riskier in relation to liabilities—often also called a "return-seeking portfolio" because it explicitly seeks return above and beyond the liability benchmark). **Liability-driven investing** (LDI) is an investment industry term that generally encompasses asset allocation that is focused on funding an investor's liabilities. Related fixed-income techniques are covered in the fixed-income sequence under liability-based mandates.

All approaches to asset allocation can be said to address goals. In investment practice and literature, however, the term "goals based" has come to be widely associated with a particular type of approach to asset allocation and investing.

Goals-based approaches to asset allocation, as discussed here, are used primarily for individuals and families, involve specifying asset allocations for sub-portfolios, each of which is aligned to specified goals ranging from supporting lifestyle needs to aspirational. Each goal is associated with regular, irregular, or bulleted cash flows; a distinct time horizon; and a risk tolerance level expressed as a required probability of achieving the goal.[7] For example, a middle-aged individual might specify a goal of maintaining his current lifestyle and require a high level of confidence that this goal will be attained. That same individual might express a goal of leaving a bequest to his alma mater. This would be a very long-term goal and might have a low required probability. Each goal is assigned to its own sub-portfolio, and an asset

---

[7]See Shefrin and Statman (2000) and Brunel (2015).

allocation strategy specific to that sub-portfolio is derived. The sum of all sub-portfolio asset allocations results in an overall strategic asset allocation for the total portfolio. **Goals-based investing** (GBI) is an investment industry term that encompasses the asset allocation focused on addressing an investor's goals.

Institutions and Goals-Based Asset Allocation

Asset segmentation as practiced by some life insurers has some similarities to goals-based investing. Asset segmentation involves notionally or actually segmenting general account assets into sub-portfolios associated with specific lines of business or blocks of liabilities. On one hand, such an approach may be distinguished from goals-based asset allocation for individual investors in being motivated by competitive concerns (to facilitate offering competitive crediting rates on groups of contracts) rather than behavioral ones. On the other hand, Fraser and Jennings (2006) described a behaviorally motivated goals-based approach to asset allocation for foundations and endowments. Following their approach, components of an overall appropriate mean–variance optimal portfolio are allocated to time-based sub-portfolios such that uncomfortably novel or risky positions for the entity's governing body are made acceptable by being placed in longer-term sub-portfolios.

Although any asset allocation approach that considers the liabilities side of the economic balance sheet might be termed "liability relative," there are several important distinctions between liabilities for an institutional investor and goals for an individual investor. These distinctions have meaningful implications for asset allocation:[8]

- Liabilities of institutional investors are legal obligations or debts, whereas goals, such as meeting lifestyle or aspirational objectives, are not. Failing to meet them does not trigger similar consequences.
- Whereas institutional liabilities, such as life insurer obligations or pension benefit obligations, are uniform in nature (all of a single type), an individual's goals may be many and varied.
- Liabilities of institutional investors of a given type (e.g., the pension benefits owed to retirees) are often numerous and so, through averaging, may often be forecast with confidence. In contrast, individual goals are not subject to the law of large numbers and averaging. Contrast an estimate of expected death benefits payable for a group of life insurance policies against an individual's uncertainty about the resources needed in retirement: For a 65-year-old individual, the number of remaining years of life is very uncertain, but insurers can estimate the average for a group of 65-year-olds with some precision.

---

[8]See Rudd and Siegel (2013), which recognizes goals-based planning as a distinct approach. This discussion draws on Brunel (2015).

Liability-Relative and Goals-Based Approaches to Investing

Various perspectives exist concerning the relationship between liability-relative and goals-based approaches to investing. Professor Lionel Martellini summarizes one perspective in the following three statements:[9]

1. Goals-based investing is related to a new paradigm that advocates more granular and investor-centric investment solutions.
2. This new investment solutions paradigm translates into goals-based investing (GBI) approaches in individual money management, in which investors' problems can be summarized in terms of their goals, and it translates into liability-driven investing (LDI) approaches in institutional money management, where the investors' liability is treated as a proxy for their goal.
3. GBI and LDI are therefore related, but each of these approaches has its own specific characteristics. For example, GBI implies the capacity to help individual investors identify a hierarchical list of goals, with a distinction between different types of goals (affordable versus non-affordable, essential versus aspirational, etc.) for which no exact counterpart exists in institutional money management.

5.1. Relevant Objectives

All three of the asset allocation approaches listed here seek to make optimal use of the amount of risk that the asset owner is comfortable bearing to achieve stated investment objectives, although they generally define risk differently. Exhibit 5 summarizes typical objectives.

EXHIBIT 5   Asset Allocation Approaches: Investment Objective

Asset Allocation Approach	Relation to Economic Balance Sheet	Typical Objective	Typical Uses and Asset Owner Types
Asset only	Does not explicitly model liabilities or goals	Maximize Sharpe ratio for acceptable level of volatility	Liabilities or goals not defined and/or simplicity is important • Some foundations, endowments • Sovereign wealth funds • Individual investors

---

[9]Communication of 3 June 2016, used with permission.

Asset Allocation Approach	Relation to Economic Balance Sheet	Typical Objective	Typical Uses and Asset Owner Types
Liability relative	Models legal and quasi-liabilities	Fund liabilities and invest excess assets for growth	Penalty for not meeting liabilities high • Banks • Defined benefit pensions • Insurers
Goals based	Models goals	Achieve goals with specified required probabilities of success	Individual investors

In a mean–variance asset-only approach, the objective is to maximize expected portfolio return per unit of portfolio volatility over some time horizon, consistent with the investor's tolerance for risk and consistent with any constraints stated in the IPS. A portfolio's Sharpe ratio is a characteristic metric for evaluating portfolios in an asset-only mean–variance approach.

The basic objective of a liability-relative asset allocation approach is to ensure payment of liabilities when they are due.

A goals-based approach is similar to a liability-relative approach in that it also seeks to ensure that there are sufficient assets to meet the desired payouts. In goals-based approaches, however, goals are generally associated with individual sub-portfolios, and an asset allocation is designed for each sub-portfolio that reflects the time horizon and required probability of success such that the sum of the sub-portfolios addresses the totality of goals satisfactorily.

5.2. Relevant Risk Concepts

Asset-only approaches focus on asset class risk and effective combinations of asset classes. The baseline asset-only approach, mean–variance optimization, uses volatility (standard deviation) of portfolio return as a primary measure of risk, which is a function of component asset class volatilities and the correlations of asset class returns. A mean–variance asset allocation can also incorporate other risk sensitivities, including risk relative to benchmarks and downside risk. Risk relative to benchmarks is usually measured by tracking risk (tracking error). Downside risk can be represented in various ways, including semi-variance, peak-to-trough maximum drawdown, and measures that focus on the extreme (tail) segment of the downside, such as value at risk.

Mean–variance results, although often the starting point for understanding portfolio risk, are regularly augmented by Monte Carlo simulation. By providing information about how an asset allocation performs when one or more variables are changed—for example, to values representing conditions of financial market stress—simulation helps complete the picture of risk, including downside and tail risk. Insights from simulation can then be incorporated as refinements to the asset allocation.

Liability-relative approaches focus on the risk of having insufficient assets to pay obligations when due, which is a kind of shortfall risk. Other risk concerns include the volatility of contributions needed to fund liabilities. Risk in a liability-relative context is generally underpinned by the differences between asset and liability characteristics (e.g., their relative size, their interest rate sensitivity, their sensitivity to inflation).

Goals-based approaches are concerned with the risk of failing to achieve goals.[10] The risk limits can be quantified as the maximum acceptable probability of not achieving a goal.[11] The plural in "liabilities" and "goals" underscores that these risks are generally related to multiple future points in time. Overall portfolio risk is thus the weighted sum of the risks associated with each goal.

Generally, a given statistical risk measure may be relevant in any of the three approaches. For example, standard deviation can be used to assess overall portfolio volatility in asset-only approaches, and it may be used to measure surplus volatility (the volatility of the difference between the values of assets and liabilities) or the volatility of the funded ratio (the ratio of the values of assets and liabilities) in liability-relative asset allocation.

5.3. Modeling Asset Class Risk

Asset classes are one of the most widely used investment concepts but are often interpreted in distinct ways. Greer (1997) defines an asset class as "a set of assets that bear some fundamental economic similarities to each other, and that have characteristics that make them distinct from other assets that are not part of that class." He specifies three "super classes" of assets:

- *Capital assets.* An ongoing source of something of value (such as interest or dividends); capital assets can be valued by net present value.
- *Consumable/transformable assets.* Assets, such as commodities, that can be consumed or transformed, as part of the production process, into something else of economic value, but which do not yield an ongoing stream of value.
- *Store of value assets.* Neither income generating nor valuable as a consumable or an economic input; examples include currencies and art, whose economic value is realized through sale or exchange.

EXAMPLE 4   Asset Classes (1)

Classify the following investments based on Greer's (1997) framework, or explain how they *do not* fit in the framework:

1. Precious metals
2. Petroleum
3. Hedge funds
4. Timberland
5. Inflation-linked fixed-income securities
6. Volatility

---

[10]See Das, Markowitz, Scheid, and Statman (2010), who call goals "mental accounts."
[11]See Brunel (2015).

Solution:

1. Precious metals are a store of value asset except in certain industrial applications (e.g., palladium and platinum in the manufacture of catalytic converters).
2. Petroleum is a consumable/transformable asset; it can be consumed to generate power or provide fuel for transport.
3. Hedge funds do not fit into Greer's (1997) super class framework; a hedge fund strategy invests in underlying asset classes.
4. Timberland is a capital asset or consumable/transformable asset. It is a capital asset in the sense that timber can be harvested and replanted cyclically to generate a stream of cash flows; it is a consumable asset in that timber can be used to produce building materials/packaging or paper.
5. Inflation-linked fixed-income securities is a capital asset because cash flows can be determined based on the characteristics of the security.
6. Volatility does not fit; it is a measurable investment characteristic. Because equity volatility is the underlying for various derivative contracts and an investable risk premium may be associated with it, it is mentioned by some as an asset.

Greer (1997) approaches the classification of asset classes in an abstract or generic sense. The next question is how to specify asset classes to support the purposes of strategic asset allocation.[12] For example, if a manager lumps together very different investments, such as distressed credit and Treasury securities, into an asset class called "fixed income," asset allocation becomes less effective in diversifying and controlling risk. Furthermore, the investor needs a logical framework for distinguishing an asset class from an investment strategy. The following are five criteria that will help in effectively *specifying asset classes for the purpose of asset allocation*:[13]

1. *Assets within an asset class should be relatively homogeneous.* Assets within an asset class should have similar attributes. In the example just given, defining equities to include both real estate and common stock would result in a non-homogeneous asset class.
2. *Asset classes should be mutually exclusive.* Overlapping asset classes will reduce the effectiveness of strategic asset allocation in controlling risk and could introduce problems in developing asset class return expectations. For example, if one asset class for a US investor is domestic common equities, then world equities ex-US is more appropriate as another asset class rather than global equities, which include US equities.
3. *Asset classes should be diversifying.* For risk control purposes, an included asset class should not have extremely high expected correlations with other asset classes or with a linear combination of other asset classes. Otherwise, the included asset class will be effectively redundant in a portfolio because it will duplicate risk exposures already present. In general, a pairwise correlation above 0.95 is undesirable (given a sufficient number of observations to have confidence in the correlation estimate).
4. *The asset classes as a group should make up a preponderance of world investable wealth.* From the perspective of portfolio theory, selecting an asset allocation from a group of asset classes satisfying this criterion should tend to increase expected return for a given level of risk.

[12]See Kritzman (1999).
[13]As opposed to criteria for asset class definition in an absolute sense.

Furthermore, the inclusion of more markets expands the opportunities for applying active investment strategies, assuming the decision to invest actively has been made. However, such factors as regulatory restrictions on investments and government-imposed limitations on investment by foreigners may limit the asset classes an investor can invest in.

5. *Asset classes selected for investment should have the capacity to absorb a meaningful proportion of an investor's portfolio.* Liquidity and transaction costs are both significant considerations. If liquidity and expected transaction costs for an investment of a size meaningful for an investor are unfavorable, an asset class may not be practically suitable for investment.

Note that Criteria 1 through 3 strictly focus on assets themselves, while Criterion 5, and to some extent Criterion 4, involve potential investor-specific considerations.

Asset Classes Should Be Diversifying

Pairwise asset class correlations are often useful information and are readily obtained. However, in evaluating an investment's value as a diversifier at the portfolio level, it is important to consider an asset in relation to all other assets as a group rather than in a one-by-one (pairwise) fashion. It is possible to reach limited or incorrect conclusions by solely considering pairwise correlations. To give an example, denote the returns to three assets by X, Y, and Z, respectively. Suppose that $Z = aX + bY$; a and b are constants, not both equal to zero. Asset Z is an exact weighted combination of X and Y and so has no value as a diversifier added to a portfolio consisting of assets X and Y. Yet, if the correlation between X and Y is -0.5, it can be shown that Z has a correlation of just 0.5 with X as well as with Y.

Examining return series' correlations during times of financial market stress can provide practically valuable insight into potential diversification benefits beyond typical correlations that average all market conditions.

In current professional practice, the listing of asset classes often includes the following:

- *Global public equity*—composed of developed, emerging, and sometimes frontier markets and large-, mid-, and small-cap asset classes; sometimes treated as several sub-asset classes (e.g., domestic and non-domestic).
- *Global private equity*—includes venture capital, growth capital, and leveraged buyouts (investment in special situations and distressed securities often occurs within private equity structures too).
- *Global fixed income*—composed of developed and emerging market debt and further divided into sovereign, investment-grade, and high-yield sub-asset classes, and sometimes inflation-linked bonds (unless included in real assets; see the following bullet). Cash and short-duration securities can be included here.
- *Real assets*—includes assets that provide sensitivity to inflation, such as private real estate equity, private infrastructure, and commodities. Sometimes, global inflation-linked bonds are included as a real asset rather than fixed income because of their sensitivity to inflation.

Emerging Market Equities and Fixed Income

Investment practice distinguishes between developed and emerging market equities and fixed income within global equities. The distinction is based on practical differences in investment characteristics, which can be related to typical market differences including the following:

- diversification potential, which is related to the degree to which investment factors driving market returns in developed and emerging markets are not identical (a topic known as "market integration");
- perceived level of informational efficiency; and
- corporate governance, regulation, taxation, and currency convertibility.

As of mid-2016, emerging markets represent approximately 10% of world equity value based on MSCI indices.[14] In fixed income, investment opportunities have expanded as governments and corporations domiciled in emerging markets have increasingly issued debt in their own currency. Markets in local currency inflation-indexed emerging market sovereign debt have become more common.[15]

"Asset classes" are, by definition, groupings of assets. Investment vehicles, such as hedge funds, that apply strategies to asset classes and/or individual investments with the objective of earning a return to investment skill or providing attractive risk characteristics may be treated as a category called "strategies" or "diversifying strategies." When that is the case, this category is assigned a percentage allocation of assets, similar to a true asset class. Economically, asset classes contrast with "strategies" by offering, in general, an inherent, non-skill-based *ex ante* expected return premium.[16]

Effective portfolio optimization and construction may be hindered by excessive asset class granularity. Consider Exhibit 6.

---

[14]MSCI uses three broad definitions to sort countries into developed, emerging, and frontier: 1) economic development, 2) size and liquidity requirements, and 3) market accessibility criteria (see the MSCI Market Classification Framework at www.msci.com/market-classification).

[15]For a discussion of their potential benefits, see Burger, Warnock, and Warnock (2012), Perry (2011), and Swinkels (2012). Kozhemiakin (2011) discusses how emerging market bonds can facilitate broader representation than an equity-only portfolio because some countries (e.g., Argentina) have small equity markets but larger bond markets.

[16]See Idzorek and Kowara (2013), p.20.

EXHIBIT 6   Examples of Asset Classes and Sub-Asset Classes

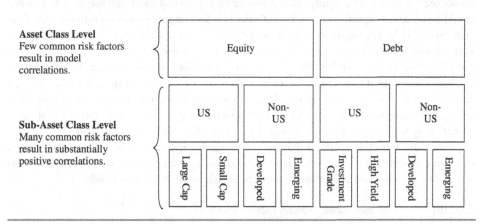

As more and more sub-asset classes are defined, they become less distinctive. In particular, the sources of risk for more broadly defined asset classes are generally better distinguished than those for narrowly defined subgroups. For example, the overlap in the sources of risk of US large-cap equity and US small-cap equity would be greater than the overlap between US and non-US equity. Using broadly defined asset classes with fewer risk source overlaps in optimization is consistent with achieving a diversified portfolio. Additionally, historical data for broadly defined asset classes may be more readily available or more reliable. The question of how much to allocate to equity versus fixed income versus other assets is far more important in strategic asset allocation than *precisely* how much to allocate to the various sub-classes of equity and fixed income. However, when the investor moves from the strategic asset allocation phase to policy implementation, sub-asset class choices become relevant.

EXAMPLE 5   Asset Classes (2)

Discuss a specification of asset classes that distinguishes between "domestic intermediate-duration fixed income" and "domestic long-duration fixed income." Contrast potential relevance in asset-only and liability-relative contexts.

Solution: These two groups share key risk factors, such as interest rate and credit risk. For achieving diversification in asset risk—for example, in an asset-only context—asset allocation using domestic fixed income, which includes intermediate and long duration, should be effective and simple. Subsequently, allocation within domestic fixed income could address other considerations, such as interest rate views. When investing in relation to liabilities, distinctions by duration could be of first-order importance and the specification could be relevant.

Any asset allocation, by whatever means arrived at, is expressed ultimately in terms of money allocations to assets. Traditionally—and still in common practice—asset allocation uses asset classes as the unit of analysis. Thus, mean–variance optimization based on four asset classes (e.g., global public equity, global private equity, global fixed income, and real assets) would be based on expected return, return volatility, and return correlation estimates for these asset classes. (The development of such capital market assumptions is the subject of chapter.) Factor-based approaches, discussed in more detail later, do not use asset classes as the basis for portfolio construction. Technically, the set of achievable investment outcomes cannot be enlarged simply by developing an asset allocation by a different means (for instance, using asset classes as the unit of analysis), all else being equal, such as constraints against short selling (non-negativity constraints).[17] Put another way, adopting a factor-based asset allocation approach does not, by default, lead to superior investment outcomes.

There are allocation methods that focus on assigning investments to the investor's desired exposures to specified risk factors. These methods are premised on the observation that asset classes often exhibit some overlaps in sources of risk, as illustrated in Exhibit 7.[18]

EXHIBIT 7   Common Factor Exposures across Asset Classes

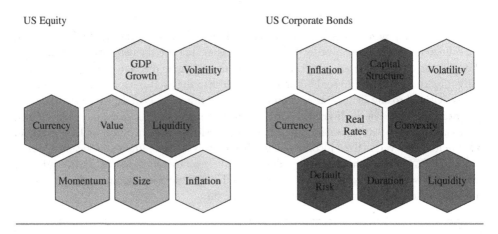

The overlaps seen in Exhibit 7 help explain the correlation of equity and credit assets. Modeling using asset classes as the unit of analysis tends to obscure the portfolio's sensitivity to overlapping risk factors, such as inflation risk in this example. As a result, controlling risk exposures may be problematic. Multifactor risk models, which have a history of use in individual asset selection, have been brought to bear on the issue of controlling systematic risk exposures in asset allocation.

In broad terms, when using factors as the units of analysis, we begin with specifying risk factors and the desired exposure to each factor. Asset classes can be described with respect to their sensitivities to each of the factors. Factors, however, are not directly investable. On that basis, asset class portfolios that isolate exposure to the risk factor are constructed; these factor portfolios involve both long and short positions. A choice of risk exposures in factor space can

[17]Stated more formally and demonstrated in Idzorek and Kowara (2013).
[18]See Podkaminer (2013).

be mapped back to asset class space for implementation. Uses of multifactor risk models in asset allocation have been labeled "factor-based asset allocation" in contrast to "asset class-based asset allocation," which uses asset classes directly as the unit of analysis.

Factor Representation

Although risk factors can be thought of as the basic building blocks of investments, most are not directly investable. In this context, risk factors are associated with expected return premiums. Long and short positions in assets (spread positions) may be needed to isolate the respective risks and associated expected return premiums. Other risk factors may be accessed through derivatives. The following are a few examples of how risk factor exposures can be achieved.

- *Inflation.* Going long nominal Treasuries and short inflation-linked bonds isolates the inflation component.
- *Real interest rates.* Inflation-linked bonds provide a proxy for real interest rates.
- *US volatility.* VIX (Chicago Board Options Exchange Volatility Index) futures provide a proxy for implied volatility.
- *Credit spread.* Going long high-quality credit and short Treasuries/government bonds isolates credit exposure.
- *Duration.* Going long 10+ year Treasuries and short 1–3 year Treasuries isolates the duration exposure being targeted.

Factor Models in Asset Allocation

The interest in using factors for asset allocation stems from a number of considerations, including the following:

- The desire to shape the asset allocation based on goals and objectives that cannot be expressed by asset classes (such as matching liability characteristics in a liability-relative approach).
- An intense focus on portfolio risk in all of its various dimensions, helped along by availability of commercial factor-based risk measurement and management tools.
- The acknowledgment that many highly correlated so-called asset classes are better defined as parts of the same high-level asset class. For example, domestic and foreign equity may be better seen as sub-classes of global public equity.
- The realization that equity risk can be the dominant risk exposure even in a seemingly well-diversified portfolio.

6. STRATEGIC ASSET ALLOCATION

An asset allocation that arises in long-term investment planning is often called the "strategic asset allocation" or "policy portfolio": It is an asset allocation that is expected to be effective in achieving an asset owner's investment objectives, given his or her investment constraints and risk tolerance, as documented in the investment policy statement.

A theoretical underpinning for quantitative approaches to asset allocation is utility theory, which uses a utility function as a mathematical representation of preferences that incorporates the investor's risk aversion. According to utility theory, the optimal asset allocation is the one that is expected to provide the highest utility to the investor at the investor's investment time horizon. The optimization program, in broad terms, is

$$\underset{\substack{\text{Maximize} \\ \text{by choice of asset class weights } w_i}}{\text{Maximize}} \quad E[U(W_T)] = f \left(\begin{array}{c} W_0, w_i, \text{asset class return distributions,} \\ \text{degree of risk aversion} \end{array} \right)$$

$$\text{subject to} \sum_{i=1}^{n} w_i = 1 \text{ and any other constraints on } w_i$$

The first line is the objective function, and the second line consists of constraints on asset class weights; other constraints besides those on weights can also be incorporated (for example, specified levels of bond duration or portfolio yield may be targeted). With W_0 and W_T (the values of wealth today and at time horizon T, respectively) the investor's problem is to select the asset allocation that maximizes the expected utility of ending wealth, $E[U(W_T)]$, subject to the constraints that asset class weights sum to 1 and that weights observe any limits the investor places on them. Beginning wealth, asset class weights, and asset class returns imply a distribution of values for ending wealth, and the utility function assigns a value to each of them; by weighting these values by their probability of occurrence, an expected utility for the asset allocation is determined.

An expected utility framework underlies many, but not all, quantitative approaches to asset allocation. A widely used group in asset allocation consists of power utility functions,[19] which exhibit the analytically convenient characteristic that risk aversion does not depend on the level of wealth. Power utility can be approximated by mean–variance utility, which underlies mean–variance optimization.

---

[19]Power utility has the form $U = \frac{w_T^{1-\lambda}}{1-\lambda}$, where $\lambda > 0$ is the parameter of risk aversion (if $\lambda \rightarrow 0$, the investor is risk neutral).

Optimal Choice in the Simplest Case

The simplest asset allocation decision problem involves one risky asset and one risk-free asset. Let λ, μ, r_f, and σ^2 represent, respectively, the investor's degree of risk aversion, the risk asset's expected return, the risk-free interest rate, and the variance of return. With mean–variance utility, the optimal allocation to the risky asset, w^*, can be shown to equal

$$w* = \tfrac{1}{\lambda} \left(\tfrac{\mu - r_f}{\sigma^2} \right)$$

The allocation to the risky asset is inversely proportional to the investor's risk aversion and directly proportional to the risk asset's expected return per unit of risk (represented by return variance).[20]

Selection of a strategic asset allocation generally involves the following steps:[21]

1. Determine and quantify the investor's objectives. What is the pool of assets meant for (e.g., paying future benefit payments, contributing to a university's budget, securing ample assets for retirement)? What is the investor trying to achieve? What liabilities or needs or goals need to be recognized (explicitly or implicitly)? How should objectives be modeled?
2. Determine the investor's risk tolerance and how risk should be expressed and measured. What is the investor's overall tolerance for risk and specific risk sensitivities? How should these be quantified in the process of developing an appropriate asset allocation (risk measures, factor models)?
3. Determine the investment horizon(s). What are the appropriate planning horizons to use for asset allocation; that is, over what horizon(s) should the objectives and risk tolerance be evaluated?
4. Determine other constraints and the requirements they impose on asset allocation choices. What is the tax status of the investor? Should assets be managed with consideration given to ESG issues? Are there any legal and regulatory factors that need to be considered? Are any political sensitivities relevant? Are there any other constraints that the investor has imposed in the IPS and other communications?
5. Determine the approach to asset allocation that is most suitable for the investor.
6. Specify asset classes, and develop a set of capital market expectations for the specified asset classes.

---

[20]See Ang (2014), Chapter 4, for further analysis.
[21]Arjan Berkelaar, CFA, contributed to this formulation of steps.

7. Develop a range of potential asset allocation choices for consideration. These choices are often developed through optimization exercises. Specifics depend on the approach taken to asset allocation.

8. Test the robustness of the potential choices. This testing often involves conducting simulations to evaluate potential results in relation to investment objectives and risk tolerance over appropriate planning horizon(s) for the different asset allocations developed in Step 7. The sensitivity of the outcomes to changes in capital market expectations is also tested.

9. Iterate back to Step 7 until an appropriate and agreed-on asset allocation is constructed.

Subsequent chapters on asset allocation in practice will address the "how." The following sections give an indication of thematic considerations. We use investors with specific characteristics to illustrate the several approaches distinguished: sovereign wealth fund for asset-only allocation; a frozen corporate DB plan for liability-relative allocation; and an ultra-high-net-worth family for goals-based allocation. In practice, any type of investor could approach asset allocation with varying degrees of focus on modeling and integrating liabilities-side balance sheet considerations. How these cases are analyzed in this chapter should not be viewed as specifying normative limits of application for various asset allocation approaches. For example, a liability-relative perspective has wide potential relevance for institutional investors because it has the potential to incorporate all information on the economic balance sheet. Investment advisers to high-net-worth investors may choose to use any of the approaches.

6.1. Asset Only

Asset-only allocation is based on the principle of selecting portfolios that make efficient use of asset risk. The focus here is mean–variance optimization, the mainstay among such approaches. Given a set of asset classes and assumptions concerning their expected returns, volatilities, and correlations, this approach traces out an efficient frontier that consists of portfolios that are expected to offer the greatest return at each level of portfolio return volatility. The Sharpe ratio is a key descriptor of an asset allocation: If a portfolio is efficient, it has the highest Sharpe ratio among portfolios with the same volatility of return.

An example of an investor that might use an asset-only approach is the (hypothetical) Government Petroleum Fund of Caflandia (GPFC) introduced next.

Investor Case Facts: GPFC, A Sovereign Wealth Fund

- *Name*: Government Petroleum Fund of Caflandia (GPFC)
- *Narrative*: The emerging country of Caflandia has established a sovereign wealth fund to capture revenue from its abundant petroleum reserves. The government's goal in setting up the fund is to promote a fair sharing of the benefits between current and future generations (intergenerational equity) from the export of the country's petroleum resources. Caflandia's equity market represents 0.50% of global equity market capitalization. Economists estimate that distributions in the interest of intergenerational equity may need to begin in 20 years. Future distribution policy is undetermined.
- *Tax status*: Non-taxable.
- *Financial assets and financial liabilities*: Financial assets are CAF$40 billion at market value, making GPFC among the largest investors in Caflandia. GPFC has no borrowings.
- *Extended assets and liabilities*: Cash inflows from petroleum exports are assumed to grow at inflation + 1% for the next 15 years and may change depending on reserves and global commodity demand. The present value of expected future income from state-owned reserves is estimated to be CAF$60 billion. Future spending needs are positively correlated with consumer inflation and population growth. In Exhibit 8, the amount for the present value (PV) of future spending, which GPFC has not yet determined, is merely a placeholder to balance assets and liabilities; as a result, no equity is shown.

EXHIBIT 8   GPFC Economic Balance Sheet (in CAF$ billions) 31 December 20x6

Assets		Liabilities and Economic Net Worth	
Financial Assets		*Financial Liabilities*	
Investments (includes cash, equities, fixed income, and other investments)	40		
Extended Assets		*Extended Liabilities*	
PV of expected future income	60	PV of future spending	100
		Economic Net Worth	
		Economic net worth	0
Total	100		100

For GPFC, the amount and timing of funds needed for future distributions to Caflandia citizens are, as yet, unclear. GPFC can currently focus on asset risk and its efficient use to grow assets within the limits of the fund's risk tolerance. In addition to considering expected return in relation to volatility in selecting an asset allocation, GPFC might include such considerations as the following:

- diversification across global asset classes (possibly quantified as a constraint on the proportion allocated to any given asset classes);
- correlations with the petroleum sources of income to GPFC;
- the potential positive correlation of future spending with inflation and population growth in Caflandia;
- long investment horizon (as a long-term investor, GPFC may be well positioned to earn any return premium that may be associated with the relatively illiquid asset classes); and
- return outcomes in severe financial market downturns.

Suppose GPFC quantifies its risk tolerance in traditional mean–variance terms as willingness to bear portfolio volatility of up to 17% per year. This risk tolerance is partly based on GPFC's unwillingness to allow the fund to fall below 90% funded. GPFC's current

EXHIBIT 9   GPFC Strategic Asset Allocation Decision

		Asset Allocation		
		Proposed		
	Current	A	B	C
Investment				
Equities				
Domestic	50%	40%	45%	30%
Global ex-domestic		10%	20%	25%
Bonds				
Nominal	30%	30%	20%	10%
Inflation linked				10%
Real estate	20%	10%	15%	10%
Diversifying strategies		10%		15%

strategic asset allocation, along with several alternatives that have been developed by its staff during an asset allocation review, are shown in Exhibit 9. The category "Diversifying strategies" consists of a diversified allocation to hedge funds.[22]

---

[22]The assumed expected returns and return volatilities are (given in that order in parentheses and expressed as decimals, rather than percentages): domestic equities (0.11, 0.25), non-domestic equities (0.09, 0.18), nominal bonds (0.05, 0.10), inflation-linked bonds (0.035, 0.06), real estate (0.075, 0.16), and diversifying strategies (0.07, 0.09). A correlation matrix with hypothetical values and a hypothetical relationship between the allocations and VaR also lies behind the exhibit. Because the purpose here is to illustrate concepts rather than mechanics, inputs are not discussed although they are very important in asset allocation.

		Asset Allocation		
			Proposed	
	Current	A	B	C
Portfolio statistics				
Expected arithmetic return	8.50%	8.25%	8.88%	8.20%
Volatility (standard deviation)	15.57%	14.24%	16.63%	14.06%
Sharpe ratio	0.353	0.369	0.353	0.370
One-year 5% VaR	−17.11%	−15.18%	−18.48%	−14.93%

Notes: The government bond rate is 3%. The acceptable level of volatility is ≤ 17% per year. The value at risk (VaR) is stated as a percent of the initial portfolio value over one year (e.g., −16% means a decline of 16%).

GPFC decides it is willing to tolerate a 5% chance of losing 22% or more of portfolio value in a given year. This risk is evaluated by examining the one-year 5% VaR of potential asset allocations.

Let us examine GPFC's decision. The current asset allocation and the alternatives developed by staff all satisfy the GPFC's tolerance for volatility and VaR limit. The staff's alternatives appear to represent incremental, rather than large-scale, changes from the current strategic asset allocation. We do not know whether capital market assumptions have changed since the current strategic asset allocation was approved.

Mix A, compared with the current asset allocation, diversifies the equity allocation to include non-domestic (global ex-domestic) equities and spreads the current allocation to real estate over real estate and diversifying strategies. Given GPFC's long investment horizon and absence of liquidity needs, an allocation to diversifying strategies at 10% should not present liquidity concerns. Because diversifying strategies are more liquid than private real estate, the overall liquidity profile of the fund improves. It is important to note that given the illiquid nature of real estate, it could take considerable time to reallocate from real estate to diversifying strategies. Mix A has a lower volatility (by 133 bps) than the current allocation and slightly lower tail risk (the 5% VaR for Mix A is −15%, whereas the 5% VaR for the current asset mix is −17%). Mix A's Sharpe ratio is slightly higher. On the basis of the facts given, Mix A appears to be an incremental improvement on the current asset allocation.

Compared with Mix A and the current asset allocation, Mix B increases the allocation to equities by 15 percentage points and pulls back from the allocation to bonds and, in relation to Mix A, diversifying strategies. Although Mix B has a higher expected return and its VaR is within GPFC's tolerance of 22%, Mix B's lower Sharpe ratio indicates that it makes inefficient use of its additional risk. Mix B does not appear to deserve additional consideration.

Compared with the current asset allocation and Mix A, Mix C's total allocation to equities, at 55%, is higher and the mix is more diversified considering the allocation of 25% non-domestic equities. Mix C's allocation to fixed income is 20% compared with 30% for Mix A and the current asset mix. The remaining fixed-income allocation has been diversified with an exposure to both nominal and inflation-linked bonds. The diversifying strategies allocation is funded by a combination of the reduced weights to fixed income and real estate. The following observations may be made:

- Mix C's increase in equity exposure (compared with the equity exposure of Mix A and the current mix) has merit because more equity-like choices in the asset allocation could be expected to give GPFC more exposure to such a factor as a GDP growth factor (see Exhibit 9); population growth is one driver of GDP.

- Within fixed income, Mix C's allocation to inflation-linked bonds could be expected to hedge the inflation risk inherent in future distributions.
- Mix C has the lowest volatility and the lowest VaR among the asset allocations, although the differences compared with Mix A are very small. Mix C's Sharpe ratio is comparable to (insignificantly higher than) Mix A's.

Based on the facts given, Mix A and Mix C appear to be improvements over the current mix. Mix C may have the edge over Mix A based on the discussion. As a further step in the evaluation process, GPFC may examine the robustness of the forecasted results by changing the capital market assumptions and simulating shocks to such variables as inflation. The discussion of Mix C shows that there are means for potential liability concerns (the probable sensitivity of spending to inflation and population growth) to enter decision-making even from a mean–variance optimization perspective.

EXAMPLE 6   Asset-Only Asset Allocation

1. Describe how the Sharpe ratio, considered in isolation, would rank the asset allocation in Exhibit 9.
2. State a limitation of basing a decision only on the Sharpe ratio addressed in Question 1.
3. An assertion is heard in an investment committee discussion that because the Sharpe ratio of diversifying strategies (0.55) is higher than real estate's (0.50), any potential allocation to real estate would be better used in diversifying strategies. Describe why the argument is incomplete.

Solution to 1: The ranking by Sharpe ratios in isolation is C (3.70), A (3.69), and current and B (both 3.53). Using only the Sharpe ratio, Mix C appears superior to the other choices, but such an approach ignores several important considerations.

Solution to 2: The Sharpe ratio, while providing a means to rank choices on the basis of return per unit of volatility, does not capture other characteristics that are likely to be important to the asset owner, such as VaR and funded ratio. Furthermore, the Sharpe ratio by itself cannot confirm that the absolute level of portfolio risk is within the investor's specified range.

Solution to 3: It is true that the higher the Sharpe ratio of an investment, the greater its contribution to the Sharpe ratio of the overall portfolio, *holding all other things equal.* However, that condition is not usually true. Diversification potential in a portfolio (quantified by correlations) may differ. For example, including both diversifying strategies and real estate in an allocation may ultimately decrease portfolio-level risk through favorable correlation characteristics. Also, as in the solution to Question 2, other risk considerations besides volatility may be relevant.

Financial theory suggests that investors should consider the global market-value weighted portfolio as a baseline asset allocation. This portfolio, which sums all investable assets (global stocks, bonds, real estate, and so forth) held by investors, reflects the balancing of supply and demand across world markets. In financial theory, it is the portfolio that minimizes diversifiable risk, which in principle is uncompensated. Because of that characteristic, theory indicates that the global market portfolio should be the available portfolio that makes the most efficient use of the risk budget.[23] Other arguments for using it as a baseline include its position as a reference point for a highly diversified portfolio and the discipline it provides in relation to mitigating any investment biases, such as home-country bias (discussed below).

At a minimum, the global market portfolio serves as a starting point for discussion and ensures that the investor articulates a clear justification for moving away from global capitalization market weights. The global market portfolio is expressed in two phases. The first phase allocates assets in proportion to the global portfolio of stocks, bonds, and real assets. The second phase disaggregates each of these broad asset classes into regional, country, and security weights using capitalization weights. The second phase is typically used within a global equity portfolio where an asset owner will examine the global capitalization market weights and either accept them or alter them. Common tilts (biases) include overweighting the home-country market, value, size (small cap), and emerging markets. For many investors, allocations to foreign fixed income have been adopted more slowly than allocations to foreign equity. Most investors have at least some amount in non-home-country equity.

Home-Country Bias

A given for GPFC was that Caflandia's equity markets represent only 0.50% of the value of world equity markets. However, in all asset allocations in Exhibit 9, the share of domestic equity ranged from 50% for the current asset allocation to 30% for Mix C. The favoring of domestic over non-domestic investment relative to global market value weights is called **home-country bias** and is very common. Even relatively small economies feature pension plans, endowments, and other funds, which are disproportionately tilted toward the equity and fixed-income offerings in the domestic market. The same tendency is true for very large markets, such as the United States and the eurozone. By biasing toward the home market, asset owners may not be optimally aligning regional weights with the global market portfolio and are implicitly implementing a market view. Investment explanations for the bias, such as offsetting liabilities that are denominated in the home currency, may be relevant in some cases, however.

For reference, the MSCI All Country World Portfolio (ACWI), a proxy for the public equities portion of the global equity market portfolio, contains the following capitalization weights as of 31 December 2015:

- Developed Europe and the Middle East: 22.8%
- Developed Pacific: 11.7%
- North America: 55.9%
- Emerging markets: 9.6%

Investing in a global market portfolio faces several implementation hurdles. First, estimating the size of each asset class on a global basis is an imprecise exercise given the uneven availability of information on non-publicly traded assets. Second, the practicality of investing proportionately

---

[23]According to the two-fund separation theorem, all investors optimally hold a combination of a risk-free asset and an optimal portfolio of all risky assets. This optimal portfolio is the global market value portfolio.

in residential real estate, much of which is held in individual homeowners' hands, has been questioned. Third, private commercial real estate and global private equity assets are not easily carved into pieces of a size that is accessible to most investors. Practically, proxies for the global market portfolio are often based only on traded assets, such as portfolios of exchange-traded funds (ETFs). Furthermore, some investors have implemented alternative weighting schemes, such as GDP weight or equal weight. However, it is a useful discipline to articulate a justification for any deviation from the capitalization-weighted global market portfolio.

6.2. Liability Relative

To illustrate the liability-relative approach, we take the defined benefit (DB) pension plan of (hypothetical) GPLE Corporation, with case facts given below.

A Frozen DB Plan, GPLE Corporation Pension

- *Name*: GPLE Corporation Pension
- *Narrative*: GPLE is a machine tool manufacturer with a market value of $2 billion. GPLE is the sponsor of a $1.25 billion legacy DB plan, which is now frozen (i.e., no new plan participants and no new benefits accruing for existing plan participants). GPLE Pension has a funded ratio (the ratio of pension assets to liabilities) of 1.15. Thus, the plan is slightly overfunded. Responsibility for the plan's management rests with the firm's treasury department (which also has responsibility for GPLE Corporation treasury operations).
- *Tax status*: Non-taxable.
- *Financial assets and financial liabilities*: Assets amount to $1.25 billion at market values. Given a funded ratio of 1.15, that amount implies that liabilities are valued at about $1.087 billion. Projected distributions to pension beneficiaries have a present value of $1.087 billion at market value.

GPLE does not reflect any extended assets or liabilities; thus, economic net worth is identical to traditional accounting net worth.

EXHIBIT 10   GPLE Pension Economic Balance Sheet (in US$ billions) 31 December 20x6

Assets		Liabilities and Economic Net Worth	
Financial Assets		*Financial Liabilities*	
Pension assets	1.250	PV of pension liability	1.087
		Economic Net Worth	
		Economic net worth	0.163
Total	1.250		1.250

GPLE, the plan sponsor, receives two asset allocation recommendations. Recommendation A does not explicitly consider GPLE's pension's liabilities but is instead based on an asset-only perspective: the mean–variance efficient frontier given a set of capital market assumptions. A second recommendation, "Recommendation B," does explicitly consider liabilities, incorporating a liability-hedging portfolio based on an analysis of GPLE pension liabilities and a return-seeking portfolio.

In evaluating asset allocation choices, consider the pensioners' and the plan sponsor's interests. Pensioners want to receive the stream of promised benefits with as little risk, or chance of interruption, as possible. Risk increases as the funded ratio declines. When the funded ratio is 1.0, pension assets just cover pension liabilities with no safety buffer. When the funded ratio is less than 1.0, the plan sponsor generally needs to make up the deficit in pension assets by contributions to the plan. For example, with a 10-year investment time horizon and a choice between two asset allocations, the allocation with the lower expected present value of cumulative contributions to Year 10 would generally be preferred by the sponsor, all else being equal. In practice, all else is usually not equal. For example, the alternative with the lower *expected* present value of contributions may involve more risk to the level of contributions in adverse market conditions. For example, the 5% of *worst outcomes* for the present value of cumulative contributions may be more severe for the lower expected contribution alternative. Thus, possible asset allocations generally involve risk trade-offs.[24] Now consider the recommendations.

Recommendation A, based on asset-only analysis, involves a 65% allocation to global equities and a 35% allocation to global fixed income. Assume that this asset allocation is mean–variance efficient and has the highest Sharpe ratio among portfolios that meet the pension's assumed tolerance for asset return volatility. Capital market assumptions indicate that equities have a significantly higher expected return and volatility than fixed income.

Recommendation B, based on a liability-relative approach to asset allocation, involves an allocation of $1.125 billion to a fixed-income portfolio that is very closely matched in interest rate sensitivity to the present value of plan liabilities (and to any other liability factor risk exposures)—the liability hedging portfolio—and a $0.125 allocation to equities (the return-seeking portfolio). This is a proportional allocation of 10% to equities and 90% to fixed income. The equities allocation is believed to provide potential for increasing the size of the buffer between pension assets and liabilities with negligible risk to funded status. Recommendation B lies below the asset-only efficient frontier with a considerably lower expected return vis-à-vis Recommendation A.

What are the arguments for and against each of these recommendations? Recommendation A is expected, given capital market assumptions, to increase the size of the buffer between pension assets and liabilities. But the sponsor does not benefit from increases in the buffer if the current buffer is adequate.[25] However, with a 0.65 × $1.25 billion = $0.8125 allocation to equities and a current buffer of assets of $1.25 billion – $1.087 billion = $0.163 billion, a decline of that amount or more in equity values (a 20% decline) would put the plan into underfunded status (assuming no commensurate changes in the liability). Thus, Recommendation A creates contribution risk for the plan sponsor without a potential upside clearly benefiting either the sponsor or beneficiaries.

---

[24]Collie and Gannon (2009) explore the contribution risk trade-off considered here in more detail.

[25]Real-world complexities, such as DB plan termination to capture a positive surplus or pension risk transfer (annuitization), are beyond the scope of this chapter; generally, there are restrictions and penalties involved in such actions, and the point made here is valid.

For Recommendation B, because the risk characteristics of the $1.125 billion fixed-income portfolio are closely matched with those of the $1.087 billion of pension liabilities with a buffer, the plan sponsor should not face any meaningful risk of needing to make further contributions to the pension. Pensioners expect the plan to be fully funded on an ongoing basis without any reliance on the sponsor's ability to make additional contributions. This is an excellent outcome for both. The pension liabilities are covered (defeased).

The example is highly stylized—the case facts were developed to make points cleanly—but does point to the potential value of managing risk in asset allocation explicitly in relation to liabilities. A typical use of fixed-income assets in liability-relative asset allocation should be noted: Liability-relative approaches to asset allocation tend to give fixed income a larger role than asset-only approaches in such cases as the one examined here because interest rates are a major financial market driver of both liability and bond values. Thus, bonds can be important in hedging liabilities, but equities can be relevant for liability hedging too. With richer case facts, as when liabilities accrue with inflation (not the case in the frozen DB example), equities may have a long-term role in matching the characteristics of liabilities. In underfunded plans, the potential upside of equities would often have greater value for the plan sponsor than in the fully funded case examined.

Liability Glide Paths

If GPLE were underfunded, it might consider establishing a liability glide path. A **liability glide path** is a technique in which the plan sponsor specifies in advance the desired proportion of liability-hedging assets and return-seeking assets and the duration of the liability hedge as funded status changes and contributions are made. The technique is particularly relevant to underfunded pensions. The idea reflects the fact that the optimal asset allocation in general is sensitive to changes in the funded status of the plan. The objective is to increase the funded status by reducing surplus risk over time. Although a higher contribution rate may be necessary to align assets with liabilities, the volatility of contributions should decrease, providing more certainty for cash flow planning purposes and decreasing risk to plan participants. Eventually, GPLE would hope to achieve and maintain a sufficiently high funded ratio so that there would be minimal risk of requiring additional contributions or transferring pension risk to an annuity provider.

The importance of such characteristics as interest rate sensitivity (duration), inflation, and credit risk in constructing a liability-hedging asset portfolio suggests the relevance of risk-factor modeling in liability-relative approaches. A risk factor approach can be extended to the return-seeking portfolio in order to minimize unintentional overlap among common factors across both portfolios—for example, credit. Exploring these topics is outside the scope of the current chapter.

The next section addresses an approach to asset allocation related to liability relative in its focus on funding needs.

6.3. Goals Based

We use the hypothetical Lee family to present some thematic elements of a goals-based approach.

Investor Case Facts: The Lee Family

- *Name*: Ivy and Charles Lee
- *Narrative*: Ivy is a 54-year-old life sciences entrepreneur. Charles is 55 years old and employed as an orthopedic surgeon. They have two unmarried children aged 25 (Deborah) and 18 (David). Deborah has a daughter with physical limitations.
- *Financial assets and financial liabilities*: Portfolio of $25 million with $1 million in margin debt as well as residential real estate of $3 million with $1 million in mortgage debt.
- *Other assets and liabilities*:
  - Pre-retirement earnings are expected to total $16 million in present value terms (human capital).
  - David will soon begin studying at a four-year private university; the present value of the expected parental contribution is $250,000.
  - The Lees desire to give a gift to a local art museum in five years. In present value terms, the gift is valued at $750,000.
  - The Lees want to establish a trust for their granddaughter with a present value of $3 million to be funded at the death of Charles.
  - The present value of future consumption expenditures is estimated at $20 million.

EXHIBIT 11   Lee Family Economic Balance Sheet (in US$ millions) 31 December 20x6

Assets		Liabilities and Economic Net Worth	
Financial Assets		*Financial Liabilities*	
Investment portfolio	25	Margin debt	1
Real estate	3	Mortgage	1
Extended Assets		*Extended Liabilities*	
Human capital	16	David's education	0.25
		Museum gift	0.75
		Special needs trust	3
		PV of future consumption	20
		Economic Net Worth	
		Economic net worth (economic assets less economic liabilities)	18
Total	44		44

The financial liabilities shown are legal liabilities. The extended liabilities include funding needs that the Lees want to meet. The balance sheet includes an estimate of the present value of future consumption, which is sometimes called the "consumption liability." The amount shown reflects expected values over their life expectancy given their ages. If they live longer, consumption needs will exceed the $20 million in the case facts and erode the $18 million in equity. If their life span is shorter, $18 million plus whatever they do not consume of the $20 million in PV of future consumption becomes part of their estate. Note that for the Lees, the value of assets exceeds the value of liabilities, resulting in a positive economic net worth (a positive difference between economic assets and economic liabilities); this is analogous to a positive owners' equity on a company's financial balance sheet.

From Exhibit 11, we can identify four goals totaling $24 million in present value terms: a lifestyle goal (assessed as a need for $20 million in present value terms), an education goal ($0.25 million), a charitable goal ($0.75 million), and the special needs trust ($3 million).

The present value of expected future earnings (human capital) at $16 million is less than the lifestyle present value of $20 million, which means that some part of the investment portfolio must fund the Lees' standard of living. It is important to note that although the Lee family has $18 million of economic net worth, most of this comes from the $16 million extended asset of human capital. Specific investment portfolio assets have not yet been dedicated to specific goals.

Goals-based asset allocation builds on several insights from behavioral finance. The approach's characteristic use of sub-portfolios is grounded in the behavioral finance insight that investors tend to ignore money's fungibility[26] and assign specific dollars to specific uses—a phenomenon known as mental accounting. Goals-based asset allocation, as described here, systemizes the fruitful use of mental accounts. This approach may help investors embrace more-optimal portfolios (as defined in an asset-only or asset–liability framework) by adding higher risk assets—that, without context, might frighten the investor—to longer-term, aspirational sub-portfolios while adopting a more conservative allocation for sub-portfolios that address lifestyle preservation.

In Exhibit 11, the Lees' lifestyle goal is split into three components: a component called "lifestyle—minimum" intended to provide protection for the Lees' lifestyle in a disaster scenario, a component called "lifestyle—baseline" to address needs outside of worst cases, and a component called "lifestyle—aspirational" that reflects a desire for a chance at a markedly higher lifestyle. These sum to the present value of future consumption shown in the preceding Exhibit 11. Exhibit 12 describes these qualitatively; a numerical characterization could be very relevant for some advisers, however. By eliciting information on the Lees' perception of the goals' importance, the investment adviser might calibrate the required probabilities of achieving the goals quantitatively. For example, the three lifestyle goals might have 99%, 90%, and 50% assigned probabilities of success, respectively.

---

[26]"Fungibility" is the property of an asset that a quantity of it may be replaced by another equal quantity in the satisfaction of an obligation. Thus, any 5,000 Japanese yen note can be used to pay a yen obligation of that amount, and the notes can be said to be fungible.

EXHIBIT 12   Lee Family: Required Probability of Meeting Goals and Goal Time Horizons

Goal	Required **Probability** of **Achieving**	**Time Horizon**
Lifestyle—minimum	Extremely high	Short to distant
Lifestyle—baseline	Very high	Short to distant
Lifestyle—aspirational	Moderate	Distant
Education	Very high	Short
Trust	High	Long
Charitable	Moderate	Short

Because the Lees might delay or forego making a gift to the museum if it would affect the trust goal, the trust goal is more urgent for the Lees. Also note that although parts of the Lees' lifestyle goals run the full time horizon spectrum from short to distant, they also have significant current earnings and human capital (which transforms into earnings as time passes). This fact puts the investment portfolio's role in funding the lifestyle goal further into the future.

Goals-based approaches generally set the strategic asset allocation in a bottom-up fashion. The Lees' lifestyle goal might be addressed with three sub-portfolios, with the longest horizon sub-portfolio being less liquid and accepting more risk than the others. Although for the GPLE pension, no risk distinction was made among different parts of the pension liability vis-à-vis asset allocation, such distinctions are made in goals-based asset allocation.

What about the Lees' other goals? Separate sub-portfolios could be assigned to the special needs and charitable goals with asset allocations that reflect the associated time horizons and required probabilities of not attaining these goals. A later chapter on asset allocation in practice addresses implementation processes in detail.

Types of Goals

As goals-based asset allocation has advanced, various classification systems for goals have been proposed. Two of those classification systems are as follows.

Brunel (2012):

- *Personal goals*—to meet current lifestyle requirements and unanticipated financial needs
- *Dynastic goals*—to meet descendants' needs
- *Philanthropic goals*

Chhabra (2005):

- *Personal risk bucket*—to provide protection from a dramatic decrease in lifestyle (i.e., safe-haven investments)
- *Market risk bucket*—to ensure the current lifestyle can be maintained (allocations for average risk-adjusted market returns)
- *Aspirational risk bucket*—to increase wealth substantially (greater than average risk is accepted)

EXAMPLE 7   Goals-Based Asset Allocation

The Lees are presented with the following optimized asset allocations:

Asset Allocation	Cash	Global Bonds	Global Equities	Diversifying Strategies
A	40%	50%	10%	0%
B	10%	30%	45%	15%

Assume that a portfolio of 70% global equities and 30% bonds reflects an appropriate balance of expected return and risk for the Lees with respect to a 10-year time horizon for most moderately important goals. Based on the information given:

1. What goal(s) may be addressed by Allocation A?
2. What goal(s) may be addressed by Allocation B?

Because of her industry connections in the life sciences, Ivy Lee is given the opportunity to be an early-stage venture capital investor in what she assesses is a very promising technology.

3. What insights does goals-based asset allocation offer on this opportunity?

Solution to 1: Allocation A stresses liquidity and stability. It may be appropriate to meet short-term lifestyle and education goals.

Solution to 2: Allocation B has a greater growth emphasis, although it is somewhat conservative in relation to a 70/30 equity/bond baseline. It may be appropriate for funding the trust because of the goal's long time horizon and the Lees' desire for a high probability of achieving it.

Solution to 3: Early-stage venture capital investments are both risky and illiquid; therefore, they belong in the longer-term and more risk-tolerant sub-portfolios. Ivy's decision about how much money she can commit should relate to how much excess capital remains after addressing goals that have a higher priority associated with them. Note that economic balance sheet thinking would stress that the life sciences opportunity is not particularly diversifying to her human capital.

Discount Rates and Longevity Risk

Although calculation of assets needed for sub-portfolios is outside the scope of this chapter, certain themes can be indicated. Consider a retiree with a life expectancy of 20 years. The retiree has two goals:

- To maintain his current lifestyle upon retirement. This goal has a high required probability of achievement that is evaluated at 95%.

- To gift $1 million to a university in five years. This is viewed as a "desire" rather than a "need" and has a required probability evaluated at 75%.

Suppose that the investor's adviser specifies sub-portfolios as follows:

- for the first decade of lifestyle spending, a 3% expected return;
- for the second decade of lifestyle spending, a 4.6% expected return; and
- for the planned gift to the university, a 5.4% expected return.

Based on an estimate of annual consumption needs and the amount of the gift and given expected returns for the assigned sub-portfolios, the assets to be assigned to each sub-portfolio could be calculated by discounting amounts back to the present using their expected returns. However, this approach does not reflect the asset owner's required probability of achieving a goal. The higher the probability requirement for a future cash need, the greater the amount of assets needed in relation to it. Because of the inverse relation between present value and the discount rate, to reflect a 95% required probability, for example, the discount rates could be set at a lower level so that more assets are assigned to the sub-portfolio, increasing the probability of achieving the goal to the required level of 95% level.

Another consideration in determining the amount needed for future consumption is longevity risk. Life expectancies are median (50th percentile) outcomes. The retiree may outlive his life expectancy. To address longevity risk, the calculation of the present value of liabilities might use a longer life expectancy, such as a 35-year life expectancy instead of his actuarial 20-year expectation. Another approach is to transfer the risk to an insurer by purchasing an annuity that begins in 20 years and makes payments to the retiree for as long as he lives. Longevity risk and this kind of deferred annuity (sometimes called a "longevity annuity") are discussed in another curriculum chapter on risk management.[27]

There are some drawbacks to the goals-based approach to asset allocation. One is that the sub-portfolios add complexity. Another is that goals may be ambiguous or may change over time. Goals-based approaches to asset allocation raise the question of how sub-portfolios coordinate to constitute an efficient whole. The subject will be taken up in a later chapter, but the general finding is that the amount of sub-optimality is small.[28]

7. IMPLEMENTATION CHOICES

Having established the strategic asset allocation policy, the asset owner must address additional strategic considerations before moving to implementation. One of these is the passive/active choice.

There are two dimensions of passive/active choices. One dimension relates to the management of the strategic asset allocation itself—for example, whether to deviate from it tactically or not. The second dimension relates to passive and active implementation choices

---

[27]See Blanchett et al. (2016) for the management of longevity risk. Milevsky (2016) is a further reference.
[28]This is addressed technically in Das et al. (2010). See also Brunel (2015).

in investing the allocation to a given asset class. Each of these are covered in the sections that follow.

In an advisory role, asset managers have an unequivocal responsibility to make implementation and asset selection choices that are initially, and on an ongoing basis, suitable for the client.[29]

7.1. Passive/Active Management of Asset Class Weights

Tactical asset allocation (TAA) involves deliberate short-term deviations from the strategic asset allocation. Whereas the strategic asset allocation incorporates an investor's long-term, equilibrium market expectations, tactical asset allocation involves short-term tilts away from the strategic asset mix that reflect short-term views—for example, to exploit perceived deviations from equilibrium.

Tactical asset allocation is active management at the asset class level because it involves intentional deviations from the strategic asset mix to exploit perceived opportunities in capital markets to improve the portfolio's risk–return trade-off. TAA mandates are often specified to keep deviations from the strategic asset allocation within rebalancing ranges or within risk budgets. Tactical asset allocation decisions might be responsive to price momentum, perceived asset class valuation, or the particular stage of the business cycle. A strategy incorporating deviations from the strategic asset allocation that are motivated by longer-term valuation signals or economic views is sometimes distinguished as **dynamic asset allocation** (DAA).

Tactical asset allocation may be limited to tactical changes in domestic stock–bond or stock–bond–cash allocations or may be a more comprehensive multi-asset approach, as in a global tactical asset allocation (GTAA) model. Tactical asset allocation inherently involves market timing as it involves buying and selling in anticipation of short-term changes in market direction; however, TAA usually involves smaller allocation tilts than an invested-or-not-invested market timing strategy.

Tactical asset allocation is a source of risk when calibrated against the strategic asset mix. An informed approach to tactical asset allocation recognizes the trade-off of any potential outperformance against this tracking error. Key barriers to successful tactical asset allocation are monitoring and trading costs. For some investors, higher short-term capital gains taxes will prove a significant obstacle because taxes are an additional trading cost. A program of tactical asset allocation must be evaluated through a cost–benefit lens. The relevant cost comparisons include the expected costs of simply following a rebalancing policy (without deliberate tactical deviations).

7.2. Passive/Active Management of Allocations to Asset Classes

In addition to active and passive decisions about the asset class mix, there are active and passive decisions about how to implement the individual allocations within asset classes. An allocation can be managed passively or actively or incorporate both active and passive sub-allocations. For investors who delegate asset management to external firms, these decisions would come under the heading of manager structure,[30] which includes decisions about how capital and

---

[29]See Standard III (C) in the Standards of Practice Handbook (CFA Institute 2014).

[30]Manager structure is defined by the number of managers, types of managers, as well as which managers are selected.

active risk are allocated to points on the passive/active spectrum and to individual external managers selected to manage the investor's assets.[31]

With a **passive management** approach, portfolio composition does not react to changes in the investor's capital market expectations or to information on or insights into individual investments. (The word *passive* means *not reacting*.) For example, a portfolio constructed to track the returns of an index of European equities might add or drop a holding in response to a change in the index composition but not in response to changes in the manager's expectations concerning the security's investment value; the market's expectations reflected in market values and index weights are taken as is. Indexing is a common passive approach to investing. (Another example would be buying and holding a fixed portfolio of bonds to maturity.)

In contrast, a portfolio manager for an active management strategy will respond to changing capital market expectations or to investment insights resulting in changes to portfolio composition. The objective of active management is to achieve, after expenses, positive excess risk-adjusted returns relative to a passive benchmark.

The range of implementation choices can be practically viewed as falling along a passive/active spectrum because some strategies use both passive and active elements. In financial theory, the pure model of a passive approach is indexing to a broad market-cap-weighted index of risky assets—in particular, the global market portfolio. This portfolio sums all investments in index components and is macro-consistent in the sense that all investors could hold it, and it is furthermore self-rebalancing to the extent it is based on market-value-weighted indices. A buy-and-hold investment as a proxy for the global market portfolio would represent a theoretical endpoint on the passive/active spectrum. However, consider an investor who indexes an equity allocation to a broad-based value equity style index. The investment could be said to reflect an active decision in tilting an allocation toward value but be passive in implementation because it involves indexing. An even more active approach would be investing the equity allocation with managers who have a value investing approach and attempt to enhance returns through security selection. Those managers would show positive tracking risk relative to the value index in general. Unconstrained active investment would be one that is "go anywhere" or not managed with consideration of any traditional asset class benchmark (i.e., "benchmark agnostic"). The degree of active management has traditionally been quantified by tracking risk and, from a different perspective, by active share.

Indexing is generally the lowest-cost approach to investing. Indexing involves some level of transaction costs because, as securities move in and out of the index, the portfolio holdings must adjust to remain in alignment with the index. Although indexing to a market-cap-weighted index is self-rebalancing, tracking an index based on other weighting schemes requires ongoing transactions to ensure the portfolio remains in alignment with index weights. An example is tracking an equally weighted index: As changes in market prices affect the relative weights of securities in the portfolio over time, the portfolio will need to be rebalanced to restore equal weights. Portfolios tracking fixed-income indices also incur ongoing transaction costs as holdings mature, default, or are called away by their issuers.

Exhibit 13 diagrams the passive/active choice as a continuum rather than binary (0 or 1) characteristic. Tracking risk and active share are widely known quantitative measures of the

---

[31]See, for example, Waring, Whitney, Pirone, and Castille (2000).

degree of active management that capture different aspects of it. Each measure is shown as tending to increase from left to right on the spectrum; however, they do not increase (or decrease) in lockstep with each other, in general.

EXHIBIT 13   Passive/Active Spectrum

	Use of information on asset classes, investment	
MOST PASSIVE	factors, and individual investments	MOST ACTIVE
(indexing to	increases is often quantified by	(unconstrained
market weights)	→ Increasing tracking risk relative to benchmark →	mandates)
	→ Increasing active share relative to benchmark →	

Asset class allocations may be managed with different approaches on the spectrum. For example, developed market equities might be implemented purely passively, whereas emerging market bonds might be invested with an unconstrained, index-agnostic approach.

Factors that influence asset owners' decisions on where to invest on the passive/active spectrum include the following:

- *Available investments.* For example, the availability of an investable and representative index as the basis for indexing.
- *Scalability of active strategies being considered.* The prospective value added by an active strategy may begin to decline at some level of invested assets. In addition, participation in it may not be available below some asset level, a consideration for small investors.
- *The feasibility of investing passively while incorporating client-specific constraints.* For example, an investor's particular ESG investing criteria may not align with existing index products.
- *Beliefs concerning market informational efficiency.* A strong belief in market efficiency for the asset class(es) under consideration would orient the investor away from active management.
- *The trade-off of expected incremental benefits relative to incremental costs and risks of active choices.* Costs of active management include investment management costs, trading costs, and turnover-induced taxes; such costs would have to be judged relative to the lower costs of index alternatives, which vary by asset class.
- *Tax status.* Holding other variables constant, taxable investors would tend to have higher hurdles to profitable active management than tax-exempt investors.[32] For taxable investors who want to hold both passive and active investments, active investments would be held, in general, in available tax-advantaged accounts.

The curriculum chapters on equity, fixed-income, and alternative investments will explore many strategies and the nature of any active decisions involved. Investors do need to understand the nature of the active decisions involved in implementing their strategic asset allocations and their appropriateness given the factors described. Exhibit 14 shows qualitatively (rather than precisely) some choices that investors may consider for equity and fixed-income allocations. In the exhibit, non-cap-weighted indexing includes such approaches as equal weighting and quantitative rules-based indexing approaches (discussed further in the equity chapters).[33]

---

[32]See Jeffrey and Arnott (1993).

[33]Podkaminer (2015) provides a survey.

EXHIBIT 14   Placement on the Passive/Active Spectrum: Examples of Possible Choices

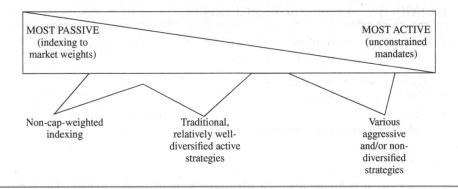

EXAMPLE 8   Implementation Choices (1)

1. Describe two kinds of passive/active choices faced by investors related to asset allocation.
2. An equity index is described as "a rules-based, transparent index designed to provide investors with an efficient way to gain exposure to large-cap and small-cap stocks with low total return variability." Compared with the market-cap weighting of the parent index (with the same component securities), the weights in the low-volatility index are proportional to the inverse of return volatility, so that the highest-volatility security receives the lowest weight. Describe the active and passive aspects of a decision to invest an allocation to equities in ETFs tracking such indices.
3. Describe how investing in a GDP-weighted global bond index involves both active and passive choices.

Solution to 1: One choice relates to whether to allow active deviations from the strategic asset allocation. Tactical asset allocation and dynamic asset allocation are examples of active management of asset allocations. A second set of choices relates to where to invest allocations to asset classes along the passive/active spectrum.

Solution to 2: The active element is the decision, relative to the parent index, to overweight securities with low volatility and underweight securities with high volatility. This management of risk is distinct from reducing portfolio volatility by combining a market-cap-weighted index with a risk-free asset proxy because it implies a belief in some risk–return advantage to favoring low-volatility equities on an individual security basis. The passive element is a transparent rules-based implementation of the weighting scheme based on inverse volatilities.

Solution to 3: The passive choice is represented by the overall selection of the universe of global bonds; however, the active choice is represented by the weighting scheme, which is to use GDP rather than capital market weights. This is a tilt toward the real economy and away from fixed-income market values.

EXAMPLE 9   Implementation Choices (2)

Describe characteristic(s) of each of the following investors that are likely to influence the decision to invest passively or actively.

1. Caflandia sovereign wealth fund
2. GPLE corporate pension
3. The Lee family
4. Auldberg University Endowment

Solution:

1. For a large investor like the Caflandia sovereign wealth fund (CAF$40 billion), the scalability of active strategies that it may wish to employ may be a consideration. If only a small percentage of portfolio assets can be invested effectively in an active strategy, for example, the potential value added for the overall portfolio may not justify the inherent costs and management time. Although the equities and fixed-income allocations could be invested using passive approaches, investments in the diversifying strategies category are commonly active.
2. The executives responsible for the GPLE corporate pension also have other, non-investment responsibilities. This is a factor favoring a more passive approach; however, choosing an outsourced chief investment officer or delegated fiduciary consultant to manage active manager selection could facilitate greater use of active investment.
3. The fact that the Lees are taxable investors is a factor generally in favor of passive management for assets not held in tax-advantaged accounts. Active management involves turnover, which gives rise to taxes.
4. According to the vignette in **Example 3**, the Auldberg University Endowment has substantial staff resources in equities, fixed income, and real estate. This fact suggests that passive/active decisions are relatively unconstrained by internal resources. By itself, it does not favor passive or active, but it is a factor that allows active choices to be given full consideration.

7.3. Risk Budgeting Perspectives in Asset Allocation and Implementation

Risk budgeting addresses the questions of which types of risks to take and how much of each to take. Risk budgeting provides another view of asset allocation—through a risk lens. Depending on the focus, the risk may be quantified in various ways. For example, a concern for volatility can be quantified as variance or standard deviation of returns, and a concern for tail risk can be quantified as VaR or drawdown. Risk budgets (budgets for risk taking) can be stated in absolute or in relative terms and in money or percent terms. For example, it is possible to state an overall risk budget for a portfolio in terms of volatility of returns, which would be an example of an absolute risk budget stated in percent terms (for example, 20% for portfolio return volatility). Risk budgeting is a tool that may be useful in a variety of contexts and asset allocation approaches.

Some investors may approach asset allocation with an exclusive focus on risk. A risk budgeting approach to asset allocation has been defined as an approach in which the investor specifies how risk (quantified by some measure, such as volatility) is to be distributed across assets in the portfolio, without consideration of the assets' expected returns.[34] An example is aiming for equal expected risk contributions to overall portfolio volatility from all included asset classes as an approach to diversification, which is a risk parity (or equal risk contribution) approach. A subsequent chapter in asset allocation addresses this in greater detail.

More directly related to the choice of passive/active implementation are active risk budgets and active risk budgeting. **Active risk budgeting** addresses the question of how much benchmark-relative risk an investor is willing to take in seeking to outperform a benchmark. This approach is risk budgeting stated in benchmark-relative terms. In parallel to the two dimensions of the passive/active decision outlined previously are two levels of active risk budgeting, which can be distinguished as follows:

- At the level of the overall asset allocation, active risk can be defined relative to the strategic asset allocation benchmark. This benchmark may be the strategic asset allocation weights applied to specified (often, broad-based market-cap-weighted) indices.
- At the level of individual asset classes, active risk can be defined relative to the asset class benchmark.

Active risk budgeting at the level of overall asset allocation would be relevant to tactical asset allocation. Active risk budgeting at the level of each asset class is relevant to how the allocation to those asset classes is invested. For example, it can take the form of expected-alpha versus tracking-error optimization in a manner similar to classic mean–variance optimization. If investment factor risks are the investor's focus, risk budgeting can be adapted to have a focus on allocating factor risk exposures instead. Later chapters revisit risk budgeting in investing in further detail.

8. REBALANCING: STRATEGIC CONSIDERATIONS

Rebalancing is the discipline of adjusting portfolio weights to more closely align with the strategic asset allocation. Rebalancing is a key part of the monitoring and feedback step of the portfolio construction, monitoring, and revision process. An investor's rebalancing policy is generally documented in the IPS.

Even in the absence of changing investor circumstances, a revised economic outlook, or tactical asset allocation views, normal changes in asset prices cause the portfolio asset mix to deviate from target weights. Industry practice defines "rebalancing" as portfolio adjustments triggered by such price changes. Other portfolio adjustments, even systematic ones, are not rebalancing.

Ordinary price changes cause the assets with a high forecast return to grow faster than the portfolio as a whole. Because high-return assets are typically also higher risk, in the absence of rebalancing, overall portfolio risk rises. The mix of risks within the portfolio becomes more concentrated as well. Systematic rebalancing maintains the original strategic risk exposures. The discipline of rebalancing serves to control portfolio risks that have become different from what the investor originally intended.

Consider the example from the internet bubble (1995–2001) in Exhibit 15. The example assumes a 60/40 stock/bond portfolio, in which stocks are represented by the large-cap US growth stocks that characterized the internet bubble. In Panel B, the left-hand scale

---

[34]See Roncalli (2013).

and upper two lines show month-by-month total portfolio *values* with and without monthly rebalancing ("wealth rebalanced" and "wealth unrebalanced," respectively). The right-hand scale and lower two lines show month-by-month portfolio *risk* as represented by the 5th percentile drawdown (in a VaR model) with and without monthly rebalancing ("risk rebalanced" and "risk unrebalanced," respectively).

EXHIBIT 15   Rebalancing

Panel A. Asset Mix

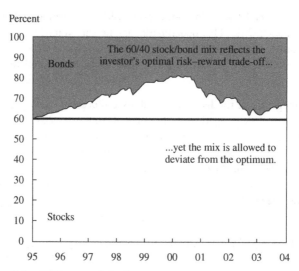

Panel B. Portfolio Value and Risk

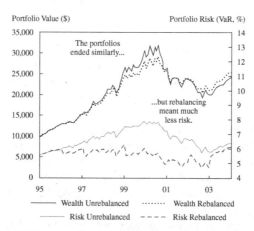

Note: The data are a 60/40 mix of the S&P 500 Growth Index and the Barclays Capital Aggregate Bond Index.

Panel A shows that, without rebalancing, the asset mix deviates dramatically from the target. Panel B shows that although the portfolios' values ended similarly (the upper two lines), disciplined rebalancing meant more-stable risks (illustrated by the lower two lines).

This risk perspective is important. Taken to the extreme, *never rebalancing* allows the high-return (and presumably higher-risk) assets to grow and dominate the portfolio. Portfolio risk rises and concentrates. Taken even further, such a philosophy of never rebalancing may suggest it would have been simpler to have invested only in the highest-expected-return asset class back when the asset mix decision was made. Not rebalancing could negate an intended level of diversification.

Because rebalancing is countercyclical, it is fundamentally a contrarian investment approach.[35] Behavioral finance tells us that such contrarianism will be uncomfortable; no one likes to sell the most recently best-performing part of the portfolio to buy the worst. Thus, rebalancing is a *discipline* of adjusting the portfolio to better align with the strategic asset allocation in both connotations of discipline—the sense of a typical practice and the sense of a strengthening regime.

8.1. A Framework for Rebalancing

The actual mechanics of rebalancing are more complex than they first appear. A number of questions arise: How often should the portfolio be rebalanced? What levels of imbalance are worth tolerating? Should the portfolio be rebalanced to the edge of the policy range or to some other point? These non-trivial questions represent the key strategic decisions in rebalancing.

The simplest approach to rebalancing is **calendar rebalancing**, which involves rebalancing a portfolio to target weights on a periodic basis—for example, monthly, quarterly, semiannually, or annually. The choice of rebalancing frequency may be linked to the schedule of portfolio reviews. Although simple, rebalancing points are arbitrary and have other disadvantages.

Percent-range rebalancing permits tighter control of the asset mix compared with calendar rebalancing. Percent-range approach involves setting rebalancing thresholds or trigger points, stated as a percentage of the portfolio's value, around target values. For example, if the target allocation to an asset class is 50% of portfolio value, **trigger points** at 45% and 55% of portfolio value define a 10 percentage point **rebalancing range** (or corridor) for the value of that asset class. The rebalancing range creates a no-trade region. The portfolio is rebalanced when an asset class's weight first passes through one of its trigger points. Focusing on percent-range rebalancing, the following questions are relevant:

- How frequently is the portfolio valued?
- What size deviation triggers rebalancing?
- Is the deviation from the target allocation fully or partially corrected?

How frequently is the portfolio valued? The percent-range discipline requires monitoring portfolio values for breaches of a trigger point at an agreed-on frequency; the more frequent the monitoring, the greater the precision in implementation. Such monitoring may be scheduled

---

[35]A quantitative interpretation of rebalancing, given by Ang (2014), is that the return to rebalancing is selling out of the money puts and calls.

daily, weekly, monthly, quarterly, or annually. A number of considerations—including governance resources and asset custodian resources—can affect valuation frequency. For many investors, monthly or quarterly evaluation efficiently balances the costs and benefits of rebalancing.

What size deviation triggers rebalancing? Trigger points take into account such factors as traditional practice, transaction costs, asset class volatility, volatility of the balance of the portfolio, correlation of the asset class with the balance of the portfolio, and risk tolerance.[36]

Before the rise of modern multi-asset portfolios, the stock/bond split broadly characterized the asset allocation and a traditional ±x% rebalancing band was common. These fixed ranges would apply no matter the size or volatility of the allocation target. For example, both a 40% domestic equity allocation and a 15% real asset allocation might have ±5% rebalancing ranges. Alternatively, proportional bands reflect the size of the target weight. For example, a 60% target asset class might have a ±6% band, whereas a 5% allocation would have a ±0.5% band. Proportional bands might also be set to reflect the relative volatility of the asset classes. A final approach is the use of cost–benefit analysis to set ranges.

Is the deviation from the target allocation fully or partially corrected? Once the portfolio is evaluated and an unacceptably large deviation found, the investor must determine rebalancing trade size, as well as the timeline for implementing the rebalancing. In practice, three main approaches are used: rebalance back to target weights, rebalance to range edge, or rebalance halfway between the range-edge trigger point and the target weight.

8.2. Strategic Considerations in Rebalancing

The four-part rebalancing framework just described highlights important questions to address in setting rebalancing policy. Strategic considerations generally include the following, all else being equal:

- Higher transaction costs for an asset class imply wider rebalancing ranges.
- More risk-averse investors will have tighter rebalancing ranges.
- Less correlated assets also have tighter rebalancing ranges.
- Beliefs in momentum favor wider rebalancing ranges, whereas mean reversion encourages tighter ranges.
- Illiquid investments complicate rebalancing.
- Derivatives create the possibility of synthetic rebalancing.
- Taxes, which are a cost, discourage rebalancing and encourage asymmetric and wider rebalancing ranges.

Asset class volatility is also a consideration in the size of rebalancing ranges. A cost–benefit approach to rebalancing sets ranges, taking transaction costs, risk aversion, asset class risks, and asset class correlations into consideration. For example, an asset that is more highly correlated with the rest of the portfolio than another would merit a wider rebalancing range, all else equal, because it would be closer to being a substitute for the balance of the portfolio; thus, larger deviations would have less impact on portfolio risk.

---

[36]See Masters (2003) for details on these factors apart from traditional factors.

EXAMPLE 10   Different Rebalancing Ranges

The table shows a simple four-asset strategic mix along with rebalancing ranges created under different approaches. The width of the rebalancing range under the proportional range approach is 0.20 of the strategic target.

State a reason that could explain why the international equity range is wider than the domestic equity range using the cost–benefit approach.

Asset Class	Strategic Target	Fixed Width Ranges	Proportional Ranges (±1,000 bps)	Cost–Benefit Ranges
Domestic equity	40%	35%–45%	36%–44%	35%–45%
International equity	25%	20%–30%	22½%–27½%	19%–31%
Emerging markets	15%	10%–20%	13½%–16½%	12%–18%
Fixed income	20%	15%–25%	18%–22%	19%–21%

Solution: Higher transaction costs for international equity compared with domestic equity could explain the wider range for international equity compared with domestic equity under the cost–benefit approach. Another potential explanation relates to the possibility that international equity has a higher correlation with the balance of the portfolio (i.e., the portfolio excluding international equity) than does domestic equity (i.e., with the portfolio excluding domestic equity). If that is the case then, all else being equal, a wider band would be justified for international equity.

Investors' perspectives on capital markets can affect their approach to rebalancing. A belief in momentum and trend following, for example, encourages wider rebalancing ranges. In contrast, a belief in mean reversion encourages stricter adherence to rebalancing, including tighter ranges.

Illiquid assets complicate rebalancing. Relatively illiquid investments, such as hedge funds, private equity, or direct real estate, cannot be readily traded without substantial trading costs and/or delays. Accordingly, illiquid investments are commonly assigned wide rebalancing ranges. However, rebalancing of an illiquid asset may be affected indirectly when a highly correlated liquid asset can be traded or when exposure can be adjusted by means of positions in derivatives. For example, public equity could be reduced to offset an overweight in private equity. Rebalancing by means of highly correlated liquid assets and derivatives, however, involves some imprecision and basis risk.

This insight about liquidity is an instance where thinking ahead about rebalancing can affect the strategic asset allocation. It is one reason that allocations to illiquid assets are often smaller than if trading were possible.

Factor-based asset allocation, liability-relative investing, and goals-based investing, each a valid approach to asset allocation, can give rise to different rebalancing considerations. Factor exposures and liability hedges require monitoring (and rebalancing) the factors weights and surplus duration in addition to asset class weights. Goals-based investing in private wealth management may require both asset class rebalancing and moving funds between different goal sub-portfolios.

Tax considerations also complicate rebalancing. Rebalancing typically realizes capital gains and losses, which are taxable events in many jurisdictions. For private wealth managers, any rebalancing benefit must be compared with the tax cost. Taxes, as a cost, are much larger than other transaction costs, which often leads to wider rebalancing ranges in taxable portfolios than in tax-exempt portfolios. Because loss harvesting generates tax savings and realizing gains triggers taxes, rebalancing ranges in taxable accounts may also be asymmetric. (For example, a 25% target asset class might have an allowable range of 24%–28%, which is −1% to +3%.)

Modern cost–benefit approaches to rebalancing suggest considering derivatives as a rebalancing tool. Derivatives can often be used to rebalance synthetically at much lower transaction costs than the costs of using the underlying stocks and bonds. Using a derivatives overlay also avoids disrupting the underlying separate accounts in a multi-manager implementation of the strategic asset allocation. Tax considerations are also relevant; it may be more cost effective to reduce an exposure using a derivatives overlay than to sell the underlying asset and incur the capital gains tax liability. Lastly, trading a few derivatives may be quicker and easier than hundreds of underlying securities. Of course, using derivatives may require a higher level of risk oversight, but then risk control is the main rationale for rebalancing.

Estimates of the benefits of rebalancing vary. Many portfolios are statistically indistinguishable from each other, suggesting that much rebalancing is unnecessary. In contrast, Willenbrock (2011) demonstrates that even zero-return assets can, in theory, generate positive returns through rebalancing, which is a demonstrable (and surprising) benefit. Whatever the return estimate for the value added from rebalancing, the key takeaway is that rebalancing is chiefly about risk control, not return enhancement.

9. SUMMARY

This chapter has introduced the subject of asset allocation. Among the points made are the following:

- Effective investment governance ensures that decisions are made by individuals or groups with the necessary skills and capacity and involves articulating the long- and short-term objectives of the investment program; effectively allocating decision rights and responsibilities among the functional units in the governance hierarchy; taking account of their knowledge, capacity, time, and position on the governance hierarchy; specifying processes for developing and approving the investment policy statement, which will govern the day-to-day operation of the investment program; specifying processes for developing and approving the program's strategic asset allocation; establishing a reporting framework to monitor the program's progress toward the agreed-on goals and objectives; and periodically undertaking a governance audit.
- The economic balance sheet includes non-financial assets and liabilities that can be relevant for choosing the best asset allocation for an investor's financial portfolio.
- The investment objectives of asset-only asset allocation approaches focus on the asset side of the economic balance sheet; approaches with a liability-relative orientation focus on funding liabilities; and goals-based approaches focus on achieving financial goals.
- The risk concepts relevant to asset-only asset allocation approaches focus on asset risk; those of liability-relative asset allocation focus on risk in relation to paying liabilities; and a goals-based approach focuses on the probabilities of not achieving financial goals.
- Asset classes are the traditional units of analysis in asset allocation and reflect systematic risks with varying degrees of overlap.
- Assets within an asset class should be relatively homogeneous; asset classes should be mutually exclusive; asset classes should be diversifying; asset classes as a group should make

up a preponderance of the world's investable wealth; asset classes selected for investment should have the capacity to absorb a meaningful proportion of an investor's portfolio.

- Risk factors are associated with non-diversifiable (i.e., systematic) risk and are associated with an expected return premium. The price of an asset and/or asset class may reflect more than one risk factor, and complicated spread positions may be necessary to identify and isolate particular risk factors. Their use as units of analysis in asset allocation is driven by considerations of controlling systematic risk exposures.
- The global market portfolio represents a highly diversified asset allocation that can serve as a baseline asset allocation in an asset-only approach.
- There are two dimensions of passive/active choices. One dimension relates to the management of the strategic asset allocation itself—for example, whether to deviate from it tactically or not. The second dimension relates to passive and active implementation choices in investing the allocation to a given asset class. Tactical and dynamic asset allocation relate to the first dimension; active and passive choices for implementing allocations to asset classes relate to the second dimension.
- Risk budgeting addresses the question of which types of risks to take and how much of each to take. Active risk budgeting addresses the question of how much benchmark-relative risk an investor is willing to take. At the level of the overall asset allocation, active risk can be defined relative to the strategic asset allocation benchmark. At the level of individual asset classes, active risk can be defined relative to the benchmark proxy.
- Rebalancing is the discipline of adjusting portfolio weights to more closely align with the strategic asset allocation. Rebalancing approaches include calendar-based and range-based rebalancing. Calendar-based rebalancing rebalances the portfolio to target weights on a periodic basis. Range-based rebalancing sets rebalancing thresholds or trigger points around target weights. The ranges may be fixed width, percentage based, or volatility based. Range-based rebalancing permits tighter control of the asset mix compared with calendar rebalancing.
- Strategic considerations in rebalancing include transaction costs, risk aversion, correlations among asset classes, volatility, and beliefs concerning momentum, taxation, and asset class liquidity.

REFERENCES

Ang, Andrew. 2014. *Asset Management: A Systematic Approach to Factor Investing*. New York: Oxford University Press.

Blanchett, David M., and Philip U. Straehl. 2015. "No Portfolio is an Island." *Financial Analysts Journal*, vol. 71, no. 3 (May/June): 15–33.

Blanchett, David M., and Philip U. Straehl. 2017. "Portfolio Implications of Job-Specific Human Capital Risk." *Journal of Asset Management*, vol. 18, no. 1: 1–15.

Blanchett, David M., David M. Cordell, Michael S. Finke, and Thomas Idzorek. 2016. "Risk Management for Individuals." CFA Institute.

Brunel, Jean L.P. 2012. "Goals-Based Wealth Management in Practice." *Conference Proceedings Quarterly*, vol. 29, no. 1 (March): 57–65.

Brunel, Jean L.P. 2015. *Goals-Based Wealth Management: An Integrated and Practical Approach to Changing the Structure of Wealth Advisory Practices*. Hoboken, NJ: John Wiley.

Burger, John D., Francis E. Warnock, and Veronica Cacdac Warnock. 2012. "Emerging Local Currency Bond Markets." *Financial Analysts Journal*, vol. 68, no. 4 (July/August): 73–93.

Chhabra, Ashvin. 2005. "Beyond Markowitz: A Comprehensive Wealth Allocation Framework for Individual Investors." *Journal of Wealth Management*, vol. 7, no. 4 (Spring): 8–34.

Collie, Bob, and James A Gannon., 2009. "Liability-Responsive Asset Allocation: A Dynamic Approach to Pension Plan Management." Russell Investments Insights (April).

Das, Sanjiv, Harry Markowitz, Jonathan Scheid, and Meir Statman. 2010. "Portfolio Optimization with Mental Accounts." *Journal of Financial and Quantitative Analysis*, vol. 45, no. 2 (April): 311–334.

Fraser, Steve P., and William W. Jennings. 2006. "Behavioral Asset Allocation for Foundations and Endowments." *Journal of Wealth Management*, vol. 9, no. 3 (Winter): 38–50.

Greer, Robert J. 1997. "What is an Asset Class, Anyway?" *Journal of Portfolio Management*, vol. 23, no. 2 (Winter): 86–91.

Ibbotson, Roger G., and Paul D., Kaplan. 2000. "Does Asset Allocation Policy Explain 40, 90, or 100 Percent of Performance?" *Financial Analysts Journal*, vol. 56, no. 1 (January/February): 26–33.

Ibbotson, Roger G., Moshe A. Milevsky, Peng Chen, and Kevin X. Zhu. 2007. *Lifetime Financial Advice: Human Capital, Asset Allocation, and Insurance.* Charlottesville, VA: CFA Institute Research Foundation.

Idzorek, Thomas M., and Maciej Kowara. 2013. "Factor-Based Asset Allocation versus Asset-Class-Based Asset Allocation." *Financial Analysts Journal*, vol. 69, no. 3 (May/June): 19–29.

Idzorek, Thomas, Jeremy Stempien, and Nathan Voris. 2013. "Bait and Switch: Glide Path Instability." *Journal of Investing*, vol. 22, no. 1 (Spring): 74–82.

Jeffrey, Robert H., and Robert D. Arnott. 1993. "Is Your Alpha Big Enough to Cover Its Taxes?" *Journal of Portfolio Management*, vol. 19, no. 3 (Spring): 15–25.

Kozhemiakin, Alexander. 2011. "Emerging Markets Local Currency Debt: Capitalizing on Improved Sovereign Fundamentals." BNY Mellon Asset Management.

Kritzman, Mark. 1999. "Toward Defining an Asset Class." *Journal of Alternative Investments*, vol. 2, no. 1 (Summer): 79–82.

Masters, Seth J. 2003. "Rebalancing." *Journal of Portfolio Management*, vol. 29, no. 3 (Spring): 52–57.

Milevsky, Moshe A. 2016. "It's Time to Retire Ruin (Probabilities)." *Financial Analysts Journal*, vol. 72, no. 2 (March/April): 8–12.

Perry, William. 2011. "The Case For Emerging Market Corporates." *Journal of Indexes*, vol. 14, no. 5 (September/October): 10–17.

Podkaminer, Eugene. 2013. "Risk Factors as Building Blocks for Portfolio Diversification: The Chemistry of Asset Allocation." CFA Institute Investment Risk and Performance papers (January).

Podkaminer, Eugene. 2015. "The Education of Beta: Can Alternative Indexes Make Your Portfolio Smarter?" *Journal of Investing*, vol. 24, no. 2 (Summer): 7–34.

Pompian, Michael M. 2011a. "The Behavioral Biases of Individuals." CFA Institute.

Pompian, Michael M. 2011b. "The Behavioral Finance Perspective." CFA Institute.

Pompian, Michael, Colin McLean, and Alistair Byrne. 2011. "Behavioral Finance and Investment Processes." CFA Institute.

Roncalli, Thierry. 2013. *Introduction to Risk Parity and Budgeting.* New York: CRC Press.

Rudd, Andrew, and Laurence B. Siegel. 2013. "Using an Economic Balance Sheet for Financial Planning." *Journal of Wealth Management*, vol. 16, no. 2 (Fall): 15–23.

Sharpe, William F. 1991. "The Arithmetic of Active Management." *Financial Analysts Journal*, vol. 47, no. 1: 7–9.

Shefrin, H., and M. Statman. 2000. "Behavioral Portfolio Theory." *Journal of Financial and Quantitative Analysis*, vol. 35, no. 2 (June): 127–151.

CFA Institute. *Standards of Practice Handbook*, 11th edition. 2014. CFA Institute.

Swinkels, Laurens. 2012. "Emerging Market Inflation-Linked Bonds." *Financial Analysts Journal*, vol. 68, no. 5 (September/October): 38–56.

Waring, M. Barton, Duane Whitney, John Pirone, and Charles Castille. 2000. "Optimizing Manager Structure and Budgeting Manager Risk." *Journal of Portfolio Management*, vol. 26, no. 3 (Spring): 90–104.

Willenbrock, Scott. 2011. "Diversification Return, Portfolio Rebalancing, and the Commodity Return Puzzle." *Financial Analysts Journal*, vol. 67, no. 4 (July/August): 42–49.

Xiong, James X., Roger G. Ibbotson, Thomas M. Idzorek, and Peng Chen. 2010. "The Equal Importance of Asset Allocation and Active Management." *Financial Analysts Journal*, vol. 66, no. 2 (March/April): 22–30.

PRACTICE PROBLEMS

The following information relates to Questions 1–8

Meg and Cramer Law, a married couple aged 42 and 44, respectively, are meeting with their new investment adviser, Daniel Raye. The Laws have worked their entire careers at Whorton Solutions (WS), a multinational technology company. The Laws have two teenage children who will soon begin college.

Raye reviews the Laws' current financial position. The Laws have an investment portfolio consisting of $800,000 in equities and $450,000 in fixed-income instruments. Raye notes that 80% of the equity portfolio consists of shares of WS. The Laws also own real estate valued at $400,000, with $225,000 in mortgage debt. Raye estimates the Laws' pre-retirement earnings from WS have a total present value of $1,025,000. He estimates the Laws' future expected consumption expenditures have a total present value of $750,000.

The Laws express a very strong desire to fund their children's college education expenses, which have an estimated present value of $275,000. The Laws also plan to fund an endowment at their alma mater in 20 years, which has an estimated present value of $500,000. The Laws tell Raye they want a high probability of success funding the endowment. Raye uses this information to prepare an economic balance sheet for the Laws.

In reviewing a financial plan written by the Laws' previous adviser, Raye notices the following asset class specifications.

Equity: US equities

Debt: Global investment-grade corporate bonds and real estate

Derivatives: Primarily large-capitalization foreign equities

The previous adviser's report notes the asset class returns on equity and derivatives are highly correlated. The report also notes the asset class returns on debt have a low correlation with equity and derivative returns.

Raye is concerned that the asset allocation approach followed by the Laws' previous financial adviser resulted in an overlap in risk factors among asset classes for the portfolio. Raye plans to address this by examining the portfolio's sensitivity to various risk factors, such as inflation, liquidity, and volatility, to determine the desired exposure to each factor.

Raye concludes that a portfolio of 75% global equities and 25% bonds reflects an appropriate balance of expected return and risk for the Laws with respect to a 20-year time horizon for most moderately important goals. Raye recommends the Laws follow a goals-based approach to asset allocation and offers three possible portfolios for the Laws to consider. Selected data on the three portfolios are presented in Exhibit 1.

EXHIBIT 1   Proposed Portfolio Allocations for the Law Family

	Cash	Fixed Income	Global Equities	Diversifying Strategies*
Portfolio 1	35%	55%	10%	0%
Portfolio 2	10%	15%	65%	10%
Portfolio 3	10%	30%	40%	20%

* Diversifying strategies consists of hedge funds

Raye uses a cost–benefit approach to rebalancing and recommends that global equities have a wider rebalancing range than the other asset classes.

1. Using the economic balance sheet approach, the Laws' economic net worth is *closest* to:
   A. $925,000.
   B. $1,425,000.
   C. $1,675,000.

2. Using an economic balance sheet, which of the Laws' current financial assets is *most* concerning from an asset allocation perspective?
   A. Equities
   B. Real estate
   C. Fixed income

3. Raye believes the previous adviser's specification for debt is incorrect given that, for purposes of asset allocation, asset classes should be:
   A. diversifying.
   B. mutually exclusive.
   C. relatively homogeneous.

4. Raye believes the previous adviser's asset class specifications for equity and derivatives are inappropriate given that, for purposes of asset allocation, asset classes should be:
   A. diversifying.
   B. mutually exclusive.
   C. relatively homogeneous.

5. To address his concern regarding the previous adviser's asset allocation approach, Raye should assess the Laws' portfolio using:
   A. a homogeneous and mutually exclusive asset class–based risk analysis.
   B. a multifactor risk model to control systematic risk factors in asset allocation.
   C. an asset class–based asset allocation approach to construct a diversified portfolio.

6. Based on Exhibit 1, which portfolio *best* meets the Laws' education goal for their children?
   A. Portfolio 1
   B. Portfolio 2
   C. Portfolio 3

7. Based on Exhibit 1, which portfolio *best* meets the Laws' goal to fund an endowment for their alma mater?
   A. Portfolio 1
   B. Portfolio 2
   C. Portfolio 3

8. Raye's approach to rebalancing global equities is consistent with:
   A. the Laws being risk averse.
   B. global equities having higher transaction costs than other asset classes.
   C. global equities having lower correlations with other asset classes.

CHAPTER 6

PRINCIPLES OF ASSET ALLOCATION

Jean L.P. Brunel, CFA
Thomas M. Idzorek, CFA
John M. Mulvey, PhD

LEARNING OUTCOMES

The candidate should be able to:

- describe and critique the use of mean–variance optimization in asset allocation;
- recommend and justify an asset allocation using mean–variance optimization;
- interpret and critique an asset allocation in relation to an investor's economic balance sheet;
- discuss asset class liquidity considerations in asset allocation;
- explain absolute and relative risk budgets and their use in determining and implementing an asset allocation;
- describe how client needs and preferences regarding investment risks can be incorporated into asset allocation;
- discuss the use of Monte Carlo simulation and scenario analysis to evaluate the robustness of an asset allocation;
- describe the use of investment factors in constructing and analyzing an asset allocation;
- recommend and justify an asset allocation based on the global market portfolio;
- describe and evaluate characteristics of liabilities that are relevant to asset allocation;
- discuss approaches to liability-relative asset allocation;
- recommend and justify a liability-relative asset allocation;
- recommend and justify an asset allocation using a goals-based approach;
- describe and critique heuristic and other approaches to asset allocation;
- discuss factors affecting rebalancing policy.

1. INTRODUCTION

Determining a strategic asset allocation is arguably the most important aspect of the investment process. This chapter builds on the "Introduction to Asset Allocation" chapter and focuses on several of the primary frameworks for developing an asset allocation, including asset-only mean–variance optimization, various liability-relative asset allocation techniques, and goals-based investing. Additionally, it touches on various other asset allocation techniques used by practitioners, as well as important related topics, such as rebalancing.

The process of creating a diversified, multi-asset class portfolio typically involves two separate steps. The first step is the asset allocation decision, which can refer to both the process and the result of determining long-term (strategic) exposures to the available asset classes (or risk factors) that make up the investor's opportunity set. Asset allocation is the first and primary step in translating the client's circumstances, objectives, and constraints into an appropriate portfolio (or, for some approaches, multiple portfolios) for achieving the client's goals within the client's tolerance for risk. The second step in creating a diversified, multi-asset-class portfolio involves implementation decisions that determine the specific investments (individual securities, pooled investment vehicles, and separate accounts) that will be used to implement the targeted allocations.

Although it is possible to carry out the asset allocation process and the implementation process simultaneously, in practice, these two steps are often separated for two reasons. First, the frameworks for simultaneously determining an asset allocation and its implementation are often complex. Second, in practice, many investors prefer to revisit their strategic asset allocation policy somewhat infrequently (e.g., annually or less frequently) in a dedicated asset allocation study, while most of these same investors prefer to revisit/monitor implementation vehicles (actual investments) far more frequently (e.g., monthly or quarterly).

Section 2 covers the traditional mean–variance optimization (MVO) approach to asset allocation. We apply this approach in what is referred to as an "asset-only" setting, in which the goal is to create the most efficient mixes of asset classes in the absence of any liabilities. We highlight key criticisms of mean–variance optimization and methods used to address them. This section also covers risk budgeting in relation to asset allocation, factor-based asset allocation, and asset allocation with illiquid assets. The observation that almost all portfolios exist to help pay for what can be characterized as a "liability" leads to the next subject.

Section 3 introduces liability-relative asset allocation—including a straightforward extension of mean–variance optimization known as surplus optimization. Surplus optimization is an economic balance sheet approach extended to the liability side of the balance sheet that finds the most efficient asset class mixes in the presence of liabilities. Liability-relative optimization is simultaneously concerned with the return of the assets, the change in value of the liabilities, and how assets and liabilities interact to determine the overall value or health of the total portfolio.

Section 4 covers an increasingly popular approach to asset allocation called goals-based asset allocation. Conceptually, goals-based approaches are similar to liability-relative asset allocation in viewing risk in relation to specific needs or objectives associated with different time horizons and degrees of urgency.

Section 5 introduces some informal (heuristic) ways that asset allocations have been determined and other approaches to asset allocation that emphasize specific objectives.

Section 6 addresses the factors affecting choices that are made in developing specific policies relating to rebalancing to the strategic asset allocation. Factors discussed include transaction costs, correlations, volatility, and risk aversion.[1]

Section 7 summarizes important points and concludes the chapter.

2. DEVELOPING ASSET-ONLY ASSET ALLOCATIONS

In this section, we discuss several of the primary techniques and considerations involved in developing strategic asset allocations, leaving the issue of considering the liabilities to Section 3 and the issue of tailoring the strategic asset allocation to meet specific goals to Section 4.

We start by introducing mean–variance optimization, beginning with unconstrained optimization, prior to moving on to the more common mean–variance optimization problem in which the weights, in addition to summing to 1, are constrained to be positive (no shorting allowed). We present a detailed example, along with several variations, highlighting some of the important considerations in this approach. We also identify several criticisms of mean–variance optimization and the major ways these criticisms have been addressed in practice.

2.1. Mean–Variance Optimization: Overview

Mean–variance optimization (MVO), as introduced by Markowitz (1952, 1959), is perhaps the most common approach used in practice to develop and set asset allocation policy. Widely used on its own, MVO is also often the basis for more sophisticated approaches that overcome some of the limitations or weaknesses of MVO.

Markowitz recognized that whenever the returns of two assets are not perfectly correlated, the assets can be combined to form a portfolio whose risk (as measured by standard deviation or variance) is less than the weighted-average risk of the assets themselves. An additional and equally important observation is that as one adds assets to the portfolio, one should focus not on the individual risk characteristics of the additional assets but rather on those assets' effect on the risk characteristics of the entire portfolio. Mean–variance optimization provides us with a framework for determining how much to allocate to each asset in order to maximize the *expected* return of the portfolio for an *expected* level of risk. In this sense, mean–variance optimization is a risk-budgeting tool that helps investors to spend their risk budget—the amount of risk they are willing to assume—wisely. We emphasize the word "expected" because the inputs to mean–variance optimization are necessarily forward-looking estimates, and the resulting portfolios reflect the quality of the inputs.

Mean–variance optimization requires three sets of inputs: returns, risks (standard deviations), and pair-wise correlations for the assets in the opportunity set. The objective function is often expressed as follows:

$$U_m = E(R_m) - 0.005\lambda\sigma_m^2 \tag{1}$$

---

[1]In this chapter, "volatility" is often used synonymously with "standard deviation."

where

  U_m = the investor's utility for asset mix (allocation) m
  R_m = the return for asset mix m
  λ = the investor's risk aversion coefficient
  σ_m^2 = the expected variance of return for asset mix m

The risk aversion coefficient (λ) characterizes the investor's risk–return trade-off; in this context, it is the rate at which an investor will forgo expected return for less variance. The value of 0.005 in Equation 1 is based on the assumption that $E(R_m)$ and σ_m are expressed as percentages rather than as decimals. (In using Equation 1, omit % signs.) If those quantities were expressed as decimals, the 0.005 would change to 0.5. For example, if $E(R_m) = 0.10$, $\lambda = 2$, and $\sigma = 0.20$ (variance is 0.04), then U_m is 0.06, or 6% [= 0.10 – 0.5(2)(0.04)]. In this case, U_m can be interpreted as a certainty-equivalent return—that is, the utility value of the risky return offered by the asset mix, stated in terms of the risk-free return that the investor would value equally. In Equation 1, 0.005 merely scales the second term appropriately.

In words, the objective function says that the value of an asset mix for an investor is equal to the expected return of the asset mix minus a penalty that is equal to one-half of the expected variance of the asset mix scaled by the investor's risk aversion coefficient. Optimization involves selecting the asset mix with the highest such value (certainty equivalent). Smaller risk aversion coefficients result in relatively small penalties for risk, leading to aggressive asset mixes. Conversely, larger risk aversion coefficients result in relatively large penalties for risk, leading to conservative asset mixes. A value of $\lambda = 0$ corresponds to a risk-neutral investor because it implies indifference to volatility. Most investors' risk aversion is consistent with λ between 1 and 10.[2] Empirically, $\lambda = 4$ can be taken to represent a moderately risk-averse investor, although the specific value is sensitive to the opportunity set in question and to market volatility.

In the absence of constraints, there is a closed-form solution that calculates, for a given set of inputs, the single set of weights (allocation) to the assets in the opportunity set that maximizes the investor's utility. Typically, this single set of weights is relatively extreme, with very large long and short positions in each asset class. Except in the special case in which the expected returns are derived using the reverse-optimization process of Sharpe (1974), the expected-utility-maximizing weights will not add up to 100%. We elaborate on reverse optimization in Section 2.4.1.

In most real-world applications, asset allocation weights must add up to 100%, reflecting a fully invested, non-leveraged portfolio. From an optimization perspective, when seeking the asset allocation weights that maximize the investor's utility, one must constrain the asset allocation weights to sum to 1 (100%). This constraint that weights sum to 100% is referred to as the "budget constraint" or "unity constraint." The inclusion of this constraint, or any other constraint, moves us from a problem that has a closed-form solution to a problem that must be solved numerically using optimization techniques.

In contrast to the single solution (single set of weights) that is often associated with unconstrained optimization (one could create an efficient frontier using unconstrained weights, but it is seldom done in practice), Markowitz's mean–variance optimization paradigm is most often identified with an efficient frontier that plots all potential efficient asset mixes subject to some common constraints. In addition to a typical budget constraint

---

[2]See Ang (2014, p. 44).

that the weights must sum to 1 (100% in percentage terms), the next most common constraint allows only positive weights or allocations (i.e., no negative or short positions).

Efficient asset mixes are combinations of the assets in the opportunity set that maximize expected return per unit of expected risk or, alternatively (and equivalently), minimize expected risk for a given level of expected return. To find all possible efficient mixes that collectively form the efficient frontier, *conceptually* the optimizer iterates through all the possible values of the risk aversion coefficient (λ) and for each value finds the combination of assets that maximizes expected utility. We have used the word *conceptually* because there are different techniques for carrying out the optimization that may vary slightly from our description, even though the solution (efficient frontier and efficient mixes) is the same. The efficient mix at the far left of the frontier with the lowest risk is referred to as the global minimum variance portfolio, while the portfolio at the far right of the frontier is the maximum expected return portfolio. In the absence of constraints beyond the budget and non-negativity constraints, the maximum expected return portfolio consists of a 100% allocation to the single asset with the highest expected return (which is not necessarily the asset with the highest level of risk).

Risk Aversion

Unfortunately, it is extremely difficult to precisely estimate a given investor's risk aversion coefficient (λ). Best practices suggest that when estimating risk aversion (or, conversely, risk tolerance), one should examine both the investor's *preference* for risk (willingness to take risk) and the investor's *capacity* for taking risk. Risk preference is a subjective measure and typically focuses on how an investor feels about and potentially reacts to the ups and downs of portfolio value. The level of return an investor hopes to earn can influence the investor's willingness to take risk, but investors must be realistic when setting such objectives. Risk capacity is an objective measure of the investor's ability to tolerate portfolio losses and the potential decrease in future consumption associated with those losses.[3] The psychometric literature has developed validated questionnaires, such as that of Grable and Joo (2004), to approximately locate an investor's risk preference, although this result then needs to be blended with risk capacity to determine risk tolerance. For individuals, risk capacity is affected by factors such as net worth, income, the size of an emergency fund in relation to consumption needs, and the rate at which the individual saves out of gross income, according to the practice of financial planners noted in Grable (2008).

With this guidance in mind, we move forward with a relatively global opportunity set, in this case defined from the point of view of an investor from the United Kingdom with an approximate 10-year time horizon. The analysis is carried out in British pounds (GBP), and none of the currency exposure is hedged. Exhibit 1 identifies 12 asset classes within the universe of available investments and a set of plausible forward-looking capital market assumptions: expected returns, standard deviations, and correlations. The chapter on capital

---

[3] *Risk preference* and *risk capacity* are sometimes referred to as the willingness and the ability to take risk, respectively.

market expectations covers how such inputs may be developed.[4] In the exhibit, three significant digits at most are shown, but the subsequent analysis is based on full precision.

Time Horizon

Mean–variance optimization is a "single-period" framework in which the single period could be a week, a month, a year, or some other time period. When working in a "strategic" setting, many practitioners typically find it most intuitive to work with annual capital market assumptions, even though the investment time horizon could be considerably longer (e.g., 10 years). If the strategic asset allocation will not be re-evaluated within a long time frame, capital market assumptions should reflect the average annual distributions of returns expected over the entire investment time horizon. In most cases, investors revisit the strategic asset allocation decision more frequently, such as annually or every three years, rerunning the analysis and making adjustments to the asset allocation; thus, the annual capital market assumption often reflects the expectations associated with the evaluation horizon (e.g., one year or three years).

EXHIBIT 1   Hypothetical UK-Based Investor's Opportunity Set with Expected Returns, Standard Deviations, and Correlations

Panel A: Expected Returns and Standard Deviations

Asset Class	Expected Return (%)	Standard Deviation (%)
UK large cap	6.6	14.8
UK mid cap	6.9	16.7
UK small cap	7.1	19.6
US equities	7.8	15.7
Europe ex UK equities	8.6	19.6
Asia Pacific ex Japan equities	8.5	20.9
Japan equities	6.4	15.2
Emerging market equities	9.0	23.0
Global REITs	9.0	22.5
Global ex UK bonds	4.0	10.4
UK bonds	2.9	6.1
Cash	2.5	0.7

---

[4]The standard deviations and correlations in Exhibit 1 are based on historical numbers, while expected returns come from reverse optimization (described later).

Panel B: Correlations

	UK Large Cap	UK Mid Cap	UK Small Cap	US Equities	Europe ex UK Equities	Asia Pacific ex Japan Equities	Japan Equities	Emerging Market Equities	Global REITs	Global ex UK Bonds	UK Bonds	Cash
UK large cap	1.00	0.86	0.79	0.76	0.88	0.82	0.55	0.78	0.64	−0.12	−0.12	−0.06
UK mid cap	0.86	1.00	0.95	0.76	0.84	0.75	0.51	0.74	0.67	−0.16	−0.10	−0.17
UK small cap	0.79	0.95	1.00	0.67	0.79	0.70	0.49	0.71	0.61	−0.22	−0.15	−0.17
US equities	0.76	0.76	0.67	1.00	0.81	0.72	0.62	0.69	0.77	0.14	0.00	−0.12
Europe ex UK equities	0.88	0.84	0.79	0.81	1.00	0.82	0.60	0.80	0.72	0.04	−0.04	−0.03
Asia Pacific ex Japan equities	0.82	0.75	0.70	0.72	0.82	1.00	0.54	0.94	0.67	0.00	−0.02	0.02
Japan equities	0.55	0.51	0.49	0.62	0.60	0.54	1.00	0.56	0.52	0.18	0.07	−0.01
Emerging market equities	0.78	0.74	0.71	0.69	0.80	0.94	0.56	1.00	0.62	−0.02	−0.03	0.04
Global REITs	0.64	0.67	0.61	0.77	0.72	0.67	0.52	0.62	1.00	0.16	0.18	−0.15
Global ex UK bonds	−0.12	−0.16	−0.22	0.14	0.04	0.00	0.18	−0.02	0.16	1.00	0.62	0.24
UK bonds	−0.12	−0.10	−0.15	0.00	−0.04	−0.02	0.07	−0.03	0.18	0.62	1.00	0.07
Cash	−0.06	−0.17	−0.17	−0.12	−0.03	0.02	−0.01	0.04	−0.15	0.24	0.07	1.00

The classification of asset classes in the universe of available investments may vary according to local practices. For example, in the United States and some other larger markets, it is common to classify equities by market capitalization, whereas the practice of classifying equities by valuation ("growth" versus "value") is less common outside of the United States. Similarly, with regard to fixed income, some asset allocators may classify bonds based on various attributes—nominal versus inflation linked, corporate versus government issued, investment grade versus non-investment grade (high yield)—and/or by maturity/duration (short, intermediate, and long). By means of the non-negativity constraint and using a reverse-optimization procedure (to be explained later) based on asset class market values to generate expected return estimates, we control the typically high sensitivity of the composition of efficient portfolios to expected return estimates (discussed further in Section 2.4). Without such precautions, we would often find that efficient portfolios are highly concentrated in a subset of the available asset classes.

Running this set of capital market assumptions through a mean–variance optimizer with the traditional non-negativity and unity constraints produces the efficient frontier depicted in Exhibit 2. We have augmented this efficient frontier with some non-traditional information that will assist with the understanding of some key concepts related to the efficient frontier. A risk-free return of 2.5% is used in calculating the reserve-optimized expected returns as well as the Sharpe ratios in Exhibit 2.

EXHIBIT 2   Efficient Frontier—Base Case

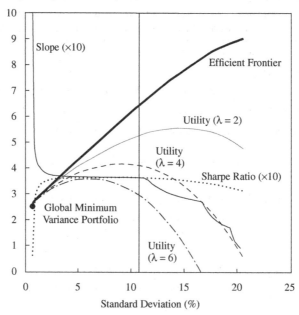

Expected Return (%)
Slope, Sharpe Ratio, Utility

Standard Deviation (%)

The slope of the efficient frontier is greatest at the far left of the efficient frontier, at the point representing the global minimum variance portfolio. Slope represents the rate at which expected return increases per increase in risk. As one moves to the right, in the direction of increasing risk, the slope decreases; it is lowest at the point representing the maximum return portfolio. Thus, as one moves from left to right along the efficient frontier, the investor takes on larger and larger amounts of risk for smaller and smaller increases in expected return. The "kinks" in the line representing the slope (times 10) of the efficient frontier correspond to portfolios (known as corner portfolios) in which an asset either enters or leaves the efficient mix.

For most investors, at the far left of the efficient frontier, the increases in expected return associated with small increases in expected risk represent a desirable trade-off. The risk aversion coefficient identifies the specific point on the efficient frontier at which the investor refuses to take on additional risk because he or she feels the associated increase in expected return is not high enough to compensate for the increase in risk. Of course, each investor makes this trade-off differently.

For this particular efficient frontier, the three expected utility curves plot the solution to Equation 1 for three different risk aversion coefficients: 2.0, 4.0, and 6.0, respectively.[5] For a given risk aversion coefficient, the appropriate efficient mix from the efficient frontier is simply the mix in which expected utility is highest (i.e., maximized). As illustrated in Exhibit 2, a lower risk aversion coefficient leads to a riskier (higher) point on the efficient frontier, while a higher risk aversion coefficient leads to a more conservative (lower) point on the efficient frontier.

---

[5]Numbers have been rounded to increase readability.

The vertical line (at volatility of 10.88%) identifies the asset mix with the highest Sharpe ratio; it intersects the Sharpe ratio line at a value of 3.7 (an unscaled value of 0.37). This portfolio is also represented by the intersection of the slope line and the Sharpe ratio line.

Exhibit 3 is an efficient frontier asset allocation area graph. Each vertical cross section identifies the asset allocation at a point along the efficient frontier; thus, the vertical cross section at the far left, with nearly 100% cash, is the asset allocation of the minimum variance portfolio, and the vertical cross section at the far right, with 45% in emerging markets and 55% in global REITs, is the optimal asset allocation for a standard deviation of 20.5%, the highest level of portfolio volatility shown. In this example, cash is treated as a risky asset; although its return volatility is very low, because it is less than perfectly correlated with the other asset classes, mixing it with small amounts of other asset classes reduces risk further. The vertical line identifies the asset mix with the highest Sharpe ratio and corresponds to the similar line shown on the original efficient frontier graph (Exhibit 2). The asset allocation mixes are well diversified for most of the first half of the efficient frontier, and in fact, for a large portion of the efficient frontier, all 12 asset classes in our opportunity set receive a positive allocation.[6]

EXHIBIT 3   Efficient Frontier Asset Allocation Area Graph—Base Case

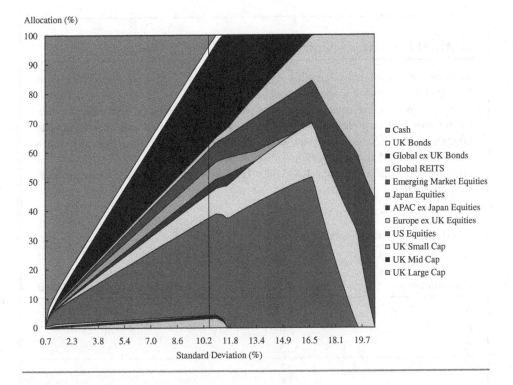

---

[6]Studying Exhibit 3 closely, one notices distinct regime shifts where the rate at which allocations are made to asset classes changes so that a line segment with a different slope begins. These regime shifts occur at what are called *corner portfolios*. The efficient mixes between two adjacent corner portfolios are simply linear combinations of those portfolios. The efficient frontier asset allocation area graph helps to clarify this result. More formally, corner portfolios are points on the efficient frontier at which an asset class either enters or leaves the efficient mix or a constraint either becomes binding or is no longer binding.

The investment characteristics of potential asset mixes based on mean–variance theory are often further investigated by means of Monte Carlo simulation, as discussed in Section 2.2. Several observations from theory and practice are relevant to narrowing the choices.

Equation 1 indicates that the basic approach to asset allocation involves estimating the investor's risk aversion parameter and then finding the efficient mix that maximizes expected utility. When the risk aversion coefficient has not been estimated, the investor may be able to identify the maximum tolerable level of portfolio return volatility. If that level is 10% per annum, for example, only the part of the efficient frontier associated with volatility less than or equal to 10% is relevant. This approach is justifiable because for a given efficient frontier, every value of the risk aversion coefficient can be associated with a value of volatility that identifies the best point on the efficient frontier for the investor; the investor may also have experience with thinking in terms of volatility. In addition, when the investor has a numerical return objective, he or she can further narrow the range of potential efficient mixes by identifying the efficient portfolios expected to meet that return objective. For example, if the return objective is 5%, one can select the asset allocation with a 5% expected return.

Example 1 illustrates the use of Equation 1 and shows the adaptability of MVO by introducing the choice problem in the context of an investor who also has a shortfall risk concern.

EXAMPLE 1   Mean–Variance-Efficient Portfolio Choice 1

An investment adviser is counseling Aimée Goddard, a client who recently inherited €1,200,000 and who has above-average risk tolerance ($\lambda = 2$). Because Goddard is young and one of her goals is to fund a comfortable retirement, she wants to earn returns that will outpace inflation in the long term. Goddard expects to liquidate €60,000 of the inherited portfolio in 12 months to fund the down payment on a house. She states that it is important for her to be able to take out the €60,000 without invading the initial capital of €1,200,000. Exhibit 4 shows three alternative strategic asset allocations.

EXHIBIT 4   Strategic Asset Allocation Choices for Goddard

Asset Allocation	Investor's Forecasts	
	Expected Return	Standard Deviation of Return
A	10.00%	20%
B	7.00	10
C	5.25	5

1. Based only on Goddard's risk-adjusted expected returns for the asset allocations, which asset allocation would she prefer?
2. Recommend and justify a strategic asset allocation for Goddard.

Note: In addressing 2, calculate the minimum return, R_L, that needs to be achieved to meet the investor's objective not to invade capital, using the expression ratio $[E(R_P) - R_L]/\sigma_P$, which reflects the probability of exceeding the minimum given a normal return distribution assumption in a safety-first approach.[7]

Solution to 1: Using Equation 1,

$$U_m = E(R_m) - 0.005\lambda\sigma_m^2$$
$$= E(R_m) - 0.005(2)\sigma_m^2$$
$$= E(R_m) - 0.01\sigma_m^2$$

So Goddard's utility for Asset Allocations A, B, and C are as follows:

$$U_A = E(R_A) - 0.01\sigma_A^2$$
$$= 10.0 - 0.01(20)^2$$
$$= 10.0 - 4.0$$
$$= 6.0 \text{ or } 6.0\%$$

$$U_B = E(R_B) - 0.01\sigma_B^2$$
$$= 7.0 - 0.01(10)^2$$
$$= 7.0 - 1.0$$
$$= 6.0 \text{ or } 6.0\%$$

$$U_C = E(R_C) - 0.01\sigma_C^2$$
$$= 5.25 - 0.01(5)^2$$
$$= 5.25 - 0.25$$
$$= 5.0 \text{ or } 5.0\%$$

Goddard would be indifferent between A and B based only on their common perceived certainty-equivalent return of 6%.

Solution to 2: Because €60,000/€1,200,000 is 5.0%, for any return less than 5.0%, Goddard will need to invade principal when she liquidates €60,000. So 5% is a threshold return level.

To decide which of the three allocations is best for Goddard, we calculate the ratio $[E(R_P) - R_L]/\sigma_P$:

Allocation A: (10% − 5%)/20% = 0.25
Allocation B: (7% − 5%)/10% = 0.20
Allocation C: (5.25% − 5%)/5% = 0.05

Both Allocations A and B have the same expected utility, but Allocation A has a higher probability of meeting the threshold 5% return than Allocation B. Therefore, A would be the recommended strategic asset allocation.

---

[7] See the Level I CFA Program chapter "Common Probability Distributions" for coverage of Roy's safety-first criterion.

There are several different approaches to determining an allocation to cash and cash equivalents, such as government bills. Exhibit 1 included cash among the assets for which we conducted an optimization to trace out an efficient frontier. The return to cash over a short time horizon is essentially certain in nominal terms. One approach to asset allocation separates out cash and cash equivalents as a (nominally) risk-free asset and calculates an efficient frontier of risky assets. Alternatively, a ray from the risk-free rate (a point on the return axis) tangent to the risky-asset efficient frontier (with cash excluded) then defines a linear efficient frontier. The efficient frontier then consists of combinations of the risk-free asset with the tangency portfolio (which has the highest Sharpe ratio among portfolios on the risky-asset efficient frontier).

A number of standard finance models (including Tobin two-fund separation) adopt this treatment of cash. According to two-fund separation, if investors can borrow or lend at the risk-free rate, they will choose the tangency portfolio for the risky-asset holdings and borrow at the risk-free rate to leverage the position in that portfolio to achieve a higher expected return, or they will split money between the tangency portfolio and the risk-free asset to reach a position with lower risk and lower expected return than that represented by the tangency portfolio. Since over horizons that are longer than the maturity of a money market instrument, the return earned would not be known, another approach that is well established in practice and reflected in Exhibit 1 is to include cash in the optimization. The amount of cash indicated by an optimization may be adjusted in light of short-term liquidity needs; for example, some financial advisers advocate that individuals hold an amount of cash equivalent to six months of expenses. All of these approaches are reasonable alternatives in practice.

Although we will treat cash as a risky asset in the following discussions, in Example 2, we stop to show the application of the alternative approach based on distinguishing a risk-free asset.

EXAMPLE 2   A Strategic Asset Allocation Based on Distinguishing a Nominal Risk-Free Asset

The Caflandia Foundation for the Fine Arts (CFFA) is a hypothetical charitable organization established to provide funding to Caflandia museums for their art acquisition programs.

CFFA's overall investment objective is to maintain its portfolio's real purchasing power after distributions. CFFA targets a 4% annual distribution of assets. CFFA has the following current specific investment policies.

Return objective
CFFA's assets shall be invested with the objective of earning an average nominal 6.5% annual return. This level reflects a spending rate of 4%, an expected inflation rate of 2%, and a 40 bp cost of earning investment returns. The calculation is $(1.04)(1.02)(1.004) - 1 = 0.065$, or 6.5%.

Risk considerations
CFFA's assets shall be invested to minimize the level of standard deviation of return subject to satisfying the expected return objective.

The investment office of CFFA distinguishes a nominally risk-free asset. As of the date of the optimization, the risk-free rate is determined to be 2.2%.

Exhibit 5 gives key outputs from a mean–variance optimization in which asset class weights are constrained to be non-negative.

EXHIBIT 5   Corner Portfolios Defining the Risky-Asset Efficient Frontier

Portfolio Number	Expected Nominal Returns	Standard Deviation	Sharpe Ratio
1	9.50%	18.00%	0.406
2	8.90	15.98	0.419
3	8.61	15.20	0.422
4	7.24	11.65	0.433
5	5.61	7.89	0.432
6	5.49	7.65	0.430
7	3.61	5.39	0.262

The portfolios shown are corner portfolios (see footnote 6), which as a group define the risky-asset efficient frontier in the sense that any portfolio on the frontier is a combination of the two corner portfolios that bracket it in terms of expected return.

Based only on the facts given, determine the most appropriate strategic asset allocation for CFFA given its stated investment policies.

Solution: An 85%/15% combination of Portfolio 4 and the risk-free asset is the most appropriate asset allocation. This combination has the required 6.5% expected return with the minimum level of risk. Stated another way, this combination defines the efficient portfolio at a 6.5% level of expected return based on the linear efficient frontier created by the introduction of a risk-free asset.

Note that Portfolio 4 has the highest Sharpe ratio and is the tangency portfolio. With an expected return of 7.24%, it can be combined with the risk-free asset, with a return of 2.2%, to achieve an expected return of 6.5%:

$$6.50 = 7.24w + 2.2(1 - w)$$
$$w = 0.853$$

Placing about 85% of assets in Portfolio 4 and 15% in the risk-free asset achieves an efficient portfolio with expected return of 6.4 with a volatility of $0.853(11.65) =$ 9.94%. (The risk-free asset has no return volatility by assumption and, also by assumption, zero correlation with any risky portfolio return.) This portfolio lies on a linear efficient frontier formed by a ray from the risk-free rate to the tangency portfolio and can be shown to have the same Sharpe ratio as the tangency portfolio, 0.433. The combination of Portfolio 4 with Portfolio 5 to achieve a 6.5% expected return would have a lower Sharpe ratio and would not lie on the efficient frontier.

Asset allocation decisions have traditionally been made considering only the investor's investment portfolio (and financial liabilities) and not the total picture that includes human capital and other non-traded assets (and liabilities), which are missing in a traditional balance sheet. Taking such extended assets and liabilities into account can lead to improved asset allocation decisions, however.

Depending on the nature of an individual's career, human capital can provide relatively stable cash flows similar to bond payments. At the other extreme, the cash flows from human capital can be much more volatile and uncertain, reflecting a lumpy, commission-based pay structure or perhaps a career in a seasonal business. For many individuals working in stable job markets, the cash flows associated with their human capital are somewhat like those of an inflation-linked bond, relatively consistent and tending to increase with inflation. If human capital is a relatively large component of the individual's total economic worth, accounting for this type of hidden asset in an asset allocation setting is extremely important and would presumably increase the individual's capacity to take on risk.

Let us look at a hypothetical example. Emma Beel is a 45-year-old tenured university professor in London. Capital market assumptions are as before (see Exhibit 1). Beel has GBP 1,500,000 in liquid financial assets, largely due to a best-selling book. Her employment as a tenured university professor is viewed as very secure and produces cash flows that resemble those of a very large, inflation-adjusted, long-duration bond portfolio. The net present value of her human capital is estimated at GBP 500,000. Beel inherited her grandmother's home on the edge of the city, valued at GBP 750,000. The results of a risk tolerance questionnaire that considers both risk preference and risk capacity suggest that Beel should have an asset allocation involving moderate risk. Furthermore, given our earlier assumption that the collective market risk aversion coefficient is 4.0, we assume that the risk aversion coefficient of a moderately risk-averse investor is approximately 4.0, from a total wealth perspective.

To account for Beel's human capital and residential real estate, these two asset classes were modeled and added to the optimization. Beel's human capital of GBP 500,000 was modeled as 70% UK long-duration inflation-linked bonds, 15% UK corporate bonds, and 15% UK equities.[8] Residential real estate was modeled based on a de-smoothed residential property index for London. (We will leave the complexities of modeling liabilities to Section 3.) Beel's assets include those shown in Exhibit 6.

Beel's UK residential real estate (representing the London house) and human capital were added to the optimization opportunity set. Additionally, working under the assumption that Beel's house and human capital are non-tradable assets, the optimizer was forced to allocate

EXHIBIT 6   Emma Beel's Assets

Asset	Value (GBP)	Percentage
Liquid financial assets	1,500,000	54.55
UK residential real estate	750,000	27.27
Human capital	500,000	18.18
	2,750,000	100

---

[8] These weights were used to create the return composite representing Beel's human capital that was used in the asset allocation optimization.

EXHIBIT 7   Efficient Frontier Asset Allocation Area Graph—Balance Sheet Approach

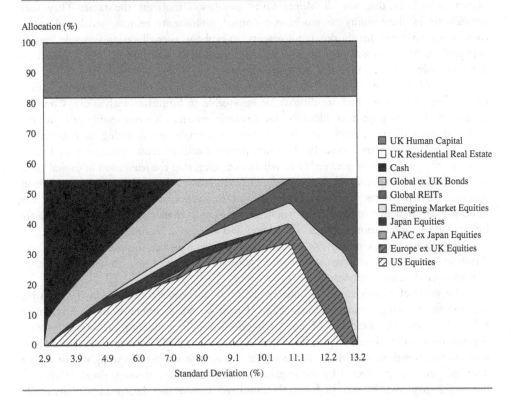

27.27% or more to UK residential real estate and 18.18% to human capital and then determined the optimal asset allocation based on a risk aversion coefficient of 4. Beel's expected utility is maximized by an efficient asset allocation with volatility of approximately 8.2%. Exhibit 7 displays the resulting asset allocation area graph.

Looking past the constrained allocations to human capital and UK residential real estate, the remaining allocations associated with Beel's liquid financial assets do not include UK equities or UK fixed income. Each of these three asset classes is relatively highly correlated with either UK residential real estate or UK human capital.[9]

2.2. Monte Carlo Simulation

Monte Carlo simulation complements MVO by addressing the limitations of MVO as a single-period framework. Additionally, in the case in which the investor's risk tolerance is either unknown or in need of further validation, Monte Carlo simulation can help paint a realistic picture of potential future outcomes, including the likelihood of meeting various goals, the distribution of the portfolio's expected value through time, and potential maximum drawdowns. Simulation also provides a tool for investigating the effects of trading/rebalancing

---

[9]For additional information on applying a total balance sheet approach, see, for example, Blanchett and Straehl (2015) or Rudd and Siegel (2013).

costs and taxes and the interaction of evolving financial markets with asset allocation. It is important to note that not all Monte Carlo simulation tools are the same: They vary significantly in their ability to model non-normal multivariate returns, serial and cross-correlations, tax rates, distribution requirements, an evolving asset allocation schedule (target-date glide path), non-traditional investments (e.g., annuities), and human capital (based on age, geography, education, and/or occupation).

Using Monte Carlo simulation, an investment adviser can effectively grapple with a range of practical issues that are difficult or impossible to formulate analytically. Consider rebalancing to a strategic asset allocation for a taxable investor. We can readily calculate the impact of taxes during a single time period. Also, in a single-period setting, as assumed by MVO, rebalancing is irrelevant. In the multi-period world of most investment problems, however, the portfolio will predictably be rebalanced, triggering the realization of capital gains and losses. Given a specific rebalancing rule, different strategic asset allocations will result in different patterns of tax payments (and different transaction costs too). Formulating the multi-period problem mathematically would be a daunting challenge. We could more easily incorporate the interaction between rebalancing and taxes in a Monte Carlo simulation.

We will examine a simple multi-period problem to illustrate the use of Monte Carlo simulation, evaluating the range of outcomes for wealth that may result from a strategic asset allocation (and not incorporating taxes).

The value of wealth at the terminal point of an investor's time horizon is a possible criterion for choosing among asset allocations. Future wealth incorporates the interaction of risk and return. The need for Monte Carlo simulation in evaluating an asset allocation depends on whether there are cash flows into or out of the portfolio over time. For a given asset allocation with no cash flows, the sequence of returns is irrelevant; ending wealth will be path independent (unaffected by the sequence or path of returns through time). With cash flows, the sequence is also irrelevant if simulated returns are independent, identically distributed random variables. We could find expected terminal wealth and percentiles of terminal wealth analytically.[10] Investors save/deposit money in and spend money out of their portfolios; thus, in the more typical case, terminal wealth is path dependent (the sequence of returns matters) because of the interaction of cash flows and returns. When terminal wealth is path dependent, an analytical approach is not feasible but Monte Carlo simulation is. Example 3 applies Monte Carlo simulation to evaluate the strategic asset allocation of an investor who regularly withdraws from the portfolio.

EXAMPLE 3   Monte Carlo Simulation for a Retirement Portfolio with a Proposed Asset Allocation

---

Malala Ali, a resident of the hypothetical country of Caflandia, has sought the advice of an investment adviser concerning her retirement portfolio. At the end of 2017, she is 65 years old and holds a portfolio valued at CAF$1 million. Ali would like to withdraw CAF$40,000 a year to supplement the corporate pension she has begun to receive. Given her health and family history, Ali believes she should plan for a retirement lasting 25 years. She is also concerned about passing along a portion of her portfolio to the families of her three children; she hopes that at least the portfolio's current real value

---

[10]Making a plausible statistical assumption, such as a lognormal distribution, for ending wealth.

can go to them. Consulting with her adviser, Ali has expressed this desire quantitatively: She wants the median value of her bequest to her children to be no less than her portfolio's current value of CAF$1 million in real terms. The median is the 50th percentile outcome. The asset allocation of her retirement portfolio is currently 50/50 Caflandia equities/Caflandia intermediate-term government bonds. Ali and her adviser have decided on the following set of capital market expectations (Exhibit 8):

EXHIBIT 8   Caflandia Capital Market Expectations

Asset Class	Investor's Forecasts	
	Expected Return	Standard Deviation of Return
Caflandia equities	9.4%	20.4%
Caflandia bonds	5.6%	4.1%
Inflation	2.6%	

The predicted correlation between returns of Caflandia equities and Caflandia intermediate-term government bonds is 0.15.

With the current asset allocation, the expected nominal return on Ali's retirement portfolio is 7.5% with a standard deviation of 11%. Exhibit 9 gives the results of the Monte Carlo simulation.[11] In Exhibit 9, the lowest curve represents, at various ages, levels of real wealth at or below which the 10% of worst real wealth outcomes lie (i.e., the 10th percentile for real wealth); curves above that represent, respectively, 25th, 50th, 75th, and 90th percentiles for real wealth.

Based on the information given, address the following:

1. Justify the presentation of ending wealth in terms of real rather than nominal wealth in Exhibit 9.
2. Is the current asset allocation expected to satisfy Ali's investment objectives?

Solution to 1: Ali wants the median real value of her bequest to her children to be "no less than her portfolio's current value of CAF$1 million." We need to state future amounts in terms of today's values (i.e., in real dollars) to assess the purchasing power of those amounts relative to CAF$1 million today. Exhibit 9 thus gives the results of the Monte Carlo simulation in real dollar terms. The median real wealth at age 90 is clearly well below the target ending wealth of real CAF$1 million.

Solution to 2: From Exhibit 9, we see that the median terminal (at age 90) value of the retirement portfolio in real dollars is less than the stated bequest goal of CAF$1 million. Therefore, the most likely bequest is less than the amount Ali has said she wants. The current asset allocation is not expected to satisfy all her investment objectives. Although one potential lever would be to invest more aggressively, given Ali's age and

---

[11]Note that the *y*-axis in this exhibit is specified using a logarithmic scale. The quantity CAF$1 million is the same distance from CAF$100,000 as CAF$10 million is from CAF$1 million because CAF$1 million is 10 times CAF$100,000, just as CAF$10 million is 10 times CAF$1 million. CAF$100,000 is 10^5, and CAF $1 million is 10^6. In Exhibit 9, a distance halfway between the CAF$100,000 and CAF$1 million hatch marks is $10^{5.5} =$ CAF$316,228.

EXHIBIT 9   Monte Carlo Simulation of Ending Real Wealth with Annual Cash Outflows

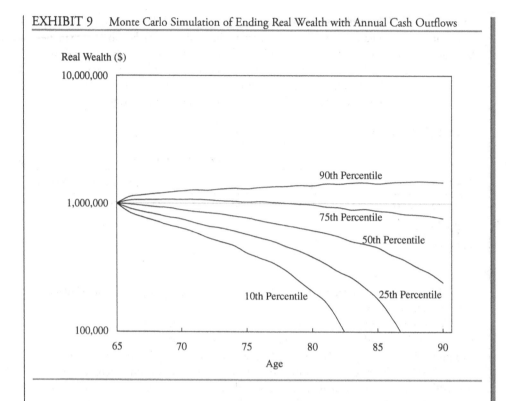

risk tolerance, this approach seems imprudent. An adviser may need to counsel that the desired size of the bequest may be unrealistic given Ali's desired income to support her expenditures. Ali will likely need to make a relatively tough choice between her living standard (spending less) and her desire to leave a CAF$1 million bequest in real terms. A third alternative would be to delay retirement, which may or may not be feasible.

2.3. Criticisms of Mean–Variance Optimization

With this initial understanding of mean–variance optimization, we can now elaborate on some of the most common criticisms of it. The following criticisms and the ways they have been addressed motivate the balance of the coverage of MVO:

1. The outputs (asset allocations) are highly sensitive to small changes in the inputs.
2. The asset allocations tend to be highly concentrated in a subset of the available asset classes.
3. Many investors are concerned about more than the mean and variance of returns, the focus of MVO.
4. Although the asset allocations may appear diversified across assets, the sources of risk may not be diversified.
5. Most portfolios exist to pay for a liability or consumption series, and MVO allocations are not directly connected to what influences the value of the liability or the consumption series.
6. MVO is a single-period framework that does not take account of trading/rebalancing costs and taxes.

In the rest of Section 2, we look at various approaches to addressing criticisms 1 and 2, giving some attention also to criticisms 3 and 4. Sections 3 and 4 present approaches to addressing criticism 5. "Asset Allocation with Real World Constraints" addresses some aspects of criticism 6.

It is important to understand that the first criticism above is not unique to MVO. Any optimization model that uses forward-looking quantities as inputs faces similar consequences of treating input values as capable of being determined with certainty. Sensitivity to errors in inputs is a problem that cannot be fully solved because it is inherent in the structure of optimization models that use as inputs forecasts of uncertain quantities.

To illustrate the importance of the quality of inputs, the sensitivity of asset weights in efficient portfolios to small changes in inputs, and the propensity of mean–variance optimization to allocate to a relatively small subset of the available asset classes, we made changes to the expected return of two asset classes in our base-case UK-centric opportunity set in Exhibit 1. We increased the expected return of Asia Pacific ex Japan equities from 8.5% to 9.0% and decreased the expected return of Europe ex UK equities from 8.6% to 8.1% (both changes are approximately 50 bps). We left all of the other inputs unchanged and reran the optimization. The efficient frontier as depicted in mean–variance space appears virtually unchanged (not shown); however, the efficient asset mixes of this new efficient frontier are dramatically different. Exhibit 10 displays the efficient frontier asset allocation area graph based on the slightly changed capital market assumptions. Notice the dramatic difference between Exhibit 10 and Exhibit 3. The small change in return assumptions has driven UK

EXHIBIT 10   Efficient Frontier Asset Allocation Area Graph—Changed Expected Returns

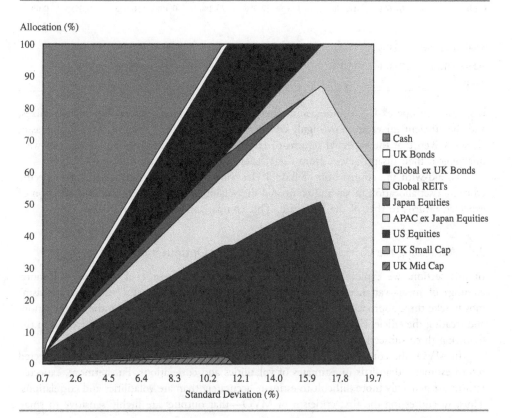

EXHIBIT 11   Comparison of Select Efficient Asset Allocations—Ad Hoc Return Modification
Allocations vs. Base-Case Allocations

	Modified 25/75	Base Case 25/75	Difference	Modified 50/50	Base Case 50/50	Difference	Modified 75/25	Base Case 75/25	Difference
UK large cap	0.0%	1.2%	−1.2%	0.0%	2.5%	−2.5%	0.0%	0.0%	0.0%
UK mid cap	0.8%	0.6%	0.3%	1.7%	0.8%	0.9%	0.0%	0.0%	0.0%
UK small cap	0.5%	0.5%	−0.1%	0.4%	0.4%	0.0%	0.0%	0.0%	0.0%
US equities	13.7%	13.8%	−0.1%	26.6%	26.8%	−0.2%	40.1%	40.5%	−0.4%
Europe ex UK equities	0.0%	2.7%	−2.7%	0.0%	6.5%	−6.5%	0.0%	13.2%	−13.2%
Asia Pacific ex Japan equities	7.5%	1.0%	6.5%	16.6%	2.3%	14.2%	26.8%	1.5%	25.3%
Japan equities	2.2%	2.3%	−0.1%	4.5%	4.5%	0.0%	4.4%	4.3%	0.1%
Emerging market equities	0.0%	2.0%	−2.0%	0.0%	4.9%	−4.9%	0.0%	10.0%	−10.0%
Global REITs	0.3%	0.9%	−0.6%	0.2%	1.4%	−1.3%	3.8%	5.6%	−1.8%
Global ex UK bonds	10.9%	10.6%	0.3%	24.7%	23.9%	0.7%	25.0%	25.0%	0.0%
UK bonds	2.5%	2.7%	−0.2%	2.4%	3.0%	−0.6%	0.0%	0.0%	0.0%
Cash	61.6%	61.7%	−0.1%	22.9%	23.1%	−0.1%	0.0%	0.0%	0.0%
Subtotal equities	25.0%	25.0%		50.0%	50.0%		75.0%	75.0%	
Subtotal fixed income	75.0%	75.0%		50.0%	50.0%		25.0%	25.0%	

large cap, Europe ex-UK equities, and emerging market equities out of the efficient mixes, and the efficient mixes are now highly concentrated in a smaller subset of the available asset classes. Given that the expected returns of UK large cap and emerging market equities were unchanged, their disappearance from the efficient frontier is not intuitive.

To aid with the comparison of Exhibit 10 with Exhibit 3, we identified three specific efficient asset allocation mixes and compared the version based on the ad hoc modification of expected returns to that of the base case. This comparison is shown in Exhibit 11.

2.4. Addressing the Criticisms of Mean–Variance Optimization

In this section, we explore several methods for overcoming some of the potential short-comings of mean–variance optimization. Techniques that address the first two criticisms mostly take three approaches: improving the quality of inputs, constraining the optimization, and treating the efficient frontier as a statistical construct. These approaches are treated in the following three subsections.

In MVO, the composition of efficient portfolios is typically more sensitive to expected return estimates than it is to estimates of volatilities and correlations. Furthermore, expected returns are generally more difficult to estimate accurately than are volatilities and correlations. Thus, in addressing the first criticism of MVO—that outputs are highly sensitive to small changes in inputs—the chapter will focus on expected return inputs. However, volatility and correlation inputs are also sources of potential error.

2.4.1. Reverse Optimization

Reverse optimization is a powerful tool that helps explain the implied returns associated with any portfolio. It can be used to estimate expected returns for use in a forward-looking optimization. MVO solves for optimal asset weights based on expected returns, covariances, and a risk aversion coefficient. Based on predetermined inputs, an optimizer solves for the optimal asset allocation weights. As the name implies, *reverse* optimization works in the opposite direction. Reverse optimization takes as its inputs a set of asset allocation weights *that are assumed to be optimal* and, with the additional inputs of covariances and the risk aversion coefficient, solves for expected returns. These reverse-optimized returns are sometimes referred to as implied or imputed returns.

When using reverse optimization to estimate a set of expected returns for use in a forward-looking optimization, the most common set of starting weights is the observed market-capitalization value of the assets or asset classes that form the opportunity set. The market capitalization of a given asset or asset classes should reflect the collective information of market participants. In representing the world market portfolio, the use of non-overlapping asset classes representing the majority of the world's investable assets is most consistent with theory.

Some practitioners will find the link between reverse optimization and CAPM equilibrium elegant, while others will see it as a shortcoming. For those who truly object to the use of market-capitalization weights in estimating inputs, the mechanics of reverse optimization can work with any set of starting weights—such as those of an existing policy portfolio, the average asset allocation policy of a peer group, or a fundamental weighting scheme. For those with more minor objections, we will shortly introduce the Black–Litterman model, which allows the expression of alternative forecasts or views.

In order to apply reverse optimization, one must create a working version of the all-inclusive market portfolio based on the constituents of the opportunity set. The market size or capitalization for most of the traditional stock and bond asset classes can be easily inferred from the various indexes that are used as asset class proxies. Many broad market-capitalization-weighted indexes report that they comprise over 95% of the securities, by market capitalization, of the asset classes they are attempting to represent. Exhibit 12 lists approximate values and weights for the 12 asset classes in our opportunity set, uses the weights associated with the asset classes to form a working version of the global market portfolio, and then uses the beta of each asset relative to our working version of the global market portfolio to infer what expected returns would be if all assets were priced by the CAPM according to their market beta. We assume a risk-free rate of 2.5% and a global market risk premium of 4%. Note that expected returns are rounded to one decimal place from the more precise values shown later (in Exhibit 13); expected returns cannot in every case be exactly reproduced based on Exhibit 12 alone because of the approximations mentioned. Also, notice in the final row of Exhibit 12 that the weighted average return and beta of the assets are 6.5% and 1, respectively.

Looking back at our original asset allocation area graph (Exhibit 3), the reason for the well-behaved and well-diversified asset allocation mixes is now clear. By using reverse optimization, we are consistently relating assets' expected returns to their systematic risk. If there isn't a consistent relationship between the expected return and systematic risk, the optimizer will see this inconsistency as an opportunity and seek to take advantage of the more attractive attributes.

EXHIBIT 12   Reverse-Optimization Example (Market Capitalization in £ billions)

Asset Class	Mkt Cap	Weight	Return $E[R_i]$		Risk-Free Rate r_f		Beta $\beta_{i,mkt}$	Market Risk Premium
UK large cap	£1,354.06	3.2%	6.62%	=	2.5%	+	1.03	(4%)
UK mid cap	£369.61	0.9%	6.92%	=	2.5%	+	1.11	(4%)
UK small cap	£108.24	0.3%	7.07%	=	2.5%	+	1.14	(4%)
US equities	£14,411.66	34.4%	7.84%	=	2.5%	+	1.33	(4%)
Europe ex UK equities	£3,640.48	8.7%	8.63%	=	2.5%	+	1.53	(4%)
Asia Pacific ex Japan equities	£1,304.81	3.1%	8.51%	=	2.5%	+	1.50	(4%)
Japan equities	£2,747.63	6.6%	6.43%	=	2.5%	+	0.98	(4%)
Emerging market equities	£2,448.60	5.9%	8.94%	=	2.5%	+	1.61	(4%)
Global REITs	£732.65	1.8%	9.04%	=	2.5%	+	1.64	(4%)
Global ex UK bonds	£13,318.58	31.8%	4.05%	=	2.5%	+	0.39	(4%)
UK bonds	£1,320.71	3.2%	2.95%	=	2.5%	+	0.112	(4%)
Cash	£83.00	0.2%	2.50%	=	2.5%	+	0.00	(4%)
	£41,840.04	100.0%	6.50%				1	

Notes: For the Mkt Cap and Weight columns, the final row is the simple sum. For the Return and Beta columns, the final row is the weighted average.

This effect was clearly visible in our second asset allocation area graph after we altered the expected returns of Asia Pacific ex Japan equities and Europe ex UK equities.

As alluded to earlier, some practitioners find that the reverse-optimization process leads to a nice starting point, but they often have alternative forecasts or views regarding the expected return of one or more of the asset classes that differ from the returns implied by reverse optimization based on market-capitalization weights. One example of having views that differ from the reverse-optimized returns has already been illustrated, when we altered the returns of Asia Pacific ex Japan equities and Europe ex UK equities by approximately 50 bps. Unfortunately, due to the sensitivity of mean–variance optimization to small changes in inputs, directly altering the expected returns caused relatively extreme and unintuitive changes in the resulting asset allocations. If one has strong views on expected returns that differ from the reverse-optimized returns, an alternative or additional approach is needed; the next section presents one alternative.

2.4.2. Black–Litterman Model
A complementary addition to reverse optimization is the Black–Litterman model, created by Fischer Black and Robert Litterman (see Black and Litterman 1990, 1991, 1992). Although the Black–Litterman model is often characterized as an asset allocation model, it is really a model for deriving a set of expected returns that can be used in an unconstrained or constrained optimization setting. The Black–Litterman model starts with excess returns (in excess of the risk-free rate) produced from reverse optimization and then provides a technique

for altering reverse-optimized expected returns in such a way that they reflect an investor's own distinctive views yet still behave well in an optimizer.

The Black–Litterman model has helped make the mean–variance optimization framework more useful. It enables investors to combine their unique forecasts of expected returns with reverse-optimized returns in an elegant manner. When coupled with a mean–variance or related framework, the resulting Black–Litterman expected returns often lead to well-diversified asset allocations by improving the consistency between each asset class's expected return and its contribution to systematic risk. These asset allocations are grounded in economic reality—via the market capitalization of the assets typically used in the reverse-optimization process—but still reflect the information contained in the investor's unique forecasts (or views) of expected return.

The mathematical details of the Black–Litterman model are beyond the scope of this chapter, but many practitioners have access to asset allocation software that includes the Black–Litterman model.[12] To assist with an intuitive understanding of the model and to show the model's ability to blend new information (views) with reverse-optimized returns, we present an example based on the earlier views regarding the expected returns of Asia Pacific ex Japan equities and Europe ex UK equities. The Black–Litterman model has two methods for accepting views: one in which an absolute return forecast is associated with a given asset class and one in which the return differential of an asset (or group of assets) is expressed relative to another asset (or group of assets). Using the relative view format of the Black–Litterman model, we expressed the view that we believe Asia Pacific ex Japan equities will outperform Europe ex UK equities by 100 bps. We placed this view into the Black–Litterman model, which blends reverse-optimized returns with such views to create a new, mixed estimate.

Exhibit 13 compares the Black–Litterman model returns to the original reverse-optimized returns (as in Exhibit 12 but showing returns to the second decimal place based on

EXHIBIT 13   Comparison of Black–Litterman and Reverse-Optimized Returns

Asset Class	Reverse-Optimized Returns	Black–Litterman Returns	Difference
UK large cap	6.62%	6.60%	–0.02%
UK mid cap	6.92	6.87	–0.05
UK small cap	7.08	7.03	–0.05
US equities	7.81	7.76	–0.05
Europe ex UK equities	8.62	8.44	–0.18
Asia Pacific ex Japan equities	8.53	8.90	0.37
Japan equities	6.39	6.37	–0.02
Emerging market equities	8.96	9.30	0.33
Global REITs	9.02	9.00	–0.01
Global ex UK bonds	4.03	4.00	–0.03
UK bonds	2.94	2.95	0.01
Cash	2.50	2.50	0.00

[12]For those interested in the mathematical details of the Black–Litterman model, see Idzorek (2007); a prepublication version is available here: http://corporate.morningstar.com/ib/documents/MethodologyDocuments/IBBAssociates/BlackLitterman.pdf.

EXHIBIT 14   Efficient Frontier Asset Allocation Area Graph, Black–Litterman Returns

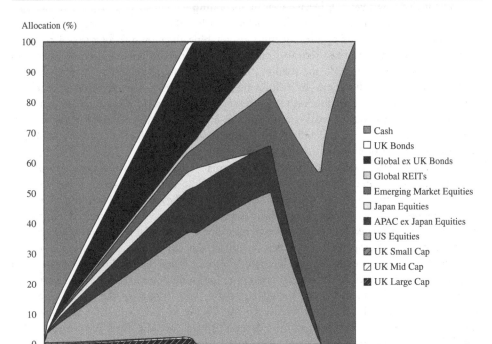

calculations with full precision). The model accounts for the correlations of the assets with each other, and as one might expect, all of the returns change slightly (the change in return on cash was extremely small).

Next, we created another efficient frontier asset allocation area graph based on these new returns from the Black–Litterman model, as shown in Exhibit 14. The allocations look relatively similar to those depicted in Exhibit 3. However, if you compare the allocations to Asia Pacific ex Japan equities and Europe ex UK equities to their allocations in the original efficient frontier asset allocation graph, you will notice that allocations to Asia Pacific ex Japan equities have increased across the frontier and allocations to Europe ex UK equities have decreased across the frontier with very little impact on the other asset allocations.

As before, to aid in the comparison of Exhibit 14 (Black–Litterman allocations) with Exhibit 3 (the base-case allocations), we identified three specific mixes in Exhibit 14 and compared those efficient asset allocation mixes based on the expected returns from the Black–Litterman model to those of the base case. The results are shown in Exhibit 15.

EXHIBIT 15   Comparison of Select Efficient Asset Allocations, Black–Litterman Allocations vs. Base-Case Allocations

	Modified 25/75	Base Case 25/75	Difference	Modified 50/50	Base Case 50/50	Difference	Modified 75/25	Base Case 75/25	Difference
UK large cap	0.4%	1.2%	–0.8%	1.4%	2.5%	–1.1%	0.0%	0.0%	0.0%
UK mid cap	0.4	0.6	–0.2	0.5	0.8	–0.3	0.0	0.0	0.0
UK small cap	0.4	0.5	–0.1	0.2	0.4	–0.2	0.0	0.0	0.0
US equities	13.8	13.8	0.0	26.8	26.8	0.0	40.0	40.5	–0.5
Europe ex UK equities	0.0	2.7	–2.7	0.0	6.5	–6.5	0.0	13.2	–13.2
Asia Pacific ex Japan equities	5.2	1.0	4.2	10.8	2.3	8.5	15.4	1.5	14.0
Japan equities	2.2	2.3	0.0	4.5	4.5	0.0	4.2	4.3	–0.1
Emerging market equities	1.8	2.0	–0.1	4.6	4.9	–0.2	9.8	10.0	–0.1
Global REITs	0.8	0.9	–0.1	1.3	1.4	–0.2	5.5	5.6	–0.1
Global ex UK bonds	10.3	10.6	–0.2	23.6	23.9	–0.3	25.0	25.0	0.0
UK bonds	3.1	2.7	0.3	3.5	3.0	0.5	0.0	0.0	0.0
Cash	61.6	61.7	–0.1	22.9	23.1	–0.1	0.0	0.0	0.0
Subtotal equities	25.0%	25.0%		50.0%	50.0%		75.0%	75.0%	
Subtotal fixed income	75.0%	75.0%		50.0%	50.0%		25.0%	25.0%	

2.4.3. Adding Constraints beyond the Budget Constraints

When running an optimization, in addition to the typical budget constraint and the non-negativity constraint, one can impose additional constraints. There are two primary reasons practitioners typically apply additional constraints: (1) to incorporate real-world constraints into the optimization problem and (2) to help overcome some of the potential shortcomings of mean–variance optimization elaborated above (input quality, input sensitivity, and highly concentrated allocations).

Most commercial optimizers accommodate a wide range of constraints. Typical constraints include the following:

1. Specify a set allocation to a specific asset—for example, 30% to real estate or 45% to human capital. This kind of constraint is typically used when one wants to include a non-tradable asset in the asset allocation decision and optimize around the non-tradable asset.
2. Specify an asset allocation range for an asset—for example, the emerging market allocation must be between 5% and 20%. This specification could be used to accommodate a constraint created by an investment policy, or it might reflect the user's desire to control the output of the optimization.

3. Specify an upper limit, due to liquidity considerations, on an alternative asset class, such as private equity or hedge funds.
4. Specify the relative allocation of two or more assets—for example, the allocation to emerging market equities must be less than the allocation to developed equities.
5. In a liability-relative (or surplus) optimization setting, one can constrain the optimizer to hold one or more assets representing the systematic characteristics of the liability short. (We elaborate on this scenario in Section 3.)

In general, good constraints are those that model the actual circumstances/context in which one is attempting to set asset allocation policy. In contrast, constraints that are simply intended to control the output of a mean–variance optimization should be used cautiously. A perceived need to add constraints to control the MVO output would suggest a need to revisit one's inputs. If a very large number of constraints are imposed, one is no longer optimizing but rather specifying an asset allocation through a series of binding constraints.

2.4.4. Resampled Mean–Variance Optimization

Another technique used by asset allocators is called resampled mean–variance optimization (or sometimes "resampling" for short).[13] Resampled mean–variance optimization combines Markowitz's mean–variance optimization framework with Monte Carlo simulation and, all else equal, leads to more-diversified asset allocations. In contrast to reverse optimization, the Black–Litterman model, and constraints, resampled mean–variance optimization is an attempt to build a better optimizer that recognizes that forward-looking inputs are inherently subject to error.

Resampling uses Monte Carlo simulation to estimate a large number of potential capital market assumptions for mean–variance optimization and, eventually, for the resampled frontier. Conceptually, resampling is a large-scale sensitivity analysis in which hundreds or perhaps thousands of variations on baseline capital market assumptions lead to an equal number of mean–variance optimization frontiers based on the Monte Carlo–generated capital market assumptions. These intermediate frontiers are referred to as simulated frontiers. The resulting asset allocations, or portfolio weights, from these simulated frontiers are saved and averaged (using a variety of methods). To draw the resampled frontier, the averaged asset allocations are coupled with the starting capital market assumptions.

To illustrate how resampling can be used with other techniques, we conducted a resampled mean–variance optimization using the Black–Litterman returns from Exhibit 10, above. Exhibit 16 provides the asset allocation area graph from this optimization. Notice that the resulting asset allocations are smoother than in any of the previous asset allocation area graphs. Additionally, relative to Exhibit 15, based on the same inputs, the smallest allocations have increased in size while the largest allocations have decreased somewhat.

The asset allocations from resampling as depicted in Exhibit 16 are appealing. Criticisms include the following: (1) Some frontiers have concave "bumps" where expected return decreases as expected risk increases; (2) the "riskier" asset allocations are over-diversified; (3) the asset allocations inherit the estimation errors in the original inputs; and (4) the approach lacks a foundation in theory.[14]

---

[13]The current embodiments of resampling grew out of the work of Jobson and Korkie (1980, 1981); Jorion (1992); DiBartolomeo (1993); and Michaud (1998).
[14]For more details, see Scherer (2002).

EXHIBIT 16   Efficient Frontier Asset Allocation Area Graph, Black–Litterman Returns with Resampling

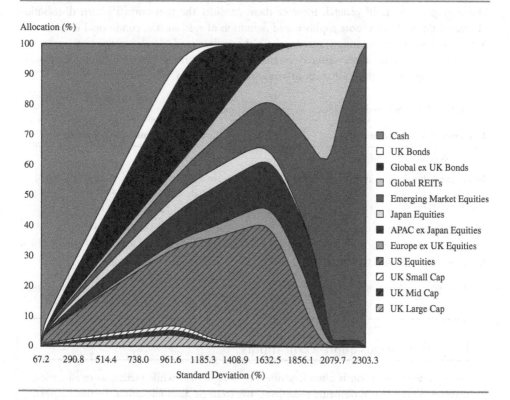

2.4.5. Other Non-Normal Optimization Approaches

From our list of shortcomings/criticisms of mean–variance optimization, the third is that investor preferences may go beyond the first two moments (mean and variance) of a portfolio's return distribution. The third and fourth moments are, respectively, skewness and kurtosis. Skewness measures the degree to which return distributions are asymmetrical, and kurtosis measures the thickness of the distributions' tails (i.e., how frequently extreme events occur). A normal distribution is fully explained by the first two moments because the skewness and (excess) kurtosis of the normal distribution are both zero.

Returning to the discussion of Equation 1, the mean–variance optimization program involves maximizing expected utility, which is equal to expected return minus a penalty for risk, where risk is measured as variance (standard deviation). Unfortunately, variance or standard deviation is an incomplete measure of risk when returns are not normally distributed. By studying historical return distributions for the major asset classes and comparing those historical distributions to normal distributions, one will quickly see that, historically, asset class returns are not normally distributed. In fact, empirically extreme returns seem to occur approximately 10 times more often than the normal distribution would suggest. Coupling this finding with the asymmetrical risk preferences observed in investors—whereby the pain of a loss is approximately twice as significant as the joy from an equivalent gain (according to Prospect theory)—has led to more complex utility functions and optimizers that expressly account for non-normal returns and asymmetric risk preference.[15] A number of variations of these more sophisticated optimization techniques have been put forth, making them challenging to cover. In general, most of them consider the non-normal return distribution characteristics and use a more sophisticated definition of risk, such as conditional value-at-risk. We view these as important advancements in the toolkit available to practitioners.

Exhibit 17 summarizes selected extensions of quantitative asset allocation approaches outside the sphere of traditional mean–variance optimization.

EXHIBIT 17   Selected Non-Mean–Variance Developments

Key Non-Normal Frameworks	Research/Recommended Reading
Mean–semivariance optimization	Markowitz (1959)
Mean–conditional value-at-risk optimization	Goldberg, Hayes, and Mahmoud (2013) Rockafellar and Uryasev (2000) Xiong and Idzorek (2011)
Mean–variance-skewness optimization	Briec, Kerstens, and Jokung (2007) Harvey, Liechty, Liechty, and Müller (2010)
Mean–variance-skewness-kurtosis optimization	Athayde and Flôres (2003) Beardsley, Field, and Xiao (2012)

Long-Term versus Short-Term Inputs

Strategic asset allocation is often described as "long term," while tactical asset allocation involves short-term movements away from the strategic asset allocation. In this context, "long term" is often defined as 10 or perhaps 20 or more years, yet in practice, very few asset allocators revisit their strategic asset allocation this infrequently. Many asset allocators update their strategic asset allocation annually, which makes it a bit more challenging to distinguish between strategic and tactical asset allocations. This frequent revisiting of the asset allocation policy brings up important questions about the time horizon associated with the inputs. In general, long-term (10-plus-year) capital market assumptions that ignore current market conditions, such as valuation levels, the business cycle, and interest rates, are often thought of as *unconditional* inputs. Unconditional inputs focus on the average capital market assumptions over the 10-plus-year time horizon. In contrast, shorter-term capital market assumptions that explicitly attempt to incorporate current market conditions (i.e., that are "conditioned" on them) are conditional inputs. For example, a practitioner who believes that the market is overvalued and that as a result we are entering a period of low returns, high volatility, and high correlations might prefer to use conditional inputs that reflect these beliefs.[16]

---

[15]For more on prospect theory, see Kahneman and Tversky (1979) and Tversky and Kahneman (1992).
[16]Relatedly, Chow, Jacquier, Kritzman, and Lowry (1999) showed a procedure for blending the optimal portfolios for periods of normal and high return volatility. The approach accounts for the tendency of asset returns to be more highly correlated during times of high volatility.

EXAMPLE 4.   Problems in Mean–Variance Optimization

In a presentation to US-based investment clients on asset allocation, the results of two asset allocation exercises are shown, as presented in Exhibit 18.

EXHIBIT 18   Asset Allocation Choices

Panel A: Area Graph 1

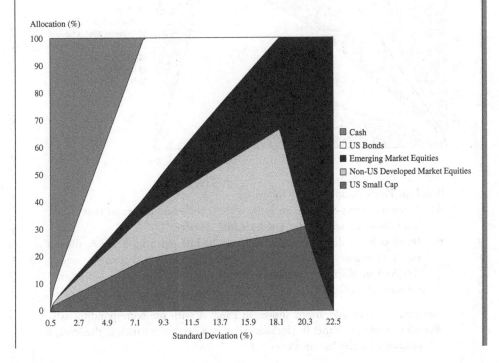

Panel B: Area Graph 2

Allocation (%)

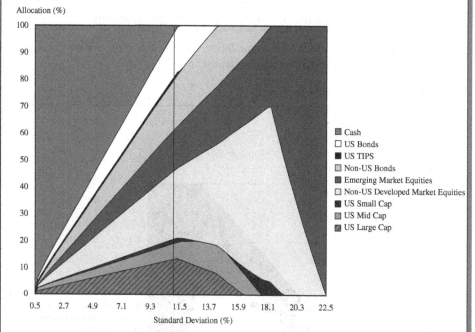

1. Based on Panel A, address the following:
   A. Based on mean–variance analysis, what is the asset allocation that would most likely be selected by a risk-neutral investor?
   B. Based only on the information that can be inferred from Panel A, discuss the investment characteristics of non-US developed market equity (NUSD) in efficient portfolios.
   C. Critique the efficient asset mixes represented in Panel A.

2. Compare the asset allocations shown in Panel A with the corresponding asset allocations shown in Panel B. (Include a comparison of the panels at the level of risk indicated by the line in Panel B.)

3.
   A. Identify three techniques that the asset allocations in Panel B might have incorporated to improve the characteristics relative to those of Panel A.
   B. Discuss how the techniques described in your answer to 3A address the high input sensitivity of MVO.

Solution to 1A: For a risk-neutral investor, the optimal asset allocation is 100% invested in emerging market equities. For a risk-neutral investor ($\lambda = 0$), expected utility is simply equal to expected return. The efficient asset allocation that maximizes expected return is the one with the highest level of volatility, as indicated on the *x*-axis. Panel A shows that that asset allocation consists entirely of emerging market equities.

Solution to 1B: The weights of NUSD as the efficient frontier moves from its minimum to its maximum risk point suggest NUSD's investment characteristics. This asset class is neither the lowest-volatility asset (which can be inferred to be cash) nor the highest-volatility asset (which is emerging market equity). At the point of the peak of NUSD, when the weight in NUSD is about to begin its decline in higher-risk efficient portfolios, US bonds drop out of the efficient frontier. Further, NUSD leaves the efficient frontier portfolio at a point at which US small cap reaches its highest weight. . These observations suggest that NUSD provided diversification benefits in portfolios including US bonds—a relatively low correlation with US bonds can be inferred—that are lost at this point on the efficient frontier. Beyond a volatility level of 20.3%, representing a corner portfolio, NUSD drops out of the efficient frontier.

Solution to 1C: Of the nine asset classes in the investor's defined opportunity set, five at most are represented by portfolios on the efficient frontier. Thus, a criticism of the efficient frontier associated with Panel A is that the efficient portfolios are highly concentrated in a subset of the available asset classes, which likely reflects the input sensitivity of MVO.

Solution to 2: The efficient asset mixes in Panels A and B cover a similar risk range: The risk levels of the two minimum-variance portfolios are similar, and the risk levels of the two maximum-return portfolios are similar. Over most of the range of volatility, however, the efficient frontier associated with Panel B is better diversified. For example, at the line in Panel B, representing a moderate level of volatility likely relevant to many investors, the efficient portfolio contains nine asset classes rather than four, as in Panel A. At that point, for example, the allocation to fixed income is spread over US bonds, non-US bonds, and US TIPS in Panel B, as opposed to just US bonds in Panel A.

Solution to 3A: To achieve the better-diversified efficient frontier shown in Panel B, several methods might have been used, including reverse optimization, the Black–Litterman model, and constrained asset class weights.

Solution to 3B: Reverse optimization and the Black–Litterman model address the issue of MVO's sensitivity to small differences in expected return estimates by anchoring expected returns to those implied by the asset class weights of a proxy for the global market portfolio. The Black–Litterman framework provides a disciplined way to tilt the expected return inputs in the direction of the investor's own views. These approaches address the problem by improving the balance between risk and return that is implicit in the inputs.

A very direct approach to the problem can be taken by placing constraints on weights in the optimization to force an asset class to appear in a constrained efficient frontier within some desired range of values. For example, non-US bonds did not appear in any efficient portfolio in Panel A. The investor could specify that the weight on non-US bonds be strictly positive. Another approach would be to place a maximum on the weight in US bonds to make the optimizer spread the fixed-income allocation over other fixed-income assets besides US bonds.

2.5. Allocating to Less Liquid Asset Classes

Large institutional investors have the ability to invest in less liquid asset classes, such as direct real estate, infrastructure, and private equity. These less liquid asset classes represent unique challenges to many of the common asset allocation techniques, such as mean–variance optimization.

For traditional, highly liquid asset classes, such as publicly listed equities and bonds, almost all of the major index providers have indexes that do an outstanding job of representing the performance characteristics of the asset class (and its various sub–asset classes). For example, over any reasonably long time period, the risk and return characteristics of a given asset class are nearly identical across the major global equity indexes and the correlations between the returns of the indexes are close to 1. Additionally, in most cases, there are passive, low-cost investment vehicles that allow investors to capture the performance of the asset class with very little tracking error.

Cash, the Risk-Free Asset, and Liquidity Needs

The so called "risk-free asset" has a special and somewhat tricky spot in the world of finance. Asset allocators typically use indexes for either 30-day or 90-day government bills to represent the characteristics associated with holding cash, which they may or may not treat as the risk-free asset. The volatility associated with these total return indexes is extremely low, but it isn't zero. An alternative to using a cash index as a proxy for the risk-free asset is to use a government bond with a duration/maturity that matches the time horizon of the investor. Some asset allocators like to include cash or another asset that could be considered a risk-free asset in the optimization and to allow the optimizer to determine how to mix it with the other asset classes included in the optimization. Other asset allocators prefer to exclude the risk-free asset from the optimization and allow real-world needs, such as liquidity needs, to determine how much to allocate to cash-like assets.

Illiquid assets may offer an expected return premium as compensation for illiquidity as well as diversification benefits. Determining an appropriate allocation to these assets is associated with various challenges, however. Common illiquid asset classes cannot be readily diversified to eliminate idiosyncratic risk, so representing an overall asset class performance is problematic. Furthermore, for less liquid asset classes, such as direct real estate, infrastructure, and private equity, there are, in general, far fewer indexes that attempt to represent aggregate performance. If one were to compare the performance characteristics of multiple indexes representing one of these less liquid asset classes, there would be noticeable risk and return differences, suggesting that it is difficult to accurately measure the risk and return characteristics of these asset classes. Also, due to the illiquid nature of the constituents that make up these asset classes, it is widely believed that the indexes don't accurately reflect their true volatility. In contrast to the more traditional, highly liquid asset classes, there are no low-cost passive investment vehicles that would allow investors to closely track the aggregate performance of these less liquid asset classes.

Thus, the problem is twofold: (1) Due to the lack of accurate indexes, it is more challenging to make capital market assumptions for these less liquid asset classes, and (2) even if there were accurate indexes, there are no low-cost passive investment vehicles to track them.

Compounding the asset allocator's dilemma is the fact that the risk and return characteristics associated with actual investment vehicles, such as direct real estate funds, infrastructure funds, and private equity funds, are typically significantly different from the characteristics of the asset classes themselves. For example, the private equity "asset class" should represent the risk and return characteristics of owning all private equity, just as the MSCI All Country World Index represents the risk and return characteristics of owning all public equity. Purchasing the exchange-traded fund (ETF) that tracks the MSCI All Country World Index completely diversifies public company-specific risk. This scenario is in direct contrast to the typical private equity fund, in which the risk and return characteristics are often dominated by company-specific (idiosyncratic) risk.

In addressing asset allocation involving less liquid asset classes, practical options include the following:

1. Exclude less liquid asset classes (direct real estate, infrastructure, and private equity) from the asset allocation decision and then consider real estate funds, infrastructure funds, and private equity funds as potential implementation vehicles when fulfilling the target strategic asset allocation.
2. Include less liquid asset classes in the asset allocation decision and attempt to model the inputs to represent the *specific risk* characteristics associated with the likely *implementation vehicles*.
3. Include less liquid asset classes in the asset allocation decision and attempt to model the inputs to represent the *highly diversified* characteristics associated with the *true asset classes*.

Related to this last option, some practitioners use listed real estate indexes, listed infrastructure, and public equity indexes that are deemed to have characteristics similar to their private equity counterparts to help estimate the risk of the less liquid asset classes and their correlation with the other asset classes in the opportunity set. It should be noted that the use of listed alternative indexes often violates the recommendation that asset classes be mutually exclusive—the securities in these indexes are likely also included in indexes representing other asset classes—and thus typically results in higher correlations among different asset classes, which has the negative impact of increasing input sensitivity in most optimization settings.

For investors who do not have access to direct real estate funds, infrastructure funds, and private equity funds—for example, small investors—the most common approach is to use one of the indexes based on listed equities to represent the asset class and then to implement the target allocation with a fund that invests similarly. Thus global REITs might be used to represent (approximately) global real estate.

2.6. Risk Budgeting

> [A] risk budget is simply a particular allocation of portfolio risk. An optimal risk budget is simply the allocation of risk such that the first order of conditions for portfolio optimization are satisfied. The risk budgeting process is the process of finding an optimal risk budget.
>
> Kurt Winkelmann (2003, p. 173)

As this quote from Kurt Winkelmann suggests, there are three aspects to risk budgeting:

- The risk budget identifies the total amount of risk and allocates the risk to a portfolio's constituent parts.
- An optimal risk budget allocates risk efficiently.
- The process of finding the optimal risk budget is risk budgeting.

Although its name suggests that risk budgeting is all about risk, risk budgeting is really using risk in relation to seeking return. The goal of risk budgeting is to maximize return per unit of risk—whether overall market risk in an asset allocation setting or active risk in an asset allocation implementation setting.

The ability to determine a position's marginal contribution to portfolio risk is a powerful tool that helps one to better understand the sources of risk. The marginal contribution to a type of risk is the partial derivative of the risk in question (total risk, active risk, or residual risk) with respect to the applicable type of portfolio holding (asset allocation holdings, active holdings, or residual holdings). Knowing a position's marginal contribution to risk allows one to (1) approximate the change in portfolio risk (total risk, active risk, or residual risk) due to a change in an individual holding, (2) determine which positions are optimal, and (3) create a risk budget. *Risk-budgeting tools assist in the optimal use of risk in the pursuit of return.*

Exhibit 19 contains risk-budgeting information for the Sharpe ratio–maximizing asset allocation from our original UK example. The betas are from Exhibit 12. The marginal contribution to total risk (MCTR) identifies the rate at which risk would change with a small (or marginal) change in the current weights. For asset class i, it is calculated as $MCTR_i =$ (Beta of asset class i with respect to portfolio)(Portfolio return volatility). The absolute contribution to total risk (ACTR) for an asset class measures how much it contributes to portfolio return volatility and can be calculated as the weight of the asset class in the portfolio times its marginal contribution to total risk: $ACTR_i = (Weight_i)(MCTR_i)$. Critically, beta takes account not only of the asset's own volatility but also of the asset's correlations with other portfolio assets.

EXHIBIT 19   Risk-Budgeting Statistics

Asset Class	Weight	MCTR	ACTR	Percent Contribution to Total Standard Deviation	Ratio of Excess Return to MCTR
UK large cap	3.2%	11.19%	0.36%	3.33%	0.368
UK mid cap	0.9	12.02	0.11	0.98	0.368
UK small cap	0.3	12.44	0.03	0.30	0.368
US equities	34.4	14.51	5.00	45.94	0.368
Europe ex UK equities	8.7	16.68	1.45	13.34	0.368
Asia Pacific ex Japan equities	3.1	16.35	0.51	4.69	0.368
Japan equities	6.6	10.69	0.70	6.46	0.368
Emerging market equities	5.9	17.51	1.02	9.42	0.368
Global REITs	1.8	17.79	0.31	2.86	0.368
Global ex UK bonds	31.8	4.21	1.34	12.33	0.368
UK bonds	3.2	1.22	0.04	0.35	0.368
Cash	0.2	0.00	0.00	0.00	0.368
	100.0		10.88	100.00	

The sum of the ACTR in Exhibit 19 is approximately 10.88%, which is equal to the expected standard deviation of this asset allocation mix. Dividing each ACTR by the total risk of 10.88% gives the percentage of total risk that each position contributes. Finally, an asset allocation is optimal from a risk-budgeting perspective when the ratio of excess return (over the risk-free rate) to MCTR is the same for all assets and matches the Sharpe ratio of the tangency portfolio. So in this case, which is based on reverse-optimized returns, we have an optimal risk budget.

For additional clarity, the following are the specific calculations used to derive the calculated values for UK large-cap equities (where we show some quantities with an extra decimal place in order to reproduce the values shown in the exhibit):

- Marginal contribution to risk (MCTR):

    Asset beta relative to portfolio × Portfolio standard deviation

    $1.0289 \times 10.876 = 11.19\%$

- ACTR:

    Asset weight in portfolio × MCTR

    $3.2\% \times 11.19\% = 0.36\%$

- Ratio of excess return to MCTR:

    (Expected return − Risk-free rate)/MCTR

    $(6.62\% - 2.5\%)/11.19\% = 0.368$

EXAMPLE 5   Risk Budgeting in Asset Allocation

1. Describe the objective of risk budgeting in asset allocation.
2. Consider two asset classes, A and B. Asset class A has two times the weight of B in the portfolio. Under what condition would B have a larger ACTR than A?
3. When is an asset allocation optimal from a risk-budgeting perspective?

Solution to 1: The objective of risk budgeting in asset allocation is to use risk efficiently in the pursuit of return. A risk budget specifies the total amount of risk and how much of that risk should be budgeted for each allocation.

Solution to 2: Because $ACTR_i = (Weight_i)(Beta\ with\ respect\ to\ portfolio)_i(Portfolio\ return\ volatility)$, the beta of B would have to be more than twice as large as the beta of A for B to contribute more to portfolio risk than A.

Solution to 3: An asset allocation is optimal when the ratio of excess return (over the risk-free rate) to MCTR is the same for all assets.

2.7. Factor-Based Asset Allocation

Until now, we have primarily focused on the mechanics of asset allocation optimization as applied to an opportunity set consisting of traditional, non-overlapping asset classes. An alternative approach used by some practitioners is to move away from an opportunity set of *asset classes* to an opportunity set consisting of investment *factors*.

In factor-based asset allocation, the factors in question are typically similar to the fundamental (or structural) factors in widely used multi-factor investment models. Factors are typically based on observed market premiums and anomalies. In addition to the all-important market (equity) exposure, typical factors used in asset allocation include size, valuation, momentum, liquidity, duration (term), credit, and volatility. Most of these factors were identified as return drivers that help to explain returns that were not explained by the CAPM. These factors can be constructed in a number of different ways, but with the exception of the market factor, typically, the factor represents what is referred to as a zero (dollar) investment, or self-financing investment, in which the underperforming attribute is sold short to finance an offsetting long position in the better-performing attribute. For example, the size factor is the combined return from shorting large-cap stocks and going long small-cap stocks (Size factor return = Small-cap stock return – Large-cap stock return). Of course, if large-cap stocks outperform small-cap stocks, the realized size return would be negative. Constructing factors in this manner removes most market exposure from the factors (because of the short positions that offset long positions); as a result, the factors generally have low correlations with the market and with one another.

We next present an example of a factor-based asset allocation optimization. Exhibit 20 shows the list of factors, how they were specified, and their historical returns and standard deviations (in excess of the risk-free rate as proxied by the return on three-month Treasury bills). The exhibit also includes historical statistics for three-month Treasury bills.

Thus far, our optimization examples have taken place in "total return space," where the expected return of each asset has equaled the expected return of the risk-free asset plus the amount of expected return in excess of the risk-free rate. In order to stay in this familiar total return space when optimizing with risk factors, the factor return needs to include the return on the assumed collateral (in this example, cash, represented by three-month Treasury bills). This adjustment is also needed if one plans to include both risk factors and some traditional asset classes in the same optimization, so that the inputs for the risk factors and traditional asset classes are similarly specified. Alternatively, one could move in the opposite direction, subtracting the return of the three-month Treasury bills from asset class returns and then conducting the optimization in excess-return space. One way to think about a self-financing allocation to a risk factor is that in order to invest in the risk factor, one must put up an equivalent amount of collateral that is invested in cash.

Because of space considerations, we have not included the full correlation matrix, but it is worth noting that the average pair-wise correlation of the risk factor–based opportunity set (in excess of the risk-free rate collateral return) is 0.31, whereas that of the asset class–based opportunity set is 0.57. Given the low pair-wise correlations of the risk factors, there has been some debate among practitioners around whether it is better to optimize using asset classes or risk factors. The issue was clarified by Idzorek and Kowara (2013), who demonstrated that in a proper comparison, neither approach is inherently superior. To help illustrate risk factor optimization and to demonstrate that if the two opportunity sets are

EXHIBIT 20   Factors/Asset Classes, Factor Definitions, and Historical Statistics (US data, January 1979 to March 2016)

Factor/Asset Class	Factor Definition	Compound Annual Factor Return	Standard Deviation	Total Return	Standard Deviation
Treasury bonds	Long-term Treasury bonds			7.77%	5.66%
Market	Total market return – Cash	7.49%	16.56%	12.97	17.33
Size	Small cap – Large cap	0.41	10.15	5.56	10.65
Valuation	Value – Growth	0.68	9.20	5.84	9.76
Credit	Corporate – Treasury	0.70	3.51	5.87	3.84
Duration	Long Treasury bonds – Treasury bills	4.56	11.29	9.91	11.93
Mortgage	Mortgage-backed – Treasury bonds	0.30	3.38	5.45	3.83
Large growth	—	—	—	12.64	19.27
Large value	—	—	—	13.23	16.52
Small growth	—	—	—	12.30	25.59
Small value	—	—	—	14.54	19.84
Mortgage-backed sec.	—	—	—	8.09	6.98
Corporate bonds	—	—	—	8.52	7.52
Treasury bonds	—	—	—	7.77	5.66
Cash	—	—	—	5.13	1.23

constructed with access to similar exposures, neither approach has an inherent advantage, we present two side-by-side optimizations. These optimizations are based on the data given in Exhibit 20.

Exhibit 21 contains the two efficient frontiers. As should be expected, given that the opportunity sets provide access to similar exposures, the two historical efficient frontiers are very similar. This result illustrates that when the same range of potential exposures is available in two opportunity sets, the risk and return possibilities are very similar.

Moving to Exhibit 22, examining the two asset allocation area graphs associated with the two efficient frontiers reveals that the efficient mixes have some relatively clear similarities. For example, in Panel A (risk factors), the combined market, size, and valuation exposures mirror the pattern (allocations) in Panel B (asset classes) of combined large value and small value exposures.

EXHIBIT 21   Efficient Frontiers Based on Historical Capital Market Assumptions (January 1979 to March 2016)

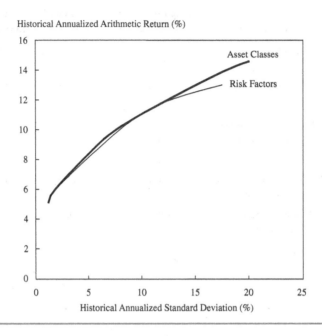

EXHIBIT 22   Asset Allocation Area Graphs—Risk Factors and Asset Classes

Panel A: Risk Factor Asset Allocation Area Graph

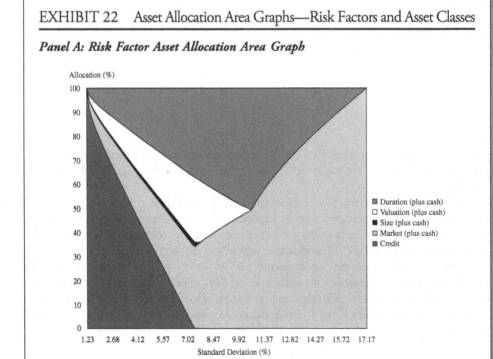

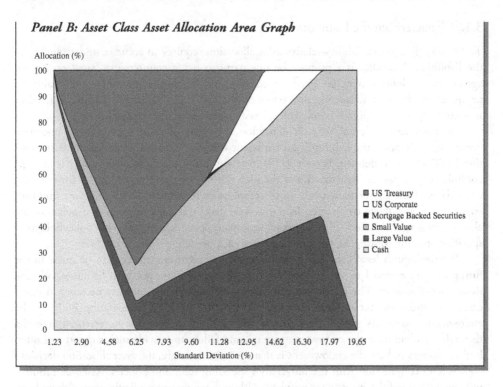

Panel B: Asset Class Asset Allocation Area Graph

Practitioners should choose to carry out asset allocation in the particular space—risk factors or asset classes—in which they are most equipped to make capital market assumptions. Regardless of which space a practitioner prefers, expanding one's opportunity set to include new, weakly correlated risk factors or asset classes should improve the potential risk–return trade-offs.

3. DEVELOPING LIABILITY-RELATIVE ASSET ALLOCATIONS

Liability-relative asset allocation is aimed at the general issue of rendering decisions about asset allocation in conjunction with the investor's liabilities. Liability-relative investors view assets as an inventory of capital, sometimes increased by additions, which is available to achieve goals and to pay future liabilities. What is the chance that an institution's capital is sufficient to cover future cash flow liabilities? This type of question is critical for liability-relative asset allocation because many large institutional investors—for example, banks, insurance companies, and pension plans—possess legal liabilities and operate in regulated environments in which an institution's inability to meet its liabilities with current capital has serious consequences. This concern gives rise to unique risk measures, such as the probability of meeting future cash flow requirements, and the restatement of traditional risk metrics, such as volatility, in relation to liabilities.

Liability-relative methods were developed in an institutional investor context, but these ideas have also been applied to individual investors. This section will focus on institutional investors. A later section addresses a thematically similar approach with behavioral finance roots—goals-based asset allocation.

3.1. Characterizing the Liabilities

To be soundly applied, liability-relative asset allocation requires an accurate understanding of the liabilities. A liability is a promise by one party to pay a counterparty based on a prior agreement. Liabilities may be fixed or contingent. When the amounts and timing of payments are fixed in advance by the terms of a contract, the liability is said to be fixed or non-contingent. A corporate bond with a fixed coupon rate is an example.

In many cases relevant to asset allocation, payments depend upon future, uncertain events. In such cases, the liability is a contingent liability.[17] An important example involves the liabilities of a defined benefit (DB) pension plan. The plan sponsor has a legal commitment to pay the beneficiaries of the plan during their retirement years. However, the exact dates of the payments depend on the employees' retirement dates, longevity, and cash payout rules. Insurance companies' liabilities—created by the sale of insurance policies—are also contingent liabilities: The insurance company promises to pay its policyholders a specified amount contingent on the occurrence of a predefined event.

We distinguish legal liabilities from cash payments that are expected to be made in the future and are essential to the mission of an institution but are not legal liabilities. We call these quasi-liabilities. The endowment of a university can fit this category because, in many cases, the endowment contributes a major part of the university's operating budget. The endowment assures its stakeholders that it will continue to support its essential activities through spending from the endowment capital, and failure to provide such support will often lead to changes in how the endowment is managed. Accordingly, the asset allocation decisions are made in conjunction with the university's spending rules and policies. Asset allocation is just one portion of the investment problem. Although we do not explicitly discuss them here, as suggested in Section 2, the spending needs of an individual represent another type of quasi-liability. Exhibit 23 summarizes the characteristics of liabilities that can affect asset allocation.

EXHIBIT 23   Characteristics of Liabilities That Can Affect Asset Allocation

1. Fixed versus contingent cash flows
2. Legal versus quasi-liabilities
3. Duration and convexity of liability cash flows
4. Value of liabilities as compared with the size of the sponsoring organization
5. Factors driving future liability cash flows (inflation, economic conditions, interest rates, risk premium)
6. Timing considerations, such as longevity risk
7. Regulations affecting liability cash flow calculations

The above liability characteristics are relevant to liability-relative asset allocation in various ways. For example, they affect the choice of appropriate discount rate(s) to establish the present value of the liabilities and thus the degree to which assets are adequate in relation

---

[17]Note that the term "contingent liability" has a specific definition in accounting. We are using the term more broadly here.

to those liabilities. Liability characteristics determine the composition of the liability-matching portfolio and that portfolio's basis risk with respect to the liabilities. (Basis risk in this context quantifies the degree of mismatch between the hedging portfolio and the liabilities.)

We will discuss the following case study in detail. It involves a frozen pension plan for LOWTECH, a hypothetical US company. The company has decided to close its defined benefit pension plan and switch to a defined contribution plan. The DB plan has the fixed liabilities (accumulated benefit obligations) shown in Exhibit 24.

In the Cash Outflow (Liability) column, the assumption is made that payments for a given year are made at the beginning of the year (in the exhibit, outflows have a positive sign). As of the beginning of 2015, the present value of these liabilities, given a 4% discount rate for high-quality corporate bonds (required in the United States by the Pension Protection Act of 2006, which applies to private DB pension plans), is US$2.261 billion. The current market value of the assets is assumed to equal US$2.5 billion, for a surplus of US$0.239 billion. On the other hand, if the discount rate is equal to the long-term government bond rate at 2% (required before the 2006 US legislation), the surplus becomes a deficit at −$0.539 billion. In many cases, regulations set the appropriate discount rates; these rates have an impact on the determination of surplus or deficit and thus on future contribution rules.

Like other institutions with legal liabilities, the LOWTECH company must analyze its legal future cash flows under its DB pension system and evaluate them in conjunction with the current market value of its assets on an annual basis. The following steps of the valuation exercise for a DB pension plan occur on a fixed annual date:

1. Calculate the market value of assets.
2. Project liability cash flows (via actuarial principles and rules).
3. Determine an appropriate discount rate for liability cash flows.
4. Compute the present value of liabilities, the surplus value, and the funding ratio.

$$\text{Surplus} = \text{Market value (assets)} - \text{Present value (liabilities)}.$$

The surplus for the LOWTECH company is US$2.500 billion − US$2.261 billion = US$0.239 billion, given the 4% discount rate assumption.

The funding ratio is another significant measure: Funding ratio = Market value (assets)/Present value (liabilities). We say that an investor is fully funded if the investor's funding ratio equals 1 (or the surplus is 0). A state of overfunding occurs when the funding ratio is greater than 1, and a state of underfunding takes place when the funding ratio is less than 1. Based on a discount rate of 4%, the funding ratio for LOWTECH = US$2.5 billion/US$2.261 billion = 1.1057, so that the company is about 10.6% overfunded.

The surplus value and the funding ratio are highly dependent upon the discount rate assumption. For example, if the discount rate is equal to 2.0% (close to the 10-year US Treasury bond rate in early 2016), the surplus drops to −US$0.539 billion and the funding ratio equals 0.8226. The company's status changes from overfunded to underfunded. The choice of discount rate is generally set by regulations and tradition. Rate assumptions are different across industries, countries, and domains. From the standpoint of economic theory, if the liability cash flows can be hedged perfectly by a set of market-priced assets, the discount rate can be determined by reference to the discount rate for the assets. For example, if the pension plan liabilities are fixed (without any uncertainty), the discount rate should be the risk-free rate with reference to the duration of the liability cash flows—for example, a five-year

EXHIBIT 24   Projected Liability Cash Flows for Company LOWTECH (US$ billions)

Beginning of Year	Cash Outflow (Liability)	PV(Liabilities) 4% Discount Rate	PV(Liabilities) 2% Discount Rate
2015	—	$2.261	$3.039
2016	$0.100	2.352	3.10
2017	0.102	2.342	3.06
2018	0.104	2.329	3.02
2019	0.106	2.314	2.97
2020	0.108	2.297	2.92
2021	0.110	2.276	2.87
2022	0.113	2.252	2.82
2023	0.115	2.225	2.76
2024	0.117	2.195	2.69
2025	0.120	2.161	2.63
2026	0.122	2.123	2.56
2027	0.124	2.081	2.49
2028	0.127	2.035	2.41
2029	0.129	1.984	2.33
2030	0.132	1.929	2.24
2031	0.135	1.869	2.15
2032	0.137	1.804	2.06
2033	0.140	1.733	1.96
2034	0.143	1.657	1.86
2035	0.146	1.575	1.75
2036	0.149	1.486	1.63
2037	0.152	1.391	1.52
2038	0.155	1.289	1.39
2039	0.158	1.180	1.26
2040	0.161	1.063	1.13
2041	0.164	0.938	0.98
2042	0.167	0.805	0.84
2043	0.171	0.663	0.68
2044	0.174	0.512	0.52
2045	0.178	0.352	0.36
2046	0.181	0.181	0.181

zero-coupon bond yield for a liability with a (modified) duration of 5. In other cases, it can be difficult to find a fully hedged portfolio because an ongoing DB pension plan's liabilities will depend upon future economic growth and inflation, which are clearly uncertain. Even a frozen pension plan can possess uncertainty due to the changing longevity of the retirees over the long-term future.

3.2. Approaches to Liability-Relative Asset Allocation

Various approaches to liability-relative asset allocation exist. These methods are influenced by tradition, regulations, and the ability of the stakeholders to understand and extend portfolio models that come from the asset-only domain.

There are several guiding principles. The first is to gain an understanding of the make-up of the investor's liabilities and especially the factors that affect the amount and timing of the cash outflows. Given this understanding, the present value of the liabilities is calculated, along with the surplus and funding ratio. These measures are used to track the results of ongoing investment and funding policies and for other tasks. Next come the decisions regarding the asset allocation taking account of the liabilities. There are a number of ways to proceed. We will discuss three major approaches:

- *Surplus optimization.* This approach involves applying mean–variance optimization (MVO) to an efficient frontier based on the volatility of the surplus ("surplus volatility," or "surplus risk") as the measure of risk. Surplus optimization is thus an extension of MVO based on asset volatility.[18] Depending on context, surplus risk may be stated in money or percentage terms ("surplus return volatility" is then another, more precise term for this measure).
- *Hedging/return-seeking portfolios approach.* This approach involves separating assets into two groups: a hedging portfolio and a return-seeking portfolio. The chapter also refers to this as the two-portfolio approach. The concept of allocating assets to two distinct portfolios can be applied for various funding ratios, but the chapter distinguishes as the basic approach the case in which there is a positive surplus available to allocate to the return-seeking portfolio.
- *Integrated asset–liability approach.* For some institutional investors, such as banks and insurance companies and long–short hedge funds, asset and liability decisions can be integrated and jointly optimized.

We cover these three approaches in turn.

3.2.1. Surplus Optimization
Surplus optimization involves adapting asset-only mean–variance optimization by substituting surplus return for asset return over any given time horizon. The quadratic optimization program involves choosing the asset allocation (mix) that maximizes expected surplus return net of a penalty for surplus return volatility at the chosen time horizon. The objective function is

$$U_m^{LR} = E(R_{s,m}) - 0.005\lambda\sigma^2(R_{s,m}) \tag{2}$$

where U_m^{LR} is the surplus objective function's expected value for a particular asset mix m; $E(R_{s,m})$ is the expected surplus return for asset mix m, with surplus return defined as

---

[18]Among the papers that discuss the surplus optimization model are Leibowitz and Henriksson (1988); Mulvey (1989, 1994); Sharpe and Tint (1990); Elton and Gruber (1992).

(Change in asset value – Change in liability value)/(Initial asset value); and the parameter λ (lambda) indicates the investor's risk aversion. The more risk averse the investor, the greater the penalty for surplus return volatility. Note that the change in liability value (liability return) measures the time value of money for the liabilities plus any expected changes in the discount rate and future cash flows over the planning horizon.

This surplus efficient frontier approach is a straightforward extension of the asset-only portfolio model. Surplus optimization assumes that the relationship between the value of liabilities and the value of assets can be approximated through a correlation coefficient. Surplus optimization exploits natural hedges that may exist between assets and liabilities as a result of their systematic risk characteristics.

The following steps describe the surplus optimization approach:

1. Select asset categories and determine the planning horizon. One year is often chosen for the planning exercise, although funding status analysis is based on an analysis of all cash flows.
2. Estimate expected returns and volatilities for the asset categories and estimate liability returns (expanded matrix).
3. Determine any constraints on the investment mix.
4. Estimate the expanded correlation matrix (asset categories and liabilities) and the volatilities.[19]
5. Compute the surplus efficient frontier and compare it with the asset-only efficient frontier.
6. Select a recommended portfolio mix.

Exhibit 25 lists LOWTECH's asset categories and current allocation for a one-year planning horizon. The current allocation for other asset categories, such as cash, is zero. LOWTECH has been following an asset-only approach but has decided to adopt a liability-relative approach. The company is exploring several liability-relative approaches. With respect to surplus optimization, the trustees want to maintain surplus return volatility at a level that tightly controls the risk that the plan will become underfunded, and they would like to keep volatility of surplus below US$0.25 billion (10%).

EXHIBIT 25   Asset Categories and Current Allocation for LOWTECH

	Private Equity	Real Estate	Hedge Funds	Real Assets	US Equities	Non-US Equities (Developed Markets)	Non-US Equities (Emerging Markets)	US Corporate Bonds
Allocation	20.0%	12.0%	18.0%	7.0%	15.0%	12.0%	8.0%	8.0%

The second step is to estimate future expected asset and liability returns, the expected present value of liabilities, and the volatility of both assets and PV(liabilities). The capital market projections can be made in several ways—based on historical data, economic analysis, or expert judgment, for example. The plan sponsor and its advisers are responsible for employing one or a blend of these approaches. Exhibit 26 shows the plan sponsor's capital market assumptions over a three- to five-year horizon. Note the inclusion of the present value of liabilities in Exhibit 26.

---

[19]A covariance matrix is computed by combining the correlation matrix and the volatilities.

EXHIBIT 26   LOWTECH's Capital Market Assumptions: Expected Annual Compound Returns and Volatilities

	Private Equity	Real Estate	Hedge Funds	Real Assets	US Equities	Non-US Equities (Developed Markets)	Emerging Markets	US Corporate Bonds	Cash	PV (Liabilities)
Expected returns	8.50%	7.50%	7.00%	6.00%	7.50%	7.20%	7.80%	4.90%	1.00%	4.90%
Volatilities	14.20%	9.80%	7.70%	6.10%	18.00%	19.50%	26.30%	5.60%	1.00%	5.60%

Typically, in the third step, the investor imposes constraints on the composition of the asset mix, including policy and legal limits on the amount of capital invested in individual assets or asset categories (e.g., a constraint that an allocation to equities must not exceed 50%). In our example, we simply constrain portfolio weights to be non-negative and to sum to 1.

The fourth step is to estimate the correlation matrix and volatilities. We assume that the liabilities have the same expected returns and volatilities as US corporate bonds; thus, the expanded matrix has a column and a row for liabilities with values equal to the corporate bond values. For simplicity, the investor may employ historical performance. Exhibit 27 shows the

EXHIBIT 27   Correlation Matrix of Returns

	Private Equity	Real Estate	Hedge Funds	Real Assets	US Equities	Non-US Equities (Developed Markets)	Non-US Equities (Emerging Markets)	US Corporate Bonds	Cash	PV (Liabilities)
Private equity	1	0.41	0.57	0.32	0.67	0.59	0.49	−0.27	0	−0.27
Real estate	0.41	1	0.45	0.41	0.31	0.33	0.17	−0.08	0	−0.08
Hedge funds	0.57	0.45	1	0.11	0.68	0.61	0.54	−0.23	0	−0.23
Real assets	0.32	0.41	0.11	1	0.04	0.06	−0.06	0.34	0	0.34
US equities	0.67	0.31	0.68	0.04	1	0.88	0.73	−0.38	0	−0.38
Non-US equities (developed)	0.59	0.33	0.61	0.06	0.88	1	0.81	−0.39	0	−0.39
Non-US equities (emerging)	0.49	0.17	0.54	−0.06	0.73	0.81	1	−0.44	0	−0.44
US corporate bonds	−0.27	−0.08	−0.23	0.34	−0.38	−0.39	−0.44	1	0	1
Cash	0	0	0	0	0	0	0	0	1	0
PV (liabilities)	−0.27	−0.08	−0.23	0.34	−0.38	−0.39	−0.44	1	0	1

correlation matrix of asset categories based on historical quarterly returns. Recall that we assume that liability returns (changes in liabilities) are driven by changes in the returns of US corporate bonds. An alternative approach is to deploy a set of underlying factors that drive the returns of the assets. Factors include changes in nominal and real interest rates, changes in economic activity (such as employment levels), and risk premiums. This type of factor investment model can be applied in an asset-only or a liability-relative asset allocation context.

Exhibit 28 shows a surplus efficient frontier that results from the optimization program based on the inputs from Exhibits 26 and 27. Surplus risk (i.e., volatility of surplus) in money terms (US$ billions) is on the x-axis, and expected surplus in money terms (US$ billions) is on the y-axis. By presenting the efficient frontier in money terms, we can associate the level of risk with the level of plan surplus, US$0.239 billion. Like the asset-only efficient frontier, the surplus efficient frontier has a concave shape.

EXHIBIT 28　　　Surplus Efficient Frontier

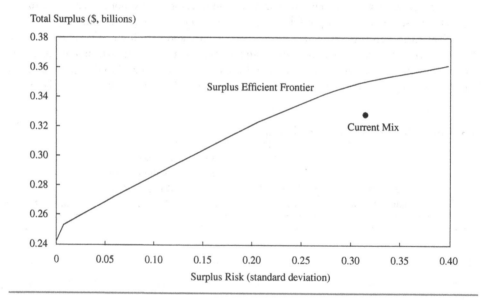

The first observation is that the current mix in Exhibit 28 lies below the surplus efficient frontier and is thus suboptimal.[20] We can attain the same expected total surplus as that of the current mix at a lower level of surplus volatility by choosing the portfolio on the efficient frontier at the current mix's level of expected total surplus. Another observation is that by uncovering the implications of asset mixes for surplus and surplus volatility, this approach allows the deliberate choice of an asset allocation in terms of the tolerable level of risk in relation to liabilities. It may be the case, for example, that neither the surplus volatility of the current mix nor that of the efficient mix with equal expected surplus is the appropriate level of surplus risk for the pension.

The surplus efficient frontier in Exhibit 28 shows efficient reward–risk combinations but does not indicate the asset class composition of the combinations. Exhibit 29 shows the asset class weights for surplus efficient portfolios.

---

[20]The current mix can also be shown to lie below the asset-only mean–variance frontier.

Exhibit 30, showing weights for portfolios on the usual *asset-only* efficient frontier based on the same capital market assumptions reflected in Exhibit 29, makes the point that efficient portfolios from the two perspectives are meaningfully different.[21]

The asset mixes are very different on the conservative side of the two frontiers. The most conservative mix for the surplus efficient frontier (in Exhibit 29) consists mostly of the US corporate bond index (the hedging asset) because it results in the lowest volatility of surplus over the one-year horizon. Bonds are positively correlated with changes in the present value of the frozen liability cash flows (because the liabilities indicate negative cash flows). In contrast, the most conservative mix for the asset-only efficient frontier (in Exhibit 30) consists chiefly of cash. As long as there is a hedging asset and adequate asset value, the investor can achieve a very low volatility of surplus, and for conservative investors, the asset value at the horizon will be uncertain but the surplus will be constant (or as constant as possible).

The two asset mixes (asset-only and surplus) become similar as the degree of risk aversion decreases, and they are identical for the most aggressive portfolio (private equity). Bonds disappear from the frontier about halfway between the most conservative and the most aggressive mixes, as shown in Exhibits 29 and 30.

EXHIBIT 29   Surplus Efficient Frontier Asset Allocation Area Graph

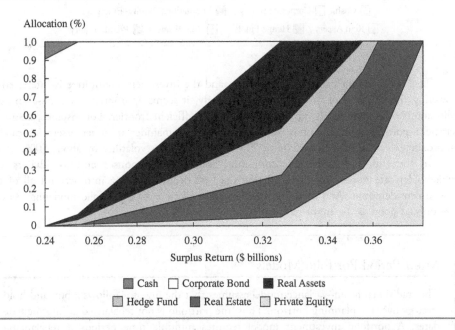

To summarize, the current asset mix is moderately aggressive and below the surplus efficient frontier. Thus, a mean–variance improvement is possible: either higher expected surplus with the same surplus risk or lower surplus risk for the same expected surplus. The current portfolio is also poorly hedged with regard to surplus volatility; the hedging asset (long bonds in this case) has a low commitment.

---

[21]In Exhibit 30, the annualized percentage returns can be equated to monetary surplus returns by multiplying by the asset value, US$2.5 billion.

EXHIBIT 30   Asset-Only Efficient Frontier Asset Allocation Area Graph

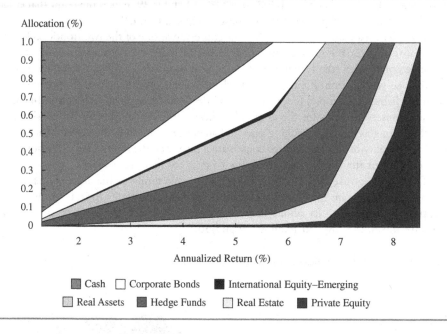

Cash ☐ Corporate Bonds ■ International Equity–Emerging
☐ Real Assets ■ Hedge Funds ☐ Real Estate ■ Private Equity

The LOWTECH plan has been frozen, and the investment committee is interested in lowering the volatility of the surplus. Accordingly, it seems appropriate to choose an asset allocation toward the left-hand side of the surplus efficient frontier. For instance, a surplus efficient portfolio with about 60% bonds and the remainder in other assets (as can be approximately identified from Exhibit 29) will drop surplus volatility by about 50%.

In the end, the investment committee for the plan sponsor and its advisers and stakeholders are responsible for rendering the best decision, taking into account all of the above considerations. And as always, the recommendations of a portfolio-modeling exercise are only as good as the input data and assumptions.

Multi-Period Portfolio Models

The traditional mean–variance model assumes that the investor follows a buy-and-hold strategy over the planning horizon. Thus, the portfolio is not rebalanced at intermediate dates. A portfolio investment model requires multiple time periods if rebalancing decisions are to be directly incorporated into the model. Mulvey, Pauling, and Madey (2003) discuss the pros and cons of building and implementing multi-period portfolio models. Applicable to both asset-only and liability-relative asset allocation, multi-period portfolio models are more comprehensive than single-period models but are more complex to implement. These models are generally implemented by means of the integrated asset–liability methods discussed in Section 3.2.1

EXAMPLE 6   Surplus Optimization

1. Explain how surplus optimization solutions differ from mean–variance optimizations based on asset class risk alone.
2. What is a liability return?
3. Compare the composition of a surplus optimal portfolio at two points on the surplus efficient frontier. In particular, take one point at the lower left of the surplus frontier (surplus return = US$0.26 billion) and the other point higher on the surplus efficient frontier (surplus return = US$0.32 billion). Refer to Exhibit 29. Explain the observed relationship in terms of the use of corporate bonds as the hedging asset for the liabilities.

Solution to 1: The surplus optimization model considers the impact of asset decisions on the (Market value of assets – Present value of liabilities) at the planning horizon.

Solution to 2: Liability returns measure the time value of money for the liabilities plus any expected changes in the discount rate over the planning horizon.

Solution to 3: Whereas the portfolio at the US$0.26 billion surplus return point on the efficient frontier has a substantial position in corporate bonds, the efficient mix with US$0.32 billion surplus return does not include them. The observed relationship that the allocation to corporate bonds declines with increasing surplus return can be explained by the positive correlation of bond price with the present value of liabilities. The hedging asset (corporate bonds) is employed to a greater degree at the low end of the surplus efficient frontier.

3.2.2. Hedging/Return-Seeking Portfolio Approach

In this approach, the liability-relative asset allocation task is divided into two parts. We distinguish as "basic" the two-portfolio approach in the case in which there is a surplus available to allocate to a return-seeking portfolio and as "variants" the approach as applied when there is not a positive surplus. In the basic case, the first part of the asset allocation task consists of hedging the liabilities through a hedging portfolio. In the second part, the surplus (or some part of it) is allocated to a return-seeking portfolio, which can be managed independently of the hedging portfolio (for example, using mean–variance optimization or another method). An essential issue involves the composition of the hedging portfolio. In some cases, such as the LOWTECH frozen DB pension plan, the hedging portfolio is straightforward to identify. The designated cash flows can be hedged via cash flow matching, duration matching, or immunization (as explained in the fixed-income chapters). This hedge will support the future cash flows with little or no risk.

In LOWTECH's application of the basic two-portfolio approach, the small surplus causes the pension plan to invest most of its capital in the hedging portfolio. The hedging portfolio can be approximated by the long-bond indexed investment as a first cut. Thus, given a 4% discount rate, US$2.261 billion is placed in long bonds. The remaining US$0.239 billion is invested in a portfolio of higher expected return assets, such as stocks, real estate, and hedge funds. This approach guarantees that the capital is adequate to pay future liabilities, as long as the hedging portfolio does not experience defaults.

Note that if the discount rate were 2% rather than 4%, the pension plan would be underfunded even if all assets were placed in a hedging portfolio. In such a case, the pension plan sponsor would either develop a strategy to increase the funding ratio so that the liabilities would be eventually paid or apply a variant of the two-portfolio approach. An underfunded plan will require higher contributions from the sponsor than a plan that is fully funded or overfunded.

The basic two-portfolio approach is most appropriate for conservative investors, such as insurance companies, and for overfunded pension plans that wish to reduce or eliminate the risk of not being able to pay future liabilities.

Several variants of the two-portfolio approach are possible. These include a partial hedge, whereby capital allocated to the hedging portfolio is reduced in order to generate higher expected returns, and dynamic versions whereby the investor increases the allotment to the hedging portfolio as the funding ratio increases. The specification of this allotment is often referred to as the liability glide path. These variants do not hedge the liabilities to the full extent possible given the assets and thus are less conservative than the basic approach discussed above. Still, there can be benefits to a partial hedge when the sponsor is able to increase contributions if the funding ratio does not increase in the future to 1 or above.

In the following discussion, we focus on determining the hedging portfolio.

Forming the Hedging Portfolio

The hedging portfolio must include assets whose returns are driven by the same factor(s) that drive the returns of the liabilities. Otherwise, even if the assets and liabilities start with equal values, the assets and liabilities will likely become inconsistent over time. One example involves promises (cash outflows) that are dependent upon future inflation. The hedging portfolio in this situation would often include index-linked (inflation-linked) Treasury bonds, again cash matched to the liabilities or immunized to the degree possible.

If there is an active market for the hedging portfolio (securities) in question, the present value of future cash flows is equal to a market value of the assets contained in the hedging portfolio. In this case, the date of valuation for the assets must be the same as the date of valuation for the liabilities. Absent market values, some form of appraised value is used.

The task of forming the hedging portfolio is complicated by the discount rate assumption and by the need to identify assets that are driven by the same factors that affect the liabilities. For example, if the discount rate is set by reference to a marketable instrument, such as the long government bond index, but the liability cash flows are driven by a factor such as inflation, the hedging task may require the use of instruments beyond nominal bonds (perhaps multiple instruments, such as interest rate swaps, inflation-linked bonds, and real assets). And in many applications, the hedge cannot be fully accomplished due to the nature of the driving factors (e.g., if they are non-marketable factors, such as economic growth).

If the uncertainties in the cash flows are related to non-market factors, such as future salary increases, the discount rate will depend upon regulations and tradition. Clearly, high discount rates lead to high funding ratios and in most cases require lower contributions from the sponsoring organization (at least in the short run). Conversely, lower discount rates give rise to lower funding ratios and thereby higher contributions. In the former case, investors with high discount rates will need to generate higher asset returns to achieve their promises if the pension plan sponsor wishes to avoid future contributions. A more conservative route is to designate a lower discount rate, as is the case in much of Europe and Asia. In all cases, it is the regulator's responsibility to set the guidelines, rules, and penalties involved in determining contribution policy.

Several issues complicate the valuation of liability cash flows. In many situations, investors must satisfy their promises without being able to go to a market and purchase a security with positive cash flows equal in magnitude to the liability cash flows.

At times, uncertain liabilities can be made more certain through the law of large numbers. For example, life insurance companies promise to pay beneficiaries when a policyholder dies. The life insurance company can minimize the risk of unexpected losses by insuring large numbers of individuals. Then, valuation of liabilities will use present value of expected cash flows based on a low (or even zero) risk premium in the discount rate. The field of application of the law of large numbers can be limited. For example, averages do not eliminate longevity risk.

Limitations
The basic two-portfolio approach cannot be directly applied under several circumstances. First, if the funding ratio is less than 1, the investor cannot create a fully hedging portfolio unless there is a sufficiently large positive cash flow (contribution). In this case, the sponsor might increase contributions enough to generate a positive surplus. As an alternative, there are conditional strategies that might help improve the investor's funding ratio, such as the glide path rules.[22]

A second barrier occurs when a true hedging portfolio is unavailable. An example involves losses due to weather-related causes, such as hurricanes or earthquakes. In these cases, the investor might be able to partially hedge the portfolio with instruments that share some of the same risks. The investor has "basis risk" when imperfect hedges are employed. (As an aside, the investor might be able to set up a contract with someone who, for a fee, will take on the liability risk that cannot be hedged. Insurance contracts have this defining characteristic.)

EXAMPLE 7   The Hedging/Return-Seeking Portfolios Approach

1. Compare how surplus optimization and the hedging/return-seeking portfolio approach take account of liabilities.
2. How does funding status affect the use of the basic hedging/return-seeking portfolio approach?

Solution to 1: The surplus optimization approach links assets and the present value of liabilities through a correlation coefficient. The two-portfolio model does not require this input. Surplus optimization considers the asset allocation problem in one step; the hedging/return-seeking portfolio approach divides asset allocation into two steps.

Solution to 2: Implementation of the basic two-portfolio approach depends on having an overfunded plan. A variant of the two-portfolio approach might be applied, however. Surplus optimization does not require an overfunded status. Both approaches address the present value of liabilities, but in different ways.

---

[22]See Gannon and Collins (2009).

3.2.3. Integrated Asset–Liability Approach

The previous two approaches are most appropriate when asset allocation decisions are made after, and relatively independently of, decisions regarding the portfolio of liabilities. However, there are numerous applications of the liability-relative perspective in which the institution must render significant decisions regarding the composition of its liabilities *in conjunction with the asset allocation*. Banks, long–short hedge funds (for which short positions constitute liabilities), insurance companies, and re-insurance companies routinely fall into this situation. Within this category, the liability-relative approaches have several names, including asset–liability management (ALM) for banks and some other investors and dynamic financial analysis (DFA) for insurance companies. These approaches are often implemented in the context of multi-period models. Using the following two cases, we review the major issues.

Integrated Asset–Liability Approach for Property/Casualty Insurance Companies

A property/casualty insurance company must make asset investment decisions in conjunction with business decisions about the portfolio of insured properties, its liabilities. To that end, asset and liability decisions are frequently integrated in an enterprise risk management system. In fact, the liability portfolio is essential to the company's long-term viability. For example, a particular property/casualty (PC) insurance company might engage (accept) liabilities for catastrophic risks such as earthquakes and hurricanes. In this case, the liabilities depend upon rare events and thus are most difficult to hedge against. Specialized firms calculate insured losses for a chosen set of properties for property/casualty insurance companies, and these firms provide liability cash flows on a probabilistic (scenario) basis. In this way information is gathered about the probability of losses over the planning horizon and the estimated losses for each loss event. An important issue involves the amount of capital needed to support the indicated liabilities. This issue is addressed by evaluating the tail risks, such as the 1% Value-at-Risk or Conditional-Value-at-Risk amount. To reduce this risk, there are major advantages to forming a diversified global portfolio of liabilities and rendering asset allocation decisions in conjunction with the liability portfolio decisions. The hedging portfolio in this case is not well defined. Therefore, it is difficult to hedge liabilities for a book of catastrophic risk policies. Liabilities might be addressed via customized products or by purchasing re-insurance. The assets and liabilities are integrated so that the worst-case events can be analyzed with regard to both sides of the balance sheet.

Integrated Asset–Liability Approach for Banks

Large global banks are often required to analyze their ability to withstand stress scenarios, in accordance with the Basel III framework. These institutions must be able to show that their current capital is adequate to withstand losses in their business units, such as asset trading, in conjunction with increases in liabilities. The chief risk officer evaluates these scenarios by means of integrated asset–liability approaches. The asset and liability decisions are linked in an enterprise manner. Both the portfolio of assets and the portfolio of liabilities have major impacts on the organization's risk. Thus, decisions to take on new products or expand an existing product—thereby generating liabilities—must take into account the associated decisions on the asset side. The integrated asset–liability management system provides a mechanism for discovering the optimal mix of assets and liabilities (products). These applications often employ multi-period models via a set of projected scenarios.

Decisions about asset allocation will affect the amount of business available to a financial intermediary, such as a bank or insurance company. Similarly, decisions about the portfolio of liabilities and concentration risks will feed back to the asset allocation decisions. Accordingly, we can set up a linked portfolio model. In a similar fashion, the performance of the assets of an institution possessing quasi-liabilities, such as a university endowment, will affect the spending rules for the institution. We can reduce worst-case outcomes by adjusting spending during crash periods, for example. Portfolio models linked to liabilities can provide significant information, helping the institution make the best compromise decisions for both the assets and the liabilities under its control. The twin goals are to maximize the growth of surplus over time subject to constraints on worst-case and other risk measures relative to the institution's surplus.

3.2.4. Comparing the Approaches

We have introduced three approaches for addressing asset allocation decisions in the context of liability issues; Exhibit 31 summarizes their characteristics. Each of these approaches has been applied in practice. The surplus optimization approach is a straightforward extension of the traditional (asset-only) mean–variance model. Surplus optimization demonstrates the importance of the hedging asset for risk-averse investors and provides choices for investors who are less risk averse in the asset mixes located on the middle and the right-hand side of the efficient frontier. The assumptions are similar to those of the traditional Markowitz model, where the inputs are expected returns and a covariance matrix. Thus, the assets and liabilities are linked through correlation conditions. The second approach, separating assets into two buckets, has the advantage of simplicity. The basic approach is most appropriate for conservative investors, such as life insurance companies, and for overfunded/fully funded institutional investors that can fully hedge their liabilities. Another advantage of this approach

EXHIBIT 31   Characteristics of the Three Liability-Relative Asset Allocation Approaches

Surplus Optimization	Hedging/Return-Seeking Portfolios	Integrated Asset–Liability Portfolios
Simplicity	Simplicity	Increased complexity
Linear correlation	Linear or non-linear correlation	Linear or non-linear correlation
All levels of risk	Conservative level of risk	All levels of risk
Any funded ratio	Positive funded ratio for basic approach	Any funded ratio
Single period	Single period	Multiple periods

is a focus on the hedging portfolio and its composition. The hedging portfolio can be constructed using a factor model and then linked to the assets via the same factors. Unfortunately, underfunded investors do not have the luxury of fully hedging their liabilities and investing the surplus in the risky portion; they must apply variants of the two-portfolio approach. The third approach, integrating the liability portfolio with the asset portfolio, is the most comprehensive of the three. It requires a formal method for selecting liabilities and for linking the asset performance with changes in the liability values. This approach can be implemented in a factor-based model, linking the assets and liabilities to the underlying driving factors. It has the potential to improve the institution's overall surplus. It does not require the linear correlation assumption and is capable of modeling transaction costs, turnover constraints, and other real-world constraints. The capital required for this approach is often determined by reference to the output of integrated asset–liability systems in banks and property/casualty insurance and re-insurance companies.

EXAMPLE 8   Liability-Relative Asset Allocation: Major Approaches

1. Discuss how the probability of not being able to pay future liabilities when they come due is or is not addressed by each of the major approaches to liability-relative asset allocation.
2. What are the advantages of the three approaches for investors who are more interested in protecting the surplus than growing their assets? Assume that the investor has a positive surplus.

Solution to 1: Such issues are best addressed by means of multi-period integrated asset–liability models. Surplus optimization and the two-portfolio approach, being single-period models, have difficulty estimating the probability of meeting future obligations.

Solution to 2: The three liability-relative approaches are appropriate for conservative investors (investors who are more interested in protecting the surplus than growing their assets). All of the three approaches force investors to understand the nature of their liabilities. This type of information can help inform the decision-making process.

3.3. Examining the Robustness of Asset Allocation Alternatives

As part of a liability-relative asset allocation study, the institutional investor can evaluate performance over selected events and "simulated" historical time periods. Each of the selected events can be interpreted as a "what if" sensitivity analysis. For example, we might wish to consider the effect of a 100 bp increase in interest rates across all maturities—that is, a parallel shift in the yield curve. This event would have a significant impact on the value of government bonds, clearly. Also, there would be a corresponding positive impact on the present discounted value of liabilities that are discounted at the government bond rate. The effect on other liability-relative asset allocation elements is less direct, and assumptions must be made. Suppose, for example, that the investor must discount at the high-quality corporate

rate. In that case, we need to estimate the effect of changing government rates on corporate rates. These designated studies are part of the stress tests required by banking and other regulators.

Another type of event study is the construction of scenarios based on carefully selected historical time periods. For example, we might select late 2008 as a reference point. In such a scenario, we are interested in the changes in the economic factors and the associated changes in the values of the institution's assets and liabilities. What would be the impact on our current (or projected) portfolio—assets and PV(liabilities)—if the conditions seen in late 2008 occurred again?

A more comprehensive method for examining robustness involves setting up a multi-stage simulation analysis. Here, we use scenarios to model uncertainty and replace decisions with "rules." The process begins with a set of scenarios for the underlying driving economic factors. Each scenario designates a path for the asset returns and the liability values at each stage of the planning horizon. The result is a set of probabilistic outcomes for the institutional investor's asset portfolio and the cash flows for its liabilities. In such modeling, one must take care to be consistent between asset returns and corresponding liabilities within a scenario; for example, if interest rates are a common factor driving both asset performance and the PV (liabilities), the interest rate effects should be based on the same assumptions.

Through the scenario analysis, the probability of both good and bad outcomes can be estimated. For example, we can measure the probability that an institutional investor will make a capital contribution in the future. Exhibit 32 shows the decision structure for the simulation of an insurance company over several periods, including modeling of the company's business strategy and the required capital rules.

To evaluate robustness, we can apply the simulation system with different assumptions. For instance, if we change the expected return of US equities, what is the effect on the probability of meeting the liabilities over an extended horizon, such as 10 years? This type of sensitivity analysis is routinely done in conjunction with the modeling exercise.

EXHIBIT 32   Simulation Analysis

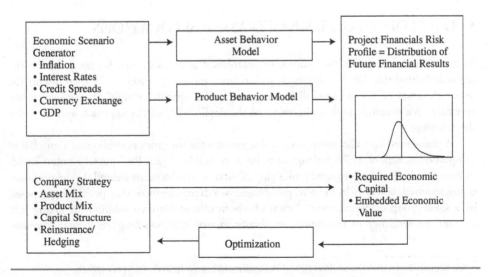

3.4. Factor Modeling in Liability-Relative Approaches

A factor-based approach for liability-relative asset allocation has gained interest and credibility for several reasons. First, in many applications, the liability cash flows are dependent on multiple uncertainties. The two primary macro factors are future economic conditions and inflation. Many pension payments to beneficiaries will be based on inflation and salary changes over the employees' work span. A fully hedged portfolio cannot be constructed when the liabilities are impacted by these uncertain factors. Recall that a hedged portfolio can be constructed for a frozen plan with fixed liabilities. For ongoing pension schemes, the best that can be done is to add asset categories to the portfolio that are positively correlated with the underlying driving risk factors, such as inflation-linked bonds. A factor-based approach can be implemented with any of the three liability-relative asset allocation methods discussed above.

EXAMPLE 9   Robustness and Risk Assessment in Liability-Relative Asset Allocation

What types of sensitivity analysis can be evaluated with a multi-period ALM simulation system?

Solution: To provide estimates of the probability of meeting future obligations and the distribution of outcomes, several types of sensitivity analysis are likely to be performed.

- For example, the expected returns could be increased or decreased to evaluate the impact on future contributions to the plan.
- Likewise, by analyzing historical events, the investor can estimate the size of losses during crash periods and make decisions about the best asset allocation to protect against these worst-case events. Multiple risk measures over time (temporal risk measures) can be readily included in a simulation system.

---

4. DEVELOPING GOALS-BASED ASSET ALLOCATIONS

In this section, we review the concept of goals-based asset allocation, focusing first on the rationale behind this different approach and its investment implications. We then discuss the major elements of the process, illustrating them with specific, simplified examples when necessary. We conclude with a discussion of the applicability of the approach and its major shortcomings.

A goals-based asset allocation process disaggregates the investor's portfolio into a number of sub-portfolios, each of which is designed to fund an individual goal (or "mental account") with its own time horizon and required probability of success. The literature behind the development of this approach is very rich. Initially, goals-based wealth management was specifically proposed by a small group of practitioners,[23] each of whom offered his own solution for taking into account the tendency of individuals to classify money into non-fungible mental accounts.

---

[23]See Brunel (2003, 2005); Nevins (2004); Pompian and Longo (2004); Chhabra (2005).

Shefrin and Statman (2000) developed the concept of the behavioral portfolio, which can be related to the Maslow (1943) hierarchy of needs. Das, Markowitz, Scheid, and Statman (2010, 2011) showed that traditional and behavioral finance could be viewed as equivalent if one were prepared to change the definition of risk from volatility of returns to the probability of not achieving a goal.[24] The essential point is that optimality requires both a suitably structured portfolio that can meet the given need *and* the correct capital allocation based on an appropriate discount rate, reflecting considerations of time horizon and the required probability of success.

Individuals have needs that are different from those of institutions. The most important difference is that individuals often have multiple goals, each with its own time horizon and its own "urgency," which can be expressed as a specific required probability of success. Exhibit 33 summarizes differences in institutional and individual investor definitions of goals. An individual's goals are not necessarily mutually compatible in two senses: The investor may not be able to address them all given the financial assets available, and there may be internal contradictions among the goals. An alternative process using one set of overall investment objectives—and thus effectively ignoring or "averaging" the different time horizons and required probabilities of success of individual goals—ostensibly loses the granular nature of client goals; as a result, the inherent complexities of the investment problem are less likely to be addressed fully. An approach that breaks the problem into sub-portfolios carries a higher chance of fully addressing an investor's goals, although it may require several iterations to ensure that the investor's portfolio is internally consistent and satisfactory.

The characteristics of individuals' goals have three major implications for an investment process that attempts to address the characteristics directly:

- The overall portfolio needs to be divided into sub-portfolios to permit each goal to be addressed individually.
- Both taxable and tax-exempt investments are important.
- Probability- and horizon-adjusted expectations (called "minimum expectations" in Exhibit 33) replace the typical use of mathematically expected average returns in determining the appropriate funding cost for the goal (or "discount rate" for future cash flows).

Compared with average return expectations—the median or average return anticipated for a combination of assets that is appropriate to address a goal—minimum expectations reflect a more complex concept. Minimum expectations are defined as the minimum return

EXHIBIT 33   Institutional and Individual Ways of Defining Goals

	Institutions	Individuals
Goals	Single	Multiple
Time horizon	Single	Multiple
Risk measure	Volatility (return or surplus)	Probability of missing goal
Return determination	Mathematical expectations[a]	Minimum expectations
Risk determination	Top-down/bottom-up	Bottom-up
Tax status	Single, often tax-exempt	Mostly taxable

[a] "Mathematical expectations" here means the weighted expected return of portfolio components.

[24]We apologize to these authors for grossly oversimplifying their work, but our aim is to make their insights more readily available without going into excruciating detail.

expected to be earned over the given time horizon with a given minimum required probability of success.

To illustrate, assume that a portfolio associated with a goal has an expected return of 7% with 10% expected volatility and the investor has indicated that the goal is to be met over the next five years with at least 90% confidence. Over the next five years, that portfolio is expected to produce returns of 35% with a volatility of 22.4%.[25] In short, this portfolio is expected to experience an average compound return of only 1.3% per year over five years with a probability of 90%; this result is quite a bit lower than the portfolio's average 7% expected return (see Exhibit 34). Thus, rather than discounting expected cash outflows by 7% to compute the dollar amount needed to defease the goal over that five-year horizon, one must use a considerably lower discount rate and by implication reserve a higher level of capital to meet that goal. Under moderate simplifying assumptions, that computation is valid whether or not return and volatility numbers are pretax or after-tax. Exhibit 34 shows, for the case of a normal distribution of returns, a return level that is expected to be exceeded 90% of the time (the 40% of the probability that lies between the vertical lines plus the 50% to the right of the median).

EXHIBIT 34   Probability-Weighted Return vs. Expected (= Median) Return

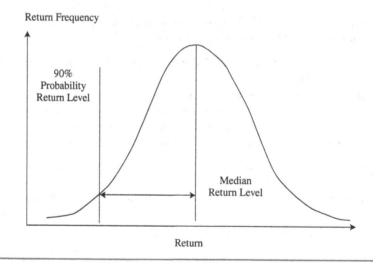

4.1. The Goals-Based Asset Allocation Process

Investment advisers taking a goals-based approach to investing client assets may implement this approach in a variety of ways. Exhibit 35 illustrates the major elements of the goals-based asset allocation process described in this chapter. Ostensibly, there are two fundamental parts to this process. The first centers on the creation of portfolio modules, while the second

---

[25]The return is the product of the annual return times the number of years, while the volatility is the product of the annual volatility times the square root of the number of years (under the assumption of independently and identically distributed returns).

EXHIBIT 35   A Stylized Representation of the Goals-Based Asset Allocation Process

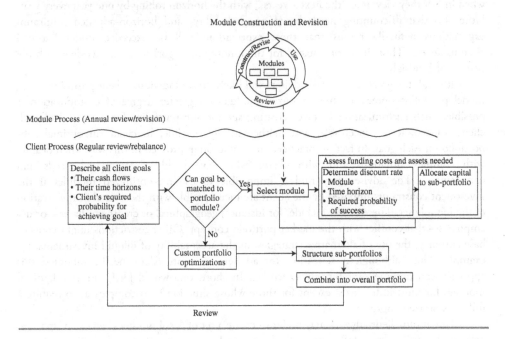

involves identifying client goals and matching each of these goals to the appropriate sub-portfolio of a suitable asset size.

Determining the lowest-cost funding for any given goal requires the formulation of an optimized portfolio that will be used to defease that goal optimally in the sense that risks are not taken for which the investor is not fairly compensated. Note that this process is most often generic and internal to the adviser and his or her firm. The adviser will typically not create a specific sub-portfolio for each goal of each client but rather will select, from a pre-established set, one of a few modules—or model portfolios—that best meet each goal.[26] As discussed above, adjusting the expected return on that portfolio to account for the time horizon and the required probability of success allows one to formulate the relevant discount rate which, when applied to the expected cash flows, will help determine the capital required at the outset. That capital will then be invested in the optimized portfolio asset allocation, where the balance will decline until the end of the horizon, when it runs out.[27] Note that the

---

[26]See the next paragraph for a discussion of when it makes sense to create specific optimal sub-portfolios.

[27]An important reason for the use of a declining-balance portfolio relates to the need for individuals and families to plan for the transfer of assets at death. In order for the income from assets to be used by an individual, these assets must be in the individual's name, or at least in a structure of which he or she is a beneficiary. Such assets would then be a part of the estate of the individual. Using a declining-balance portfolio allows the individual to receive the income—and some of the principal liquidated every year—while still ensuring that the amount of assets kept in the individual's name remains as low as appropriate given the individual's goals. An exception to this scenario would be the case of families whose income needs are so modest in relation to total assets that there is no need to provide income in planning for generational transfers or families that have such large eventual philanthropic intentions that assets kept in some beneficiaries' names are meant to be transferred to charity at death.

process is somewhat iterative because individual investors may describe a certain horizon as set when in fact they view it as "the next x years," with the horizon rolling by one year every year. Note also that discounting needs based on probability- and horizon-adjusted minimum expectations naturally means that these expectations will be exceeded under "normal circumstances." Thus, it is not unusual for the funding for a goal to seem excessive with the benefit of hindsight.

Although the great majority of advisers will likely create individual client portfolios using model portfolios—precisely, pre-optimized modules—a greater degree of customization is possible. Such customization involves creating specific sub-portfolios for each goal of each client. Indeed, it is conceivable, and mathematically possible, to create an optimal sub-portfolio for each goal. In fact, in practice, one would often proceed in this way when dealing with complex situations and with clients who have highly differentiated needs and constraints.[28] The adviser may find it impossible to use pre-optimized modules if the investment constraints imposed by the client are incompatible with those used in the creation of the module set. These might include, for instance, geographical or credit emphases—or de-emphases—that conflict with the market portfolio concept. Other restrictions might concern base currency, the use of alternative strategies, or the acceptability of illiquid investments, for example. Thus, although it is feasible for advisers to create client-specific modules, this approach can become prohibitively expensive. In short, one would likely use standardized modules for most individuals, except for those whose situation is so complex as to require a fully customized approach.

Many multi-client advisers may prefer to create a set of "goal modules" whose purpose is, collectively, to cover a full range of capital market opportunities and, individually, to represent a series of return–risk trade-offs that are sufficiently differentiated to offer adequate but not excessive choices to meet all the goals they expect their clients to express. These modules should therefore collectively appear to create a form of efficient frontier, though the frontier they depict in fact does not exist because the modules may well be based on substantially different sets of optimization constraints.

The two most significant differences from one module to the next, besides the implied return–risk trade-offs, are liquidity requirements and the eligibility of certain asset classes or strategies. Additionally, while intra–asset class allocation to individual sub–asset classes or strategies may typically be guided by the market portfolio for that asset class, one can conceive of instances where the selection of a specific sub–asset class or strategy is justified, even though the asset class per se may seem inappropriate. For instance, one might agree to hold high-yield bonds in an equity-dominated portfolio because of the equity risk factor exposure inherent in lower-credit fixed income. Conversely, the fixed-income market portfolio might be limited to investment-grade bonds and possibly the base-currency-hedged variant of non-domestic investment-grade bonds. We will return to the construction of these modules in Section 4.5.

4.2. Describing Client Goals

At this point, it is important to note that individual investors do not always consider all goals as being equal and similarly well-formulated in their own minds. Thus, while certain investors

---

[28]Note that such an approach, being more complex, is also costlier. It would therefore be more likely to be economically feasible for those advisory clients who also have the ability to pay a higher fee.

will have a well-thought-out set of goals—which may at times not be simultaneously achievable given the financial assets available—others will focus only on a few "urgent" goals and keep other requirements in the background.

Thus, a first step is to distinguish between goals for which anticipated cash flows are available—whether regularly or irregularly timed across the horizon or represented by a bullet payment at some future point—and those we call "labeled goals," for which details are considerably less precise. The term "labeled" here simply means that the individual has certain "investment features" in mind—such as minimal risk, capital preservation, purchasing power preservation, and long-term growth—but has not articulated the actual need that stands behind each label. The individual may already have mentally allocated some portion of his or her assets, in currency or percentage terms, to one or several of these labels. For cash flow-based goals,[29] the time horizon over which the goal is to be met is usually not difficult to ascertain: It is either the period over which cash outflows are expected to be made or the point in time at which a bullet payment is expected. More complex, however, is the issue of the urgency of the goal and thus of the required minimum probability of success.

By working to preserve a human (as opposed to a technical) tone in the advisory conversations, the adviser can serve the client without forcing him or her to come up with a quantified probability of success. The adviser may start with the simple observation that there are two fundamental types of goals: those that one seeks to achieve and those whose consequences one seeks to avoid. Dividing the goals the investor seeks to achieve into "needs, wants, wishes, and dreams" provides the adviser with an initial sense of the urgency of each goal. A need typically must be met and so should command a 90%–99% probability of success, while at the other end of the spectrum, it is an unfortunate fact that we all live with unfulfilled dreams, whose required probabilities of success probably fall below 60%. A parallel—and analogous—structure can be created to deal with goals one seeks to avoid:[30] "nightmares, fears, worries, and concerns," with similar implications in terms of required probabilities of success. In short, while some discussion of probability level may well take place, it can be informed and guided by the use of commonly accepted everyday words that will ensure that the outcome is internally consistent. The adviser avoids the use of jargon, which many clients dislike, and yet is able to provide professional advice.[31]

The simplest way to bring this concept to life is to work with a basic case study. Imagine a family, the Smiths, with financial assets of US$25 million. (For the sake of simplicity, we are assuming that they do not pay taxes and that all assets are owned in a single structure.) The parents are in their mid-fifties, and the household spends about US$500,000 a year. They expect that inflation will average about 2% per year for the foreseeable future. They express four important goals and are concerned that they may not be able to meet all of them:

---

[29]Note that all cash flows do not have to be negative (i.e., outflows). One can easily imagine circumstances where certain future inflows are anticipated and yet are not seen, individually, as sufficient to meet the specified goal.

[30]Although negative goals may sound surprising, they do exist and play a double role. First, when a negative goal is explicitly stated, it can be "replaced" by a specific positive goal: Avoiding the nightmare of running out of capital, for example, can be turned into the need to meet a certain expense budget. Second, negative goals serve as a useful feedback loop to check the internal consistency of the investor's goal set.

[31]Note that the adviser can also identify a series of "secondary" words to help determine whether a need, for instance, means that the required probability of success should be set at 99%, 95%, or 90%. An *indispensable* need could require a 99% probability of being met, while an *urgent* need might require only a 95% probability of success, and a *serious* need a 90% probability.

1. They *need* a 95% chance of being able to maintain their current expenditures over the next five years.
2. They *want* an 85% chance of being able to maintain their current expenditures over the ensuing 25 years, which they see as a reasonable estimate of their joint life expectancy.
3. They *need* a 90% chance of being able to transfer US$10 million to their children in 10 years.
4. They *wish* to have a 75% chance to be able to create a family foundation, which they wish to fund with US$10 million in 20 years.

EXAMPLE 10 Understanding Client Goals

1. A client describes a desire to have a reserve of €2 million for business opportunities that may develop when he retires in five years. What are the important features of this goal?
2. A 70-year-old client discusses the need to be able to maintain her lifestyle for the balance of her life and wishes to leave US$3 million to be split among her three grandchildren at her death. What are the important features of this situation?

Solution to 1: The time horizon is five years. Words such as "desire" in describing a goal, compared with expressions indicating "need," indicate that there is room for "error" in the event that capital markets are not supportive. The portfolio required to meet the goal described as a desire will likely be able to involve a riskier profile. One would want to verify this assumption by comparing the size of that goal compared with the total financial assets available to the client.

Solution to 2: The key takeaway is that although the two goals have the same time horizon, the two portfolios designed to defease them will have potentially significantly different risk profiles. The time horizon is approximately 20 years. The first goal relates to maintaining the client's lifestyle and must be defeased with an appropriately structured portfolio. The second goal, relating to the wish to leave some money to grandchildren, will allow more room for risk taking.

4.3. Constructing Sub-Portfolios

Having defined the needs of the investor in as much detail as possible, the next step in the process is to identify the amount of money that needs to be allocated to each goal and the asset allocation that will apply to that sum. For most advisers, the process will start with a set of sub-portfolio modules (such as those we briefly discussed in Section 4.1 and will study in more depth in Section 4.5). When using a set of pre-optimized modules, the adviser will then need to identify the module best suited to each of the specific goals of the client. That process is always driven by the client's time horizon and required probability of success, and it involves identifying the module that offers the highest possible return given the investor's risk tolerance as characterized by a given required probability of success over a given time horizon.

EXHIBIT 36   "Highest Probability- and Horizon-Adjusted Return" Sub-Portfolio Module under
Different Horizon and Probability Scenarios

	A	B	C	D	E	F
Portfolio Characteristics						
Expected return	4.3%	5.5%	6.4%	7.2%	8.0%	8.7%
Expected volatility	2.7%	4.5%	6.0%	7.5%	10.0%	12.5%
		Annualized Minimum Expectation Returns				
Time Horizon (years)			5			
Required Success						
99%	1.5%	0.9%	0.2%	–0.6%	–2.4%	–4.3%
95	2.3	2.2	2.0	1.7	0.7	–0.5
90	2.7	3.0	3.0	2.9	2.3	1.5
75	3.5	4.2	4.6	4.9	5.0	4.9
Time Horizon (years)			10			
Required Success						
99%	2.3%	2.2%	2.0%	1.7%	0.7%	–0.5%
90	3.2	3.7	4.0	4.1	4.0	3.6
75	3.7	4.6	5.1	5.6	5.9	6.0
60	4.1	5.2	5.9	6.6	7.2	7.7
Time Horizon (years)			20			
Required Success						
95%	3.3%	3.9%	4.2%	4.4%	4.4%	4.1%
90	3.5	4.3	4.7	5.0	5.2	5.1
85	3.7	4.5	5.0	5.4	5.7	5.8
75	3.9	4.9	5.5	6.0	6.5	6.8
Time Horizon (years)			25			
Required Success						
95%	3.4%	4.1%	4.4%	4.7%	4.7%	4.6%
90	3.6	4.4	4.9	5.2	5.5	5.5
85	3.7	4.6	5.2	5.6	6.0	6.1
75	3.9	4.9	5.6	6.2	6.7	7.0

To illustrate, consider the set of six modules shown in Exhibit 36;[32] these modules result
from an optimization process that will be explained later.[33] In the exhibit, the entries for

---

[32]The different ranges of required probabilities of success for various time horizons reflect the fact that the
differentiation across modules can occur more or less rapidly, reflecting the different ratios of return per unit
of risk.

[33]Exhibit 38 presents the details of the asset allocation of these modules and the constraints underpinning
their optimization.

minimum expected return are shown rounded to one decimal place; subsequent calculations for required capital are based on full precision.

In Exhibit 36, the top section, on portfolio characteristics, presents the expected return and expected volatility of each module. Below that are four sections, one for each of four time horizons: 5, 10, 20, and 25 years. In a given section, the entries are the returns that are expected for a given required probability of achieving success. For example, at a 10-year horizon and a 90% required probability of success, Modules A, B, C, D, E, and F are expected to return, respectively, 3.2%, 3.7%, 4.0%, 4.1%, 4.0%, and 3.6%. In this case, Module D would be selected to address a goal with this time horizon and required probability of success because its 4.1% expected return is higher than those of all the other modules. Thus, Module D offers the lowest "funding cost" for the given goal. The highest expected return translates to the lowest initially required capital when the expected cash flows associated with the goal are discounted using that expected return.

EXAMPLE 11   Selecting a Module

Address the following module selection problems using Exhibit 36:

1. A client describes a desire to have a reserve of €2 million for business opportunities that may develop when he retires in five years. Assume that the word "desire" points to a wish to which the adviser will ascribe a probability of 75%.
2. A 70-year-old client with a 20-year life expectancy discusses the need to be able to maintain her lifestyle for the balance of her life and wishes to leave US$3 million to be split among her three grandchildren at her death.

Solution to 1: The time horizon is five years. Exhibit 36 shows that Module E has the highest expected return (5.0%) over the five-year period and with the assumed 75% required probability of success.

Solution to 2: The time horizon is 20 years. The first goal is a need, while the second is a wish. We assume a required probability of success of 95% for a need and 75% for a wish. Exhibit 36 shows that Module D provides the highest horizon- and required-probability-adjusted return (4.4%) for the first goal. Module F is better suited to the second goal because, even though the second goal has the same time horizon, it involves only a 75% required probability of success; the appropriately adjusted return is 6.8%, markedly the highest, which means the initially required capital is lower.

Returning to the Smiths, let us use that same set of modules to look at their four specific goals. The results of our analysis are presented in Exhibit 37.

1. The first goal is a need, with a five-year time horizon and a 95% required probability of success. Looking at the 95% required probability line in the five-year time horizon section of Exhibit 36, we can see that the module with the highest expected return on a time horizon- and required probability-adjusted basis is Module A and that the appropriately adjusted expected return for that module is 2.3%. Discounting a US $500,000 annual cash flow,

EXHIBIT 37   Module Selection and Dollar Allocations (US$ thousands)

| | Total Financial Assets | | | | 25,000 | |
| | Goals | | | | | Overall Asset |
	1	2	3	4	Surplus	Allocation
Horizon (years)	5	25	10	20		
Required probability of success	95%	85%	90%	75%	$E(R_t)$	7.2%
Discount rate	2.3%	6.1%	4.1%	6.8%	$\sigma(R_t)$	8.0%
Module	**A**	**F**	**D**	**F**	**C**	
Required capital						
In currency	2,430	6,275	6,671	2,679	6,945	25,000
As a % of total	9.7%	25.1%	26.7%	10.7%	27.8%	100.0%

inflated by 2% a year from Year 2 onwards, required a US$2,430,000 initial investment. This amount represents 9.7% of the total financial wealth of the Smiths.

2. The second goal is a want, with a 25-year time horizon and an 85% required probability of success. The corresponding line of the table in Exhibit 36 points to Module F and a discount rate of 6.1%. Discounting their current expenses with the same assumption over the 25 years starting in Year 6 with a 6.1% rate points to an initially required capital of US$6,275,000, representing 25.1% of the Smiths' wealth.

3. The third goal is another need, with a 10-year time horizon and a 90% required probability of success. Module D is the best module, and the US$6,671,000 required capital reflects the discounting of a US$10 million payment in 10 years at the 4.1% indicated in Exhibit 36.

4. Finally, the fourth goal is a wish with a 20-year time horizon and a 75% required probability of success. Module F is again the best module, and the discounting of a US $10 million payment 20 years from now at the 6.8% expected return from Exhibit 36 points to a required capital of US$2,679,000 today.

Note that different goals may, in fact, be optimally addressed using the same module; thus, an individual module may be used more than once in the allocation of the individual's overall financial assets. Here, Goals 2 and 4 can both be met with the riskiest of the six modules, although their time horizons differ, as do the required probabilities of success, with Goal 2 being characterized as a want and Goal 4 as a wish.

Note also that the Smiths' earlier worry, that they might not be able to meet all their goals, can be addressed easily. Our assumptions suggest that, in fact, they have excess capital representing 27.8% of their total financial wealth. They can either revisit their current goals and bring the timing of payments forward or raise their probability of success. The case suggests that they would rather think of additional goals but will want to give themselves some time to refine their intentions. Their adviser then suggests that a "middle of the road" module be used as a "labeled goal" for that interim period, and they call this module (Module C) "capital preservation."

4.4. The Overall Portfolio

Assuming the same six modules, with their detailed composition shown in Exhibit 38, one can then derive the overall asset allocation by aggregating the individual exposures to the various modules. In short, the overall allocation is simply the weighted average exposure to each of the asset classes or strategies within each module, with the weight being the percentage of financial assets allocated to each module. Exhibit 39 presents these computations and the overall asset allocation, which is given in bold in the right-most column. The overall portfolio's expected return and volatility are also shown. In Exhibit 38, liquidity[34] is measured as one minus the ratio of the average number of days that might be needed to liquidate a position to the number of trading days in a year. (Note that the column B values add up to 101 because of rounding.)

EXHIBIT 38   Asset Allocation of Each Module

	A	B	C	D	E	F
Portfolio Characteristics						
Expected return	4.3%	5.5%	6.4%	7.2%	8.0%	8.7%
Expected volatility	2.7%	4.5%	6.0%	7.5%	10.0%	12.5%
Expected liquidity	100.0%	96.6%	90.0%	86.1%	83.6%	80.0%
Portfolio Allocations						
Cash	80%	26%	3%	1%	1%	1%
Global investment-grade bonds	20	44	45	25	0	0
Global high-yield bonds	0	5	11	25	34	4
Lower-volatility alternatives	0	9	13	0	0	0
Global developed equities	0	9	13	19	34	64
Global emerging equities	0	2	2	3	6	11
Equity-based alternatives	0	0	0	8	0	0
Illiquid global equities	0	0	5	10	15	20
Trading strategy alternatives	0	1	3	6	7	0
Global real estate	0	5	5	3	3	0
Total	100%	100%	100%	100%	100%	100%

---

[34]Note that we need to incorporate some estimate of liquidity for all asset classes and strategies to ensure that the client's and the goals' liquidity constraints can be met.

EXHIBIT 39   Goals-Based Asset Allocation (US$ thousands)

	Total Financial Assets				25,000	
	Goals				Surplus	Overall Asset Allocation
	1	2	3	4		
Horizon	5	25	10	20		
Required success	95%	85%	90%	75%	$E(R_t)$	7.2%
Discount rate	2.3%	6.1%	4.1%	6.8%	$\sigma(R_t)$	8.0%
Module	**A**	**F**	**D**	**F**	**C**	
Required capital						
In currency	2,430	6,275	6,671	2,679	6,945	25,000
As a % of total	9.7	25.1	26.7	10.7	27.8	100.0
Cash	80%	1%	1%	1%	3%	**9%**
Global investment-grade bonds	20	0	25	0	45	**24**
Global high-yield bonds	0	4	25	4	11	**12**
Lower-volatility alternatives	0	0	0	0	13	**4**
Global developed equities	0	64	19	64	13	**28**
Global emerging equities	0	11	3	11	2	**5**
Equity-based alternatives	0	0	8	0	0	**2**
Illiquid global equities	0	20	10	20	5	**10**
Trading strategy alternatives[a]	0	0	6	0	3	**3**
Global real estate	0	0	3	0	5	**2**
Total	100	100	100	100	100	**100**

[a] "Trading strategy alternatives" refers to discretionary or systematic trading strategies such as global macro and managed futures.

4.5. Revisiting the Module Process in Detail

Having explained and illustrated the client process in Exhibit 35, we now explore how modules are developed. Creating an appropriate set of optimized modules starts with the formulation of capital market assumptions. Exhibit 40 presents a possible set of forward-looking pretax capital market expectations for expected return, volatility, and liquidity[35] in Panel A and a historical 15-year correlation matrix in Panel B.[36]

---

[35] For clients who might invest in traditional asset classes by means of vehicles such as mutual funds or ETFs, these asset classes can be treated as providing virtually instant liquidity. For clients with particularly large asset pools who might use separately managed accounts, the liquidity factor for high-yield or emerging market bonds, small-capitalization equities, and certain real assets might be adjusted downward.

[36] For illiquid equities, data availability reduces the time period to seven years. The correlation matrix is based on the 15 years ending with March 2016.

EXHIBIT 40   Example of Capital Market Expectations for a Possible
Asset Class Universe

Panel A

	Expected		
	Return	Volatility	Liquidity
Cash	4.0%	3.0%	100%
Global investment-grade bonds	5.5	6.5	100
Global high-yield bonds	7.0	10.0	100
Lower-volatility alternatives	5.5	5.0	65
Global developed equities	8.0	16.0	100
Global emerging equities	9.5	22.0	100
Equity-based alternatives	6.0	8.0	65
Illiquid global equities	11.0	30.0	0
Trading strategy alternatives	6.5	10.0	80
Global real estate	7.0	15.0	100

Panel B

	Cash	Global IG Bonds	Global HY Bonds	Lower-Volatility Alts	Global Developed Equities	Global Emerging Equities	Equity-Based Alts	Trading Strategy Alts	Illiquid Equities	Global Real Estate
Cash	1.00	0.00	−0.12	0.08	−0.06	−0.04	0.02	0.04	−0.26	−0.01
Global investment-grade bonds	0.00	1.00	0.27	0.14	0.28	0.09	0.07	0.16	0.20	0.24
Global high-yield bonds	−0.12	0.27	1.00	0.46	0.70	0.17	0.31	−0.08	0.35	0.28
Lower-volatility alternatives	0.08	0.14	0.46	1.00	0.44	0.61	0.86	0.12	0.65	0.47
Global developed equities	−0.06	0.28	0.70	0.44	1.00	0.17	0.32	−0.03	0.47	0.38
Global emerging equities	−0.04	0.09	0.17	0.61	0.17	1.00	0.72	−0.03	0.67	0.49
Equity-based alternatives	0.02	0.07	0.31	0.86	0.32	0.72	1.00	0.11	0.72	0.45
Trading strategy alternatives	0.04	0.16	−0.08	0.12	−0.03	−0.03	0.11	1.00	−0.09	0.07
Illiquid global equities	−0.26	0.20	0.35	0.65	0.47	0.67	0.72	−0.09	1.00	0.88
Global real estate	−0.01	0.24	0.28	0.47	0.38	0.49	0.45	0.07	0.88	1.00

Ostensibly, in the real world, the process ought to be associated with a set of after-tax expectations, which usually cannot be limited to broad asset classes or sub–asset classes. Indeed, the tax impact of management processes within individual asset classes or strategies (for instance, index replication, index replication with systematic tax-loss harvesting, broadly diversified portfolios, or concentrated portfolios) requires that each management process within each asset class or strategy be given its own expected return and volatility. We will dispense with that step here for the sake of simplicity, both in absolute terms and with respect to jurisdictional differences.

Exhibit 41 presents a possible set of such modules based on the capital market expectations from Exhibit 40. The optimization uses a mean–variance process and is subject to a variety of constraints that are meant to reflect both market portfolio considerations and reasonable asset class or strategy suitability given the goals that we expect to correspond to various points on the frontier. Note that the frontier is not "efficient" in the traditional sense of the term because the constraints applied to the portfolios differ from one to the next. Three elements within the set of constraints deserve special mention. The first is the need to be concerned with the liquidity of the various strategies: It would make little sense, even if it were appropriate based on other considerations, to include any material exposure to illiquid equities in a declining-balance portfolio expected to "mature" within 10 years, for instance. Any exposure thus selected would be bound to increase through time because portfolio liquidation focuses on more-liquid assets. The second relates to strategies whose return distributions are known not to be "normal." This point applies particularly to a number of alternative strategies that suffer from skew and kurtosis,[37] which a mean–variance optimization process does not take into account (see Section 2.4.4). Finally, the constraints contain a measure of drawdown control to alleviate the problems potentially associated with portfolios that, although apparently optimal, appear too risky in overly challenging market circumstances. Drawdown controls are an important element in that they help deal with the often-observed asymmetric tolerance of investors for volatility: upward volatility is much preferred to downward volatility.

The six sub-portfolios shown in Exhibit 41 satisfy two major design goals: First, they cover a wide spectrum of the investment universe, ranging from a nearly all-cash portfolio (Portfolio A) to an all-equity alternative (Portfolio F). Second, they are sufficiently differentiated to avoid creating distinctions without real differences. These portfolios are graphed in Exhibit 42.

Returning to an earlier point about "labeled goals," one can easily imagine "aspirations" to describe each of these modules, ranging from "immediate- to short-term lifestyle" for Module A to "aggressive growth" for Module F. Module B might be labeled "long-term lifestyle," while C and D might represent forms of capital preservation and E a form of "balanced growth."

A final point deserves special emphasis: Modules need to be revisited on a periodic basis. While equilibrium assumptions will likely not change much from one year to the next, the need to identify one's position with respect to a "normal" market cycle can lead to modest changes in forward-looking assumptions. It would indeed be foolish to keep using long-term equilibrium assumptions when it becomes clear that one is closer to a market top than to a market bottom. The question of the suitability of revisions becomes moot when using a

---

[37] Kat (2003) described the challenge, and Davies, Kat, and Lu (2009) presented a solution that involves the use of mean–variance-skew-kurtosis optimization, which is typically too complex for most real-life circumstances.

EXHIBIT 41   Six Possible Sub-Portfolio Modules

	A	B	C	D	E	F
Portfolio Characteristics						
Expected return	4.3%	5.5%	6.4%	7.2%	8.0%	8.7%
Expected volatility	2.7	4.5	6.0	7.5	10.0	12.5
Expected liquidity	100.0	96.6	90.0	86.1	83.6	80.0
Portfolio Allocations						
Cash	80%	26%	3%	1%	1%	1%
Global investment-grade bonds	20	44	45	25	0	0
Global high-yield bonds	0	5	11	25	34	4
Lower-volatility alternatives	0	9	13	0	0	0
Global developed equities	0	9	13	19	34	64
Global emerging equities	0	2	2	3	6	11
Equity-based alternatives	0	0	0	8	0	0
Illiquid global equities	0	0	5	10	15	20
Trading strategy alternatives	0	1	3	6	7	0
Global real estate	0	5	5	3	3	0
Total	100%	100%	100%	100%	100%	100%
Constraints						
Maximum volatility	3.0%	4.5%	6.0%	7.5%	10.0%	12.5%
Minimum liquidity	100.0	95.0	90.0	85.0	80.0	70.0
Maximum alternatives	0.0	10.0	20.0	30.0	30.0	30.0
Minimum cash	80.0	20.0	0.3	0.5	0.7	1.0
Maximum HY as a percent of total fixed income	0.0	10.0	20.0	50.0	100.0	100.0
Maximum equity spectrum	0.0	10.0	20.0	40.0	75.0	100.0
Maximum EM as a percent of public equities	15.0	15.0	15.0	15.0	15.0	15.0
Maximum illiquid equities	0.0	0.0	5.0	10.0	15.0	20.0
Maximum trading as a percent of equity spectrum	0.0	10.0	15.0	15.0	20.0	25.0
Maximum real estate	0.0	5.0	10.0	15.0	20.0	25.0
Escrow cash as a percent of illiquid equities	5.0	5.0	5.0	5.0	5.0	5.0
Maximum probability of return < drawdown	1.0	1.5	2.0	2.0	2.5	2.5
Drawdown horizon	3	3	3	3	3	3
Drawdown amount	0.0	−5.0	−7.5	−10.0	−15.0	−20.0

systematic approach such as the Black–Litterman model. One may also need to review the continued suitability of constraints, not to mention (when applicable) the fact that the make-up of the market portfolio may change in terms of geography or credit distribution.

EXHIBIT 42   Sub-Portfolio Modules Cover a Full Range

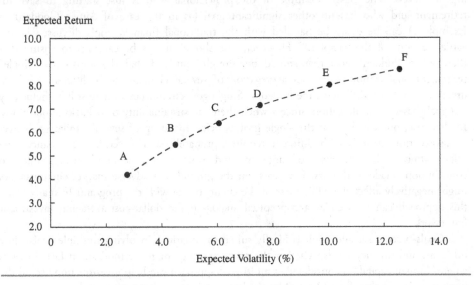

4.6. Periodically Revisiting the Overall Asset Allocation

Once set, the goals-based allocation must be regularly reviewed. Two considerations dominate:

1. Goals with an initially fixed time horizon are not necessarily one year closer to maturity after a year. Superficially, one would expect that someone who says that his or her need is to meet lifestyle expenditures over the next five years, for instance, means exactly this. Accordingly, next year, the time horizon should shift down to four years. Yet experience suggests that certain horizons are "placeholders": One year on, the time horizon remains five years. This is particularly—and understandably—relevant when the horizon reflects the anticipated death of an individual.
2. The preference for upward rather than downward volatility, combined with perceptions that goals may have higher required probabilities of success than is truly the case, leads to portfolios that typically outperform the discount rate used to compute the required initial capital. Thus, one would expect there to be some need for portfolio rebalancing when the assets allocated to certain goals appear excessive, at least in probability- and horizon-adjusted terms. This situation gives rise to important discussions with taxable clients because any form of portfolio rebalancing is inherently more complex and costly in a taxable environment than when taxes do not come into consideration.

4.7. Issues Related to Goals-Based Asset Allocation

Although goals-based asset allocation offers an elegant and mathematically sound way to deal with the circumstances of individuals, it is not a panacea. By definition, goals-based asset allocation applies best to individuals who have multiple goals, time horizons, and urgency levels. The classic example of the professional who is just starting to save for retirement and who has no other significant goal (as in the case of Aimée Goddard in Example 1) can be easily be handled with the traditional financial tools discussed in the earlier sections of this chapter.[38] However, one should always be cautious to ensure that there is no "hidden" goal that should be brought out and that the apparently "single" retirement goal is not in fact an aggregation of several elements with different levels of urgency, if not also different time horizons. Single-goal circumstances may still be helped by the goals-based asset allocation process when there are sustainability or behavioral questions. In that case, one can look at the single goal as being made up of several similar goals over successive time periods with different required probabilities of success. For instance, one might apply a higher sense of urgency—and thus require a lower risk profile—to contributions made in the first few years, on the ground that adverse market circumstances might negatively affect the willingness of the client to stay with the program. In many ways, this approach can be seen as a conceptual analog to the dollar-cost-averaging investment framework.

Goals-based asset allocation is ideally suited to situations involving multiple goals, time horizons, and urgency levels, whether the assets are large or more modest. In fact, in cases where "human capital" is considered, a multi-goal approach can help investors understand the various trade-offs they face. Ostensibly, the larger the assets, the more complex the nature of the investment problem, the more diverse the list of investment structures, and the more one should expect a client-focused approach to offer useful benefits. However, the ratio of cash outflows to assets under consideration is a more germane issue than the overall size of the asset pool.

Advisers using goals-based wealth management must contend with a considerably higher level of business management complexity. They will naturally expect to have a different policy for each client and potentially more than one policy per client. Thus, managing these portfolios day to day and satisfying the usual regulatory requirement that all clients be treated in an equivalent manner can appear to be a major quandary.

Typically, the solution would involve developing a systematic approach to decision-making such that it remains practical for advisers to formulate truly individual policies that reflect their investment insights. Exhibit 43 offers a graphical overview of advisers' activities, divided into those that involve "firm-wide" processes, defined as areas where no real customization is warranted, and those that must remain "client focused." The result is analogous to a customized racing bicycle, whose parts are mass produced but then combined into a truly unique bike custom-designed for the individual racer.

---

[38]However, an adviser may find it appropriate to help the individual divide the funds he or she believes are needed for retirement into several categories. For instance, there may be some incompressible lifestyle expenditure that represents a minimum required spending level, but there may also be some luxury or at least compressible spending that does not have such a high level of urgency or that applies over a different time frame (say, the early or late years). Thus, one could still describe the problem as involving multiple goals, multiple time horizons, and multiple urgency levels. Then, one could compare the costs associated with the funding of these goals and have the individual weigh potential future satisfaction against the loss of current purchasing power.

EXHIBIT 43   Goals-Based Wealth Management Advisory Overview

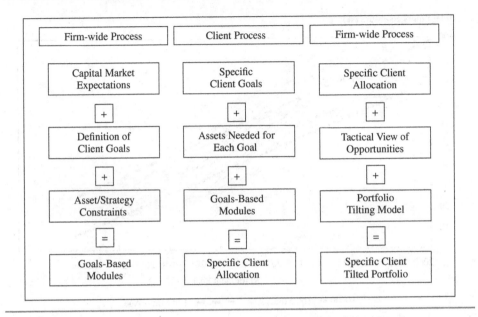

5. HEURISTICS AND OTHER APPROACHES TO ASSET ALLOCATION

In addition to the various asset allocation approaches already covered, a variety of heuristics (rules that provide a reasonable but not necessarily optimal solution) and other techniques deserve mention:

5.1. The "120 minus your age" rule.

The phrase "120 minus your age" is a heuristic for inferring a hidden, age-driven risk tolerance coefficient that then leads directly to an age-based stock versus fixed income split: 120 – Age = Percentage allocated to stocks. Thus, a 25-year-old man would allocate 95% of his investment portfolio to stocks. Although we are aware of no theoretic basis for this heuristic—or its older and newer cousins, "100 minus your age" and "125 minus your age," respectively—it results in a linear decrease in equity exposure that seems to fit the general equity glide paths associated with target-date funds, including those that are based on a total balance sheet approach that includes human capital. A number of target-date funds (sometimes called life-cycle or age-based funds) and some target-date index providers report that their glide path (the age-based change in equity exposure) is based on the evolution of an individual's human capital. For example, one set of indexes[39] explicitly targets an investable proxy for the world market portfolio in which the glide path is the result of the evolving relationship of financial capital to human capital.[40]

---

[39]Morningstar's Lifetime Allocation (target-date) indexes.
[40]See Idzorek (2008).

EXHIBIT 44   Target-Date Funds and Age Heuristics (as of January 2016)

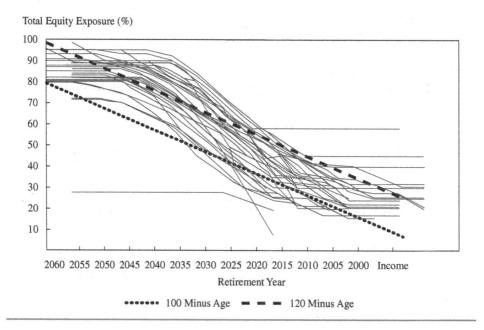

Exhibit 44 displays the glide paths of the 60 largest target-date fund families in the United States. The retirement year (typically part of the fund's name) on the *x*-axis denotes the year in which the investor is expected to retire, which is almost always assumed to be the year the investor turns 65. Thus, as of 2016, the 2060 allocations correspond to a 21-year-old investor (79% equity, using the heuristic), whereas the 2005 allocation corresponds to a 76-year-old investor (24% equity, using the heuristic).[41] One dashed line represents the equity allocation based on the "100 minus your age" heuristic, while another dashed line represents the "120 minus your age" heuristic. The heuristic lines lack some of the nuances of the various glide path lines, but it would appear that an age-based heuristic leads to asset allocations that are broadly similar to those used by target-date funds.

5.2. The 60/40 stock/bond heuristic.

Some investors choose to skip the various optimization techniques and simply adopt an asset allocation consisting of 60% equities and 40% fixed income.

The equity allocation is viewed as supplying a long-term growth foundation, and the fixed-income allocation as supplying risk reduction benefits. If the stock and bond allocations are themselves diversified, an overall diversified portfolio should result.

There is some evidence that the global financial asset market portfolio is close to this prototypical 60/40 split. Exhibit 45 displays the estimated market value of eight major components of the market portfolio from 1990 to 2012. In approximately 7 of the 23 years,

---

[41]Many target-date funds continue to offer a "2005" vintage that would have been marketed/sold to people retiring in 2005.

EXHIBIT 45   Global Market Portfolio, 1990 to 2012

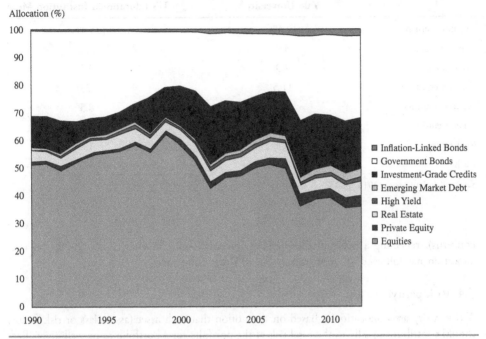

Source: Doeswijk, Lam, and Swinkels (2014).

equities, private equity, and real estate account for slightly more than 60%, while for the rest of the time, the combined percentage is slightly less.

5.3. The endowment model.

An approach to asset allocation that emphasizes large allocations to non-traditional investments, including equity-oriented investments driven by investment manager skill (e.g., private equities), has come to be known as the endowment model or Yale model. The label "Yale model" reflects the fact that the Yale University Investments Office under David Swensen pioneered the approach in the 1990s; the label "endowment model" reflects the influence of this approach among US university endowments. Swensen (2009) stated that most investors should not pursue the Yale model but should instead embrace a simpler asset allocation implemented with low-cost funds. Besides high allocations to non-traditional assets and a commitment to active management, the approach characteristically seeks to earn illiquidity premiums, which endowments with long time horizons are well positioned to capture. Exhibit 46, showing the Yale endowment asset allocation, makes these points. In the exhibit, "absolute return" indicates investment in event-driven and value-driven strategies.

In almost diametrical contrast to the endowment model is the asset allocation approach of Norway's Government Pension Fund Global (Statens pensjonsfond Utland), often called the Norway model.[42] This model's asset allocation is highly committed to passive investment in publicly traded securities (subject to environmental, social, and governance [ESG]

---

[42]See Curtis (2012).

EXHIBIT 46   Yale University Endowment Asset Allocation as of June 2014

	Yale University	US Educational Institution Mean
Absolute return	17.4%	23.3%
Domestic equity	3.9	19.3
Fixed income	4.9	9.3
Foreign equity	11.5	22.0
Natural resources	8.2	8.5
Private equity	33.0	10.0
Real estate	17.6	4.2
Cash	3.5	3.5

Source: Yale University (2014, p. 13).

concerns), reflecting a belief in the market's informational efficiency. Since 2009, the asset allocation has followed an approximate 60/40 stock/bond mix.

5.4. Risk parity.

A risk parity asset allocation is based on the notion that each asset (asset class or risk factor) should contribute equally to the total risk of the portfolio for a portfolio to be well diversified. Recall that in Section 2, we identified various criticisms and potential shortcomings of mean–variance optimization, one of which was that, while the resulting asset allocations may appear diversified across assets, the sources of risk may not be diversified. In the section on risk budgeting, Exhibit 19 contained a risk decomposition of a reverse-optimization-based asset allocation from a United Kingdom–based investor. There, we noted that the overall equity/fixed-income split was approximately 54% equities and 46% fixed income, yet of the 10% standard deviation, approximately 74% of the risk came from equities while only 26% came from fixed income.

Risk parity is a relatively controversial approach. Although there are several variants, the most common risk parity approach has the following mathematical form:

$$w_i \times \text{Cov}(r_i, r_P) = \frac{1}{n}\sigma_P^2 \tag{3}$$

where

$$w_i = \text{the weight of asset } i$$
$$\text{Cov}(r_i, r_P) = \text{the covariance of asset } i \text{ with the portfolio}$$
$$n = \text{the number of assets}$$
$$\sigma_P^2 = \text{the variance of the portfolio}$$

In general, there is not a closed-form solution to the problem, and it must be solved using some form of optimization (mathematical programming). Prior to Markowitz's development of mean–variance optimization, which simultaneously considered both risk and return, most asset allocation approaches focused only on return *and ignored risk* (or accounted for it in an ad hoc manner). The primary criticism of risk parity is that it makes the opposite mistake: It *ignores expected returns*. In general, most of the rules-based risk approaches—such as other forms of volatility weighting, minimum volatility, and target volatility—suffer from this shortcoming.

With risk parity, the contribution to risk is highly dependent on the formation of the opportunity set. For example, if the opportunity set consists of seven equity asset classes and three fixed-income asset classes, intuitively, 70% of risk will come from the equities and 30% of risk will come from fixed income. Conversely, if the opportunity set consists of three equity asset classes and seven fixed-income asset classes, intuitively, 70% of risk will come from fixed income and 30% of risk will come from equities. The point is that practitioners of risk parity must be very cognizant of the formation of their opportunity set.

Exhibit 47 gives a US-centric example consisting of five equity asset classes and three fixed-income asset classes. A constrained optimization routine (weights must sum to 100%) was used to determine the weight to each asset class, such that all asset classes contributed the same amount to total risk. In this case, each asset class contributed 0.8%, resulting in an asset allocation with a total standard deviation of 6.41%. In this example, 5/8 of total risk comes from equity asset classes and 3/8 comes from fixed-income asset classes. Earlier, we explained that reverse optimization can be used to infer the expected return of any set of presumed efficient weights. In Exhibit 47, based on a total market risk premium of 2.13% and a risk-free rate of 3%, we inferred the reverse-optimized total returns (final column). In this case, these seem to be relatively reasonable expected returns.

After deriving a risk parity–based asset allocation, the next step in the process is to borrow (use leverage) or to lend (save a portion of wealth, presumably in cash) so that the overall portfolio corresponds to the investor's risk appetite. Continuing with our example, the market risk premium is 2.13% (above the assumed risk-free rate of 3%) and the market variance is 0.41% (i.e., 6.41% squared); thus, the implied market trade-off of expected return (in excess of the risk-free rate) for risk is 2.13% divided by 0.41%, which equals approximately 5.2. Investors with a greater appetite for risk than the market as a whole would

EXHIBIT 47   Risk Parity Portfolio Weights and Risk-Budgeting Statistics Based on Reverse-Optimized Returns

Asset Class	Weight	Marginal Contribution to Total Risk (MCTR)	ACTR	Percentage Contribution to Total Standard Deviation	Reverse-Optimized Total Returns
US large-cap equities	7.7%	10.43%	0.80%	12.50%	6.47%
US mid-cap equities	6.1	13.03	0.80	12.50	7.33
US small-cap equities	5.9	13.61	0.80	12.50	7.52
Non-US developed market equities	5.6	14.38	0.80	12.50	7.78
Emerging market equities	4.5	17.74	0.80	12.50	8.89
Non-US bonds	15.5	5.17	0.80	12.50	4.72
US TIPS	23.9	3.36	0.80	12.50	4.12
US bonds	30.8	2.60	0.80	12.50	3.86
Total	100.0%		6.41%	100.00%	5.13%

borrow money to lever up the risk parity portfolios, while investors with a lower appetite for risk would invest a portion of their wealth in cash.

Back tests of levered risk parity portfolios have produced promising results, although critics of these back tests argue that they suffer from look-back bias and are very dependent on the ability to use extremely large amounts of leverage at low borrow rates (which may not have been feasible); see, for example, Anderson, Bianchi, and Goldberg (2012). Proponents of risk parity have suggested that the idea of "leverage aversion" contributes to the success of the strategy. Black (1972) suggested that restrictions on leverage and a general aversion to leverage may cause return-seeking investors to pursue higher-returning assets, such as stocks. All else equal, this behavior would reduce the price of bonds, thus allowing the investor to buy bonds at a small discount, hold them to maturity, and realize the full value of the bond. Asness, Frazzini, and Pedersen (2012) have offered this idea as a potential explanation for why a levered (bond-centric) asset allocation might outperform an equity-centric asset allocation with equivalent or similar risk.

5.5. The $1/N$ rule.

One of the simplest asset allocation heuristics involves equally weighting allocations to assets. DeMiguel, Garlappi, and Uppal (2009) define an approach in which $1/N$ of wealth is allocated to each of N assets available for investment at each rebalancing date. Calendar rebalancing to equal weighting at quarterly intervals is one common rebalancing discipline used. By treating all assets as indistinguishable in terms of mean returns, volatility, and correlations, in principle, $1/N$ rule portfolios should be dominated by methods that optimize asset class weights to exploit differences in investment characteristics. In empirical studies comparing approaches, however, the $1/N$ rule has been found to perform considerably better, based on Sharpe ratios and certainty equivalents, than theory might suggest. One possible explanation is that the $1/N$ rule sidesteps problems caused by optimizing when there is estimation error in inputs.

6. PORTFOLIO REBALANCING IN PRACTICE

The chapter "Introduction to Asset Allocation" provided an introduction to rebalancing, including some detailed comments on strategic considerations. This section aims to present useful additional insight and information.

Meanings of "Rebalancing"

Rebalancing has been defined as the discipline of adjusting portfolio weights to more closely align with the strategic asset allocation. In that sense, rebalancing includes policy regarding the correction of any drift away from strategic asset allocation weights resulting from market price movements and the passage of time for finite-lived assets, such as bonds. In liability-relative asset allocation, adjusting a liability-hedging portfolio to account for changes in net duration exposures from the passage of time, for example, would fall under the rubric of rebalancing.

Some use the term "rebalancing" more expansively, to include the combined effects on asset class weights not only of rebalancing in the above sense but also of active allocation activities. In that sense, rebalancing would include tactical allocations.

> Although rebalancing policy can be established to accommodate tactical adjustments, tactical asset allocation per se is not covered under "rebalancing" as the term is used here.
>
> Changes in asset allocation weights in response to changes in client circumstances, goals, or other client factors are sometimes also referred to as "rebalancing" (especially if the adjustments are minor). These activities fall under the scope of client monitoring and asset allocation review, as described elsewhere in the CFA curriculum.

An appropriate rebalancing policy involves a weighing of benefits and costs. Benefits depend on the idea that if an investor's strategic asset allocation is optimal, then any divergence in the portfolio from that asset allocation represents an expected utility loss to the investor. Rebalancing benefits the investor by reducing the present value of expected losses from not tracking the optimum. In theory, the basic cost of not rebalancing is this present value of expected utility losses from straying from the optimum.[43]

Apart from the above considerations of trade-offs, disciplined rebalancing has tended to reduce risk while incrementally adding to returns. Several interpretations of this empirical finding have been offered, including the following:

- *Rebalancing earns a diversification return.* The compound growth rate of a portfolio is greater than the weighted average compound growth rates of the component portfolio holdings (given positive expected returns and positive asset weights). Given sufficiently low transaction costs, this effect leads to what has been called a *diversification return* to frequent rebalancing to a well-diversified portfolio.[44]
- *Rebalancing earns a return from being short volatility.* In the case of a portfolio consisting of a risky asset and a risk-free asset, the return to a rebalanced portfolio can be replicated by creating a buy-and-hold position in the portfolio, writing out-of-the-money puts and calls on the risky asset, and investing the premiums in risk-free bonds.[45] As the value of puts and calls is positively related to volatility, such a position is called being short volatility (or being short gamma, by reference to the option Greeks).

Practice appears not to have produced a consensus on the most appropriate rebalancing discipline. "Introduction to Asset Allocation" defined and discussed calendar rebalancing[46]— sometimes mentioned as common in portfolios managed for individual investors—and percent-range rebalancing. Calendar rebalancing involves lower overhead because of lower monitoring costs. Percent-range rebalancing is a more disciplined risk control policy, however, because it makes rebalancing contingent on market movements. Without weighing costs and benefits in the abstract, Exhibit 48 assumes percent-range rebalancing and summarizes the effects of each of several key factors on the corridor width of an asset class, holding all else equal, except for the factor of the asset class's own volatility.[47] For taxable

---

[43]See Leland (2000).

[44]See Willenbrock (2011). This phenomenon was called *rebalancing return* by Mulvey and Kim (2009). Luenberger (2013) suggests that the phenomenon could be exploited by a strategy of buying high-volatility assets and rebalancing often, a process he called *volatility pumping*.

[45]As shown in Ang (2014, pp. 135–139).

[46]Rebalancing a portfolio to target weights on a periodic basis—for example, monthly, quarterly, semiannually, or annually.

[47]See Masters (2003).

EXHIBIT 48   Factors Affecting the Optimal Corridor Width of an Asset Class

Factor	Effect on Optimal Width of Corridor (All Else Equal)	Intuition
Factors Positively Related to Optimal Corridor Width		
Transaction costs	The higher the transaction costs, the wider the optimal corridor.	High transaction costs set a high hurdle for rebalancing benefits to overcome.
Risk tolerance	The higher the risk tolerance, the wider the optimal corridor.	Higher risk tolerance means less sensitivity to divergences from the target allocation.
Correlation with the rest of the portfolio	The higher the correlation, the wider the optimal corridor.	When asset classes move in sync, further divergence from target weights is less likely.
Factors Inversely Related to Optimal Corridor Width		
Volatility of the rest of the portfolio	The higher the volatility, the narrower the optimal corridor.	Higher volatility makes large divergences from the strategic asset allocation more likely.

investors, transactions trigger capital gains in jurisdictions that tax them; therefore, for such investors, higher tax rates on capital gains should also be associated with wider corridors.

Among positive factors, the cases of transaction costs and risk tolerance are obvious. Transaction costs can be reduced to the extent that portfolio cash flows can be used to rebalance. The case of correlation is less obvious. Because of correlations, the rebalancing triggers among different asset classes are linked.

Consider correlation in a two–asset class scenario. Suppose one asset class is above its target weight, so the other asset class is below its target weight. A further increase in the value of the overweight asset class implies, on average, a smaller divergence in the asset mix if the asset classes' returns are more highly positively correlated (because the denominator in computing the overweight asset class's weight is the sum of the values of the two asset classes). In a multi-asset-class scenario, all pair-wise asset class correlations would need to be considered, making the interpretation of correlations complex. To expand the application of the two-asset case's intuition, one simplification involves considering the balance of a portfolio to be a single hypothetical asset and computing an asset class's correlation with it.

As indicated in Exhibit 48, the higher the volatility of the rest of the portfolio, excluding the asset class being considered, the more likely a large divergence from the strategic asset allocation becomes. That consideration should point to a narrower optimal corridor, all else being equal.

In the case of an asset class's own volatility, "holding all else equal" is not practically meaningful. If rebalancing did not involve transaction costs, then higher volatility would lead to a narrower corridor, all else equal, for a risk-averse investor.[48] Higher volatility implies that if an asset class is not brought back into the optimal range after a given move away from it, the chance of an even further divergence from optimal is greater. In other words, higher volatility makes large divergence from the strategic asset allocation more likely. However, reducing a corridor's width means more frequent rebalancing and higher transaction costs. Thus, the effect of volatility on optimal corridor width involves a trade-off between

---

[48]As in Masters (2003).

controlling transaction costs and controlling risk. Conclusions also depend on the assumptions made about asset price return dynamics.

In practice, corridor width is often specified to be proportionally greater, the higher an asset class's volatility, with a focus on transaction cost control. In *volatility-based rebalancing*, corridor width is set proportionally to the asset class's own volatility. In one variation of *equal probability rebalancing* (McCalla 1997), the manager specifies a corridor for each asset class in terms of a common multiple of the standard deviation of the asset class's returns such that, under a normal probability assumption, each asset class is equally likely to trigger rebalancing.

EXAMPLE 12   Tolerance Bands for an Asset Allocation

An investment committee is reviewing the following strategic asset allocation:

Domestic equities 50% ± 5% (i.e., 45% to 55% of portfolio value)
International equities 15% ± 1.5%
Domestic bonds 35% ± 3.5%

The market for the domestic bonds is relatively illiquid. The committee views the above corridors as appropriate *if* each asset class's risk and transaction cost characteristics remain unchanged. The committee now wants to account for differences among the asset classes in setting the corridors.

Evaluate the implications of the following sets of facts for the stated tolerance bands, given an all-else-equal assumption in each case:

1. Tax rates for international equities increase by 10 percentage points.
2. Transaction costs in international equities increase by 20% relative to domestic equities, but the correlation of international equities with domestic equities and bonds declines. What is the expected effect on the tolerance band for international equities?
3. The volatility of domestic bonds increases. What is the expected effect on their tolerance band? Assume that domestic bonds are relatively illiquid.

Solution to 1: The tolerance band for international equities should increase if the entity is a taxable investor.

Solution to 2: Increased transaction costs point to widening the tolerance band for international equities, but declining correlations point to narrowing it. The overall effect is indeterminate.

Solution to 3: Given that the market for domestic bonds is relatively illiquid, the increase in volatility suggests widening the rebalancing band. Containing transaction costs is more important than the expected utility losses from allowing a larger divergence from the strategic asset allocation.

One decision involved in rebalancing policy is whether to adjust asset class holdings to their target proportions, to the limits of the corridors, or to within the corridors but not to target weights. Compared with rebalancing to target weights, rebalancing to the upper or lower limit of the allowed range results in less close alignment with target proportions but lower transaction costs—an especially important consideration in the case of relatively illiquid assets. The choice among alternatives may be influenced by judgmental tactical considerations.

Because one rebalancing decision affects later rebalancing decisions, the optimal rebalancing decisions at different points in time are linked. However, optimal rebalancing in a multi-period, multi-asset case is an unsolved problem.

The analysis of Dybvig (2005) suggests that fixed transaction costs favor rebalancing to the target weights and variable transaction costs favor rebalancing to the nearest corridor border (the interior of the corridor being therefore a "no trade zone"). A number of studies have contrasted rebalancing to target weights and rebalancing to the allowed range based on particular asset classes, time periods, and measures of the benefits of rebalancing. These studies have reached a variety of conclusions, suggesting that no simple, empirically based advice can be provided.

Rebalancing in a Goals-Based Approach

The use of probability- and horizon-adjusted discount rates to size the various goal-defeasing sub-portfolios means that portfolios will usually produce returns that are higher than assumed. Thus, as time passes, the dollars allocated to the various sub-portfolios—other than labeled-goal portfolios—may be expected to exceed the actual requirements. For example, in average markets, returns should exceed the conservative requirements of a goal associated with a 90% required probability of success. Sub-portfolios with shorter time horizons for goals with high required probabilities of success will tend to contain relatively low-risk assets, whereas riskier assets may have high allocations in longer-horizon portfolios for goals with lower required probabilities of success. Thus, there is a greater chance that the exposure to lower-risk assets will creep up before one experiences the same for riskier assets. Thus, failing to rebalance the portfolio will gradually move it down the risk axis—and the defined efficient frontier—and thus lead the client to take less risk than he or she can bear.

---

7. CONCLUSIONS

This chapter has surveyed how appropriate asset allocations can be determined to meet the needs of a variety of investors. Among the major points made have been the following:

- The objective function of asset-only mean–variance optimization is to maximize the expected return of the asset mix minus a penalty that depends on risk aversion and the expected variance of the asset mix.
- Criticisms of MVO include the following:
  - o The outputs (asset allocations) are highly sensitive to small changes in the inputs.
  - o The asset allocations are highly concentrated in a subset of the available asset classes.
  - o Investors are often concerned with characteristics of asset class returns such as skewness and kurtosis that are not accounted for in MVO.

- o While the asset allocations may appear diversified across assets, the sources of risk may not be diversified.
- o MVO allocations may have no direct connection to the factors affecting any liability or consumption streams.
- o MVO is a single-period framework that tends to ignore trading/rebalancing costs and taxes.
- Deriving expected returns by reverse optimization or by reverse optimization tilted toward an investor's views on asset returns (the Black–Litterman model) is one means of addressing the tendency of MVO to produce efficient portfolios that are not well diversified.
- Placing constraints on asset class weights to prevent extremely concentrated portfolios and resampling inputs are other ways of addressing the same concern.
- For some relatively illiquid asset classes, a satisfactory proxy may not be available; including such asset classes in the optimization may therefore be problematic.
- Risk budgeting is a means of making optimal use of risk in the pursuit of return. A risk budget is optimal when the ratio of excess return to marginal contribution to total risk is the same for all assets in the portfolio.
- Characteristics of liabilities that affect asset allocation in liability-relative asset allocation include the following:
  - o Fixed versus contingent cash flows
  - o Legal versus quasi-liabilities
  - o Duration and convexity of liability cash flows
  - o Value of liabilities as compared with the size of the sponsoring organization
  - o Factors driving future liability cash flows (inflation, economic conditions, interest rates, risk premium)
  - o Timing considerations, such longevity risk
  - o Regulations affecting liability cash flow calculations

- Approaches to liability-relative asset allocation include surplus optimization, a hedging/return-seeking portfolios approach, and an integrated asset–liability approach.
  - o Surplus optimization involves MVO applied to surplus returns.
  - o A hedging/return-seeking portfolios approach assigns assets to one of two portfolios. The objective of the hedging portfolio is to hedge the investor's liability stream. Any remaining funds are invested in the return-seeking portfolio.
  - o An integrated asset–liability approach integrates and jointly optimizes asset and liability decisions.
- A goals-based asset allocation process combines into an overall portfolio a number of sub-portfolios, each of which is designed to fund an individual goal with its own time horizon and required probability of success.
- In the implementation, there are two fundamental parts to the asset allocation process. The first centers on the creation of portfolio modules, while the second relates to the identification of client goals and the matching of these goals to the appropriate sub-portfolios to which suitable levels of capital are allocated.
- Other approaches to asset allocation include "120 minus your age," 60/40 stocks/bonds, the endowment model, risk parity, and the $1/N$ rule.
- Disciplined rebalancing has tended to reduce risk while incrementally adding to returns. Interpretations of this empirical finding include that rebalancing earns a diversification

return, that rebalancing earns a return from being short volatility, and that rebalancing earns a return to supplying liquidity to the market.

- Factors positively related to optimal corridor width include transaction costs, risk tolerance, and an asset class's correlation with the rest of the portfolio. The higher the correlation, the wider the optimal corridor, because when asset classes move in sync, further divergence from target weights is less likely.
- The volatility of the rest of the portfolio (outside of the asset class under consideration) is inversely related to optimal corridor width.
- An asset class's own volatility involves a trade-off between transaction costs and risk control. The width of the optimal tolerance band increases with transaction costs for volatility-based rebalancing.

REFERENCES

Anderson, Robert M., Stephen W. Bianchi, and Lisa R. Goldberg. 2012. "Will My Risk Parity Strategy Outperform?" *Financial Analysts Journal*, vol. 68, no. 6 (November/December): 75–93.

Ang, Andrew. 2014. *Asset Management*. New York: Oxford University Press.

Asness, Clifford S., Andrea Frazzini, and Lasse H. Pedersen. 2012. "Leverage Aversion and Risk Parity." *Financial Analysts Journal*, vol. 68, no. 1 (January/February): 47–59.

Athayde, Gustavo M. de, and Renato G. Flôres Jr. 2003. "Incorporating Skewness and Kurtosis in Portfolio Optimization: A Multideminsional Efficient Set." In *Advances in Portfolio Construction and Implementation*, edited by Stephen Satchell and Alan Scowcroft. Oxford, UK: Butterworth–Heinemann.

Beardsley, Xiaoxin W., Brian Field, and Mingqing Xiao. 2012. "Mean–Variance-Skewness-Kurtosis Portfolio Optimization with Return and Liquidity." *Communications in Mathematical Finance*, vol. 1, no. 1: 13–49.

Black, Fischer. 1972. "Capital market equilibrium with restricted borrowing." *Journal of Business*, vol. 45, no. 3: 444–455.

Black, Fischer, and Robert Litterman. 1990. "Asset Allocation: Combining Investors Views with Market Equilibrium." Fixed Income Research, Goldman, Sachs & Company, September.

Black, Fischer, and Robert Litterman. 1991. "Global Asset Allocation with Equities, Bonds, and Currencies." Fixed Income Research, Goldman, Sachs & Company, October.

Black, Fischer, and Robert Litterman. 1992. "Global Portfolio Optimization." *Financial Analysts Journal*, vol. 48, no. 5 (September/October): 28–43.

Blanchett, David M., and Philip U. Straehl. 2015. "No Portfolio is an Island." *Financial Analysts Journal*, vol. 71, no. 3 (May/June): 15–33.

Briec, W., K. Kerstens, and O. Jokung. 2007. "Mean–Variance-Skewness Portfolio Performance Gauging: A General Shortage Function and Dual Approach." *Management Science*, vol. 53, no. 1 (January): 135–149.

Brunel, Jean L.P. 2003. "Revisiting the Asset Allocation Challenge through a Behavioral Finance Lens." *Journal of Wealth Management*, vol. 6, no. 2 (Fall): 10–20.

Brunel, Jean L.P. 2005. "A Behavioral Finance Approach to Strategic Asset Allocation—A Case Study." *Journal of Investment Consulting*, vol. 7, no. 3 (Winter): 61–69.

Chhabra, Ashvin. 2005. "Beyond Markowitz: A Comprehensive Wealth Allocation Framework for Individual Investors." *Journal of Wealth Management*, vol. 7, no. 4 (Spring): 8–34.

Chow, George, Eric Jacquier, Mark Kritzman, and Kenneth Lowry. 1999. "Optimal Portfolios in Good Times and Bad." *Financial Analysts Journal*, vol. 55, no. 3 (May/June): 65–73.

Curtis, Gregory. 2012. "Yale versus Norway." White Paper 55, Greycourt (September).

Das, Sanjiv, Harry Markowitz, Jonathan Scheid, and Meir Statman. 2010. "Portfolio Optimization with Mental Accounts." *Journal of Financial and Quantitative Analysis*, vol. 45, no. 2 (April): 311–334.

Das, Sanjiv, Harry Markowitz, Jonathan Scheid, and Meir Statman. 2011. "Portfolios for Investors Who Want to Reach Their Goals While Staying on the Mean–Variance Efficient Frontier." *Journal of Wealth Management*, vol. 14, no. 2 (Fall): 25–31.

Davies, Ryan, Harry M. Kat, and Sa Lu. 2009. "Fund of Hedge Funds Portfolio Selection: A Multiple-Objective Approach." *Journal of Derivatives & Hedge Funds*, vol. 15, no. 2: 91–115.

DeMiguel, V., L. Garlappi, and R. Uppal. 2009. "Optimal versus Naive Diversification: How Inefficient Is the 1/*N* Portfolio Strategy?" *Review of Financial Studies*, vol. 22, no. 5: 1915–1953.

DiBartolomeo, Dan. 1993. "Portfolio Optimization: The Robust Solution." Prudential Securities Quantitative Conference. Available online at http://www.northinfo.com/documents/45.pdf.

Doeswijk, Ronald, Trevin Lam, and Laurens Swinkels. 2014. "The Global Multi-Asset Market Portfolio, 1959–2012." *Financial Analysts Journal*, vol. 70, no. 2 (March/April): 26–41.

Dybvig, Philip H. 2005. "Mean-variance portfolio rebalancing with transaction costs." Working paper, Washington University in Saint Louis.

Elton, Edwin J., and Martin J. Gruber. 1992. "Optimal Investment Strategies with Investor Liabilities." *Journal of Banking & Finance*, vol. 16, no. 5: 869–890.

Gannon, James A., and Bob Collins. 2009. "Liability-Responsive Asset Allocation." Russell Research Viewpoint.

Goldberg, Lisa R., Michael Y. Hayes, and Ola Mahmoud. 2013. "Minimizing Shortfall." *Quantitative Finance*, vol. 13, no. 10: 1533–1545.

Grable, John E. 2008. "RiskCAT: A Framework for Identifying Maximum Risk Thresholds in Personal Portfolios." *Journal of Financial Planning*, vol. 21, no. 10: 52–62.

Grable, John E., and Soo-Hyun Joo. 2004. "Environmental and Biopsychosocial Factors Associated with Financial Risk Tolerance." *Financial Counseling and Planning*, vol. 15, no. 1: 73–88.

Harvey, Campbell R., John C. Liechty, Merrill W. Liechty, and Peter Müller. 2010. "Portfolio Selection with Higher Moments." *Quantitative Finance*, vol. 10, no. 5 (May): 469–485.

Idzorek, Thomas. 2008. "Lifetime Asset Allocations: Methodologies for Target Maturity Funds." Ibbotson Associates Research Report.

Idzorek, Thomas M., and Maciej Kowara. 2013. "Factor-Based Asset Allocation vs. Asset-Class-Based Asset Allocation." *Financial Analysts Journal*, vol. 69, no. 3 (May/June): 19–29.

Jobson, David J., and Bob Korkie. 1980. "Estimation for Markowitz Efficient Portfolios." *Journal of the American Statistical Association*, vol. 75, no. 371 (September): 544–554.

Jobson, David J., and Bob Korkie. 1981. "Putting Markowitz Theory to Work." *Journal of Portfolio Management*, vol. 7, no. 4 (Summer): 70–74.

Jorion, Phillipe. 1992. "Portfolio Optimization in Practice." *Financial Analysts Journal*, vol. 48, no. 1 (January/February): 68–74.

Kahneman, Daniel, and Amos Tversky. 1979. "Prospect Theory: An Analysis of Decision under Risk." *Econometrica*, vol. 47, no. 2: 263–292.

Kat, Harry M. 2003. "10 Things That Investors Should Know about Hedge Funds." *Journal of Wealth Management*, vol. 5, no. 4 (Spring): 72–81.

Leibowitz, Martin L., and Roy D. Henriksson. 1988. "Portfolio Optimization Within a Surplus Framework." *Financial Analysts Journal*, vol. 44, no. 2: 43–51.

Leland, Hayne. 2000. "Optimal Portfolio Implementation with Transaction Costs and Capital Gains Taxes." Working paper, University of California, Berkeley.

Luenberger, David G. 2013. *Investment Science*, 2nd ed. New York: Oxford University Press.

Markowitz, Harry M. 1952. "Portfolio Selection." *Journal of Finance*, vol. 7, no. 1 (March): 77–91.

Markowitz, Harry M. 1959. *Portfolio Selection: Efficient Diversification of Investments*. New York: John Wiley & Sons.

Maslow, A. H. 1943. "A Theory of Human Motivation." *Psychological Review*, vol. 50, no. 4: 370–396.

Masters, Seth J. 2003. "Rebalancing." *Journal of Portfolio Management*, vol. 29, no. 3: 52–57.

McCalla, Douglas B. 1997. "Enhancing the Efficient Frontier with Portfolio Rebalancing." *Journal of Pension Plan Investing*, vol. 1, no. 4: 16–32.

Michaud, Richard O. 1998. *Efficient Asset Management*. Boston: Harvard Business School Press.

Mulvey, John M. 1989. "A Surplus Optimization Perspective." *Investment Management Review*, vol. 3: 31–39.

Mulvey, John M. 1994. "An Asset-Liability System." *Interfaces*, vol. 24, no. 3: 22–33.

Mulvey, J.M., and W. Kim. 2009. "Constantly Rebalanced Portfolio—Is Mean-Reverting Necessary?" in Rama Cont, ed. *Encyclopedia of Quantitative Finance*, vol 2, Hoboken, NJ: John Wiley & Sons.

Mulvey, John M., Bill Pauling, and Ron E. Madey. 2003. "Advantages of Multi-Period Portfolio Models." *Journal of Portfolio Management*, vol. 29, no. 2 (Winter): 35–45.

Nevins, Daniel. 2004. "Goal-Based Investing: Integrating Traditional and Behavioral Finance." *Journal of Wealth Management*, vol. 6, no. 4 (Spring): 8–23.

Pompian, Michael M., and John B. Longo. 2004. "A New Paradigm for Practical Application of Behavioral Finance." *Journal of Wealth Management*, vol. 7, no. 2 (Fall): 9–15.

Rockafellar, R. Tyrrell, and Stanislav Uryasev. 2000. "Optimization of Conditional Value-at-Risk." *Journal of Risk*, vol. 2, no. 3 (Spring): 21–41.

Rudd, Andrew, and Laurence B. Siegel. 2013. "Using an Economic Balance Sheet for Financial Planning." *Journal of Wealth Management*, vol. 16, no. 2 (Fall): 15–23.

Scherer, Bernd. 2002. "Portfolio Resampling: Review and Critique." *Financial Analysts Journal*, vol. 58, no. 6 (November/December): 98–109.

Sharpe, William. 1974. "Imputing Expected Security Returns from Portfolio Composition." *Journal of Financial and Quantitative Analysis*, vol. 9, no. 3 (June): 463–472.

Sharpe, William, and Lawrence G. Tint. 1990. "Liabilities: A New Approach." *Journal of Portfolio Management*, vol. 16, no. 2: 5–10.

Shefrin, H., and M. Statman. 2000. "Behavioral Portfolio Theory." *Journal of Financial and Quantitative Analysis*, vol. 35, no. 2: 127–151.

Swensen, D. 2009. *Pioneering Portfolio Management: An Unconventional Approach to Institutional Investment*, 2nd ed. New York: Free Press.

Tversky, Amos, and Daniel Kahneman. 1992. "Advances in prospect theory: Cumulative representation of uncertainty." *Journal of Risk and Uncertainty*, vol. 5, no. 4: 297–323.

Willenbrock, Scott. 2011. "Diversification Return, Portfolio Rebalancing, and the Commodity Return Puzzle." *Financial Analysts Journal*, vol. 67, no. 4 (July/August): 42–49.

Winkelmann, Kurt. 2003. "Developing an Optimal Active Risk Budget," in *Modern Investment Management: An Equilibrium Approach*, Bob Litterman, ed. New York: John Wiley & Sons.

Xiong, James X., and Thomas M. Idzorek. 2011. "The Impact of Skewness and Fat Tails on the Asset Allocation Decision." *Financial Analysts Journal*, vol. 67, no. 2 (March/April): 23–35.

Yale University. 2014. "The Yale Endowment 2014" (http://investments.yale.edu/s/Yale_Endowment_14.pdf).

PRACTICE PROBLEMS

The following information relates to questions 1–8

Megan Beade and Hanna Müller are senior analysts for a large, multi-divisional money management firm. Beade supports the institutional portfolio managers, and Müller does the same for the private wealth portfolio managers.

EXHIBIT 1   Asset Allocation and Market Weights (in percent)

Asset Classes	Asset Allocation	Investable Global Market Weights
Cash	0	—
US bonds	30	17
US TIPS	0	3
Non-US bonds	0	22
Emerging market equity	25	5
Non-US developed equity	20	29
US small- and mid-cap equity	25	4
US large-cap equity	0	20

Beade reviews the asset allocation in Exhibit 1, derived from a mean–variance optimization (MVO) model for an institutional client, noting that details of the MVO are lacking.

The firm's policy is to rebalance a portfolio when the asset class weight falls outside of a corridor around the target allocation. The width of each corridor is customized for each client and proportional to the target allocation. Beade recommends wider corridor widths for high-risk asset classes, narrower corridor widths for less liquid asset classes, and narrower corridor widths for taxable clients with high capital gains tax rates.

One client sponsors a defined benefit pension plan where the present value of the liabilities is $241 million and the market value of plan assets is $205 million. Beade expects interest rates to rise and both the present value of plan liabilities and the market value of plan assets to decrease by $25 million, changing the pension plan's funding ratio.

Beade uses a surplus optimization approach to liability-relative asset allocation based on the objective function

$$U_m^{LR} = E(R_{s,m}) - 0.005\lambda\sigma^2(R_{s,m})$$

where $E(R_{s,m})$ is the expected surplus return for portfolio m, λ is the risk aversion coefficient, and $\sigma^2(R_{s,m})$ is the variance of the surplus return. Beade establishes the expected surplus return and surplus variance for three different asset allocations, shown in Exhibit 2. Given $\lambda = 1.50$, she chooses the optimal asset mix.

Client Haunani Kealoha has a large fixed obligation due in 10 years. Beade assesses that Kealoha has substantially more funds than are required to meet the fixed obligation.

EXHIBIT 2   Expected Surplus Return and Volatility for Three Portfolios

	Return	Standard Deviation
Portfolio 1	13.00%	24%
Portfolio 2	12.00%	18%
Portfolio 3	11.00%	19%

EXHIBIT 3   Characteristics of Sub-Portfolios

Sub-Portfolio	A	B	C	D	E
Expected return, in percent	4.60	5.80	7.00	8.20	9.40
Expected volatility, in percent	3.46	5.51	8.08	10.80	13.59
Required Success Rate	**Minimum Expected Return for Success Rate**				
99%	1.00	0.07	−1.40	−3.04	−4.74
95%	2.05	1.75	1.06	0.25	−0.60
90%	2.62	2.64	2.37	2.01	1.61
85%	3.00	3.25	3.26	3.19	3.10
75%	3.56	4.14	4.56	4.94	5.30

The client wants to earn a competitive risk-adjusted rate of return while maintaining a high level of certainty that there will be sufficient assets to meet the fixed obligation.

In the private wealth area, the firm has designed five sub-portfolios with differing asset allocations that are used to fund different client goals over a five-year horizon. Exhibit 3 shows the expected returns and volatilities of the sub-portfolios and the probabilities that the sub-portfolios will exceed an expected minimum return. Client Luis Rodríguez wants to satisfy two goals. Goal 1 requires a conservative portfolio providing the highest possible minimum return that will be met at least 95% of the time. Goal 2 requires a riskier portfolio that provides the highest minimum return that will be exceeded at least 85% of the time.

Müller uses a risk parity asset allocation approach with a client's four–asset class portfolio. The expected return of the domestic bond asset class is the lowest of the asset classes, and the returns of the domestic bond asset class have the lowest covariance with other asset class returns. Müller estimates the weight that should be placed on domestic bonds.

Müller and a client discuss other approaches to asset allocation that are not based on optimization models or goals-based models. Müller makes the following comments to the client:

Comment 1:   An advantage of the "120 minus your age" heuristic over the 60/40 stock/ bond heuristic is that it incorporates an age-based stock/bond allocation.

Comment 2:   The Yale model emphasizes traditional investments and a commitment to active management.

Comment 3:   A client's asset allocation using the 1/N rule depends on the investment characteristics of each asset class.

1. The asset allocation in Exhibit 1 *most likely* resulted from a mean–variance optimization using:
   A.   historical data.
   B.   reverse optimization.
   C.   Black–Litterman inputs.

2. For clients concerned about rebalancing-related transactions costs, which of Beade's suggested changes in the corridor width of the rebalancing policy is correct? The change with respect to:
   A.   high-risk asset classes.
   B.   less liquid asset classes.
   C.   taxable clients with high capital gains tax rates.

3. Based on Beade's interest rate expectations, the pension plan's funding ratio will:
   A. decrease.
   B. remain unchanged.
   C. increase.

4. Based on Exhibit 2, which portfolio provides the greatest objective function expected value?
   A. Portfolio 1
   B. Portfolio 2
   C. Portfolio 3

5. The asset allocation approach most appropriate for client Kealoha is *best* described as:
   A. a surplus optimization approach.
   B. an integrated asset–liability approach.
   C. a hedging/return-seeking portfolios approach.

6. Based on Exhibit 3, which sub-portfolios *best* meet the two goals expressed by client Rodríguez?
   A. Sub-Portfolio A for Goal 1 and Sub-Portfolio C for Goal 2
   B. Sub-Portfolio B for Goal 1 and Sub-Portfolio C for Goal 2
   C. Sub-Portfolio E for Goal 1 and Sub-Portfolio A for Goal 2

7. In the risk parity asset allocation approach that Müller uses, the weight that Müller places on domestic bonds should be:
   A. less than 25%.
   B. equal to 25%.
   C. greater than 25%.

8. Which of Müller's comments about the other approaches to asset allocation is correct?
   A. Comment 1
   B. Comment 2
   C. Comment 3

The following information relates to questions 9–13

Investment adviser Carl Monteo determines client asset allocations using quantitative techniques such as mean–variance optimization (MVO) and risk budgets. Monteo is reviewing the allocations of three clients. Exhibit 1 shows the expected return and standard deviation of returns for three strategic asset allocations that apply to several of Monteo's clients.

Monteo interviews client Mary Perkins and develops a detailed assessment of her risk preference and capacity for risk, which is needed to apply MVO to asset allocation. Monteo estimates the risk aversion coefficient (λ) for Perkins to be 8 and uses the following utility function to determine a preferred asset allocation for Perkins:

$$U_m = E(R_m) - 0.005\lambda\sigma_m^2$$

EXHIBIT 1   Strategic Asset Allocation Alternatives

	Adviser's Forecasts	
Asset Allocation	Expected Return (%)	Standard Deviation of Returns (%)
A	10	12.0
B	8	8.0
C	6	2.0

Another client, Lars Velky, represents Velky Partners (VP), a large institutional investor with $500 million in investable assets. Velky is interested in adding less liquid asset classes, such as direct real estate, infrastructure, and private equity, to VP's portfolio. Velky and Monteo discuss the considerations involved in applying many of the common asset allocation techniques, such as MVO, to these asset classes. Before making any changes to the portfolio, Monteo asks Velky about his knowledge of risk budgeting. Velky makes the following statements:

Statement 1:   An optimum risk budget minimizes total risk.

Statement 2:   Risk budgeting decomposes total portfolio risk into its constituent parts.

Statement 3:   An asset allocation is optimal from a risk-budgeting perspective when the ratio of excess return to marginal contribution to risk is different for all assets in the portfolio.

Monteo meets with a third client, Jayanta Chaterji, an individual investor. Monteo and Chaterji discuss mean–variance optimization. Chaterji expresses concern about using the output of MVOs for two reasons:

Criticism 1: The asset allocations are highly sensitive to changes in the model inputs.

Criticism 2: The asset allocations tend to be highly dispersed across all available asset classes.

Monteo and Chaterji also discuss other approaches to asset allocation. Chaterji tells Monteo that he understands the factor-based approach to asset allocation to have two key characteristics:

Characteristic 1:   The factors commonly used in the factor-based approach generally have low correlations with the market and with each other.

Characteristic 2:   The factors commonly used in the factor-based approach are typically different from the fundamental or structural factors used in multifactor models.

Monteo concludes the meeting with Chaterji after sharing his views on the factor-based approach.

9. Based on Exhibit 1 and the risk aversion coefficient, the preferred asset allocation for Perkins is:
   A. Asset Allocation A.
   B. Asset Allocation B.
   C. Asset Allocation C.

10. In their discussion of the asset classes that Velky is interested in adding to the VP portfolio, Monteo should tell Velky that:
    A. these asset classes can be readily diversified to eliminate idiosyncratic risk.
    B. indexes are available for these asset classes that do an outstanding job of representing the performance characteristics of the asset classes.
    C. the risk and return characteristics associated with actual investment vehicles for these asset classes are typically significantly different from the characteristics of the asset classes themselves.

11. Which of Velky's statements about risk budgeting is correct?
    A. Statement 1
    B. Statement 2
    C. Statement 3

12. Which of Chaterji's criticisms of MVO is/are valid?
    A. Only Criticism 1
    B. Only Criticism 2
    C. Both Criticism 1 and Criticism 2

13. Which of the characteristics put forth by Chaterji to describe the factor-based approach is/are correct?
    A. Only Characteristic 1
    B. Only Characteristic 2
    C. Both Characteristic 1 and Characteristic 2

14. John Tomb is an investment advisor at an asset management firm. He is developing an asset allocation for James Youngmall, a client of the firm. Tomb considers two possible allocations for Youngmall. Allocation A consists of four asset classes: cash, US bonds, US equities, and global equities. Allocation B includes these same four asset classes, as well as global bonds.

    Youngmall has a relatively low risk tolerance with a risk aversion coefficient (λ) of 7. Tomb runs mean–variance optimization (MVO) to maximize the following utility function to determine the preferred allocation for Youngmall:

    $$U_m = E(R_m) - 0.005\lambda\sigma_m^2$$

    The resulting MVO statistics for the two asset allocations are presented in Exhibit 1.

EXHIBIT 1   MVO Portfolio Statistics

	Allocation A	Allocation B
Expected return	6.7%	5.9%
Expected standard deviation	11.9%	10.7%

Determine which allocation in Exhibit 1 Tomb should recommend to Youngmall. **Justify** your response.

Determine which allocation in Exhibit 1 Tomb should recommend to Youngmall. (circle one)

Allocation A	Allocation B

Justify your response.

15. Walker Patel is a portfolio manager at an investment management firm. After successfully implementing mean–variance optimization (MVO), he wants to apply reverse optimization to his portfolio. For each asset class in the portfolio, Patel obtains market capitalization data, betas computed relative to a global market portfolio, and expected returns. This information, along with the MVO asset allocation results, are presented in Exhibit 1.

EXHIBIT 1   Asset Class Data and MVO Asset Allocation Results

Asset Class	Market Cap (trillions)	Beta	Expected Returns	MVO Asset Allocation
Cash	$4.2	0.0	2.0%	10%
US bonds	$26.8	0.5	4.5%	20%
US equities	$22.2	1.4	8.6%	35%
Global equities	$27.5	1.7	10.5%	20%
Global bonds	$27.1	0.6	4.7%	15%
Total	$107.8			

The risk-free rate is 2.0%, and the global market risk premium is 5.5%.

Contrast, using the information provided above, the results of a reverse optimization approach with that of the MVO approach for each of the following:
i.   The asset allocation mix
ii. The values of the expected returns for US equities and global bonds
Justify your response.

16. Viktoria Johansson is newly appointed as manager of ABC Corporation's pension fund. The current market value of the fund's assets is $10 billion, and the present value of the fund's liabilities is $8.5 billion. The fund has historically been managed using an asset-only approach, but Johansson recommends to ABC's board of directors that they adopt a liability-relative approach, specifically the hedging/return-seeking portfolios approach. Johansson assumes that the returns of the fund's liabilities are driven by changes in the returns of index-linked government bonds. Exhibit 1 presents three potential asset allocation choices for the fund.

EXHIBIT 1   Potential Asset Allocations Choices for ABC Corp's Pension Fund

Asset Class	Allocation 1	Allocation 2	Allocation 3
Cash	15%	5%	0%
Index-linked government bonds	70%	15%	85%
Corporate bonds	0%	30%	5%
Equities	15%	50%	10%
Portfolio Statistics			
Expected return	3.4%	6.2%	3.6%
Expected standard deviation	7.0%	12.0%	8.5%

Determine which asset allocation in Exhibit 1 would be *most appropriate* for Johansson given her recommendation. **Justify** your response.

Determine which asset allocation in Exhibit 1 would be *most appropriate* for Johansson given her recommendation.
(circle one)

Allocation 1	Allocation 2	Allocation 3

Justify your response.

The following information relates to Questions 17 and 18

Mike and Kerry Armstrong are a married couple who recently retired with total assets of $8 million. The Armstrongs meet with their financial advisor, Brent Abbott, to discuss three of their financial goals during their retirement.

Goal 1: An 85% chance of purchasing a vacation home for $5 million in five years.
Goal 2: A 99% chance of being able to maintain their current annual expenditures of $100,000 for the next 10 years, assuming annual inflation of 3% from Year 2 onward.
Goal 3: A 75% chance of being able to donate $10 million to charitable foundations in 25 years.

Abbott suggests using a goals-based approach to construct a portfolio. He develops a set of sub-portfolio modules, presented in Exhibit 1. Abbott suggests investing any excess capital in Module A.

EXHIBIT 1   "Highest Probability- and Horizon-Adjusted Return" Sub-Portfolio Modules under
Different Horizon and Probability Scenarios

	A	B	C	D
Portfolio Characteristics				
Expected return	6.5%	7.9%	8.5%	8.8%
Expected volatility	6.0%	7.7%	8.8%	9.7%
Annualized Minimum Expectation Returns				
Time Horizon	5 Years			
Required Success				
99%	0.3%	−0.1%	−0.7%	−1.3%
85%	3.7%	4.3%	4.4%	4.3%
75%	4.7%	5.6%	5.8%	5.9%
Time Horizon	10 Years			
Required Success				
99%	2.1%	2.2%	2.0%	1.7%
85%	4.5%	5.4%	5.6%	5.6%
75%	5.2%	6.3%	6.6%	6.7%
Time Horizon	25 Years			
Required Success				
99%	3.7%	4.3%	4.4%	4.3%
85%	5.3%	6.3%	6.7%	6.8%
75%	5.7%	6.9%	7.3%	7.5%

17. **Select**, for each of Armstrong's three goals, which sub-portfolio module from Exhibit 1
     Abbott should choose in constructing a portfolio. **Justify** each selection.

Select, for each of Armstrong's three goals, which sub-portfolio module from Exhibit 1 Abbott should
choose in constructing a portfolio. (circle one module for each goal)

Goal 1	Goal 2	Goal 3
Module A	Module A	Module A
Module B	Module B	Module B
Module C	Module C	Module C
Module D	Module D	Module D

Justify each selection.

18. **Construct** the overall goals-based asset allocation for the Armstrongs given their three goals and Abbott's suggestion for investing any excess capital. **Show** your calculations.

Construct the overall goals-based asset allocation for the Armstrongs given their three goals and Abbott's suggestion for investing any excess capital.
(insert the percentage of the total assets to be invested in each module)

Module A	Module B	Module C	Module D

Show your calculations.

CHAPTER 7

ASSET ALLOCATION WITH REAL-WORLD CONSTRAINTS

Peter Mladina
Brian J. Murphy, CFA
Mark Ruloff, FSA, EA, CERA

LEARNING OUTCOMES

The candidate should be able to:

- discuss asset size, liquidity needs, time horizon, and regulatory or other considerations as constraints on asset allocation;
- discuss tax considerations in asset allocation and rebalancing;
- recommend and justify revisions to an asset allocation given change(s) in investment objectives and/or constraints;
- discuss the use of short-term shifts in asset allocation;
- identify behavioral biases that arise in asset allocation and recommend methods to overcome them.

1. INTRODUCTION

This chapter illustrates ways in which the asset allocation process must be adapted to accommodate specific asset owner circumstances and constraints. It addresses adaptations to the asset allocation inputs given an asset owner's asset size, liquidity, and time horizon as well as external constraints that may affect the asset allocation choice (Section 2). We also discuss the ways in which taxes influence the asset allocation process for the taxable investor (Section 3). In addition, we discuss the circumstances that should trigger a re-evaluation of the long-term strategic asset allocation (Section 4), when and how an asset owner might want to make short-term shifts in asset allocation (Section 5), and how innate investor behaviors can interfere with successful long-term planning for the investment portfolio (Section 6). Throughout the chapter, we illustrate the application of these concepts using a series of hypothetical investors.

2. CONSTRAINTS IN ASSET ALLOCATION

General asset allocation principles assume that all asset owners have equal ability to access the entirety of the investment opportunity set, and that it is merely a matter of finding that combination of asset classes that best meets the wants, needs, and obligations of the asset owner. In practice, however, it is not so simple. An asset owner must consider a number of constraints when modeling and choosing among asset allocation alternatives. Some of the most important are asset size, liquidity needs, taxes, and time horizon. Moreover, regulatory and other external considerations may influence the investment opportunity set or the optimal asset allocation decision.

2.1. Asset Size

The size of an asset owner's portfolio has implications for asset allocation. It may limit the opportunity set—the asset classes accessible to the asset owner—by virtue of the scale needed to invest successfully in certain asset classes or by the availability of investment vehicles necessary to implement the asset allocation.

Economies and diseconomies of scale are perhaps the most important factors relevant to understanding asset size as a constraint. The size of an asset owner's investment pool may be too small—or too large—to capture the returns of certain asset classes or strategies efficiently. Asset owners with larger portfolios can generally consider a broader set of asset classes and strategies. On the one hand, they are more likely to have sufficient governance capacity—sophistication and staff resources—to develop the required knowledge base for the more complex asset classes and investment vehicles. They also have sufficient size to build a diversified portfolio of investment strategies, many of which have substantial minimum investment requirements. On the other hand, some asset owners may have portfolios that are *too* large; their desired minimum investment may exhaust the capacity of active external investment managers in certain asset classes and strategies. Although "too large" and "too small" are not rigidly defined, the following example illustrates the difficulty of investing a very large portfolio. Consider an asset owner with an investment portfolio of US$25 billion who is seeking to make a 5% investment in global small-cap stocks:

- The median total market capitalization of the stocks in the S&P Global SmallCap is approximately US$555 million.
- Assume a small-cap manager operates a 50-stock portfolio and is willing to own 3% of the market cap of any one of its portfolio companies. Their average position size would be US$17 million, and an effective level of assets under management (AUM) would be on the order of US$850 million. Beyond that level, the manager may be forced to expand the portfolio beyond 50 stocks or to hold position sizes greater than 3% of a company's market cap, which could then create liquidity issues for the manager.
- Now, our US$25 billion fund is looking to allocate US$1.25 billion to small-cap stocks (US$25 billion × 5%). They want to diversify this allocation across three or four active managers—a reasonable allocation of governance resources in the context of all of the

fund's investment activities. The average allocation per manager is approximately US$300 to US$400 million, which would constitute between 35% and 50% of each manager's AUM. This exposes both the asset owner and the investment manager to an undesirable level of operational risk.

Although many large asset owners have found effective ways to implement a small-cap allocation, this example illustrates some of the issues associated with managing a large asset pool. These include such practical considerations as the number of investment managers that might need to be hired to fulfill an investment allocation and the ability of the asset owner to identify and monitor the required number of managers.

Research has shown that investment managers tend to incur certain disadvantages from increasing scale: Growth in AUM leads to larger trade sizes, incurring greater price impact; capital inflows may cause active investment managers to pursue ideas outside of their core investment theses; and organizational hierarchies may slow down decision-making and reduce incentives.[1] Asset *owners*, however, are found to have *increasing* returns to scale, as discussed below.

A study of pension plan size and performance (using data spanning 1990–2008) found that large defined benefit plans outperformed smaller ones by 45–50 basis points per year on a risk-adjusted basis.[2] The gains are derived from a combination of cost savings related to internal management, a greater ability to negotiate fees with external managers, and the ability to support larger allocations to private equity and real estate investments. As fund size increases, the "per participant" costs of a larger governance infrastructure decline and the plan sponsor can allocate resources away from such asset classes as small-cap stocks, which are sensitive to diseconomies of scale, to such other areas as private equity funds or co-investments where they are more likely to realize scale-related benefits.

Whereas owners of large asset pools may achieve these operating efficiencies, scale may also impose obstacles related to the liquidity and trading costs of the underlying asset. Above some size, it becomes difficult to deploy capital effectively in certain active investment strategies. As illustrated in Exhibit 1, owners of very large portfolios may face size constraints in allocating to active equity strategies. The studies referenced earlier noted that these asset owners frequently choose to invest passively in developed equity markets where their size inhibits alpha potential. The asset owner's finite resources can then be allocated instead toward such strategies as private equity, hedge funds, and infrastructure, where their scale and resources provide a competitive advantage.

Even in these strategies, very large asset owners may be constrained by scale. In smaller or less liquid markets, can a large asset owner invest enough that the exposure contributes a material benefit to the broader portfolio? For example, a sovereign wealth fund or large public pension plan may not find enough attractive hedge fund managers to fulfill their desired allocation to hedge funds. True alpha is rare, limiting the opportunity set. Asset owners who find that they have to split their mandate into many smaller pieces may end up with an index-like portfolio but with high active management fees; one manager's active bets may cancel out those of another active manager. A manager mix with no true alpha becomes index-like because the uncompensated, idiosyncratic return variation is diversified away. A much smaller allocation may be achievable, but it may be too small to meaningfully affect the risk and return characteristics of the overall portfolio. More broadly, a very large size makes it more

---

[1]See Stein (2002); Chen, Hong, Huang, and Kubik (2004); and Pollet and Wilson (2008).
[2]See Dyck and Pomorski (2011). The median plan in this study was just over US$2 billion. The 25th percentile plan was US$780 million, and the 75th percentile plan was US$6.375 billion.

EXHIBIT 1   Asset Size and Investor Constraints

Asset Class	Investor Constraints by Size
• Cash equivalents and money market funds	No size constraints.
• Large-cap developed market equity • Small-cap developed market equity • Emerging market equity	Generally accessible to large and small asset owners, although the very large asset owner may be constrained in the amount of assets allocated to certain active strategies and managers.
• Developed market sovereign bonds • Investment-grade bonds • Non-investment-grade bonds • Private real estate equity	Generally accessible to large and small asset owners, although to achieve prudent diversification, smaller asset owners may need to implement via a commingled vehicle.
Alternative Investments • Hedge funds • Private debt • Private equity • Infrastructure • Timberland and farmland	May be accessible to large and small asset owners, although if offered as private investment vehicles, there may be legal minimum qualifications that exclude smaller asset owners. The ability to successfully invest in these asset classes may also be limited by the asset owner's level of investment understanding/expertise. Prudent diversification may require that smaller asset owners implement via a commingled vehicle, such as a fund of funds, or an ancillary access channel, such as a liquid alternatives vehicle or an alternatives ETF. For very large funds, the allocation may be constrained by the number of funds available.

difficult to benefit from opportunistic investments in smaller niche markets or from skilled investment managers who have a small set of unique ideas or concentrated bets. No hard and fast rules exist to determine whether a particular asset owner is too small or too large to effectively access an asset class. Greater governance resources more commonly found among owners of larger asset pools create the capacity to pursue the more complex investment opportunities, but the asset owner may still need to find creative ways to implement the desired allocation. Each asset owner has a unique set of knowledge and constraints that will influence the opportunity set.

Smaller asset owners (typically institutions with less than US$500 million in assets, and private wealth investors with less than US$25 million in assets) also find that their opportunity set may be constrained by the size of their investment portfolio. This is primarily a function of the more limited governance infrastructure typical of smaller asset owners: They may be too small to adequately diversify across the range of asset classes and investment managers or may have staffing constraints (insufficient asset size to justify a dedicated internal staff). Complex strategies may be beyond the reach of asset owners that have chosen not to develop investment expertise internally or where the oversight committee lacks individuals with sufficient investment understanding. In some asset classes and strategies, commingled investment vehicles can be used to achieve the needed diversification, provided the governing documents do not prohibit their use.

Access to other asset classes and strategies—private equity, private real estate, hedge funds, and infrastructure—may still be constrained for smaller asset owners. The commingled vehicles through which these strategies are offered typically require high minimum investments. For successful private equity and hedge fund managers, in particular, minimum investments can be in the tens of millions of (US) dollars, even for funds of funds.

Regulatory restrictions can also impose a size constraint. In the United Kingdom, for example, an asset owner in a private investment vehicle must qualify as an elective professional client, meaning they must meet two of the following three conditions:

1. The client has carried out transactions, in significant size, on the relevant market at an average frequency of 10 per quarter over the previous four quarters.
2. The size of the client's financial instrument portfolio exceeds €500,000.
3. The client works or has worked in the financial sector for at least one year in a professional position, which requires knowledge of the transactions or services envisaged.

In the United States, investors must be either accredited or qualified purchasers to invest in many private equity and hedge fund vehicles. To be a qualified purchaser, a natural person must have at least US$5 million in investments, a company must have at least US$25 million in investable assets, and an investment manager must have at least US$25 million under management. In Hong Kong SAR, the Securities and Futures Commission requires that an investor must meet the qualifications of a "Professional Investor" to invest in certain categories of assets. A Professional Investor is generally defined as a trust with total assets of not less than HK$40 million, an individual with a portfolio not less than HK$8 million, or a corporation or partnership with a portfolio not less than HK$8 million or total assets of not less than HK $40 million. The size constraints related to these asset classes suggest that smaller asset owners have real challenges achieving an effective private equity or hedge fund allocation.

Asset size as a constraint is often a more acute issue for individual investors than institutional asset owners. Wealthy families may pool assets through such vehicles as family limited partnerships, investment companies, fund of funds, or other forms of commingled vehicles to hold their assets. These pooled vehicles can then access investment vehicles, asset classes, and strategies that individual family members may not have portfolios large enough to access on their own.

Where Asset Size Constrains Investment Opportunity

As of early 2016, the 10 largest sovereign wealth funds globally each exceed US$400 billion in assets. For a fund of this size, a 5% allocation to hedge funds (the average sovereign wealth fund allocation) would imply US$20 *billion* to be deployed. The global hedge fund industry manages approximately US$2.8 trillion in total; 73% of the funds manage less than US$100 million. The remaining 27% of the funds (roughly 3,000) manage 72% of the industry's AUM; their implied average AUM is therefore US$670 million. If we assume that the asset owner would want to be no more than 20% of a firm's AUM, we can infer that the average investment might be approximately US$130 million. With US$20 billion to deploy, the fund would need to invest with nearly 150 funds to achieve a 5% allocation to hedge funds.

Sources: Sovereign Wealth Fund Institute, BarclayHedge, Eurekahedge (2016).

EXAMPLE 1   Asset Size Constraints in Asset Allocation

1. Akkarat Aromdee is the recently retired president of Alpha Beverage, a producer and distributor of energy drinks throughout Southeast Asia. Upon retiring, the company provided a lump sum retirement payment of THB880,000,000 (equivalent to €20 million), which was rolled over to a tax-deferred individual retirement savings plan. Aside from these assets, Aromdee owns company stock worth about THB70,000,000. The stock is infrequently traded. He has consulted with an investment adviser, and they are reviewing the following asset allocation proposal:

Global equities	40%
Global high-yield bonds	15%
Domestic intermediate bonds	30%
Hedge funds	10%
Private equity	5%

Describe asset size constraints that Aromdee might encounter in implementing this asset allocation. Discuss possible means to address them.

2. The CAF$40 billion Government Petroleum Fund of Caflandia is overseen by a nine-member Investment Committee. The chief investment officer has a staff with sector heads in global equities, global bonds, real estate, hedge funds, and derivatives. The majority of assets are managed by outside investment managers. The Investment Committee, of which you are a member, approves the asset allocation policy and makes manager selection decisions. Staff has recommended an increase in the private equity allocation from its current 0% to 15%, to be implemented over the next 12 to 36 months. The head of global equities will oversee the implementation of the private equity allocation.

   Given the asset size of the fund, formulate a set of questions regarding the feasibility of this recommendation that you would like staff to address at the next Investment Committee meeting.

3. The Courneuve University Endowment has US$250 million in assets. The current allocation is 65% global large-capitalization stocks and 35% high-quality bonds, with a duration target of 5.0 years. The University has adopted a 5% spending policy. University enrollment is stable and expected to remain so. A capital spending initiative of US$100 million for new science buildings in the next three to seven years is being discussed, but it has not yet been approved. The University has no dedicated investment staff and makes limited use of external resources. Investment recommendations are formulated by the University's treasurer and approved by the Investment Committee, composed entirely of external board members.

The new president of the University has stated that he feels the current policy is overly restrictive, and he would like to see a more diversified program that takes advantage of the types of investment strategies used by large endowment programs. Choosing from among the following asset classes, propose a set of asset classes to be considered in the revised asset allocation. Justify your response.

- Cash equivalents and money market funds
- Large-cap developed market equity
- Small-cap developed market equity
- Emerging market equity
- Developed market sovereign bonds
- Investment-grade bonds

- Non-investment-grade bonds
- Private real estate equity
- Hedge funds
- Private debt
- Private equity

Solution to 1: With a THB88 million (€2 million) allocation to hedge funds and a THB44 million (€1 million) allocation to private equity funds, Aromdee may encounter restrictions on his eligibility to invest in the private investment vehicles typically used for hedge fund and private equity investment. To the extent he is eligible to invest in hedge funds and/or private equity funds, a fund-of-funds or similar commingled arrangement would be essential to achieving an appropriate level of diversification. Additionally, it is essential that he and his adviser develop the necessary level of expertise to invest in these alternative assets. To achieve a prudent level of diversification, the allocation to global high-yield bonds would most likely need to be accomplished via a commingled investment vehicle.

Solution to 2: Questions regarding the feasibility of the recommendation include the following:

- How many private equity funds do you expect to invest in to achieve the 15% allocation to private equity?
- What is the anticipated average allocation to each fund?
- Are there a sufficient number of high-quality private equity funds willing to accept an allocation of that size?
- What expertise exists at the staff or board level to conduct due diligence on private equity investment funds?
- What resources does the staff have to oversee the increased allocation to private equity?

Solution to 3: Asset size and limited governance resources are significant constraints on the investment opportunity set available to the Endowment. The asset allocation should emphasize large and liquid investments, such as cash equivalents, developed and emerging market equity, and sovereign and investment-grade bonds. Some small portion of assets, however, could be allocated to commingled investments in real estate, private equity, or hedge funds. Given the University's limited staff resources, it is necessary to ensure that the board members have the level of expertise necessary to select and monitor these more complex asset classes. The Endowment might also consider engaging an outside expert to advise on investment activities in these asset classes.

2.2. Liquidity

Two dimensions of liquidity must be considered when developing an asset appropriate allocation solution: the liquidity needs of the asset owner and the liquidity characteristics of the asset classes in the opportunity set. Integrating the two dimensions is an essential element of successful investment planning.

The need for liquidity in an investment portfolio will vary greatly by asset owner and by the goals the assets are set aside to achieve. For example, a bank will typically have a very large portfolio supporting its day-to-day operations. That portfolio is likely to experience very high turnover and a very high need for liquidity; therefore, the investment portfolio must hold high-quality, very short-term, and highly liquid assets.

The same bank may have another designated investment pool one level removed from operating assets. Although the liquidity requirements for this portfolio may be lower, the investments most likely feature a high degree of liquidity—a substantial allocation to investment-grade bonds, perhaps with a slight extension of maturity. For its longer-term investment portfolio, the bank may choose to allocate some portion of its portfolio to less liquid investments. The opportunity set for each portfolio will be constrained by applicable banking laws and regulations.

Long-term investors, such as sovereign wealth funds and endowment funds, can generally exploit illiquidity premiums available in such asset classes as private equity, real estate, and infrastructure investments. However, pension plans may be limited in the amount of illiquidity they can absorb. For example, a frozen pension plan may anticipate the possibility of eliminating its pension obligation completely by purchasing a group annuity and relinquishing the responsibility for making pension payments to an insurance company. If there is a significant probability that the company will take this step in the near term, liquidity of plan assets will become a primary concern; and if there is a substantial allocation to illiquid assets, the plan sponsor may be unable to execute the desired annuity purchase transaction.

Liquidity needs must also consider the particular circumstances and financial strength of the asset owner and what resources they may have beyond those held in the investment portfolio. The following examples illustrate this point:

- A university must consider its prospects for future enrollments and the extent to which it relies on tuition to meet operating needs. If the university experiences a significant drop in enrollment, perhaps because of a poor economic environment, or takes on a new capital improvement project, the asset allocation policy for the endowment should reflect the increased probability of higher outflows to support university operations.
- A foundation whose mission supports medical research in a field in which a breakthrough appears imminent may desire a higher level of liquidity to fund critical projects than would a foundation that supports ongoing community efforts.
- An insurance company whose business is predominantly life or auto insurance, where losses are actuarially predictable, can absorb more liquidity risk than a property/casualty reinsurer whose losses are subject to unpredictable events, such as natural disasters.
- A family with several children nearing college age will have higher liquidity needs than a couple of the same age and circumstances with no children.

When assessing the appropriateness of any given asset class for a given asset owner, it is wise to evaluate potential liquidity needs in the context of an extreme market stress event. The market losses of the 2008–2009 global financial crisis were extreme. Simultaneously, other forces exacerbated investors' distress: Many university endowments were called upon to provide an increased level of operating support; insurers dipped into reserves to offset operating losses; community foundations found their beneficiaries in even greater need of financial support; and some individual investors experienced setbacks that caused them to move, if only temporarily, from being net contributors to net spenders of financial wealth. A successful asset allocation effort will stress the proposed allocation; it will anticipate, where possible, the likely behavior of other facets of the saving/spending equation during times of stress.

It is also important to consider the intersection of asset class and investor liquidity in the context of the asset owner's governance capacity. Although the mission of the organization or trust may allow for a certain level of illiquidity, if those responsible for the oversight of the investment program do not have the mental fortitude or discipline to maintain course through the crisis, illiquid and less liquid investments are unlikely to produce the rewards typically expected of these exposures. Although rates of return may be mean-reverting, wealth is not. Losses resulting from panic selling during times of stress become permanent losses; there are fewer assets left to earn returns in a post-crash recovery.

The Case of Vanishing Liquidity

In the global financial crisis of 2008–2009, many investors learned painful truths about liquidity. When most needed—whether to rebalance or to meet spending obligations— it can evaporate. As investors liquidated their most liquid assets to meet financial obligations (or to raise cash in fear of further market declines), the remaining less liquid assets in their portfolios became an ever-larger percentage of the portfolio. Many investors were forced to sell private partnership interests on the secondary market at steeply discounted prices. Others defaulted on outstanding private fund capital commitments by refusing to honor future obligations.

Similarly, illiquidity became a substantial problem during the Asian currency crisis of 1997–1998 and again with the Russian debt default and Long-Term Capital Management (LTCM) crisis of 1998. In the following paragraphs, we describe several "liquidity crises" that are often used in stress testing asset allocation choices.

The Asian Currency Crisis of 1997
In the spring of 1997, Thailand spent billions to defend the Thai baht against speculative attacks, finally capitulating and devaluing the baht in July 1997. This triggered a series of moves throughout the region to defend currencies against speculators. Ultimately, these efforts were unsuccessful and many countries abandoned the effort and allowed their currencies to float freely. The Philippines, Indonesia, and South Korea abandoned their pegs against the US dollar. On 27 October 1997, rattled by the currency crisis, Asian and European markets declined sharply in advance of the opening of the US markets. The S&P 500 declined nearly 7%, and trading on US stock markets was suspended.

The Russian Debt/LTCM Crisis of August 1998
On 17 August 1998, the Russian government defaulted on its short-term debt. This unprecedented default of a sovereign debtor roiled the global bond markets. A global flight-to-quality ensued, which caused credit spreads to widen and liquidity to evaporate. Highly levered investors experienced significant losses. Long-Term Capital

Management, with reported notional exposure of over US$125 billion (a 25-to-1 leverage ratio), exacerbated these price declines as they faced their own liquidity crisis and were forced to liquidate large relative value, distressed, convertible arbitrage, merger arbitrage, and equity positions. Ultimately, the magnitude of the liquidity squeeze for LTCM and the risk of potential disruption to global markets caused the New York branch of the Federal Reserve Bank to orchestrate a disciplined, structured bailout of the LTCM fund.

Financial markets are increasingly linked across borders and asset classes; as a result, changes in liquidity conditions in one country can directly affect liquidity conditions elsewhere. These linkages do improve access to financing and capital markets, but they also show that a liquidity problem in one part of the world can ripple across the globe—increasing volatility, creating higher execution costs for investors, and possibly leading to a reduction in credit availability and a decline in economic activity.

EXAMPLE 2   Liquidity Constraints in Asset Allocation

The Frentel Furniture Pension Fund has £200 million frozen in a defined benefit pension plan that is 85% funded. The plan has a provision that allows employees to elect a lump sum distribution of their pension benefit at retirement. The company is strong financially and is committed to fully funding the pension obligations over time. However, they also want to minimize cash contributions to the plan. Few governance resources are allocated to the pension fund, and there is no dedicated staff for pension investment activities. The current asset allocation is as shown:

Global equities	20%
Private equity	10%
Real estate	10%
Infrastructure	5%
Hedge funds	15%
Bonds	40%

The company expects to reduce their employee headcount sometime in the next three to five years, and they are tentatively planning incentives to encourage employees to retire early.

Discuss the appropriateness of the current asset allocation strategy for the pension fund, including benefits and concerns.

Solution: In addition to the size constraints a £200 million (≈ US$250 million) plan faces when attempting to invest in real estate, private equity, infrastructure, and hedge funds, the likelihood of early retirement incentives and lump-sum distribution requests in the next three to five years indicates a need for increased sensitivity to liquidity concerns. Investments in private equity, infrastructure, and real estate may be unsuitable for the plan given their less liquid nature. Although hedge fund investments would likely be accessible via a commingled vehicle, the liquidity of the commingled vehicle should be evaluated to determine if it is consistent with the liquidity needs of the plan.

2.3. Time Horizon

An asset owner's time horizon is a critical constraint that must be considered in any asset allocation exercise. A liability to be paid at a given point in the future or a goal to be funded by a specified date each define the asset owner's horizon, thus becoming a basic input to the asset allocation solution. The changing composition of the asset owner's assets and liabilities must also be considered. As time progresses, the character of both *assets* (human capital) and *liabilities* changes.

2.3.1. Changing Human Capital

When asset allocation considers such extended portfolio assets as human capital, the optimal allocation of financial capital can change through time (Bodie, Merton, and Samuelson 1992). Assuming no change in the investor's utility function, as human capital—with its predominately bond-like risk—declines over time, the asset allocation for financial capital would reflect an increasing allocation to bonds. This is a prime example of how time horizon can influence asset allocation.

2.3.2. Changing Character of Liabilities

The changing character of liabilities through time will also affect the asset allocation aligned to fund those liabilities.

As an example, the term structure of liabilities changes as they approach maturity. A pension benefit program is a simple way to illustrate this point. When the employee base is young and retirements are far into the future, the liability can be hedged with long-term bonds. As the employee base ages and prospective retirements are not so far into the future, the liability is more comparable to intermediate- or even short-term bonds. When retirements are imminent, the structure of the liabilities can be characterized as cash-like, and an optimal asset allocation would also have cash-like characteristics.

Similarly, the overall profile of an individual investor's liabilities changes with the progression of time, particularly for investors with finite investment horizons. Nearer-term goals and liabilities move from partially funded to fully funded, while other, longer-term goals and liabilities move progressively closer to funding. As the relative weights of the goals to be funded shift and the time horizon associated with certain goals shortens, the aggregate asset allocation must be adapted if it is to remain aligned with the individual's goals.

Time horizon is also likely to affect the manner in which an investor prioritizes certain goals and liabilities. This will influence the desired risk profile of the assets aligned to fund them. Consider a 75-year-old retired investor with two goals:

1. Fund consumption needs through age 95
2. Fund consumption needs from age 95 through age 105

He most likely assigns a much higher priority to funding goal 1, given the lower probability that he will live beyond age 95.[3] Let's also assume that he has sufficient assets to fund goal 1 and to partially fund goal 2. The higher priority assigned to goal 1 indicates he is less willing to take risk, and this sub-portfolio will be invested more conservatively. Now consider goal 2: Given the low probability of living past 95 and the fact that he does not currently have sufficient assets to fund that goal, the sub-portfolio assigned to goal 2 is likely to have a more growth-oriented asset allocation. The priority of a given goal can change as the investor's time horizon shortens—or lengthens.

Consider the hypothetical investors Ivy and Charles Lee from the chapter "Introduction to Asset Allocation." Ivy is a 54-year-old life science entrepreneur. Charles is a 55-year-old orthopedic surgeon. They have two unmarried children aged 25 (Deborah) and 18 (David). Deborah has a daughter with physical limitations. Four goals have been identified for the Lees:

1. Lifestyle/future consumption needs
2. College education for son David, 18 years old
3. Charitable gift to a local art museum in 5 years
4. Special needs trust for their granddaughter, to be funded at the death of Charles

The lifestyle/consumption goal is split into three components: required minimum consumption requirements (a worst-case scenario of reduced lifestyle), baseline consumption needs (maintaining current standard of living), and aspirational consumption needs (an improved standard of living). At age 54, the risk preferences assigned to these goals might look something like the following:

Lifestyle Goals	Risk Preference	Asset Allocation	Sub-Portfolio as % of Total*
Required minimum	Conservative	100% bonds and cash	65%
Baseline	Moderate	60% equities/40% bonds	10%
Aspirational	Aggressive	100% equities	4%
College education	Conservative	100% bonds and cash	1%
Charitable gift (aspirational)	Aggressive	100% equities	5%
Special needs trust	Moderate	60% equities/40% bonds	15%
Aggregate portfolio		≈ 25% equities/75% bonds and cash	100%

* The present value of each goal as a proportion of the total portfolio.

The asset allocation for the total portfolio aggregates the asset allocations for each of the goal-aligned sub-portfolios, weighted by the present value of each goal. For the Lees, this is an

---

[3] A 75-year-old US American male has a life expectancy of 11.1 years, per the Social Security Administration's 2014 "Actuarial Life Tables," https://www.ssa.gov/oact/STATS/table4c6_2014.html (Accessed 22 Nov 2018).

overall asset allocation of about 25% equities and 75% bonds and cash. (Each goal is discounted to its present value by expected return of its respective goal-aligned sub-portfolio.)

Move forward 20 years. The Lees are now in their mid-70s, and their life expectancy is about 12 years. Their son has completed his college education and is successfully established in his own career. The charitable gift has been made. These two goals have been realized. The assets needed to fund the baseline consumption goal are significantly reduced because fewer future consumption years need to be funded. The special needs trust for their granddaughter remains a high priority. Although the Lee's risk preferences for these goals have not changed, the overall asset allocation *will* change because the total portfolio is an aggregated mix of the remaining goal-aligned sub-portfolios, weighted by their current present values:

Lifestyle Goals	Risk Preference	Asset Allocation	Sub-Portfolio as % of Total*
Required minimum	Conservative	100% bonds and cash	54%
Baseline	Moderate	60% equities/40% bonds	9%
Aspirational	Aggressive	100% equities	3%
Special needs trust	Moderate	60% equities/40% bonds	34%
Aggregate portfolio		≈ 30% equities/70% bonds and cash	100%

* The present value of each goal as a proportion of the total portfolio. The implied assumption is that current assets are sufficient to fund all goals, provided the Lees adopt an aggressive asset allocation strategy for the aspirational and charitable gifting goals. If the value of current assets exceeds the present value of all goals, the Lees would have greater flexibility to adopt a lower risk preference for some or all goals.

Although for ease of illustration our example assumed the Lee's risk preferences remained the same, this is not likely to be the case in the real world. Required minimum and baseline consumption goals would remain very important; there is less flexibility to withstand losses caused by either reduced earnings potential or lower likelihood of the market regaining lost ground within the shorter horizon. The aspirational lifestyle goal is likely to be a much lower priority, and it may have been eliminated altogether. The special needs trust may have a higher (or lower) priority as the needs of the granddaughter and the ability of her parents to provide for her needs after their death become more evident. The preferred asset allocation for each of these goals will shift over the course of the investor's lifetime.

As an investor's time horizon shifts, both human capital and financial market considerations, along with changes in the investor's priorities, will most likely lead to different asset allocation decisions.

EXAMPLE 3   Time Horizon Constraints in Asset Allocation

Akkarat Aromdee, the recently retired president of Alpha Beverage, is 67 years old with a remaining life expectancy of 15 years. Upon his retirement two years ago, he established a charitable foundation and funded it with THB600 million (≈ US$17.3 million). The remaining financial assets, THB350 million (≈ US$10 million), were transferred to a trust that will allow him to draw a lifetime income. The assets are invested 100% in fixed-income securities, consistent with Aromdee's desire for a high level of certainty in meeting his goals. He is a widower with no children. His consumption needs are estimated at THB20 million annually. Assets remaining in the trust at his death will pass to the charities named in the trust.

While vacationing in Ko Samui, Aromdee met and later married a 45-year-old woman with two teenage children. She has limited financial assets of her own. Upon returning from his honeymoon, Aromdee meets with his investment adviser. He intends to pay the college expenses of his new stepchildren—THB2 million annually for eight years, beginning five years from now. He would also like to ensure that his portfolio can provide a modest lifetime income for his wife after his death.

Discuss how these changed circumstances are likely to influence Aromdee's asset allocation.

Solution: At the time Aromdee established the trust, the investment horizon was 15 years and his annual consumption expenditures could easily be funded from the trust. His desire to support his new family introduces two new horizons to be considered: In five years, the trust will begin making annual payments of THB2 million to fund college expenses, and the trust will continue to make distributions to his wife after his death, though at a reduced rate. When the trust needed to support only his consumption requirements, a conservative asset allocation was appropriate. However, the payment of college expenses will reduce his margin of safety and the lengthening of the investment horizon suggests that he should consider adding equity-oriented investments to the asset mix to provide for growth in assets over time.

Time Diversification of Risk

In practice, investors often align lower risk/lower return assets with short-term goals and liabilities and higher risk/higher return assets with long-term goals and liabilities. It is generally believed that longer-horizon goals can tolerate the higher volatility associated with higher risk/higher return assets as below average and above average returns even out over time. This is the notion of time diversification.

Mean–variance optimization, typically conducted using a multi-year time horizon, assumes that asset returns follow a random walk; returns in Year X are independent of returns in Year X − 1. Under this baseline assumption, there *is* no reduction in risk with longer time horizons.[4] Although the *probability* of reduced wealth or of a shortfall in funding a goal or liability (based on the mean of the distribution of possible outcomes) may be lower at longer time horizons, the dispersion of possible outcomes widens as the investment horizon expands. Thus, the *magnitude* of potential loss or shortfall can be greater.

Consider the choice of investing US$100,000 in an S&P 500 Index fund with a 10% expected return and 15% standard deviation versus a risk-free asset with a 3% annual return.[5] The table below compares the return of the risk-free asset over various time horizons, with the range of predicted returns for the S&P 500 Index fund at a 95% confidence interval. Although the *mean* return of the distribution of S&P 500

---

[4]See Samuelson (1963) and Samuelson (1969).
[5]This example is drawn from Kritzman (2015).

returns exceeds that of the risk-free asset in each time period (thus the notion that the volatility of higher risk, higher return assets evens out over time), the lower boundary of expected S&P 500 returns is less than the initial investment for all periods less than 10 years! The lower boundary of the S&P 500 outcomes does not exceed the ending wealth of the risk-free investment until the investment horizon is extended to 20 years. If the confidence interval is expanded to 99%, the lower boundary of S&P 500 outcomes falls below the initial investment up until and through 20 years!

| | Ending Wealth (US$) | | |
| | S&P 500 95% Confidence Interval | | |
	Lower Boundary	Upper Boundary	Risk-Free Asset
1 year	81,980	147,596	103,000
5 years	83,456	310,792	115,927
10 years	102,367	657,196	134,392
15 years	133,776	130,4376	155,797
20 years	180,651	2,565,345	180,611

Although one-year returns are largely independent, there is some evidence that risky asset returns can display mean-reverting tendencies over intermediate to longer time horizons. An assumption of mean-reverting risky asset returns would support the conventional arguments for funding long-term goals and liabilities with higher risk/ higher return assets, and it would also support a reduction in the allocation to these riskier assets as the time horizon shortens.

2.4. Regulatory and Other External Constraints

Just as an integrated asset/liability approach to asset allocation is likely to result in a different allocation decision than what might have been selected in an asset-only context, external considerations may also influence the asset allocation decision. Local laws and regulations can have a material effect on an investor's asset allocation decisions.

Pension funds, insurance companies, sovereign wealth funds, and endowments and foundations are each subject to externally imposed constraints that are likely to tilt their asset allocation decision away from what may have been selected in a pure asset/liability context.

2.4.1. Insurance Companies

Unlike pension fund or endowment assets—which are legally distinct from the assets of the sponsoring entity—insurance companies' investment activities are an integral part of their day-to-day operations. Although skilled underwriting may be the focus of the firm as the key to profitability, investment returns are often a material contributor to profits or losses. Regulatory requirements and accounting treatment vary from country to country, but insurers are most often highly focused on matching assets to the projected, probabilistic cash flows of the risks they are underwriting. Fixed-income assets, therefore, are typically the largest component of an insurance company's asset base, and investing with skill in this asset class is a key to competitive pricing and success. In some regions, the relevant accounting treatment may be a book value approach, rendering variability in the market pricing of assets to be a secondary consideration as long as an asset does not have to have its book value written down as "other than temporarily impaired" ("OTTI"). Risk considerations for an insurance company include the need for capital to pay policyholder benefits and other factors that directly influence the company's financial strength ratings. Some of the key considerations are risk-based capital measures, yield, liquidity, the potential for forced liquidation of assets to fund negative claims development, and credit ratings.

Additionally, allocations to certain asset classes are often constrained by a regulator. For example, the maximum limit on equity exposure is often 10%, but it ranges as high as 30% in Switzerland and 50% in Mexico. Israel and Korea impose a limit of 15% on real estate investments.[6] Restrictions on non-publicly traded securities might also limit the allocation to such assets as private equity, for example, and there may also be limits on the allocation to high-yield bonds. Insurance regulators generally set a minimum capital level for each insurer based on that insurer's mix of assets, liabilities, and risk. Many countries are moving to Solvency II regulatory standards designed to harmonize risk-based capital requirements for insurance companies across countries.[7] Asset classes are often treated differently for purposes of determining whether an insurer meets risk-based capital requirements.

2.4.2. Pension Funds

Pension fund asset allocation decisions may be constrained by regulation and influenced by tax rules.[8] Some countries regulate maximum or minimum percentages in certain asset classes. For example, Japanese pension funds must hold a certain minimum percentage of assets in Japanese bonds in order to maintain their tax-exempt status. Canada allows a maximum of 10% of market value invested in any one entity or related entities; Switzerland generally limits real estate investments to 30%; Estonia allows a maximum of 75% of assets invested in public equity with no limit on foreign investments; and Brazil allows a maximum of 70% in public equity with a maximum of 10% in foreign public equity.[9] Ukraine limits bond investments to no more than 40%.

Pension funds are also subject to a wide array of funding, accounting, reporting, and tax constraints that may influence the asset allocation decision. (For example, US public pension funding and public and corporate accounting rules favor equity investments—higher equity allocations support a higher discount rate—and thus lower pension cost. Loss recognition is deferred until later through the smoothing mechanism.) The plan sponsor's appetite for risk is defined in part by these constraints, and the choice among asset allocation alternatives is often influenced by funding and financial statement considerations, such as the anticipated

---

[6]https://www.oecd.org/finance/private-pensions/Regulation-of-Insurance-Company-and-Pension-Fund-Investment.pdf (September 2015)–accessed 23 November 2018.

[7]Solvency II is an EU legislative program implemented in all 28 member states, including the United Kingdom, in January 2016. It introduces a new, harmonized EU-wide insurance regulatory regime.

[8]Information in this section is based on the OECD "Annual Survey of Investment Regulation of Pension Funds" (2017).

[9]Foreign investment is restricted to MERCOSUR countries for equities (other asset classes are more flexible).

contributions, the volatility of anticipated contributions, or the forecasted pension expense or income under a given asset allocation scenario. The specific constraints vary by jurisdiction, and companies with plans in multiple jurisdictions must satisfy the rules and regulations of each jurisdiction while making sound financial decisions for the organization as a whole.

Exhibit 2 illustrates how funding considerations may affect the asset allocation decision. In this chart, risk is defined as the probability of contributions exceeding some threshold amount. In this case, the risk threshold is specified as the 95th percentile of the present value of contributions—that point on the distribution of possible contributions (using Monte Carlo simulation) where the plan sponsor can be 95% certain that contributions will not exceed that amount.

Assume that an allocation of 70% equities/30% aggregate bonds represents the most efficient portfolio for the plan sponsor's desired level of risk in an asset optimization framework. In Exhibit 2, we can see that the 70% equity/30% aggregate bond mix (Portfolio A) is associated with a present value (PV) of expected contributions of approximately US$51 million (y-axis) and a 95% confidence level that contributions will not exceed approximately US$275 million (x-axis)—Portfolio A in Exhibit 2. If the plan sponsor were to shift to longer-duration bonds (from aggregate to long bonds) to better match the duration of liabilities—Portfolio D_1 on Exhibit 2—the PV of expected contributions declines by approximately US$5 million and the 95% confidence threshold improves to approximately US$265 million. In fact, Portfolio D_1 results in nearly the lowest PV of contributions for this plan sponsor. (Note that the vertical axis is ordered from highest contributions at the bottom and lowest contributions at the top, consistent with the notion of lower contributions as a better outcome.)

EXHIBIT 2   Efficient Frontiers Where Risk Is Defined as the Risk of Large Contributions

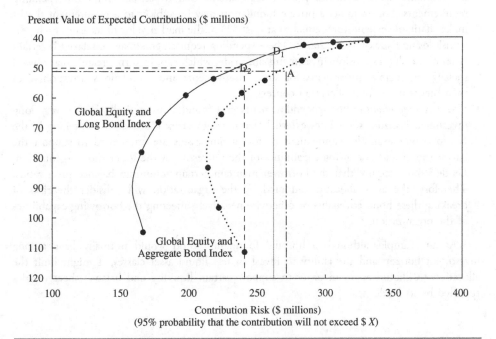

Present Value of Expected Contributions ($ millions)

Contribution Risk ($ millions)
(95% probability that the contribution will not exceed $ X)

Now consider Portfolio D_2, 60% equities/40% long bonds. Reducing the equity exposure from 70% to 60% lowers the contribution risk significantly, with only marginally higher expected PV of contributions than Portfolio A. (A lower equity allocation implies a lower expected rate of return, which increases the PV of contributions. However, the lower equity allocation also reduces the probability that less-than-expected returns will lead to unexpectedly large contributions.) The sponsor that wishes to reduce contribution risk substantially is likely to give serious consideration to moving from Portfolio A to Portfolio D_2.

By iterating through various efficient frontiers using different definitions of risk, the sponsor is able to better understand the risk and reward trade-offs of alternative asset allocation choices. The regulatory or tax constraints on minimum and maximum contributions, or on minimum required funded levels, or other values that are important to the plan sponsor, can be factored into the simulations so the sponsor can better understand how these constraints might affect the risk and reward trade-offs.

2.4.3. Endowments and Foundations

Endowments and foundations are often established with the expectation that they will exist in perpetuity and thus can invest with a long investment horizon. In addition, the sponsoring entity often has more flexibility over payments from the fund than does a pension plan sponsor or insurance company. As a result, endowments and foundations generally can adopt a higher-risk asset allocation than other institutions. However, two categories of externally imposed constraints may influence the asset allocation decisions of an endowment or foundation: tax incentives and credit-worthiness considerations.

- *Tax incentives.* Although some endowments and foundations—US public foundations and some Austrian and Asian foundations, for example—are not required to make minimum distributions, many countries provide tax benefits tied to certain minimum spending requirements. For example, a private foundation may be subject to a requirement that it make charitable expenditures equal to at least 5% of the market value of its assets each year or risk losing its tax-favored status. These spending requirements may be relaxed if certain types of socially responsible investments are made, which can, in turn, create a bias toward socially responsible investments for some endowments and foundations, irrespective of their merits in an asset allocation context.
- *Credit considerations.* Although endowments and foundations typically have a very long investment horizon, sometimes external factors may restrict the level of risk-taking in the portfolio. For example, endowment or foundation assets are often used to support the balance sheet and borrowing capabilities of the university or the foundation organization. Lenders often require that the borrower maintain certain minimum balance sheet ratios. Therefore, the asset allocation adopted by the organization will consider the risks of breaking these bond covenants or otherwise negatively affecting the borrowing capabilities of the organization.

As an example, although a hospital foundation fund would normally have a long investment horizon and the ability to invest in less liquid asset classes, it might limit the allocation to illiquid assets in order to support certain liquidity and balance sheet metrics specified by its lender(s).

2.4.4. Sovereign Wealth Funds

Although every sovereign wealth fund (SWF) is unique with respect to its mission and objectives, some broad generalizations can be made with respect to the external constraints that may affect a fund's asset allocation choices. In general, SWFs are government-owned pools of capital invested on behalf of the peoples of their states or countries, investing with a long-term orientation. They are not generally seeking to defease a set of liabilities or known obligations as is common with pension funds and, to a lesser extent, endowment funds.

The governing entities adopt regulations that constrain the opportunity set for asset allocation. For example, the Korean SWF KIC cannot invest in Korean won-denominated domestic assets;[10] and the Norwegian SWF NBIM is not permitted to invest in any alternative asset class other than real estate, which is limited to no more than 7% of assets.[11] Furthermore, as publicly owned entities, SWFs are typically subject to broad public scrutiny and tend to adopt a lower-risk asset allocation than might otherwise be considered appropriate given their long-term investment horizon in order to avoid reputation risk.

In addition to the broad constraints of asset size, liquidity, time horizon, and regulations, there may be cultural or religious factors which also constrain the asset allocation choices. Environmental, social, and governance (ESG) considerations are becoming increasingly important to institutional and individual investors alike. Sharia law, for example, prohibits investment in any business that has links to pork, alcohol, tobacco, pornography, prostitution, gambling, or weaponry, and it constrains investments in most businesses that operate on interest payments (like major Western banks and mortgage providers) and in businesses that transfer risk (such as major Western insurers).[12]

ESG goals are not typically modeled during the asset allocation decision process. Instead, these goals may be achieved through the implementation of the asset allocation, or the asset owner may choose to set aside a targeted portion of the assets for these missions. The asset allocation process would treat this "set-aside" in much the same way that a concentrated stock position might be handled: The risk, return, and correlation characteristics of this holding are specified; the "set aside" asset becomes an asset class in the investor's opportunity set; and the asset allocation constraints will designate a certain minimum investment in this asset class.

EXAMPLE 4   External Constraints and Asset Allocation

1. An insurance company has traditionally invested its pension plan using the asset allocation strategy adopted for its insurance assets: The pension assets are 95% invested in high-quality intermediate duration bonds and 5% in global equities. The duration of pension liabilities is approximately 25 years. Until now, the company has always made contributions sufficient to maintain a fully funded status. Although the company has a strong capability to fund the plan adequately and a relatively high tolerance for variability in asset returns, as part of a refinement

---

[10]https://mpra.ub.uni-muenchen.de/44028/1/MPRA_paper_44028.pdf (accessed 23 November 2018). Note: In principle, KIC must invest only in assets denominated in foreign currencies. If KIC manages KRW-denominated assets temporarily for an unavoidable reason, it must be either in the form of bank deposits or passively held public debt.

[11]https://www.nbim.no/en/investments/investment-strategy/ (accessed 23 November 2018).

[12]Islamic Investment Network (www.islamicinvestmentnetwork.com/sharialaw.php).

in corporate strategy, management is now seeking to reduce long-term expected future cash contributions. Management is willing to accept more risk in the asset return, but they would like to limit contribution risk and the risk to the plan's funded status. The Investment Committee is considering three asset allocation proposals for the pension plan:

A. Maintain the current asset allocation with the same bond portfolio duration.

B. Increase the equity allocation and lengthen the bond portfolio duration to increase the hedge of the duration risk in the liabilities.

C. Maintain the current asset allocation of 95% bonds and 5% global equities, but increase the duration of bond investments.

Discuss the merits of each proposal.

2. A multinational corporation headquartered in Mexico has acquired a former competitor in the United States. It will maintain both the US pension plan with US$250 million in assets and the Mexican pension plan with MXN$18,600 million in assets ($\approx$ US$1 billion). Both plans are 95% funded and have similar liability profiles. The Mexican pension trust has an asset allocation policy of 30% equities (10% invested in the Mexican equity market and 20% in equity markets outside Mexico), 10% hedge funds, 10% private equity, and 50% bonds. The treasurer has proposed that the company adopt a consistent asset allocation policy across all of the company's pension plans worldwide.

Critique the treasurer's proposal.

Solution to 1: Given the intermediate duration bond allocation, Proposal A fails to consider the mismatch between pension assets and liabilities and risks a reduction in the funded status and *increased* contributions if bond yields decline. (If yields decline across the curve, the shorter duration bond portfolio will fail to hedge the increase in liabilities.) To meet the objective of lower future contributions, the asset allocation must include a higher allocation to equities. Proposal B has this higher allocation, and the extension of duration in the bond portfolio in Proposal B reduces balance sheet and surplus risk relative to the pension liabilities. The net effect could be a reduction in short-term contribution risk; moreover, if the greater expected return on equities is realized, it should result in reduced contributions to the plan over the long term. Proposal C improves the hedging of the liabilities, and it may result in a modest improvement in the expected return on assets if the yield curve is upward-sloping. However, the expected return on Proposal C is likely lower than the expected return of Proposal B and is therefore unlikely to achieve the same magnitude of reduction in future cash contributions. Proposal C would be appropriate if the goal was focused on reducing surplus risk rather than reducing long-term contributions.

Solution to 2: The treasurer's proposal fails to consider the relative asset size of the two pension plans as well as the likelihood that plans in different jurisdictions may be subject to different funding, regulatory, and financial reporting requirements. The US pension plan may be unable to effectively access certain alternative asset classes, such as private equity, infrastructure, and hedge funds. Although economies of scale may be realized if management of the pension assets is consolidated under one team, the legal and regulatory differences of the markets in which they operate mean that the asset allocation policy must be customized to each plan.

3. ASSET ALLOCATION FOR THE TAXABLE INVESTOR

Portfolio theory developed in a frictionless world. But in the real world, taxes on income and capital gains can erode the returns achieved by taxable investors. The asset owner who ignores taxes during the asset allocation process is overlooking an economic variable that can materially alter the outcome. Although tax adjustments can be made after the asset allocation has been determined, this is a suboptimal approach because the pre-tax and after-tax risk and return characteristics of each asset class can be materially different.

Some assets are less tax efficient than others because of the character of their returns—the contribution of interest, dividends, and realized or unrealized capital gains to the total return. Interest income is usually taxed in the tax year it is received, and it often faces the highest tax rates. Therefore, assets that generate returns largely comprised of interest income tend to be less tax efficient in many countries.[13] Jurisdictional rules can also affect how the returns of certain assets are taxed. In the United States, for example, the interest income from state and local government bonds is generally exempt from federal income taxation. As a result, these bonds often constitute a large portion of a US high-net-worth investor's bond allocation. Preferred stocks, often used in lieu of bonds as an income-producing asset, are also eligible for more favorable tax treatment in many jurisdictions, where the income from preferred shares may be taxed at more favorable dividend tax rates.

The tax environment is complex. Different countries have different tax rules and rates, and these rules and rates can change frequently. However, looking across the major economies, there are some high-level commonalities in how investment returns are taxed. Interest income is taxed typically (but not always) at progressively higher income tax rates. Dividend income and capital gains are taxed typically (but not always) at lower tax rates than those applied to interest income and earned income (wages and salaries, for example). Capital losses can be used to offset capital gains (and sometimes income). Generally, interest income incurs the highest tax rate, with dividend income taxed at a lower rate in some countries, and long-term capital gains receive the most favorable tax treatment in many jurisdictions. Once we move beyond these general commonalities, however, the details of tax treatment among countries quickly diverge.

Entities and accounts can be subject to different tax rules. For example, retirement savings accounts may be tax deferred or tax exempt, with implications for the optimal asset allocation solution. These rules provide opportunities for strategic asset *location*—placing less tax-efficient assets in tax-advantaged accounts.

We will provide a general framework for considering taxes in asset allocation. We will not survey global tax regimes or incorporate all potential tax complexities into the asset allocation solution. When considering taxes in asset allocation, the objective is to model material investment-related taxes, thereby providing a closer approximation to economic reality than is represented when ignoring taxes altogether.

For simplicity, we will assume a basic tax regime that represents no single country but includes the key elements of investment-related taxes that are roughly representative of what a typical taxable asset owner in the major developed economies must contend with.

3.1. After-Tax Portfolio Optimization

After-tax portfolio optimization requires adjusting each asset class's expected return and risk for expected tax. The expected after-tax return is defined in Equation 1:

---

[13]See Deloitte's tax guides and country highlights: https://dits.deloitte.com/#TaxGuides.

$$r_{at} = r_{pt}(1 - t) \tag{1}$$

where
$\quad$ r_{at} = the expected after-tax return
$\quad$ r_{pt} = the expected pre-tax (gross) return
$\quad$ t = the expected tax rate

This can be straightforward for bonds in cases where the expected return is driven by interest income. Take, for example, an investment-grade par bond with a 3% coupon expected to be held to maturity. If interest income is subject to a 40% expected tax rate, the bond has an expected after-tax return of 1.80% [0.03(1 − 0.40) = 0.018].

The expected return for equity typically includes both dividend income and price appreciation (capital gains). Equation 2 expands Equation 1 accordingly:

$$r_{at} = p_d r_{pt}(1 - t_d) + p_a r_{pt}(1 - t_{cg}) \tag{2}$$

where
$\quad$ p_d = the proportion of r_{pt} attributed to dividend income
$\quad$ p_a = the proportion of r_{pt} attributed to price appreciation
$\quad$ t_d = the dividend tax rate
$\quad$ t_{cg} = the capital gains tax rate

The treatment of the capital gains portion of equity returns can be more complex. Assuming no dividend income, a stock with an 8% expected pre-tax return that is subject to a 25% capital gains tax rate has an expected after-tax return of 6% [0.08(1 − 0.25) = 0.06]. This is an approximation satisfactory for modeling purposes.[14]

Taxable assets may have existing unrealized capital gains or losses (i.e., the cost basis is below or above market value), which come with embedded tax liabilities (or tax assets). Although there is not a clear consensus on how best to deal with existing unrealized capital gains (losses), many approaches adjust the asset's current market value for the value of the embedded tax liability (asset) to create an after-tax value. Reichenstein (2006) approximates the after-tax value by subtracting the value of the embedded capital gains tax from the market value, as if the asset were sold today. Horan and Al Zaman (2008) assume the asset is sold in the future and discount the tax liability to its present value using the asset's after-tax return as the discount rate. Turvey, Basu, and Verhoeven (2013) argue that the after-tax risk-free rate is the more appropriate discount rate because the embedded tax liability is analogous to an interest-free loan from the government, where the tax liability can be arbitraged away by dynamically investing in the risk-free asset. We will discuss how to incorporate after-tax values into the portfolio optimization process in Section 3.3, where we address strategies to reduce the impact of taxes.

The ultimate purpose of an asset can be a consideration when modeling tax adjustments. In the preceding material on asset allocation, we discussed goals-based investing. If the purpose of a given pool of assets is to fund consumption in 10 years, then that 10-year holding period may influence the estimated implied annual capital gains tax rate. If the purpose of the specified pool of assets is to fund a future gift of appreciated stock to a

---

[14]A more precise estimation of the expected after-tax return also takes into account the effect of the holding period on the capital gains tax. For those interested in a more detailed discussion of these issues, see Mladina (2011).

tax-exempt charity, then capital gains tax may be ignored altogether. Through this alignment of goals with assets, goals-based investing facilitates more-precise tax adjustments.

Although correlation assumptions need not be adjusted when modeling asset allocation choices for the taxable asset owner (taxes are proportional to return, after-tax co-movements are the same as pre-tax co-movements), taxes do affect the standard deviation assumption for each asset class. The expected after-tax standard deviation is defined in Equation 3:

$$\sigma_{at} = \sigma_{pt}(1 - t) \tag{3}$$

where
  σ_{at} = the expected after-tax standard deviation
  σ_{pt} = the expected pre-tax standard deviation

Taxes alter the distribution of returns by both reducing the expected mean return and muting the dispersion of returns. Taxes truncate both the high and low ends of the distribution of returns, resulting in lower highs and higher lows. The effect of taxes is intuitive when considering a positive return, but the same economics apply to a negative return: Losses are muted by the same $(1 - t)$ tax adjustment. The investor is not taxed on losses but instead receives the economic benefit of a capital loss, whether realized or not. In many countries, a realized capital loss can offset a current or future realized capital gain. An unrealized capital loss captures the economic benefit of a cost basis that is above the current market value, making a portion of expected future appreciation tax free.

How does the optimal asset allocation along a pre-tax efficient frontier compare with the optimal asset allocation along an after-tax efficient frontier? Let's assume all investment assets are taxable and that cost bases equal current market values. Assume also that interest income is taxed at 40%, and dividend income and capital gains are taxed at 25%.

The asset classes we will consider include investment-grade (IG) bonds, high-yield (HY) bonds, and equity. Exhibit 3 shows the expected pre-tax returns and standard deviations for each asset class as well as the correlation matrix. Note that for ease of illustration, we have assumed that the IG bonds and HY bond returns are comprised of 100% interest income. In practice, some portion of the expected return would be eligible for capital gains tax treatment.

EXHIBIT 3   Expected Pre-Tax Return and Risk

	Return	Std. Dev.	
IG bonds	3.0%	4.0%	
HY bonds	5.0%	10.0%	
Equity	8.0%	20.0%	
Correlations	**IG Bonds**	**HY Bonds**	**Equity**
IG bonds	1.0	0.2	0.0
HY bonds	0.2	1.0	0.7
Equity	0.0	0.7	1.0

Employing mean–variance portfolio optimization with these pre-tax inputs, we obtain the optimal asset allocations in Exhibit 4, which shows the allocations for portfolios P1 (lowest risk), P25, P50 (median risk), P75, and P100 (highest risk)—each on an efficient frontier comprised of 100 portfolios.

EXHIBIT 4   Optimal Pre-Tax Asset Mixes

	$P1_{pt}$	$P25_{pt}$	$P50_{pt}$	$P75_{pt}$	$P100_{pt}$
IG bonds	93%	52%	25%	0%	0%
HY bonds	5%	18%	26%	33%	0%
Equity	2%	30%	49%	67%	100%

Using Equations 1, 2, and 3, we calculate the expected after-tax returns and standard deviations displayed in Exhibit 5. No adjustments are made to correlations.

EXHIBIT 5   Expected After-Tax Return and Risk

	Return	Std. Dev.
IG bonds	1.8%	2.4%
HY bonds	3.0%	6.0%
Equity	6.0%	15.0%

Portfolio optimization using these after-tax inputs produces the optimal asset allocations shown in Exhibit 6.

EXHIBIT 6   Optimal After-Tax Asset Mixes

	$P1_{at}$	$P25_{at}$	$P50_{at}$	$P75_{at}$	$P100_{at}$
IG bonds	92%	60%	38%	16%	0%
HY bonds	7%	7%	7%	7%	0%
Equity	1%	33%	55%	77%	100%

In Exhibit 7, we compare the pre-tax and after-tax efficient frontiers from these previous exhibits. Note that the portfolios at either extreme (P1 and P100) are essentially unchanged after taxes are factored into the assumptions. In portfolios P25, P50, and P75, however, you can see a significant reduction in the allocation to high-yield bonds. This is because of the heavier tax burden imposed on high-yield bonds. Although investment-grade bonds receive the same tax treatment, they are less risky than high-yield bonds and demonstrate a lower correlation with equity, so they continue to play the important role of portfolio risk reduction.

EXHIBIT 7   Pre-Tax and After-Tax Asset Allocation Comparisons

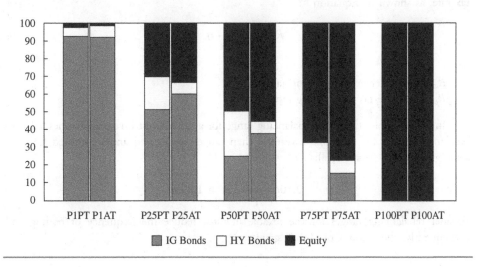

The optimal after-tax asset allocation depends on the interaction of after-tax returns, after-tax risk, and correlations. If an asset class or strategy is tax inefficient, it can still play a diversifying role in an optimal after-tax asset allocation if the asset or strategy offers sufficiently low correlations. After-tax portfolio optimization helps answer that question.

3.2. Taxes and Portfolio Rebalancing

Among tax-exempt institutional asset owners, periodic portfolio rebalancing—reallocating assets to return the portfolio to its target strategic asset allocation—is an integral part of sound portfolio management. This is no less true for taxable asset owners, but with the important distinction that more frequent rebalancing exposes the taxable asset owner to realized taxes that could have otherwise been deferred or even avoided. Whereas the tax burden incurred by liquidating assets to fund-required consumption cannot be avoided, rebalancing is discretionary; thus, the taxable asset owner should consider the trade-off between the benefits of tax minimization and the merits of maintaining the targeted asset allocation by rebalancing. The decision to rebalance and incur taxes is driven by each asset owner's unique circumstances.

Because after-tax volatility is less than pre-tax volatility (Equation 3) and asset class correlations remain the same, it takes larger asset class movements to materially alter the risk profile of the taxable portfolio. This suggests that rebalancing ranges for a taxable portfolio can be wider than those of a tax-exempt portfolio with a similar risk profile.

For example, consider a portfolio with a 50% allocation to equity, where equity returns are subject to a 25% tax rate. A tax-exempt investor may establish a target allocation to equities of 50%, with an acceptable range of 40% to 60% (50% plus or minus 10%). A taxable investor with the same target equity allocation can achieve a similar risk constraint with a range of 37% to 63% (50% plus or minus 13%). The equivalent rebalancing range for the taxable investor is derived by adjusting the permitted 10% deviation (up or down) by the tax rate, as shown in Equation 4:

$$R_{at} = R_{pt}/(1 - t) \qquad (4)$$

where

R_{at} = the after-tax rebalancing range
R_{pt} = the pre-tax rebalancing range

In our example, the 10% rebalancing range for a tax-exempt investor becomes a 13.3% rebalancing range for a taxable investor (when ranges are viewed and monitored from the same gross return perspective):

$$0.10/(1 - 0.25) = 13.3\%$$

Broader rebalancing ranges for the taxable investor reduce the frequency of trading and, consequently, the amount of taxable gains.

3.3. Strategies to Reduce Tax Impact

Additional strategies can be used to reduce taxes, including tax-loss harvesting and choices in the placement of certain types of assets in taxable or tax-exempt accounts (strategic asset location). Tax-loss harvesting is intentionally trading to realize a capital loss, which is then used to offset a current or future realized capital gain in another part of the portfolio, thereby reducing the taxes owned by the investor. It is discussed elsewhere in the curriculum, but we address strategic asset location strategies here.

Strategic asset location refers to placing (or locating) less tax-efficient assets in accounts with more favorable tax treatment, such as retirement savings accounts.

Aggregating assets across accounts with differing tax treatment requires modifying the asset value inputs to the portfolio optimization. Assets held in tax-*exempt* accounts require no tax adjustment to their market values. Assets in tax-*deferred* accounts grow tax free but are taxed upon distribution. Because these assets cannot be distributed (and consumed) without incurring the tax, the tax burden is inseparable from the economic value of the assets. Thus, the after-tax value of assets in a tax-deferred account is defined by Equation 5:

$$v_{at} = v_{pt}(1 - t_i) \qquad (5)$$

where

v_{at} = the after-tax value of assets
v_{pt} = the pre-tax market value of assets
t_i = the expected income tax rate upon distribution

In our earlier example, we had three asset classes: investment-grade bonds, high-yield bonds, and equities. If we assume that each of these three asset classes can be held in either of two account types—taxable or tax-deferred—then our optimization uses six different after-tax asset classes (three asset classes times two account types). The three asset classes in taxable accounts use the after-tax return and risk inputs derived earlier. The three asset classes in tax-deferred accounts (which grow tax free) use expected pre-tax return and risk inputs. The optimization adds constraints based on the after-tax value of the assets currently available in each account type and derives the optimal after-tax asset allocation and asset location simultaneously.

As a general rule, the portion of a taxable asset owner's assets that are eligible for lower tax rates and deferred capital gains tax treatment should first be allocated to the investor's taxable accounts. For example, equities should generally be held in taxable accounts, while taxable bonds and high-turnover trading strategies should generally be located in tax-exempt and tax-deferred accounts to the extent possible.

One important exception to this general rule regarding asset location applies to assets held for near-term liquidity needs. Because tax-exempt and tax-deferred accounts may not be immediately accessible without tax penalty, a portion of the bond allocation may be held in taxable accounts if its role is to fund near-term consumption requirements.

EXAMPLE 5   Asset Allocation and the Taxable Investor

1. Sarah Moreau, 45 years old, is a mid-level manager at a consumer products company. Her investment portfolio consists entirely of tax-deferred retirement savings accounts. Through careful savings and investments, she is on track to accumulate sufficient assets to retire at age 60. Her portfolio is currently allocated as indicated below:

Investment-grade bonds	20%
High-yield bonds	20%
Common stock–dividend income strategy	30%
Common stock–total return (capital gain) strategy	30%
Total portfolio	100%

   The common stock–dividend income strategy focuses on income-oriented, high-dividend-paying stocks; the common stock–total return strategy focuses on stocks that represent good, long-term opportunities but pay little to no dividend. For the purposes of this example, we will assume that the expected long-term return is equivalent between the two strategies. Moreau has a high comfort level with this portfolio and the overall level of risk it entails.

   Moreau has recently inherited additional monies, doubling her investable assets. She intends to use this new, taxable portfolio to support causes important to her personally over her lifetime. There is no change in her risk tolerance. She is interviewing prospective investment managers and has asked each to recommend an asset allocation strategy for the new portfolio using the same set of asset classes. She has received the following recommendations:

	Recommendation		
	A	**B**	**C**
Investment-grade bonds	20%	40%	30%
High-yield bonds	20%	0%	0%
Common stock–dividend income strategy	30%	30%	0%
Common stock–total return (capital gain) strategy	30%	30%	70%
Total portfolio	100%	100%	100%

Which asset allocation is *most* appropriate for the new portfolio? Justify your response.

2. How should Moreau distribute these investments among her taxable and tax-exempt accounts?

3. You are a member of the Investment Committee for a multinational corporation, responsible for the supervision of two portfolios. Both portfolios were established to fund retirement benefits: One is a tax-exempt defined benefit pension fund, and the other is taxable, holding assets intended to fund non-exempt retirement benefits. The pension fund has a target allocation of 70% equities and 30% fixed income, with a +/– 5% rebalancing range. There is no formal asset allocation policy for the taxable portfolio; it has simply followed the same allocation adopted by the pension portfolio. Because of recent strong equity market returns, both portfolios are now allocated 77% to equities and 23% to bonds. Management expects that the equity markets will continue to produce strong returns in the near term. Staff has offered the following options for rebalancing the portfolios:

   A. Do not rebalance.

   B. Rebalance both portfolios to the 70% equity/30% fixed-income target allocation.

   C. Rebalance the tax-exempt portfolio to the 70% equity/30% fixed-income target allocation, but expand the rebalancing range for the taxable portfolio.

   Which recommendation is *most* appropriate? Justify your response.

Solution to 1: Recommendation C would be the most appropriate asset allocation for the new portfolio. The high-yield bond and common stock–dividend income strategies are tax disadvantaged in a taxable portfolio. (Although investment-grade bonds are also tax disadvantaged, they maintain the role of controlling portfolio risk to maintain Moreau's risk preference.) By shifting this equity-like risk to the total return common stock strategy, Moreau should achieve a greater after-tax return. Given the lower standard deviation characteristics of after-tax equity returns when held in the taxable portfolio, a higher allocation to common stocks may be justified without exceeding Moreau's desired risk level. Recommendations A and B do not consider the negative tax implications of holding the high-yield and/or common stock–dividend income strategies in a taxable portfolio. Recommendation B also fails to consider Moreau's overall risk tolerance: The volatility of the common stock–capital gain strategy is lower when held in a taxable portfolio, thus a higher allocation to this strategy can enhance returns while remaining within Moreau's overall risk tolerance.[15]

Solution to 2: If Moreau is willing to think of her investable portfolio as a single portfolio, rather than as independent "retirement" and "important causes" portfolios, she should hold the allocation to high-yield bonds and dividend-paying stocks in her tax-exempt retirement portfolio. In addition, subject to the overall volatility of the individual tax-exempt and taxable portfolios, it would be sensible to bear any increased stock risk in the taxable portfolio. A new optimization for *all* of Moreau's assets—using pre-tax and after-tax risk and return assumptions and subject to the constraint that half of the assets are held in a taxable portfolio and half are held in the tax-exempt portfolio—would more precisely allocate investments across portfolio (account) types.

Asset Location for Optimal Tax Efficiency

	Tax Advantaged Retirement Account	Taxable Account
Investment-grade bonds	X	
High-yield bonds	X	
Common stock–dividend income strategy	X	
Common stock–total return (capital gain) strategy		X

Solution to 3: Recommendation C is the most appropriate course of action. Rebalancing of the tax-exempt portfolio is unencumbered by tax considerations, and rebalancing maintains the desired level of risk. The rebalancing range for the taxable portfolio can be wider than that of the tax-exempt portfolio based on the desire to minimize avoidable taxes and the lower volatility of after-tax equity returns. Recommendation A (no rebalancing) does not address the increased level of risk in the tax-exempt portfolio that results from the increase in the stock allocation. Recommendation B would create an unnecessary tax liability for the company, given that the portfolio is still operating in a reasonable range of risk when adjusted for taxes.

Increasing Allocations to Fixed Income in Corporate Pension Plans

Increasing allocations to fixed income by defined benefit pension funds worldwide have been driven largely by a desire to better hedge plan liabilities. In some countries, accounting standards discourage de-risking. De-risking, however, is not the only argument in favor of a higher fixed-income allocation.

De-risking
There has been much discussion globally of pension plans "de-risking"—moving toward larger fixed-income allocations to better hedge liabilities, thereby reducing

---

[15]Investment-grade bonds also have lower after-tax volatility. The equivalent risk portfolios in pre-tax and after-tax environments are a function of a complex interaction of after-tax returns, standard deviations, and correlations.

contribution uncertainty. Some countries' accounting rules, however—most notably those in the United States—discourage companies from moving in that direction. Under US GAAP accounting rules, for example, a higher allocation to equities allows the plan sponsor to employ a higher return assumption, thereby reducing pension cost, a non-cash expense that directly affects reported income.

For underfunded pension plans, de-risking leads to higher pension contributions. If a company has a weak core business with a higher-than-average probability of going bankrupt and makes only the minimum required contribution, it might be argued that the asset allocation decision was contrary to the interests of plan participants. If the company were to go bankrupt, the participants would get only the benefits covered by any government guaranty program. Had the company taken equity risk in the plan, there would have been a possibility of closing the funding gap, resulting in higher benefit payments.

Efficient Allocation of Risk

A higher allocation to fixed income—and a lower allocation to equity—might also be driven by corporate governance considerations. Pension investment activities are not a core competency of many companies, especially non-financial companies. Assuming that the company has a limited appetite for risk, shareholders might prefer that management allocate its risk budget to the core business of the company where they are expected to have skill, rather than to the pension fund. The rewards per unit of risk should presumably be greater in the company's core business, and the improved profitability should offset the increase in pension contributions required as a result of the lower equity allocation.

A Holistic Approach to Asset Location

Finally, some have argued that an asset allocation of 100% fixed-income securities can be justified on the premise that the company is acting as an agent for the benefit of all stakeholders, including shareholders and plan participants. This argument centers on tax-efficient asset location. A taxable investor—the shareholder and plan participant—should prefer to take his long-term equity risk in that portion of his overall portfolio where he will receive the benefit of lower capital gains rates rather than in tax-deferred accounts, the proceeds of which will be taxed at income tax rates. Consider a small business owner with US$3 million in total assets. The assets are split between a pension fund of which he is the sole participant (US$1 million) and a taxable portfolio (US$2 million). Assume that the asset allocation that represents his preferred level of risk is 67% equities and 33% fixed income. Where should this individual hold his equity exposure? As discussed, the more favorable tax treatment of equity returns argues for holding the equity exposure in his taxable account, while the investments subject to the higher tax rate should be held in the tax-deferred account—the pension plan. Theoretically, this tax efficiency argument can be extended to pension funds operated by publicly traded companies.[16]

---

[16]For those interested in a more detailed discussion of this concept, see "The Case against Stock in Public Pension Funds" (Bader and Gold 2007) or the UBS Q-Series article, "Pension Fund Asset Allocation" (Cooper and Bianco 2003).

4. REVISING THE STRATEGIC ASSET ALLOCATION

An asset owner's strategic asset allocation is not a static decision. Circumstances often arise that justify revisiting the original decision, either to confirm its appropriateness or to consider a change to the current allocation strategy. It is sound financial practice to periodically re-examine the asset allocation strategy even in the absence of one of the external factors discussed next. Many institutional asset owners typically re-visit the asset allocation policy at least once every five years through a formal asset allocation study, and all asset owners should affirm annually that the asset allocation remains appropriate given their needs and circumstances.

The circumstances that might trigger a special review of the asset allocation policy can generally be classified as relating to a change in *goals*, a change in *constraints*, or a change in *beliefs*. Among the reasons to review the strategic asset allocation are the following:

4.1. Goals

- Changes in business conditions affecting the organization supporting the fund and, therefore, expected changes in the cash flows
- A change in the investor's personal circumstances that may alter her risk appetite or risk capacity

Over an individual's lifespan, or throughout the course of an institutional fund's lifespan, it is unlikely that the investment goals and objectives will remain unchanged. An individual may get married, have children, or become disabled, for example, each of which may have implications for the asset allocation strategy.

Significant changes in the core business of an organization supporting or benefiting from the trust might prompt a re-examination of the asset allocation strategy. For example, an automobile manufacturer that has historically generated a significant portion of its revenues from its consumer finance activities may find that technology is disrupting this source of revenue as more online tools become available to car buyers. With greater uncertainty in its revenue stream, company management may move to reduce risk-taking in the pension fund in order to achieve a goal of reducing the variability in year-to-year contributions.

A university may embark on a long-term capital improvement plan that is reliant on the endowment fund for financial support. Or the university may be experiencing declining enrollments and must lean more heavily on the endowment fund to support its ongoing operational expenditures. The source of funds to a sovereign wealth fund may shrink considerably or even evaporate. When any of these, or similar, events occur or are anticipated, the existing asset allocation policy should be re-evaluated.

4.2. Constraints

A material change in any one of the constraints mentioned earlier—time horizon, liquidity needs, asset size, or regulatory or other external constraints—is also reason to re-examine the existing asset allocation policy. Some of these changes might include the following:

- Changes in the expected payments from the fund
- A significant cash inflow or unanticipated expenditure
- Changes in regulations governing donations or contributions to the fund
- Changes in time horizon resulting from the adoption of a lump sum distribution option at retirement
- Changes in asset size as a result of the merging of pension plans

Changes in the expected payments from the fund can materially affect the asset allocation strategy. For example, a university reduces its spending policy from 5% to 4% of assets annually; an individual retires early, perhaps for health reasons or an involuntary late-career layoff; or a US corporate pension sponsor reduces or freezes pension benefits because it can no longer afford increasing Pension Benefit Guaranty Corporation[17] premiums. Faced with lower payouts, the university endowment may have greater latitude to invest in less liquid segments of the market. Decisions as to how and where to invest given this greater flexibility should be made within the framework of an asset allocation study to ensure the resulting allocation achieves the optimal trade-off of risk and return.

Similarly, a significant cash inflow has the potential to materially affect the asset allocation strategy. If a university endowment fund with £500 million in assets receives a gift of £100 million, the new monies *could* be invested in parallel with the existing assets, but that fails to consider the increased earning potential of the fund and any spending requirements associated with the donation. Pausing to formally reassess the fund's goals, objectives, constraints, and opportunities through an asset allocation study allows the asset owner to consider more broadly how best to maximize this additional wealth.

A change in regulations may also give rise to a change in asset allocation policy. Examples of regulatory changes that could trigger a re-examination of the asset allocation include the following:

- Regulatory changes in the United States in 2006 mandated a change in the liability discount rate, which resulted in larger pension contributions. With higher required contributions, there was less need to reach for higher investment returns. Many US corporate pension plans began de-risking (adopting an asset allocation strategy focused on hedging the liabilities) to reduce contribution volatility.
- UK tax incentives (30% of social impact investment costs can be deducted from income tax) and relaxed regulations for institutional investors were instituted to encourage socially responsible (impact) investing.

Again, an asset allocation study to objectively evaluate the effect of these changes on the investment opportunity set can help ensure that any new investment strategies adopted are consistent with the fund's overarching goals and objectives.

4.3. Beliefs

Investment beliefs are a set of guiding principles that govern the asset owner's investment activities. Beliefs are not static, however, and changes in the economic environment and capital market expectations or a change in trustees or committee members are two factors that may lead to an altering of the principles that guide investment activities.[18]

An integral aspect of any asset allocation exercise is the forecasting of expected returns, volatilities, and correlations of the asset classes in the opportunity set. It follows, then, that a material change in the outlook for one or more of the asset classes may heavily influence the asset allocation outcome.

Consider the 2015–2016 environment relative to the environment that prevailed in 1984–2014. The 1984–2014 investing environment was characterized by declining inflation and interest rates (from the extraordinarily high levels of the 1970s and early 1980s); strong global

---

[17]The Pension Benefit Guaranty Corporation insures certain US pension plan benefits.

[18]For an example of an investment belief statement, see www.uss.co.uk/how-uss-invests/investment-approach/investment-beliefs-and-principles.

GDP growth, aided by favorable demographics; gains in productivity; and rapid growth in China. Corporate profit growth was extremely robust, reflecting revenue growth from new markets, declining corporate taxes over the period, and improved efficiencies. Despite increased market turbulence, returns on US and Western European equities and bonds during the past 30 years were considerably higher than the long-run trend.

The environment of 2015–2016 was much less favorable for investors. The dramatic decline in inflation and interest rates ended, and labor force expansion and productivity gains stalled, with negative implications for GDP growth. The largest developed-country companies that generated much of the profits of the past 30 years were faced with competitive pressures as emerging-market companies expanded and technology advances changed the competitive landscape. In April 2016, McKinsey Global Institute published a projection of stocks and bonds under two growth scenarios—a slow growth scenario and a moderate growth scenario (Exhibit 8). In neither instance do the expected returns of the next 30 years come close to the returns of the past 30 years.[19] Clearly, an asset allocation developed in 2010 built on return expectations based on the prior 26 years would look materially different than an asset allocation developed using more current, forward-looking return assumptions.

EXHIBIT 8   A Major Shift in Underlying Return Assumptions

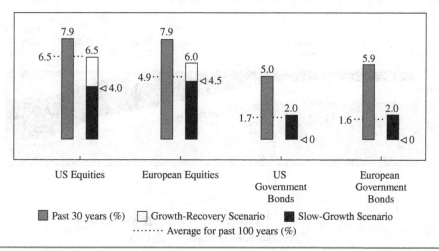

Notes:

Numbers for growth-recovery and slow-growth scenarios reflect the range between the low end of the slow-growth scenario and the high end of the growth-recovery scenario.

European equities: Weighted average real returns based on each year's Geary-Khamis purchasing power parity GDP for 14 countries in Western Europe.

US and European government bonds: Bond duration for United States is primarily 10 years; for Europe, duration varies by country but is typically 20 years.

Source: McKinsey Global Institute (www.mckinsey.com/industries/private-equity-and-principal-investors/our-insights/why-investors-may-need-to-lower-their-sights).

---

[19]McKinsey Global Institute, "Diminishing Returns: Why Investors May Need to Lower Their Expectations" (May 2016).

Finally, as new advisers or members join the Investment Committee, they bring their own beliefs and biases regarding certain investment activities. Conducting an asset allocation study to educate these new members of the oversight group and introduce them to the investment philosophy and process that has been adopted by the organization will smooth their integration into the governance system and ensure that they have a holistic view of the asset owner's goals and objectives.

In some instances, a change to an asset allocation strategy may reasonably be implemented without a formal asset allocation study. Certain milestones are reasonable points at which to implement a change in the policy, in most instances, reducing the level of risk. (For pension funds, these "milestones" are typically related to changes in the plan's funded status.) Anticipating these milestones by putting an asset allocation policy in place that anticipates these changes allows the investor to respond more quickly to changing circumstances and in a non-reactive and objective manner. This rebalancing policy is frequently referred to as a "glide path." Target-date mutual funds common in retirement investing for individuals are one example of this approach to asset allocation. Exhibit 9 illustrates one fund company's approach to migrating the asset allocation away from equities and towards bonds as retirement approaches.

EXHIBIT 9   An Asset Allocation Glide Path

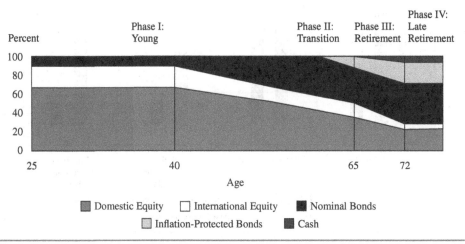

Source: Vanguard, "Target-Date Funds: A Solid Foundation for Retirement Investors" (May 2009): www.vanguard.com/jumppage/targetretirement/TRFCOMM.pdf.

In an institutional framework, the Investment Committee may specify certain funding levels it seeks to achieve. At the start of the period, an underfunded pension plan might adopt a higher equity allocation in an attempt to reduce the underfunding. If this is successful, the plan becomes better funded and there is less of a desire or need to take the higher level of equity risk. A pension fund may quickly implement "pre-programmed" asset allocation changes as the funded status of a pension plan improves. Typically, these planned reallocations are spelled out in an Investment Policy Statement.

EXAMPLE 6   Revising the Strategic Asset Allocation

1. Auldberg University Endowment Fund (AUE) has assets totaling CAF$200 million. The current asset allocation is as follows:
   - CAF$100 million in domestic equities
   - CAF$60 million in domestic government debt
   - CAF$40 million in Class B office real estate

   AUE has historically distributed to the University 5% of the 36-month moving average of net assets, contributing approximately CAF$10 million of Auldberg University's CAF$60 million annual operating budget. Real estate income (from the University's CAF$350 million direct investment in domestic commercial real estate assets, including office buildings and industrial parks, much of it near the campus) and provincial subsidies have been the main source of income to the University. Admission is free to all citizens who qualify academically.

   Growth in the Caflandia economy has been fueled by low interest rates, encouraging excess real estate development. There is a strong probability that the economy will soon go into recession, negatively impacting both the property values and the income potential of the University's real estate holdings.

   Gizi Horvath, a University alumnus, has recently announced an irrevocable CAF$200 million gift to AUE, to be paid in equal installments over the next five years. AUE employs a well-qualified staff with substantial diverse experience in equities, fixed income, and real estate. Staff has recommended that the gift from Ms. Horvath be invested using the same asset allocation policy that the endowment has been following successfully for the past five years. They suggest that the asset allocation policy should be revisited once the final installment has been received.

   Critique staff's recommendation, and identify the case facts that support your critique.

2. The Government Petroleum Fund of Caflandia (GPFC) is operating under the following asset allocation policy, which was developed with a 20-year planning horizon. Target weights and actual weights are given:

	Target Asset Allocation	Current Asset Allocation
Global equities	30%	38%
Global high-yield bonds	10%	15%
Domestic intermediate bonds	30%	25%
Hedge funds	15%	15%
Private equity	15%	7%

When this asset allocation policy was adopted 5 years ago, the petroleum revenues that support the sovereign wealth fund were projected to continue to grow for at least the next 25 years and intergenerational distributions were expected to begin in 20 years. However, since the adoption of this policy, alternate fuel sources have eroded both the price and quantity of oil exports, the economy is undergoing significant restructuring, inflows to the fund have been suspended, and distributions are expected to begin within 5 years.

What are the implications of this change in the liquidity constraints for the current asset allocation policy?

3. O-Chem Corp has a defined benefit pension plan with US$1.0 billion in assets. The plan is closed, the liabilities are frozen, and the plan is currently 65% funded. The company intends to increase cash contributions to improve the funded status of the plan and then purchase annuities to fully address all of the plan's pension obligations. As part of an asset allocation analysis conducted every five years, the company has recently decided to allocate 80% of assets to liability-matching bonds and the remaining 20% to a mix of global equities and real estate. An existing private equity portfolio is in the midst of being liquidated. This allocation reflects a desired reduction in the level of investment risk.

O-Chem has just announced an ambitious US$15 billion capital investment program to build new plants for refining and production. The CFO informed the Pension Committee that the company will be contributing to the plan only the minimum funding required by regulations for the foreseeable future. It is estimated that achieving fully funded status for the pension plan under minimum funding requirements and using the current asset allocation approach will take at least 10 years.

What are the implications of this change in funding policy for the pension plan's asset allocation strategy?

Solution to 1: The size of the anticipated contributions will double AUE's assets over the next five years, potentially increasing the opportunity set of asset classes suitable for their investment program. Given that a typical asset allocation study encompasses a long investment horizon—10 years, 20 years, or more—staff should begin to evaluate the opportunities available to them today in *anticipation* of the future cash flows. Given the material change in the economic balance sheet along with changes in the asset size, liquidity, and time horizon constraints, AUE should plan on a regular, more frequent, formal review of the asset allocation policy until the situation stabilizes. The asset allocation study should explore the feasibility of adding new asset classes as well as the ability to improve diversification within existing categories, perhaps by including non-domestic equities and bonds. Furthermore, the forecast economic environment may materially alter the outflows from the fund in support of the University's day-to-day operations. Cash flows from the University's real estate holdings are likely to decline, as are the values of those real estate assets. Given the outlook for real estate, a strong case can be made to limit or reduce the endowment's investment in real estate; moreover, consideration should be given to the effect of declining income from the current real estate investment.

Solution to 2: GPFC had adopted a long-range asset allocation policy under the expectation of continuing net cash inflows and no immediate liquidity constraints. With the change in circumstances, the need for liquidity in the fund has increased significantly. The current asset allocation policy allocates 40% of the fund's assets to less liquid asset classes—high-yield bonds, hedge funds, and private equity. Although the allocation to private equity has not been fully implemented, the fund is overweight high-yield bonds and at the target weight for hedge funds. These asset classes—or the size of the allocation to these asset classes—may no longer be appropriate for the fund given the change in circumstances.

Solution to 3: The Investment Committee should conduct a new asset allocation study to address the changes in cash flow forecasts. The lower contributions imply that the pension plan will need to rely more heavily on investment returns to reach its funding objectives. A higher allocation to return-seeking assets, such as public and private equities, is warranted. The company should suspend the current private equity liquidation plan until the new asset allocation study has been completed. A liability-matching bond portfolio is still appropriate, although less than the current 80% of assets should be allocated to this portfolio.

5. SHORT-TERM SHIFTS IN ASSET ALLOCATION

Strategic asset allocation (SAA), or policy asset allocation, represents long-term investment policy targets for asset class weights, whereas tactical asset allocation (TAA) allows short-term deviations from SAA targets.[20] TAA moves might be justified based on cyclical variations within a secular trend (e.g., stage of business or monetary cycle) or temporary price dislocations in capital markets. TAA has the objective of increasing return, or risk-adjusted return, by taking advantage of short-term economic and financial market conditions that appear more favorable to certain asset classes. In seeking to capture a short-term return opportunity, TAA decisions move the investor's risk away from the targeted risk profile. TAA is predicated on a belief that investment returns, in the short run, are predictable. (This contrasts with the random walk assumption more strongly embedded in most SAA processes.) Using either short-term views or signals, the investor actively re-weights broad asset classes, sectors, or risk factor premiums. TAA is not concerned with individual security selection. In other words, generating alpha through TAA decisions is dependent on successful market or factor timing rather than security selection. TAA is an asset-only approach. Although tactical asset allocation shifts must still conform to the risk constraints outlined in the investment policy statement, they do not expressly consider liabilities (or goals in goals-based investing).

The SAA policy portfolio is the benchmark against which TAA decisions are measured. Tactical views are developed and bets are sized relative to the asset class targets of the SAA policy portfolio. The sizes of these bets are typically subject to certain risk constraints. The most common risk constraint is a pre-established allowable range around each asset class's policy target. Other risk constraints may include either a predicted tracking error budget versus the SAA or a range of targeted risk (e.g., an allowable range of predicted volatility).

The success of TAA decisions can be evaluated in a number of ways. Three of the most common are

• a comparison of the Sharpe ratio realized under the TAA relative to the Sharpe ratio that would have been realized under the SAA;

---

[20]SAA and TAA are distinct from GTAA (global tactical asset allocation), an opportunistic investment strategy that seeks to take advantage of pricing or valuation anomalies across multiple asset classes, typically equities, fixed income, and currencies.

- evaluating the information ratio or the *t*-statistic of the average excess return of the TAA portfolio relative to the SAA portfolio; and
- plotting the realized return and risk of the TAA portfolio versus the realized return and risk of portfolios along the SAA's efficient frontier. This approach is particularly useful in assessing the risk-adjusted TAA return. The TAA portfolio may have produced a higher return or a higher Sharpe ratio than the SAA portfolio, but it could be less optimal than other portfolios along the investor's efficient frontier of portfolio choices.

The composition of the portfolio's excess return over the SAA portfolio return can also be examined more closely using attribution analysis, evaluating the specific overweights and underweights that led to the performance differential.

Tactical investment decisions may incur additional costs—higher trading costs and taxes (in the case of taxable investors). Tactical investment decisions can also increase the concentration of risk relative to the policy portfolio. For example, if the tactical decision is to overweight equities, not only is the portfolio risk increased but also the diversification of risk contributions is reduced. This is particularly an issue when the SAA policy portfolio relies on uncorrelated asset classes. These costs should be weighed against the predictability of short-term returns.

There are two broad approaches to TAA. The first is discretionary, which relies on a qualitative interpretation of political, economic, and financial market conditions. The second is systematic, which relies on quantitative signals to capture documented return anomalies that may be inconsistent with market efficiency.

5.1. Discretionary TAA

Discretionary TAA is predicated on the existence of manager skill in predicting and timing short-term market moves away from the expected outcome for each asset class that is embedded in the SAA policy portfolio. In practice, discretionary TAA is typically used in an attempt to mitigate or hedge risk in distressed markets while enhancing return in positive return markets (i.e., an asymmetric return distribution).

Short-term forecasts consider a large number of data points that provide relevant information about current and expected political, economic, and financial market conditions that may affect short-term asset class returns. Data points might include valuations, term and credit spreads, central bank policy, GDP growth, earnings expectations, inflation expectations, and leading economic indicators. Price-to-earnings ratios, price-to-book ratios, and the dividend yield are commonly used valuation measures that can be compared to historical averages and across similar assets to inform short-to-intermediate-term tactical shifts. Term spreads provide information about the business cycle, inflation, and potential future interest rates. Credit spreads gauge default risk, borrowing conditions, and liquidity. Other data points are more directly related to current and expected GDP and earnings growth.

Short-term forecasts may also consider economic sentiment indicators. TAA often assumes a close relationship between the economy and capital market returns. Because consumer spending is a major driver of GDP in developed countries, consumer sentiment is a key consideration. Consumer confidence surveys provide insight as to the level of optimism regarding the economy and personal finances.

TAA also considers market sentiment—indicators of the optimism or pessimism of financial market participants. Data points considered in gauging market sentiment include margin borrowing, short interest, and a volatility index.

- Margin borrowing measures give an indication of the current level of bullishness, and the capacity for more or less margin borrowing has implications for future bullishness. Higher prices tend to inspire confidence and spur more buying; similarly, more buying on margin tends to spur higher prices. The aggregate level of margin can be an indicator that bullish sentiment is overdone, although the level of borrowing must be considered in the context of the rate of change in borrowing.
- Short interest measures give an indication of current bearish sentiment and also have implications for future bearishness. Although rising short interest indicates increasing negative sentiment, a high short interest ratio may be an indication of the extreme pessimism that often occurs at market lows.
- The volatility index, commonly known as the fear index, is a measure of market expectations of near-term volatility. VDAX-NEW in Germany, V2X in the United Kingdom, and VIX in the United States each measure the level of expected volatility of their respective indexes as implied by the bid/ask quotations of index options; it rises when put option buying increases and falls when call buying activity increases.

Different approaches to discretionary TAA may include different data points and relationships and also may prioritize and weight those data points differently depending on both the approach and the prevailing market environment. Despite the plethora of data inputs, the interpretation of this information is qualitative at its core.

5.2. Systematic TAA

Using signals, systematic TAA attempts to capture asset class level return anomalies that have been shown to have some predictability and persistence. Value and momentum, for example, are factors that have been determined to offer some level of predictability, both among securities within asset classes (for security selection) and at the asset class level (for asset class timing).

The value factor is the return of value stocks over the return of growth stocks. The momentum factor is the return of stocks with higher prior returns over the return of stocks with lower prior returns. Value and momentum (and size) factors have been determined to have some explanatory power regarding the relative returns of equity securities within the equity asset class. Value and momentum phenomena are also present at the asset class level and can be used in making tactical asset allocation decisions across asset classes.

Valuation ratios have been shown to have some explanatory power in predicting variation in future equity returns. Predictive measures for equities include dividend yield, cash flow yield, and Shiller's earnings yield (the inverse of Shiller's P/E[21]). Sometimes these yield measures are defined as the excess of the yield over the local risk-free rate or inflation.[22]

Other asset classes have their own value signals, such as yield and carry in currencies, commodities, and/or fixed income. Carry in currencies uses short-term interest rate differentials to determine which currencies (or currency-denominated assets) to overweight (or own) and which to underweight (or sell short). Carry in commodities compares positive (backwardation) and negative (contango) roll yields to determine which commodities to own

---

[21]A price-to-earnings ratio based on the average inflation-adjusted earnings of the previous 10 years.

[22]Return predictability for equity markets is driven by historical mean-reversion, which tends to occur over the intermediate-term. These valuation measures are often used as signals for TAA, but they can also be used to shape return expectations for SAA.

or short. And for bonds, yields-to-maturity and term premiums (yields in excess of the local risk-free rate) signal the relative attractiveness of different fixed-income markets.

Asset classes can trend positively or negatively for some time before changing course. Trend following is an investment or trading strategy based on the expectation that asset class (or asset) returns will continue in the same upward or downward trend that they have most recently exhibited.[23] A basic trend signal is the most recent 12-month return: The expectation is that the direction of the most recent 12-month returns can be expected to persist for the next 12 months. Shorter time frames and different weighting schemes can also be used. For example, another trend signal is the moving-average crossover, where the moving average price of a shorter time frame is compared with the moving average price of a longer time frame. This signals an upward (downward) trend when the moving average of the shorter time frame is above (below) the moving average of the longer time frame. Trend signals are widely used in systematic TAA. Asset classes may be ranked or categorized into positive or negative buckets based on their most recent prior 12-month performance and over- or underweighted accordingly. More-complex signals for both momentum/trend signals (such as those that use different lookback periods or momentum signals correlated with earnings momentum) and value/carry are also used.

EXAMPLE 7   Short-Term Shifts in Asset Allocation

1. The investment policy for Alpha Beverage Corporation's pension fund allows staff to overweight or underweight asset classes, within pre-established bands, using a TAA model that has been approved by the Investment Committee. The asset allocation policy is reflected in Exhibit 10, and the output of the TAA model is

EXHIBIT 10   Strategic Asset Allocation Policy

SAA Policy	Current Weight	Target Allocation	Upper Policy Limit	Lower Policy Limit
Investment-grade bonds	45%	40%	45%	35%
High-yield bonds	10%	10%	15%	5%
Developed markets equity	35%	40%	45%	35%
Emerging markets equity	10%	10%	15%	5%

EXHIBIT 11   Trend Signal (the positive or negative trailing 12-month excess return)

	12-Month Return	Risk-Free Return	Excess Return	Signal
Investment-grade bonds	4%	1%	3%	Long
High-yield bonds	−2%	1%	−3%	Short
Developed markets equity	5%	1%	4%	Long
Emerging markets equity	−10%	1%	−11%	Short

---

[23]Trend following is also called time-series momentum. Cross-sectional momentum describes the relative momentum returns of securities within the same asset class.

given in Exhibit 11. Using the data presented in Exhibits 10 and 11, recommend a TAA strategy for the pension fund and justify your response.

2. One year later, the Investment Committee for Alpha Beverage Corporation is conducting its year-end review of pension plan performance. Staff has prepared the following exhibits regarding the tactical asset allocation decisions taken during the

EXHIBIT 12A

Asset Class	Asset Allocation	Calendar Year Return
Investment-grade bonds	45%	3.45%
High-yield bonds	5%	−6.07%
Developed markets equity	45%	−0.32%
Emerging markets equity	5%	−14.60%

EXHIBIT 12B

	Policy Portfolio	Realized Results
12-month return	−0.82%	0.38%
Risk-free rate	0.50%	0.50%
Standard deviation	5.80%	6.20%
Sharpe ratio	−0.23	−0.02

EXHIBIT 12C

Calendar Year Return (%)

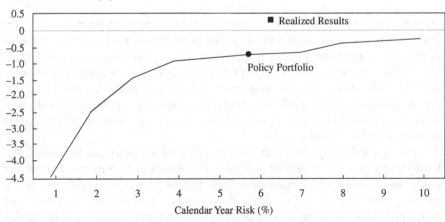

past year. Assume that all investments are implemented using passively managed index funds. Evaluate the effectiveness of the TAA decisions.

Solution to 1: The TAA decision must be taken in the context of the SAA policy constraints. Thus, although the signals for high-yield bonds and emerging market equities are negative, the minimum permissible weight in each is 5%. Similarly, although the signals for investment-grade bonds and developed markets equities are positive, the maximum permissible weight in each is 45%. Asset classes can be over- or underweighted to the full extent of the policy limits. Based on the trend signals and the policy constraints, the recommended tactical asset allocation is as follows:

- Investment-grade bonds   45% *(overweight by 5%)*
- High-yield bonds   5% *(underweight by 5%)*
- Developed markets equity   45% *(overweight by 5%)*
- Emerging markets equity   5% *(underweight by 5%)*

Solution to 2: The decision to overweight investment grade bonds and underweight emerging markets equity and high-yield bonds was a profitable one. The chosen asset allocation added approximately 120 basis points to portfolio return over the year. Although portfolio risk was elevated relative to the policy portfolio (standard deviation of 6.2% versus 5.8% for the policy portfolio), the portfolio positioning improved the fund's Sharpe ratio relative to allocations they might have selected along the efficient frontier.

A Silver Lining to the 2008–2009 Financial Crisis

Prior to 2008, corporate pension plans had begun to shift the fixed-income component of their policy portfolios from an intermediate maturity bond index to a long bond index. Despite the relatively low interest rates at the time, this move was made to better align the plans' assets with the long duration liability payment stream. The fixed-income portfolios were typically benchmarked against a long government and credit index that included both government and corporate bonds. Swaps or STRIPS* were sometimes used to extend duration.

During the financial crisis that began in 2008, these heavier and longer-duration fixed-income positions performed well relative to equities (the long government and credit index was up 8%, whereas the S&P 500 Index was down 37% in 2008), providing plan sponsors with a level of investment protection that had not been anticipated. Additionally, with its exposure to higher-returning government bonds that benefited from investors' flight to safety, this fixed-income portfolio often outperformed the liabilities. (Recall from the earlier discussion on pension regulation that pension liabilities are typically measured using corporate bond yields. Thus, liabilities rose in the face of declining corporate bond yields while the liability-hedging asset rose even further given its overall higher credit quality.) This was an unintended asset/ liability mismatch that had very positive results. Subsequent to this rally in bonds, some plan sponsors made a tactical asset allocation decision—to move out of swaps and government bonds and into physical corporate bonds (non-derivative fixed-income exposure)—locking in the gains and better hedging the liability.

*Treasury STRIPS are fixed-income securities with no interest payments that are sold at a discount to face value and mature at par. STRIPS is an acronym for Separate Trading of Registered Interest and Principal of Securities.

6. DEALING WITH BEHAVIORAL BIASES IN ASSET ALLOCATION

Although global capital markets are competitive pricing engines, human behavior can be less rational than most economic models assume. Behavioral finance—the hybrid study of financial economics and psychology—has documented a number of behavioral biases that commonly arise in investing. The CFA Program chapter "The Behavioral Biases of Individuals" discusses 16 common behavioral biases. The biases most relevant in asset allocation include loss aversion, the illusion of control, mental accounting, representativeness bias, framing, and availability bias. An effective investment program will address these decision-making risks through a formal asset allocation process with its own objective framework, governance, and controls. An important first step toward mitigating the negative effects of behavioral biases is simply acknowledging that they exist; just being aware of them can reduce their influence on decision-making. It is also possible to incorporate certain behavioral biases into the investment decision-making process to produce better outcomes. This is most commonly practiced in goals-based investing. We will discuss strategies that help deal with these common biases.

6.1. Loss Aversion

Loss-aversion bias is an emotional bias in which people tend to strongly prefer avoiding losses as opposed to achieving gains. A number of studies on loss aversion suggest that, psychologically, losses are significantly more powerful than gains. The utility derived from a gain is much lower than the utility given up with an equivalent loss. This behavior is related to the marginal utility of wealth, where each additional dollar of wealth is valued incrementally less with increasing levels of wealth.

A diversified multi-asset class portfolio is generally thought to offer an approximately symmetrical distribution of returns around a positive expected mean return. Financial market theory suggests that a rational investor would think about risk as the dispersion or uncertainty (variance) around the mean (expected) outcome. However, loss aversion suggests the investor assigns a greater weight to the negative outcomes than would be implied by the actual shape of the distribution. Looking at this another way, risk is not measured relative to the expected mean return but rather on an absolute basis, relative to a 0% return. The loss-aversion bias may interfere with an investor's ability to maintain his chosen asset allocation through periods of negative returns.

In goals-based investing, loss-aversion bias can be mitigated by framing risk in terms of shortfall probability or by funding high-priority goals with low-risk assets.

Shortfall probability is the probability that a portfolio will not achieve the return required to meet a stated goal. Where there are well-defined, discrete goals, sub-portfolios can be established for each goal and the asset allocation for that sub-portfolio would use shortfall probability as the definition of risk.

Similarly, by segregating assets into sub-portfolios aligned to goals designated by the client as high-priority and investing those assets in risk-free or low risk assets of similar duration, the adviser mitigates the loss-aversion bias associated with this particular goal—freeing up other assets to take on a more appropriate level of risk. Riskier assets can then be used to fund lower-priority and aspirational goals.

In institutional investing, loss aversion can be seen in the herding behavior among plan sponsors. Adopting an asset allocation not too different from the allocation of one's peers minimizes reputation risk.

6.2. Illusion of Control

The illusion of control is a cognitive bias—the tendency to overestimate one's ability to control events. It can be exacerbated by overconfidence, an emotional bias. If investors believe they have more or better information than what is reflected in the market, they have (excessive) confidence in their ability to generate better outcomes. They may perceive *information* in what are random price movements, which may lead to more frequent trading, greater concentration of portfolio positions, or a greater willingness to employ tactical shifts in their asset allocation. The following investor behaviors might be attributed to this illusion of control:

- Alpha-seeking behaviors, such as attempted market timing in the form of extreme tactical asset allocation shifts or all in/all out market calls—the investor who correctly anticipated a market reversal now believes he has superior insight on valuation levels.
- Alpha-seeking behaviors based on a belief of superior resources—the institutional investor who believes her internal resources give her an edge over other investors in active security selection and/or the selection of active investment managers.
- Excessive trading, use of leverage, or short selling—the long/short equity investor who moves from a normal exposure range of 65% long/20% short to 100% long/50% short.
- Reducing, eliminating, or even shorting asset classes that are a significant part of the global market portfolio based on non-consensus return and risk forecasts—the chair of a foundation's investment committee who calls for shortening the duration of the bond portfolio from six years to six months based on insights drawn from his position in the banking industry.
- Retaining a large, concentrated legacy asset that contributes diversifiable risk—the employee who fails to diversify her holding of company stock.

Hindsight bias—the tendency to perceive past investment outcomes as having been predictable—exacerbates the illusion of control.

In the asset allocation process, an investor who believes he or she has better information than others may use estimates of return and risk that produce asset allocation choices that are materially different from the market portfolio. This can result in undiversified portfolios with outsized exposures to just one or two minor asset classes, called extreme corner portfolios.

Using such biased risk and return estimates results in a biased asset allocation decision—precisely what an objective asset allocation process seeks to avoid.

The illusion of control can be mitigated by using the global market portfolio as the starting point in developing the asset allocation. Building on the basic principles of CAPM, Markowitz's mean–variance theory, and efficient market theory, the global market portfolio offers a theoretically sound benchmark for asset allocation. Deviations from this baseline portfolio must be thoughtfully considered and rigorously vetted, ensuring the asset allocation process remains objective. A formal asset allocation process that employs long-term return and risk forecasts, optimization constraints anchored around asset class weights in the global market portfolio, and strict policy ranges will significantly mitigate the illusion of control bias in asset allocation.

6.3. Mental Accounting

Mental accounting is an information-processing bias in which people treat one sum of money differently from another sum based solely on the mental account the money is assigned to. Investors may separate assets or liabilities into buckets based on subjective criteria. For example, an investor may consider his retirement investment portfolio independent of the portfolio that funds his child's education, even if the combined asset allocation of the two portfolios is sub-optimal. Or an employee with significant exposure to her employer's stock through vested stock options may fail to consider this exposure alongside other assets when establishing a strategic asset allocation.

Goals-based investing incorporates mental accounting directly into the asset allocation solution. Each goal is aligned with a discrete sub-portfolio, and the investor can specify the acceptable level of risk for each goal. Provided each of the sub-portfolios lies along the same efficient frontier, the sum of the sub-portfolios will also be efficient.[24]

Concentrated stock positions also give rise to another common mental accounting issue that affects asset allocation. For example, the primary source of an entrepreneur's wealth may be a concentrated equity position in the publicly traded company he founded. The entrepreneur may prefer to retain a relatively large exposure to this one security within his broader investment portfolio despite the inherent risk. Although there may be rational reasons for this preference—including ownership control, an information advantage, and tax considerations—the desire to retain this riskier exposure is more often the result of a psychological loyalty to the asset that generated his wealth. This mental accounting bias is further reinforced by the endowment effect—the tendency to ascribe more value to an asset already owned rather than another asset one might purchase to replace it.

The concentrated stock/mental accounting bias can be accommodated in goals-based asset allocation by assigning the concentrated stock position to an aspirational goal—one that the client would *like* to achieve but to which he or she is willing to assign a lower probability of success. Whereas lifetime consumption tends to be a high-priority goal requiring a well-diversified portfolio to fund it with confidence, an aspirational goal such as a charitable gift may be an important but much less highly valued goal. It can reasonably be funded with the concentrated stock position. (This could have the additional benefit of avoiding capital gains tax altogether!)

---

[24]This condition holds when the asset allocation process is unconstrained. With a long-only constraint, some efficiency is lost but the effect is much less significant than the loss of efficiency from inaccurately specifying risk aversion (which goals-based approaches to asset allocation attempt to mitigate). See Das, Markowitz, Scheid, and Statman (2010) and Das et al. (2011).

6.4. Representativeness Bias

Representativeness, or recency, bias is the tendency to overweight the importance of the most recent observations and information relative to a longer-dated or more comprehensive set of long-term observations and information. Tactical shifts in asset allocation, those undertaken in response to recent returns or news—perhaps shifting the asset allocation toward the highest or lowest allowable ends of the policy ranges—are particularly susceptible to recency bias. Return chasing is a common manifestation of recency bias, and it results in overweighting asset classes with good recent performance.

It is believed that asset prices largely follow a random walk; past prices cannot be used to predict future returns. If this is true, then shifting the asset allocation in response to recent returns, or allowing recent returns to unduly influence the asset class assumptions used in the asset allocation process, will likely lead to sub-optimal results. *If*, however, asset class returns exhibit trending behavior, the recent past *may* contain information relevant to tactical shifts in asset allocation. And if asset class returns are mean-reverting, comparing current valuations to historical norms may signal the potential for a reversal or for above-average future returns.

Recency bias is not uniformly negative. Random walk, trending, and mean-reversion may be simultaneously relevant to the investment decision-making process, although their effect on asset prices will unfold over different time horizons. The strongest defenses against recency bias are an objective asset allocation process and a strong governance framework. It is important that the investor objectively evaluate the motivation underlying the response to recent market events. A formal asset allocation policy with pre-specified allowable ranges will constrain recency bias. A strong governance framework with the appropriate level of expertise and well-documented investment beliefs increases the likelihood that shifts in asset allocation are made objectively and in accordance with those beliefs.

6.5. Framing Bias

Framing bias is an information-processing bias in which a person may answer a question differently based solely on the way in which it is asked. One example of framing bias is common in committee-oriented decision-making processes. In instances where one individual frequently speaks first and speaks with great authority, the views of other committee members may be suppressed or biased toward this first position put on the table.

A more nuanced form of framing bias can be found in asset allocation. The investor's choice of an asset allocation may be influenced merely by the manner in which the risk-to-return trade-off is presented.

Risk can mean different things to different investors: volatility, tail risk, the permanent loss of capital, or a failure to meet financial goals. These definitions are all closely related, but the relative importance of each of these aspects can influence the investor's asset allocation choice. Further, the investor's perception of each of these risks can be influenced by the manner in which they are presented—gain and loss potential framed in money terms versus percentages, for example.

Investors are often asked to evaluate portfolio choices using expected return, with standard deviation as the sole measure of risk. Standard deviation measures the dispersion or volatility around the mean (expected) return. Other measures of risk may also be used. Value at risk (VaR) is a loss threshold: "If I choose this asset mix, I can be pretty sure that my losses will not exceed X, most of the time." More formally, VaR is the minimum loss that would be expected a certain percentage of the time over a certain period of time given the assumed market conditions. Conditional value at risk (CVaR) is the probability-weighted average of losses when the VaR threshold is breached. VaR and CVaR both measure downside or tail risk.

Exhibit 13 shows the expected return and risk for five portfolios that span an efficient frontier from P1 (lowest risk) to P100 (highest risk). A normal distribution of returns is assumed; therefore, the portfolio's VaR and CVaR are a direct function of the portfolio's expected return and standard deviation. In this case, standard deviation, VaR, and CVaR measure precisely the same risk but frame that risk differently. Standard deviation presents that risk as volatility, while VaR and CVaR present it as risk of loss. When dealing with a normal distribution, as this example presumes, the 5% VaR threshold is simply the point on the distribution 1.65 standard deviations below the expected mean return.

EXHIBIT 13   There's More Than One Way to Frame Risk

	P1	P25	P50	P75	P100
Return	3.2%	4.9%	6.0%	7.0%	8.0%
Std. Dev.	3.9%	7.8%	11.9%	15.9%	20.0%
VaR (5%)	−3.2%	−8.0%	−13.6%	−19.3%	−25.0%
CVaR (5%)	−4.8%	−11.2%	−18.5%	−25.8%	−33.2%

When viewing return and volatility alone, many investors may gravitate to P50 with its 6.0% expected return and 11.9% standard deviation. P50 represents the median risk portfolio that appeals to many investors in practice because it balances high-risk and low-risk choices with related diversification benefits. However, loss-aversion bias suggests that some investors who gravitate to the median choice might actually find the −18.5% CVaR of P50 indicative of a level of risk they find very uncomfortable. The CVaR frame intuitively communicates a different perspective of exactly the same risk that is already fully explained by standard deviation—namely, the downside or tail-risk aspects of the standard deviation and mean. With this example, you can see that how risk is framed and presented can affect the asset allocation decision.

The framing effect can be mitigated by presenting the possible asset allocation choices with multiple perspectives on the risk/reward trade-off. The most commonly used risk measure—standard deviation—can be supplemented with additional measures, such as **shortfall probability** (the probability of failing to meet a specific liability or goal)[25] and tail-risk measures (e.g., VaR and CVaR). Historical stress tests and Monte Carlo simulations can also be used to capture and communicate risk in a tangible way. These multiple perspectives of the risk and reward trade-offs among a set of asset allocation choices compel the investor to consider more carefully what outcomes are acceptable or unacceptable.

---

[25]Shortfall risk and shortfall probability are often used to refer to the same concept. This author prefers shortfall probability because the measure refers to the probability of shortfall, not the magnitude of the potential shortfall. For example, you may have a low probability of shortfall but the size of the shortfall could be significant. In this case, it could be misleading to say the shortfall risk is low.

6.6. Availability Bias

Availability bias is an information-processing bias in which people take a mental shortcut when estimating the probability of an outcome based on how easily the outcome comes to mind. Easily recalled outcomes are often perceived as being more likely than those that are harder to recall or understand. For example, more recent events or events in which the investor has personally been affected are likely to be assigned a higher probability of occurring again, regardless of the objective odds of the event actually occurring.

As an example, many private equity investors experienced a liquidity squeeze during the financial crisis that began in 2008. Their equity portfolios had suffered large losses, and their private equity investments were illiquid. Worse yet, they were contractually committed to additional capital contributions to those private equity funds. At the same time, their financial obligations continued at the same or an even higher pace. Investors who personally experienced this confluence of negative events are likely to express a strong preference for liquid investments, assigning a higher probability to such an event occurring again than would an investor who had cash available to acquire the private equity interests that were sold at distressed prices.

Familiarity bias stems from availability bias: People tend to favor the familiar over the new or different because of the ease of recalling the familiar. In asset allocation, familiarity bias most commonly results in a **home bias**—a preference for securities listed on the exchanges of one's home country. However, concentrating portfolio exposure in home country securities, particularly if the home country capital markets are small, results in a less diversified, less efficient portfolio. Familiarity bias can be mitigated by using the global market portfolio as the starting point in developing the asset allocation, where deviations from this baseline portfolio must be thoughtfully considered and rigorously vetted.

Familiarity bias may also cause investors to fall into the trap of comparing their investment decisions (and performance) to others', without regard for the appropriateness of those decisions for their own specific facts and circumstances. By avoiding comparison of investment returns or asset allocation decisions with others, an organization is more capable of identifying the asset allocation that is best tailored to their needs.

Investment decision-making is subject to a wide range of potential behavioral biases. This is true in both private wealth *and* institutional investing. Employing a formal asset allocation process using the global market portfolio as the starting point for asset allocation modeling is a key component of ensuring the asset allocation decision is as objective as possible.

A strong governance structure, such as that discussed in the overview chapter on asset allocation, is a necessary first step to mitigating the effect that these behavioral biases may have on the long-term success of the investment program. Bringing a diverse set of views to the deliberation process brings more tools to the table to solve any problem and leads to better and more informed decision-making. A clearly stated mission—a common goal—and a commitment from committee members and other stakeholders to that mission are critically important in constraining the influence of these biases on investment decisions.

Effective Investment Governance

Six critical elements of effective investment governance are

1. clearly articulated long- and short-term investment objectives of the investment program;
2. allocation of decision rights and responsibilities among the functional units in the governance hierarchy, taking account of their knowledge, capacity, time, and position in the governance hierarchy;
3. established processes for developing and approving the investment policy statement that will govern the day-to-day operation of the investment program;
4. specified processes for developing and approving the program's strategic asset allocation;
5. a reporting framework to monitor the program's progress toward the agreed-upon goals and objectives; and
6. periodic governance audits.

EXAMPLE 8   Mitigating Behavioral Biases in Asset Allocation

Ivy Lee, the retired founder of a publicly traded company, has two primary goals for her investment assets. The first goal is to fund lifetime consumption expenditures of US$1 million per year for herself and her husband; this is a goal the Lees want to achieve with a high degree of certainty. The second goal is to provide an end-of-life gift to Auldberg University. Ivy has a diversified portfolio of stocks and bonds totaling US$5 million and a sizable position in the stock of the company she founded. The following table summarizes the facts.

Investor Profile	
Annual consumption needs	US$1,000,000
Remaining years of life expectancy	40
Diversified stock holdings	US$3,000,000
Diversified bond holdings	US$2,000,000
Concentrated stock holdings	US$15,000,000
Total portfolio	US$20,000,000

Assume that a 60% equity/40% fixed-income portfolio represents the level of risk Ivy is willing to assume with respect to her consumption goal. This 60/40 portfolio offers an expected return of 6.0%. (For simplicity, this illustration ignores inflation and taxes.)

The present value of the expected consumption expenditures is US$15,949,075. This is the amount needed on hand today, which, if invested in a portfolio of 60% equities and 40% fixed income, would fully fund 40 annual cash distributions of US$1,000,000 each.[26]

The concentrated stock has a highly uncertain expected return and comes with significant idiosyncratic (stock-specific) risk. A preliminary mean–variance optimization using three "asset classes"—stocks, bonds, and the concentrated stock—results in a zero allocation to the concentrated stock position. But Ivy prefers to retain as much concentrated stock as possible because it represents her legacy and she has a strong psychological loyalty to it.

1. Describe the behavioral biases most relevant to developing an asset allocation recommendation for Ivy.
2. Recommend and justify an asset allocation for Ivy given the facts presented above.

Solution to 1: Two behavioral biases that the adviser must be aware of in developing an asset allocation recommendation for Ivy are illusion of control and mental accounting. Because Ivy was the founder of the company whose stock comprises 75% of her investment portfolio, she may believe she has more or better information about the return prospects for this portion of the portfolio. The belief that she has superior information may lead to a risk assessment that is not reflective of the true risk in the holding. Using a goals-based approach to asset allocation may help Ivy more fully understand the risks inherent in the concentrated stock position. The riskier, concentrated stock position can be assigned to a lower-priority goal, such as the gift to Auldberg University.

Solution to 2: It is recommended that Ivy fully fund her high-priority lifestyle consumption needs (US$15,949,075) with US$16 million in a diversified portfolio of stocks and bonds. To achieve this, US$11 million of the concentrated stock position should be sold and the proceeds added to the diversified portfolio that supports lifestyle consumption needs. The remaining US$4 million of concentrated stock can be retained to fund the aspirational goal of an end-of-life gift to Auldberg University. In this example, the adviser has employed the mental accounting bias to achieve a suitable outcome: By illustrating the dollar value needed to fund the high-priority lifetime

	Beginning Asset Allocation	Recommended Asset Allocation
Diversified stocks	US$3,000,000	US$9,600,000
Diversified bonds	US$2,000,000	US$6,400,000
Funding of lifestyle goal		*US$16,000,000*
Concentrated stock	US$15,000,000	US$4,000,000
Total portfolio	US$20,000,000	US$20,000,000

---

[26]Assumes cash distributions occur at the beginning of the year and the expected return is the geometric average.

consumption needs goal, the adviser was able to clarify for Ivy the risks in retaining the concentrated stock position. The adviser might also simulate portfolio returns and the associated probability of achieving Ivy's goals using a range of scenarios for the performance of the concentrated stock position. Framing the effect this one holding may have on the likelihood of achieving her goals may help Ivy agree to reduce the position size. Consideration of certain behavioral biases like mental accounting can improve investor outcomes when they are incorporated in an objective decision-making framework.

7. SUMMARY

- The primary constraints on an asset allocation decision are asset size, liquidity, time horizon, and other external considerations, such as taxes and regulation.
- The size of an asset owner's portfolio may limit the asset classes accessible to the asset owner. An asset owner's portfolio may be too small—or too large—to capture the returns of certain asset classes or strategies efficiently.
- Complex asset classes and investment vehicles require sufficient governance capacity.
- Large-scale asset owners may achieve operating efficiencies, but they may find it difficult to deploy capital effectively in certain active investment strategies given liquidity conditions and trading costs.
- Smaller portfolios may also be constrained by size. They may be too small to adequately diversify across the range of asset classes and investment managers, or they may have staffing constraints that prevent them from monitoring a complex investment program.
- Investors with smaller portfolios may be constrained in their ability to access private equity, private real estate, hedge funds, and infrastructure investments because of the high required minimum investments and regulatory restrictions associated with those asset classes. Wealthy families may pool assets to meet the required minimums.
- The liquidity needs of the asset owner and the liquidity characteristics of the asset classes each influence the available opportunity set.
- Liquidity needs must also take into consideration the financial strength of the investor and resources beyond those held in the investment portfolio.
- When assessing the appropriateness of any given asset class for a given investor, it is important to evaluate potential liquidity needs in the context of an extreme market stress event.
- An investor's time horizon must be considered in any asset allocation exercise. Changes in human capital and the changing character of liabilities are two important time-related constraints of asset allocation.
- External considerations—such as regulations, tax rules, funding, and financing needs—are also likely to influence the asset allocation decision.
- Taxes alter the distribution of returns by both reducing the expected mean return and muting the dispersion of returns. Asset values and asset risk and return inputs to asset allocation should be modified to reflect the tax status of the investor. Correlation assumptions do not need to be adjusted, but taxes do affect the return and the standard deviation assumptions for each asset class.

- Periodic portfolio rebalancing to return the portfolio to its target strategic asset allocation is an integral part of sound portfolio management. Taxable investors must consider the tax implications of rebalancing.
- Rebalancing thresholds may be wider for taxable portfolios because it takes larger asset class movements to materially alter the risk profile of the taxable portfolio.
- Strategic asset location is the placement of less tax-efficient assets in accounts with more-favorable tax treatment.
- An asset owner's strategic asset allocation should be re-examined periodically, even in the absence of a change in the asset owner's circumstances.
- A special review of the asset allocation policy may be triggered by a change in goals, constraints, or beliefs.
- In some situations, a change to an asset allocation strategy may be implemented without a formal asset allocation study. Anticipating key milestones that would alter the asset owner's risk appetite, and implementing pre-established changes to the asset allocation in response, is often referred to as a "glide path."
- Tactical asset allocation (TAA) allows short-term deviations from the strategic asset allocation (SAA) targets and are expected to increase risk-adjusted return. Using either short-term views or signals, the investor actively re-weights broad asset classes, sectors, or risk-factor premiums. The sizes of these deviations from the SAA are often constrained by the Investment Policy Statement.
- The success of TAA decisions is measured against the performance of the SAA policy portfolio by comparing Sharpe ratios, evaluating the information ratio or the t-statistic of the average excess return of the TAA portfolio relative to the SAA portfolio, or plotting outcomes versus the efficient frontier.
- TAA incurs trading and tax costs. Tactical trades can also increase the concentration of risk.
- Discretionary TAA relies on a qualitative interpretation of political, economic, and financial market conditions and is predicated on a belief of persistent manager skill in predicting and timing short-term market moves.
- Systematic TAA relies on quantitative signals to capture documented return anomalies that may be inconsistent with market efficiency.
- The behavioral biases most relevant in asset allocation include loss aversion, the illusion of control, mental accounting, recency bias, framing, and availability bias.
- An effective investment program will address behavioral biases through a formal asset allocation process with its own objective framework, governance, and controls.
- In goals-based investing, loss-aversion bias can be mitigated by framing risk in terms of shortfall probability or by funding high-priority goals with low-risk assets.
- The cognitive bias, illusion of control, and hindsight bias can all be mitigated by using a formal asset allocation process that uses long-term return and risk forecasts, optimization constraints anchored around asset class weights in the global market portfolio, and strict policy ranges.
- Goals-based investing incorporates the mental accounting bias directly into the asset allocation solution by aligning each goal with a discrete sub-portfolio.
- A formal asset allocation policy with pre-specified allowable ranges may constrain recency bias.
- The framing bias effect can be mitigated by presenting the possible asset allocation choices with multiple perspectives on the risk/reward trade-off.

- Familiarity bias, a form of availability bias, most commonly results in an overweight in home country securities and may also cause investors to inappropriately compare their investment decisions (and performance) to other organizations. Familiarity bias can be mitigated by using the global market portfolio as the starting point in developing the asset allocation and by carefully evaluating any potential deviations from this baseline portfolio.
- A strong governance framework with the appropriate level of expertise and well-documented investment beliefs increases the likelihood that shifts in asset allocation are made objectively and in accordance with those beliefs. This will help to mitigate the effect that behavioral biases may have on the long-term success of the investment program.

REFERENCES

Bader, Lawrence N., and Jeremy Gold. 2007. "The Case against Stock in Public Pension Funds." *Financial Analysts Journal*, vol. 63, no. 1 (January/February): 55–62.

Bodie, Zvi, Robert C. Merton, and William F. Samuelson. 1992. "Labor Supply Flexibility and Portfolio Choice in a Life Cycle Model." *Journal of Economic Dynamics & Control*, vol. 16: 427–449.

Chen, Joseph, Harrison Hong, Ming Huang, and Jeffrey Kubik. 2004. "Does Fund Size Erode Mutual Fund Performance? The Role of Liquidity and Organization." *American Economic Review*, vol. 94, no. 5: 1276–1302.

Cooper, Stephen, and David Bianco. 2003. "Q-Series™: Pension Fund Asset Allocation." UBS Investment Research (September).

Das, Sanjiv, Harry Markowitz, Jonathan Scheid, and Meir Statman. 2010. "Portfolio Optimization with Mental Accounts." *Journal of Financial and Quantitative Analysis*, vol. 45, no. 2: 311–334.

Das, Sanjiv, Harry Markowitz, Jonathan Scheid, and Meir Statman. 2011. "Portfolios for Investors Who Want to Reach Their Goals While Staying on the Mean–Variance Efficient Frontier." *Journal of Wealth Management*, vol. 14, no. 2 (Fall): 25–31.

Dyck, Alexander, and Lukasz Pomorski. 2011. "Is Bigger Better? Size and Performance in Pension Plan Management." Rotman School of Management Working Paper No. 1690724.

Horan, Stephen, and Ashraf Al Zaman. 2008. "Tax-Adjusted Portfolio Optimization and Asset Location: Extensions and Synthesis." *Journal of Wealth Management*, vol. 11, no. 3: 56–73.

Kritzman, Mark. 2015. "What Practitioners Need to Know about Time Diversification (corrected March 2015)." *Financial Analysts Journal*, vol. 71, no. 1 (January/February): 29–34.

Mladina, Peter. 2011. "Portfolio Implications of Triple Net Returns." *Journal of Wealth Management*, vol. 13, no. 4 (Spring): 51–59.

Pollet, Joshua, and Mungo Wilson. 2008. "How Does Size Affect Mutual Fund Behavior?" *Journal of Finance*, vol. 63, no. 6 (December): 2941–2969.

Reichenstein, William. 2006. "After-Tax Asset Allocation." *Financial Analysts Journal*, vol. 62, no. 4 (July/August): 14–19.

Samuelson, Paul A. 1963. "Risk and Uncertainty: A Fallacy of Large Numbers." *Scientia*, vol. 57, no. 98: 108–113.

Samuelson, Paul A. 1969. "Lifetime Portfolio Selection by Dynamic Stochastic Programming." *Review of Economics and Statistics*, vol. 51, no. 3: 239–246.

Stein, Jeremy. 2002. "Information Production and Capital Allocation: Decentralized versus Hierarchical Firms." *Journal of Finance*, vol. 57, no. 5 (October): 1891–1921.

Turvey, Philip, Anup Basu, and Peter Verhoeven. 2013. "Embedded Tax Liabilities and Portfolio Choice." *Journal of Portfolio Management*, vol. 39, no. 3: 93–101.

PRACTICE PROBLEMS

The following information relates to questions 1–6

Rebecca Mayer is an asset management consultant for institutions and high-net-worth individuals. Mayer meets with Sebastian Capara, the newly appointed Investment Committee chairman for the Kinkardeen University Endowment (KUE), a very large tax-exempt fund.

Capara and Mayer review KUE's current and strategic asset allocations, which are presented in Exhibit 1. Capara informs Mayer that over the last few years, Kinkardeen University has financed its operations primarily from tuition, with minimal need of financial support from KUE. Enrollment at the University has been rising in recent years, and the Board of Trustees expects enrollment growth to continue for the next five years. Consequently, the board expects very modest endowment support to be needed during that time. These expectations led the Investment Committee to approve a decrease in the endowment's annual spending rate starting in the next fiscal year.

EXHIBIT 1   Kinkardeen University Endowment—Strategic Asset Allocation Policy

Asset Class	Current Weight	Target Allocation	Lower Policy Limit	Upper Policy Limit
Developed markets equity	30%	30%	25%	35%
Emerging markets equity	28%	30%	25%	35%
Investment-grade bonds	15%	20%	15%	25%
Private real estate equity	15%	10%	5%	15%
Infrastructure	12%	10%	5%	15%

As an additional source of alpha, Mayer proposes tactically adjusting KUE's asset-class weights to profit from short-term return opportunities. To confirm his understanding of tactical asset allocation (TAA), Capara tells Mayer the following:

Statement 1.   The Sharpe ratio is suitable for measuring the success of TAA relative to SAA.
Statement 2.   Discretionary TAA attempts to capture asset-class-level return anomalies that have been shown to have some predictability and persistence.
Statement 3.   TAA allows a manager to deviate from the IPS asset-class upper and lower limits if the shift is expected to produce higher expected risk-adjusted returns.

Capara asks Mayer to recommend a TAA strategy based on excess return forecasts for the asset classes in KUE's portfolio, as shown in Exhibit 2.

EXHIBIT 2   Short-Term Excess Return Forecast

Asset Class	Expected Excess Return
Developed markets equity	2%
Emerging markets equity	5%
Investment-grade bonds	−3%
Private real estate equity	3%
Infrastructure	−1%

Following her consultation with Capara, Mayer meets with Roger Koval, a member of a wealthy family. Although Koval's baseline needs are secured by a family trust, Koval has a personal portfolio to fund his lifestyle goals.

In Koval's country, interest income is taxed at progressively higher income tax rates. Dividend income and long-term capital gains are taxed at lower tax rates relative to interest and earned income. In taxable accounts, realized capital losses can be used to offset current or future realized capital gains. Koval is in a high tax bracket, and his taxable account currently holds, in equal weights, high-yield bonds, investment-grade bonds, and domestic equities focused on long-term capital gains.

Koval asks Mayer about adding new asset classes to the taxable portfolio. Mayer suggests emerging markets equity given its positive short-term excess return forecast. However, Koval tells Mayer he is not interested in adding emerging markets equity to the account because he is convinced it is too risky. Koval justifies this belief by referring to significant losses the family trust suffered during the recent economic crisis.

Mayer also suggests using two mean–variance portfolio optimization scenarios for the taxable account to evaluate potential asset allocations. Mayer recommends running two optimizations: one on a pre-tax basis and another on an after-tax basis.

1. The change in the annual spending rate, in conjunction with the board's expectations regarding future enrollment and the need for endowment support, could justify that KUE's target weight for:
    A. infrastructure be increased.
    B. investment-grade bonds be increased.
    C. private real estate equity be decreased.

2. Which of Capara's statements regarding tactical asset allocation is correct?
    A. Statement 1
    B. Statement 2
    C. Statement 3

3. Based on Exhibits 1 and 2, to attempt to profit from the short-term excess return forecast, Capara should increase KUE's portfolio allocation to:
    A. developed markets equity and decrease its allocation to infrastructure.
    B. emerging markets equity and decrease its allocation to investment-grade bonds.
    C. developed markets equity and increase its allocation to private real estate equity.

4. Given Koval's current portfolio and the tax laws of the country in which he lives, Koval's portfolio would be more tax efficient if he reallocated his taxable account to hold more:
    A. high-yield bonds.
    B. investment-grade bonds.
    C. domestic equities focused on long-term capital gain opportunities.

5. Koval's attitude toward emerging markets equity reflects which of the following behavioral biases?
    A. Hindsight bias
    B. Availability bias
    C. Illusion of control

6. In both of Mayer's optimization scenarios, which of the following model inputs could be used without adjustment?
    A. Expected returns
    B. Correlation of returns
    C. Standard deviations of returns

The following information relates to questions 7–13

Elsbeth Quinn and Dean McCall are partners at Camel Asset Management (CAM). Quinn advises high-net-worth individuals, and McCall specializes in retirement plans for institutions.

Quinn meets with Neal and Karina Martin, both age 44. The Martins plan to retire at age 62. Twenty percent of the Martins' $600,000 in financial assets is held in cash and earmarked for funding their daughter Lara's university studies, which begin in one year. Lara's education and their own retirement are the Martins' highest-priority goals. Last week, the Martins learned that Lara was awarded a four-year full scholarship for university. Quinn reviews how the scholarship might affect the Martins' asset allocation strategy.

The Martins have assets in both taxable and tax-deferred accounts. For baseline retirement needs, Quinn recommends that the Martins maintain their current overall 60% equity/40% bonds (± 8% rebalancing range) strategic asset allocation. Quinn calculates that given current financial assets and expected future earnings, the Martins could reduce future retirement savings by 15% and still comfortably retire at 62. The Martins wish to allocate that 15% to a sub-portfolio with the goal of making a charitable gift to their alma mater from their estate. Although the gift is a low-priority goal, the Martins want the sub-portfolio to earn the highest return possible. Quinn promises to recommend an asset allocation strategy for the Martins' aspirational goal.

Next, Quinn discusses taxation of investments with the Martins. Their interest income is taxed at 35%, and capital gains and dividends are taxed at 20%. The Martins want to minimize taxes. Based on personal research, Neal makes the following two statements:

Statement 1.   The after-tax return volatility of assets held in taxable accounts will be less than the pre-tax return volatility.

Statement 2.   Assets that receive more favorable tax treatment should be held in tax-deferred accounts.

The equity portion of the Martins' portfolios produced an annualized return of 20% for the past three years. As a result, the Martins' equity allocation in both their taxable and tax-deferred portfolios has increased to 71%, with bonds falling to 29%. The Martins want to keep the strategic asset allocation risk levels the same in both types of retirement portfolios. Quinn discusses rebalancing; however, Neal is somewhat reluctant to take money out of stocks, expressing confidence that strong investment returns will continue.

Quinn's CAM associate, McCall, meets with Bruno Snead, the director of the Katt Company Pension Fund (KCPF). The strategic asset allocation for the fund is 65% stocks/ 35% bonds. Because of favorable returns during the past eight recession-free years, the KCPF is now overfunded. However, there are early signs of the economy weakening. Since Katt Company is in a cyclical industry, the Pension Committee is concerned about future market and economic risk and fears that the high-priority goal of maintaining a fully funded status may be adversely affected. McCall suggests to Snead that the KCPF might benefit from an updated IPS. Following a thorough review, McCall recommends a new IPS and strategic asset allocation.

The proposed IPS revisions include a plan for short-term deviations from strategic asset allocation targets. The goal is to benefit from equity market trends by automatically increasing (decreasing) the allocation to equities by 5% whenever the S&P 500 Index 50-day moving average crosses above (below) the 200-day moving average.

7. Given the change in funding of Lara's education, the Martins' strategic asset allocation would *most likely* decrease exposure to:
   A.   cash.
   B.   bonds.
   C.   equities.

8. The *most* appropriate asset allocation for the Martins' new charitable gift sub-portfolio is:
   A.   40% equities/60% bonds.
   B.   70% equities/30% bonds.
   C.   100% equities/0% bonds.

9. Which of Neal's statements regarding the taxation of investments is correct?
   A.   Statement 1 only
   B.   Statement 2 only
   C.   Both Statement 1 and Statement 2

10. Given the Martins' risk and tax preferences, the taxable portfolio should be rebalanced:
    A.   less often than the tax-deferred portfolio.
    B.   as often as the tax-deferred portfolio.
    C.   more often than the tax-deferred portfolio.

11. During the rebalancing discussion, which behavioral bias does Neal exhibit?
    A.   Framing bias
    B.   Loss aversion
    C.   Representativeness bias

12. Given McCall's IPS recommendation, the *most* appropriate new strategic asset allocation for the KCPF is:
    A.   40% stocks/60% bonds.
    B.   65% stocks/35% bonds.
    C.   75% stocks/25% bonds.

13. The proposal for short-term adjustments to the KCPF asset allocation strategy is known as:
    A. de-risking.
    B. systematic tactical asset allocation.
    C. discretionary tactical asset allocation.

The following information relates to questions 14–18

Emma Young, a 47-year-old single mother of two daughters, ages 7 and 10, recently sold a business for $5.5 million net of taxes and put the proceeds into a money market account. Her other assets include a tax-deferred retirement account worth $3.0 million, a $500,000 after-tax account designated for her daughters' education, a $400,000 after-tax account for unexpected needs, and her home, which she owns outright.

Her living expenses are fully covered by her job. Young wants to retire in 15 years and to fund her retirement from existing assets. An orphan at eight who experienced childhood financial hardships, she places a high priority on retirement security and wants to avoid losing money in any of her three accounts.

14. **Identify** the behavioral biases Young is *most likely* exhibiting. **Justify** each response.

Identify the behavioral biases Young is *most likely* exhibiting. (Circle the correct answers.)
Justify each response.

Bias	Justification
Loss Aversion	
Illusion of Control	
Mental Accounting	
Representative Bias	
Framing Bias	
Availability Bias	

A broker proposes to Young three portfolios, shown in Exhibit 1. The broker also provides Young with asset class estimated returns and portfolio standard deviations in Exhibit 2 and Exhibit 3, respectively. The broker notes that there is a $500,000 minimum investment requirement for alternative assets. Finally, because the funds in the money market account are readily investible, the broker suggests using that account only for this initial investment round.

EXHIBIT 1   Proposed Portfolios

Asset Class	Portfolio 1	Portfolio 2	Portfolio 3
Municipal Bonds	5%	35%	30%
Small-Cap Equities	50%	10%	35%
Large-Cap Equities	35%	50%	35%
Private Equity	10%	5%	0%
Total	100%	100%	100%

EXHIBIT 2   Asset Class Pre-Tax Returns

Asset Class	Pre-Tax Return
Municipal Bonds	3%
Small-Cap Equities	12%
Large-Cap Equities	10%
Private Equity	25%

EXHIBIT 3   Portfolio Standard Deviations

Proposed Portfolio	Post-Tax Standard Deviation
Portfolio 1	28.2%
Portfolio 2	16.3%
Portfolio 3	15.5%

Young wants to earn at least 6.0% after tax per year, without taking on additional incremental risk. Young's capital gains and overall tax rate is 25%.

15. **Determine** which proposed portfolio *most closely* meets Young's desired objectives. **Justify** your response.

Determine which proposed portfolio *most closely* meets Young's desired objectives. (Circle one.)

Portfolio 1	Portfolio 2	Portfolio 3

Justify your response.

The broker suggests that Young rebalance her $5.5 million money market account and the $3.0 million tax-deferred retirement account periodically in order to maintain their targeted allocations. The broker proposes the same risk profile for the equity positions with two potential target equity allocations and rebalancing ranges for the two accounts as follows:

• Alternative 1: 80% equities +/− 8.0% rebalancing range
• Alternative 2: 75% equities +/− 10.7% rebalancing range

16. **Determine** which alternative *best* fits each account. **Justify** each selection.

Determine which alternative (circle one) *best* fits each account.		
Account	**Alternative**	**Justify** each selection.
$5.5 Million Account	Alternative 1	
	Alternative 2	
$3.0 Million Account	Alternative 1	
	Alternative 2	

Ten years later, Young is considering an early-retirement package offer. The package would provide continuing salary and benefits for three years. The broker recommends a special review of Young's financial plan to assess potential changes to the existing allocation strategy.

17. **Identify** the *primary* reason for the broker's reassessment of Young's circumstances. **Justify** your response.

Identify the *primary* reason for the broker's reassessment of Young's circumstances. (Circle one.)		
Change in goals	**Change in constraints**	**Change in beliefs**

Justify your response.

Young decides to accept the retirement offer. Having very low liquidity needs, she wants to save part of the retirement payout for unforeseen costs that might occur more than a decade in the future. The broker's view on long-term stock market prospects is positive and recommends additional equity investment.

18. **Determine** which of Young's accounts (education, retirement, reallocated money market, or unexpected needs) is *best* suited for implementing the broker's recommendation.

Determine which of Young's accounts is *best* suited for implementing the broker's recommendation. (Circle one.)	
Account	**Justification**
Education	
Reallocated Money Market	
Retirement	
Unexpected Needs	

The following information relates to questions 19–20

Mark DuBord, a financial adviser, works with two university foundations, the Titan State Foundation (Titan) and the Fordhart University Foundation (Fordhart). He meets with each university foundation investment committee annually to review fund objectives and constraints.

Titan's portfolio has a market value of $10 million. After his annual meeting with its investment committee, DuBord notes the following points:

- Titan must spend 3% of its beginning-of-the-year asset value annually to meet legal obligations.
- The investment committee seeks exposure to private equity investments and requests DuBord's review of the Sun-Fin Private Equity Fund as a potential new investment.
- A recent declining trend in enrollment is expected to continue. This is a concern because it has led to a loss of operating revenue from tuition.
- Regulatory sanctions and penalties are likely to result in lower donations over the next five years.

DuBord supervises two junior analysts and instructs one to formulate new allocations for Titan. This analyst proposes the allocation presented in Exhibit 1.

EXHIBIT 1   Fund Information for Titan

Fund Name	Existing Allocation	Proposed Allocation	Fund Size in Billions (AUM)	Fund Minimum Investment
Global Equity Fund	70%	70%	$25	$500,000
Investment-Grade Bond Fund	27%	17%	$50	$250,000
Sun-Fin Private Equity Fund	0%	10%	$0.40	$1,000,000
Cash Equivalent Fund	3%	3%	$50	$100,000

19. **Discuss** *two* reasons why the proposed asset allocation is inappropriate for Titan.

The Fordhart portfolio has a market value of $2 billion. After his annual meeting with its investment committee, DuBord notes the following points:

- Fordhart must spend 3% of its beginning-of-the-year asset value annually to meet legal obligations.
- The investment committee seeks exposure to private equity investments and requests that DuBord review the CFQ Private Equity Fund as a potential new investment.
- Enrollment is strong and growing, leading to increased operating revenues from tuition.
- A recent legal settlement eliminated an annual obligation of $50 million from the portfolio to support a biodigester used in the university's Center for Renewable Energy.

DuBord instructs his second junior analyst to formulate new allocations for Fordhart. This analyst proposes the allocation presented in Exhibit 2.

EXHIBIT 2   Fund Information for Fordhart

Fund Name	Existing Allocation	Proposed Allocation	Fund Size in Billions (AUM)	Fund Minimum Investment
Large-Cap Equity Fund	49%	29%	$50	$250,000
Investment-Grade Bond Fund	49%	59%	$80	$500,000
CFQ Private Equity Fund	0%	10%	$0.5	$5,000,000
Cash Equivalent Fund	2%	2%	$50	$250,000

20. **Discuss** *two* reasons why the proposed asset allocation is inappropriate for Fordhart.

CHAPTER 8

CURRENCY MANAGEMENT: AN INTRODUCTION

William A. Barker, PhD, CFA

LEARNING OUTCOMES

The candidate should be able to:

- analyze the effects of currency movements on portfolio risk and return;
- discuss strategic choices in currency management;
- formulate an appropriate currency management program given financial market conditions and portfolio objectives and constraints;
- compare active currency trading strategies based on economic fundamentals, technical analysis, carry-trade, and volatility trading;
- describe how changes in factors underlying active trading strategies affect tactical trading decisions;
- describe how forward contracts and FX (foreign exchange) swaps are used to adjust hedge ratios;
- describe trading strategies used to reduce hedging costs and modify the risk–return characteristics of a foreign-currency portfolio;
- describe the use of cross-hedges, macro-hedges, and minimum-variance-hedge ratios in portfolios exposed to multiple foreign currencies;
- discuss challenges for managing emerging market currency exposures.

1. INTRODUCTION

Globalization has been one of the most persistent themes in recent history, and this theme applies equally to the world of finance. New investment products, deregulation, worldwide financial system integration, and better communication and information networks have

---

opened new global investment opportunities. At the same time, investors have increasingly shed their "home bias" and sought investment alternatives beyond their own borders.

The benefits of this trend for portfolio managers have been clear, both in terms of the broader availability of higher-expected-return investments as well as portfolio diversification opportunities. Nonetheless, investments denominated in foreign currencies also bring a unique set of challenges: measuring and managing foreign exchange risk. Buying foreign-currency denominated assets means bringing currency risk into the portfolio. Exchange rates are volatile and, at least in the short to medium term, can have a marked impact on investment returns and risks—*currency matters*. The key to the superior performance of global portfolios is the effective management of this currency risk.

This chapter explores basic concepts and tools of currency management. Section 2 reviews some of the basic concepts of foreign exchange (FX) markets. The material in subsequent sections presumes an understanding of these concepts. Section 3 examines some of the basic mathematics involved in measuring the effects of foreign-currency investments on portfolio return and risk. Section 4 discusses the *strategic* decisions portfolio managers face in setting the target currency exposures of the portfolio. The currency exposures that the portfolio can accept range from a fully hedged position to active management of currency risk. Section 5 discusses some of the *tactical* considerations involving active currency management if the investment policy statement (IPS) extends some latitude for active currency management. A requisite to any active currency management is having a market view; so this section includes various methodologies by which a manager can form directional views on future exchange rate movements and volatility. Section 6 covers a variety of trading tools available to implement both hedging and active currency management strategies. Although the generic types of FX derivatives tools are relatively limited—spot, forward, option, and swap contracts—the number of variations within each and the number of combinations in which they can be used is vast. Section 7 examines some of the issues involved in managing the currency exposures of emerging market currencies—that is, those that are less liquid than the major currencies. Section 8 presents a summary.

2. REVIEW OF FOREIGN EXCHANGE CONCEPTS

We begin with a review of the basic trading tools of the foreign exchange market: spot, forward, FX swap, and currency option transactions. The concepts introduced in this section will be used extensively in our discussion of currency management techniques in subsequent sections.

Most people think only of spot transactions when they think of the foreign exchange market, but in fact the spot market accounts for less than 40% of the average daily turnover in currencies.[1] Although cross-border *business* may be transacted in the spot market (making and receiving foreign currency payments), the *risk management* of these flows takes place in FX derivatives markets (i.e., using forwards, FX swaps, and currency options). So does the hedging of foreign currency assets and liabilities. It is unusual for market participants to engage in any foreign currency transactions without also managing the currency risk they create. Spot transactions typically generate derivative transactions. As a result, understanding

---

[1]2013 Triennial Survey, Bank for International Settlements (2013).

these FX derivatives markets, and their relation to the spot market, is critical for understanding the currency risk management issues examined in this chapter.

2.1. Spot Markets

In professional FX markets, exchange rate quotes are described in terms of the three-letter currency codes used to identify individual currencies. Exhibit 1 shows a list of some of the more common currency codes.

EXHIBIT 1	Currency Codes
USD	US dollar
EUR	Euro
GBP	British pound
JPY	Japanese yen
MXN	Mexican peso
CHF	Swiss franc
CAD	Canadian dollar
SEK	Swedish krona
AUD	Australian dollar
KRW	Korean won
NZD	New Zealand dollar
BRL	Brazilian real
RUB	Russian ruble
CNY	Chinese yuan
INR	Indian rupee
ZAR	South African rand

An exchange rate is the number of units of one currency (called the *price currency*) that one unit of another currency (called the *base currency*) will buy. For example, in the notation we will use a USD/EUR rate of 1.3650, which means that one euro buys $1.3650; equivalently, the price of one euro is 1.3650 US dollars. Thus, the euro here is the base currency and the US dollar is the price currency. The exact notation used to represent exchange rates can vary widely between sources, and occasionally the same exchange rate notation will be used by different sources to mean completely different things. The reader should be aware that the notation used here may not be the same as that encountered elsewhere. To avoid confusion, this chapter will identify exchange rates using the convention of "P/B," which refers to the price of one unit of the base currency "B" expressed in terms of the price currency "P."

How the professional FX market quotes exchange rates—which is the base currency, and which is the price currency, in any currency pair—is not arbitrary but follows conventions that are broadly agreed on throughout the market. Generally, there is a hierarchy as to which currency will be quoted as the base currency in any given P/B currency pair:

1. Currency pairs involving the EUR will use the EUR as the base currency (for example, GBP/EUR).
2. Currency pairs involving the GBP, other than those involving the EUR, will use the GBP as the base currency (for example, CHF/GBP).
3. Currency pairs involving either the AUD or NZD, other than those involving either the EUR or GBP, will use these currencies as the base currency (for example, USD/AUD and NZD/AUD). The market convention between these two currencies is for a NZD/AUD quote.
4. All other currency quotes involving the USD will use USD as the base currency (for example, MXN/USD).

Readers are encouraged to familiarize themselves with the quoting conventions used in the professional FX market because they are the currency quotes that will be experienced in practice. Exhibit 2 lists some of the most commonly traded currency pairs in global FX markets and their market-standard quoting conventions. These market-standard conventions will be used for the balance of this chapter.

EXHIBIT 2   Select Market-Standard Currency Pair Quotes

Quote convention	Market name
USD/EUR	Euro-dollar
GBP/EUR	Euro-sterling
USD/GBP	Sterling-dollar
JPY/USD	Dollar-yen
USD/AUD	Aussie-dollar
CHF/USD	Dollar-Swiss
CAD/USD	Dollar-Canada
JPY/EUR	Euro-yen
CHF/EUR	Euro-Swiss
JPY/GBP	Sterling-yen

Another convention used in professional FX markets is that most spot currency quotes are priced out to four decimal places: for example, a typical USD/EUR quote would be 1.3500 and not 1.35. The price point at the fourth decimal place is commonly referred to as a "pip." Professional FX traders also refer to what is called the "big figure" or the "handle," which is the integer to the left side of the decimal place as well as the first two decimal places of the quote. For example, for a USD/EUR quote of 1.3568, 1.35 is the handle and there are 68 pips.

There are exceptions to this four decimal place rule. First, forward quotes—discussed later—will often be quoted out to five and sometimes six decimal places. Second, because of the relative magnitude of some currency values, some currency quotes will only be quoted out to two decimal places. For example, because it takes many Japanese yen to buy one US dollar, the typical spot quote for JPY/USD is priced out to only two decimal places (for example, 86.35 and not 86.3500).[2]

The spot exchange rate is usually for settlement on the second business day after the trade date, referred to as $T + 2$ settlement.[3] In foreign exchange markets—as in other financial markets—market participants confront a two-sided price in the form of a bid price and an offer price (also called an ask price) being quoted by potential counterparties. The **bid price** is the price, defined in terms of the price currency, at which the counterparty providing a two-sided price quote is willing to buy one unit of the **base** currency. Similarly, **offer price** is the price, in terms of the price currency, at which that counterparty is willing to sell one unit of the base currency. For example, given a price request from a client, a dealer might quote a two-sided price on the spot USD/EUR exchange rate of 1.3648/1.3652. This quote means that the dealer is willing to pay USD1.3648 to buy one euro (bid) and that the dealer will sell one euro (offer) for USD1.3652. The market width, usually referred to as dealer's spread or the bid–offer spread, is the difference between the bid and the offer. When transacting on a dealer's bid-offer two-sided price quote, a client is said to either "hit the bid" (selling the base currency) or "pay the offer" (buying the base currency).

An easy check to see whether the bid or offer should be used for a specific transaction is that the party *asking* the dealer for a price should be on the more expensive side of the market. For example, if one wants to buy 1 EUR, 1.3652 is more USD per EUR than 1.3648. Hence, paying the offer involves paying more EUR. Similarly, when selling 1 EUR, hitting the bid at 1.3648 means less USD received than 1.3652.

2.2. Forward Markets

Forward contracts are agreements to exchange one currency for another on a future date at an exchange rate agreed on today.[4] In contrast to spot rates, forward contracts are any exchange rate transactions that occur with settlement longer than the usual $T + 2$ settlement for spot delivery.

In professional FX markets, forward exchange rates are typically quoted in terms of "points." The points on a forward rate quote are simply the difference between the forward exchange rate quote and the spot exchange rate quote; that is, the forward premium or discount, with the points scaled so that they can be related to the last decimal place in the spot quote. Forward points are adjustments to the spot price of the base currency, using our standard price/base (P/B) currency notation.

This means that forward rate quotes in professional FX markets are typically shown as the bid–offer on the spot rate and the number of forward points at each maturity.[5] For illustration purposes, assume that the bid–offer for the spot and forward points for the USD/EUR exchange rate are as shown in Exhibit 3.

---

[2]Many electronic dealing platforms in the FX market are moving to five decimal place pricing for spot quotes, using what are referred to as "deci-pips." In this case, for example, a USD/EUR spot quote might be shown as 1.37645. Spot quotes for JPY/USD on these systems will be given out to three decimal places.

[3]The exception among the major currencies is CAD/USD, for which standard spot settlement is $T + 1$.

[4]These are sometimes called outright forwards to distinguish them from FX swaps, which are discussed later.

[5]Maturity is defined in terms of the time between spot settlement, usually $T + 2$, and the settlement of the forward contract.

EXHIBIT 3   Sample Spot and Forward Quotes (Bid–Offer)

Maturity	Spot Rate or Forward Points
Spot (USD/EUR)	1.3549/1.3651
One month	−5.6/−5.1
Three months	−15.9/−15.3
Six months	−37.0/−36.3
Twelve months	−94.3/−91.8

To convert any of these quoted forward points into a forward rate, one would divide the number of points by 10,000 (to scale down to the fourth decimal place, the last decimal place in the USD/EUR spot quote) and then add the result to the spot exchange rate quote.[6] But one must be careful about which side of the market (bid or offer) is being quoted. For example, suppose a market participant was *selling* the EUR forward against the USD. Given the USD/EUR quoting convention, the EUR is the base currency. This means the market participant must use the *bid* rates (i.e., the market participant will "hit the bid") given the USD/EUR quoting convention. Using the data in Exhibit 3, the three-month forward *bid* rate in this case would be based on the bid for both the spot and the forward points, and hence would be:

$$1.3549 + \left(\frac{-15.9}{10,000}\right) = 1.35331$$

This result means that the market participant would be selling EUR three months forward at a price of USD1.35331 per EUR. Note that the quoted points are already scaled to each maturity—they are not annualized—so there is no need to adjust them.

Although there is no cash flow on a forward contract until settlement date, it is often useful to do a mark-to-market valuation on a forward position before then to (1) judge the effectiveness of a hedge based on forward contracts (i.e., by comparing the change in the mark-to-market of the underlying asset with the change in the mark-to-market of the forward), and (2) to measure the profitability of speculative currency positions at points before contract maturity.

As with other financial instruments, the mark-to-market value of forward contracts reflects the profit (or loss) that would be realized from closing out the position at current market prices. To close out a forward position, it must be offset with an equal and opposite forward position using the spot exchange rate and forward points available in the market when the offsetting position is created. When a forward contract is initiated, the forward rate is such that no cash changes hands (i.e., the mark-to-market value of the contract at initiation is zero). From that moment onward, however, the mark-to-market value of the forward contract will change as the spot exchange rate changes as well as when interest rates change in either of the two currencies.

---

[6]Because the JPY/USD exchange rate is only quoted to two decimal places, forward points for the dollar/yen currency pair are divided by 100.

Consider an example. Suppose that a market participant bought GBP10,000,000 for delivery against the AUD in six months at an "all-in" forward rate of 1.6100 AUD/GBP. (The all-in forward rate is simply the sum of the spot rate and the forward points, appropriately scaled to size.) Three months later, the market participant wants to close out this forward contract. To do that would require selling GBP10,000,000 three months forward using the AUD/GBP spot exchange rate and forward points in effect at that time. Assume the bid–offer for spot and forward points three months prior to the settlement date are as follows:

Spot rate (AUD/GBP)	1.6210/1.6215
Three-month points	130/140

To sell GBP (the base currency in the AUD/GBP quote) means calculating the *bid* side of the market. Hence, the appropriate all-in three-month forward rate to use is

$$1.6210 + 130/10,000 = 1.6340$$

Thus, the market participant originally bought GBP10,000,000 at an AUD/GBP rate of 1.6100 and subsequently sold them at a rate of 1.6340. These GBP amounts will net to zero at settlement date (GBP10 million both bought and sold), but the AUD amounts will not net to zero because the forward rate has changed. The AUD cash flow at settlement date will be equal to

$$(1.6340 - 1.6100) \times 10,000,000 = \text{AUD240,000}$$

This amount is a cash *inflow* because the market participant was long the GBP with the original forward position and the GBP subsequently appreciated (the AUD/GBP rate increased).

This cash flow is paid at settlement day, which is still three months away. To calculate the mark-to-market value on the dealer's position, this cash flow must be discounted to the present. The present value of this amount is found by discounting the settlement day cash flow by the three-month discount rate. Because it is an AUD amount, the three-month AUD discount rate is used. If Libor is used and the three-month AUD Libor is 4.80% (annualized), the present value of this future AUD cash flow is then

$$\frac{\text{AUD240,000}}{1 + 0.048\left[\frac{90}{360}\right]} = \text{AUD237,154}$$

This is the mark-to-market value of the original long GBP10 million six-month forward contract when it is closed out three months prior to settlement.

To summarize, the process for marking-to-market a forward position is relatively straightforward:

1. Create an equal and offsetting forward position to the original forward position. (In the example earlier, the market participant is long GBP10 million forward, so the offsetting forward contract would be to sell GBP10 million.)

2. Determine the appropriate all-in forward rate for this new, offsetting forward position. If the base currency of the exchange rate quote is being sold (bought), then use the bid (offer) side of the market.

3. Calculate the cash flow at settlement day. This calculation will be based on the original contract size times the difference between the original forward rate and the rate calculated in Step 2. If the currency the market participant was originally long (short) subsequently appreciated (depreciated), then there will be a cash *inflow*. Otherwise, there will be a cash outflow. (In the earlier example, the market participant was long the GBP and it subsequently appreciated; this appreciation led to a cash inflow at the settlement day.)

4. Calculate the present value of this cash flow at the future settlement date. The currency of the cash flow and the discount rate must match. (In the example earlier, the cash flow at the settlement date is in AUD, so an AUD Libor rate is used to calculate the present value.)

Finally, we note that in the example, the mark-to-market value is given in AUD. It would be possible to translate this AUD amount into any other currency value using the current spot rate for the relevant currency pair. In the example above, this would be done by redenominating the mark-to-market in USD, by selling 240,000 AUD 90-days forward against the USD at the prevailing USD/AUD 90-day forward bid rate. This will produce a USD cash flow in 90 days. This USD amount can then be present-valued at the 90-day US rate to get the USD mark-to-market value of the AUD/GBP forward position. The day-count convention used here is an "actual/360" basis.

2.3. FX Swap Markets

An FX swap transaction consists of offsetting and simultaneous spot and forward transactions, in which the base currency is being bought (sold) spot and sold (bought) forward. These two transactions are often referred to as the "legs" of the swap. The two legs of the swap can either be of equal size (a "matched" swap) or one can be larger than the other (a "mismatched" swap). FX swaps are distinct from currency swaps. Similar to currency swaps, FX swaps involve an exchange of principal amounts in different currencies at swap initiation that is reversed at swap maturity. Unlike currency swaps, FX swaps have no interim interest payments and are nearly always of much shorter term than currency swaps.

FX swaps are important for managing currency risk because they are used to "roll" forward contracts forward as they mature. For example, consider the case of a trader who *bought* GBP1,000,000 one month forward against the CHF in order to set up a currency hedge. One month later, the forward contract will expire. To maintain this long position in the GBP against the CHF, two days prior to contract maturity, given $T + 2$ settlement, the trader must (1) sell GBP1,000,000 against the CHF spot, to settle the maturing forward contract; and (2) buy GBP1,000,000 against the CHF forward. That is, the trader is engaging in an FX swap (a matched swap in this case because the GBP currency amounts are equal).

If a trader wanted to adjust the size of the currency hedge (i.e., the size of the outstanding forward position), the forward leg of the FX swap can be of a different size than the spot transaction when the hedge is rolled. Continuing the previous example, if the trader wanted to increase the size of the long-GBP position by GBP500,000 as the outstanding forward contract expires, the transactions required would be to (1) sell GBP1,000,000 against the CHF spot, to settle the maturing forward contract; and (2) buy GBP1,500,000 against the CHF forward. This would be a mismatched swap.

The pricing of swaps will differ slightly depending on whether they are matched or mismatched swaps. If the amount of the base currency involved for the spot and forward legs of the swap are equal (a matched swap), then these are exactly offsetting transactions; one is a buy, the other a sell, and both are for the same amount. Because of this equality, a common *spot* exchange rate is typically applied to both legs of the swap transaction; it is standard practice to use the mid-market spot exchange rate for a matched swap transaction. However, the *forward* points will still be based on either the bid or offer, depending on whether the market participant is buying or selling the base currency forward. In the earlier example, the trader is *buying* the GBP (the base currency) forward and would hence pay the *offer* side of the market for forward points.

If the FX swap is mismatched, then pricing will need to reflect the difference in trade sizes between the two legs of the transaction. Continuing the example in which the trader increased the size of the long-GBP position by GBP500,000, this mismatched swap is equivalent to (1) a matched swap for a size of GBP1,000,000, and (2) an outright forward contract buying GBP500,000. Pricing for the mismatched swap must reflect this net GBP purchase amount. Because the matched swap would already price the forward points on the offer side of the market, typically this mismatched size adjustment would be reflected in the *spot* rate quoted as the base for the FX swap. Because a net amount of GBP is being *bought*, the spot quote would now be on the *offer* side of the CHF/GBP spot rate quote. (In addition, the trader would still pay the offer side of the market for the forward points.)

We will return to these topics later in the chapter when discussing in more depth the use of forward contracts and FX swaps to adjust hedge ratios. (A **hedge ratio** is the ratio of the nominal value of the derivatives contract used as a hedge to the market value of the hedged asset.)

2.4. Currency Options

The final product type within FX markets is currency options. The market for currency options is, in many ways, similar to option markets for other asset classes, such as bonds and equities. As in other markets, the most common options in FX markets are call and put options, which are widely used for both risk management and speculative purposes. However, in addition to these vanilla options, the FX market is also characterized by active trading in exotic options. ("Exotic" options have a variety of features that make them exceptionally flexible risk management tools, compared with vanilla options.)

The risk management uses of both vanilla and exotic currency options will be examined in subsequent sections. Although daily turnover in FX options market is small in *relative* terms compared with the overall daily flow in global spot currency markets, because the overall currency market is so large, the *absolute* size of the FX options market is still very considerable.

3. CURRENCY RISK AND PORTFOLIO RETURN AND RISK

In this section, we examine the effect of currency movements on asset returns and portfolio risk. We then turn to how these effects help determine construction of a foreign asset portfolio.

3.1. Return Decomposition

In this section, we examine how international exposure affects a portfolio's return. A **domestic asset** is an asset that trades in the investor's **domestic currency** (or **home currency**). From a portfolio manager's perspective, the domestic currency is the one in which portfolio valuation and returns are reported. *Domestic* refers to a relation between the currency denomination of the asset and the investor; it is not an inherent property of either the asset or the currency. An example of a domestic asset is a USD-denominated bond portfolio from the perspective of a US-domiciled investor. The return on a domestic asset is not affected by exchange rate movements of the domestic currency.

   Foreign assets are assets denominated in currencies other than the investor's home currency. An example of a foreign asset is a USD-denominated bond portfolio from the perspective of a eurozone-domiciled investor (and for whom the euro is the home currency). The return on a foreign asset will be affected by exchange rate movements in the home currency against the **foreign currency**. Continuing with our example, the return to the eurozone-domiciled investor will be affected by the USD return on the USD-denominated bond as well as movements in the exchange rate between the home currency and the foreign currency, the EUR and USD respectively.

   The return of the foreign asset measured in foreign-currency terms is known as the **foreign-currency return**. Extending the example, if the value of the USD-denominated bond increased by 10%, measured in USD, that increase is the foreign-currency return to the eurozone-domiciled investor. The **domestic-currency return** on a foreign asset will reflect both the foreign-currency return on that asset as well as percentage movements in the spot exchange rate between the home and foreign currencies. The domestic-currency return is multiplicative with respect to these two factors:

$$R_{DC} = (1 + R_{FC})(1 + R_{FX}) - 1 \tag{1}$$

where R_{DC} is the domestic-currency return (in percent), R_{FC} is the foreign-currency return, and R_{FX} is the percentage change of the foreign currency against the domestic currency.

   Returning to the example, the domestic-currency return for the eurozone-domiciled investor on the USD-denominated bond will reflect both the bond's USD-denominated return as well as movements in the exchange rate between the USD and the EUR. Suppose that the foreign-currency return on the USD-denominated bond is 10% and the USD appreciates by 5% against the EUR. In this case, the domestic-currency return to the eurozone investor will be:

$$(1 + 10\%)(1 + 5\%) - 1 = (1.10)(1.05) - 1 = 0.155 = 15.5\%$$

   Although the concept is seemingly straightforward, the reader should be aware that Equation 1 hides a subtlety that must be recognized. The term R_{FX} is defined as the percentage change in the foreign currency against the domestic currency. However, this change is *not* always the same thing as the percentage change in the spot rate using market standard P/B quotes (for example, as shown in Exhibit 2). Specifically, it is not always the case that $R_{FX} = \%\Delta S_{P/B}$, where the term on the right side of the equal sign is defined in standard FX market convention (note that $\%\Delta$ is percentage change).

   In other words, R_{FX} is calculated as the change in the directly quoted exchange rate, where the domestic currency is defined as the investor's home currency. Because market quotes are not always in direct terms, analysts will need to convert to direct quotes before calculating percentage changes.

With this nuance in mind, what holds for the domestic-currency return of a single foreign asset also holds for the returns on a multi-currency portfolio of foreign assets, except now the portfolio weights must be considered. More generally, the domestic-currency return on a portfolio of multiple foreign assets will be equal to

$$R_{DC} = \sum_{i=1}^{n} \omega_i(1 + R_{FC,i})(1 + R_{FX,i}) - 1 \tag{2}$$

where $R_{FC,i}$ is the foreign-currency return on the i-th foreign asset, $R_{FX,i}$ is the appreciation of the i-th foreign currency against the domestic currency, and ω_i are the portfolio weights of the foreign-currency assets (defined as the percentage of the aggregate domestic-currency value of the portfolio) and $\sum_{i=1}^{n} \omega_i = 1$. (Note that if short selling is allowed in the portfolio, some of the ω_i can be less than zero.) Again, it is important that the exchange rate notation in this expression (used to calculate $R_{FX,i}$) must be consistently defined with the domestic currency as the price currency.

Assume the following information for a portfolio held by an investor in India. Performance is measured in terms of the Indian rupee (INR) and the weights of the two assets in the portfolio, at the beginning of the period, are 80% for the GBP-denominated asset and 20% for the EUR-denominated asset, respectively. (Note that the portfolio weights are measured in terms of a common currency, the INR, which is the investor's domestic currency in this case.)

	One Year Ago	Today*
INR/GBP spot rate	84.12	85.78
INR/EUR spot rate	65.36	67.81
GBP-denominated asset value, in GBP millions	43.80	50.70
EUR-denominated asset value, in EUR millions	14.08	12.17
GBP-denominated asset value, in INR millions	3,684,46	
EUR-denominated asset value, in INR millions	920.27	
GBP-denominated assets, portfolio weight (INR)	80%	
EUR-denominated assets, portfolio weight (INR)	20%	

* Today's asset values are prior to rebalancing.

The domestic-currency return (R_{DC}) is calculated as follows:

$$R_{DC} = 0.80(1 + R_{FC,GBP})(1 + R_{FX,GBP}) + 0.20(1 + R_{FC,EUR})(1 + R_{FX,EUR}) - 1$$

Note that given the exchange rate quoting convention, the INR is the price currency in the P/B quote for both currency pairs. Adding the data from the table leads to:

$$R_{DC} = 0.80 \left(\frac{50.70}{43.80} \right) \left(\frac{85.78}{84.12} \right) + 0.20 \left(\frac{12.17}{14.08} \right) \left(\frac{67.81}{65.36} \right) - 1$$

This solves to 0.124 or 12.4%.

To get the *expected* future return on a foreign-currency asset portfolio, based on Equation 2, the portfolio manager would need a market opinion for the expected price movement in each of the foreign assets ($R_{A,i}$) and exchange rates ($R_{FX,i}$) in the portfolio. There are typically correlations between all of these variables—correlations between the foreign asset price movements across countries, correlations between movements among various currency pairs, and correlations between exchange rate movements and foreign-currency asset returns. The portfolio manager would need to account for these correlations when forming expectations about future asset price and exchange rate movements.

3.2. Volatility Decomposition

Now we will turn to examining the effect of currency movements on the volatility of domestic-currency returns. Equation 1 can be rearranged as

$$R_{DC} = (1 + R_{FC})(1 + R_{FX}) - 1 = R_{FC} + R_{FX} + R_{FC}R_{FX}$$

When R_{FC} and R_{FX} are small, then the cross-term ($R_{FC}R_{FX}$) is small, and as a result this equation can be approximated as

$$R_{DC} \approx R_{FC} + R_{FX} \tag{3}$$

We return to the example in which the foreign-currency return on the USD-denominated bond was 10% and the USD appreciated by 5% against the EUR. In this example, the domestic-currency return for the Eurozone investor's holding in the USD-denominated bond was approximately equal to 10% + 5% = 15% (which is close to the exact value of 15.5%). We can combine the approximation of Equation 3 with the statistical rule that:

$$\sigma^2(\omega_x X + \omega_y Y) = \omega_x^2 \sigma^2(X) + \omega_y^2 \sigma^2(Y) + 2\omega_x \omega_y \sigma(X)\sigma(Y)\rho(X,Y) \tag{4}$$

where X and Y are random variables, ω are weights attached to X and Y, σ^2 is variance of a random variable, σ is the corresponding standard deviation, and ρ represents the correlation between two random variables. Applying this result to the domestic-currency return approximation of Equation 3 leads to:

$$\sigma^2(R_{DC}) \approx \sigma^2(R_{FC}) + \sigma^2(R_{FX}) + 2\sigma(R_{FC})\sigma(R_{FX})\rho(R_{FC},R_{FX}) \tag{5}$$

This equation is for the variance of the domestic-currency returns (R_{DC}), but risk is more typically defined in terms of standard deviation because mean and standard deviation are measured in the same units (percent, in this case). Hence, the total risk for domestic-currency returns—that is, $\sigma(R_{DC})$—is the square root of the results calculated in Equation 5.

Note as well that because Equation 5 is based on the addition of all three terms on the right side of the equal sign, exchange rate exposure will generally cause the variance of domestic-currency returns, $\sigma^2(R_{DC})$, to increase to more than that of the foreign-currency returns, $\sigma^2(R_{FC})$, considered on their own. That is, if there was no exchange rate risk, then it would be the case that $\sigma^2(R_{DC}) = \sigma^2(R_{FC})$. Using this as our base-case scenario, adding exchange rate risk exposure to the portfolio usually adds to domestic-currency return variance (the effect is indeterminate if exchange rate movements are negatively correlated with foreign asset returns).

These results on the variance of domestic-currency return can be generalized to a portfolio of foreign-currency assets. If we define the random variables X and Y in Equation 4 in terms of the domestic-currency return (R_{DC}) of two different foreign-currency investments, and the ω_i as portfolio weights that sum to one, then the result is the variance of the domestic-currency returns for the overall foreign asset portfolio:

$$\sigma^2(\omega_1 R_1 + \omega_2 R_2) \approx \omega_1^2 \sigma^2(R_1) + \omega_2^2 \sigma^2(R_2) + 2\omega_1 \omega_2 \sigma(R_1)\sigma(R_2)\rho(R_1,R_2) \qquad (6)$$

where R_i is the domestic-currency return of the i-th foreign-currency asset. But as shown in Equation 3, the domestic-currency return of a foreign-currency asset (R_{DC}) is itself based on the sum of two random variables: R_{FC} and R_{FX}. This means that we would have to embed the variance expression shown in Equation 5 in *each* of the $\sigma^2(R_i)$ shown in Equation 6 to get the complete solution for the domestic-currency return variance of the overall portfolio. (We would also have to calculate the correlations between *all* of the R_i.) These requirements would lead to a very cumbersome mathematical expression for even a portfolio of only two foreign-currency assets; the expression would be far more complicated for a portfolio with many foreign currencies involved.

Thus, rather than attempt to give the complete mathematical formula for the variance of domestic-currency returns for a multi-currency portfolio, we will instead focus on the key intuition behind this expression. Namely, that the domestic-currency risk exposure of the overall portfolio—that is, $\sigma(R_{DC})$—will depend not only on the variances of *each* of the foreign-currency returns (R_{FC}) and exchange rate movements (R_{FX}) but also on how each of these *interacts* with the others. Generally speaking, negative correlations among these variables will help reduce the overall portfolio's risk through diversification effects.

Note as well that the overall portfolio's risk exposure will depend on the portfolio weights (ω_i) used. If short-selling is allowed in the portfolio, some of these ω_i can be negative as long as the total portfolio weights sum to one. So, for two foreign assets with a strong positive return correlation, short selling one can create considerable diversification benefits for the portfolio. (This approach is equivalent to trading movements in the price spread between these two assets.)

As before with the difference between realized and expected domestic-currency portfolio returns (R_{DC}), there is a difference between realized and expected domestic-currency portfolio risk, $\sigma(R_{DC})$. For Equation 6 to apply to the expected future volatility of the domestic-currency return of a multi-currency foreign asset portfolio, we would need to replace the observed, historical values of the variances and covariances in Equation 6 with their expected future values. This can be challenging, not only because it potentially involves a large number of variables but also because historical price patterns are not always a good guide to future price behavior. Variance and correlation measures are sensitive to the time period used to estimate them and can also vary over time. These variance and correlation measures can either drift randomly with time, or they can be subject to abrupt movements in times of market stress. It should also be clear that these observed, historical volatility and correlation measures need not be the same as the forward-looking *implied* volatility (and correlation) derived from option prices. Although sometimes various survey or consensus forecasts can be used, these too can be sensitive to sample size and composition and are not always available on a timely basis or with a consistent starting point. As with any forecast, they are also not necessarily an accurate guide to future developments; judgment must be used.

Hence, to calculate the expected future risk of the foreign asset portfolio, the portfolio manager would need a market opinion—however derived—on the variance of each of the foreign-currency asset returns (R_{FC}) over the investment horizon as well the variance of future exchange rate movements (R_{FX}) for each currency pair. The portfolio manager would also need a market opinion of how each of these future variables would interact with each other (i.e., their expected correlations). Historical price patterns can serve as a guide, and with computers and large databases, this modeling problem is daunting but not intractable. But the portfolio manager must always be mindful that historical risk patterns may not repeat going forward.

EXAMPLE 1   Portfolio Risk and Return Calculations

The following table shows current and future expected asset prices, measured in their domestic currencies, for both eurozone and Canadian assets (these can be considered "total return" indexes). The table also has the corresponding data for the CAD/EUR spot rate.

	Eurozone		Canada	
	Today	Expected	Today	Expected
Asset price	100.69	101.50	101.00	99.80
CAD/EUR	1.2925	1.3100		

1. What is the expected domestic-currency return for a eurozone investor holding the Canadian asset?
2. What is the expected domestic-currency return for a Canadian investor holding the eurozone asset?
3. From the perspective of the Canadian investor, assume that $\sigma(R_{FC}) = 3\%$ (the expected risk for the foreign-currency asset is 3%) and the $\sigma(R_{FX}) = 2\%$ (the expected risk of exchange rate movements is 2%). Furthermore, the expected correlation between movements in foreign-currency asset returns and movements in the CAD/EUR rate is +0.5. What is the expected risk of the domestic-currency return [$\sigma(R_{DC})$]?

Solution to 1: For the eurozone investor, the $R_{FC} = (99.80/101.00) - 1 = -1.19\%$. Note that, given we are considering the eurozone to be "domestic" for this investor and given the way the R_{FX} expression is defined, we will need to convert the CAD/EUR exchange rate quote so that the EUR is the *price* currency. This leads to $R_{FX} = [(1/1.3100)/(1/1.2925)] - 1 = -1.34\%$. Hence, for the eurozone investor, $R_{DC} = (1 - 1.19\%)(1 - 1.34\%) - 1 = -2.51\%$.

Solution to 2: For the Canadian investor, the $R_{FC} = (101.50/100.69) - 1 = +0.80\%$. Given that in the CAD/EUR quote the CAD is the price currency, for this investor the $R_{FX} = (1.3100/1.2925) - 1 = +1.35\%$. Hence, for the Canadian investor the $R_{DC} = (1 + 0.80\%)(1 + 1.35\%) - 1 = 2.16\%$.

Solution to 3: Because this is a single foreign-currency asset we are considering (not a portfolio of such assets), we can use Equation 5:

$$\sigma^2(R_{DC}) \approx \sigma^2(R_{FC}) + \sigma^2(R_{FX}) + 2\sigma(R_{FC})\sigma(R_{FX})\rho(R_{FC}, R_{FX})$$

Inserting the relevant data leads to

$$\sigma^2(R_{DC}) \approx (3\%)^2 + (2\%)^2 + 2(3\%)(2\%)(0.50) = 0.0019$$

Taking the square root of this leads to $\sigma(R_{DC}) \approx 4.36\%$. (Note that the units in these expressions are all in percent, so in this case 3% is equivalent to 0.03 for calculation purposes.)

4. CURRENCY MANAGEMENT: STRATEGIC DECISIONS

There are a variety of approaches to currency management, ranging from trying to avoid all currency risk in a portfolio to actively seeking foreign exchange risk in order to manage it and enhance portfolio returns.

There is no firm consensus—either among academics or practitioners—about the most effective way to manage currency risk. Some investment managers try to hedge all currency risk, some leave their portfolios unhedged, and others see currency risk as a potential source of incremental return to the portfolio and will actively trade foreign exchange. These widely varying management practices reflect a variety of factors including investment objectives, investment constraints, and beliefs about currency markets.

Concerning beliefs, one camp of thought holds that in the long run currency effects cancel out to zero as exchange rates revert to historical means or their fundamental values. Moreover, an efficient currency market is a zero-sum game (currency "A" cannot appreciate against currency "B" without currency "B" depreciating against currency "A"), so there should not be any long-run gains overall to speculating in currencies, especially after netting out management and transaction costs. Therefore, both currency hedging and actively trading currencies represent a cost to a portfolio with little prospect of consistently positive active returns.

At the other extreme, another camp of thought notes that currency movements can have a dramatic impact on short-run returns and return volatility and holds that there are pricing inefficiencies in currency markets. They note that much of the flow in currency markets is related to international trade or capital flows in which FX trading is being done on a need-to-do basis and these currency trades are just a spinoff of the other transactions. Moreover, some market participants are either not in the market on a purely profit-oriented basis (e.g., central banks, government agencies) or are believed to be "uninformed traders" (primarily retail accounts). Conversely, speculative capital seeking to arbitrage inefficiencies is finite. In short, marketplace diversity is believed to present the potential for "harvesting alpha" through active currency trading.

This ongoing debate does not make foreign-currency risk in portfolios go away; it still needs to managed, or at least, recognized. Ultimately, each portfolio manager or investment oversight committee will have to reach their own decisions about how to manage risk and whether to seek return enhancement through actively trading currency exposures.

Fortunately, there are a well-developed set of financial products and portfolio management techniques that help investors manage currency risk no matter what their individual objectives, views, and constraints. Indeed, the potential combinations of trading tools and strategies are almost infinite, and can shape currency exposures to custom-fit individual circumstance and market opinion. In this section, we explore various points on a spectrum reflecting currency exposure choices (a risk spectrum) and the guidance that portfolio managers use in making strategic decisions about where to locate their portfolios on this continuum. First, however, the implication of investment objectives and constraints as set forth in the investment policy statement must be recognized.

4.1. The Investment Policy Statement

The Investment Policy Statement (IPS) mandates the degree of discretionary currency management that will be allowed in the portfolio, how it will be benchmarked, and the limits on the type of trading polices and tools (e.g., such as leverage) than can be used.

The starting point for organizing the investment plan for any portfolio is the IPS, which is a statement that outlines the broad objectives and constraints of the beneficial owners of the assets. Most IPS specify many of the following points:

- the general objectives of the investment portfolio;
- the risk tolerance of the portfolio and its capacity for bearing risk;
- the time horizon over which the portfolio is to be invested;
- the ongoing income/liquidity needs (if any) of the portfolio; and
- the benchmark against which the portfolio will measure overall investment returns.

The IPS sets the guiding parameters within which more specific portfolio management policies are set, including the target asset mix; whether and to what extent leverage, short positions, and derivatives can be used; and how actively the portfolio will be allowed to trade its various risk exposures.

For most portfolios, currency management can be considered a sub-set of these more specific portfolio management policies within the IPS. The currency risk management policy will usually address such issues as the

- target proportion of currency exposure to be passively hedged;
- latitude for active currency management around this target;

- frequency of hedge rebalancing;
- currency hedge performance benchmark to be used; and
- hedging tools permitted (types of forward and option contracts, etc.).

Currency management should be conducted within these IPS-mandated parameters.

4.2. The Portfolio Optimization Problem

Having described the IPS as the guiding framework for currency management, we now examine the strategic choices that have to be made in deciding the benchmark currency exposures for the portfolio, and the degree of discretion that will be allowed around this benchmark. This process starts with a decision on the optimal foreign-currency asset and FX exposures.

Optimization of a multi-currency portfolio of foreign assets involves selecting portfolio weights that locate the portfolio on the efficient frontier of the trade-off between risk and expected return defined in terms of the investor's domestic currency. As a simplification of this process, consider the portfolio manager examining the expected return and risk of the multi-currency portfolio of foreign assets by using different combinations of portfolio weights (ω_i) that were shown in Equations 2 and 6, respectively, which are repeated here:

$$R_{DC} = \sum_{i=1}^{n} \omega_i (1 + R_{FC,i})(1 + R_{FX,i}) - 1$$

$$\sigma^2(\omega_1 R_1 + \omega_2 R_2) \approx \omega_1^2 \sigma^2(R_1) + \omega_2^2 \sigma^2(R_2) + 2\omega_1 \sigma(R_1)\omega_2 \sigma(R_2)\rho(R_1, R_2)$$

Recall that the R_i in the equation for variance are the R_{DC} for each of the foreign-currency assets. Likewise, recall that the R_{FX} term is defined such that the investor's "domestic" currency is the price currency in the P/B exchange rate quote. In other words, this calculation may require using the algebraic reciprocal of the standard market quote convention. These two equations together show the domestic-currency return and risk for a multi-currency portfolio of foreign assets.

When deciding on an optimal investment position, these equations would be based on the *expected* returns and risks for each of the foreign-currency assets; and hence, including the *expected* returns and risks for each of the foreign-currency exposures. As we have seen earlier, the number of market parameters for which the portfolio manager would need to have a market opinion grows geometrically with the complexity (number of foreign-currency exposures) in the portfolio. That is, to calculate the expected efficient frontier, the portfolio manager must have a market opinion for *each* of the $R_{FC,i}$, $R_{FX,i}$, $\sigma(R_{FC,i})$, $\sigma(R_{FX,i})$, and $\rho(R_{FC,i} R_{FX,i})$, as well as for each of the $\rho(R_{FC,i} R_{FC,j})$ and $\rho(R_{FX,i} R_{FX,j})$. This would be a daunting task for even the most well-informed portfolio manager.

In a perfect world with complete (and costless) information, it would likely be optimal to *jointly* optimize all of the portfolio's exposures—over all currencies and all foreign-currency assets—simultaneously. In the real world, however, this can be a much more difficult task. Confronted with these difficulties, many portfolio managers handle asset allocation with currency risk as a two-step process: (1) portfolio optimization over fully hedged returns; and (2) selection of active currency exposure, if any. Derivative strategies can allow the various risk exposures in a portfolio to be "unbundled" from each other and managed separately. The same applies for currency risks. Because the use of derivatives allows the price risk ($R_{FC,i}$) and exchange rate risk ($R_{FX,j}$) of foreign-currency assets to be unbundled and managed separately, a starting point for the selection process of portfolio weights would be to assume a complete currency hedge. That is, the portfolio manager will choose the exposures to the foreign-currency assets first, and then decide on the appropriate currency exposures afterward (i.e., decide whether to relax the full currency hedge). These decisions are made to simplify the portfolio construction process.

If the currency exposures of foreign assets could be perfectly and costlessly hedged, the hedge would completely neutralize the effect of currency movements on the portfolio's domestic-currency return (R_{DC}).[7] In Equation 2, this would set $R_{FX} = 0$, meaning that the domestic-currency return is then equal to the foreign-currency return ($R_{DC} = R_{FC}$). In Equation 5, this would set $\sigma^2(R_{DC}) = \sigma^2(R_{FC})$, meaning that the domestic-currency return risk is equal to the foreign-currency return risk.

Removing the currency effects leads to a simpler, two-step process for portfolio optimization. First the portfolio manager could pick the set of portfolio weights (w_i) for the foreign-currency assets that optimize the expected foreign-currency asset risk–return trade-off (assuming there is no currency risk). Then the portfolio manager could choose the desired currency exposures for the portfolio and decide whether and by how far to relax the constraint to a full currency hedge for each currency pair.

4.3. Choice of Currency Exposures

A natural starting point for the strategic decisions is the "currency-neutral" portfolio resulting from the two-step process described earlier. The question then becomes, How far along the risk spectrum between being fully hedged and actively trading currencies should the portfolio be positioned?

4.3.1. Diversification Considerations

The time horizon of the IPS is important. Many investment practitioners believe that in the long run, adding unhedged foreign-currency exposure to a portfolio does not affect expected long-run portfolio returns; hence in the long run, it would not matter if the portfolio was hedged. (Indeed, portfolio management costs would be reduced without a hedging process.) This belief is based on the view that in the long run, currencies "mean revert" to either some fair value equilibrium level or a historical average; that is, that the *expected* %$\Delta S = 0$ for a sufficiently long time period. This view typically draws on the expectation that purchasing power parity (PPP) and the other international parity conditions that link movements in exchange rates, interest rates, and inflation rates will eventually hold over the long run.

Supporting this view, some studies argue that in the long-run currencies will in fact mean revert, and hence that currency risk is lower in the long run than in the short run (an early example is Froot 1993). Although much depends on how long run is defined, an investor (IPS) with a very long investment horizon and few immediate liquidity needs—which could potentially require the liquidation of foreign-currency assets at disadvantageous exchange rates—might choose to forgo currency hedging and its associated costs. Logically, this would require a portfolio benchmark index that is also unhedged against currency risk.

Although the international parity conditions may hold in the long run, it can be a *very* long time—possibly decades. Indeed, currencies can continue to drift away from the fair value

---

[7]A "costless" hedge in this sense would not only mean zero transaction costs, but also no "roll yield."

mean reversion level for much longer than the time period used to judge portfolio performance. Such time periods are also typically longer than the patience of the portfolio manager's oversight committee when portfolio performance is lagging the benchmark. If this very long-run view perspective is not the case, then the IPS will likely impose some form of currency hedging.

Diversification considerations will also depend on the *asset composition* of the foreign-currency asset portfolio. The reason is because the foreign-currency asset returns (R_{FC}) of different asset classes have different correlation patterns with foreign-currency returns (R_{FX}). If there is a negative correlation between these two sets of returns, having at least some currency exposure may help portfolio diversification and moderate the domestic-currency return risk, $\sigma(R_{DC})$. (Refer to Equation 5 in Section 3.3.)

It is often asserted that the correlation between foreign-currency returns and foreign-currency asset returns tends to be greater for fixed-income portfolios than for equity portfolios. This assertion makes intuitive sense: both bonds and currencies react strongly to movements in interest rates, whereas equities respond more to expected earnings. As a result, the implication is that currency exposures provide little diversification benefit to fixed-income portfolios and that the currency risk should be hedged. In contrast, a better argument can be made for carrying currency exposures in global equity portfolios.

To some degree, various studies have corroborated this relative advantage to currency hedging for fixed-income portfolios. But the evidence seems somewhat mixed and depends on which markets are involved. One study found that the hedging advantage for fixed-income portfolios is not always large or consistent (Darnell 2004). Other studies (Campbell 2010; Martini 2010) found that the optimal hedge ratio for foreign-currency equity portfolios depended critically on the investor's domestic currency. (Recall that the hedge ratio is defined as the ratio of the nominal value of the hedge to the market value of the underlying.) For some currencies, there was no risk-reduction advantage to hedging foreign equities (the optimal hedge ratio was close to 0%), whereas for other currencies, the optimal hedge ratio for foreign equities was close to 100%.

Other studies indicate that the optimal hedge ratio also seems to depend on *market conditions* and longer-term trends in currency pairs. For example, Campbell, Serfaty-de Medeiros, and Viceira (2007) found that there were no diversification benefits from currency exposures in foreign-currency bond portfolios, and hence to minimize the risk to domestic-currency returns these positions should be fully hedged. The authors also found, however, that during the time of their study (their data spanned 1975 to 2005), the US dollar seemed to be an exception in terms of its correlations with foreign-currency asset returns. Their study found that the US dollar tended to appreciate against foreign currencies when global bond prices fell (for example, in times of global financial stress there is a tendency for investors to shift investments into the perceived safety of reserve currencies). This finding would suggest that keeping some exposure to the US dollar in a global bond portfolio would be beneficial. For non-US investors, this would mean under-hedging the currency exposure to the USD (i.e., a hedge ratio less than 100%), whereas for US investors it would mean over-hedging their foreign-currency exposures back into the USD. Note that some currencies—the USD, JPY, and CHF in particular—seem to act as a safe haven and appreciate in times of market stress. Keeping some of these currency exposures in the portfolio—having hedge ratios that are not set at 100%–can help hedge losses on riskier assets, especially for foreign currency equity portfolios (which are more risk exposed than bond portfolios).

Given this diversity of opinions and empirical findings, it is not surprising to see actual hedge ratios vary widely in practice among different investors. Nonetheless, it is still more likely to see currency hedging for fixed-income portfolios rather than equity portfolios, although actual hedge ratios will often vary between individual managers.

4.3.2. Cost Considerations

The costs of currency hedging also guide the strategic positioning of the portfolio. Currency hedges are not a "free good" and they come with a variety of expenses that must be borne by the overall portfolio. Optimal hedging decisions will need to balance the benefits of hedging against these costs.

Hedging costs come mainly in two forms: trading costs and opportunity costs. The most immediate costs of hedging involve trading expenses, and these come in several forms:

- Trading involves dealing on the bid–offer spread offered by banks. Their profit margin is based on these spreads, and the more the client trades and "pays away the spread," the more profit is generated by the dealer. Maintaining a 100% hedge and rebalancing frequently with every minor change in market conditions would be expensive. Although the bid–offer spreads on many FX-related products (especially the spot exchange rate) are quite narrow, "churning" the hedge portfolio would progressively add to hedging costs and detract from the hedge's benefits.

- Some hedges involve currency options; a long position in currency options requires the payment of up-front premiums. If the options expire out of the money (OTM), this cost is unrecoverable.

- Although forward contracts do not require the payment of up-front premiums, they do eventually mature and have to be "rolled" forward with an FX swap transaction to maintain the hedge. Rolling hedges will typically generate cash inflows or outflows. These cash flows will have to be monitored, and as necessary, cash will have to be raised to settle hedging transactions. In other words, even though the currency hedge may *reduce* the volatility of the domestic mark-to-market value of the foreign-currency asset portfolio, it will typically *increase* the volatility in the organization's cash accounts. Managing these cash flow costs can accumulate to become a significant portion of the portfolio's value, and they become more expensive (for cash outflows) the higher interest rates go.

- One of the most important trading costs is the need to maintain an administrative infrastructure for trading. Front-, middle-, and back-office operations will have to be set up, staffed with trained personnel, and provided with specialized technology systems. Settlement of foreign exchange transactions in a variety of currencies means having to maintain cash accounts in these currencies to make and receive these foreign-currency payments. Together all of these various overhead costs can form a significant portion of the overall costs of currency trading.

A second form of costs associated with hedging are the opportunity cost of the hedge. To be 100% hedged is to forgo any possibility of favorable currency rate moves. If skillfully handled, accepting and managing currency risk—or any financial risk—can potentially add value to the portfolio, even net of management fees. (We discuss the methods by which this might be done in Section 5.)

These opportunity costs lead to another motivation for having a strategic hedge ratio of less than 100%: regret minimization. Although it is not possible to accurately predict foreign exchange movements in advance, it is certainly possible to judge after the fact the results of the decision to hedge or not. Missing out on an advantageous currency movement because of a currency hedge can cause *ex post* regret in the portfolio manager or client; so too can having a foreign-currency loss if the foreign-currency asset position was unhedged. Confronted with this *ex ante* dilemma of whether to hedge, many portfolio managers decide simply to "split the difference" and have a 50% hedge ratio (or some other rule-of-thumb number). Both survey evidence and anecdotal evidence show that there is a wide variety of hedge ratios actually used in practice by managers, and that these variations cannot be explained by more "fundamental" factors alone. Instead, many managers appear to incorporate some degree of regret minimization into hedging decisions (for example, see Michenaud and Solnik 2008).

All of these various hedging expenses—both trading and opportunity costs—will need to be managed. Hedging is a form of insurance against risk, and in purchasing any form of insurance the buyer matches their needs and budgets with the policy selected. For example, although it may be possible to buy an insurance policy with full, unlimited coverage, a zero deductible, and no co-pay arrangements, such a policy would likely be prohibitively expensive. Most insurance buyers decide that it is not necessary to insure against every outcome, no matter how minor. Some minor risks can be accepted and "self-insured" through the deductible; some major risks may be considered so unlikely that they are not seen as worth paying the extra premium. (For example, most ordinary people would likely not consider buying insurance against being kidnapped.)

These same principles apply to currency hedging. The portfolio manager (and IPS) would likely not try to hedge every minor, daily change in exchange rates or asset values, but only the larger adverse movements that can materially affect the overall domestic-currency returns (R_{DC}) of the foreign-currency asset portfolio. The portfolio manager will need to balance the benefits and costs of hedging in determining both strategic positioning of the portfolio as well as any latitude for active currency management. However, around whatever strategic positioning decision taken by the IPS in terms of the benchmark level of currency exposure, hedging cost considerations alone will often dictate a *range* of permissible exposures instead of a single point. (This discretionary range is similar to the deductible in an insurance policy.)

4.4. Locating the Portfolio Along the Currency Risk Spectrum

The strategic decisions encoded in the IPS with regard to the trade-off between the benefits and costs of hedging, as well as the potential for incremental return to the portfolio from active currency management, are the foundation for determining specific currency management strategies. These strategies are arrayed along a spectrum from very risk-averse passive hedging, to actively seeking out currency risk in order to manage it for profit. We examine each in turn.

4.4.1. Passive Hedging
In this approach, the goal is to keep the portfolio's currency exposures close, if not equal to, those of a benchmark portfolio used to evaluate performance. Note that the benchmark portfolio often has no foreign exchange exposure, particularly for fixed-income assets; the benchmark index is a "local currency" index based only on the foreign-currency asset return (R_{FC}). However, benchmark indexes that have some foreign exchange risk are also possible.

Passive hedging is a rules-based approach that removes almost all discretion from the portfolio manager, regardless of the manager's market opinion on future movements in exchange rates or other financial prices. In this case, the manager's job is to keep portfolio exposures as close to "neutral" as possible and to minimize tracking errors against the benchmark portfolio's performance. This approach reflects the belief that currency exposures that differ from the benchmark portfolio inject risk (return volatility) into the portfolio without any sufficiently compensatory return. Active currency management—taking positional views on future exchange rate movements—is viewed as being incapable of consistently adding incremental return to the portfolio.

But the hedge ratio has a tendency to "drift" with changes in market conditions, and even passive hedges need periodic rebalancing to realign them with investment objectives. Often the management guidance given to the portfolio manager will specify the rebalancing period—for example, monthly. There may also be allowance for intra-period rebalancing if there have been large exchange rate movements.

4.4.2. Discretionary Hedging

This approach is similar to passive hedging in that there is a "neutral" benchmark portfolio against which actual portfolio performance will be measured. However, in contrast to a strictly rules-based approach, the portfolio manager now has some limited discretion on how far to allow actual portfolio risk exposures to vary from the neutral position. Usually this discretion is defined in terms of percentage of foreign-currency market value (the portfolio's currency exposures are allowed to vary plus or minus x% from the benchmark). For example, a eurozone-domiciled investor may have a US Treasury bond portfolio with a mandate to keep the hedge ratio within 95% to 105%. Assuming no change in the foreign-currency return (R_{FC}), but allowing exchange rates (R_{FX}) to vary, this means the portfolio can tolerate exchange rate movements between the EUR and USD of up to 5% before the exchange rate exposures in the portfolio are considered excessive. The manager is allowed to manage currency exposures within these limits without being considered in violation of the IPS.

This discretion allows the portfolio manager at least some limited ability to express directional opinions about future currency movements—to accept risk in an attempt to earn reward—in order to add value to the portfolio performance. Of course, the portfolio manager's actual performance will be compared with that of the benchmark portfolio.

4.4.3. Active Currency Management

Further along the spectrum between extreme risk aversion and purely speculative trading is active currency management. In principle, this approach is really just an extension of discretionary hedging: the portfolio manager is allowed to express directional opinions on exchange rates, but is nonetheless kept within mandated risk limits. The performance of the manager—the choices of risk exposures assumed—is benchmarked against a "neutral" portfolio. But for all forms of active management (i.e., having the discretion to express directional market views), there is no allowance for unlimited speculation; there are risk management systems in place for even the most speculative investment vehicles, such as hedge funds. These controls are designed to prevent traders from taking unusually large currency exposures and risking the solvency of the firm or fund.

In many cases, the difference between discretionary hedging and active currency management is one of emphasis more than degree. The primary duty of the discretionary hedger is to protect the portfolio from currency risk. As a secondary goal, within limited bounds, there is some scope for directional opinion in an attempt to enhance overall portfolio returns. If the manager lacks any firm market conviction, the natural neutral position for the discretionary hedger is to be flat—that is, to have no meaningful currency exposures. In contrast, the active currency manager is supposed to take currency risks and manage them for profit. The primary goal is to add alpha to the portfolio through successful trading. Leaving actual portfolio exposures near zero for extended periods is typically not a viable option.

4.4.4. Currency Overlay

Active management of currency exposures can extend beyond limited managerial discretion within hedging boundaries. Sometimes accepting and managing currency risk for profit can be considered a portfolio objective. Active currency management is often associated with what are called **currency overlay programs**, although this term is used differently by different sources.

- In the most limited sense of the term, currency overlay simply means that the portfolio manager has outsourced managing currency exposures to a firm specializing in FX management. This could imply something as limited as merely having the external party implement a fully passive approach to currency hedges. If dealing with FX markets and managing currency hedges is beyond the professional competence of the investment manager, whose focus is on managing foreign equities or some other asset class, then hiring such external professional help is an option. Note that typically currency overlay programs involve external managers. However, some large, sophisticated institutional investors may have in-house currency overlay programs managed by a separate group of specialists within the firm.

- A broader view of currency overlay allows the externally hired currency overlay manager to take directional views on future currency movements (again, with the caveat that these be kept within predefined bounds). Sometimes a distinction is made between currency overlay and "foreign exchange as an asset class." In this classification, currency overlay is limited to the currency exposures already in the foreign asset portfolio. For example, if a eurozone-domiciled investor has GBP- and CHF-denominated assets, currency overlay risks are allowed only for these currencies.

- In contrast, the concept of foreign exchange as an asset class does not restrict the currency overlay manager, who is free to take FX exposures in any currency pair where there is value-added to be harvested, regardless of the underlying portfolio. In this sense, the currency overlay manager is very similar to an FX-based hedge fund. To implement this form of active currency management, the currency overlay manager would have a *joint* opinion on a range of currencies, and have market views not only on the expected movements in the spot rates but also the likelihood of these movements (the variance of the expected future spot rate distribution) as well as the expected correlation between future spot rate movements. Basically, the entire portfolio of currencies is actively managed and optimized over all of the expected returns, risks, and correlations among all of the currencies in the portfolio.

We will focus on this latter form of currency overlay in this chapter: active currency management conducted by external, FX-specialized sub-advisors to the portfolio.

It is quite possible to have the foreign-currency asset portfolio fully hedged (or allow some discretionary hedging internally) but then also to add an external currency overlay manager to the portfolio. This approach separates the hedging and alpha function mandates of the portfolio. Different organizations have different areas of expertise; it often makes sense to allocate managing the hedge (currency "beta") and managing the active FX exposures (currency "alpha") to those individuals with a comparative advantage in that function.

Adding this form of currency overlay to the portfolio (FX as an asset class) is similar in principle to adding any type of alternative asset class, such as private equity funds or farmland. In each case, the goal is the search for alpha. But to be most effective in adding value to the portfolio, the currency overlay program should add incremental returns (alpha) and/or greater diversification opportunities to improve the portfolio's risk–return profile. To do this, the currency alpha mandate should have minimum correlation with both the major asset classes and the other alpha sources in the portfolio.

Once this FX as an asset class approach is taken, it is not necessary to restrict the portfolio to a single overlay manager any more than it is necessary to restrict the portfolio to a single private equity fund. Different overlay managers follow different strategies (these are described in more detail in Section 5). Within the overall portfolio allocation to "currency as an alternative asset class," it may be beneficial to diversify across a range of active management styles, either by engaging several currency overlay managers with different styles or by applying a fund-of-funds approach, in which the hiring and management of individual currency overlay managers is delegated to a specialized external investment vehicle.

Whether managed internally or externally (via a fund of funds) it will be necessary to monitor, or benchmark, the performance of the currency overlay manager: Do they generate the returns expected from their stated trading strategy? Many major investment banks as well as specialized market-information firms provide a wide range of proprietary indexes that track the performance of the investible universe of currency overlay managers; sometimes they also offer sub-indexes that focus on specific trading strategies (for example, currency positioning based on macroeconomic fundamentals). However, the methodologies used to calculate these various indexes vary between suppliers. In addition, different indexes show different aspects of active currency management. Given these differences between indexes, there is no simple answer for which index is most suitable as a benchmark; much depends on the specifics of the active currency strategy.

EXAMPLE 2   Currency Overlay

Windhoek Capital Management is a South Africa-based investment manager that runs the Conservative Value Fund, which has a mandate to avoid all currency risk in the portfolio. The firm is considering engaging a currency overlay manager to help with managing the foreign exchange exposures of this investment vehicle. Windhoek does not consider itself to have the in-house expertise to manage FX risk.

Brixworth & St. Ives Asset Management is a UK-based investment manager, and runs the Aggressive Growth Fund. This fund is heavily weighted toward emerging market equities, but also has a mandate to seek out inefficiencies in the global foreign exchange market and exploit these for profit. Although Brixworth & St. Ives manages the currency hedges for all of its investment funds in-house, it is also considering engaging a currency overlay manager.

1. Using a currency overlay manager for the Conservative Value Fund is *most likely* to involve:
    A. joining the alpha and hedging mandates.
    B. a more active approach to managing currency risks.
    C. using this manager to passively hedge their foreign exchange exposures.

2. Using a currency overlay manager for the Aggressive Growth Fund is *most likely* to involve:
   A. separating the alpha and hedging mandates.
   B. a less discretionary approach to managing currency hedges.
   C. an IPS that limits active management to emerging market currencies.

3. Brixworth & St. Ives is *more likely* to engage multiple currency overlay managers if:
   A. their returns are correlated with asset returns in the fund.
   B. the currency managers' returns are correlated with each other.
   C. the currency managers use different active management strategies.

Solution to 1: C is correct. The Conservative Value Fund wants to avoid all currency exposures in the portfolio and Windhoek believes that it lacks the currency management expertise to do this.

Solution to 2: A is correct. Brixworth & St. Ives already does the FX hedging in house, so a currency overlay is more likely to be a pure alpha mandate. This should not change the way that Brixworth & St. Ives manages its hedges, and the fund's mandate to seek out inefficiencies in the global FX market is unlikely to lead to a restriction to actively manage only emerging market currencies.

Solution to 3: C is correct. Different active management strategies may lead to a more diversified source of alpha generation, and hence reduced portfolio risk. Choices A and B are incorrect because a higher correlation with foreign-currency assets in the portfolio or among overlay manager returns is likely to lead to less diversification.

4.5. Formulating a Client-Appropriate Currency Management Program

We now try to bring all of these previous considerations together in describing how to formulate an appropriate currency management program given client objectives and constraints, as well as overall financial market conditions. Generally speaking, the *strategic* currency positioning of the portfolio, as encoded in the IPS, should be biased toward a more-fully hedged currency management program the more

- short term the investment objectives of the portfolio;
- risk averse the beneficial owners of the portfolio are (and impervious to *ex post* regret over missed opportunities);
- immediate the income and/or liquidity needs of the portfolio;
- fixed-income assets are held in a foreign-currency portfolio;
- cheaply a hedging program can be implemented;
- volatile (i.e., risky) financial markets are;[8] and
- skeptical the beneficial owners and/or management oversight committee are of the expected benefits of active currency management.

---

[8]As we will see, this also increases hedging costs when currency options are used.

The relaxation of any of these conditions creates latitude to allow a more proactive currency risk posture in the portfolio, either through wider tolerance bands for discretionary hedging, or by introducing foreign currencies as a separate asset class (using currency overlay programs as an alternative asset class in the overall portfolio). In the latter case, the more currency overlay is expected to generate alpha that is uncorrelated with other asset or alpha-generation programs in the portfolio, the more it is likely to be allowed in terms of strategic portfolio positioning.

Investment Policy Statement

Kailua Kona Advisors runs a Hawaii-based hedge fund that focuses on developed market equities located outside of North America. Its investor base consists of local high-net-worth individuals who are all considered to have a long investment horizon, a high tolerance for risk, and no immediate income needs. In its prospectus to investors, Kailua Kona indicates that it actively manages both the fund's equity and foreign-currency exposures, and that the fund uses leverage through the use of loans as well as short-selling.

Exhibit 4 presents the hedge fund's currency management policy included in the IPS for this hedge fund.

EXHIBIT 4   Hedge Fund Currency Management Policy: An Example

Overall Portfolio Benchmark:	MSCI EAFE Index (local currency)
Currency Exposure Ranges:	Foreign-currency exposures, based on the USD market value of the equities actually held by the fund at the beginning of each month, will be hedged back into USD within the following tolerance ranges of plus or minus:
	• EUR: 20%
	• GBP: 15%
	• JPY: 10%
	• CHF: 10%
	• AUD: 10%
	• SEK: 10%
	Other currency exposures shall be left unhedged.
Rebalancing:	The currency hedges will be rebalanced at least monthly, to reflect changes in the USD-denominated market value of portfolio equity holdings.
Hedging Instruments:	• Forward contracts up to 12 months maturity;
	• European put and call options can be bought or written, for maturities up to 12 months; and
	• Exotic options of up to 12 months maturity can be bought or sold.
Reporting:	Management will present quarterly reports to the board detailing net foreign-currency exposures and speculative trading results. Speculative trading results will be benchmarked against a 100% hedged currency exposure.

With this policy, Kailua Kona Advisors is indicating that it is willing to accept foreign-currency exposures within the portfolio but that these exposures must be kept within pre-defined limits. For example, suppose that at the beginning of the month the portfolio held EUR10 million of EUR-denominated assets. Also suppose that this EUR10 million exposure, combined with all the other foreign-currency exposures in the portfolio, matches Kailua Kona Advisors' desired portfolio weights by currency (as a US-based fund, these desired percentage portfolio allocations across all currencies will be based in USD).

The currency-hedging guidelines indicate that the hedge (for example, using a short position in a USD/EUR forward contract) should be between EUR8 million and EUR12 million, giving some discretion to the portfolio manager on the size of the net exposure to the EUR. At the beginning of the next month, the USD values of the foreign assets in the portfolio are measured again, and the process repeats. If there has been either a large move in the foreign-currency value of the EUR-denominated assets and/or a large move in the USD/EUR exchange rate, it is possible that Kailua Kona Advisors' portfolio exposure to EUR-denominated assets will be too far away from the desired percentage allocation.[9] Kailua Kona Advisors will then need to either buy or sell EUR-denominated assets. If movements in the EUR-denominated value of the assets or in the USD/EUR exchange rate are large enough, this asset rebalancing may have to be done before month's end. Either way, once the asset rebalancing is done, it establishes the new EUR-denominated asset value on which the currency hedge will be based (i.e., plus or minus 20% of this new EUR amount).

If the portfolio is not 100% hedged—for example, continuing the Kailua Kona illustration, if the portfolio manager only hedges EUR9 million of the exposure and has a residual exposure of being long EUR1 million—the success or failure of the manager's tactical decision will be compared with a "neutral" benchmark. In this case, the comparison would be against the performance of a 100% fully hedged portfolio—that is, with a EUR10 million hedge.

5. CURRENCY MANAGEMENT: TACTICAL DECISIONS

The previous section discussed the *strategic* decisions made by the IPS on locating the currency management practices of the portfolio along a risk spectrum ranging from a very conservative approach to currency risk to very active currency management. In this section, we consider the case in which the IPS has given the portfolio manager (or currency overlay manager) at least some limited discretion for actively managing currency risk within these mandated strategic bounds. This then leads to *tactical* decisions: which FX exposures to accept and manage within these discretionary limits. In other words, tactical decisions involve active currency management.

A market view is a prerequisite to any form of active management. At the heart of the trading decision in FX (and other) markets, lies a view on future market prices and

---

[9] The overall portfolio percentage allocations by currency will also depend on the price moves of all *other* foreign-currency assets and exchange rates as well, but we will simplify our example by ignoring this nuance.

conditions. This market opinion guides all decisions with respect to currency risk exposures, including whether currency hedges should be implemented and, if so, how they should be managed.

In what follows, we will explore some of the methods used to form directional views about the FX market. However, a word of caution that cannot be emphasized enough: *There is no simple formula, model, or approach that will allow market participants to precisely forecast exchange rates (or any other financial prices) or to be able to be confident that any trading decision will be profitable.*

5.1. Active Currency Management Based on Economic Fundamentals

This section sets out a broad framework for developing a view about future exchange rate movements based on underlying fundamentals. In contrast to other methods for developing a market view (which are discussed in subsequent sections), at the heart of this approach is the assumption that, in a flexible exchange rate system, exchange rates are determined by logical economic relationships and that these relationships can be modeled.

The simple economic framework is based on the assumption that in the long run, the real exchange rate will converge to its "fair value," but short- to medium-term factors will shape the convergence path to this equilibrium.[10]

Recall that the real exchange rate reflects the ratio of the real purchasing power between two countries; that is, the once nominal purchasing power in each country is adjusted by its respective price level as well as the spot exchange rate between the two countries. The long-run equilibrium level for the real exchange rate is determined by purchasing power parity or some other model of an exchange rate's fair value, and serves as the anchor for longer-term movements in exchange rates.

Over shorter time frames, movements in real exchange rates will also reflect movements in the real interest rate differential between countries. Recall that the real interest rate (r) is the nominal interest rate adjusted by the expected inflation rate, or $r = i - \pi^\varepsilon$, where i is the nominal interest rate and π^ε is the expected inflation rate over the same term as the nominal and real interest rates. Movements in risk premiums will also affect exchange rate movements over shorter-term horizons. The riskier a country's assets are perceived to be by investors, the more likely they are to move their investments out of that country, thereby depressing the exchange rate. Finally, the framework recognizes that there are two currencies involved in an exchange rate quote (the price and base currencies) and hence movements in exchange rates will reflect movements in the *differentials* between these various factors.

As a result, all else equal, the base currency's real exchange rate should appreciate if there is an upward movement in

- its long-run equilibrium real exchange rate;
- either its real or nominal interest rates, which should attract foreign capital;
- expected foreign inflation, which should cause the foreign currency to depreciate; and
- the foreign risk premium, which should make foreign assets less attractive compared with the base currency nation's domestic assets.

The real exchange rate should also increase if it is currently below its long-term equilibrium value. All of this makes intuitive sense.

---

[10]This model was derived and explained by Rosenberg and Barker (2017).

In summary, the exchange rate forecast is a mix of long-term, medium-term, and short-term factors. The long-run equilibrium real exchange rate is the anchor for exchange rates and the point of long-run convergence for exchange rate movements. Movements in the short- to medium-term factors (nominal interest rates, expected inflation) affect the timing and path of convergence to this long-run equilibrium. A stylized depiction of the price dynamics generated by this interaction between short-, medium-, and longer-term pricing factors is shown in Exhibit 5.

EXHIBIT 5   Interaction of Long-Term and Short-Term Factors in Exchange Rates

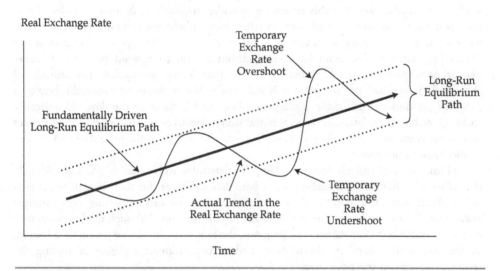

Source: Based on Rosenberg (2002), page 32.

It needs to be stressed that it can be very demanding to model how each of these separate effects—nominal interest rate, expected inflation, and risk premium differentials—change over time and affect exchange rates. It can also be challenging to model movements in the long-term equilibrium real exchange rate. A broad variety of factors, such as fiscal and monetary policy, will affect all of these variables in our simple economic model.[11]

5.2. Active Currency Management Based on Technical Analysis

Another approach to forming a market view is based on technical analysis. This approach is based on quite different assumptions compared with modeling based on economic fundamentals. Whereas classical exchange rate economics tends to view market participants as rational, markets as efficient, and exchange rates as driven by underlying economic factors, technical analysis ignores economic analysis. Instead, technical analysis is based on three broad themes.[12]

---

[11]A broader discussion of exchange rate economics can be found in Rosenberg and Barker (2017).
[12]Some material in this section is based on Sine and Strong (2012).

First, market technicians believe that in a liquid, freely traded market the historical price data can be helpful in projecting future price movements.[13] The reason is because many traders have already used any useful data external to the market to generate their trading positions, so this information is already reflected in current prices. Therefore, it is not necessary to look outside of the market to form an opinion on future price movements. This means it is not necessary to examine interest rates, inflation rates, or risk premium differentials (the factors in our fundamentally based model) because exchange rates already incorporate these factors.

Second, market technicians believe that historical patterns in the price data have a tendency to repeat, and that this repetition provides profitable trade opportunities. These price patterns repeat because market prices reflect human behavior and human beings have a tendency to react in similar ways to similar situations, even if this repetitive behavior is not always fully rational. For example, when confronted with an upward price trend, many market participants eventually come to believe that it will extrapolate (an attitude of "irrational exuberance" or "this time it is different"). When the trend eventually breaks, a panicked position exit can cause a sharp overshoot of fair value to the downside. Broadly speaking, technical analysis can be seen as the study of market psychology and how market participant emotions—primarily greed and fear—can be read from the price data and used to predict future price moves.

Third, technical analysis does not attempt to determine where market prices *should* trade (fair value, as in fundamental analysis) but where they *will* trade. Because these price patterns reflect trader emotions, they need not reflect—at least immediately—any cool, rational assessment of the underlying economic or fundamental situation. Although market prices may eventually converge to fair value in the long run, the long run can be a very long time indeed. In the meanwhile, there are shorter-term trading opportunities available in trading the technical patterns in the price data.

Combined, these three principles of technical analysis define a discipline dedicated to identifying patterns in the historical price data, especially as it relates to identifying market trends and market turning points. (Technical analysis is less useful in a trendless market.) Technical analysis tries to identify when markets have become **overbought** or **oversold**, meaning that they have trended too far in one direction and are vulnerable to a trend reversal, or correction. Technical analysis also tries to identify what are called **support levels** and **resistance levels**, either within ongoing price trends or at their extremities (i.e., turning points). These support and resistance levels are price points on dealers' order boards where one would expect to see clustering of bids and offers, respectively. At these exchange rate levels, the price action is expected to get "sticky" because it will take more order flow to pierce the wall of either bids or offers. But once these price points are breached, the price action can be expected to accelerate as **stops** are triggered. (Stops, in this sense, refer to stop-loss orders, in which traders leave resting bids or offers away from the current market price to be filled if the market reaches those levels. A stop-loss order is triggered when the price action has gone against a trader's position, and it gets the trader out of that position to limit further losses.)

Technical analysis uses visual cues for market patterns as well as more quantitative technical indicators. There is a wide variety of technical indexes based on market prices that

---

[13]In many other asset classes, technical analysis is based on trade volume data as well as price data. But there are no reliable, timely, and high-frequency trade volume data that are publicly available for over-the-counter (OTC) FX markets.

are used in this context. Some technical indicators are as simple as using moving averages of past price points. The 200-day moving average of daily exchange rates is often seen as an important indicator of likely support and resistance. Sometimes two moving averages are used to establish when a price trend is building momentum. For example, when the 50-day moving average crosses the 200-day moving average, this is sometimes seen as a price "break out" point.

Other technical indicators are based on more complex mathematical formulae. There is an extremely wide variety of these more mathematical indicators, some of them very esoteric and hard to connect intuitively with the behavior of real-world financial market participants.

In summary, many FX active managers routinely use technical analysis—either alone or in conjunction with other approaches—to form a market opinion or to time position entry and exit points. Even though many technical indicators lack the intellectual underpinnings provided by formal economic modeling, they nonetheless remain a prominent feature of FX markets.

5.3. Active Currency Management Based on the Carry Trade

The **carry trade** is a trading strategy of borrowing in low-yield currencies and investing in high-yield currencies. The term "carry" is related to what is known as the cost of carry—that is, of carrying or holding an investment. This investment has either an implicit or explicit cost (borrowing cost) but may also produce income. The net cost of carry is the difference between these two return rates.

If technical analysis is based on ignoring economic fundamentals, then the carry trade is based on exploiting a well-recognized violation of one of the international parity conditions often used to describe these economic fundamentals: uncovered interest rate parity. Recall that uncovered interest rate parity asserts that, *on a longer-term average*, the return on an unhedged foreign-currency asset investment will be the same as a domestic-currency investment. Assuming that the base currency in the P/B quote is the low-yield currency, stated algebraically uncovered interest rate parity asserts that

$$\%\Delta S_{H/L} \approx i_H - i_L$$

where $\%\Delta S_{H/L}$ is the percentage change in the $S_{H/L}$ spot exchange rate (the low-yield currency is the base currency), i_H is the interest rate on the high-yield currency, and i_L is the interest rate on the low-yield currency. If uncovered interest rate parity holds, the yield spread *advantage* for the high-yielding currency (the right side of the equation) will, on average, be matched by the *depreciation* of the high-yield currency (the left side of the equation; the low-yield currency is the base currency and hence a positive value for $\%\Delta S_{H/L}$ means a depreciation of the high-yield currency). According to the uncovered interest rate parity theorem, it is this offset between (1) the yield advantage and (2) the currency depreciation that equates, on average, the unhedged currency returns.

But in reality, the historical data show that there are persistent deviations from uncovered interest rate parity in FX markets, at least in the short to medium term. Indeed, high-yield countries often see their currencies *appreciate*, not depreciate, for extended periods of time. The positive returns from a combination of a favorable yield differential plus an appreciating currency can remain in place long enough to present attractive investment opportunities.

This persistent violation of uncovered interest rate parity described by the carry trade is often referred to as the **forward rate bias**. An implication of uncovered interest rate parity is that the forward rate should be an unbiased predictor of future spot rates. The historical data, however, show that the forward rate is not the center of the distribution for future spot rates; in fact, it is a *biased* predictor (for example, see Kritzman 1999). Hence the name "forward rate bias." With the forward rate premium or discount defined as $F_{P/B} - S_{P/B}$ the "bias" in the forward rate bias is that the premium typically overstates the amount of appreciation of the base currency, and the discount overstates the amount of depreciation. Indeed, the forward discount or premium often gets even the *direction* of future spot rate movements wrong.

The carry trade strategy (borrowing in low-yield currencies, investing in high-yield currencies) is equivalent to a strategy based on trading the forward rate bias. Trading the forward rate bias involves buying currencies selling at a forward discount, and selling currencies trading at a forward premium. This makes intuitive sense: It is desirable to buy low and sell high.

To show the equivalence of the carry trade and trading the forward rate bias, recall that covered interest rate parity (which is enforced by arbitrage) is stated as

$$\frac{F_{P/B} - S_{P/B}}{S_{P/B}} = \frac{(i_P - i_B)\left(\frac{t}{360}\right)}{1 + i_B\left(\frac{t}{360}\right)}$$

This equation shows that when the base currency has a lower interest rate than the price currency (i.e., the right side of the equality is positive) the base currency will trade at a forward premium (the left side of the equality is positive). That is, being low-yield currency and trading at a forward premium is synonymous. Similarly, being a high-yield currency means trading at a forward discount. Borrowing in the low-yield currency and investing in the high-yield currency (the carry trade) is hence equivalent to selling currencies that have a forward premium and buying currencies that have a forward discount (trading the forward rate bias). We will return to these concepts in Section 6.1.2 when we discuss the roll yield in hedging with forward contracts. Exhibit 6 summarizes several key points about the carry trade.

EXHIBIT 6   The Carry Trade: A Summary

	Buy/Invest	Sell/Borrow
Implementing the carry trade	High-yield currency	Low-yield currency
Trading the forward rate bias	Forward discount currency	Forward premium currency

The gains that one can earn through the carry trade (or equivalently, through trading the forward rate bias) can be seen as the risk premiums earned for carrying an unhedged position—that is, for absorbing currency risk. (In efficient markets, there is no extra reward without extra risk.) Long periods of market stability can make these extra returns enticing to many investors, and the longer the yield differential persists between high-yield and low-yield currencies, the more carry trade positions will have a tendency to build up. But these high-yield currency advantages can be erased quickly, particularly if global financial markets are subject to sudden bouts of stress. This is especially true because the carry trade is a *leveraged* position: borrowing in the low-yielding currency and investing in the high-yielding currency.

These occasional large losses mean that the return distribution for the carry trade has a pronounced negative skew.

This negative skew derives from the fact that the **funding currencies** of the carry trade (the low-yield currencies in which borrowing occurs) are typically the safe haven currencies, such as the USD, CHF, and JPY. In contrast, the **investment currencies** (the high-yielding currencies) are typically currencies perceived to be higher risk, such as several emerging market currencies. Any time global financial markets are under stress there is a flight to safety that causes rapid movements in exchange rates, and usually a panicked unwinding of carry trades. As a result, traders running carry trades often get caught in losing positions, with the leverage involved magnifying their losses. Because of the tendency for long periods of relatively small gains in the carry trade to be followed by brief periods of large losses, the carry trade is sometimes characterized as "picking up nickels in front of a steamroller." One guide to the riskiness of the carry trade is the volatility of spot rate movements for the currency pair; all else equal, lower volatility is better for a carry trade position.

We close this section by noting that although the carry trade can be based on borrowing in a single funding currency and investing in a single high-yield currency, it is more common for carry trades to use multiple funding and investment currencies. The number of funding currencies and investment currencies need not be equal: for example, there could be five of one and three of the other. Sometimes the portfolio weighting of exposures between the various funding and investment currencies are simply set equal to each other. But the weights can also be optimized to reflect the trader's market view of the expected movements in each of the exchange rates, as well as their individual risks ($\sigma[\%\Delta S]$) and the expected correlations between movements in the currency pairs. These trades can be dynamically rebalanced, with the relative weights among both funding and investment currencies shifting with market conditions.

5.4. Active Currency Management Based on Volatility Trading

Another type of active trading style is unique to option markets and is known as volatility trading (or simply "vol trading").[14] To explain this trading style, we will start with a quick review of some option basics.

The derivatives of the option pricing model show the sensitivity of the option's premium to changes in the factors that determine option value. These derivatives are often referred to as the "Greeks" of option pricing. There is a very large number of first, second, third, and cross-derivatives that can be taken of an option pricing formula, but the two most important Greeks that we will consider here are the following:

- **Delta:** The sensitivity of the option premium to a small change in the price of the underlying[15] of the option, typically a financial asset. This sensitivity is an indication of *price* risk.
- **Vega:** The sensitivity of the option premium to a small change in implied volatility. This sensitivity is an indication of *volatility* risk.

---

[14]In principle, this trading style can be applied to all asset classes with options, not just FX trading. But FX options are the most liquid and widely traded options in the world, so it is in FX where most of volatility trading likely takes place in global financial markets.

[15]The underlying asset of a derivative is typically referred to simply as the "underlying."

The most important concept to grasp in terms of volatility trading is that the use of options allows the trader, through a variety of trading strategies, to *unbundle* and isolate all of the various risk factors (the Greeks) and trade them separately. Once an initial option position is taken (either long or short), the trader has exposure to *all* of the various Greeks/risk factors. The unwanted risk exposures, however, can then be hedged away, leaving *only* the desired risk exposure to express that specific directional view.

Delta hedging is the act of hedging away the option position's exposure to delta, the price risk of the underlying (the FX spot rate, in this case). Because delta shows the sensitivity of the option price to changes in the spot exchange rate, it thus defines the option's hedge ratio: The size of the offsetting hedge position that will set the *net* delta of the combined position (option plus delta hedge) to zero. Typically implementing this delta hedge is done using either forward contracts or a spot transaction (spot, by definition, has a delta of one, and no exposure to any other of the Greeks; forward contracts are highly correlated with the spot rate). For example, if a trader was long a call option on USD/EUR with a nominal value of EUR1 million and a delta of +0.5, the delta hedge would involve a short forward position in USD/EUR of EUR0.5 million. That is, the size of the delta hedge is equal to the option's delta times the nominal size of the contract. This hedge size would set the net delta of the overall position (option and forward) to zero.[16] Once the delta hedge has set the net delta of the position to zero, the trader then has exposure *only* to the other Greeks, and can use various trading strategies to position in these (long or short) depending on directional views.

Although one could theoretically trade *any* of the other Greeks, the most important one traded is vega; that is, the trader is expressing a view on the future movements in implied volatility, or in other words, is engaged in volatility trading. Implied volatility is not the same as realized, or observed, historical volatility, although it is heavily influenced by it. By engaging in volatility trading, the trader is expressing a view about the future volatility of exchange rates *but not their direction* (the delta hedge set the net delta of the position to zero).

One simple option strategy that implements a volatility trade is a **straddle**, which is a combination of both an at-the-money (ATM) put and an ATM call. A long straddle buys both of these options. Because their deltas are −0.5 and +0.5, respectively, the net delta of the position is zero; that is, the long straddle is delta neutral. This position is profitable in more volatile markets, when either the put or the call go sufficiently in the money to cover the up-front cost of the two option premiums paid. Similarly, a short straddle is a bet that the spot rate will stay relatively stable. In this case, the payout on any option exercise will be less than the twin premiums the seller has collected; the rest is net profit for the option seller. A similar option structure is a **strangle** position for which a long position is buying out-of-the-money (OTM) puts and calls with the same expiry date and the same degree of being out of the money (we elaborate more on this subject later). Because OTM options are being bought, the cost of the position is cheaper—but conversely, it also does not pay off until the spot rate passes the OTM strike levels. As a result, the risk–reward for a strangle is more moderate than that for a straddle.

The interesting thing to note is that by using delta-neutral trading strategies, volatility is turned into a product that can be actively traded like any other financial product or asset class, such as equities, commodities, fixed-income products, and so on. Volatility is not constant nor are its movements completely random. Instead volatility is determined by a wide variety

---

[16]Strictly speaking, the net delta would be *approximately* equal to zero because forward contracts do not have identical price properties to those of the spot exchange rate. But it is close enough for our purposes here, and we will ignore this small difference.

of underlying factors—both fundamental and technical—that the trader can express an opinion on. Movements in volatility are cyclical, and typically subject to long periods of relative stability punctuated by sharp upward spikes in volatility as markets come under periodic bouts of stress (usually the result of some dramatic event, financial or otherwise). Speculative vol traders—for example, among currency overlay managers—often want to be net-short volatility. The reason is because most options expire out of the money, and the option writer then gets to keep the option premium without delivery of the underlying currency pair. The amount of the option premium can be considered the risk premium, or payment, earned by the option writer for absorbing volatility risk. It is a steady source of income under "normal" market conditions. Ideally, these traders would want to "flip" their position and be long volatility ahead of volatility spikes, but these episodes can be notoriously difficult to time. Most hedgers typically run options positions that are net-long volatility because they are buying protection from unanticipated price volatility. (Being long the option means being exposed to the time decay of the option's time value; that is similar to paying insurance premiums for the protection against exchange rate volatility.)

We can also note that just as there are *currency overlay* programs for actively trading the portfolio's currency exposures (as discussed in Section 4.4.4) there can also be *volatility overlay* programs for actively trading the portfolio's exposures to movements in currencies' implied volatility. Just as currency overlay programs manage the portfolio's exposure to currency delta (movements in spot exchange rates), volatility overlay programs manage the portfolio's exposure to currency vega. These volatility overlay programs can be focused on earning speculative profits, but can also be used to hedge the portfolio against risk (we will return to this concept in the discussion of macro hedges in Section 6.4.2).

Enumerating all the potential strategies for trading foreign exchange volatility is beyond the scope of this chapter. Instead, the reader should be aware that this dimension of trading FX volatility (not price) exists and sees a large amount of active trading. Moreover, the best traders are able to think and trade in both dimensions simultaneously. Movements in volatility are often correlated with directional movements in the price of the underlying. For example, when there is a flight to safety as carry trades unwind, there is typically a spike in volatility (and options prices) at the same time. Although pure vol trading is based on a zero-delta position, this need not always be the case; a trader can express a market opinion on volatility (vega exposure) and still have a directional exposure to the underlying spot exchange rate as well (delta exposure). That is, the overall trading position has net vega and delta exposures that reflect the *joint* market view.

We end this section by explaining how currency options are quoted in professional FX markets. (This information will be used in Section 6 when we discuss other option trading strategies.) Unlike exchanged-traded options, such as those used in equity markets, OTC options for currencies are not described in terms of specific strike levels (i.e., exchange rate levels). Instead, in the interdealer market, options are described in terms of their "delta." Deltas for puts can range from a minimum of −1 to a maximum of 0, with a delta of −0.5 being the point at which the put option is ATM; OTM puts have deltas between 0 and −0.5. For call options, delta ranges from 0 to +1, with 0.5 being the ATM point. In FX markets, these delta values are quoted both in *absolute* terms (i.e., in positive rather than negative values) and as percentages, with standard FX option quotes usually in terms of 25-delta and 10-delta options (i.e., a delta of 0.25 and 0.10, respectively; the 10-delta option is deeper OTM and hence cheaper than the 25-delta option). The FX options market is the most liquid around these standard delta quoting points (ATM, 25-delta, 10-delta), but of course, as a flexible OTC market, options of any delta/strike price can be traded. The 25-delta put option (for example) will still go in the money if the spot price dips below a *specific* exchange rate level; this *implied* strike price is *backed out* of an option pricing model once all the other pricing factors, including the current spot rate and the 25-delta of the option, are put into the option pricing model. (The specific option pricing model used is agreed on by both parties to the trade.)

These standard delta price points are often used to define option trading strategies. For example, a 25-delta strangle would be based on 25-delta put and call options. Similarly, a 10-delta strangle would be based on 10-delta options (and would cost less and have a more moderate payoff structure than a 25-delta strangle). Labeling option structures by their delta is common in FX markets.

EXAMPLE 3   Active Strategies

Annie McYelland works as an analyst at Scotland-based Kilmarnock Advisors, an investment firm that offers several investment vehicles for its clients. McYelland has been put in charge of formulating the firm's market views for some of the foreign currencies that these vehicles have exposures to. Her market views will be used to guide the hedging and discretionary positioning for some of the actively managed portfolios.

McYelland begins by examining yield spreads between various countries and the implied volatility extracted from the option pricing for several currency pairs. She collects the following data:

One-Year Yield Levels	
Switzerland	0.103%
United States	0.162%
Poland	4.753%
Mexico	4.550%
One-Year Implied Volatility	
PLN/CHF	8.4%
MXN/CHF	15.6%
PLN/USD	20.3%
MXN/USD	16.2%

Note: PLN = Polish zloty; the Swiss yields are negative because of Swiss policy actions.

McYelland is also examining various economic indicators to shape her market views. After studying the economic prospects for both Japan and New Zealand, she expects that the inflation rate for New Zealand is about to accelerate over the next few years, whereas the inflation rate for Japan should remain relatively stable. Turning her attention to the economic situation in India, McYelland believes that the Indian authorities are about to tighten monetary policy, and that this change has not been fully priced into the market. She reconsiders her short-term view for the Indian rupee (i.e., the INR/USD spot rate) after conducting this analysis.

McYelland also examines the exchange rate volatility for several currency pairs to which the investment trusts are exposed. Based on her analysis of the situation, she believes that the exchange rate between Chilean peso and the US dollar (CLP/USD) is about to become much more volatile than usual, although she has no strong views about whether the CLP will appreciate or depreciate.

One of McYelland's colleagues, Catalina Ortega, is a market technician and offers to help McYelland time her various market position entry and exit points based on chart patterns. While examining the JPY/NZD price chart, Ortega notices that the 200-day moving average is at 62.0405 and the current spot rate is 62.0315.

1. Based on the data she collected, all else equal, McYelland's *best* option for implementing a carry trade position would be to fund in:
   A. USD and invest in PLN.
   B. CHF and invest in MXN.
   C. CHF and invest in PLN.

2. Based on McYelland's inflation forecasts, all else equal, she would be *more likely* to expect a(n):
   A. depreciation in the JPY/NZD.
   B. increase in capital flows from Japan to New Zealand.
   C. more accommodative monetary policy by the Reserve Bank of New Zealand.

3. Given her analysis for India, McYelland's short-term market view for the INR/USD spot rate is now *most likely* to be:
   A. biased toward appreciation.
   B. biased toward depreciation.
   C. unchanged because it is only a short-run view.

4. Using CLP/USD options, what would be the *cheapest* way for McYelland to implement her market view for the CLP?
   A. Buy a straddle
   B. Buy a 25-delta strangle
   C. Sell a 40-delta strangle

5. Based on Ortega's analysis, she would *most likely* expect:
   A. support near 62.0400.
   B. resistance near 62.0310.
   C. resistance near 62.0400.

Solution to 1: C is correct. The yield spread between the funding and investment currencies is the widest and the implied volatility (risk) is the lowest. The other choices have a narrower yield spread and higher risk (implied volatility).

Solution to 2: A is correct. All else equal, an increase in New Zealand's inflation rate will decrease its real interest rate and lead to the real interest rate differential favoring Japan over New Zealand. This would likely result in a depreciation of the JPY/NZD rate over time. The shift in the relative real returns should lead to reduced capital flows from Japan to New Zealand (so Choice B is incorrect) and the RBNZ—New Zealand's central bank—is more likely to tighten monetary policy than loosen it as inflation picks up (so Choice C is incorrect).

Solution to 3: B is correct. Tighter monetary policy in India should lead to higher real interest rates (at least in the short run). This increase will cause the INR to appreciate against the USD, but because the USD is the base currency, this will be represented as depreciation in the INR/USD rate. Choice C is incorrect because a tightening of monetary policy that is not fully priced-in to market pricing is likely to move bond yields and hence the exchange rate in the short run (given the simple economic model in Section 5.1).

Solution to 4: B is correct. Either a long straddle or a long strangle will profit from a marked increase in volatility in the spot rate, but a 25-delta strangle would be cheaper (because it is based on OTM options). Writing a strangle—particularly one that is close to being ATM, which is what a 40-delta structure is—is likely to be exercised in favor of the counterparty if McYelland's market view is correct.

Solution to 5: C is correct. The 200-day moving average has not been crossed yet, and it is higher than the current spot rate. Hence this technical indicator suggests that resistance lies above the current spot rate level, likely in the 62.0400 area. Choice A is incorrect because the currency has not yet appreciated to 62.0400, so it cannot be considered a "support" level. Given that the currency pair has already traded through 62.0310 and is still at least 90 pips away from the 200-day moving average, it is more likely to suspect that resistance still lies above the current spot rate.

6. TOOLS OF CURRENCY MANAGEMENT

In this section, we focus on how the portfolio manager uses financial derivatives to implement both the *strategic* positioning of the portfolio along the risk spectrum (i.e., the performance benchmark) as well as the *tactical* decisions made in regard to variations around this "neutral" position. The manager's market view—whether based on carry, fundamental, currency volatility, or technical considerations—leads to this active management of risk positioning around the strategic benchmark point. Implementing both strategic and tactical viewpoints requires the use of trading tools, which we discuss in this section.

The balance of this chapter will assume that the portfolio's strategic foreign-currency asset exposures and the maximum amount of currency risk desired have already been determined by the portfolio's IPS. We begin at the conservative end of the risk spectrum by describing a passive hedge for a single currency (with a 100% hedge ratio). After discussing the costs and limitations of this approach, we move out further along the risk spectrum by describing strategies in which the basic "building blocks" of financial derivatives can be combined to implement the manager's tactical positioning and construct much more customized risk–return profiles. Not surprisingly, the basic trading tools themselves—forwards, options, FX swaps— are used for both strategic and tactical risk management and by both hedgers and speculators alike (although for different ends). Note that the instruments covered as tools of currency management are not nearly an exhaustive list. For example, exchange-traded funds for currencies are a vehicle that can be useful in managing currency risk.

6.1. Forward Contracts

In this section, we consider the most basic form of hedging: a 100% hedge ratio for a single foreign-currency exposure. Futures or forward contracts on currencies can be used to obtain full currency hedges, although most institutional investors prefer to use forward contracts for the following reasons:

1. Futures contracts are standardized in terms of settlement dates and contract sizes. These may not correspond to the portfolio's investment parameters.
2. Futures contracts may not always be available in the currency pair that the portfolio manager wants to hedge. For example, the most liquid currency futures contracts trade on the Chicago Mercantile Exchange (CME). Although there are CME futures contracts for all major exchange rates (e.g., USD/EUR, USD/GBP) and many cross rates (e.g., CAD/EUR, JPY/CHF), there are not contracts available for all possible currency pairs. Trading these cross rates would need multiple futures contracts, adding to portfolio management costs. In addition, many of the "second tier" emerging market currencies may not have liquid futures contracts available against any currency, let alone the currency pair in which the portfolio manager is interested.
3. Futures contracts require up-front margin (initial margin). They also have intra-period cash flow implications, in that the exchange will require the investor to post additional variation margin when the spot exchange rate moves against the investor's position. These initial and ongoing margin requirements tie up the investor's capital and require careful monitoring through time, adding to the portfolio management expense. Likewise, margin flows can go in the investor's favor, requiring monitoring and reinvestment.

In contrast, forward contracts do not suffer from any of these drawbacks. Major global investment dealers (such as Deutsche Bank, Royal Bank of Scotland, UBS, etc.) will quote prices on forward contracts for practically every possible currency pair, settlement date, and transaction amount. They typically do not require margin to be posted or maintained.

Moreover, the daily trade volume globally for OTC currency forward and swap contracts dwarfs that for exchange-traded currency futures contracts; that is, forward contracts are more liquid than futures for trading in large sizes. Reflecting this liquidity, forward contracts are the predominant hedging instrument in use globally. For the balance of this section, we will focus only on currency forward contracts. However, separate side boxes discuss exchange-traded currency futures contracts and currency-based exchange-traded funds (ETFs).

6.1.1. Hedge Ratios with Forward Contracts

In principle, setting up a full currency hedge is relatively straightforward: match the current market value of the foreign-currency exposure in the portfolio with an equal and offsetting position in a forward contract. In practice, of course, it is not that simple because the market value of the foreign-currency assets will change with market conditions. This means that the actual hedge ratio will typically *drift* away from the desired hedge ratio as market conditions change. A **static hedge** (i.e., unchanging hedge) will avoid transaction costs, but will also tend to accumulate unwanted currency exposures as the value of the foreign-currency assets change. This characteristic will cause a mismatch between the market value of the foreign-currency asset portfolio and the nominal size of the forward contract used for the currency hedge; this is pure currency risk. For this reason, the portfolio manager will typically need to implement a **dynamic hedge** by rebalancing the portfolio periodically. This hedge rebalancing will mean adjusting some combination of the size, number, and maturities of the forward currency contracts.

A simple example will illustrate this rebalancing process. Suppose that an investor domiciled in Switzerland has a EUR-denominated portfolio that, at the start of the period, is worth EUR1,000,000. Assume a monthly hedge-rebalancing cycle. To hedge this portfolio, the investor would sell EUR1,000,000 one month forward against the CHF. Assume that one month later, the EUR-denominated investment portfolio is then actually worth only EUR950,000. To roll the hedge forward for the next month, the investor will engage in a mismatched FX swap. (Recall that a "matched" swap means that both the spot and forward transactions—the near and far "legs" of the swap, respectively—are of equal size). For the near leg of the swap, EUR1 million will be bought at spot to settle the expiring forward contract. (The euro amounts will then net to zero, but a Swiss franc cash flow will be generated, either a loss or a gain for the investor, depending on how the CHF/EUR rate has changed over the month). For the far leg of the swap, the investor will sell EUR950,000 forward for one month.

Another way to view this rebalancing process is to consider the case in which the original short forward contract has a three-month maturity. In this case, rebalancing after one month would mean that the manager would have to *buy* 50,000 CHF/EUR two months forward. There is no cash flow at the time this second forward contract is entered, but the *net* amount of euro for delivery at contract settlement two months into the future is now the euro hedge amount desired (i.e., EUR950,000). There will be a net cash flow (denominated in CHF) calculated over these two forward contracts on the settlement date two months hence.

Although rebalancing a dynamic hedge will keep the actual hedge ratio close to the target hedge ratio, it will also lead to increased transaction costs compared with a static hedge. The manager will have to assess the cost–benefit trade-offs of how frequently to dynamically rebalance the hedge. These will depend on a variety of idiosyncratic factors (manager risk aversion, market view, IPS guidelines, etc.), and so there is no single "correct" answer— different managers will likely make different decisions.

However, we can observe that the higher the degree of risk aversion, the more frequently the hedge is likely to be rebalanced back to the "neutral" hedge ratio. Similarly, the greater the tolerance for active trading, and the stronger the commitment to a particular market view, the more likely it is that the actual hedge ratio will be allowed to vary from a "neutral" setting, possibly through entering into new forward contracts. (For example, if the P/B spot rate was seen to be oversold and likely to rebound higher, an actively traded portfolio might buy the base currency through forward contracts to lock in this perceived low price—and thus change the actual hedge ratio accordingly.) The sidebar on executing a hedge illustrates the concepts of rolling hedges, FX swaps and their pricing (bid–offer), and adjusting hedges for market views and changes in market values.

Executing a Hedge

Jiao Yang works at Hong Kong SAR-based Kwun Tong Investment Advisors; its reporting currency is the Hong Kong Dollar (HKD). She has been put in charge of managing the firm's foreign-currency hedges. Forward contracts for two of these hedges are coming due for settlement, and Yang will need to use FX swaps to roll these hedges forward three months.

Hedge #1: Kwun Tong has a short position of JPY800,000,000 coming due on a JPY/HKD forward contract. The market value of the underlying foreign-currency assets has not changed over the life of the contract, and Yang does not have a firm opinion on the expected future movement in the JPY/HKD spot rate.

Hedge #2: Kwun Tong has a short position of EUR8,000,000 coming due on a HKD/EUR forward contract. The market value of the EUR-denominated assets has increased (measured in EUR). Yang expects the HKD/EUR spot rate to decrease.

The following spot exchange rates and three-month forward points are in effect when Yang transacts the FX swaps necessary to roll the hedges forward:

	Spot Rate	Three-Month Forward Points
JPY/HKD	10.80/10.82	−20/−14
HKD/EUR	10.0200/10.0210	125/135

Note: The JPY/HKD forward points will be scaled by 100; the HKD/EUR forward points will be scaled by 10,000.

As a result, Yang undertakes the following transactions:

For **Hedge #1**, the foreign-currency value of the underlying assets has not changed, and she does not have a market view that would lead her to want to either over- or under-hedge the foreign-currency exposure. Therefore, to roll these hedges forward, she uses a matched swap. For matched swaps (see Section 2.3), the convention is to base pricing on the mid-market spot exchange rate. Thus, the spot leg of the swap would be to buy JPY800,000,000 at the mid-market rate of 10.81 JPY/HKD. The forward leg of the swap would require selling JPY800,000,000 forward three months. Selling JPY (the price currency in the JPY/HKD quote) is equivalent to buying HKD (the base currency). Therefore, she uses the offer-side forward points, and the all-in forward rate for the forward leg of the swap is as follows:

$$10.81 + \frac{-14}{100} = 10.67$$

For **Hedge #2**, the foreign-currency value of the underlying assets has increased; Yang recognizes that this implies that she should increase the size of the hedge greater than EUR8,000,000. She also believes that the HKD/EUR spot rate will decrease, and recognizes that this implies a hedge ratio of more than 100% (Kwun Tong Advisors has given her discretion to over- or under-hedge based on her market views). This too means that the size of the hedge should be increased more than EUR8,000,000, because Yang will want a larger short position in the EUR to take advantage of its expected depreciation. Hence, Yang uses a mismatched swap, buying EUR8,000,000 at spot rate against the HKD, to settle the maturing forward contract and then *selling* an amount *more* than EUR8,000,000 forward to increase the hedge size. Because the EUR is the base currency in the HKD/EUR quote, this means using the *bid* side for both the spot rate and the forward points when calculating the all-in forward rate:

$$10.0200 + \frac{125}{10,000} = 10.0325$$

The spot leg of the swap—buying back EUR8,000,000 to settle the outstanding forward transaction—is also based on the bid rate of 10.0200. This is because Yang is selling an amount larger than EUR8,000,000 forward, and the all-in forward rate of the swap is already using the bid side of the market (as it would for a matched swap). Hence, to pick up the net increase in forward EUR sales, the dealer Yang is transacting with would price the swap so that Yang also has to use bid side of the *spot* quote for the spot transaction used to settle the maturing forward contract.

6.1.2. Roll Yield

The roll yield (also called the roll return) on a hedge results from the fact that forward contracts are priced at the spot rate adjusted for the number of forward points at that maturity (see the example shown in Exhibit 3). This forward point adjustment can either benefit or detract from portfolio returns (positive and negative roll yield, respectively) depending on whether the forward points are at a premium or discount, and what side of the market (buying or selling) the portfolio manager is on.

The concept of roll yield is illustrated with the simplified example shown in Exhibit 7.

EXHIBIT 7   The Forward Curve and Roll Yield

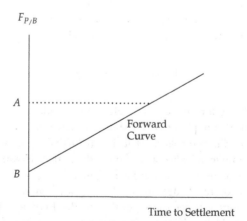

The magnitude of roll yield is given by $|(F_{P/B} - S_{P/B})/S_{P/B}|$ where "||" indicates absolute value. The sign depends on whether the investor needs to buy or to sell the base currency forward in order to maintain the hedge. A *positive* roll yield results from buying the base currency at a forward discount or selling it at a forward premium (the intuition here is that it is profitable to "buy low and sell high"). Otherwise, the roll yield is negative (i.e., a positive cost). Examining the case of negative roll yield, assume that to implement the hedge requires buying the base currency in the P/B quote, and that the base currency is trading at a forward premium (as shown in Exhibit 7). By using a long position in a forward contract to implement this hedge, it means paying the forward price of A. All else equal, as time passes the price of the forward contract will "roll down the curve" toward Price B as the forward contract's settlement date approaches. (Note that in reality the curve is not always linear.) At the settlement date of the forward contract, it is necessary to roll the hedging position forward to extend the currency hedge. This rolling forward will involve selling the base currency at the then-current spot exchange rate to settle the forward contract, and then going long another far-dated forward contract (i.e., an FX swap transaction). Note that the portfolio manager originally bought the base currency at Price A and then subsequently sold it at a lower Price B —and that buying high and selling low will be a cost to the portfolio. Or put differently, all else equal, the roll yield would be negative in this case. Note that the "all else equal" caveat refers to the fact that the all-in price of the forward contract consists of the spot rate and forward points, and both are likely to change over the life of the forward contract. It is possible that at the settlement date the spot rate would have moved higher than A, in which case the roll yield would be positive. But the larger the gap between A and B at contract initiation, the less likely this is to occur.

The concept of roll yield is very similar to the concept of forward rate bias (and the carry trade) introduced in Section 5. Indeed, a negative roll yield typically indicates that the hedger was trading *against* the forward rate bias by buying a currency at a forward premium (as in Exhibit 7) or selling a currency at a forward discount. This is the exact opposite of trading the forward rate bias, which is to buy at a discount and sell at a premium. Given the equivalence between the forward rate bias and the carry trade, by trading against the forward rate bias the hedger with a negative roll yield is also essentially entering into *negative* carry trade, in effect borrowing at high rates and investing at low rates. On average, this will not be a winning strategy. Given the equivalence between implementing a carry trade, trading the forward rate bias, and earning positive roll yield, we can now complete Exhibit 6 introduced in Section 5.3 on the carry trade:

EXHIBIT 8   The Carry Trade and Roll Yield

	Buy/Invest	**Sell/Borrow**	
Implementing the carry trade	High-yield currency	Low-yield currency	Earning a positive roll yield
Trading the forward rate bias	Forward discount currency	Forward premium currency	

Note as well that this concept of roll yield applies to forward and futures contracts used to trade *any* asset class, not just currencies: It applies equally well to forwards and futures on equities, fixed-income securities, commodities, and indeed, any financial product. For example, consider the case of a commodity processor that hedges the costs of its production process by going long corn futures contracts. If the futures curve for corn futures contracts is in contango (upward sloping, as in Exhibit 7), then this hedging position will also face the potential for negative roll yield.

To be fair, it is also possible for the level of, and movement in, forward points to be in the portfolio manager's favor. Extending our previous example, consider the case of a portfolio manager that has to *sell* the base currency to implement the currency hedge. In this case, the manager would be selling the base currency forward at Price A in Exhibit 7 and, all else equal and through entering an FX swap at settlement date, buying the currency back at the lower Price B—essentially, short selling a financial product with a declining price. In this case, the roll yield is positive.

Because the level of and movements in forward points can either enhance or reduce currency-hedged returns, it explains an observed tendency in foreign exchange markets for the amount of currency hedging to generally vary with movements in forward points. As forward points move against the hedger, the amount of hedging activity typically declines as the cost/benefit ratio of the currency hedge deteriorates. The opposite occurs when movements in forward points reduce hedging costs. Essentially the tendency to hedge will vary depending on whether implementing the hedge happens to be trading in the same direction of the forward rate bias strategy or against it. It is easier to sell a currency forward if there is a "cushion" when it is selling at a forward premium. Likewise, it is more attractive to buy a currency when it is trading at a forward discount. This swings the forward rate bias (and carry trade advantage) in favor of the hedge.

Combined with the manager's market view of future spot rate movements, what this concept implies is that, when setting the hedge ratio, the portfolio manager must balance the effect of expected future exchange rate movements on portfolio returns against the expected effect of the roll yield (i.e., the expected cost of the hedge).

A simple example can illustrate this effect. Consider a portfolio manager that needs to sell forward the base currency of a currency pair (P/B) to implement a currency hedge. Clearly, the manager would prefer to sell this currency at as high a price as possible. Assume that given the forward points for this currency pair and the time horizon for the hedge, the expected roll yield (cost of the hedge) is −3%. Suppose the portfolio manager had a market view that the base currency would depreciate by 4%. In this case, the hedge makes sense: It is better to pay 3% for the hedge to avoid an expected 4% loss.

Now, suppose that with a movement in forward points the new forward discount on the base currency is 6% away from the current spot rate. If the manager's market view is unchanged (an expected depreciation of the base currency of 4%), then now the use of the hedge is less clear: Does it make sense to pay 6% for the hedge to avoid an expected 4% loss? A *risk-neutral* manager would not hedge under these circumstances because the net expected value of the hedge is negative. But a *risk-averse* manager might still implement the hedge regardless of the negative net expected value. The reason is because it is possible that the market forecast is wrong and that the *actual* depreciation of the base currency (and realized loss to the portfolio) may be higher than the 6% cost of the hedge. The risk-averse manager must then weigh the *certainty* of a hedge that costs 6% against the *risk* that actual unhedged currency losses might be much higher than that.

Clearly, the cost/benefit analysis has shifted against hedging in this case, but many risk-averse investors would still undertake the hedge anyway. The risk-averse manager would likely only take an unhedged currency position if the difference between the expected cost of the hedge and the expected return on an unhedged position was so great as to make the risk acceptable. Balancing these two considerations would depend on the type of market view the manager held and the degree of conviction in it, as well as the manager's degree of risk aversion. The decision taken will vary among investors, so no definitive answer can be given as to what would be the appropriate hedging choice (different portfolio managers will make different choices given the same opportunity set). But hedging costs will vary with market conditions and the higher the expected cost of the hedge (negative roll yield) the more the cost/benefit calculation moves against using a fully hedged position. Or put another way, if setting up the hedge involves selling the low-yield currency and buying the high-yield currency in the P/B pair (i.e., an implicit carry position), then the more likely the portfolio will be fully hedged or even over-hedged. The opposite is also true: Trading against the forward rate bias is likely to lead to lower hedge ratios, all else equal.

EXAMPLE 4   The Hedging Decision

The reporting currency of Hong Kong SAR-based Kwun Tong Investment Advisors is the Hong Kong dollar (HKD). The investment committee is examining whether it should implement a currency hedge for the firm's exposures to the GBP and the ZAR (the firm has long exposures to both of these foreign currencies). The hedge would use forward contracts. The following data relevant to assessing the expected cost of the hedge and the expected move in the spot exchange rate has been developed by the firm's market strategist.

	Current Spot Rate	Six-Month Forward Rate	Six-Month Forecast Spot Rate
HKD/GBP	12.4610	12.6550	12.3000
HKD/ZAR	0.9510	0.9275	0.9300

1. Recommend whether to hedge the firm's long GBP exposure. Justify your recommendation.
2. Discuss the trade-offs in hedging the firm's long ZAR exposure.

Solution to 1: Kwun Tong is long the GBP against the HKD, and HKD/GBP is selling at a forward premium of +1.6% compared with the current spot rate. All else equal, this is the expected roll yield—which is in the firm's favor, in this case, because to implement the hedge Kwun Tong would be *selling* GBP, the base currency in the quote, at a price *higher* than the current spot rate. Moreover, the firm's market strategist expects the GBP to *depreciate* by 1.3% against the HKD. Both of these considerations argue for hedging this exposure.

Solution to 2: Kwun Tong is long the ZAR against the HKD, and HKD/ZAR is selling at a forward discount of −2.5% compared with the current spot rate. Implementing the hedge would require the firm to *sell* the base currency in the quote, the ZAR, at a price *lower* than the current spot rate. This would imply that, all else equal, the roll yield would go against the firm; that is, the expected cost of the hedge would be 2.5%. But the firm's strategist also forecasts that the ZAR will depreciate against the HKD by 2.2%. This makes the decision to hedge less certain. A risk-neutral investor would not hedge because the expected cost of the hedge is more than the expected depreciation of the ZAR. But this is only a point forecast and comes with a degree of uncertainty— there is a risk that the HKD/ZAR spot rate might depreciate by more than the 2.5% cost of the hedge. In this case, the decision to hedge the currency risk would depend on the trade-offs between (1) the level of risk aversion of the firm; and (2) the conviction the firm held in the currency forecast—that is, the level of certainty that the ZAR would not depreciate by more than 2.5%.

6.2. Currency Options

One of the costs of forward contracts is the opportunity cost. Once fully hedged, the portfolio manager forgoes any upside potential for future currency moves in the portfolio's favor. Currency options remove this opportunity cost because they provide the manager the right, but not the obligation, to buy or sell foreign exchange at a future date at a rate agreed on today. The manager will only exercise the option at the expiry date if it is favorable to do so.[17]

Consider the case of a portfolio manager who is long the base currency in the P/B quote and needs to sell this currency to implement the hedge. One approach is to simply buy an at-the-money put option on the P/B currency pair. Matching a long position in the underlying with a put option is known as a **protective put** strategy. Suppose the current spot rate is 1.3650 and the strike price on the put option bought is 1.3650. If the P/B rate subsequently goes down (P appreciates and B depreciates) by the expiry date, the manager can exercise the option, implement the hedge, and guarantee a selling price of 1.3650. But if the P/B rate increases (P depreciates and B appreciates), the manager can simply let the option expire and collect the currency gains.

Unfortunately, like forward contracts, currency options are not "free goods" and, like any form of insurance, there is always a price to be paid for it. Buying an option means paying an up-front premium. This premium is determined, first, by its **intrinsic value**, which is the difference between the spot exchange rate and the strike price of the option (i.e., whether the option is in the money, at the money, or out of the money, respectively). ATM options are more expensive than OTM options, and frequently these relatively expensive options expire without being exercised.

The second determinant of an option's premium is its **time value**, which in turn is heavily influenced by the volatility in exchange rates. Regardless of exchange rate volatility, however, options are always moving toward expiry. In general, the time value of the option is always declining. This is the time decay of the option's value (theta, one of the "Greeks" of option prices, describes this effect) and is similar in concept to that of negative roll yield on forward contracts described earlier. Time decay always works against the owner of an option.

---

[17]Almost all options in the FX market are European-style options, which only allow for exercise at the expiry date.

As with forward contracts, a portfolio manager will have to make judgments about the cost/benefit trade-offs of options-based strategies. Although options do allow the portfolio upside potential from favorable currency movements, options can also be a very expensive form of insurance. The manager will have to balance any market view of potential currency gains against hedging costs and the degree of risk aversion. There is no "right" answer; different managers will make different decisions about the cost/benefit trade-offs when given the same opportunity set.

EXAMPLE 5   Hedging Problems

Brixworth & St. Ives Asset Management is a UK-based firm managing a dynamic hedging program for the currency exposures in its Aggressive Growth Fund. One of the fund's foreign-currency asset holdings is denominated in the Mexican peso (MXN), and one month ago Brixworth & St. Ives fully hedged this exposure using a two-month MXN/GBP forward contract. The following table provides the relevant information.

	One Month Ago	Today
Value of assets (in MXN)	10,000,000	9,500,000
MXN/GBP spot rate (bid–offer)	20.0500/20.0580	19.5985/20.0065
One-month forward points (bid–offer)	625/640	650/665
Two-month forward points (bid–offer)	875/900	900/950

The Aggressive Growth Fund also has an unhedged foreign-currency asset exposure denominated in the South African rand (ZAR). The current mid-market spot rate in the ZAR/GBP currency pair is 5.1050.

1. One month ago, Brixworth & St. Ives *most likely* sold:
   A. MXN9,500,000 forward at an all-in forward rate of MXN/GBP 19.6635.
   B. MXN10,000,000 forward at an all-in forward rate of MXN/GBP 20.1375.
   C. MXN10,000,000 forward at an all-in forward rate of MXN/GBP 20.1480.

2. To rebalance the hedge today, the firm would *most likely* need to:
   A. buy MXN500,000 spot.
   B. buy MXN500,000 forward.
   C. sell MXN500,000 forward.

3. Given the data in the table, the roll yield on this hedge at the forward contracts' maturity date is *most likely* to be:
   A. zero.
   B. negative.
   C. positive.

4. Assuming that all ZAR/GBP options considered have the same notional amount and maturity, the *most* expensive hedge that Brixworth & St. Ives could use to hedge its ZAR exposure is a long position in a(n):
    A. ATM call.
    B. 25-delta call.
    C. put with a strike of 5.1050.

Solution to 1: C is correct. Brixworth & St. Ives is long the MXN and hence must sell the MXN forward against the GBP. Selling MXN against the GBP means buying GBP, the base currency in the MXN/GBP quote. Therefore, the offer side of the market must be used. This means the all-in rate used one month ago would have been 20.0580 + 900/10,000, which equals 20.1480. Choice A is incorrect because it uses today's asset value and the bid side of the spot and one-month forward quotes and Choice B is incorrect because it uses the wrong side of the market (the bid side).

Solution to 2: B is correct. The foreign investment went down in value in MXN terms. Therefore Brixworth & St. Ives must reduce the size of the hedge. Previously it had sold MXN10,000,000 forward against the GBP, and this amount must be reduced to MXN9,500,000 by buying MXN500,000 forward. Choice A is incorrect because hedging is done with forward contracts not spot deals. Choice C is incorrect because selling MXN forward would increase the size of the hedge, not decrease it.

Solution to 3: B is correct. To implement the hedge, Brixworth & St. Ives must sell MXN against the GBP, or equivalently, buy GBP (the base currency in the P/B quote) against the MXN. The base currency is selling forward at a premium, and—all else equal—its price would "roll down the curve" as contract maturity approached. Having to settle the forward contract means then selling the GBP spot at a lower price. Buying high and selling low will define a negative roll yield. Moreover, the GBP has depreciated against the MXN, because the MXN/GBP spot rate declined between one month ago and now, which will also add to the negative roll yield.

Solution to 4: A is correct. The Aggressive Growth Fund is long the ZAR through its foreign-currency assets, and to hedge this exposure it must sell the ZAR against the GBP, or equivalently, buy GBP—the base currency in the P/B quote—against the ZAR. Hedging a required purchase means a long position in a call option (not a put, which is used to hedge a required sale of the base currency in the P/B quote). An ATM call option is more expensive than a 25-delta call option.

6.3. Strategies to Reduce Hedging Costs and Modify a Portfolio's Risk Profile

In the previous sections, we showed that completely hedging currency risk is possible—but can also be expensive. It can be even more expensive when trying to avoid all downside risk while keeping the full upside potential for favorable currency movements (i.e., a protective put strategy with ATM options). Hedging can be seen as a form of insurance, but it is possible to overpay for insurance. Judgments have to be made to determine at what point the costs outweigh the benefits.

As with any form of insurance, there are always steps that can be taken to reduce hedging costs. For most typical insurance products, these cost-reduction measures include such things as higher deductibles, co-pay arrangements, and lower maximum payouts. The same sorts of measures exist in the FX derivatives market; we will explore these various alterative measures in this section. The key point to keep in mind is that all of these various cost-reduction measures invariably involve some combination of *less downside protection* and/or *less upside potential* for the hedge. In efficient markets, lower insurance premiums mean lower insurance.

These cost-reduction measures also start moving the portfolio away from a passively managed 100% hedge ratio toward discretionary hedging in which the manager is allowed to take directional positions. Once the possibility of accepting some downside risk, and some upside potential, is introduced into the portfolio, the manager is moving away from a rules-based approach to hedging toward a more active style of trading. The portfolio manager can then use the trading tools and strategies described in the following sections to express a market view and/or cut hedging costs.

The variety of trading strategies—involving various combinations of forwards, options, and swaps—that can be deployed to this end is almost infinite. We will not attempt to explore all of them in this chapter, but rather to give a sense of the range of trading tools and strategies available for managing currency risk. We begin with Exhibit 9, which gives a high-level description of some of these various trading strategies that will then be explained in more detail in subsequent sections. Note that as this section progresses, we will be describing strategies at different points along the risk spectrum described in Section 4, moving in turn from passive hedge-based approaches to strategies used in more active currency management schemes.

EXHIBIT 9   Select Currency Management Strategies

Forward Contracts	Over-/under-hedging	Profit from market view
Option Contracts	OTM options	Cheaper than ATM
	Risk reversals	Write options to earn premiums
	Put/call spreads	Write options to earn premiums
	Seagull spreads	Write options to earn premiums
Exotic Options	Knock-in/out features	Reduced downside/upside exposure
	Digital options	Extreme payoff strategies

We will make one simplifying assumption for the following sections. Currency management strategies will differ fundamentally depending on whether the base currency of the P/B price quote must be bought or sold to decrease the foreign-currency exposure. To simplify the material and impose consistency on the discussions that follow, we will assume that the portfolio manager must sell the base currency in the P/B quote to reduce currency risk. In addition, unless otherwise noted, the notional amounts and expiration dates on all forward and options contracts are the same.[18]

---

[18]Examples of implementing a hedge by *buying* the base currency will be provided in some of the practice examples.

6.3.1. Over-/Under-Hedging Using Forward Contracts

When the IPS gives the manager discretion either to over- or under-hedge the portfolio, relative to the "neutral" benchmark, there is the possibility to add incremental value based on the manager's market view. Profits from successful tactical positioning help reduce net hedging costs. For example, if the neutral benchmark hedge ratio is 100% for the base currency being hedged, and the portfolio manager has a market opinion that the base currency is likely to depreciate, then *over*-hedging through a short position in P/B forward contracts might be implemented—that is, the manager might use a hedge ratio higher than 100%. Similarly, if the manager's market opinion is that the base currency is likely to appreciate, the currency exposure might be *under*-hedged.

A variant of this approach would be to adjust the hedge ratio based on exchange rate movements: to increase the hedge ratio if the base currency depreciated, but decrease the hedge ratio if the base currency appreciated. Essentially, this approach is a form of "delta hedging" that tries to mimic the payoff function of a put option on the base currency. That is, this form of dynamic hedging with forward contracts tries to increasingly participate in any upside moves of the base currency, but increasingly hedge any downside moves. Doing so adds "convexity" to the portfolio, meaning that the hedge's payoff function will be a convex curve when this function is graphed with profit on the vertical axis and the spot rate on the horizontal axis. (Note that this concept of convexity is identical in intent to the concept of convexity describing bonds; as convexity increases the price of a bond rises more quickly in a declining yield environment and drops more slowly in a rising yield environment. Convexity is a desirable characteristic in both the fixed-income and currency-hedging contexts.)

6.3.2. Protective Put Using OTM Options

In the previous section, we examined a dynamic hedging strategy using forward contracts that tries to mimic the payoff function of an option and put convexity into the hedge's payoff function. The payoff functions for options are naturally convex to begin with. However, this can be a costly form of convexity (relatively high option premiums), and fully hedging a currency position with a protective put strategy using an ATM option is the most expensive means of all to buy convexity.

One way to reduce the cost of using options is to accept some downside risk by using an OTM option, such as a 25- or 10-delta option. These options will be less costly, but also do not fully protect the portfolio from adverse currency movements. Conversely, it makes sense to insure against larger risks but accept some smaller day-to-day price movements in currencies. As an analogy, it may be possible to buy a home or car insurance policy with a zero deductible—but the premiums would be exorbitant. It may be more rational to have a cheaper insurance policy and accept responsibility for minor events, but insure against extreme damage.

6.3.3. Risk Reversal (or Collar)

Another set of option strategies involves *selling* options (also known as writing options) to earn income that can be used to offset the cost of buying a put option, which forms the "core" of the hedge. Recall that in this section, we are using the simplifying convention that the manager is long the base currency in the P/B quote; hence puts and not calls would be used for hedging in this case.

One strategy to obtain downside protection at a lower cost than a straight protective put position is to *buy* an OTM put option and *write* an OTM call option. Essentially, the portfolio manager is selling some of the upside potential for movements in the base currency (writing a call) and using the option's premiums to help pay the cost of the long put option being purchased. This approach is similar to creating a collar in fixed-income markets. The portfolio is protected against downside movements, but its upside is limited to the strike price on the OTM call option; the exchange rate risk is confined to a corridor or "collar."

In professional FX markets, having a long position in a call option and a short position in a put option is called a **risk reversal**. For example, buying a 25-delta call and writing a 25-delta put is referred to as a *long* position in a 25-delta risk reversal. The position used to create the collar position we just described (buying a put, writing a call) would be a *short* position in a risk reversal.

The majority of currency hedging for foreign-currency asset portfolios and corporate accounts is based on the use of forward contracts and simple option strategies (protective puts/covered calls and risk reversals/collars). We now begin to transition to more active trading strategies that are designed to express market views for speculative profit.

6.3.4. Put Spread

A variation of the short risk reversal position is a **put spread**, which is also used to reduce the up-front cost of buying a protective put. The short risk reversal is structured by buying a put option and writing a call option: the premiums received by writing the call help cover the cost of the put. Similarly, the put spread position involves buying a put option and writing another put option to help cover the cost of the long put's premiums. This position is typically structured by buying an OTM put, and writing a deeper-OTM put to gain income from premiums; both options involved have the same maturity.

To continue our previous example, with the current spot rate at 1.3550, the portfolio manager might set up the following put spread: buy a put with a strike of 1.3500 and write a put with a strike of 1.3450. The payoff on the put spread position will then be as follows: there is no hedge protection between 1.3550 and 1.3500; the portfolio is hedged from 1.3500 down to 1.3450; at spot rates below 1.3450, the portfolio becomes unhedged again. The put spread reduces the cost of the hedge, but at the cost of more limited downside protection. The portfolio manager would then use this spread only for cases in which a modest decline in the spot exchange rate was expected, and this position would have to be closely monitored against adverse exchange rate movements.

Note that the put spread structure will not be zero-cost because the deeper-OTM put (1.3450) being written will be cheaper than the less-OTM put (1.3500) being bought. However, there are approaches that will make the put spread (or almost any other option spread position) cheaper or possibly zero-cost: the manager could alter: (a) the strike prices of the options; (b) the notional amounts of the options; or (c) some combination of these two measures.

Altering the strike prices of the put options would mean moving them closer together (and hence more equal in cost). However, this would reduce the downside protection on the hedge. Instead, the portfolio manager could write a larger notional amount for the deeper-OTM option; for example, the ratio for the notionals for the options written versus bought might be 1:2. (In standard FX market notation, this would be a 1×2 put spread—the option with exercise price closest to being ATM is given first. However, to avoid confusion it is good practice to specify explicitly in the price quote which is the long and short positions, and what their deltas/strike prices are.) Although this structure may now be (approximately) zero-cost it is not without risks: for spot rates below 1.3450 the portfolio has now seen its exposure to the base currency double-up (because of the 1:2 proportion of notionals) and at a

worse spot exchange rate for the portfolio on top of it. Creating a zero-cost structure with a
1 × 2 put spread is equivalent to adding leverage to the options position, because you are
selling more options than you are buying. This means that this put spread position will have
to be carefully managed. For example, the portfolio manager might choose to close out the
short position in the deep-OTM put (by going long/buying an equivalent put option) before
the base currency depreciates to the 1.3450 strike level. This may be a costly position exit,
however, as the market moves against the manager's original positioning. Because of this, this
sort of 1 × 2 structure may be more appropriate for expressing directional opinions rather
than as a pure hedging strategy.

6.3.5. Seagull Spread

An alternative, and somewhat safer approach, would be to combine the original put spread
position (1:1 proportion of notionals) with a covered call position. This is simply an extension
of the concept behind risk reversals and put spreads. The "core" of the hedge (for a manager
long the base currency) is the long position in a put option. This is expensive. To reduce the
cost, a short risk reversal position writes a call option while a put spread writes a deep-OTM
put option. Of course, the manager can always do both: that is, be long a protective put and
then write *both* a call and a deep-OTM put. This option structure is sometimes referred to as
a **seagull spread**.

As with the names for other option strategies based on winged creatures, the "seagull"
indicates an option structure with at least three individual options, and in which the options
at the most distant strikes—the wings—are on the opposite side of the market from the
middle strike(s)—the body. For example, if the current spot price is 1.3550, a seagull could
be constructed by going *long* an ATM put at 1.3550 (the middle strike is the "body"), *short*
an OTM put at 1.3500, and *short* an OTM call at 1.3600 (the latter two options are the
"wings"). Because the options in the "wings" are being written (sold) this is called a *short*
seagull position. The risk/return profile of this structure gives full downside protection from
1.3550 to 1.3500 (at which point the short put position neutralizes the hedge) and
participation in the upside potential in spot rate movements to 1.3600 (the strike level for the
short call option).

Note that because *two* options are now being written to gain premiums instead of one,
this approach allows the strike price of the long put position to be ATM, increasing the
downside protection. The various strikes and/or notional sizes of these options (and hence
their premiums) can always be adjusted up or down until a zero-cost structure is obtained.
However, note that this particular seagull structure gives away some upside potential (the
short call position) as well as takes on some downside risk (if the short put position is
triggered, it will disable the hedge coverage coming from the long put position). As always,
lower structure costs come with some combination of lower downside protection and/or less
upside potential.

There are many variants of these seagull strategies, each of which provides a different
risk–reward profile (and net cost). For example, for the portfolio manager wishing to hedge a
long position in the base currency in the P/B quote when the current spot rate is 1.3550,
another seagull structure would be to write an ATM call at 1.3550 and use the proceeds to
buy an OTM put option at 1.3500 and an OTM call option at 1.3600. Note that in this
seagull structure, the "body" is now a *short* option position, not a long position as in the
previous example, and the "wings" are the long position. Hence, it is a *long* seagull spread.
This option structure provides cheap downside protection (the hedge kicks in at the put's

1.3500 strike) while providing the portfolio manager with unlimited participation in any rally in the base currency beyond the 1.3600 strike of the OTM call option. As before, the various option strikes and/or notional sizes on the options bought and written can be adjusted so that a zero-cost structure is obtained.

6.3.6. Exotic Options

In this section, we move even further away from derivatives and trading strategies used mainly for hedging, and toward the more speculative end of the risk spectrum dominated by active currency management. Exotic options are often used by more sophisticated players in the professional trading market—for example, currency overlay managers—and are less frequently used by institutional investors, investment funds, or corporations for hedging purposes. There are several reasons for this relatively light usage of "exotics" for hedging purposes, some related to the fact that many smaller entities lack familiarity with these products. Another reason involves the difficulty of getting hedge accounting treatment in many jurisdictions, which is more advantageous for financial reporting reasons. Finally, the specialized terms of such instruments make them difficult to value for regulatory and accounting purposes.

In general, the term "exotic" refers to all options that are not "vanilla." In FX, vanilla refers essentially to European-style put and call options. The full range of exotic options is both very broad and constantly evolving; many are extraordinarily complex both to price and even to understand. However, all exotics, no matter how complex, typically share one defining feature in common: They are designed to customize the risk exposures desired by the client and provide them at the lowest possible price.[19] Much like the trading strategies described previously, they usually involve some combination of lower downside protection and/or lower upside potential while providing the client with the specific risk exposures they are prepared to manage, and to do so at what is generally a lower cost than vanilla options.

The two most common types of exotic options encountered in foreign exchange markets are those with **knock-in/knock-out** features and digital options.

An option with a knock-in feature is essentially a vanilla option that is created only when the spot exchange rate touches a pre-specified level (this trigger level, called the "barrier," is not the same as the strike price). Similarly a knock-out option is a vanilla option that ceases to exist when the spot exchange rate touches some pre-specified barrier level. Because these options only exist (i.e., get knocked-in or knocked-out) under certain circumstances, they are more restrictive than vanilla options and hence are cheaper. But again, the knock-in/out features provide less upside potential and/or downside protection.

Digital options are also called binary options, or all-or-nothing options. They are called this because they pay a *fixed* amount if they "touch" their exercise level at any time before expiry (even if by a single pip). This characteristic of "extreme payoff" options makes them almost akin to a lottery ticket. Because of these large payoffs, digital options usually cost more than vanilla options with the same strike price. But digitals also provide highly leveraged exposure to movements in the spot rate. This makes these exotic products more appropriate as trading tools for active currency management, rather than as hedging tools. In practice, digital options are typically used by more sophisticated speculative accounts in the FX market to express directional views on exchange rates.

---

[19]Although the price is low for the client compared with vanilla options, exotics are typically nonetheless high profit margin items for investment dealers.

A full exposition of exotic options is beyond the scope of this chapter, but the reader should be aware of their existence and why they exist.

6.3.7. Section Summary

Clearly, loosening the constraint of a fully hedged portfolio begins to introduce complicated active currency management decisions. The following steps can be helpful to sort things out:

a. First, identify the *base* currency in the P/B quote (currency pair) you are dealing with. Derivatives are typically quoted in terms of either buying or selling the *base* currency when the option is exercised. A move upward in the P/B quote is an appreciation of the base currency.

b. Then, identify whether the base currency must be *bought* or *sold* to establish the hedge. These are the price movements you will be protecting against.

c. If *buying* the base currency is required to implement the hedge, then the core hedge structure will be based on some combination of a long call option and/or a long forward contract. The cost of this core hedge can be reduced by buying an OTM call option or writing options to earn premiums. (But keep in mind, lower hedging costs equate to less downside protection and/or upside potential.)

d. If *selling* the base currency is required to implement the hedge, then the core hedge structure will be based on some combination of a long put option and/or a short forward contract. The cost of this core hedge can be reduced by buying an OTM put option or writing options to earn premiums.

e. The higher the allowed discretion for active management, the lower the risk aversion; and the firmer a particular market view is held, the more the hedge is likely to be structured to allow risk exposures in the portfolio. This approach involves positioning in derivatives that "lean the same way" as the market view. (For example, a market view that the base currency will depreciate would use some combination of short forward contracts, writing call options, buying put options, and using "bearish" exotic strategies.) This directional bias to the trading position would be superimposed on the core hedge position described in steps "c" and "d," creating an active-trading "tilt" in the portfolio.

f. For these active strategies, varying the strike prices and notional amounts of the options involved can move the trading position toward a zero-cost structure. But as with hedges, keep in mind that lower cost implies less downside protection and/or upside potential for the portfolio.

A lot of different hedging tools and strategies have been named and covered in this section. Rather than attempting to absorb all of them by rote memorization (a put spread is "X" and a seagull is "Y"), the reader is encouraged instead to focus on the intuition behind a hedge, and how and why it is constructed. It matters less what name (if any) is given to any specific approach; what is important is understanding how all the moving parts fit together. The reader should focus on a "building blocks" approach in understanding how and why the parts of the currency hedge are assembled in a given manner.

EXAMPLE 6   Alternative Hedging Strategies

Brixworth & St. Ives Asset Management, the UK-based investment firm, has hedged the exposure of its Aggressive Growth Fund to the MXN with a long position in a

MXN/GBP forward contract. The fund's foreign-currency asset exposure to the ZAR is hedged by buying an ATM call option on the ZAR/GBP currency pair. The portfolio managers at Brixworth & St. Ives are looking at ways to modify the risk–reward trade-offs and net costs of their currency hedges.

Jasmine Khan, one of the analysts at Brixworth & St. Ives, proposes an option-based hedge structure for the long-ZAR exposure that would replace the hedge based on the ATM call option with either long or short positions in the following three options on ZAR/GBP:

a. ATM put option
b. 25-delta put option
c. 25-delta call option

Khan argues that these three options can be combined into a hedge structure that will have some limited downside risk, but provide complete hedge protection starting at the relevant 25-delta strike level. The structure will also have unlimited upside potential, although this will not start until the ZAR/GBP exchange rate moves to the relevant 25-delta strike level. Finally, this structure can be created at a relatively low cost because it involves option writing.

1. The *best* method for Brixworth & St. Ives to gain some upside potential for the hedge on the Aggressive Growth Fund's MXN exposure using MXN/GBP options is to replace the forward contract with a:
   A. long position in an OTM put.
   B. short position in an ATM call.
   C. long position in a 25-delta risk reversal.

2. While keeping the ATM call option in the ZAR/GBP, the method that would lead to *greatest* cost reduction on the hedge would be to:
   A. buy a 25-delta put.
   B. write a 10-delta call.
   C. write a 25-delta call.

3. Setting up Khan's proposed hedge structure would *most likely* involve being:
   A. long the 25-delta options and short the ATM option.
   B. long the 25-delta call, and short both the ATM and 25-delta put options.
   C. short the 25-delta call, and long both the ATM and 25-delta put options.

Solution to 1: C is correct. The Aggressive Growth Fund has a long foreign-currency exposure to the MXN in its asset portfolio, which is hedged by selling the MXN against the GBP, or equivalently, buying the GBP—the base currency in the P/B quote—against the MXN. This need to protect against an *appreciation* in the GBP is why the hedge is using a *long* position in the forward contract. To set a collar around the MXN/GBP rate, Brixworth & St. Ives would want a long call option position with a strike greater than the current spot rate (this gives upside potential to the hedge) and a short put position with a strike less than the current spot rate (this reduces net cost of the hedge). A long call and a short put defines a long position in a risk reversal.

Choice A is incorrect because, if exercised, buying a put option would increase the fund's exposure to the MXN (sell GBP, buy MXN). Similarly, Choice B is incorrect because, if exercised, the ATM call option would increase the MXN exposure (the GBP is "called" away from the fund at the strike price with MXN delivered). Moreover, although writing the ATM call option would gain some income from premiums, writing options (on their own) is never considered the "best" hedge because the premium income earned is fixed but the potential losses on adverse currency moves are potentially unlimited.

Solution to 2: C is correct. As before, the hedge is implemented in protecting against an *appreciation* of the base currency of the P/B quote, the GBP. The hedge is established with an ATM call option (a long position in the GBP). Writing an OTM call option (i.e., with a strike that is more than the current spot rate of 5.1050) establishes a call spread (although hedge protection is lost if ZAR/GBP expires at or above the strike level). Writing a 25-delta call earns more income from premiums than a deeper-OTM 10-delta call (although the 25-delta call has less hedge protection). Buying an option would increase the cost of the hedge, and a put option on the ZAR/GBP would increase the fund's ZAR exposure if exercised (the GBP is "put" to the counterparty at the strike price and ZAR received).

Solution to 3: A is correct. Once again, the hedge is based on hedging the need to sell ZAR/buy GBP, and GBP is the base currency in the ZAR/GBP quote. This means the hedge needs to protect against an *appreciation* of the GBP (an appreciation of the ZAR/GBP rate). Based on Khan's description, the hedge provides protection after a certain loss point, which would be a long 25-delta call. Unlimited upside potential after favorable (i.e., down) moves in the ZAR/GBP past a certain level means a long 25-delta put. Getting the low net cost that Khan refers to means that the cost of these two long positions is financed by selling the ATM option. (Together these three positions define a long seagull spread.) Choice B is incorrect because although the first two legs of the position are right, a short position in the put does not provide any unlimited upside potential (from a down-move in ZAR/GBP). Choice C is incorrect because any option-based hedge, given the need to hedge against an up-move in the ZAR/GBP rate, is going to be based on a long call position. C does not contain any of these.

6.4. Hedging Multiple Foreign Currencies

We now expand our discussion to hedging a portfolio with multiple foreign-currency assets. The hedging tools and strategies are very similar to those discussed for hedging a single foreign-currency asset, except now the currency hedge must consider the *correlation* between the various foreign-currency risk exposures.

For example, consider the case of a US-domiciled investor who has exposures to foreign-currency assets in Australia and New Zealand. These two economies are roughly similar in that they are resource-based and closely tied to the regional economy of the Western Pacific, especially the large emerging markets in Asia. As a result, the movements in their currencies are often closely correlated; the USD/AUD and USD/NZD currency pairs will tend to move together. If the portfolio manager has the discretion to take short positions, the portfolio may (for example) possibly have a net long position in the Australian foreign-currency asset and a net short position in the New Zealand foreign-currency asset. In this case, there may be less need to hedge away the AUD and NZD currency exposures separately because the portfolio's long exposure to the AUD is diversified by the short position on the NZD.

6.4.1. Cross Hedges and Macro Hedges

A **cross hedge** occurs when a position in one asset (or a derivative based on the asset) is used to hedge the risk exposures of a different asset (or a derivative based on it). Normally, cross hedges are not needed because, as we mentioned earlier, forward contracts and other derivatives are widely available in almost every conceivable currency pair. However, if the portfolio already has "natural" cross hedges in the form of negatively correlated residual currency exposures—as in the long-AUD/short-NZD example in Section 6.4—this helps moderate portfolio risk ($\sigma[R_{DC}]$) without having to use a direct hedge on the currency exposure.

Sometimes a distinction is made between a "proxy" hedge and a "cross" hedge. When this distinction is made, a *proxy hed*ge removes the foreign currency risk by hedging it back to the investor's domestic currency—such as in the example with USD/AUD and USD/NZD discussed in the text. In contrast, a *cross hed*ge moves the currency risk from one foreign currency to another foreign currency. For example, a US-domiciled investor may have an exposure to both the Indonesian rupiah (IDR) and the Thai baht (THB), but based on a certain market view, may only want exposure to the THB. In this context, the manager might use currency derivatives as a cross hedge to convert the IDR/USD exposure to a THB/USD exposure. But not all market participants make this sharp of a distinction between proxy hedges and cross hedges, and these terms are often used interchangeably. The most common term found among practitioners in most asset classes is simply a cross hedge, as we are using the term here: hedging an exposure with a closely correlated product (i.e., a proxy hedge when this distinction is made). The cross hedge of moving currency exposures between various *foreign* currencies is more of a special-case application of this concept. In our example, a US investor wanting to shift currency exposures between the IDR and THB would only need to shift the relative size of the IDR/USD and THB/USD forward contracts *already* being used. As mentioned earlier, forwards are available on almost every currency pair, so a cross hedge from foreign currency "A" to foreign currency "B" would be a special case when derivatives on one of the currencies are not available.

EXAMPLE 7   Cross Hedges

Mai Nguyen works at Cape Henlopen Advisors, which runs a US-domiciled fund that invests in foreign-currency assets of Australia and New Zealand. The fund currently has equally weighted exposure to one-year Australian and New Zealand treasury bills (i.e., both of the portfolio weights, $\omega_i = 0.5$). Because the foreign-currency return on these treasury bill assets is risk-free and known in advance, their expected $\sigma(R_{FC})$ is equal to zero.

Nguyen wants to calculate the USD-denominated returns on this portfolio as well as the cross hedging effects of these investments. She collects the following information:

Expected Values	Australia	New Zealand
Foreign-currency asset return R_{FC}	4.0%	6.0%
Foreign-currency return R_{FX}	5.0%	5.0%
Asset risk $\sigma(R_{FC})$	0%	0%
Currency risk $\sigma(R_{FX})$	8.0%	10.0%
Correlation (USD/AUD; USD/NZD)	+0.85	

Using Equation 1, Nguyen calculates that the expected domestic-currency return for the Australian asset is

$$(1.04)(1.05) - 1 = 0.092$$

or 9.2%. Likewise, she determines that the expected domestic-currency return for the New Zealand asset is

$$(1.06)(1.05) - 1 = 0.113$$

or 11.3%. Together, the result is that the expected domestic-currency return (R_{DC}) on the equally weighted foreign-currency asset portfolio is the weighted average of these two individual country returns, or

$$R_{DC} = 0.5(9.2\%) + 0.5(11.3\%) = 10.3\%$$

Nguyen now turns her attention to calculating the portfolio's investment risk $[\sigma(R_{DC})]$. To calculate the expected risk for the domestic-currency return, the currency risk of R_{FX} needs to be multiplied by the *known* return on the treasury bills. The portfolio's investment risk, $\sigma(R_{DC})$, is found by calculating the standard deviation of the right-hand-side of:

$$R_{DC} = (1 + R_{FC})(1 + R_{FX}) - 1$$

Although R_{FX} is a random variable—it is not known in advance—the R_{FC} term is in fact known in advance because the asset return is risk-free. Because of this Nguyen can make use of the statistical rules that, first, $\sigma(kX) = k\sigma(X)$, where X is a random variable and k is a constant; and second, that the correlation between a random variable and a constant is zero. These results greatly simplify the calculations because, in this case, she does not need to consider the correlation between exchange rate movements and foreign-currency asset returns. Instead, Nguyen needs to calculate the risk only on the currency side. Applying these statistical rules to the above formula leads to the following results:

A.   The expected risk (i.e., standard deviation) of the domestic-currency return for the Australian asset is equal to $(1.04) \times 8\% = 8.3\%$.
B.   The expected risk (i.e., standard deviation) of the domestic-currency return for the New Zealand asset is equal to $(1.06) \times 10\% = 10.6\%$.

Adding all of these numerical values into Equation 4 leads Nguyen to calculate:

$$\sigma^2(R_{DC}) = (0.5)^2(8.3\%)^2 + (0.5)^2(10.6\%)^2 + [(2)0.5(8.3\%)0.5(10.6\%)0.85]$$
$$= 0.8\%$$

The standard deviation of this amount—that is, $\sigma(R_{DC})$—is 9.1%. Note that in the expression, all of the units are in percent, so for example, 8.3% is equivalent to 0.083 for calculation purposes. The careful reader may also note that Nguyen is able to use an exact expression for calculating the variance of the portfolio returns, rather than the approximate expressions shown in Equations 3 and 5. This is because, with risk-free foreign-currency assets, the variance of these foreign-currency returns $\sigma^2(R_{FC})$ is equal to zero.

Nguyen now considers an alternative scenario in which, instead of an equally weighted portfolio (where the $\omega_i = 0.5$), the fund has a long exposure to the New Zealand asset and a short exposure to the Australian asset (i.e., the ω_i are +1 and −1, respectively; this is similar to a highly leveraged carry trade position). Putting these weights into Equations 2 and 4 leads to

$$R_{DC} = -1.0(9.2\%) + 1.0(11.3\%) = 2.1\%$$

$$\sigma^2(R_{DC}) = (1.0)^2(8.3\%)^2 + (1.0)^2(10.6\%)^2 + [-2.0(8.3\%)(10.6\%)0.85]$$
$$= 0.3\%$$

The standard deviation—that is, $\sigma(R_{DC})$—is now 5.6%, less than either of the expected risks for foreign-currency asset returns (results A and B). Nguyen concludes that having long and short positions in positively correlated currencies can lead to much lower portfolio risk, through the benefits of cross hedging. (Nguyen goes on to calculate that if the expected correlation between USD/AUD and USD/NZD increases to 0.95, with all else equal, the expected domestic-currency return risk on the long–short portfolio drops to 3.8%.)

Some types of cross hedges are often referred to as macro hedges. The reason is because the hedge is more focused on the entire portfolio, particularly when individual asset price movements are highly correlated, rather than on individual assets or currency pairs. Another way of viewing a macro hedge is to see the portfolio not just as a collection of financial assets, but as a collection of risk exposures. These various risk exposures are typically defined in categories, such as term risk, credit risk, and liquidity risk. These risks can also be defined in terms of the potential financial scenarios the portfolio is exposed to, such as recession, financial sector stress, or inflation. Often macro hedges are defined in terms of the financial scenario they are designed to protect the portfolio from.

Putting gold in the portfolio sometimes serves this purpose by helping to provide broad portfolio protection against extreme market events. Using a volatility overlay program can also hedge the portfolio against such risks because financial stress is typically associated with a spike in exchange rates' implied volatility. Using a derivative product based on an index, rather than specific assets or currencies, can also define a macro hedge. One macro hedge specific to foreign exchange markets uses derivatives based on fixed-weight baskets of currencies (such derivatives are available in both exchange-traded and OTC form). In a multi-currency portfolio, it may not always be cost efficient to hedge each single currency separately, and in these situations a macro hedge using currency basket derivatives is an alternative approach.

6.4.2. Minimum-Variance Hedge Ratio

A mathematical approach to determining the optimal cross hedging ratio is known as the minimum-variance hedge ratio. Recall that regression analysis based on ordinary least squares (OLS) is used to minimize the variance of $\hat{\varepsilon}$, the residual between actual and fitted values of the regression

$$y_t = \alpha + \beta x_t + \varepsilon_t \text{ where } \hat{\varepsilon}_t = y_t - (\hat{\alpha} + \hat{\beta}x_t)$$

This same principle can be used to minimize the tracking error between the value of the hedged asset and the hedging instrument. In the regression formula, we substitute the percentage change in the value of the asset to be hedged for y_t, and the percentage change in the value of the hedging instrument for x_t (both of these values are measured in terms of the investor's domestic currency). The calculated coefficient in this regression $(\hat{\beta})$ gives the optimal hedging ratio, which means it minimizes the variance of $\hat{\varepsilon}$ and minimizes the tracking error between changes in the value of the hedge and changes in the value of the asset it is hedging. It can be shown that the formula for the minimum-variance hedge ratio—the formula for calculating the $\hat{\beta}$ coefficient in the regression—is mathematically equal to:

$$\frac{\text{covariance } (y,x)}{\text{variance } (x)} = \text{correlation } (y,x) \times \left[\frac{\text{std. dev. } (y)}{\text{std. dev. } (x)}\right]$$

where y and x are defined as before, the change in the domestic-currency value of the asset and the hedge, respectively.

Calculating the minimum-variance hedge ratio typically applies only for "indirect" hedges based on cross hedging or macro hedges; it is not typically applied to a "direct" hedge in which exposure to a spot rate is hedged with a forward contract in that same currency pair. This is because the correlation between movements in the spot rate and its forward contract is likely to be very close to +1. Likewise, the variance in spot price movements and movements in the price of the forward contract are also likely to be approximately equal. Therefore, calculating the minimum-variance hedge ratio by regressing changes in the spot exchange rate against changes in the forward rate will almost always result is a $\hat{\beta}$ regression estimate very close to 1, and hence a minimum-variance hedge ratio close to 100%. So, undertaking the regression analysis is superfluous.

But the minimum-variance hedge ratio can be quite different from 100% when the hedge is *jointly* optimized over *both* exchange rate movements R_{FX} and changes in the foreign-currency value of the asset R_{FC}. A sidebar discusses this case.

There can also be cases when the optimal hedge ratio may not be 100% because of the market characteristics of a specific currency pair. For example, a currency pair may not have a (liquid) forward contract available and hence an alternative cross hedging instrument or a macro hedge must be used instead. We examine when such situations might come up in Section 7.

6.4.3. Basis Risk

The portfolio manager must be aware that any time a direct currency hedge (i.e., a spot rate hedged against its own forward contract) is replaced with an indirect hedge (cross hedge, macro hedge), **basis risk** is brought into the portfolio. This risk reflects the fact that the price movements in the exposure being hedged and the price movements in the cross hedge instrument are not perfectly correlated, and that the correlation will change with time—and sometimes both dramatically and unexpectedly. For a minimum-variance hedge ratio, this risk is expressed as instability in the $\widehat{\beta}$ coefficient estimate as more data become available.

For an example of basis risk, return to the illustration earlier of the foreign-currency asset portfolio that cross hedged a long USD/AUD exposure with a short USD/NZD exposure. It is not only possible, but highly likely, that the correlation between movements in the USD/AUD and the USD/NZD spot rates will vary with time. This varying correlation would reflect movements in the NZD/AUD spot rate. Another example of basis risk would be that the correlation between a multi-currency portfolio's domestic-currency market value and the value of currency basket derivatives being used as a macro hedge will neither be perfect nor constant.

At a minimum, this means that all cross hedges and macro hedges will have to be carefully monitored and, as needed, rebalanced to account for the drift in correlations. It also means that minimum-variance hedge ratios will have to be re-estimated as more data become available. The portfolio manager should beware that sudden, unexpected spikes in basis risk can sometimes turn what was once a minimum-variance hedge or an effective cross hedge into a position that is highly correlated with the underlying assets being hedged—the opposite of a hedge.

Basis risk is also used in the context of forward and futures contracts because the price movements of these derivatives products do not always correspond exactly with those of the underlying currency. This is because the price of the forward contract also reflects the interest rate differential between the two countries in the currency pair as well as the term to contract maturity. But with futures and forwards, the derivatives price converges to the price of the underlying as maturity approaches, which is enforced by arbitrage. This convergence is not the case with cross hedges, which potentially can go disastrously wrong with sudden movements in market risk (price correlations), credit risk, or liquidity risk.

Optimal Minimum-Variance Hedges

For simple foreign-currency asset portfolios, it may be possible to use the single-variable OLS regression technique to do a *joint* optimization of the hedge over both the foreign-currency value of the asset R_{FC} and the foreign-currency risk exposure R_{FX}. This approach will reduce the variance of the all-in domestic-currency return R_{DC}, which is the risk that matters most to the investor, not just reducing the variance of the foreign exchange risk R_{FX}.

Calculating the minimum-variance hedge for the foreign exchange risk R_{FX} proceeds by regressing changes in the spot rate against changes in the value of the hedging instrument (i.e., the forward contract). But as indicated in the text, performing this regression is typically unnecessary; for all intents and purposes, the minimum-variance hedge for a spot exchange rate using a forward contract will be close to 100%.

But when there is only a *single* foreign-currency asset involved, one can perform a joint optimization over both of the foreign-currency risks (i.e., both R_{FC} and R_{FX}) by regressing changes in the domestic-currency return (R_{DC}) against percentage changes in the value of the hedging instrument. Basing the optimal hedge ratio on the OLS estimate for β in this regression will minimize the variance of the domestic-currency return $\sigma^2(R_{DC})$. The result will be a better hedge ratio than just basing the regression on R_{FX} alone because this joint approach will also pick up any *correlations* between R_{FX} and R_{FC}. (Recall from Section 4.3.1 that the asset mix in the portfolio, and hence the correlations between R_{FX} and R_{FC}, can affect the optimal hedge ratio.) This single-variable OLS approach, however, will only work if there is a single foreign-currency asset in the portfolio.

Work by Campbell (2010) has shown that the optimal hedge ratio based jointly on movements in R_{FC} and R_{FX} for international *bond* portfolios is almost always close to 100%. However, the optimal hedge ratio for single-country foreign *equity* portfolios varies widely between currencies, and will depend on *both* the investor's domestic currency and the currency of the foreign investment. For example, the optimal hedge ratio for a US equity portfolio will be different for UK and eurozone-based investors; and for eurozone investors, the optimal hedge ratio for a US equity portfolio can be different from that of a Canadian equity portfolio. The study found that the optimal hedge ratio for foreign equity exposures can vary widely from 100% between countries. But as the author cautions, these optimal hedge ratios are calculated on historical data that may not be representative of future price dynamics.

Minimum-Variance Hedge Ratio Example

Annie McYelland is an analyst at Scotland-based Kilmarnock Capital. Her firm is considering an investment in an equity index fund based on the Swiss Stock Market Index (SMI). The SMI is a market-cap weighted average of the twenty largest and most liquid Swiss companies, and captures about 85% of the overall market capitalization of the Swiss equity market.

McYelland is asked to formulate a currency-hedging strategy. Because this investment involves only one currency pair and one investment (the SMI), she decides to calculate the minimum-variance hedge ratio for the entire risk exposure, not just the currency exposure. McYelland collects 10 years of monthly data on the CHF/GBP spot exchange rate and movements in the Swiss Market Index.

McYelland notes that the GBP is the base currency in the CHF/GBP quote and that the formula for domestic-currency returns (R_{DC}) shown in Equation 1 requires that the domestic currency be the price currency. Accordingly, she starts by inverting the CHF/GBP quote to a GBP/CHF quote ($S_{GBP/CHF}$). Then she calculates the monthly percentage changes for this adjusted currency series (%$\Delta S_{GBP/CHF}$) as well as for the SMI (%ΔSMI). This allows her to calculate the monthly returns of an unhedged investment in the SMI with these unhedged returns measured in the "domestic" currency, the GBP:

$$R_{DC} = (1 + R_{FC})(1 + R_{FX}) - 1$$

where R_{FC} = %ΔSMI and R_{FX} = %$\Delta S_{GBP/CHF}$. Because McYelland wants to minimize the variance of these unhedged domestic-currency returns, she calculates the minimum-variance hedge ratio with the following OLS regression:

$$R_{DC} = \alpha + \beta(\%\Delta S_{GBP/CHF}) + \varepsilon$$

The calculated regression coefficients show that $\widehat{\alpha} = -0.21$ and $\widehat{\beta} = 1.35$. McYelland interprets these results to mean that the estimated $\widehat{\beta}$-coefficient is the minimum-variance hedge ratio. This conclusion makes sense because $\widehat{\beta}$ represents the sensitivity of the domestic-currency return on the portfolio to percentage changes in the spot rate. In this case, the return on the SMI seems very sensitive to the appreciation of the CHF. Indeed, over the 10 years of data she collected, McYelland notices that the correlation between %ΔSMI and %$\Delta S_{GBP/CHF}$ is equal to +0.6.

On the basis of these calculations, she recommends that the minimum-variance hedge ratio for Kilmarnock Capital's exposure to the SMI be set at approximately 135%. This recommendation means that a *long* CHF1,000,000 exposure to the SMI should be hedged with a *short* position in CHF against the GBP of approximately CHF1,350,000. Because forward contracts in professional FX markets are quoted in terms of CHF/GBP for this currency pair, this would mean a *long* position in the forward contract ($F_{CHF/GBP}$)—that is, *selling* the CHF means *buying* the base currency GBP.

McYelland cautions the Investment Committee at Kilmarnock Capital that this minimum-variance hedge ratio is only approximate and must be closely monitored because it is estimated over historical data that may not be representative of future price dynamics. For example, the +0.6 correlation estimated between %ΔSMI and %$\Delta S_{GBP/CHF}$ is the 10-year *average* correlation; future market conditions may not correspond to this historical average.

6.5. Basic Intuitions for Using Currency Management Tools

This section has covered only some of the most common currency management tools and strategies used in FX markets—there are a great many other derivatives products and strategies that have not been covered. The key points are that there are *many* different hedging and active trading strategies, there are many possible *variations* within each of these strategies, and these strategies can be used in *combination* with each other. There is no need to cover all of what would be a very large number of possible permutations and combinations. Instead, we will close this section with a key thought: Each of these many approaches to either hedging or expressing a directional view on currency movements has its advantages and disadvantages, its risks, and its costs.

As a result, there is no single "correct" approach to initiating and managing currency exposures. Instead, at the strategic level, the IPS of the portfolio sets guidelines for risk exposures, permissible hedging tools, and strategies, which will vary among investors. At the tactical level, at which the portfolio manager has discretion on risk exposures, currency strategy will depend on the manager's management style, market view, and risk tolerance. It will also depend on the manager's perceptions of the relative costs and benefit of any given strategy. Market conditions will affect the cost/benefit calculations behind the hedging decision, as movements in forward points (expected roll yield) or exchange rate volatility (option premiums) affect the expected cost of the hedge; the same hedge structure can be "rich" or "cheap" depending on current market conditions.

Reflecting all of these considerations, different managers will likely make different decisions when confronted with the same opportunity set; and each manager will likely have a good reason for their individual decision. The most important point is that the portfolio manager be aware of all the benefits, costs, and risks of the chosen strategy and be comfortable that any remaining residual currency risks in the hedge are acceptable.

To summarize the key insights of Section 6—and continuing our example of a portfolio manager who is long the base currency in the P/B quote and wants to hedge that price risk—the manager needs to understand the following:

1. Because the portfolio has a *long* exposure to base currency, to neutralize this risk the hedge will attempt to build a *short* exposure out of that currency's derivatives using some combination of forward and/or option contracts.

2. A currency hedge is not a free good, particularly a complete hedge. The hedge cost, real or implied, will consist of some combination of lost upside potential, potentially negative roll yield (forward points at a discount or time decay on long option positions), and up-front payments of option premiums.

3. The cost of any given hedge structure will vary depending on market conditions (i.e., forward points and implied volatility).

4. The cost of the hedge is focused on its "core." For a manager with a long exposure to a currency, the cost of this "core" hedge will be the implicit costs of a short position in a forward contract (no upside potential, possible negative roll yield) or the up-front premium on a long position in a put option. Either of these two forms of insurance can be expensive. However, there are various cost mitigation methods that can be used alone or in combination to reduce these core hedging costs:

   a. Writing options to gain up-front premiums.
   b. Varying the strike prices of the options written or bought.
   c. Varying the notional amounts of the derivative contracts.
   d. Using various "exotic" features, such as knock-ins or knock-outs.

5. There is nothing inherently wrong with any of these cost mitigation approaches—but the manager *must* understand that these invariably involve some combination of reduced upside potential and/or reduced downside protection. A reduced cost (or even a zero-cost) hedge structure is perfectly acceptable, but only as long as the portfolio manager fully understands all of the residual risks in the hedge structure and is prepared to accept and manage them.

6. There are often "natural" hedges within the portfolio, in which some residual risk exposures are uncorrelated with each other and offer portfolio diversification effects. Cross hedges and macro hedges bring basis risk into the portfolio, which will have to be monitored and managed.

7. There is no single or "best" way to hedge currency risk. The portfolio manager will have to perform a due diligence examination of potential hedge structures and make a rational decision on a cost/benefit basis.

EXAMPLE 8   Hedging Strategies

Ireland-based Old Galway Capital runs several investment trusts for its clients. Fiona Doyle has just finished rebalancing the dynamic currency hedge for Overseas Investment Trust III, which has an IPS mandate to be fully hedged using forward contracts. Shortly after the rebalancing, Old Galway receives notice that one of its largest investors in the Overseas Investment Trust III has served notice of a large withdrawal from the fund.

Padma Bhattathiri works at Malabar Coast Capital, an India-based investment company. Her mandate is to seek out any alpha opportunities in global FX markets and aggressively manage these for speculative profit. The Reserve Bank of New Zealand (RBNZ) is New Zealand's central bank, and is scheduled to announce its policy rate decision within the week. The consensus forecast among economists is that the RBNZ will leave rates unchanged, but Bhattathiri believes that the RBNZ will surprise the markets with a rate hike.

Jasmine Khan, analyst at UK-based Brixworth & St. Ives Asset Management, has been instructed by the management team to reduce hedging costs for the firm's Aggressive Growth Fund, and that more currency exposure—both downside risk and upside potential—will have to be accepted and managed. Currently, the fund's ZAR-denominated foreign-currency asset exposures are being hedged with a 25-delta risk reversal (on the ZAR/GBP cross rate). The current ZAR/GBP spot rate is 13.1350.

Bao Zhang is a market analyst at South Korea–based Kwangju Capital, an investment firm that offers several actively managed investment trusts for its clients. She notices that the exchange rate for the Philippines Peso (PHP/USD) is increasing (PHP is depreciating) toward its 200-day moving average located in the 42.2500 area (the current spot rate is 42.2475). She mentions this to Akiko Takahashi, a portfolio manager for one of the firm's investment vehicles. Takahashi's view, based on studying economic fundamentals, is that the PHP/USD rate should continue to increase, but after speaking with Zhang she is less sure. After further conversation, Zhang and Takahashi come to the view that the PHP/USD spot rate will either break through the 42.2500 level and gain upward momentum through the 42.2600 level, or stall at the 42.2500 level and then drop down through the 42.2400 level as frustrated long positions exit the market. They decide that either scenario has equal probability over the next month.

Annie McYelland is an analyst at Scotland-based Kilmarnock Capital. The firm is considering a USD10,000,000 investment in an S&P 500 Index fund. McYelland is asked to calculate the minimum-variance hedge ratio. She collects the following statistics based on 10 years of monthly data:

$\sigma(\%\Delta S_{GBP/USD})$	$\sigma(R_{DC})$	$\rho(R_{DC},\%\Delta S_{GBP/USD})$
2.7%	4.4%	0.2

Source: Data are from Bloomberg.

1. Given the sudden liquidity need announced, Doyle's *best* course of action with regard to the currency hedge is to:
   A. do nothing.
   B. reduce the hedge ratio.
   C. over-hedge by using currency options.

2. Given her market view, Bhattathiri would *most likely* choose which of the following long positions?
   A. 5-delta put option on NZD/AUD
   B. 10-delta put option on USD/NZD
   C. Put spread on JPY/NZD using 10-delta and 25-delta options

3. Among the following, replacing the current risk reversal hedge with a long position in which of the following would *best* meet Khan's instructions? (All use the ZAR/GBP.)
   A. 10-delta risk reversal
   B. Put option with a 13.1300 strike
   C. Call option with a 13.1350 strike

4. Which of the following positions would *best* implement Zhang's and Takahashi's market view?
   A. Long a 42.2450 put and long a 42.2550 call
   B. Long a 42.2450 put and short a 42.2400 put
   C. Long a 42.2450 put and short a 42.2550 call

5. Which of the following positions would *best* implement Kilmarnock Capital's minimum-variance hedge?
   A. Long a USD/GBP forward contract with a notional size of USD1.2 million
   B. Long a USD/GBP forward contract with a notional size of USD3.3 million
   C. Short a USD/GBP forward contract with a notional size of USD2.0 million

Solution to 1: A is correct. After rebalancing, the Overseas Investment Trust III is fully hedged; currency risk is at a minimum, which is desirable if liquidity needs have increased. Choices B and C are incorrect because they increase the currency risk exposures.

Solution to 2: A is correct. The surprise rate hike should cause the NZD to appreciate against most currencies. This appreciation would mean a depreciation of the NZD/AUD rate, which a put option can profit from. A 5-delta option is deep-OTM, but the price reaction on the option premiums will be more extreme than a higher-delta option. That is to say, the *percentage* change in the premiums for a 5-delta option for a given percentage change in the spot exchange rate will be higher than the percentage change in premiums for a 25-delta option. In a sense, a very low delta option is like a highly leveraged lottery ticket on the event occurring. With a surprise rate hike, the odds would swing in Bhattathiri's favor. Choice B is incorrect because the price reaction in the USD/NZD spot rate after the surprise rate hike would likely cause the NZD to appreciate; so Bhattathiri would want a call option on the USD/NZD currency pair. Choice C is incorrect because an appreciation of the NZD after the surprise rate hike would best be captured by a call spread on the JPY/NZD rate, which will likely increase (the NZD is the base currency).

Solution to 3: A is correct. Moving to a 10-delta risk reversal will be cheaper (these options are deeper-OTM than 25-delta options) and widen the bands in the corridor being created for the ZAR/GBP rate. Choice B is incorrect because a long put provides no protection against an upside movement in the ZAR/GBP rate, which Brixworth & St. Ives is trying to hedge (recall that the fund is long ZAR in its foreign-currency asset exposure and hence needs to sell ZAR/buy GBP to hedge). Also, if Brixworth & St. Ives exercises the option, they would "put" GBP to the counterparty at the strike price and receive ZAR in return. Although this option position may be considered profitable in its own right, it nonetheless causes the firm to double-up its ZAR exposure. Choice C is incorrect because although an ATM call option on ZAR/GBP will provide complete hedge protection, it will be expensive and clearly more expensive than the current 25-delta risk reversal.

Solution to 4: A is correct. Zhang's and Takahashi's market view is that, over the next month, a move in PHP/USD to either 42.2400 or 42.2600 is equally likely. A strangle would express this view of heightened volatility but without a directional bias, and would require a long put and a long call positions. Choice B is incorrect because it is a put spread; it will profit by a move in PHP/USD between 42.2450 and 42.2400. If it moves below 42.2400 the short put gets exercised by the counterparty and neutralizes the long put. Although less costly than an outright long put position, this structure is not positioned to profit from a move higher in PHP/USD. Choice C is incorrect because it is a short risk reversal position. It provides relatively cheap protection for a down-move in PHP/USD but is not positioned to profit from an up-move in PHP/USD.

Solution to 5: B is correct. The formula for the minimum-variance hedge ratio (*h*) is:

$$h = \rho(R_{DC}; R_{FX}) \times \left[\frac{\sigma(R_{DC})}{\sigma(R_{FX})} \right]$$

After inputting the data from the table, this equation solves to 0.33. This means that for a USD10 million investment in the S&P 500 (long position), Kilmarnock Capital would want to be *short* approximately USD3.3 million in a forward contract. Because the standard market quote for this currency pair is USD/GBP, to be short the USD means one would have to buy the GBP; that is, a *long* position in a USD/GBP forward contract. Choice A is incorrect because it inverts the ratio in the formula. Choice C is incorrect because it shows a short position in the USD/GBP forward, and because it only uses the correlation to set the contract size.

7. CURRENCY MANAGEMENT FOR EMERGING MARKET CURRENCIES

Most of the material in this chapter has focused on what might be described as the major currencies, such as the EUR, GBP, or JPY. This focus is not a coincidence: The vast majority of daily flow in global FX markets is accounted for by the top half dozen currencies. Moreover, the vast majority of investable assets globally, as measured by market capitalization, are denominated in the major currencies. Nonetheless, more investors are looking at emerging markets, as well as "frontier markets," for potential investment opportunities. And many developing economies are beginning to emerge as major forces in the global economy. In the following sections, we survey the challenges for currency management and the use of non-deliverable forwards as one tool to address them.

7.1. Special Considerations in Managing Emerging Market Currency Exposures

Managing emerging market currency exposure involves unique challenges. Perhaps the two most important considerations are (1) higher trading costs than the major currencies under "normal" market conditions, and (2) the increased likelihood of extreme market events and severe illiquidity under stressed market conditions.

Many emerging market currencies are thinly traded, causing higher transaction costs (bid–offer spreads). There may also be fewer derivatives products to choose from, especially exchange-traded products. Although many global investment banks will quote spot rates and

OTC derivatives for almost any conceivable currency pair, many of these are often seen as "specialty" products and often come with relatively high mark-ups. This mark-up increases trading and hedging costs. (In addition, the underlying foreign-currency asset in emerging markets can be illiquid and lack the full array of derivatives products.)

These higher currency trading costs would especially be the case for "crosses" in these currency pairs. For example, there is no reason why an investor in Chile (which uses the Chilean peso, currency code CLP) could not have an investment in assets denominated in the Thai baht (THB). But the CLP/THB cross is likely to be very thinly traded; there simply are not enough trade or capital flows between these two countries. Typically, any trade between these two currencies would go through a major intermediary currency, usually the USD. Hence, the trade would be broken into two legs: a trade in the CLP/USD pair and another in the THB/USD pair. These trades might go through different traders or trading desks at the same bank; or perhaps one leg of the trade would be done at one bank and the other leg through a different bank. There may also be time zone issues affecting liquidity; one leg of the trade may be relatively liquid at the same time as the other leg of the trade may be more thinly traded. The reason is because liquidity in most emerging market currencies is typically deepest in their domestic time zones. In any event, there are two bid–offer spreads—one for each leg of the trade—to be covered. This is often the case for many of the cross-rate currency pairs among developed market currencies as well. However, the bid–offer spreads are usually tighter for major currency pairs.

The liquidity issue is especially important when trades in these less-liquid currencies get "crowded," for example, through an excessive build-up of carry trades or through a fad-like popularity among investors for investing in a particular region or trading theme. Trades can be much easier to gradually enter into than to quickly exit, particularly under stressed market conditions. For example, after a long period of slow build-up, carry trades into these currencies can occasionally be subject to panicked unwinds as market conditions suddenly turn. This situation typically causes market liquidity to evaporate and leaves traders locked into positions that continue to accumulate losses.

The investment return probability distributions for currency (and other) trades subject to such relatively frequent extreme events have fatter tails than the normal distribution as well as a pronounced negative skew. Risk measurement and control tools (such as value at risk, or VaR) that depend on normal distributions can be misleading under these circumstances and greatly understate the risks the portfolio is actually exposed to. Many investment performance measures are also based on the normal distribution. Historical investment performance measured by such indexes as the Sharpe ratio can look very attractive during times of relative tranquility; but this seeming outperformance can disappear into deep losses faster than most investors can react (investors typically do a poor job of timing crises). As mentioned in the prior section on volatility trading, price volatility in financial markets is very cyclical and implied volatility can be subject to sharp spikes. These volatility spikes can severely affect both option prices and hedging strategies based on options. Even if the initial option protection is in place, it will eventually have to be rolled as options expire—but then at much higher prices for the option buyer.

The occurrence of currency crises can also affect hedging strategies based on forward contracts. Recall that hedging a long exposure to a foreign currency typically involves selling the foreign currency forward. However, when currencies are under severe downward pressure, central banks often react by hiking the policy rate to support the domestic currency. But recall that the higher interest rates go in a country, then, all else equal, the deeper the forward discount for its currency (enforced by the arbitrage conditions of covered interest rate parity). Having to sell the currency forward at increasingly deep discounts will cause losses through negative roll yield and undermine the cost effectiveness of the hedging program.

Extreme price movements in financial markets can also undermine many hedging strategies based on presumed diversification. Crises not only affect the volatility in asset prices but also their correlations, primarily through "contagion" effects. The history of financial markets (circa 2012) has been characterized by a "risk-on, risk-off" environment dominated by swings in investor sentiment between speculative enthusiasm and pronounced flight-to-safety flows. In the process, there is often little differentiation between individual currencies, which tend to get traded together in broader baskets (such as "haven currencies"—USD, JPY, and CHF—and "commodity currencies"—AUD, NZD, and ZAR). Investors who may have believed that they had diversified their portfolio through a broad array of exposures in emerging markets may find instead in crises that they doubled-up their currency exposures. (Likewise, there can be correlated and extreme movements in the underlying assets of these foreign-currency exposures.)

Another potential factor affecting currency management in these "exotic" markets is government involvement in setting the exchange rate through such measures as foreign exchange market intervention, capital controls, and pegged (or at least tightly managed) exchange rates. These measures too can lead to occasional extreme events in markets; for example, when central banks intervene or when currency pegs change or get broken. Short-term stability in these government-influenced markets can lull traders into a false sense of overconfidence and over-positioning. When currency pegs break, the break can happen quickly. Assuming that investment returns will be normally distributed according to parameters estimated on recent historical data, or that correlation factors and liquidity will not change suddenly, can be lethal.

It bears noting that currency crises and government involvement in FX markets is not limited to emerging market currencies, but often occur among the major currencies as well. The central banks of major currencies will, on occasion, intervene in their own currencies or use other polices (such as sharp movements in policy rates) to influence exchange rate levels. These too can lead to extreme events in currency markets.

7.2. Non-Deliverable Forwards

Currencies of many emerging market countries trade with some form of capital controls. Where capital controls exist and delivery in the controlled currency is limited by the local government, it is often possible to use what are known as **non-deliverable forwards** (NDFs). These are similar to regular forward contracts, but they are cash settled (in the non-controlled currency of the currency pair) rather than physically settled (the controlled currency is neither delivered nor received). The non-controlled currency for NDFs is usually the USD or some other major currency. A partial list of some of the most important currencies with NDFs would include the Chinese yuan (CNY), Korean won (KRW), Russian ruble (RUB), Indian rupee (INR), and Brazilian real (BRL). The NDF is essentially a cash-settled "bet" on the movement in the spot rate of these currencies.

For example, a trader could enter into a long position in a three-month NDF for the BRL/USD. Note that the BRL—the currency with capital controls—is the price currency and the base currency, the USD is the currency that settlement of the NDF will be made in. Assume that the current all-in rate for the NDF is 2.0280 and the trader uses an NDF with a notional size of USD1,000,000. Suppose that three months later the BRL/USD spot rate is 2.0300 and the trader closes out the existing NDF contract with an equal and offsetting spot transaction at this rate. Settlement proceeds by noting that the USD amounts net to zero (USD1,000,000 both bought and sold on settlement date), so the net cash flow generated would normally be in BRL if this was an ordinary forward contract. The net cash flow to the long position in this case would be calculated as

$$(2.0300 - 2.0280) \times 1,000,000 = BRL2,000$$

But with an NDF, there is no delivery in the controlled currency (hence the name *non-deliverable* forward). Settlement must be in USD, so this BRL amount is converted to USD at the then-current spot rate of 2.0300. This leads to a USD cash inflow for the long position in the NDF of

$$BRL2,000 \div 2.0300 \ BRL/USD = USD985.22$$

The credit risk of an NDF is typically lower than for the outright forward because the principal sums in the NDF do not move, unlike with an outright "vanilla" forward contract. For example, in the illustration the cash pay-off to the "bet" was the relatively small amount of USD985.22—there was no delivery of USD1,000,000 against receipt of BRL2,028,000. Conversely, as noted previously, NDFs exist because of some form of government involvement in foreign exchange markets. Sudden changes in government policy can lead to sharp movements in spot and NDF rates, often reversing any investment gains earned during long periods of seeming (but artificial) market calm. The implicit market risk of the NDF embodies an element of "tail risk."

Finally, we note that when capital controls exist, the free cross-border flow of capital that enforces the arbitrage condition underlying covered interest rate parity no longer functions consistently. Therefore, the pricing on NDFs need not be exactly in accord with the covered interest rate parity theorem. Instead, NDF pricing will reflect the individual supply and demand conditions (and risk premia) in the offshore market, which need not be the same as the onshore market of the specific emerging market country. Some of the most active participants in the NDF market are offshore hedge funds and proprietary traders making directional bets on the emerging market currency, rather than corporate or institutional portfolio managers hedging currency exposures. Volatility in the net speculative demand for emerging market exposure can affect the level of forward points. We also note that the type and strictness of capital controls can vary among emerging markets; hence, the need for knowledge of local market regulations is another factor influencing currency risk management in these markets.

8. SUMMARY

In this chapter, we have examined the basic principles of managing foreign exchange risk within the broader investment process. International financial markets create a wide range of opportunities for investors, but they also create the need to recognize, measure, and control exchange rate risk. The management of this risk starts with setting the overall mandate for the portfolio, encoding the investors' investment objectives and constraints into the investment policy statement, and providing strategic guidance on how currency risk will be managed in the portfolio. It extends to tactical positioning when portfolio managers translate market views into specific trading strategies within the overall risk management guidelines set by the IPS. We have examined some of these trading strategies, and how a range of portfolio management tools—positions in spot, forward, option, and FX swap contracts—can be used either to hedge away currency risk, or to express a market opinion on future exchange rate movements.

What we have emphasized throughout this chapter is that there is no simple or single answer for the "best" currency management strategies. Different investors will have different strategic mandates (IPS), and different portfolio managers will have different market opinions and risk tolerances. There is a near-infinite number of possible currency trading strategies, each with its own benefits, costs, and risks. Currency risk management—both at the strategic and tactical levels—means having to manage the trade-offs between all of these various considerations.

Some of the main points covered in this chapter are as follows:

- In professional FX markets, currencies are identified by standard three-letter codes, and quoted in terms of a price and a base currency (P/B).
- The spot exchange rate is typically for $T + 2$ delivery, and forward rates are for delivery for later periods. Both spot and forward rates are quoted in terms of a bid–offer price. Forward rates are quoted in terms of the spot rate plus forward points.
- An FX swap is a simultaneous spot and forward transaction; one leg of the swap is buying the base currency and the other is selling it. FX swaps are used to renew outstanding forward contracts once they mature, to "roll them forward."
- The domestic-currency return on foreign-currency assets can be broken into the foreign-currency asset return and the return on the foreign currency (the percentage appreciation or depreciation of the foreign currency against the domestic currency). These two components of the domestic-currency return are multiplicative.
- When there are several foreign-currency assets, the portfolio domestic-currency return is the weighted average of the individual domestic-currency returns (i.e., using the portfolio weights, which should sum to one).
- The risk of domestic-currency returns (its standard deviation) can be approximated by using a variance formula that recognizes the individual variances and covariances (correlations) among the foreign-currency asset returns and exchange rate movements.
- The calculation of the domestic-currency risk involves a large number of variables that must be estimated: the risks and correlations between all of the foreign-currency asset returns and their exchange rate risks.
- Guidance on where to target the portfolio along the risk spectrum is part of the IPS, which makes this a *strategic* decision based on the investment goals and constraints of the beneficial owners of the portfolio.
- If the IPS allows currency risk in the portfolio, the amount of desired currency exposure will depend on both portfolio diversification considerations and cost considerations.
  - Views on the diversifying effects of foreign-currency exposures depend on the time horizon involved, the type of foreign-currency asset, and market conditions.
  - Cost considerations also affect the hedging decision. Hedging is not free: It has both direct transactional costs as well as opportunity costs (the potential for favorable outcomes is foregone). Cost considerations make a perfect hedge difficult to maintain.
- Currency management strategies can be located along a spectrum stretching from:

- ■ passive, rules-based, complete hedging of currency exposures;
- ■ discretionary hedging, which allows the portfolio manager some latitude on managing currency exposures;
- ■ active currency management, which seeks out currency risk in order to manage it for profit; and to
- ■ currency overlay programs that aggressively manage currency "alpha."

- There are a variety of methods for forming market views.
  - ■ The use of macroeconomic fundamentals to predict future currency movements is based on estimating the "fair value" for a currency with the expectation that spot rates will eventually converge on this equilibrium value.
  - ■ Technical market indicators assume that, based on market psychology, historical price patterns in the data have a tendency to repeat. Technical indicators can be used to predict support and resistance levels in the market, as well as to confirm market trends and turning points.
  - ■ The carry trade is based on violations of uncovered interest rate parity, and is also based on selling low-yield currencies in order to invest in high-yield currencies. This approach is equivalent to trading the forward rate bias, which means selling currencies trading at a forward premium and buying currencies trading at a forward discount.
  - ■ Volatility trading uses the option market to express views on the distribution of future exchange rates, not their levels.

- Passive hedging will typically use forward contracts (rather than futures contracts) because they are more flexible. However, currency futures contracts are an option for smaller trading sizes and are frequently used in private wealth management.
- Forward contracts have the possibility of negative roll yield (the forward points embedded in the forward price can work for or against the hedge). The portfolio manager will have to balance the advantages and costs of hedging with forward contracts.
- Foreign-currency options can reduce opportunity costs (they allow the upside potential for favorable foreign-currency movements). However, the up-front option premiums must be paid.
- There are a variety of means to reduce the cost of the hedging with either forward or option contracts, but these cost-reduction measures always involve some combination of less downside protection and/or less upside potential.
- Hedging multiple foreign currencies uses the same tools and strategies used in hedging a single foreign-currency exposure, except now the correlation between residual currency exposures in the portfolio should be considered.
- Cross hedges introduce basis risk into the portfolio, which is the risk that the correlation between exposure and its cross hedging instrument may change in unexpected ways. Forward contracts typically have very little basis risk compared with movements in the underlying spot rate.
- The number of trading strategies that can be used, for hedging or speculative purposes, either for a single foreign currency or multiple foreign currencies, is near infinite. The manager must assess the costs, benefits, and risks of each in the context of the investment goals and constraints of the portfolio. There is no single "correct" approach.

REFERENCES

Bank for International Settlements. 2013. "Triennial Central Bank Survey of Foreign Exchange and Derivatives Market Activity."

Campbell, John Y. 2010. "Global Currency Hedging: What Role Should Foreign Currency Play in a Diversified Investment Portfolio?" *CFA Institute Conference Proceedings Quarterly*, vol. 27, no. 4 (December): 8–18.

Campbell, John Y., Karine Serfaty-de Medeiros, and Luis. M. Viceira. 2007. "Global Currency Hedging," NBER Working Paper 13088 (May).

Darnell, R. Max. 2004. "Currency Strategies to Enhance Returns." In *Fixed-Income Tools for Enhancing Return and Meeting Client Objectives*. Charlottesville, VA: Association for Investment Management and Research.

Froot, Kenneth A. 1993. "Currency Hedging Over Long Horizons." NBER Working Paper 4355 (April): www.people.hbs.edu/kfroot/oldwebsite/cvpaperlinks/currency_hedging.pdf.

Hnatkovska, Viktoria, and Martin Evans. 2005. "International Capital Flows in a World of Greater Financial Integration." NBER Working Paper 11701 (October).

Kritzman, Mark P. 1999. "The Forward-Rate Bias." In *Currency Risk in Investment Portfolios*. Charlottesville, VA: Association for Investment Management and Research.

Martini, Giulio. 2010. "The Continuum from Passive to Active Currency Management." *CFA Institute Conference Proceedings Quarterly*, vol. 27, no. 1 (March): 1–11.

Michenaud, Sébastien, and Bruno Solnik. 2008. "Applying Regret Theory to Investment Choices: Currency Hedging Decisions." *Journal of International Money and Finance*, vol. 27, no. 5: 677–694.

Rosenberg, Michael R. 2002. *Deutsche Bank Guide to Exchange-Rate Determination*. London: Irwin Professional Publishing (May).

Rosenberg, Michael R., and William A. Barker. 2017. "Currency Exchange Rates: Understanding Equilibrium Value." CFA Program Curriculum, Level II.

Sine, Barry M., and Robert A. Strong. 2012. "Technical Analysis." CFA Program Curriculum, Level I.

US Department of the Treasury. 2007. "Semiannual Report on International Economic and Exchange Rate Policies, Appendix I." (December).

PRACTICE PROBLEMS

The following information relates to Questions 1–9

Kamala Gupta, a currency management consultant, is hired to evaluate the performance of two portfolios. Portfolio A and Portfolio B are managed in the United States and performance is measured in terms of the US dollar (USD). Portfolio A consists of British pound (GBP) denominated bonds and Portfolio B holds euro (EUR) denominated bonds.

Gupta calculates a 19.5% domestic-currency return for Portfolio A and 0% domestic-currency return for Portfolio B.

1. **Analyze** the movement of the USD against the foreign currency for Portfolio A. **Justify** your choice.

Template for Question 1

Asset	Foreign-Currency Portfolio Return	USD Relative to Foreign-Currency (circle one)
Portfolio A	15%	appreciated
		depreciated

Justification

2. **Analyze** the foreign-currency return for Portfolio B. **Justify** your choice.

Template for Question 2

Asset	Percentage Movement in the Spot Exchange Rate	Foreign-Currency Portfolio Return (circle one)
Portfolio B	EUR appreciated 5% against the USD	positive
		negative

Justification

The fund manager of Portfolio B is evaluating an internally-managed 100% foreign-currency hedged strategy.

3. **Discuss** *two* forms of trading costs associated with this currency management strategy.

   Gupta tells the fund manager of Portfolio B:

   "We need to seriously consider the potential costs associated with favorable currency rate movements, given that a 100% hedge-ratio strategy is being applied to this portfolio."

4. **Explain** Gupta's statement in light of the strategic choices in currency management available to the portfolio manager.

   The investment policy statement (IPS) for Portfolio A provides the manager with discretionary authority to take directional views on future currency movements. The fund manager believes the foreign currency assets of the portfolio could be fully hedged internally. However, the manager also believes existing firm personnel lack the expertise to actively manage foreign-currency movements to generate currency alpha.

5. **Recommend** a solution that will provide the fund manager the opportunity to earn currency alpha through active foreign exchange management.

Gupta and the fund manager of Portfolio A discuss the differences among several active currency management methods.

6. **Evaluate** each statement independently and select the active currency approach it *best* describes. **Justify** each choice.

Template for Question 6

Gupta's Statements	Active Currency Approach (circle one)	Justification
"Many traders believe that it is not necessary to examine factors like the current account deficit, inflation, and interest rates because current exchange rates already reflect the market view on how these factors will affect future exchange rates."	carry trade technical analysis economic fundamental	
"The six-month interest rate in India is 8% compared to 1% in the United States. This presents a yield pick-up opportunity."	carry trade technical analysis economic fundamental	
"The currency overlay manager will estimate the fair value of the currencies with the expectation that observed spot rates will converge to long-run equilibrium values described by parity conditions."	carry trade technical analysis economic fundamental	

The following information is used for Question 7

Gupta interviews a currency overlay manager on behalf of Portfolio A. The foreign currency overlay manager describes volatility-based trading, compares volatility-based trading strategies and explains how the firm uses currency options to establish positions in the foreign exchange market. The overlay manager states:

Statement 1.   "Given the current stability in financial markets, several traders at our firm take advantage of the fact that most options expire out-of-the money and therefore are net-short volatility."

Statement 2.   "Traders that want to minimize the impact of unanticipated price volatility are net-long volatility."

7. **Compare** Statement 1 and Statement 2 and **identify** which *best* explains the view of a speculative volatility trader and which best explains the view of a hedger of volatility. **Justify** your response.

The following information is used for Questions 8 and 9

The fund manager of Portfolio B believes that setting up a full currency hedge requires a simple matching of the *current* market value of the foreign-currency exposure in the portfolio with an equal and offsetting position in a forward contract.

8. **Explain** how the hedge, as described by the fund manager, will eventually expose the portfolio to currency risk.
9. **Recommend** an alternative hedging strategy that will keep the hedge ratio close to the target hedge ratio. **Identify** the main disadvantage of implementing such a strategy.

The following information relates to Questions 10–15

Guten Investments GmbH, based in Germany and using the EUR as its reporting currency, is an asset management firm providing investment services for local high-net-worth and institutional investors seeking international exposures. The firm invests in the Swiss, UK, and US markets, after conducting fundamental research in order to select individual investments. Exhibit 1 presents recent information for exchange rates in these foreign markets.

EXHIBIT 1   Exchange Rate Data

	One Year Ago	Today
Euro-dollar (USD/EUR)*	1.2730	1.2950
Euro-sterling (GBP/EUR)	0.7945	0.8050
Euro-Swiss (CHF/EUR)	1.2175	1.2080

* The amount of USD required to buy one EUR

In prior years, the correlation between movements in the foreign-currency asset returns for the USD-denominated assets and movements in the exchange rate was estimated to be +0.50. After analyzing global financial markets, Konstanze Ostermann, a portfolio manager at Guten Investments, now expects that this correlation will increase to +0.80, although her forecast for foreign-currency asset returns is unchanged.

Ostermann believes that currency markets are efficient and hence that long-run gains cannot be achieved from active currency management, especially after netting out management and transaction costs. She uses this philosophy to guide hedging decisions for her discretionary accounts, unless instructed otherwise by the client.

Ostermann is aware, however, that some investors hold an alternative view on the merits of active currency management. Accordingly, their portfolios have different investment guidelines. For these accounts, Guten Investments employs a currency specialist firm, Umlauf Management, to provide currency overlay programs specific to each client's investment objectives. For most hedging strategies, Umlauf Management develops a market view based on underlying fundamentals in exchange rates. However, when directed by clients, Umlauf Management uses options and a variety of trading strategies to unbundle all of the various risk factors (the "Greeks") and trade them separately.

Ostermann conducts an annual review for three of her clients and gathers the summary information presented in Exhibit 2.

EXHIBIT 2   Select Clients at Guten Investments

Client	Currency Management Objectives
Adele Kastner – A high-net-worth individual with a low risk tolerance.	Keep the portfolio's currency exposures close, if not equal to, the benchmark so that the domestic-currency return is equal to the foreign-currency return.
Braunt Pensionskasse – A large private-company pension fund with a moderate risk tolerance.	Limited discretion, which allows the actual portfolio currency risk exposures to vary plus or minus 5% from the neutral position.
Franz Trading GmbH – An exporting company with a high risk tolerance.	Discretion with respect to currency exposure is allowed in order to add alpha to the portfolio.

10. Based on Exhibit 1, the domestic-currency return over the last year (measured in EUR terms) was *higher* than the foreign-currency return for:
    A. USD-denominated assets.
    B. GBP-denominated assets.
    C. CHF-denominated assets.

11. Based on Ostermann's correlation forecast, the expected domestic-currency return (measured in EUR terms) on USD-denominated assets will *most* likely:
    A. increase.
    B. decrease.
    C. remain unchanged.

12. Based on Ostermann's views regarding active currency management, the percentage of currency exposure in her discretionary accounts that is hedged is *most likely:*
    A. 0%.
    B. 50%.
    C. 100%.

13. The active currency management approach that Umlauf Management is *least* likely to employ is based on:
    A. volatility trading.
    B. technical analysis.
    C. economic fundamentals.

14. Based on Exhibit 2, the currency overlay program *most* appropriate for Braunt Pensionskasse would:
   A. be fully passive.
   B. allow limited directional views.
   C. actively manage foreign exchange as an asset class.

15. Based on Exhibit 2, the client *most likely* to benefit from the introduction of an additional overlay manager is:
   A. Adele Kastner.
   B. Braunt Pensionskasse.
   C. Franz Trading GmbH.

The following information relates to Questions 16–19

Li Jiang is an international economist operating a subscription website through which she offers financial advice on currency issues to retail investors. One morning she receives four subscriber e-mails seeking guidance.

Subscriber 1   "As a French national now working in the United States, I hold US dollar-denominated assets currently valued at USD 700,000. The USD/EUR exchange rate has been quite volatile and now appears oversold based on historical price trends. With my American job ending soon, I will return to Europe. I want to protect the value of my USD holdings, measured in EUR terms, before I repatriate these funds back to France. To reduce my currency exposure I am going to use currency futures contracts. Can you explain the factors most relevant to implementing this strategy?"

Subscriber 2   "I have observed that many of the overseas markets for Korean export goods are slowing, while the United States is experiencing a rise in exports. Both trends can combine to possibly affect the value of the won (KRW) relative to the US dollar. As a result, I am considering a speculative currency trade on the KRW/USD exchange rate. I also expect the volatility in this exchange rate to increase."

Subscriber 3   "India has relatively high interest rates compared to the United States and my market view is that this situation is likely to persist. As a retail investor actively trading currencies, I am considering borrowing in USD and converting to the Indian rupee (INR). I then intend to invest these funds in INR-denominated bonds, but without using a currency hedge."

Subscriber 4   "I was wondering if trading in emerging market currencies provides more opportunities for superior returns through active management than trading in Developed Market currencies."

16. For Subscriber 1, the *most* significant factor to consider would be:
   A. margin requirements.
   B. transaction costs of using futures contracts.
   C. different quoting conventions for future contracts.

17. For Subscriber 2, and assuming all of the choices relate to the KRW/USD exchange rate, the *best* way to implement the trading strategy would be to:

    A. write a straddle.

    B. buy a put option.

    C. use a long NDF position.

18. Which of the following market developments would be *most* favorable for Subscriber 3's trading plan?

    A. A narrower interest rate differential.

    B. A higher forward premium for INR/USD.

    C. Higher volatility in INR/USD spot rate movements.

19. Jiang's *best* response to Subscriber 4 would be that active trading in trading in emerging market currencies:

    A. typically leads to return distributions that are positively skewed.

    B. should not lead to higher returns because FX markets are efficient.

    C. often leads to higher returns through carry trades, but comes with higher risks and trading costs.

The following information relates to Questions 20–23

Rika Björk runs the currency overlay program at a large Scandinavian investment fund, which uses the Swedish krona (SEK) as its reporting currency. She is managing the fund's exposure to GBP-denominated assets, which are currently hedged with a GBP 100,000,000 forward contract (on the SEK/GBP cross rate, which is currently at 10.6875 spot). The maturity for the forward contract is December 1, which is still several months away. However, since the contract was initiated the value of the fund's assets has declined by GBP 7,000,000. As a result, Björk wants to rebalance the hedge immediately.

Next Björk turns her attention to the fund's Swiss franc (CHF) exposures. In order to maintain some profit potential Björk wants to hedge the exposure using a currency option, but at the same time, she wants to reduce hedging costs. She believes that there is limited upside for the SEK/CHF cross rate.

Björk then examines the fund's EUR-denominated exposures. Due to recent monetary tightening by the Riksbank (the Swedish central bank) forward points for the SEK/EUR rate have swung to a premium. The fund's EUR-denominated exposures are hedged with forward contracts.

Finally Björk turns her attention to the fund's currency exposures in several emerging markets. The fund has large positions in several Latin American bond markets, but Björk does not feel that there is sufficient liquidity in the related foreign exchange derivatives to easily hedge the fund's Latin American bond markets exposures. However, the exchange rates for these countries, measured against the SEK, are correlated with the MXN/SEK exchange rate. (The MXN is the Mexican peso, which is considered to be among the most liquid Latin American currencies). Björk considers using forward positions in the MXN to cross-hedge the fund's Latin American currency exposures.

20. To rebalance the SEK/GBP hedge, and assuming all instruments are based on SEK/ GBP, Björk would buy:

    A. GBP 7,000,000 spot.

    B. GBP 7,000,000 forward to December 1.

    C. SEK 74,812,500 forward to December 1.

21. Given her investment goals and market view, and assuming all options are based on SEK/CHF, the *best* strategy for Björk to manage the fund's CHF exposure would be to buy an:

    A. ATM call option.

    B. ITM call option and write an OTM call option.

    C. OTM put option and write an OTM call option.

22. Given the recent movement in the forward premium for the SEK/EUR rate, Björk can expect that the hedge will experience higher:

    A. basis risk.

    B. roll yield.

    C. premia income.

23. The *most* important risk to Björk's Latin American currency hedge would be changes in:

    A. forward points.

    B. exchange rate volatility.

    C. cross-currency correlations.

The following information relates to Question 24

Kalila Al-Khalili has been hired as a consultant to a Middle Eastern sovereign wealth fund. The fund's oversight committee has asked her to examine the fund's financial characteristics and recommend an appropriate currency management strategy given the fund's Investment Policy Statement. After a thorough study of the fund and its finances, Al-Khalili reaches the following conclusions:

- The fund's mandate is focused on the long-term development of the country, and the royal family (who are very influential on the fund's oversight committee) are prepared to take a long-term perspective on the fund's investments.
- The fund's strategic asset allocation is tilted toward equity rather than fixed-income assets.
- Both its fixed-income and equity portfolios have a sizeable exposure to emerging market assets.
- Currently, about 90% of exchange rate exposures are hedged, although the IPS allows a range of hedge ratios.
- Liquidity needs of the fund are minimal, since the government is running a balanced budget and is unlikely to need to dip into the fund in the near term to cover fiscal deficits. Indeed, the expected lifetime of country's large oil reserves has been greatly extended by recent discoveries, and substantial oil royalties are expected to persist into the future.

24. Based on her investigation, Al-Khalili would *most* likely recommend:

    A. active currency management.

    B. a hedging ratio closer to 100%.

    C. a narrow discretionary band for currency exposures.

The following information relates to Questions 25–27

Mason Darden is an adviser at Colgate & McIntire (C&M), managing large-cap global equity separate accounts. C&M's investment process restricts portfolio positions to companies based in the United States, Japan, and the eurozone. All C&M clients are US-domiciled, with client reporting in US dollars.

Darden manages Ravi Bhatt's account, which had a total (US dollar) return of 7.0% last year. Darden must assess the contribution of foreign currency to the account's total return. Exhibit 1 summarizes the account's geographic portfolio weights, asset returns, and currency returns for last year.

EXHIBIT 1   Performance Data for Bhatt's Portfolio Last Year

Geography	Portfolio Weight	Asset Return	Currency Return
United States	50%	10.0%	NA
Eurozone	25%	5.0%	2.0%
Japan	25%	–3.0%	4.0%
Total	100%		

25. **Calculate** the contribution of foreign currency to the Bhatt account's total return. **Show** your calculations.

Darden meets with Bhatt and learns that Bhatt will be moving back to his home country of India next month to resume working as a commodity trader. Bhatt is concerned about a possible US recession. His investment policy statement (IPS) allows for flexibility in managing currency risk. Overall returns can be enhanced by capturing opportunities between the US dollar and the Indian rupee (INR) within a range of plus or minus 25% from the neutral position using forward contracts on the currency pair. C&M has a currency overlay team that can appropriately manage currency risk for Bhatt's portfolio.

26. **Determine** the *most appropriate* currency management strategy for Bhatt. **Justify** your response.

Determine the *most appropriate* currency management strategy for Bhatt. (Circle one.)

Passive hedging	Discretionary hedging	Active currency management

---

Justify your response.

Following analysis of Indian economic fundamentals, C&M's currency team expects continued stability in interest rate and inflation rate differentials between the United States and India. C&M's currency team strongly believes the US dollar will appreciate relative to the Indian rupee.

C&M would like to exploit the perceived alpha opportunity using forward contracts on the USD10,000,000 Bhatt portfolio.

27. **Recommend** the trading strategy C&M should implement. **Justify** your response.

The following information relates to Questions 28–29

Renita Murimi is a currency overlay manager and market technician who serves institutional investors seeking to address currency-specific risks associated with investing in international assets. Her firm also provides volatility overlay programs. She is developing a volatility-based strategy for Emil Konev, a hedge fund manager focused on option trading. Konev seeks to implement an "FX as an asset class" approach distinct to his portfolio to realize speculative gains and believes the long-term strength of the US dollar is peaking.

28. **Describe** how a volatility-based strategy for Konev would *most likely* contrast with Murimi's other institutional investors. **Justify** your response.
29. **Discuss** how Murimi can use her technical skills to devise the strategy.

30. Carnoustie Capital Management, Ltd. (CCM), a UK-based global investment advisory firm, is considering adding an emerging market currency product to its offerings. CCM has for the past three years managed a "model" portfolio of emerging market currencies using the same investment approach as its developed economy currency products. The risk and return measures of the "model" portfolio compare favorably with the one- and three-year emerging market benchmark performance net of CCM's customary advisory fee and estimated trading costs. Mindful of the higher volatility of emerging market currencies, CCM management is particularly pleased with the "model" portfolio's standard deviation, Sharpe ratio, and value at risk (VAR) in comparison to those of its developed economy products.

Recognizing that market conditions have been stable since the "model" portfolio's inception, CCM management is sensitive to the consequences of extreme market events for emerging market risk and return.

Evaluate the application of emerging market and developed market investment return probability distributions for CCM's potential new product.

The following information relates to Questions 31–32

Wilson Manufacturing (Wilson) is an Australian institutional client of Ethan Lee, who manages a variety of portfolios across asset classes. Wilson prefers a neutral benchmark over a rules-based approach, with its investment policy statement (IPS) requiring a currency hedge ratio between 97% and 103% to protect against currency risk. Lee has assessed various currency management strategies for Wilson's US dollar-denominated fixed-income portfolio to optimally locate it along the currency risk spectrum. The portfolio is currently in its flat natural neutral position because of Lee's lack of market conviction.

31. **Identify** the *most likely* approach for Lee to optimally locate Wilson's portfolio on the currency risk spectrum, consistent with the IPS. **Justify** your response with *two* reasons supporting the approach.

Identify the *most likely* approach for Lee to optimally locate Wilson's portfolio on the currency risk spectrum, consistent with IPS. (Circle one.)

Passive Hedging   Discretionary Hedging   Active Currency Management   Currency Overlay

---

Justify your response with *two* reasons supporting the approach.

Lee and Wilson recently completed the annual portfolio review and determined the IPS is too short-term focused and excessively risk averse. Accordingly, the IPS is revised and foreign currency is introduced as a separate asset class. Lee hires an external foreign exchange sub-adviser to implement a currency overlay program, emphasizing that it is important to structure the program so that the currency overlay is allowed in terms of strategic portfolio positioning.

32. **Discuss** a key attribute of the currency overlay that would *increase* the likelihood it would be allowed in terms of strategic portfolio positioning.

The following information relates to Questions 33–35

Rosario Delgado is an investment manager in Spain. Delgado's client, Max Rivera, seeks assistance with his well-diversified investment portfolio denominated in US dollars.

Rivera's reporting currency is the euro, and he is concerned about his US dollar exposure. His portfolio IPS requires monthly rebalancing, at a minimum. The portfolio's market value is USD2.5 million. Given Rivera's risk aversion, Delgado is considering a monthly hedge using either a one-month forward contract or one-month futures contract.

33. **Determine** which type of hedge instrument combination is *most* appropriate for Rivera's situation. **Justify** your selection.

Determine which type of hedge instrument combination is *most* appropriate for Rivera's situation. (Circle one.)

| Static Forward | Static Futures | Dynamic Forward | Dynamic Futures |

Justify your selection.

Assume Rivera's portfolio was perfectly hedged. It is now time to rebalance the portfolio and roll the currency hedge forward one month. The relevant data for rebalancing are provided in Exhibit 1.

EXHIBIT 1   Portfolio and Relevant Market Data

	One Month Ago	Today
Portfolio value of assets (USD)	2,500,000	2,650,000
USD/EUR spot rate (bid–offer)	0.8913/0.8914	0.8875/0.8876
One-month forward points (bid–offer)	25/30	20/25

34. **Calculate** the net cash flow (in euros) to maintain the desired hedge. **Show** your calculations.

With the US dollar currently trading at a forward premium and US interest rates lower than Spanish rates, Delgado recommends trading against the forward rate bias to earn additional return from a positive roll yield.

35. **Identify** *two* strategies Delgado should use to earn a positive roll yield. **Describe** the specific steps needed to execute each strategy.

Identify *two* strategies Delgado should use to earn a positive roll yield.	**Describe** the specific steps needed to execute *each* strategy.
1.	
2.	

CHAPTER 9

OVERVIEW OF FIXED-INCOME PORTFOLIO MANAGEMENT

Bernd Hanke, PhD, CFA
Brian J. Henderson, PhD, CFA

LEARNING OUTCOMES

The candidate should be able to:

- discuss roles of fixed-income securities in portfolios;
- describe how fixed-income mandates may be classified and compare features of the mandates;
- describe bond market liquidity, including the differences among market sub-sectors, and discuss the effect of liquidity on fixed-income portfolio management;
- describe and interpret a model for fixed-income returns;
- discuss the use of leverage, alternative methods for leveraging, and risks that leverage creates in fixed-income portfolios;
- discuss differences in managing fixed-income portfolios for taxable and tax-exempt investors.

1. INTRODUCTION

Globally, fixed-income markets represent the largest asset class in financial markets, and most investors' portfolios include fixed-income investments. Fixed-income markets include publicly traded securities (such as commercial paper, notes, and bonds) and non-publicly traded instruments (such as loans and privately placed securities). Loans may be securitized and become part of the pool of assets supporting an asset-backed security.

This chapter discusses why investor portfolios include fixed-income securities and provides an overview of fixed-income portfolio management. Section 2 discusses different roles of fixed-income securities in portfolios, including diversification, regular cash flows, and

Portfolio Management, Second Edition, by Bernd Hanke, PhD, CFA, and Brian J. Henderson, PhD, CFA. Copyright © 2017 by CFA Institute.

inflation hedging potential. Section 3 describes the two main types of fixed-income portfolio mandates: liability-based (or structured) mandates and total return mandates. It also describes approaches to implementing these mandates. Section 4 discusses bond market liquidity and its effects on pricing and portfolio construction. Section 5 introduces a model of how a bond position's total expected return can be decomposed. The model provides a better understanding of the driving forces behind expected returns to fixed-income securities. Section 6 discusses the use of leverage in fixed-income portfolios. Section 7 describes considerations in managing fixed-income portfolios for both taxable and tax-exempt investors. A summary of key points completes the chapter.

2. ROLES OF FIXED-INCOME SECURITIES IN PORTFOLIOS

Fixed-income securities serve important roles in investment portfolios, including diversification, regular cash flows, and possible inflation hedging. The correlations of fixed-income securities with equity securities vary, but adding fixed-income securities to portfolios that include equity securities is usually an effective way to obtain diversification benefits. Fixed-income securities typically specify schedules for principal repayments and interest payments. The scheduled nature of their cash flows enables investors—both individual and institutional —to fund, with some degree of predictability, known future obligations such as tuition payments or corporate pension obligations. Some fixed-income securities, such as inflation-linked bonds, may also provide a hedge for inflation.

2.1. Diversification Benefits

In a portfolio context, fixed-income investments can provide diversification benefits when combined with other asset classes. Recall that a major reason that portfolios can effectively reduce risk is that combining securities whose returns are not perfectly correlated (i.e., a correlation coefficient of less than +1.0) provides risk diversification. Lower correlations are associated with lower risk. The challenge in diversifying risk is to find assets that have a correlation that is much lower than +1.0.

Exhibit 1 shows the correlation matrix across several bond market sectors and the S&P 500 Index (an index of large-cap US equity securities) for the period January 2003 to September 2015. The bond market sectors in the matrix are represented by indexes of four investment-grade bond sub-sectors of the US bond market:

1. The Bloomberg Barclays US Aggregate (US dollar–denominated bonds with maturity greater than 1 year, including Treasuries, government-related and corporate securities, mortgage-backed securities, asset-backed securities, and commercial mortgage-backed securities);
2. The Bloomberg Barclays US Treasury Bond 10-Year Term (US Treasury bonds with maturities of 7–10 years);
3. The Bloomberg Barclays US Corporate (US dollar–denominated corporate bonds with maturity greater than 1 year); and
4. The Bloomberg Barclays US TIPS (Series-L) (US Treasury Inflation-Protected Securities [TIPS] with maturity greater than 1 year).

In addition to investment-grade bonds, the matrix includes a high-yield (non-investment-grade) bond market index: the Bloomberg Barclays US Corporate High-Yield

EXHIBIT 1   Correlation Matrix

Index	Bloomberg Barclays US Aggregate	Bloomberg Barclays US Treasury 10-Year Term	Bloomberg Barclays US Corporate	Bloomberg Barclays US TIPS	Bloomberg Barclays Global Aggregate	Bloomberg Barclays US Corporate High Yield	JP Morgan GBI-EM Global	S&P 500
Bloomberg Barclays US Aggregate	1.00	0.95	0.92	0.81	0.54	0.03	−0.01	−0.27
Bloomberg Barclays US Treasury 10-Year Term	0.95	1.00	0.88	0.79	0.50	−0.13	−0.12	−0.35
Bloomberg Barclays US Corporate	0.92	0.88	1.00	0.77	0.50	0.16	0.04	−0.25
Bloomberg Barclays US TIPS	0.81	0.79	0.77	1.00	0.49	0.07	0.08	−0.21
Bloomberg Barclays Global Aggregate	0.54	0.50	0.50	0.49	1.00	0.09	0.46	0.04
Bloomberg Barclays US Corporate High Yield	0.03	−0.13	0.16	0.07	0.09	1.00	0.47	0.32
JP Morgan GBI-EM Global	−0.01	−0.12	0.04	0.08	0.46	0.47	1.00	0.36
S&P 500	−0.27	−0.35	−0.25	−0.21	0.04	0.32	0.36	1.00

Sources: Authors' calculations for the period January 2003 to September 2015, based on data from Barclays Risk Analytics and Index Solutions; J.P. Morgan Index Research; S&P Dow Jones Indices.

(US dollar–denominated high-yield corporate bonds with maturity greater than one year). The matrix also includes two international bond indexes: the Bloomberg Barclays Global Aggregate (international investment-grade bonds) and the JP Morgan Government Bond Index–Emerging Markets Global (GBI–EM Global).

For the period January 2003 to September 2015, the correlation matrix shows the following:

- The US bond market's investment-grade sub-sectors were highly correlated with each other, as evidenced by the correlations ranging from 0.77 to 0.95.
- International investment-grade bonds, which include US investment-grade bonds, show a 0.54 correlation with the overall US investment-grade bond sector. Because the US Aggregate Index and the US Aggregate Index portion of the Global Aggregate Index have a correlation of 1.0, the non-US investment-grade bonds must have had an even lower correlation with US investment-grade bonds. During this period, significant diversification benefits existed for including both US and non-US bonds in portfolios.

- The US investment-grade bond sub-sectors exhibited low (and in some cases, negative) correlations with equities, US high-yield bonds, and emerging market bonds. International investment-grade bonds also exhibited low correlations with equities and US high-yield bonds but were moderately correlated with emerging market bonds. The low or negative correlations indicate that investment-grade bonds would have provided significant diversification benefits if combined with these other, more-volatile asset classes.
- High-yield bonds, emerging market bonds, and equities exhibited positive correlations with each other, ranging from 0.32 to 0.47.

Based on Exhibit 1, it appears that combining investment-grade, high-yield, and emerging market bonds and equities can result in portfolio diversification benefits. Fixed-income investments may also provide diversification benefits through their low correlations with other asset classes, such as real estate and commodities.

Importantly, these correlations are not constant over time. During a long historical period, the average correlation of returns between two asset classes may be low, but in any particular period, the correlation can differ from the average correlation. Correlation estimates can vary based on the capital market dynamics during the period when the correlations are measured. The correlation between the asset classes may increase or decrease, depending on the circumstances. During periods of market stress, investors may exhibit a "flight to quality" by buying safer assets such as government bonds (increasing their prices) and selling riskier assets such as equity securities and high-yield bonds (lowering their prices). These actions may decrease the correlation between government bonds and equity securities, as well as between government bonds and high-yield bonds. At the same time, the correlation between riskier assets such as equity securities and high-yield bonds may increase.

Correlation among assets is the primary determinant of diversification benefits and a reduction in portfolio risk, but volatility of each asset class also affects portfolio risk. Bonds are generally less volatile than other major asset classes such as equity securities. Consider the standard deviation of daily returns to the indexes shown in Exhibit 1, covering the same period (January 2003 to September 2015). The Bloomberg Barclays US Aggregate (Bond) Index exhibited annualized return standard deviations of approximately 4%. The Bloomberg Barclays US Corporate High-Yield Index and the JP Morgan GBI–EM Index, which are higher-risk sectors of the bond market, exhibited 6.3% and 9.8% annualized return standard deviations, respectively. By comparison, the S&P 500 exhibited an annualized return standard deviation of 19.4%. Including diversified fixed-income positions in an investment portfolio, combined with exposure to other major asset classes, may significantly lower portfolio risk.

It is important to note that similar to correlations, volatility (standard deviation) of asset class returns may also vary over time. If interest rate volatility increases, bonds, particularly those with long maturities, can exhibit higher near-term volatility relative to the average volatility during a long historical period. The standard deviation of returns for lower credit quality (high-yield) bonds can rise significantly during times of financial stress, because as credit quality declines and the probability of default increases, investors often view these bonds as being more similar to equities.

2.2. Benefits of Regular Cash Flows

Fixed-income investments typically produce regular cash flows to a portfolio. Regular cash flows allow investors—both individual and institutional—to plan how to meet, with some degree of predictability, known future obligations such as tuition payments, pension obligations, or payouts on life insurance policies. In these cases, future liabilities can be estimated with some reasonable certainty. Fixed-income securities are often acquired and "dedicated" to funding those future liabilities. In dedicated portfolios, fixed-income securities are selected such that the timing and magnitude of their cash flows match the timing and magnitude of the projected future liabilities.

Frequently, investors will "ladder" bond portfolios by staggering the maturity dates of portfolio bonds throughout the investment horizon. This approach can help to balance price risk and reinvestment risk. Buy-and-hold portfolios can also be tailored to fit an investor's specific investment horizon. For example, if an investor seeks regular income over a 10-year horizon, coupon-paying bonds that mature approximately 10 years in the future are good building blocks for such a portfolio.

It is important to note that reliance on regular cash flows assumes that no credit event (such as an issuer missing a scheduled interest or principal payment) or other market event (such as a decrease in interest rates increasing prepayments of mortgages underlying mortgage-backed securities) will occur. These events may cause actual cash flows of fixed-income securities to differ from expected cash flows. If any credit or market event occurs, a portfolio manager may need to adjust the portfolio.

2.3. Inflation Hedging Potential

Some fixed-income securities can provide a hedge for inflation. Bonds with floating-rate coupons protect interest income from inflation because the reference rate should adjust for inflation. The principal payment at maturity is unadjusted for inflation. Inflation-linked bonds provide investors with valuable inflation hedging benefits by paying a return that is directly linked to an index of consumer prices and adjusting the principal for inflation. There are several different structures for inflation-linked bonds, such as zero-coupon bonds with the inflation adjustment made to the principal payment, and capital-indexed bonds where a fixed coupon rate is applied to a principal amount that is adjusted for inflation throughout the bond's life.

The return on inflation-linked bonds includes a real return plus an additional component that is tied directly to the inflation rate. Inflation-linked bonds typically exhibit lower return volatility than conventional bonds and equities because the volatility of the returns on inflation-linked bonds depends on the volatility of *real*, rather than *nominal*, interest rates. The volatility of real interest rates is typically lower than the volatility of nominal interest rates that drive the returns of conventional bonds and equities.

Many governments in developed countries have issued inflation-linked bonds, including the United States, United Kingdom, France, Germany, Sweden, and Canada, as well as some in developing countries such as Brazil, Chile, and Argentina. Corporate issuers of inflation-linked bonds have included both financial and non-financial companies. For investors with long investment horizons, especially institutions facing long-term liabilities (for example, defined benefit pension plans and life insurance companies), inflation-linked bonds are particularly useful.

Exhibit 2 illustrates inflation protection provided by type of bond.

EXHIBIT 2   Protection against Inflation

	Coupon	Principal
Fixed-coupon bonds	Inflation unprotected	Inflation unprotected
Floating-coupon bonds	Inflation protected	Inflation unprotected
Inflation-linked bonds	Inflation protected	Inflation protected

Adding inflation-indexed bonds to diversified portfolios of bonds and equities typically results in superior risk-adjusted real portfolio returns. This improvement occurs because inflation-linked bonds can effectively represent a separate asset class, as they offer returns that differ from other asset classes and add to market completeness. Introducing inflation-linked bonds to an asset allocation strategy can result in a superior mean-efficient frontier.

EXAMPLE 1   Adding Fixed-Income Securities to a Portfolio

Mary Baker is anxious about the level of risk in her portfolio based on a recent period of increased equity market volatility. Most of her wealth is invested in a diversified global equities portfolio.

Baker contacts two wealth management firms, Atlantic Investments (AI) and West Coast Capital (WCC), for advice. In conversation with each adviser, she expresses her desire to reduce her portfolio's risk and to have a portfolio that generates a cash flow stream with consistent purchasing power over her 15-year investment horizon.

The correlation coefficient of Baker's diversified global equities portfolio with a diversified fixed-coupon bond portfolio is −0.10 and with a diversified inflation-linked bond portfolio is 0.10. The correlation coefficient between a diversified fixed-coupon bond portfolio and a diversified inflation-linked bond portfolio is 0.65.

The adviser from AI suggests diversifying half of her investment assets into nominal fixed-coupon bonds. The adviser from WCC also suggests diversification but recommends that Baker invest 25% of her investment assets into fixed-coupon bonds and 25% into inflation-linked bonds.

Evaluate the advice given to Baker by each adviser based on her stated desires regarding portfolio risk reduction and cash flow stream. Recommend which advice Baker should follow, making sure to discuss the following concepts in your answer:

a. Diversification benefits
b. Cash flow benefits
c. Inflation hedging benefits

Solution:

Advice from AI:
Diversifying into fixed-coupon bonds would offer substantial diversification benefits in lowering overall portfolio volatility (risk) given the negative correlation of −0.10. The portfolio's volatility, measured by standard deviation, would be lower than the weighted

standard deviations of the diversified global equities portfolio and the diversified fixed-coupon bond portfolio. The portfolio will generate regular cash flows because it includes fixed-coupon bonds. This advice, however, does not address Baker's desire to have the cash flows maintain purchasing power over time and thus serve as an inflation hedge.

Advice from WCC:
Diversifying into both fixed-coupon bonds and inflation-linked bonds offers additional diversification benefits beyond that offered by fixed-coupon bonds only. The correlation between diversified global equities and inflation-linked bonds is only 0.10. The correlation between nominal fixed-coupon bonds and inflation-linked bonds is 0.65, which is also less than 1.0. The portfolio will generate regular cash flows because of the inclusion of fixed-coupon and inflation-linked bonds. Adding the inflation-linked bonds helps to at least partially address Baker's desire for consistent purchasing power over her investment horizon.

Based on her stated desires and the analysis above, Baker should follow the advice provided by WCC.

3. FIXED-INCOME MANDATES

The previous section discussed the roles of fixed-income securities in portfolios and the benefits these securities provide. When investment mandates include an allocation to fixed income, investors need to decide how to add fixed-income securities to portfolios. Fixed-income mandates can be broadly classified into liability-based mandates and total return mandates. Liability-based mandates are managed to match or cover expected liability payments with future projected cash inflows. As such, they are also referred to as structured mandates, asset/liability management (ALM), or liability-driven investments (LDI). These types of mandates are structured in a way to ensure that a liability or a stream of liabilities (e.g., a company's pension liabilities) can be covered and that any risk of shortfalls or deficient cash inflows is minimized.

Total return mandates are generally managed in an attempt to either track or outperform a market-weighted fixed-income benchmark such as the Bloomberg Barclays Global Aggregate Index. Both liability-based and total return mandates exhibit common features, such as the attempt by investors to achieve the highest risk-adjusted returns (or perhaps highest yields) given a set of constraints. The two types of mandates have fundamentally different objectives, however.

Some fixed-income mandates include a requirement that environmental, social, and governance (ESG) factors are considered during the investment process. When considering these factors, an analyst or portfolio manager may look for evidence on whether the portfolio contains companies whose operations are favorable or unfavorable in the context of ESG, and whether such companies' actions and resource management practices reflect a sustainable business model. For example, the analyst or portfolio manager may consider whether a company experienced incidents involving significant environmental damage, instances of unfair labor practices, or lapses in corporate governance integrity. For companies that do not fare favorably in an ESG analysis, investors may assume that these companies are more likely to encounter future ESG-related incidents that could cause serious reputational and financial damage to the company. Such incidents could impair a company's credit quality and result in a decline in both the price of the company's bonds and the performance of a portfolio containing those bonds.

3.1. Liability-Based Mandates

Users of liability-based mandates include individuals funding specific cash flow and lifestyle needs as well as institutions such as banks, insurance companies, and pension funds. These types of institutions have a need to match future liabilities, such as payouts on life insurance policies and pension benefits, with corresponding cash inflows. Pension funds are perhaps the largest users of liability-based mandates based on assets invested. Regulators in many jurisdictions impose minimum funding levels on pension liabilities to ensure the safety of retiree pensions. Insurance companies project future cash outflows based on expected claims from policyholders. Additionally, life insurance companies may offer annuities and guaranteed investment contracts, both of which require cash outflows for extended periods.

There are two main approaches to liability-based mandates: **cash flow matching** and **duration matching**, which are immunization approaches. Immunization is the process of structuring and managing a fixed-income portfolio to minimize the variance in the realized rate of return over a known time horizon. This variance arises from the volatility of future interest rates. Immunization is an asset/liability management approach that structures investments in bonds to reduce or eliminate the risks associated with a change in market interest rates. In addition, several variations use or combine elements of these approaches, including contingent immunization and horizon matching.[1] The following discussion provides an overview of these approaches.

3.1.1. Cash Flow Matching

Cash flow matching is an immunization approach that may be the simplest and most intuitive way to match a liability stream and a stream of cash inflows. This approach, unlike duration matching, essentially has no underlying assumptions. Cash flow matching attempts to ensure that all future liability payouts are matched precisely by cash flows from bonds or fixed-income derivatives, such as interest rate futures, options, or swaps. Exhibit 3 shows the results of a cash flow matching approach for a liability stream and a bond portfolio. Future liability payouts are exactly mirrored by coupon and principal payments arising from the bond portfolio. Bond cash inflows coincide with liability cash outflows. Therefore, there is no need for reinvestment of cash inflows.

EXHIBIT 3   Cash Flow Matching

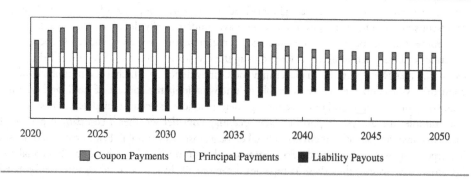

| Coupon Payments | Principal Payments | Liability Payouts |

---

[1]Leibowitz (1986a and 1986b) provides an insightful summary of the main approaches.

In practice, perfect matching of cash flows is difficult to achieve. It is rare that a combination of fixed-income securities can be found that exactly matches the timing and amount of the required cash outflows. Further, implementing a cash flow matching approach may result in relatively high transaction costs, even if quantitative optimization techniques are used to construct a cash flow matching portfolio at the lowest possible cost. Timing mismatches, such as some cash inflows preceding corresponding cash outflows, tend to exist because it may be less costly and more practical to not match cash flows precisely. Such a mismatch, however, results in some reinvestment risk.

Although in theory a cash flow matching portfolio does not need to be rebalanced once in place, it is often desirable or necessary to do so. As market conditions change, the lowest-cost cash flow matching portfolio may change because the universe of securities eligible for inclusion into the portfolio changes and the characteristics of securities change. A portfolio manager, therefore, has an incentive to rebalance the portfolio periodically despite incurring transaction costs.

For some types of fixed-income securities, the timing or amount of cash flows may change. For example, a corporate bond issuer may default and subsequent cash flows cease, or a bond with an embedded option may be called before maturity. Although these types of "imperfections" can often be avoided by restricting the universe of eligible securities and including only certain types of bonds (e.g., government bonds) in the portfolio, it is usually not optimal to do so. Securities that are not included in a smaller restricted universe might provide better return-to-risk tradeoffs.

3.1.2. Duration Matching

Duration matching is an immunization approach that is based on the duration of assets and liabilities. Ideally, the liabilities being matched (the liability portfolio) and the portfolio of assets (the bond portfolio) should be affected similarly by a change in interest rates. Conditions that need to be satisfied to achieve immunization using duration matching include the following: (1) A bond portfolio's duration must equal the duration of the liability portfolio; and (2) the present value of the bond portfolio's assets must equal the present value of the liabilities at current interest rate levels. The idea is that changes in the bond portfolio's market value closely match changes in the liability portfolio, whether interest rates rise or fall.

If interest rates increase or decrease, changes in reinvestment income and changes in bond prices immunize against the effect of interest rate changes. If interest rates decrease, reduced reinvestment income is offset by an increase in bond prices. If interest rates increase, higher reinvestment income offsets the decrease in bond prices. A crucial limitation of immunization is that it protects against only a parallel change in the yield curve—that is, the same yield change across the entire maturity spectrum of the yield curve. In practice, however, changes in the bond market environment may lead to changes in yield curve shape, such as steepening, flattening, or changes in the curvature.[2] Hence immunization remains imperfect, and the strategy design needs to incorporate some margin for error.

It is important to note other considerations for an immunized portfolio:

---

[2]There are extensions to the classical immunization approach (Redington 1952) that can incorporate non-parallel yield curve shifts (see, for example, Fong and Vasicek 1984). These approaches are more complex, however, and are not discussed here.

- A portfolio is an immunized portfolio only at a given point in time. As market conditions change, the immunization conditions will be violated, and the portfolio therefore needs to be rebalanced periodically to continue to achieve its immunization objective.
- The need to rebalance makes liquidity considerations important. Moreover, if bond portfolio cash flows (e.g., scheduled coupon and principal payments) are not perfectly matched with liability cash flows under immunization, bond positions may need to be liquidated in order to satisfy the liability outflows.
- Rebalancing and the need to liquidate positions can result in high portfolio turnover.
- Immunization assumes that bond issuers do not default, and it does not protect against issuer- or bond-specific interest rate changes such as those resulting from an individual bond issuer's change in credit quality.
- Immunization can accommodate bonds with embedded options (such as certain corporate bonds and mortgage-backed securities) to the extent that a bond's duration is replaced by its effective duration as an input to the methodology. Effective duration takes into account that future interest rate changes can affect the expected cash flows for a bond with embedded options.

In summary, the duration matching approach requires that reinvestment risk and the risk of bond price movements in a portfolio are offset. In practice, however, some immunization risk always remains. An exception would be a portfolio of zero-coupon bonds that are designed to match liability cash flows. In this case, because the zero-coupon bonds are held to maturity, the effect of interest rate changes on price are irrelevant and there are no interim cash flows to reinvest. In effect, there is no price risk, no reinvestment risk, and therefore no immunization risk, although credit risk remains.

Exhibit 4 gives an overview of key features of duration matching and cash flow matching.

EXHIBIT 4   Liability-Based Mandates: Key Features

	Duration Matching	**Cash Flow Matching**
Yield curve assumptions	Parallel yield curve shifts	None
Mechanism	Risk of shortfall in cash flows is minimized by matching duration and present value of liability stream	Bond portfolio cash flows match liabilities
Basic principle	Cash flows come from coupon and principal repayments of the bond portfolio and offset liability cash flows	Cash flows, coupons, and principal repayments of the bond portfolio offset liability cash flows
Rebalancing	Frequent rebalancing required	Not required but often desirable
Complexity	High	Low

3.1.3. Contingent Immunization
Variations of both duration and cash flow matching approaches exist. A commonly used hybrid approach is known as **contingent immunization**, which combines immunization with an active management approach when the asset portfolio's value exceeds the present value of the liability portfolio. In other words, there is a surplus. The portfolio manager is allowed to actively manage the asset portfolio, or some portion of the asset portfolio, as long as the value of the actively managed portfolio exceeds a specified value (threshold). The actively managed

portfolio can potentially be invested into any asset category, including equity, fixed-income, and alternative investments. If the actively managed portfolio value falls to the specified threshold, active management ceases and a conventional duration matching or a cash flow matching approach is put in place.

3.1.4. Horizon Matching

Another hybrid approach, **horizon matching**, combines cash flow and duration matching approaches. Under this approach, liabilities are categorized as short- and long-term liabilities. The short-term liability portion (usually liabilities up to about four or five years) is covered by a cash flow matching approach, whereas the long-term liabilities are covered by a duration matching approach. This approach combines desirable features of both approaches—a portfolio manager has more flexibility over the less certain, longer horizon and can still meet more certain, shorter-term obligations.

EXAMPLE 2   Liability-Based Mandates (1)

Dave Wilson, a fixed-income analyst, has been asked by his manager to analyze different liability-based mandates for a pension fund client. The pension plan currently has a very large surplus of assets over liabilities. Evaluate whether an immunization or contingent immunization approach would be most suitable for the pension fund.

Solution: Because the pension fund currently has a large surplus of assets over liabilities, a contingent immunization approach would be most suitable. A pure immunization approach would not be appropriate, because a key assumption under this approach is that the present value of the fund's assets equals the present value of its liabilities. The contingent immunization approach allows the pension fund's portfolio manager to follow an active management approach as long as the portfolio remains above a specified value. If the pension fund's portfolio decreases to the specified value, a duration matching or even a cash flow matching approach would be put in place to ensure adequate funding of the pension plan's liabilities.

EXAMPLE 3   Liability-Based Mandates (2)

If the yield curve experiences a one-time parallel shift of 1%, what is the likely effect on the match between a portfolio's assets and liabilities for a duration matching approach and a cash flow matching approach?

Solution: There should be no effect on the match between assets and liabilities for either a duration matching or cash flow matching portfolio. Duration matching insures against any adverse effects of a one-time parallel shift in the yield curve. By contrast, non-parallel shifts would cause mismatches between assets and liabilities in a duration matching approach. In a cash flow matching approach, asset and liability matching remains in place even if market conditions change.

3.2. Total Return Mandates

In contrast to liability-based mandates, total return mandates do not attempt to match future liabilities. Total return mandates can establish objectives based on a specified absolute return or a relative return. Generally structured to either track or outperform a specified bond index, total return mandates are the focus of this discussion. Total return and risk are both critical considerations for these types of mandates, with **active return** and **active risk** representing key metrics. Active return is defined as the portfolio return minus the benchmark return. Active risk is the annualized standard deviation of active returns, which may also be referred to as **tracking error** (also sometimes called **tracking risk**).

Total return mandates can be classified into different approaches based on their target active return and active risk levels. Approaches range from a pure indexing approach that has targeted active return and active risk (tracking error) of zero to fully active approaches that substantially deviate from the benchmarks and attempt to generate significant excess (or active) returns. Portfolios that attempt to closely match a bond index, as compared with an equity index, are more challenging to construct and monitor.

3.2.1. Pure Indexing

A pure indexing approach attempts to replicate a bond index as closely as possible. Under this approach, the targeted active return and active risk are both zero. In practice, even if the tracking error is zero, the portfolio return will almost always be lower than the corresponding index return because of trading costs and management fees. Theoretically, the portfolio should include all of the underlying securities in the same proportions as the index. It is generally very difficult and costly, however, to precisely replicate most bond indexes because many bonds included in standard indexes are illiquid. Illiquidity is typically higher for bonds with small issuance size, less familiarity of the bond issuer among investors, and longer period outstanding. To help deal with bond market illiquidity, portfolio managers are generally allowed some flexibility around index holdings in an attempt to reduce costs and make the portfolio more implementable in practice.

An index manager, who is allowed some flexibility in holdings, is expected to match the risk factor exposures of the benchmark index, such as duration, credit (or quality) risk, sector risk, call risk, and prepayment risk. In this way, all or most of the known systematic risk factors can be matched to the extent possible. The risk that remains is then mostly issuer-specific (or idiosyncratic) risk, which can be largely mitigated if both the benchmark index and the portfolio are sufficiently diversified. Overall, a pure indexing approach that allows some flexibility in holdings is generally less costly and easier to implement than precise replication of an index. Portfolio turnover for pure indexing approaches is normally consistent with benchmark turnover but considerably lower than that of most active management approaches.[3]

---

[3]In general, bond index turnover is considerably higher than equity index turnover. This is true because higher cash flows are received as a result of bonds maturing or being called by issuers and also as a result of coupon payments. Cash flows from equity indexes are typically lower than those of bond indexes, and they mostly come from dividends as well as corporate actions. Bond index turnover depends to a large extent on the index's average maturity as well as its duration. Shorter-term bond indexes incur more-frequent principal repayments as bonds mature, which need to be reinvested in new bonds being added to these indexes. As a result, turnover for shorter-term bond indexes tends to be high.

3.2.2. Enhanced Indexing

An enhanced indexing approach maintains a close link to the benchmark but attempts to generate at least a modest amount of outperformance relative to the benchmark. As with the pure indexing approach in practice, enhanced indexing allows small deviations in portfolio holdings from the benchmark index but tracks the benchmark's primary risk factor exposures very closely (particularly duration). Unlike the pure indexing approach, however, minor risk factor mismatches (e.g., sector or quality bets) are allowed under enhanced indexing. The intent of the mismatches is to generate higher returns than the benchmark. A target active risk or tracking error of less than 50 bps per year is typical. The turnover of this type of approach is generally only marginally higher than that of a pure indexing portfolio. Any potential outperformance of an enhanced indexing approach is likely to be modest. As a result, managers need to monitor turnover and the associated transaction costs closely in order to achieve positive active returns net of fees and costs. Management fees for an enhanced indexing approach are normally higher than those of a pure indexing approach portfolio. The higher fees largely reflect the manager's efforts to outperform the index. Management fees for an enhanced indexing approach are considerably lower than those of a fully active management approach.

3.2.3. Active Management

Active management allows larger risk factor mismatches relative to a benchmark index. These mismatches may cause significant return differences between the active portfolio and the underlying benchmark. Most notably, portfolio managers may take views on portfolio duration that differ markedly from the duration of the underlying benchmark. To take advantage of potential opportunities in changing market environments, active managers may incur significant portfolio turnover—often considerably higher than the underlying benchmark's turnover. Active portfolio managers normally charge higher management fees than pure or enhanced index managers. The higher fees and transaction costs increase the rate of return necessary to achieve positive active returns net of fees and costs.

As with enhanced indexing, actively managed portfolios seek to outperform the underlying benchmark. In practice, however, most active managers (in both fixed income and equity) have historically underperformed their benchmarks after fees and transaction costs. Bond index funds have also historically underperformed their benchmark indexes, but to a lesser extent than active fixed-income portfolios, because of lower turnover and management fees in bond index funds. A key challenge for investors is identifying, in advance, portfolio managers that will outperform their benchmarks.

Exhibit 5 summarizes the key features of the total return approaches discussed here.

EXHIBIT 5 Total Return Approaches: Key Features

	Pure Indexing	Enhanced Indexing	Active Management
Objective	Match benchmark return and risk as closely as possible	Modest outperformance (generally 20 bps to 30 bps) of benchmark while active risk is kept low (typically around 50 bps or lower)	Higher outperformance (generally around 50 bps or more) of benchmark and higher active risk levels
Portfolio weights	Ideally the same as benchmark or only slight mismatches	Small deviations from underlying benchmark	Significant deviations from underlying benchmark
Risk factor matching	Risk factors are matched exactly	Most primary risk factors are closely matched (in particular, duration)	Large risk factor deviations from benchmark (in particular, duration)
Turnover	Similar to underlying benchmark	Slightly higher than underlying benchmark	Considerably higher turnover than the underlying benchmark

---

EXAMPLE 4 The Characteristics of Different Total Return Approaches

Diane Walker is a consultant for a large corporate pension plan. She is looking at three funds (Funds X, Y, and Z) as part of the pension plan's global fixed-income allocation. All three funds use the Bloomberg Barclays Global Aggregate Index as a benchmark. Exhibit 6 provides characteristics of each fund and the index as of February 2016.

Identify the approach (pure indexing, enhanced indexing, or active management) that is *most likely* used by each fund, and support your choices by referencing the information in Exhibit 6.

EXHIBIT 6 Characteristics of Funds X, Y, and Z and the Bloomberg Barclays Global Aggregate Index

Risk and Return Characteristics	Fund X	Fund Y	Fund Z	Bloomberg Barclays Global Aggregate Index
Average maturity (years)	8.61	8.35	9.45	8.34
Modified duration (years)	6.37	6.35	7.37	6.34
Average yield (%)	1.49	1.42	1.55	1.43
Convexity	0.65	0.60	0.72	0.60
Quality				
AAA	41.10	41.20	40.11	41.24
AA	15.32	15.13	14.15	15.05
A	28.01	28.51	29.32	28.78
BBB	14.53	14.51	15.23	14.55

Risk and Return Characteristics	Fund X	Fund Y	Fund Z	Bloomberg Barclays Global Aggregate Index
BB	0.59	0.55	1.02	0.35
Not rated	0.45	0.10	0.17	0.05
Maturity Exposure				
0–3 Years	21.43	21.67	19.20	21.80
3–5 Years	23.01	24.17	22.21	24.23
5–10 Years	32.23	31.55	35.21	31.67
10+ Years	23.33	22.61	23.38	22.30
Country Exposure				
United States	42.55	39.44	35.11	39.56
Japan	11.43	18.33	13.33	18.36
France	7.10	6.11	6.01	6.08
United Kingdom	3.44	5.87	4.33	5.99
Germany	6.70	5.23	4.50	5.30
Italy	4.80	4.01	4.43	4.07
Canada	4.44	3.12	5.32	3.15
Other	19.54	17.89	26.97	17.49

Notes: Quality, Maturity Exposure, and Country Exposure are shown as a percentage of the total for each fund and the index. Weights do not always sum to 100 because of rounding.
Source: Barclays Research.

Solution: Fund X most likely uses an enhanced indexing approach. Fund X's modified duration and convexity are very close to those of the benchmark but still differ slightly. The average maturity of Fund X is slightly longer than that of the benchmark, whereas Fund X's average yield is slightly higher than that of the benchmark. Fund X also has deviations in quality, maturity exposure, and country exposures from the benchmark, providing further evidence of an enhanced indexing approach. Some of these deviations are meaningful; for example, Fund X has a relatively strong underweight in Japan.

Fund Y most likely uses a pure indexing approach because it provides the closest match to the Bloomberg Barclays Global Aggregate Index. The risk and return characteristics are almost identical between Fund Y and the benchmark. Furthermore, quality, maturity exposure, and country exposure deviations from the benchmark are very minor.

Fund Z most likely uses an active management approach because risk and return characteristics, quality, maturity exposure, and country exposure differ markedly from the index. The difference can be seen most notably with the mismatch in modified duration (7.37 for Fund Z versus 6.34 for the benchmark). Other differences exist between Fund Z and the index, but a sizable duration mismatch provides the strongest evidence of an active management approach.

4. BOND MARKET LIQUIDITY

A liquid security is one that may be transacted quickly with little effect on the security's price. Fixed-income securities vary greatly in their liquidity. Recently issued "on-the-run" sovereign government bonds may be very liquid and trade frequently at narrow bid–ask spreads. Other bonds, such as corporate and non-sovereign government bonds, may be very illiquid. These bonds may trade infrequently, in small quantities, or possibly never; and bid–ask spreads, if they are available, may be very wide.

Compared with equities, fixed-income markets are generally less liquid. The global fixed-income universe contains a multitude of individual bonds with varying features. Many issuers have multiple bonds outstanding with their own unique maturity dates, coupon rates, early redemption features, and other specific features. In other words, even for a single issuer, bonds are very heterogeneous. In contrast, each share of a single issuing company's common stock has identical features. Investors must understand the implications of varying features on bond values.

An important structural feature affecting liquidity is that fixed-income markets are typically over-the-counter dealer markets. Search costs (the costs of finding a willing counterparty) exist in bond markets because investors may have to locate desired bonds. In addition, when either buying or selling, investors may have to obtain quotes from various dealers to obtain the most advantageous pricing. With limited, although improving, sources for transaction prices and quotes, bond markets are ordinarily less transparent than equity markets. Liquidity, search costs, and price transparency are closely related to the type of issuer and its credit quality. An investor is likely to find that bonds of a highly creditworthy government issuer are more liquid, have greater price transparency, and have lower search costs than bonds of, for example, a corporate issuer with a lower credit quality.

Bond liquidity is typically highest right after issuance. For example, an on-the-run bond issue of a highly creditworthy sovereign entity is typically more liquid than a bond with similar features—including maturity—that was issued previously (an off-the-run bond). This difference in liquidity is typically found even if the off-the-run bond was issued only one or two months earlier. One reason for this phenomenon is that soon after bonds are issued, dealers normally have a supply of the bonds in inventory, but as time goes by and bonds are traded, many are purchased by buy-and-hold investors. Once in the possession of such investors, those bonds are no longer available for trading. Typically, after issuance, the available supply of bonds in an issue is reduced and liquidity is impaired.

Liquidity typically affects bond yields. Bond investors require higher yields for investing in illiquid securities relative to otherwise identical securities that are more liquid. The higher yield compensates investors for the costs they may encounter if they try to sell illiquid bonds prior to maturity. These costs include the opportunity costs associated with the delays in finding trading counterparties, as well as the bid–ask spread (which is a direct loss of wealth). The incremental yield investors require for holding illiquid bonds instead of liquid bonds is referred to as a liquidity premium. The magnitude of the liquidity premium normally varies depending on such factors as the issuer, the issue size, and date of maturity. For example, the off-the-run 10-year US Treasury bond typically trades at several basis points higher yield than the on-the-run bond.

4.1. Liquidity among Bond Market Sub-Sectors

Bond market liquidity varies across sub-sectors. These sub-sectors can be categorized by key features such as issuer type, credit quality, issue size, and maturity. The global bond market includes sovereign government bonds, non-sovereign government bonds, government-related bonds, corporate bonds, and securitized bonds (such as asset-backed securities and commercial mortgage-backed securities). For simplicity, in this section we focus on sovereign government and corporate bonds.

Sovereign government bonds are typically more liquid than corporate and non-sovereign government bonds. Their superior liquidity relates to their large issuance size, use as benchmark bonds, acceptance as collateral in the repo market, and well-recognized issuers. Sovereign government bonds of countries with high credit quality are typically more liquid than bonds of lower-credit-quality countries.

In contrast to sovereign government bonds, corporate bonds are issued by many different companies and represent a wide spectrum of credit quality. For corporate bonds with low credit quality, it can be difficult to find a counterparty dealer with the securities in inventory or willing to take them into inventory. Bonds of infrequent issuers are often less liquid than the bonds of issuers with many outstanding issues because market participants are less familiar with companies that seldom issue debt.

Liquidity among sub-sectors can vary across additional dimensions, such as issue size and maturity. For example, in the corporate bond market, smaller issues are generally less liquid than larger issues because small bond issues are typically excluded from major bond indexes with minimum issue size requirements. Further, market participants generally have less incentive to dedicate resources to monitoring smaller issuers, whose bonds may constitute a small proportion of an investor's portfolio. Bonds with longer maturities tend to be less liquid than nearer-term bonds because investors frequently purchase bonds with the intention to hold them until maturity, so such bonds may be unavailable for trading for a long period.

4.2. The Effects of Liquidity on Fixed-Income Portfolio Management

Liquidity concerns influence fixed-income portfolio management in multiple ways, including pricing, portfolio construction, and consideration of alternatives to bonds (such as derivatives).

4.2.1. Pricing

As mentioned earlier, pricing in bond markets is generally less transparent than pricing in equity markets. Sources for recent bond transactions—notably corporate bonds—are not always readily available. It should be noted that price transparency is improving in some bond markets. For example, in the United States, the Financial Industry Regulatory Authority's (FINRA) Trade Reporting and Compliance Engine (TRACE) and the Municipal Securities Rulemaking Board's Electronic Municipal Market Access (EMMA) are electronic systems that help to increase transparency in US corporate and municipal bond markets. Outside the United States, corporate bonds traded on market exchanges serve a similar role as TRACE in increasing pricing transparency. In most bond markets, however, the lack of transparency in corporate bond trading presents a challenge.

Because many bonds do not trade, or trade infrequently, using recent transaction prices to represent current value is not practical. Reliance on last traded prices, which may be out-of-date prices that do not incorporate current market conditions, could result in costly trading decisions. The determinants of corporate bond value, including interest rates, credit spreads, and liquidity premiums, change frequently.

For bonds that trade infrequently, a common investor approach is matrix pricing. Matrix pricing uses the recent transaction prices of comparable bonds to estimate the market discount rate or required rate of return on less frequently traded bonds. The comparable bonds have similar features such as credit quality, time to maturity, and coupon rate to the illiquid bond. A benefit of matrix pricing is that it does not require sophisticated financial modeling of bond market characteristics such as term structure and credit spreads. A disadvantage is that some value-relevant features between different bonds (for example, call features) may be ignored.

4.2.2. Portfolio Construction

Investors' liquidity needs directly influence portfolio construction. In constructing a portfolio, investors must consider an important trade-off between yield and liquidity. As mentioned previously, illiquid bonds typically have higher yields; a buy-and-hold investor that seeks yield will likely prefer less liquid bonds for these higher yields. By contrast, investors that emphasize liquidity will likely give up some yield and choose more-liquid bonds. Some investors may restrict their portfolio holdings to bonds within a certain maturity range. This restriction reduces the need to sell bonds to generate needed cash inflows. In such cases, the investors that anticipate their liquidity needs may give up the higher yield typically available to longer-term bonds. In addition to avoiding longer-term bonds, investors that have liquidity concerns may also avoid bonds with generally lower liquidity, such as small issues and private placements of corporate bonds.

A challenge in bond portfolio construction relates to the dealer market. Bond dealers often carry an inventory of bonds because buy and sell orders do not arrive simultaneously. A dealer is not certain how long bonds will remain in its inventory. Less liquid bonds are likely to remain in inventory longer than liquid bonds. A dealer provides bid–ask quotes (prices at which it will buy and sell) on bonds of its choice. Some illiquid bonds will not have quotes, particularly bid quotes, from any dealer. A number of different factors determine the bid–ask spread. Riskier bonds often have higher bid–ask spreads because of dealers' aversion to hold those bonds in inventory. Because bond dealers must finance their inventories, the dealers incur costs in both obtaining funding and holding those bonds. Dealers seek to cover their costs and make a profit through the bid–ask spread, and therefore the spread will be higher on illiquid bonds that are likely to remain in inventory longer.

A bond's bid–ask spread is also a function of the bond's complexity and how easily market participants can analyze the issuer's creditworthiness. Bid–ask spreads in government bonds are generally lower than spreads in corporate bonds or structured financial instruments, such as asset-backed securities. Conventional (plain vanilla) corporate bonds normally have lower spreads than corporate bonds with non-standard or complex features, such as embedded options. Bonds of large, high-credit-quality corporations that have many outstanding bond issues are the most liquid among corporate bonds, and thus they have relatively low bid–ask spreads compared with smaller, less creditworthy companies.

Illiquidity directly increases bid–ask spreads on bonds, which increases the cost of trading. Higher transaction costs reduce the benefits to active portfolio decisions and may decrease portfolio managers' willingness to adjust their portfolios to take advantage of opportunities that present themselves.

4.2.3. Alternatives to Direct Investment in Bonds

As we have discussed, transacting in fixed-income securities may present challenges because of low liquidity in many global bond markets. As an alternative, investors can use fixed-income derivatives, which are often more liquid than their underlying bonds. Such fixed-income derivatives include those traded on an exchange (for example, futures and options on futures) and those traded over the counter (for example, interest rate swaps and credit default swaps). In particular, bond futures, which are exchange traded and standardized, provide a liquid alternative for investors to gain exposure to the underlying bond(s).

Based on notional amount outstanding, interest rate swaps are the most widely used over-the-counter derivative worldwide. Some interest rate swaps are liquid, with multiple swaps dealers posting competitive two-way quotes. In addition to interest rate swaps, fixed-income portfolio managers use inflation swaps, total return swaps, and credit swaps to alter their portfolio exposure. Because they trade over the counter, swaps may be tailored to an investor's specific needs.

Fixed-income exchange-traded funds (ETFs) and pooled investment vehicles (such as mutual funds) have emerged as another alternative to transacting in individual bonds. ETF shares tend to be more liquid than the underlying individual securities and have thus provided new opportunities for investors seeking liquid fixed-income investments. ETFs may allow certain qualified financial institutions (authorized participants) to transact through in-kind deposits and redemptions (delivering and receiving a portfolio of securities, such as a portfolio of bonds). In the more illiquid bond market sectors, such as high-yield corporate bonds, fixed-income portfolio managers may purchase ETF shares and then redeem those shares for the actual underlying portfolio of bonds. In this redemption process, an ETF authorized participant generally acts as the intermediary between the portfolio managers redeeming their ETF shares and the ETF sponsor supplying the portfolio of bonds.

5. A MODEL FOR FIXED-INCOME RETURNS

Investors often have views on future changes in the yield curve and (re)structure their portfolios accordingly. Investment strategies should be evaluated in terms of expected returns rather than just yields. A bond position's yield provides an incomplete measure of its expected return. Instead, expected fixed-income returns consist of a number of different components in addition to yield. Examining these components leads to a better understanding of the driving forces behind expected returns. The focus is on *expected* as opposed to *realized* returns, but realized returns can be decomposed in a similar manner.

5.1. Decomposing Expected Returns[4]

Decomposing expected fixed-income returns allows an investor to differentiate among several important return components. At the most general level, expected returns (denoted as E(R) below) can be decomposed (approximately) in the following manner:

---

[4]Some of this material has been adapted from Hanke and Seals (2010). A more detailed analysis of expected returns of US government bonds can be found in Ilmanen (1995a, 1995b, and 2011).

E(R) ≈ Yield income

    + Rolldown return

    + E(Change in price based on investor's views of yields and yield spreads)

    − E(Credit losses)

    + E(Currency gains or losses)

where E(…) represents effects on expected returns based on expectations of the bracketed item. The decomposition holds only approximately and can be a better or worse approximation of reality depending on the type of bond. It has very general applicability for all types of fixed-income securities, however, ranging from high-credit-quality, home currency sovereign government bonds to lower-credit-quality (high-yield) corporate bonds denominated in a currency other than an investor's home currency. The decomposition should help investors better understand their own investment positions and any assumptions reflected in those positions. The following discussion assumes the model is being applied to an annual period, but the same model can be generalized to other periods. In addition, for simplification, the model does not reflect taxes.

Yield income is the income that an investor receives from coupon payments relative to the bond's price as well as interest on reinvestment income. Assuming there is no reinvestment income, yield income equals a bond's annual current yield.

Yield income (or Current yield) = Annual coupon payment/Current bond price

The rolldown return results from the bond "rolling down" the yield curve as the time to maturity decreases, assuming zero interest rate volatility. Bond prices change as time passes even if the market discount rate remains the same. As time passes, a bond's price typically moves closer to par. This price movement is illustrated by the constant-yield price trajectory, which shows the "pull to par" effect on the price of a bond trading at a premium or a discount to par value. If the issuer does not default, the price of a bond approaches par value as its time to maturity approaches zero.

The rolldown return equals the bond's percentage price change assuming an unchanged yield curve over the strategy horizon. Bonds trading at a premium to their par value will experience capital losses during their remaining life, and bonds trading at a discount relative to their par value will experience capital gains during their remaining life.

To compute the rolldown return, the bond has to be revalued at the end of the strategy horizon assuming an unchanged yield curve. Then the annualized rolldown return is as follows:

$$\text{Rolldown Return} = \frac{\left(\text{Bond price}_{\text{End-of-horizon period}} - \text{Bond price}_{\text{Beginning-of-horizon period}}\right)}{\text{Bond price}_{\text{Beginning-of-horizon period}}}$$

The sum of the yield income and the rolldown return may be referred to as the bond's rolling yield.

The expected change in price based on investor's views of yields and yield spreads reflects an investor's expectation of changes in yields and yield spreads over the investment horizon. This expected change is zero if the investor expects yield curves and yield spreads to remain unchanged. Assuming the investor does expect a change in the yield curve, this expected return component is computed as follows:

$$\text{E(Change in price based on investor's views of yields and yield spreads)} = [-\text{MD} \times \text{Yield}] + [\tfrac{1}{2} \times \text{Convexity} \times (\text{Yield})^2]$$

where MD is the modified duration of a bond, Yield is the expected change in yield based on expected changes to both the yield curve and yield spread, and convexity estimates the effect of the non-linearity of the yield curve.[5] It should be noted that for bonds with embedded options, the duration and convexity measures used in the expected return decomposition need to be effective duration and effective convexity. Also, in contrast to fixed-coupon bonds, floating-rate notes have modified duration near zero.

Expected credit losses represent the expected percentage of par value lost to default for a bond. The expected credit loss equals the bond's probability of default (also called expected default rate) multiplied by its expected loss severity (also known as loss given default). Expected credit losses may be low based on past experience of default rates and resulting credit losses. For example, US investment-grade bonds experienced an average annual default rate of around 0.1% from 1980 to 2015.[6]

If an investor holds bonds denominated in a currency other than her home currency, she also needs to factor in any expected fluctuations in the currency exchange rate or expected currency gains or losses over the investment horizon. This quantity could simply be a reflection of her own views, or it could be based on survey information or some kind of quantitative model. It could also be based on the exchange rate that can be locked in over the investment horizon using currency forwards.

The following discussion shows an application of the fixed-income model described here. Expected return and its components are on an annualized basis, and any potential coupons are assumed to be paid annually.

EXAMPLE 5   Decomposing Expected Returns

Ann Smith works for a US investment firm in its London office. She manages the firm's British pound–denominated corporate bond portfolio. Her department head in New York has asked Smith to make a presentation on the next year's total expected return of her portfolio in US dollars and the components of this return. Exhibit 7 shows information on the portfolio and Smith's expectations for the next year. Calculate the total expected return of Smith's bond portfolio, assuming no reinvestment income.

---

[5]Leibowitz, Krasker, and Nozari (1990) offer a detailed analysis of spread duration.

[6]As reported by Vazza and Kraemer (2016), for the period 1981 to 2015, the average one-year cumulative global corporate default rates were 0.10% for investment-grade issues, 3.80% for speculative-grade (high-yield) issues, and 1.49% for all rated issues. Yearly default rates vary, however, and during the period 1981 to 2015, one-year cumulative global corporate default rates ranged between 0.14% (1981) and 4.18% (2009) for all rated issues.

EXHIBIT 7   Portfolio Characteristics and Expectations

Notional principal of portfolio (in millions)	£100
Average bond coupon payment (per £100)	£2.75
Coupon frequency	Annual
Investment horizon	1 year
Current average bond price	£97.11
Expected average bond price in one year (assuming an unchanged yield curve)	£97.27
Average bond convexity	18
Average bond modified duration	3.70
Expected average yield and yield spread change	0.26%
Expected credit losses	0.10%
Expected currency losses (£ depreciation versus US$)	0.50%

Solution: The portfolio's yield income is 2.83%. The portfolio has an average coupon of £2.75 on a £100 notional principal and currently trades at £97.11. The yield income over a one-year horizon is 2.83% = £2.75/£97.11.

In one year's time, assuming an unchanged yield curve and zero interest rate volatility, the rolldown return is 0.16% = (£97.27 − £97.11)/£97.11.

The rolling yield, which is the sum of the yield income and the rolldown return, is 2.99% = 2.83% + 0.16%.

The expected change in price based on Smith's views of yields and yield spreads is −0.96%. The bond portfolio has a modified duration of 3.70 and a convexity statistic of 0.18. Smith expects an average yield and yield spread change of 0.26%. Smith expects to incur a decrease in prices and a reduction in return based on her yield view. The expected change in price based on Smith's views of yields and yield spreads is thus $-0.0096 = [-3.70 \times 0.0026] + [\frac{1}{2} \times 18 \times (0.0026)^2]$. So the expected reduction in return based on Smith's yield view is 0.96%.

Smith expects 0.1% of credit losses in her well-diversified investment-grade bond portfolio.

Smith expects the British pound, the foreign currency in which her bond position is denominated, to depreciate by an annualized 50 bps (or 0.5%) over the investment horizon against the US dollar, the home country currency. The expected currency loss to the portfolio is thus 0.50%.

After combining the foregoing return components, the total expected return on Smith's bond position is 1.43%. For ease of reference, Exhibit 8 summarizes the calculations.

EXHIBIT 8   Return Component Calculations

Return Component	Formula	Calculation
Yield income	Annual coupon payment/Current bond price	£2.75/£97.11 = 2.83%
+ Rolldown return	$\frac{(\text{Bond price}_{End-of-horizon\ period} - \text{Bond price}_{Beginning-of-horizon\ period})}{\text{Bond price}_{Beginning-of-horizon\ period}}$	(£97.27 − £97.11)/ £97.11 = 0.16%
= Rolling yield	Yield income + Rolldown return	2.83% + 0.16% = 2.99%
+ E(Change in price based on Smith's yield and yield spread view)	$[-MD \times \text{Yield}]$ $+ [\frac{1}{2} \times \text{Convexity} \times (\text{Yield})^2]$	$[-3.70 \times 0.0026]$ $+ [\frac{1}{2} \times 18 \times (0.0026)^2]$ = −0.96%
− E(Credit losses)	given	−0.10%
+ E(Currency gains or losses)	given	−0.50%
= **Total expected return**		**1.43%**

5.2. Estimation of the Inputs

In the model for fixed-income returns discussed earlier, some of the individual expected return components can be more easily estimated than others. The easiest component to estimate is the yield income. The rolldown return, although still relatively straightforward to estimate, depends on the curve-fitting technique used.

The return model's most uncertain individual components are the investor's views of changes in yields and yield spreads, expected credit losses, and expected currency movements. These components are normally based on purely qualitative (subjective) criteria, on survey information, or on a quantitative model. Although a quantitative approach may seem more objective, the choice of quantitative model is largely subjective given the multitude of such models available.

5.3. Limitations of the Expected Return Decomposition

The return decomposition described in Section 5.1 is an approximation; only duration and convexity are used to summarize the price–yield relationship. In addition, the model implicitly assumes that all intermediate cash flows of the bond are reinvested at the yield to maturity, which results in different coupon reinvestment rates for different bonds.

The model also ignores other factors, such as local richness/cheapness effects as well as potential financing advantages. Local richness/cheapness effects are deviations of individual maturity segments from the fitted yield curve, which was obtained using a curve estimation technique. Yield curve estimation techniques produce relatively smooth curves, and there are likely slight deviations from the curve in practice. There may be financing advantages to certain maturity segments in the repo market. The repo market provides a form of short-term borrowing for dealers in government securities who sell government bonds to other market participants overnight and buy them back, typically on the following day. In most cases, local richness/cheapness effects and financing advantages tend to be relatively small and are thus not included in the expected return decomposition model.

EXAMPLE 6   Components of Expected Return

Kevin Tucker manages a global bond portfolio. At a recent investment committee meeting, Tucker discussed his portfolio's domestic (very high credit quality) government bond allocation with another committee member. The other committee member argued that if the yield curve is expected to remain unchanged, the only determinants of a domestic government bond's expected return are its coupon payment and its price.

Explain why the other committee member is incorrect, including a description of the additional expected return components that need to be included.

Solution: A bond's coupon payment and its price allow only its yield income to be computed. Yield income is an incomplete measure of a bond's expected return. For domestic government bonds, in addition to yield income, the rolldown return needs to be considered. The rolldown return results from the fact that bonds are pulled to par as the time to maturity decreases, even if the yield curve is expected to remain unchanged over the investment horizon. Currency gains and losses would also need to be considered in a global portfolio. Because the portfolio consists of government bonds with very high credit quality, the view on credit spreads and expected credit losses are less relevant for Tucker's analysis. For government and corporate bonds with lower credit quality, however, credit spreads and credit losses would also need to be considered as additional return components.

---

6. LEVERAGE

Leverage is the use of borrowed capital to increase the magnitude of portfolio positions, and it is an important tool for fixed-income portfolio managers. By using leverage, fixed-income portfolio managers may be able to increase portfolio returns relative to what they can achieve in unleveraged portfolios.

Managers often have mandates that place limits on the types of securities they may hold. Simultaneously, managers may have return objectives that are difficult to achieve, especially during low interest rate environments. Through the use of leverage, a manager can increase his investment exposure and may be able to increase the returns to fixed-income asset classes that typically have low returns. The increased return potential, however, comes at the cost of increased risk: If losses occur, these would be higher than in unleveraged positions.

6.1. Using Leverage

Leverage increases portfolio returns if the securities in the portfolio have higher returns than the cost of borrowing. In an unleveraged portfolio, the return on the portfolio (r_p) equals the return on invested funds (r_I). When the manager uses leverage, however, the invested funds exceed the portfolio's equity by the amount that is borrowed.

The leveraged portfolio return, r_p, can be expressed as the total investment gains per unit of invested capital:

$$r_P = \frac{\text{Portfolio return}}{\text{Portfolio equity}} = \frac{[r_I \times (V_E + V_B) - (V_B \times r_B)]}{V_E}$$

where

V_E = value of the portfolio's equity
V_B = borrowed funds
r_B = borrowing rate (cost of borrowing)
r_I = return on the invested funds (investment returns)
r_p = return on the levered portfolio

The numerator represents the total return on the portfolio assets, $r_I \times (V_E + V_B)$, minus the cost of borrowing, $V_B \times r_B$, divided by the portfolio's equity.

The leveraged portfolio return can be decomposed further to better identify the effect of leverage on returns:

$$r_P = \frac{[r_I \times (V_E + V_B) - (V_B \times r_B)]}{V_E}$$
$$= \frac{(r_I \times V_E) + [V_B \times (r_I - r_B)]}{V_E}$$
$$= r_I + \frac{V_B}{V_E}(r_I - r_B)$$

This expression decomposes the leveraged portfolio return into the return on invested funds and a portion that accounts for the effect of leverage. If $r_I > r_B$, then the second term is positive because the rate of return on invested funds exceeds the borrowing rate—in this case, leverage increases the portfolio's return. If $r_I < r_B$, then the second term is negative because the rate of return on invested funds is less than the borrowing rate—in this case, the use of leverage decreases the portfolio's return. The degree to which the leverage increases or decreases portfolio returns is proportional to the use of leverage (amount borrowed), V_B/V_E, and the amount by which investment return differs from the cost of borrowing, $(r_I - r_B)$.

6.2. Methods for Leveraging Fixed-Income Portfolios

Fixed-income portfolio managers have a variety of tools available to create leveraged portfolio exposures, notably the use of financial derivatives as well as borrowing via collateralized money markets. Derivatives or borrowing are explicit forms of leverage. Other forms of leverage, such as the use of structured financial instruments, are more implicit.

6.2.1. Futures Contracts

Futures contracts embed significant leverage because they permit the counterparties to gain exposure to a large quantity of the underlying asset without having to actually transact in the underlying. Futures contracts can be obtained for a modest investment that comes in the form of a margin deposit. A futures contract's notional value equals the current value of the underlying asset multiplied by the multiplier, or the quantity of the underlying asset controlled by the contract.

The futures leverage is the ratio of the futures exposure (in excess of the margin deposit) normalized by the amount of margin required to control the notional amount. We can calculate the futures leverage using the following equation:

$$\text{Leverage}_{\text{Futures}} = \frac{\text{Notional value} - \text{Margin}}{\text{Margin}}$$

6.2.2. Swap Agreements

Interest rate swaps can be viewed as a portfolio of bonds. In an interest rate swap, the fixed-rate payer is effectively short a fixed-rate bond and long a floating-rate bond. When interest rates increase, the value of the swap to the fixed-rate payer increases because the present value of the fixed-rate liability decreases and the floating-rate payments received increase. The fixed-rate receiver in the interest rate swap agreement effectively has a long position in a fixed-rate bond and a short position in a floating-rate bond. If interest rates decline, the value of the swap to the fixed-rate receiver increases because the present value of the fixed-rate asset increases and the floating-rate payments made decrease.

Because interest rate swaps are economically equivalent to a long–short bond portfolio, they provide leveraged exposure to bonds; the only capital required to enter into swap agreements is collateral required by the counterparties. Collateral for interest rate swap agreements has historically occurred between the two (or more) counterparties in the transaction. Increasingly, collateral for interest rate and other swaps occurs through central clearinghouses. The most significant driver of this shift has been regulation enacted after the 2008–2009 global financial crisis. Clearing of interest rate swaps through central clearinghouses has increased standardization and has reduced counterparty risk.

6.2.3. Structured Financial Instruments

Structured financial instruments (or structured products) are designed to repackage and redistribute risks. Many structured financial instruments have embedded leverage. An example of such a structured financial instrument is an inverse floating-rate note, also known as an inverse floater. An inverse floater's defining feature is that its coupon has an inverse relationship to a market interest rate such as Libor. As an example, the coupon rate for an inverse floater may be as follows:

$$\text{Coupon rate} = 15\% - (1.5 \times \text{Libor}_{\text{3-month}})$$

The inverse floater exacerbates the magnitude of the inverse relationship between bond prices and interest rates. The coupon rate in the example above can range from 0% to 15%. If three-month Libor increases to at least 10%, the coupon rate is 0%. At the other extreme, if three-month Libor decreases to 0%, the coupon rate is 15%. It should be noted that the inverse floater's structure would specify that the coupon rate cannot be less than 0%. A long position in an inverse floater is ideal for a fixed-income manager looking to express a strong view that interest rates will remain low or possibly decline over the life of the bond. However, the embedded leverage adds an additional source of price volatility to a fixed-income investor's portfolio.

6.2.4. Repurchase Agreements

Repurchase agreements (repos) are an important source of short-term financing for fixed-income securities dealers and other financial institutions, as evidenced by the trillions of dollars of repo transactions that take place annually. In a repurchase agreement, a security owner agrees to sell a security for a specific cash amount while simultaneously agreeing to repurchase the security at a specified future date (typically one day later) and price. Repos are thus effectively collateralized loans. When referring to a repo, the transaction normally refers to the borrower's standpoint; from the standpoint of the lender, these agreements are referred to as **reverse repos**.

The interest rate on a repurchase agreement, called the **repo rate**, is the difference between the security's selling price and its repurchase price. For example, consider a dealer wishing to finance a $15 million bond position with a repurchase agreement. The dealer enters into an overnight repo at a repo rate of 5%. We can compute the price at which she agrees to repurchase this bond after one day as the $15 million value today plus one day of interest. The interest amount is computed as follows:

$$\text{Dollar interest} = \text{Principal amount} \times \text{Repo rate} \times (\text{Term of repo in days}/360)$$

Continuing with the example, the dollar interest = $2,083.33 = $15 million × 5% × (1/360). Thus, the dealer will repurchase the bond the next day for $15,002,083.33.

The term, or length, of a repurchase agreement is measured in days. Overnight repos are common, although they are often rolled over to create longer-term funding. A repo agreement may be cash driven or security driven. Cash-driven transactions feature one party that owns bonds and wants to borrow cash, as in the foregoing example. Cash-driven transactions usually feature "general collateral," which are securities commonly accepted by investors and dealers, such as Treasury bonds. In a security-driven transaction, the lender typically seeks a particular security. The motives may be for hedging, arbitrage, or speculation.

Credit risk is a concern in a repo agreement, in particular for the counterparty that lends capital. Protection against a default by the borrower is provided by the underlying collateral bonds. Additional credit protection comes from the "haircut," the amount by which the collateral's value exceeds the repo principal amount. For example, haircuts for high-quality government bonds typically range from 1% to 3% and are higher for other types of bonds. The size of the haircut serves to not only protect the lender against a potential default by the borrower but also to limit the borrower's net leverage capacity. Generally, the size of the haircut increases as the price volatility of the underlying collateral increases.

Repos are categorized as bilateral repos or tri-party repos based on the way they are settled. Bilateral repos are conducted directly between two institutions, and settlement is typically conducted as "delivery versus payment," meaning that the exchanges of cash and collateral occur simultaneously through a central custodian (for example, the Depository Trust Company in the United States). Bilateral repos are usually used for security-driven transactions. Tri-party repo transactions involve a third party that provides settlement and collateral management services. Most cash-motivated repo transactions against general collateral are conducted as tri-party repo transactions.

6.2.5. Securities Lending

Securities lending is another form of collateralized lending, and is closely linked to the repo market. The primary motive of securities lending transactions is to facilitate short sales, which involve the sale of securities the seller does not own. A short seller must borrow the securities he has sold short in order to deliver them upon trade settlement. Another motive for securities lending transactions is financing, or collateralized borrowing. In a financing-motivated security loan, a bond owner lends the bond to another investor in exchange for cash.

Security lending transactions are collateralized by cash or high-credit-quality bonds. In the United States, most transactions feature cash collateral, although in many other countries, highly rated bonds are used as collateral. Typically, security lenders require collateral valued in excess of the value of the borrowed securities when bonds are used as collateral. For example, if high-quality government bonds are used as collateral, the lender may require bonds valued at 102% of the value of the borrowed securities. The extra 2% functions in the same way as the haircut in the repo market, providing extra protection against borrower default. The collateral required will increase if lower-quality bonds are used as collateral.

In security lending transactions with cash collateral, the security borrower typically pays the security lender a fee equal to a percentage of the value of the securities loaned. For securities that are readily available for lending, that fee is small. The security lender earns an additional return by reinvesting the cash collateral. In cases where the securities loan is initiated for financing purposes, the lending fee is typically negative, indicating that the security lender pays the security borrower a fee in exchange for its use of the cash.

When bonds are posted as collateral, the income earned on the collateral usually exceeds the security lending rate; the security lender (who is in possession of the bonds as collateral) usually repays the security borrower a portion of the interest earned on the bond collateral. The term **rebate rate** refers to the portion of the collateral earnings rate that is repaid to the security borrower by the security lender. This relationship can be expressed as follows:

$$\text{Rebate rate} = \text{Collateral earnings rate} - \text{Security lending rate}$$

When securities are difficult to borrow, the rebate rate may be negative, which means the fee for borrowing the securities is greater than the return earned on the collateral. In this case, the security borrower pays a fee to the security lender in addition to forgoing the interest earned on the collateral.

There are important differences between repurchase agreements and securities lending transactions. Unlike repurchase agreements, security lending transactions are typically open-ended. The securities lender may recall the securities at any time, forcing the borrower to deliver the bonds by buying them back or borrowing from another lender. Similarly, the borrower may deliver the borrowed securities back to the lender at any time, forcing the lender, or its agent, to return the collateral (cash or bonds) and search for another borrower.

6.3. Risks of Leverage

Leverage alters the risk–return properties of an investment portfolio. A heavily leveraged portfolio may incur significant losses even when portfolio assets suffer only moderate valuation declines.

Leverage can lead to forced liquidations. If the value of the portfolio decreases, the portfolio's equity relative to borrowing levels is reduced and the portfolio's leverage increases. Portfolio assets may be sold in order to pay off borrowing and reduce leverage. If portfolio assets are not liquidated, then the overall leverage increases, corresponding to higher levels of risk. Decreases in portfolio value can lead to forced liquidations even if market conditions are unfavorable for selling—for example, during crisis periods. The term "fire sale" refers to forced liquidations at prices that are below fair value as a result of the seller's need for immediate liquidation. Reducing leverage, declining asset values, and forced sales have the potential to create spiraling effects that can result in severe declines in values and reduction in market liquidity.

Additionally, reassessments of counterparty risk typically occur during extreme market conditions, such as occurred in the 2008–2009 financial crisis. During periods of financial crisis, counterparties to short-term financing arrangements, such as credit lines, repurchase agreements, and securities lending agreements, may withdraw their financing. These withdrawals undermine the ability of leveraged market participants to maintain their investment exposures. Thus, the leveraged investor may be forced to reduce their investment exposure at exactly the worst time—that is, when prices are depressed.

7. FIXED-INCOME PORTFOLIO TAXATION

A tax-exempt investor's objective is to achieve the highest possible risk-adjusted returns net of fees and transaction costs. A taxable investor needs to also consider the effects of taxes on both expected and realized net investment returns. Taxes typically complicate investment decisions.

The investment management industry has traditionally made investment decisions based on pretax returns as though investors are tax exempt (such as pension funds in many countries).[7] The majority of the world's investable assets, however, is owned by taxable investors, who are concerned with after-tax rather than pretax returns.

Taxes may differ across investor types, among countries, and based on income source, such as interest or capital gains. In many countries, pension funds are exempt from taxes but corporations generally have to pay tax on their investments. Many countries make some allowance for tax-sheltered investments that individuals can use (up to certain limits). These types of tax shelters generally offer either an exemption from tax on investment income or a deferral of taxes until an investor draws money from the shelter (usually after retirement). Such shelters allow returns to accrue on a pretax basis until retirement, which can provide substantial benefits. In a fixed-income context for taxable investors, coupon payments (interest income) are typically taxed at the investor's normal income tax rate. Capital gains,

---

[7]See, for example, Rogers (2006).

however, may be taxed at a lower effective rate than an investor's normal income tax rate. In some countries, income from special types of fixed-income securities, such as bonds issued by the sovereign government, a non-sovereign government, or various government agencies, may be taxed at a lower effective rate or even not taxed.

It is beyond the scope of this chapter to discuss specific tax rules because these vary across countries. Any discussion of the effect of taxes on investor returns—and therefore on how portfolios should optimally be managed for taxable investors—is especially challenging if it needs to apply on a global level. Although accounting standards have become more harmonized globally, any kind of tax harmonization among countries is not likely to occur anytime soon. An investor should consider how taxes affect investment income in the country where the income is earned and how the investment income is treated when it is repatriated to the investor's home country. Treaties between countries may affect tax treatment of investment income. Taxes are complicated and can make investment decisions difficult. Portfolio managers who manage assets for taxable individual investors, as opposed to tax-exempt investors, need to consider a number of issues.

7.1. Principles of Fixed-Income Taxation

Although tax codes differ across countries, there are certain principles that most tax codes have in common with regard to taxation of fixed-income investments:

- The two primary sources of investment income that affect taxes for fixed-income securities are coupon payments (interest income) and capital gains or losses.
- In general, tax is payable only on capital gains and interest income that have actually been received. In some countries, an exception to this rule applies to zero-coupon bonds. Imputed interest may be calculated that is taxed throughout a zero-coupon bond's life. This method of taxation ensures that tax is paid over the bond's life and that the return on a zero-coupon bond is not taxed entirely as a capital gain.
- Capital gains are frequently taxed at a lower effective tax rate than interest income.
- Capital losses generally cannot be used to reduce sources of income other than capital gains. Capital losses reduce capital gains in the tax year in which they occur. If capital losses exceed capital gains in the year, they can often be "carried forward" and applied to gains in future years; in some countries, losses may also be "carried back" to reduce capital gains taxes paid in prior years. Limits typically exist on the number of years that capital losses can be carried forward or back.
- In some countries, short-term capital gains are taxed at a different (usually higher) rate than long-term capital gains.

An investor or portfolio manager generally has no control over the timing of when coupon income is received and the related income tax must be paid. However, he or she can generally decide the timing of sale of investments and therefore has some control over the timing of realized capital gains and losses. This control can be valuable for a taxable investor because it may be optimal to delay realizing gains and related tax payments and to realize losses as early as possible. This type of tax-driven strategic behavior is referred to as tax-loss harvesting.

Key points for managing taxable fixed-income portfolios include the following:

- Selectively offset capital gains and losses for tax purposes.

- If short-term capital gains tax rates are higher than long-term capital gains tax rates, then be judicious when realizing short-term gains.
- Realize losses taking into account tax consequences. They may be used to offset current or future capital gains for tax purposes.
- Control turnover in the fund. In general, the lower the turnover, the longer capital gains tax payments can be deferred.
- Consider the trade-off between capital gains and income for tax purposes.

7.2. Investment Vehicles and Taxes

The choice of investment vehicle often affects how investments are taxed at the final investor level. In a pooled investment vehicle (sometimes referred to as a collective investment scheme) such as a mutual fund, interest income is generally taxed at the final investor level when it occurs—regardless of whether the fund reinvests interest income or pays it out to investors. In other words, for tax purposes the fund is considered to have distributed interest income for tax purposes in the year it is received even if it does not actually pay it out to investors. Taxation of capital gains arising from the individual investments within a fund is often treated differently in different countries.

Some countries, such as the United States, use what is known as *pass-through treatment* of capital gains in mutual funds. Realized net capital gains in the underlying securities of a fund are treated as if distributed to investors in the year that they arise, and investors need to include the gains on their tax returns. Other countries, such as the United Kingdom, do not use pass-through treatment. Realized capital gains arising within a fund increase the net asset value of the fund shares that investors hold. Investors pay taxes on the net capital gain when they sell their fund shares. This tax treatment leads to a deferral in capital gains tax payments. The UK portfolio manager's decisions on when to realize capital gains or losses do not affect the timing of tax payments on capital gains by investors.

In a separately managed account, an investor typically pays tax on realized gains in the underlying securities at the time they occur. The investor holds the securities directly rather than through shares in a fund. For separately managed accounts, the portfolio manager needs to consider tax consequences for the investor when making investment decisions.

Tax-loss harvesting, which we defined earlier as deferring the realization of gains and realizing capital losses early, allows investors to accumulate gains on a pretax basis. The deferral of taxes increases the present value of investments to the investor.

EXAMPLE 7   Managing Taxable and Tax-Exempt Portfolios

A bond portfolio manager needs to raise €10,000,000 in cash to cover outflows in the portfolio she manages. To satisfy her cash demands, she considers one of two corporate bond positions for potential liquidation: Position A and Position B. For tax purposes, capital gains receive pass-through treatment; realized net capital gains in the underlying securities of a fund are treated as if distributed to investors in the year that they arise. Assume that the capital gains tax rate is 28% and the income tax rate for interest is 45%. Exhibit 9 provides relevant data for the two bond positions.

EXHIBIT 9   Selected Data for Two Bonds

	Position A	Position B
Current market value	€10,000,000	€10,000,000
Capital gain/loss	€1,000,000	–€1,000,000
Coupon rate	5.00%	5.00%
Remaining maturity	10 years	10 years
Income tax rate	45%	
Capital gains tax rate	28%	

The portfolio manager considers Position A to be slightly overvalued and Position B to be slightly undervalued. Assume that the two bond positions are identical with regard to all other relevant characteristics. How should the portfolio manager optimally liquidate bond positions if she manages a portfolio for:

1. tax-exempt investors?
2. taxable investors?

Solution to 1: The taxation of capital gains and capital losses has minimal consequences to tax-exempt investors. Consistent with the portfolio manager's investment views, the portfolio manager would likely liquidate Position A, which she considers slightly overvalued rather than liquidating Position B, which she considers slightly undervalued.

Solution to 2: All else equal, portfolio managers for taxable investors should have an incentive to defer capital gains taxes and realize capital losses early (tax-loss harvesting) so that losses can be used to offset current or future capital gains. Despite the slight undervaluation of the position, the portfolio manager might want to liquidate Position B because of its embedded capital loss, which will result in a lower realized net capital gain being distributed to investors. This decision is based on the assumption that there are no other capital losses in the portfolio that can be used to offset other capital gains. Despite the slight overvaluation of Position A, its liquidation would be less desirable for a taxable investor because of the required capital gains tax.

8. SUMMARY

This chapter describes the roles of fixed-income securities in an investment portfolio and introduces fixed-income portfolio management. Key points of the chapter include the following:

- Fixed-income investments provide diversification benefits in a portfolio context. These benefits arise from the generally low correlations of fixed-income investments with other major asset classes such as equities.

- Fixed-income investments have regular cash flows, which is beneficial for the purposes of funding future liabilities.
- Floating-rate and inflation-linked bonds can be used to hedge inflation risk.
- Liability-based fixed-income mandates are managed to match or cover expected liability payments with future projected cash inflows.
- For liability-based fixed-income mandates, portfolio construction follows two main approaches—cash flow matching and duration matching—to match fixed-income assets with future liabilities.
- Cash flow matching is an immunization approach based on matching bond cash flows with liability payments.
- Duration matching is an immunization approach based on matching the duration of assets and liabilities.
- Hybrid forms of duration and cash flow matching include contingent immunization and horizon matching.
- Total return mandates are generally structured to either track or outperform a benchmark.
- Total return mandates can be classified into different approaches based on their target active return and active risk levels. Approaches range from pure indexing to enhanced indexing to active management.
- Liquidity is an important consideration in fixed-income portfolio management. Bonds are generally less liquid than equities, and liquidity varies greatly across sectors.
- Liquidity affects pricing in fixed-income markets because many bonds either do not trade or trade infrequently.
- Liquidity affects portfolio construction because there is a trade-off between liquidity and yield. Less liquid bonds have higher yields, all else being equal, and may be more desirable for buy-and-hold investors. Investors anticipating liquidity needs may forgo higher yields for more-liquid bonds.
- Fixed-income derivatives, as well as fixed-income exchange-traded funds and pooled investment vehicles, are often more liquid than their underlying bonds and provide investment managers with an alternative to trading in illiquid underlying bonds.
- When evaluating fixed-income investment strategies, it is important to consider expected returns and to understand the different components of expected returns.
- Decomposing expected fixed-income returns allows investors to understand the different sources of returns given expected changes in bond market conditions.
- A model for expected fixed-income returns can decompose them into the following components: yield income, rolldown return, expected change in price based on investor's views of yields and yield spreads, expected credit losses, and expected currency gains or losses.
- Leverage is the use of borrowed capital to increase the magnitude of portfolio positions. By using leverage, fixed-income portfolio managers may be able to increase portfolio returns relative to what they can achieve in unleveraged portfolios. The potential for increased returns, however, comes with increased risk.
- Methods for leveraging fixed-income portfolios include the use of futures contracts, swap agreements, structured financial instruments, repurchase agreements, and securities lending.
- Taxes can complicate investment decisions in fixed-income portfolio management. Complications result from the difference in taxation across investor types, countries, and income sources (interest income or capital gains).

REFERENCES

Chen, Y., W. Ferson, and H. Peters. 2010. "Measuring the Timing Ability and Performance of Bond Mutual Funds." *Journal of Financial Economics*, vol. 98, no. 1: 72–89.

Davidson, R.B. 1999. "Bond Management for Taxable Investors." Association for Investment Management and Research Conference Proceedings no. 2 (August): 59–68.

Fong, H.G., and O.A. Vasicek. 1984. "A Risk Minimizing Strategy for Portfolio Immunization." *Journal of Finance*, vol. 39, no. 5 (December): 1541–1546.

Gorton, G., and A. Metrick. 2012. "Securitized Banking and the Run on Repo." *Journal of Financial Economics*, vol. 104, no. 3 (June): 425–451.

Hanke, B., and G. Seals. 2010. "Fixed-Income Analysis: Yield Curve Construction, Trading Strategies, and Risk Analysis." CFA Institute online course.

Ilmanen, A. 1995a. "Convexity Bias and the Yield Curve." *Understanding the Yield Curve: Part 5.* New York: Salomon Brothers.

Ilmanen, A. 1995b. "A Framework for Analyzing Yield Curve Trades." *Understanding the Yield Curve: Part 6.* New York: Salomon Brothers.

Ilmanen, A. 2011. *Expected Returns: An Investor's Guide to Harvesting Market Rewards.* Hoboken, NJ: John Wiley & Sons.

Kothari, S.P., and J. Shanken. 2004. "Asset Allocation with Inflation-Protected Bonds." *Financial Analysts Journal*, vol. 60, no. 1 (January–February): 54–70.

Leibowitz, M.L. 1986a. "The Dedicated Bond Portfolio in Pension Funds – Part I: Motivations and Basics." *Financial Analysts Journal*, vol. 42, no. 1 (January–February): 68–75.

Leibowitz, M. L. 1986b. "The Dedicated Bond Portfolio in Pension Funds – Part II: Immunization, Horizon Matching and Contingent Procedures." *Financial Analysts Journal*, vol. 42, no. 2 (March–April): 47–57.

Leibowitz, M., W. Krasker, and A. Nozari. 1990. "Spread Duration: A New Tool for Bond Management." *Journal of Portfolio Management*, vol. 16, no. 3 (Spring): 46–53.

Lin, H., J. Wang, and C. Wu. 2011. "Liquidity Risk and Expected Corporate Bond Returns." *Journal of Financial Economics*, vol. 99, no. 3: 628–650.

Redington, F.M. 1952. "Review of the Principles of Life Insurance Valuations." *Journal of the Institute of Actuaries*, vol. 78: 286–340.

Rogers, D. 2006. *Tax-Aware Investment Management: The Essential Guide.* New York: Bloomberg Press.

Roll, R. 2004. "Empirical TIPS." *Financial Analysts Journal*, vol. 60, no. 1 (January–February): 31–53.

Vazza, D, and N. Kraemer. 2016. "2015 Annual Global Corporate Default Study and Rating Transitions." *Standard & Poor's Ratings Services*, 2 May.

Wilcox, J., J. Horvitz, and D. diBartolomeo. 2006. *Investment Management for Taxable Private Investors.* Charlottesville, VA: Research Foundation of CFA Institute.

PRACTICE PROBLEMS

The following information relates to Questions 1–6

Cécile Perreaux is a junior analyst for an international wealth management firm. Her supervisor, Margit Daasvand, asks Perreaux to evaluate three fixed-income funds as part of the firm's global fixed-income offerings. Selected financial data for the funds Aschel, Permot, and

EXHIBIT 1   Selected Data on Fixed-Income Funds

	Aschel	Permot	Rosaiso
Current average bond price	$117.00	$91.50	$94.60
Expected average bond price in one year (end of Year 1)	$114.00	$96.00	$97.00
Average modified duration	7.07	7.38	6.99
Average annual coupon payment	$3.63	$6.07	$6.36
Present value of portfolio's assets (millions)	$136.33	$68.50	$74.38
Bond type*			
Fixed-coupon bonds	95%	38%	62%
Floating-coupon bonds	2%	34%	17%
Inflation-linked bonds	3%	28%	21%
Quality*			
AAA	65%	15%	20%
BBB	35%	65%	50%
B	0%	20%	20%
Not rated	0%	0%	10%
Value of portfolio's equity (millions)	$94.33		
Value of borrowed funds (millions)	$42.00		
Borrowing rate	2.80%		
Return on invested funds	6.20%		

* Bond type and Quality are shown as a percentage of total for each fund.

Rosaiso are presented in Exhibit 1. In Perreaux's initial review, she assumes that there is no reinvestment income and that the yield curve remains unchanged.

After further review of the composition of each of the funds, Perreaux notes the following.

Note 1.   Aschel is the only fund of the three that uses leverage.
Note 2.   Rosaiso is the only fund of the three that holds a significant number of bonds with embedded options.

Daasvand asks Perreaux to analyze immunization approaches to liability-based mandates for a meeting with Villash Foundation. Villash Foundation is a tax-exempt client. Prior to the meeting, Perreaux identifies what she considers to be two key features of a cash flow–matching approach.

Feature 1   It requires no yield curve assumptions.
Feature 2   Cash flows come from coupons and liquidating bond portfolio positions.

Two years later, Daasvand learns that Villash Foundation needs $5,000,000 in cash to meet liabilities. She asks Perreaux to analyze two bonds for possible liquidation. Selected data on the two bonds are presented in Exhibit 2.

EXHIBIT 2   Selected Data for Bonds 1 and 2

	Bond 1	Bond 2
Current market value	$5,000,000	$5,000,000
Capital gain/loss	400,000	–400,000
Coupon rate	2.05%	2.05%
Remaining maturity	8 years	8 years
Investment view	Overvalued	Undervalued
Income tax rate	39%	
Capital gains tax rate	30%	

1. Based on Exhibit 1, which fund provides the highest level of protection against inflation for coupon payments?
   A. Aschel
   B. Permot
   C. Rosaiso

2. Based on Exhibit 1, the rolling yield of Aschel over a one-year investment horizon is *closest* to:
   A. –2.56%.
   B. 0.54%.
   C. 5.66%.

3. The levered portfolio return for Aschel is *closest* to:
   A. 7.25%.
   B. 7.71%.
   C. 8.96%.

4. Based on Note 2, Rosaiso is the only fund for which the expected change in price based on the investor's views of yields and yield spreads should be calculated using:
   A. convexity.
   B. modified duration.
   C. effective duration.

5. Is Perreaux correct with respect to key features of cash flow matching?
   A. Yes.
   B. No, only Feature 1 is correct.
   C. No, only Feature 2 is correct.

6. Based on Exhibit 2, the optimal strategy to meet Villash Foundation's cash needs is the sale of:
    A. 100% of Bond 1.
    B. 100% of Bond 2.
    C. 50% of Bond 1 and 50% of Bond 2.

The following information relates to Questions 7–12

Celia Deveraux is chief investment officer for the Topanga Investors Fund, which invests in equities and fixed income. The clients in the fund are all taxable investors. The fixed-income allocation includes a domestic (US) bond portfolio and an externally managed global bond portfolio.

The domestic bond portfolio has a total return mandate, which specifies a long-term return objective of 25 basis points (bps) over the benchmark index. Relative to the benchmark, small deviations in sector weightings are permitted, such risk factors as duration must closely match, and tracking error is expected to be less than 50 bps per year.

The objectives for the domestic bond portfolio include the ability to fund future liabilities, protect interest income from short-term inflation, and minimize the correlation with the fund's equity portfolio. The correlation between the fund's domestic bond portfolio and equity portfolio is currently 0.14. Deveraux plans to reduce the fund's equity allocation and increase the allocation to the domestic bond portfolio. She reviews two possible investment strategies.

Strategy 1 Purchase AAA rated fixed-coupon corporate bonds with a modified duration of two years and a correlation coefficient with the equity portfolio of –0.15.

Strategy 2 Purchase US government agency floating-coupon bonds with a modified duration of one month and a correlation coefficient with the equity portfolio of –0.10.

Deveraux realizes that the fund's return may decrease if the equity allocation of the fund is reduced. Deveraux decides to liquidate $20 million of US Treasuries that are currently owned and to invest the proceeds in the US corporate bond sector. To fulfill this strategy, Deveraux asks Dan Foster, a newly hired analyst for the fund, to recommend Treasuries to sell and corporate bonds to purchase.

Foster recommends Treasuries from the existing portfolio that he believes are overvalued and will generate capital gains. Deveraux asks Foster why he chose only overvalued bonds with capital gains and did not include any bonds with capital losses. Foster responds with two statements.

Statement 1.   Taxable investors should prioritize selling overvalued bonds and always sell them before selling bonds that are viewed as fairly valued or undervalued.

Statement 2.   Taxable investors should never intentionally realize capital losses.

Regarding the purchase of corporate bonds, Foster collects relevant data, which are presented in Exhibit 1.

EXHIBIT 1   Selected Data on Three US Corporate Bonds

Bond Characteristics	Bond 1	Bond 2	Bond 3
Credit quality	AA	AA	A
Issue size ($ millions)	100	75	75
Maturity (years)	5	7	7
Total issuance outstanding ($ millions)	1,000	1,500	1,000
Months since issuance	New issue	3	6

Deveraux and Foster review the total expected 12-month return (assuming no reinvestment income) for the global bond portfolio. Selected financial data are presented in Exhibit 2.

EXHIBIT 2   Selected Data on Global Bond Portfolio

Notional principal of portfolio (in millions)	€200
Average bond coupon payment (per €100 par value)	€2.25
Coupon frequency	Annual
Current average bond price	€98.45
Expected average bond price in one year (assuming an unchanged yield curve)	€98.62
Average bond convexity	22
Average bond modified duration	5.19
Expected average yield and yield spread change	0.15%
Expected credit losses	0.13%
Expected currency gains (€ appreciation vs. $)	0.65%

Deveraux contemplates adding a new manager to the global bond portfolio. She reviews three proposals and determines that each manager uses the same index as its benchmark but pursues a different total return approach, as presented in Exhibit 3.

EXHIBIT 3   New Manager Proposals Fixed-Income Portfolio Characteristics

Sector Weights (%)	Manager A	Manager B	Manager C	Index
Government	53.5	52.5	47.8	54.1
Agency/quasi-agency	16.2	16.4	13.4	16.0
Corporate	20.0	22.2	25.1	19.8
MBS	10.3	8.9	13.7	10.1
Risk and Return Characteristics	**Manager A**	**Manager B**	**Manager C**	**Index**
Average maturity (years)	7.63	7.84	8.55	7.56
Modified duration (years)	5.23	5.25	6.16	5.22
Average yield (%)	1.98	2.08	2.12	1.99
Turnover (%)	207	220	290	205

7. Which approach to its total return mandate is the fund's domestic bond portfolio *most likely* to use?
   A. Pure indexing
   B. Enhanced indexing
   C. Active management

8. Strategy 2 is *most likely* preferred to Strategy 1 for meeting the objective of:
   A. protecting inflation.
   B. funding future liabilities.
   C. minimizing the correlation of the fund's domestic bond portfolio and equity portfolio.

9. Are Foster's statements to Deveraux supporting Foster's choice of bonds to sell correct?
   A. Only Statement 1 is correct.
   B. Only Statement 2 is correct.
   C. Neither Statement 1 nor Statement 2 is correct.

10. Based on Exhibit 1, which bond *most likely* has the highest liquidity premium?
    A. Bond 1
    B. Bond 2
    C. Bond 3

11. Based on Exhibit 2, the total expected return of the fund's global bond portfolio is *closest* to:
    A. 0.90%.
    B. 2.20%.
    C. 3.76%.

12. Based on Exhibit 3, which manager is *most likely* to have an active management total return mandate?
    A. Manager A
    B. Manager B
    C. Manager C

CHAPTER 10

LIABILITY-DRIVEN AND INDEX-BASED STRATEGIES

James F. Adams, PhD, CFA
Donald J. Smith, PhD

James F. Adams is a contributing author and his contributions solely represent his views and can in no way be taken to reflect the views of JPMorgan Chase & Co.

LEARNING OUTCOMES

The candidate should be able to:

- describe liability-driven investing;
- evaluate strategies for managing a single liability;
- compare strategies for a single liability and for multiple liabilities, including alternative means of implementation;
- evaluate liability-based strategies under various interest rate scenarios and select a strategy to achieve a portfolio's objectives;
- explain risks associated with managing a portfolio against a liability structure;
- discuss bond indexes and the challenges of managing a fixed-income portfolio to mimic the characteristics of a bond index;
- compare alternative methods for establishing bond market exposure passively;
- discuss criteria for selecting a benchmark and justify the selection of a benchmark;
- describe construction, benefits, limitations, and risk–return characteristics of a laddered bond portfolio.

Portfolio Management, Second Edition, by James F. Adams, PhD, CFA, and Donald J. Smith, PhD. Copyright © 2017 by CFA Institute.

1. INTRODUCTION

Fixed-income instruments make up nearly three-quarters of all global financial assets available to investors, so it is not surprising that bonds are a critical component of most investment portfolios. This chapter focuses on structured and passive total return fixed-income investment strategies. "Passive" does not necessarily mean "buy and hold" because the primary strategies discussed—immunization and indexation—can entail frequent rebalancing of the bond portfolio. "Passive" stands in contrast to "active" fixed-income strategies that are based on the asset manager's particular view on interest rate and credit market conditions.

Sections 2 through 6 address how to best structure a fixed-income portfolio when considering both the asset and liability sides of the investor's balance sheet. It is first important to have a thorough understanding of both the timing and relative certainty of future financial obligations. Because it is rare to find a bond investment whose characteristics perfectly match one's obligations, we introduce the idea of structuring a bond portfolio to match the future cash flows of one or more liabilities that have bond-like characteristics. Asset–liability management (ALM) strategies are based on the concept that investors incorporate both rate-sensitive assets and liabilities into the portfolio decision-making process. When the liabilities are given and assets are managed, liability-driven investing (LDI) may be used to ensure adequate funding for an insurance portfolio, a pension plan, or an individual's budget after retirement.[1] The techniques and risks associated with LDI are introduced using a single liability, and then expanded to cover both cash flow and duration matching techniques and multiple liabilities. This strategy, known as immunization, may be viewed simply as a special case of interest rate hedging. It is important to note that when funds exceed a predetermined threshold, investors can also use interest rate derivatives as a tool to manage their liabilities in addition to choosing a specific asset portfolio to achieve the management of their liabilities. This contingent form of immunization involves active management above a pre-specified funding threshold while retaining a more passive approach at lower funding levels. Section 5 reviews these concepts in detail using the example of a defined benefit pension plan. Section 6 reviews risks associated with these strategies, such as model risk and measurement risk.

Investors often use an index-based investment strategy to gain a broader exposure to fixed-income markets rather than tailoring investments to match a specific liability profile. Sections 7 through 9 cover this approach. Advantages of index-based investing include greater diversification and lower cost when compared with active management. That said, the depth and breadth of bond markets make both creating and tracking an index more challenging than in the equity markets. Fixed-income managers face a variety of alternatives in matching a bond index, from full replication to enhanced indexing using primary risk factors. We describe how portfolio managers and investors in general can gain fixed-income exposure through mutual funds or exchange-traded funds, as well as via synthetic means. Given the wide variety of fixed-income instruments available, it is critical to select a benchmark that is most relevant to a specific investor based on factors such as the targeted duration profile and risk appetite. In the area of private wealth management, establishing a laddered portfolio of bonds is often an effective strategy to match an individual investor's duration and risk preferences. The final section discusses this approach.

---

[1] In this chapter, we use the terms "liability driven" and "liability based" interchangeably.

2. LIABILITY-DRIVEN INVESTING

Let us start with the example of a 45-year-old investor who plans to retire at age 65 and would like to secure a stable stream of income thereafter. It is quite probable that he currently has a diversified portfolio that includes bonds, equities, and possibly other asset classes. Our focus here is on the fixed-income portion of his overall portfolio. We will assume that the investor builds the bond portfolio and adds to it year by year. Upon retirement, he plans to sell the bonds and buy an annuity that will pay a fixed benefit for his remaining lifetime. This investor's initial 20-year time horizon is critical to identifying and measuring the impact on retirement income arising from future interest rate volatility, and it forms the initial frame of reference for understanding and dealing with interest rate risk.

More generally, the frame of reference is in the form of a balance sheet of rate-sensitive assets and liabilities. In the example of the 45-year-old investor, the asset is the growing bond portfolio and the liability is the present value of the annuity that the investor requires to satisfy the fixed lifetime benefit. Asset–liability management strategies consider both assets and liabilities in the portfolio decision-making process. ALM strategies became popular in the 1970s following the surge in oil prices and inflation. As rising inflation led to US interest rate volatility, bank managers began to implement ALM strategies in order to better balance the interest rate exposure of assets and liabilities. Before ALM, bank managers often made loans and deposit rate decisions independently, leading to unexpected gaps between the maturity profiles of loan assets and deposit liabilities. Managers realized that coordinated rate decisions and measurement of gaps between asset and liability maturities would reduce interest rate risk. These institutions set up asset–liability committees (ALCOs) to monitor and manage the maturity gaps and set rates in a coordinated manner. For example, if the bank acquired long-term fixed-rate assets, it would raise rates on long-term deposits so as to make such deposits attractive to savers, allowing the bank to maintain a balance in the maturities. The use of derivatives such as interest rate swaps to manage these maturity gaps through synthetic ALM strategies became widespread in the 1980s.

Liability-driven investing (LDI) and asset-driven liabilities (ADL) are special cases of ALM. The key difference is that with ADL, the assets are given and the liabilities are structured to manage interest rate risk; whereas with LDI, the liabilities are given and the assets are managed. As an example of LDI, a life insurance company acquires a liability portfolio based on the insurance policies underwritten by its sales force. Another example involves the future employee benefits promised by a defined benefit pension plan, which create a portfolio of rate-sensitive liabilities. In each circumstance, the liabilities are defined and result from routine business and financial management decisions. The present value of those liabilities depends on current interest rates. A life insurance or pension manager will use the estimated interest rate sensitivity of plan liabilities as a starting point when making investment portfolio decisions. This process often requires building a model for the liabilities, as discussed in Section 5 of this chapter.

With ADL, the asset side of the balance sheet results from a company's underlying businesses, and the debt manager seeks a liability structure to reduce interest rate risk. One example might be a leasing company with short-term contracts that chooses to finance itself with short-term debt. The company is aiming to match the maturities of its assets and liabilities to minimize risk. Alternatively, a manufacturing company might identify that its operating revenues are highly correlated with the business cycle. Monetary policy is typically managed so there is positive correlation between interest rates and the business cycle. Central banks lower policy rates when the economy is weak and raise them when it is strong. Therefore, this company has a natural preference for variable-rate liabilities so that operating revenue and interest expense rise and fall together.[2]

An LDI strategy starts with analyzing the size and timing of the entity's liabilities. Exhibit 1 shows a classification scheme for this analysis.[3]

EXHIBIT 1   Classification of Liabilities

Liability Type	Amount of Cash Outlay	Timing of Cash Outlay
I	Known	Known
II	Known	Uncertain
III	Uncertain	Known
IV	Uncertain	Uncertain

The same scheme also applies to financial assets, but our focus here is on liabilities and on LDI, which is much more common than ADL. Type I liabilities arise from financial contracts that specify certain amounts due on scheduled future dates. An example is a traditional fixed-income bond having no embedded options. How much one pays (or receives) in coupon interest and principal redemption, as well as the timing of the payments, are known in advance. The next two sections assume Type I liabilities, first for only a single payment and then for multiple bonds. An advantage to knowing the size and timing of cash flows is that yield duration statistics—that is, Macaulay duration, modified duration, money duration, and the present value of a basis point (PVBP)—can be used to measure the interest rate sensitivity of the liabilities.

Type II liabilities have known amounts, but the timing of those payments is uncertain. Examples of this type of liability are callable and putable bonds. The call price payable upon exercise of the option is known in advance, but when or if the bond will be called is uncertain. Similarly, the issuer of a putable bond does not know when or if the investor will exercise the option. Another example is a term life insurance policy. Although the timing of the insured's death is unknown, a life insurance company holding a large portfolio of policies can benefit from the "law of large numbers." This means that the insurance company can use actuarial science to predict, on average, the amount of total liabilities due for each year and so can gain a very good sense of the amount of cash flow it will have to pay out in a given year.

Type III liabilities have known payment dates but an uncertain amount. A floating-rate note is an obvious example because the interest payments depend on future money market rates. Moreover, some structured notes have principal redemption amounts tied to a commodity price or interest rate index. Inflation-indexed bonds issued by many governments are another example. In the United States, the US Treasury issues Treasury inflation-protected securities (TIPS). The principal redemption amount is adjusted for the changes in the Consumer Price Index realized over the security's lifetime, making interest and principal payment amounts uncertain.

Type IV liabilities present the most difficult setting for an LDI strategy because both the amount and timing of the future obligations are uncertain. A property and casualty insurance

---

[2]See Adams and Smith (2013) for further examples and the use of interest rate swaps to transform fixed-rate debt into a synthetic-floating rate liability.
[3]This classification scheme is taken from Fabozzi (2013).

company offers a good example. Although the amount and timing of some claims might follow a known pattern (for instance, automobile insurance), others such as damages from catastrophic weather events (e.g., tornados, cyclones, and floods) are inherently difficult to predict.

With Types II, III, and IV liabilities, a curve duration statistic known as effective duration is needed to estimate interest rate sensitivity.[4] This statistic is calculated using a model for the uncertain amount and/or timing of the cash flows and an initial assumption about the yield curve. Then the yield curve is shifted up and down to obtain new estimates for the present value of the liabilities. We demonstrate this process in Section 5 for the sponsor of a defined benefit pension plan, which is another example of an entity with Type IV liabilities.

EXAMPLE 1

Modern Mortgage, a savings bank, decides to establish an ALCO to improve risk management and coordination of its loan and deposit rate-setting processes. Modern's primary assets are long-term, fixed-rate, monthly payment, fully amortizing residential mortgage loans. The mortgage loans are prime quality and have loan-to-value ratios that average 80%. The loans are pre-payable at par value by the homeowners at no fee. Modern also holds a portfolio of non-callable, fixed-income government bonds (considered free of default risk) of varying maturities to manage its liquidity needs. The primary liabilities are demand and time deposits that are fully guaranteed by a government deposit insurance fund. The demand deposits are redeemable by check or debit card. The time deposits have fixed rates and maturities ranging from 90 days to three years and are redeemable before maturity at a small fee. The banking-sector regulator in the country in which Modern operates has introduced a new capital requirement for savings banks. In accordance with the requirement, contingent convertible long-term bonds are issued by the savings bank and sold to institutional investors. The key feature is that if defaults on the mortgage loans reach a certain level or the savings bank's capital ratio drops below a certain level, as determined by the regulator, the bonds convert to equity at a specified price per share.

As a first step, the ALCO needs to identify the types of assets and liabilities that comprise its balance sheet using the classification scheme in Exhibit 1. Type I has certain amounts and dates for its cash flows; Type II has known amounts but uncertain dates; Type III has specified dates but unknown amounts; and Type IV has uncertain amounts and dates.

Specify and explain the classification scheme for the following:

1. Residential mortgage loans
2. Government bonds
3. Demand and time deposits
4. Contingent convertible bonds

---

[4]In this chapter, we discuss only the use of yield and curve duration statistics for a fixed-income bond. In academic literature, duration is often calculated by discounting each cash flow with the spot (or zero-coupon) rate corresponding with the date. The resulting duration statistic is known as Fisher–Weil duration. Although theoretically correct, it is difficult to calculate in practice because of the lack of observable spot rates for risky bonds.

Solution to 1: Residential mortgage loans are Type IV assets to the savings bank. The timing of interest and principal cash flows is uncertain because of the prepayment option held by the homeowner. This type of call option is complex. Homeowners might elect to prepay for many reasons, including sale of the property as well as the opportunity to refinance if interest rates come down. Therefore, a prepayment model is needed to project the timing of future cash flows. Default risk also affects the projected amount of the cash flow for each date. Even if the *average* loan-to-value ratio is 80%, indicating high-quality mortgages, some loans could have higher ratios and be more subject to default, especially if home prices decline.

Solution to 2: Fixed-rate government bonds are Type I assets because the coupon and principal payment dates and amounts are determined at issuance.

Solution to 3: Demand and time deposits are Type II liabilities from the savings bank's perspective. The deposit amounts are known, but the depositor can redeem the deposits prior to maturity, creating uncertainty about timing.

Solution to 4: The contingent convertible bonds are Type IV liabilities. The presence of the conversion option makes both the amount and timing of cash flows uncertain.

3. INTEREST RATE IMMUNIZATION—MANAGING THE INTEREST RATE RISK OF A SINGLE LIABILITY

Liability-driven investing in most circumstances is used to manage the interest rate risk on multiple liabilities. In this section, we focus on only a single liability to demonstrate the techniques and risks of the classic investment strategy known as interest rate **immunization**.[5] Immunization is the process of structuring and managing a fixed-income bond portfolio to minimize the variance in the realized rate of return over a known time horizon.[6] This variance arises from the volatility of future interest rates. Default risk is neglected at this point because the portfolio bonds are assumed to have default probabilities that approach zero.

The most obvious way to immunize the interest rate risk on a single liability is to buy a zero-coupon bond that matures on the obligation's due date. The bond's face value matches the liability amount. There is no cash flow reinvestment risk because there are no coupon payments to reinvest, and there is no price risk because the bond is held to maturity. Any interest rate volatility over the bond's lifetime is irrelevant in terms of the asset's ability to pay off the liability. The problem is that in many financial markets, zero-coupon bonds are not available. Nevertheless, the perfect immunization provided by a zero-coupon bond sets a standard to measure the performance of immunizing strategies using coupon-bearing bonds.

Exhibit 2 illustrates the connection between immunization and the duration of a traditional coupon-bearing fixed-income bond.

---

[5]This section is based on Smith (2014, ch. 9–10).
[6]The British actuary F.M. Redington coined the term "immunization" in his article, "Review of the Principles of Life-Office Valuations," *Journal of the Institute of Actuaries*, 1952.

EXHIBIT 2   Interest Rate Immunization with a Single Fixed-Income Bond

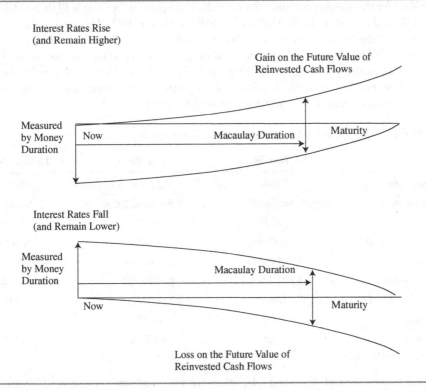

Assume that the bond is currently priced at par value. Then, an instantaneous, one-time, upward shift occurs in the yield curve. The bond's value falls, as shown in the upper panel. That drop in value is estimated by the money duration of the bond. The money duration is the bond's modified duration statistic multiplied by the price. Subsequently, the bond price will be "pulled to par" as the maturity date nears (assuming no default, of course). But there is another factor at work. Assuming that interest rates remain higher, the future value of reinvested coupon payments goes up. It is a rising line as more and more payments are received and reinvested at the higher interest rates.

The key detail to note in Exhibit 2 is that at some point in time, the two effects—the price effect and the coupon reinvestment effect—cancel each other. The lower panel shows the same cancellation for an immediate downward shift in interest rates. The remarkable result is that this point in time turns out to be the bond's Macaulay duration (for a zero-coupon bond, its Macaulay duration is its maturity). Therefore, an investor having an investment horizon equal to the bond's Macaulay duration is effectively protected, or immunized, from interest rate risk in that price, and coupon reinvestment effects offset for either higher or lower rates.

A numerical example is useful to show that the strategy of matching the Macaulay duration to the investment horizon works for a bond portfolio as well as for an individual security. Suppose that some entity has a single liability of EUR 250 million due 15 February 2023. The current date is 15 February 2017, so the investment horizon is six years. The asset manager for the entity seeks to build a three-bond portfolio to earn a rate of return sufficient to pay off the obligation.

Exhibit 3 reports the prices, yields, risk statistics (Macaulay duration and convexity), and par values for the chosen portfolio. The portfolio's current market value is EUR 200,052,250 (= EUR 47,117,500 + EUR 97,056,750 + EUR 55,878,000). The semi-annual coupon payments on the bonds occur on 15 February and 15 August of each year. The price is per 100 of par value, and the yield to maturity is on a street-convention semi-annual bond basis (meaning an annual percentage rate having a periodicity of two). Both the Macaulay duration and the convexity are annualized. (Note that in practice, some bond data vendors [such as Bloomberg] report the convexity statistic divided by 100.)

EXHIBIT 3   The Bond Portfolio to Immunize the Single Liability

	2.5-Year Bond	7-Year Bond	10-Year Bond
Coupon rate	1.50%	3.25%	5.00%
Maturity date	15 August 2019	15 February 2024	15 February 2027
Price	100.25	99.75	100.50
Yield to maturity	1.3979%	3.2903%	4.9360%
Par value	47,000,000	97,300,000	55,600,000
Market value	47,117,500	97,056,750	55,878,000
Macaulay duration	2.463	6.316	7.995
Convexity	7.253	44.257	73.747
Allocation	23.55%	48.52%	27.93%

Exhibit 4 shows the cash flows and calculations used to obtain the relevant portfolio statistics. The third column aggregates the coupon and principal payments received for each date from the three bonds.

EXHIBIT 4   Portfolio Statistics

Time	Date	Cash Flow	PV of Cash Flow	Weight	Time × Weight	Dispersion	Convexity
0	15-Feb-17	−200,052,250					
1	15-Aug-17	3,323,625	3,262,282	0.0163	0.0163	1.9735	0.0326
2	15-Feb-18	3,323,625	3,202,071	0.0160	0.0320	1.6009	0.0960
3	15-Aug-18	3,323,625	3,142,971	0.0157	0.0471	1.2728	0.1885
4	15-Feb-19	3,323,625	3,084,962	0.0154	0.0617	0.9871	0.3084
5	15-Aug-19	50,323,625	45,847,871	0.2292	1.1459	11.2324	6.8754
6	15-Feb-20	2,971,125	2,656,915	0.0133	0.0797	0.4782	0.5578
7	15-Aug-20	2,971,125	2,607,877	0.0130	0.0913	0.3260	0.7300
8	15-Feb-21	2,971,125	2,559,744	0.0128	0.1024	0.2048	0.9213
9	15-Aug-21	2,971,125	2,512,500	0.0126	0.1130	0.1131	1.1303
10	15-Feb-22	2,971,125	2,466,127	0.0123	0.1233	0.0493	1.3560
11	15-Aug-22	2,971,125	2,420,610	0.0121	0.1331	0.0121	1.5972
12	15-Feb-23	2,971,125	2,375,934	0.0119	0.1425	0.0000	1.8527

Time	Date	Cash Flow	PV of Cash Flow	Weight	Time × Weight	Dispersion	Convexity
13	15-Aug-23	2,971,125	2,332,082	0.0117	0.1515	0.0116	2.1216
14	15-Feb-24	100,271,125	77,251,729	0.3862	5.4062	1.5434	81.0931
15	15-Aug-24	1,390,000	1,051,130	0.0053	0.0788	0.0473	1.2610
16	15-Feb-25	1,390,000	1,031,730	0.0052	0.0825	0.0825	1.4028
17	15-Aug-25	1,390,000	1,012,688	0.0051	0.0861	0.1265	1.5490
18	15-Feb-26	1,390,000	993,997	0.0050	0.0894	0.1788	1.6993
19	15-Aug-26	1,390,000	975,651	0.0049	0.0927	0.2389	1.8533
20	15-Feb-27	56,990,000	39,263,380	0.1963	3.9253	12.5585	82.4316
			200,052,250	1.0000	12.0008	33.0378	189.0580

For instance, EUR 3,323,625 is the sum of the coupon payments for the first four dates:

$$(1.50\% \times 0.5 \times EUR\ 47,000,000) + (3.25\% \times 0.5 \times EUR\ 97,300,000) + (5.00\% \times 0.5 \times EUR\ 55,600,000) = EUR\ 352,500 + EUR\ 1,581,125 + EUR\ 1,390,000 = EUR\ 3,323,625$$

On 15 August 2019, the principal of EUR 47,000,000 is redeemed so that the total cash flow is EUR 50,323,625. The next eight cash flows represent the coupon payments on the second and third bonds, and so forth.

The internal rate of return on the cash flows in column 3 for the 20 semi-annual periods, including the portfolio's initial market value on 15 February 2017, is 1.8804%. Annualized on a semi-annual bond basis, the portfolio's cash flow yield is 3.7608% (= 2 × 1.8804%). This yield is significantly higher than the market value weighted average of the individual bond yields presented in Exhibit 3, which equals 3.3043%.

$$(1.3979\% \times 0.2355) + (3.2903\% \times 0.4852) + (4.9360\% \times 0.2793) = 3.3043\%$$

This difference arises because of the steepness in the yield curve. The key point is that the goal of the immunization strategy is to achieve a rate of return close to 3.76%, not 3.30%.

The fourth column in Exhibit 4 shows the present values for each of the aggregate cash flows, calculated using the internal rate of return per period (1.8804%) as the discount rate. For example, the combined payment of EUR 100,271,125 due on 15 February 2024 has a present value of EUR 77,251,729. [*Note: Calculations in this chapter are carried out on a spreadsheet that preserves precision. For readability and to avoid clutter, the exhibits and text report rounded results. For example, the following calculation gives 77,251,498 with the numbers shown on the left-hand side, but it gives 77,251,729, the amount shown on the right-hand side, when the precise semi-annual cash flow yield, 1.0188037819%, is used.*]

$$\frac{100,271,125}{(1.018804)^{14}} = 77,251,729$$

The sum of the present values in column 4 is EUR 200,052,250, the current market value for the bond portfolio.

The sixth column is used to obtain the portfolio's Macaulay duration. This duration statistic is the weighted average of the times to the receipt of cash flow, whereby the share of total market value for each date is the weight. Column 5 shows the weights, which are the PV of each cash flow divided by the total PV of EUR 200,052,250. The times to receipt of cash flow (the times from column 1) are multiplied by the weights and then summed. For example, the contribution to total portfolio duration for the second cash flow on 15 February 2018 is 0.0320 ($= 2 \times 0.0160$). The sum of column 6 is 12.0008. That is the Macaulay duration for the portfolio in terms of semi-annual periods. Annualized, it is 6.0004 ($= 12.0008/2$). It is now clear why the asset manager for the entity chose this portfolio: The portfolio Macaulay duration matches the investment horizon of six years.

In practice, it is common to estimate the portfolio duration using the market value weighted average of the individual durations for each bond.[7] Exhibit 3 shows those individual durations and the allocation percentages for each bond. The average Macaulay duration is $(2.463 \times 0.2355) + (6.316 \times 0.4852) + (7.995 \times 0.2793) = 5.8776$.

The difference, as with the cash flow yield and the market value weighted average yield, arises because the yield curve is not flat. When the yield curve is upwardly sloped, average duration (5.8776) is less than the portfolio duration (6.0004). This difference in duration statistics is important because using the average duration in building the immunizing portfolio instead of the portfolio duration would introduce model risk to the strategy. Section 6 of this chapter discusses model risk.

The sum of the seventh column in Exhibit 4 is the portfolio **dispersion** statistic. Whereas Macaulay duration is the weighted *average* of the times to receipt of cash flow, dispersion is the weighted *variance*. It measures the extent to which the payments are spread out around the duration. For example, the contribution to total portfolio dispersion for the fifth cash flow on 15 August 2019 is 11.2324: $(5 - 12.0008)^2 \times 0.2292 = 11.2324$.

This portfolio's dispersion is 33.0378 in terms of semi-annual periods. Annualized, it is 8.2594 ($= 33.0378/4$). The Macaulay duration statistic is annualized by dividing by the periodicity of the bonds (two payments per year); dispersion (and convexity, which follows) is annualized by dividing by the periodicity squared.

The portfolio convexity is calculated with the eighth column. It is the sum of the times to the receipt of cash flow, multiplied by those times plus one, multiplied by the shares of market value for each date (weight), and all divided by one plus the cash flow yield squared. For example, the contribution to the sum for the 14th payment on 15 February 2024 is 81.0931 ($= 14 \times 15 \times 0.3862$). The sum of the column is 189.0580. The convexity in semi-annual periods is 182.1437:

$$\frac{189.0580}{(1.018804)^2} = 182.1437$$

The annualized convexity for the portfolio is 45.5359 ($= 182.1437/4$). This result is slightly higher than the market value weighted average of the individual convexity statistics reported in Exhibit 3:

$$(7.253 \times 0.2355) + (44.257 \times 0.4852) + (73.747 \times 0.2793) = 43.7786$$

---

[7]Another, and more theoretically correct, way to obtain the portfolio duration would be to discount the cash flows using spot (or zero-coupon) rates. As mentioned in Footnote 4, this duration calculation is difficult to implement in practice.

As with the average yield and duration, this difference results from the slope of the yield curve. The convexity statistic can be used to improve the estimate for the change in portfolio market value following a change in interest rates than is provided by duration alone. That is, convexity is the second-order effect, whereas duration is the first-order effect.

There is an interesting connection among the portfolio convexity, Macaulay duration, dispersion, and cash flow yield.[8]

$$\text{Convexity} = \frac{\text{Macaulay duration}^2 + \text{Macaulay duration} + \text{Dispersion}}{(1 + \text{Cash flow yield})^2} \tag{1}$$

In terms of semi-annual periods, the Macaulay duration for this portfolio is 12.0008, the dispersion is 33.0378, and the cash flow yield is 1.8804%.

$$\text{Convexity} = \frac{12.0008^2 + 12.0008 + 33.0378}{(1.018804)^2} = 182.1437$$

The portfolio dispersion and convexity statistics are used to assess the structural risk to the interest rate immunization strategy. Structural risk arises from the potential for shifts and twists to the yield curve. This risk is discussed later in this section.

Exhibit 5 demonstrates how matching the Macaulay duration for the portfolio to the investment horizon leads to interest rate immunization.

EXHIBIT 5   Interest Rate Immunization

Time	Date	Cash Flow	Total Return at 3.7608%	Total Return at 2.7608%	Total Return at 4.7608%
0	15-Feb-17	−200,052,250			
1	15-Aug-17	3,323,625	4,079,520	3,864,613	4,305,237
2	15-Feb-18	3,323,625	4,004,225	3,811,992	4,205,138
3	15-Aug-18	3,323,625	3,930,319	3,760,088	4,107,366
4	15-Feb-19	3,323,625	3,857,777	3,708,891	4,011,868
5	15-Aug-19	50,323,625	57,333,230	55,392,367	59,332,093
6	15-Feb-20	2,971,125	3,322,498	3,225,856	3,421,542
7	15-Aug-20	2,971,125	3,261,175	3,181,932	3,341,989
8	15-Feb-21	2,971,125	3,200,984	3,138,607	3,264,286
9	15-Aug-21	2,971,125	3,141,904	3,095,871	3,188,390
10	15-Feb-22	2,971,125	3,083,914	3,053,718	3,114,258
11	15-Aug-22	2,971,125	3,026,994	3,012,138	3,041,850
12	15-Feb-23	2,971,125	2,971,125	2,971,125	2,971,125
13	15-Aug-23	2,971,125	2,916,287	2,930,670	2,902,045
14	15-Feb-24	100,271,125	96,603,888	97,559,123	95,662,614
15	15-Aug-24	1,390,000	1,314,446	1,333,991	1,295,282

[8]The derivation of Equation 1, as well as additional examples of calculating dispersion and convexity for fixed-income bonds, are included in Smith (2014).

Time	Date	Cash Flow	Total Return at 3.7608%	Total Return at 2.7608%	Total Return at 4.7608%
16	15-Feb-25	1,390,000	1,290,186	1,315,827	1,265,166
17	15-Aug-25	1,390,000	1,266,373	1,297,911	1,235,750
18	15-Feb-26	1,390,000	1,242,999	1,280,238	1,207,018
19	15-Aug-26	1,390,000	1,220,058	1,262,806	1,178,955
20	15-Feb-27	56,990,000	49,099,099	51,070,094	47,213,270
			250,167,000	250,267,858	250,265,241

The fourth column shows the values of the cash flows as of the horizon date of 15 February 2023, assuming that the cash flow yield remains unchanged at 3.7608%. For instance, the future value of the EUR 3,323,625 in coupon payments received on 15 August 2017 is EUR 4,079,520.

$$3,323,625 \times \left(1 + \frac{0.037608}{2}\right)^{11} = 4,079,520$$

The value of the last cash flow for EUR 56,990,000 on 15 February 2027 is EUR 49,099,099 as of the horizon date of 15 February 2023.

$$\frac{56,990,000}{\left(1 + \frac{0.037608}{2}\right)^{8}} = 49,099,099$$

All of the payments received before the horizon date are reinvested at the cash flow yield. All of the payments received after the horizon date are sold at their discounted values. The sum of the fourth column is EUR 250,167,000, which is more than enough to pay off the EUR 250 million liability. The six-year holding period rate of return (ROR), also called the horizon yield, is 3.7608%. It is based on the original market value and the total return and is the solution for ROR:

$$200,052,250 = \frac{250,167,000}{\left(1 + \frac{ROR}{2}\right)^{12}}, ROR = 0.037608$$

The holding period rate of return equals the cash flow yield for the portfolio. This equivalence is the multi-bond version of the well-known result for a single bond: The realized rate of return matches the yield to maturity only if coupon payments are reinvested at that same yield and if the bond is held to maturity or sold at a point on the constant-yield price trajectory.

The fifth column in Exhibit 5 repeats the calculations for the assumption of an instantaneous, one-time, 100 bp drop in the cash flow yield on 15 February 2017. The future values of all cash flows received are now lower because they are reinvested at 2.7608% instead of 3.7608%. For example, the payment of EUR 50,323,625 on 15 August 2019, which contains the principal redemption on the 2.5-year bond, grows to only EUR 55,392,367.

$$50,323,625 \times \left(1 + \frac{0.027608}{2}\right)^{7} = 55,392,367$$

The value of the last cash flow is now higher because it is discounted at the lower cash flow yield.

$$\frac{56,990,000}{\left(1 + \frac{0.027608}{2}\right)^8} = 51,070,094$$

The important result is that the total return as of the horizon date is EUR 250,267,858, demonstrating that the cash flow reinvestment effect is balanced by the price effect, as illustrated for a single bond in Exhibit 2. The holding-period rate of return is 3.7676%.

$$200,052,250 = \frac{250,267,858}{\left(1 + \frac{ROR}{2}\right)^{12}}, ROR = 0.037676$$

To complete the example, the sixth column reports the results for an instantaneous, one-time, 100 bp jump in the cash flow yield, up to 4.7608% from 3.7608%. In this case, the future values of the reinvested cash flows are higher and the discounted values of cash flows due after the horizon date are lower. Nevertheless, the total return of EUR 250,265,241 for the six-year investment horizon is enough to pay off the liability. The horizon yield is 3.7674%.

$$200,052,250 = \frac{250,265,241}{\left(1 + \frac{ROR}{2}\right)^{12}}, ROR = 0.037674$$

This numerical exercise demonstrates interest rate immunization using a portfolio of fixed-income bonds. The total returns and holding period rates of return are virtually the same—in fact, slightly higher because of convexity—whether the cash flow yield goes up or down. Exhibit 4 is somewhat misleading, however, because it suggests that immunization is a buy-and-hold passive investment strategy. It suggests that the entity will (a) hold on the horizon date of 15 February 2023 the same positions in what then will be one-year, 3.25% and four-year, 5% bonds and (b) sell the bonds on that date. This suggestion is misleading because the portfolio must be frequently rebalanced to stay on its target duration. As time passes, the portfolio's Macaulay duration changes but not in line with the change in the remainder of the investment horizon. For example, after five years, the investment horizon as of 15 February 2022 is just one remaining year. The portfolio Macaulay duration at that time needs to be 1.000. The asset manager will have had to execute some trades by then, substantially reducing the holdings in what is then the five-year, 5% bond.

Exhibit 6 offers another way to illustrate interest rate immunization. An immunization strategy is essentially "zero replication." We know that the perfect bond to lock in the six-year holding period rate of return is a six-year zero-coupon bond having a face value that matches the EUR 250 million liability. The idea is to originally structure and then manage over time a portfolio of coupon-bearing bonds that replicates the period-to-period performance of the zero-coupon bond. Therefore, immunization is essentially just an interest rate hedging strategy. As the yield on the zero-coupon bond rises and falls, there will be unrealized losses and gains. In Exhibit 6, this is illustrated by the zero-coupon bond's value moving below and above the constant-yield price trajectory. Two paths for the zero-coupon yield are presented: Path A for generally lower rates (and higher values) and Path B for higher rates (and lower values). Regardless, the market value of the zero-coupon bond will be "pulled to par" as maturity nears.

EXHIBIT 6   Interest Rate Immunization as Zero Replication

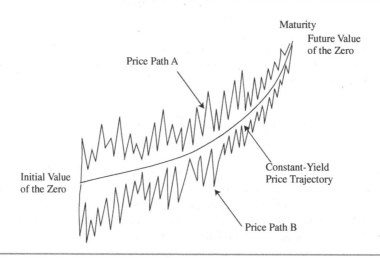

Immunizing with coupon-bearing bonds entails continuously matching the portfolio Macaulay duration with the Macaulay duration of the zero-coupon bond over time and as the yield curve shifts, even though the zero-coupon bond could be hypothetical and not exist in reality. Also, the bond portfolio's initial market value has to match or exceed the present value of the zero-coupon bond. The Macaulay duration of that, perhaps hypothetical, zero-coupon bond always matches the investment horizon. Immunization will be achieved if any ensuing change in the cash flow yield on the bond portfolio is equal to the change in the yield to maturity on the zero-coupon bond. That equivalence will ensure that the change in the bond portfolio's market value is close to the change in the market value of the zero-coupon bond. Therefore, at the end of the six-year investment horizon, the bond portfolio's market value should meet or exceed the face value of the zero-coupon bond, regardless of the path for interest rates over the six years.

The key assumption to achieve immunization is the statement that "any ensuing change in the cash flow yield on the bond portfolio is equal to the change in the yield to maturity on the zero-coupon bond." A *sufficient*, but not *necessary*, condition for that statement is a parallel (or shape-preserving) shift to the yield curve whereby all yields change by the same amount. *Sufficient* means that if the yield curve shift is parallel, the change in the bond portfolio's cash flow yield will equal the change in yield to maturity of the zero-coupon bond, which is enough to ensure immunization. To achieve immunization, however, it is not *necessary* that the yield curve shifts in a parallel manner. That is, in some cases, the immunization property can prevail even with non-parallel yield curve movements such as an upward and steepening shift (sometimes called a "bear steepener"), an upward and flattening shift (a "bear flattener"), a downward and steepening shift (a "bull steepener"), or a downward and flattening shift (a "bull flattener").

Exhibit 7 demonstrates this observation. Panel A of Exhibit 7 presents three different upward yield curve shifts. The first is a parallel shift of 102.08 bps for each of the three bond yields. The second is a steepening shift of 72.19 bps for the 2.5-year bond, 94.96 bps for the 7-year bond, and 120.82 bps for the 10-year bond. The third is a flattening shift whereby the yields on the three bonds increase by 145.81 bps, 109.48 bps, and 79.59 bps, respectively.

The key point is that each of these yield curve shifts results in the same 100 bp increase in the cash flow yield from 3.7608% to 4.7608%. Moreover, each shift in the yield curve produces virtually the same reduction in the portfolio's market value.

Panel B of Exhibit 7 shows the results for three downward shifts in the yield curve. The first is a parallel shift of 102.06 bps. The second and third are downward and steepening (–129.00 bps, –104.52 bps, and –92.00 bps for the 2.5-year, 7-year, and 10-year bonds) and downward and flattening (–55.76 bps, –86.32 bps, and –134.08 bps). Each shift results in the same 100 bp decrease in the cash flow yield from 3.7608% to 2.7608% and virtually the same increase in the market value of the portfolio.

EXHIBIT 7   Some Yield Curve Shifts That Achieve Interest Rate Immunization

Panel A Yield Curve Shift

	Change in 2.5-Year Yield	Change in 7-Year Yield	Change in 10-Year Yield	Change in Cash Flow Yield	Change in Market Value
Upward and parallel	+102.08 bps	+102.08 bps	+102.08 bps	+100 bps	–11,340,537
Upward and steepening	+72.19 bps	+94.96 bps	+120.82 bps	+100 bps	–11,340,195
Upward and flattening	+145.81 bps	+109.48 bps	+79.59 bps	+100 bps	–11,340,183

Panel B Yield Curve Shift

	Change in 2.5-Year Yield	Change in 7-Year Yield	Change in 10-Year Yield	Change in Cash Flow Yield	Change in Market Value
Downward and parallel	–102.06 bps	–102.06 bps	–102.06 bps	–100 bps	12,251,212
Downward and steepening	–129.00 bps	–104.52 bps	–92.00 bps	–100 bps	12,251,333
Downward and flattening	–55.76 bps	–86.32 bps	–134.08 bps	–100 bps	12,251,484

Notice that the interest rate immunization property shown in Exhibit 5 rests only on the change in the cash flow yield going up or down by 100 bps. It is not necessary to assume that the change in the value of the immunizing portfolio arises only from a parallel shift in the yield curve. In the same manner, the immunization property illustrated in Exhibit 6 requires only that the change in the value of the immunizing portfolio, one that has a Macaulay duration matching the investment horizon, is close to the change in the value of the zero-coupon bond that provides perfect immunization. Exhibit 7 demonstrates that non-parallel as well as parallel shifts can satisfy those conditions. Of course, there are many other non-parallel shifts for which those conditions are not met.

In general, the interest rate risk to an immunization strategy is that the change in the cash flow yield on the portfolio is not the same as on the ideal zero-coupon bond. This difference can occur with twists to the shape of the yield curve, in addition to some non-parallel shifts.[9] Exhibit 8 portrays two such twists. To exaggerate the risk, assume that the immunizing portfolio has a "barbell" structure in that it is composed of half short-term bonds and half long-term bonds. The portfolio Macaulay duration for the barbell is six years. The zero-coupon bond that provides perfect immunization has a maturity (and Macaulay duration) also of six years.

EXHIBIT 8   Immunization Risk and Twists to the Yield Curve

A. Steepening Twist

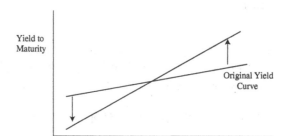

B. Positive Butterfly Twist

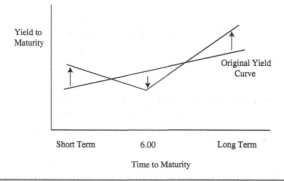

The upper panel of Exhibit 8 shows a steepening twist to the yield curve. The twist is assumed to occur at the six-year point to indicate that the value of the zero-coupon bond does not change. Short-term yields go down and long-term yields go up by approximately the same amount. The value of the barbell portfolio goes down because the losses on the long-term

---

[9]In this chapter, we distinguish "non-parallel shift" and "twist" to the yield curve. With a non-parallel shift, all yields rise or fall to varying degrees. With a twist to the yield curve, some yields rise while others fall.

positions exceed the gains on the short-term holdings as a result of the difference in duration between the holdings and the equivalence in the assumed changes in yield. Therefore, this portfolio does not track the value of the zero-coupon bond.

The lower panel of Exhibit 8 illustrates a dramatic twist in the shape of the yield curve. Short-term and long-term yields go up while the six-year yields go down. This type of twist is named a "positive butterfly." (In a "negative butterfly" twist, short-term and long-term yields go down and intermediate-term yields go up.) The immunizing portfolio decreases in value as its yields go up and the zero-coupon bond goes up in value. Again, the portfolio does not track the change in the value of the bond that provides perfect immunization. Fortunately for those entities that pursue interest rate immunization, these types of twists are rare. Most yield curve shifts are generally parallel, with some steepening and flattening, especially for maturities beyond a few years.

Exhibit 8 also illustrates how to reduce **structural risk** to an immunizing strategy. Structural risk arises from portfolio design, particularly the choice of the portfolio allocations. The risk is that yield curve twists and non-parallel shifts lead to changes in the cash flow yield that do not match the yield to maturity of the zero-coupon bond that provides for perfect immunization. Structural risk is reduced by minimizing the dispersion of the bond positions, going from a barbell design to more of a bullet portfolio that concentrates the component bonds' durations around the investment horizon. At the limit, a zero-coupon bond that matches the date of the single obligation has, by design, no structural risk.

Equation 1 indicates that minimizing portfolio dispersion is the same as minimizing the portfolio convexity for a given Macaulay duration and cash flow yield. An advantage to using convexity to measure the extent of structural risk is that the portfolio statistic can be approximated by the market value weighted average of the individual bonds' convexities. A problem with estimating portfolio dispersion using the dispersion statistics for individual bonds is that it can be misleading. Consider a portfolio of all zero-coupon bonds of varying maturities. Each individual bond has zero dispersion (because it has only one payment), so the market value weighted average is also zero. Clearly, the portfolio overall can have significant (non-zero) dispersion.

In summary, the characteristics of a bond portfolio structured to immunize a single liability are that it (1) has an initial market value that equals or exceeds the present value of the liability; (2) has a portfolio Macaulay duration that matches the liability's due date; and (3) minimizes the portfolio convexity statistic. This portfolio must be regularly rebalanced over the horizon to maintain the target duration, because the portfolio Macaulay duration changes as time passes and as yields change. The portfolio manager needs to weigh the trade-off between incurring transactions costs from rebalancing and allowing some duration gap. This and other risks to immunization—for instance, those arising from the use of interest rate derivatives to match the duration of assets to the investment horizon—are covered in Section 6.

EXAMPLE 2

An institutional client asks a fixed-income investment adviser to recommend a portfolio to immunize a single 10-year liability. It is understood that the chosen portfolio will need to be rebalanced over time to maintain its target duration. The adviser proposes two portfolios of coupon-bearing government bonds because zero-coupon bonds are not available. The portfolios have the same market value. The institutional client's objective is to minimize the variance in the realized rate of return over the 10-year horizon. The two portfolios have the following risk and return statistics:

	Portfolio A	Portfolio B
Cash flow yield	7.64%	7.65%
Macaulay duration	9.98	10.01
Convexity	107.88	129.43

These statistics are based on aggregating the interest and principal cash flows for the bonds that constitute the portfolios; they are not market value weighted averages of the yields, durations, and convexities of the individual bonds. The cash flow yield is stated on a semi-annual bond basis, meaning an annual percentage rate having a periodicity of two; the Macaulay durations and convexities are annualized.

Indicate the portfolio that the investment adviser should recommend, and explain the reasoning.

Solution: The adviser should recommend Portfolio A. First, notice that the cash flow yields of both portfolios are virtually the same and that both portfolios have Macaulay durations very close to 10, the horizon for the liability. It would be wrong and misleading to recommend Portfolio B because it has a "higher yield" and a "duration closer to the investment horizon of 10 years." In practical terms, a difference of 1 bp in yield is not likely to be significant, nor is the difference of 0.03 in annual duration.

Given the fact that the portfolio yields and durations are essentially the same, the choice depends on the difference in convexity. The difference between 129.43 and 107.88, however, is meaningful. In general, convexity is a desirable property of fixed-income bonds. All else being equal (meaning the same yield and duration), a more convex bond gains more if the yield goes down and loses less if the yield goes up than a less convex bond.

The client's objective, however, is to minimize the variance in the realized rate of return over the 10-year horizon. That objective indicates a conservative immunization strategy achieved by building the duration matching portfolio and minimizing the portfolio convexity. Such an approach minimizes the dispersion of cash flows around the Macaulay duration and makes the portfolio closer to the zero-coupon bond that would provide perfect immunization; see Equation 1.

The structural risk to the immunization strategy is the potential for non-parallel shifts and twists to the yield curve, which lead to changes in the cash flow yield that do not track the change in the yield on the zero-coupon bond. This risk is minimized by selecting the portfolio with the lower convexity (and dispersion of cash flows).

Note that default risk is neglected in this discussion because the portfolio consists of government bonds that presumably have default probabilities approaching zero.

4. INTEREST RATE IMMUNIZATION—MANAGING THE INTEREST RATE RISK OF MULTIPLE LIABILITIES

The principle of interest rate immunization applies to multiple liabilities in addition to a single liability. For now, we continue to assume that these are Type I cash flows in that the scheduled amounts and payment dates are known to the asset manager. In particular, we assume that the same three bonds from Exhibits 3 and 4, which were assets in the single-liability immunization, are now themselves liabilities to be immunized. This assumption allows us to use the same portfolio statistics as in the previous section. The entity in the examples that follow seeks to immunize the cash flows in column 3 (the cash flow column) of Exhibit 4 from Dates 1 through 20, and so needs to build a portfolio of assets that will allow it to pay those cash flows. The present value of the (now) corporate debt liabilities is EUR 200,052,250. As in Section 3, the cash flow yield is 3.76%; the Macaulay duration is 6.00; and the convexity is 45.54. We use the portfolio statistics rather than the market value weighted averages because they better summarize Type I liabilities.

In this section, we discuss several approaches to manage these liabilities:

- *Cash flow matching*, which entails building a dedicated portfolio of zero-coupon or fixed-income bonds to ensure that there are sufficient cash inflows to pay the scheduled cash outflows;
- *Duration matching*, which extends the ideas of the previous section to a portfolio of debt liabilities;
- *Derivatives overlay*, in particular using futures contracts on government bonds in the immunization strategy; and
- *Contingent immunization*, which allows for active bond portfolio management until a minimum threshold is reached and that threshold is identified by the interest rate immunization strategy.

4.1. Cash Flow Matching

A classic strategy to eliminate the interest rate risk arising from multiple liabilities is to build a dedicated asset portfolio of high-quality fixed-income bonds that, as closely as possible, matches the amount and timing of the scheduled cash outflows. "Dedicated" means that the bonds are placed in a held-to-maturity portfolio. A natural question is, if the entity has enough cash to build the dedicated bond portfolio, why not just use that cash to buy back and retire the liabilities? The answer is that the buyback strategy is difficult and costly to implement if the bonds are widely held by buy-and-hold institutional and retail investors. Most corporate bonds are rather illiquid, so buying them back on the open market is likely to drive up the purchase price. Cash flow matching can be a better use of the available cash assets.

A corporate finance motivation for cash flow matching is to improve the company's credit rating. The entity has sufficient cash assets to retire the debt liabilities, and dedicating the bonds effectively accomplishes that objective. Under some circumstances, a corporation might even be able to remove both the dedicated asset portfolio and the debt liabilities from its balance sheet through the process of **accounting defeasance**. Also called in-substance defeasance, accounting defeasance is a way of extinguishing a debt obligation by setting aside sufficient high-quality securities, such as US Treasury notes, to repay the liability.[10]

---

[10]Note that the mention of defeasance is intended to motivate the passive fixed-income strategies and not to teach the accounting for such transactions.

Panel A in Exhibit 9 illustrates the dedicated cash flow matching asset portfolio. These assets could be zero-coupon bonds or traditional fixed-income securities. Panel B represents the amount and timing of the debt liabilities. The amounts come from the third column in Exhibit 4 and are the sum of the coupon and principal payments on the three debt securities.

EXHIBIT 9   Cash Flow Matching

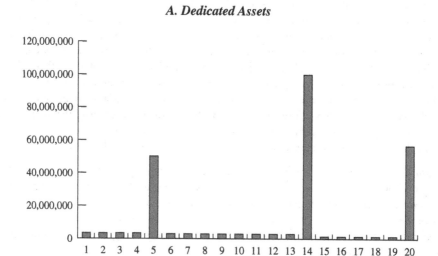

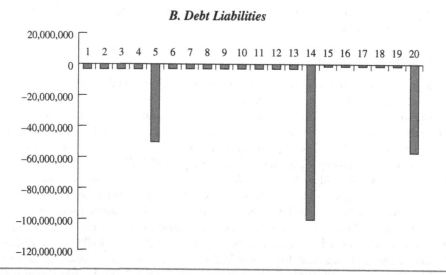

A concern when implementing this strategy is the *cash-in-advance constraint*. That means securities are not sold to meet obligations; instead sufficient funds must be available on or before each liability payment date to meet the obligation. The design of traditional bonds—a fixed coupon rate and principal redemption at maturity—is a problem if the liability stream, unlike in Exhibit 9, is a level payment annuity. That scenario could lead to large cash holdings between payment dates and, therefore, cash flow reinvestment risk, especially if yields on high-quality, short-term investments are low (or worse, negative).

EXAMPLE 3

Alfred Simonsson is assistant treasurer at a Swedish lumber company. The company has sold a large tract of land and now has sufficient cash holdings to retire some of its debt liabilities. The company's accounting department assures Mr. Simonsson that its external auditors will approve of a defeasement strategy if Swedish government bonds are purchased to match the interest and principal payments on the liabilities. Following is the schedule of payments due on the debt as of June 2017 that the company plans to defease:

June 2018	SEK 3,710,000
June 2019	SEK 6,620,000
June 2020	SEK 4,410,000
June 2021	SEK 5,250,000

The following Swedish government bonds are available. Interest on the bonds is paid annually in May of each year.

Coupon Rate	Maturity Date
2.75%	May 2018
3.50%	May 2019
4.75%	May 2020
5.50%	May 2021

How much in par value for each government bond will Mr. Simonsson need to buy to defease the debt liabilities, assuming that the minimum denomination in each security is SEK 10,000?

Solution: The cash flow matching portfolio is built by starting with the last liability of SEK 5,250,000 in June 2021. If there were no minimum denomination, that liability could be funded with the 5.50% bonds due May 2021 having a par value of SEK 4,976,303 (= SEK 5,250,000/1.0550). To deal with the constraint, however, Mr. Simonsson buys SEK 4,980,000 in par value. That bond pays SEK 5,253,900 (= SEK 4,980,000 × 1.0550) at maturity. This holding also pays SEK 273,900 (= SEK 4,980,000 × 0.0550) in coupon interest in May 2018, 2019, and 2020.

Then move to the June 2020 obligation, which is SEK 4,136,100 after subtracting the SEK 273,900 received on the 5.50% bond: SEK 4,410,000 − SEK 273,900 = SEK 4,136,100. Mr. Simonsson buys SEK 3,950,000 in par value of the 4.75% bond due May 2020. That bond pays SEK 4,137,625 (= SEK 3,950,000 × 1.0475) at maturity and SEK 187,625 in interest in May 2018 and 2019.

The net obligation in June 2019 is SEK 6,158,475 (= SEK 6,620,000 − SEK 273,900 − SEK 187,625) after subtracting the interest received on the longer-maturity bonds. The company can buy SEK 5,950,000 in par value of the 3.50% bond due May 2019. At maturity, this bond pays SEK 6,158,250 (= SEK 5,950,000 × 1.0350). The small shortfall of SEK 225 (= SEK 6,158,475 − SEK 6,158,250) can be made up because the funds received in May are reinvested until June. This bond also pays SEK 208,250 in interest in May 2018.

Finally, Mr. Simonsson needs to buy SEK 2,960,000 in par value of the 2.75% bond due May 2018. This bond pays SEK 3,041,400 (= SEK 2,960,000 × 1.0275) in May 2018. The final coupon and principal, plus the interest on the 5.50%, 4.75%, and 3.50% bonds, total SEK 3,711,175 (= SEK 3,041,400 + SEK 273,900 + SEK 187,625 + SEK 208,250). That amount is used to pay off the June 2018 obligation of SEK 3,710,000. Note that the excess could be kept in a bank account to cover the 2019 shortfall.

In sum, Mr. Simonsson buys the following portfolio:

Bond	Par Value
2.75% due May 2018	SEK 2,960,000
3.50% due May 2019	SEK 5,950,000
4.75% due May 2020	SEK 3,950,000
5.50% due May 2021	SEK 4,980,000

The following chart illustrates the cash flow matching bond portfolio: Each bar represents the par amount of a bond maturing in that year plus coupon payments from bonds maturing in later years. For example, the 2018 bar has SEK 2.96 million of the 2.75% bond maturing that year, plus coupon payments from the 2019 3.5% bond, 2020 4.75% bond, and 2021 5.5% bond.

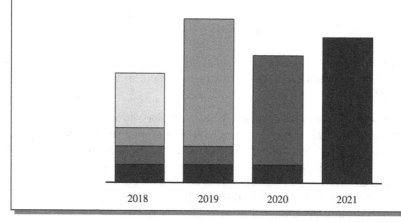

4.2. Duration Matching

Duration matching to immunize multiple liabilities is based on similar principles to those covered in the previous section for a single liability. A portfolio of fixed-income bonds is structured and managed to track the performance of the zero-coupon bonds that would perfectly lock in the rates of return needed to pay off the corporate debt liabilities identified in Exhibit 4. In the case of a single liability, the immunization strategy is to match the portfolio Macaulay duration with the investment horizon. Also, the initial investment needs to match (or exceed) the present value of the liability. These two conditions can be combined to prescribe that the money duration of the immunizing portfolio matches the money duration of the debt liabilities. Money duration, often called "dollar duration" in North America, is the portfolio modified duration multiplied by the market value. The modified duration is the portfolio Macaulay duration divided by one plus the cash flow yield per period. With multiple liabilities, matching money durations is useful because the market values and cash flow yields of the assets and liabilities are not necessarily equal.

The money duration for the debt liabilities is EUR 1,178,237,935:

$$\left[\frac{6.0004}{\left(1 + \frac{0.037608}{2}\right)} \right] \times 200,052,250 = 1,178,237,935$$

The term in brackets is the annualized modified duration for the bond portfolio. To keep the numbers manageable, we use the basis point value (BPV) measure for money duration. This measure is the money duration multiplied by 1 bp. The BPV is EUR 117,824 (= EUR 1,178,237,935 × 0.0001). For each 1 bp change in the cash flow yield, the market value changes by approximately EUR 117,824. It is an approximation because convexity is not included. A closely related risk measure is the present value of a basis point (PVBP), also called the PV01 (present value of an "01", meaning 1 bp) and, in North America, the DV01 (dollar value of an "01").

Exhibit 10 shows the three bonds purchased by the asset manager on 15 February 2017. The total cash outlay on that date is EUR 202,224, 094 (= EUR 41,772,719 + EUR 99,750,000 + EUR 60,701,375 = the market values of the three bonds). Exhibit 11 presents the table used to calculate the cash flow yield and the risk statistics. The annualized cash flow yield is 3.5822%. It is the internal rate of return on the cash flows in the second column of Exhibit 11, multiplied by two. The annualized Macaulay duration for the portfolio is 5.9308 (= 11.8615/2) and the modified duration is 5.8264 (= 5.9308/[1 + 0.035822/2]). The annualized dispersion and convexity statistics are 12.3048 (= 49.2194/4) and 48.6846 (= {201.7767/[1 + 0.035822/2]²}/4), respectively. Notice that the first few cash flows for the assets in Exhibit 11 are less than the liability payments in Exhibit 4. That disparity indicates that some of the bonds held in the asset portfolio will need to be sold to meet the obligations.

EXHIBIT 10 The Bond Portfolio to Immunize the Multiple Liabilities

	1.5-Year Bond	6-Year Bond	11.5-Year Bond
Coupon rate	1.00%	2.875%	4.50%
Maturity date	15 August 2018	15 February 2023	15 August 2028
Price	99.875	99.75	100.25
Yield to maturity	1.0842%	2.9207%	4.4720%
Par value	41,825,000	100,000,000	60,550,000
Market value	41,772,719	99,750,000	60,701,375
Macaulay duration	1.493	5.553	9.105
Convexity	2.950	34.149	96.056
Allocation	20.657%	49.326%	30.017%

EXHIBIT 11   Portfolio Statistics

Time	Date	Cash Flow	PV of Cash Flow	Weight	Time × Weight	Dispersion	Convexity
0	15-Feb-17	−202,224,094					
1	15-Aug-17	3,009,000	2,956,054	0.0146	0.0146	1.7245	0.0292
2	15-Feb-18	3,009,000	2,904,040	0.0144	0.0287	1.3966	0.0862
3	15-Aug-18	44,834,000	42,508,728	0.2102	0.6306	16.5068	2.5225
4	15-Feb-19	2,799,875	2,607,951	0.0129	0.0516	0.7970	0.2579
5	15-Aug-19	2,799,875	2,562,062	0.0127	0.0633	0.5965	0.3801
6	15-Feb-20	2,799,875	2,516,981	0.0124	0.0747	0.4276	0.5228
7	15-Aug-20	2,799,875	2,472,692	0.0122	0.0856	0.2890	0.6847
8	15-Feb-21	2,799,875	2,429,183	0.0120	0.0961	0.1791	0.8649
9	15-Aug-21	2,799,875	2,386,440	0.0118	0.1062	0.0966	1.0621
10	15-Feb-22	2,799,875	2,344,449	0.0116	0.1159	0.0402	1.2753
11	15-Aug-22	2,799,875	2,303,196	0.0114	0.1253	0.0085	1.5034
12	15-Feb-23	102,799,875	83,075,901	0.4108	4.9297	0.0079	64.0865
13	15-Aug-23	1,362,375	1,081,607	0.0053	0.0695	0.0069	0.9734
14	15-Feb-24	1,362,375	1,062,575	0.0053	0.0736	0.0240	1.1034
15	15-Aug-24	1,362,375	1,043,878	0.0052	0.0774	0.0508	1.2389
16	15-Feb-25	1,362,375	1,025,510	0.0051	0.0811	0.0869	1.3794
17	15-Aug-25	1,362,375	1,007,465	0.0050	0.0847	0.1315	1.5245
18	15-Feb-26	1,362,375	989,738	0.0049	0.0881	0.1844	1.6738
19	15-Aug-26	1,362,375	972,323	0.0048	0.0914	0.2450	1.8271
20	15-Feb-27	1,362,375	955,214	0.0047	0.0945	0.3129	1.9839
21	15-Aug-27	1,362,375	938,406	0.0046	0.0974	0.3875	2.1439
22	15-Feb-28	1,362,375	921,894	0.0046	0.1003	0.4686	2.3067
23	15-Aug-28	61,912,375	41,157,805	0.2035	4.6811	25.2505	112.3462
			202,224,094	1.0000	11.8615	49.2194	201.7767

The market value of the immunizing fixed-income bonds is EUR 202,224,094. That amount is higher than the value of the liabilities, which is EUR 200,052,250. The reason for the difference in market values as of 15 February 2017 is the difference in the cash flow yields. The high-quality assets needed to immunize the corporate liabilities have a cash flow yield of 3.5822%, which is lower than the cash flow yield of 3.7608% on the debt obligations. The assets grow at a lower rate and, therefore, need to start at a higher level. If we discount the debt liabilities scheduled in the third column of Exhibit 4 at 3.5822%, the present value is EUR 202,170,671, indicating that initially, the immunizing portfolio is slightly overfunded. Importantly, the asset portfolio BPV is EUR 117,824 (= 202,224,094 × 5.8264 × 0.0001), matching the BPV for the debt liabilities.

There is another meaningful difference in the structure of the asset and liability portfolios. Although the money durations are the same, the dispersion and convexity statistics for the assets are greater than for the liabilities—12.30 compared with 8.26 for dispersion, and 48.68 compared with 45.54 for convexity. This difference is required to achieve immunization for multiple liabilities. (Mathematically, in the optimization problem to minimize the difference in the change in the values of assets and liabilities, the first derivative leads to matching money duration [or BPV] and the second derivative to having a higher dispersion.) Intuitively, this condition follows from the general result that, for equal durations, a more convex portfolio generally outperforms a less convex portfolio (higher gains if yields fall, lower losses if yields rise). But, as in the case of immunizing a single liability, the dispersion of the assets should be as low as possible subject to being greater than or equal to the dispersion of the liabilities to mitigate the effect of non-parallel shifts in the yield curve. Note that from Equation 1, higher dispersion implies higher convexity when the Macaulay durations and cash flow yields are equal.

Some numerical examples are useful to illustrate that immunization of multiple liabilities is essentially an interest rate risk hedging strategy. The idea is that changes in the market value of the asset portfolio closely match changes in the debt liabilities whether interest rates rise or fall. Exhibit 12 demonstrates this dynamic.

EXHIBIT 12   Immunizing Multiple Liabilities

Upward Parallel Shift	Immunizing Assets	Debt Liabilities	Difference
ΔMarket value	−2,842,408	−2,858,681	16,273
ΔCash flow yield	0.2437%	0.2449%	−0.0012%
ΔPortfolio BPV	−2,370	−2,207	−163
Downward Parallel Shift	**Immunizing Assets**	**Debt Liabilities**	**Difference**
ΔMarket value	2,900,910	2,913,414	−12,504
ΔCash flow yield	−0.2437%	−0.2449%	0.0012%
ΔPortfolio BPV	2,429	2,256	173
Steepening Twist	**Immunizing Assets**	**Debt Liabilities**	**Difference**
ΔMarket value	−1,178,071	−835,156	−342,915
ΔCash flow yield	0.1004%	0.0711%	0.0293%
ΔPortfolio BPV	−984	−645	−339
Flattening Twist	**Immunizing Assets**	**Debt Liabilities**	**Difference**
ΔMarket value	1,215,285	850,957	364,328
ΔCash flow yield	−0.1027%	−0.0720%	−0.0307%
ΔPortfolio BPV	1,016	658	358

First, we allow the yield curve to shift upward in a parallel manner. The yields on the bonds in Exhibit 10 go up instantaneously by 25 bps on 15 February 2017, immediately after the asset portfolio is purchased. That increase results in a drop in market value of EUR 2,842,408. The yields on the debt liabilities in Exhibit 4 also go up by 25 bps, dropping the market value by EUR 2,858,681. The difference is EUR 16,273, a small amount given that the size of portfolios exceeds EUR 200 million. This scenario implicitly assumes no change in the corporate entity's credit risk. Next, we shift the yield curve downward by 25 bps. Both the asset and liability portfolios gain market value by almost the same amount. The difference is only EUR 12,504.

The driving factor behind the success of the strategy given these upward and downward shifts is that the portfolio durations are matched and changes in the cash flow yields are very close: 24.37 bps for the assets and 24.49 bps for the liabilities.[11] As explained in the previous section, a parallel shift is a sufficient but not necessary condition for immunization. Although not shown in Exhibit 12, an upward non-parallel shift of 15.9 bps in the 1.5-year bond, 23.6 bps in the 6-year bond, and 27.5 bps in the 11.5-year bond leads to virtually the same change in market value (EUR 2,842,308) as the 25 bp parallel shift. Those particular changes are chosen because they result in the same change in the cash flow yield of 24.37 bps.

The structural risk to the immunization strategy is apparent in the third scenario in Exhibit 12. This scenario is the steepening twist in which short-term yields on high-quality bonds go down while long-term yields go up. The 1.5-year yield is assumed to drop by 25 bps. The 6-year yield remains the same, and the 11.5-year yield goes up by 25 bps. These changes lead to a loss of EUR 1,178,071 in the asset portfolio as the cash flow yield increases by 10.04 bps. The maturities of the debt liabilities differ from those of the assets. For simplicity, we assume that those yields change in proportion to the differences in maturity around the six-year pivot point for the twist. The 2.5-year yield drops by 19.44 bps (= 25 bps × 3.5/4.5), the 7-year yield goes up by 4.55 bps (= 25 bps × 1/5.5), and the 10-year by 18.18 bps (= 25 bps × 4/5.5). The market value of the liabilities drops by only EUR 835,156 because the cash flow yield increases by only 7.11 bps. The value of the assets goes down by more than the liabilities—the difference is EUR 342,915. The steepening twist to the shape of the yield curve is the source of the loss.

The results of the fourth scenario show that a flattening twist can lead to a comparable gain if long-term high-quality yields fall while short-term yields rise. We make the same assumptions about proportionate changes in the yields. In this case, the cash flow yield of the assets goes down more and the market value rises higher than the debt liabilities. Clearly, an entity that pursues immunization of multiple liabilities hopes that steepening twists are balanced out by flattening twists and that most yield curve shifts are more or less parallel.

Exhibit 12 also reports the changes in the portfolio BPVs for the assets and liabilities. Before the yield curve shifts and twists, the BPVs are matched at EUR 117,824. Afterward, there is a small money duration mismatch. In theory, the asset manager needs to rebalance the portfolio immediately. In practice, the manager likely waits until the mismatch is large enough to justify the transactions' costs in selling some bonds and buying others. Another method to rebalance the portfolio is to use interest rate derivatives.

---

[11]The astute reader might have noticed in Exhibit 12 that the asset portfolio rises slightly less than the liabilities when the yield curve shifts down in a parallel manner by 25 bps. Hence, the loss is EUR 12,504 despite the greater convexity of the assets. That disparity is explained by the slightly higher decrease in the cash flow yield on the liabilities.

EXAMPLE 4

A Japanese corporation recently sold one of its lines of business and would like to use the cash to retire the debt liabilities that financed those assets. Summary statistics for the multiple debt liabilities, which range in maturity from three to seven years, are market value, JPY 110.4 billion; portfolio modified duration, 5.84; portfolio convexity, 46.08; and BPV, JPY 64.47 million.

An investment bank working with the corporation offers three alternatives to accomplish the objective:

1. **Bond tender offer.** The corporation would buy back the debt liabilities on the open market, paying a premium above the market price. The corporation currently has a single-A rating and hopes for an upgrade once its balance sheet is improved by retiring the debt. The investment bank anticipates that the tender offer would have to be at a price commensurate with a triple-A rating to entice the bondholders to sell. The bonds are widely held by domestic and international institutional investors.

2. **Cash flow matching.** The corporation buys a portfolio of government bonds that matches, as closely as possible, the coupon interest and principal redemptions on the debt liabilities. The investment bank is highly confident that the corporation's external auditors will agree to accounting defeasement because the purchased bonds are government securities. That agreement will allow the corporation to remove both the defeasing asset portfolio and the liabilities from the balance sheet.

3. **Duration matching.** The corporation buys a portfolio of high-quality corporate bonds that matches the duration of the debt liabilities. Interest rate derivative contracts will be used to keep the duration on its target as time passes and yields change. The investment bank thinks it is very unlikely that the external auditors will allow this strategy to qualify for accounting defeasement. The corporation can explain to investors and the rating agencies in the management section of its annual report, however, that it is aiming to "effectively defease" the debt. To carry out this strategy, the investment bank suggests three different portfolios of investment-grade corporate bonds that range in maturity from 2 years to 10 years. Each portfolio has a market value of about JPY 115 billion, which is considered sufficient to pay off the liabilities.

	Portfolio A	Portfolio B	Portfolio C
Modified duration	5.60	5.61	5.85
Convexity	42.89	50.11	46.09
BPV (in millions)	JPY 64.50	JPY 64.51	JPY 67.28

After some deliberation and discussion with the investment bankers and external auditors, the corporation's CFO chooses Strategy 3, duration matching.

1. Indicate the likely trade-offs that led the corporate CFO to choose the duration matching strategy over the tender offer and cash flow matching.

2. Indicate the portfolio that the corporation should choose to carry out the duration matching strategy.

Solution to 1: The likely trade-offs are between removing the debt liabilities from the balance sheet, either by directly buying the bonds from investors or by accounting defeasement via cash flow matching, and the cost of the strategy. The tender offer entails buying the bonds at a triple-A price, which would be considerably higher than at a single-A price. Cash flow matching entails buying even more expensive government bonds. The duration matching strategy can be implemented at a lower cost because the asset portfolio consists of less expensive investment-grade bonds. The CFO has chosen the lowest-cost strategy, even though the debt liabilities will remain on the balance sheet.

Solution to 2: The corporation should recommend Portfolio B. Portfolio C closely matches the modified duration (as well as the convexity) of the liabilities. Duration matching when the market values of the assets and liabilities differ, however, entails matching the money durations, in particular the BPVs. The choice then comes down to Portfolios A and B. Although both have BPVs close to the liabilities, it is incorrect to choose A based on its BPV being "closer."

The important difference between Portfolios A and B lies in the convexities. To immunize multiple liabilities, the convexity (and dispersion of cash flows) of the assets needs to be greater than the liabilities. Therefore, Portfolio A does not meet that condition.

Recall that in Example 2, the correct immunizing portfolio is the one with the lower convexity, which minimizes the structural risk to the strategy. But, that bond portfolio still has a convexity greater than the zero-coupon bond that would provide perfect immunization. This greater convexity of the immunizing portfolio is because the dispersion of the zero-coupon bond is zero and the durations are the same. As seen in Equation 1, that dispersion implies a lower convexity statistic.

4.3. Derivatives Overlay

Interest rate derivatives can be a cost-effective method to rebalance the immunizing portfolio to keep it on its target duration as the yield curve shifts and twists and as time passes. Suppose that in the duration matching example in Section 4.2, there is a much larger instantaneous upward shift in the yield curve on 15 February 2017. In particular, all yields shift up by 100 bps. Because yields and duration are inversely related, the portfolio duration statistics go down, as does the market value. The BPV of the immunizing asset portfolio decreases from EUR 117,824 to EUR 108,679, a drop of EUR 9,145. The BPV for the debt liabilities goes down to EUR 109,278, a drop of EUR 8,546. There is now a duration gap of –EUR 599 (= EUR 108,679 – EUR 109,278). The asset manager could sell some of the 1%, 1.5-year bonds and buy some more of the 4.50%, 11-year bonds to close the money duration gap. A more efficient and lower-cost rebalancing strategy, however, is likely to buy, or go long, a few interest rate futures contracts to rebalance the portfolio.

To address the question of the required number of contracts to close, or reduce, a duration gap, we change the example from euros to US dollars. Doing so allows us to illustrate the calculations for the required number of futures contracts using the actively traded 10-year US Treasury note futures contract offered at the CME Group. The present value of corporate debt liabilities shown in Exhibits 3 and 4 now is assumed to be USD 200,052,250. Risk and return statistics are invariant to currency denomination, so the portfolio Macaulay duration is still 6.0004 and the BPV is USD 117,824.

Unlike the previous example for duration matching of multiple liabilities, however, we assume that the asset manager buys a portfolio of high-quality, short-term bonds. This portfolio has a market value of USD 222,750,000, Macaulay duration of 0.8532, and cash flow yield of 1.9804%. Discounting the debt liabilities in the third column of Exhibit 4 at 1.9804% gives a present value of USD 222,552,788. This value indicates that the immunizing portfolio is overfunded on 15 February 2017. The BPV for the asset portfolio is USD 18,819:

$$\left[\frac{0.8532}{\left(1 + \frac{0.019804}{2}\right)} \right] \times 222{,}750{,}000 \times 0.0001 = 18{,}819$$

There are a number of reasons why the asset manager might elect to hold a portfolio of short-term bonds rather than intermediate-term and long-term securities. Perhaps there is much greater liquidity and the perception of finer pricing in the short-term market. Another possibility is that the entity faces liquidity constraints and needs to hold these short-term bonds to meet regulatory requirements. A derivatives overlay strategy is then used to close the duration gap while keeping the underlying portfolio unchanged. In general, a derivatives overlay transforms some aspect of the underlying portfolio—the currency could be changed with foreign exchange derivatives or the credit risk profile with credit default swap contracts. Here, interest rate derivatives are used to change the interest rate risk profile, increasing the portfolio BPV from USD 18,819 to USD 117,824.

Although the details of interest rate futures contracts are covered in other chapters, some specific features of the 10-year US Treasury note contract traded at the CME Group are important for this example. Each contract is for USD 100,000 in par value and has delivery dates in March, June, September, and December. The T-notes qualifying for delivery range from 6.5 to 10 years in maturity. (In January 2016, the CME Group introduced the Ultra 10-year contract for which the qualifying T-notes have maturities from 9 years and 5 months to 10 years.) Conversion factors that are used to make the qualifying T-notes roughly equivalent for delivery by the contract seller, or short position, are based on an arbitrary yield to maturity of 6.00%. If the eligible T-note has a coupon rate below (above) 6.00%, the conversion factor is less (more) than 1.0000. The invoice price paid by the buyer of the contract, the long position, at the expiration of the contract is the futures price multiplied by the conversion factor, plus accrued interest. The logic of this design is that if the contract seller chooses to deliver a qualifying T-note having a lower (higher) coupon rate than 6.00%, the buyer pays a lower (higher) price.

The key point is that, although the eligible T-notes are roughly equivalent, one will be identified as the cheapest-to-deliver (CTD) security. Importantly, the duration of the 10-year T-note futures contract is assumed to be the duration of the CTD T-note. A factor in determining the CTD T-note is that the conversion factors for each qualifying security are based on the arbitrary assumption of a 6.00% yield to maturity. In practice, when yields are below 6.00% the CTD security typically is the qualifying T-note having the lowest duration. Therefore, the 10-year T-note futures contract essentially has been acting as a 6.5-year contract. (That explains the motivation for introducing the Ultra 10-year contract—to provide a hedging instrument more closely tied to the 10-year T-note traded in the cash market.)

To illustrate the importance of using the risk statistics for the CTD T-note, Exhibit 13 reports two hypothetical qualifying securities for the March 2017 10-year futures contract. One is designated the 6.5-year T-note. It has a coupon rate of 2.75% and matures on 15 November 2023. As of 15 February 2017, it is assumed to be priced to yield 3.8088%. Its BPV per USD 100,000 in par value is USD 56.8727, and its conversion factor is 0.8226. The other is the on-the-run 10-year T-note. Its coupon rate is 4.00%, and it matures on 15 February 2027. Its BPV is USD 81.6607, and its conversion factor is 0.8516.

EXHIBIT 13   Two Qualifying T-Notes for the March 2017 10-Year T-Note Futures Contract as of 15 February 2017

	6.5-Year T-Note	10-Year T-Note
Coupon rate	2.75%	4.00%
Maturity date	15 November 2023	15 February 2027
Full price per 100,000 in par value	USD 94,449	USD 99,900
Yield to maturity	3.8088%	4.0122%
Modified duration	6.0215	8.1742
BPV per 100,000 in par value	56.8727	81.6607
Conversion factor	0.8226	0.8516

The calculation of the required number of futures contract, denoted N_f comes from this relationship:

$$\text{Asset portfolio BPV} + (N_f \times \text{Futures BPV}) = \text{Liability portfolio BPV} \qquad (2)$$

Inherent in this expression is the important idea that, although futures contracts have a market value of zero as a result of daily mark-to-market valuation and settlement, they can add to or subtract from the asset portfolio BPV. This equation can be rearranged to isolate N_f:

$$N_f = \frac{\text{Liability portfolio BPV} - \text{Asset portfolio BPV}}{\text{Futures BPV}} \qquad (3)$$

If N_f is a positive number, the asset manager buys, or goes long, the required number of futures contracts. Doing so raises the money duration of the assets to match that of the liabilities. If N_f is a negative number, the asset manager sells, or goes short, futures contracts to reduce the money duration. In our problem, the asset portfolio BPV is USD 18,819 and the liability portfolio BPV is USD 117,824. Therefore, N_f is a large positive number and depends on the BPV for the futures contract. The exact formulation for the Futures BPV is complicated, however, and goes beyond the scope of this chapter. It involves details such as the number of days until the expiration of the contract, the interest rate for that period, and the accrued interest on the deliverable bond. To simplify, we use an approximation formula that is common in practice:

$$\text{Futures BPV} \approx \frac{\text{BPV}_{\text{CTD}}}{\text{CF}_{\text{CTD}}} \quad (4)$$

where CF_{CTD} is the conversion factor for the CTD security. (In interest futures markets that do not have a CTD security, the Futures BPV is simply the BPV of the deliverable bond.)

If the CTD security is the 6.5-year T-note shown in Exhibit 13, the Futures BPV is estimated to be USD 69.1377 (= 56.8727/0.8226). Then the required number of contracts is approximately 1,432:

$$\frac{117,824 - 18,819}{69.1377} = 1,432$$

But, if the CTD security is the 10-year T-note, the Futures BPV is USD 95.8909 (= 81.6607/0.8516). To close the money duration gap, the required number of contracts is only 1,032.

$$\frac{117,824 - 18,819}{95.8909} = 1,032$$

Clearly, the asset manager must know the CTD T-note to use in the derivatives overlay strategy. The difference of 400 futures contracts is significant.

The asset manager has established a synthetic "barbell" strategy having positions in the short-term and longer-term segments of the yield curve. The term "synthetic" means "created with derivatives." The underlying asset portfolio is concentrated in the short-term market. The derivatives portfolio is either at the 6.5-year or 10-year segment of the yield curve. There also are actively traded two-year and five-year Treasury futures contracts at CME Group. Therefore, the asset manager could choose to spread out the futures contracts across other segments of the yield curve. That diversification reduces the structural risk to the immunization strategy arising from non-parallel shifts and twists to the curve.

EXAMPLE 5

A Frankfurt-based asset manager uses the Long Bund contract traded at the Intercontinental Exchange (ICE) futures exchange to manage the gaps that arise from "duration drift" in a portfolio of German government bonds that are used to immunize a portfolio of corporate debt liabilities. This futures contract has a notional principal of EUR 100,000 and a 6% coupon rate. The German government bonds that are eligible for delivery have maturities between 8.5 years and 10.5 years.

Currently, the corporate debt liabilities have a market value of EUR 330,224,185, a modified duration of 7.23, and a BPV of EUR 238,752. The asset portfolio has a market value of EUR 332,216,004, a modified duration of 7.42, and a BPV of EUR 246,504. The duration drift has arisen because of a widening spread between corporate and government bond yields as interest rates in general have come down. The lower yields on government bonds have increased the modified durations relative to corporates.

Based on the deliverable bond, the asset manager estimates that the BPV for each futures contract is EUR 65.11.

1. Does the asset manager go long (buy) or go short (sell) the futures contract?
2. How many contracts does the manager buy or sell to close the duration gap?

Solution to 1: The money duration of the assets, as measured by the BPV, is greater than the money duration of debt liabilities. This relationship is true of the modified duration statistics as well, but the money duration is a better measure of the gap because the market values differ. The asset manager needs to go short (or sell) Long Bund futures contracts.

Solution to 2: Use Equation 3 to get the requisite number of futures contracts to sell.

$$N_f = \frac{\text{Liability portfolio BPV} - \text{Asset portfolio BPV}}{\text{Futures BPV}}$$

where Liability portfolio BPV = 238,752, Asset portfolio BPV = 246,504, and Futures BPV = 65.11.

$$N_f = \frac{238,752 - 246,504}{65.11} = -119.06$$

The minus sign indicates the need to go short (or sell) 119 contracts to close the duration gap.

4.4. Contingent Immunization

The last two examples illustrate that the initial market value for the immunizing asset portfolio can vary according to the strategy chosen by the asset manager. In the duration matching example, the initial market value of the asset portfolio is EUR 202,224,094, while the liabilities are EUR 200,052,250. The derivatives overlay example is to hold a portfolio of short-term bonds having a market value of USD 222,750,000 and 1,432 10-year futures contracts (assuming that the CTD eligible security is the 6.5-year T-note) to immunize the liability of USD 200,052,250.

The difference between the market values of the assets and liabilities is the **surplus**. The initial surplus in the duration matching example is EUR 2,171,844 (= EUR 202,224,094 − EUR 200,052,250); the surplus in the derivatives overlay example is USD 22,697,750 (= EUR 222,750,000 − EUR 200,052,250). The presence of a significant surplus allows the asset manager to consider a hybrid passive–active strategy known as **contingent immunization**. The idea behind contingent immunization is that the asset manager can pursue active investment strategies, as if operating under a total return mandate, as long as the surplus is above a designated threshold. If the actively managed assets perform poorly, however, and the surplus evaporates, the mandate reverts to the purely passive strategy of building a duration matching portfolio and then managing it to remain on duration target.

In principle, the available surplus can be deployed into any asset category, including equity, fixed income, and alternative investments. The surplus could be used to buy out-of-the-money commodity option contracts or credit default swaps. The objective is to attain gains on the actively managed funds in order to reduce the cost of retiring the debt obligations. Obviously, liquidity is an important criterion in selecting the investments because the positions would need to be unwound if losses cause the surplus to near the threshold.

A natural setting for contingent immunization is in the fixed-income derivatives overlay strategy. Instead of buying, or going long, 1,432 10-year T-note futures contracts, the asset manager could intentionally over-hedge or under-hedge, depending on the held view on rate volatility at the 6.5-year segment of the Treasury yield curve. That segment matters because the 10-year T-note futures contract price responds to changes in the yield of the CTD security. The asset manager could buy more (less) than 1,432 contracts if she expects the 6.5-year Treasury yield to go down (up) and the futures price to go up (down).

Suppose that on 15 February 2017, the price of the March 10-year T-note futures contract is quoted to be 121-03. The price is 121 and 3/32 percent of USD 100,000, which is the contract size. Therefore, the delivery price in March would be USD 121,093.75 multiplied by the conversion factor, plus the accrued interest. What matters to the asset manager is the change in the settlement futures price from day to day. For each futures contract, the gain or loss is USD 31.25 for each 1/32nd change in the futures price, calculated as 1/32 percent of USD 100,000.

Now suppose that the asset manager anticipates an upward shift in the yield curve. Such a shift would cause bond prices to drop in both the Treasury cash and futures markets. Suppose that the quoted March futures price drops from 121-03 to 119-22. That is a 45/32nd change in the price and causes a loss of USD 1,406.25 (= 45 × USD 31.25) per contract. If the asset manager holds 1,432 long contracts, the loss that day is USD 2,013,750 (= USD 1,406.25 × 1,432). But if the asset manager is allowed to under-hedge, he could have dramatically reduced the number of long futures contracts and maybe even gone short in anticipation of the upward shift. The presence of the surplus allows the manager the opportunity to take a view on interest rates and save some of the cost of the strategy to retire the debt liabilities. The objective is to be over-hedged when yields are expected to fall and under-hedged when they are expected to rise.

EXAMPLE 6

An asset manager is asked to build and manage a portfolio of fixed-income bonds to retire multiple corporate debt liabilities. The debt liabilities have a market value of GBP 50,652,108, a modified duration of 7.15, and a BPV of GBP 36,216.

The asset manager buys a portfolio of British government bonds having a market value of GBP 64,271,055, a modified duration of 3.75, and a BPV of GBP 24,102. The initial surplus of GBP 13,618,947 and the negative duration gap of GBP 12,114 are intentional. The surplus allows the manager to pursue a contingent immunization strategy to retire the debt at, hopefully, a lower cost than a more conservative duration matching approach. The duration gap requires the manager to buy, or go long, interest rate futures contracts to close the gap. The manager can choose to over-hedge or under-hedge, however, depending on market circumstances.

The futures contract that the manager buys is based on 10-year gilts having a par value of GBP 100,000. It is estimated to have a BPV of GBP 98.2533 per contract. Currently, the asset manager has purchased, or gone long, 160 contracts.

Which statement *best* describes the asset manager's hedging strategy and the held view on future 10-year gilt interest rates? The asset manager is:

A. over-hedging because the rate view is that 10-year yields will be rising.
B. over-hedging because the rate view is that 10-year yields will be falling.
C. under-hedging because the rate view is that 10-year yields will be rising.
D. under-hedging because the rate view is that 10-year yields will be falling.

Solution: B is correct. The asset manager is over-hedging because the rate view is that 10-year yields will be falling. First calculate the number of contracts (N_f) needed to fully hedge (or immunize) the debt liabilities. The general relationship is Equation 2:
Asset portfolio BPV $+ (N_f \times$ Futures BPV$) =$ Liability portfolio BPV.

Asset portfolio BPV is GBP 24,102; Futures BPV is 98.2533; and Liability portfolio BPV is 36,216.

$24,102 + (N_f \times 98.2533) = 36,216$

$N_f = 123.3$

The asset manager is over-hedging because a position in 160 long futures contracts is more than what is needed to close the duration gap. Long, or purchased, positions in interest rate futures contracts gain when futures prices rise and rates go down. The anticipated gains from the strategic decision to over-hedge in this case further increase the surplus and reduce the cost of retiring the debt liabilities.

5. LIABILITY-DRIVEN INVESTING—AN EXAMPLE OF A DEFINED BENEFIT PENSION PLAN

In Section 2, we introduced four types of liabilities: Types I, II, III, and IV. In Sections 3 and 4, we looked at Type I liabilities for which the amount and timing of cash flows are known to the asset manager. That knowledge allows the manager to consider immunization strategies using yield duration statistics such as Macaulay, modified, and money duration. An example of a Type II liability is a callable bond. The corporate issuer knows that the bond can be repurchased at the preset call prices on the call dates and, if it is not called, that it will be redeemed at par value at maturity. A floating-rate note is an example of a Type III liability. The issuer knows the interest payment dates but not the amounts, which are linked to future rates. Models are needed to project the amounts and dates of the cash flows and to calculate the effective durations of the callable and floating-rate securities. Because there are no well-defined yields to maturity as a result of the uncertain amounts and timing of cash flows, yield duration statistics such as Macaulay and modified duration do not apply.

Defined benefit pension plan obligations are a good example of Type IV liabilities for which both the amounts and dates are uncertain.[12] An LDI strategy for this entity starts with a model for these liabilities. We reveal some of the assumptions that go into this complex financial modeling problem by assuming the work history and retirement profile for a representative employee covered by the pension plan. We assume that this employee has worked for G years, a sufficient length of time to ensure that the retirement benefits are vested. The employee is expected to work for another T years and then to retire and live for Z years. Exhibit 14 illustrates this time line.

---

[12]This section is based on Adams and Smith (2009).

EXHIBIT 14   Time Line Assumptions for the Representative Employee

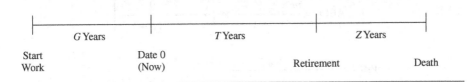

Although there are many types of pension plans worldwide, here we model a final-pay US defined benefit plan. In principle, the same type of model can be built to illustrate retirement obligations in other countries. In this example, the retired employee receives a fixed lifetime annuity based on her wage at the time of retirement, denoted W_T. Some pension plans index the annual retirement benefit to inflation. Our example assumes an annuity fixed in nominal terms, calculated as the final wage, W_T, multiplied by a multiplier, m, multiplied by the total number of years worked, $G + T$.

There are two general measures of the retirement obligations as of Time 0—the accumulated benefit obligation (ABO) and the projected benefit obligation (PBO). The ABO calculates the liability based on the G years worked and the current annual wage, denoted W_0, even though the annuity paid in retirement is based on W_T and $G + T$ years. The use of the current annual wage and the number of years worked is because the ABO represents the *legal liability* today of the plan sponsor if the plan were to be closed or converted to another type of plan, such as a defined contribution plan. The ABO is the present value of the annuity, discounted at an annual rate r on high-quality corporate bonds,[13] which for simplicity we assume applies for all periods (a flat yield curve).

$$\text{ABO} = \frac{1}{(1+r)^T} \times \left[\frac{m \times G \times W_0}{1+r} + \frac{m \times G \times W_0}{(1+r)^2} + \cdots + \frac{m \times G \times W_0}{(1+r)^Z} \right]$$

The term in brackets is the value of the Z-year annuity as of year T, and that sum is discounted back over T years to Time 0.

The PBO liability measure uses the projected wage for year T instead of the current wage in the Z-year annuity.

$$\text{PBO} = \frac{1}{(1+r)^T} \times \left[\frac{m \times G \times W_T}{1+r} + \frac{m \times G \times W_T}{(1+r)^2} + \cdots + \frac{m \times G \times W_T}{(1+r)^Z} \right]$$

Although the ABO is the legal obligation to the plan sponsor, the PBO is the liability reported in financial statements and used to assess the plan's funding status. The plan is over-funded (under-funded) if the current fair value of assets is more (less) than the present value of the promised retirement benefits.

The next step is to consider how wages evolve between dates 0 and T. We denote w to be the average annual wage growth rate for the employee's remaining work life of T years. Therefore, the relationship between W_0 and W_T is $W_T = W_0 \times (1 + w)^T$.

After some algebraic manipulation and substitution, the two liability measures can be written more compactly as follows:

---

[13]In the United States, government regulators and the accounting authorities allow high-quality corporate bonds to be used to discount the future liabilities.

$$\text{ABO} = \frac{m \times G \times W_0}{(1+r)^T} \times \left[\frac{1}{r} - \frac{1}{r \times (1+r)^Z} \right]$$

$$\text{PBO} = \frac{m \times G \times W_0 \times (1+w)^T}{(1+r)^T} \times \left[\frac{1}{r} - \frac{1}{r \times (1+r)^Z} \right]$$

Note that the PBO always will be larger than the ABO by the factor of $(1+w)^T$, assuming positive wage growth in nominal terms.[14]

We see in this simple model several of the important assumptions that go into using an LDI strategy to manage these Type IV liabilities. The assumed post-retirement lifetime (Z years) is critical. A higher value for Z increases both the ABO and PBO measures of liability. The pension plan faces *longevity risk*, which is the risk that employees live longer in their retirement years than assumed in the models. Some plans have become under-funded and have had to increase assets because regulators required that they recognize longer life expectancies. Another important assumption is the time until retirement (T years). In the ABO measure, increases in T reduce the liability. That result also holds for the PBO as long as w is less than r. Assuming w is less than r is reasonable if it can be assumed that employees over time generally are compensated for price inflation and some part of real economic growth, as well as for seniority and productivity improvements, but overall the labor income growth rate does not quite keep pace with the nominal return on high-quality financial assets.

We now use a numerical example to show how the effective durations of ABO and PBO liability measures are calculated. Assume that $m = 0.02$, $G = 25$, $T = 10$, $Z = 17$, $W_0 =$ USD 50,000, and $r = 0.05$. We also assume that the wage growth rate w is an arbitrarily chosen constant fraction of the yield on high-quality corporate bonds r—in particular, that $w = 0.9 \times r$ so that $w = 0.045 \ (= 0.9 \times 0.05)$. Based on these assumptions, the ABO and PBO for the representative employee are USD 173,032 and USD 268,714, respectively.

$$\text{ABO} = \frac{0.02 \times 25 \times 50,000}{(1.05)^{10}} \times \left[\frac{1}{0.05} - \frac{1}{0.05 \times (1.05)^{17}} \right] = 173,032$$

$$\text{PBO} = \frac{0.02 \times 25 \times 50,000 \times (1.045)^{10}}{(1.05)^{10}} \times \left[\frac{1}{0.05} - \frac{1}{0.05 \times (1.05)^{17}} \right] = 268,714$$

If the plan covers 10,000 similar employees, the total liability is approximately USD 1.730 billion ABO and USD 2.687 billion PBO. Assuming that the pension plan has assets with a market value of USD 2.700 billion, the plan currently is overfunded by both measures of liability.

In general, the effective durations for assets or liabilities are obtained by raising and lowering the assumed yield curve in the valuation model and recalculating the present values.

$$\text{Effective duration} = \frac{(\text{PV}_-) - (\text{PV}_+)}{2 \times \Delta\text{Curve} \times (\text{PV}_0)} \tag{5}$$

[14]The second term to the right of the equal sign in the foregoing expressions may be familiar to readers as the present value factor for an annuity.

PV_0 is the initial value, PV_- is the new value after the yield curve is lowered by $\Delta Curve$, and PV_+ is the value after the yield curve is raised. In this simple model with a flat yield curve, we raise r from 0.05 to 0.06 (and w from 0.045 to 0.054) and lower r from 0.05 to 0.04 (and w from 0.045 to 0.036). Therefore, $\Delta Curve = 0.01$. A more realistic model would have shape to the yield curve and include the interaction of a yield change on other variables. For example, an increase in yields on high-quality financial assets could be modeled to shorten the time to retirement.

Given our assumptions, ABO_0 is USD 173,032. Redoing the calculations for the higher and lower values for r and w gives USD 146,261 for ABO_+ and USD 205,467 for ABO_-. The ABO effective duration is 17.1.

$$ABO \text{ duration} = \frac{205,467 - 146,261}{2 \times 0.01 \times 173,032} = 17.1$$

Repeating the calculations for the PBO liability measure gives USD 247,477 for PBO_+ and USD 292,644 for PBO_-. Given that PBO_0 is 268,714, the PBO duration is 8.4.

$$PBO = \frac{292,644 - 247,477}{2 \times 0.01 \times 268,714} = 8.4$$

These calculations indicate the challenge facing the fund manager. There is a significant difference between having liabilities of USD 1.730 billion and an effective duration of 17.1, as measured by the ABO, and liabilities of USD 2.687 billion and an effective duration of 8.4, as measured by the PBO. The ABO BPV is USD 2,958,300 (= USD 1.730 billion × 17.1 × 0.0001), and the PBO BPV is USD 2,257,080 (= USD 2.687 billion × 8.4 × 0.0001). The plan sponsor must decide which liability measure to use for risk management and asset allocation. For example, if the corporation anticipates that it might be a target for an acquisition and that the acquirer likely would want to convert the retirement plan from defined benefit to defined contribution, the ABO measure matters more than the PBO.

We assume that the corporate sponsor sees itself as an ongoing independent institution that preserves the pension plan's current design. Therefore, PBO is the appropriate measure for pension plan liabilities. The plan is fully funded in that the market value of assets, assumed to be USD 2.700 billion, exceeds the PBO of USD 2.687 billion. Currently, the surplus is only USD 13 million (= 2.700 billion – 2.687 billion). That surplus disappears quickly if yields on high-quality corporate bonds that are used to discount the projected benefits drop by about 5 bps to 6 bps. Note that the surplus divided by the PBO BPV is 5.76 (= 13,000,000/2,257,080). Interest rate risk is a major concern to the plan sponsor because changes in the funding status flow through the income statement, thereby affecting reported earnings per share.

Lower yields also raise the market value of assets depending on how those assets are allocated. We assume that the current asset allocation is 50% equity, 40% fixed income, and 10% alternatives. The fixed-income portfolio is managed to track an index of well-diversified corporate bonds—such indexes are covered in a later section of this chapter. Relevant at this point is that the chosen bond index reports a modified duration of 5.5.

The problem is to assign a duration for the equity and alternative investments. To be conservative, we assume that there is no stable and predictable relationship between valuations on those asset classes and market interest rates. Therefore, equity duration and alternatives duration are assumed to be zero. Assuming zero duration does not imply that equity and alternatives have no interest rate risk. Effective duration estimates the percentage change in value arising from a change in nominal interest rates. The effect on equity and alternatives depends on *why* the nominal rate changes, especially if that rate change is not widely anticipated in the market. Higher or lower interest rates can arise from a change in expected inflation, a change in monetary policy, or a change in macroeconomic conditions. Only fixed-income securities have a well-defined connection between market values and the yield curve. Nevertheless, assumptions are a source of model risk, as discussed in the next section.

Given these assumptions, we conclude that the asset BPV is USD 594,000 = USD 2.700 billion × [(0.50 × 0) + (0.40 × 5.5) + (0.10 × 0)] × 0.0001. The term in brackets is the estimated effective duration for the asset portfolio, calculated using the shares of market value as the weights. Clearly, the pension plan is running a significant duration gap—the asset BPV of USD 594,000 is much lower than the liability BPV of USD 2,257,080, using the PBO measure. If all yields go down by 10 bps, the market value of assets goes up by approximately USD 5.940 million and the present value of liabilities goes up by USD 22.571 million. The pension plan would have a deficit and be deemed under-funded.

The pension fund manager can choose to reduce, or even eliminate, the duration gap using a derivatives overlay. For example, suppose the Ultra 10-year Treasury futures contract at the Chicago Mercantile Exchange (CME) has a BPV of USD 95.8909 because the on-the-run T-note is the CTD security, as discussed in Section 4.3. Using Equation 3, the pension plan would need to buy, or go long, 17,343 contracts to fully hedge the interest rate risk created by the duration gap:

$$\frac{2,257,080 - 594,000}{95.8909} = 17,343$$

We discuss the risks to derivatives overlay strategies associated with LDI in the next section. One concern with hedging with futures is the need for daily oversight of the positions. That need arises because futures contracts are marked to market and settled at the end of each trading day into the margin account. Suppose that the fund did buy 17,343 futures contracts and 10-year Treasury yields go up by 5 bps. Given that the Futures BPV is USD 95.8909 per contract, the *realized* loss that day is more than USD 8.315 million: USD 95.8909 × 5 × 17,343 = 8,315,179. That amount is offset by the *unrealized* reduction in the present value of liabilities. Such a large position in futures contracts would lead to significant daily cash inflows and outflows. For that reason, hedging problems such as the one facing the pension fund often are addressed with over-the-counter interest rate swaps rather than exchange-traded futures contracts.

Suppose that the pension fund manager can enter a 30-year, receive-fixed, interest rate swap against three-month Libor. The fixed rate on the swap is 4.16%. Its effective duration is +16.73, and its BPV is +0.1673 per USD 100 of notional principal. Exhibit 15 illustrates this swap.

EXHIBIT 15   Interest Rate Swap

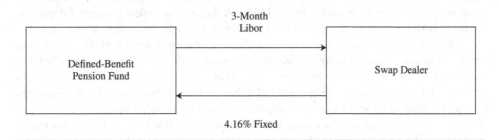

The risk statistics for an interest rate swap can be obtained from interpreting the contract as a combination of bonds. From the pension fund's perspective, the swap is viewed as buying a 30-year, 4.16% fixed-rate bond from the swap dealer and financing that purchase by issuing a 30-year floating-rate note (FRN) that pays three-month Libor.[15] The swap's duration is taken to be the (high) duration of the fixed-rate bond minus the (low) duration of the FRN. That explains why a receive-fixed swap has positive duration. From the swap dealer's perspective, the contract is viewed as purchasing a (low duration) FRN that is financed by issuing a (high duration) fixed-rate bond. Hence, the swap has negative duration to the dealer.

The notional principal (NP) on the interest rate swap needed to close the duration gap to zero can be calculated with this expression:

$$\text{Asset BPV} + \left[\text{NP} \times \frac{\text{Swap BPV}}{100}\right] = \text{Liability BPV} \qquad (6)$$

This is similar to Equation 2 for futures contracts. Given that the Asset BPV is USD 594,000 and the Liability BPV is USD 2,257,080 using the PBO measure, the required notional principal for the receive-fixed swap having a BPV of 0.1673 is about USD 994 million.

$$594,000 + \left[\text{NP} \times \frac{0.1673}{100}\right] = 2,257,080, \text{NP} = 994,070,532$$

We use the term "hedging ratio" to indicate the extent of interest rate risk management. A hedging ratio of 0% indicates no hedging at all. The pension plan retains the significant negative duration gap and the risk of lower corporate bond yields if it does not hedge. A hedging ratio of 100% indicates an attempt to fully balance, or to immunize, the assets and liabilities. In this case, the plan manager enters the receive-fixed swap for a notional principal of USD 994 million. In practice, partial hedges are common—the manager's task is to select the hedging ratio between 0% and 100%. The initial use of derivatives entails moving up a substantial learning curve. It is important that all stakeholders to the retirement plan understand the hedging strategy. These stakeholders include the plan sponsor, the regulatory authorities, the auditors, the employees covered by the plan, and perhaps even the employees' union representatives. Interest rate swaps typically have a value of zero at initiation. If swap rates rise, the value of the receive-fixed swap becomes negative and stakeholders will need an

---

[15]Swaps are typically quoted as a fixed rate against Libor flat, meaning no spread. The spread over Libor is put into the fixed rate. For instance, a swap of 4.00% against Libor flat is the same as a swap of 4.25% against Libor + 0.25%.

explanation of those losses. If the contract is collateralized, the pension fund will have to post cash or marketable securities with the swap dealer. We discuss collateralization further in the next section. The key point is that in all likelihood, the prudent course of action for the plan manager is to use a partial hedge rather than attempt to reduce the duration gap to zero.

One possibility is that the plan sponsor allows the manager some flexibility in selecting the hedging ratio. This flexibility in selecting the hedging ratio can be called strategic hedging. For example, the mandate could be to stay within a range of 25% to 75%. When the manager anticipates lower market rates and gains on receive-fixed interest rate swaps, the manager prefers to be at the top of an allowable range. On the other hand, if market (swap) rates are expected to go up, the manager could reduce the hedging ratio to the lower end of the range. The performance of the strategic hedging decisions can be measured against a strategy of maintaining a preset hedging ratio, for instance, 50%. That strategy means entering the receive-fixed swap for a notional principal of USD 497 million, which is about half of the notional principal needed to attempt to immunize the plan from interest rate risk (we assume that if the plan manager chooses to enter the receive-fixed swap, its notional principal would be USD 497 million, a 50% hedging ratio).

Another consideration for the plan manager is whether to use an option-based derivatives overlay strategy. Instead of entering a 30-year, receive-fixed interest rate swap against three-month Libor, the pension fund could purchase an option to enter a similar receive-fixed swap. This contract is called a receiver swaption. Suppose that the strike rate on the swaption is 3.50%. Given that the current 30-year swap fixed rate is assumed to be 4.16%, this receiver swaption is out of the money. The swap rate would have to fall by 66 bps (= 4.16% − 3.50%) for the swap contract to have intrinsic value. Suppose that the swaption premium is 100 bps, an amount based on the assumed level of interest rate volatility and the time to expiration (the next date that liabilities are measured and reported). Given a notional principal of USD 497 million, the pension plan pays USD 4.97 million (= USD 497 million × 0.0100) up front to buy the swaption. (This example neglects that the 3.50% swap has a somewhat higher effective duration and BPV than the 4.16% swap.)

When the expiration date arrives, the plan exercises the swaption if 30-year swap rates are below 3.50%. The plan could "take delivery" of the swap and receive what has become an above-market fixed rate for payment of three-month Libor. Or, the plan could close out the swap with the counterparty to capture the present value of the annuity based on the difference between the contractual fixed rate of 3.50% and the fixed rate in the swap market, multiplied by the notional principal. This gain partially offsets the loss incurred on the higher value for the pension plan liabilities. If 30-year swap rates are equal to or above 3.50% at expiration, the plan lets the swaption expire.

Another derivatives overlay is a swaption collar. The plan buys the same receiver swaption, but instead of paying the premium of USD 4.97 million in cash, the plan writes a payer swaption. Suppose that a strike rate of 5.00% on the payer swaption generates an up-front premium of 100 bps. Therefore, the combination is a "zero-cost" collar, at least in terms of the initial expense. If 30-year swap rates are below 3.50% at expiration, the purchased receiver swaption is in the money and the option is exercised. If the swap rate is between 3.50% and 5.00%, both swaptions are out of the money. But if the swap rate exceeds 5.00%, the payer swaption is in the money to the counterparty. As the writer of the contract, the pension plan is obligated to receive a fixed rate of only 5.00% when the going market rate is higher. The plan could continue with the swap but, in practice, would more likely seek to close it out by making a payment to the counterparty for the fair value of the contract.

Hedging decisions involve a number of factors, including accounting and tax treatment for the derivatives used in the overlay strategy. An important consideration is the various stakeholders' sensitivity to losses on the derivatives. Obviously, the plan manager is a "hero" if yields suddenly go down and if any of the three strategies—enter the receive-fixed swap, buy the receiver swaption, or enter the swaption collar—are undertaken. Note that swap rates do not need to go below 3.50% for the receiver swaption to generate an immediate gain. Its market value would go up if market rates fall (an increase in the value of the option) and it could be sold for more than the purchase price. The problem for the manager, however, occurs if yields suddenly and unexpectedly go up, leading to a significant loss on the hedge. Will being hedged be deemed a managerial mistake by some of the stakeholders? An advantage to buying the receiver swaption is that, like an insurance contract, its cost is a known amount paid up front. Potential losses on the receive-fixed swap and swaption collar are *time-deferred* and *rate-contingent* and therefore are uncertain.

A factor in the choice of derivatives overlay is the plan manager's view on future interest rates, particularly on high-quality corporate bond yields at the time of the next reporting for liabilities. An irony to interest rate risk management is that the view on rates is part of decision-making even when uncertainty about future rates is the motive for hedging. Exhibit 16 illustrates the payoffs on the three derivatives and the breakeven rates that facilitate the choice of contract.

EXHIBIT 16   Payoffs on Received-Fixed Swap, Receiver Swaption, and Swaption Collar

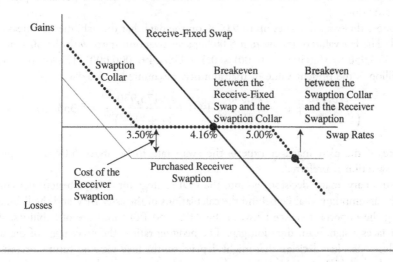

Consider first the downward-sloping payoff line for the received-fixed swap, which we assume has a notional principal of USD 497 million (a 50% hedging ratio). There are gains (losses) if rates on otherwise comparable 30-year swaps are below (above) 4.16%. In reality, the payoff line is not linear as shown in the exhibit. Suppose the swap rate moves down to 4.10%. The gain is the present value of the 30-year annuity of USD 149,100 (= [0.0416 – 0.0410] × 0.5 × USD 497,000,000) per period, assuming semi-annual payments. Assuming that 4.10% is the correct rate for discounting, the gain is about USD 5.12 million:

$$\frac{149{,}100}{\left(1+\frac{0.0410}{2}\right)^{1}}+\frac{149{,}100}{\left(1+\frac{0.0410}{2}\right)^{2}}+\cdots+\frac{149{,}100}{\left(1+\frac{0.0410}{2}\right)^{60}}=5{,}120{,}670$$

If the swap rate moves up to 4.22%, the annuity is still USD 149,100. But the loss is about USD 5.05 million using 4.22% to discount the cash flows.

$$\frac{149,100}{\left(1 + \frac{0.0422}{2}\right)^1} + \frac{149,100}{\left(1 + \frac{0.0422}{2}\right)^2} + \cdots + \frac{149,100}{\left(1 + \frac{0.0422}{2}\right)^{60}} = 5,047,526$$

The payoffs for the purchased 3.50% receiver swaption are shown as the thin line in Exhibit 16. The payoff line includes the cost to buy the swaption. The premium paid at purchase is USD 4.97 million, assuming that the quoted price is 100 bps and the notional principal is USD 497 million. The dotted line shows the payoffs on the swaption collar. It is composed of the long position in the 3.50% receiver swaption and the short position in the 5.00% payer swaption. There is a gain if the swap rate is below 3.50% and a loss if the rate is above 5.00%.

Decision-making is facilitated by breakeven numbers. It is easier to ask "do we expect the rate to be above or below a certain number?" than to state a well-articulated probability distribution for the future rate. Exhibit 16 shows two breakeven rates. If the plan manager expects the swap rate to be at or below 4.16%, the receive-fixed swap is preferred. Its gains are higher than the other two derivative overlays. If the manager expects the swap rate to be above 4.16%, however, the swaption collar is attractive because the swap would be incurring a loss. At some point above 5.00%, the purchased receiver swaption is better because it limits the loss. That breakeven rate can be found by trial-and-error search. The task is to find the swap rate that generates a loss that is more than the USD 4.97 million purchase price for the receiver swaption.

Suppose the swap rate goes up to 5.07% on the date that the liabilities are measured and reported. The fair value of the written 5.00% payer swaption starts with the 30-year annuity of USD 173,950 [= (0.0507 − 0.0500) × 0.5 × USD 497,000,000]. The loss of about USD 5.33 million is the present value of that annuity, discounted at 5.07%.

$$\frac{173,950}{\left(1 + \frac{0.0507}{2}\right)^1} + \frac{173,950}{\left(1 + \frac{0.0507}{2}\right)^2} + \cdots + \frac{173,950}{\left(1 + \frac{0.0507}{2}\right)^{60}} = 5,333,951$$

Therefore, if the plan manager expects the swap rate to be above 5.07%, the purchased receiver swaption is preferred.

In summary, many decisions go into the LDI strategy for defined benefit pension plans. Given the assumptions that lie behind the calculations of the asset BPV and the liability BPV, including the important choice between the ABO and PBO measure of liabilities, the plan manager faces a significant duration gap. The hedging ratio—the percentage of the duration gap to close—is a key decision that might depend on the held view on future interest rates—in particular, on high-quality corporate bond yields that are used to measure the liabilities. Then, given the determined hedging ratio, the choice of derivatives overlay is made. That decision once again depends on many factors, including the view on future rates.

EXAMPLE 7

A corporation is concerned about the defined benefit pension plan that it sponsors for its unionized employees. Because of recent declines in corporate bond yields and weak performance in its equity investments, the plan finds itself to be only about 80% funded. That fact is raising concerns with its employees as well as with the rating agencies. Currently, the present value of the corporation's retirement obligations is estimated by the plan's actuarial advisers to be about USD 1.321 billion using the PBO measure of liabilities. The corporation has no plans to close the defined benefit plan but is concerned about having to report the funding status in its financial statements. The market value of its asset portfolio is USD 1.032 billion—the plan is underfunded by USD 289 million.

The pension fund's asset allocation is rather aggressive: 70% equity, 10% alternative assets, and 20% fixed income. The fund manager hopes that a recovering equity market will reverse the deficit and ultimately return the plan to a fully funded position. Still, the manager is concerned about tightening corporate spreads as the economy improves. That scenario could lead to lower discount rates that are used to calculate the present value of the liabilities and offset any gains in the stock market.

The pension plan has hired a qualified professional asset manager (QPAM) to offer advice on derivatives overlay strategies and to execute the contracts with a commercial bank. The QPAM suggests that the pension plan consider the use of interest rate derivatives to partially close the duration gap between its assets and liabilities. The actuarial advisers to the plan estimate that the effective duration of the liabilities is 9.2, so that the BPV is USD 1.215 million. The corporate sponsor requires that the manager assume an effective duration of zero on equity and alternative assets. The fixed-income portfolio consists mostly of long-term bonds, including significant holdings of zero-coupon government securities. Its effective duration is estimated to be 25.6. Taken together, the asset BPV is USD 528,384. The negative money duration gap is substantial.

The QPAM has negotiated three interest rate derivatives with the commercial bank. The first is a 30-year, 3.80% receive-fixed swap referencing three-month Libor. The swap's effective duration is +17.51 and its BPV is 0.1751 per USD 100 of notional principal. The second is a receiver swaption having a strike rate of 3.60%. The plan pays a premium of 145 bps up front to buy the right to enter a 30-year swap as the fixed-rate receiver. The expiration date is set to match the date when the pension plan next reports its funding status. The third is a swaption collar, the combination of buying the 3.60% receiver swaption and writing a 4.25% payer swaption. The premiums on the two swaptions offset, so this is a "zero-cost" collar.

After some discussions with the rates desk at the commercial bank and a conversation with the bank's strategy group, the plan manager instructs the QPAM to select the 3.80% receive-fixed interest rate swap. Moreover, the manager chooses a hedging ratio of 75%.

1. Calculate the notional principal on the interest rate swap to achieve the 75% hedging ratio.
2. Indicate the plan manager's likely view on future 30-year swap fixed rates given the decision to choose the swap rather than the purchased receiver swaption or the swaption collar.

Solution to 1: First calculate the notional principal needed to close the duration gap between assets and liabilities to zero using Equation 6.

$$\text{Asset BPV} + \left(\text{NP} \times \frac{\text{Swap BPV}}{100} \right) = \text{Liability BPV}$$

Asset BPV is USD 528,384; Swap BPV is 0.1751 per 100 of notional principal; and Liability BPV is USD 1.215 million.

$$528{,}384 + \left(NP \times \frac{0.1751}{100} \right) = 1{,}215{,}000; NP = 392{,}127{,}927$$

A 100% hedging ratio requires a receive-fixed interest rate swap having a notional principal of about USD 392 million. For a hedging ratio of 75%, the notional principal needs to be about USD 294 million (= 392 × 0.75).

Solution to 2: The plan manager's likely view is that the 30-year swap rate will be less than 3.80%. Then the gains on the receive-fixed interest rate swap exceed those on the swaption collar (i.e., not profitable until the swap rate falls below 3.60%) and on the purchased receiver swaption (i.e., not profitable until the swap rate falls sufficiently below 3.60% to recover the premium paid) as illustrated in Exhibit 16. Note that if the 30-year swap rate exceeds 3.80%, then the receive-fixed interest rate swap will begin losing immediately. Losses on the swaption collar will not begin until the rate rises above 4.25%, while losses on the purchased receiver swaption (at any swap rate above 3.60%) are limited to the premium paid.

Notice that this rate view is also consistent with the concern about lower corporate bond yields and the relatively high hedging ratio.

6. RISKS IN LIABILITY-DRIVEN INVESTING

We have mentioned in previous sections some of the risks to LDI strategies for single and multiple liabilities. In this section, we review those risks and introduce some new ones. The essential relationship for full interest rate hedging is summarized in this expression:

Asset BPV × ΔAsset yields + Hedge BPV × ΔHedge yields

≈ Liability BPV × ΔLiability yields   (7)

ΔAsset yields, ΔHedge yields, and ΔLiability yields are measured in basis points. This equation describes an immunization strategy (a hedging ratio of 100%) whereby the intent is to match the changes in market value on each side of the balance sheet when yields change. Doing so entails matching the money duration of assets and liabilities. We know, however, that entities also choose to partially hedge interest rate risk by selecting a hedging ratio less than 100%. In any case, Equation 7 serves to indicate the source of the risks to LDI. The "approximately equals" sign (≈) in the equation results from ignoring higher-order terms such as convexity.

We encounter model risk in financial modeling whenever assumptions are made about future events and approximations are used to measure key parameters. The risk is that those assumptions turn out to be wrong and the approximations are inaccurate. For example, in the defined benefit pension plan example in Section 5, we assumed that the effective durations for investments in equity and alternative assets are zero. That assumption introduces the risk that

Asset BPV is mis-measured if in fact those market values change as the yield curve shifts. The modeling problem is that the effect on those asset classes is not predictable or stable because it depends on the reason for the change in nominal interest rates. Unlike fixed-income bonds, an increase in expected inflation can have a very different effect on equity and alternative asset valuations than an increase in the real rate.

Measurement error for Asset BPV can even arise in the classic immunization strategy for Type I cash flows, which have set amounts and dates. In practice, it is common to approximate the asset portfolio duration using the weighted average of the individual durations for the component bonds. A better approach to achieve immunization, however, uses the cash flow yield to discount the future coupon and principal payments.[16] This error is minimized when the underlying yield curve is flat or when future cash flows are concentrated in the flattest segment of the curve.

A similar problem arises in measuring Hedge BPV. In Section 4.3 on using derivatives overlays to immunize, we used a common approximation for the Futures BPV. Equation 4 estimates it to be the BPV for the CTD qualifying security divided by its conversion factor. A more developed calculation involving short-term rates and accrued interest, however, could change the number of contracts needed to hedge the interest rate risk. Although the error introduced by using an approximation might not be large, it still can be a source of underperformance in the hedging strategy.

Model risk in obtaining a measure of Liability BPV is evident in the defined benefit pension plan example in Section 5. Measuring a defined benefit pension plan's liability is clearly a difficult financial modeling problem. Even the simple models for the two liability measures (the ABO and PBO) necessarily require many assumptions about the future, including the dates when employees retire and their wage levels at those times. The difficulty in projecting life spans of retirees covered by the pension plan leads to longevity risk. The risk is the sponsor has not provided sufficient assets to make the longer-than-expected payout stream. More, and harder-to-make, assumptions are needed to deal with Type IV liabilities and lead to greater uncertainty regarding the models' outputs.

Implicit in Equation 7 is the assumption that all yields change by the same number of basis points—that is, ΔAsset Yields, ΔHedge Yields, and ΔLiability Yields are equal. That is a strong assumption—and a source of risk—if the particular fixed-income assets, the derivatives, and the liabilities are positioned at varying points along the benchmark bond yield curve and at varying spreads to that curve. In Section 3 on immunizing the interest rate risk on a single liability by structuring and managing a portfolio of fixed-income bonds, we point out that a parallel yield curve shift is a sufficient, but not necessary, condition to achieve the desired outcome. Non-parallel shifts as well as twists to the yield curve can result in changes to the cash flow yield on the immunizing portfolio that do not match the change in the yield on the zero-coupon bond that provides perfect immunization. Minimizing dispersion of the cash flows in the asset portfolio mitigates this risk.

Generally, the framework for thinking about interest rate risk rests on changes in the benchmark bond yield curve, which usually is the yield curve for government bonds. In practice, however, ΔAsset Yields and ΔLiability Yields often refer to various classes of corporate bonds. In the example in Section 5, the pension fund holds a portfolio of fixed-income bonds that tracks a well-diversified index of corporate bonds that may include non-investment-grade securities. The present value of retirement benefits, however, depends on

---

[16]See also Footnotes 4 and 7.

yields on high-quality corporate bonds. Therefore, a risk is that the respective spreads on the broad index and the high-quality sector do not move in unison with a shift in the government bond yield curve. A similar spread risk is present in Section 4.2 in the example of immunizing multiple Type I liabilities. The difference is that the assets in that example are of higher quality than the liabilities.

Spread risk also is apparent in the derivatives overlay LDI strategies. In Sections 4.3 and 4.4, we illustrated how futures contracts can be used to hedge the interest rate risk of the multiple liabilities, either passively or contingently. In particular, the futures contracts are on 10-year US Treasury notes whereas the liabilities are corporate obligations. Movements in the corporate–Treasury yield spread introduce risk to the hedging strategy. Usually, yields on high-quality corporate bonds are less volatile than on more-liquid Treasuries. Government bonds are used in a wide variety of hedging as well as speculative trading strategies by institutional investors. Also, inflows of international funds typically are placed in government bonds, at least until they are allocated to other asset classes. Those factors lead to greater volatility in Treasury yields than comparable-maturity corporate bonds.

Another source of spread risk is the use of interest rate swap overlays. In Section 5, we showed how receive-fixed swaps, purchased receiver swaptions, and swaption collars can reduce the duration gap between pension plan assets and liabilities. In that example, ΔHedge Yields refers to fixed rates on interest rate swaps referencing three-month Libor. The spread risk is between high-quality corporate bond yields and swap rates. Typically, there is less volatility in the corporate/swap spread than in the corporate/Treasury spread because both Libor and corporate bond yields contain credit risk vis-à-vis Treasuries. Therefore, one of the usual advantages to hedging corporate bond risk with interest rate swaps is that those derivatives pose less spread risk than Treasury futures contracts.

Counterparty credit risk is a concern if the interest rate swap overlays are uncollateralized, as was common before the 2008–2009 financial crisis. Suppose that the interest rate swap portrayed in Exhibit 15 does not have a collateral agreement, or Credit Support Annex (CSA), to the standard International Swaps and Derivatives Association (ISDA) contract. The credit risk facing the pension plan is that the swap dealer defaults at a time when the replacement swap fixed rate is below 4.16%. In the same manner, the credit risk facing the dealer is that the pension plan defaults at the time when the market rate on a comparable swap is above 4.16%. Therefore, credit risk entails the joint probability of default by the counterparty and movement in market rates that results in the swap being valued as an asset.

Since the 2008–2009 financial crisis, over-the-counter derivatives increasingly include a CSA to the ISDA contract to mitigate counterparty credit risk. Collateral provisions vary. A typical CSA calls for a zero threshold, meaning that only the counterparty for which the swap has negative market value posts collateral, which usually is cash but can be highly marketable securities. The CSA can be one way (only the "weaker" counterparty needs to post collateral when the swap has negative market value from its perspective) or two way (either counterparty is obligated to post collateral when the swap has negative market value). The threshold could be positive, meaning that the swap has to have a certain negative value before collateral needs to be exchanged. Another possibility is that one or both counterparties are required to post a certain amount of collateral, called an independent amount, even if the swap has zero or positive value. This provision makes the CSA similar to the use of margin accounts with exchange-traded futures contracts.

Collateralization on derivatives used in an LDI strategy introduces a new risk factor—the risk that available collateral becomes exhausted. That risk is particularly important for the example in Section 5, in which the pension plan would need to enter a sizable derivatives overlay to even use a 50% hedging ratio, let alone to fully hedge the interest rate risk. That is because the duration gap between assets and liabilities is often large, especially for plans having a significant equity allocation. Therefore, the probability of exhausting collateral is a factor in determining the hedging ratio and the permissible range in the ratio if strategic hedging is allowed.

The same concern about cash management and collateral availability arises with the use of exchange-traded futures contracts. These contracts entail daily mark-to-market valuation and settlement into a margin account. This process requires daily oversight because cash moves into or out of the margin account at the close of each trading day. In contrast, the CSA on a collateralized swap agreement typically allows the party a few days to post additional cash or marketable securities. Also, there usually is a *minimum transfer amount* to mitigate the transactions costs for small inconsequential payments.

Asset liquidity becomes a risk factor in strategies that combine active investing to the otherwise passive fixed-income portfolios. This risk is particularly important with contingent immunization, as in the example in Section 4.4. Then, some or all of the surplus is actively managed. But if losses reduce the surplus to some minimum amount, the positions need to be sold off to revert to a passive duration matching fixed-income portfolio of high-quality bonds. One of the lessons from the 2008–2009 financial crisis is that distressed assets that become hard to value, such as tranches of subprime mortgage-backed securities, also become illiquid.

In summary, an LDI manager has a fundamental choice between managing interest rate risk with asset allocation and with derivatives overlays. As with all financial management decisions, the choice depends on a thorough evaluation of risk and return trade-offs. In some circumstances, derivatives might be deemed too expensive or risky, particularly with regard to available collateral and cash holdings. Then the manager might choose to increase holdings of long-term, high-quality bonds that have high duration statistics. The growth of government zero-coupon bonds, such as US Treasury STRIPS (Separate Trading of Registered Interest and Principal of Securities), facilitates that asset reallocation process.

EXAMPLE 8

A derivatives consultant, a former head of interest rate swaps trading at a major London bank, is asked by a Spanish corporation to devise an overlay strategy to "effectively defease" a large debt liability. That means that there are dedicated assets to retire the debt even if both assets and the liability remain on the balance sheet. The corporation currently has enough euro-denominated cash assets to retire the bonds, but its bank advises that acquiring the securities via a tender offer at this time will be prohibitively expensive.

The 10-year fixed-rate bonds are callable at par value in three years. This is a one-time call option. If the issuer does not exercise the option, the bonds are then non-callable for the remaining time to maturity. The corporation's CFO anticipates higher benchmark interest rates in the coming years. Therefore, the strategy of investing the available funds for three years and then calling the debt is questionable because the embedded call option might be "out of the money" when the call date arrives. Moreover, it is likely that the cost to buy the bonds on the open market at that time will still be prohibitive.

The corporation has considered a cash flow matching approach by buying a corporate bond having the same credit rating and a call structure (call date and call price) close to the corporation's own debt liability. The bank working with the CFO has been unable to identify an acceptable bond, however. Instead, the bank suggests that the corporation buy a 10-year non-callable, fixed-rate corporate bond and use a swaption to mimic the characteristics of the embedded call option. The idea is to transform the callable bond (the liability) into a non-callable security synthetically using the swaption. Then the newly purchased non-callable bond "effectively" defeases the transformed "non-callable" debt liability.

To confirm the bank's recommendation for the derivatives overlay, the CFO turns to the derivatives consultant, asking if the corporation should (1) buy a payer swaption, (2) buy a receiver swaption, (3) write a payer swaption, or (4) write a receiver swaption. The time frames for the swaptions correspond to the embedded call option. They are "3y7y" contracts, an option to enter a seven-year interest rate swap in three years. The CFO also asks the consultant about the risks to the recommended swaption position.

1. Indicate the swaption position that the derivatives consultant should recommend to the corporation.
2. Indicate the risks in using the derivatives overlay.

Solution to 1: The derivatives consultant should recommend that the corporation choose the fourth option and write a receiver swaption—that is, an option that gives the swaption buyer the right to enter into a swap to receive fixed and pay floating. When the corporation issued the callable bond, it effectively bought the call option, giving the corporation the flexibility to refinance at a lower cost of borrowed funds if benchmark rates and/or the corporation's credit spread narrows. Writing the receiver swaption "sells" that call option, and the corporation captures the value of the embedded call option by means of the premium received. Suppose that market rates in three years are higher than the strike rate on the swaption and the yield on the debt security. Then both options—the embedded call option in the bond liability, as well as the swaption—expire out of the money. The asset and liability both have seven years until maturity and are non-callable. Suppose instead that market rates fall and bond prices go up. Both options are now in the money. The corporation sells the seven-year bonds (the assets) and uses the proceeds to call the debt liabilities at par value. The gain on that transaction offsets the loss on closing out the swaption with the counterparty.

Solution to 2: Potential risks to using swaptions include (1) credit risk if the swaption is not collateralized, (2) "collateral exhaustion risk" if it is collateralized, and (3) spread risk between swap fixed rates and the corporation's cost of funds. First, suppose the receiver swaption is not collateralized. In general, the credit risk on an option is unilateral, meaning that the buyer bears the credit risk of the writer. That unilateral risk assumes the premium is paid in full upon entering the contract; in other words, the buyer has met their entire obligation. Therefore, the corporation as the swaption writer would have no additional credit exposure to the buyer. Second, assume that the swaption is collateralized. As the writer of the option, the corporation would need to regularly post cash collateral or marketable securities with either the counterparty or a third-party clearinghouse. The risk is that the corporation exhausts its available cash or holdings of marketable securities and cannot maintain the hedge. Spread risk arises because the value of the embedded call option in three years depends on the corporation's cost of funds at that time, including its credit risk. The value of the swaption depends only on seven-year swap fixed rates at that time. In particular, the risk is that the corporate/swap spread widens when benchmark rates are low and both options can be exercised. If the corporate spread over the benchmark rate goes up, the gain in the embedded call option is reduced. If the swap spread over the same benchmark rate goes down, the loss on the swaption increases. Fortunately, corporate and swap spreads over benchmark rates are usually positively correlated, but still the risk of an unexpected change in the spread should be identified.

7. BOND INDEXES AND THE CHALLENGES OF MATCHING A FIXED-INCOME PORTFOLIO TO AN INDEX

Though the need to offset liabilities through immunization requires a specific bond portfolio, many investors seek a broader exposure to the fixed-income universe. These investors may be attracted to the risk versus return characteristics available in bond markets, or they may seek to allocate a portion of their investable assets to fixed income as part of a well-diversified multi-asset portfolio. In either case, an investment strategy based on a bond market index offers an investor the ability to gain broad exposure to the fixed-income universe. Index-based investments generally offer investors the possibility of greater diversification and lower fees as well as avoiding the downside risk from seeking positive excess returns over time from active management.

An investor seeking to offset a specific liability through immunization gauges the success of his strategy based on how closely the chosen bonds offset the future liability or liabilities under different interest rate scenarios. In contrast, an investor seeking to match the returns of a bond market index will gauge an investment strategy's success in terms of how closely the chosen market portfolio mirrors the return of the underlying bond market index. Deviation of returns on the selected portfolio from bond market index returns are referred to as **tracking risk** or tracking error. Kenneth Volpert (2012) identifies several methods investors use to match an underlying market index.[17] The first of these is **pure indexing**, in which the investor aims to replicate an existing market index by purchasing all of the constituent securities in the index to minimize tracking risk. The purchase of all securities within an index is known as the **full replication approach**. In **enhanced indexing strategy**, the investor purchases fewer securities than the full set of index constituents but matches primary risk factors (discussed later) reflected in the index. This strategy aims to replicate the index performance under different market scenarios more efficiently than the full replication of a pure indexing approach. **Active management** involves taking positions in primary risk factors that deviate from those of the index in order to generate excess return.

Casual financial market observers usually refer to an equity market index to gauge overall financial market sentiment. Examples often consist of a small set of underlying securities, such as the Dow Jones Industrial Average of 30 US stocks, the CAC 40 traded on Euronext in Paris, or the 50 constituent companies in the Hang Seng Index, which represent more than

---

[17]Volpert (2012).

half the market capitalization of the Hong Kong stock market. When bond markets are mentioned at all, the price and yield of the most recently issued benchmark government bond is typically referenced rather than a bond market index. This contrast reflects the unwieldy nature of bond markets for both the average investor and financial professionals alike.

Although rarely highlighted in the financial press, investments based on bond market indexes form a very substantial proportion of financial assets held by investors. Fixed-income markets have unique characteristics that make them difficult to track, and investors therefore face significant challenges in replicating a bond market index. These challenges include the size and breadth of bond markets, the wide array of fixed-income security characteristics, unique issuance and trading patterns of bonds versus other securities, and the effect of these patterns on index composition and construction, pricing, and valuation. We will tackle each of these issues and their implications for fixed-income investors.

Fixed-income markets are much larger and broader than equity markets. According to the Global McKinsey Institute, global financial instruments reached a total value of USD 212 trillion in 2010, with nearly three-quarters of this total consisting of fixed-income instruments and loans, whereas only USD 54 trillion were equity securities.[18] In addition to the relative size of market capitalization between debt and equity, the number of fixed-income securities outstanding is vastly larger as reflected in broad market indexes. For instance, the MSCI World Index, capturing equities in 23 developed market countries and 85% of the available market capitalization in each market, consists of 1,642 securities, whereas the Bloomberg Barclays Global Aggregate Index, covering global investment-grade debt from 24 local currency markets, consists of more than 16,000 securities. Those fixed-income issuers represent a much wider range of borrowers than the relatively narrow universe of companies issuing equity securities. For example, the oldest and most widely recognized US bond market index, the Bloomberg Barclays US Aggregate Index (one of four regional aggregate benchmarks that constitute the Bloomberg Barclays Global Aggregate Index), includes US Treasuries, government agency securities, corporate bonds, mortgage-backed securities, asset-backed securities, and commercial mortgage-backed securities. Although the large number of index constituents provides a means of risk diversification, in practice it is neither feasible nor cost-effective for investors to pursue a full replication approach with a broad fixed-income market index.

Different maturities, ratings, call/put features, and varying levels of security and subordination give rise to a much wider array of public and private bonds available to investors. Exhibit 17 illustrates the number of publicly traded fixed-income and equity securities outstanding for a select group of major global issuers.

EXHIBIT 17   Debt and Equity Securities Outstanding for Select Issuers

Issuer	Fixed-Income Securities	Common Equity Securities	Preferred Equity Securities
Royal Dutch Shell PLC	39	1	0
BHP Billiton Limited	36	1	0
Johnson & Johnson	26	3	0
Ford Motor Company	243	2	0

Source: Bloomberg as of 28 February 2015.

---

[18]Roxburgh, Lund, and Piotrowski (2011, p, 2), based on a sample of 79 countries.

At the end of 2015, Royal Dutch Shell had 39 bonds outstanding across four currencies, some of which were both fixed and floating rate, with a range of maturities from under a year to bonds maturing in 2045. The existence of many debt securities for a particular issuer suggests that many near substitutes may exist for an investor seeking to pursue an enhanced index strategy. That said, the relative liquidity and performance characteristics of those bonds may differ greatly depending on how recently the bond was issued and how close its coupon is to the yield currently required to price the bond at par.

Unlike equity securities, which trade primarily over an exchange, fixed-income markets are largely over-the-counter markets that rely on broker/dealers as principals to trade in these securities using a quote-based execution process rather than the order-based trading systems common in equity markets. The traditional over-the-counter trading model in fixed-income markets has changed since the 2008 financial crisis.[19] The rising cost of maintaining risk-weighted assets on dealer balance sheets as a result of Basel III capital requirements has had an adverse effect on fixed-income trading and liquidity for a number of reasons. Broker/dealers have reduced bond inventories because of higher capital costs. With lower trading inventories, dealers have both a limited appetite to facilitate trading at narrow bid–offer spreads and are less willing to support larger "block" trades, preferring execution in smaller trade sizes. Finally, a significant decline in proprietary trading among dealers has had a greater pricing effect on less liquid or "off-the-run" bonds. Although many see these structural changes in fixed-income trading acting as a catalyst for more electronic trading, this trend will likely be most significant for the most liquid fixed-income securities in developed markets, with a more gradual effect on less frequently traded fixed-income securities worldwide.

Although fixed-income trading in many markets is difficult to track, in the United States, the world's largest global bond market, regulators developed a vehicle known as the Trade Reporting and Compliance Engine (TRACE) to facilitate mandatory reporting of over-the-counter transactions in eligible fixed-income securities starting in 2001. All broker/dealers that are Financial Industry Regulatory Authority (FINRA) member firms must report corporate bond transactions within 15 minutes of occurrence. Analysis of TRACE trading data demonstrates the distinct nature of fixed-income trading versus equities. For example, in 2012, 38% of the 37,000 TRACE-eligible fixed-income securities did not trade at all, with another 23% trading only a few times during the year, compared with the 1% that traded every business day, according to MarketAxess, a leading electronic trading provider.[20] It is also important to note that the average trade size in dollar terms in the US investment-grade bond market is roughly 70 times the size of the average stock trade.

The illiquid nature of most fixed-income instruments gives rise to pricing and valuation challenges for asset managers. For fixed-income instruments that are not actively traded and therefore do not have an observable price, it is common to use an estimation process known as **matrix pricing** or **evaluated pricing**. Matrix pricing makes use of observable liquid benchmark yields such as Treasuries of similar maturity and duration as well as the benchmark spreads of bonds with comparable times to maturity, credit quality, and sector or security type in order to estimate the current market yield and price. In practice, asset managers will typically outsource this function to a global custodian or external vendor. This estimation analysis is another potential source of variation between index performance and portfolio returns.

---

[19]McKinsey & Company and Greenwich Associates, *Corporate Bond E-Trading: Same Game, New Playing Field*, August 2013.

[20]McKinsey & Company and Greenwich Associates (2013, pp. 10–11).

The complexity of trading and valuing individual fixed-income securities further underscores the challenges associated with managing an index-based bond portfolio. Early bond indexes, such as those from Standard & Poor's and Citigroup dating back to the 1920s, simply measured the average yield of corporate bonds. Not until the significant advances in computing power of the 1970s did the first broad-based, rate of return–based fixed-income index (now known as the Bloomberg Barclays US Aggregate Index) come into being.[21] Fixed-income indexes change frequently as a result of both new debt issuance and the maturity of outstanding bonds. Bond index eligibility is also affected by changes in ratings and bond callability. As a result, rebalancing of bond market indexes usually occurs monthly rather than semi-annually or annually as it does for equity indexes. Fixed-income investors pursuing a pure indexing strategy therefore must also incur greater transaction costs associated with maintaining a bond portfolio consistent with the index.

Given the significant hurdles involved in bond index matching, asset managers typically seek to target the primary risk factors present in a fixed-income index through a diversified portfolio. Volpert (2012) summarized these primary indexing risk factors as follows:[22]

- **Portfolio modified adjusted duration.** Effective duration, or the sensitivity of a bond's price to a change in a benchmark yield curve, is an important primary factor as a first approximation of an index's exposure to interest rate changes. It is important to factor in option-adjusted duration so that the analysis reflects securities with embedded call risk. Larger rate moves should incorporate the second-order convexity adjustment to increase accuracy.
- **Key rate duration.** Although effective duration may be a sufficient measure for small rate changes and parallel yield curve shifts, the **key rate duration** takes into account rate changes in a specific maturity along the yield curve while holding the remaining rates constant. This measure of duration gauges the index's sensitivity to non-parallel yield curve shifts. By effectively matching the key rate durations between the portfolio and the underlying index, a manager can significantly reduce the portfolio's exposure to changes in the yield curve.
- **Percent in sector and quality.** Index yield is most effectively matched by targeting the same percentage weights across fixed-income sectors and credit quality, assuming that maturity parameters have also been met.
- **Sector and quality spread duration contribution.** The portfolio manager can minimize deviations from the benchmark by matching the amounts of index duration associated with the respective issuer sectors and quality categories. The former refers to the issuer type and/ or industry segment of the bond issuer. In the case of the latter, the risk that a bond's price will change in response to an idiosyncratic rate move rather than an overall market yield change is known as spread risk. For non-government fixed-income securities, we separate the yield to maturity into a benchmark yield (typically the most recently issued or on-the-run government bond with the closest time to maturity) and a spread reflecting the difference between the benchmark yield and the security-specific yield. **Spread duration** refers to the change in a non-Treasury security's price given a widening or narrowing of the spread compared with the benchmark. Matching the relative quality between the portfolio and the fixed-income index will minimize this risk.

---

[21]The index was created in 1973 by Lehman Brothers, and its sale to Bloomberg LP was announced in December 2015.
[22]This section is derived from Volpert (2012, pp. 1133–1138).

- **Sector/coupon/maturity cell weights.** Asset managers face a number of challenges in matching price/yield sensitivity beyond the use of effective duration. Although convexity is a useful second-order condition that should be used to improve this approximation, the negative convexity of callable bonds may distort the call exposure of an index and lead to costly rebalancing when rates shift. As a result, managers should seek to match the sector, coupon, and maturity weights of callable bonds by sector. Doing so is particularly important in the mortgage sector because of the refinancing of high-coupon securities with lower-coupon bonds.
- **Issuer exposure.** Concentration of issuers within a portfolio exposes the asset manager to issuer-specific event risk. The manager should therefore seek to match the portfolio duration effect from holdings in each issuer.

Another method used to address a portfolio's sensitivity to rate changes along the yield curve is referred to as the **present value of distribution of cash flows methodology**. This approach seeks to approximate and match the yield curve risk of an index over discrete time periods referred to as cash flow vertices, and it involves several steps as follows:

1. The manager divides the cash flows for each non-callable security in the index into discrete semi-annual periods, aggregates them, and then adds the cash flows for callable securities in the index based on the probability of call for each given period.
2. The present value of aggregated cash flows for each semi-annual period is computed, with the total present value of all such aggregated cash flows equal to the index's present value. The percentage of the present value of each cash flow vertex is calculated.
3. The time period is then multiplied by the present value of each cash flow. Because each cash flow represents an effective zero-coupon payment in the corresponding period, the time period reflects the duration of each cash flow. For example, the third period's contribution to duration might be 1.5 years × 3.0%, or 0.045.
4. Finally, each period's contribution to duration is added to arrive at a total representing the bond index's duration. The portfolio being managed will be largely protected from deviations from the benchmark associated with yield curve changes by matching the percentage of the portfolio's present value that comes due at specific points in time with that of the index.

The goal of matching these primary indexing risk factors is to minimize the difference between a given portfolio's return and that of an underlying benchmark index, known as **tracking error**. Tracking error is defined as the standard deviation of a portfolio's active return for a given period, whereby active return is defined as follows:

$$\text{Active return} = \text{Portfolio return} - \text{Benchmark index return}$$

If we assume that returns are normally distributed around the mean, then from a statistical perspective, 68% of those returns will lie within one standard deviation of the mean. Therefore, if a fund's tracking error is 50 bps, then for approximately two-thirds of the time period observations, we would expect the fund's return to be less than 50 bps above or below the index's return.

EXAMPLE 9

Cindy Cheng, a Hong Kong–based portfolio manager, has established the All Asia Dragon Fund, a fixed-income fund designed to outperform the Markit iBoxx Asian Local Bond Index (ALBI). The ALBI tracks the total return performance of liquid bonds denominated in local currencies in the following markets: Chinese mainland, Hong Kong SAR, India, Indonesia, Korea, Malaysia, the Philippines, Singapore, Taiwan Region, and Thailand. The index includes both government and non-government bond issues, with constituent selection criteria by government as well as weights designed to balance the desire for liquidity and stability.[23]

Individual bond weightings are based on market capitalization, and market weights, reviewed annually, are designed to reflect the investability of developing Asian local currency bonds available to international investors. These weights are driven by local market size and market capitalization, secondary bond market liquidity, accessibility to foreign investors, and development of infrastructure that supports fixed-income investment and trading such as credit ratings, yield curves, and derivative products.

Given the large number of bonds in the index, Cheng uses a representative sample of the bonds to construct the fund. She chooses bonds so that the fund's duration, market weights, and sector/quality percentage weights closely match the ALBI. Given the complexity of managing bond investments in these local markets, Cheng is targeting a 1.25% tracking error for the fund.

1. Interpret Cheng's tracking error target for the All Asia Dragon Fund.
2. One of Cheng's largest institutional investors has encouraged her to reduce tracking error. Suggest steps Cheng could take to minimize this risk in the fund.

Solution to 1: The target tracking error of 1.25% means that assuming normally distributed returns, in 68% or two-thirds of time periods, the All Asia Dragon Fund should have a return that is within 1.25% of the ALBI.

Solution to 2: Cheng could further reduce tracking error beyond her choice of duration, market, and sector/quality weightings to mirror the index by using the present value of distribution of cash flows methodology outlined earlier. By doing so, she can better align the contribution to portfolio duration that comes from each market, sector, and issuer type based on credit quality.

Cheng should consider matching the amount of index duration that comes from each sector, as well as matching the amount of index duration that comes from various quality categories across government and non-government bonds, to minimize tracking error.

Finally, Cheng should evaluate the portfolio duration coming from each issuer to minimize event risk. Again, this evaluation should occur on a duration basis rather than as a percentage of market value to quantify the exposure more accurately versus the benchmark ALBI.

---

[23]Markit iBoxx ALBI™ Index Guide, January 2016, Markit Ltd.

8. ALTERNATIVE METHODS FOR ESTABLISHING PASSIVE BOND MARKET EXPOSURE

Why is passive bond market exposure attractive for investors? A **passive investment** in the fixed-income market may be defined as one that seeks to mimic the prevailing characteristics of the overall investments available in terms of credit quality, type of borrower, maturity, and duration rather than express a specific market view. This approach is consistent with the efficient markets hypothesis in that the portfolio manager seeks to simply replicate broader fixed-income market performance rather than outperform the market. Stated differently, establishing passive bond market exposure does not require the in-depth analysis necessary to achieve an above-market return nor does it require the high trading frequency of active management, which should lead to lower costs for managing and servicing a portfolio. Finally, the stated goal of matching the performance of a broad-based bond index is consistent with the highest degree of portfolio diversification.

Several methods exist for establishing a passive bond market exposure. In what follows, we will explore both full index replication as well as an enhanced indexing strategy and compare the risks, costs, and relative liquidity of these strategies when applied to the bond market.

Bond market index replication is the most straightforward strategy that a manager can use to mimic index performance. Use of full replication reflects the belief or expectation that an active manager cannot consistently outperform the index on a risk-adjusted basis. Initial index replication does not require manager analysis but rather involves sourcing a wide range of securities in exact proportion to the index, many of which may be thinly traded. The manager's ongoing task under full replication is to purchase or sell bonds when there are changes to the index in addition to managing inflows and outflows for a specific fund. For example, the manager may have to sell when a security no longer meets the index criteria, such as when a security either matures or is downgraded.[24] On the other hand, managers must purchase newly issued securities that meet index criteria to maintain full replication, which, depending on the index, may occur quite frequently. Rolling bond maturities, as well as frequent new issuance eligible for inclusion in the index, drive a monthly rebalancing for most fixed-income indexes. The number of purchases and sales required to maintain an exact proportional allocation would be very significant for most bond indexes. As a result, although the large number of index constituents may well provide the best means of risk diversification, in practice it is neither feasible nor cost-effective for investors to pursue full replication for broad-based fixed-income indexes.

Many limitations of the full replication approach are addressed by an enhanced indexing strategy. This approach's goal is to mirror the most important index characteristics and still closely track index performance over time while purchasing fewer securities. This general approach is referred to as a **stratified sampling** or **cell approach** to indexing. First, each cell or significant index portfolio characteristic is identified and mapped to the current index. Second, the fixed-income portfolio manager identifies a subset of bonds or bond-linked exposures, such as derivatives, with characteristics that correspond to the index. Finally, the positions in each cell are adjusted over time given changes to the underlying index versus

---

[24]For the Bloomberg Barclays US Aggregate Bond Index, a fixed-income security becomes ineligible when it either has a maturity of less than one year or is downgraded below the minimum rating (Baa3, BBB–, and BBB– for Moody's Investors Service, Standard & Poor's, and Fitch Ratings, respectively). https://index.barcap.com.

existing portfolio positions. For example, say a fixed-income index contains 1,000 fixed-income securities, 10% of which are AAA rated. The portfolio manager might choose five to 10 AAA rated securities within a cell in order to mimic the performance of the AAA rated bonds within the index.

Enhanced indexing is also of critical importance to investors who consider environmental, social, or other factors when selecting a fixed-income portfolio. **Environmental, social, and corporate governance (ESG)**, also called socially responsible investing, refers to the explicit inclusion of ethical, environmental, or social criteria when selecting a portfolio.[25] For example, ESG investors may shun entire sectors such as alcohol-related, gambling, or tobacco companies, or alternatively, they may evaluate underlying issuers based on non-financial criteria such as their adherence to environmental, human rights, or labor standards.

Volpert (2012) outlines a number of enhancement strategies available to portfolio managers seeking to reduce the component of tracking error associated with the expenses and transactions costs of portfolio management as follows:[26]

- **Lower cost enhancements.** The most obvious enhancement is in the area of cost reduction, whether this involves minimizing fund expenses or introducing a more competitive trading process to reduce the bid–offer cost of trading.
- **Issue selection enhancements.** The use of bond valuation models to identify specific issues that are undervalued or "cheap" to their implied value provides another opportunity to enhance return.
- **Yield curve enhancements.** The use of analytical models to gauge and calculate relative value across the term structure of interest rates allows managers to develop strategies to both overweight maturities that are considered undervalued and underweight those that appear to be richly priced.
- **Sector/quality enhancements.** This strategy involves overweighting specific bond and credit sectors across the business cycle to enhance returns. Other sectors are underweighted as a result. This approach may tilt exposure toward corporates given a greater yield spread per unit of duration exposure or shorter maturities or it may over- or underweight specific sectors or qualities based on analysis of the business cycle.

For example, a manager may increase her allocation to Treasuries over corporates when significant spread widening is anticipated, or reverse this allocation if spread narrowing is deemed more likely.

- **Call exposure enhancements.** Because effective duration is a sufficient risk measure only for relatively small rate changes, anticipated larger yield changes may affect bond performance significantly, especially when a bond shifts from trading to maturity to trading to an earlier call date. Large expected yield changes increase the value of call protection, and any significant differences from index exposure should incorporate potentially large tracking risk implications, as well as the implicit market view that this difference implies. For example, an anticipated drop in yields might cause a callable bond to shift from being priced on a yield-to-maturity basis to a yield-to-call basis. Callable fixed-income securities (priced on a yield-to-call basis) trading above par tend to be less price sensitive for a given effective duration than those priced on a yield-to-maturity basis, suggesting a manager should use metrics other than effective duration in this case when changing exposure.

---

[25]See Hayat and Orsagh (2015).
[26]Volpert (2012), pp. 1138–1145.

The stratified sampling approach provides an asset manager the ability to optimize portfolio performance across these characteristics with fewer securities than would be required through full index replication. By matching portfolio performance as closely as possible, investment managers also seek to minimize tracking error, limit the need to purchase or sell thinly traded securities, and/or frequently rebalance the portfolio as would be required when precisely matching the index.

EXAMPLE 10

Adelaide Super, a superannuation fund, offers a range of fixed interest (or fixed-income) investment choices to its members. Superannuation funds are Australian government-supported arrangements for Australian workers to save for retirement, which combine a government-mandated minimum percentage of wages contributed by employers with a voluntary employee contribution that offers tax benefits. Superannuation plans are similar to defined contribution plans common in the United States, Europe, and Asia.

Three of the bond fund choices Adelaide Super offers are as follows:

- **Dundee Australian Fixed-Income Fund.** The investment objective is to outperform the Bloomberg AusBond Composite Index in the medium to long term. The index includes investment-grade fixed-interest bonds with a minimum of one month to maturity issued in the Australian debt market under Australian law, including the government, semi-government, credit, and supranational/sovereign sectors. The index includes AUD-denominated bonds only. The investment strategy is to match index duration but add value through fundamental and model-driven return strategies.
- **Newcastleton Australian Bond Fund.** The fund aims to outperform the Bloomberg AusBond Composite Index over any three-year rolling period, before fees, expenses, and taxes, and uses multiple strategies such as duration, curve positioning, and credit and sector rotation rather than one strategy, allowing the fund to take advantage of opportunities across fixed-income markets under all market conditions.
- **Paisley Fixed-Interest Fund.** The fund aims to provide investment returns after fees in excess of the fund's benchmark, which is the Bloomberg AusBond Bank Bill Index and the Bloomberg AusBond Composite Index (equally weighted) by investing in a diversified portfolio of Australian income-producing assets. Paisley seeks to minimize transaction costs via a buy-and-hold strategy, as opposed to active management. The AusBond Bank Bill Index is based on the bank bill market, which is the short-term market (90 days or less) in which Australian banks borrow from and lend to one another via bank bills.

Rank the three fixed-income funds in order of risk profile, and suggest a typical employee for whom this might be a suitable investment.

Solution: The Paisley Fixed-Interest Fund represents the lowest risk of the three fund choices, given both its choice of underlying bond index (half of which is in short-term securities) and lack of active management strategies. The Paisley Fund could be a suitable choice for an investor near retirement who is seeking income with a minimum risk profile.

The Dundee Fund represents a medium risk profile given the choice of the composite benchmark and suggests an enhanced approach to indexing. This fund may be the best choice for a middle-aged worker seeking to add a fixed-income component with moderate risk to his portfolio.

The Newcastleton Fund has the highest risk of the three choices and is an example of an actively managed fund that has a mandate to take positions in primary risk factors such as duration and credit that deviate from those of the index in order to generate excess return. This fund could be an appropriate choice for a younger worker who is seeking exposure to fixed income but willing to accommodate higher risk.

Investment managers have several alternatives to investing directly in fixed-income securities in order to seek a passive index-based exposure, including indirectly through a bond mutual fund or a fixed-income **exchange-traded fund** (ETF), as well as through synthetic means such as index-based total return swaps. In considering direct versus indirect investments, the asset manager must weigh the ongoing fees associated with mutual funds and ETFs against the bid–offer cost of direct investment in the underlying securities in the index. In addition, the asset manager can target individual issuers, maturities, and other characteristics in order to meet specific requirements, and the manager faces known interest and principal cash flows as long as the bond is not called or the issuer does not default through the stated maturity date. The indirect alternatives introduce a tradeoff between greater cost and diversification, as well as other factors outlined as follows.

Mutual funds are pooled investment vehicles whose shares or units represent a proportional share in the ownership of the assets in an underlying portfolio. In the case of open-ended mutual funds, new shares may be redeemed or issued at the fund's **net asset value** (NAV) established at the end of each trading day based on the fund's valuation of all existing assets minus liabilities, divided by the total number of shares outstanding. Mutual fund purchases or sales received after a pre-specified cutoff time take place at the NAV on the following business day.

Open-ended bond mutual funds have several additional characteristics that distinguish them from direct investment in fixed-income instruments. The benefit from economies of scale is usually the overriding factor for smaller investors in their choice of a bond mutual fund over direct investment. Because bonds often trade at a minimum lot size of USD 1 million or higher per bond, successful replication of a broad index could easily require hundreds of millions of dollars in investments. Therefore, the additional cost in terms of an up-front load in some instances and an annual management fee may be well worth the greater diversification achievable across fixed-income markets within a larger fund. Although investors benefit from increased diversification, the fund must outline its stated investment objectives and periodic fees, but actual securities holdings are available only on a retroactive basis. Unlike the underlying securities, the bond mutual fund has no maturity date, as the fund manager continuously purchases and sells bonds to track index performance, and monthly interest payments fluctuate based on fund holdings. Finally, although many funds have early redemption penalties for investors who choose to liquidate within 90 days of share purchase, bond mutual fund investors enjoy the advantage of being able to redeem holdings at the fund's NAV rather than facing a need to sell illiquid positions.

Exchange-traded funds share some mutual fund characteristics but have more tradability features. ETFs solicit broker/dealers, referred to as **authorized participants**, who enter into an agreement with the distributor of the fund, purchasing shares from or selling ETF shares to the fund in what are known as **creation units**—large blocks of ETF shares often traded against a basket of underlying securities. Authorized participants may invest longer-term in the ETF, or they may act as market makers by exchanging creation units with underlying bonds to provide liquidity and ensure the intraday price is a close approximation of the NAV.

Investors benefit from greater bond ETF liquidity versus mutual funds given their availability to be purchased or sold throughout the trading day at a discount or premium relative to the NAV of the underlying bonds. A significant spread between the market price of the underlying fixed-income securities portfolio and an ETF's NAV should drive an authorized participant to engage in arbitrage to profit from a divergence between the two prices. That said, the fact that many fixed-income securities are either thinly traded or not traded at all might allow such a divergence to persist to a much greater degree for a bond ETF than might be the case in the equity market.

Synthetic strategies provide another means of gaining exposure to an index. As in the case of portfolio immunization outlined earlier, both over-the-counter and exchanged-traded alternatives are available to portfolio managers in managing index exposure. Over-the-counter solutions entail customized arrangements between two counterparties that reference an underlying market price or index, and exchange-traded products involve financial instruments with standardized terms, documentation, and pricing traded on an organized exchange.

A **total return swap** (TRS) is the most common over-the-counter portfolio derivative strategy, combining elements of interest rate swaps and credit derivatives. Similar to an interest rate swap, a total return swap involves the periodic exchange of cash flows between two parties for the life of the contract. Unlike an interest rate swap, in which counterparties exchange a stream of fixed cash flows versus a floating-rate benchmark such as Libor (the London Interbank Offered Rate) to transform fixed assets or liabilities to a variable exposure, a TRS has a periodic exchange based on a reference obligation that is an underlying equity, commodity, or bond index. Exhibit 18 outlines the most basic TRS structure. The **total return receiver** receives both the cash flows from the underlying index as well as any appreciation in the index over the period in exchange for paying Libor plus a pre-determined spread. The **total return payer** is responsible for paying the reference obligation cash flows and return to the receiver but will also be compensated by the receiver for any depreciation in the index or default losses incurred on the portfolio.

EXHIBIT 18   Total Return Swap Mechanics

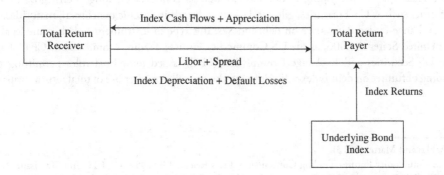

The TRS transaction is an over-the-counter derivative contract based on an ISDA master agreement. This contract specifies a notional amount, periodic cash flows, and final maturity, as well as the credit and other legal provisions related to the transaction. The historical attractiveness of using TRS stemmed from the efficient risk transfer on the reference obligation from one counterparty to another on a confidential basis without requiring the full cash outlay associated with the mutual fund or ETF purchase. In fact, another way to think of the TRS is as a synthetic secured financing transaction in which the investor (the total return receiver) benefits from more-advantageous funding terms faced by a dealer (typically the total return payer) offering to facilitate the transaction.

The potential for both a smaller initial cash outlay and lower swap bid–offer costs, when compared with the transaction costs of direct purchase or use of a mutual fund or ETF, are the most compelling reasons to consider a TRS to add fixed-income exposure. That said, several considerations may offset these benefits in a number of instances. First, the investor does not legally own the underlying assets but rather has a combined synthetic long position in both the market and credit risk of the index that is contingent upon the performance of the total return payer. Given the shorter nature of these contracts compared with an investor's typical longer-term time horizon, the total return receiver must both perform the necessary credit due diligence on its counterparty and also face the rollover risk upon maturity of having the ability to renew the contract with reasonable pricing and business terms in the future. Second, as a funding cost arbitrage transaction, the TRS can allow investors to gain particular access to subsets of the fixed-income markets, such as bank loans or high-yield instruments for which cash markets are relatively illiquid or the cost and administrative complexity of maintaining a portfolio of these instruments is prohibitive for the investor. Finally, structural changes to the market, greater regulatory oversight of derivatives markets, and changes to Basel III capital rules affecting dealers have raised the cost and operational burden of these transactions. The need to collateralize mark-to-market positions significantly increases the operational risks of TRS, including more-frequent collateralization within a $T + 1$ timeframe, or shorter, as well as the need for expertise in execution and settlement.[27]

The availability of exchange-traded interest rate products continues to evolve with the shifting market landscape and changes in investor demand. For many years, the most prevalent liquid interest rate futures and option contracts available on global futures exchanges such as Eurex, the Intercontinental Exchange, and the Chicago Mercantile Exchange were limited to individual fixed-income securities. Examples include money market instruments such as Eurodollar futures and options contracts, as well as contracts on longer-term government securities such as US Treasuries, gilts, and German bunds in specific benchmark maturities. As for exchange-traded derivatives on debt indexes, this type of instrument only became legal in the United States in 2006, as the US Commodity Futures Trading Commission (CFTC) and the US Securities and Exchange Commission (SEC) issued joint final rules permitting the trading of futures on debt indexes.[28] Although the over-the-counter use of total return swaps on

---

[27]Aakko and Martel (2013).
[28]US Commodity Futures Trading Commission, Press Release PR5195-06, CFTC and SEC Issue Rules for Trading Futures on Debt Security Index Contracts, 10 July 2006, available at www.cftc.gov and www.sec.gov.

debt indexes continues, the use of exchange-traded futures on debt indexes has proven less popular, and the CME Group delisted its Barclays US Aggregate Bond Index contract in June 2015.[29] Other exchanges have been slow to adopt such instruments. Similarly, although the launch of ETF futures on equity indexes at the CME Group in 2005 marked a shift toward these instruments to gain broad-based index exposure, the exchange stopped listing new ETF contracts in 2010 in response to a lack of liquidity in these instruments.[30] In contrast to futures market developments, the exchange-traded options market for interest rate–related ETFs remains active. As of the end of 2015, the Chicago Board Options Exchange offered options with physical settlement and American-style exercise on a range of interest rate ETFs across Treasury funds, high-yield, investment grade corporate, and inflation-protected securities.[31] Frequent changes in the availability of specific exchange-traded derivative instruments on fixed-income indexes make it challenging for investors to rely on such strategies, versus an over-the-counter hedge, over time.

9. BENCHMARK SELECTION

The choice of a benchmark is perhaps an investment manager's most important decision beyond the passive versus active decision or the form that the investment takes, as described earlier. Benchmark selection is one of the final steps in the broader asset allocation process.

The asset allocation process starts with a clear delineation of the portfolio manager's investment goals and objectives. Examples of such goals might include the protection of funds (especially against inflation), broad market replication, predictable returns within acceptable risk parameters, or maximum absolute returns through opportunistic means. The manager must agree on an investment policy with the asset owners, beneficiaries, and other constituents outlining return objectives, risk tolerance, and constraints to narrow choices available in the broader capital markets to meet these objectives. A **strategic asset allocation** targeting specific weightings for each permissible asset class is the result of this process, while a **tactical asset allocation** range often provides the investment manager some short-term flexibility to deviate from these weightings in response to anticipated market changes.

Bonds figure prominently in most asset allocations given that they represent the largest fraction of global capital markets, capture a wide range of issuers and, as borrowed funds, represent claims that should theoretically involve lower risk than common equity. Choosing a fixed-income benchmark is unique, however, in that the investor usually has some degree of fixed-income exposure embedded within its asset/liability portfolio, as outlined in the foregoing immunization and liability-driven investing examples. The investment manager must therefore consider these implicit or explicit duration preferences when choosing a fixed-income benchmark.

---

[29]CME Group, Advisory Notice #15-156, Product Modification Summary: Delist Barclays US Aggregate Bond Index Contracts, 8 June 2015, available at www.cmegroup.com.
[30]Yesalavich (2010).
[31]See www.cboe.com/InterestRateETF for the full range of available contracts.

Benchmark selection must factor in the broad range of issuers and characteristics available in the fixed-income markets. In general, the use of an index as a widely accepted benchmark requires clear, transparent rules for security inclusion and weighting, investability, daily valuation and availability of past returns, and turnover. Unlike in equity indexes, fixed-income market dynamics can drive deviation from a stable benchmark sought by investors for a number of reasons. First, the finite maturity of bonds in a static portfolio implies that duration will drift downward over time. Second, market dynamics and issuer preferences tend to dictate both issuer composition for broad-based indexes as well as maturity selection for narrower indexes. For example, as shown in Exhibit 19, the composition of the Bloomberg Barclays US Aggregate Bond Index changed significantly during the years prior to and after the 2008 financial crisis, with a large increase in securitized debt pre-crisis and a significant rise in government debt thereafter:

EXHIBIT 19   Bloomberg Barclays US Aggregate Bond Index Sector Allocation, Selected Years

Year	Government	Corporate	Securitized
1993	53.0%	17.0%	30.0%
1998	46.0%	22.0%	32.0%
2000	38.0%	24.0%	39.0%
2005	40.2%	19.5%	40.2%
2008	38.6%	17.7%	43.7%
2010	45.8%	18.8%	35.5%
2015	44.8%	24.2%	31.0%

Source: Lehman Brothers, Barclays.

Separately, a corporate debt index investor might find her benchmark choice no longer desirable if issuers refinance maturing bonds for longer maturities and extend overall debt duration. Third, value-weighted indexes assign a larger share of the index to borrowers with the largest amount of outstanding debt, leading a more leveraged issuer or sector to receive a higher weight. Creditworthiness and leverage tend to be negatively correlated. As a particular issuer or sector of the economy borrows more, investors tracking a value-weighted index will automatically increase their fixed-income exposure to these borrowers. The greater allocation to more-levered borrowers is known as the "bums problem."[32] Examples of the bums problem for entire sectors of the fixed-income market include the large increase in global telecoms–related debt financing in 2000 and the increase in US mortgage-backed financing prior to the 2008 financial crisis, both of which negatively affected investors who faced higher allocation to these sectors through a value-weighted index.

The dynamics of fixed-income markets require investors to more actively understand and define their underlying duration preferences as well as a desired risk and return profile within their fixed-income allocation when conducting benchmark selection. Expressed differently, the desired duration profile may be considered the portfolio "beta," with the

----

[32]See Siegel (2003).

targeted duration equal to an investor's preferred duration exposure. Once these parameters are clear, investors may wish to combine several well-defined sub-benchmark categories into an overall benchmark. Examples of sub-benchmark categories might include Treasuries (or domestic sovereign bonds), US agencies or other asset-backed securities, corporate bonds, high-yield bonds, bank loans, developed markets global debt, or emerging markets debt.

For fixed-income investors seeking to reduce the cost of active management while addressing systematic biases such as the bums problem, a third alternative known as **smart beta** has emerged. Smart beta involves the use of simple, transparent, rules-based strategies as a basis for investment decisions. The starting point for smart beta investors is an analysis of the well-established, static strategies that tend to drive excess portfolio returns. In theory, asset managers who are able to isolate and pursue such strategies can capture a significant proportion of these excess returns without the significantly higher fees associated with active management. Although the use of smart beta strategies is more established among equity managers, fixed-income managers are increasing their use of these techniques as well.[33]

EXAMPLE 11

Given the significant rise in regional bond issuance following the 2008 financial crisis, Next Europe Asset Management Limited aims to grow its assets under management by attracting a variety of new local Eurozone investors to the broader set of alternatives available in the current fixed-income market. Several of the indexes that Next Europe offers as a basis for investment are as follows:

- **S&P Eurozone Sovereign Bond Index.** This index consists of fixed-rate, sovereign debt publicly issued by Eurozone national governments for their domestic markets with various maturities including 1 to 3 years, 3 to 5 years, 5 to 7 years, 7 to 10 years, and 10+ years. For example, the one- to three-year index had a weighted average maturity of 1.88 years and a modified duration of 1.82 as of 31 December 2015.[34]
- **Bloomberg EUR Investment Grade European Corporate Bond Index (BERC).** The BERC index consists of local, EUR-based corporate debt issuance in Eurozone countries and had an effective duration of 5.39 as of January 2016.
- **Bloomberg EUR High Yield Corporate Bond Index (BEUH).** This index consists of sub-investment grade, EUR-denominated bonds issued by Eurozone-based corporations. It had an effective duration of 4.44 as of January 2016.[35]
- **FTSE Pfandbrief Index.** The Pfandbrief, which represents the largest segment of the German private debt market, is a bond issued by German mortgage banks, collateralized by long-term assets such as real estate or public sector loans. These securities are also referred to as covered bonds, and are being used as a model for similar issuance in other European countries.

---

[33]See Staal et al. (2015).
[34]www.us.spindices.com
[35]www.bloombergindexes.com

The FTSE Pfandbrief indexes include jumbo Pfandbriefs from German issuers, as well as those of comparable structure and quality from other Eurozone countries. The sub-indexes offer a range of maturities including 1 to 3 years, 3 to 5 years, 5 to 7 years, 7 to 10 years and 10+ years.[36]

Which of the above indexes would be suitable for the following investor portfolios?

1. A highly risk-averse investor who is sensitive to fluctuations in portfolio value.
2. A new German private university that has established an endowment with a very long-term investment horizon.
3. A Danish life insurer relying on the fixed-income portfolio managed by Next Europe to meet both short-term claims as well as offset long-term obligations.

Solution to 1: Given this investor's high degree of risk aversion, an index with short or intermediate duration with limited credit risk would be most appropriate to limit market value risk. Of the alternatives listed above, the S&P Eurozone Sovereign Bond 1–3 Years Index or the FTSE 1–3 Year Pfandbrief Index (given the high credit quality of covered bonds) would be appropriate choices.

Solution to 2: This investor's very long investment horizon suggests that the BERC is an appropriate index, because it has the longest duration of the indexes given. In addition, the long-term S&P Eurozone Sovereign Bond or FTSE Pfandbrief indexes (10+ years) could be appropriate choices as well. Next Europe should consider the tradeoff between duration and risk in its discussion with the endowment.

Solution to 3: The Danish life insurer faces two types of future obligation, namely a short-term outlay for expected claims and a long-term horizon for future obligations. For the short-term exposure, stability of market value is a primary consideration, and the insurer would seek an index with low market risk. Of the above alternatives, the 1–3 Years S&P Sovereign Bond or the FTSE Pfandbrief 1–3 Year alternatives would be the best choices. The longer-term alternatives in the Solution to 2 would be most appropriate for the long-term future obligations.

10. LADDERED BOND PORTFOLIOS

A popular fixed-income investment strategy in the wealth management industry is to build a "laddered" portfolio for clients. Exhibit 20 illustrates this approach, along with two other maturity-based strategies—a "bullet" portfolio and a "barbell" portfolio. The laddered portfolio spreads the bonds' maturities and par values more or less evenly along the yield curve. The bullet portfolio concentrates the bonds at a particular point on the yield curve, whereas the barbell portfolio places the bonds at the short-term and long-term ends of the curve. In principle, each can have the same portfolio duration statistic and approximately the same change in value for a parallel shift in the yield curve. A non-parallel shift or a twist in the curve, however, leads to very different outcomes for the bullet and barbell structures. An obvious

---

[36]www.ftse.com/products/indices

advantage to the laddered portfolio is protection from shifts and twists—the cash flows are essentially "diversified" across the time spectrum.

EXHIBIT 20   Laddered, Bullet, and Barbell Fixed-Income Portfolios

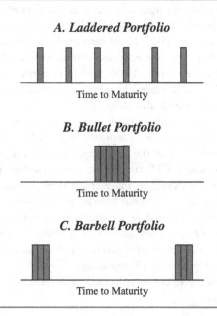

A. Laddered Portfolio

Time to Maturity

B. Bullet Portfolio

Time to Maturity

C. Barbell Portfolio

Time to Maturity

This "diversification" over time provides the investor a balanced position between the two sources of interest rate risk—cash flow reinvestment and market price volatility. Bonds mature each year and are reinvested at the longer-term end of the ladder, typically at higher rates than short-term securities. Over time, the laddered portfolio likely includes bonds that were purchased at high interest rates as well as low interest rates. Investors familiar with "dollar cost averaging" will see the similarity. In addition, by reinvesting funds as bonds mature maintains the duration of the overall portfolio.

Another attractive feature to the laddered portfolio apparent in Exhibit 20 is in convexity. Convexity, technically, is the second-order effect on the value of an asset or liability given a change in the yield to maturity. Importantly, it is affected by the dispersion of cash flows, as indicated in Equation 1 repeated here:

$$\text{Convexity} = \frac{\text{Macaulay duration}^2 + \text{Macaulay duration} + \text{Dispersion}}{(1 + \text{Cash flow yield})^2}$$

If the three portfolios have the same duration (and cash flow yield), then the barbell clearly has the highest convexity and the bullet the lowest. The laddered portfolio also has high convexity because its cash flows by design are spread over the time line. Compared with the barbell, the laddered portfolio has much less cash flow reinvestment risk.

In practice, perhaps the most desirable aspect of the laddered portfolio is in liquidity management. This aspect is particularly relevant if the bonds are not actively traded, as is the case for many corporate securities. As time passes, there is always a bond that is close to redemption. Its duration will be low so that its price is fairly stable even in a time of interest rate volatility. If the client needs immediate cash, the soon-to-mature bond makes for high-quality collateral on a personal loan or, for an institution, a repo contract. As the bonds mature, the final coupon and principal can be deployed for consumption or reinvested in a long-term bond at the back of the ladder.

Another way for a wealth manager to build a laddered portfolio for a client is to use fixed-maturity corporate bond ETFs. These ETFs have a designated year of maturity and credit risk profile—for instance, 2021 investment-grade corporate bonds. This ETF is a passively managed (and, therefore, low-administrative-cost) fund that seeks to replicate the performance of an index of, for instance, 50 held-to-maturity investment-grade corporate bonds that mature in 2021. As discussed in previous sections, the ETF manager can use a stratified sampling approach to track the index.

Suppose that in 2017, the wealth manager buys for the client roughly equal positions in the 2018 through 2025 fixed-maturity corporate bond ETFs. These purchases create a laddered portfolio that should provide the same benefits as holding the bonds directly—price stability in the soonest-to-mature ETF and greater convexity than holding more of a bullet portfolio. Moreover, the ETFs should be more liquid than positions in the actual bonds.

But laddered portfolios are not without limitations. For many investors, the decision to build a laddered bond portfolio should be weighed against buying shares in a fixed-income mutual fund, especially if the portfolio consists of a limited number of corporate bonds. Clearly, the mutual fund provides greater diversification of default risk. Moreover, actual bonds can entail a much higher cost of acquisition. If the entire investment needs to be liquidated, the mutual fund shares can be redeemed more quickly than the bonds can be sold, and likely at a better price.

EXAMPLE 12

Zheng Zilong, CFA, is a Shanghai-based wealth adviser. A major client of his, the Wang family, holds most of its assets in residential property and equity investments. Mr. Zheng recommends that the Wang family also have a laddered portfolio of Chinese government bonds. He suggests the following portfolio, priced for settlement on 1 January 2017:

Coupon Rate	Payment Frequency	Maturity	Flat Price	Yield (s.a.)	Par Value	Market Value
3.22%	Annual	26-Mar-18	101.7493	1.758%	10 Million	10,422,826
3.14%	Annual	8-Sept-20	102.1336	2.508%	10 Million	10,312,292
3.05%	Annual	22-Oct-22	101.4045	2.764%	10 Million	10,199,779
2.99%	Semi-annual	15-Oct-25	101.4454	2.803%	10 Million	10,208,611
					40 Million	41,143,508

The yields to maturity on the first three bonds have been converted from a periodicity of one to two in order to report them on a consistent semi-annual bond basis, as indicated by "(s.a.)." The total market value of the portfolio is CNY 41,143,508.

The cash flow yield for the portfolio is 2.661%, whereas the market value weighted average yield is 2.455%.

Most important for his presentation to the senior members of the Wang family is the schedule for the 30 cash flows:

1	26-Mar-17	322,000	16	8-Sep-20	10,314,000
2	15-Apr-17	149,500	17	15-Oct-20	149,500
3	8-Sep-17	314,000	18	22-Oct-20	305,000
4	15-Oct-17	149,500	19	15-Apr-21	149,500
5	22-Oct-17	305,000	20	15-Oct-21	149,500
6	26-Mar-18	10,322,000	21	22-Oct-21	305,000
7	15-Apr-18	149,500	22	15-Apr-22	149,500
8	8-Sep-18	314,000	23	15-Oct-22	149,500
9	15-Oct-18	149,500	24	22-Oct-22	10,305,000
10	22-Oct-18	305,000	25	15-Apr-23	149,500
11	15-Apr-19	149,500	26	15-Oct-23	149,500
12	8-Sep-19	314,000	27	15-Apr-24	149,500
13	15-Oct-19	149,500	28	15-Oct-24	149,500
14	22-Oct-19	305,000	29	15-Apr-25	149,500
15	15-Apr-20	149,500	30	15-Oct-25	10,149,500

Indicate the main points that Mr. Zheng should emphasize in this presentation about the laddered portfolio to senior members of the Wang family.

Solution: Mr. Zheng should emphasize three features of the portfolio:

1. **High credit quality.** Given that the family already has substantial holdings in residential property and equity, which are subject to price volatility and risk, investments in government bonds provide the Wang family with holdings in a very low-risk asset class.
2. **Liquidity.** The schedule of payments shows that coupon payments are received each year. These funds can be used for any cash need, including household expenses. The large principal payments can be reinvested in longer-term government bonds at the back of the ladder.
3. **Yield curve diversification.** The bond investments are spread out along four segments of the government bond yield curve. If they were concentrated at a single point, the portfolio would have the risk of higher yields at that point. By spreading out the maturities in the ladder formation, the portfolio has the benefit of diversification.

11. SUMMARY

This chapter covers structured and passive total return fixed-income strategies: immunization of single and multiple liabilities, indexation, and laddering. The chapter makes the following main points:

- Passive fixed-income investing requires a frame of reference, such as a balance sheet, to structure the bond portfolio. This frame of reference can be as simple as the time to retirement for an individual or as complex as a balance sheet of rate-sensitive assets and liabilities for a company.
- Asset–liability management strategies consider both assets and liabilities.
- Liability-driven investing takes the liabilities as given and builds the asset portfolio in accordance with the interest rate risk characteristics of the liabilities.
- Asset-driven liabilities take the assets as given and structures debt liabilities in accordance with the interest rate characteristics of the assets.
- Assets and liabilities can be categorized by the degree of certainty surrounding the amount and timing of cash flows. Type I assets and liabilities, such as traditional fixed-rate bonds with no embedded options, have known amounts and payment dates. For Type I assets and liabilities, yield duration statistics such as Macaulay, modified, and money duration apply. Type II, III, and IV assets and liabilities have uncertain amounts and/or uncertain timing of payment. For Type II, III, and IV assets and liabilities, curve duration statistics such as effective duration are needed. A model is used to obtain the estimated values when the yield curve shifts up and down by the same amount.
- Immunization is the process of structuring and managing a fixed-income portfolio to minimize the variance in the realized rate of return over a known investment horizon.
- In the case of a single liability, immunization is achieved by matching the Macaulay duration of the bond portfolio to the horizon date. As time passes and bond yields change, the duration of the bonds changes and the portfolio needs to be rebalanced. This rebalancing can be accomplished by buying and selling bonds or using interest rate derivatives such as futures contracts and interest rate swaps.
- An immunization strategy aims to lock in the cash flow yield on the portfolio, which is the internal rate of return on the cash flows. It is not the weighted average of the yields to maturity on the bonds that constitute the portfolio.
- Immunization can be interpreted as "zero replication" in that the performance of the bond portfolio over the investment horizon replicates the zero-coupon bond that provides for perfect immunization. This zero-coupon bond has a maturity that matches the date of the single liability—there is no coupon reinvestment risk nor price risk as the bond is held to maturity (assuming no default).
- The risk to immunization is that as the yield curve shifts and twists, the cash flow yield on the bond portfolio does not match the change in the yield on the zero-coupon bond that would provide for perfect immunization.
- A sufficient, but not necessary, condition for immunization is a parallel (or shape-preserving) shift whereby all yields change by the same amount in the same direction. If the change in the cash flow yield is the same as that on the zero-coupon bond being replicated, immunization can be achieved even with a non-parallel shift to the yield curve.
- Structural risk to immunization arises from some non-parallel shifts and twists to the yield curve. This risk is reduced by minimizing the dispersion of cash flows in the portfolio, which can be accomplished by minimizing the convexity statistic for the portfolio. Concentrating the cash flows around the horizon date makes the immunizing portfolio closely track the zero-coupon bond that provides for perfect immunization.
- For multiple liabilities, one method of immunization is cash flow matching. A portfolio of high-quality zero-coupon or fixed-income bonds is purchased to match as closely as possible the amount and timing of the liabilities.

- A motive for cash flow matching can be accounting defeasance, whereby both the assets and liabilities are removed from the balance sheet.
- Immunization of multiple liabilities can be achieved by structuring and managing a portfolio of fixed-income bonds. Because the market values of the assets and liabilities differ, the strategy is to match the money durations. The money duration is the modified duration multiplied by the market value. The basis point value is a measure of money duration calculated by multiplying the money duration by 0.0001.
- The conditions to immunize multiple liabilities are that (1) the market value of assets is greater than or equal to the market value of the liabilities, (2) the asset basis point value (BPV) equals the liability BPV, and (3) the dispersion of cash flows and the convexity of assets are greater than those of the liabilities.
- A derivatives overlay—for example, interest rate futures contracts—can be used to immunize single or multiple liabilities.
- The number of futures contracts needed to immunize is the liability BPV minus the asset BPV, divided by the futures BPV. If the result is a positive number, the entity buys, or goes long, futures contracts. If the result is a negative number, the entity sells, or goes short, futures contracts. The futures BPV can be approximated by the BPV for the cheapest-to-deliver security divided by the conversion factor for the cheapest-to-deliver security.
- Contingent immunization adds active management of the surplus, which is the difference between the asset and liability market values, with the intent to reduce the overall cost of retiring the liabilities. In principle, any asset classes can be used for the active investment. The entity can choose to over-hedge or under-hedge the number of futures contracts needed for passive immunization.
- Liability-driven investing (LDI) often is used for complex rate-sensitive liabilities, such as those for a defined benefit pension plan. The retirement benefits for covered employees depend on many variables, such as years of employment, age at retirement, wage level at retirement, and expected lifetime. There are different measures for the liabilities: for instance, the accumulated benefit obligation (ABO) that is based on current wages and the projected benefit obligation (PBO) that is based on expected future wages. For each liability measure (ABO or PBO), a model is used to extract the effective duration and BPV.
- Interest rate swap overlays can be used to reduce the duration gap as measured by the asset and liability BPVs. There often is a large gap because pension funds hold sizable asset positions in equities that have low or zero effective durations and their liability durations are high.
- The hedging ratio is the percentage of the duration gap that is closed with the derivatives. A hedging ratio of zero implies no hedging. A hedging ratio of 100% implies immunization —that is, complete removal of interest rate risk.
- Strategic hedging is the active management of the hedging ratio. Because asset BPVs are less than liability BPVs in typical pension funds, the derivatives overlay requires the use of receive-fixed interest rate swaps. Because receive-fixed swaps gain value as current swap market rates fall, the fund manager could choose to raise the hedging ratio when lower rates are anticipated. If rates are expected to go up, the manager could strategically reduce the hedging ratio.
- An alternative to the receive-fixed interest rate swap is a purchased receiver swaption. This swaption confers to the buyer the right to enter the swap as the fixed-rate receiver. Because of its negative duration gap (asset BPV is less than liability BPV), the typical pension plan

suffers when interest rates fall and could become underfunded. The gain on the receiver swaption as rates decline offsets the losses on the balance sheet.

- Another alternative is a swaption collar, the combination of buying the receiver swaption and writing a payer swaption. The premium received on the payer swaption that is written offsets the premium needed to buy the receiver swaption.

- The choice among hedging with the receive-fixed swap, the purchased receiver swaption, and the swaption collar depends in part on the pension fund manager's view on future interest rates. If rates are expected to be low, the receive-fixed swap typically is the preferred derivative. If rates are expected to go up, the swaption collar can become attractive. And if rates are projected to reach a certain threshold that depends on the option costs and the strike rates, the purchased receiver swaption can become the favored choice.

- Model risks arise in LDI strategies because of the many assumptions in the models and approximations used to measure key parameters. For example, the liability BPV for the defined benefit pension plan depends on the choice of measure (ABO or PBO) and the assumptions that go into the model regarding future events (e.g., wage levels, time of retirement, and time of death).

- Spread risk in LDI strategies arises because it is common to assume equal changes in asset, liability, and hedging instrument yields when calculating the number of futures contracts, or the notional principal on an interest rate swap, to attain a particular hedging ratio. The assets and liabilities are often on corporate securities, however, and their spreads to benchmark yields can vary over time.

- The Credit Support Annex to the standard ISDA swap agreement often calls for collateralization by one or both counterparties to the contract. This requirement introduces the risk of exhausting available securities or cash assets to serve as collateral.

- Investing in a fund that tracks a bond market index offers the benefits of both diversification and low administrative costs. The deviation of the returns between the index and the fund is called tracking risk, or tracking error. Tracking risk arises when the fund manager chooses to buy only a subset of the index, a strategy called enhanced indexing, because fully replicating the index can be impractical as a result of the large number of bonds in the fixed-income universe.

- Corporate bonds are often illiquid. Capital requirements have reduced the incentive for broker/dealers to maintain inventory in thinly traded securities. The lack of active trading is a challenge for valuation. Matrix pricing uses available data on comparable securities to estimate the fair value of the illiquid bonds.

- The primary risk factors encountered by an investor tracking a bond index include decisions regarding duration (option-adjusted duration for callable bonds, convexity for possible large yield shifts, and key rate durations for non-parallel shifts) and portfolio weights (assigned by sector, credit quality, maturity, coupon rate, and issuer).

- Index replication is one method to establish a passive exposure to the bond market. The manager buys or sells bonds only when there are changes to the index. Full replication can be expensive, however, as well as infeasible for broad-based fixed-income indexes that include many illiquid bonds.

- Several enhancement strategies can reduce the costs to track a bond index: lowering trading costs, using models to identify undervalued bonds and to gauge relative value at varying points along the yield curve, over/under weighting specific credit sectors over the business cycle, and evaluating specific call features to identify value given large yield changes.

- Investors can obtain passive exposure to the bond market using mutual funds and exchange-traded funds that track a bond index. Shares in mutual funds are redeemable at the net asset value with a one-day time lag. Exchange-traded fund (ETF) shares have the advantage of trading on an exchange.
- A total return swap, an over-the-counter derivative, allows an institutional investor to transform an asset or liability from one asset category to another—for instance, from variable-rate cash flows referencing Libor to the total return on a particular bond index.
- A total return swap (TRS) can have some advantages over a direct investment in a bond mutual fund or ETF. As a derivative, it requires less initial cash outlay than direct investment in the bond portfolio for similar performance. A TRS also carries counterparty credit risk, however. As a customized over-the-counter product, a TRS can offer exposure to assets that are difficult to access directly, such as some high-yield and commercial loan investments.
- Selecting a particular bond index is a major decision for a fixed-income investment manager. Selection is guided by the specified goals and objectives for the investment. The decision should recognize several features of bond indexes: (1) Given that bonds have finite maturities, the duration of the index drifts down over time; (2) the composition of the index changes over time with the business cycle and maturity preferences of issuers; and (3) value-weighted indexes assign larger shares to borrowers having more debt, leading to the "bums problem" that bond index investors can become overly exposed to leveraged firms.
- A laddered bond portfolio is a common investment strategy in the wealth management industry. The laddered portfolio offers "diversification" over the yield curve compared with "bullet" or "barbell" portfolios. This structure is especially attractive in stable, upwardly sloped yield curve environments as maturing short-term debt is replaced with higher-yielding long-term debt at the back of the ladder.
- A laddered portfolio offers an increase in convexity because the cash flows have greater dispersions than a more concentrated (bullet) portfolio.
- A laddered portfolio provides liquidity in that it always contains a soon-to-mature bond that could provide high-quality, low-duration collateral on a repo contract if needed.
- A laddered portfolio can be constructed with fixed-maturity corporate bond ETFs that have a designated maturity and credit risk profile.

REFERENCES

Aakko, Markus, and Rene Martel. 2013. "Understanding Derivative Overlays, in All Their Forms." PIMCO (February).

Adams, James, and Donald J. Smith. 2009. "Mind the Gap: Using Derivatives Overlays to Hedge Pension Duration." *Financial Analysts Journal*, vol. 65, no. 4 (July/August): 60–67.

Adams, James, and Donald J. Smith. 2013. "Synthetic Floating-Rate Debt: An Example of an Asset-Driven Liability Structure." *Journal of Applied Corporate Finance*, vol. 25, no. 4 (Fall): 50–59.

Fabozzi, Frank J. 2013. *Bond Markets, Analysis, and Strategies*, 8th ed. Upper Saddle River, NJ: Prentice Hall.

Hayat, Usman, and Matt Orsagh. 2015. *Environmental, Social and Governance Issues in Investing: A Guide for Investment Professionals*. Charlottesville, VA: CFA Institute.

Roxburgh, Charles, Susan Lund, and John Piotrowski. 2011. "Mapping Global Capital Markets 2011." McKinsey Global Institute.

Siegel, L.B. 2003. *Benchmarks and Investment Management*. Charlottesville, VA: Research Foundation of the Association for Investment Management and Research.

Smith, Donald J. 2014. *Bond Math: The Theory behind the Formulas*, 2nd ed. Hoboken, NJ: Wiley Finance.

Staal, Arne, Marco Corsi, Sara Shores, and Chris Woida. 2015. "A Factor Approach to Smart Beta Development in Fixed Income." *Journal of Index Investing*, vol. 6, no. 1: 98–110.

Volpert, Kenneth E. 2012. "Introduction to Bond Portfolio Management." In *Handbook of Fixed-Income Securities*, 8th ed. Edited by Frank J. Fabozzi. New York: McGraw Hill: 1123–1150.

Yesalavich, Donna K. 2010. "CME Pulls Back on ETF Futures." *Wall Street Journal*, 16 December.

PRACTICE PROBLEMS

The following information relates to Questions 1–8

Serena Soto is a risk management specialist with Liability Protection Advisors. Trey Hudgens, CFO of Kiest Manufacturing, enlists Soto's help with three projects. The first project is to defease some of Kiest's existing fixed-rate bonds that are maturing in each of the next three years. The bonds have no call or put provisions and pay interest annually. Exhibit 1 presents the payment schedule for the bonds.

EXHIBIT 1   Kiest Manufacturing Bond Payment Schedule
As of 1 October 2017

Maturity Date	Payment Amount
1 October 2018	$9,572,000
1 October 2019	$8,392,000
1 October 2020	$8,200,000

The second project for Soto is to help Hudgens immunize a $20 million portfolio of liabilities. The liabilities range from 3.00 years to 8.50 years with a Macaulay duration of 5.34 years, cash flow yield of 3.25%, portfolio convexity of 33.05, and basis point value (BPV) of $10,505. Soto suggested employing a duration-matching strategy using one of the three AAA rated bond portfolios presented in Exhibit 2.

EXHIBIT 2   Possible AAA Rated Duration-Matching Portfolios

	Portfolio A	Portfolio B	Portfolio C
Bonds (term, coupon)	4.5 years, 2.63%	3.0 years, 2.00%	1.5 years, 1.25%
	7.0 years, 3.50%	6.0 years, 3.25%	11.5 years, 4.38%
		8.5 years, 3.88%	
Macaulay duration	5.35	5.34	5.36
Cash flow yield	3.16%	3.33%	3.88%
Convexity	31.98	34.51	50.21
BPV	$10,524	$10,506	$10,516

Soto explains to Hudgens that the underlying duration-matching strategy is based on the following three assumptions.

1. Yield curve shifts in the future will be parallel.
2. Bond types and quality will closely match those of the liabilities.
3. The portfolio will be rebalanced by buying or selling bonds rather than using derivatives.

The third project for Soto is to make a significant direct investment in broadly diversified global bonds for Kiest's pension plan. Kiest has a young workforce, and thus, the plan has a long-term investment horizon. Hudgens needs Soto's help to select a benchmark index that is appropriate for Kiest's young workforce and avoids the "bums" problem. Soto discusses three benchmark candidates, presented in Exhibit 3.

EXHIBIT 3   Global Bond Index Benchmark Candidates

Index Name	Effective Duration	Index Characteristics
Global Aggregate	7.73	Market cap weighted; Treasuries, corporates, agency, securitized debt
Global Aggregate GDP Weighted	7.71	Same as Global Aggregate, except GDP weighted
Global High Yield	4.18	GDP weighted; sovereign, agency, corporate debt

With the benchmark selected, Hudgens provides guidelines to Soto directing her to (1) use the most cost-effective method to track the benchmark and (2) provide low tracking error.

After providing Hudgens with advice on direct investment, Soto offered him additional information on alternative indirect investment strategies using (1) bond mutual funds, (2) exchange-traded funds (ETFs), and (3) total return swaps. Hudgens expresses interest in using bond mutual funds rather than the other strategies for the following reasons.

Reason 1.   Total return swaps have much higher transaction costs and initial cash outlay than bond mutual funds.

Reason 2.   Unlike bond mutual funds, bond ETFs can trade at discounts to their underlying indexes, and those discounts can persist.

Reason 3.   Bond mutual funds can be traded throughout the day at the net asset value of the underlying bonds.

1. Based on Exhibit 1, Kiest's liabilities would be classified as:
   A. Type I.
   B. Type II.
   C. Type III.

2. Based on Exhibit 2, the portfolio with the greatest structural risk is:
   A. Portfolio A.
   B. Portfolio B.
   C. Portfolio C.

3. Which portfolio in Exhibit 2 fails to meet the requirements to achieve immunization for multiple liabilities?
   A. Portfolio A
   B. Portfolio B
   C. Portfolio C

4. Based on Exhibit 2, relative to Portfolio C, Portfolio B:
   A. has higher cash flow reinvestment risk.
   B. is a more desirable portfolio for liquidity management.
   C. provides less protection from yield curve shifts and twists.

5. Soto's three assumptions regarding the duration-matching strategy indicate the presence of:
   A. model risk.
   B. spread risk.
   C. counterparty credit risk.

6. The global bond benchmark in Exhibit 3 that is *most* appropriate for Kiest to use is the:
   A. Global Aggregate Index.
   B. Global High Yield Index.
   C. Global Aggregate GDP Weighted Index.

7. To meet both of Hudgens's guidelines for the pension's bond fund investment, Soto should recommend:
   A. pure indexing.
   B. enhanced indexing.
   C. active management.

8. Which of Hudgens's reasons for choosing bond mutual funds as an investment vehicle is correct?
   A. Reason 1
   B. Reason 2
   C. Reason 3

The following information relates to questions 9–17

SD&R Capital (SD&R), a global asset management company, specializes in fixed-income investments. Molly Compton, chief investment officer, is meeting with a prospective client, Leah Mowery of DePuy Financial Company (DFC).

Mowery informs Compton that DFC's previous fixed-income manager focused on the interest rate sensitivities of assets and liabilities when making asset allocation decisions. Compton explains that, in contrast, SD&R's investment process first analyzes the size and timing of client liabilities, then builds an asset portfolio based on the interest rate sensitivity of those liabilities.

Compton notes that SD&R generally uses actively managed portfolios designed to earn a return in excess of the benchmark portfolio. For clients interested in passive exposure to fixed-income instruments, SD&R offers two additional approaches.

Approach 1.   Seeks to fully replicate the Bloomberg Barclays US Aggregate Bond Index.

Approach 2.   Follows an enhanced indexing process for a subset of the bonds included in the
               Bloomberg Barclays US Aggregate Bond Index. Approach 2 may also be
               customized to reflect client preferences.

To illustrate SD&R's immunization approach for controlling portfolio interest rate risk,
Compton discusses a hypothetical portfolio composed of two non-callable, investment-grade
bonds. The portfolio has a weighted average yield-to-maturity of 9.55%, a weighted average
coupon rate of 10.25%, and a cash flow yield of 9.85%.

Mowery informs Compton that DFC has a single $500 million liability due in nine
years, and she wants SD&R to construct a bond portfolio that earns a rate of return sufficient
to pay off the obligation. Mowery expresses concern about the risks associated with an
immunization strategy for this obligation. In response, Compton makes the following
statements about liability-driven investing:

Statement 1.   Although the amount and date of SD&R's liability is known with certainty,
                measurement errors associated with key parameters relative to interest rate
                changes may adversely affect the bond portfolios.
Statement 2.   A cash flow matching strategy will mitigate the risk from non-parallel shifts in
                the yield curve.

Compton provides the four US dollar–denominated bond portfolios in Exhibit 1 for
consideration. Compton explains that the portfolios consist of non-callable, investment-grade
corporate and government bonds of various maturities because zero-coupon bonds are
unavailable.

EXHIBIT 1   Proposed Bond Portfolios to Immunize SD&R Single Liability

	Portfolio 1	Portfolio 2	Portfolio 3	Portfolio 4
Cash flow yield	7.48%	7.50%	7.53%	7.51%
Average time to maturity	11.2 years	9.8 years	9.0 years	10.1 years
Macaulay duration	9.8	8.9	8.0	9.1
Market value weighted duration	9.1	8.5	7.8	8.6
Convexity	154.11	131.75	130.00	109.32

The discussion turns to benchmark selection. DFC's previous fixed-income manager used a
custom benchmark with the following characteristics:

Characteristic 1.   The benchmark portfolio invests only in investment-grade bonds of US
                     corporations with a minimum issuance size of $250 million.
Characteristic 2.   Valuation occurs on a weekly basis, because many of the bonds in the
                     index are valued weekly.
Characteristic 3.   Historical prices and portfolio turnover are available for review.

Compton explains that, in order to evaluate the asset allocation process, fixed-income
portfolios should have an appropriate benchmark. Mowery asks for benchmark advice
regarding DFC's portfolio of short-term and intermediate-term bonds, all denominated in US
dollars. Compton presents three possible benchmarks in Exhibit 2.

EXHIBIT 2   Proposed Benchmark Portfolios

Benchmark	Index	Composition	Duration
1	Bloomberg Barclays US Bond Index	80% US government bonds 20% US corporate bonds	8.7
2 Index Blend	50% Bloomberg Barclays US Corporate Bond Index	100% US corporate bonds	7.5
	50% Bloomberg Barclays Short-Term Treasury Index	100% short-term US government debt	0.5
3	Bloomberg Barclays Global Aggregate Bond Index	60% EUR-denominated corporate bonds	12.3
		40% US-denominated corporate debt	

9. The investment process followed by DFC's previous fixed-income manager is *best* described as:
    A. asset-driven liabilities.
    B. liability-driven investing.
    C. asset–liability management.

10. Relative to Approach 2 of gaining passive exposure, an advantage of Approach 1 is that it:
    A. reduces the need for frequent rebalancing.
    B. limits the need to purchase bonds that are thinly traded.
    C. provides a higher degree of portfolio risk diversification.

11. Relative to Approach 1 of gaining passive exposure, an advantage of Approach 2 is that it:
    A. minimizes tracking error.
    B. requires less risk analysis.
    C. is more appropriate for socially responsible investors.

12. The two-bond hypothetical portfolio's immunization goal is to lock in a rate of return equal to:
    A. 9.55%.
    B. 9.85%.
    C. 10.25%.

13. Which of Compton's statements about liability-driven investing is (are) correct?
    A. Statement 1 only.
    B. Statement 2 only.
    C. Both Statement 1 and Statement 2.

14. Based on Exhibit 1, which of the portfolios will *best* immunize SD&R's single liability?
    A. Portfolio 1
    B. Portfolio 2
    C. Portfolio 3

15. Which of the portfolios in Exhibit 1 *best* minimizes the structural risk to a single-liability immunization strategy?
    A. Portfolio 1
    B. Portfolio 3
    C. Portfolio 4

16. Which of the custom benchmark's characteristics violates the requirements for an appropriate benchmark portfolio?
    A. Characteristic 1
    B. Characteristic 2
    C. Characteristic 3

17. Based on DFC's bond holdings and Exhibit 2, Compton should recommend:
    A. Benchmark 1.
    B. Benchmark 2.
    C. Benchmark 3.

The following information relates to questions 18–23

Doug Kepler, the newly hired chief financial officer for the City of Radford, asks the deputy financial manager, Hui Ng, to prepare an analysis of the current investment portfolio and the city's current and future obligations. The city has multiple liabilities of different amounts and maturities relating to the pension fund, infrastructure repairs, and various other obligations.

Ng observes that the current fixed-income portfolio is structured to match the duration of each liability. Previously, this structure caused the city to access a line of credit for temporary mismatches resulting from changes in the term structure of interest rates.

Kepler asks Ng for different strategies to manage the interest rate risk of the city's fixed-income investment portfolio against one-time shifts in the yield curve. Ng considers two different strategies:

Strategy 1: Immunization of the single liabilities using zero-coupon bonds held to maturity.
Strategy 2: Immunization of the single liabilities using coupon-bearing bonds while continuously matching duration.

The city also manages a separate, smaller bond portfolio for the Radford School District. During the next five years, the school district has obligations for school expansions and renovations. The funds needed for those obligations are invested in the Bloomberg Barclays US Aggregate Index. Kepler asks Ng which portfolio management strategy would be most efficient in mimicking this index.

A Radford School Board member has stated that she prefers a bond portfolio structure that provides diversification over time, as well as liquidity. In addressing the board member's inquiry, Ng examines a bullet portfolio, a barbell portfolio, and a laddered portfolio.

18. A disadvantage of Strategy 1 is that:
    A. price risk still exists.
    B. interest rate volatility introduces risk to effective matching.
    C. there may not be enough bonds available to match all liabilities.

19. Which duration measure should be matched when implementing Strategy 2?
    A. Key rate
    B. Modified
    C. Macaulay

20. An upward shift in the yield curve on Strategy 2 will *most likely* result in the:
    A. price effect canceling the coupon reinvestment effect.
    B. price effect being greater than the coupon reinvestment effect.
    C. coupon reinvestment effect being greater than the price effect.

21. The effects of a non-parallel shift in the yield curve on Strategy 2 can be reduced by:
    A. minimizing the convexity of the bond portfolio.
    B. maximizing the cash flow yield of the bond portfolio.
    C. minimizing the difference between liability duration and bond-portfolio duration.

22. Ng's response to Kepler's question about the most efficient portfolio management strategy should be:
    A. full replication.
    B. active management.
    C. an enhanced indexing strategy.

23. Which portfolio structure should Ng recommend that would satisfy the school board member's preference?
    A. Bullet portfolio
    B. Barbell portfolio
    C. Laddered portfolio

The following information relates to questions 24–26

Chaopraya Av is an investment advisor for high-net-worth individuals. One of her clients, Schuylkill Cy, plans to fund her grandson's college education and considers two options:

Option 1. Contribute a lump sum of $300,000 in 10 years.
Option 2. Contribute four level annual payments of $76,500 starting in 10 years.

The grandson will start college in 10 years. Cy seeks to immunize the contribution today.
   For Option 1, Av calculates the present value of the $300,000 as $234,535. To immunize the future single outflow, Av considers three bond portfolios given that no zero-coupon government bonds are available. The three portfolios consist of non-callable, fixed-rate, coupon-bearing government bonds considered free of default risk. Av prepares a comparative analysis of the three portfolios, presented in Exhibit 1.

EXHIBIT 1   Results of Comparative Analysis of Potential Portfolios

	Portfolio A	Portfolio B	Portfolio C
Market value	$235,727	$233,428	$235,306
Cash flow yield	2.504%	2.506%	2.502%
Macaulay duration	9.998	10.002	9.503
Convexity	119.055	121.498	108.091

Av evaluates the three bond portfolios and selects one to recommend to Cy.

24. **Recommend** the portfolio in Exhibit 1 that would *best* achieve the immunization. **Justify** your response.

Template for Question 24

Recommend the portfolio in Exhibit 1 that would *best* achieve the immunization. (circle one)	**Justify** your response.
Portfolio A	
Portfolio B	
Portfolio C	

Cy and Av now discuss Option 2.

Av estimates the present value of the four future cash flows as $230,372, with a money duration of $2,609,700 and convexity of 135.142. She considers three possible portfolios to immunize the future payments, as presented in Exhibit 2.

EXHIBIT 2   Data for Bond Portfolios to Immunize Four Annual Contributions

	Portfolio 1	**Portfolio 2**	**Portfolio 3**
Market value	$245,178	$248,230	$251,337
Cash flow yield	2.521%	2.520%	2.516%
Money duration	2,609,981	2,609,442	2,609,707
Convexity	147.640	139.851	132.865

25. **Determine** the *most appropriate* immunization portfolio in Exhibit 2. **Justify** your decision.

Template for Question 25

Determine the *most appropriate* immunization portfolio in Exhibit 2. (circle one)	**Justify** your decision.
Portfolio 1	
Portfolio 2	
Portfolio 3	

After selecting a portfolio to immunize Cy's multiple future outflows, Av prepares a report on how this immunization strategy would respond to various interest rate scenarios. The scenario analysis is presented in Exhibit 3.

EXHIBIT 3   Projected Portfolio Response to Interest Rate Scenarios

	Immunizing Portfolio	Outflow Portfolio	Difference
Upward parallel shift			
ΔMarket value	−6,410	−6,427	18
ΔCash flow yield	0.250%	0.250%	0.000%
ΔPortfolio BPV	−9	−8	−1
Downward parallel shift			
ΔMarket value	6,626	6,622	4
ΔCash flow yield	−0.250%	−0.250%	0.000%
ΔPortfolio BPV	9	8	1
Steepening twist			
ΔMarket value	−1,912	347	−2,259
ΔCash flow yield	0.074%	−0.013%	0.087%
ΔPortfolio BPV	−3	0	−3
Flattening twist			
ΔMarket value	1,966	−343	2,309
ΔCash flow yield	−0.075%	0.013%	−0.088%
ΔPortfolio BPV	3	0	3

26.   **Discuss** the effectiveness of Av's immunization strategy in terms of duration gaps.

CHAPTER 11

OVERVIEW OF EQUITY PORTFOLIO MANAGEMENT

James Clunie, PhD, CFA
James Alan Finnegan, CAIA, RMA, CFA

LEARNING OUTCOMES

The candidate should be able to:

- describe the roles of equities in the overall portfolio;
- describe how an equity manager's investment universe can be segmented;
- describe the types of income and costs associated with owning and managing an equity portfolio and their potential effects on portfolio performance;
- describe the potential benefits of shareholder engagement and the role an equity manager might play in shareholder engagement;
- describe rationales for equity investment across the passive–active spectrum.

1. INTRODUCTION

Equities represent a sizable portion of the global investment universe and thus often represent a primary component of investors' portfolios. Rationales for investing in equities include potential participation in the growth and earnings prospects of an economy's corporate sector as well as an ownership interest in a range of business entities by size, economic activity, and geographical scope. Publicly traded equities are generally more liquid than other asset classes and thus may enable investors to more easily monitor price trends and purchase or sell securities with low transaction costs.

This chapter provides an overview of equity portfolio management. Section 2 discusses the roles of equities in a portfolio. Section 3 discusses the equity investment universe, including several ways the universe can be segmented. Section 4 covers the income and costs in an equity portfolio. Section 5 discusses shareholder engagement between equity investors and the companies in which they invest. Section 6 discusses equity investment across the passive–active investment spectrum. A summary of key points completes the chapter.

2. THE ROLES OF EQUITIES IN A PORTFOLIO

Equities provide several roles in (or benefits to) an overall portfolio, such as capital appreciation, dividend income, diversification with other asset classes, and a potential hedge against inflation. In addition to these benefits, client investment considerations play an important role for portfolio managers when deciding to include equities in portfolios.

2.1. Capital Appreciation

Long-term returns on equities, driven predominantly by capital appreciation, have historically been among the highest among major asset classes. Exhibit 1 demonstrates the average annual real returns on equities versus bonds and bills—both globally and within various countries— from 1967–2016. With a few exceptions, equities outperformed both bonds and bills, in particular, during this period across the world.

EXHIBIT 1   Real Returns on Equities (1967–2016)

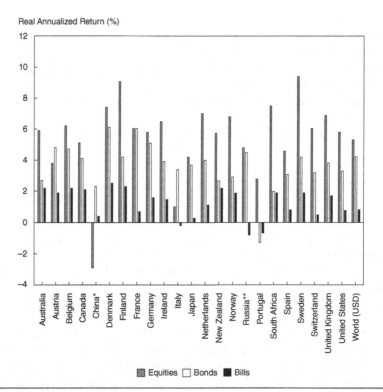

* China data are from 1993 to 2016.

** Russia data are from 1995 to 2016.

Source: Credit Suisse Global Investment Returns Yearbook 2017, Summary Edition.

Equities tend to outperform other asset classes during periods of strong economic growth, and they tend to underperform other asset classes during weaker economic periods. Capital (or price) appreciation of equities often occurs when investing in companies with growth in earnings, cash flows, and/or revenues—as well as in companies with competitive success. Capital appreciation can occur, for example, in such growth-oriented companies as small technology companies as well as in large, mature companies where management successfully reduces costs or engages in value-added acquisitions.

2.2. Dividend Income

The most common sources of income for an equity portfolio are dividends. Companies may choose to distribute internally generated cash flows as common dividends rather than reinvest the cash flows in projects, particularly when suitable projects do not exist or available projects have a high cost of equity or a low probability of future value creation. Large, well-established corporations often provide dividend payments that increase in value over time, although there are no assurances that common dividend payments from these corporations will grow or even be maintained. In addition to common dividends, preferred dividends can provide dividend income to those shareholders owning preferred shares.

Dividends have comprised a significant component of long-term total returns for equity investors. Over shorter periods of time, however, the proportion of equity returns from dividends (reflected as dividend yield) can vary considerably relative to capital gains or losses. Exhibit 2 illustrates this effect of dividend returns relative to annual total returns on the S&P 500 Index from 1936 through 2016. Since 1990, the dividend yield on the S&P 500 has been in the 1–3% range; thus, the effect of dividends can clearly be significant during periods of weak equity market performance. Also note that the dividend yield may vary considerably by sector within the S&P 500.

EXHIBIT 2   S&P 500 Dividend Contribution (1936–2016)

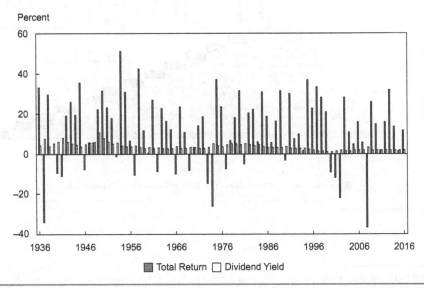

Source: Bloomberg.

2.3. Diversification with Other Asset Classes

Individual equities clearly have unique characteristics, although the correlation of returns among equities is often high. In a portfolio context, however, equities can provide meaningful diversification benefits when combined with other asset classes (assuming less than perfect correlation). Recall that a major reason why portfolios can effectively reduce risk (typically expressed as standard deviation of returns) is that combining securities whose returns are less than perfectly correlated reduces the standard deviation of the diversified portfolio below the weighted average of the standard deviations of the individual investments. The challenge in diversifying risk is to find assets that have a correlation that is much lower than +1.0.

Exhibit 3 provides a correlation matrix across various global equity indexes and other asset classes using total monthly returns from January 2001 to February 2017.[1] The correlation matrix shows that during this period, various broad equity indexes and, to a lesser extent, country equity indexes were highly correlated with each other. Conversely, both the broad and country equity indexes were considerably less correlated with indexes in other asset classes, notably global treasury bonds and gold. Overall, Exhibit 3 indicates that combining equities with other asset classes can result in portfolio diversification benefits.

EXHIBIT 3   Correlation Matrix, January 2001 to February 2017

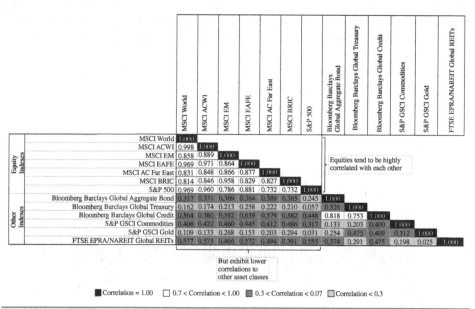

Source: Morningstar Direct.

---

[1]Monthly return data cover January 2001 to February 2017 for all indexes except the FTSE EPRA/NAREIT Global Real Estate Index (whose inception date was November 2008).

It is important to note that correlations are not constant over time. During a long historical period, the correlation of returns between two asset classes may be low, but in any given period, the correlation can differ from the long term. Correlation estimates can vary based on the capital market dynamics during the period when the correlations are measured. During periods of market crisis, correlations across asset classes and among equities themselves often increase and reduce the benefit of diversification. As with correlations, volatility (standard deviation) of asset class returns may also vary over time.

2.4. Hedge Against Inflation

Some individual equities or sectors can provide some protection against inflation, although the ability to do so varies. For example, certain companies may be successful at passing along higher input costs (such as raw materials, energy, or wages) to customers. This ability to pass along costs to customers can protect a company's or industry's profit margin and cash flow and can be reflected in their stock prices. As another example, companies within sectors that produce broad-based commodities (e.g., oil or industrial metals producers) can more directly benefit from increases in commodity prices. Although individual equities or sectors can protect against inflation, the success of equities as an asset class in hedging inflation has been mixed. Certain empirical studies have indeed shown that real returns on equities and inflation have positive correlation over the long-term, thus in theory forming a hedge. However, the degree of correlation typically varies by country and is dependent on the time period assessed. In fact, for severe inflationary periods, some studies have shown that real returns on equities and inflation have been *negatively* correlated. When assessing the relationship between equity returns and inflation, investors should be aware that inflation is typically a lagging indicator of the business cycle, while equity prices are often a leading indicator.

2.5. Client Considerations for Equities in a Portfolio

The inclusion of equities in a portfolio can be driven by a client's goals or needs. A client's investment considerations are typically described in an investment policy statement (IPS), which establishes, among other things, a client's return objectives, risk tolerance, constraints, and unique circumstances. By understanding these client considerations, a financial adviser or wealth manager can determine whether—and how much—equities should be in a client's portfolio.

Equity investments are often characterized by such attributes as growth potential, income generation, risk and return volatility, and sensitivity to various macro-economic variables (e.g., energy prices, GDP growth, interest rates, and inflation). As a result, a portfolio manager can adapt such specific factors to an equity investor's investment goals and risk tolerance. For example, a risk-averse and conservative investor may prefer some exposure to well-established companies with strong and stable cash flow that pay meaningful dividends. Conversely, a growth-oriented investor with an aggressive risk tolerance may prefer small or large growth-oriented companies (e.g., those in the social media or alternative energy sectors).

Wealth managers and financial advisers often consider the following investment objectives and constraints when deciding to include equities (or asset classes in general, for that matter) in a client's portfolio:

- *Risk objective* addresses how risk is measured (e.g., in absolute or relative terms); the investor's willingness to take risk; the investor's ability to take risk; and the investor's specific risk objectives.
- *Return objective* addresses how returns are measured (e.g., in absolute or relative terms); stated return objectives.
- *Liquidity requirement* is a constraint in which cash is needed for anticipated or unanticipated events.
- *Time horizon* is the time period associated with an investment objective (e.g., short term, long term, or some combination of the two).
- *Tax concerns* include tax policies that can affect investor returns; for example, dividends may be taxed at a different rate than capital gains.
- *Legal and regulatory factors* are external factors imposed by governmental, regulatory, or oversight authorities.
- *Unique circumstances* are an investor's considerations other than liquidity requirements, time horizon, or tax concerns that may constrain portfolio choices. These considerations may include environmental, social, and governance (ESG) issues or religious preferences.

ESG considerations often occur at the request of clients because interest in sustainable investing has grown. With regard to equities, these considerations often determine the suitability of certain sectors or individual company stocks for designated investor portfolios. Historically, ESG approaches used by portfolio managers have largely represented **negative screening** (or exclusionary screening), which refers to the practice of excluding certain sectors or companies that deviate from accepted standards in such areas as human rights or environmental concerns. More recently, portfolio managers have increasingly focused on **positive screening** or **best-in-class** approaches, which attempt to identify companies or sectors that score most favorably with regard to ESG-related risks and/or opportunities. **Thematic investing** is another approach that focuses on investing in companies within a specific sector or following a specific theme, such as energy efficiency or climate change. **Impact investing** is a related approach that seeks to achieve targeted social or environmental objectives along with measurable financial returns through engagement with a company or by direct investment in projects or companies.

EXAMPLE 1 Roles of Equities

Alex Chang, Lin Choi, and Frank Huber manage separate equity portfolios for the same investment firm. Chang's portfolio objective is conservative in nature, with a regular stream of income as the primary investment objective. Choi's portfolio is more aggressive in nature, with a long-term horizon and with growth as the primary objective. Finally, Huber's portfolio consists of wealthy entrepreneurs who are concerned about rising inflation and wish to preserve the purchasing power of their wealth.

Discuss the investment approach that each portfolio manager would likely use to achieve his or her portfolio objectives.

Solution: Given that his portfolio is focused on a regular stream of income, Chang is likely to focus on companies with regular dividend income. More specifically, Chang is likely to invest in large, well-established companies with stable or growing dividend payments. With a long-term horizon, Choi is most interested in capital appreciation of her portfolio, so she is likely to focus on companies with earnings growth and competitive success. Finally, Huber's clients are concerned about the effects of inflation, so he will likely seek to invest in shares of companies that can provide an inflation hedge. Huber would likely seek companies that can successfully pass on higher input costs to their customers, and he may also seek commodity producers that may benefit from rising commodity prices.

3. EQUITY INVESTMENT UNIVERSE

Given the extensive range of companies in which an equity portfolio manager may invest, an important task for the manager is to segment companies or sectors according to similar characteristics. This segmentation enables portfolio managers to better evaluate and analyze their equity investment universe, and it can help with portfolio diversification. Several approaches to segmenting the equity investment universe are discussed in the following sections.

3.1. Segmentation by Size and Style

A popular approach to segmenting the equity universe incorporates two factors: (1) size and (2) style. Size is typically measured by market capitalization and often categorized by large cap, mid cap, and small cap. Style is typically classified as value, growth, or a combination of value and growth (typically termed "blend" or "core"). In addition, style is often determined through a "scoring" system that incorporates multiple metrics or ratios, such as price-to-book ratios, price-to-earnings ratios, earnings growth, dividend yield, and book value growth. These metrics are then typically "scored" individually for each company, assigned certain weights, and then aggregated. The result is a composite score that determines where the company's stock is positioned along the value–growth spectrum. A combination of growth and value style is not uncommon, particularly for large corporations that have both mature and higher growth business lines.

Exhibit 4 illustrates a common matrix that reflects size and style dimensions. Each category in the matrix can be represented by companies with considerably different business activities. For example, both a small, mature metal fabricating business and a small health care services provider may fall in the Small Cap Value category. In practice, individual stocks may not clearly fall into one of the size/style categories. As a result, the size/style matrix tends to be more of a scatter plot than a simple set of nine categories. An example of a scatter plot is demonstrated in Exhibit 5, which includes all listed equities on the New York Stock Exchange as of March 2017. Each company represents a single dot in Exhibit 5. This more granular representation enables the expansion of size and style categories, such as blue chip and micro-cap companies in size and deep value and high growth in style. It should be noted that Morningstar applies the term "core" for those stocks in which neither value nor growth characteristics dominate, and the term "blend" for those funds with a combination of both growth and value stocks or mostly core stocks.

EXHIBIT 4   Equity Size and Style Matrix

		Investment Style		
		Value	Core	Growth
Company Size (Market Cap)	Large Cap	Large Cap value	Large Cap core	Large Cap growth
	Mid Cap	Mid Cap value	Mid Cap core	Mid Cap growth
	Small Cap	Small Cap value	Small Cap core	Small Cap growth

Source: Morningstar.

EXHIBIT 5   Equity Size and Style Scatter Plot

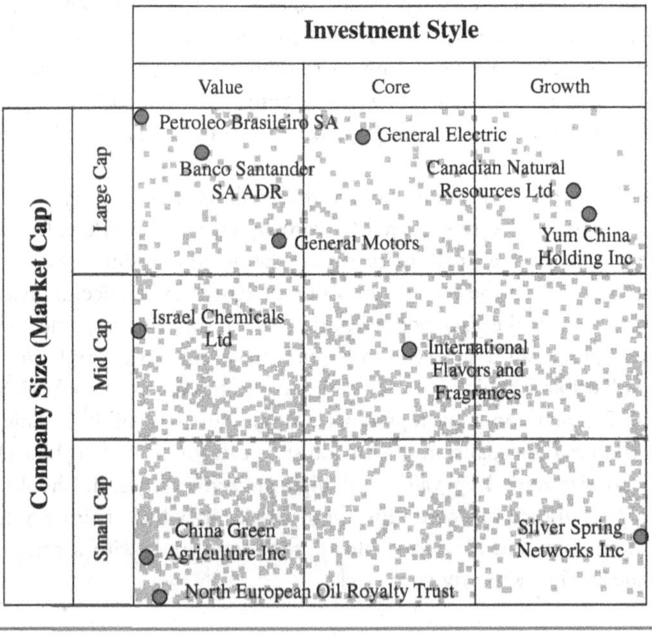

Source: Morningstar Direct.

Segmentation by size/style can provide several advantages for portfolio managers. First, portfolio managers can construct an overall equity portfolio that reflects desired risk, return, and income characteristics in a relatively straightforward and manageable way. Second, given the broad range of companies within each segment, segmentation by size/style results in diversification across economic sectors or industries. Third, active equity managers—that is, those seeking to outperform a given benchmark portfolio—can construct performance benchmarks for specific size/style segments. Generally, large investment management firms may have sizable teams dedicated toward specific size/style categories, while small firms may specialize in a specific size/style category, particularly mid-cap and small-cap companies, seeking to outperform a standard benchmark or comparable peer group.

The final advantage of segmentation by size/style is that it allows a portfolio to reflect a company's maturity and potentially changing growth/value orientation. Specifically, many companies that undertake an IPO (initial public offering) are small and in a growth phase, and thus they may fall in the small-cap growth category. If these companies can successfully grow, their size may ultimately move to mid cap or even large cap, while their style may conceivably shift from high growth to value or a combination of growth and value (e.g., a growth and income stock). Accordingly, over the life cycle of companies, investor preferences for these companies may shift increasingly from capital appreciation to dividend income. In addition, segmentation also helps fund managers adjust holdings over time—for example, when stocks that were previously considered to be in the growth category mature and possibly become value stocks. The key disadvantages of segmentation by size/style are that the categories may change over time and may be defined differently among investors.

3.2. Segmentation by Geography

Another common approach to equity universe segmentation is by geography. This approach is typically based on the stage of markets' macroeconomic development and wealth. Common geographic categories are *developed markets*, *emerging markets*, and *frontier markets*. Exhibit 6 demonstrates the commonly used geographic segmentation of international equity indexes according to MSCI. Other major index providers—such as FTSE, Standard & Poor's, and Russell—also provide similar types of international equity indexes.

Geographic segmentation is useful to equity investors who have considerable exposure to their domestic market and want to diversify by investing in global equities. A key weakness of geographic segmentation is that investing in a specific market (e.g., market index) may provide lower-than-expected exposure to that market. As an example, many large companies domiciled in the United States, Europe, or Asia may be global in nature as opposed to considerable focus on their domicile. Another key weakness of geographic segmentation is potential currency risk when investing in different global equity markets.

EXHIBIT 6   MSCI International Equity Indexes (as of November 2016)

Developed Markets

Americas	Europe and Middle East	Pacific
Canada	Austria	Australia
United States	Belgium	Hong Kong SAR
	Denmark	Japan
	Finland	New Zealand
	France	Singapore
	Germany	
	Ireland	
	Israel	
	Italy	
	Netherlands	
	Norway	
	Portugal	
	Spain	
	Sweden	
	Switzerland	
	United Kingdom	

Emerging Markets

Americas	Europe, Middle East, and Africa	Asia Pacific
Brazil	Czech Republic	Chinese mainland
Chile	Egypt	India
Colombia	Greece	Indonesia
Mexico	Hungary	Korea
Peru	Poland	Malaysia
	Qatar	Philippines
	Russia	Taiwan Region
	South Africa	Thailand
	Turkey	Pakistan
	United Arab Emirates	

Frontier Markets

Americas	Europe and CIS	Africa	Middle East	Asia
Argentina	Croatia	Kenya	Bahrain	Bangladesh
	Estonia	Mauritius	Jordan	Sri Lanka
	Lithuania	Morocco	Kuwait	Vietnam
	Kazakhstan	Nigeria	Lebanon	
	Romania	Tunisia	Oman	
	Serbia			
	Slovenia			

Notes:

1. The following markets are not included in the developed, emerging, or frontier indexes but have their own market-specific indexes: Saudi Arabia, Jamaica, Trinidad & Tobago, Bosnia Herzegovina, Bulgaria, Ukraine, Botswana, Ghana, Zimbabwe, and Palestine.
2. Pakistan was reclassified from the frontier market to the emerging market category as of May 2017.
3. CIS: Commonwealth of Independent States (formerly the USSR).

3.3. Segmentation by Economic Activity

Economic activity is another approach that portfolio managers may use to segment the equity universe. Most commonly used equity classification systems group companies into industries/sectors using either a *production-oriented* approach or a *market-oriented* approach. The production-oriented approach groups companies that manufacture similar products or use similar inputs in their manufacturing processes. The market-oriented approach groups companies based on the markets they serve, the way revenue is earned, and the way customers use companies' products. For example, using a production-oriented approach, a coal company may be classified in the basic materials or mining sector. However, using a market-oriented approach, this same coal company may be classified in the energy sector given the primary market (heating) for the use of coal. As another example, a commercial airline carrier may be classified in the transportation sector using the production-oriented approach, while the same company may be classified in the travel and leisure sector using the market-oriented approach.

Four main global classification systems segment the equity universe by economic activity: (1) the Global Industry Classification Standard (GICS); (2) the Industrial Classification Benchmark (ICB); (3) the Thomson Reuters Business Classification (TRBC); and (4) the Russell Global Sectors Classification (RGS). The GICS uses a market-oriented approach, while the ICB, TRBC, and RGS all use a production-oriented approach. These classification systems help standardize industry definitions so that portfolio managers can compare and analyze companies and industries/sectors. In addition, the classification systems are useful in the creation of industry performance benchmarks.

Exhibit 7 compares the four primary classification systems mentioned. Each system is classified broadly and then increasingly more granular to compare companies and their underlying businesses.

EXHIBIT 7   Primary Sector Classification Systems

Level/System	GICS	ICB	TRBC	RGS
1st	11 Sectors	10 Industries	10 Economic Sectors	9 Economic Sectors
2nd	24 Industry Groups	19 Super Sectors	28 Business Sectors	33 Sub-Sectors
3rd	68 Industries	41 Sectors	54 Industry Groups	157 Industries
4th	157 Sub-Industries	114 Sub-Sectors	136 Industries	Not Applicable

Source: Thomson Reuters, S&P/MSCI, FTSE/Dow Jones.

To illustrate how segmentation of the classification systems may be used in practice, Exhibit 8 demonstrates how GICS, perhaps the most prominent classification system, subdivides selected sectors—in this case, Consumer Discretionary, Consumer Staples, and Information Technology—into certain industry group, industry, and sub-industry levels.

EXHIBIT 8   GICS Classification Examples

Sector	Consumer Discretionary	Consumer Staples	Information Technology
Industry Group Example	Automobiles & Components	Food, Beverage & Tobacco	Technology Hardware & Equipment
Industry Example	Automobiles	Beverages	Electronic Equipment, Instruments & Components
Sub-Industry Example	Motorcycle Manufacturers	Soft Drinks	Electronic Manufacturing Services

Source: MSCI.

As with other segmentation approaches mentioned previously, segmentation by economic activity enables equity portfolio managers to construct performance benchmarks for specific sectors or industries. Portfolio managers may also obtain better industry representation (diversification) by segmenting their equity universe according to economic activity. The key disadvantage of segmentation by economic activity is that the business activities of companies—particularly large ones—may include more than one industry or subindustry.

EXAMPLE 2   Segmenting the Equity Investment Universe

A portfolio manager is initiating a new fund that seeks to invest in the Chinese robotics industry, which is experiencing rapidly accelerating earnings. To help identify appropriate company stocks, the portfolio manager wants to select an approach to segment the equity universe.

Recommend which segmentation approach would be most appropriate for the portfolio manager.

> *Solution:* Based on his desired strategy to invest in companies with rapidly accelerating (growing) earnings, the portfolio manager would most likely segment his equity universe by size/style. The portfolio manager would most likely use an investment style that reflects growth, with size (large cap, mid cap, or small cap) depending on the company being analyzed. Other segmentation approaches, including those according to geography and economic activity, would be less appropriate for the portfolio manager given the similar geographic and industry composition of the Chinese robotics industry.

3.4. Segmentation of Equity Indexes and Benchmarks

Segmentation of equity indexes or benchmarks reflects some of or all the approaches previously discussed in this section. For example, the MSCI Europe Large Cap Growth Index, the MSCI World Small Cap Value Index, the MSCI Emerging Markets Large Cap Growth Index, or the MSCI Latin America Midcap Index combine various geographic, size, and style dimensions. This combination of geography, size, and style also sometimes applies to individual countries—particularly those in large, developed markets.

A more focused approach to segmentation of equity indexes uses industries or sectors. Because many industries and sectors are global in scope, the most common types of these indexes are comprised of companies in different countries. A few examples include the following:

- Global Natural Resources—the *S&P Global Natural Resources Index* includes 90 of the largest publicly traded companies in natural resources and commodities businesses across three primary commodity-related sectors: agribusiness; energy; and metals and mining.
- Worldwide Oil and Natural Gas—the *MSCI World Energy Index* includes the large-cap and mid-cap segments of publicly traded oil and natural gas companies within the developed markets.
- Multinational Financials—the *Thomson Reuters Global Financials Index* includes the 100 largest publicly traded companies within the global financial services sector as defined by the TRBC classification system.

Finally, some indexes reflect specific investment approaches, such as ESG. Such ESG indexes are comprised of companies that reflect certain considerations, such as sustainability or impact investing.

4. INCOME AND COSTS IN AN EQUITY PORTFOLIO

Dividends are the primary source of income for equity portfolios. In addition, some portfolio managers may use securities lending or option-writing strategies to generate income. On the cost side, equity portfolios incur various fees and trading costs that adversely affect portfolio returns. The primary types of income and costs are discussed in this section.

4.1. Dividend Income

Investors requiring regular income may prefer to invest in stocks with large or frequent dividend payments, whereas growth-oriented investors may have little interest in dividends. Taxation is an important consideration for dividend income received, particularly for individuals. Depending on the country where the investor is domiciled, where dividends are issued, and the type of investor, dividends may be subject to withholding tax and/or income tax.

Beyond regular dividends, equity portfolios may receive **special dividends** from certain companies. Special dividends occur when companies decide to distribute excess cash to shareholders, but the payments may not be maintained over time. **Optional stock dividends** are another type of dividend in which shareholders may elect to receive either cash or new shares. When the share price used to calculate the number of stock dividend shares is established before the shareholder's election date, the choice between a cash or stock dividend may be important. This choice represents "optionality" for the shareholder, and the optionality has value. Some market participants, typically investment banks, may offer to purchase this "option," providing an additional, if modest, source of income to an equity investor.

4.2. Securities Lending Income

For some investors, **securities lending**—a form of collateralized lending—may be used to generate income for portfolios. Securities lending can facilitate short sales, which involve the sale of securities the seller does not own. When a securities lending transaction involves the transfer of equities, the transaction is generally known as **stock lending** and the securities are generally known as *stock loans*. Stock loans are collateralized with either cash or other high-quality securities to provide some financial protection to the lender. Stock loans are usually open-ended in duration, but the borrower must return the shares to the lender on demand.

Stock lenders generally receive a fee from the stock borrower as compensation for the loaned shares. Most stock loans in developed markets earn a modest fee, approximately 0.2–0.5% on an annualized basis. In emerging markets, fees are typically higher, often 1–2% annualized for large-cap stocks. In many equity markets, certain stocks—called "specials"—are in high demand for borrowing. These specials can earn fees that are substantially higher than average (typically 5–15% annualized), and in cases of extreme demand, they could be as high as 25–100% annually. However, such high fees do not normally persist for long periods of time.

In addition to fees earned, stock lenders can generate further income by reinvesting the cash collateral received (assuming a favorable interest rate environment). However, as with virtually any other investment, the collateral would be subject to market risk, credit risk, liquidity risk, and operational risk. The administrative costs of a securities lending program, in turn, will reduce the collateral income generated. Dividends on loaned stock are "manufactured" by the stock borrower for the stock lender—that is, the stock borrower ensures that the stock lender is compensated for any dividends that the lender would have received had the stock not been loaned.

Index funds are frequent stock lenders because of their large, long-term holdings in stocks. In addition, because index funds merely seek to replicate the performance of an index, portfolio managers of these funds are normally not concerned that borrowed stock used for short-selling purposes might decrease the prices of the corresponding equities. Large, actively managed pension funds, endowments, and institutional investors are also frequent stock lenders, although these investors are likely more concerned with the effect on their returns if the loaned shares are used to facilitate short-selling. The evidence on the impact of stock lending on asset prices has, however, been mixed (see, for example, Kaplan, Moskowitz, and Sensoy 2013).

4.3. Ancillary Investment Strategies

Additional income can be generated for an equity portfolio through a trading strategy known as **dividend capture**. Under this strategy, an equity portfolio manager purchases stocks just before their ex-dividend dates, holds these stocks through the ex-dividend date to earn the right to receive the dividend, and subsequently sells the shares. Once a stock goes ex-dividend, the share price should, in theory, decrease by the value of the dividend. In this way, capturing dividends would increase portfolio income, although the portfolio would, again in theory, experience capital losses of similar magnitude. However, the share price movement could vary from this theoretical assumption given income tax considerations, stock-specific supply/demand conditions, and general stock market moves around the ex-dividend date.

Selling (writing) options can also generate additional income for an equity portfolio. One such options strategy is writing a *covered call*, whereby the portfolio manager already owns the underlying stock and sells a call option on that stock. Another options strategy is writing a *cash-covered put* (also called a *cash-secured put*), whereby the portfolio manager writes a put option on a stock and simultaneously deposits money equal to the exercise price into a designated account. Under both covered calls and cash-covered puts, income is generated through the writing of options, but clearly the risk profile of the portfolio would be altered. For example, writing a covered call would limit the upside from share price appreciation of the underlying shares.

EXAMPLE 3   Equity Portfolio Income

Isabel Cordova is an equity portfolio manager for a large multinational investment firm. Her portfolio consists of several dividend-paying stocks, and she is interested in generating additional income to enhance the portfolio's total return. Describe potential sources of additional income for Cordova's equity portfolio.

Solution: Cordova's primary source of income for her portfolio would likely be "regular" and, in some cases, special dividends from those companies that pay them. Another potential source of income for Cordova is securities (stock) lending, whereby eligible equities in her portfolio can be loaned to other market participants, including those seeking to sell short securities. In this case, income would be generated from fees received from the stock borrower as well as from reinvesting the cash collateral received. Another potential income-generating strategy available to Cordova is dividend capture, which entails purchasing stocks just before their ex-dividend dates, holding the stocks through the ex-dividend date to earn the right to receive the dividend, and subsequently selling the shares. Selling (writing) options, including covered call and cash-covered put (cash-secured put) strategies, is another way Cordova can generate additional income for her equity portfolio.

4.4. Management Fees

Management fees are typically determined as a percentage of the funds under management (an *ad-valorem* fee) at regular intervals. For actively managed portfolios, the level of management fees involves a balance between fees that are high enough to fund investment research but low enough to avoid detracting too much from investor returns. Management fees for actively managed portfolios include direct costs of research (e.g., remuneration and expenses for investment analysts and portfolio managers) and the direct costs of portfolio management (e.g., software, trade processing costs, and compliance). For passively managed portfolios, management fees are typically low because of lower direct costs of research and portfolio management relative to actively managed portfolios.

4.5. Performance Fees

In addition to management fees, portfolio managers sometimes earn performance fees (also known as incentive fees) on their portfolios. Performance fees are generally associated with hedge funds and long/short equity portfolios, rather than long-only portfolios. These fees are an incentive for portfolio managers to achieve or outperform return objectives, to the benefit of both the manager and investors. As an example, a performance fee might represent 10–20% of any capital appreciation in a portfolio that exceeds some stated annual absolute return threshold (e.g., 8%). Several performance fee structures exist, although performance fees tend to be "upwards only"—that is, fees are earned by the manager when performance objectives are met, but fund investors are not reimbursed when performance is negative. However, performance fees could be reduced following a period of poor performance. Fee calculations also reflect high-water marks. A **high-water mark** is the highest value, net of fees, that the fund has reached. The use of high-water marks protects clients from paying twice for the same performance. For example, if a fund performed well in a given year, it might earn a performance fee. If the value of the same fund fell the following year, no performance fee would be payable. Then, if the fund's value increased in the third year to a point just below the value achieved at the end of the first year, no performance fee would be earned because the fund's value did not exceed the high-water mark. This basic fee structure is used by many alternative investment funds and partnerships, including hedge funds.

Investment managers typically present a standard schedule of fees to a prospective client, although actual fees can be negotiated between the manager and investors. For a fund, fees are established in the prospectus, although investors could negotiate special terms (e.g., a discount for being an early investor in a fund).

4.6. Administration Fees

Equity portfolios are subject to administration fees. These fees include the processing of corporate actions, such as rights issues; the measurement of performance and risk of a portfolio; and voting at company meetings. Generally, these functions are provided by an investment management firm itself and are included as part of the management fee.

Some functions, however, are provided by external parties, with the fees charged to the client in addition to management fees. These externally provided functions include:

- *Custody fees* paid for the safekeeping of assets by a custodian (often a subsidiary of a large bank) that is independent of the investment manager.
- *Depository fees* paid to help ensure that custodians segregate the assets of the portfolio and that the portfolio complies with any investment limits, leverage requirements, and limits on cash holdings.
- *Registration fees* that are associated with the registration of ownership of units in a mutual fund.

4.7. Marketing and Distribution Costs

Most investment management firms market and distribute their services to some degree. Marketing and distribution costs typically include the following:

- Costs of employing marketing, sales, and client servicing staff
- Advertising costs
- Sponsorship costs, including costs associated with sponsoring or presenting at conferences
- Costs of producing and distributing brochures or other communications to financial intermediaries or prospective clients
- "Platform" fees, which are costs incurred when an intermediary offers an investment management firm fund services on the intermediary's platform of funds (e.g., a "funds supermarket")
- Sales commissions paid to such financial intermediaries as financial planners, independent financial advisers, and brokers to facilitate the distribution of funds or investment services

When marketing and distribution services are performed by an investment management firm, the costs are likely included as part of the management fee. However, those marketing and distribution services that are performed by external parties (e.g., consultants) typically incur additional costs to the investor.

4.8. Trading Costs

Buying and selling equities incurs a series of trading (or transaction) costs. Some of these trading costs are explicit, including brokerage commission costs, taxes, stamp duties, and stock exchange fees. In addition, many countries charge a modest regulatory fee for certain types of equity trading.

In contrast to explicit costs, some trading costs are implicit in nature. These implicit costs include the following:

- Bid–offer spread
- Market impact (also called price impact), which measures the effect of the trade on transaction prices
- Delay costs (also called slippage), which arise from the inability to complete desired trades immediately because of order size or lack of market liquidity

In an equity portfolio, total trading costs are a function of the size of trades, the frequency of trading, and the degree to which trades demand liquidity from the market. Unlike many other equity portfolio costs, such as management fees, the total cost of trading is generally not revealed to the investor. Rather, trading costs are incorporated into a portfolio's total return and presented as overall performance data. One final trading cost relates to stock lending transactions that were previously discussed. Equity portfolio managers who borrow shares in these transactions must pay fees on shares borrowed.

4.9. Investment Approaches and Effects on Costs

Equity portfolio costs tend to vary depending on their underlying strategy or approach. As mentioned previously, passively managed strategies tend to charge lower management fees than active strategies primarily because of lower research costs to manage the portfolios. Passively managed equity portfolios also tend to trade less frequently than actively managed equity portfolios, with trading in passive portfolios typically involving rebalancing or changes to index constituents. Index funds, however, do face a "hidden" cost from potential predatory trading. As an illustration, a predatory trader may purchase (or sell short) shares prior to their effective inclusion (or deletion) from an index, resulting in price movement and potential profit for a predatory trader. Such predatory trading strategies can be regarded as a cost to investors in index funds, albeit a cost that is not necessarily evident to a portfolio manager or investor.

Some active investing approaches "demand liquidity" from the market. For example, in a momentum strategy, the investor seeks to buy shares that are already rising in price (or sell those that are already falling). In contrast, some active investing approaches are more likely to "provide liquidity" to the market, such as deep value strategies (i.e., those involving stocks that are deemed to be significantly undervalued). Investment strategies that involve frequent trading and demand liquidity are, unsurprisingly, likely to have higher trading costs than long-term, buy-and-hold investment strategies.

5. SHAREHOLDER ENGAGEMENT

Shareholder engagement refers to the process whereby investors actively interact with companies. Shareholder engagement often includes voting on corporate matters at general meetings as well as other forms of communication (e.g., quarterly investor calls or in-person meetings) between shareholders and representatives of a company. Generally, shareholder engagement concerns issues that can affect the value of a company and, by extension, an investor's shares.

When shareholders engage with companies, several issues may be discussed. Some of these issues include the following:

- *Strategy*—a company's strategic goals, resources, plans for growth, and constraints. Also of interest may be a company's research, product development, culture, sustainability and corporate responsibility, and industry and competitor developments. Shareholders may ask the company how it balances short-term requirements and long-term goals and how it prioritizes the interests of its various stakeholders.

- *Allocation of capital*—a company's process for selecting new projects as well as its mergers and acquisitions strategy. Shareholders may be interested to learn about policies on dividends, financial leverage, equity raising, and capital expenditures.
- *Corporate governance* and regulatory and political risk—including internal controls and the operation of its audit and risk committees.
- *Remuneration*—compensation structures for directors and senior management, incentives for certain behaviors, and alignment of interests between directors and shareholders. In some cases, investors may be able to influence future remuneration structures. Such influence, especially regarding larger companies, often involves the use of remuneration consultants and an iterative process with large, long-term shareholders.
- *Composition of the board of directors*—succession planning, director expertise and competence, culture, diversity, and board effectiveness.

5.1. Benefits of Shareholder Engagement

Shareholder engagement can provide benefits for both shareholders and companies. From a company's perspective, shareholder engagement can assist in developing a more effective corporate governance culture. In turn, shareholder engagement may lead to better company performance to the benefit of shareholders (as well as other stakeholders).

Investors may also benefit from engagement because they will have more information about companies or the sectors in which companies operate. Such information may include a company's strategy, culture, and competitive environment within an industry. Shareholder engagement is particularly relevant for active portfolio managers given their objective to outperform a benchmark portfolio. By contrast, passive (or index) fund managers are primarily focused on tracking a given benchmark or index while minimizing costs to do so. Any process, such as shareholder engagement, that takes up management time (and adds to cost) would detract from the primary goal of a passive manager. This would be less of an issue for very large passively managed portfolios, where any engagement costs could be spread over a sizable asset base.

In theory, some investors could benefit from the shareholder engagement of others under the so-called "free rider problem." Specifically, assume that a portfolio manager using an active strategy actively engages with a company to improve its operations and was successful in increasing the company's stock price. The manager's actions in this case improved the value of his portfolio and also benefitted other investors who own the same stock in their portfolios. Investors who did not participate in shareholder engagement benefitted from improved performance but without the costs necessary for engagement.

In addition to shareholders, other stakeholders of a company may also have an interest in the process and outcomes of shareholder engagement. These stakeholders may include creditors, customers, employees, regulators, governmental bodies, and certain other members of society (e.g., community organizations and citizen groups). These other stakeholders can gain or lose influence with companies depending on the outcomes of shareholder engagement. For example, employees can be affected by cost reduction programs requested by shareholders. Another example is when creditors of a company are affected by a change in a company's vendor payment terms, which can impact the company's working capital and cash flow. Such external forces as the media, the academic community, corporate governance consultants, and proxy voting advisers can also influence the process of shareholder engagement.

Shareholders that also have non-financial interests, such as ESG considerations, may also benefit from shareholder engagement. However, these benefits are difficult to quantify. Empirical evidence relating shareholder returns to a company's adherence to corporate governance and ESG practices is mixed. This mixed evidence could be partly attributable to the fact that a company's management quality and effective ESG practices may be correlated with one another. As a result, it is often difficult to isolate non-financial factors and measure the direct effects of shareholder engagement.

5.2. Disadvantages of Shareholder Engagement

Shareholder engagement also has several disadvantages. First, shareholder engagement is time consuming and can be costly for both shareholders and companies. Second, pressure on company management to meet near-term share price or earnings targets could be made at the expense of long-term corporate decisions. Third, engagement can result in selective disclosure of important information to a certain subset of shareholders, which could lead to a breach of insider trading rules while in possession of specific, material, non-public information about a company. Finally, conflicts of interest can result for a company. For example, a portfolio manager could engage with a company that also happens to be an investor in the manager's portfolio. In such a situation, a portfolio manager may be unduly influenced to support the company's management so as not to jeopardize the company's investment mandate with the portfolio manager.

5.3. The Role of an Equity Manager in Shareholder Engagement

Active managers of equity portfolios typically engage, to some degree, with companies in which they currently (or potentially) invest. In fact, investment firms in some countries have legal or regulatory responsibilities to establish written policies on stewardship and/or shareholder engagement. Engagement activities for equity portfolio managers often include regular meetings with company management or investor relations teams. Such meetings can occur at any time but are often held after annual, semi-annual, or quarterly company results have been published.

For such non-financial issues as ESG, large investment firms, in particular, sometimes employ an analyst (or team of analysts) who focuses on ESG issues. These ESG-focused analysts normally work in conjunction with traditional fundamental investment analysts, with primary responsibility for shareholder voting decisions or environmental or social issues that affect equity investments. In lieu of—or in addition to—dedicated ESG analyst teams, some institutional investors have retained outside experts to assist with corporate governance monitoring and proxy voting. In response to this demand, an industry that provides corporate governance services, including governance ratings and proxy advice, has developed.

5.3.1. Activist Investing

A distinct and specialized version of engagement is known as activist investing. Activist investors (or activists) specialize in taking stakes in companies and creating change to generate a gain on the investment. Hedge funds are among the most common activists, possibly because of the potential for, in many cases, high performance fees. In addition, because hedge funds are subject to limited regulation, have fewer investment constraints, and can often leverage positions, these investors often have more flexibility as activists.

Engagement through activist investing can include meetings with management as well as shareholder resolutions, letters to management, presentations to other investors, and media campaigns. Activists may also seek representation on a company's board of directors as a way of exerting influence. Proxy contests are one method used to obtain board representation. These contests represent corporate takeover mechanisms in which shareholders are persuaded to vote for a group seeking a controlling position on a company's board of directors. Social media and other communication tools can help activists coordinate the actions of other shareholders.

5.3.2. Voting

The participation of shareholders in general meetings, also known as general assemblies, and the exercise of their voting rights are among the most influential tools available for shareholder engagement. General meetings enable shareholders to participate in discussions and to vote on major corporate matters and transactions that are not delegated to the board of directors. By engaging in general meetings, shareholders can exercise their voting rights on major corporate issues and better monitor the performance of the board and senior management.

Proxy voting enables shareholders who are unable to attend a meeting to authorize another individual (e.g., another shareholder or director) to vote on their behalf. Proxy voting is the most common form of investor participation in general meetings. Although most resolutions pass without controversy, sometimes minority shareholders attempt to strengthen their influence at companies via proxy voting. Occasionally, multiple shareholders may use this process to collectively vote their shares in favor of or in opposition to a certain resolution.

Some investors use external proxy advisory firms that provide voting recommendations and reduce research efforts by investors. Portfolio managers need not follow the recommendations of proxy advisory firms, but these external parties can highlight potential controversial issues. An investor's voting instructions are typically processed electronically via third-party proxy voting agents.

When an investor loans shares, the transaction is technically an assignment of title with a repurchase option; that is, the voting rights are transferred to the borrower. The transfer of voting rights with stock lending could potentially result in the borrower having different voting opinions from the lending investor. To mitigate this problem, some stock lenders recall shares ahead of voting resolutions to enable exercise of their voting rights. The downside of this action would be the loss of stock lending revenue during the period of stock loan recall and potential reputation risk as an attractive lender. Investors, in some cases, may borrow shares explicitly to exercise the voting rights attached. This process is called *empty voting*, whereby no capital is invested in the voted shares.

EXAMPLE 4   Shareholder Engagement

An investor manages a fund with a sizable concentration in the transportation sector and is interested in meeting with senior management of a small aircraft manufacturer. Discuss how the investor may benefit from his/her shareholder engagement activities, as well as from the shareholder engagement of other investors, with this manufacturer.

Solution: The investor may benefit from information obtained about the aircraft manufacturer, such as its strategy, allocation of capital, corporate governance, remuneration of directors and senior management, culture, and competitive environment within the aerospace industry. The investor may also benefit as a "free rider," whereby other investors may improve the manufacturer's operating performance through shareholder engagement—to the benefit of all shareholders. Finally, if the investor has non-financial interests, such as ESG, he or she may address these considerations as part of shareholder engagement.

---

6. EQUITY INVESTMENT ACROSS THE PASSIVE–ACTIVE SPECTRUM

The debate between passive management and active management of equity portfolios has been a longstanding one in the investment community. In reality, the decision between passive management and active management is not an "either/or" (binary) alternative. Instead, equity portfolios tend to exist across a passive–active spectrum, ranging from portfolios that closely track an equity market index or benchmark to unconstrained portfolios that are not subject to any benchmark or index. In some cases, portfolios may resemble a "closet index" in which the portfolio is advertised as actively managed but essentially resembles a passively managed fund. For an equity manager (or investment firm), several rationales exist for positioning a portfolio along the passive–active spectrum. Each of these rationales is discussed further.

6.1. Confidence to Outperform

An active investment manager typically needs to be confident that she can adequately outperform her benchmark. This determination requires an understanding of the manager's equity investment universe as well as a competitive analysis of other managers that have a similar investment universe.

6.2. Client Preference

For equity portfolio managers, client preference is a primary consideration when deciding between passive or active investing. Portfolio managers must assess whether their passive or active investment strategies will attract sufficient funds from clients to make the initiatives viable. Another consideration reflects investors' beliefs regarding the potential for active strategies to generate positive alpha. For example, in some equity market categories, such as large-cap/developed markets, companies are widely known and have considerable equity analyst coverage. For such categories as these, investors often believe that potential alpha is substantially reduced because all publicly available information is efficiently disseminated, analyzed, and reflected in stock prices.

A comparison of passive and active equities is illustrated in Exhibit 9. The exhibit demonstrates the relative proportion of investment passive and active equities in US open-ended mutual funds and exchange-traded funds (ETFs) by equity category. Nearly all equities in some categories, such as foreign small/mid-cap growth, are managed on an active basis. Conversely, equities in other categories, such as large-cap blend, are predominantly managed on a passive basis.

EXHIBIT 9   Passive versus Active Equities in US Open-Ended Mutual Funds and ETFs

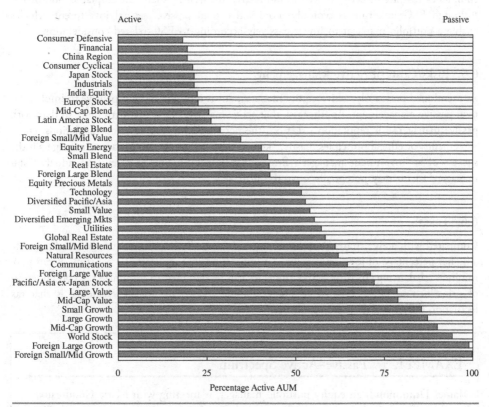

Source: Morningstar Direct. Data as of August 2016.

6.3. Suitable Benchmark

An investor or equity manager's choice of benchmark can play a meaningful role in the ability to attract new funds. This choice is particularly relevant in the institutional equity market, where asset owners (and their consultants) regularly screen new managers in desired equity segments. As part of the selection process in desired equity segments, active managers normally must have benchmarks with sufficient liquidity of underlying securities (thus maintaining a reasonable cost of trading). In addition, the number of securities underlying the benchmark typically must be broad enough to generate sufficient alpha. For this reason, many country or sector-specific investment strategies (e.g., consumer defensive companies) are managed passively rather than actively.

6.4. Client-Specific Mandates

Client-specific investment mandates, such as those related to ESG considerations, are typically managed actively rather than passively. This active approach occurs because passive management may not be particularly efficient or cost effective when managers must meet a client's desired holdings (or holdings to avoid). For example, a mandate to avoid investments in companies involved in certain "unacceptable" activities (e.g., the sale of military technology or weapons, tobacco/alcohol, or gambling) requires ongoing monitoring and management. As part of this *exclusionary (or negative) screening* process, managers need to determine those companies that are directly, as well as indirectly, involved in such "unacceptable" industries. Although ESG investing is typically more active than passive, several investment vehicles enable a portfolio manager to invest passively according to ESG-related considerations.

6.5. Risks/Costs of Active Management

As mentioned previously, active equity management is typically more expensive to implement than passive management. Another risk that active managers face—perhaps more so than with passive managers—is reputation risk from the potential violation of rules, regulations, client agreements, or ethical principles. Lastly, "key person" risk is relevant for active managers if the success of an investment manager's firm is dependent on one or a few individuals ("star managers") who may potentially leave the firm.

6.6. Taxes

Compared with active strategies, passive strategies generally have lower turnover and generate a higher percentage of long-term gains. An index fund that replicates its benchmark can have minimal rebalancing. In turn, active strategies can be designed to minimize tax consequences of gains/income at the expense of higher trading costs. One overall challenge is that tax legislation differs widely across countries.

EXAMPLE 5 Passive–Active Spectrum

James Drummond, an equity portfolio manager, is meeting with Marie Goudreaux, a wealthy client of his investment firm. Goudreaux is very cost conscious and believes that equity markets are highly efficient. Goudreaux also has a narrow investment focus, seeking stocks in specific country and industry sectors.

Discuss where Goudreaux's portfolio is likely to be positioned across the passive–active spectrum.

Solution: Goudreaux's portfolio is likely to be managed passively. Because she believes in market efficiency, Goudreaux likely believes that Drummond's ability to generate alpha is limited. Goudreaux's cost consciousness also supports passive management, which is typically less expensive to implement than active management. Finally, Goudreaux's stated desire to invest in specific countries and sectors would likely be better managed passively.

SUMMARY

This chapter provides an overview of the roles equity investments may play in the client's portfolio, how asset owners and investment managers segment the equity universe for purposes of defining an investment mandate, the costs and obligations of equity ownership (including shareholder engagement) and issues relevant to the decision to pursue active or passive management of an equity portfolio. Among the key points made in this chapter are the following:

- Equities can provide several roles or benefits to an overall portfolio, including capital appreciation, dividend income, diversification with other asset classes, and a potential hedge against inflation.
- The inclusion of equities in a portfolio can be driven by a client's goals or needs. Portfolio managers often consider the following investment objectives and constraints when deciding to include equities (or asset classes in general, for that matter) in a client's portfolio: *risk objective; return objective; liquidity requirement; time horizon; tax concerns; legal and regulatory factors*; and *unique circumstances.*
- Investors often segment the equity universe according to (1) size and style; (2) geography; and (3) economic activity.
- Sources of equity portfolio income include dividends; securities lending fees and interest; dividend capture; covered calls; and cash-covered puts (or cash-secured puts).
- Sources of equity portfolio costs include management fees; performance fees; administration fees; marketing/distribution fees; and trading costs.
- Shareholder engagement is the process whereby companies engage with their shareholders. The process typically includes voting on corporate matters at general meetings and other forms of communication, such as quarterly investor calls or in-person meetings.
- Shareholder engagement can provide benefits for both shareholders and companies. From a company's perspective, shareholder engagement can assist in developing a more effective corporate governance culture. In turn, shareholder engagement may lead to better company performance to the benefit of shareholders (as well as other stakeholders).
- Disadvantages of shareholder engagement include costs and time involved, pressure on a company to meet near-term share price or earnings targets, possible selective disclosure of information, and potential conflicts of interest.

- Activist investors (or activists) specialize in taking stakes in companies and creating change to generate a gain on the investment.
- The participation of shareholders in general meetings, also known as general assemblies, and the exercise of their voting rights are among the most influential tools available for shareholder engagement.
- The choice of using active management or passive management is not an "either/or" (binary) alternative but rather a decision involving a passive–active spectrum. Investors may decide to position their portfolios across the passive–active spectrum based on their confidence to outperform, client preference, suitable benchmarks, client-specific mandates, risks/costs of active management, and taxes.

REFERENCES

Chincarini, Ludwig, and Kim Daehwan. 2006. *Quantitative Equity Portfolio Management*. New York, NY: McGraw-Hill.

Kaplan, Steven, Tobias Moskowitz, and Berk Sensoy. 2013. "The Effects of Stock Lending on Security Prices: An Experiment." *Journal of Finance*, vol. 68, no. 5: 1891–1936.

McMillan, Michael, Jerald Pinto, Wendy Pirie, and Gerhard Van de Venter. 2011. *Investments: Principles of Portfolio and Equity Analysis*. CFA Institute Investment Series. Hoboken, NJ: John Wiley & Sons.

Weigand, Robert. 2014. *Applied Equity Analysis and Portfolio Management*. Hoboken, NJ: John Wiley & Sons.

Zhou, Xinfeng, and Sameer Jain. 2014. *Active Equity Management*. 1st ed. Cambridge, MA: MIT University Press.

PRACTICE PROBLEMS

The following information relates to questions 1–8

Three years ago, the Albright Investment Management Company (Albright) added four new funds—the Barboa Fund, the Caribou Fund, the DoGood Fund, and the Elmer Fund—to its existing fund offering. Albright's new funds are described in Exhibit 1.

EXHIBIT 1   Albright Investment Management Company New Funds

Fund	Fund Description
Barboa Fund	Invests solely in the equity of companies in oil production and transportation industries in many countries.
Caribou Fund	Uses an aggressive strategy focusing on relatively new, fast-growing companies in emerging industries.
DoGood Fund	Investment universe includes all US companies and sectors that have favorable environmental, social, and governance (ESG) ratings and specifically excludes companies with products or services related to aerospace and defense.
Elmer Fund	Investments selected to track the S&P 500 Index. Minimizes trading based on the assumption that markets are efficient.

Hans Smith, an Albright portfolio manager, makes the following notes after examining these funds:

Note 1. The fee on the Caribou Fund is a 15% share of any capital appreciation above a 7% threshold and the use of a high-water mark.

Note 2. The DoGood Fund invests in Fleeker Corporation stock, which is rated high in the ESG space, and Fleeker's pension fund has a significant investment in the DoGood Fund. This dynamic has the potential for a conflict of interest on the part of Fleeker Corporation but not for the DoGood Fund.

Note 3. The DoGood Fund's portfolio manager has written policies stating that the fund does not engage in shareholder activism. Therefore, the DoGood Fund may be a free-rider on the activism by these shareholders.

Note 4. Of the four funds, the Elmer Fund is most likely to appeal to investors who want to minimize fees and believe that the market is efficient.

Note 5. Adding investment-grade bonds to the Elmer Fund will decrease the portfolio's short-term risk.

Smith discusses means of enhancing income for the three funds with the junior analyst, Kolton Frey, including engaging in securities lending or writing covered calls. Frey tells Smith the following:

Statement 1. Securities lending would increase income through reinvestment of the cash collateral but would require the fund to miss out on dividend income from the lent securities.

Statement 2. Writing covered calls would generate income, but doing so would limit the upside share price appreciation for the underlying shares.

1. The Barboa Fund can be *best* described as a fund segmented by:
    A. size/style.
    B. geography.
    C. economic activity.

2. The Caribou Fund is *most likely* classified as a:
    A. large-cap value fund.
    B. small-cap value fund.
    C. small-cap growth fund.

3. The DoGood Fund's approach to the aerospace and defense industry is *best* described as:
    A. positive screening.
    B. negative screening.
    C. thematic investing.

4. The Elmer fund's management strategy is:
    A. active.
    B. passive.
    C. blended.

5. Based on Note 1, the fee on the Caribou Fund is *best* described as a:
    A. performance fee.
    B. management fee.
    C. administrative fee.

6. Which of the following notes about the DoGood Fund is correct?
   A. Only Note 2
   B. Only Note 3
   C. Both Note 2 and Note 3

7. Which of the notes regarding the Elmer Fund is correct?
   A. Only Note 4
   B. Only Note 5
   C. Both Note 4 and Note 5

8. Which of Frey's statements about securities lending and covered call writing is correct?
   A. Only Statement 1
   B. Only Statement 2
   C. Both Statement 1 and Statement 2

CHAPTER 12

PASSIVE EQUITY INVESTING

David M. Smith, PhD, CFA
Kevin K. Yousif, CFA

LEARNING OUTCOMES

The candidate should be able to:

- discuss considerations in choosing a benchmark for a passively managed equity portfolio;
- compare passive factor-based strategies to market-capitalization-weighted indexing;
- compare different approaches to passive equity investing;
- compare the full replication, stratified sampling, and optimization approaches for the construction of passively managed equity portfolios;
- discuss potential causes of tracking error and methods to control tracking error for passively managed equity portfolios;
- explain sources of return and risk to a passively managed equity portfolio.

1. INTRODUCTION

This chapter provides a broad overview of passive equity investing, including index selection, portfolio management techniques, and the analysis of investment results.

Although they mean different things, passive equity investing and indexing have become nearly synonymous in the investment industry. Indexing refers to strategies intended to replicate the performance of benchmark indexes, such as the S&P 500 Index, the Topix 100, the FTSE 100, and the MSCI All-Country World Index. The main advantages of indexing include low costs, broad diversification, and tax efficiency. Indexing is the purest form of a more general idea: passive investing. Passive investing refers to any rules-based, transparent, and investable strategy that does not involve identifying mispriced individual securities. Unlike indexing, however, passive investing can include investing in a changing set of market segments that are selected by the portfolio manager.

Studies over the years have reported support for passive investing. Renshaw and Feldstein (1960) observe that the returns of professionally managed portfolios trailed the returns on the principal index of that time, the Dow Jones Industrial Average. They also conclude that the index would be a good basis for what they termed an "unmanaged investment company." French (2008) indicates that the cost of passive investing is lower than the cost of active management.

Further motivation for passive investing comes from studies that examine the return and risk consequences of stock selection, which involves identifying mispriced securities. This differs from asset allocation, which involves selecting asset class investments that are, themselves, essentially passive indexed-based portfolios. Brinson, Hood, and Beebower (1986) find a dominant role for asset allocation rather than security selection in explaining return variability. With passive investing, portfolio managers eschew the idea of security selection, concluding that the benefits do not justify the costs.

The efficient market hypothesis gave credence to investors' interest in indexes by theorizing that stock prices incorporate all relevant information—implying that after costs, the majority of active investors could not consistently outperform the market. With this backdrop, investment managers began to offer strategies to replicate the returns of stock market indexes as early as 1971.

In comparison with passive investing strategies, active management of an investment portfolio requires a substantial commitment of personnel, technological resources, and time spent on analysis and management that can involve significant costs. Consequently, passive portfolio fees charged to investors are generally much lower than fees charged by their active managers. This fee differential represents the most significant and enduring advantage of passive management.

Another advantage is that passive managers seeking to track an index can generally achieve their objective. Passive managers model their clients' portfolios to the benchmark's constituent securities and weights as reported by the index provider, thereby replicating the benchmark. The skill of a passive manager is apparent in the ability to trade, report, and explain the performance of a client's portfolio. Gross-of-fees performance among passive managers tends to be similar, so much of the industry views passive managers as undifferentiated apart from their scope of offerings and client-servicing capabilities.

Investors of passively managed funds may seek market return, otherwise known as beta exposure, and do not seek outperformance, known as alpha. A focus on beta is based on a single-factor model: the capital asset pricing model.

Since the turn of the millennium, passive factor-based strategies, which are based on more than a single factor, have become more prevalent as investors gain a different understanding of what drives investment returns. These strategies maintain the low-cost advantage of index funds and provide a different expected return stream based on exposure to such factors as style, capitalization, volatility, and quality.

This chapter contains the following sections. Section 2 focuses on how to choose a passive benchmark, including weighting considerations. Section 3 looks at how to gain exposure to the desired index, whether through a pooled investment, a derivatives-based approach, or a separately managed account. Section 4 describes passive portfolio construction techniques. Section 5 discusses how a portfolio manager can control tracking error against the benchmark, including the sources of tracking error. Section 6 introduces methods a portfolio manager can use to attribute the sources of return in the portfolio, including country returns, currency returns, sector returns, and security returns. This section also describes sources of portfolio risk. A summary of key points concludes the chapter.

2. CHOOSING A BENCHMARK

Investors initially used benchmark indexes solely to compare the performance of an active portfolio manager against the performance of an unmanaged market portfolio. Indexes are now used as a basis for investment strategies. Many investment vehicles try to replicate index performance, which has contributed to a proliferation of indexes. Indeed, many indexes are developed specifically as a basis for new investment securities.

Successful investors choose their performance benchmarks with care. It is surprising that investors who spend countless hours analyzing the investment process and past performance of an active management strategy may accept a strategy based on a benchmark index without question. A comprehensive analysis of the creation methodology and performance of an index is just as important to investors as the analysis of an active strategy.

2.1. Indexes as a Basis for Investment

For an index to become the basis for an equity investment strategy, it must meet three initial requirements. It must be rules-based, transparent, and investable.

Examples of rules include criteria for including a constituent stock and the frequency with which weights are rebalanced. An active manager may use rules and guidelines, but it is often impossible for others to replicate the active manager's decision process. Index rules, on the other hand, must be objective, consistent, and predictable.

Transparency may be the most important requirement because passive investors expect to understand the rules underlying their investment choices. Benchmark providers disclose the rules used and constituents in creating their indexes without any black-box methodologies, which assures investors that indexes will continue to represent the intended strategy.

Equity index benchmarks are investable when their performance can be replicated in the market. For example, the FTSE 100 Index is an investable index because its constituent securities can be purchased easily on the London Stock Exchange. In contrast, most investors cannot track hedge fund-of-funds indexes, such as the HFRI series of indexes, because of the difficulty of buying the constituent hedge funds. Another example of a non-investable index is the Value Line Geometric Index, which is a multiplicative average price. In other words, the value of the index is obtained by multiplying the prices and taking a root corresponding to the number of stocks. This index is not useful for investing purposes because it cannot be replicated.

Certain features of individual securities make them non-investable as index constituents. Many stock indexes "free-float adjust" their shares outstanding, which means that they count only shares available for trade by the public, excluding those shares that are held by founders, governments, or other companies. When a company's shares that are floated in the market are a small fraction of the total shares outstanding, trading can result in disproportionate effects. Similarly, stocks for which trading volume is a small fraction of the total shares outstanding are likely to have low liquidity and commensurately high trading costs. Many indexes consequently require that stocks have float and average shares traded above a certain percent of shares outstanding.

Equity index providers include CRSP, FTSE Russell, Morningstar, MSCI, and S&P Dow Jones. These index providers publicize the rules underlying their indexes, communicate changes in the constituent securities, and report performance. For a fee, they may also provide data to investors who want to replicate the underlying basket of securities.

Index providers have taken steps to make their indexes more investable. One key decision concerns when individual stocks will migrate from one index to another. As a stock increases in market capitalization (market cap) over time, it might move from small-cap to mid-cap to large-cap status. Some index providers have adopted policies intended to limit stock migration problems and keep trading costs low for investors who replicate indexes. Among these policies are buffering and packeting. **Buffering** involves establishing ranges around breakpoints that define whether a stock belongs in one index or another. As long as stocks remain within the buffer zone, they stay in their current index. For example, the MSCI USA Large Cap Index contains the 300 largest companies in the US equity market. But a company currently in the MSCI USA Mid Cap Index must achieve a rank as the 200th largest stock to move up to the Large Cap Index. Similarly, a large-cap constituent must shrink and be the 451st largest stock to move down to the Mid Cap Index. Size rankings may change almost every day with market price movements, so buffering makes index transitions a more gradual and orderly process.

The effect of buffering is demonstrated with the MSCI USA Large Cap Index during the regularly scheduled May 2016 reconstitution. The MSCI USA Large Cap Index consists of stocks of US-based companies that meet the criterion to be considered for large cap. Further, the MSCI USA Large Cap Index is intended to represent the largest 70% of the market capitalization of the US equity market.

At each rebalance date, MSCI sets a cutoff value for the smallest company in the index and then sets the buffer value at 67% of the cutoff value. During the May 2016 rebalance, the cutoff market capitalization (market cap) of the smallest company in the index was USD 15,707 million; so, the buffer value was USD 10,524 million or approximately USD 10.5 billion.

Whole Foods Market, a grocery store operating primarily in the United States, had experienced a drop in market value from USD 15.3 billion in May of 2015 to USD 10.4 billion in May of 2016. The drop in value put the market cap of Whole Foods Market at a lower value than the acceptable buffer. That is, Whole Foods Market was valued at USD 10.4 billion, which was below the buffer point of USD 10.5 billion. Per the stated rules, Whole Foods Market was removed from the MSCI USA Large Cap Index and was added to the MSCI USA Mid Cap Index.

Packeting involves splitting stock positions into multiple parts. Let us say that a stock is currently in a mid-cap index. If its capitalization increases and breaches the breakpoint between mid-cap and large-cap indexes, a portion of the total holding is transferred to the large-cap index but the rest stays in the mid-cap index. On the next reconstitution date, if the stock value remains large-cap and all other qualifications are met, the remainder of the shares are moved out of the mid-cap and into the large-cap index. A policy of packeting can keep portfolio turnover and trading costs low. The Center for Research in Security Prices (CRSP) uses packeting in the creation of the CRSP family of indexes.

2.2. Considerations When Choosing a Benchmark Index

The first consideration when choosing a benchmark index is the desired *market exposure*, which is driven by the objectives and constraints in the investor's investment policy statement

(IPS). For equity portfolios, the choices to be made include the market segment (broad versus sectors; domestic versus international), equity capitalization (large, mid, or small), style (value, growth, or blend/core), exposure, and other constituent characteristics (e.g., high or low momentum, low volatility, and quality) that are considered risk factors.

The choice of market depends on the investor's perspective. The investor's domicile, risk tolerance, liquidity needs, and legal considerations all influence the decision. For example, the decision will proceed differently for an Indian institutional investor than for a US-based individual investor. In India, the domestic equity universe is much smaller than in the United States, making the Indian investor more likely to invest globally. But a domestic investment does not carry with it the complexities of cross-border transactions.

A common way to implement the domestic/international investment decision is to use country indexes. Some indexes cover individual countries, and others encompass multiple country markets. For example, the global equity market can also be broken into geographic regions or based on development status (developed, emerging, or frontier markets). The US market is frequently treated as distinct from other developed markets because of its large size.

Another decision element is the *risk-factor exposure* that the index provides. As described later, equity risk factors can arise from several sources, including the holdings' market capitalization (the Size factor), investment style (growth vs. value, or the Value factor), price momentum (the Momentum factor), and liquidity (the Liquidity factor).

The Size factor is perhaps the best known of these. Market history and empirical studies show that small-cap stocks tend to be riskier and provide a higher long-term return than large-cap stocks. This return difference is considered a risk factor. To the extent that a benchmark's return is correlated with this risk factor, the benchmark has exposure to the Size factor. A similar argument applies to the Value factor, which is calculated as the return on value stocks less the return on growth stocks.

Practically speaking, some investors consider certain size ranges (e.g., small cap) to be more amenable to alpha generation using active management and others (e.g., large cap) amenable to lower-cost passive management. Size classifications range from mega cap to micro cap. Classifications are not limited to individual size categories. For example, many indexes seek to provide equity exposure to both small- and mid-cap companies ("smid-cap" indexes). Investors who desire exposure across the capitalization spectrum may use an "all-cap" index. Such indexes do not necessarily contain all stocks in the market; they usually just combine representative stocks from each of the size ranges. Note that a large-cap stock in an emerging market may have the same capitalization as a small-cap stock in a developed country. Accordingly, index providers usually classify company capitalizations in the context of the local market environment.

Equity benchmark selection also involves the investor's preference for exposure on the growth vs. value style spectrum. Growth stocks exhibit such characteristics as high price momentum, high P/Es, and high EPS growth. Value stocks, however, may exhibit high dividend yields, low P/Es, and low price-to-book value ratios. Depending on their basic philosophy and market outlook, investors may have a strong preference for growth or value.

Exhibit 1 shows the number of available total-return equity indexes[1] in various classifications available worldwide. Broad market exposure is provided by nearly two-thirds of all indexes, while the others track industry sectors. Developed market indexes are about twice

---

[1]Total-return indexes account for both price and income (e.g., from cash dividends) returns to the constituent securities. The value of price-return indexes changes only because of return from the constituents' price changes.

as common as emerging-market indexes. The majority of broad market indexes cover the all-cap space or are otherwise focused on large-cap and mid-cap stocks.

EXHIBIT 1   Characteristics of Equity Indexes

Equity indexes	9,165
Broad market indexes	5,658
Sector indexes	3,479
Not classified	28
Of the 5,658 broad market indexes:	
Developed markets	2,903
Emerging markets	1,701
Developed & emerging markets	1,050
Not classified	4
Of the 5,658 broad market indexes:	
All-cap stocks	1,892
Large-cap stocks	121
Large-cap and mid-cap stocks	2,100
Mid-cap stocks	657
Mid- and small-cap stocks	39
Small-cap stocks	846
Not classified	3

Source: Morningstar Direct, May 2017.

Once the investor has settled on the market, capitalization, and style of benchmark, the next step is to explore the method used in constructing and maintaining the benchmark index.

2.3. Index Construction Methodologies

Equity index providers differ in their stock inclusion methods, ranging from **exhaustive** to **selective** in their investment universes. Exhaustive stock inclusion strategies are those that select every constituent of a universe, while selective approaches target only those securities with certain characteristics. The CRSP US Total Market Index has perhaps the most exhaustive set of constituents in the US market. This market-cap-weighted index includes approximately 4,000 publicly traded stocks from across the market-cap spectrum. In contrast, the S&P 500 Index embodies a selective approach and aims to provide exposure to US large-cap stocks. Its constituent securities are selected using a committee process and are based on both size and broad industry affiliation.

The weighting method used in constructing an index influences its performance. One of the most common weighting methods is market-cap weighting. The equity market cap of a constituent company is its stock price multiplied by the number of shares outstanding. Each constituent company's weight in the index is calculated as its market capitalization divided by the total market capitalization of all constituents of the index. In the development of the capital asset pricing model, the capitalization-weighted market portfolio is mean–variance efficient, meaning that it offers the highest return for a given level of risk. To the extent a capitalization-weighted equity index is a reasonable proxy for the market portfolio, the tracking portfolio may be close to mean–variance efficient.

A further advantage of the capitalization-weighted approach is that it reflects a strategy's investment capacity. A cap-weighted index can be thought of as a liquidity-weighted index because the largest-cap stocks tend to have the highest liquidity and the greatest capacity to handle investor flows at a manageable cost. Many investor portfolios tend to be biased toward large-cap stocks and use benchmarks that reflect that bias.

The most common form of market-cap weighting is free-float weighting, which adjusts each constituent's shares outstanding for closely held shares that are not generally available to the investing public. The process to determine the free-float-adjusted shares outstanding relies on publicly available information to determine the holders of the shares and whether those shares would be available for purchase in the marketplace. One reason to adjust a company's share count may include strategic holdings by governments, affiliated companies, founders, and employees. Another less common reason is to account for limitations on foreign ownership of a company; these limitations typically represent rules that are generally set up by a governmental entity through regulation.

Adjusting a company's shares outstanding for float can be a complex task and often requires an index provider to reach out to the company's shareholder services unit or to rely on analytical judgments. Although all data used in determining a company's free-float-adjusted shares outstanding are public information, the various index providers often report a different number of shares outstanding for the same security. This variation in reported shares outstanding can often be attributed to small differences in their methodologies.

In a *price-weighted* index, the weight of each stock is its price per share divided by the sum of all share prices in the index. A price-weighted index can be interpreted as a portfolio that consists of one share of each constituent company. Although some price-weighted indexes, such as the Dow Jones Industrial Average and the Nikkei 225, have high visibility as indicators of day-to-day market movements, price-weighted investment approaches are not commonly used by portfolio managers. A stock split for any constituent of the index complicates the index calculation. The weight in the index of the stock that split decreases, and the index divisor decreases as well. With its divisor changed, the index ceases to be a simple average of the constituent stocks' prices. For price-weighted indexes, the assumption that the same number of shares is held in each component stock is a shortcoming, because very few market participants invest in that way.

Equally weighted indexes produce the least-concentrated portfolios. Such indexes have constituent weights of $1/n$, where n represents the number of stocks in the index. Equal weighting of stocks within an index is considered a naive strategy because it does not show preference toward any single stock. The reduction of single stock concentration risk and slow-changing sector exposures make equal weighting attractive to many investors.

As noted by Zeng and Luo (2013), broad market equally weighted indexes are factor-indifferent and the weighting randomizes factor mispricing. Equal weighting also produces higher volatility than cap weighting, one reason being that it imparts a small-cap bias to the portfolio. Equal weights deviate from market weights most dramatically for large-cap indexes, which contain mega-cap stocks. Constrained market-cap ranges such as mid-cap indexes, even if market weighted, tend to have relatively uniform weights.

Equally weighted indexes require regular rebalancing because immediately after trading in the constituent stocks begins, the weights are no longer equal. Most investors use a regular reweighting schedule. Standard & Poor's offers its S&P 500 Index in an equally weighted format and rebalances the index to equal weights once each quarter. Therein would appear to lie a misleading aspect of equally weighted indexes. For a 91-day quarter, the index is not equally weighted for $90/91 = 99\%$ of the time.

Another drawback of equal weighting is its limited investment capacity. The smallest-cap constituents of an equally weighted index may have low liquidity, which means that investors cannot purchase a large number of shares without causing price changes. Zeng and Luo (2013) address this issue by assuming that 10% of shares in the cap-weighted S&P 100 and 500 and 5% of shares in the cap-weighted S&P 400 and 600 indexes are currently held in cap-weighted indexing strategies without any appreciable liquidity problems. They then focus on the smallest-cap constituent of each index as of December 2012, and they determine the value that 10% (5%) of its market capitalization represents. Finally, they multiply this amount by the number of stocks in the index to estimate the total investment capacity for tracking each of the S&P equally weighted equity indexes. Zeng's and Luo's estimates are shown in Exhibit 2.

EXHIBIT 2   Estimated Investment Capacity of Equally Weighted (EW) Equity Indexes

Index	Capitalization Category	Estimated Capacity
S&P 100 EW	Mega cap	USD 176 billion
S&P 500 EW	Large cap	USD 82 billion
S&P 400 EW	Mid cap	USD 8 billion
S&P 600 EW	Small cap	USD 2 billion

Source: Zeng and Luo (2013).

Qin and Singal (2015) show that equally weighted portfolios have a natural advantage over cap-weighted portfolios. To the extent that any of the constituent stocks are mispriced, equally weighted portfolios will experience return superiority as the stock prices move up or down toward their correct intrinsic value. Because of the aforementioned need to rebalance back to equal weights, Qin and Singal find that the advantage largely vanishes when taxes and transaction costs are considered. However, based on their results, tax-exempt institutional investors could experience superior returns from equal weighting.

Other non-cap-weighted indexes are weighted based on such attributes as a company or stock's fundamental characteristics (e.g., sales, income, or dividends). Discussed in more detail later, fundamental weighting delinks a constituent stock's portfolio weight from its market value. The philosophy behind fundamental weighting is that although stock prices may become over- or undervalued, the market price will eventually converge to a level implied by the fundamental attributes.

Market-cap-weighted indexes and fundamentally weighted indexes share attractive characteristics, including low cost, rules-based construction, transparency, and investability. Their philosophies, however, are different. Market-cap-weighted portfolios are based on the efficient market hypothesis, while fundamentally weighted indexes look to exploit possible inefficiencies in market pricing.

An important concern in benchmark selection relates to how concentrated the index is. In this case, the concept of the effective number of stocks, which is an indication of portfolio concentration, can provide important information. An index that has a high degree of stock concentration or a low effective number of stocks may be relatively undiversified. Woerheide and Persson (1993) show that the Herfindahl–Hirschman Index (HHI) is a valid measure of stock-concentration risk in a portfolio, and Hannam and Jamet (2017) demonstrate its use by practitioners. The HHI is calculated as the sum of the constituent weightings squared, as shown in Equation 1:

$$HHI = \sum_{i=1}^{n} w_i^2 \tag{1}$$

where w_i is the weight of stock i in the portfolio.

The HHI can range in value from $1/n$, where n is equal to the number of securities held, to 1.0. An HHI of $1/n$ would signify an equally weighted portfolio, and a value of 1.0 would signify portfolio concentration in a single security.

Using the HHI, one can estimate the effective (or equivalent) number of stocks, held in equal weights, that would mimic the concentration level of the chosen index. The effective number of stocks for a portfolio is calculated as the reciprocal of the HHI, as shown in Equation 2.

$$Effective\ number\ of\ stocks = \frac{1}{\sum_{i=1}^{n} w_i^2} = 1/HHI \tag{2}$$

Malevergne, Santa-Clara, and Sornette (2009) demonstrate that cap-weighted indexes have a surprisingly low effective number of stocks. Consider the NASDAQ 100, a US-based market-cap-weighted index consisting of 100 stocks. If the index were weighted uniformly, each stock's weight would be 0.01 (1%). In May 2017, the constituent weights ranged from 0.123 for Apple, Inc., to 0.0016 for Liberty Global plc, a ratio of 77:1. Weights for the top five stocks totaled almost 0.38 (38%), a significant allocation to those securities. Across all stocks in the index, the median weight was 0.0039 (that is, 0.39%). The effective number of stocks can be estimated by squaring the weights for the stocks, summing the results, and calculating the reciprocal of that figure. The squared weights for the NASDAQ 100 stocks summed to 0.0404, the reciprocal of which is $1/0.0404 = 24.75$, the effective number of stocks. Thus, the 100 stocks in the index had a concentration level that can be thought of as being equivalent to approximately 25 stocks held in equal weights.

EXAMPLE 1   Effective Number of Stocks

A market-cap-weighted index contains 50 stocks. The five largest-cap stocks have weights of 0.089, 0.080, 0.065, 0.059, and 0.053. The bottom 45 stocks represent the remaining weight of 0.654, and the sum of the squares of those weights is 0.01405. What are the portfolio's Herfindahl–Hirschman Index and effective number of stocks held?

Solution: The stocks, their weights, and their squared weights are shown in Exhibit 3.

EXHIBIT 3   Calculations for Effective Number of Stocks

Stock	Weight	Squared Weight
1	0.089	0.00792
2	0.080	0.00640
3	0.065	0.00423
4	0.059	0.00348
5	0.053	0.00281
Stocks 6–50	0.654	Sum of squared weights for stocks 6–50: 0.01405
Total for stocks 1–50	1.000	0.03889

The HHI is shown in the final row: 0.03889. The reciprocal of the HHI is 1/0.03889 = 25.71. Thus, the effective number of stocks is approximately 26. The fact that the portfolio weights are far from being a uniform 2% across the 50 stocks makes the effective number of stocks held in equal weights less than 26.

The stock market crises of 2000 and 2008 brought heightened attention to investment strategies that are defensive or volatility reducing. For example, some income-oriented investors are drawn to strategies that weight benchmark constituents based on the dividend yield of each stock. Volatility weighting calculates the volatility of each constituent stock and weights the index based on the inverse of each stock's relative volatility. A related method produces a minimum-variance index using mean–variance optimization.

Exhibit 4 shows the various methods for weighting the constituent securities of broad-based, non-industry-sector, total-return equity indexes.

EXHIBIT 4   Equity Index Constituent Weighting Methods

Weighting Method	Number of Indexes
Market-cap, free-float adjusted	5,182
Market-cap-weighted	169
Multi-factor-weighted	143
Equal-weighted	63
Dividend-weighted	36

Source: Morningstar Direct, May 2017.

Another consideration in how an index is constructed involves its periodic rebalancing and reconstitution schedule. Reconstitution of an index frequently involves the addition and deletion of index constituents, while rebalancing refers to the periodic reweighting of those constituents. Index reconstitution and rebalancing create turnover. The turnover for developed-market, large-cap indexes that are infrequently reconstituted tends to be low, while benchmarks constructed using stock selection rather than exhaustive inclusion have higher turnover. As seen in Exhibit 5, both rebalancing and reconstitution occur with varied frequency, although the former is slightly more frequent.

EXHIBIT 5   Index Rebalancing/Reconstitution Frequency for Broad Equity Market Total-Return Indexes

Frequency	Rebalancing	Reconstitution
Daily	3	2
Monthly	4	3
Quarterly	2,481	1,379
Semi-annually	2,743	3,855
Annually	260	308
As needed	74	13

Note: The totals for the Rebalancing and Reconstitution columns differ slightly, as does the index total in Exhibit 4.
Source: Morningstar Direct, May 2017.

The method of reconstitution may produce additional effects. When reconstitution occurs, index-tracking portfolios, mutual funds, and ETFs will want to hold the newly included names and sell the deleted names. The demand created by investors seeking to track an index can push up the stock prices of added companies while depressing the prices of the deleted ones. Research shows that this produces a significant price effect in each case. Depending on the reconstitution method used by index publishers, arbitrageurs may be able to anticipate the changes and front-run the trades that will be made by passive investors. In some cases, the index rules are written so that the decision to add or remove an index constituent is voted on by a committee maintained by the index provider. Where a committee makes the final decision, the changes become difficult to guess ahead of time. In other cases, investors know the precise method used for reconstitution, so guessing is often successful.

Chen, Noronha, and Singal (2004) find that constituent changes for indexes that reconstitute using subjective criteria are often more difficult for arbitrageurs to predict than indexes that use objective criteria. Even indexes that use objective criteria for reconstitution often announce the changes several weeks before they are implemented. Stocks near the breakpoint between small-cap and large-cap indexes are especially vulnerable to reconstitution-induced price changes. The smallest-cap stocks in the Russell 1000 Large-Cap Index have a low weight in that cap-weighted index. After any of those stocks are demoted to the Russell 2000 Small-Cap Index, they are likely to have some of the highest weights. Petajisto (2010) shows that the process of moving in that direction tends to be associated with increases in stock prices, while movements into the large-cap index tend to have negative effects. He also concludes that transparency in reconstitution is a virtue rather than a drawback.

A final consideration is investability. As stated in a prior section, an effective benchmark must be investable in that its constituent stocks are available for timely purchase in a liquid trading environment. Indexes that represent the performance of a market segment that is not available for direct ownership by investors must be replicated through derivatives strategies, which for reasons explained later may be sub-optimal for many investors.

2.4. Factor-Based Strategies

Traditional indexing generally involves tracking the returns to a market-cap-weighted benchmark index. Yet most benchmark returns are driven by factors, which are risk exposures that can be identified and isolated. An investor who wants access only to specific aspects of an index's return stream can invest in a subset of constituent securities that best reflect the investor's preferred risk factors, such as Size, Value, Quality, and Momentum. The goal of being exposed to one or more specific risk factors will also drive the choice of a benchmark index.

Factor-based strategies are an increasingly popular variation on traditional indexing, and they have important implications for benchmark selection. Some elaboration on the topic is warranted. The origin of passive factor-based strategies dates to at least the observation by Banz (1981) that small-cap stocks tend to outperform large-cap stocks. Work by Fama and French (2015) shows that at least five risk factors explain US equity market returns. Their asset pricing model incorporates the market risk premium from the CAPM plus factors for a company's size, book-to-market (value or growth style classification), operating profitability, and investment intensity. Consistent with prior research, they find a positive risk premium for small companies and value stocks over large companies and growth stocks. They measure operating profitability as the previous year's gross profit minus selling, general, and administrative expenses as well as interest expense—all divided by the beginning book value of equity. Investment intensity is measured as the growth rate in total assets in the previous year.

Although the concepts underlying passive factor investing, sometimes marketed as "smart beta," have been known for a long time, investors' use of the technique increased dramatically over time. There presently exist many passive investment vehicles and indexes that allow access to such factors as Value, Size, Momentum, Volatility, and Quality, which are described in Exhibit 6. Many investors use their beliefs about market conditions to apply factor tilts to their portfolios. This is the process of intentionally overweighting and underweighting certain risk factors. Passive factor-based strategies can be used in place of or to complement a market-cap-weighted indexed portfolio.

EXHIBIT 6   Common Equity Risk Factors

Factor	Description
Growth	Growth stocks are generally associated with high-performing companies with an above-average net income growth rate and high P/Es.
Value	Value stocks are generally associated with mature companies that have stable net incomes or are experiencing a cyclical downturn. Value stocks frequently have low price-to-book and price-to-earnings ratios as well as high dividend yields.
Size	A tilt toward smaller size involves buying stocks with low float-adjusted market capitalization.
Yield	Yield is identified as dividend yield relative to other stocks. High dividend-yielding stocks may provide excess returns in low interest rate environments.
Momentum	Momentum attempts to capture further returns from stocks that have experienced an above-average increase in price during the prior period.
Quality	Quality stocks might include those with consistent earnings and dividend growth, high cash flow to earnings, and low debt-to-equity ratios.
Volatility	Low volatility is generally desired by investors seeking to lower their downside risk. Volatility is often measured as the standard deviation of stock returns.

Passive factor-based equity strategies use passive rules, but they frequently involve active decision-making: Decisions on the timing and degree of factor exposure are being made. As Jacobs and Levy (2014) note, the difference between passive factor investing and conventional active management is that with the former, active management takes place up front rather than continuously. Relative to broad-market-cap-weighting, passive factor-based strategies tend to concentrate risk exposures, leaving investors exposed during periods when a chosen risk factor is out of favor. The observation that even strong risk factors experience periods of underperformance has led many investors toward multi-factor approaches. Passive factor-based strategies tend to be transparent in terms of factor selection, weighting, and rebalancing. Possible risks include ease of replication by other investors, which can produce overcrowding and reduce the realized advantages of a strategy.

Fundamental Factor Indexing

Capitalization weighting of indexes and index-tracking portfolios involve treating each constituent stock as if investors were buying all the available shares. Arnott, Hsu, and Moore (2005) developed an alternative weighting method based on the notion that if stock market prices deviate from their intrinsic value, larger-cap stocks will exhibit this tendency more than smaller-cap stocks. Thus, traditional cap weighting is likely to overweight overpriced stocks and underweight underpriced stocks. The combination is intended to make cap-weighting inferior to a method that does not use market prices as a basis for weighting.

The idea advanced by Arnott, Hsu, and Moore is to use a cluster of company fundamentals—book value, cash flow, revenue, sales, dividends, and employee count—as a basis for weighting each company. A separate weighting is developed for each fundamental measure. In the case of a large company, its sales might be 1.3% of the total sales for all companies in the index, so its weight for this criterion would be 0.013. For each company, the weightings are averaged across all of the fundamental measures, and those average values represent the weight of each stock in a "composite fundamentals" index.

The authors show that over a 43-year period, a fundamental index would have outperformed a related cap-weighted index by an average of almost 200 basis points per year. They hasten to add that the result should not necessarily be considered alpha, because the fundamental portfolio provides heightened exposure to the Value and Size factors.

Since the time of the seminal article's publication, fundamental-weighted indexing strategies for country markets as well as market segments have gained in popularity and attracted a large amount of investor funds.

No matter the style of a passive factor-based strategy, its ultimate goal is to improve upon the risk or return performance of the market-cap-weighted strategy. Passive factor-based approaches gain exposure to many of the same risk factors that active managers seek to exploit. The strategies can be return oriented, risk oriented, or diversification oriented.

Return-oriented factor-based strategies include dividend yield strategies, momentum strategies, and fundamentally weighted strategies. Dividend yield strategies can include dividend growth as well as absolute dividend yield. The low interest rate environment, which followed the 2008–2009 global financial crisis, led to an increase in dividend yield strategies as investors sought reliable income streams. An example index is the S&P 1500 High Yield Dividend Aristocrats Index. This index selects securities within the S&P 1500 that increased dividends in each of the past 20 years and then weights those securities by their dividend yield, with the highest dividend-yielding stocks receiving the highest weight.

Another return-oriented strategy is momentum, which is generally defined by the amount of a stock's excess price return relative to the market over a specified time period. Momentum can be determined in various ways. One example is MSCI's Momentum Index family, in which a stock's most recent 12-month and 6-month price performance are determined and then used to weight the securities in the index.[2]

Risk-oriented strategies take several forms, seeking to reduce downside volatility and overall portfolio risk. For example, risk-oriented factor strategies include volatility weighting, where all of an index's constituents are held and then weighted by the inverse of their relative price volatility. Price volatility is defined differently by each index provider, but two common methods include using standard deviation of price returns for the past 252 trading days (approximately one calendar year) or the weekly standard deviation of price returns for the past 156 weeks (approximately three calendar years).

Volatility weighting can take other forms as well. Minimum variance investing is another risk-reducing strategy, and it requires access to a mean–variance optimizer. Minimum variance weights are those that minimize the volatility of the portfolio's returns based on historical price returns, subject to certain constraints on the index's construction. Constraints can include limitations on sector over/under weights, country selection limits, and limits on single stock concentration levels. Mean–variance optimizer programs can be accessed from such vendors as Axioma, BARRA, and Northfield.

Risk weighting has the advantages of being simple to understand and providing a way to reduce absolute volatility and downside returns. However, the development of these strategies is based on past return data, which may not reflect future returns. Thus, investors will not always achieve their objectives despite the strategy's stated goal.

Diversification-oriented strategies include equally weighted indexes and maximum-diversification strategies. Equal weighting is intuitive and is discussed elsewhere in the chapter as having a low amount of single-stock risk. The low single-stock risk comes by way of the weighting structure of $1/n$, where n is equal to the number of securities held. Choueifaty and Coignard (2008) define maximum diversification by calculating a "diversification ratio" as the ratio of the weighted average volatilities divided by the portfolio volatility. Diversification strategies then can attempt to maximize future diversification by determining portfolio weights using past price return volatilities.

Portfolio managers who pursue factor-based strategies often use multiple benchmark indexes, including a factor-based index and a broad market-cap-weighted index. This mismatch in benchmarks can also produce an unintended mismatch in returns, known as tracking error, from the perspective of the end investor who has modeled a portfolio against a broad market-cap-weighted index. Tracking error indicates how closely the portfolio behaves like its benchmark and is measured as the standard deviation of the differences between a portfolio's returns and its benchmark returns. The concept of tracking error is discussed in detail later.

---

[2]The indexes are rebalanced semi-annually. More information can be found at www.msci.com/eqb/methodology/meth_docs/MSCI_Momentum_Indices_Methodology.pdf.

Finally, passive factor-based strategies can involve higher management fees and trading commissions than broad-market indexing. Factor-based index providers and managers demand a premium price for the creation and management of these strategies, and those fees decrease performance. Also, commission costs can be higher in factor-based strategies than they are in market-cap-weighted strategies. All else equal, higher costs will lead to lower net performance.

Passive factor-based approaches may offer an advantage for those investors who believe it is prudent to seek out groups of stocks that are poised to have desirable return patterns. Active managers also believe in seeking those stocks, but active management brings the burden of higher fees that can eat into any outperformance. Active managers may also own stocks that are outside the benchmark and are, thus, incompatible with the investment strategy. In contrast, passive factor-based strategies can provide nearly pure exposure to specific market segments, and there are numerous benchmarks against which to measure performance. Fees are restricted because factor-based strategies are rules based and thus do not require constant monitoring. An investor's process of changing exposures to specific risk factors as market conditions change is known as factor rotation. With factor rotation, investors can use passive vehicles to make active bets on future market conditions.

3. APPROACHES TO PASSIVE EQUITY INVESTING

Passive equity investment strategies may be implemented using several approaches, from the do-it-yourself method of buying stocks to hiring a subadviser to create and maintain the investment strategy. Passively managed investment strategies can be replicated by any internal or external portfolio manager who has the index data, trading tools, and necessary skills. In contrast, actively managed funds each, in theory, have a unique investment strategy developed by the active portfolio manager.

This section discusses different approaches to gain access to an investment strategy's desired performance stream: pooled investments (e.g., mutual funds and exchange-traded funds), derivatives-based portfolios (using options, futures, and swaps contracts), and direct investment in the stocks underlying the strategy.

Some passive investments are managed to establish a target beta, and managers are judged on how closely they meet that target. Portfolio managers commonly use futures and open-end mutual funds to transform a position (in cash, for example) and obtain the desired equity exposure. This process is known as "equitizing." The choice of which method to use is largely determined by the financing costs of rolling the futures contracts over time.[3] With multinational indexes, it can be expedient to buy a set of complementary exchange-traded funds to replicate market returns for the various countries.

3.1. Pooled Investments

Pooled investments are the most convenient approach for the average investor because they are easy to purchase, hold, and sell. This section covers conventional open-end mutual funds and exchange-traded funds (ETFs).

---

[3]Rolling a futures contract involves closing out a contract prior to its last trading day before expiration while taking a similar position in the next month's contract. Contracts that are cash-settled are marked to market, and any resulting funds in the account are available as margin that is used to initiate a position in the next month's contract.

The Qualidex Fund, started in 1970, was the first open-end index mutual fund available to retail investors. It was designed to track the Dow Jones Industrial Average. The Vanguard S&P 500 Index Fund, started in 1975, was the first retail fund to attract investors on a large scale. The primary advantage provided by a mutual fund purchase is its ease of investing and record keeping.

Investors who want to invest in a passively managed mutual fund must take the same steps as those investing in actively managed ones. First, a needs analysis must be undertaken to decide on the investor's return and risk objectives as well as investment constraints, and then to find a corresponding strategy. For example, risk-averse equity investors may seek a low volatility strategy, while investors looking to match the broad market may prefer an all-cap market-cap-weighted strategy. Once the need has been identified, it is likely that a mutual fund-based strategy can be built to match that need.

Traditional mutual fund shares can be purchased directly from the adviser who manages the fund, through a fund marketplace, or through an individual financial adviser. The process is the same for any mutual fund whether passively or actively managed. Investment companies generally have websites and call centers to help their prospective investors transact shares.

A fund marketplace is a brokerage company that offers funds from different providers. The advantage of buying a mutual fund from a fund marketplace is the ease of purchasing a mutual fund from different providers while maintaining a single account for streamlined record keeping.

A financial adviser can also help in purchasing a fund by offering the guidance needed to identify the strategy, providing the single account to house the fund shares, and gaining access to lower-cost share classes that may not be available to all investors.

No matter how mutual fund shares are purchased, the primary benefits of investing passively using mutual funds are low costs and the convenience of the fund structure. The manager of the passively managed fund handles all of the needed rebalancing, reconstitution, and other changes that are required to keep the investment portfolio in line with the index. Passively managed strategies require constant maintenance and care to reinvest cash from dividends and to execute the buys and sells required to match the additions and deletions of securities to the index. The portfolio manager of a passively managed mutual fund also has most of the same responsibilities as a direct investor. These include trading securities, managing cash, deciding how to proceed with corporate actions, voting proxies, and reporting performance. Moreover, index-replicating mutual funds bear costs in such areas as registration, custodial, and audit, which are similar to those for actively managed mutual funds.

Record-keeping functions for a mutual fund include maintaining a record of who owns the shares and when and at what price those shares were purchased. Record keepers work closely with both the custodian of the fund shares to ensure that the security is safely held in the name of the investor and the mutual fund sponsor who communicates those trades.

In the United States, mutual funds are governed by provisions of the Investment Company Act of 1940. In Europe, Undertakings for Collective Investment in Transferable Securities (UCITS) is an agreement among countries in the European Union that governs the management and sale of collective investment funds (mutual funds) across European borders.

ETFs are another form of pooled investment vehicle. The first ETF was launched in the Canadian market in 1990 to track the return of 35 large stocks listed on the Toronto Stock Exchange. ETFs were introduced in the US market in 1993. They are registered funds that can be bought and sold throughout the trading day and change hands like stocks. Advantages of the ETF structure include ease of trading, low management fees, and tax efficiency. Unlike with traditional open-end mutual funds, ETF shares can be bought by investors using margin borrowing; moreover, investors can take short positions in an ETF. ETFs offer flexibility in that they track a wide array of indexes.

ETFs have a unique structure that requires a fund manager as well as an authorized participant who can deliver the assets to the manager. The role of the authorized participant is to be the market maker for the ETF and the intermediary between investors and the ETF fund manager when shares are created or redeemed. To create shares of the ETF, the authorized participant delivers a basket of the underlying stocks to the fund manager and, in exchange, receives shares of the ETF that can be sold to the public. When an authorized participant needs to redeem shares, the process is reversed so that the authorized participant delivers shares of the ETF in exchange for a basket of the underlying stocks that can then be sold in the market.

The creation/redemption process is used when the authorized participant is either called upon to deliver new shares of the ETF to meet investor needs or when large redemptions are requested. The redemption process occurs when an authorized participant needs to reduce its exposure to the ETF holding and accepts shares of the underlying securities in exchange for shares of the ETF.

All else equal, taxable investors in an ETF will have a smaller taxable event than those in a similarly managed mutual fund. Managers of mutual funds must sell their portfolio holdings to fulfill shareholder redemptions, creating a taxable event where gains and losses are realized. ETFs have the advantage of accommodating those redemptions through an in-kind delivery of stock, which is the redemption process. Capital gains are not recorded when a redemption is fulfilled through an in-kind delivery of securities, so the taxable gain/loss passed to the investor becomes smaller.

Disadvantages of the ETF structure include the need to buy at the offer and sell at the bid price, commission costs, and the risk of an illiquid market when the investor needs to buy or sell the actual ETF shares.

ETFs that track indexes are used to an increasing degree by financial advisers to provide targeted exposure to different sectors of the investable market. Large investors find it more cost effective to build their own portfolios through replication, stratified sampling, and optimization, concepts to be introduced later. Other investors find ETFs to be a relatively low-cost method of tracking major indexes. Importantly, like traditional open-end mutual funds, ETFs are an integrated approach in that portfolio management and accounting are conducted by the fund adviser itself. A limitation is that there are far more benchmark indexes than ETFs, so not all indexes have an exchange-traded security that tracks them, although new ETFs are constantly being created. Exhibit 7 depicts the strong global trend in investor net flows into index-tracking equity ETFs since 1998. The exhibit does not reflect changes in value caused by market fluctuations, but rather purely investments and redemptions.

Exhibit 7 also shows that, over time, factor-based ETFs have become a large segment of the market. Factor-based ETFs provide exposure to such single factors as Size, Value, Momentum, Quality, Volatility, and Yield. Among the most important innovations are ETFs that track multiple factors simultaneously. For example, the iShares Edge MSCI Multifactor USA ETF emphasizes exposure to Size, Value, Momentum, and Quality factors. Meanwhile, the ETF attempts to maintain characteristics that are similar to the underlying MSCI USA Diversified Multiple-Factor Index, including industry sector exposure. As of 2017, the fund's expense ratio is 0.20% and it holds all 139 of the stocks in the index.

EXHIBIT 7   Cumulative Monthly Flows (USD millions) into Index-Tracking Equity ETF Shares
Listed in 33 Markets, January 1997–April 2017

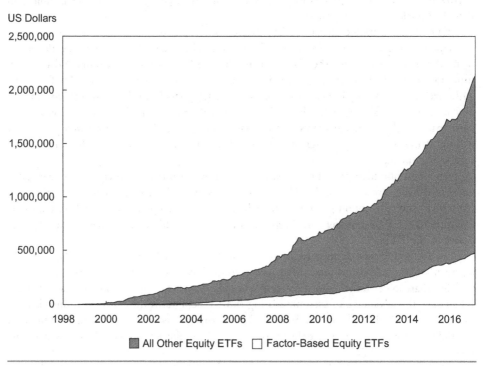

Source: Morningstar Direct, May 2017.

Exhibit 8 shows that, among 33 major exchange locations, the market value of equity
ETFs that track indexes approaches USD 3 trillion. US exchanges have about one-third of the
individual ETFs and more than 75% of the total market value as of May 2017. Japan, the

EXHIBIT 8   Number of Index-Tracking Equity ETFs and Their Market Values (in USD millions)
May 2017

Exchange Location	ETFs	Market Value
United States	1,104	2,236,166
Japan	99	200,965
United Kingdom	365	139,900
Switzerland	272	104,025
Germany	205	81,047
France	260	66,680
Canada	252	47,625

Exchange Location	ETFs	Market Value
Netherlands	24	22,350
South Korea	177	12,162
Hong Kong SAR	63	9,605
Italy	22	3,724
Singapore	41	3,451
Australia	55	2,873
Mexico	12	2,319
Sweden	4	1,922
Spain	6	1,654
Brazil	13	1,411
South Africa	27	1,347
New Zealand	11	566
Finland	1	234
Next 13 Locations	52	794
Total for 33 Locations	3,166	2,940,818

Source: Morningstar Direct, May 2017.

United Kingdom, and Switzerland have more than half of the remaining market value. These numbers reflect purely passive ETFs, including factor-based securities.

The decision of whether to use a conventional open-end mutual fund versus an ETF often comes down to cost and flexibility. Investors who seek to mimic an index must identify a suitable tracking security. According to Morningstar, in the United States, ETFs track 1,354 distinct equity indexes while conventional open-end mutual funds track only 184. Of the ETFs, 38 benchmarks are for price-only returns and the remainder are for total returns, which also include the return from reinvested dividends. Long-term investors benefit from the slightly lower expense ratios of ETFs than otherwise equivalent conventional open-end mutual funds. However, the brokerage fees associated with frequent investor trades into ETF shares can negate the expense ratio advantage and thus make ETFs less economical.

3.2. Derivatives-Based Approaches

Beyond purchasing a third-party-sponsored pooled investment and building it themselves, investors can access index performance through such derivatives as options, swaps, or futures contracts. Derivative strategies are advantageous in that they can be low cost, easy to implement, and provide leverage. However, they also present a new set of risks, including counterparty default risk for derivatives that are not traded on exchanges or cleared through a clearing house. Derivatives can also be relatively difficult to access for individual investors.

Options, swaps, and futures contracts can be found on many of the major indexes, such as the MSCI EAFE Index (EAFE stands for Europe, Australasia, and the Far East) and the S&P 500 Index. Options and futures are traded on exchanges and so are processed through a clearing house. This is important because a clearing house eliminates virtually all of the default risk present in having a contract with a single counterparty. Equity swaps, on the other hand, are generally executed with a single counterparty and so add the risk of default by that counterparty.

Derivatives allow for leverage through their notional value amounts. Notional value of the contracts can be many times greater than the initial cash outlay. However, derivatives expire, whereas stocks can be held indefinitely. The risk of an expiring options contract is a complete loss of the relatively small premium paid to acquire the exposure. Futures and swaps can be extended by "rolling" the contract forward, which means selling the expiring contract and buying a longer dated one.

Futures positions must be initiated with a futures commission merchant (FCM), a clearing house member assigned to trade on behalf of the investor. The FCM posts the initial margin required to open the position and then settles on a daily basis to comply with the maintenance margin required by the clearing house. The FCM also helps close the position upon expiration. However, futures accounts are not free of effort on the client's part. Having a futures account requires the management of daily cash flows, sometimes committing additional money and sometimes drawing it down.

It is uncommon for passive portfolio managers to use derivatives in the long term to synthetically mimic the return from physical securities. Derivatives are typically used to adjust a pre-existing portfolio to move closer to meeting its objectives. These derivative positions are often referred to as an **overlay**. A **completion overlay** addresses an indexed portfolio that has diverged from its proper exposure. A common example is a portfolio that has built up a surplus of cash from investor flows or dividends, causing the portfolio's beta to be significantly less than that of the benchmark. Using derivatives can efficiently restore the overall portfolio beta to its target. A **rebalancing overlay** addresses a portfolio's need to sell certain constituent securities and buy others. Particularly in the context of a mixed stock and bond portfolio, using equity index derivatives to rebalance toward investment policy target weights can be efficient and cost-effective. A **currency overlay** assists a portfolio manager in hedging the returns of securities that are held in a foreign currency back to the home country's currency.

Equity index derivatives offer several advantages over cash-based portfolio construction approaches. A passive portfolio manager can increase or decrease exposure to the entire index portfolio in a single transaction. Managers who want to make tactical adjustments to portfolio exposure often find derivatives to be a more efficient tool than cash-market transactions for achieving their goals. Many derivatives contracts are highly liquid, sometimes more so than the underlying cash assets. Especially in this case, portfolio exposures can be tactically adjusted quickly and at low cost.

For the longer term, strategic changes to portfolios are usually best made using cash instruments, which have indefinite expirations and do not necessitate rolling over expiring positions. Futures markets, for example, can impose position limits on such instruments that constrain the scale of use. Derivatives usage is also sometimes restricted by regulatory bodies or investment policy statement stipulations, so in this case cash could be a preferred approach. Finally, depending on the index that is being tracked by the passive portfolio manager, a suitable exchange-traded futures contract may not be available.

In addition to options, which have nonlinear payoffs,[4] the two primary types of equity index derivatives contracts are futures and swaps. Equity index futures provide exposure to a

---

[4]The nonlinearity of option payoffs arises because all prices of the underlying that cause the option to be out-of-the-money at expiration produce zero payoff for the investor who holds the option. When an option is in the money, the investor holding it experiences a linearly increasing payoff at all prices of the underlying in that range. In the case of futures and swaps, the payoffs are two-sided and linear for price changes in the underlying that are in the investor's favor as well as those that are against the investor.

specific index. Unlike many commodity futures contracts, index futures are cash-settled, which means the counterparties exchange cash rather than the underlying shares.

The buyer of an equity index futures contract obtains the right to buy the underlying (in this case, an index) on the expiration date of the contract at the futures price prevailing at the time the derivative was purchased. For exchange-traded futures, the buyer is required to post margin (collateral) in the account to decrease the credit risk to the exchange, which is the effective counterparty. For S&P 500 Index futures contracts as traded on the Chicago Mercantile Exchange, every USD change in the futures price produces a USD 250 change in the contract value (thus a "multiplier" of 250). On 4 August 2016, the September S&P 500 futures contract settled at a price of 2,159.30, after settling at 2,157 the day before. The change in contract value was thus $250 \times USD (2,159.30 - 2,157) = USD 575$.

Equity index futures contracts for various global markets are shown in Exhibit 9.

EXHIBIT 9   Representative Equity-Index Futures Contracts

Index Futures Contract	Market	Contract Currency and Multiplier
Americas		
Dow Jones mini	United States	USD 5
S&P 500	United States	USD 250
S&P 500 mini	United States	USD 50
NASDAQ 100 mini	United States	USD 20
Mexican IPC	Mexico	MXN 10
S&P/TSX Composite mini	Canada	CAD 5
S&P/TSX 60	Canada	CAD 200
Ibovespa	Brazil	BRL 1
Europe, Middle East, and Africa		
Euro STOXX 50	Europe	EUR 10
FTSE 100	United Kingdom	GBP 10
DAX 30	Germany	EUR 25
CAC 40	France	EUR 10
FTSE/Athens 20	Greece	EUR 5
OMX Stockholm 30	Sweden	SEK 100
Swiss Market	Switzerland	CHF 10
OMX Copenhagen 20	Denmark	DKK 100
PSI-20	Portugal	EUR 1
IBEX 35	Spain	EUR 10
WIG20	Poland	PLN 10
BIST 30	Turkey	TRY 100
FTSE/JSE Top 40	South Africa	ZAR 10

Index Futures Contract	Market	Contract Currency and Multiplier
Asia Pacific		
S&P/ASX 200	Australia	AUD 25
CSI 300	Chinese mainland	CNY 300
Hang Seng	Hong Kong SAR	HKD 50
H-Shares	Hong Kong SAR	HKD 50
Nifty 50	India	INR 50
Nikkei 225	Japan	JPY 1,000
Topix	Japan	JPY 10,000
KOSPI 200	Korea	KRW 500,000

Given that futures can be traded using only a small amount of margin, it is clear that futures provide a significant degree of potential leverage to a portfolio. Leverage can be considered either a positive or negative characteristic, depending on the manner with which the derivative instrument is used. Unlike some institutional investors' short-sale constraints on stock positions, many investors do not face constraints on opening a futures position with a sale of the contracts. Among other benefits of futures is the high degree of liquidity in the market, as evidenced by low bid–ask spreads. Both commission and execution costs also tend to be low relative to the exposure achieved. The low cost of transacting makes it easy for portfolio managers to use futures contracts to modify the equity risk exposure of their portfolios.

Equity index futures do come with some disadvantages. Futures are used by index fund managers because the instruments are expected to move in line with the underlying index. To the extent that the futures and spot prices do not move in concert, the portfolio may not track the benchmark perfectly. The extent to which futures prices do not move with spot prices is known as basis risk. Basis risk results from using a hedging instrument that is imperfectly matched to the investment being hedged. Basis risk can arise when the underlying securities pay dividends, while the futures contract tracks only the price of the underlying index. The difference can be partially mitigated when futures holders combine that position with interest-bearing securities.

As noted, futures account holders also must post margin. The margin amount varies by trading exchange. In the case of an ASX-200 futures contract, the initial margin required by the Sydney Futures Exchange in January 2017 for an overnight position is AUD 6,700. The minimum maintenance margin for one contract is AUD 5,300.

By way of example, assume an investor buys an ASX-200 futures contract priced at AUD 5,700, and the futures contract has a multiplier of 25. The investor controls AUD 142,500 [= 25 × AUD 5,700] in value. This currency amount is known as the contract unit value. With the initial margin of AUD 6,700 and a maintenance margin of AUD 5,300, a margin call will be triggered if the contract unit value decreases by more than AUD 1,400. A decrease of AUD 1,400 in the margin is associated with a contract unit value of AUD 142,500 – AUD 1,400 = AUD 141,100. This corresponds to an ASX-200 futures price of AUD 5,644 [= AUD 141,100/25]. Thus, a futures price decrease of 0.98% [= (AUD 5,644 – AUD 5,700)/ AUD 5,700] is associated with a decrease in the margin account balance of 20%. This example demonstrates how even a small change in the index value can result in a margin call once the mark-to-market process occurs.

Another derivatives-based approach is the use of equity index swaps. Equity index swaps are negotiated arrangements in which two counterparties agree to exchange cash flows in the future. For example, consider an investor who has a EUR 20 million notional amount and wants to be paid the return on her benchmark index, the Euro STOXX 50, during the coming year. In exchange, the investor agrees to pay a floating rate of return of Libor + 0.20% per year, with settlement occurring semi-annually. Assuming a six-month stock index return of 2.3% and annualized Libor of 0.18% per year, the first payment on the swap agreement would be calculated as follows. The investor would receive EUR 20 million × 0.023 = EUR 460,000. The investor would be liable to the counterparty for EUR 20 million × (0.0018 + 0.0020) × (180/360) = EUR 38,000; so, when the first settlement occurs the investor would receive EUR 460,000 − EUR 38,000 = EUR 422,000. In this case, the payment received by the passive portfolio manager is from the first leg of the swap, and the payment made by that manager is from the second leg. Libor is used in this example, but the second leg can also involve the return on a different index, stock, or other asset, or even a fixed currency amount per period.

Disadvantages of swaps include counterparty, liquidity, interest rate, and tax policy risks. Relatively frequent settlement decreases counterparty risk and reduces the potential loss from a counterparty's failure to perform. Equity swaps tend to be non-marketable instruments, so once the agreement is made there is not a highly liquid market that allows them to be sold to another party (though it is usually possible to go back to the dealer and enter into an offsetting position). Although the equity index payment recipient is an equity investor, this investor must deliver an amount linked to Libor; the investor bears interest rate risk. One prime motivation for initiating equity swaps is to avoid paying high taxes on the full return amount from an equity investment. This advantage is dependent on tax laws remaining favorable, which means that equity swaps carry tax policy risk.

There are a number of advantages to using an equity swap to gain synthetic exposure to index returns. Exchange-traded futures contracts are available only on a limited number of equity indexes. Yet as long as there is a willing counterparty, a swap can be initiated on virtually any index. So swaps can be customized with respect to the underlying as well as to settlement frequency and maturity. Although most swap agreements are one year or shorter in maturity, they can be negotiated for as long a tenor as the counterparties are willing. If a swap is used, it is not necessary for an investor to pay transaction costs associated with buying all of the index constituents. Like futures, a swap can help a portfolio manager add leverage or hedge a portfolio, which is usually done on a tactical or short-term basis.

3.3. Separately Managed Equity Index-Based Portfolios

Building an index-based equity portfolio as a separately managed portfolio requires a certain set of capabilities and tools. An equity investor who builds an indexed portfolio will need to subscribe to certain data on the index and its constituents. The investor also requires a robust trading and accounting system to manage the portfolio, broker relationships to trade efficiently and cheaply, and compliance systems to meet applicable laws and regulations.

The data subscription can generally be acquired directly from the index provider and may be offered on a daily or less-frequent basis. Generally, the data are provided for analysis only and a separate license must be purchased for index replication strategies. The index subscription data should include company and security identifiers, weights, cash dividend, return, and corporate action information. Corporate actions can include stock dividends and splits, mergers and acquisitions, liquidations, and other reasons for index constituent inclusion and exclusion. These data are generally provided in electronic format and can be delivered via file downloads or fed through a portfolio manager's analytical systems, such as Bloomberg or FactSet. The data are then used as the basis for the indexed portfolio.

Certain trading systems, such as those provided by Charles River Investment Management Solution, SS&C Advent (through Moxy), and Eze Castle Integration, allow the manager to see her portfolio and compare it to the chosen benchmark. Common features of trading systems include electronic communication with multiple brokers and exchanges, an ability to record required information on holdings for taxable investors, and modeling tools so that a portfolio can be traded to match its benchmark.

Accounting systems should be able to report daily performance, record historical transactions, and produce statements. Portfolio managers rely heavily on their accounting systems and teams to help them understand the drivers of portfolio performance.

Broker relationships are an often-overlooked advantage of portfolio managers that are able to negotiate better commission rates. Commissions are a negative drag on a portfolio's returns. The commission rates quoted to a manager can differ on the basis of the type of securities being traded, the size of the trade, and the magnitude of the relationship between the manager and broker.

Finally, compliance tools and teams are necessary. Investors must adhere to a myriad of rules and regulations, which can come from client agreements and regulatory bodies. Sanctions for violating compliance-related rules can range from losing a client to losing the registration to participate in the investment industry; thus, a robust compliance system is essential to the success of an investment manager.

Compliance rules can be company-wide or specific to an investor's account. Company-wide rules take such forms as restricting trades in stocks of affiliated companies. Rules specific to an account involve such matters as dealing with a directed broker or steps to prevent cash overdrafts. Compliance rules should also be written to prohibit manager misconduct, such as front-running in a personal account prior to executing client trades.

To ensure that their portfolios closely match the return stream of the chosen index, indexed portfolio managers must review their holdings and their weightings versus the index each day. Although a perfect match is a near impossibility because of rounding errors and trading costs, the manager must always weigh the benefits and costs of maintaining a close match.

To establish the portfolio, the manager creates a trading file and transmits the file to an executing broker, who buys the securities using a program trade. **Program trading** is a strategy of buying or selling many stocks simultaneously. Index portfolio managers may trade thousands of positions in a single trade file and are required to deliver the orders and execute the trades quickly. The creation of trades may be done on something as rudimentary as an Excel spreadsheet, but it is more likely to be created on an order management system (OMS), such as Charles River

Portfolio managers use their OMS to model their portfolios against the index, decide which trades to execute, and transmit the orders. Transmitting an order in the United States is generally done on a secure communication line, such as through FIX Protocol. FIX Protocol is an electronic communication protocol to transmit the orders from the portfolio manager to the broker or directly to the executing market place. The orders are first transmitted via FIX Protocol to a broker who executes the trade and then delivers back pricing and settlement instructions to the OMS. International trading is usually communicated using a similar protocol through SWIFT. SWIFT stands for "Society for Worldwide Interbank Financial Telecommunication," and is a service that is used to securely transmit trade instructions.

Index-based strategies seek to replicate an index that is priced at the close of business each day. Therefore, most index-based trade executions take place at the close of the business day using market-on-close (MOC) orders. Matching the trade execution to the benchmark price helps the manager more closely match the performance of the index.

Beyond the portfolio's initial construction, managers maintain the portfolio by trading any index changes, such as adds/deletes, rebalances, and reinvesting cash dividend payments. These responsibilities require the manager to commit time each day to oversee the portfolio and create the necessary trades. Best practice would be to review the portfolio's performance each day and its composition at least once a month.

Dividends paid over time can accumulate to significant amounts that must be reinvested into the securities in the index. Index fund managers must determine when the cash paid out by dividends should be reinvested and then create trades to purchase the required securities.

4. PORTFOLIO CONSTRUCTION

This section discusses the principal approaches that equity portfolio managers use when building a passive-indexed portfolio by transacting in individual securities. The three approaches are full replication, stratified sampling, and optimization. According to Morningstar, among index-tracking equity ETF portfolios globally:

- 38% of funds (representing 42% of July 2016 assets) use full replication;
- 41% of funds (representing 54% of assets) use stratified sampling or optimization techniques; and
- 21% of funds (representing only about 4% of assets) use synthetic replication, using over-the-counter derivatives.

4.1. Full Replication

Full replication in index investing occurs when a manager holds all securities represented by the index in weightings that closely match the actual index weightings. Advantages of full replication include the fact that it usually accomplishes the primary goal of matching the index performance, and it is easy to comprehend. Full replication, however, requires that the asset size of the mandate is sufficient and that the index constituents are available for trading.

Not all indexes lend themselves to full replication. For example, the MSCI ACWI Investable Markets Index consists of over 8,000 constituents,[5] but not all securities need be

---

[5]The MSCI ACWI Investable Markets Index captures large, mid-, and small-cap stocks across developed and emerging market countries and represents 8,609 securities as of April 2016.

held to closely match the characteristics and performance of that index. Other indexes, such as the S&P 500, have constituents that are readily available for trading and can be applied to portfolios as small as USD 10 million.

With respect to the choice between index replication versus sampling, as the number of securities held increases, tracking error decreases because the passive portfolio gets closer to replicating the index perfectly. Yet as the portfolio manager adds index constituent stocks that are smaller and more thinly traded than average, trading costs increase. The trading costs can take the form of brokerage fees and upward price pressure as a result of the portfolio's purchases. These transaction costs can depress performance and start to impose a small negative effect on tracking effectiveness. As the portfolio manager moves to the least liquid stocks in the index, transaction costs begin to dominate and tracking error increases again. Thus, for an index that has some constituent securities that are relatively illiquid, the conceptual relationship between tracking error and the number of securities held is U-shaped. The relation can be depicted as shown in Exhibit 10.

EXHIBIT 10   Relation between Tracking Error and Transaction Costs versus Number of Benchmark Index Constituent Stocks Held

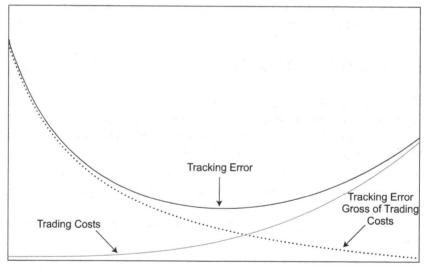

Number of Securities Held

Source: Author team.

Many managers attempt to match an index's characteristics and performance through a full replication technique, but how does a manager create the portfolio? As mentioned in a prior section, the passive equity manager needs data from the index provider to construct the portfolio. This includes the constituent stocks, their relevant identifiers (ticker, CUSIP, SEDOL, or ISIN), shares outstanding, and price. Additional data, such as constituents' dividends paid and total return, facilitate management of the portfolio.

The manager then uses the index data to create the portfolio by replicating as closely as possible the index constituents and weights. The portfolio construction method may vary by investor, but the most common method is to import the provided data into a data compiler such as Charles River, Moxy, or some other external or internally created OMS. The imported data show the manager the trades that are needed to match the index. Exhibit 11 contains an example for a portfolio that has an initial investment of USD 10 million.

Exhibit 11 shows a current portfolio made up of one security and a cash holding that needs to be traded to match a two-security index. The index becomes the model for the portfolio, and that model is used to match the portfolio. This type of modeling can easily and cheaply be conducted using spreadsheet and database programs, such as Excel and Access. However, the modeling is only a part of the portfolio management process.

EXHIBIT 11   Sample Index Portfolio Positions and Transactions

Identifier	Security Description	Current Price	Current Weight	Model Weight	Current Weight – Model Weight = Variance	Current Shares	New Shares	Shares to Trade
Cash	Cash	1	50%	0%	50%	5,000,000	0	−5,000,000
SECA	Security 1	100	50%	50%	0%	50,000	50,000	0
SECB	Security 2	50	0%	50%	−50%	0	100,000	100,000

The OMS should also be programmed to provide the investor with pre-trade compliance to check for client-specific restrictions, front-running issues, and other compliance rules. The OMS is also used to deliver the buy and sell orders for execution using FIX or SWIFT Protocol, as described previously.

After initial creation of the indexed portfolio, the manager must maintain the portfolio according to any changes in the index. The changes are announced publicly by the index provider. Index fund managers use those details to update their models in the OMS and to determine the number of shares to buy or sell. A fully replicated portfolio must make those changes in a timely manner to maintain its performance tracking with the index. Again, a perfectly replicated index portfolio must trade at the market-on-close price where available to match the price used by the index provider in calculating the index performance.

4.2. Stratified Sampling

Despite their preference to realize the benefits of pure replication of an index, portfolio managers often find it impractical to hold all the constituent securities. Some equity indexes have a large number of constituents, and not all constituents offer high trading liquidity. This can make trading expensive, especially if a portfolio manager needs to scale up the portfolio. Brokerage fees can also become excessive if the number of constituents is large.

Holding a limited sample of the index constituents can produce results that track the index return and risk characteristics closely. But such sampling is not done randomly. Rather, portfolio managers use stratified sampling. To stratify is to arrange a population into distinct strata or subgroupings. Arranged correctly, the various strata will be mutually exclusive and also exhaustive (a complete set), and they should closely match the characteristics and performance of the index. Common stratification approaches include using industry membership and equity style characteristics. Investors who use stratified sampling to track the S&P 500 commonly assign each stock to one of the eleven sectors designated by the Global Industry Classification Standard (GICS). For multinational indexes, stratification is often done first on the basis of country affiliation. Indexes can be stratified along multiple dimensions (e.g., country affiliation and then industry affiliation) within each country. An advantage of stratifying along multiple dimensions is closer index tracking.

In equity indexing, stratified sampling is most frequently used when the portfolio manager wants to track indexes that have many constituents or when dealing with a relatively low level of assets under management. Indexes with many constituents are usually multi-country or multi-cap indexes, such as the S&P Global Broad Market Index that consists of more than 11,000 constituents. Most investors are reluctant to trade and maintain 11,000 securities when a significantly smaller number of constituents would achieve most portfolios' tracking objectives. Regardless of the stratified sampling approach used, passive equity managers tend to weight portfolio holdings proportionately to each stratum's weight in the index.

EXAMPLE 2   Stratified Sampling

A portfolio manager responsible for accounts of high-net-worth individuals is asked to build an index portfolio that tracks the S&P 500 Value Index, which has more than 300 constituents. The manager and the client agree that the minimum account size will be USD 750,000, but the manager explains to the client that full replication is not feasible at a reasonable cost because of the mandate size. How can the manager use stratified sampling to achieve her goal of tracking the S&P 500 Value Index?

Solution: The manager recommends that the client set a maximum number of constituents (for example, 200) to limit the average lot size and to reduce commission costs. Next, the manager seeks to identify the constituents to hold based on their market capitalization. That is, the manager selects the 200 securities with the largest market capitalizations. Then the manager seeks to more closely match the performance of the index by matching the sector weightings of the sampled portfolio to the sector weightings of the index. After comparing sector weights, the manager reweights the sampled portfolio. Using this method of stratified sampling meets the manager's stated goal of closely tracking the performance of the index at a reasonable cost.

4.3. Optimization

Optimization approaches for index portfolio construction, such as full replication and stratified sampling, have index-tracking goals. Optimization typically involves maximizing a desirable characteristic or minimizing an undesirable characteristic, subject to one or more constraints. For an indexed portfolio, optimization could involve minimizing index tracking error, subject to the constraint that the portfolio holds 50 constituent securities or fewer. The desired output from the optimization process is identification of the 50 securities and their weights that results in the lowest possible tracking error. The number of security holdings is not the only possible constraint. Other common constraints include limiting portfolio membership to stocks that have a market capitalization above a certain specified level, style characteristics that mimic those of the benchmark, restricting trades to round lots, and using only stocks that will keep rebalancing costs low.

Roll (1992) and Jorion (2003) demonstrate that running an optimization to minimize tracking error can lead to portfolios that are mean–variance inefficient versus the benchmark. That is, the optimized portfolio may exhibit higher risk than the benchmark it is being optimized against. They show that a useful way to address this problem is to add a constraint on total portfolio volatility. Accordingly, the manager of an optimized passive fund would aim to make its total volatility equal to that of the benchmark index.

Fabozzi, Focardi, and Kolm (2010) note that in practice, passive portfolio managers often conduct a mean–variance optimization using all the index constituents, the output from which shows highly diverse weightings for the stocks. Given that investing in the lowest-weight stocks may involve marginal transaction costs that exceed marginal diversification benefits, in a second, post-optimization stage, the managers may then delete the lowest-weighted stocks.

Optimization can be conducted in conjunction with stratified sampling or alone. Optimization programs, when run without constraints, do not consider country or industry affiliation but rather use security-level data. Optimization requires an analyst who has a high level of technical sophistication, including familiarity with computerized optimization software or algorithms, and a good understanding of the output.

Advantages of optimization involve a lower amount of tracking error than stratified sampling. Also, the optimization process accounts explicitly for the covariances among the portfolio constituents. Although two securities from different industry sectors may be included in a passive portfolio under stratified sampling, if their returns move strongly together, one will likely be excluded from an optimized portfolio.

Usually the constituents and weights of an optimized portfolio are determined based on past market data; however, returns, variances, and correlations between securities tend to vary over time. Thus, the output from an optimization program may apply only to the period from which the data are drawn and not to a future period. Even if current results apply to the future, they might not be applicable for long. This means that optimization would need to be run frequently and adjustments made to the portfolio, which can be costly.

4.4. Blended Approach

For indexes that have few constituent securities or for which the constituents are homogeneous, full replication is typically advisable. When the reverse is true, sampling or optimization are likely to be the preferred methods. But such indexes as the Russell 3000, the S&P 1500, and the Wilshire 5000 span the capitalization spectrum from large to small. For these indexes, the 1,000 or so largest constituents are quite liquid, which means that brokerage fees, bid–ask spreads, and trading costs are low. For the largest-cap portion of an indexed portfolio, full replication is a sensible and desirable approach. For the index constituents that have smaller market capitalizations or less liquidity, however, a stratified sampling or optimization approach can be useful for all the reasons mentioned previously in this section. Thus, an indexed portfolio can actually be managed using a blended approach consisting of full replication for more-liquid issues and one of the other methods for less-liquid issues.

5. TRACKING ERROR MANAGEMENT

As discussed previously, managers of passive strategies use a variety of approaches to track indexes in cost-efficient ways. To the extent the portfolio manager's skills are ineffective, tracking error results. This section discusses the measurement and management of tracking error.

5.1. Tracking Error and Excess Return

Tracking error and excess return are two measures that enable investors to differentiate performance among passive portfolio managers. Tracking error indicates how closely the portfolio behaves like its benchmark and measures a manager's ability to replicate the benchmark return. Tracking error is calculated as the standard deviation of the difference between the portfolio return and its benchmark index return. Excess return measures the difference between the portfolio returns and benchmark returns. Tracking error for portfolio p then can be expressed by Equation 3.

$$\text{Tracking error}_p = \sqrt{\text{Variance}_{(R_p - R_b)}} \tag{3}$$

where R_p is the return on the portfolio and R_b is the return on the benchmark index. Excess return for portfolio p is calculated as in Equation 4.

$$\text{Excess return}_p = R_p - R_b \tag{4}$$

Tracking error and excess return are distinct measures; the terms should not be used interchangeably. Tracking error measures the manager's ability to closely track the benchmark over time. In principle, a manager whose return is identical to that of the index could have arrived at that point by lagging and subsequently leading the index, producing a net difference of zero. But being a standard deviation, tracking error cannot be zero in cases such as the one described. Excess returns can be positive or negative and tell the investor how the manager performed relative to the benchmark. Tracking error, which is a standard deviation, is always presented as a non-negative number.

Index fund managers endeavor to have low tracking error and excess returns that are not negative. Low tracking error is important in measuring the skill of the index fund manager because the investor's goal is to mimic the return stream of the index. Avoiding negative excess returns versus the benchmark is also important because the manager will want to avoid underperforming the stated index.

Tracking error varies according to the manager's approach to tracking the index. An index that contains a large number of constituents will tend to create higher tracking error than those with fewer constituents. This is because a large number of constituents may prevent the manager from fully replicating the index.

For an index fund, the degree of tracking error fluctuates over time. Also, the value will differ depending on whether the data frequency is daily or less frequent.

EXAMPLE 3   Tracking Error and Excess Return

Exhibit 12 illustrates key portfolio metrics for three of the older and larger conventional open-end funds in the Australian and South Korean markets. Based on the levels of tracking error and excess return figures provided in the exhibit, explain whether the funds are likely replicating or sampling.

EXHIBIT 12   Major Conventional Index Mutual Funds in Australia and South Korea

Fund Name (Holdings)	Holdings	Annual Management Fee (bps)	3-Year Annualized Tracking Error	3-Year Annualized Excess Return
Australian market benchmark for the following funds is the S&P/ASX 300 Index. Number of securities in the index: 300.				
BlackRock Indexed Australian Equity Fund	296	20	0.0347%	−0.1684%
Macquarie True Index Australian Shares	259	0	0.0167%	0.0111%
Vanguard Australian Shares Index	293	18	0.1084%	−0.1814%
South Korean market benchmark for the funds below is the KRX KOSPI 200 Korea Index. Number of securities in the index: 200.				
KB Star Korea Index Equity CE	190	36	1.2671%	0.3356%
KIM Cruise Index F2.8 Equity-Deriv A	178	9	1.5019%	1.7381%
Samsung Index Premium Equity-Deriv A	204	40	1.3325%	1.1097%

Solution: Based on the number of stocks in the fund compared to the index constituent number, it appears most funds are attempting to replicate. Two of the funds (Macquarie True Index and KIM Cruise Index) have 80% to 90% of the stocks in the index, which indicates they are more likely to be using sampling. One fund (Samsung Index Premium) actually holds more than the index, which can happen if buffering is used. No fund contains the same number of stocks as constituents in the index. Thus, it is not surprising that the funds failed to track their respective indexes perfectly. On an annualized basis, tracking error for the Australian funds is less than one-tenth the level of the Korean funds. However, the Korean funds' excess return—which is fund return less the benchmark index return—is positive in all three cases. The negative excess returns for two of the Australian funds are relatively close and possibly attributable to their management fees of 18–20 basis points.

5.2. Potential Causes of Tracking Error and Excess Return

Tracking error in an indexed equity fund can arise for several reasons. A major reason involves the fees charged. Although tracking error is expressed as an absolute value, fees are always negative because they represent a cost and drive down the excess return. Therefore, higher fees will contribute to lower excess returns and higher tracking error.

A second issue to consider is the number of securities held by the portfolio versus the benchmark index. Stock indexes that are liquid and investable may be fully replicated, while indexes with hard-to-find securities or a great number of securities are sampled. Sampled portfolios typically report greater tracking error than those that are fully replicated.

The intra-day trading of the constituent stocks of an indexed portfolio also presents an important issue to consider when attributing tracking error. The effect of intra-day trading can be positive or negative for a portfolio's returns compared to its benchmark index. The price levels used to report index returns are struck at the close of the trading day, so any securities that are bought or sold at a different price than that of the index will contribute to portfolio tracking error. Index fund managers can minimize this type of tracking error by transacting at the market-on-close price or as near to the closing time as feasible.

A secondary component of trading costs that contributes to tracking error is the trading commission paid to brokers. Commission costs make excess returns more negative and also affect tracking error. According to Perold and Salomon (1991), the trading cost for passive portfolio managers is likely to be lower than the trading cost for active managers who are suspected by their counterparties to possess an information advantage.

Another issue to consider is the cash holding of the portfolio. Equity indexes do not have a cash allocation, so any cash balance creates tracking error for the index fund manager. Cash can be accumulated in the portfolio from a variety of sources, such as dividends received, sale proceeds, investor contributions, and other sources of income. Cash flows from investors and from the constituent companies may not be invested immediately, and investing them often entails a commission cost. Both may affect tracking error. The tracking error caused by temporarily uninvested cash is known as **cash drag**. The effect of cash drag on portfolio value is negative when the market is rising and positive when it is falling.

Hill and Cheong (1996) discuss how to equitize a portfolio that would otherwise suffer from cash drag. One method is to use futures contracts. ETFs have been used widely for this purpose. Some portfolio managers establish a futures commission merchant relationship to offset their cash positions with a futures contract that represents the replicated index. When a manager does this, she will calculate the accrued dividends as well to hedge the dividend drag, which is cash drag attributable to accrued cash dividends paid to shareholders.

5.3. Controlling Tracking Error

The process of controlling tracking error involves trade-offs between the benefits and costs of maintaining complete faithfulness to the benchmark index, as illustrated in Exhibit 10. Portfolio managers who are unconstrained would keep the number of constituent securities and their weights as closely aligned to the benchmark index as possible. Even so, trading costs and other fees cause actual investment performance to deviate from index performance. Passive investing does not mean that the fund does not trade. Managers trade to accommodate inflows and outflows of cash from investors, to reinvest dividends, and to reflect changes in constituents of the underlying index.

As discussed in Section 5.2, most passive portfolio managers attempt to minimize cash held because a cash position generally creates undesirable tracking error. To keep tracking error low, portfolio managers need to invest cash flows received at the same valuations used by the benchmark index provider. Of course, because this is not always feasible, portfolio managers aim to maintain a beta of 1.0 relative to the benchmark index, while keeping other risk factor exposures similar to those of the index.

6. SOURCES OF RETURN AND RISK IN PASSIVE EQUITY PORTFOLIOS

Indexed portfolios began as a representation of market performance, and some investors accept the returns of the indexed portfolio without judgment. However, understanding both positive and negative sources of return through attribution analysis is an important step in the passive equity investment process.

6.1. Attribution Analysis

An investor has many choices across the investable spectrum of assets. An investor must first choose between stocks, bonds, and other asset classes and then partition each asset class by its sub-categories. In partitioning stocks, the process begins with choosing what countries to invest in, what market-cap sizes and investment style to use, and whether to weight the constituents using market cap or an alternative weighting method.

The return on an indexed portfolio can come from any of the aforementioned criteria. Return analyses are conducted ex-post, which means that the returns of the portfolio are studied after they have been experienced.

The sources of return for an equity index replication portfolio are the same as for any actively managed fund and include company-specific returns, sector returns, country returns, and currency returns. Beyond the traditional methods of grouping the risk and returns of the indexed portfolio, portfolio managers can group their indexed portfolios according to the stated portfolio objective. For example, a high dividend yield indexed portfolio may be grouped against the broad market benchmark by dividend yield. A low volatility portfolio could be grouped by volatility buckets to show how the lowest volatility stocks performed in the indexed portfolio as well as the broad market.

Most portfolio managers will rely on their portfolio attribution system to help them in understanding the sources of return. Index fund managers who track a broad market index need to understand what factors are driving the returns of that portfolio and its underlying index. Index fund managers of passive factor-based strategies should understand both the sources of return for their indexed portfolios and how those returns relate to the broad market index from which the constituents were chosen. In this way, passive factor-based strategies are very similar to actively managed funds in the sense that they are actively chosen.

Exhibit 13 shows an example of a portfolio attribution analysis using annual returns. Portfolio X is an index fund that seeks to replicate the performance of its benchmark. The manager of Portfolio X confirms that the portfolio, which has a return of 5.62%, is closely replicating the performance of the benchmark, which has a return of 5.65%.

EXHIBIT 13   Example of Sector Attribution Analysis (All figures in %)

Sector	Sector Return (A)	Portfolio X Sector Weight (B)	Portfolio X Contribution to Return (C) = (A) × (B)	Benchmark for Portfolio X Sector Weight (D)	Benchmark for Portfolio X Contribution to Return (E) = (A) × (D)	Attribution Analysis Difference (F) = (C) − (E)
Total	5.62	100.00	5.62	100.00	5.65	−0.03
Telecom. Services	16.94	2.25	0.38	2.34	0.40	−0.02
Utilities	15.45	12.99	2.01	13.03	2.01	−0.01
Consumer Discretionary	12.09	3.89	0.47	3.90	0.47	0.00
Materials	9.61	2.08	0.20	2.08	0.20	0.00
Information Technology	7.03	2.82	0.20	2.85	0.20	0.00
Consumer Staples	6.82	15.07	1.03	15.09	1.03	0.00
Industrials	3.93	16.08	0.63	16.15	0.63	0.00
Financials	0.50	19.85	0.10	19.32	0.10	0.00
Health Care	0.31	12.70	0.04	12.77	0.04	0.00
Real Estate	0.80	5.04	0.04	5.23	0.04	0.00
Energy	7.21	7.23	0.52	7.24	0.52	0.00
[Cash]	0.00	0.00	0.00	0.00	0.00	0.00

Using Exhibit 13, the manager analyzes the relative sector weights and sources of the three basis points of return difference. A portfolio that is within three basis points of its benchmark index is undoubtedly tracking the index closely. Beyond seeking the source of the tracking error, the portfolio manager will also seek to understand the source of the positive returns.

Attribution analyses like the one in Exhibit 13 can be structured in many ways. This analysis is grouped by economic sector. Sector attribution can help an investor develop expectations about how a portfolio might perform in different market conditions. For example, during an era of low interest rates, high-dividend stocks such as utilities are likely to outperform while financial stocks such as banks are likely to underperform, other things held equal. To the extent the portfolio holds financial stocks in a lower concentration than the benchmark, the portfolio will likely outperform if interest rates stay low.

Column A in Exhibit 13 shows the total return for each sector. For example, the Telecommunications sector posted a return of 16.94% over this period.

Column B shows Portfolio's X's sector weight. The portfolio is heavily invested in Financials, because this is the largest sector in the benchmark index.

Column C shows each sector's contribution to the overall return of Portfolio X, obtained by multiplying each sector weight in Portfolio X by the sector's total return. The sum of the eleven sectors' contributions to return is equal to the total return of the portfolio.

Column D shows the benchmark's sector weights.

Column E shows the contribution to return of each sector held by the benchmark, obtained by multiplying each sector's weight in the benchmark by the sector's total return. The sum of the eleven sectors' contributions to return is equal to the total return of the benchmark.

Finally, column F shows the difference in contribution to returns between Portfolio X and the benchmark. Column F is the difference between columns C and E.

Portfolio X has 15.07% invested in Consumer Staples, which compares to the benchmark index's 15.09% weight in that sector. The negligible underweighting combined with a sector return of 6.82% enabled the portfolio to closely match the contribution to return of the portfolio to that of the index.

The Telecommunications and Utilities sectors were the best-performing sectors over the period. Telecommunications and Utilities holdings made up 15.24% of the portfolio's holdings and contributed 2.39 percentage points (or 239 basis points) of the 5.62% total return.

Companies in the Telecommunications and Utilities sectors are high-dividend payers and are positively affected by falling interest rates. Given this information, the manager could then connect the positive performance of the sectors to the prevailing interest rate environment. The manager would also note in the attribution analysis that the same interest rate environment, in part, caused the Financials sector to underperform the market. These opposing forces act as a good hedge against interest rate movements in either direction and are part of a robust portfolio structure.

The portfolio manager of the strategy may use the attribution analysis to determine the sources of tracking error. In this case, the analysis confirmed that the portfolio is meeting its goal of closely tracking the composition and performance of its benchmark. Further, the portfolio manager is able to determine the sources of return, which in this case are in large part from the high-dividend-yielding Telecommunications and Utilities sectors.

6.2. Securities Lending

Investors who hold long equity positions usually keep the shares in their brokerage accounts, so they are ready to sell when the time arises. But there is a demand for those shares independent of fellow investors who may wish to buy them. Investors who want to sell short may need to borrow the shares, and they are willing to pay for the right to borrow. The securities-lending income received by long portfolio managers can be a valuable addition to portfolio returns. At the very least, the proceeds can help offset the other costs of managing the portfolio. In the case of low-cost indexed portfolios, securities lending income can actually make net expenses negative—meaning that in addition to tracking the benchmark index, the portfolio earns a return in excess of the index.

An investor who wants to lend securities often uses a lending agent. In the case of institutional investors (e.g., mutual funds, pension funds, and hedge funds), the custodian (i.e., custody bank) is frequently used. Occasionally, the asset management firm will offer securities lending services. Two legal documents are usually put in place, including a securities lending authorization agreement between the lender and the agent and a master securities lending agreement between the agent and borrowers.

The lending agent identifies a borrower who posts collateral (typically 102–105% of the value of the securities). When the collateral is in securities rather than cash, the lending agent holds them as a guarantee. The lending agent evaluates the collateral daily to ensure that it is sufficient. When the collateral is in the form of cash, the lending agent invests it in money market instruments and receives interest income. In this case, the borrower sometimes receives a rebate that partially defrays its lost interest income. Regardless, the borrower pays a fee to the lender when borrowing the securities, and the lender typically splits part of this fee with the lending agent.

According to the International Securities Lending Association (ISLA) (2016), the 30 June 2016 global value of securities made available for lending by institutional investors was EUR 14 trillion. Of this, EUR 1.9 trillion in value was actually loaned, 53% of which was in equity securities. Of global securities on loan, US and Canadian lenders represented 67% of value. Mutual funds and pension funds accounted for 66% of the total value of equity securities loaned. In North America, cash represents approximately 70% of all collateral; in Europe, noncash collateral is more than 80% of the total. ISLA reports that over 60 countries have issued formal legal opinions on the responsibilities of securities lending counterparties.

Securities lending carries risks that can offset the benefits. The main risks are the credit quality of the borrower (credit risk) and the value of the posted collateral (market risk), although liquidity risk and operational risk are additional considerations. Lenders are permitted to sell loaned securities at any time under the normal course of the portfolio management mandate, and the borrowed shares must be returned in time for normal settlement of that sale. However, there is no guarantee that the borrower can deliver on a timely basis.

An additional risk is that lenders can invest cash held as collateral; and if a lender elects to invest the cash in long-term or risky securities, the collateral value is at risk of erosion. As long as the cash is invested in low-risk securities, risk is kept low. Typically, an agreed return on the invested cash is rebated by the lender to the borrower. Similarly, borrowers must pay cash to lenders in lieu of any cash dividends received because the dividends paid by the issuers of the shares will go to the holders. According to Duffie, Gârleanu, and Pedersen (2002), institutional investors such as index mutual funds and pension funds are viewed as preferred lenders because they are long-term holders of shares and unlikely to claim their shares back abruptly from borrowers.

The example of Sigma Finance Company illustrates collateral investment risk. Sigma Finance was a structured investment vehicle that primarily held long-term debt financed by short-term borrowings, and profit came from the interest differential. During the credit 2008–2009 global financial crisis, Sigma was downgraded by the rating agencies and lost its ability to borrow in the short-term markets, which led to default. Investors in Sigma's credit offerings, many of them security lenders, suffered substantial losses because of the default.

Borrowers take formal legal title to the securities, receive all cash flows and voting rights, and pay an annualized cost of borrowing (typically 2–10%). The borrowing cost depends on the borrower's credit quality and how difficult it is to borrow the security in question. Some securities are widely recognized as "easy to borrow" (ETB).

A popular exchange-traded fund (ETF) represents a good example of how securities lending revenue can provide a benefit to investment beneficiaries. As of 31 March 2016, the USD 25.344 billion iShares Russell 2000 ETF had loaned out USD 4.273 billion in securities to 19 counterparties. This amount was 100% collateralized with cash. An affiliated party, BlackRock Institutional Trust Company, served as the securities lending agent in exchange for 4 basis points of collateral investment fees annually, totaling USD 29 million for the year ending 31 March 2016. IWM's net securities lending income for the year was slightly above USD 10 million, which nearly offset the approximately USD 14 million in investment advisory fees charged by the portfolio managers.

6.3. Investor Activism and Engagement by Passive Managers

Institutional investors, especially index fund managers, are among the largest shareholders of many companies. The shares that they vote can have a large influence on corporate elections and outcomes of the proxy process. Their status as large shareholders often gives such investors access to private meetings with corporate management to discuss their concerns and preferences regarding corporate policies on board structure and composition, management compensation, operational risk management, the integrity of accounting statements, and other matters. Goldstein (2014) reports that in a survey, about two-thirds of public companies indicate investor engagement in 2014 was higher than it had been three years earlier. The typical points of contact were investor relations specialists, general counsel/corporate secretary, the board chair, and the CEO or CFO of the company. The respondents also reported that engagement is now covering more topics, but the subject matter is not principally financial. Governance policies, executive compensation, and social, environmental, and strategy issues are dominant.

Ferguson (2010) argues that institutional investors—who are themselves required to act in a fiduciary capacity—have a key responsibility to carry out their duties as voting shareholders. Lambiotte, Gibney, and Hartley (2014) assert that if done in an enlightened way, voting and engagement with company management by passive investors can be a return-enhancing activity. Many hedge funds and other large investors even specialize in activism to align governance in their invested companies with shareholder interests.

Activist investors are usually associated with active portfolio management. If their activism efforts do not produce the desired result, they can express their dissatisfaction by selling their shares. In contrast, passive investors hold index-constituent stocks directly or indirectly. If they are attempting to match an index's performance, they do not have the flexibility to sell. Yet both types of investors usually have the opportunity to vote their shares and participate in governance improvements.

Why should governance matter for passive investors in broadly diversified portfolios? Across such portfolios, governance quality is broadly diversified; moreover, by definition, passive investors do not try to select the best-performing companies or avoid the worst. However, corporate governance improvements are aimed at improving the effectiveness of the operations, management, and board oversight of the business. If the resulting efficiency improvements are evidenced in higher returns to index-constituent stocks, the index performance rises and so does the performance of an index-tracking portfolio. Thus, a goal of activism is to increase returns.

Passive investors may even have a higher duty than more-transient active managers to use their influence to improve governance. As long as a stock has membership in the benchmark index, passive managers can be considered permanent shareholders. Such investors might benefit from engaging with company management and boards, even outside the usual proxy season. Reinforcing the concept of permanence, some companies even give greater voting rights to long-term shareholders. Dallas and Barry (2016) examine 12 US companies with voting rights that increase to four, five, or even ten votes per share if the holding period is greater than three and sometimes four years.

Most passive managers have a fiduciary duty to their clients that includes the obligation to vote proxy ballots on behalf of investors. Although shareholder return can be enhanced by engagement, the costs of these measures must also be considered. Among the more significant costs are staff resources required to become familiar with key issues and to engage management, regulators, and other investors. Researching and voting thousands of proxy ballots becomes problematic for many managers. They frequently hire a proxy voting service, such as Institutional Shareholder Services or Broadridge Financial Services, to achieve their goal of voting the proxy ballots in their clients' favor.

Although a strong argument can be made in favor of even passive managers voting their shares in an informed way and pursuing governance changes when warranted, potential conflicts of interest may limit investors' propensity to challenge company management. Consider the hypothetical case of a large financial firm that earns substantial fees from its business of administering corporate retirement plans, including the pension plan of Millheim Corp. Let us say that the financial firm also manages index funds, and Millheim's stock is one of many index constituents. If Millheim becomes the target of shareholder activism, the financial firm's incentives are structured to support Millheim's management on any controversial issue.

Some may question the probable effectiveness of activist efforts by passive investors. Management of the company targeted by activist investors is likely to see active portfolio managers as skillful and willing users of the proxy process to effect changes and accordingly will respond seriously. In contrast, passive investors are required to hold the company's shares to fulfill their tracking mandate (without the flexibility to sell or take a short position), and management may be aware of this constrained position and thus take passive investors' activist activities less seriously.

SUMMARY

This chapter explains the rationale for passive investing as well as the construction of equity market indexes and the various methods by which investors can track the indexes. Passive portfolio managers must understand benchmark index construction and the advantages and disadvantages of the various methods used to track index performance.

Among the key points made in this chapter are the following:

- Active equity portfolio managers who focus on individual security selection have long been unsuccessful at beating benchmarks and have charged high management fees to their end investors. Consequently, passive investing has increased in popularity.
- Passive equity investors seek to track the return of benchmark indexes and construct their portfolios to reflect the characteristics of the chosen benchmarks.

- Selection of a benchmark is driven by the equity investor's objectives and constraints as presented in the investment policy statement. The benchmark index must be rules-based, transparent, and investable. Specific important characteristics include the domestic or foreign market covered, the market capitalization of the constituent stocks, where the index falls in the value–growth spectrum, and other risk factors.
- The equity benchmark index weighting scheme is another important consideration for investors. Weighting methods include market-cap weighting, price weighting, equal weighting, and fundamental weighting. Market cap-weighting has several advantages, including the fact that weights adjust automatically.
- Index rebalancing and reconstitution policies are important features. Rebalancing involves adjusting the portfolio's constituent weights after price changes, mergers, or other corporate events have caused those weights to deviate from the benchmark index. Reconstitution involves deleting names that are no longer in the index and adding names that have been approved as new index members.
- Increasingly, passive investors use index-based strategies to gain exposure to individual risk factors. Examples of known equity risk factors include Capitalization, Style, Yield, Momentum, Volatility, and Quality.
- For passive investors, portfolio tracking error is the standard deviation of the portfolio return net of the benchmark return.
- Indexing involves the goal of minimizing tracking error subject to realistic portfolio constraints.
- Methods of pursuing passive investing include the use of such pooled investments as mutual funds and exchange-traded funds (ETFs), a do-it-yourself approach of building the portfolio stock-by-stock, and using derivatives to obtain exposure.
- Conventional open-end index mutual funds generally maintain low fees. Their expense ratios are slightly higher than for ETFs, but a brokerage fee is usually required for investor purchases and sales of ETF shares.
- Index exposure can also be obtained through the use of derivatives, such as futures and swaps.
- Building a passive portfolio by full replication, meaning to hold all the index constituents, requires a large-scale portfolio and high-quality information about the constituent characteristics. Most equity index portfolios are managed using either a full replication strategy to keep tracking error low, are sampled to keep trading costs low, or use optimization techniques to match as closely as possible the characteristics and performance of the underlying index.
- The principal sources of passive portfolio tracking error are fees, trading costs, and cash drag. Cash drag refers to the dilution of the return on the equity assets because of cash held. Cash drag can be exacerbated by the receipt of dividends from constituent stocks and the delay in getting them converted into shares.
- Portfolio managers control tracking error by minimizing trading costs, netting investor cash inflows and redemptions, and using equitization tools like derivatives to compensate for cash drag.
- Many index fund managers offer the constituent securities held in their portfolios for lending to short sellers and other market participants. The income earned from lending those securities helps offset portfolio management costs, often resulting in lower net fees to investors.

- Investor activism is engagement with portfolio companies and recognizing the primacy of end investors. Forms of activism can include expressing views to company boards or management on executive compensation, operational risk, board governance, and other value-relevant matters.
- Successful passive equity investment requires an understanding of the investor's needs, benchmark index construction, and methods available to track the index.

REFERENCES

Arnott, Robert, Jason Hsu, and Philip Moore. 2005. "Fundamental Indexation." *Financial Analysts Journal*, vol. 61, no. 2: 83–99.

Banz, Rolf W. 1981. "The Relationship between Return and Market Value of Common Stocks." *Journal of Financial Economics*, vol. 9, no. 1: 3–18.

Brinson, Gary P., L. Randolph Hood, and Gilbert L. Beebower. 1986. "Determinants of Portfolio Performance." *Financial Analysts Journal*, vol. 42, no. 4: 39–44.

Chen, Honghui, Gregory Noronha, and Vijay Singal. 2004. "The Price Response to S&P 500 Index Additions and Deletions: Evidence of Asymmetry and a New Explanation." *Journal of Finance*, vol. 63, no. 4: 1537–1573.

Choueifaty, Yves, and Yves Coignard. 2008. "Toward Maximum Diversification." *Journal of Portfolio Management*, vol. 35, no. 1: 40–51.

Dallas, Lynne, and Jordan M. Barry. 2016. "Long-Term Shareholders and Time-Phased Voting." *Delaware Journal of Corporate Law*, vol. 40, no. 2: 541–646.

Duffie, Darrell, Nicolae Gârleanu, and Lasse Heje Pedersen. 2002. "Securities Lending, Shorting, and Pricing." *Journal of Financial Economics*, vol. 66, no. 2–3: 307–339.

Fabozzi, Frank J., Sergio M. Focardi, and Petter N. Kolm. 2010. *Quantitative Equity Investing: Techniques and Strategies.* Hoboken, NJ: John Wiley & Sons.

Fama, Eugene F. and Kenneth R. French. 2015. "A Five-Factor Asset Pricing Model." *Journal of Financial Economics*, vol. 116, no. 1: 1–22.

Ferguson, Roger W., Jr. 2010. "Riding Herd on Company Management." *Wall Street Journal* (27 April).

French, Kenneth R. 2008. "The Cost of Active Investing." *Journal of Finance*, vol. 63, no. 4: 1537–1573.

Goldstein, Marc. 2014. "Defining Engagement: An Update on the Evolving Relationship between Shareholders, Directors, and Executives." Institutional Shareholder Services for the Investor Responsibility Research Center Institute: 1–48.

Hannam, Richard, and Frédéric Jamet. 2017. "IQ Insights: Equal Weighting and Other Forms of Size Tilting." SSGA white paper (January).

Hill, Joanne M., and Rebecca K. Cheong. 1996. "Minimizing Cash Drag with S&P 500 Index Tools." Goldman Sachs New York working paper.

International Securities Lending Association. 2015. "Establishing an Agency Securities Lending Program." ISLA white paper available at www.isla.co.uk.

International Securities Lending Association. 2016. "ISLA Securities Lending Market Report" (September): http://www.isla.co.uk/wp-content/uploads/2016/10/ISLA-SL-REPORT-9-16-final.pdf.

Jacobs, Bruce I., and Kenneth N. Levy. 2014. "Smart Beta versus Smart Alpha." *Journal of Portfolio Management*, vol. 40, no. 4: 4–7.

Jorion, Philippe. 2003. "Portfolio Optimization with Tracking-Error Constraints." *Financial Analysts Journal*, vol. 59, no. 5: 70–82.

Lambiotte, Clay, Paul Gibney, and Joel Hartley. 2014. "Activist Equity Investing: Unlocking Value by Acting as a Catalyst for Corporate Change." LCP: Insight-Clarity-Advice. Lane, Clark, and Peacock LLP (August): 1–2.

Malevergne, Yannick, Pedro Santa-Clara, and Didier Sornette. 2009. "Professor Zipf Goes to Wall Street." NBER Working Paper 15295 (August).

MSCI. 2017. "MSCI US Equity Indexes Methodology": www.msci.com/eqb/methodology/meth_docs/ MSCI_Feb17_USEI_Methodology.pdf.

Perold, André, and Robert S. Salomon Jr. 1991. "The Right Amount of Assets under Management." *Financial Analysts Journal*, vol. 47, no. 3: 31–39.

Petajisto, Antti. 2010. "The Index Premium and Its Hidden Cost for Index Funds." NYU Stern Working paper.

Podkaminer, Gene. 2015. "The Education of Beta—Revisited." Callan Investments Institute white paper.

Qin, Nan, and Vijay Singal. 2015. "Investor Portfolios When Stocks Are Mispriced: Equally-Weighted or Value-Weighted?" Virginia Tech working paper.

Renshaw, Edward F., and Paul J. Feldstein. 1960. "The Case for an Unmanaged Investment Company." *Financial Analysts Journal*, vol. 16, no. 1: 43–46.

Roll, Richard. 1992. "A Mean/Variance Analysis of Tracking Error." *Journal of Portfolio Management*, vol. 18, no. 4: 13–22.

Soe, Aye M., and Ryan Poirer. 2016. "SPIVA U.S. Scorecard." S&P Dow Jones Indices Report.

Woerheide, Walt, and Don Persson. 1993. "An Index of Portfolio Diversification." *Financial Services Review*, vol. 2, no. 2: 73–85.

Zeng, Liu, and Frank Luo. 2013. "10 Years Later: Where in the World Is Equal Weight Indexing Now?" Standard & Poor's white paper.

PRACTICE PROBLEMS

The following information relates to questions 1–8

Evan Winthrop, a senior officer of a US-based corporation, meets with Rebecca Tong, a portfolio manager at Cobalt Wealth Management. Winthrop recently moved his investments to Cobalt in response to his previous manager's benchmark-relative underperformance and high expenses.

Winthrop resides in Canada and plans to retire there. His annual salary covers his current spending needs, and his vested defined benefit pension plan is sufficient to meet retirement income goals. Winthrop prefers passive exposure to global equity markets with a focus on low management costs and minimal tracking error to any index benchmarks. The fixed-income portion of the portfolio may consist of laddered maturities with a home-country bias.

Tong proposes using an equity index as a basis for an investment strategy and reviews the most important requirements for an appropriate benchmark. With regard to investable indexes, Tong tells Winthrop the following:

Statement 1.   A free-float adjustment to a market-capitalization weighted index lowers its liquidity.

Statement 2.   An index provider that incorporates a buffering policy makes the index more investable.

Winthrop asks Tong to select a benchmark for the domestic stock allocation that holds all sectors of the Canadian equity market and to focus the portfolio on highly liquid, well-known companies. In addition, Winthrop specifies that any stock purchased should have a relatively low beta, a high dividend yield, a low P/E, and a low price-to-book ratio (P/B).

Winthrop and Tong agree that only the existing equity investments need to be liquidated. Tong suggests that, as an alternative to direct equity investments, the new equity portfolio be composed of the exchange-traded funds (ETFs) shown in Exhibit 1.

EXHIBIT 1   Available Equity ETFs

Equity Benchmark	ETF Ticker	Number of Constituents	P/B	P/E	Fund Expense Ratio
S&P/TSX 60	XIU	60	2.02	17.44	0.18%
S&P 500	SPY	506	1.88	15.65	0.10%
MSCI EAFE	EFA	933	2.13	18.12	0.33%

Winthrop asks Tong about the techniques wealth managers and fund companies use to create index-tracking equity portfolios that minimize tracking error and costs. In response, Tong outlines two frequently used methods:

Method 1.   One process requires that all index constituents are available for trading and liquid, but significant brokerage commissions can occur when the index is large.

Method 2.   When tracking an index with a large number of constituents and/or managing a relatively low level of assets, a relatively straightforward and technically unsophisticated method can be used to build a passive portfolio that requires fewer individual securities than the index and reduces brokerage commission costs.

Tong adds that portfolio stocks may be used to generate incremental revenue, thereby partially offsetting administrative costs but potentially creating undesirable counterparty and collateral risks.

After determining Winthrop's objectives and constraints, the CAD147 million portfolio's new strategic policy is to target long-term market returns while being fully invested at all times. Tong recommends quarterly rebalancing, currency hedging, and a composite benchmark composed of equity and fixed-income indexes. Currently the USD is worth CAD1.2930, and this exchange rate is expected to remain stable during the next month. Exhibit 2 presents the strategic asset allocation and benchmark weights.

EXHIBIT 2   Composite Benchmark and Policy Weights

Asset Class	Benchmark Index	Policy Weight
Canadian equity	S&P/TSX 60	40.0%
US equity	S&P 500	15.0%
International developed markets equity	MSCI EAFE	15.0%
Canadian bonds	DEX Universe	30.0%
Total portfolio		100.0%

In one month, Winthrop will receive a performance bonus of USD5,750,000. He believes that the US equity market is likely to increase during this timeframe. To take advantage of Winthrop's market outlook, he instructs Tong to immediately initiate an equity transaction using the S&P 500 futures contract with a current price of 2,464.29 while respecting the policy weights in Exhibit 2. The S&P 500 futures contract multiplier is 250, and the S&P 500 E-mini multiplier is 50.

Tong cautions Winthrop that there is a potential pitfall with the proposed request when it comes time to analyze performance. She discloses to Winthrop that equity index futures returns can differ from the underlying index, primarily because of corporate actions such as the declaration of dividends and stock splits.

1. Which of Tong's statements regarding equity index benchmarks is (are) correct?
   A. Only Statement 1
   B. Only Statement 2
   C. Both Statement 1 and Statement 2

2. To satisfy Winthrop's benchmark and security selection specifications, the Canadian equity index benchmark Tong selects should be:
   A. small-capitalization with a core tilt.
   B. large-capitalization with a value tilt.
   C. mid-capitalization with a growth tilt.

3. Based on Exhibit 1 and assuming a full-replication indexing approach, the tracking error is expected to be highest for:
   A. XIU.
   B. SPY.
   C. EFA.

4. Method 1's portfolio construction process is *most likely*:
   A. optimization.
   B. full replication.
   C. stratified sampling.

5. Method 2's portfolio construction process is *most likely*:
   A. optimization.
   B. full replication.
   C. stratified sampling.

6. The method that Tong suggests to add incremental revenue is:
   A. program trading.
   B. securities lending.
   C. attribution analysis.

7. In preparation for receipt of the performance bonus, Tong should immediately:
   A. buy two US E-mini equity futures contracts.
   B. sell nine US E-mini equity futures contracts.
   C. buy seven US E-mini equity futures contracts.

8. The risk that Tong discloses regarding the equity futures strategy is *most likely*:
   A. basis risk.
   B. currency risk.
   C. counterparty risk.

The following information relates to questions 9–14

The Mackenzie Education Foundation funds educational projects in a four-state region of the United States. Because of the investment portfolio's poor benchmark-relative returns, the foundation's board of directors hired a consultant, Stacy McMahon, to analyze performance and provide recommendations.

McMahon meets with Autumn Laubach, the foundation's executive director, to review the existing asset allocation strategy. Laubach believes the portfolio's underperformance is attributable to the equity holdings, which are allocated 55% to a US large-capitalization index fund, 30% to an actively managed US small-cap fund, and 15% to an actively managed developed international fund.

Laubach states that the board is interested in following a passive approach for some or all of the equity allocation. In addition, the board is open to approaches that could generate returns in excess of the benchmark for part of the equity allocation. McMahon suggests that the board consider following a passive factor-based momentum strategy for the allocation to international stocks.

McMahon observes that the benchmark used for the US large-cap equity component is a price-weighted index containing 150 stocks. The benchmark's Herfindahl–Hirschman Index (HHI) is 0.0286.

McMahon performs a sector attribution analysis based on Exhibit 1 to explain the large-cap portfolio's underperformance relative to the benchmark.

EXHIBIT 1   Trailing 12-Month US Large-Cap Returns and Foundation/Benchmark Weights

Sector	Sector Returns	Foundation Sector Weights	Benchmark Sector Weights
Information technology	10.75%	18.71%	19.06%
Consumer staples	12.31%	16.52%	16.10%
Energy	8.63%	9.38%	9.53%
Utilities	−3.92%	8.76%	8.25%
Financials	7.05%	6.89%	6.62%

The board decides to consider adding a mid-cap manager. McMahon presents candidates for the mid-cap portfolio. Exhibit 2 provides fees and cash holdings for three portfolios and an index fund.

EXHIBIT 2   Characteristics of US Mid-Cap Portfolios and Index Fund

	Portfolio 1	Portfolio 2	Portfolio 3	Index Fund
Fees	0.10%	0.09%	0.07%	0.03%
Cash holdings	6.95%	3.42%	2.13%	0.51%

9. Compared with broad-market-cap weighting, the international equity strategy suggested by McMahon is *most likely* to:
   A. concentrate risk exposure.
   B. be based on the efficient market hypothesis.
   C. overweight stocks that recently experienced large price decreases.

10. The international strategy suggested by McMahon is *most likely* characterized as:
    A. risk based.
    B. return oriented.
    C. diversification oriented.

11. The initial benchmark used for the US large-cap allocation:
    A. is unaffected by stocks splits.
    B. is essentially a liquidity-weighted index.
    C. holds the same number of shares in each component stock.

12. Based on its HHI, the initial US large-cap benchmark *most likely* has:
    A. a concentration level of 4.29.
    B. an effective number of stocks of approximately 35.
    C. individual stocks held in approximately equal weights.

13. Using a sector attribution analysis based on Exhibit 1, which US large-cap sector is the primary contributor to the portfolio's underperformance relative to the benchmark?
    A. Utilities
    B. Consumer staples
    C. Information technology

14. Based on Exhibit 2, which portfolio will *most likely* have the lowest tracking error?
    A. Portfolio 1
    B. Portfolio 2
    C. Portfolio 3

CHAPTER 13

ACTIVE EQUITY INVESTING: STRATEGIES

Bing Li, PhD, CFA

Yin Luo, CPA, PStat, CFA

Pranay Gupta, CFA

LEARNING OUTCOMES

The candidate should be able to:

- compare fundamental and quantitative approaches to active management;
- analyze bottom-up active strategies, including their rationale and associated processes;
- analyze top-down active strategies, including their rationale and associated processes;
- analyze factor-based active strategies, including their rationale and associated processes;
- analyze activist strategies, including their rationale and associated processes;
- describe active strategies based on statistical arbitrage and market microstructure;
- describe how fundamental active investment strategies are created;
- describe how quantitative active investment strategies are created;
- discuss equity investment style classifications.

1. INTRODUCTION

This chapter provides an overview of active equity investing and the major types of active equity strategies. The chapter is organized around a classification of active equity strategies into two broad approaches: fundamental and quantitative. Both approaches aim at outperforming a passive benchmark (for example, a broad equity market index), but they tend to make investment decisions differently. Fundamental approaches stress the use of human judgment in processing information and making investment decisions, whereas quantitative approaches tend to rely more heavily on rules-based quantitative models. As a result, some practitioners and academics refer to the fundamental, judgment-based approaches as "discretionary" and to the rules-based, quantitative approaches as "systematic."

This chapter is organized as follows. Section 2 introduces fundamental and quantitative approaches to active management. Section 3 discusses bottom-up, top-down, factor-based, and activist investing strategies. Section 4 describes the process of creating fundamental active investment strategies, including the parameters to consider as well as some of the pitfalls. Section 5 describes the steps required to create quantitative active investment strategies, as well as the pitfalls in a quantitative investment process. Section 6 discusses style classifications of active strategies and the uses and limitations of such classifications. A summary of key points completes the chapter.

2. APPROACHES TO ACTIVE MANAGEMENT

Active equity investing may reflect a variety of ideas about profitable investment opportunities. However, with regard to how these investment ideas are implemented—for example, how securities are selected—active strategies can be divided into two broad categories: fundamental and quantitative. Fundamental approaches are based on research into companies, sectors, or markets and involve the application of analyst discretion and judgment. In contrast, quantitative approaches are based on quantitative models of security returns that are applied systematically with limited involvement of human judgment or discretion. The labels *fundamental* and *quantitative* in this context are an imperfect shorthand that should not be misunderstood. The contrast with quantitative approaches does not mean that fundamental approaches do not use quantitative tools. Fundamental approaches often make use of valuation models (such as the free cash flow model), quantitative screening tools, and statistical techniques (e.g., regression analysis). Furthermore, quantitative approaches often make use of variables that relate to company fundamentals. Some investment disciplines may be viewed as hybrids in that they combine elements of both fundamental and quantitative disciplines. In the next sections, we examine these two approaches more closely.

Fundamental research forms the basis of the fundamental approach to investing. Although it can be organized in many ways, fundamental research consistently involves and often begins with the analysis of a company's financial statements. Through such an analysis, this approach seeks to obtain a detailed understanding of the company's current and past profitability, financial position, and cash flows. Along with insights into a company's business model, management team, product lines, and economic outlook, this analysis provides a view on the company's future business prospects and includes a valuation of its shares. Estimates are typically made of the stock's intrinsic value and/or its relative value compared to the shares of a peer group or the stock's own history of market valuations. Based on this valuation and other factors (including overall portfolio considerations), the portfolio manager may conclude that the stock should be bought (or a position increased) or sold (or a position reduced). The decision can also be stated in terms of overweighting, market weighting, or underweighting relative to the portfolio's benchmark.

In the search for investment opportunities, fundamental strategies may have various starting points. Some strategies start at a top or macro level—with analyses of markets, economies, or industries—to narrow the search for likely areas for profitable active investment. These are called top-down strategies. Other strategies, often referred to as bottom-up strategies, make little or no use of macro analysis and instead rely on individual stock analysis to identify areas of opportunity. Research distributed by investment banks and reports produced by internal analysts, organized by industry or economic sector, are also potential sources of investment ideas. The vetting of such ideas may be done by portfolio managers, who may themselves be involved in fundamental research, or by an investment committee.

Quantitative strategies, on the other hand, involve analyst judgment at the design stage, but they largely replace the ongoing reliance on human judgment and discretion with systematic processes that are often dependent on computer programming for execution. These systematic processes search for security and market characteristics and patterns that have predictive power in order to identify securities or trades that will earn superior investment returns. ("Superior" in the sense of expected added value relative to risk or expected return relative to a benchmark—for example, an index benchmark or peer benchmark). Variables that might be considered include valuation metrics (e.g., earnings yield), size (e.g., market capitalization), profitability metrics (e.g., return on equity), financial strength metrics (e.g., debt-to-equity ratio), market sentiment (e.g., analyst consensus on companies' long-term earnings growth), industry membership (e.g., stocks' GICS classification), and price-related attributes (e.g., price momentum).

Once a pattern or relationship between a given variable (or set of variables) and security prices has been established by analysis of past data, a quantitative model is used to predict future expected returns of securities or baskets of securities. Security selection then flows from expected returns, which reflect securities' exposures to the selected variables with predictive power.[1] From a quantitative perspective, investment success depends not on individual company insights but on model quality.

EXHIBIT 1   Differences between Fundamental and Quantitative Approaches

	Fundamental	**Quantitative**
Style	Subjective	Objective
Decision-making process	Discretionary	Systematic, non-discretionary
Primary resources	Human skill, experience, judgment	Expertise in statistical modeling
Information used	Research (company/industry/ economy)	Data and statistics
Analysis focus	Conviction (high depth) in stock-, sector-, or region-based selection	A selection of variables, subsequently applied broadly over a large number of securities
Orientation to data	Forecast future corporate parameters and establish views on companies	Attempt to draw conclusions from a variety of historical data
Portfolio construction	Use judgment and conviction within permissible risk parameters	Use optimizers

---

[1]A wide range of security characteristics have been used to define "factors." Some factors (most commonly, size, value, momentum, and quality) have been shown to be positively associated with a long-term return premium. These we call *rewarded* factors. Many other factors are used in portfolio construction but have not been empirically proven to offer a persistent return premium. Some call these *unrewarded* factors. The average investor doesn't typically distinguish between rewarded and unrewarded factors, but it is important to draw that distinction for the sake of clarity across curriculum chapters.

Exhibit 1 presents typical differences between the main characteristics of fundamental and quantitative methodologies.

In the following section, we take a closer look at some of the distinguishing characteristics listed in Exhibit 1 and how they are evolving with the advent of new technologies available to investors.

2.1. Differences in the Nature of the Information Used

To contrast the information used in fundamental and quantitative strategies, we can start by describing typical activities for fundamental investors with a bottom-up investment discipline. Bottom-up fundamental analysts research and analyze a company, using data from company financial statements and disclosures to assess attributes such as profitability, leverage, and absolute or peer-relative valuation. They typically also assess how those metrics compare to their historical values to identify trends and scrutinize such characteristics as the company's management competence, its future prospects, and the competitive position of its product lines. Such analysts usually focus on the more recent financial statements (which include current and previous years' accounting data), notes to the financial statements and assumptions in the accounts, and management discussion and analysis disclosures. Corporate governance is often taken into consideration as well as wider environmental, social, and governance (ESG) characteristics.

Top-down fundamental investors' research focuses first on region, country, or sector information (e.g., economic growth, money supply, and market valuations). Some of the data used by fundamental managers can be measured or expressed numerically and therefore "quantified." Other items, such as management quality and reputation, cannot.

Quantitative approaches often use large amounts of historical data from companies' financial reports (in addition to other information, such as return data) but process those data in a systematic rather than a judgmental way. Judgment is used in model building, particularly in deciding which variables and signals are relevant. Typically, quantitative approaches use historical stock data and statistical techniques to identify variables that may have a statistically significant relationship with stock returns; then these relationships are used to predict individual security returns. In contrast to the fundamental approach, the quantitative approach does not normally consider information or characteristics that cannot be quantified. In order to minimize survivorship and look-ahead biases, historical data used in quantitative research should include stocks that are no longer listed, and accounting data used should be the original, un-restated numbers that were available to the market at that point in time.

Investment Process: Fundamental vs. Quantitative

The goal of the investment process is to construct a portfolio that best reflects the stated investment objective and risk tolerance, with an optimal balance between expected return and risk exposure, subject to the constraints imposed by the investment policy. The investment processes under both fundamental and quantitative approaches involve a number of considerations, such as the methodology and valuation process, which are the subject of this chapter. Other considerations, such as portfolio construction and risk

	Fundamental	**Quantitative**
Methodology	Determine methodology to evaluate stocks (bottom-up or top-down, value or growth, income or deep value, intrinsic or relative value, etc.)	Define model to estimate expected stock returns (choose time-series macro-level factors or cross-sectional stock-level factors, identify factors that have a stable positive information coefficient IC, use a factor combination algorithm, etc.)
Valuation process	• Prescreen to identify potential investment candidates with stringent financial and market criteria • Perform in-depth analysis of companies to derive their intrinsic values • Determine buy or sell candidates trading at a discount or premium to their intrinsic values	• Construct factor exposures across all shares in the same industry • Forecast IC and/or its volatility for each factor by using algorithms (such as artificial intelligence or time-series analysis) or fundamental research • Combine factor exposures to estimate expected returns
Portfolio construction and rebalancing	• Allocate assets by determining industry and country/region exposures • Set limits on maximum sector, country, and individual stock positions • Determine buy-and-sell list • Monitor portfolio holdings continuously	• Determine which factors to underweight or overweight • Use risk model to measure *ex ante* active risk • Run portfolio optimization with risk model, investment, and risk constraints, as well as the structure of transaction costs • Rebalance at regular intervals

management, trade execution, and ongoing performance monitoring, are the subjects of subsequent curriculum chapters.

2.2. Differences in the Focus of the Analysis

Fundamental investors usually focus their attention on a relatively small group of stocks and perform in-depth analysis on each one of them. This practice has characteristically given fundamental (or "discretionary") investors an edge of depth in understanding individual companies' businesses over quantitative (or "systematic") investors, who do not focus on individual stocks. Quantitative investors instead usually focus on factors across a potentially very large group of stocks. Therefore, fundamental investors tend to take larger positions in their selected stocks, while quantitative investors tend to focus their analysis on a selection of factors but spread their selected factor bets across a substantially larger group of holdings.[2]

---

[2]The implications for portfolio risk of using individual stocks or factors will be considered in the chapter on portfolio construction.

2.3. Difference in Orientation to the Data: Forecasting the Future vs. Analyzing the Past

Fundamental analysis places an emphasis on forecasting future prospects, including the future earnings and cash flows of a company. Fundamental investors use judgment and in-depth analysis to formulate a view of the company's outlook and to identify the catalysts that will generate future growth. They rely on knowledge, experience, and their ability to predict future conditions in a company to make investment decisions. Conceptually, the fundamental approach aims at forecasting forward parameters in order to make investment decisions.

In contrast, quantitative analysis uses a company's history to arrive at investment decisions. Quantitative investors construct models by backtesting past data, using what is known about or has been reported by a company, including future earnings estimates that have been published by analysts, to search for the best company characteristics for purposes of stock selection. Once a model based on historical data has been finalized, it is applied to the latest available data to determine investment decisions. Conceptually, the quantitative approach aims to predict future returns using conclusions derived from analyzing historical data.

Forestalling Look-Ahead Bias

Satyam Computers is an India-based company that provides IT consulting and solutions to its global customers. In the eight years preceding 2009, Satyam overstated its revenues and profits and reported a cash holdings total of approximately $1.04 billion that did not exist. The falsification of the accounts came to light in early 2009, and Satyam was removed from the S&P CNX Nifty 50 index on 12 January.

If a quantitative analyst runs a simulation benchmarked against the S&P CNX Nifty 50 index on 31 December 2008, he or she should include the 50 stocks that were in the index on 31 December 2008 and use only the data for the included stocks that were available to investors as of that date. The analyst should therefore include Satyam as an index constituent and use the original accounting data that were published by the company at that time. While it was subsequently proved that these accounting data were fraudulent, this fact was not known to analysts and investors on 31 December 2008. As a result, it would not have been possible for any analyst to incorporate the true accounting data for Satyam on that date.

2.4. Differences in Portfolio Construction: Judgment vs. Optimization

Fundamental investors typically select stocks by performing extensive research on individual companies, which results in a list of high-conviction stocks. Thus, fundamental investors see risk at the company level. There is a risk that the assessment of the company's fair value is inaccurate, that the business's performance will differ from the analyst's expectations, or that the market will fail to recognize the identified reason for under- or overvaluation. Construction of a fundamental portfolio therefore often depends on judgment, whereby the absolute or index-relative sizes of positions in stocks, sectors, or countries are based on the manager's conviction of his or her forecasts. The portfolio must, of course, still comply with the risk parameters set out in the investment agreements with clients or in the fund prospectus.

In quantitative analysis, on the other hand, the risk is that factor returns will not perform as expected. Because the quantitative approach invests in baskets of stocks, the risks lie at the portfolio level rather than at the level of specific stocks. Construction of a quantitative portfolio is therefore generally done using a portfolio optimizer, which controls for risk at the portfolio level in arriving at individual stock weights.

The two approaches also differ in the way that portfolio changes or rebalancings are performed. Managers using a fundamental approach usually monitor the portfolio's holdings continuously and may increase, decrease, or eliminate positions at any time. Portfolios managed using a quantitative approach are usually rebalanced at regular intervals, such as monthly or quarterly. At each interval, the program or algorithm, using pre-determined rules, automatically selects positions to be sold, reduced, added, or increased.

EXAMPLE 1   Fundamental vs. Quantitative Approach

Consider two equity portfolios with the same benchmark index, the MSCI Asia ex Japan. The index contains 627 stocks as of December 2016. One portfolio is managed using a fundamental approach, while the other is managed using a quantitative approach. The fundamental approach–based portfolio is made up of 50 individually selected stocks, which are reviewed for potential sale or trimming on an ongoing basis. In the fundamental approach, the investment universe is first pre-screened by valuation and by the fundamental metrics of earnings yield, dividend yield, earnings growth, and financial leverage. The quantitative approach–based portfolio makes active bets on 400 stocks with monthly rebalancing. The particular approach used is based on a five-factor model of equity returns.

Contrast fundamental and quantitative investment processes with respect to the following:

1. Constructing the portfolio
2. Rebalancing the portfolio

Solution to 1: Fundamental: Construct the portfolio by overweighting stocks that are expected to outperform their peers or the market as a whole. Where necessary for risk reduction, underweight some benchmark stocks that are expected to underperform. The stocks that fell out in the pre-screening process do not have explicit forecasts and will not be included in the portfolio.

Quantitative: Construct the portfolio by maximizing the objective function (such as portfolio alpha or information ratio) with risk models.

Solution to 2: Fundamental: The manager monitors each stock continuously and sells stocks when their market prices surpass the target prices (either through appreciation of the stock price or through reduction of the target price due to changes in expectations).

Quantitative: Portfolios are usually rebalanced at regular intervals, such as monthly.

3. TYPES OF ACTIVE MANAGEMENT STRATEGIES

Equity investors have developed many different techniques for processing all the information necessary to arrive at an investment decision. Multiple approaches may be taken into account in formulating an overall opinion of a stock; however, each analyst will have his or her own set of favorite techniques based on his or her experience and judgment. Depending on the specifics of the investment discipline, most fundamental and quantitative strategies can be characterized as either bottom-up or top-down.

3.1. Bottom-Up Strategies

Bottom-up strategies begin the asset selection process with data at the individual asset and company level, such as price momentum and profitability. Bottom-up quantitative investors harness computer power to apply their models to this asset- and company-level information (with the added requirement that the information be quantifiable). The balance of this section illustrates the bottom-up process as used by fundamental investors. These investors typically begin their analysis at the company level before forming an opinion on the wider sector or market. The ability to identify companies with strong or weak fundamentals depends on the analyst's in-depth knowledge of each company's industry, product lines, business plan, management abilities, and financial strength. After identifying individual companies, the bottom-up approach uses economic and financial analysis to assess the intrinsic value of a company and compares that value with the current market price to determine which stocks are undervalued or overvalued. The analyst may also find companies operating efficiently with good prospects even though the industry they belong to is deteriorating. Similarly, companies with poor prospects may be found in otherwise healthy and prosperous industries.

Fundamental investors often focus on one or more of the following parameters for a company, either individually or in relation to its peers:

- business model and branding
- competitive advantages
- company management and corporate governance

Valuation is based on either a discounted cash flow model or a preferred market multiple, often earnings-related. We address each of these parameters and valuation approaches in turn.

Business Model and Branding
The business model of a company refers to its overall strategy for running the business and generating profit. The business model details how a company converts its resources into products or services and how it delivers those products or services to customers. Companies with a superior business model compete successfully, have scalability, and generate significant earnings. Further, companies with a robust and adaptive business model tend to outperform their peers in terms of return on shareholder equity. The business model gives investors insight into a company's value proposition, its operational flow, the structure of its value chain, its branding strategy, its market segment, and the resulting revenue generation and profit margins. This insight helps investors evaluate the sustainability of the company's competitive advantages and make informed investment decisions.

Corporate branding is a way of defining the company's business for the market in general and retail customers in particular and can be understood as the company's identity as well as its promise to its customers. Strong brand names convey product quality and can give the company an edge over its competitors in both market share and profit margin. It is widely recognized that brand equity plays an important role in the determination of product price, allowing companies to command price premiums after controlling for observed product differentiation. Apple in consumer technology and BMW in motor vehicles, for example, charge more for their products, but customers are willing to pay the premium because of brand loyalty.

Competitive Advantages

A competitive advantage typically allows a company to outperform its peers in terms of the return it generates on its capital. There are many types of competitive advantage, such as access to natural resources, superior technology, innovation, skilled personnel, corporate reputation, brand strength, high entry barriers, exclusive distribution rights, and superior product or customer support.

For value investors, who search for companies that appear to be trading below their intrinsic value (often following earnings disappointments), it is important to understand the sustainability of the company's competitive position when assessing the prospects for recovery.

Company Management

A good management team is crucial to a company's success. Management's role is to allocate resources and capital to maximize the growth of enterprise value for the company's shareholders. A management team that has a long-term rather than a short-term focus is more likely to add value to an enterprise over the long term.

To evaluate management effectiveness, one can begin with the financial statements. Return on assets, equity, or invested capital (compared either to industry peers or to historical rates achieved by the company) and earnings growth over a reasonable time period are examples of indicators used to gauge the value added by management.

Qualitative analysis of the company's management and governance structures requires attention to (1) the alignment of management's interests with those of shareholders to minimize agency problems; (2) the competence of management in achieving the company's objectives (as described in the mission statement) and long-term plans; (3) the stability of the management team and the company's ability to attract and retain high-performing executives; and (4) increasingly, risk considerations and opportunities related to a company's ESG attributes. Analysts also monitor management insider purchases and sales of the company's shares for potential indications of the confidence of management in the company's future.

The above qualitative considerations and financial statement analysis will help in making earnings estimates, cash flow estimates, and evaluations of risk, providing inputs to company valuation. Fundamental strategies within the bottom-up category may use a combination of approaches to stock valuation. Some investors rely on discounted cash flow or dividend models. Others focus on relative valuation, often based on earnings-related valuation metrics such as a P/E, price to book (P/B), and enterprise value (EV)/EBITDA. A conclusion that a security's intrinsic value is different from its current market price means the valuation is using estimates that are different from those reflected in current market prices. Conviction that the analyst's forecasts are, over a particular time period, more accurate than the market's is therefore important, as is the belief that the market will reflect the more accurate estimates within a time frame that is consistent with the strategy's investment horizon.

Bottom-up strategies are often broadly categorized as either value-based (or value-oriented) or growth-based (or growth-oriented), as the following section explains.

3.1.1. Value-Based Approaches

Benjamin Graham is regarded as the father of value investing. Along with David Dodd, he wrote the book *Security Analysis* (1934), which laid the basic framework for value investing. Graham posited that buying earnings and assets relatively inexpensively afforded a "margin of safety" necessary for prudent investing. Consistent with that idea, value-based approaches aim to buy stocks that are trading at a significant discount to their estimated intrinsic value. Value investors typically focus on companies with attractive valuation metrics, reflected in low earnings (or asset) multiples. In their view, investors' sometimes irrational behavior can make stocks trade below the intrinsic value based on company fundamentals. Such opportunities may arise due to a variety of behavioral biases and often reflect investors' overreaction to negative news. Various styles of value-based investing are sometimes distinguished; for example, "relative value" investors purchase stocks on valuation multiples that are high relative to historical levels but that compare favorably to those of the peer group.

3.1.1.1. Relative Value

Investors who pursue a relative value strategy evaluate companies by comparing their value indicators (e.g., P/E or P/B multiples) to the average valuation of companies in the same

EXHIBIT 2 Key Financial Ratios of Hang Seng Index (30 December 2016)

	Weight	Dividend Yield	Price-to-Earnings Ratio (P/E)	Price-to-Cash-Flow Ratio (P/CF)	Price-to-Book Ratio (P/B)	Total Debt to Common Equity (%)	Current Ratio
Hang Seng Index	**100.0**	**3.5**	**12.2**	**6.1**	**1.1**	**128.4**	**1.3**
Consumer discretionary	2.9	4.1	21.3	12.5	3.0	26.3	1.4
Consumer staples	1.6	2.6	16.8	14.3	3.3	62.1	1.4
Energy	7.0	2.6	39.5	3.7	0.9	38.5	1.0
Financials	47.5	4.3	10.1	5.0	1.1	199.8	1.1
Industrials	5.5	3.8	11.8	6.0	0.9	158.7	1.2
Information technology	11.4	0.6	32.7	19.9	8.2	60.2	1.0
Real estate	10.6	3.9	8.3	8.0	0.7	30.3	2.5
Telecommunication services	7.8	3.2	13.3	4.6	1.4	11.5	0.7
Utilities	5.6	3.7	14.2	10.8	1.7	47.0	1.3

Source: Bloomberg.

industry sector with the aim of identifying stocks that offer value relative to their sector peers. As different sectors face different market structures and different competitive and regulatory conditions, average sector multiples vary.

Exhibit 2 lists the key financial ratios for sectors in the Hang Seng Index on the last trading day of 2016. The average P/E for companies in the energy sector is almost five times the average P/E for those in real estate. A consumer staples company trading on a P/E of 12 would appear undervalued relative to its sector, while a real estate company trading on the same P/E multiple of 12 would appear overvalued relative to its sector.

Investors usually recognize that in addition to the simple comparison of a company's multiple to that of the sector, one needs a good understanding of why the valuation is what it is. A premium or discount to the industry may well be justified by the company's fundamentals.

3.1.1.2. Contrarian Investing

Contrarian investors purchase and sell shares against prevailing market sentiment. Their investment strategy is to go against the crowd by buying poorly performing stocks at valuations they find attractive and then selling them at a later time, following what they expect to be a recovery in the share price. Companies in which contrarian managers invest are frequently depressed cyclical stocks with low or even negative earnings or low dividend payments. Contrarians expect these stocks to rebound once the company's earnings have turned around, resulting in substantial price appreciation.

Contrarian investors often point to research in behavioral finance suggesting that investors tend to overweight recent trends and to follow the crowd in making investment decisions. A contrarian investor attempts to determine whether the valuation of an individual company, industry, or entire market is irrational—that is, undervalued or overvalued at any time—and whether that irrationality represents an exploitable mispricing of shares. Accordingly, contrarian investors tend to go against the crowd.

Both contrarian investors and value investors who do not describe their style as contrarian aim to buy shares at a discount to their intrinsic value. The primary difference between the two is that non-contrarian value investors rely on fundamental metrics to make their assessments, while contrarian investors rely more on market sentiment and sharp price movements (such as 52-week high and low prices as sell and buy prices) to make their decisions.

3.1.1.3. High-Quality Value

Some value-based strategies give valuation close attention but place at least equal emphasis on financial strength and demonstrated profitability. For example, one such investment discipline requires a record of consistent earnings power, above-average return on equity, financial strength, and exemplary management. There is no widely accepted label for this value style, the refinement of which is often associated with investor Warren Buffett.[3]

3.1.1.4. Income Investing

The income investing approach focuses on shares that offer relatively high dividend yields and positive dividend growth rates. Several rationales for this approach have been offered. One argument is that a secure, high dividend yield tends to put a floor under the share price in the case of companies that are expected to maintain such a dividend. Another argument points to

---

[3]See Greenwald, Kahn, Sonkin, and Biema (2001).

empirical studies that demonstrate the higher returns to equities with these characteristics and their greater ability to withstand market declines.

3.1.1.5. Deep-Value Investing

A value investor with a deep-value orientation focuses on undervalued companies that are available at extremely low valuation relative to their assets (e.g., low P/B). Such companies are often those in financial distress. The rationale is that market interest in such securities may be limited, increasing the chance of informational inefficiencies. The deep-value investor's special area of expertise may lie in reorganizations or related legislation, providing a better position from which to assess the likelihood of company recovery.

3.1.1.6. Restructuring and Distressed Investing

While the restructuring and distressed investment strategies are more commonly observed in the distressed-debt space, some equity investors specialize in these disciplines. Opportunities in restructuring and distressed investing are generally countercyclical relative to the overall economy or to the business cycle of a particular sector. A weak economy generates increased incidence of companies facing financial distress. When a company is having difficulty meeting its short-term liabilities, it will often propose to restructure its financial obligations or change its capital structure.

Restructuring investors seek to purchase the debt or equity of companies in distress. A distressed company that goes through restructuring may still have valuable assets, distribution channels, or patents that make it an attractive acquisition target. Restructuring investing is often done before an expected bankruptcy or during the bankruptcy process. The goal of restructuring investing is to gain control or substantial influence over a company in distress at a large discount and then restructure it to restore a large part of its intrinsic value.

Effective investment in a distressed company depends on skill and expertise in identifying companies whose situation is better than the market believes it to be. Distressed investors assume that either the company will survive or there will be sufficient assets remaining upon liquidation to generate an appropriate return on investment.

3.1.1.7. Special Situations

The "special situations" investment style focuses on the identification and exploitation of mispricings that may arise as a result of corporate events such as divestitures or spinoffs of assets or divisions or mergers with other entities. In the opinion of many investors, such situations represent short-term opportunities to exploit mispricing that result from such special situations. According to Greenblatt (2010), investors often overlook companies that are in such special situations as restructuring (involving asset disposals or spinoffs) and mergers, which may create opportunities to add value through active investing. To take advantage of such opportunities, this type of investing requires specific knowledge of the industry and the company, as well as legal expertise.

3.1.2. Growth-Based Approaches

Growth-based investment approaches focus on companies that are expected to grow faster than their industry or faster than the overall market, as measured by revenues, earnings, or cash flow. Growth investors usually look for high-quality companies with consistent growth or companies with strong earnings momentum. Characteristics usually examined by growth investors include historical and estimated future growth of earnings or cash flows, underpinned by attributes such as a solid business model, cost control, and exemplary management able to execute long-term plans to achieve higher growth. Such companies typically feature above-average return on equity, a large part of which they retain and reinvest in funding future growth. Because growth companies may also have volatile earnings and cash flows going forward, the intrinsic values calculated by discounting expected future cash flows are subject to relatively high uncertainty. Compared to value-focused investors, growth-focused investors have a higher tolerance for above-average valuation multiples.

GARP (growth at a reasonable price) is a sub-discipline within growth investing. This approach is used by investors who seek out companies with above-average growth that trade at reasonable valuation multiples, and is often referred to as a hybrid of growth and value investing. Many investors who use GARP rely on the P/E-to-growth (PEG) ratio—calculated as the stock's P/E divided by the expected earnings growth rate (in percentage terms)—while also paying attention to variations in risk and duration of growth.

EXAMPLE 2   Characteristic Securities for Bottom-Up Investment Disciplines

---

The following table provides information on four stocks.

Company	Price	12-Month Forward EPS	3-Year EPS Growth Forecast	Dividend Yield	Industry Sector	Sector Average P/E
A	50	5	20%	1%	Industrial	10
B	56	2	2%	0%	Information technology	35
C	22	10	–5%	2%	Consumer staples	15
D	32	2	2%	8%	Utilities	16

Using only the information given in the table above, for each stock, determine which fundamental investment discipline would most likely select it.

Solution:

- Company A's forward P/E is 50/5 = 10, and its P/E-to-growth ratio (PEG) is 10/20 = 0.5, which is lower than the PEGs for the other companies (28/2 = 14 for Company B, negative for Company C, and 16/2 = 8 for Company D). Given the favorable valuation relative to growth, the company is a good candidate for investors who use GARP.
- Company B's forward P/E is 56/2 = 28, which is lower than the average P/E of 35 for its sector peers. The company is a good candidate for the relative value approach.
- Company C's forward P/E is 22/10 = 2.2, which is considered very low in both absolute and relative terms. Assuming the investor pays attention to company circumstances, the stock could be a good candidate for the deep-value approach.

- Company D's forward P/E is 32/2 = 16, which is the same as its industry average. Company D's earnings are growing slowly at 2%, but the dividend yield of 8% appears high. This combination makes the company a good candidate for income investing.

EXAMPLE 3   Growth vs. Value

Tencent Holdings Limited is a leading provider of value-added internet services in China. The company's services include social networks, web portals, e-commerce, and multiplayer online games.

Exhibit 3 shows an excerpt from an analyst report on Tencent published following the release of the company's Q3 2016 results on 16 November 2016.

EXHIBIT 3   Financial Summary and Valuation for Tencent Holdings Limited

Market Data: 16 November 2016			2014	2015	2016E	2017E	2018E
Closing price	196.9	Revenue (RMB millions)	78,932	102,863	150,996	212,471	276,538
Price target	251.5	YOY (%)	30.60	30.32	46.79	40.71	30.15
HSCEI	9,380	Net income (RMB millions)	23,810	28,806	42,292	56,533	68,994
HSCCI	3,669	YOY (%)	53.49	21.85	46.76	32.87	22.04
52-Week high/low	132.10/ 220.8	EPS (RMB)	2.58	3.10	4.56	6.05	7.39
Market cap (USD millions)	240,311	Diluted EPS (RMB)	2.55	3.06	4.51	5.99	7.31
Market cap (HKD millions)	1,864,045	ROE (%)	29.09	23.84	26.11	26.18	24.71
Shares outstanding (millions)	9,467	Debt/Assets (%)	52.02	60.20	61.33	61.26	60.37
Exchange rate (RMB/HKD)	0.8857	Dividend yield (%)	0.20	0.20	0.28	0.38	0.46
		P/E	54.78	55.17	38.27	28.80	23.60
		P/B	22.31	19.35	13.39	9.99	7.54
		EV/EBITDA	40.79	35.88	28.06	20.09	15.39

Notes: Market data are quoted in HKD; the company's filing is in RMB. Diluted EPS is calculated as if all outstanding convertible securities (such as convertible preferred shares, convertible debentures, stock options, and warrants) were exercised. P/E is calculated as closing price divided by each year's EPS.
Source: SWS Research.

From the perspective of the date of Exhibit 3:

1. Which metrics would support a decision to invest by a growth investor?

2. Which characteristics would a growth investor tend to weigh less heavily than a high-quality value investor?

Solution to 1: A growth investor would focus on the following:

- The year-over-year change in revenue exceeded 30% in 2014 and 2015 and is expected to accelerate over 2016–2018.
- Past and expected net income growth rates are also high.

Solution to 2: A growth investor would tend to be less concerned about the relatively high valuation levels (high P/E, P/B, and EV/EBITDA) and low dividend yield.

3.2. Top-Down Strategies

As the name suggests, in contrast to bottom-up strategies, top-down strategies use an investment process that begins at a top or macro level. Instead of focusing on individual company- and asset-level variables in making investment decisions, top-down portfolio managers study variables affecting many companies, such as the macroeconomic environment, demographic trends, and government policies. These managers often use instruments such as futures contracts, ETFs, swaps, and custom baskets of individual stocks to capture macro dynamics and generate portfolio return. Some bottom-up stock pickers also incorporate top-down analysis as part of their process for arriving at investment decisions. A typical method of incorporating both top-down macroeconomic and bottom-up fundamental processes is to have the portfolio strategist set the target country and sector weights. Portfolio managers then construct stock portfolios that are consistent with these preset weights.

3.2.1. Country and Geographic Allocation to Equities

Investors using country allocation strategies form their portfolios by investing in different geographic regions depending on their assessment of the regions' prospects. For example, the manager may have a preference for a particular region and may establish a position in that region while limiting exposure to others. Managers of global equity funds may, for example, make a decision based on a tradeoff between the US equity market and the European equity market, or they may allocate among all investable country equity markets using futures or ETFs. Such strategies may also seek to track the overall supply and demand for equities in regions or countries by analyzing the aggregate volumes of share buybacks, investment fund flows, the volumes of initial public offerings, and secondary share issuance.

The country or geographic allocation decision itself can be based on both top-down macroeconomic and bottom-up fundamental analysis. For example, just as economic data for a given country are available, the market valuation of a country can be calculated by aggregating all company earnings and market capitalization.

3.2.2. Sector and Industry Rotation

Just as one can formulate a strategy that allocates to different countries or regions in an investment universe, one can also have a view on the expected returns of various sectors and industries across borders. Industries that are more integrated on a global basis—and therefore subject to global supply and demand dynamics—are more suitable to global sector allocation decisions. Examples of such industries include information technology and energy. On the other hand, sectors and industries that are more local in nature to individual countries are more suitable to sector allocation within a country. Examples of these industries are real estate and consumer staples. The availability of sector and industry ETFs greatly facilitates the implementation of sector and industry rotation strategies for those portfolio managers who cannot or do not wish to implement such strategies by investing in individual stocks.

As with country and geographic allocation, both top-down macroeconomic and bottom-up fundamental variables can be used to predict sector/industry returns. Many bottom-up portfolio managers also add a top-down sector overlay to their portfolios.

3.2.3. Volatility-Based Strategies

Another category of top-down equity strategies is based on investors' view on volatility and is usually implemented using derivative instruments. Those managers who believe they have the skill to predict future market volatility better than option-implied volatility (reflected, for example, in the VIX Index) can trade the VIX futures listed on the CBOE Futures Exchange (CFE), trade instruments such as index options, or enter into volatility swaps (or variance swaps).

Let's assume that an investor predicts a major market move, not anticipated by others, in the near term. The investor does not have an opinion on the direction of the move and only expects the index volatility to be high. The investor can use an index straddle strategy to capitalize on his or her view. Entering into an index straddle position involves the purchase of call and put options (on the same underlying index) with the same strike price and expiry date. The success of this long straddle strategy depends on whether or not volatility turns out to be higher than anticipated by the market; the strategy incurs losses when the market stays broadly flat. Exhibit 4 shows the payoff of such an index straddle strategy. The maximum loss of the long straddle is limited to the total call and put premiums paid.

3.2.4. Thematic Investment Strategies

Thematic investing is another broad category of strategies. Thematic strategies can use broad macroeconomic, demographic, or political drivers, or bottom-up ideas on industries and sectors,

EXHIBIT 4   Payoff Pattern of a Classic Long Straddle Strategy

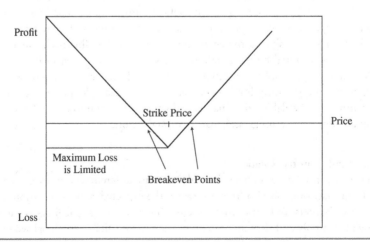

to identify investment opportunities. Disruptive technologies, processes, and regulations; innovations; and economic cycles present investment opportunities and also pose challenges to existing companies. Investors constantly search for new and promising ideas or themes that will drive the market in the future.

It is also important to determine whether any new trend is structural (and hence long-term) or short-term in nature. Structural changes can have long-lasting impacts on the way people behave or a market operates. For example, the development of smartphones and tablets and the move toward cloud computing are probably structural changes. On the other hand, a manager might attempt to identify companies with significant sales exposure to foreign countries as a way to benefit from short-term views on currency movements. The success of a structural thematic investment depends equally on the ability to take advantage of future trends and the ability to avoid what will turn out to be merely fashionable for a limited time, unless the strategy specifically focuses on short-term trends. Further examples of thematic investment drivers include new technologies, mobile communication and computing devices, clean energy, fintech, and advances in medicine.

Implementation of Top-Down Investment Strategies

A global equity portfolio manager with special insights into particular countries or regions can tactically choose to overweight or underweight those countries or regions on a short-term basis. Once the country or region weights are determined by a top-down process, the portfolio can be constructed by selecting stocks in the relevant countries or regions.

A portfolio manager with expertise in identifying drivers of sector or industry returns will establish a view on those drivers and will set weights for those sectors in a portfolio. For example, the performance of the energy sector is typically driven by the price of crude oil. The returns of the materials sector rest on forecasts for commodity prices. The consumer and industrials sectors require in-depth knowledge of the customer–supplier chains and a range of other dynamics. Once a view is established on the return and risk of each sector, a manager can then decide which industries to invest in and what weightings to assign to those industries relative to the benchmark.

The significant growth of passive factor investing—sometimes marketed as "smart beta" products—has given portfolio managers more tools and flexibility for investing in different equity styles. One can exploit the fact, for example, that high-quality stocks tend to perform well in recessions, or that cyclical deep-value companies are more likely to deliver superior returns in a more "risk-on" environment, in which the market becomes less risk-averse. For example, where the investment mandate permits, top-down managers can choose among different equity style ETFs and structured products to obtain risk exposures that are consistent with their views on different stages of the economic cycle or their views on market sentiment.

Portfolio Overlays

Bottom-up fundamental strategies often lead to unintended macro (e.g., sector or country) risk exposures. However, bottom-up fundamental investors can incorporate some of the risk control benefits of top-down investment strategies via portfolio overlays. (A **portfolio overlay** is an array of derivative positions managed separately from the securities portfolio to achieve overall portfolio characteristics that are desired by the portfolio manager.) The fundamental investor's sector weights, for example, may vary from the benchmark's weights as a result of the stock selection process even though the investor did not intend to make sector bets. In that case, the investor may be able to adjust the sector weights to align with the benchmark's weights via long and short positions in derivatives. In this way, top-down strategies can be effective in controlling risk exposures. Overlays can also be used to attempt to add active returns that are not correlated with those generated by the underlying portfolio strategy.

3.3. Factor-Based Strategies

A factor is a variable or characteristic with which individual asset returns are correlated. It can be broadly defined as any variable that is believed to be valuable in ranking stocks for investment and in predicting future returns or risks. A wide range of security characteristics have been used to define "factors." Some factors (most commonly, size, value, momentum, and quality) have been shown to be positively associated with a long-term return premium and are often referred to as *rewarded* factors. In fact, hundreds of factors have been identified and used in portfolio construction, but a large number have not been empirically proven to offer a persistent return premium (some call these *unrewarded* factors).

Broadly defined, a factor-based strategy aims to identify significant factors that can predict future stock returns and to construct a portfolio that tilts toward such factors. Some strategies rely on a single factor, are transparent, and maintain a relatively stable exposure to that factor with regular rebalancing (as is explained in the curriculum chapter on passive equity investing). Other strategies rely on a selection of factors. Yet other strategies may attempt to time the exposure to factors, recognizing that factor performance varies over time.

For new factor ideas, analysts and managers of portfolios that use factor strategies often rely on academic research, working papers, in-house research, and external research performed by entities such as investment banks. The following exhibits illustrate how some of the traditional style factors performed in recent decades, showing the varying nature of returns. Exhibit 5 shows the cumulative performance of large-cap versus small-cap US equities, using the S&P 500 and Russell 2000 total return indexes. Exhibit 6 presents the total returns of value (Russell 1000 Value Index) versus growth (Russell 1000 Growth Index) styles. Over the 28 years from January 1988 to April 2016, small-cap stocks earned marginally higher returns than large-cap stocks, but with significantly higher risk. Value and growth styles produce about the same return, but growth equities seem to be slightly more volatile (see Exhibit 7).

Equity style rotation strategies, a subcategory of factor investing, are based on the belief that different factors—such as size, value, momentum, and quality—work well during some time periods but less well during other time periods. These strategies use an investment process that allocates to stock baskets representing each of these styles when a particular style is expected to offer a positive excess return compared to the benchmark. While style rotation as a strategy can be used in both fundamental and quantitative investment processes, it is generally more in the domain of quantitative investing. Unlike sector or country allocation, discussed earlier, the classification of securities into style categories is less standardized.

EXHIBIT 5   Large-Cap vs. Small-Cap Equities

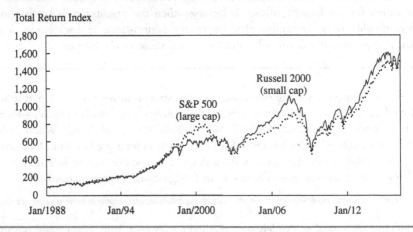

Sources: S&P, FTSE Russell.

EXHIBIT 6   Value vs. Growth Equities

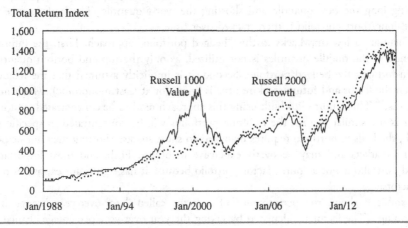

Sources: S&P, FTSE Russell.

EXHIBIT 7   Summary Statistics

	S&P 500	**Russell 2000**	**Russell 1000 Value**	**Russell 1000 Growth**
Annual return (%)	10.7	11.1	10.9	10.7
Annual volatility (%)	14.4	18.7	14.2	16.4
Sharpe Ratio	0.74	0.59	0.77	0.65

Sources: S&P, FTSE Russell.

The most important test, however, is the "smell" test: Does the factor make intuitive sense? A factor can often pass statistical backtesting, but if it does not make common sense—if justification for the factor's efficacy is lacking—then the manager may be data-mining. Investors should always remember that impressive performance in backtesting does not necessarily imply that the factor will continue to add value in the future.

> An important step is choosing the appropriate investment universe. Practitioners mostly define their investment universe in terms of well-known broad market indexes—for the United States, for example, the S&P 500, Russell 3000, and MSCI World Index. Using a well-defined index has several benefits: Such indexes are free from look-ahead and survivorship biases, the stocks in the indexes are investable with sufficient liquidity, and the indexes are also generally free from foreign ownership restrictions.

The most traditional and widely used method for implementing factor-based portfolios is the hedged portfolio approach, pioneered and formulated by Fama and French (1993). In this approach, after choosing the factor to be scrutinized and ranking the investable stock universe by that factor, investors divide the universe into groups referred to as *quantiles* (typically quintiles or deciles) to form quantile portfolios. Stocks are either equally weighted or capitalization weighted within each quantile. A long/short hedged portfolio is typically formed by going long the best quantile and shorting the worst quantile. The performance of the hedged long/short portfolio is then tracked over time.

There are a few drawbacks to this "hedged portfolio" approach. First, the information contained in the middle quantiles is not utilized, as only the top and bottom quantiles are used in forming the hedged portfolio. Second, it is implicitly assumed that the relationship between the factor and future stock returns is linear (or at least monotonic), which may not be the case.[4] Third, portfolios built using this approach tend to be concentrated, and if many managers use similar factors, the resulting portfolios will be concentrated in specific stocks. Fourth, the hedged portfolio requires managers to short stocks. Shorting may not be possible in some markets and may be overly expensive in others. Fifth, and most important, the hedged portfolio is not a "pure" factor portfolio because it has significant exposures to other risk factors.

Exhibit 8 shows the performance of a factor called "year-over-year change in debt outstanding." The factor is calculated by taking the year-over-year percentage change in the per share long-term debt outstanding on the balance sheet, using all stocks in the Russell 3000 universe. The portfolio is constructed by buying the top 10% of companies that reduce their debt and shorting the bottom 10% of companies that issue the most debt. Stocks in both the long and short portfolios are equally weighted.[5] The bars in the chart indicate the monthly portfolio returns. The average monthly return of the strategy is about 0.22% (or 2.7% per year), and the Sharpe ratio is 0.53 over the test period. All cumulative performance is computed on an initial investment in the factor of $100, with monthly rebalancing and excluding transaction costs.

---

[4]The payoff patterns between factor exposures and future stock returns are becoming increasingly non-linear, especially in the United States and Japan.
[5]Stocks can also be weighted based on their market capitalization.

EXHIBIT 8   Hedged Portfolio Return, "Year-over-Year Change in Debt Outstanding" Strategy

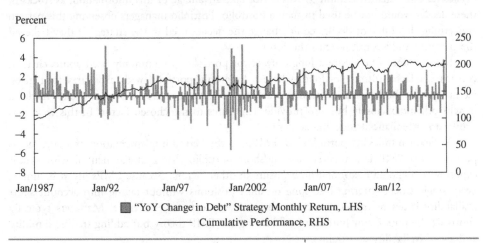

Sources: Compustat, FTSE Russell.

EXHIBIT 9   Average Decile Portfolio Return Based on Year-over-Year Change in Debt Outstanding

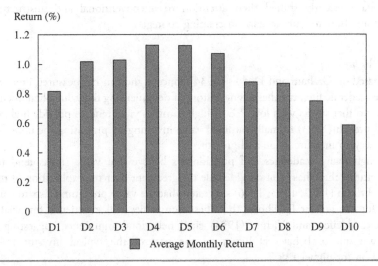

Sources: Compustat, FTSE Russell.

Exhibit 9 shows the average monthly returns of the 10 decile portfolios. It shows that companies with the highest year-over-year increase in debt financing (D10 category) marginally underperform companies with the lowest year-over-year increase in debt financing (average monthly return of 0.6% versus average monthly return of 0.8%). However, it can also be seen that the best-performing companies are the ones with reasonable financial leverage in Deciles 3 to 6. A long/short hedged portfolio approach based on the 1st and 10th deciles (as illustrated in Exhibit 9) would not take advantage of this information, as stocks in these deciles would not be used in such a portfolio. Portfolio managers observing this pattern concerning the different deciles could change the deciles used in the strategy if they believed the pattern would continue into the future.

For investors who desire a long-only factor portfolio, a commonly used approach is to construct a factor-tilting portfolio, where a long-only portfolio with exposures to a given factor can be built with controlled tracking error. The factor-tilting portfolio tracks a benchmark index closely but also provides exposures to the chosen factor. In this way, it is similar to an enhanced indexing strategy.

A "factor-mimicking portfolio," or FMP, is a theoretical implementation of a pure factor portfolio. An FMP is a theoretical long/short portfolio that is dollar neutral with a unit exposure to a chosen factor and no exposure to other factors. Because FMPs invest in almost every single stock, entering into long or short positions without taking into account short availability issues or transaction costs, they are very expensive to trade. Managers typically construct the pure factor portfolio by following the FMP theory but adding trading liquidity and short availability constraints.

3.3.1. Style Factors

Factors are the raw ingredients of quantitative investing and are often referred to as signals. Quantitative managers spend a large amount of time studying factors. Traditionally, factors have been based on fundamental characteristics of underlying companies. However, many investors have recently shifted their attention to unconventional and unstructured data sources in an effort to gain an edge in creating strategies.

3.3.1.1. Value

Value is based on Graham and Dodd's (1934) concept and can be measured in a number of ways. The academic literature has a long history of documenting the value phenomenon. Basu (1977) found that stocks with low P/E or high earnings yield tend to provide higher returns. Fama and French (1993) formally outlined value investing by proposing the book-to-market ratio as a way to measure value and growth.

Although many academics and practitioners believe that value stocks tend to deliver superior returns, there has been considerable disagreement over the explanation of this effect. Fama and French (1992, 1993, 1996) suggested that the value premium exists to compensate investors for the greater likelihood that these companies will experience financial distress. Lakonishok, Shleifer, and Vishny (1994) cited behavioral arguments, suggesting that the effect is a result of behavioral biases on the part of the typical investor rather than compensation for higher risk.

Value factors can also be based on other fundamental performance metrics of a company, such as dividends, earnings, cash flow, EBIT, EBITDA, and sales. Investors often add two more variations on most value factors by adjusting for industry (and/or country) and historical differences. Most valuation ratios can be computed using either historical (also called *trailing*) or forward metrics. Exhibit 10 shows the performance of the price-to-earnings multiple factor implemented as a long/short decile portfolio.

EXHIBIT 10   Performance of the P/E Factor (Long/Short Decile Portfolio)

Percent

P/E Factor Strategy Monthly Performance, LHS
Cumulative Performance, RHS

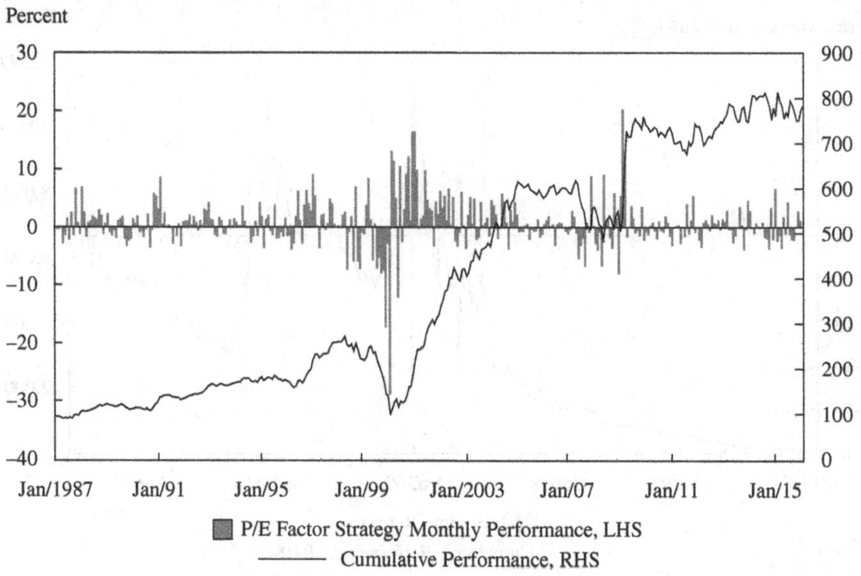

Sources: Compustat, FTSE Russell.

3.3.1.2. Price Momentum

Researchers have also found a strong price momentum effect in almost all asset classes in most countries. In fact, value and price momentum have long been the two cornerstones of quantitative investing.

Jegadeesh and Titman (1993) first documented that stocks that are "winners" over the previous 12 months tend to outperform past "losers" (those that have done poorly over the previous 12 months) and that such outperformance persists over the following 2 to 12 months. The study focused on the US market during the 1965–1989 period. The authors also found a short-term reversal effect, whereby stocks that have high price momentum in the previous month tend to underperform over the next 2 to 12 months. This price momentum anomaly is commonly attributed to behavioral biases, such as overreaction to information.[6] It is interesting to note that since the academic publication of these findings, the performance of the price momentum factor has become much more volatile (see Exhibit 11). Price momentum is, however, subject to extreme tail risk. Over the three-month March–May 2009 time period, the simple price momentum strategy (as measured by the long/short decile portfolio) lost 56%. For this data period, some reduction in downside risk can be achieved by removing the effect of sector exposure from momentum factor returns: We will call this modified version the "sector-neutralized price momentum factor."[7] The results are shown in Exhibits 12 and 13 for US, European, and Japanese markets.

---

[6]Behavioral biases are covered in the Level III chapters on behavioral finance.

[7]The methods for removing sector exposure are beyond the scope of this chapter.

EXHIBIT 11   Performance of the Price Momentum Factor (Long/Short Decile Portfolio)

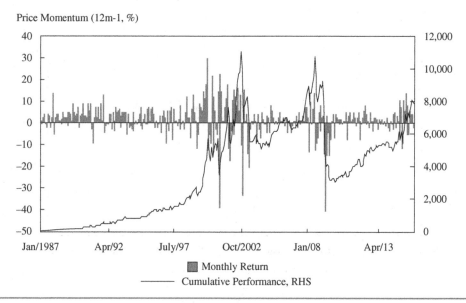

Sources: Compustat, FTSE Russell.

EXHIBIT 12   Performance of the Sector-Neutralized Price Momentum Factor (Long/Short Decile Portfolio)

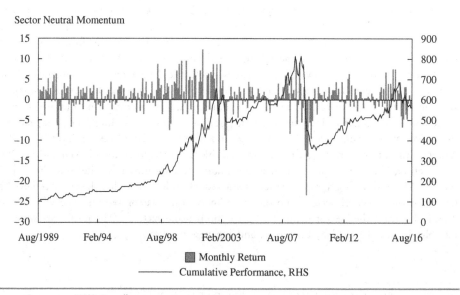

Sources: Compustat, FTSE Russell.

EXHIBIT 13   Performance of the Sector-Neutralized Price Momentum Factor in US, European, and Japanese Markets (Long/Short Decile Portfolio)

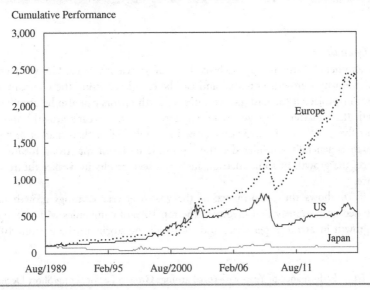

Sources: Compustat, FTSE Russell.

Exhibit 13 extends the analysis to include European and Japanese markets, where a similar effect on downside risk can be shown to have been operative over the period.

EXAMPLE 4   Factor Investing

A quantitative manager wants to expand his current strategy from US equities into international equity markets. His current strategy uses a price momentum factor. Based on Exhibit 13:

1. State whether momentum has been a factor in European and Japanese equity returns overall in the time period examined.
2. Discuss the potential reasons why neutralizing sectors reduces downside risk.

Solution to 1: As shown in Exhibit 13, price momentum has performed substantially better in Europe than in the United States. On the other hand, there does not appear to be any meaningful pattern of price momentum in Japan. Exhibit 13 suggests that the price momentum factor could be used for a European portfolio but not for a Japanese portfolio. However, managers need to perform rigorous backtesting before they can confidently implement a factor model in a market that they are not familiar with. Managers should be aware that what appears to be impressive performance in backtests does not necessarily imply that the factor will continue to add value in the future.

Solution to 2: Using the simple price momentum factor means that a portfolio buys past winners and shorts past losers. The resulting portfolio could have exposure to potentially significant industry bets. Sector-neutral price momentum focuses on stock selection without such risk exposures and thus tends to reduce downside risk.

3.3.1.3. Growth

Growth is another investment approach used by some style investors. Growth factors aim to measure a company's growth potential and can be calculated using the company's historical growth rates or projected forward growth rates. Growth factors can also be classified as short-term growth (last quarter's, last year's, next quarter's, or next year's growth) and long-term growth (last five years' or next five years' growth). While higher-than-market or higher-than-sector growth is generally considered to be a possible indicator for strong future stock price performance, the growth of some metrics, such as assets, results in weaker future stock price performance.

Exhibit 14 shows the performance of the year-over-year earnings growth factor. The exhibit is based on a strategy that invests in the top 10% of companies with the highest year-over-year growth in earnings per share and shorts all the stocks in the bottom 10%.

EXHIBIT 14   Performance of Year-over-Year Earnings Growth Factor (Long/Short Decile Portfolio)

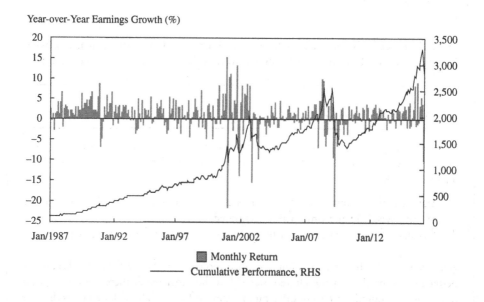

Sources: Compustat, FTSE Russell.

3.3.1.4. Quality

In addition to using accounting ratios and share price data as fundamental style factors, investors have continued to create more complex factors based on the variety of accounting

EXHIBIT 15   Performance of Earnings Quality Factor

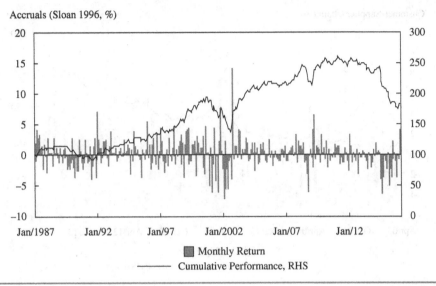

Accruals (Sloan 1996, %)

Monthly Return
Cumulative Performance, RHS

Sources: Compustat, FTSE Russell.

information available for companies. One of the best-known examples of how in-depth accounting knowledge can impact investment performance is Richard Sloan's (1996) seminal paper on earnings quality, with its proposition of the accruals factor. Sloan suggests that stock prices fail to reflect fully the information contained in the accrual and cash flow components of current earnings.[8] The performance of the accruals anomaly factor, however, appears to be quite cyclical.

In addition to the accruals anomaly, there are many other potential factors based on a company's fundamental data, such as profitability, balance sheet and solvency risk, earnings quality, stability, sustainability of dividend payout, capital utilization, and management efficiency measures. Yet another, analyst sentiment, refers to the phenomenon of sell-side analysts revising their forecasts of corporate earnings estimates, which is called *earnings revision*. More recently, with the availability of more data, analysts have started to include cash flow revisions, sales revisions, ROE revisions, sell-side analyst stock recommendations, and target price changes as variables in the "analyst sentiment" category.

A new and exciting area of research involves news sentiment. Rather than just relying on the output of sell-side analysts, investors could use natural language processing (NLP) algorithms to analyze the large volume of news stories and quantify the news sentiment on stocks.

---

[8]Sloan (1996) argues that in the long term, cash flows from operations and net income (under accruals-based accounting) should converge and be consistent. In the short term, they could diverge. Management has more discretion in accruals-based accounting; therefore, the temporary divergence between cash flows and net income reflects how conservative a company chooses to be in reporting its net income.

EXHIBIT 16   Performance of Customer–Supplier-Chain Factor

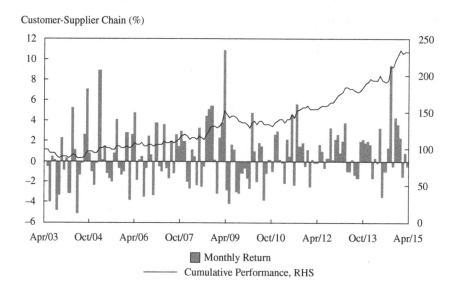

Customer-Supplier Chain (%)

■ Monthly Return
——— Cumulative Performance, RHS

Sources: Compustat, FactSet Revere, FTSE Russell.

3.3.2. Unconventional Factors Based on Unstructured Data

With the rapid growth in technology and computational algorithms, investors have been embracing big data. "Big data" is a broad term referring to extremely large datasets that may include structured data—such as traditional financial statements and market data—as well as unstructured or "alternative" data that has previously not been widely used in the investment industry because it lacks recognizable structure. Examples of such alternative data include satellite images, textual information, credit card payment information, and the number of online mentions of a particular product or brand.

Exhibit 16 shows the performance (as measured by the long/short quintile portfolio) of a factor based on customer–supplier chain data.[9] The signal is based on the trailing one-month stock price return of a company's largest customer. Stocks are ranked by largest customer performance, and the portfolio goes long the top quintile and shorts the lowest quintile. The positions are held until the following month's stock ranking and rebalancing. The intuition is that the positive performance of customers is likely to benefit the supplier company in subsequent periods. Indeed, compared to many traditional factors, the supply-chain signal seems to have shown more consistent returns, especially in recent years.

Portfolio construction is covered in the curriculum chapter titled "Active Equity Portfolio Construction."

---

[9]These data can be obtained from FactSet Revere's historical point-in-time supply chain dataset.

EXAMPLE 5   Researching Factor Timing

An analyst is exploring the relationship between interest rates and style factor returns for the purpose of developing equity style rotation strategies for the US equity market. The analysis takes place in early 2017. The first problem the analyst addresses is how to model the interest rate variable. The data in Exhibit 17 show an apparent trend of declining US government bond yields over the last 30 years. Trends may or may not continue into the future. The analyst decides to normalize the yield data so that they do not incorporate a prediction on continuation of the trend and makes a simple transformation by subtracting the yield's own 12-month moving average:

$$\text{Normalized yield}_t = \text{Nominal yield}_t - \frac{1}{12}\sum_{\tau=1}^{12}\text{Nominal yield}_{t-\tau+1}$$

The normalized yield data are shown in Exhibit 18. Yields calculated are as of the beginning of the month. Do the fluctuations in yield have any relationship with style factor returns? The analyst explores possible contemporaneous (current) and lagged relationships by performing two regressions (using the current month's and the next month's factor returns, respectively) against the normalized long-term bond yield:

$$f_{i,t} = \beta_{i,0} + \beta_{i,1}\text{Normalized yield}_t + \varepsilon_{i,t}$$

and

$$f_{i,t+1} = \beta_{i,0} + \beta_{i,1}\text{Normalized yield}_t + \varepsilon_{i,t}$$

EXHIBIT 17   Current and Expected Bond Yield, US

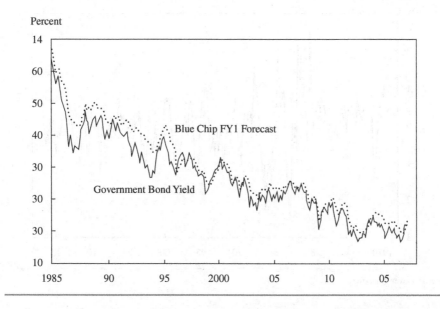

where $f_{i,t}$ is the return of style factor i at time t and $f_{i,t+1}$ is the subsequent (next) month's return to style factor i. The first regression reveals the contemporaneous relationship between interest rate and factor performance—that is, how well the current interest rate relates to the current factor performance. The second equation states whether the current interest rate can predict the next month's factor return. Exhibit 19 shows the findings.

Using only the information given, address the following:

1. Interpret Exhibit 19.
2. Discuss the relevance of contemporaneous and forward relationships in an equity factor rotation strategy.
3. What concerns could the analyst have in relation to an equity factor rotation strategy, and what possible next steps could the analyst take to address those concerns?

Solution to 1: Exhibit 19 suggests an inverse relationship between concurrent bond yields and returns to the dividend yield, price reversal, and ROE factors. For some factors (such as earnings quality), the relationship between bond yields and forward (next month's) factor returns is in the same direction as the contemporaneous relationship.

Solution to 2: Attention needs to be given to the timing relationship of variables to address this question. A contemporaneous style factor return becomes known as of the end of the month. If the known value of bond yields at the beginning of the month is correlated with factor returns, the investor may be able to gain some edge relative to

EXHIBIT 18 · Normalized 10-Year Treasury Bond Yield, US

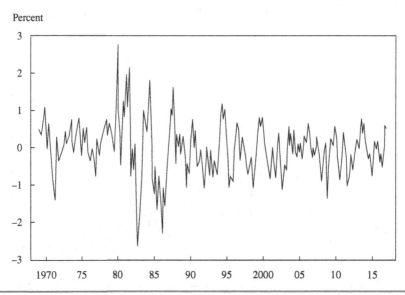

Source: Haver Analytics.

EXHIBIT 19   Normalized Bond Yield and Style Factor Returns

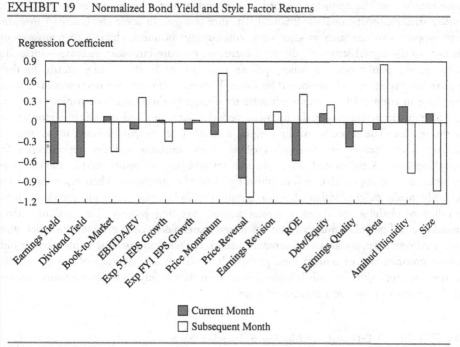

Source: Haver Analytics.

investors who do not use that information. The same conclusion holds concerning the forward relationship. If the contemporaneous variable were defined so that it is realized at the same time as the variable we want to predict, the forward but not the contemporaneous variable would be relevant.

Solution to 3: The major concern is the validity of the relationships between normalized interest rates and the style variables. Among the steps the analyst can take to increase his or her conviction in the relationships' validity are the following:

- Establish whether the relationships have predictive value out of sample (that is, based on data not used to model the relationship).
- Investigate whether or not there are economic rationales for the relationships such that those relationships could be expected to persist into the future.

Exhibit 19 shows both weak relationships (e.g., for earnings revision) and strong relationships (e.g., for size and beta) in relation to the subsequent month's returns. This fact suggests some priorities in examining this question.

3.4. Activist Strategies

Activist investors specialize in taking stakes in listed companies and advocating changes for the purpose of producing a gain on the investment. The investor may wish to obtain representation on the company's board of directors or use other measures in an effort to initiate strategic, operational, or financial structure changes. In some cases, activist investors may support activities such as asset sales, cost-cutting measures, changes to management, changes to the capital structure, dividend increases, or share buybacks. Activists—including hedge funds, public pension funds, private investors, and others—vary greatly in their approaches, expertise, and investment horizons. They may also seek different outcomes. What they have in common is that they advocate for change in their target companies.

Shareholder activism typically follows a period of screening and analysis of opportunities in the market. The investor usually reviews a number of companies based on a range of parameters and carries out in-depth analysis of the business and the opportunities for unlocking value. Activism itself starts when an investor buys an equity stake in the company and starts advocating for change (i.e., pursuing an activist campaign). These equity stakes are generally made public. Stakes above a certain threshold must be made public in most jurisdictions. Exhibit 20 shows a typical activist investing process. The goal of activist investing could be either financial gain (increased shareholder value) or a non-financial cause (e.g., environmental, social, and governance issues). Rather than pursuing a full takeover bid, activist investors aim to achieve their goals with smaller stakes, typically of less than 10%. Activist investors' time horizon is often shorter than that of buy-and-hold investors, but the whole process can last for a number of years.

EXHIBIT 20   A Typical Shareholder Activist Investing Process

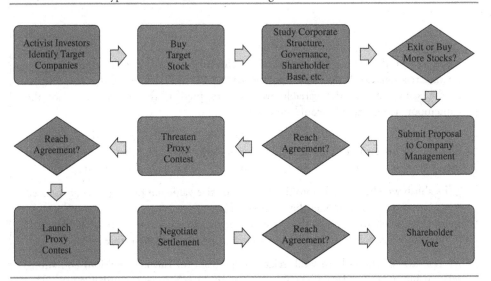

Source: Deutsche Bank.

3.4.1. The Popularity of Shareholder Activism

Shareholder (or investor) activism is by no means a new investment strategy. Its foundations go back to the 1970s and 1980s, when investors known as corporate raiders took substantial stakes in companies in order to influence their operations, unlock value in the target companies, and thereby raise the value of their shares. Proponents of activism argue that it is an important and necessary activity that helps monitor and discipline corporate management to the benefit of all shareholders. Opponents argue that such interventionist tactics can cause distraction and negatively impact management performance.

Activist hedge funds—among the most prominent activist investors—saw growing popularity for a number of years, with assets under management (AUM) reaching $50 billion in 2007[10] before falling sharply during the global financial crisis. Activist hedge fund investing has since strongly recovered, with AUM close to $120 billion in 2015.[11] The activity of such investors can be tracked by following the activists' announcements that they are launching a campaign seeking to influence companies. Exhibit 21 shows the number of activist events reported by the industry. Hedge funds that specialize in activism benefit from lighter regulation than other types of funds, and their fee structure, offering greater rewards, justifies concerted campaigns for change at the companies they hold. The popularity and viability of investor activism are influenced by the legal frameworks in different jurisdictions, shareholder structures, and cultural considerations. The United States has seen the greatest amount of activist activity initiated by hedge funds, individuals, and pension funds, but there have been a number of activist events in Europe too. Other regions have so far seen more limited activity on the part of activist investors. Cultural reasons and more concentrated shareholder ownership of companies are two frequently cited explanations.

EXHIBIT 21   Number of Global Activist Events

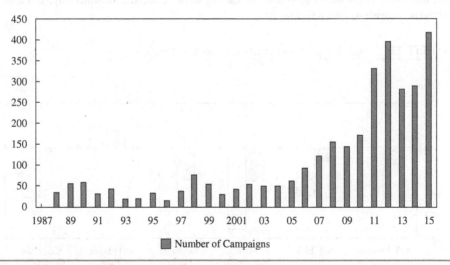

Source: Thomson Reuters Activism database.

3.4.2. Tactics Used by Activist Investors

Activists use a range of tactics on target companies in order to boost shareholder value. These tactics include the following:

- Seeking board representation and nominations

---

[10]Hedge Fund Research.
[11]See "Activist Funds: An Investor Calls," *Economist* (7 February 2015).

- Engaging with management by writing letters to management calling for and explaining suggested changes, participating in management discussions with analysts or meeting the management team privately, or launching proxy contests whereby activists encourage other shareholders to use their proxy votes to effect change in the organization
- Proposing significant corporate changes during the annual general meeting (AGM)
- Proposing restructuring of the balance sheet to better utilize capital and potentially initiate share buybacks or increase dividends
- Reducing management compensation or realigning management compensation with share price performance
- Launching legal proceedings against existing management for breach of fiduciary duties
- Reaching out to other shareholders of the company to coordinate action
- Launching a media campaign against existing management practices
- Breaking up a large conglomerate to unlock value

The effectiveness of shareholder activism depends on the response of the existing management team and the tools at that team's disposal. In many countries, defense mechanisms can be employed by management or a dominant shareholder to hinder activist intervention. These techniques include multi-class share structures whereby a company founder's shares are typically entitled to multiple votes per share; "poison pill" plans allowing the issuance of shares at a deep discount, which causes significant economic and voting dilution; staggered board provisions whereby a portion of the board members are not elected at annual shareholders meetings and hence cannot all be replaced simultaneously; and charter and bylaw provisions and amendments.

EXHIBIT 22   Fundamental Characteristics of Target Companies

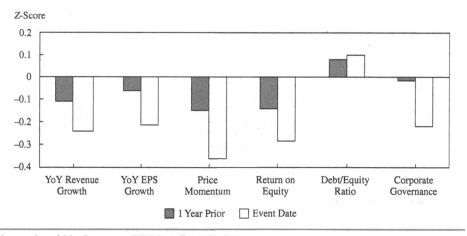

Sources: Capital IQ, Compustat, FTSE Russell, MSCI, S&P.

3.4.3. Typical Activist Targets

Activist investors look for specific characteristics in deciding which companies to target. Exhibit 22 shows the characteristics of target companies relative to the market as a whole. The exhibit provides a measure of these characteristics on the event day as well as a year before the announcement, giving a flavor of the dynamics of these attributes. It shows that, on average,[12] target companies feature slower revenue and earnings growth than the market, suffer negative share price momentum, and have weaker-than-average corporate governance.[13] By building stakes and initiating change in underperforming companies, activists hope to unlock value. In addition, by targeting such companies, activist investors are more likely to win support for their actions from other shareholders and the wider public. Traditionally, the target companies have been small and medium-sized listed stocks. This has changed as a number of larger companies have become subject to activism.[14]

Do Activists Really Improve Company Performance?

Exhibit 23 shows that, on average, fundamental characteristics of targeted companies do improve in subsequent years following activists' efforts, with evidence that revenue and earnings growth increase, profitability improves, and corporate governance indicators become more robust. There is evidence, however, that the financial leverage of such companies increases significantly.

EXHIBIT 23   Fundamentals of Target Companies Improve

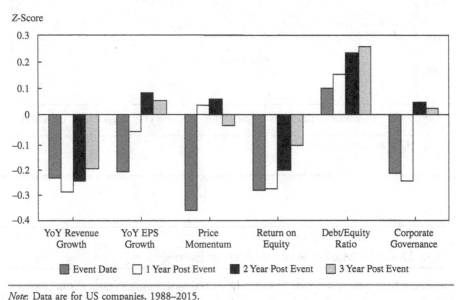

Note: Data are for US companies, 1988–2015.

Sources: Capital IQ, Compustat, FTSE Russell, MSCI, S&P.

---

[12]The fundamental characteristics of all companies in the investment universe (i.e., the Russell 3000) are standardized using Z-scores (by subtracting the mean and dividing by the standard deviation) every month from 1988 until 2015. Thus, we can compare the average exposure to each fundamental characteristic over time.

[13]We normalize all target and non-target companies' factor exposures using Z-scores (i.e., subtracting the sample mean and dividing by the sample standard deviation).

[14]Trian Fund Management proposed splitting PepsiCo into standalone public companies; Third Point called for leadership change at Yahoo!.

Do Activist Investors Generate Alpha?

Activist hedge funds are among the major activist investors. Based on the HFRX Activist Index, in the aggregate, activist hedge funds have delivered an average annual return of 7.7% with annual volatility of 13.7% and therefore a Sharpe ratio of 0.56—slightly higher than the Sharpe ratio of the S&P 500 Index of 0.54 (see Exhibit 24). However, it is difficult to conclude how much value activist investors add because the HFRX index does not include a large enough number of managers. Furthermore, managers themselves vary in their approaches and the risks they take.

EXHIBIT 24   Performance of HFRX Activist Index vs. S&P 500

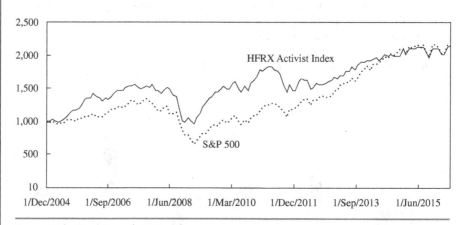

Sources: Hedge Fund Research, S&P.

How Does the Market React to Activist Events?

Investors have generally reacted positively to activism announcements: On average, target company stocks go up by 2% on the announcement day (based on all activist events in the Thomson Reuters Corporate Governance Intelligence database from 1987 to 2016).[15] Interestingly, the positive reaction comes on top of stock appreciation prior to activism announcements (see Exhibit 25). According to the model of Maug (1998), activist investors trade in a stock prior to the announcement to build up a stake, assert control, and profit from the value creation. It may also be argued that there must be information leakage about the activists' involvement, driving the stock higher even before the first public announcement. There is a modest post-announcement drift:

---

[15]All returns are excess returns, adjusted for the market and sector. For details, see Jussa, Webster, Zhao, and Luo (2016).

In the month after the activist announcement date, target share prices move up by 0.6%, on average, relative to the market.

EXHIBIT 25   Market Reactions to Activist Events

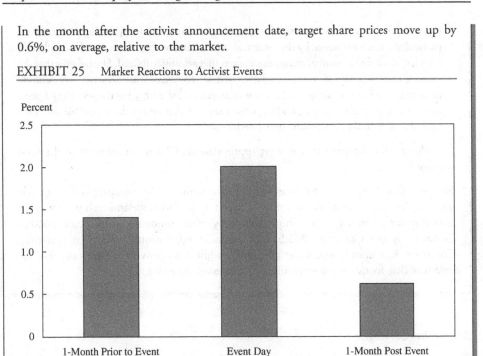

Sources: Capital IQ, Compustat, FTSE Russell, S&P.

EXAMPLE 6   Activist Investing

Kendra Cho is an analyst at an investment firm that specializes in activist investing and manages a concentrated portfolio of stocks invested in listed European companies. Cho and her colleagues hope to identify and buy stakes in companies with the potential to increase their value through strategic, operational, or financial change. Cho is considering the following three companies:

- Company A is a well-established, medium-sized food producer. Its profitability, measured by operating margins and return on assets, is ahead of industry peers. The company is recognized for its high corporate governance standards and effective communication with existing and potential investors. Cho's firm has invested in companies in this sector in the past and made gains on those positions.

- Company B is a medium-sized engineering business that has experienced a significant deterioration in profitability in recent years. More recently, the company has been unable to pay interest on its debt, and its new management team has recognized the need to restructure the business and negotiate with its creditors. Due to the company's losses, Cho cannot use earnings-based price multiples to assess upside potential, but based on sales and asset multiples, she believes there is significant upside potential in the stock if the company's current difficulties can be overcome and the debt can be restructured.

- Company C is also a medium-sized engineering business, but its operating performance, particularly when measured by the return on assets, is below that of the rest of the industry. Cho has identified a number of company assets that are underutilized. She believes that the management has significant potential to reduce fixed-asset investments, concentrate production in fewer facilities, and dispose of assets, in line with what the company's peers have been doing. Such steps could improve asset turnover and make it possible to return capital to shareholders through special dividends.

Identify the company that is most appropriate for Cho to recommend to the fund managers:

Solution: Company C is the most appropriate choice. The company offers upside potential because of its ability to improve operating performance and cash payout using asset disposals, a strategy being implemented by other companies in its sector. Neither Company A nor Company B offers an attractive opportunity for activist investing: Company A is already operating efficiently, while Company B is more suitable for investors that focus on restructuring and distressed investing.

3.5. Other Strategies

There are many other strategies that active portfolio managers employ in an attempt to beat the market benchmark. In this section, we explain two other categories of active strategies that do not fit neatly into our previous categorizations—namely, statistical arbitrage and event-driven strategies. Both rely on extensive use of quantitative data and are usually implemented in a systematic, rules-based way but can also incorporate the fund manager's judgment in making investment decisions.

3.5.1. Strategies Based on Statistical Arbitrage and Market Microstructure

Statistical arbitrage (or "stat arb") strategies use statistical and technical analysis to exploit pricing anomalies. Statistical arbitrage makes extensive use of data such as stock price, dividend, trading volume, and the limit order book for this purpose. The analytical tools used include (1) traditional technical analysis, (2) sophisticated time-series analysis and econometric models, and (3) machine-learning techniques. Portfolio managers typically take advantage of either mean reversion in share prices or opportunities created by market microstructure issues.

Pairs trading is an example of a popular and simple statistical arbitrage strategy. Pairs trading uses statistical techniques to identify two securities that are historically highly correlated with each other. When the price relationship of these two securities deviates from its long-term average, managers that expect the deviation to be temporary go long the underperforming stock and simultaneously short the outperforming stock. If the prices do converge to the long-term average as forecast, the investors close the trade and realize a profit. This kind of pairs trading therefore bets on a mean-reversion pattern in stock prices. The biggest risk in pairs trading and most other mean-reversion strategies is that the observed price divergence is not temporary; rather, it might be due to structural reasons.[16] Because risk management is critical for the success of such strategies, investors often employ stop-loss rules to exit trades when a loss limit is reached.

---

[16] For example, the outperformance of one stock might be due to the fact that the company has developed a new technology or product that cannot be easily replicated by competitors.

The most difficult aspect of a pairs-trading strategy is the identification of the pairs of stocks. This can be done either by using a quantitative approach and creating models of stock prices or by using a fundamental approach to judge the two stocks whose prices should move together for qualitative reasons.

Consider Canadian National Railway (CNR) and Canadian Pacific Railway (CP). These are the two dominant railways in Canada. Their business models are fairly similar, as both operate railway networks and transport goods throughout the country. Exhibit 26 shows that the prices of the two stocks have been highly correlated.[17] The *y*-axis shows the log price differential, referred to as the spread.[18] The exhibit also shows the moving average of the spread computed on a rolling 130-day window and bands at two standard deviations above and two standard deviations below the moving average. A simple pairs-trading strategy would be to enter into a trade when the spread is more than (or less than) two standard deviations from the moving average. The trade would be closed when the spread reaches the moving average again. Exhibit 26 shows the three trades based on our decision rules. The first trade was opened on 2 October 2014, when the spread between CNR and CP crossed the –2 standard deviation mark.[19] This trade was closed on 18 November 2014, when the spread reached the moving average. The first trade was profitable, and the position was maintained for slightly more than a month. The second trade was also profitable but lasted much longer. After the third trade was entered on 21 July 2015, however, there was a structural break, in that CP's decline further intensified while CNR stayed relatively flat; therefore, the spread continued to widen. The loss on the third trade could have been significantly greater than the profits made from the first two transactions if the positions had been closed prior to mean reversion in the spring of 2016. This example highlights the risk inherent in mean-reversion strategies.

EXHIBIT 26   Pairs Trade between CNR and CP

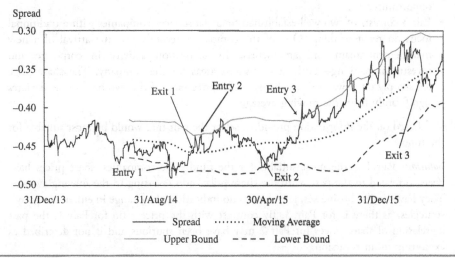

Sources: Bloomberg, Wolfe Research.

---

[17]The correlation coefficient between the two stocks was 69% based on daily returns from 2 January 2014 to 26 May 2016.

[18]ln(Price of CNR/Price of CP).

[19]The position is long CNR and short CP.

In the United States, many market microstructure–based arbitrage strategies take advantage of the NYSE Trade and Quote (TAQ) database and often involve extensive analysis of the limit order book to identify very short-term mispricing opportunities. For example, a temporary imbalance between buy and sell orders may trigger a spike in share price that lasts for only a few milliseconds. Only those investors with the analytical tools and trading capabilities for high-frequency trading are in a position to capture such opportunities, usually within a portfolio of many stocks designed to take advantage of very short-term discrepancies.

EXAMPLE 7

An analyst is asked to recommend a pair of stocks to be added to a statistical arbitrage fund. She considers the following three pairs of stocks:

- Pair 1 consists of two food-producing companies. Both are mature companies with comparable future earnings prospects. Both typically trade on similar valuation multiples. The ratio of their share prices shows mean reversion over the last two decades. The ratio is currently more than one standard deviation above its moving average.
- Pair 2 consists of two consumer stocks: One is a food retailer, and the other is a car manufacturer. Although the two companies operate in different markets and have different business models, statistical analysis performed by the analyst shows strong correlation between their share prices that has persisted for more than a decade. The stock prices have moved significantly in opposite directions in recent days. The analyst, expecting mean reversion, believes this discrepancy represents an investment opportunity.
- Pair 3 consists of two well-established financial services companies with a traditional focus on retail banking. One of the companies recently saw the arrival of a new management team and an increase in acquisition activity in corporate and investment banking—both new business areas for the company. The share price fell sharply on news of these changes. The price ratio of the two banks now deviates significantly from the moving average.

Based on the information provided, select the pair that would be most suitable for the fund.

Solution: Pair 1 is the most suitable for the fund. The companies' share prices have been correlated in the past, with the share price ratio reverting to the moving average. They have similar businesses, and there is no indication of a change in either company's strategies, as there is for Pair 3. By contrast with the price ratio for Pair 1, the past correlation of share prices for Pair 2 may have been spurious and is not described as exhibiting mean reversion.

3.5.2. Event-Driven Strategies

Event-driven strategies exploit market inefficiencies that may occur around corporate events such as mergers and acquisitions, earnings or restructuring announcements, share buybacks, special dividends, and spinoffs.

Risk arbitrage associated with merger and acquisition (M&A) activity is one of the most common examples of an event-driven strategy.

In a cash-only transaction, the acquirer proposes to purchase the shares of the target company for a given price. The stock price of the target company typically remains below the offered price until the transaction is completed. Therefore, an arbitrageur could buy the stock of the target company and earn a profit if and when the acquisition closes.

In a share-for-share exchange transaction, the acquirer uses its own shares to purchase the target company at a given exchange ratio. A risk arbitrage trader normally purchases the target share and simultaneously short-sells the acquirer's stock at the same exchange ratio. Once the acquisition is closed, the arbitrageur uses his or her long positions in the target company to exchange for the acquirer's stocks, which are further used to cover the arbitrageur's short positions.

The first challenge in managing risk arbitrage positions is to accurately estimate the risk of the deal failing. An M&A transaction, for example, may not go through for numerous reasons. A regulator may block the deal because of antitrust concerns, or the acquirer may not be able to secure the approval from the target company's shareholders. If a deal fails, the price of the target stock typically falls sharply, generating significant loss for the arbitrageur. Hence, this strategy has the label "risk arbitrage."

Another important consideration that an arbitrageur has to take into account is the deal duration. At any given point in time, there are many M&A transactions outstanding, and the arbitrageur has to decide which ones to participate in and how to weight each position, based on the predicted premium and risk. The predicted premium has to be annualized to enable the arbitrageur to compare different opportunities. Therefore, estimating deal duration is important for accurately estimating the deal premium.

4. CREATING A FUNDAMENTAL ACTIVE INVESTMENT STRATEGY

Fundamental (or discretionary) investing remains one of the prevailing philosophies of active management. In the following sections, we discuss how fundamental investors organize their investment processes.

4.1. The Fundamental Active Investment Process

The broad goal of active management is to outperform a selected benchmark on a risk-adjusted basis, net of fees and transaction costs. Value can be added at different stages of the investment process. For example, added value may come from the use of proprietary data, from special skill in security analysis and valuation, or from insight into industry/sector allocation.

Many fundamental investors use processes that include the following steps:

1. Define the investment universe and the market opportunity—the perceived opportunity to earn a positive risk-adjusted return to active investing, net of costs—in accordance with the investment mandate. The market opportunity is also known as the investment thesis.
2. Prescreen the investment universe to obtain a manageable set of securities for further, more detailed analysis.
3. Understand the industry and business for this screened set by performing:
   • industry and competitive analysis and
   • analysis of financial reports.

4. Forecast company performance, most commonly in terms of cash flows or earnings.
5. Convert forecasts to valuations and identify *ex ante* profitable investments.
6. Construct a portfolio of these investments with the desired risk profile.
7. Rebalance the portfolio with buy and sell disciplines.

The investment universe is mainly determined by the mandate agreed on by the fund manager and the client. The mandate defines the market segments, regions, and/or countries in which the manager will seek to add value. For example, if an investment mandate specifies Hong Kong's Hang Seng Index as the performance benchmark, the manager's investment universe will be primarily restricted to the 50 stocks in that index. However, an active manager may also include non-index stocks that trade on the same exchange or whose business activities significantly relate to this region. It is important for investors who seek to hold a diversified and well-constructed portfolio to understand the markets in which components of the portfolio will be invested. In addition, a clear picture of the market opportunity to earn positive active returns is important for active equity investment. The basic question is, what is the opportunity and why is it there? The answer to this two-part question can be called the investment thesis. The "why" part involves understanding the economic, financial, behavioral, or other rationale for a strategy's profitability in the future.

Practically, the investment thesis will suggest a set of characteristics that tend to be associated with potentially profitable investments. The investor may prescreen the investment universe with quantitative and/or qualitative criteria to obtain a manageable subset that will be analyzed in greater detail. Prescreening criteria can often be associated with a particular investment style. A value style manager, for example, may first exclude those stocks with high P/E multiples and high debt-to-equity ratios. Growth style managers may first rule out stocks that do not have high enough historical or forecast EPS growth. Steps 3 to 5 cover processes of in-depth analysis described in the Level II CFA Program chapters on industry and company analysis and equity valuation. Finally, a portfolio is constructed in which stocks that have high upside potential are overweighted relative to the benchmark and stocks that are expected to underperform the benchmark are underweighted, not held at all, or (where relevant) shorted.[20]

As part of the portfolio construction process (step 6), the portfolio manager needs to decide whether to take active exposures to particular industry groups or economic sectors or to remain sector neutral relative to the benchmark. Portfolio managers may have top-down

---

[20]A portfolio that is benchmarked against an index that contains hundreds or thousands of constituents will most likely have zero weighting in most of them.

views on the business trends in some industries. For example, innovations in medical technology may cause an increase in earnings in the health care sector as a whole, while a potential central bank interest rate hike may increase the profitability of the banking sector. With these views, assuming the changed circumstances are not already priced in by the market, a manager could add extra value to the portfolio by overweighting the health care and financial services sectors. If the manager doesn't have views on individual sectors, he or she should, in theory, establish a neutral industry position relative to the benchmark in constructing the portfolio. However, a manager who has very strong convictions on the individual names in a specific industry may still want to overweight the industry that those names belong to. The potential high excess return from overweighting individual stocks can justify the risk the portfolio takes on the active exposure to that industry.

In addition to the regular portfolio rebalancing that ensures that the investment mandate and the desired risk exposures are maintained, a stock sell discipline needs to be incorporated into the investment process. The stock sell discipline will enable the portfolio to take profit from a successful investment and to exit from an unsuccessful investment at a prudent time.

In fundamental analysis, each stock is typically assigned a target price that the analyst believes to be the fair market value of the stock. The stock will be reclassified from undervalued to overvalued if the stock price surpasses this target price. Once this happens, the upside of the stock is expected to be limited, and holding that stock may not be justified, given the potential downside risk. The sell discipline embedded within an investment process requires the portfolio manager to sell the stock at this point. In practice, recognizing that valuation is an imprecise exercise, managers may continue to hold the stock or may simply reduce the size of the position rather than sell outright. This flexibility is particularly relevant when, in relative valuation frameworks where the company is being valued against a peer group, the valuations of industry peers are also changing. The target price of a stock need not be a constant but can be updated by the analyst with the arrival of new information. Adjusting the target price downward until it is lower than the current market price would also trigger a sale or a reduction in the position size.

Other situations could arise in which a stock's price has fallen and continues to fall for what the analyst considers to be poorly understood reasons. If the analyst remains positive on the stock, he or she should carefully consider the rationale for maintaining the position; if the company fundamentals indeed worsened, the analyst must also consider his or her own possible behavioral biases. The portfolio manager needs to have the discipline to take a loss by selling the stock if, for example, the price touches some pre-defined stop-loss trigger point. The stop-loss point is intended to set the maximum loss for each asset, under any conditions, and limit such behavioral biases.

EXAMPLE 8   Fundamental Investing

A portfolio manager uses the following criteria to prescreen his investment universe:

1. The year-over-year growth rate in earnings per share from continuing operations has increased over each of the last four fiscal years.
2. Growth in earnings per share from continuing operations over the last 12 months has been positive.

3. The percentage difference between the actual announced earnings and the consensus earnings estimate for the most recent quarter is greater than or equal to 10%.
4. The percentage change in stock price over the last four weeks is positive.
5. The 26-week relative price strength is greater than or equal to the industry's 26-week relative price strength.
6. The average daily volume for the last 10 days is in the top 50% of the market.

Describe the manager's investment mandate.

Solution: The portfolio manager has a growth orientation with a focus on companies that have delivered EPS growth in recent years and that have maintained their earnings and price growth momentum. Criterion 1 specifies accelerating EPS growth rates over recent fiscal years, while criterion 2 discards companies for which recent earnings growth has been negative. Criterion 3 further screens for companies that have beaten consensus earnings expectations—have had a positive earnings surprise—in the most recent quarter. A positive earnings surprise suggests that past earnings growth is continuing. Criteria 4 and 5 screen for positive recent stock price momentum. Criterion 6 retains only stocks with at least average market liquidity. Note the absence of any valuation multiples among the screening criteria: A value investor's screening criteria would typically include a rule to screen out issues that are expensively valued relative to earnings or assets.

4.2. Pitfalls in Fundamental Investing

Pitfalls in fundamental investing include behavioral biases, the value trap, and the growth trap.

4.2.1. Behavioral Bias

Fundamental, discretionary investing in general and stock selection in particular depend on subjective judgments by portfolio managers based on their research and analysis. However, human judgment, though potentially more insightful than a purely quantitative method, can be less rational and is often susceptible to human biases. The CFA Program curriculum chapters on behavioral finance divide behavioral biases into two broad groups: cognitive errors and emotional biases. Cognitive errors are basic statistical, information-processing, or memory errors that cause a decision to deviate from the rational decisions of traditional finance, while emotional biases arise spontaneously as a result of attitudes and feelings that can cause a decision to deviate from the rational decisions of traditional finance. Several biases that are relevant to active fundamental equity management are discussed here.

4.2.1.1. Confirmation Bias

A cognitive error, confirmation bias—sometimes referred to as "stock love bias"—is the tendency of analysts and investors to look for information that confirms their existing beliefs about their favorite companies and to ignore or undervalue any information that contradicts their existing beliefs. This behavior creates selective exposure, perception, and retention and may be thought of as a selection bias. Some of the consequences are a poorly diversified portfolio, excessive risk exposure, and holdings in poorly performing securities. Actively seeking out the opinions of other investors or team members and looking for information from a range of sources to challenge existing beliefs may reduce the risk of confirmation bias.

4.2.1.2. Illusion of Control

The basic philosophy behind active equity management is that investors believe they can control or at least influence outcomes. Skilled investors have a healthy confidence in their own ability to select stocks and influence outcomes, and they expect to outperform the market. The illusion of control bias refers to the human tendency to overestimate these abilities. Langer (1983) defines the illusion of control bias as "an expectancy of a personal success probability inappropriately higher than the objective probability would warrant." The illusion of control is a cognitive error.

Having an illusion of control could lead to excessive trading and/or heavy weighting on a few stocks. Investors should seek contrary viewpoints and set and enforce proper trading and portfolio diversification rules to try to avoid this problem.

4.2.1.3. Availability Bias

Availability bias is an information-processing bias whereby individuals take a mental shortcut in estimating the probability of an outcome based on the availability of the information and how easily the outcome comes to mind. Easily recalled outcomes are often perceived as being more likely than those that are harder to recall or understand. Availability bias falls in the cognitive error category. In fundamental equity investing, this bias may reduce the investment opportunity set and result in insufficient diversification as the portfolio manager relies on familiar stocks that reflect a narrow range of experience. Setting an appropriate investment strategy in line with the investment horizon, as well as conducting a disciplined portfolio analysis with a long-term focus, will help eliminate any short-term over-emphasis caused by this bias.

4.2.1.4. Loss Aversion

Loss aversion is an emotional bias whereby investors tend to prefer avoiding losses over achieving gains. A number of studies on loss aversion suggest that, psychologically, losses are significantly more powerful than gains. In absolute value terms, the utility derived from a gain is much lower than the utility given up in an equivalent loss.

Loss aversion can cause investors to hold unbalanced portfolios in which poorly performing positions are maintained in the hope of potential recovery and successful investments are sold (and the gains realized) prematurely in order to avoid further risk. A disciplined trading strategy with firmly established stop-loss rules is essential to prevent fundamental investors from falling into this trap.

4.2.1.5. Overconfidence Bias

Overconfidence bias is an emotional bias whereby investors demonstrate unwarranted faith in their own intuitive reasoning, judgment, and/or cognitive abilities. This overconfidence may be the result of overestimating knowledge levels, abilities, and access to information. Unlike the illusion of control bias, which is a cognitive error, overconfidence bias is an illusion of exaggerated knowledge and abilities. Investors may, for example, attribute success to their own ability rather than to luck. Such bias means that the portfolio manager underestimates risks and overestimates expected returns. Regularly reviewing actual investment records and seeking constructive feedback from other professionals can help investors gain awareness of such self-attribution bias.

4.2.1.6. Regret Aversion Bias

An emotional bias, regret aversion bias causes investors to avoid making decisions that they fear will turn out poorly. Simply put, investors try to avoid the pain of regret associated with bad decisions. This bias may actually prevent investors from making decisions. They may instead hold on to positions for too long and, in the meantime, lose out on profitable investment opportunities.

A carefully defined portfolio review process can help mitigate the effects of regret aversion bias. Such a process might, for example, require investors to periodically review and justify existing positions or to substantiate the decision not to have exposure to other stocks in the universe.

4.2.2. Value and Growth Traps

Value- and growth-oriented investors face certain distinctive risks, often described as "traps."

4.2.2.1. The Value Trap

A value trap is a stock that appears to be attractively valued—with a low P/E multiple (and/or low price-to-book-value or price-to-cash-flow multiples)—because of a significant price fall but that may still be overpriced given its worsening future prospects. For example, the fact that a company is trading at a low price relative to earnings or book value might indicate that the company or the entire sector is facing deteriorating future prospects and that stock prices may stay low for an extended period of time or decline even further. Often, a value trap appears to be such an attractive investment that investors struggle to understand why the stock fails to perform. Value investors should conduct thorough research before investing in any company that appears to be cheap so that they fully understand the reasons for what appears to be an attractive valuation. Stock prices generally need catalysts or a change in perceptions in order to advance. If a company doesn't have any catalysts to trigger a reevaluation of its prospects, there is less of a chance that the stock price will adjust to reflect its fair value. In such a case, although the stock may appear to be an attractive investment because of a low multiple, it could lead the investor into a value trap.

HSBC Holdings is a multinational banking and financial services holding company headquartered in London. It has a dual primary listing on the Hong Kong Stock Exchange (HKSE) and the London Stock Exchange (LSE) and is a constituent of both the Hang Seng Index (HSI) and the FTSE 100 Index (UKX).

The stock traded on the HKSE at a price of over $80 at the end of 2013 and dropped below $50 in mid-June 2016. It declined by 43.7% in two and a half years, while the industry index (the Hang Seng Financial Index) lost only 5.4% over the same period. At the start of the period, HSBC Holdings looked cheap compared to peers and its own history, with average P/E and P/B multiples of 10.9x and 0.9x, respectively. Despite appearing undervalued, the stock performed poorly over the subsequent two-and-a-half-year period (see Exhibit 27) for reasons that included the need for extensive cost cutting. The above scenario is an illustration of a value trap.

EXHIBIT 27   Performance of HSBC vs. Its Value Indicators

Panel A

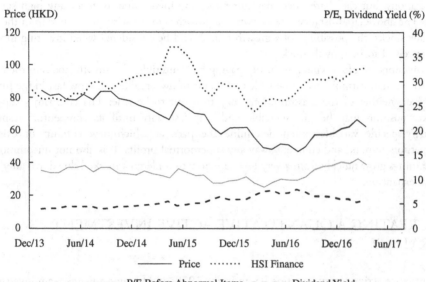

Panel B

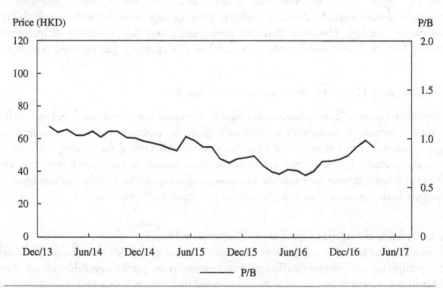

Source: Bloomberg.

4.2.2.2. The Growth Trap

Investors in growth stocks do so with the expectation that the share price will appreciate when the company experiences above-average earnings (or cash flow) growth in the future. However, if the company's results fall short of these expectations, stock performance is affected negatively. The stock may also turn out to have been overpriced at the time of the purchase. The company may deliver above-average earnings or cash flow growth, in line with expectations, but the share price may not move any higher due to its already high starting level. The above circumstances are known as a growth trap. As with the value trap in the case of value stocks, the possibility of a growth trap should be considered when investing in what are perceived to be growth stocks.

Investors are often willing to justify paying high multiples for growth stocks in the belief that the current earnings are sustainable and that earnings are likely to grow fast in the future. However, neither of these assumptions may turn out to be true: The company's superior market position may be unsustainable and may last only until its competitors respond. Industry-specific variables often determine the pace at which new entrants or existing competitors respond and compete away any supernormal profits. It is also not uncommon to see earnings grow quickly from a very low base only to undergo a marked slowdown after that initial expansion.

5. CREATING A QUANTITATIVE ACTIVE INVESTMENT STRATEGY

Quantitative active equity investing began in the 1970s and became a mainstream investment approach in the subsequent decades. Many quantitative equity funds suffered significant losses in August 2007, an event that became known as the "quant meltdown." The subsequent global financial crisis contributed to growing suspicions about the sustainability of quantitative investing. However, both the performance and the perception of quantitative investing have recovered significantly since 2012 as this approach has regained popularity.

5.1. Creating a Quantitative Investment Process

Quantitative (systematic, or rules-based) investing generally has a structured and well-defined investment process. It starts with a belief or hypothesis. Investors collect data from a wide range of sources. Data science and management are also critical for dealing with missing values and outliers. Investors then create quantitative models to test their hypothesis. Once they are comfortable with their models' investment value, quantitative investors combine their return-predicting models with risk controls to construct their portfolios.

5.1.1. Defining the Market Opportunity (Investment Thesis)

Like fundamental active investing, quantitative active investing is based on a belief that the market is competitive but not necessarily efficient. Fund managers use publicly available information to predict future returns of stocks, using factors to build their return-forecasting models.

5.1.2. Acquiring and Processing Data

Data management is probably the least glamorous part of the quantitative investing process. However, investors often spend most of their time building databases, mapping data from different sources, understanding the data availability, cleaning up the data, and reshaping the data into a usable format. The most commonly used data in quantitative investing typically fall into the following categories:

- **Company mapping** is used to track many companies over time and across data vendors. Each company may also have multiple classes of shares. New companies go public, while some existing companies disappear due to bankruptcies, mergers, or takeovers. Company names, ticker symbols, and other identifiers can also change over time. Different data vendors have their own unique identifiers.
- **Company fundamentals** include company demographics, financial statements, and other market data (e.g., price, dividends, stock splits, trading volume). Quantitative portfolio managers almost never collect company fundamental data themselves. Instead, they rely on data vendors, such as Capital IQ, Compustat, Worldscope, Reuters, FactSet, and Bloomberg.
- **Survey data** include details of corporate earnings, forecasts, and estimates by various market participants, macroeconomic variables, sentiment indicators, and information on funds flow.
- **Unconventional data,** or unstructured data, include satellite images, measures of news sentiment, customer–supplier chain metrics, and corporate events, among many other types of information.

Data are almost never in the format that is required for quantitative investment analysis. Hence, investors spend a significant amount of time checking data for consistency, cleaning up errors and outliers, and transforming the data into a usable format.

5.1.3. Backtesting the Strategy

Once the required data are available in the appropriate form, strategy backtesting is undertaken. Backtesting is a simulation of real-life investing. For example, in a standard monthly backtest, one can build a portfolio based on a value factor as of a given month-end—perhaps 10 years ago—and then track the return of this portfolio over the subsequent month. Investors normally repeat this process (i.e., rebalance the portfolio) according to a predefined frequency or rule for multiple years to evaluate how such a portfolio would perform and assess the effectiveness of a given strategy over time.

5.1.3.1. Information Coefficient

Under the assumption that expected returns are linearly related to factor exposures, the correlation between factor exposures and their holding period returns for a cross section of securities has been used as a measure of factor performance in quantitative backtests. This correlation for a factor is known in this context as the factor's information coefficient (IC). An advantage of the IC is that it aggregates information about factors from all securities in the investment universe, in contrast to an approach that uses only the best and worst deciles (a quantile-based approach), which captures only the top and bottom extremes.

The Pearson IC is the simple correlation coefficient between the factor scores (essentially standardized exposures) for the current period's and the next period's stock returns. As it is a correlation coefficient, its value is always between −1 and +1 (or, expressed in percentage terms, between −100% and +100%). The higher the IC, the higher the predictive power of the factor for subsequent returns. As a simple rule of thumb, in relation to US equities, any factor with an average monthly IC of 5%–6% is considered very strong. The coefficient is sensitive to outliers, as is illustrated below.

A similar but more robust measure is the Spearman rank IC, which is often preferred by practitioners. The Spearman rank IC is essentially the Pearson correlation coefficient between the ranked factor scores and ranked forward returns.

In the example shown in Exhibit 28 for earnings yield, the Pearson IC is negative at –0.8%, suggesting that the signal did not perform well and was negatively correlated with the subsequent month's returns. Looking more carefully, however, we can see that the sample factor is generally in line with the subsequent stock returns, with the exception of Stock I, for which the factor predicts the highest return but which turns out to be the worst performer. A single outlier can therefore turn what may actually be a good factor into a bad one, as the Pearson IC is sensitive to outliers. In contrast, the Spearman rank IC is at 40%, suggesting that the factor has strong predictive power for subsequent returns. If three equally weighted portfolios had been constructed, the long basket (Stocks G, H, and I) would have outperformed the short basket (Stocks A, B, and C) by 56 bps in this period.

5.1.3.2. Creating a Multifactor Model

After studying the efficacy of single factors, managers need to decide which factors to include in a multifactor model. Factor selection and weighting is a fairly complex subject. Managers can select and weight each factor using either qualitative or systematic processes. For example, Qian, Hua, and Sorensen (2007) propose treating each factor as an asset; therefore, factor

EXHIBIT 28   Pearson Correlation Coefficient IC and Spearman Rank IC

Stock	Factor Score	Subsequent Month Return (%)	Rank of Factor Score	Rank of Return
A	−1.45	−3.00%	9	8
B	−1.16	−0.60%	8	7
C	−0.60	−0.50%	7	6
D	−0.40	−0.48%	6	5
E	0.00	1.20%	5	4
F	0.40	3.00%	4	3
G	0.60	3.02%	3	2
H	1.16	3.05%	2	1
I	1.45	−8.50%	1	9
Mean	0.00	−0.31%		
Standard deviation	1.00	3.71%		
Pearson IC		−0.80%		
Spearman rank IC				40.00%
Long/short tercile portfolio return				0.56%

Note: The portfolio is split into terciles, with each tercile containing one-third of the stocks.
Source: QES (Wolfe Research).

weighting becomes an asset allocation decision. A standard mean–variance optimization can also be used to weight factors. Deciding on which factors to include and their weight is a critical piece of the strategy. Investors should bear in mind that factors may be effective individually but not add material value to a factor model because they are correlated with other factors.

5.1.4. Evaluating the Strategy

Once backtesting is complete, the performance of the strategy can be evaluated. An out-of-sample backtest, in which a different set of data is used to evaluate the model's performance, is generally done to confirm model robustness. However, even strategies with great out-of-sample performance may perform poorly in live trading. Managers generally compute various statistics—such as the t-statistic, Sharpe ratio, Sortino ratio, VaR, conditional VaR, and drawdown characteristics—to form an opinion on the outcome of their out-of-sample backtest.

5.1.5. Portfolio Construction Issues in Quantitative Investment

Most quantitative managers spend the bulk of their time searching for and exploring models that can predict stock returns, and may overlook the importance of portfolio construction to the quantitative investment process. While portfolio construction is covered in greater detail in other chapters, the following aspects are particularly relevant to quantitative investing:

- **Risk models:** Risk models estimate the variance–covariance matrix of stock returns—that is, the risk of every stock and the correlation among stocks. Directly estimating the variance–covariance matrix using sample return data typically is infeasible and suffers from significant estimation errors.[21] Managers generally rely on commercial risk model vendors[22] for these data.
- **Trading costs:** There are two kinds of trading costs—explicit (e.g., commissions, fees, and taxes) and implicit (e.g., bid–ask spread and market impact). When two stocks have similar expected returns and risks, normally the one with lower execution costs is preferred.[23]

Unconventional Big Data and Machine-Learning Techniques

Rohal, Jussa, Luo, Wang, Zhao, Alvarez, Wang, and Elledge (2016) discuss the implications and applications of big data and machine-learning techniques in investment management. The rapid advancement in computing power today allows for the collection and processing of data from sources that were traditionally impossible or overly expensive to access, such as satellite images, social media, and payment-processing systems.

---

[21]One problem with a sample covariance matrix is the curse of dimensionality. For a portfolio of N assets, we need to estimate $N \times (N + 1)/2$ parameters—that is, $N \times (N - 1)/2$ covariance parameters and N estimates of stock-specific risk. For a universe of 3,000 stocks, we would have to estimate about 4.5 million parameters.

[22]MSCI Barra and Axioma are examples of data providers.

[23]Trading costs are covered in depth in separate curriculum chapters.

Investors now have access to data that go far beyond the traditional company fundamentals metrics. There are also many data vendors providing increasingly specialized or unique data content. Processing and incorporating unconventional data into existing investment frameworks, however, remains a challenge. With the improvements in computing speed and algorithms, significant successes in machine-learning techniques have been achieved. Despite concerns about data mining, machine learning has led to significant improvement in strategy performance.

5.2. Pitfalls in Quantitative Investment Processes

All active investment strategies have their pros and cons. There are many pitfalls that investors need to be aware of when they assess any quantitative strategy. Wang, Wang, Luo, Jussa, Rohal, and Alvarez (2014) discuss some of the common issues in quantitative investing in detail.

5.2.1. Survivorship Bias, Look-Ahead Bias, Data Mining, and Overfitting

Survivorship bias is one of the most common issues affecting quantitative decision-making. While investors are generally aware of the problem, they often underestimate its significance. When backtests use only those companies that are currently in business today, they ignore the stocks that have left the investment universe due to bankruptcy,[24] delisting, or acquisition. This approach creates a bias whereby only companies that have survived are tested and it is assumed that the strategy would never have invested in companies that have failed. Survivorship bias often leads to overly optimistic results and sometimes even causes investors to draw wrong conclusions.

The second major issue in backtesting is look-ahead bias. This bias results from using information that was unknown or unavailable at the time an investment decision was made. An example of this bias is the use of financial accounting data for a company at a point in time before the data were actually released by the company.

In computer science, data mining refers to automated computational processes for discovering patterns in large datasets, often involving sophisticated statistical techniques, computation algorithms, and large-scale database systems. In finance, data mining can refer to such a process and can introduce a bias that results in model overfitting. It can be described as excessive search analysis of past financial data to uncover patterns and to conform to a pre-determined model for potential use in investing.

5.2.2. Turnover, Transaction Costs, and Short Availability

Backtesting is often conducted in an ideal, but unrealistic world without transaction costs, constraints on turnover, or limits on the availability of long and short positions. In reality, managers may face numerous constraints, such as limits on turnover and difficulties in establishing short positions in certain markets. Depending on how fast their signal decays, they may or may not be able to capture their model's expected excess return in a live trading process.

---

[24]In the United States, companies may continue to trade after filing for bankruptcy as long as they continue to meet listing requirements. However, their stocks are normally removed from most equity indexes.

EXHIBIT 29   Annualized Returns with Different Transaction Cost Assumptions

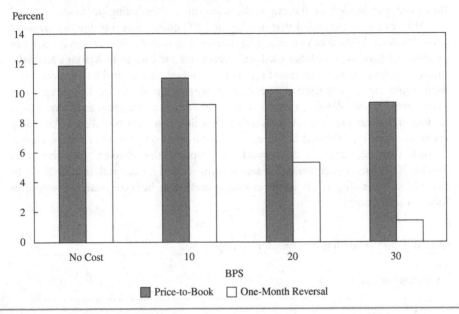

Sources: Compustat, Capital IQ, Thomson Reuters.

More importantly, trading is not free. Transaction costs can easily erode returns significantly. An example is the use of short-term reversal as a factor: Stocks that have performed well recently (say, in the last month) are more likely to revert (underperform) in the subsequent month. This reversal factor has been found to be a good stock selection signal in the Japanese equity market (before transaction costs). As shown in Exhibit 29, in a theoretical world with no transaction costs, a simple long/short strategy (buying the top 20% dividend-paying stocks in Japan with the worst performance in the previous month and shorting the bottom 20% stocks with the highest returns in the previous month) has generated an annual return of 12%, beating the classic value factor of price to book. However, if the transaction cost assumption is changed from 0 bps to 30 bps per trade, the return of the reversal strategy drops sharply, while the return of the price-to-book value strategy drops only modestly.

Quant Crowding

In the first half of 2007, despite some early signs of the US subprime crisis, the global equity market was relatively calm. Then, in August 2007, many of the standard factors used by quantitative managers suffered significant losses,[25] and quantitative equity

---

[25]The average performance of many common factors was strong and relatively stable in 2003–2007. Actually, value and momentum factors suffered more severe losses in late 2002 and around March 2009.

managers' performance suffered. These losses have been attributed to crowding among quantitative managers following similar trades (see Khandani and Lo 2008). Many of these managers headed for the exit at the same time, exacerbating the losses.

How can it be concluded that the August 2007 quant crisis was due to crowding? More importantly, how can crowding be measured so that the next crowded trade can be avoided? Jussa et al (2016a) used daily short interest data from Markit's securities finance database to measure crowding. They proposed that if stocks with poor price momentum are heavily shorted[26] relative to outperforming stocks, it indicates that many investors are following a momentum style. Hence, momentum as an investment strategy might get crowded. A measure of crowding that may be called a "crowding coefficient" can be estimated by regressing short interest on price momentum. Details of such regression analysis are beyond the scope of this chapter.[27] As shown in Exhibit 30, the level of crowding for momentum reached a local peak in mid-2007. In the exhibit, increasing values of the crowding coefficient indicate greater crowding in momentum strategies.

EXHIBIT 30   Crowding in Momentum Strategies

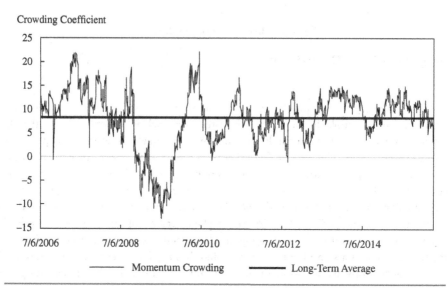

Sources: Compustat, FTSE Russell, Markit.

---

[26]Short interest can be defined as the ratio of the number of stocks shorted to the number of stocks in the available inventory for lending.
[27]For more on this subject, see Jussa, Rohal, Wang, Zhao, Luo, Alvarez, Wang, and Elledge (2016) and Cahan and Luo (2013).

EXAMPLE 9   How to Start a Quantitative Investment Process

An asset management firm that traditionally follows primarily a fundamental value investing approach wants to diversify its investment process by incorporating a quantitative element. Discuss the potential benefits and hurdles involved in adding quantitative models to a fundamental investment approach.

Solution: Quantitative investing is based on building models from attributes of thousands of stocks. The performance of quantitative strategies is generally not highly correlated with that of fundamental approaches. Therefore, in theory, adding a quantitative overlay may provide some diversification benefit to the firm.

In practice, however, because the processes behind quantitative and fundamental investing tend to be quite different, combining these two approaches is not always straightforward. Quantitative investing requires a large up-front investment in data, technology, and model development. It is generally desirable to use factors and models that are different from those used by most other investors to avoid potential crowded trades.

Managers need to be particularly careful with their backtesting so that the results do not suffer from look-ahead and survivorship biases. Transaction costs and short availability (if the fund involves shorting) should be incorporated into the backtesting.

---

6. EQUITY INVESTMENT STYLE CLASSIFICATION

An investment style classification process generally splits the stock universe into two or three groups, such that each group contains stocks with similar characteristics. The returns of stocks within a style group should therefore be correlated with one another, and the returns of stocks in different style groups should have less correlation. The common style characteristics used in active management include value, growth, blend (or core), size, price momentum, volatility, income (high dividend), and earnings quality. Stock membership in an industry, sector, or country group—for example, the financial sector or emerging markets—is also used to classify the investment style. Exhibit 31 lists a few mainstream categories of investment styles in use today.

EXHIBIT 31   Examples of Investment Styles

Characteristics based	Value, Growth or Blend/Core
	Capitalization
	Volatility
Membership based	Sector
	Country
	Market (developed or emerging)
Position based	Long/short (net long, short, or neutral)

Investment style classification is important for asset owners who seek to select active strategies. It allows active equity managers with similar styles to be compared with one another. Further, comparing the active returns or positions of a manager with those of the right style index can provide more information about the manager's active strategy and approach. A manager's portfolio may appear to have active positions when compared with the general market benchmark index; however, that manager may actually follow a style index and do so passively. Identifying the actual investment style of equity managers is important for asset owners in their decision-making process.

6.1. Different Approaches to Style Classification

Equity styles are defined by pairs of common attributes, such as value and growth, large cap and small cap, high volatility and low volatility, high dividend and low dividend, or developed markets and emerging markets. Style pairs need not be mutually exclusive. Each pair interprets the stock performance from a different perspective. A combination of several style pairs may often give a more complete picture of the sources of stock returns.

Identifying the investment styles of active managers helps to reveal the sources of added value in the portfolio. Modern portfolio theory advocates the use of efficient portfolio management of a diversified portfolio of stocks and bonds. Gupta, Skallsjö, and Li (2016) detail how the concept of diversification, when extended to different strategies and investment processes, can have a significant impact on the risk and reward of an investor's portfolio. A portfolio's risk–return profile is improved not only by including multiple asset classes but also by employing managers with different investment styles. An understanding of the investment style of a manager helps in evaluating the manager and confirming whether he or she sticks with the claimed investment style or deviates from it.

Two main approaches are often used in style analysis: a holdings-based approach and a returns-based approach. Each approach has its own strengths and weaknesses.

6.1.1. Holdings-Based Approaches

An equity investment style is actually the aggregation of attributes from individual stocks in the portfolio. Holdings-based approaches to style analysis are done bottom-up, but they are executed differently by the various commercial investment information providers. Using different criteria or different sources of underlying value and growth numbers may lead to slightly different classifications for stocks and therefore may result in different style characterizations for the same portfolio. In the style classification process followed by Morningstar and Thomson Reuters Lipper, the styles of individual stocks are clearly defined in that a stock's attribute for a specific style is 1 if it is included in that style index; otherwise, it is 0. The methodology used by MSCI and FTSE Russell, on the other hand, assumes that a stock can have characteristics of two styles, such as value and growth, at the same time. This methodology uses a multifactor approach to assign style inclusion factors to each stock. So a particular stock can belong to both value and growth styles by a pre-determined fraction. A portfolio's active exposure to a certain style equals the sum of the style attributes from all the individual stocks, weighted by their active positions.

The Morningstar Style Box

The Morningstar Style Box first appeared in 1992 to help investors and advisers determine the investment style of a fund. In a style box, each style pair splits the stock universe into two to three groups, such as value, core (or "blend"), and growth. The same universe can be split by another style definition—for example, large cap, mid cap, and small cap. The Morningstar Style Box splits the stock universe along both style dimensions, creating a grid of nine squares. It uses holdings-based style analysis and classifies about the same number of stocks in each of the value, core, and growth styles. Morningstar determines the value and growth scores by using five stock attributes (see Exhibit 33). The current Morningstar Style Box, as shown in Exhibit 32, is a nine-square grid featuring three stock investment styles for each of three size categories: large, mid, and small. Two of the three style categories are "value" and "growth," common to both stocks and funds. However, the third, central column is labeled "core" for stocks (i.e., those stocks for which neither value nor growth characteristics dominate) and "blend" for funds (meaning that the fund holds a mixture of growth and value stocks).

EXHIBIT 32   Morningstar Fund Style Classification

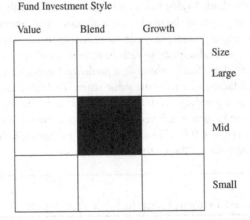

Source: Morningstar.

6.1.1.1. Large-Cap, Mid-Cap, and Small-Cap Classifications
The size classification is determined by the company's market capitalization. There is no consensus on what the size thresholds for the different categories should be, and indeed, different data and research providers use different criteria for size classification purposes. Large-cap companies tend to be well-established companies with a strong market presence, good levels of information disclosure, and extensive scrutiny by the investor community and

the media. While these attributes may not apply universally across different parts of the world, large-cap companies are recognized as being lower risk than smaller companies and offering more limited future growth potential. Small-cap companies, on the other hand, tend to be less mature companies with potentially greater room for future growth, higher risk of failure, and a lower degree of analyst and public scrutiny.

Mid-cap companies tend to rank between the two other groups on many important parameters, such as size, revenues, employee count, and client base. In general, they are in a more advanced stage of development than small-cap companies but provide greater growth potential than large-cap companies.

There is no consensus on the boundaries that separate large-, mid-, and small-cap companies. One practice is to define large-cap stocks as those that account for the top ~70% of the capitalization of all stocks in the universe, with mid-cap stocks representing the next ~20% and small-cap stocks accounting for the balance.

6.1.1.2. Measuring Growth, Value, and Core Characteristics

Equity style analysis starts with assigning a style score to each individual stock. Taking the value/growth style pair as an example, each stock is assigned a value score based on the combination of several value and growth characteristics or factors of that stock. The simplest value scoring model uses one factor, price-to-book ratio, to rank the stock. The bottom half of the stocks in this ranking (smaller P/Bs) constitute the value index, while the stocks ranked in the top half (higher P/Bs) constitute the growth index. Weighting the stocks by their market capitalization thus creates both a value index and a growth index, with the condition that each style index must represent 50% of the market capitalization of all stocks in the target universe. A comprehensive value scoring model may use more factors in addition to price to book, such as price to earnings, price to sales, price to cash flow, return on equity, dividend yield, and so on. The combination of these factors through a predefined process, such as assigning a fixed weight to each selected factor, generates the value score. The value score is usually a number between 0 and 1, corresponding to 0% and 100% contribution to the value index. Depending on the methodologies employed by the vendors, the value score may be a fraction. A security with a value score of 0.6 will have 60% of its market capitalization allocated to the value index and the remaining 40% to the growth index.

Morningstar's Classification Criteria for Value Stocks

For each stock, Morningstar assigns a growth score and a value score, each based on five components that are combined with pre-determined weights, as shown in Exhibit 33.

EXHIBIT 33   Morningstar Value and Growth Scoring Scheme

Value Score Components and Weights		Growth Score Components and Weights	
Forward-looking measures	**50.0%**	*Forward-looking measures*	**50.0%**
*Price to projected earnings		*Long-term projected earnings growth	

Value Score Components and Weights		Growth Score Components and Weights	
Historical measures	**50.0%**	*Historical measures*	**50.0%**
*Price to book	12.5%	*Historical earnings growth	12.5%
*Price to sales	12.5%	*Sales growth	12.5%
*Price to cash flow	12.5%	*Cash flow growth	12.5%
*Dividend yield	12.5%	*Book value growth	12.5%

The scores are scaled to a range of 0 to 100, and the difference between the stock's growth and value scores is called the net style score. If this net style score is strongly negative, approaching –100, the stock's style is classified as value. If the result is strongly positive, the stock is classified as growth. If the scores for value and growth are similar in strength, the net style score will be close to zero and the stock will be classified as core. On average, value, core, and growth stocks each account for approximately one-third of the total capitalization in a given row of the Morningstar Style Box.

MSCI World Value and Growth Indexes

MSCI provides a range of indexes that include value and growth. In order to construct those indexes, the firm needs to establish the individual stocks' characteristics. The following (simplified) process is used to establish how much of each stock's market capitalization should be included in the respective indexes.

EXHIBIT 34   Cumulative Return of MSCI World Value and Growth Indexes since 1975

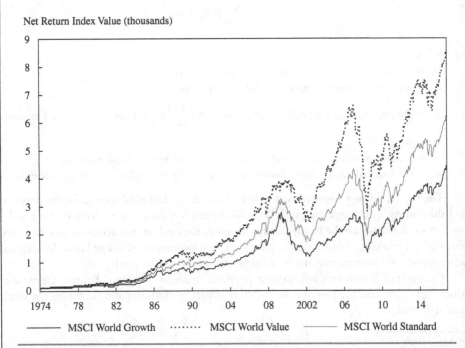

Source: MSCI.

The value investment style characteristics for index construction are defined using three variables: book-value-to-price ratio, 12-month forward-earnings-to-price ratio, and dividend yield. The growth investment style characteristics for index construction are defined using five variables: long-term forward EPS growth rate, short-term forward EPS growth rate, current internal growth rate, long-term historical EPS growth trend, and long-term historical sales-per-share growth trend. Z-scores for each variable are calculated and aggregated for each security to determine the security's overall style characteristics. For example, a stock is assigned a so-called "value inclusion factor" of 0.6, which means that the stock could have both value and growth characteristics and contributes to the performance of the value and growth indexes by 60% and 40%, respectively. Exhibit 34 shows the cumulative return of the MSCI World Value and MSCI World Growth indexes since 1975.

6.1.2. Returns-Based Style Analysis

Many investment managers do not disclose the full details of their portfolios, and therefore a holdings-based approach cannot be used to assess their strategies. The investment style of these portfolio managers is therefore analyzed by using a returns-based approach to compare the returns of the employed strategy to those of a set of style indexes.

The objective of a returns-based style analysis is to find the style concentration of underlying holdings by identifying the style indexes that provide significant contributions to fund returns with the help of statistical tools. Such an analysis attributes fund returns to selected investment styles by running a constrained multivariate regression:[28]

$$r_t = \alpha + \sum_{s=1}^{m} \beta^s R_t^s + \varepsilon_t$$

where

r_t = the fund return within the period ending at time t

R_t^s = the return of style index s in the same period

β^s = the fund exposure to style s (with constraints $\sum_{s=1}^{m} \beta^s = 1$ and $\beta^s > 0$ for a long-only portfolio)

α = a constant often interpreted as the value added by the fund manager

ε_t = the residual return that cannot be explained by the styles used in the analysis

The key inputs to a returns-based style analysis are the historical returns for the portfolio and the returns for the style indexes. The critical part, however, is the selection of the styles used, as stock returns can be highly correlated within the same sector, across sectors, and even across global markets. If available, the manager's own description of his or her style is a good starting point for determining the investment styles that can be used.

Commercial investment information providers, such as Thomson Reuters Lipper and Morningstar, perform the role of collecting and analyzing fund data and classifying the funds into style groups.

---

[28]Sharpe (1992).

Data Sources

The success of a returns-based style analysis depends, to some extent, on the choice of style indexes. The component-based style indexes provided by investment information providers enable analysts to identify the style that is closest to the investment strategy employed by the fund manager.

EXHIBIT 35   Lipper's Style Classification

	OPEN-END EQUITY FUNDS		
	General Domestic Equity	**World Equity**	**Sector Equity**
Prospectus-Based Classifications	**All** prospectus-based classifications in this group are considered diversified.	**Some** prospectus-based classifications in this group are considered diversified (global and international types only).	**No** prospectus-based classifications in this group are considered diversified.
	Capital Appreciation	Gold	Health/Biotech
	Growth	European Region	Natural Resources
	Micro Cap	Pacific Region	Technology
	Mid Cap	Japan	Telecom
	Small Cap	Pacific ex-Japan	Utilities
	Growth & Income	China	Financial Services
	S&P 500	Emerging Markets	Real Estate
	Equity	Latin America	Specialty & Miscellaneous
	Income	Global	
		Global Small Cap	
		International	
		International Small Cap	
Portfolio-Based Classifications	Large-Cap Growth	Global Large-Cap Growth	
	Large-Cap Core	Global Large-Cap Core	
	Large-Cap Value	Global Large-Cap Value	
	Multi-Cap Growth	Global Multi-Cap Growth	
	Multi-Cap Core	Global Multi-Cap Core	
	Multi-Cap Value	Global Multi-Cap Value	
	Mid-Cap Growth	Global Small-/Mid-Cap Growth	
	Mid-Cap Core	Global Small-/Mid-Cap Core	
	Mid-Cap Value	Global Small-/Mid-Cap Value	
	Small-Cap Growth	International Large-Cap Growth	
	Small-Cap Core	International Large-Cap Core	
	Small-Cap Value	International Large-Cap Value	
	S&P 500	International Multi-Cap Growth	
	Equity Income	International Multi-Cap Core	
		International Multi-Cap Value	
		International Small-/Mid-Cap Growth	
		International Small-/Mid-Cap Core	
		International Small-/Mid-Cap Value	

Source: Thomson Reuters Lipper.

Thomson Reuters Lipper provides mutual and hedge fund data as well as analytical and reporting tools to institutional and retail investors. All funds covered by Lipper are given a classification based on statements in the funds' prospectuses. Funds that are considered "diversified," because they invest across economic sectors and/or countries, also have a portfolio-based classification. Exhibit 35 shows the Lipper fund classifications for US-listed open-end equity funds.

6.1.3. Manager Self-Identification

Equity strategy investment styles result from the active equity manager's employment of a particular strategy to manage the fund. The fund's investment strategy is usually described in the fund prospectus and can be used to identify the fund's investment objective. This objective can be regarded as the manager's self-identification of the investment style.

Returns-based or holdings-based style analysis is commonly used to identify the investment style—such as value/growth or large cap/small cap—and to determine whether it corresponds to the manager's self-identified style. Some other styles, however, cannot be easily identified by such methods. For example, the styles of equity hedge funds, equity income funds, and special sector funds can be more efficiently identified using a combination of manager self-identification and holdings- or returns-based analysis.

Some equity hedge fund styles are non-standard and do not fit into any of the established style categories. Examples include long/short equity, equity market neutral, and dedicated short bias. For such funds, the investment objective is often laid out in the prospectus, which explains the fund's investment strategy. The prospectus becomes the key source of information for those assigning styles to such funds.

6.2. Strengths and Limitations of Style Analysis

Holdings-based style analysis is generally more accurate than returns-based analysis because it uses the actual portfolio holdings. Portfolio managers (and those who assess their strategies and performance) can see how each portfolio holding contributes to the portfolio's style, verify that the style is in line with the stated investment philosophy, and take action if they wish to prevent the portfolio's style from moving away from its intended target. Unlike returns-based style analysis, holdings-based style analysis is able to show the styles that any portfolio is exposed to, thus providing input for style allocation decisions.

Holdings-based style analysis requires the availability of all the portfolio constituents as well as the style attributes of each stock in the portfolio. While this information may be accessible for current portfolios, an analyst who wants to track the historical change in investment styles may face some difficulty. In this case, point-in-time databases are required for both the constituents of the fund and the stocks' style definitions.

As investment style research uses statistical and empirical methods to arrive at conclusions, it can produce inaccurate results due to limitations of the data or flaws in the application design. Kaplan (2011) argued that most returns-based style analysis models impose unnecessary constraints that limit the results within certain boundaries, making it difficult to detect more aggressive positions, such as deep value or micro cap. Furthermore, the limited availability of data on derivatives often makes holdings-based style analysis less effective for funds with substantial positions in derivatives. It is therefore important to understand the strengths and limitations of style analysis models in order to interpret the results correctly. Morningstar studies have concluded that holdings-based style analysis generally produces more accurate results than returns-based style analysis, although there may be exceptions. Ideally, practitioners should use both approaches: Returns-based models can often be more widely applied, while holdings-based models allow deeper style analysis.

Variation of Fund Characteristics within a Style Classification

Consider the Morningstar Style Box, in which funds are classified along two dimensions: value/growth and size (market capitalization). Within the same value style box, funds can be classified as large cap or small cap. To keep the classification map simple and concise, Morningstar omits other styles and characteristics, such as performance volatility and sector or market/region exposure. It is important to note that style classification provides only a reference to the key investment styles that may contribute to performance. The funds within the same style classification can be quite different in other characteristics, which may also contribute to fund returns and lead to differences in performance.

EXAMPLE 10   Equity Investment Styles

Consider an actively managed equity fund that has a five-year track record. An analyst performed both holdings-based and returns-based style analysis on the portfolio. She used the current portfolio holdings to perform the holdings-based style analysis and five-year historical monthly returns to carry out the returns-based analysis. The analyst found the following:

- Holdings-based style analysis on the current portfolio shows that the fund has value and growth exposures of 0.85 and 0.15, respectively.
- Returns-based style analysis with 60 months' historical returns shows that the value and growth exposures of the fund are equal to 0.4 and 0.6, respectively.

Explain possible reason(s) for the inconsistency between the holdings-based and returns-based style analyses.

Solution: Some active equity managers may maintain one investment style over time in the belief that that particular style will outperform the general market. Others may rotate or switch between styles to accommodate the then-prevailing investment thesis. Returns-based style analysis regresses the portfolio's historical returns against the returns of the corresponding style indexes (over 60 months in this example). Its output indicates the average effect of investment styles employed during the period. While the holdings-based analysis suggests that the current investment style of the equity fund is value oriented, the returns-based analysis indicates that the style actually employed was likely in the growth category for a period of time within the past five years.

7. SUMMARY

This chapter discusses the different approaches to active equity management and describes how the various strategies are created. It also addresses the style classification of active approaches.

- Active equity management approaches can be generally divided into two groups: fundamental (also referred to as discretionary) and quantitative (also known as systematic or rules-based). Fundamental approaches stress the use of human judgment in arriving at an investment decision, whereas quantitative approaches stress the use of rules-based, quantitative models to arrive at a decision.
- The main differences between fundamental and quantitative approaches include the following characteristics: approach to the decision-making process (subjective versus objective); forecast focus (stock returns versus factor returns); information used (research versus data); focus of the analysis (depth versus breadth); orientation to the data (forward looking versus backward looking); and approach to portfolio risk (emphasis on judgment versus emphasis on optimization techniques).
- The main types of active management strategies include bottom-up, top-down, factor-based, and activist.
- Bottom-up strategies begin at the company level, and use company and industry analyses to assess the intrinsic value of the company and determine whether the stock is undervalued or overvalued relative to its market price.
- Fundamental managers often focus on one or more of the following company and industry characteristics: business model and branding, competitive advantages, and management and corporate governance.
- Bottom-up strategies are often divided into value-based approaches and growth-based approaches.
- Top-down strategies focus on the macroeconomic environment, demographic trends, and government policies to arrive at investment decisions.
- Top-down strategies are used in several investment decision processes, including the following: country and geographic allocation, sector and industry rotation, equity style rotation, volatility-based strategies, and thematic investment strategies.
- Quantitative equity investment strategies often use factor-based models. A factor-based strategy aims to identify significant factors that drive stock prices and to construct a portfolio with a positive bias toward such factors.
- Factors can be grouped based on fundamental characteristics—such as value, growth, and price momentum—or on unconventional data.
- Activist investors specialize in taking meaningful stakes in listed companies and influencing those companies to make changes to their management, strategy, or capital structures for the purpose of increasing the stock's value and realizing a gain on their investment.
- Statistical arbitrage (or "stat arb") strategies use statistical and technical analysis to exploit pricing anomalies and achieve superior returns. Pairs trading is an example of a popular and simple statistical arbitrage strategy.
- Event-driven strategies exploit market inefficiencies that may occur around corporate events such as mergers and acquisitions, earnings announcements, bankruptcies, share buybacks, special dividends, and spinoffs.
- The fundamental active investment process includes the following steps: define the investment universe; prescreen the universe; understand the industry and business; forecast

the company's financial performance; convert forecasts into a target price; construct the portfolio with the desired risk profile; and rebalance the portfolio according to a buy and sell discipline.

- Pitfalls in fundamental investing include behavioral biases, the value trap, and the growth trap.
- Behavioral biases can be divided into two groups: cognitive errors and emotional biases. Typical biases that are relevant to active equity management include confirmation bias, illusion of control, availability bias, loss aversion, overconfidence, and regret aversion.
- The quantitative active investment process includes the following steps: define the investment thesis; acquire, clean, and process the data; backtest the strategy; evaluate the strategy; and construct an efficient portfolio using risk and trading cost models.
- The pitfalls in quantitative investing include look-ahead and survivorship biases, overfitting, data mining, unrealistic turnover assumptions, transaction costs, and short availability.
- An investment style generally splits the stock universe into two or three groups, such that each group contains stocks with similar characteristics. The common style characteristics used in active management include value, size, price momentum, volatility, high dividend, and earnings quality. A stock's membership in an industry, sector, or country group is also used to classify the investment style.
- Two main approaches are often used in style analysis: a returns-based approach and a holdings-based approach. Holdings-based approaches aggregate the style scores of individual holdings, while returns-based approaches analyze the investment style of portfolio managers by comparing the returns of the strategy to those of a set of style indexes.

REFERENCES

Basu, S. 1977. "Investment Performance of Common Stocks in Relation to Their Price-Earnings Ratios: A Test of the Efficient Market Hypothesis." *Journal of Finance* 32 (3): 663–82.

Cahan, R., and Y. Luo. 2013. "Standing Out From the Crowd: Measuring Crowding in Quantitative Strategies." *Journal of Portfolio Management* 39 (4): 14–23.

Fama, E., and K.R. French. 1992. "The Cross-Section of Expected Stock Returns." *Journal of Finance* 47 (2): 427–65.

Fama, E., and K.R. French. 1993. "Common Risk Factors in the Returns on Stocks and Bonds." *Journal of Financial Economics* 33 (1): 3–56.

Fama, E., and K.R. French. 1996. "Multifactor Explanations of Asset Pricing Anomalies." *Journal of Finance* 51 (1): 55–84.

Graham, B., and D.L. Dodd. 1934. *Security Analysis.* New York: McGraw-Hill.

Greenblatt, J. 2010. *The Little Book That Still Beats the Market.* Hoboken, NJ: John Wiley & Sons.

Greenwald, B., J. Kahn, P. Sonkin, and M. Biema. 2001. *Value Investing: From Graham to Buffett and Beyond.* Hoboken, NJ: John Wiley & Sons.

Gupta, P., S. Skallsjö, and B. Li. 2016. *Multi-Asset Investing: A Practitioner's Framework.* Chichester, UK: John Wiley & Sons.

Jegadeesh, N., and S. Titman. 1993. "Returns to Buying Winners and Selling Losers: Implications for Stock Market Efficiency." *Journal of Finance* 48 (1): 65–91.

Jussa, J., G. Rohal, S. Wang, G. Zhao, Y. Luo, M. Alvarez, A. Wang, and D. Elledge. 2016a. "*Strategy Crowding.*" Deutsche Bank (16 May).

Jussa, J., K. Webster, G. Zhao, and Y. Luo. 2016b. *"Activism, Alpha and Action Heroes."* Deutsche Bank (6 January).

Kaplan, P. 2011. *Frontiers of Modern Asset Allocation.* Hoboken, NJ: John Wiley & Sons.

Khandani, A., and A. Lo. 2008. "What Happened to the Quants in August 2007? Evidence from Factors and Transactions Data." NBER Working Paper 14465.

Lakonishok, J., A. Shleifer, and R.W. Vishny. 1994. "Contrarian Investment, Extrapolation, and Risk." *Journal of Finance* 49 (5): 1541–78.

Langer, E.J. 1983. *The Psychology of Control.* Beverly Hills, CA: Sage Publications.

Maug, E. 1998. "Large Shareholders as Monitors: Is There a Trade-Off between Liquidity and Control?" *Journal of Finance* 53 (1): 65–98.

Qian, E.E., R.H. Hua, and E.H. Sorensen. 2007. *Quantitative Equity Portfolio Management: Modern Techniques and Applications.* Boca Raton, FL: Chapman & Hall/CRC.

Rohal, G., J. Jussa, Y. Luo, S. Wang, G. Zhao, M. Alvarez, A. Wang, and D. Elledge. 2016. *"Big Data in Investment Management."* Deutsche Bank (17 February).

Sharpe, W.F. 1992. "Asset Allocation, Management Style, and Performance Measurement." *Journal of Portfolio Management* 18 (2): 7–19.

Sloan, R.G. 1996. "Do Stock Prices Fully Reflect Information in Accruals and Cash Flows about Future Earnings?" *Accounting Review* 71 (3): 289–315.

Wang, S., A. Wang, Y. Luo, J. Jussa, G. Rohal, and M. Alvarez. 2014. *Seven Sins of Quantitative Investing.* Deutsche Bank Market Research (September).

PRACTICE PROBLEMS

The following information relates to questions 1–6

James Leonard is a fund-of-funds manager with Future Generation, a large sovereign fund. He is considering whether to pursue more in-depth due diligence processes with three large-cap long-only funds proposed by his analysts. Although the funds emphasize different financial metrics and use different implementation methodologies, they operate in the same market segment and are evaluated against the same benchmark. The analysts prepared a short description of each fund, presented in Exhibit 1.

EXHIBIT 1   Description of Each Candidate Fund

Fund	Description
Furlings	Furlings Investment Partners combines sector views and security selection. The firm's head manager uses several industry and economic indicators identified from his own experience during the last two decades, as well as his personal views on market flow dynamics, to determine how to position the fund on a sector basis. Sector deviations from the benchmark of 10% or more are common and are usually maintained for 12 to 24 months. At the same time, sector managers at Furlings use their expertise in dissecting financial statements and their understanding of the corporate branding and competitive landscape within sectors to build equally weighted baskets of securities within sectors. Each basket contains their 7 to 10 highest-conviction securities, favoring firms that have good governance, strong growth potential, competitive advantages such as branding, and attractive relative valuations. The Furlings master fund holds approximately 90 securities.

Fund	Description
Asgard	Asgard Investment Partners is a very large asset manager. It believes in investing in firms that have a strong business model and governance, reasonable valuations, solid capital structures with limited financial leverage, and above-average expected earnings growth for the next three years. Although the Asgard master fund invests in fewer than 125 securities, each sector analyst builds financial models that track as many as 50 firms. To support them in their task, analysts benefit from software developed by the Asgard research and technology group that provides access to detailed market and accounting information on 5,000 global firms, allowing for the calculation of many valuation and growth metrics and precise modeling of sources of cash-flow strengths and weaknesses within each business. Asgard analysts can also use the application to backtest strategies and build their own models to rank securities' attractiveness according to their preferred characteristics. Security allocation is determined by a management team but depends heavily on a quantitative risk model developed by Asgard. Asgard has a low portfolio turnover.
Tokra	Tokra Capital uses a factor-based strategy to rank securities from most attractive to least attractive. Each security is scored based on three metrics: price-to-book value (P/B), 12-month increase in stock price, and return on assets. Tokra's managers have a strong risk management background. Their objective is to maximize their exposure to the most attractive securities using a total scoring approach subject to limiting single-security concentration below 2%, sector deviations below 3%, active risk below 4%, and annual turnover less than 40%, while having a market beta close to 1. The master fund holds approximately 400 positions out of a possible universe of more than 2,000 securities evaluated.

When Leonard's analysts met with Asgard, they inquired whether its managers engage in activist investing because Asgard's portfolio frequently holds significant positions, because of their large asset size, and because of their emphasis on strong governance and their ability to model sources of cash-flow strengths and weaknesses within each business. The manager indicated that Asgard engages with companies from a long-term shareholder's perspective, which is consistent with the firm's low portfolio turnover, and uses its voice, and its vote, on matters that can influence companies' long-term value.

Leonard wants to confirm that each manager's portfolios are consistent with its declared style. To this end, Exhibit 2 presents key financial information associated with each manager's portfolio and also with the index that all three managers use.

EXHIBIT 2   Key Financial Data

Fund	Index	Furlings	Asgard	Tokra
Dividend/price (trailing 12-month)	2.3%	2.2%	2.2%	2.6%
P/E (trailing 12-month)	26.5	24.7	26.6	27.3
Price/cash flows (12-month forward)	12.5	13.8	12.5	11.6
P/B	4.8	4.30	4.35	5.4
Average EPS growth (three to five years forward)	11.9%	11.0%	13.1%	10.8%
Net income/assets	2.8%	4.5%	4.3%	3.2%
Average price momentum (trailing 12 months)	10.5%	14.0%	10.0%	12.0%

1. Which fund manager's investing approach is most consistent with fundamental management?
   A. Furlings
   B. Asgard
   C. Tokra

2. Which of the following statements about the approaches and styles of either Furlings, Asgard, or Tokra is incorrect?
   A. Furlings is a top-down sector rotator with a value orientation within sectors.
   B. Asgard is a bottom-up manager with a GARP (growth at a reasonable price) style.
   C. Tokra is a factor-based manager using value, growth, and profitability metrics.

3. Which manager is most likely to get caught in a value trap?
   A. Furlings
   B. Asgard
   C. Tokra

4. Which activist investing tactic is Asgard *least likely* to use?
   A. Engaging with management by writing letters to management, calling for and explaining suggested changes, and participating in management discussions with analysts or meeting the management team privately
   B. Launching legal proceedings against existing management for breach of fiduciary duties
   C. Proposing restructuring of the balance sheet to better utilize capital and potentially initiate share buybacks or increase dividends

5. Based on the information provided in Exhibits 1 and 2, which manager's portfolio characteristics is most likely at odds with its declared style?
   A. Furlings
   B. Asgard
   C. Tokra

6. Leonard is looking at the style classification from Asgard as reported by Morningstar and Thomson Reuters Lipper. He is surprised to find that Asgard is classified as a blend fund by Morningstar and a value fund by Lipper. Which of the following statements is correct?
   A. Although the Morningstar methodology classifies securities as either value, growth, or core, the Lipper methodology assumes a stock can have the characteristics of many styles. This approach can result in a different classification for the same portfolio.
   B. The Lipper methodology can only lead to a value or growth classification. It does not offer a core/blend component.
   C. The Morningstar methodology classifies securities as either value, growth, or core by looking at the difference between their respective growth and value scores. It is possible that the Asgard funds hold a balanced exposure to both value and growth and/or core stocks.

The following information relates to questions 7–14

Aleksy Nowacki is a new portfolio manager at Heydon Investments. The firm currently offers a single equity fund, which uses a top-down investment strategy based on fundamentals. Vicky Knight, a junior analyst at Heydon, assists with managing the fund.

Nowacki has been hired to start a second fund, the Heydon Quant Fund, which will use quantitative active equity strategies. Nowacki and Knight meet to discuss distinct characteristics of the quantitative approach to active management, and Knight suggests three such characteristics:

Characteristic 1.   The focus is on factors across a potentially large group of stocks.
Characteristic 2.   The decision-making process is systematic and non-discretionary.
Characteristic 3.   The approach places an emphasis on forecasting the future prospects of underlying companies.

Nowacki states that quantitative investing generally follows a structured and well-defined process. Knight asks Nowacki:

"What is the starting point for the quantitative investment process?"

The new Heydon Quant Fund will use a factor-based strategy. Nowacki assembles a large dataset with monthly standardized scores and monthly returns for the strategy to back-test a new investment strategy and calculates the information coefficient. $FS(t)$ is the factor score for the current month, and $FS(t + 1)$ is the score for the next month. $SR(t)$ is the strategy's holding period return for the current month, and $SR(t + 1)$ is the strategy's holding period return for the next month.

As an additional step in backtesting of the strategy, Nowacki computes historical price/book ratios (P/Bs) and price/earnings ratios (P/Es) using calendar year-end (31 December) stock prices and companies' financial statement data for the same calendar year. He notes that the financial statement data for a given calendar year are not typically published until weeks after the end of that year.

Because the Heydon Quant Fund occasionally performs pairs trading using statistical arbitrage, Nowacki creates three examples of pairs trading candidates, presented in Exhibit 1. Nowacki asks Knight to recommend a suitable pair trade.

EXHIBIT 1   Possible Pairs Trades Based on Statistical Arbitrage

Stock Pair	Current Price Ratio Compared with Long-Term Average	Historical Price Ratio Relationship	Historical Correlation between Returns
1 and 2	Not significantly different	Mean reverting	High
3 and 4	Significantly different	Mean reverting	High
5 and 6	Significantly different	Not mean reverting	Low

Knight foresees a possible scenario in which the investment universe for the Heydon Quant Fund is unchanged but a new factor is added to its multifactor model. Knight asks Nowacki whether this scenario could affect the fund's investment-style classifications using either the returns-based or holdings-based approaches.

7. Which of the following asset allocation methods would *not likely* be used by Nowacki and Knight to select investments for the existing equity fund?
   A. Sector and industry rotation
   B. Growth at a reasonable price
   C. Country and geographic allocation

8. Relative to Heydon's existing fund, the new fund will *most likely*:
   A. hold a smaller number of stocks.
   B. rebalance at more regular intervals.
   C. see risk at the company level rather than the portfolio level.

9. Which characteristic suggested by Knight to describe the quantitative approach to active management is *incorrect*?
   A. Characteristic 1
   B. Characteristic 2
   C. Characteristic 3

10. Nowacki's *most appropriate* response to Knight's question about the quantitative investment process is to:
    A. backtest the new strategy.
    B. define the market opportunity.
    C. identify the factors to include and their weights.

11. In Nowacki's backtesting of the factor-based strategy for the new fund, the calculated information coefficient should be based on:
    A. $FS(t)$ and $SR(t)$.
    B. $FS(t)$ and $SR(t + 1)$.
    C. $SR(t)$ and $FS(t + 1)$.

12. Nowacki's calculated price/book ratios (P/Bs) and price/earnings ratios (P/Es), in his backtesting of the new strategy, are a problem because of:
    A. data mining.
    B. look-ahead bias.
    C. survivorship bias.

13. Based on Exhibit 1, which stock pair should Knight recommend as the best candidate for statistical arbitrage?
    A. Stock 1 and Stock 2
    B. Stock 3 and Stock 4
    C. Stock 5 and Stock 6

14. The *most appropriate* response to Knight's question regarding the potential future scenario for the Heydon Quant Fund is:
    A. only the returns-based approach.
    B. only the holdings-based approach.
    C. both the returns-based approach and the holdings-based approach.

The following information relates to questions 15–19

Jack Dewey is managing partner of DC&H, an investment management firm, and Supriya Sardar is an equity analyst with the firm. Dewey recently took over management of the firm's Purity Fund. He is developing a fundamental active investment process for managing this fund that emphasizes financial strength and demonstrated profitability of portfolio companies. At his previous employer, Dewey managed a fund for which his investment process involved taking active exposures in sectors based on the macroeconomic environment and demographic trends.

Dewey and Sardar meet to discuss developing a fundamental active investment process for the Purity Fund. They start by defining the investment universe and market opportunity for the fund, and then they pre-screen the universe to obtain a manageable set of securities for further, more detailed analysis. Next, Dewey notes that industry and competitive analysis of the list of securities must be performed. He then asks Sardar to recommend the next step in development of the fundamental active management process.

During the next few months, Dewey rebalances the Purity Fund to reflect his fundamental active investment process. Dewey and Sardar meet again to discuss potential new investment opportunities for the fund. Sardar recommends the purchase of AZ Industrial, which she believes is trading below its intrinsic value, despite its high price-to-book value (P/B) relative to the industry average.

Dewey asks Sardar to perform a bottom-up style analysis of the Purity Fund based on the aggregation of attributes from individual stocks in the portfolio. Dewey plans to include the results of this style analysis in a profile he is preparing for the fund.

15. In managing the fund at his previous employer, Dewey's investment process can be *best* described as:
    A. an activist strategy.
    B. a top-down strategy.
    C. a bottom-up strategy.

16. Sardar's recommendation for the next step should be to:
    A. review results from backtesting the strategy.
    B. make recommendations for rebalancing the portfolio.
    C. forecast companies' performances and convert those forecasts into valuations.

17. Based upon Dewey's chosen investment process for the management of the Purity Fund, rebalancing of the fund will *most likely* occur:
    A. at regular intervals.
    B. in response to changes in company-specific information.
    C. in response to updated output from optimization models.

18. Which investment approach is the *most likely* basis for Sardar's buy recommendation for AZ Industrial?
    A. Relative value
    B. High-quality value
    C. Deep-value investing

19. The analysis performed by Sardar on the Purity Fund can be *best* described as being based on:
    A. a holdings-based approach.
    B. manager self-identification.
    C. a returns-based style analysis.

CHAPTER 14

HEDGE FUND STRATEGIES

Barclay T. Leib, CFE, CAIA
Kathryn M. Kaminski, PhD, CAIA
Mila Getmansky Sherman, PhD

LEARNING OUTCOMES

The candidate should be able to:

- discuss how hedge fund strategies may be classified;
- discuss investment characteristics, strategy implementation, and role in a portfolio of *equity-related* hedge fund strategies;
- discuss investment characteristics, strategy implementation, and role in a portfolio of *event-driven* hedge fund strategies;
- discuss investment characteristics, strategy implementation, and role in a portfolio of *relative value* hedge fund strategies;
- discuss investment characteristics, strategy implementation, and role in a portfolio of *opportunistic* hedge fund strategies;
- discuss investment characteristics, strategy implementation, and role in a portfolio of *specialist* hedge fund strategies;
- discuss investment characteristics, strategy implementation, and role in a portfolio of *multi-manager* hedge fund strategies;
- describe how factor models may be used to understand hedge fund risk exposures;
- evaluate the impact of an allocation to a hedge fund strategy in a traditional investment portfolio.

1. INTRODUCTION

Hedge funds form an important subset of the alternative investments opportunity set, but they come with many pros and cons in their use and application across different asset classes and investment approaches. The basic tradeoff is whether the added fees typically involved

Portfolio Management, Second Edition, by Barclay T. Leib, CFE, CAIA, Kathryn M. Kaminski, PhD, CAIA, and Mila Getmansky Sherman, PhD. Copyright © 2019 by CFA Institute.

with hedge fund investing result in sufficient additional alpha and portfolio diversification benefits to justify the high fee levels. This is an ongoing industry debate.

Some argue that investing in hedge funds is a key way to access the very best investment talent—those individuals who can adroitly navigate investment opportunities across a potentially wider universe of markets. Others argue that hedge funds are important because the alpha that may be produced in down markets is hard to source elsewhere.

The arguments against hedge funds are also non-trivial. In addition to the high fee levels, the complex offering memorandum documentation needs to be understood by investors (i.e., the limited partners). Other issues include lack of full underlying investment transparency/attribution, higher cost allocations associated with the establishment and maintenance of the fund investment structures, and generally longer–lived investment commitment periods with limited redemption availability.

In addition, each hedge fund strategy area tends to introduce different types of added portfolio risks. For example, to achieve meaningful return objectives, arbitrage-oriented hedge fund strategies tend to utilize significant leverage that can be dangerous to limited partner investors, especially during periods of market stress. Long/short equity and event-driven strategies may have less beta exposure than simple, long-only beta allocations, but the higher hedge fund fees effectively result in a particularly expensive form of embedded beta. Such strategies as managed futures or global macro investing may introduce natural benefits of asset class and investment approach diversification, but they come with naturally higher volatility in the return profiles typically delivered. Extreme tail risk in portfolios may be managed with the inclusion of relative value volatility or long volatility strategies, but it comes at the cost of a return drag during more normal market periods. In other words, some hedge fund strategies may have higher portfolio diversification benefits, while others may simply be return enhancers rather than true portfolio diversifiers.

Also, the hedge fund industry continues to evolve in its overall structure. Over the past decade, traditional limited partnership formats have been supplemented by offerings of liquid alternatives (liquid alts)—which are mutual fund, closed-end fund, and ETF-type vehicles that invest in various hedge fund-like strategies. Liquid alts are meant to provide daily liquidity, transparency, and lower fees while opening hedge fund investing to a wider range of investors. However, empirical evidence shows that liquid alts significantly underperform similar strategy hedge funds, which suggests that traditional hedge funds may be benefiting from an illiquidity premium phenomenon that cannot be easily transported into a mutual fund format.

Investors must understand the various subtleties involved with investing in hedge funds. Although secular bull market trends have arguably made "hedged" strategies less critical for inclusion in portfolio allocations than they were during the mid-to-late 2000s, the overall popularity of hedge funds tends to be somewhat cyclical. Notably, as demonstrated by the endowment model of investing, placing hedge funds as a core allocation can increase net returns and reduce risk.

This chapter presents the investment characteristics and implementation for the major categories of hedge fund strategies. It also provides a framework for classifying and evaluating these strategies based on their risk profiles. Section 2 summarizes some distinctive regulatory and investment characteristics of hedge funds and discusses ways to classify hedge fund strategies. Sections 3 through 8 present investment characteristics and strategy implementation for each of the following six hedge fund strategy categories: equity-related; event-driven; relative value; opportunistic; specialist; and multi-manager strategies. Section 9 introduces a conditional factor model as a unifying framework for understanding and analyzing the risk exposures of these strategies. Section 10 evaluates the contributions of each hedge fund strategy to the return and risk profile of a traditional portfolio of stocks and bonds. The chapter concludes with a summary.

2. CLASSIFICATION OF HEDGE FUNDS AND STRATEGIES

The most important characteristics of hedge funds are summarized as follows:

1. **Legal/Regulatory Overview:** Different countries have varying requirements for investor eligibility to access hedge fund investments. These regulations are typically intended to limit access to traditional hedge funds to sophisticated investors with a minimum income or net-worth requirement, and they allow hedge fund managers to accept only a limited number of investment subscriptions. Most traditional hedge funds in the United States are offered effectively as private placement offerings. Whether the underlying fund manager must register with regulatory authorities depends on assets under management (AUM); however, regardless of AUM, all US hedge funds are subject to regulatory oversight against fraudulent conduct. Hedge funds offered in other jurisdictions— attractive, tax-neutral locales like the Cayman Islands, the British Virgin Islands, or Bermuda—are typically presented to investors as stand-alone corporate entities subject to the rules and regulations of the particular locality.

   From a regulatory perspective, the advent of liquid alts has likely caused the greatest shift in the industry over the past decade. Some of the more liquid hedge fund strategies that meet certain liquidity and diversification requirements (generally long/short equity and managed futures strategies) are offered by many fund sponsors in mutual fund-type structures in the United States and in the undertakings for collective investment in transferable securities (UCITs) format in Europe and Asia. By law, these liquid alts vehicles can be more widely marketed to retail investors. Whereas traditional hedge funds typically offer only limited periodic liquidity, liquid alts funds may be redeemed by investors on a daily basis. Also, traditional hedge funds typically involve both a management fee and an incentive fee; however, liquid alts in most countries are prohibited from charging an incentive fee.

   Finally, the overall regulatory constraints for hedge funds are far less than those for regulated investment vehicles—except for the liquid alts versions, which have much higher constraints to provide liquidity to investors.

2. **Flexible Mandates—Few Investment Constraints:** Given the relatively low legal and regulatory constraints faced by hedge funds, their mandates are flexible; thus, they are relatively unhindered in their trading and investment activities in terms of investable asset classes and securities, risk exposures, and collateral. The fund prospectus (i.e., offering memorandum) will specify the hedge fund's mandate and objectives and will include constraints, if any, on investment in certain asset classes as well as in the use of leverage, shorting, and derivatives.

3. **Large Investment Universe:** Lower regulatory constraints and flexible mandates give hedge funds access to a wide range of assets outside the normal set of traditional investments. Examples include private securities, non-investment-grade debt, distressed securities, derivatives, and more-esoteric contracts, such as life insurance contracts and even music or film royalties.

4. **Aggressive Investment Styles:** Hedge funds may use their typically flexible investment mandates to undertake strategies deemed too risky for traditional investment funds. These strategies may involve significant shorting and/or concentrated positions in domestic and foreign securities that offer exposure to credit, volatility, and liquidity risk premiums.

5. **Relatively Liberal Use of Leverage:** Hedge funds generally use leverage more extensively than regulated investment funds. Their leveraged positions are implemented either by borrowing securities from a prime broker or by using implied leverage via derivatives. In many instances, such leverage is necessary to make the return profile of the strategy meaningful. In other instances, derivatives may be used to hedge away unwanted risks (e.g., interest rate or credit risk) that may create high "notional leverage" but result in a less risky portfolio. Within long/short equity trading, leverage is most often applied to quantitative approaches in which small statistical valuation aberrations—typically over short windows of time—are identified by a manager or an algorithm. Such quant managers will typically endeavor to be market neutral but will apply high leverage levels to make the opportunities they identify meaningful from a return perspective.

6. **Hedge Fund Liquidity Constraints:** Limited partnership-format hedge funds involve initial lock-up periods, liquidity gates, and exit windows. These provide hedge fund managers with a greater ability to take and maintain positions than vehicles that allow investors to withdraw their investment essentially at will. It is thus not surprising that empirical evidence shows that such privately-placed hedge funds significantly outperform similar-strategy liquid alts products by approximately 100 bps–200 bps, on average, per year.

7. **Relatively High Fee Structures:** Hedge funds have traditionally imposed relatively high investment fees on investors, including both management fees and incentive fees. These have historically been 1% or more of AUM for management fees and 10%–20% of annual returns for incentive fees. The incentive fee structure is meant to align the interests of the hedge fund manager with those of the fund's investors.

With this background, we now address how hedge funds are classified. One distinction is between single manager hedge funds and multi-manager hedge funds. A **single-manager fund** is a fund in which one portfolio manager or team of portfolio managers invests in one strategy or style. A **multi-manager fund** can be of two types. One type is a **multi-strategy fund**, in which teams of portfolio managers trade and invest in multiple different strategies within the same fund. The second type, a fund-of-hedge funds, often simply called a **fund-of-funds** (FoF), is a fund in which the fund-of-funds manager allocates capital to separate, underlying hedge funds (e.g., single manager and/or multi-manager funds) that themselves run a range of different strategies.

At the single manager and single strategy level, hedge fund strategies can be classified in various ways. The taxonomy is often based on some combination of:

1. the instruments in which the managers invest (e.g., equities, commodities, foreign exchange, convertible bonds);
2. the trading philosophy followed by the managers (e.g., systematic, discretionary); and
3. the types of risk the managers assume (e.g., directional, event driven, relative value).

Most prominent hedge fund data vendors use a combination of these criteria to classify hedge fund strategies. For example, Hedge Fund Research, Inc. (HFR) reports manager performance statistics on more than 30 strategies and divides funds into six single strategy groupings that are widely used in the hedge fund industry. HFR's six main single strategy groupings are 1) equity hedge; 2) event driven; 3) fund-of-funds; 4) macro; 5) relative value; and 6) risk parity.

Lipper TASS, another well-known data vendor, classifies funds into the following ten categories: 1) dedicated short bias; 2) equity market neutral; 3) long/short equity hedge; 4) event driven; 5) convertible arbitrage; 6) fixed-income arbitrage; 7) global macro; 8) managed futures; 9) fund-of-funds; and 10) multi-strategy.

Morningstar CISDM goes even further and separates hedge funds in its database into finer categories, like merger arbitrage and systematic futures, among others. In addition, the Morningstar CISDM Database separates fund-of-funds strategies into several different sub-categories, such as debt, equity, event driven, macro/systematic, multi-strategy, and relative value.

Eurekahedge, an important index provider with its roots in Asia, has grown to include many smaller hedge fund managers globally. Its main strategy indexes include nine categories: 1) arbitrage; 2) commodity trading adviser (CTA)/managed futures; 3) distressed debt; 4) event driven; 5) fixed income; 6) long/short equities; 7) macro; 8) multi-strategy; and 9) relative value.

A final example of a prominent hedge fund data vendor is Credit Suisse. Its Credit Suisse Hedge Fund Index is an asset-weighted index that monitors approximately 9,000 funds and consists of funds with a minimum of US$50 million AUM, a 12-month track record, and audited financial statements. The index is calculated and rebalanced monthly, and it reflects performance net of all performance fees and expenses. Credit Suisse also subdivides managers into nine main sub-indexes for strategy areas: 1) convertible arbitrage; 2) emerging markets; 3) equity market neutral; 4) event driven; 5) fixed income; 6) global macro; 7) long/short equity; 8) managed futures; and 9) multi-strategy.

These different data providers use different methodologies for index calculation. HFR produces both the HFRX Index of equally weighted hedge funds, which includes those that are open or closed to new investment, and its HFRI index series, which tracks only hedge funds open to new investment. Because managers who have closed their funds to new investment are typically superior managers who are limited in their capacity to manage additional funds, the HFRX series regularly outperforms the HFRI series. However, the mix of managers represented by the HFRX Index would obviously not be replicable in real-time by an investor, thus limiting its usefulness. Meanwhile, the Credit Suisse Hedge Fund Index is weighted by fund size (i.e., AUM), so its overall performance is more reflective of the performance of the larger hedge funds, such as the multi-strategy managers.

Notably, less overlap exists in manager reporting to the different index providers than one might expect or is likely optimal. In fact, less than 1% of hedge fund managers self-report to all the index service providers mentioned. Clearly, no single index is all-encompassing.

Generally consistent with the above data vendor groupings and with a practice-based risk factor perspective, this chapter groups single hedge fund strategies into the following six categories: 1) equity; 2) event-driven; 3) relative value; 4) opportunistic; 5) specialist; and 6) multi-manager.

- **Equity-related hedge fund strategies** focus primarily on the equity markets, and the majority of their risk profiles involve equity-oriented risk. Within this equity-related bucket, long/short equity, dedicated short bias, and equity market neutral are the main strategies that will be discussed further.

- **Event-driven hedge fund strategies** focus on corporate events, such as governance events, mergers and acquisitions, bankruptcy, and other key events for corporations. The primary risk for these strategies is event risk, the possibility that an unexpected event will negatively affect a company or security. Unexpected events include unforeseen corporate reorganization, a failed merger, credit rating downgrades, or company bankruptcy. The most common event-driven hedge fund strategies, merger arbitrage and distressed securities, will be discussed in detail.
- **Relative value hedge fund strategies** focus on the relative valuation between two or more securities. These strategies are often exposed to credit and liquidity risks because the valuation differences from which these strategies seek to benefit often are due to differences in credit quality and/or liquidity across different securities. The two common relative value hedge fund strategies to be covered further are fixed-income arbitrage and convertible bond arbitrage.
- **Opportunistic hedge fund strategies** take a top-down approach, focusing on a multi-asset (often macro-oriented) opportunity set. The risks for opportunistic hedge fund strategies depend on the opportunity set involved and can vary across time and asset classes. The two common opportunistic hedge fund strategies that are discussed in further detail are global macro and managed futures.
- **Specialist hedge fund strategies** focus on special or niche opportunities that often require a specialized skill or knowledge of a specific market. These strategies can be exposed to unique risks that stem from particular market sectors, niche securities, and/or esoteric instruments. We will explore two specialist strategies in further detail: volatility strategies involving options and reinsurance strategies.
- **Multi-manager hedge fund strategies** focus on building a portfolio of diversified hedge fund strategies. Managers in this strategy bucket use their skills to combine diverse strategies and dynamically re-allocate among them over time. The two most common types of multi-manager hedge funds are multi-strategy funds and fund-of-funds, which we will discuss in further detail.

Exhibit 1 shows the five single strategy hedge fund buckets that will be covered individually. Multi-strategy funds and fund-of funds—two types of multi-manager strategies—will also be covered. A discussion of each strategy's contributions to portfolio risk and return will follow.

EXHIBIT 1   Hedge Fund Strategies by Category

Equity	Event-Driven	Relative Value	Opportunistic	Specialist	Multi-Manager
• Long/Short Equity • Dedicated Short Bias • Equity Market Neutral	• Merger Arbitrage • Distressed Securitites	• Fixed-Income Arbitrage • Convertible Bond Arbitrage	• Global Macro • Managed Futures	• Volatility Strategies • Reinsurance Strategies	• Multi-strategy • Fund-of-Funds

3. EQUITY STRATEGIES

Equity hedge fund strategies invest primarily in equity and equity-related instruments. As mentioned previously, the alpha related to equity strategies tends to derive from the wide variety of equity investments available globally combined with astute long and short stock picking. The size and sign of equity market exposure often dictate the classification of equity hedge fund strategies. As the name suggests, long-only equity hedge fund strategies focus on holding only long positions in equities, and they sometimes use leverage. Long/short equity hedge fund strategies hold both long and short positions in equities that typically result in more-hedged, less-volatile overall portfolios. Short-biased strategies focus on strategic short selling of companies that are expected to lose value in the future (sometimes with an activist inclination, sometimes with long positions in other securities as an offset). Equity market-neutral strategies hold balanced long and short equity exposures to maintain zero (or close to zero) net exposure to the equity market and such factors as sector and size (i.e., market cap). They then focus on, for example, pairs of long and short securities whose prices are out of historical alignment and are expected to experience mean reversion. The following sections discuss long/short equity, dedicated short bias, and equity market-neutral hedge fund strategies.

3.1. Long/Short Equity

Long/short (L/S) equity managers buy equities of companies they expect will rise in value (i.e., they take long positions in undervalued companies) and sell short equities of companies they think will fall in value (i.e., they take short positions in overvalued companies). The objective of long/short equity strategies is to be flexible in finding attractive opportunities on both the long and short sides of the market and to size them within a portfolio. Depending on their specific mandates, long/short equity strategies can shift between industry sectors (e.g., from technology to consumer goods), factors (e.g., from value to growth), and geographic regions (e.g., from Europe to Asia). In practice, however, managers tend to maintain their philosophical biases and areas of focus, typically with a heavy emphasis on fundamental research.

Although market timing using "beta tilts" can play a factor in manager performance, studies have shown that most fundamental long/short equity managers offer little added alpha from such adjustments. They are typically either too net long at market highs or not net long enough at market lows. Most L/S equity managers are not known for their portfolio-level market-timing abilities, but those with such market-timing skills may be particularly valuable from a portfolio allocation perspective.

L/S equity managers also are typically able to take concentrated positions in high conviction buys or sells and can readily apply leverage to increase these positions (although higher levels of leverage are used mostly by quantitatively-oriented managers, not fundamental managers). As a result, stock selection defines manager skill for most L/S equity managers—with market-timing ability being an additive, but generally secondary, consideration. L/S equity is one of the most prevalent hedge fund strategies. It accounts for about 30% of all hedge funds.

3.1.1. Investment Characteristics

Because manager skill derives mainly from stock selection, it is not surprising that individual long/short equity managers tend to have a focus based on their own unique skill sets. As a result, many long/short equity managers specialize in either a specific geographic region, sector, or investment style. However, several key characteristics define long/short equity managers: their strategy focus, their flexibility in holding long and short positions over time, and their use of leverage. Given the specific mandate for a long/short equity manager, his/her exposures to various equity factors can be very different from other long/short equity managers. For example, a manager focusing on small-cap growth stocks would have a positive exposure to the size factor and a negative exposure to the value factor. Conversely, a manager with a focus on large-cap value stocks would have a negative exposure to the size factor and a positive exposure to the value factor.

Given that equity markets tend to rise over the long run, most long/short equity managers typically hold net long equity positions. Some managers maintain their short positions as a hedge against unexpected market downturns. Other managers are more opportunistic; they tend to take on more short positions after uncovering negative issues with a company's management, strategies, and/or financial statements or whenever their valuation models suggest selling opportunities in certain stocks or sectors. As a result, performance during market crisis periods is important for differentiating between hedge fund managers. Given that hedge funds typically carry high fees, it is important to avoid paying such added fees just for embedded beta exposure that could be achieved more cheaply by investing in traditional long-only strategies. The goal in long/short equity investing is generally to find more sources of idiosyncratic alpha (primarily via stock picking and secondarily by market timing) rather than embedded systematic beta. Exhibit 2 presents some key aspects of this important strategy area.

EXHIBIT 2   Long/Short Equity—Risk, Liquidity, Leverage, and Benchmarking

Risk Profile and Liquidity

- Diverse opportunities globally create a wide universe from which to create alpha through astute stock picking.
- Diverse investment styles include value/growth, large cap/small cap, discretionary/ quantitative, and industry specialized.
- They typically have average exposures of 40%–60% net long, composed of gross exposures of 70%–90% long vs. 20%–50% short, but they can vary widely. Return profiles are typically aimed to achieve average annual returns roughly equivalent to a long-only approach but with a standard deviation 50% lower than a long-only approach.
- Some managers use index-based short hedges to reduce market risk, but most search for single-name shorts for portfolio alpha and added absolute return.
- Some managers are able to add alpha via market timing of portfolio beta tilt, but evidence suggests that most L/S managers do this poorly.
- This strategy can typically be handled by both limited partner and mutual fund-type vehicles.

- Attractiveness: Liquid, diverse, with mark-to-market pricing driven by public market quotes; added short-side exposure typically reduces beta risk and provides an additional source of potential alpha and reduced portfolio volatility.

Leverage Usage

- Variable: The more market-neutral or quantitative the strategy approach, the more levered the strategy application tends to be to achieve a meaningful return profile.

Benchmarking

- L/S equity benchmarks include HFRX and HFRI Equity Hedge Indices; Lipper TASS L/S Equity Hedge; Morningstar/CISDM Equity L/S Index; and Credit Suisse L/S Equity Index.

3.1.2. Strategy Implementation

When long and short stock positions are placed together into a portfolio, the market exposure is the net of the beta-adjusted long and short exposures. For example, with many strong sells and a relatively large short position, the strategy could be net short for brief periods of time. Typically, most long/short equity managers end up with modest net long exposures averaging between 40%–60% net long. Many long/short equity managers are naturally sector-specific, often designing their funds around their industry specialization. Such specialist L/S fund managers analyze fundamental situations that they know well from both a top-down and bottom-up analytical perspective. Natural areas of specialization include potentially more complex sectors, such as telecom/media/technology (TMT), financial, consumer, health care, and biotechnology sectors. Conversely, generalist L/S managers search further afield, thus having flexibility to invest across multiple industry groups. Typically, these generalists avoid complex sectors; for example, they may avoid biotechnology because corporate outcomes may be deemed too binary depending on the success or failure of drug trials. Although generalist managers do take a more balanced and flexible approach, they may miss detailed industry subtleties that are increasingly important to understand in a world where news flows 24/7 and is increasingly nuanced.

Overall, long/short equity investing in most instances is a mix of extracting alpha on the long and short sides from single-name stock selection combined with some naturally net long embedded beta.

EXAMPLE 1   Long/Short Equity Investing Dilemma

The Larson family office views L/S equity investing as a significant portion of the hedge fund universe and would like to access managers talented not only at long investing but also at short selling. However, it does not want to pay high hedge fund fees just for long-biased beta because it has access to long-biased beta at lower fees elsewhere in its portfolio. But, Larson will pay hedge fund fees for strategies that can produce strong risk-adjusted performance in a unique and differentiated fashion.

1. Discuss some potential hedge fund strategies the Larson family office should consider adding to its existing portfolio.
2. Discuss some of the problems and risks that it may encounter.

Solution to 1: The Larson family office should consider managers focused on an L/S equity strategy with a sector-specialization as opposed to a generalist fundamental L/S strategy. Generalist L/S managers can benefit from the flexibility to scan a wide universe of stocks to find investments, but they may not be able to develop a sufficient information edge in their analysis to dependably deliver sufficient alpha relative to their fees and natural long beta positioning. However, managers running specialist L/S equity strategies—especially in such complex sectors as technology, finance, and biotechnology/health care—are more likely to have the specialized capabilities to perform the "deep-dive" differentiated analysis required to develop more original views and stronger portfolio performance.

Solution to 2: A key problem with selecting sector-specialist L/S equity hedge funds is that they are more difficult to analyze and assess. There are also fewer to choose from compared to generalist L/S hedge funds. Sectors can fall out of favor, risking an allocation to a good fund but in the wrong area given dynamic macroeconomic and financial market conditions. Moreover, generalist L/S strategies, by definition, can readily reallocate capital more efficiently as opportunities emerge in different sectors. Put another way, the Larson family office could potentially find itself with too much single sector, short-sided, or idiosyncratic exposure at the wrong time if it chooses a sector-specialist L/S equity fund.

3.2. Dedicated Short Selling and Short-Biased

Dedicated short-selling hedge fund managers take short-only positions in equities deemed to be expensively priced versus their deteriorating fundamental situations. Such managers may vary their short exposures only in terms of portfolio sizing by, at times, holding higher levels of cash. **Short-biased** hedge fund managers use a less extreme version of this approach. They also search for opportunities to sell expensively priced equities, but they may balance short exposure with some modest value-oriented, or possibly index-oriented, long exposure. This latter approach can potentially help short-biased hedge funds cope with long bull market periods in equities. Both types of short sellers actively aim to create an uncorrelated or negatively correlated source of return by seeking out failing business models, fraudulent accounting, corporate mismanagement, or other factors that may sour the market's perception of a given equity. Because of the overall secular up-trend in global equity markets, especially across the past several decades, it has been very difficult to be a successful short seller. As a result, fewer such managers are in existence today than in the 1990s.

One exception is the emergence of **activist short selling**, whereby managers take a short position in a given security and then publicly present their research backing the short thesis. Typically, if the hedge fund manager has a solid reputation from its past activist short-selling forays, the release of such research causes a significant stock price plunge into which the activist short seller might cover a portion of its short position. In the United States, this practice has not been deemed to be market manipulation by securities' regulators as long as the activist short seller is not publishing erroneous information, is not charging for such information (which might create potential conflicts of interest between subscribers and investors), and is acting only in the best interests of its limited partner investors.

3.2.1. Investment Characteristics

Short-selling managers focus on situations involving overvalued equities of companies facing deteriorating fundamentals that typically have not yet been perceived by the market. They also attempt to maximize returns during periods of market declines. If these short-selling managers can achieve success with their approaches, they can provide a unique and useful source of negatively correlated returns compared to many other strategy areas.

Short selling involves borrowing securities, selling them "high," and then after prices have declined, buying the same securities back "low" and returning them to the lender. To borrow the securities to short sell, the manager must post collateral with the securities lender to cover potential losses. The manager must also pay interest on the securities loan, which can be high if the securities are difficult for the lender to locate. One key risk is that the lender may want the securities back at an inopportune time—such as before the expected price decline has materialized, which could be disadvantageous for the hedge fund manager.

Short selling in general is a difficult investment practice to master in terms of risk management because of the natural phenomenon that positions will grow if prices advance against the short seller but will shrink if prices decline. This is the opposite of what occurs with long-only investing, and it is more difficult to manage. Additionally, access to company management for research purposes can be blocked for fund managers who become known as active short sellers.

From a regulatory perspective, many countries limit or impose stringent rules on short selling. In the United States, the "uptick rule" states that when a stock decreases by 10% or more from its prior closing price, a short sale order can be executed only at a price higher than the current best (i.e., highest) bid. This means the stock's price must be rising to execute the short sale. Although many emerging markets have allowed short selling, particularly to enhance market liquidity (e.g., the Saudi Stock Exchange allowed short sales beginning in 2016), there is always concern that limits could be placed on short selling during extreme market environments or that regulations could change. For example, for a brief period during the global financial crisis of 2007–2009, new short sales on a designated list of financial stocks were banned by the US SEC to lessen systematic market stress.

Given the difficult operational aspects of short selling, and because equity markets tend to secularly rise over time, successful short-selling managers typically have something of a short-term "attack and retreat" style. The return profile for a successful short-biased manager might best be characterized by increasingly positive returns as the market declines and the risk-free return when the market rises. In some idealized short-selling world, this would entail being short the market during down periods and investing in low-risk government debt when the market is not declining. But, the actual goal of a short seller is to pick short-sale stocks that can still generate positive returns even when the general market trend is up. Skillful, dedicated short-biased managers look for possible short-selling targets among companies that are overvalued, that are experiencing declining revenues and/or earnings, or that have internal management conflicts, weak corporate governance, or even potential accounting frauds. Other possible short-sale candidates are companies that may have single products under development that the short seller believes will ultimately either be unsuccessful or non-repeatable. Exhibit 3 shows some important aspects of this strategy area.

EXHIBIT 3   Dedicated Short Sellers and Short-Biased—Risk, Liquidity, Leverage, and Benchmarking

---

Risk Profile and Liquidity

- Dedicated short sellers: They only trade with short-side exposure, although they may moderate short beta by also holding cash.
- Short-biased managers: They are focused on good short-side stock picking, but they may moderate short beta with some value-oriented long exposure or index-oriented long exposure as well as cash.
- Dedicated short sellers tend to be 60%–120% short at all times. Short-biased managers are typically around 30%–60% net short. The focus in both cases tends to be on single equity stock picking as opposed to index shorting.
- Return goals are typically less than those for most other hedge fund strategies but with a negative correlation benefit. They are more volatile than a typical L/S equity hedge fund given short beta exposure.
- Managers have some ability to add alpha via market timing of portfolio beta tilt, but it is difficult to do with consistency or added alpha.
- This strategy is typically handled best in a limited partnership because of difficult operational aspects of short selling.
- Attractiveness: Liquid, negatively correlated alpha to that of most other strategies, with mark-to-market pricing from public prices. Historic returns have been lumpy and generally disappointing.

Leverage Usage

- Low: There is typically sufficient natural volatility that short-selling managers do not need to add much leverage.

Benchmarking

- Short-biased indexes include Eurekahedge Equity Short Bias Hedge Fund Index and Lipper TASS Dedicated Short-Bias Index. Some investors also compare short-biased funds' returns to the inverse of returns on related stock indexes.

Note: Each index has different methodologies for fund inclusion. Because there are fewer short-selling managers, the construction of an acceptably diverse index is particularly difficult. The Lipper TASS Dedicated Short-Bias Index, for example, includes just four managers.

3.2.2. Strategy Implementation

Because finding strategic selling opportunities is key to dedicated short-biased strategies, stock selection is an important part of the investment process. Short-selling managers typically take a bottom-up approach by scanning the universe of potential sell targets to uncover and sell short those companies whose shares are most likely to substantially decline in value over the relevant time horizon. Managers search for, among other factors, inherently flawed business models, unsustainable levels of corporate leverage, and indications of poor corporate governance and/or accounting gimmickry. Tools that may be helpful to dedicated short-biased managers in finding potential sell candidates include monitoring single-name credit default swap spreads, corporate bond yield spreads, and/or implied volatility of exchange-traded put options. Traditional technical analysis and/or pattern recognition techniques may assist the manager in the market timing of short sales. Various accounting ratios and measures, such as the Altman *Z*-score for judging a company's bankruptcy potential and the Beneish *M*-score for identifying potentially fraudulent financial statements, may also be useful. Because of the inherent difficulty and dangers of short selling, most successful short sellers do significant "deep-dive" forensic work on their short-portfolio candidates. As such, short sellers serve as a valuable resource in creating more overall pricing efficiency in the market.

EXAMPLE 2   Candidate for Short-Biased Hedge Fund Strategy

Kit Stone, a short-biased hedge fund manager, is researching Generic Inc. (GI) for possible addition to his portfolio. GI was once a drug industry leader, but for the past 10 years its R&D budgets have declined. Its drug patents have all expired, so it now operates in the competitive generic drug business. GI has staked its future on a new treatment for gastro-intestinal disease. R&D was financed by debt, so GI's leverage ratio is twice the industry average. Early clinical trials were inconclusive. Final clinical trial results for GI's new drug are to be revealed within one month. Although the market is constructive, many medical experts remain doubtful of the new drug's efficacy. Without any further insights into the trial results, Stone reviews the following information.

Generic Inc. (GI)			Industry Average		
PE (X)	PB (X)	T12M EPS Growth	PE (X)	PB (X)	T12M EPS Growth
30	3.5	3%	20	2.5	18%

Additionally, Stone notes that GI shares are very thinly traded, with a high short-interest ratio of 60%. Stone's broker has informed him that it is expensive to borrow GI shares for shorting; they are on "special" (i.e., difficult to borrow), with a high borrowing cost of 20% per year. Moreover, there is an active market for exchange-traded options on GI's shares. Prices of one-month GI options appear to reflect a positive view of the company.

1. Discuss whether Stone should add GI shares to his short-biased portfolio.
2. Discuss how Stone might instead take advantage of the situation using GI options.

Solution to 1: Generic Inc. appears to be substantially overvalued. Its main business relies on the competitive generic drug market; it has taken on substantial debt to fund R&D; and skepticism surrounds its new drug. GI's P/Es and P/Bs are higher than industry averages by 50% and 40%, respectively, and its trailing 12-month EPS growth is meager (3% vs. 18% industry average). However, although Stone would normally decide to add GI to his short-biased portfolio, the stock's high short-interest ratio and high cost to borrow (for shorting) are very concerning. Both factors suggest significant potential that a dangerous short-squeeze situation could develop if clinical results really do show efficacy of GI's new drug. So, based on the negative demand/supply dynamics for the stock, Stone decides not to add GI to his portfolio.

Solution to 2: Stone might instead consider expressing his negative view on GI by simply purchasing put options. Alternatively, Stone could purchase a long put calendar spread, where he would buy a put with expiry beyond and sell a put with expiry before the expected release date of the clinical trial results. In that case, the premium received from writing the shorter tenor put would finance, in part, the cost of buying the longer tenor put. As a third possibility, Stone might even consider buying GI shares and then lending them at the attractive 20% rate. In that case, he would need to hedge this long stock position with the purchase of out-of-the-money puts, thereby creating a protective put position. As a final possibility, if out-of-the-money calls are deemed to be expensive because of positive sentiment, Stone could sell such calls to finance the purchase of out-of-the-money puts, creating a short risk reversal that provides synthetic short exposure.

3.3. Equity Market Neutral

Equity market-neutral (EMN) hedge fund strategies take opposite (i.e., long and short) positions in similar or related equities that have divergent valuations, and they also attempt to maintain a near net zero portfolio exposure to the market. EMN managers neutralize market risk by constructing their portfolios such that the expected portfolio beta is approximately equal to zero. Moreover, managers often choose to set the betas for sectors or industries as well as for such common risk factors as market size, price-to-earnings ratio, or book-to-market ratio, which are also equal to zero. Because these portfolios do not take beta risk but do attempt to neutralize so many other factor risks, they typically must apply leverage to the long and short positions to achieve a meaningful expected return from their individual stock selections. Approaches vary, but equity market-neutral portfolios are often constructed using highly quantitative methodologies; the portfolios end up being more diverse in their holdings; and the portfolios are typically modified and adjusted over shorter time horizons. The condition of zero market beta can also be achieved with the use of derivatives, including stock index futures and options. Whichever way they are constructed, the overall goal of equity market-neutral portfolios is to capture alpha while minimizing portfolio beta exposure.

Although **pairs trading** is just one subset of equity market-neutral investing, it is an intuitively easy example to consider. With this strategy, pairs are identified of similar under- and overvalued equities, divergently valued shares of a holding company and its subsidiaries, or different share classes of the same company (multi-class stocks typically having different voting rights) in which their prices are out of alignment.

In whatever manner they are created, the pairs are monitored for their typical trading patterns relative to each other—conceptually, the degree of co-integration of the two securities' prices. Positions are established when unusually divergent spread pricing between the two paired securities is observed. Underpinning such a strategy is the expectation that the differential valuations or trading relationships will revert to their long-term mean values or their fundamentally-correct trading relationships, with the long position rising and the short position declining in value. Situations will obviously vary, but strictly quantitative EMN pairs trading, while attempting to minimize overall beta exposure, may still have effective short volatility "tail risk" exposure to abnormal market situations of extreme stress. This is less the case if a fundamental pricing discrepancy is being exploited in anticipation of a possible event that would cause that discrepancy to correct.

Another type of EMN trading is **stub trading**, which entails buying and selling stock of a parent company and its subsidiaries, typically weighted by the percentage ownership of the parent company in the subsidiaries. Assume parent company A owns 90% and 75% of subsidiaries B and C, respectively, and shares of A are determined to be overvalued while shares of B and C are deemed undervalued, all relative to their historical mean valuations. Then, for each share of A sold short, the EMN fund would buy 0.90 and 0.75 shares of B and C, respectively.

Yet another type of EMN approach may involve **multi-class trading**, which involves buying and selling different classes of shares of the same company, such as voting and non-voting shares. As with pairs trading, the degree of co-integration of returns and the valuation metrics for the multi-class shares are determined. If/when prices move outside of their normal ranges, the overvalued shares are sold short while the undervalued shares are purchased. The goal is to gain on the change in relative pricing on the two securities as market pricing reverts to more normal ranges.

Fundamental trade setups—although not per se "equity market neutral" but still designed to be market neutral—may be created that are long or short equity hedged against offsetting bond exposures if relative pricing between the stocks and bonds is deemed to be out of alignment. Such pairs trading is referred to as capital structure arbitrage and will be discussed in the event-driven strategies section. In these situations, attractive expected outcomes are often created from relative security mispricings designed to exploit potential event situations (e.g., a potential merger or bankruptcy) that would have an impact on relative pricing. Moreover, when two bonds are positioned relative to each other (e.g., to exploit a misunderstood difference in bond covenants or a potential differential asset recovery), a market-neutral strategy can also be employed.

When building market-neutral portfolios, sometimes large numbers of securities are traded and positions are adjusted on a daily or even an hourly basis using algorithm-based models. Managers following this approach are referred to as **quantitative market-neutral** managers. The frequent adjustments implemented by such managers are driven by the fact that market prices change faster than company fundamental factors. This price movement triggers a rebalancing of the EMN portfolio back to a market neutrality. When the time horizon of EMN trading shrinks to even shorter intervals and mean reversion and relative momentum characteristics of market behavior are emphasized, quantitative market-neutral trading becomes what is known as statistical arbitrage trading. With EMN and statistical arbitrage trading, a natural push/pull occurs between maintaining an optimal beta-neutral portfolio and the market impacts and brokerage costs of nearly continuous adjusting of the portfolio. So, many EMN managers use trading-cost hurdle models to determine if and when they should rebalance a portfolio.

Overall, the main source of skill for an EMN manager is in security selection, with market timing being of secondary importance. Sector exposure also tends to be constrained, although this can vary by the individual manager's approach. Managers that are overall beta neutral and specialize in sector rotation exposure as their source of alpha are known as market-neutral tactical asset allocators or macro-oriented market-neutral managers.

3.3.1. Investment Characteristics

Equity market-neutral fund managers seek to insulate their portfolios from movements in the overall market, and they can take advantage of divergent valuations by trading specific securities. As discussed, this is often a quantitatively driven process that uses a substantial amount of leverage to generate meaningful return objectives. However, many discretionary EMN managers implement their positions with significantly less leverage.

Overall, EMN managers generally are more useful for portfolio allocation during periods of non-trending or declining markets because they typically deliver returns that are steadier and less volatile than those of many other hedge strategy areas. Over time, their conservative and constrained approach typically results in less-volatile overall returns than those of managers who accept beta exposure. The exception to this norm is when the use of significant leverage may cause forced portfolio downsizing. By using portfolio margining techniques offered by prime brokers, market-neutral managers may run portfolios with up to 300% long versus 300% short exposures. Prime broker portfolio margining rules generally allow managers to maintain such levered positioning until a portfolio loss of a specified magnitude (i.e., excess drawdown) is incurred. At the time of such excess drawdown, the prime broker can force the manager to downsize his/her overall portfolio exposure. This is a key strategy risk, particularly for quantitative market-neutral managers.

Despite the use of substantial leverage and because of their more standard and overall steady risk/return profiles, equity market-neutral managers are often considered as preferred replacements for (or at least a complement to) fixed-income managers during periods when fixed-income returns are unattractively low/and or the yield curve is flat. EMN managers are, of course, sourcing a very different type of alpha with very different risks than in fixed-income investing. EMN managers must deal with leverage risk, including the issues of availability of leverage and at what cost, and tail risk, particularly the performance of levered portfolios during periods of market stress. Exhibit 4 presents important aspects of this strategy area.

EXHIBIT 4   Equity Market Neutral—Risk, Liquidity, Leverage, and Benchmarking

Risk Profile and Liquidity
- They have relatively modest return profiles, with portfolios aimed to be market neutral, and differing constraints to other factors and sector exposures are allowed.
- They generally have high levels of diversification and liquidity and lower standard deviation of returns than many other strategies across normal market conditions.
- Many different types of EMN managers exist, but many are purely quantitative managers (vs. discretionary managers).
- Time horizons vary, but EMN strategies are typically oriented toward mean reversion, with shorter horizons than other strategies and more active trading.
- Because of often high leverage, EMN strategies typically do not meet regulatory leverage limits for mutual fund vehicles. So, limited partnerships are the preferred vehicle.

- Attractiveness: EMN strategies typically take advantage of idiosyncratic short-term mispricing between securities whose prices should otherwise be co-integrated. Their sources of return and alpha, unlike those of many other strategies, do not require accepting beta risk. So, EMN strategies are especially attractive during periods of market vulnerability and weakness.

Leverage Usage

- High: As many beta risks (e.g., market, sector) are hedged away, it is generally deemed acceptable for EMN managers to apply higher levels of leverage while striving for meaningful return targets.

Benchmarking

- Market-neutral indexes include HFRX and HFRI Equity Market Neutral Indices; Lipper TASS Equity Market Neutral Index; Morningstar/CISDM Equity Market Neutral Index; and Credit Suisse Equity Market Neutral Index.

3.3.2. Strategy Implementation

Equity market-neutral portfolios are constructed in four main steps. First, the investment universe is evaluated to include only tradable securities with sufficient liquidity and adequate short-selling potential. Second, securities are analyzed for buy and sell opportunities using fundamental models (which use company, industry, and economic data as inputs for valuation) and/or statistical and momentum-based models. Third, a portfolio is constructed with constraints to maintain market risk neutrality, whereby the portfolio's market value-weighted beta is approximately zero and there is often dollar (i.e., money), sector, or other factor risk neutrality. Fourth, the availability and cost of leverage are considered in terms of desired return profile and acceptable potential portfolio drawdown risk. The execution costs of the strategy rebalancing are also introduced as a filter for decision-making as to how often the portfolio should be rebalanced. Markets are dynamic because volatility and leverage are always changing; therefore, the exposure to the market is always changing. Consequently, EMN managers must actively manage their funds' exposures to remain neutral over time. However, costs are incurred every time the portfolio is rebalanced. So, EMN managers must be very careful to not allow such costs to overwhelm the security-selection alpha that they are attempting to capture.

Note that the following is a simplified example. In reality, most EMN managers would likely not hedge beta on a stock-by-stock basis but rather would hedge beta on an overall portfolio basis. They would also likely consider other security factor attributes.

EXAMPLE 3   Equity Market-Neutral Pairs Trading:

Ling Chang, a Hong Kong-based EMN manager, has been monitoring PepsiCo Inc. (PEP) and Coca-Cola Co. (KO), two global beverage industry giants. After examining the Asia marketing strategy for a new PEP drink, Chang feels the marketing campaign is too controversial and the overall market is too narrow. Although PEP has relatively weak earnings prospects compared to KO, 3-month valuation metrics show PEP shares are substantially overvalued versus KO shares (relative valuations have moved beyond their historical ranges). As part of a larger portfolio, Chang wants to allocate $1 million to the PEP versus KO trade and notes the historical betas and S&P 500 Index weights, as shown in the following table.

Stock	Beta	S&P 500 Index Weight
PEP	0.65	0.663
KO	0.55	0.718

Discuss how Chang might implement an EMN pairs trading strategy.

Solution: Chang should take a short position in PEP and a long position in KO with equal beta-weighted exposures. Given Chang wants to allocate $1 million to the trade, she would take on a long KO position of $1 million. Assuming realized betas will be similar to historical betas, to achieve an equal beta-weighted exposure for the short PEP position, Chang needs to short $846,154 worth of PEP shares [= –$1,000,000 / (0.65/0.55)]. Only the overall difference in performance between PEP and KO shares would affect the performance of the strategy because it will be insulated from the effect of market fluctuations. If over the next 3 months the valuations of PEP and KO revert to within normal ranges, then this pairs trading EMN strategy should reap profits.

Note: The S&P 500 Index weights are not needed to answer this question.

4. EVENT-DRIVEN STRATEGIES

Event-driven (ED) hedge fund strategies take positions in corporate securities and derivatives that are attempting to profit from the outcome of mergers and acquisitions, bankruptcies, share issuances, buybacks, capital restructurings, re-organizations, accounting changes, and similar events. ED hedge fund managers analyze companies' financial statements and regulatory filings and closely examine corporate governance issues (e.g., management structure, board composition, issues for shareholder consideration, proxy voting) as well as firms' strategic objectives, competitive position, and other firm-specific issues. Investments can be made either proactively in anticipation of an event that has yet to occur (i.e., a **soft-catalyst event-driven approach**), or investments can be made in reaction to an already announced corporate event in which security prices related to the event have yet to fully converge (i.e., a **hard-catalyst event-driven approach**). The hard approach is generally less volatile and less risky than soft-catalyst investing. Merger arbitrage and distressed securities are among the most common ED strategies.

4.1. Merger Arbitrage

Mergers and acquisitions can be classified by the method of purchase: cash-for-stock or stock-for-stock. In a cash-for-stock acquisition, the acquiring company (A) offers the target company (T) a cash price per share to acquire T. For example, assume T's share price is $30 and A decides to purchase T for $40 per share (i.e., A is offering a 33% premium to purchase T's shares). In a stock-for-stock acquisition, A offers a specific number of its shares in exchange for 1 T share. So, if A's share price is $20 and it offers 2 of its shares in exchange for 1 T share, then T's shareholders would receive a value of $40 per T share, assuming A's share price is constant until the merger is completed. Although merger deals are structured in different ways for many reasons (e.g., tax implications, corporate structure, or provisions to dissuade a merger, such as a "poison pill"[1]), acquiring companies are generally more likely to offer cash for their target companies when cash surpluses are high. However, if the stock prices are high and acquiring companies' shares are considered richly valued by management, then stock-for-stock acquisitions can take advantage of potentially overvalued shares as a "currency" to acquire target companies.

4.1.1. Investment Characteristics

In a cash-for-stock acquisition, the merger-arb manager may choose to buy just the target company (T), expecting it to increase in value once the acquisition is completed. In a stock-for-stock deal, the fund manager typically buys T and sells the acquiring company (A) in the same ratio as the offer, hoping to earn the spread on successful deal completion. If the acquisition is unsuccessful, the manager faces losses if the price of T (A) has already risen (fallen) in anticipation of the acquisition. Less often, managers take the view that the acquisition will fail—usually due to anti-competition or other regulatory concerns. In this case, he/she would sell T and buy A.

For most acquisitions, the initial announcement of a deal will cause the target company's stock price to rise toward the acquisition price and the acquirer's stock price to fall (either because of the potential dilution of its outstanding shares or the use of cash for purposes other than a dividend payment). The considerable lag time between deal announcement and closing means that proposed merger deals can always fail for any variety of reasons, including lack of financing, regulatory hurdles, and not passing financial due diligence. Hostile takeover bids, where the target company's management has not already agreed to the terms of a merger, are typically less likely to be successfully completed than friendly takeovers, where the target's management has already agreed to merger terms.

Approximately 70%–90% of announced mergers in the United States eventually close successfully. Given the probability that some mergers will not close for whatever reason as well as the costs of establishing a merger arbitrage position (e.g., borrowing the acquiring stock, commissions) and the risk that merger terms might be changed because of market conditions (especially in stressed market environments), merger arbitrage typically offers a 3%–7% return spread depending on the deal-specific risks. Of course, a particularly risky deal might carry an even larger spread. If the average time for merger deal completion is 3-4 months—with managers recycling capital into new deals several times a year and typically applying some leverage to their portfolio positions—then attractive return/risk profiles can be

---

[1]A poison pill is a pre-offer takeover defense mechanism that gives target company bondholders the right to sell their bonds back to the target at a pre-specified redemption price, typically at or above par; this defense increases the acquirer's need for cash and raises the cost of the acquisition.

created, earning net annualized returns in the range of 7%–12%, with little correlation to non-deal-specific factors. Diversifying across a variety of mergers, deals, and industries can further help hedge the risk of any one deal failing. So overall, this strategy can be a good uncorrelated source of alpha.

When merger deals do fail, the initial price rise (fall) of the target (acquirer) company is typically reversed. Arbitrageurs who jumped into the merger situation after its initial announcement stand to incur substantial losses on their long (short) position in the target (acquirer)—often as large as negative 20% to 40%. So, the strategy thus does have left-tail risk associated with it.

Corporate events are typically binary: An acquisition either succeeds or fails. The merger arbitrage strategy can be viewed as selling insurance on the acquisition. If the acquisition succeeds (no adverse event occurs), then the hedge fund manager collects the spread (like the premium an insurance company receives for selling insurance) for taking on event risk. If the acquisition fails (an adverse event occurs), then he/she faces the losses on the long and short positions (similar to an insurance company paying out a policy benefit after an insured event has occurred). Thus, the payoff profile of the merger arbitrage strategy resembles that of a riskless bond and a short put option. The merger arbitrage investor also can be viewed as owning an additional call option that becomes valuable if/when another interested acquirer (i.e., White Knight) makes a higher bid for the target company before the initial merger proposal is completed. Exhibit 5 shows risk and return attributes of merger arbitrage investing.

EXHIBIT 5   Event-Driven Merger Arbitrage—Risk, Liquidity, Leverage, and Benchmarking

Risk Profile and Liquidity

- Merger arbitrage is a relatively liquid strategy—with defined gains from idiosyncratic single security takeover situations but occasional downside shocks when merger deals unexpectedly fail.
- To the extent that deals are more likely to fail in market stress periods, this strategy has market sensitivity and left-tail risk attributes. Its return profile is insurance-like plus a short put option.
- Because cross-border merger and acquisition (M&A) usually involves two sets of governmental approvals and M&A deals involving vertical integration often face anti-trust scrutiny, these situations carry higher risks and offer wider merger spread returns.
- Some merger arbitrage managers invest only in friendly deals trading at relatively tight spreads, while others embrace riskier hostile takeovers trading at wider spreads. In the latter case, there may be expectations of a higher bid from a White Knight.
- The preferred vehicle is limited partnership because of merger arbitrage's use of significant leverage, but some low-leverage, low-volatility liquid alts merger arbitrage funds do exist.
- Attractiveness: Relatively high Sharpe ratios with typically low double-digit returns and mid–single digit standard deviation (depending on specific levels of leverage applied), but left-tail risk is associated with an otherwise steady return profile.

> ### *Leverage Usage*
>
> - Moderate to high: Managers typically apply 3 to 5 times leverage to this strategy to generate meaningful target return levels.
>
> ### *Benchmarking*
>
> - Sub-indexes include HFRX or HFRI Merger Arbitrage Index; CISDM Hedge Fund Merger Arbitrage Index; and Credit Suisse Merger Arbitrage Index.

4.1.2. Strategy Implementation

Merger arbitrage strategies are typically established using common equities; however, a range of other corporate securities, including preferred stock, senior and junior debt, convertible securities, options, and other derivatives, may also be used for positioning and hedging purposes. Often for a cash-for-stock acquisition, a hedge fund manager may choose to use leverage to buy the target firm. For a stock-for-stock acquisition, leverage may also often be used, but short selling the acquiring firm may be difficult due to liquidity issues or short-selling constraints, especially in emerging markets. Merger arbitrage strategies can utilize derivatives to overcome some short-sale constraints or to manage risks if the deal were to fail. For example, the manager could buy out-of-the money (O-T-M) puts on T and/or buy O-T-M call options on A (to cover the short position).

Convertible securities also provide exposure with asymmetrical payoffs. For example, the convertible bonds of T would also rise in value as T's shares rise because of the acquisition; the convertibles' bond value would provide a cushion if the deal fails and T's shares fall. When the acquiring company's credit is superior to the target company's credit, trades may be implemented using credit default swaps (CDS). In this case, protection would be sold (i.e., shorting the CDS) on the target company to benefit from its improved credit quality (and decline in price of protection and the CDS) once a merger is completed. If the pricing is sufficiently cheap, buying protection (i.e., going long the CDS) on the target may also be used as a partial hedge against a merger deal failing. Overall market risk (that could potentially disrupt a merger's consummation) might also be hedged by using added short equity index ETFs/futures or long equity index put positions.

In sum, the true source of return alpha for a merger arbitrage hedge fund manager is in the initial decision as to which deals to embrace and which to avoid. However, once involved with a given merger situation, there may be multiple ways to implement a position depending on the manager's deal-specific perspectives.

EXAMPLE 4   Merger Arbitrage Strategy Payoffs

An acquiring firm (A) is trading at $45/share and has offered to buy target firm (T) in a stock-for-stock deal. The offer ratio is 1 share of A in exchange for 2 shares of T. Target firm T was trading at $15 per share just prior to the announcement of the offer. Shortly thereafter, T's share price jumps up to $19 while A's share price falls to $42 in anticipation of the merger receiving required approvals and the deal closing successfully.

A hedge fund manager is confident this deal will be completed, so he buys 20,000 shares of T and sells short 10,000 shares of A.

What are the payoffs of the merger arbitrage strategy if the deal is successfully completed or if the merger fails?

Solution: At current prices it costs $380,000 to buy 20,000 shares of T, and $420,000 would be received for short selling 10,000 shares of A. This provides a net spread of $40,000 to the hedge fund manager if the merger is successfully completed. If the merger fails, then prices should revert to their pre-merger announcement levels. The manager would need to buy back 10,000 shares of A at $45 (costing $450,000) to close the short position, while the long position in 20,000 shares of T would fall to $15 per share (value at $300,000). This would cause a total loss of $110,000 [= (A: +$420,000 − $450,000) + (T: −$380,000 + $300,000)]. In sum, this merger strategy is equivalent to holding a riskless bond with a face value of $40,000 (the payoff for a successful deal) and a short binary put option, which expires worthless if the merger succeeds but pays out $110,000 if the merger fails.

4.2. Distressed Securities

Distressed securities strategies focus on firms that either are in bankruptcy, facing potential bankruptcy, or under financial stress. Firms face these circumstances for a wide variety of reasons, including waning competitiveness, excessive leverage, poor governance, accounting irregularities, or outright fraud. Often the securities of such companies have been sold out of long-only portfolios and may be trading at a significant discount to their eventual work-out value under proper stewardship and guidance. Because hedge funds are not constrained by institutional requirements on minimum credit quality, hedge fund managers are often natural candidates to take positions in such situations. Hedge funds, generally, also provide their investors only periodic liquidity (typically quarterly or sometimes only annually), making the illiquid nature of such securities less problematic than if such positions were held within a mutual fund. Hedge fund managers may find inefficiently priced securities before, during, or after the bankruptcy process, but typically they will be looking to realize their returns somewhat faster than the longer-term orientation of private equity firms. However, this is not always the case; for example, managers that invest in some distressed sovereign debt (e.g., Puerto Rico, Venezuela) often must face long time horizons to collect their payouts.

At times, distressed hedge fund managers may seek to own the majority or all of a certain class of securities within the capital structure, which enables them to exert creditor control in the corporate bankruptcy or reorganization process. Such securities will vary by country depending on individual bankruptcy laws and procedures. Some managers are active in their distressed investing by building concentrated positions and placing representatives on the boards of the companies they are seeking to turn around. Other distressed managers may be more "passive" in their orientation, relying on others to bear the often substantial legal costs of a corporate capital structure reorganization that may at times involve expensive proxy contests.

By nature, distressed debt and other illiquid assets may take several years to resolve, and they are generally difficult to value. Therefore, hedge fund managers running portfolios of distressed securities typically require relatively long initial lock-up periods (e.g., no redemptions allowed for the first two years) from their investors. Distressed investment managers may also impose fund-level or investor-level redemption gates that are meant to limit the amount of money that investors (i.e., limited partners) may withdraw from a partnership during any given quarter. As for valuing distressed securities, external valuation specialists may be needed to provide an independent estimate of fair value. Valuations of distressed securities with little or no liquidity (e.g., those deemed Level 3 assets for US accounting purposes) are subject to the smoothing effect of "mark-to-model" price determination.

The bankruptcy process typically results in one or two outcomes: liquidation or firm re-organization. In a liquidation, the firm's assets are sold off over some time period; then, based on the priority of their claim, debt- and equity-holders are paid off sequentially. In this case, claimants on the firm's assets are paid in order of priority from senior secured debt, junior secured debt, unsecured debt, convertible debt, preferred stock, and finally common stock. In a re-organization, a firm's capital structure is re-organized and the terms for current claims are negotiated and revised. Current debtholders may agree to extend the maturity of their debt contracts or even to exchange their debt for new equity shares. In this case, existing equity would be canceled (so existing shareholders would be left with nothing) and new equity issued, which would also be sold to new investors to raise funds to improve the firm's financial condition.

4.2.1. Investment Characteristics

Distressed securities present new sets of risks and opportunities and thus require special skills and increased monitoring. As previously mentioned, many institutional investors, like banks and insurance companies, by their mandates cannot hold non-investment-grade securities in their portfolios. As a result, many such investors must sell off investments in firms facing financial distress. This situation may result in illiquidity and significant price discounting when trades do occur, but it also creates potentially attractive opportunities for hedge funds. Moreover, the movement from financial distress to bankruptcy can unfold over long periods and because of the complexities of legal proceedings, informational inefficiencies cause securities to be improperly valued.

To successfully invest in distressed securities, hedge fund managers require specific skills for analyzing complicated legal proceedings, bankruptcy processes, creditor committee discussions, and re-organization scenarios. They also must be able to anticipate market reactions to these actions. At times, and depending on relative pricing, managers may establish "capital structure arbitrage" positions: For the same distressed entity, they may be long securities where they expect to receive acceptable recoveries but short other securities (including equity) where the value-recovery prospects are dim.

Current market conditions also affect the success of distressed securities strategies. In liquidation, assets may need to be sold quickly, and discounted selling prices will lower the total recovery rate. When illiquid assets must be sold quickly, forced sales and liquidity spirals may lead to fire-sale prices. For re-organizations, current market conditions partly determine whether (and how much) a firm can raise capital from asset sales and/or from the issuance of new equity. Exhibit 6 provides some key attributes of distressed securities investing.

EXHIBIT 6   Distressed Securities—Risk, Liquidity, Leverage, and Benchmarking

Risk Profile and Liquidity

- The return profile for distressed securities investing is typically at the higher end of event-driven strategies but with more variability.
- Outright shorts or hedged positions are possible, but distressed securities investing is usually long-biased. It is subject to security-specific outcomes but still impacted by the health of the macro-economy.
- Distressed securities investing typically entails relatively high levels of illiquidity, especially if using a concentrated activist approach. Pricing may involve "mark-to-model" with return smoothing. Ultimate results are generally binary: either very good or very bad.
- Attractiveness: Returns tend to be "lumpy" and somewhat cyclical. Distressed investing is particularly attractive in the early stages of an economic recovery after a period of market dislocation.

Usage

- Moderate to low: Because of the inherent volatility and long-biased nature of distressed securities investing, hedge fund managers utilize modest levels of leverage, typically with 1.2 to 1.7 times NAV invested, and with some of the nominal leverage from derivatives hedging.

Benchmarking

- Hedge fund sub-indexes include HFRX and HFRI Distressed Indices; CISDM Distressed Securities Index; Lipper TASS Event-Driven Index; and Credit Suisse Event Driven Distressed Hedge Fund Index.

Note: Alpha produced by distressed securities managers tends to be idiosyncratic. Also, the strategy capitalizes on information inefficiencies and structural inabilities of traditional managers to hold such securities.

4.2.2. Strategy Implementation

Hedge fund managers take several approaches when investing in distressed securities. In a liquidation situation, the focus is on determining the recovery value for different classes of claimants. If the fund manager's estimate of recovery value is higher than market expectations, perhaps due to illiquidity issues, then he/she can buy the undervalued debt securities in hopes of realizing the higher recovery rate. For example, assume bankrupt company X's senior secured debt is priced at 50% of par. By conducting research on the quality of the collateral and by estimating potential cash flows (and their timing) in liquidation, the hedge fund manager estimates a recovery rate of 75%. He/she can buy the senior secured debt and expect to realize the positive difference in recovery rates. However, even assuming the manager is correct, if the liquidation process drags on and/or market conditions deteriorate, then this premium may be only partly realized, if at all.

In a reorganization situation, the hedge fund manager's focus is on how the firm's finances will be restructured and on assessing the value of the business enterprise and the future value of different classes of claims. There are various avenues for investing in a re-organization. The manager will evaluate the different securities of the company in question and purchase those deemed to be undervalued given the likely re-organization outcome. The selection of security will also depend on whether the manager seeks a control position or not. If so, he/she will be active in the negotiating process and will seek to identify fulcrum securities that provide leverage (or even liquidation) in the reorganization. **Fulcrum securities** are partially-in-the-money claims (not expected to be repaid in full) whose holders end up owning the reorganized company. Assuming the re-organization is caused by excessive financial leverage but the company's operating prospects are still good, a financial restructuring may be implemented whereby senior unsecured debt purchased by the hedge fund manager is swapped for new shares (existing debt and equity are canceled) and new equity investors inject fresh capital into the company. As financial distress passes and the intrinsic value of the reorganized company rises, an initial public offering (IPO) would likely be undertaken. The hedge fund manager could then exit and earn the difference between what was paid for the undervalued senior unsecured debt and the proceeds received from selling the new shares of the revitalized company in the IPO.

EXAMPLE 5   Capital Structure Arbitrage in the Energy Crisis of 2015–2016

With a sudden structural increase in US energy reserves caused by modern fracking techniques, oil prices tumbled dramatically from more than $60/barrel in mid-2015 to less than $30/barrel in early 2016. Debt investors suddenly became concerned about the very survivability of the smaller, highly levered exploration and production (E&P) companies if such low energy prices were to persist. Prices of many energy-related, junior, unsecured, non-investment-grade debt securities fell dramatically. However, retail equity investors generally reacted more benignly. As a result, the shares of several such E&P companies still carried significant implied enterprise value while their debt securities traded as if bankruptcy was imminent.

1. Discuss why such a divergence in the valuation of the debt and equity securities of these E&P companies might have occurred.
2. Discuss how a hedge fund manager specializing in distressed securities might take advantage of this situation.

Solution to 1: This divergence in valuation occurred because of structural differences between the natural holders of debt and equity securities. Institutional holders of the debt likely felt more compelled, or in some cases were required by investment policy, to sell these securities as credit ratings on these bonds were slashed. Retail equity investors were likely less informed as to the potential seriousness of the impact of such a sharp energy price decline on corporate survivability. With equity markets overall still moving broadly higher, retail equityholders may have been expressing a "buy the dip" mentality. Such cross-asset arbitrage situations represent a significant opportunity for nimble and flexible hedge fund managers that are unrestrained by a single asset class perspective or other institutional constraints.

Solution to 2: An astute hedge fund manager would have realized three key points: 1) the junior unsecured debt securities were temporarily undervalued; 2) although bankruptcy in certain specific companies was indeed possible (depending on how long energy prices stayed low), detailed research could uncover those E&P companies for which bankruptcy was less likely; and 3) the unsecured debt securities could be purchased with some safety by shorting the still overvalued equities (or buying put options on those equities) as a hedge.

If energy prices subsequently remained low for too long and bankruptcy was indeed encountered, the equities would become worthless. However, the unsecured debt might still have some recovery value from corporate asset sales, or these securities might become the fulcrum securities that would be converted in a bankruptcy reorganization into new equity in an ongoing enterprise. Alternatively, if oil prices were to recover (as indeed transpired; oil prices closed 2017 at more than $60/barrel), the unsecured debt securities of many of these companies would rebound far more substantially than their equity shares would rise.

In sum, a distressed securities hedge fund arbitrageur willing to take a position in the unsecured debt hedged against short equity (or long puts on the equity) could make money under a variety of possible outcomes.

5. RELATIVE VALUE STRATEGIES

We have previously described equity market-neutral investing as one specific equity-oriented relative value hedge fund approach, but other types of relative value strategies are common for hedge funds involving fixed-income securities and hybrid convertible debt. Like equity market-neutral trading, many of these strategies involve the significant use of leverage. Changes in credit quality, liquidity, and implied volatility (for securities with embedded options) are some of the causes of relative valuation differences. During normal market conditions, successful relative value strategies can earn credit, liquidity, or volatility premiums over time. But, in crisis periods—when excessive leverage, deteriorating credit quality, illiquidity, and volatility spikes come to the fore—relative value strategies can result in losses. Fixed-income arbitrage and convertible bond arbitrage are among the most common relative value strategies.

5.1. Fixed-Income Arbitrage

Fixed-income arbitrage strategies attempt to exploit pricing inefficiencies by taking long and short positions across a range of debt securities, including sovereign and corporate bonds, bank loans, and consumer debt (e.g., credit card loans, student loans, mortgage-backed securities). Arbitrage opportunities between fixed-income instruments may develop because of variations in duration, credit quality, liquidity, and optionality.

5.1.1. Investment Characteristics

In its simplest form, fixed-income arbitrage involves buying the relatively undervalued securities and short selling the relatively overvalued securities with the expectation that the mispricing will resolve itself (reversion back to normal valuations) within the specified investment horizon. Valuation differences beyond normal historical ranges can result from differences in credit quality (investment-grade versus non-investment-grade securities), differences in liquidity (on-the-run versus off-the-run securities), differences in volatility expectations (especially for securities with embedded options), and even differences in issue sizes. More generally, fixed-income arbitrage can be characterized as exploiting price differences relative to expected future price relationships, with mean reversion being one important aspect. In many instances, realizing a net positive relative carry over time may also be the goal of the relative security positioning, which may involve exploiting kinks in a yield curve or an expected shift in the shape of a yield curve.

Where positioning may involve the acceptance of certain relative credit risks across different security issuers, fixed-income arbitrage morphs into what is more broadly referred to as L/S credit trading. This version of trading tends to be naturally more volatile than the exploitation of small pricing differences within sovereign debt alone.

Unless trading a price discrepancy directly involves establishing a desired yield curve exposure, fixed-income arbitrageurs will typically immunize their strategies, which involve both long and short positions, from interest rate risk by taking duration-neutral positions. However, duration neutrality provides a hedge against only small shifts in the yield curve. To hedge against large yield changes and/or non-parallel yield curve movements (i.e., steepening or flattening), the manager might employ a range of fixed-income derivatives, including futures, forwards, swaps, and swaptions (i.e., options on a swap). Moreover, fixed-income securities also vary in their complexity. For example, in addition to interest rate risk, straight government debt is exposed to sovereign risk (and potentially currency risk), which can be substantial in many countries, while asset-backed and mortgaged-backed securities are subject to credit risk and pre-payment risk. Derivatives are also useful for hedging such risks.

Fixed-income security pricing inefficiencies are often quite small, especially in the more-efficient developed capital markets, but the correlation aspects across different securities is typically quite high. Consequently, it may be necessary and acceptable to utilize substantial amounts of leverage to exploit these inefficiencies. Typical leverage ratios in fixed-income arbitrage strategies can be 4 to 5 times (assets to equity). In the case of some market-neutral multi-strategy funds, where fixed-income arbitrage may form just a portion of total risk, fixed-income arbitrage leverage levels can sometimes be as high as 12 to 15 times assets to equity. Of course, leverage will magnify the myriad risks to which fixed-income strategies are exposed, especially during stressed market conditions.

Another factor that has compounded the risks of fixed-income arbitrage strategies has been the inclination of financial engineers to create tranched, structured products around certain fixed-income cash flows—particularly involving residential mortgages—to isolate certain aspects of credit risk and prepayment risk. For example, within a pool of mortgages, cash flows may be divided such that some credit tranche holders have seniority over others or so that interest-only income payments flow to one set of holders and principal-only payoffs flow to another set of holders. The risks of relative value strategies involving mortgage-related securities, which are especially relevant during periods of market stress, include negative convexity aspects of many mortgage-backed securities and some of the structured products built around them; underlying default rates potentially exceeding expectations and resulting in a high-volatility environment; balance sheet leverage of hedge funds; and hedge fund investor redemption pressures.

Globally, fixed-income markets are substantially larger in total issuance size and scale than equity markets and come in a myriad of different securities types. Away from on-the-run government securities and other sovereign-backed debt securities, which in most developed financial markets are generally very liquid, the liquidity aspects of many fixed-income securities are typically poor. This creates relative value arbitrage opportunities for hedge fund managers, but it also entails positioning and liquidity risks in portfolio management. Natural price opaqueness must often be overcome—particularly for "off-the-run" securities that may trade only occasionally. Liquidity in certain municipal bond markets and corporate debt markets, for example, can be particularly thin. Some key points of fixed-income arbitrage appear in Exhibit 7.

EXHIBIT 7   Fixed-Income Arbitrage—Risk, Liquidity, Leverage, and Benchmarking

Risk Profile and Liquidity

- The risk/return profile of fixed-income arbitrage trading derives from the high correlations found across different securities, the yield spread pick-up to be captured, and the sheer number of different types of debt securities across different markets with different credit quality and convexity aspects in their pricing. Structured products built around debt securities introduce added complexity that may result in mispricing opportunities.
- Yield curve and carry trades within the US government universe tend to be very liquid but typically have the fewest mispricing opportunities. Liquidity for relative value positions generally decreases in other sovereign markets, mortgage-related markets, and especially across corporate debt markets.
- Attractiveness: A function of correlations between different securities, the yield spread available, and the high number and wide diversity of debt securities across different markets.

Leverage Usage

- High: This strategy has high leverage usage, but leverage availability typically diminishes with product complexity. To achieve the desired leverage, prime brokers offer collateralized repurchase agreements with associated leverage "haircuts" depending on the types of securities being traded. The haircut is the prime broker's cushion against market volatility and illiquidity if posted collateral ever needs to be liquidated.

Benchmarking

- This is a broad category that encompasses the following sub-indexes: HFRX and HFRI Fixed Income Relative Value Indices; Lipper TASS Fixed Income Arbitrage Index; CISDM Debt Arbitrage Index; and Credit Suisse Fixed Income Arbitrage Index.

Note: HFRX and HFRI also offer more granular hedge fund fixed-income, relative value indexes related to sovereign bonds trading, credit trading, and asset-backed trading.

5.1.2. Strategy Implementation

The most common types of fixed-income arbitrage strategies include yield curve trades and carry trades. Considering yield curve trades, the prevalent calendar spread strategy involves taking long and short positions at different points on the yield curve where the relative mispricing of securities offers the best opportunities, such as in a curve flattening or steepening, to profit. Perceptions and forecasts of macroeconomic conditions are the backdrop for these types of trades. The positions can be in fixed-income securities of the same issuer; in that case, most credit and liquidity risks would likely be hedged, making interest rate risk the main concern. Alternatively, longs and shorts can be taken in the securities of different issuers—but typically ones operating in the same industry or sector. In this case, differences in credit quality, liquidity, volatility, and issue-specific characteristics would likely drive the relative mispricing. In either case, the hedge fund manager aims to profit as the mispricing reverses (mean reversion occurs) and the longs rise and shorts fall in value within the targeted time frame.

Carry trades involve going long a higher yielding security and shorting a lower yielding security with the expectation of receiving the positive carry and of profiting on long and short sides of the trade when the temporary relative mispricing reverts to normal. A classic example of a fixed-income arbitrage trade involves buying lower liquidity, off-the-run government securities and selling higher liquidity, duration matched, on-the-run government securities. Interest rate and credit risks are hedged because long and short positions have the same duration and credit exposure. So, the key concern is liquidity risk. Under normal conditions, as time passes the more (less) expensive on- (off-) the-run securities will decrease (increase) in price as the current on-the-runs are replaced by a more liquid issue of new on-the-run bonds that then become off-the-run bonds.

The payoff profile of this fixed-income arbitrage strategy resembles a short put option. If the strategy unfolds as expected, it returns a positive carry plus a profit from spread narrowing. But, if the spread unexpectedly widens, then the payoff becomes negative. Mispricing of government securities is generally small, so substantial leverage would typically be used to magnify potential profits. But, with highly levered positions, even a temporary negative price shock can be sufficient to set off a wave of margin calls that force fund managers to sell at significant losses. Such a scenario in the wake of the 1997 Asian Financial Crisis and the 1998 Russian Ruble Crisis led to the collapse and subsequent US Federal Reserve-supervised bailout of legendary hedge fund Long-Term Capital Management. It is important to note that there are far more complex relative value fixed-income strategies beyond just yield curve trades, carry trades, or relative credit trades.

EXAMPLE 6 Fixed-Income Arbitrage: Treasuries vs. Inflation Swap + TIPS

Guernsey Shore Hedge Fund closely monitors government bond markets and looks for valuation discrepancies among the different issues.

Portfolio manager Nick Landers knows that Treasury Inflation-Protected Securities (TIPS) pay a coupon (i.e., real yield) while accruing inflation into the principal, which is paid at maturity. This insulates the TIPS owner from inflation risk.

Landers also understands that because the US government issues both TIPS and Treasuries that have the same maturity, they should trade at similar yields after adjusting for inflation. Landers knows that by using OTC inflation swaps, the inflation-linked components of TIPS can be locked in, thereby fixing all payments to be similar to those of a Treasury bond.

After accounting for expected inflation in normal periods, global investors often prefer Treasuries to inflation-indexed bonds. This may be because market participants do not fully trust the way inflation may be measured over time. As such, inflation-hedged TIPS (as a package with the associated offsetting inflation swap) have typically yielded about 25 bps to 35 bps more than similar maturity Treasuries.

During a period of extreme market distress, in November 2XXX, Landers keenly observed that TIPS were particularly mispriced. Their yields, adjusted for inflation, were substantially higher than straight Treasuries, while inflation swaps were priced as if outright deflation was imminent. Landers notes the information on the relative pricing of these different products and considers whether to implement the follow trade:

November 2XXX	Fixed Rate	Inflation Rate	Cost
Buy 5-year TIPS	Receive 3.74%	Receive inflation	−1,000,000
Short 5-year Treasuries	Pay 2.56%	—	+1,000,000
Inflation swap: receive fixed rate and pay inflation index	Receive 1.36%	Pay inflation	0
Net of three trades	Receive 2.54%	—	0

Discuss whether Landers has uncovered a risk-free arbitrage, and if so, discuss some of the risks he may still face with its execution.

Solution: The situation observed by Landers occurred during a period of extreme market stress. In such turbulent times, instances of very attractive, near risk-free arbitrage can occur, as in this case. Often these periods are characterized by a fear of deflation, so straight Treasury bonds are in high demand for flight-to-quality reasons. But there would be some operational hurdles to overcome. For Landers to short the expensive Treasuries and buy the more attractive TIPS, Guernsey Shore would need access as a counterparty to the interbank repurchase market to borrow the Treasury bonds. Bank credit approval [via an International Swaps and Derivatives Association (ISDA) relationship] would also be required for accessing the inflation swap market for yield enhancement and to lock in the inflation hedge. Unfortunately, during periods of extreme market distress, credit lines to hedge funds typically shrink (or are withdrawn), not expand. Moreover, there is potential for "losing the borrow" on the short Treasuries (i.e., the lender demanding return of his/her Treasuries), which makes the trade potentially difficult to maintain. Assuming Guernsey Shore met these operational requirements, Landers would need to act quickly to capture the fixed-income arbitrage profit of 2.54%. Such extreme levels of arbitrage rarely persist for very long.

5.2. Convertible Bond Arbitrage

Convertible bonds are hybrid securities that can be viewed as a combination of straight debt plus a long equity call option with an exercise price equal to the strike price times the conversion ratio (also known as conversion value). The conversion ratio is the number of shares for which the bond can be exchanged. The bond's current conversion price is the current stock price times the conversion ratio. If the bond's current conversion price is significantly below the conversion value, the call is out-of-the-money and the convertible bond will behave more like a straight bond. Conversely, if the conversion price is significantly above the conversion value, the call is in-the-money and the convertible bond will behave more like the underlying equity.

5.2.1. Investment Characteristics

Convertible securities are naturally complex and thus generally not well understood. They are impacted by numerous factors, including overall interest rate levels, corporate credit spreads, bond coupon and principal cash flows, and the value of the embedded stock option (which itself is influenced by dividend payments, stock price movements, and equity volatility). Convertibles are often issued sporadically by companies in relatively small sizes compared to straight debt issuances, and thus they are typically thinly-traded securities. Moreover, most convertibles are non-rated and typically have fewer covenants than straight bonds. Because the equity option value is embedded within such thinly-traded, complex securities, the embedded options within convertibles tend to trade at relatively low implied volatility levels compared to the historical volatility level of the underlying equity. Convertibles also trade cyclically relative to the amount of new issuance of such securities in the overall market. The higher the new convertible issuance that the market must absorb, the cheaper their pricing and the more attractive the arbitrage opportunities for a hedge fund manager.

The key problem for the convertible arbitrage manager is that to access and extract the relatively cheap embedded optionality of the convertible, he/she must accept or hedge away other risks that are embedded in the convertible security. These include interest rate risk, credit risk of the corporate issuer, and market risk (i.e., the risk that the stock price will decline and thus render the embedded call option less valuable). Should the convertible manager desire, all these risks can be hedged using a combination of interest rate derivatives, credit default swaps, and short sales of an appropriate delta-adjusted amount of the underlying stock. The purchase of put options can also be a stock-sale substitute. The use of any such hedging tools may also erode the very attractiveness of the targeted convertible holding.

Convertible managers who are more willing to accept credit risk may choose to not hedge the credit default risk of the corporate issuer; instead, they will take on the convertible position more from a credit risk perspective. Such managers are known as credit-oriented convertible managers. Other managers may hedge the credit risk but will take a more long-biased, directional view of the underlying stock and then underhedge the convertible's equity exposure. Yet other managers may overhedge the equity risk to create a bearish tilt with respect to the underlying stock, thus providing a more focused exposure to increased volatility. These managers are referred to as volatility-oriented convertible managers. In sum, several different ways and styles can be utilized to set up convertible arbitrage exposures. Exhibit 8 presents some key aspects of convertible bond arbitrage.

EXHIBIT 8   Convertible Bond Arbitrage—Risk, Liquidity, Leverage, and Benchmarking

Risk Profile and Liquidity

- Convertible arbitrage managers strive to extract and benefit from this structurally cheap source of implied volatility by delta hedging and gamma trading short equity hedges against their long convertible holdings.
- Liquidity issues surface for convertible arbitrage strategies in two ways: 1) naturally less-liquid securities because of their relatively small issue sizes and inherent complexities; 2) availability and cost to borrow underlying equity for short selling.
- Attractiveness: Convertible arbitrage works best during periods of high convertible issuance, moderate volatility, and reasonable market liquidity. It fares less well in periods of acute credit weakness and general illiquidity, when the pricing of convertible securities is unduly impacted by supply/demand imbalances.

Leverage Usage

- High: Because of many legs needed to implement convertible arbitrage trades (e.g., short sale, CDS transaction, interest rate hedge), relatively high levels of leverage are used to extract a modest ultimate gain from delta hedging. Managers typically run convertible portfolios at 300% long vs. 200% short, the lower short exposure being a function of the delta-adjusted equity exposure needed from short sales to balance the long convertible.

Benchmarking

- Sub-indexes include HFRX and HFRI FI-Convertible Arbitrage Indices; Lipper TASS Convertible Arbitrage Index; CISDM Convertible Arbitrage Index; and Credit Suisse Convertible Arbitrage Index.

Note: Convertible bond arbitrage is a core hedge fund strategy area that is run within many multi-strategy hedge funds together with L/S equity, merger arbitrage, and other event-driven distressed strategies.

5.2.2. Strategy Implementation

A classic convertible bond arbitrage strategy is to buy the relatively undervalued convertible bond and take a short position in the relatively overvalued underlying stock. The number of shares to sell short to achieve a delta neutral overall position is determined by the delta of the convertible bond. For convertible bonds with high bond conversion prices relative to the conversion value, the delta will be close to 1. For convertibles with low bond conversion prices relative to the conversion value, the delta will be closer to 0. The combination of a long convertible and short equity delta exposure would create a situation where for small changes in the equity price, the portfolio will remain essentially balanced. As the underlying stock price moves further, however, the delta hedge of the convertible will change because the convertible is an instrument with the natural positive convexity attributes of positive gamma.

Because stock gamma is always zero, the convertible arbitrage strategy will leave the convertible arbitrageur "synthetically" longer in total equity exposure as the underlying security price rises and synthetically less long as the equity price falls. This added gamma-driven exposure can then be hedged at favorable levels with appropriate sizing adjustments of the underlying short stock hedge—selling more stock at higher levels and buying more stock at lower levels. The convertible arbitrage strategy will be profitable given sufficiently large stock price swings and proper periodic rebalancing (assuming all else equal). If realized equity volatility exceeds the implied volatility of the convertible's embedded option (net of hedging costs), an overall gain is achieved by the arbitrageur.

Several circumstances can create concerns for a convertible arbitrage strategy. First, when short selling, shares must be located and borrowed; as a result, the stock owner may subsequently want his/her shares returned at a potentially inopportune time, such as during stock price run-ups or more generally when supply for the stock is low or demand for the stock is high. This situation, particularly a short squeeze, can lead to substantial losses and a suddenly unbalanced exposure if borrowing the underlying equity shares becomes too difficult or too costly for the arbitrageur (of course, initially locking in a "borrow" over a "term period" can help the arbitrageur avoid short squeezes, but this may be costly to execute). Second, credit issues may complicate valuation given that bonds have exposure to credit risk; so when credit spreads widen or narrow, there would be a mismatch in the values of the stock and convertible bond positions that the convertible manager may or may not have attempted to hedge away. Third, the strategy can lose money because of time decay of the convertible bond's embedded call option during periods of reduced realized equity volatility and/or from a general compression of market implied volatility levels.

Convertible arbitrage strategies have performed best when convertible issuance is high (implying a wider choice among convertible securities and generally cheaper prices), general market volatility levels are moderate, and the liquidity to trade and adjust positions is ample. On the other hand, extreme market volatility also typically implies heightened credit risks; given that convertibles are naturally less-liquid securities, convertible managers generally do not fare well during such periods. The fact that hedge funds have become the natural market makers for convertibles and they typically face significant redemption pressures from investors during crises implies further unattractive left-tail risk attributes to the strategy during periods of market stress.

EXAMPLE 7   Convertible Arbitrage Strategy

Cleopatra Partners is a Dubai-based hedge fund engaging in convertible bond arbitrage. Portfolio manager Shamsa Khan is considering a trade involving the euro-denominated convertible bonds and stock of QXR Corporation. She has assembled the following information:

QXR Convertible Bond		
Price (% of par)	120	—
Coupon (%)	5.0	—
Remaining maturity (years)	1.0	

QXR Convertible Bond

Conversion ratio	50	—
S&P Rating	BBB	—
QXR Inc.		**Industry Average**
Price (per share)	30	–
P/E (x)	30	20
P/BV (x)	2.25	1.5
P/CF (x)	15	10

- It costs 2 to borrow each QXR share (paid to the stock lender) to carry the short position for a year.
- The stock pays a 1 dividend.

1. Discuss (using only the information in the table) the basic trade setup that Khan should implement.
2. Demonstrate (without using the additional information) that potential profits earned are the same whether QXR's share price falls to 24, rises to 36, or remains flat at 30.
3. Discuss (using also the additional information) how the results of the trade will change.

Solution to 1: QXR's convertible bond price is 1,200 [= 1,000 × (120/100)], and its conversion ratio is 50; so, the conversion price is 24 (1,200/50). This compares with QXR's current share price of 30. QXR's share valuation metrics are all 50% higher than its industry's averages. It can be concluded that in relative terms, QXR's shares are overvalued and its convertible bonds are undervalued. Thus, Khan should buy the convertibles and short sell the shares.

Solution to 2: By implementing this trade and buying the bond at 1,200, exercising the bond's conversion option, and selling her shares at the current market price, Khan can lock in a profit of 6 per share under any of the scenarios mentioned, as shown in the following table:

	Profit on:		
QXR Share Price	**Long Stock via Convertible Bond**	**Short Stock**	**Total Profit**
24	0	6	6
36	12	–6	6
30	6	0	6

Solution to 3: The 2 per share borrowing costs and the 1 dividend payable to the lender together represent a 3 per share outflow that Khan must pay. But, the convertible bond pays a 5% coupon or 50, which equates to an inflow of 1 per share equivalent (50 coupon/50 shares per bond). Therefore, the total profit outcomes, as indicated in the table, would each be reduced by 2. In sum, Khan would realize a total profit of 4 per each QXR share.

6. OPPORTUNISTIC STRATEGIES

Opportunistic hedge fund strategies seek to profit from investment opportunities across a wide range of markets and securities using a variety of techniques. They invest primarily in asset classes, sectors, regions, and across macro themes and multi-asset relationships on a global basis (as opposed to focusing on the individual security level). So, broad themes, global relationships, market trends, and cycles affect their returns.

Although opportunistic hedge funds can sometimes be difficult to categorize and may use a variety of techniques, they can generally be divided by 1) the type of analysis and approach that drives the trading strategy (technical or fundamental), 2) how trading decisions are implemented (discretionary or systematic), and 3) the types of instruments and/markets in which they trade. Fundamental-based strategies use economic data as inputs and focus on fair valuation of securities, sectors, markets, and intra-market relationships. Technical analysis utilizes statistical methods to predict relative price movements based on past price trends.

Discretionary implementation relies on manager skills to interpret new information and make investment decisions, and it may be subject to such behavioral biases as overconfidence and loss aversion. Systematic implementation is rules-based and executed by computer algorithms with little or no human intervention; however, it may encounter difficulty coping with new, complex situations (not seen historically). As the absolute size of systematic trend-following funds has increased in significance, so too has the issue of negative execution slippage caused by the simultaneous reversal of multiple trend-following models that sometimes create a "herding effect." Such effects can temporarily overwhelm normal market liquidity and at times temporarily distort fundamental market pricing of assets (i.e., trend-following "overshoots" caused by momentum-signal triggers). We now discuss the two most common hedge fund stategies: global macro and managed futures.

6.1. Global Macro Strategies

Global macro strategies focus on global relationships across a wide range of asset classes and investment instruments, including derivative contracts (e.g., futures, forwards, swaps, and options) on commodities, currencies, precious and base metals, and fixed-income and equity indexes—as well as on sovereign debt securities, corporate bonds, and individual stocks. Given the wide range of possibilities to express a global macro view, these strategies tend to focus on certain themes (e.g., trading undervalued emerging market currencies versus overvalued US dollar using OTC currency swaps), regions (e.g., trading stock index futures on Italy's FTSE MIB versus Germany's DAX to capitalize on differences in eurozone equity valuations), or styles (e.g., systematic versus discretionary spread trading in energy futures).

Global macro managers typically hold views on the relative economic health and central bank policies of different countries, global yield curve relationships, trends in inflation and relative purchasing power parity, and capital trade flow aspects of different countries (typically expressed through relative currency or rate-curve positioning).

Global macro managers tend to be anticipatory and sometimes contrarian in setting their strategies. Some macro managers may try to extract carry gains or ride momentum waves, but most have a tendency to be early in their positioning and then benefit when some rationality eventually returns to relative market pricing. This can make an allocation to global macro strategies particularly useful when a sudden potential reversal in markets is feared. For example, many global macro managers sensed the developing sub-prime mortgage crisis in the United States as early as 2006. They took on long positions in credit default swaps (CDS) (i.e., they purchased protection) on mortgage bonds, on tranches of mortgage structured products, or simply on broader credit indexes that they deemed particularly vulnerable to weakening credit conditions. Although they had to wait until 2007–2008 for these CDS positions to pay off, some global macro managers performed spectacularly well as market conditions morphed into the global financial crisis. Including global macro managers with significant subprime mortgage-focused CDS positions within a larger portfolio turned out to be a very valuable allocation.

It is important to note that because global macro managers trade a wide variety of instruments and markets and typically do so by different methods, these managers are fairly heterogeneous as a group. Thus, global macro funds are not as consistently dependable as a source of short alpha when compared to pure systematic, trend-following managed futures funds that typically attempt to capture any significant market trend. But, as noted earlier, global macro managers tend to be more anticipatory (compared to managed futures managers), which can be a useful attribute.

6.1.1. Investment Characteristics

Global macro managers use fundamental and technical analysis to value markets, and they use discretionary and systematic modes of implementation. The view taken by global macro portfolio managers can be directional (e.g., buy bonds of banks expected to benefit from "normalization" of US interest rates) or thematic (e.g., buy the "winning" companies and short sell the "losing" companies from Brexit). Because of their heterogeneity, added due diligence and close attention to the current portfolio of a macro manager may be required by an allocator to correctly anticipate the factor risks that a given global macro manager will deliver.

Despite their heterogeneity, a common feature among most global macro managers is the use of leverage, often obtained through the use of derivatives, to magnify potential profits. A margin-to-equity ratio typically of 15% to 25% posted against futures or forward positions allows a manager to control face amounts of assets up to 6 to 7 times a fund's assets. The use of such embedded leverage naturally allows the global macro manager ease and flexibility in relative value and directional positioning.

Generally, the key source of returns in global macro strategies revolves around correctly discerning and capitalizing on trends in global markets. As such, mean-reverting low volatility markets are the natural bane of this strategy area. Conversely, steep equity market sell-offs, interest rate regime changes, currency devaluations, volatility spikes, and geopolitical shocks caused by such events as trade wars and terrorism are examples of global macro risks; however, they can also provide some of the opportunities that global macro managers often attempt to exploit. Of course, the exposures selected in any global macro strategy may not react to the global risks as expected because of either unforeseen contrary factors or global risks that simply do not materialize. Thus, macro managers tend to produce somewhat lumpier and uneven return streams than other hedge fund strategies, and generally higher levels of volatility are associated with their returns.

Notably, the prevalence of quantitative easing since the global financial crisis of 2007–2009 resulted in generally benign market conditions for most of the subsequent decade, which was an especially imperfect environment for global macro managers. Although equity and fixed-income markets generally trended higher during this period, overall volatility levels across these and many other markets, such as currencies and commodities, were relatively low. In some cases, central bankers intervened to curtail undesirable market outcomes, thereby preventing certain global macro trends from fully materializing. Because such intervention substantially moderates the trendiness and the volatility of markets, which are the lifeblood of global macro strategies, some hedge fund allocators began avoiding these strategies. This may be shortsighted, however, because such opportunistic strategies as global macro can be very useful over a full market cycle in terms of portfolio diversification and alpha generation.

6.1.2. Strategy Implementation

Global macro strategies are typically top-down and employ a range of macroeconomic and fundamental models to express a view regarding the direction or relative value of an asset or asset class. Positions may comprise a mix of individual securities, baskets of securities, index futures, foreign exchange futures/forwards, precious or base metals futures, agricultural futures, fixed-income products or futures, and derivatives or options on any of these. If the hedge fund manager is making a directional bet, then directional models will use fundamental data regarding a specific market or asset to determine if it is undervalued or overvalued relative to history and the expected macro trend. Conversely, if the manager's proclivity is toward relative value positioning, then that manager will consider which assets are under- or overvalued relative to each other given historical and expected macro conditions.

For example, if currencies of the major ASEAN block countries (i.e., Indonesia, Malaysia, Philippines, Singapore, and Thailand) are depreciating against the US dollar, a directional model might conclude that the shares of their key exporting companies are undervalued and thus should be purchased. However, further investigation might signal that the public bonds of these exporters are cheap relative to their shares, so the bonds should be bought and the shares sold short. This situation might occur in the likely scenario that the share prices react quickly to the currency depreciation and bond prices take longer to react to the trend.

Successful global macro trading requires the manager to have both a correct fundamental view of the selected market(s) and the proper methodology and timing to express tactical views. Managers who repeatedly implement a position too early/unwind one too late or who choose an inappropriate method for implementation will likely face redemptions from their investors. Given the natural leverage used in global macro strategies, managers may be tempted to carry many (possibly too many) positions simultaneously; however, the diversification benefits of doing so are typically less than those derived from more idiosyncratic long/short equity strategies. This is because of the nature of "risk-on" or "risk-off" market conditions (often caused by central bank policies) that impact a variety of asset classes in a correlated manner.

EXAMPLE 8   Global Macro Strategy

Consider the following (hypothetical) macroeconomic scenario: Emerging market (EM) countries have been growing rapidly (in fact, overheating) and accumulating both historically large government budget deficits and trade deficits as expanding populations demand more public services and foreign goods. EM central banks have been intervening to support their currencies for some time, and electoral support for candidates promoting exorbitant business taxes and vast social welfare schemes in many EM countries has risen dramatically. These trends are expected to continue.

Melvin Chu, portfolio manager at Bermuda-based Global Macro Advisers (GMA), has been considering how to position his global macro hedge fund. After meeting with a senior central banker of a leading EM country, GMA's research director informs Chu that it appears this central bank may run out of foreign exchange reserves soon and thus may be unable to continue its supportive currency intervention.

Discuss a global macro strategy Chu might implement to profit from these trends by using options.

Solution: Assuming this key EM country runs out of foreign currency reserves, then it is likely its currency will need to be devalued. This initial devaluation might reasonably be expected to trigger a wave of devaluations and economic and financial market turbulence in other EM countries in similar circumstances. So, Chu should consider trades based on anticipated EM currency depreciation (maybe even devaluation) as well as trades benefitting from rising interest rates, downward pressure on equities, and spikes in volatility in the EM space.

A reasonable way for Chu to proceed would be to buy put options. If his expectations fail to materialize, his losses would then be capped at the total of the premiums paid for the options. Chu should consider buying puts on the following: a variety of EM currencies, EM government bond futures, and EM equity market indexes. He should buy in-the-money puts to implement his high conviction trades and out-of-the money puts for trades where he has a lower degree of confidence. Moreover, to take advantage of a possible flight-to-safety, Chu should consider buying call options on developed market (DM) reserve currencies as well as call options on bond futures for highly-rated DM government issuers.

6.2. Managed Futures

Managed futures, which gained its first major academic backing in a classic paper by John Lintner in 1983, is a hedge fund strategy that focuses on investments using futures, options on futures, and sometimes forwards and swaps (primarily on stock and fixed-income indexes) and commodities and currencies. As futures markets have evolved over time and in different countries—gaining in size (i.e., open interest) and liquidity—some managers have also engaged in trading sector and industry index futures as well as more exotic contracts, such as futures on weather (e.g., temperature, rainfall) and derivatives contracts on carbon emissions.

6.2.1. Investment Characteristics

The uncorrelated nature of managed futures with stocks and bonds generally makes them a potentially attractive addition to traditional portfolios for improved risk-adjusted return profiles (i.e., improved efficient frontiers in a mean–variance framework). The value added from managed futures has typically been demonstrated during periods of market stress; for example, in 2007–2009 managers using this strategy benefited from short positions in equity futures and long positions in fixed-income futures at a time when equity indexes were falling and fixed-income indexes were rising. Put another way, managed futures demonstrated natural positive skewness that has been useful in balancing negatively-skewed strategies.

The return profile of managed futures tends to be very cyclical. Between 2011 and 2018, the trendiness (i.e., directionality) of foreign exchange and fixed-income markets deteriorated, volatility levels in many markets dissipated, and periods of acute market stress temporarily disappeared. Except for equity markets in some developed countries, many markets became range-bound or mean-reverting, which hurt managed futures performance. The diversification benefit of trend following strong equity markets is also (by definition) less diversifying to traditional portfolios than if such trends existed in other non-equity markets.

In a world where sovereign bonds have approached the zero-yield boundary, the correlation benefit of managed futures has also changed. The past practice of trend following the fixed-income markets as they get higher may likely not be as repeatable going forward. Assuming managed futures managers begin to trend follow fixed-income markets as they get lower (i.e., as developed market interest rates "normalize"), then positive returns may still be realized—although with a very different type of correlation behavior to equity markets (i.e., not as valuable). Also, given the upward sloping nature of most global yield curves, less natural fixed-income "carry" contribution may occur from trend following the fixed-income markets to the downside (i.e., higher interest rates and lower prices).

Managed futures strategies are typically characterized as highly liquid, active across a wide range of asset classes, and able to go long or short with relative ease. High liquidity results from futures markets being among the most actively traded markets in the world. For example, the E-mini S&P 500 futures contract on the Chicago Mercantile Exchange has 3 to 4 times the daily dollar volume of the SPDR S&P 500 ETF (SPY), the world's most actively traded equity index fund. Futures contracts also provide highly liquid exposures to a wide range of asset classes that can be traded across the globe 24 hours a day. Because futures contracts require relatively little collateral to take positions as a result of the exchanges' central clearinghouse management of margin and risk, it is easier to take long and short positions with higher leverage than traditional instruments.

For example, futures contracts require margin from 0.1% to 10% of notional value for both long and short positions, as compared to standard equity market margin levels in the United States of 50%. Thus, the capital efficiency of futures contracts makes it easier for managed futures managers to be dynamic in both their long and short exposures. A traditional long-only portfolio is levered by borrowing funds to purchase additional assets. Futures portfolios do not own assets; they acquire asset exposures based on the notional value of the futures contracts held. The majority (typically 85% to 90%) of capital in a managed futures account is invested in short-term government debt (or other highly liquid collateral acceptable to the futures clearing house). The remainder (10% to 15%) is used to collateralize long and short futures contracts.

6.2.2. Strategy Implementation

Highly liquid contracts allow managed futures funds the flexibility to incorporate a wide range of investment strategies. Most managed futures strategies involve some "pattern recognition" trigger that is either momentum/trend driven or based on a volatility signal. Managers trade these signals across different time horizons, often with short-term mean reversion filters imposed on top of their core longer-term models. For example, a manager might have traded using a long-term horizon model that suggested gold prices would trend lower; as a result, the manager established a short position in gold futures some time ago. A short-term moving average of gold prices crossing below a longer-term moving average could have triggered this view. But later, that manager might also trade using a second, shorter time horizon model, which suggests that the downside momentum in gold prices has temporarily subsided and a mean-reverting bounce is likely. The results of these two models would be weighted and combined into an adjusted net position, typically with the longer-term model weighted more heavily than the shorter-term filter.

Such fundamental factors as carry relationships or volatility factors are often added to the core momentum and breakout signal methodologies, and they can be particularly useful regarding position sizing. Many managed futures managers implement their portfolios' relative position sizing by assessing both the volatility of each underlying futures position as well as the correlation of their return behaviors against one another. Generally, the greater the volatility of an asset, the smaller its portfolio sizing; and the greater its correlation to other futures being positioned, the smaller its portfolio sizing. Being attentive to correlation aspects between different futures contracts would then become a second step of analysis for most managed futures traders as a portfolio sizing risk constraint.

Besides core position sizing and sizing adjustments for volatility and correlation, managed futures managers will have either a price target exit methodology, a momentum reversal exit methodology, a time-based exit methodology, a trailing stop-loss exit methodology, or some combination thereof. A key to successful managed futures strategies is to have a consistent approach and to avoid overfitting of a model when backtesting performance across different markets and time periods. The goal is to have a model that performs well in a future "out of sample" period. Of course, trading models have a natural tendency to degrade in effectiveness over time as more and more managers use similar signals and the market opportunity being exploited consequently diminishes. Managed futures traders are thus constantly searching for new and differentiated trading signals. In today's world, many new signals are increasingly being developed using nontraditional, unstructured data and other types of "big data" analysis.

Apart from this accelerating search for more unique nonprice signals, the most common type of managed futures approach is typically referred to as **time-series momentum** (TSM) trend following. Momentum trading strategies are driven by the past returns of the individual assets. Simply put, managers go long assets that are rising in price and go short assets that are falling in price. TSM strategies are traded on an absolute basis, meaning the manager can be net long or net short depending on the current price trend of an asset. Such TSM strategies work best when an asset's (or market's) own past returns are a good predictor of its future returns.

A second, less common approach is using **cross-sectional momentum** (CSM) strategies, which are implemented with a cross-section of assets (generally within an asset class) by going long those that are rising in price the most and by shorting those that are falling the most. Such CSM strategies generally result in holding a net zero or market-neutral position. CSM strategies work well when a market's out- or underperformance relative to other markets is a reliable predictor of its future performance. However, CSM may be constrained by limited futures contracts available for a cross section of assets at the asset class level.

Global macro strategies and managed futures strategies often involve trading the same subset of markets but in different ways. It is important to understand the respective attributes of these two strategies. Exhibit 9 provides such a comparison.

EXHIBIT 9   Managed Futures and Global Macro Strategies—Comparison of Risk, Liquidity, Leverage, and Benchmarking

Risk Profile and Liquidity

- Both global macro and managed futures strategies are highly liquid but with some crowding aspects and execution slippage in managed futures as AUM have grown rapidly. Being more heterogeneous in approaches used, global macro strategies face less significant execution crowding effects.
- Typically, managed futures managers tend to take a more systematic approach to implementation than global macro managers, who are generally more discretionary in their application of models and tools.
- Returns of managed futures strategies typically exhibit positive right-tail skewness in periods of market stress, which is very useful for portfolio diversification. Global macro strategies have delivered similar diversification in such stress periods but with more heterogeneous outcomes.
- Despite positive skewness, managed futures and global macro managers are somewhat cyclical and at the more volatile end of the spectrum of hedge fund strategies (with volatility positively related to the strategy's time horizon). In addition, macro managers can also be early and overly anticipatory in their positioning.

Leverage Usage

- High: High leverage is embedded in futures contracts. Notional amounts up to 6 to 7 times fund assets can be controlled with initial margin-to-equity of just 10%–20% (with individual futures margin levels being a function of the volatility of the underlying assets). Active use of options by many global macro managers adds natural elements of leverage and positive convexity.

Benchmarking

- Managed futures are best tracked by such sub-indexes as HFRX and HFRI Macro Systematic Indices; CISDM CTA Equal-Weighted Index; Lipper TASS Managed Futures Index; and Credit Suisse Managed Futures Index.
- Global macro strategies are best tracked by HFRX and HFRI Macro Discretionary Indices; CISDM Hedge Fund Global Macro Index; Lipper TASS Global Macro Index; and Credit Suisse Global Macro Index.

EXAMPLE 9   Cross-Sectional and Time-Series Momentum

An institutional investor is considering adding an allocation to a managed futures strategy that focuses on medium-term momentum trading involving precious metals. This investor is evaluating two different managed futures funds that both trade precious metals futures, including gold, silver, platinum, and palladium futures. Of the two funds being considered, one is run using a cross-sectional momentum (CSM) strategy, and the other is managed using a time-series momentum (TSM) strategy. Both funds use trailing 6-month returns for developing their buy/sell signals, and they both volatility-weight their futures positions to have equal impact on their overall portfolios.

Explain how the CSM and TSM strategies would work and compare their risk profiles.

Solution: For the CSM strategy, each day the manager will examine the returns for the four metals in question and then take a long position in the two metals futures with the best performance (i.e., the top 50%) in terms of trailing 6-month risk-adjusted returns and a short position in the two metals contracts with the worst performance (i.e., the bottom 50%) of returns. According to this strategy, the top (bottom) 50% will continue their relative value out- (under-) performance. Note that it is possible for metals contracts (or markets more generally) in the top (bottom) 50% to have negative (positive) absolute returns—for example, during bear (bull) markets. The CSM strategy is very much a relative momentum strategy, with the established positions acting as a quasi-hedge relative to each other in terms of total sector exposure. This CSM-run fund would likely deliver an overall return profile with somewhat less volatility than the TSM strategy.

For the TSM strategy, each day the manager will take a long position in the precious metals futures with positive trailing 6-month returns and sell short those metals contracts with negative trailing 6-month returns. According to this TSM strategy, the metals futures (or markets, more generally) with positive (negative) returns will continue to rise (fall) in absolute value, resulting in an expected profit on both long and short positions. However, by utilizing a TSM strategy, the fund might potentially end up with long positions in all four metals contracts or short positions in all these precious metals futures at the same time.

Consequently, the CSM strategy typically results in a net zero market exposure during normal periods, while the TSM strategy can be net long or net short depending on how many metal (or markets, generally) have positive and negative absolute returns. The return profile of the TSM managed fund is thus likely to be more volatile than that of the CSM managed fund and also far more sensitive to periods when the precious metals sector is experiencing strong trends (i.e., directionality).

7. SPECIALIST STRATEGIES

Specialist hedge fund strategies require highly specialized skill sets for trading in niche markets. Two such typical specialist strategies are volatility trading and reinsurance/life settlements.

7.1. Volatility Trading

Over the past several decades, volatility trading has become an asset class unto itself. Niche hedge fund managers specialize in trading relative volatility strategies globally across different geographies and asset classes. For example, given the plethora of structured product offerings in Asia with inexpensive embedded options that can be stripped out and resold (usually by investment banks), volatility pricing in Asia is often relatively cheap compared to the more expensive implied volatility of options traded in North American and European markets. In these latter markets, there is a proclivity to buy out-of-the-money options as a protective hedge (i.e., insurance). The goal of **relative value volatility arbitrage** strategies is to source and buy cheap volatility and sell more expensive volatility while netting out the time decay aspects normally associated with options portfolios. Depending on the instruments used (e.g., puts and calls or variance swaps), these strategies may also attempt to extract value from active gamma trading adjustments when markets move.

7.1.1. Investment Characteristics and Strategy Implementation

The easiest way to understand relative value volatility trading is through a few examples. Throughout the 1980s and 1990s, options on the Japanese yen consistently traded at lower volatility levels within Asian time zones than similar options were traded in London, New York, or Chicago (i.e., IMM futures market). Capturing the volatility spread between these options is a type of relative value volatility trading known as time-zone arbitrage—in this case of a single underlying fungible global asset, the Japanese yen. As a second arbitrage example, managers in today's markets may periodically source Nikkei 225 implied volatility in Asia at cheaper levels than S&P 500 implied volatility is being traded in New York, even though the Nikkei 225 typically has realized volatility higher than that of the S&P 500. This type of relative value volatility trading is known as cross-asset volatility trading, which may often involve idiosyncratic, macro-oriented risks.

Of course, another simpler type of volatility trading involves outright long volatility traders who may trade against consistent volatility sellers. Equity volatility is approximately 80% *negatively* correlated with equity market returns. Otherwise stated, volatility levels tend to go up when equity markets fall, with options pricing skew reflecting such a tendency. Clearly, this makes the long volatility strategy a useful potential diversifier for long equity investments, albeit at the cost to the option premium paid by the volatility buyer. Selling volatility provides a volatility risk premium or compensation for taking on the risk of providing insurance against crises for holders of equities and other securities.

In the United States, the most liquid volatility contracts are short-term VIX Index futures contracts, which track the 30-day implied volatility of S&P 500 Index options as traded on the Chicago Board Options Exchange (CBOE). Because volatility is non-constant but high levels of volatility are difficult to perpetuate over long periods of time (markets eventually calm down after sudden jump shifts), VIX futures are often prone to mean reversion. Given this fact and the fact that VIX futures prices typically slide down a positively sloped implied volatility curve as expiration approaches, many practitioners prefer trading simple exchange-traded options, over-the-counter (OTC) options, variance swaps, and volatility swaps. The general mean-reverting nature of volatility still impacts these products, but it does so in a less explicit fashion than with the futures.

Multiple paths can be taken to implement a volatility trading strategy. If a trader uses simple exchange-traded options, then the maturity of such options typically extends out to no more than approximately two years. In terms of expiry, the longer-dated options will have more absolute exposure to volatility levels (i.e., vega exposure) than shorter-dated options, but the shorter-dated options will exhibit more delta sensitivity to price changes (i.e., gamma exposure). Traders need to monitor the following: the term structure of volatility, which is typically upward sloping but can invert during periods of crisis; the volatility smile across different strike prices, whereby out-of-the-money options will typically trade at higher implied volatility levels than at-the-money options; and the volatility skew, whereby out-of-the-money puts may trade at higher volatility levels than out-of-the-money calls. Volatility traders strive to capture relative timing and strike pricing opportunities using various types of option spreads, such as bull and bear spreads, straddles, and calendar spreads.

To extract an outright long volatility view, options are purchased and delta hedging of the gamma exposure is required. How the embedded gamma of the long options position is managed is also important. For example, one could have a positive view of a volatility expansion but then fail to capture gains in a volatility spike during an adverse market move by poorly managing gamma exposure. Conversely, some managers may use options to extract a more intermediate-term, directional insurance protection-type view of both price and volatility and not engage in active delta hedging.

A second, similar path might be to implement the volatility trading strategy using OTC options. Then the tenor and strike prices of the options can be customized, and the tenor of expiry dates can be extended beyond what is available with exchange-traded options. However, by utilizing OTC options, the strategy is subject to counterparty credit risk as well as added illiquidity risk.

Migrating to the use of VIX Index futures (or options on VIX futures) can more explicitly express a pure volatility view without the need for constant delta hedging of an equity put or call for isolating the volatility exposure. However, as just mentioned, volatility pricing tends to be notoriously mean reverting. Also, an abundant supply of traders and investors typically are looking to sell volatility to capture the volatility premium and the volatility roll down payoff. Roll down refers to the fact that the term structure of volatility tends to be positively sloped, so the passage of time causes added option price decay. In other words, the theta of a long option position is always negative, and if shorter-dated options have a lower implied volatility, then the passage of time increases the rate of natural theta decay.

A fourth path for implementing a volatility trading strategy would be to purchase an OTC volatility swap or a variance swap from a creditworthy counterparty. A volatility swap is a forward contract on future realized price volatility. Similarly, a variance swap is a forward contract on future realized price variance, where variance is the square of volatility. In both cases, at inception of the trade the strike is typically chosen such that the fair value of the swap is zero. This strike is then referred to as fair volatility or fair variance, respectively. At expiry of the swaps, the receiver of the floating leg pays the difference between the realized volatility (or variance) and the agreed-on strike times some prespecified notional amount that is not initially exchanged. Both volatility and variance swaps provide "pure" exposure to volatility alone—unlike standardized options in which the volatility exposure depends on the price of the underlying asset and must be isolated and extracted via delta hedging. These swaps can thus be used to take a view on future realized volatility, to trade the spread between realized and implied volatility, or to hedge the volatility exposure of other positions. These OTC products also offer the advantage of longer-dated, tailored maturities and strikes.

A long volatility strategy utilizing OTC volatility or variance swaps, options, or swaptions requires finding undervalued instruments. This is accomplished by being in frequent contact with options dealers around the world in a variety of asset classes. Once implemented, positions are held until they are either exercised, sold during a volatility event, actively delta hedged (in the case of a long options position), or expire. A long volatility strategy is a convex strategy because the movement of volatility pricing is typically asymmetric and skewed to the right. Also, strike prices of options may be set such that the cost of the options is small, but their potential payoffs are often many multiples of the premiums paid for the options.

Long volatility strategies are potentially attractive but also come with key challenges and risks for implementation. Given that OTC options, as well as volatility and variance swaps, are not exchange-traded, they must be negotiated. These contracts are typically structured under ISDA documentation; they are subject to bilateral margin agreements (as negotiated within an ISDA Credit Support Annex document), but they still carry more counterparty risk and liquidity risk to both establish and liquidate than instruments traded on an exchange. Also, smaller hedge funds may not even be able to access ISDA-backed OTC derivatives with banking counterparts until surpassing a minimum AUM threshold, generally $100 million. Above all, although the purchase of volatility assets provides positively convex outcomes, it almost always involves some volatility curve roll down risk and premium expense. Key aspects of volatility trading are presented in Exhibit 10.

EXHIBIT 10   Volatility Trading Strategies—Risk, Liquidity, Leverage, and Benchmarking

Risk Profile and Liquidity

- Long volatility positioning exhibits positive convexity, which can be particularly useful for hedging purposes. On the short side, option premium sellers generally extract steadier returns in normal market environments.
- Relative value volatility trading may be a useful source of portfolio return alpha across different geographies and asset classes.
- Liquidity varies across the different instruments used for implementation. VIX Index futures and options are very liquid; exchange-traded index options are generally liquid, but with the longest tenors of about two years (with liquidity decreasing as tenor increases); OTC contracts can be customized with longer maturities but are less liquid and less fungible between different counterparties.

Leverage Usage

- The natural convexity of volatility instruments typically means that outsized gains may be earned at times with very little up-front risk. Although notional values appear nominally levered, the asymmetric nature of long optionality is an attractive aspect of this strategy.

Benchmarking

- Volatility trading is a niche strategy that is difficult to benchmark.
- CBOE Eurekahedge has the following indexes:
    Long (and Short) Volatility Index, composed of 11 managers with a generally long (short) volatility stance; Relative Value Volatility Index (composed of 35 managers); and Tail Risk Index (composed of 8 managers), designed to perform best during periods of market stress.

EXAMPLE 10   Long Volatility Strategy Payoff

Consider the following scenario: Economic growth has been good, equity markets have been rising, and interest rates have been low. However, consumer debt (e.g., subprime mortgages, credit card debt, personal loans) has been rising rapidly, surpassing historic levels. In mid-January, Serena Ortiz, a long volatility hedge fund manager, purchased a basket of long-dated (one-year), 10% out-of-the money put options on a major stock index for $100 per contract at an implied volatility level of 12%.

As of mid-April, consumer debt is still at seemingly dangerous levels and financial markets appear ripe for a major correction. However, the stock index has risen another 20% above its mid-January levels, and volatility is low. So, Ortiz's options are priced even more cheaply than before, at $50 per contract.

Now jump forward in time by another three months to mid-July, when a crisis—unexpected by many participants—has finally occurred. Volatility has spiked, and the stock index has fallen to 25% below its April level and 10% below its starting January level. Ortiz's put options are now trading at an implied volatility pricing of 30%.

1. Discuss the time, volatility, and price impact on Ortiz's long volatility exposure in put options as of mid-July.
2. Discuss what happens if the market subsequently moves broadly sideways between July and January of the next year.

Solution to 1: Despite an initial 50% mark-to-market loss on her put exposure as of mid-April, Ortiz likely has substantial unrealized profits by mid-July. As six months passed (other things being equal), Ortiz would have suffered some time decay loss in her long put position, but her options have also gone from being 10% out-of-the-money to now being at-the-money. Implied volatility has increased 2.5 times (from 12% to 30%), which on a six-month, at-the-money put will have a significant positive impact on the option's pricing (the closer an option is to being at-the-money, the greater the impact that changes in implied volatility will have on its price). So, as of mid-July, Ortiz will likely have a significant mark-to-market gain.

Solution to 2: If the market subsequently moves broadly sideways until January of the next year, Ortiz's at-the-money option premium will slowly erode because of time decay. Assuming the puts remain at-the-money, their volatility value will eventually dissipate; Ortiz will ultimately lose all of her original $100 investment per contract unless she has nimbly traded against the position with active delta hedging of the underlying stock index futures. This would entail buying and selling the index futures over time to capture small profitable movements to offset the time decay and volatility erosion in the puts.

7.2. Reinsurance/Life Settlements

Although still somewhat nascent, hedge funds have also entered the world of insurance, reinsurance, life settlements, and catastrophe reinsurance. Underlying insurance contracts provide a payout to the policyholder (or their beneficiaries) on the occurrence of a specific insured event in exchange for a stream of cash flows (periodic premiums) paid by the policyholder. Common types of insurance contracts sold by insurance providers include vehicle and home insurance, life insurance, and catastrophe insurance, which covers damage from such events as floods, hurricanes, or earthquakes. The insurance market encompasses a wide range of often highly specific and detailed contracts that are less standardized than other financial contracts. As a result, insurance contracts are generally not liquid and are difficult to sell or purchase after contract initiation.

Although the primary market for insurance has existed for centuries, the secondary market for insurance has grown substantially in the last several decades. Individuals who purchased whole or universal life policies and who no longer want or need the insurance can surrender their policies to the original insurance issuer. However, such policyholders are increasingly finding that higher cash values (i.e., significantly above surrender value) are being paid for their policies by third-party brokers, who, in turn, offer these policies as investments to hedge funds. Hedge funds may formulate a differentiated view of individual or group life expectancy; if correct, investment in such life policies can provide attractive uncorrelated returns.

Reinsurance of catastrophe risk has also increasingly attracted hedge fund capital. These new secondary markets have improved liquidity and enhanced the value of existing insurance contracts. For insurance companies, the reinsurance market allows for risk transfer, capital management, and solvency management. For hedge funds, the reinsurance market offers a source of uncorrelated return alpha.

7.2.1. Investment Characteristics and Strategy Implementation
Life insurance protects the policyholder's dependents in the case of his/her death. The secondary market for life insurance involves the sale of a life insurance contract to a third party—a **life settlement**. The valuation of a life settlement typically requires detailed biometric analysis of the individual policyholder and an understanding of actuarial analysis. So, a hedge fund manager specialized in investing in life settlements would require such expert knowledge and skills or would need to source such knowledge from a trusted partner/actuarial adviser.

A hedge fund strategy focusing on life settlements involves analyzing pools of life insurance contracts being offered for sale, typically being sold by a third-party broker who purchased the insurance contracts from the original policyholders. The hedge fund would look for the following policy characteristics: 1) the surrender value being offered to an insured individual is relatively low; 2) the ongoing premium payments to keep the policy active are also relatively low; and, yet, 3) the probability is relatively high that the designated insured person is indeed likely to die within a certain period of time (i.e., earlier than predicted by standard actuarial methods).

On finding the appropriate policy (or, more typically, a pool of policies), the hedge fund manager pays a lump sum (via a broker) to the policyholder(s), who transfers the right to the eventual policy benefit to the hedge fund. The hedge fund is then responsible for making ongoing premium payments on the policy in return for receiving the future death benefit. This strategy is successful when the present value of the future benefit payment received by the hedge fund exceeds the present value of intervening payments made by the hedge fund. The two key inputs in the hedge fund manager's analysis are the expected policy cash flows (i.e., up-front, lump-sum payment to buy the policy; ongoing premium payments to the insurance company; and the eventual death benefit to be received) and the time to mortality. Neither of these factors has anything to do with the overall behavior of financial markets. Thus, this strategy area is unrelated and uncorrelated with other hedge fund strategies.

Catastrophe insurance protects the policyholder in case of such events as floods, hurricanes, and earthquakes, which are highly idiosyncratic and also unrelated and uncorrelated with financial market behavior. Insurance companies effectively reinsure portions of their exposure (typically above a given threshold and for a limited amount) with reinsurance companies, who, in turn, deal with hedge funds as a source of capital. An attractive and uncorrelated return profile may be achieved if by making such reinsurance investments a hedge fund can do the following: 1) obtain sufficient policy diversity in terms of geographic exposure and type of insurance being offered; 2) receive a sufficient buffer in terms of loan loss reserves from the insurance company; and 3) receive enough premium income.

Valuation methods for catastrophe insurance may require the hedge fund manager to consider global weather patterns and make forecasts using sophisticated prediction models that involve a wide range of geophysical inputs. But, more generally, assumptions are made as to typical weather patterns; the worst-case loss potentials are made from different reinsurance structures. These assumptions are then weighed against the reinsurance income to be received. If a catastrophic event does occur, then hedge fund managers hope to have enough geographic diversity that they are not financially harmed by a single event, thereby continuing to benefit when insurance premiums are inevitably increased to cover future catastrophic events.

Organized markets for catastrophe bonds and catastrophe risk futures continue to develop. These bonds and financial futures can be used to take long positions or to hedge catastrophe risk in a portfolio of insurance contracts. Their issuance and performance tend to be seasonal. Many such catastrophe bonds are issued before the annual North American hurricane season begins (May/June) and may perform particularly well if a given hurricane season is benign.

EXAMPLE 11   Investing in Life Settlements

Mikki Tan runs specialty hedge fund SingStar Pte. Ltd. (SingStar), based in Singapore, that focuses on life settlements. SingStar is staffed with biometric and actuarial science experts who perform valuation analysis on pools of life insurance policies offered for sale by insurance broker firms. These intermediaries buy the policies from individuals who no longer need the insurance and who want an up-front cash payment that is higher than the surrender value offered by their insurance companies.

Tan knows that Warwick Direct has been buying many individuals' life insurance policies that were underwritten by NextLife, an insurance company with a reputation in industry circles for relatively weak underwriting procedures (i.e., charging low premiums for insuring its many relatively unhealthy policyholders) and for paying low surrender values. Tan is notified that Warwick Direct is selling a pool of life settlements heavily weighted with policies that were originated by NextLife. Parties wishing to bid will be provided with data covering a random sample of the life insurance policies in the pool.

Tan asks SingStar's experts to analyze the data, and they report that many of the policies in the pool were written on individuals who have now developed early-onset Alzheimer's and other debilitating diseases and thus required the up-front cash for assisted living facilities and other special care. Moreover, the analysts indicate that early-onset Alzheimer's patients have a life expectancy, on average, that is 10 years shorter than persons without the disease.

Discuss how Tan and SingStar's team might proceed given this potential investment.

Solution: SingStar's financial, biometric, and actuarial experts need to work together to forecast expected cash flows from this potential investment and then value it using an appropriate risk-adjusted discount rate. The cash flows would include the following:

- The ongoing premium payments that SingStar would need to make to the originating insurance companies (in this case, mainly to NextLife) to keep the policies active. The low premiums NextLife is known to charge as well as the shorter average life expectancy of many individuals represented in the pool are important factors to consider in making this forecast.
- The timing of future benefit payments to be received by SingStar on the demise of the individuals (the formerly insured). The prevalence of early-onset Alzheimer's disease and other debilitating diseases as well as the shorter average life expectancy of many individuals in the pool are key factors to consider in formulating this forecast.

Once an appropriate discount rate is decided on—one that compensates for the risks of the investment—then its present value can be determined. The difference between the PV and any minimum bid price set by Warwick Direct, as well as Tan's perceptions of the competition in bidding, will determine Tan's proposed purchase price. If SingStar ultimately buys the pool of life settlement policies and the forecasts (e.g., biometric, actuarial, and financial) of Tan's team are met or exceeded, then this investment should yield attractive returns to SingStar that are uncorrelated to other financial markets.

8. MULTI-MANAGER STRATEGIES

The previous sections examined individual hedge fund strategies. In practice, most investors invest in a range of hedge fund strategies. Three main approaches are used to combine individual hedge fund strategies into a portfolio: 1) *creating one's own mix of managers* by investing directly into individual hedge funds running different strategies; 2) *fund-of-funds,* which involves investing in a single fund-of-funds manager who then allocates across a set of individual hedge fund managers running different strategies; and 3) *multi-strategy funds*, which entails investing in a single fund that includes multiple internal management teams running different strategies under the same roof. Of course, approaches (1) and (2) are not specific to combinations of strategies; they apply to individual strategies too.

8.1. Fund-of-Funds

Fund-of-funds (FoF) managers aggregate investors' capital and allocate it to a portfolio of separate, individual hedge funds following different, less correlated strategies. The main roles of the FoF manager are to provide diversification across hedge fund strategies; to make occasional tactical, sector-based reallocation decisions; to engage in underlying manager selection and due diligence; and to perform ongoing portfolio management, risk assessment, and consolidated reporting. FoF managers can provide investors with access to certain closed hedge funds, economies of scale for monitoring, currency hedging capabilities, the ability to obtain and manage leverage at the portfolio level, and such other practical advantages as better liquidity terms than would be offered by an individual hedge fund manager.

Disadvantages of the FoF approach include a double layer of fees the investor must pay; a lack of transparency into individual hedge fund manager processes and returns; the inability to net performance fees on individual managers; and an additional principal–agent relationship. Regarding fees, in addition to management and incentive fees charged by the individual hedge funds (with historical norms of 1%–2% and 10%–20%, respectively) in which the FoF invests, investors in a fund-of-funds historically paid an additional 1% management fee and 10% incentive fee (again, historical norms) on the performance of the total FoF portfolio. As the performance of funds of funds has generally waned, fees have become more negotiable; management fees of 50 bps and incentive fees of 5% (or simply just a 1% flat total management fee) are becoming increasingly prevalent.

Occasionally, liquidity management of FoF can result in liquidity squeezes for FoF managers. Most FoFs require an initial one-year lock-up period, and then they offer investors monthly or quarterly liquidity thereafter, typically with a 30- to 60-day redemption notice also being required. However, the underlying investments made by the FoF may not fit well with such liquidity needs. Some underlying managers or newer underlying investments may have their own lock-up provisions or liquidity (i.e., redemption) gates. So, the FoF manager must stagger his/her underlying portfolio investments to create a conservative liquidity profile while carefully assessing the probability and potential magnitude of any FoF-level redemptions that he/she might face. FoFs may also arrange a reserve line of credit as an added liquidity backstop to deal with the potential mismatch between cash flows available from underlying investments and cash flows required to meet redemptions.

8.1.1. Investment Characteristics

FoFs are important hedge fund "access vehicles" for smaller high-net-worth investors and smaller institutions. Most hedge funds require minimum initial investments that range from $500,000 to $5,000,000 (with $1,000,000 being the most typical threshold). To create a reasonably diversified portfolio of 15–20 managers, $15–20 million would be required, which is a large amount even for most wealthy families and many small institutions. Selecting the 15–20 different hedge fund managers would itself require substantial time and resources that most such investors may lack. In addition, investors may potentially face substantial tax reporting requirements for each separate hedge fund investment owned. By comparison, a high-net-worth investor or small institution can typically start FoF investments with just $100,000, effectively achieving a portfolio that includes a diversified mix of talented hedge fund managers. Through their network of relationships and their large scale, FoFs may also provide access to successful managers whose funds are otherwise closed to new investment. Overall, FoFs may thus be considered convenient for access, diversification, liquidity, and operational tax reporting reasons.

But FoFs are also designed to provide other attractive features, even for such institutional investors as endowments, foundations, and pension plans. Such institutional clients may initially turn to FoFs as their preferred path to navigate their way into the hedge fund space. FoFs offer expertise not only in individual manager selection and due diligence but also in strategic allocation, tactical allocation, and style allocation into individual hedge fund strategies. The FoF strategic allocation is the long-term allocation to different hedge fund styles. For example, a FoF may have a strategic allocation of 20% to long/short equity strategies, 30% to event-driven strategies, 30% to relative value strategies, and 20% to global macro strategies. Tactical allocations include periodically overweighting and underweighting different hedge fund styles across different market environments depending on the level of conviction of the FoF manager. The overall capital or risk exposure can also be geared up or down to reflect the opportunity set in different market conditions.

Through their prime brokerage services, commercial banks provide levered capital to FoFs. Such leverage is typically collateralized by the existing hedge fund assets held in custody by these banks. Because hedge funds often deliver full funds back to redeeming investors with some substantial time lag (a 10% holdback of the total redemption amount until audit completion is typical), access to leverage can often be useful from a bridge loan point of view. In this way, capital not yet returned can be efficiently redeployed for the benefit of remaining investors.

Another attractive aspect of larger FoFs is that by pooling smaller investor assets into a larger single investment commitment, the FoF may be able to extract certain fee breaks, improved liquidity terms, future capacity rights, and/or added transparency provisions from an underlying hedge fund. The FoF may also be able to secure a commitment from the underlying fund to receive the best terms that might subsequently be offered to any future investor. These can all be valuable concessions that a smaller investor would most likely be unable to obtain by investing directly. Some FoFs have argued that these concessions made at the underlying fund manager level can be worth more than the added layering of fees by the FoF.

Overall, by combining different and ideally less correlated strategies, a FoF portfolio should provide more diversification, less extreme risk exposures, lower realized volatility, and generally less single manager tail risk than direct investing in individual hedge fund strategies. FoFs may also achieve economies of scale, manager access, research expertise, potential liquidity efficiencies, useful portfolio leverage opportunities, and potentially valuable concessions from the underlying funds.

8.1.2. Strategy Implementation

Implementing a FoF portfolio is typically a multi-step process that transpires over several months. First, FoF managers will become acquainted with different hedge fund managers via the use of various databases and introductions at prime broker-sponsored capital introduction events, where hedge fund managers present their perceived opportunity sets and qualifications to potential investors. Then, the FoF manager must decide the desired strategic allocation of the portfolio across the different hedge fund strategy groupings.

Next, with both quantitative and qualitative top-down and bottom-up approaches, the formal manager selection process is initiated. For each strategy grouping, the FoF manager screens the available universe of hedge funds with the goal to formulate a select "peer group" of potential investment candidates. This is followed by direct interviews of each hedge fund manager as well as a review of their relevant materials, such as presentation booklets, Alternative Investment Management Association Due Diligence Questionnaires (AIMA DDQs), recent quarterly letters and risk reports, as well as past audits. Typically, FoF managers will meet with prospective hedge fund managers on several different occasions (with at least one onsite visit at their offices). FoF managers will have an increasingly granular focus not only on the hedge fund managers' investment philosophy and portfolio construction but also on the firms' personnel, operational, and risk management processes.

Once an individual hedge fund is deemed a true candidate for investment, the fund's Offering Memorandum and Limited Partnership Agreement will be fully reviewed. The fund's service providers (e.g., auditor, legal adviser, custodian bank, prime broker) will be verified and other background checks and references obtained. At some larger FoF firms, these more operational aspects of the due diligence process will be performed by a dedicated team of specialists who validate the original FoF team's investment conclusions or cite concerns that may need to be addressed prior to an allocation. At this point, the FoF manager may endeavor to obtain certain concessions, agreed to in "side letters," from the hedge fund manager entitling the FoF to reduced fees, added transparency provisions, capacity rights to build an investment in the future, and/or improved redemption liquidity provisions. The larger the potential investment, the greater the FoF's negotiation advantage.

After a hedge fund is approved and the strategy is included in the FoF portfolio, then the process moves into the ongoing monitoring and review phases. The main concerns are monitoring for performance consistency with investment objectives and for any style drift, personnel changes, regulatory issues, or other correlation/return shifts that may transpire when compared to other managers both within the portfolio and when compared to similar hedge fund peers.

8.2. Multi-Strategy Hedge Funds

Multi-strategy hedge funds combine multiple hedge fund strategies under the same hedge fund structure. Teams of managers dedicated to running different hedge fund strategies share operational and risk management systems under the same roof.

8.2.1. Investment Characteristics

A key advantage to this approach is that the multi-strategy manager can reallocate capital into different strategy areas more quickly and efficiently than would be possible by the FoF manager. The multi-strategy manager has full transparency and a better picture of the interactions of the different teams' portfolio risks than would ever be possible for the FoF manager to achieve. Consequently, the multi-strategy manager can react faster to different real-time market impacts—for example, by rapidly increasing or decreasing leverage within different strategies depending on the perceived riskiness of available opportunities. Teams within a multi-strategy manager also can be fully focused on their respective portfolios because the business, operational, and regulatory aspects of running the hedge fund are handled by other administrative professionals. Many talented portfolio managers decide to join a multi-strategy firm for this reason.

The fees paid by investors in a multi-strategy fund can be structured in many ways, some of which can be very attractive when compared to the FoF added fee layering and netting risk attributes. Conceptually, the FoF investor always faces netting risk, whereby he/she is responsible for paying performance (i.e., incentive) fees due to winning underlying funds while suffering return drag from the performance of losing underlying funds. Even if the FoF's overall performance (aggregated across all funds) is flat or down, FoF investors must still pay incentive fees due to the managers of the winning underlying funds.

The fee structure is more investor-friendly at multi-strategy hedge funds where the general partner absorbs the netting risk arising from the divergent performances of his/her fund's different strategy teams. This is an attractive outcome for the multi-strategy fund investor because 1) the GP is responsible for netting risk; and 2) the only investor-level incentive fees paid are those due on the total fund performance after netting the positive and negative performances of the various strategy teams. Although beneficial to investors, this structure can at times cause discord within a multi-strategy fund. Because the GP is responsible for netting risk, the multi-strategy fund's overall bonus pool may shrink; thus, high-performing strategy teams will be disaffected if they do not receive their full incentive amounts, which ultimately results in personnel losses.

However, some multi-strategy hedge fund firms operate with a "pass-through" fee model. Using this model, they may charge no management fee but instead pass through the costs of paying individual teams (inclusive of salary and incentive fees earned by each team) before an added manager level incentive fee is charged to the investor on total fund performance. In this instance, the investor does implicitly pay for a portion of netting risk between the different teams (in place of a management fee), while the multi-strategy fund's GP bears a portion of that netting risk (via the risk that the total fund-level incentive fee may not cover contractual obligations that the GP is required to pay individual teams).

The main risk of multi-strategy funds is that they are generally quite levered: Position transparency is closely monitored in-house, and fee structures are typically tilted toward performance (due to high costs of the infrastructure requirements). Leverage applied to tight risk management is usually benign, but in market stress periods, risk management miscalibrations can certainly matter. The left-tail, risk-induced implosions of prominent multi-strategy funds, such as Ritchie Capital (2005) and Amaranth Advisors (2006), are somewhat legendary. Moreover, the operational risks of a multi-strategy firm, by definition, are not well diversified because all operational processes are performed under the same fund structure. Finally, multi-strategy funds can be somewhat limited in the scope of strategies offered because they are constrained by the available pool of in-house manager talent and skills (and are often staffed by managers with similar investment styles and philosophies).

8.2.2. Strategy Implementation

Multi-strategy funds invest in a range of individual hedge fund strategies. As mentioned, the breadth of strategies they can access is a function of the portfolio management skills available within the particular multi-strategy fund. Similar to a FoF manager, a multi-strategy fund will engage in both strategic and tactical allocations to individual hedge fund strategies. Given that multi-strategy fund teams manage each strategy directly and operate under the same fund roof, compared to FoF managers, they are more likely to be well informed about when to tactically reallocate to a particular strategy and more capable of shifting capital between strategies quickly. Conversely, multi-strategy funds may also be less willing to exit strategies in which core expertise is in-house. Common risk management systems and processes are also more likely to reveal interactions and correlations between the different strategies run by the various portfolio management teams. Such nuanced aspects of risk might be far harder to detect within a FoF structure.

Exhibit 11 compares some key attributes of fund-of-funds and multi-strategy funds that investors must consider when deciding which of these two multi-manager types best fits their needs.

EXHIBIT 11   Fund-of-Funds and Multi-Strategy Funds—Comparison of Risk, Liquidity, Leverage, and Benchmarking

---

Risk Profile and Liquidity

- FoF and multi-strategy funds are designed to offer steady, low-volatility returns via their strategy diversification. Multi-strategy funds have generally outperformed FoFs but with more variance and occasional large losses often related to their higher leverage.
- Multi-strategy funds offer potentially faster tactical asset allocation and improved fee structure (netting risk handled at strategy level) but with higher manager-specific operational risks. FoFs offer a potentially more diverse strategy mix but with less transparency and slower tactical reaction time.
- Both groups typically have similar initial lock-up and redemption periods, but multi-strategy funds also often impose investor-level or fund-level gates on maximum redemptions allowed per quarter.

Leverage Usage

- Multi-strategy funds tend to use significantly more leverage than most FoFs, which gravitate to modest leverage usage. Thus, multi-strategy funds are somewhat more prone to left-tail blow-up risk in stress periods. Still, better strategy transparency and shorter tactical reaction time make multi-strategy funds overall more resilient than FoFs in preserving capital.

Benchmarking

- FoFs can be tracked using such sub-indexes as HFRX and HFRI Fund of Funds Composite Indices; Lipper/TASS Fund-of-Funds Index; CISDM Fund-of-Funds Multi-Strategy Index; and the broad Credit Suisse Hedge Fund Index as a general proxy for a diversified pool of managers.
- Multi-strategy managers can be tracked via HFRX and HFRI Multi-Strategy Indices; Lipper/TASS Multi-Strategy Index; CISDM Multi-Strategy Index; and CS Multi-Strategy Hedge Fund Index.

Note: The FoF business model has been under significant pressure since 2008 because of fee compression and increased investor interest in passive, long-only investing and the advent of liquid alternatives for retail investors. Conversely, multi-strategy funds have grown as many institutional investors prefer to invest directly in such funds and avoid FoF fee layering.

EXAMPLE 12   Fund-of-Funds: Net-of-Fee Returns

Squaw Valley Fund of Funds (SVFOF) charges a 1% management fee and 10% incentive fee and invests an equal amount of its assets into two individual hedge funds: Pyrenees Fund (PF) and Ural Fund (UF), each charging a 2% management fee and a 20% incentive fee. For simplicity in answering the following questions, please ignore fee compounding and assume that all fees are paid at year-end.

1. If the managers of both PF and UF generate 20% gross annual returns, what is the net-of-fee return for an investor in SVFOF?
2. If PF's manager earns a gross return of 20% but UF's manager loses 5%, what is the net-of-fee return for an investor in SVFOF?

Solution to 1:

Incentive fees are deducted only from gross gains net of management fees and expenses. Thus, the answer becomes:

Net of Fees Return for PF and UF Investor = (20% − 2% − 3.6%) = 14.4%, where 3.6% = 20% × (20% − 2%);

Net of Fees Return for SVFOF Investor = (14.4% − 1% − 1.34%) = **12.06%**, where 1.34% = 10% × (14.4% − 1%).

Solution to 2:

Net of Fees Return for PF Investor = (20% − 2% − 3.6%) = 14.4%;

Net of Fees Return for UF Investor = (−5% − 2% − 0%) = −7.0%;

Gross Return for SVFOF Investor = (0.5 × 14.4% + 0.5 × −7.0%) = 3.7%;

Net of Fees Return for SVFOF Investor = (3.7% − 1% − 0.27%) = **2.43%**, where 0.27% = 10% × (3.7% − 1%).

In conclusion, if both PF and UF managers generate gross returns of 20%, then the net-of-fee return for SVFOF's investor is 12.06%, with fees taking up 39.7% of the total gross investment return [(2% + 3.6% + 1% + 1.34%)/20% = 39.7%] and the remainder going to the SVFOF investor.

But, if PF's manager earns a 20% gross return and UF's manager loses 5%, then the net-of-fee return for the SVFOF investor is a meager 2.43%. In this case, most (67.6%) of the original gross return of 7.5% [= 20% × 0.50 + (−5% × 0.50)] goes to PF, UF, and SVFOF managers as fees. Note that {[0.50 × (2% + 3.6% + 2% + 0%)] + (1% + 0.27%)}/7.5% equals 67.6%. This is an example of fee netting risk that comes with investing in FoFs.

EXAMPLE 13   Fund-of-Funds or Multi-Strategy Funds—Which to Choose?

The Leonardo family office in Milan manages the 435 million fortune of the Da Vinci family. Mona, the family's matriarch, trained as an economist and worked at Banca d'Italia for many years. She is now retired but still monitors global financial markets. The portfolio that Leonardo manages for the Da Vinci family consists of traditional long-only stocks and bonds, real estate, private equity, and single manager hedge funds following distressed securities and merger arbitrage strategies.

Mona believes global financial markets are about to enter a prolonged period of heightened volatility, so she asks Leonardo's senior portfolio manager to sell some long-only stocks and the merger arbitrage hedge fund and then buy a multi-manager hedge fund. Mona's objectives are to increase the portfolio's diversification, flexibility, and transparency while maximizing net-of-fees returns during the volatile period ahead.

Discuss advantages and disadvantages that Leonardo's portfolio manager should consider in choosing between a FoF and a multi-strategy fund.

Solution: Leonardo's portfolio manager understands that both multi-strategy funds and FoFs are designed to offer steady, low-volatility returns via their strategy diversification.

However, digging deeper he sees that multi-strategy funds have generally out-performed FoFs. This may be because of such key advantages as their enhanced flexibility and the fast pace of tactical asset allocation (important in dynamic, volatile markets) given that the different strategies are executed within the same fund structure. Another advantage of this set-up of multi-strategy funds is increased transparency regarding overall positions and exposures being carried. Moreover, many multi-strategy funds have an investor-friendly fee structure, in which fee netting risk is handled at the strategy level and absorbed (or partially absorbed) by the general partner of the multi-strategy fund. As for disadvantages, Leonardo's portfolio manager should consider that multi-strategy funds entail higher manager-specific operational risks, so detailed due diligence is important; moreover, they tend to use relatively high leverage, which may increase the variance of returns.

The main advantages of FoFs are that they offer a potentially more diverse strategy mix with lower leverage (and somewhat less return variance), and they have less operational risk (i.e., each separate underlying hedge fund is responsible for its own risk management). Leonardo's portfolio manager realizes that FoFs also entail reduced transparency into the portfolio decisions made at the underlying hedge funds as well as a slower tactical reaction time. Another key disadvantage is that FoFs require a double layer of fees to be paid, with netting risk borne by the investor, which imposes a substantial drag on net-of-fees returns.

9. ANALYSIS OF HEDGE FUND STRATEGIES

From the foregoing discussion, it is reasonable to conclude the following: L/S equity and event-driven managers tend to be exposed to some natural equity market beta risk; arbitrage managers often are exposed to credit spread risk and market volatility tail risk; opportunistic managers tend to have risk exposures to the trendiness (or directionality) of markets; and relative value managers do not expect trendiness but are typically counting on mean reversion. Each strategy has unique sources of factor exposures and resulting vulnerabilities. Moreover, risk factor exposures in many strategies arise from simply holding financial instruments whose prices are directly impacted by those risk factors. That is, long and short exposures to a given risk factor in different securities are not equal, thereby giving rise to a non-zero *net* exposure. Following a practice-based risk factor perspective, this chapter uses a conditional linear factor model to uncover and analyze hedge fund strategy risk exposures. While this is just one way to go about explaining hedge fund strategies' risks and returns, it is representative of the widely used risk factor approach.

One may ask why it is necessary to use such a model to investigate hedge fund strategies. It is because a linear factor model can provide insights into the intrinsic characteristics and risks in a hedge fund investment. Moreover, given the dynamic nature of hedge fund strategies, a conditional model allows for the analysis in a specific market environment to determine, for example, whether hedge fund strategies are exposed to certain risks under abnormal market conditions. A conditional model can show whether hedge fund risk exposures (e.g., to credit or volatility) that are insignificant during calm market periods may become significant during turbulent market periods. The importance of using a conditional factor model is underscored by the fact that the hedge fund industry is dynamic; for example, it experienced a huge decline in AUM during the global financial crisis. Specifically, after recording more than a 25% CAGR (compound annual growth rate) in assets between 2000 and 2007, the global hedge fund industry's aggregate AUM declined by 17% CAGR between 2007 and 2009 (the period of the global financial crisis) from a high of more than $2.6 trillion. Moreover, global AUM did not surpass the 2007 high until 2014. In short, thousands of hedge funds were shuttered during this time as performance plunged when many managers were caught off guard by their funds' actual risk exposures during the crisis period and in its aftermath.

9.1. Conditional Factor Risk Model

A simple conditional linear factor model applied to a hedge fund strategy's returns can be represented as:

$$\text{(Return on HF}_i)_t = \alpha_i + \beta_{i,1}(\text{Factor 1})_t + \beta_{i,2}(\text{Factor 2})_t + \ldots + \beta_{i,K}(\text{Factor } K)_t + D_t\beta_{i,1}(\text{Factor 1})_t + D_t\beta_{i,2}(\text{Factor 2})_t + \ldots + D_t\beta_{i,K}(\text{Factor } K)_t + (\text{error})_{i,t}$$

where

- (Return on HF$_i$)$_t$ is the return of hedge fund i in period t;
- $\beta_{i,1}$(Factor 1)$_t$ represents the exposure to risk factor 1 (up to risk factor K) for hedge fund i in period t during normal times;
- $D_t\beta_{i,1}$(Factor 1)$_t$ represents the *incremental* exposure to risk factor 1 (up to risk factor K) for hedge fund i in period t during financial crisis periods, where D_t is a dummy variable that equals 1 during financial crisis periods (i.e., June 2007 to February 2009) and 0 otherwise;
- α_i is the intercept for hedge fund i; and
- (error)$_{i,t}$ is random error with zero mean and standard deviation of σ_i.

Each factor beta represents the expected change in hedge fund returns for a one-unit increase in the specific risk factor, holding all other factors (independent variables) constant. The portion of hedge fund returns not explained by the risk factors is attributable to three sources: 1) alpha, the hedge fund manager's unique investment skills; 2) omitted factors; and 3) random errors. The starting point for building this model is the identification of a comprehensive set of asset class and macro-oriented, market-based risks, including the behavior of stocks, bonds, currencies, commodities, credit spreads, and volatility. Following Hasanhodzic and Lo (2007) and practice, the model starts with the following six factors:

- **Equity risk (SNP500):** monthly total return of the S&P 500 Index, including dividends.
- **Interest rate risk (BOND):** monthly return of the Bloomberg Barclays Corporate AA Intermediate Bond Index.
- **Currency risk (USD):** monthly return of the US Dollar Index.
- **Commodity risk (CMDTY):** monthly total return of the Goldman Sachs Commodity Index (GSCI).
- **Credit risk (CREDIT):** difference between monthly seasoned Baa and Aaa corporate bond yields provided by Moody's.
- **Volatility risk (VIX):** first-difference of the end-of-month value of the CBOE Volatility Index (VIX).

Once these potentially relevant macro risk factors were identified for analysis, the next consideration was the appropriateness of using them together in the model. To address the issue of highly correlated risk factors and to avoid potential multi-collinearity problems, a four-step "stepwise regression" process was used to build a conditional linear factor model that is less likely to include highly correlated risk factors. This process is described briefly in the accompanying sidebar.

Practical Steps for Building Hedge Fund Risk Factor Models

The following four-step procedure describes a stepwise regression process that can help build linear conditional factor models that are less likely to include highly correlated risk factors, thereby avoiding multi-collinearity issues.

Step 1: Identify potentially important risk factors.

Step 2: Calculate pairwise correlations across all risk factors. If two-state conditional models are used, calculate correlations across all risk factors for both states—for example, during normal market conditions (state 1) and during market crisis conditions (state 2). For illustration purposes, risk factors A and B can be assumed to be highly correlated if the correlation coefficient between them exceeds 60%.

Step 3: For highly correlated risk factors A and B, regress the return series of interest (e.g., hedge fund returns) on all risk factors excluding factor A. Then, regress the same returns on all risk factors, but this time exclude factor B. Given the adjusted R^2 for regressions without A and without B, keep the risk factor that results in the highest adjusted R^2.

Step 4: Repeat step 3 for all other highly correlated factor pairs, with the aim of eliminating the least useful (in terms of explanatory power) factors and thereby avoiding multi-collinearity issues.

To address the multi-collinearity problem, the stepwise regression procedure was implemented using two of the hedge fund databases mentioned previously: Lipper TASS (TASS) and Morningstar Hedge/CISDM (CISDM). The accompanying sidebar provides useful background for practitioners on these two important sources of hedge fund information.

Hedge Fund Databases

The analysis in this chapter uses two well-known hedge fund databases to evaluate hedge fund strategies: Lipper TASS (TASS) and Morningstar Hedge/CISDM (CISDM) databases. These databases are among the ones most widely used for hedge fund research.

The analysis covers the period of 2000–2016. Each database is separated into "live" (operating/open), "defunct" (non-operating/shut down or operating/closed to new investment or operating/delisted and relisted with another database), and "all" funds (live + defunct) groups. Hedge fund return data are filtered to exclude funds that 1) do not report net-of-fee returns; 2) report returns in currencies other than US dollar; 3) report returns less frequently than monthly; 4) do not provide AUM or estimates; and 5) have less than 36 months of return data. TASS and CISDM databases have a total of 6,352 and 7,756 funds, respectively. Importantly, 82% (18%) and 80% (20%) of all TASS and CISDM funds, respectively, are defunct (live). This is consistent with the relatively high attrition rate of hedge funds and the relatively short life of a typical hedge fund.

Databases that include defunct funds can be highly useful for asset allocators because the historical track record of managers that may be starting new funds might be found to include defunct funds. Then, further analysis could be conducted to determine if such funds became defunct because of the managers' poor performance and/or excessive redemptions, so they were shut down, or because of the managers' initial success, such that an overabundance of inflows caused subsequent investment capacity issues. From a data analysis point of view, including defunct funds also helps to appropriately adjust for database survivorship bias that might otherwise yield incorrect analytical conclusions.

Live, Defunct, and All Funds in TASS Database from 2000–2016

Grouping	TASS Primary Categories	Number of Live Funds	Number of Defunct Funds	Total Number of Funds
Equity	Dedicated short bias	4	38	42
Equity	Equity market neutral	38	270	308
Equity	Long/short equity hedge	350	1,705	2,055
Event driven	Event driven	87	465	552
Relative value	Convertible arbitrage	17	162	179
Relative value	Fixed-income arbitrage	42	167	209
Opportunistic	Global macro	59	266	325
Opportunistic	Managed futures	1	2	3
Multi-manager	Fund of funds	454	1,711	2,165
Multi-manager	Multi-strategy	100	414	514
Total		1,152	5,200	6,352

Live, Defunct, and All Funds in CISDM Database from 2000–2016

Grouping	CISDM Categories	Number of Live Funds	Number of Defunct Funds	Total Number of Funds
Equity	Asia/Pacific long/short equity	31	203	234
Equity	Bear market equity	2	36	38
Equity	Equity market neutral	40	272	312
Equity	Europe long/short equity	47	161	208
Equity	Global long/short equity	86	406	492
Equity	US long/short equity	218	849	1,067
Equity	US small-cap long/short equity	67	171	238
Event driven	Merger arbitrage	22	16	38
Event driven	Distressed securities	46	159	205
Event driven	Event driven	63	228	291
Relative value	Convertible arbitrage	25	125	150
Relative value	Debt arbitrage	32	141	173
Opportunistic	Global macro	84	380	464
Opportunistic	Systematic futures	182	518	700
Multi-manager	Fund of funds – debt	20	97	117
Multi-manager	Fund of funds – equity	104	592	696
Multi-manager	Fund of funds – event	10	124	134
Multi-manager	Fund of funds – macro/systematic	30	163	193
Multi-manager	Fund of funds – multi-strategy	164	789	953
Multi-manager	Fund of funds – relative value	12	83	95
Multi-manager	Multi-strategy	111	395	506
Specialist	Volatility	28	30	58
Specialist	Long/short debt	115	279	394
Total		1,539	6,217	7,756

Using TASS and CISDM datasets, the stepwise regression procedure resulted in both BOND and CMDTY factors being dropped from the final conditional linear risk model because of multi-collinearity issues. This is because retaining CREDIT and SNP500 factors produced higher adjusted R^2s compared to retaining BOND and CMDTY factors.

Exhibit 12 provides useful information for interpreting the effects of the factor exposures included in the conditional risk model on hedge fund strategy returns. For both normal and crisis periods, it shows the four risk factors, the typical market trend during these periods, the hedge fund manager's desired position (long or short), and the desired factor exposure for benefitting from a particular market trend.

EXHIBIT 12   Interpretation of Conditional Risk Factor Exposures

Period/Risk Factor	Typical Market Trend	Desired Position	Desired Factor Exposure	Comments
Normal				
SNP500	Equities Rising	Long	Positive	Aims to add risk, increase return
CREDIT	Spreads Flat/Narrowing	Long	Positive	Aims to add risk, increase return
USD	USD Flat/Depreciating	Short	Negative	Sells USD to boost returns
VIX	Volatility Falling	Short	Negative	Sells volatility to boost returns
Crisis				
DSNP500	Equities Falling Sharply	Short	Negative	Aims to reduce risk
DCREDIT	Spreads Widening	Short	Negative	Aims to reduce risk
DUSD	USD Appreciating	Long	Positive	USD is haven in crisis periods
DVIX	Volatility Rising	Long	Positive	Negative correlation with equities

9.2. Evaluating Equity Hedge Fund Strategies

Using data from the CISDM and TASS databases from 2000 to 2016, this section discusses key return and risk characteristics for hedge funds pursuing equity-related strategies. More specifically, the conditional factor model is used to assess average risk exposures (during both normal and crisis market periods) for all "live" funds in each of the equity-related categories in these databases. Finally, the heterogeneity among funds, which is masked in the average exposures, is then revealed in an analysis showing the percentage of all hedge funds in each category that have significant factor exposures (positive and negative) during normal and crisis periods.

Note that the results of such a risk factor analysis may vary somewhat based on the hedge fund database used, the time period examined, and the specification of the factor model. However, the key takeaway is that such an analysis can uncover unintended adverse risk exposures to a hedge fund—stemming from the strategy it pursues—that may assert themselves only during turbulent market periods. As mentioned previously, unintended adverse risk exposures that revealed themselves during the global financial crisis resulted in the demise of literally thousands of hedge funds worldwide. Thus, understanding how to interpret the results of such a risk factor analysis is a key practical competency for any practitioner involved in advising on the strategies followed by hedge funds or in managing or owning the hedge funds themselves. First, we describe how the factor model can be used to understand risk exposures of equity-related hedge fund strategies. Then, we turn to understanding risks of multi-manager strategies.

The key return characteristics are shown for equity-related hedge fund strategies by category in Exhibit 13. In addition to the Sharpe ratio, we calculate the Sortino ratio.[2] The Sortino ratio replaces standard deviation in the Sharpe ratio with downside deviation, so it concentrates on

---

[2]In addition to Sharpe and Sortino ratios, other performance measures can be used, such as the Treynor ratio, information ratio, return on VaR, Jensen's alpha, M^2, maximum drawdown, and gain-to-loss ratio.

returns below a specified threshold. For example, if the threshold return is zero, then the Sortino ratio uses downside deviation based on losses. Because hedge funds potentially invest in illiquid securities (which artificially smooth returns, thus lowering the measured standard deviation), besides measuring risk and return one should also investigate the autocorrelation of returns. Rho is a measure of first order serial autocorrelation, the correlation between a fund's return and its own lagged returns. High Rho signals smoothed returns and thus is an indicator of potential liquidity issues (specifically, illiquidity and infrequent trading) in the underlying securities.

Exhibit 13 shows that L/S Equity Hedge (TASS) has the highest mean return (11.30%) but also the highest standard deviation (22.86%). Among categories with more than four funds, EMN (TASS) has the highest Sharpe ratio; notably, despite having the highest standard deviation, L/S Equity Hedge (TASS) also has the highest Sortino ratio; and Global L/S Equity (CISDM) shows the largest Rho. Overall, these results indicate that by accepting some beta and illiquidity exposure, L/S equity managers generally outperform equity market-neutral managers in terms of total returns delivered. Returns of L/S equity managers, however, are also more volatile than those of EMN managers and so produce lower Sharpe ratios. Intuitively, these results are in line with expectations.

EXHIBIT 13   Key Return Characteristics for Equity Hedge Fund Strategies (2000–2016)

Database	Category	Sample Size	Annualized Mean (%)		Annualized Sharpe Ratio		Annualized Sortino Ratio		Rho (%)	
			Mean	SD	Mean	SD	Mean	SD	Mean	SD
TASS	Dedicated short bias	4	2.91	14.75	2.27	4.36	1.35	1.07	20.0	45.7
CISDM	Bear market equity	2	2.04	7.37	0.29	1.18	0.70	1.47	9.15	1.79
TASS	Equity market neutral	38	7.81	10.20	0.83	0.56	0.80	0.53	9.3	15.8
CISDM	Equity market neutral	40	7.48	8.82	0.79	0.81	0.65	0.92	16.29	8.88
TASS	Long/short equity hedge	350	11.30	22.86	0.62	0.64	1.33	1.04	11.0	13.5
CISDM	Global long/short equity	86	8.83	16.93	0.44	0.57	0.76	1.09	17.43	15.63
CISDM	Asia/Pacific long/short equity	31	8.87	20.27	0.45	0.36	0.73	0.57	16.72	10.49
CISDM	Europe long/short equity	47	7.05	11.59	0.56	0.37	0.69	1.08	13.92	10.53
CISDM	US long/short equity	218	9.41	17.50	0.62	0.46	0.60	0.55	12.76	8.98
CISDM	US small cap long/short equity	67	9.88	19.60	0.65	0.48	1.14	0.86	11.71	7.44

Taking a more granular view of factor risks, Exhibit 14 presents average risk exposures (equity, credit, currency, and volatility) for equity-related hedge fund strategies using the conditional risk factor model from 2000 to 2016. The crisis period is from June 2007 to February 2009, and crisis period factors are preceded by the letter "D" (e.g., the crisis period equity factor is DSNP500). Light (dark) shaded coefficients have t-statistics greater than 1.96 (1.67) and are significant at the 5% (10%) level.

EXHIBIT 14   Risk Exposures for Equity Hedge Funds Using the Conditional Risk Factor Model (2000–2016)

Strategy	Dedicated Short Bias	Bear Market Equity	Equity Market Neutral	Equity Market Neutral	Asia/ Pacific Long/ Short Equity	Europe Long/ Short Equity	Global Long/ Short Equity	US Long/ Short Equity	US Small Cap Long/ Short Equity	Long/ Short Equity Hedge
Database	TASS	CISDM	TASS	CISDM	CISDM	CISDM	CISDM	CISDM	CISDM	TASS
Sample Size	4	2	38	40	31	47	86	218	67	350
Normal Times Exposures										
Intercept	−0.02	0.00	0.01	0.01	0.01	0.01	0.02	−0.01	0.01	0.01
SNP500	−0.28	−0.46	0.11	0.09	0.42	0.24	0.52	0.58	0.58	0.41
USD	−0.13	−0.07	−0.02	0.00	−0.02	0.06	−0.01	−0.03	−0.01	−0.04
CREDIT	1.24	0.22	−0.12	−0.07	−0.26	−0.23	−0.77	0.63	−0.09	−0.20
VIX	0.04	−0.05	0.01	0.00	−0.01	0.02	−0.01	−0.03	0.03	0.07
Crisis Times Exposures (Incremental)										
DSNP500	0.04	0.11	0.04	0.05	−0.02	−0.14	−0.04	0.03	−0.02	−0.03
DUSD	−0.08	−0.06	−0.17	−0.02	0.15	−0.42	−0.07	−0.07	−0.09	−0.17
DCREDIT	0.02	0.05	0.06	0.10	−0.01	0.07	0.16	0.03	−0.20	0.07
DVIX	0.00	−0.02	−0.06	−0.04	−0.04	−0.09	−0.04	0.02	−0.02	−0.02

On average, funds following EMN strategies maintain low exposure to equity market risk (0.11, significant at 10%) as well as a neutral exposure to the other risk factors in the model in both normal and crisis periods. L/S equity strategies maintain significant (at the 5% level) average beta loadings to equity risk during normal periods. The equity risk betas range from 0.24 for Europe L/S Equity to 0.58 for both US and US Small Cap L/S Equity strategies. Although there are no significant incremental (i.e., additional) exposures to equity risk (DSNP500) during crisis periods, total exposures during crisis periods (normal + crisis) are positive and significant for all L/S equity strategies. For example, the total equity exposure in crisis times for US L/S Equity is 0.61 (= 0.58 + 0.03). Because they show average exposures across all live funds in the given strategy category, these results mask significant heterogeneity between funds in their exposures to the four risk factors.

Exhibit 15 highlights this heterogeneity by presenting the percentage of funds experiencing significant (at the 10% level or better) factor exposures within each strategy category. The (T) indicates funds from the TASS database, and all other funds are from CISDM; gray (white) bars signify positive (negative) factor exposures. The *y*-axis indicates the percentage of funds within each strategy category that experienced the significant risk exposures.

EXHIBIT 15   Significant Positive and Negative Factor Exposures for Funds by Equity Hedge Strategy During Normal and Crisis Periods (2000–2016)

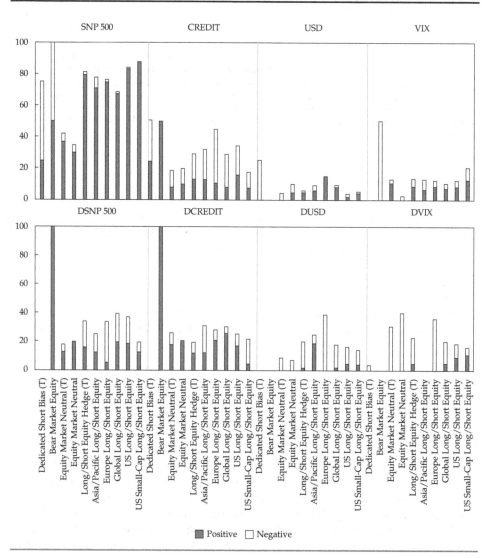

For example, with the exception of dedicated short-biased funds, most equity-related hedge funds have significant positive exposure to equity risk during normal market periods (30%+ for EMN funds and 70%+ for L/S equity funds). However, during crisis periods, less than 40% of L/S equity funds have any significant incremental equity exposure; for those that do, their added exposure is mixed (negative and positive). This suggests that managers were able to decrease adverse crisis period effects on their returns—likely by deleveraging, outright selling of stock (short sales, too) and equity index futures, and/or by buying index put options. This also indicates that although they did not reduce long beta tilting by much, on average L/S equity managers did not make things worse by trying to aggressively "bottom pick" the market. Finally, these results are consistent with the average incremental equity exposure during crisis periods of approximately zero, as seen in the previous exhibit.

As one might intuitively expect, most L/S equity managers do not have significant exposure to CREDIT. Only about one-third of L/S equity funds have significant exposure to CREDIT— mainly negative exposure, indicating that they are unlikely to benefit from moderating credit risk (spreads narrowing, credit upgrades). Interestingly, for the 25% of funds with significant incremental crisis period CREDIT exposure, these exposures become more positive, which would tend to hurt returns as spreads widen and credit downgrades accelerate during market sell-offs. Similarly, exposures to USD and VIX for L/S equity funds are marginal during normal times, with few funds having any significant exposures. However, in most cases during crisis periods, any significant additional exposures are mainly negative. For example, about 40% of Europe L/S Equity funds show significant negative exposure to USD—perhaps expecting a crisis-induced flight to quality into the euro or Japanese yen as opposed to USD. Again, nearly 40% of these funds show negative added VIX exposure (i.e., short volatility) during crisis times. Returns of some high-profile hedge funds have been hurt by being unexpectedly short volatility during crisis periods, which underscores why understanding the heterogeneity of factor exposures is important to understanding risk profiles of hedge funds.

EXAMPLE 14   Dedicated Short-Biased Hedge Fund

Bearish Asset Management (BAM) manages a short-biased hedge fund that varies its portfolio's short tilt depending on perceived opportunities. Using the fund's monthly returns for the past 10 years, which include periods of financial market crisis, a conditional risk factor model was estimated. The following table provides factor beta estimates with corresponding t-statistics [dark (light) shaded are significant at the 5% (10%) level].

Interpret the factor loadings. Also, what can you infer about BAM's overall risk exposure during crisis periods?

Coefficient	Estimate	t-Statistic
Normal Times Exposures		
Intercept	0.005	1.10
USD	0.072	0.72
CREDIT	−0.017	−0.07
SNP500	−0.572	−9.65
VIX	−0.164	−2.19
Crisis Times Exposures (Incremental)		
DUSD	0.456	1.31
DCREDIT	−0.099	−0.40
DSNP500	0.236	1.74
DVIX	0.105	1.03

Solution: BAM's fund has highly significant negative loadings on equity risk (SNP500) and volatility risk (VIX). The negative equity risk exposure is as expected for a short-biased strategy. But the negative VIX loading is consistent with short volatility exposure. This suggests that BAM's manager may be selling puts against some of its short exposures, thereby attempting to also capture a volatility premium. During crisis periods, the equity beta rises from –0.572 to –0.336 (= –0.572 + 0.236 = –0.336). This negative exposure is still significant and suggests that despite being a short-biased fund, BAM had less negative equity risk exposure during crisis periods. In this case, the manager may be purposefully harvesting some of its short exposure into market weakness.

9.3. Evaluating Multi-Manager Hedge Fund Strategies

It is important to understand the risks of multi-manager hedge fund strategies. Exhibit 16 shows that multi-strategy hedge funds outperform funds-of-funds: They have higher mean returns (7.85%/TASS and 8.52%/CISDM) and among the highest Sharpe ratios and Sortino ratios. Multi-strategy funds have higher Rho (more than 20%) compared to FoF, indicating relatively high serial autocorrelation. This is reasonable because multi-strategy funds may be simultaneously running strategies using less liquid instruments, such as convertible arbitrage, fixed-income arbitrage, and other relative value strategies. That is why, unlike FoFs, they often impose investor-level or fund-level gates on maximum quarterly redemptions.

EXHIBIT 16   Key Return Characteristics for Multi-Manager Hedge Fund Strategies (2000–2016)

Database	Category	Sample Size	Annualized Mean (%)		Annualized Sharpe Ratio		Annualized Sortino Ratio		Rho (%)	
			Mean	SD	Mean	SD	Mean	SD	Mean	SD
CISDM	Fund of funds – debt	20	6.52	7.94	0.89	0.66	0.68	1.17	13.89	4.24
CISDM	Fund of funds – equity	104	4.69	9.15	0.41	0.28	0.44	0.91	12.27	10.61
CISDM	Fund of funds – event	10	4.59	4.99	0.75	0.51	0.56	1.19	13.76	6.71
CISDM	Fund of funds – macro/ systematic	30	5.09	10.16	0.39	0.39	0.57	0.60	8.15	3.52
CISDM	Fund of funds – multi-strategy	164	4.47	7.18	0.54	1.84	1.34	1.43	12.43	9.31
CISDM	Fund of funds – relative value	12	5.31	8.58	0.70	0.42	1.31	0.63	15.86	13.77
TASS	Fund of funds	454	5.73	10.03	0.38	0.71	0.52	0.62	19.9	18.1
CISDM	Multi-strategy	111	8.52	11.01	0.89	1.36	1.32	1.58	20.09	16.24
TASS	Multi-strategy	100	7.85	11.51	0.86	1.40	1.00	1.05	22.7	24.3

Exhibit 17 presents average risk exposures for multi-manager hedge fund strategies using the conditional risk factor model. The crisis period is from June 2007 to February 2009, and light (dark) shaded betas have *t*-statistics of more than 1.96 (1.67).

EXHIBIT 17   Risk Exposures for Multi-Manager Hedge Funds Using the Conditional Risk Factor Model (2000–2016)

Strategy	Fund of Funds – Debt	Fund of Funds – Equity	Fund of Funds – Event	Fund of Funds – Macro/ Systematic	Fund of Funds – Multi- Strategy	Fund of Funds – Relative Value	Fund of Funds	Multi- Strategy	Multi- Strategy
Database	CISDM	CISDM	CISDM	CISDM	CISDM	CISDM	TASS	CISDM	TASS
Sample Size	20	104	10	30	163	12	454	111	100
Normal Times Exposures									
Intercept	0.01	0.01	0.01	0.01	0.01	0.01	0.01	0.10	0.01
SNP500	0.16	0.33	0.14	−0.02	0.21	0.12	0.24	−0.14	0.22
USD	−0.01	0.01	0.01	−0.07	0.00	0.01	0.01	−0.41	−0.01
CREDIT	−0.36	−0.43	−0.22	−0.10	−0.28	−0.14	−0.45	−5.71	−0.03
VIX	0.00	0.03	0.00	0.04	0.01	0.02	0.01	−0.03	0.01
Crisis Times Exposures (Incremental)									
DSNP500	−0.02	0.02	−0.01	−0.01	0.00	0.02	0.00	0.05	0.06
DUSD	0.03	−0.09	−0.19	−0.21	−0.20	−0.27	−0.05	−0.05	−0.05
DCREDIT	−0.10	0.09	−0.13	0.01	0.03	−0.10	0.09	0.07	−0.05
DVIX	0.03	−0.09	−0.03	−0.05	−0.07	−0.06	−0.05	−0.02	−0.05

Results show that all FoF strategies (except macro/systematic) have significant positive exposure to equity risk (ranging from 0.14 to 0.33) for the full period. The finding for macro/systematic is consistent with results presented earlier for opportunistic hedge funds, which show they tend not to be exposed to equity risks in aggregate. Interestingly, multi-strategy funds have significant equity exposure but differing signs—negative (positive) for CISDM (TASS)—which highlights the heterogeneity between the two databases.

Multi-manager funds as a group do not appear to provide significant hedging benefits (via diversification) in crisis times. If they did, then significant negative exposures to DSNP500 would be observed. This is consistent with the research findings that in the 2007–2009 global financial crisis, diversification across hedge fund strategies did not decrease total portfolio risk. These researchers conclude that during crises, simple diversification is insufficient; rather, it is important to focus on such other risks as liquidity, volatility, and credit—particularly because these risks may be magnified by the application of leverage.

Exhibit 18 tells a different story when individual funds are studied. The majority of multi-manager funds have significant positive exposure to the equity factor, but around 30% of funds show a mix of negative and positive incremental exposures (DSNP 500) to equities during the crisis period. This suggests that at least some funds (ones with negative loadings) were able to shield their investors from substantial market declines by either deleveraging, selling equity pre-crisis, and/or short selling. About 40% of all multi-manager funds have significant, mostly negative, exposure to CREDIT, indicating that they generally were not positioned to benefit from improving credit spreads. In crisis times, they took on additional (mostly negative) CREDIT exposure. For example, about 50% of FoF-Debt and FoF-Relative Value funds experienced incremental negative CREDIT exposure during turbulent periods, which hedged them from deteriorating credit conditions.

EXHIBIT 18   Significant Positive and Negative Factor Exposures for Multi-Manager Hedge Funds During Normal and Crisis Periods (2000–2016)

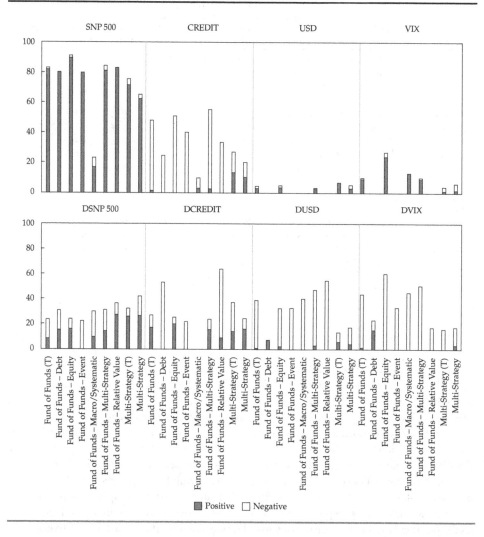

For the full period, multi-manager funds have minimal exposures to USD and VIX. Notably, these exposures increase dramatically, becoming significantly negative during financial crises. For example, only 2% of FoF-Equity have negative exposure to VIX overall. But, 60% of these funds show additional significant negative VIX exposure in crisis times. A similar pattern is revealed for USD exposure. Such negative exposures would seem undesirable during times when volatility is spiking and the USD is likely appreciating. Natural embedded leverage may be a partial explanation for these seemingly undesirable exposures during crisis times. In sum, as crisis periods generate potentially unexpected exposures to systematic risks, it is essential to use conditional factor models to understand risks of hedge fund strategies.

10. PORTFOLIO CONTRIBUTION OF HEDGE FUND STRATEGIES

This section examines the return and risk contributions of the hedge fund strategies previously covered when added to a traditional 60% stock/40% bond investment portfolio.

10.1. Performance Contribution to a 60/40 Portfolio

For each hedge fund strategy category that has been discussed, we now consider an equal-weighted portfolio of the individual funds in that category. We examine the impact of a 20% allocation to such a hedge fund strategy portfolio when combined with a traditional investment portfolio consisting of 60% stocks and 40% bonds. The S&P 500 Total Return Index and the Bloomberg Barclays Corporate AA Intermediate Bond Index are used to proxy the 60%/40% portfolio. When the hedge fund strategy portfolio is added to the traditional portfolio, the resulting allocations for the combined portfolio are 48% stocks, 32% bonds, and 20% in the particular hedge fund strategy portfolio. Please note this exercise is for illustrating the portfolio performance contribution of hedge fund strategies; practically speaking, it is unlikely an investor would hold an allocation (here 20%) that included an equal weighting of all live funds in one particular hedge fund strategy category.

Exhibit 19 provides performance and risk metrics for the combined portfolios from 2000 to 2016. It shows that when added to a traditional 60%/40% portfolio (with a mean return of 6.96%), a 20% allocation to the US Small Cap L/S Equity strategy generates the highest mean return (7.53%) of all the combined portfolios—an improvement of 57 bps. Adding a 20% allocation of an equal-weighted portfolio of funds in any of the following hedge fund categories to the traditional portfolio produces average annual returns of more than 7.30%: fixed-income arbitrage, distressed securities, or systematic futures. Adding a 20% allocation of any of the hedge fund strategies shown in Exhibit 19 to the traditional portfolio almost always decreases total portfolio standard deviation while increasing Sharpe and Sortino ratios (and also decreasing maximum drawdown in about one-third of the combined portfolios). These results demonstrate that hedge funds act as both risk-adjusted return enhancers and diversifiers for the traditional stock/bond portfolio.

EXHIBIT 19   Performance and Risk of 48/32/20 Portfolio, Where 20% Allocation Is to an Equal-Weighted Portfolio for Each Hedge Fund Strategy Category (2000–2016)

Category	Type	Database	Mean Return (%)	SD (%)	Sharpe Ratio	Sortino Ratio	Maximum Drawdown (%)
60% Stocks/40% Bonds	*Traditional Portfolio*	*—*	*6.96*	*8.66*	*0.62*	*1.13*	*14.42*
Long/Short Equity Hedge	Equity	TASS	7.22	8.29	0.68	1.45	21.34
Global Long/Short Equity	Equity	CISDM	7.06	8.17	0.67	1.22	22.51
U.S. Long/Short Equity	Equity	CISDM	7.17	8.22	0.68	1.24	16.77

Category	Type	Database	Mean Return (%)	SD (%)	Sharpe Ratio	Sortino Ratio	Maximum Drawdown (%)
U.S. Small Cap Long/Short Equity	Equity	CISDM	7.53	8.75	0.68	1.23	27.02
Asia/Pacific Long/Short Equity	Equity	CISDM	6.44	8.12	0.60	1.07	21.74
Europe Long/Short Equity	Equity	CISDM	6.79	7.69	0.67	1.24	15.20
Dedicated Short Bias	Equity	TASS	6.02	5.59	0.79	1.02	16.06
Bear Market Equity	Equity	CISDM	5.97	5.68	0.77	1.43	16.62
Equity Market Neutral	Equity	TASS	6.81	7.17	0.73	1.80	10.72
Equity Market Neutral	Equity	CISDM	6.79	7.13	0.73	1.36	4.99
Event Driven	Event Driven	TASS	7.13	7.76	0.71	1.44	20.96
Event Driven	Event Driven	CISDM	7.19	7.83	0.71	1.31	20.57
Distressed Securities	Event Driven	CISDM	7.40	7.67	0.75	1.38	20.00
Merger Arbitrage	Event Driven	CISDM	6.85	7.22	0.73	1.35	5.60
Convertible Arbitrage	Relative Value	TASS	6.76	7.75	0.66	1.27	31.81
Fixed-Income Arbitrage	Relative Value	TASS	7.50	7.82	0.75	1.39	12.68
Convertible Arbitrage	Relative Value	CISDM	6.91	7.68	0.69	1.25	27.91
Global Macro	Opportunistic	TASS	6.96	7.36	0.73	1.29	5.14
Global Macro	Opportunistic	CISDM	6.97	7.29	0.74	1.38	5.19
Systematic Futures	Opportunistic	CISDM	7.34	6.94	0.83	1.68	8.04
Fund of Funds	Multi-Manager	TASS	6.43	7.53	0.64	1.23	18.92
Multi-Strategy	Multi-Manager	TASS	6.98	7.57	0.71	1.13	17.35
Fund of Funds – Debt	Multi-Manager	CISDM	6.56	7.40	0.67	1.22	17.77
Fund of Funds – Equity	Multi-Manager	CISDM	6.39	7.76	0.62	1.11	21.63
Fund of Funds – Event	Multi-Manager	CISDM	6.35	7.48	0.63	1.15	21.37
Fund of Funds - Macro/ Systematic	Multi-Manager	CISDM	6.47	7.05	0.69	1.31	10.65
Fund of Funds – Multi- Strategy	Multi-Manager	CISDM	6.36	7.41	0.64	1.17	18.17
Fund of Funds - Relative Value	Multi-Manager	CISDM	6.46	7.22	0.67	1.23	17.16
Multi-Strategy	Multi-Manager	CISDM	7.00	7.47	0.72	1.34	13.83

The Sharpe ratio measures risk-adjusted performance, where risk is defined as standard deviation, so it penalizes both upside and downside variability. The Sortino ratio measures risk-adjusted performance, where risk is defined as downside deviation, so it penalizes only downside variability below a minimum target return. For hedge fund strategies with large negative events, the Sortino ratio is considered a better performance measure. The combined portfolio with the highest Sharpe ratio (0.83) includes a 20% allocation to systematic futures hedge funds. High Sharpe ratios are also achieved from allocations to distressed securities, fixed-income arbitrage, and global macro or equity market-neutral strategies. Adding allocations of 20% consisting of hedge funds from equity market-neutral (TASS), systematic futures, L/S equity hedge, or event-driven (TASS) categories to the traditional portfolio produces combined portfolios with by far the best Sortino ratios.

Exhibit 20 plots the Sharpe and Sortino ratios for 48/32/20 portfolios, where the 20% allocation is to an equal-weighted portfolio of the funds in each hedge fund strategy category. As a point of reference, the Sharpe and Sortino ratios for the 60/40 portfolio are 0.62 and 1.13, respectively. This graphic visually demonstrates that adding allocations of systematic futures, equity market-neutral, global macro, or event-driven hedge fund strategies, among others, to the traditional portfolio is effective in generating superior risk-adjusted performance—as evidenced by their relatively high Sharpe and Sortino ratios. Moreover, the implication is that despite the flexibility to invest in a wide range of strategies, fund-of-funds and multi-manager funds do not enhance risk-adjusted performance very much.

EXHIBIT 20   Sharpe and Sortino Ratios for 48/32/20 Portfolios, Where 20% Allocation Is to an Equal-Weighted Portfolio for Each Hedge Fund Strategy Category

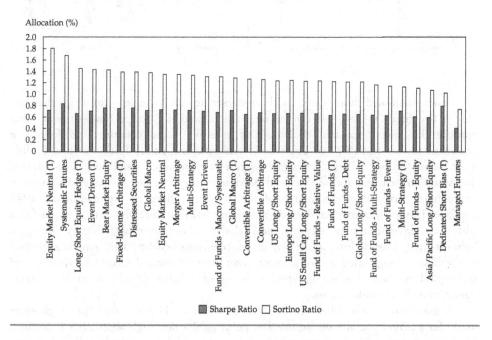

10.2. Risk Metrics

Considering the different risk exposures and investments that hedge fund strategies entail, many investors consider these strategies for portfolio risk reduction or risk mitigation. Exhibit 21 illustrates which strategies may be most effective in reducing risk in a traditional portfolio (with standard deviation of 8.66%). The exhibit presents the standard deviation of returns for 48/32/20 portfolios, where the 20% allocation is to an equal-weighted portfolio for each hedge fund strategy category.

EXHIBIT 21   Standard Deviations for 48/32/20 Portfolios, Where 20% Allocation Is to an Equal-Weighted Portfolio for Each Hedge Fund Strategy Category

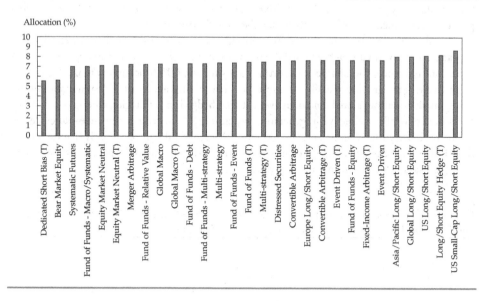

Besides dedicated short-biased and bear market-neutral strategies—for which there are only 6 live funds in total—it can be seen that among the hedge fund strategies that produce the lowest standard deviations of returns in the combined portfolios are systematic futures (6.94%) and FoF-macro/systematic and equity market neutral (a little more than 7.0%). These strategies appear to provide significant risk-reducing diversification benefits; and as discussed previously, they are also the same categories of hedge funds that enhance risk-adjusted returns when added to the traditional 60/40 portfolio. It is evident that standard deviations are relatively high for combined portfolios with event-driven/distressed securities and relative value/convertible arbitrage strategies, indicating they provide little in the way of risk-reduction benefits. This may be attributed to the binary, long-biased nature of most event-driven/distressed securities investing and the typical leverage downsizing/liquidity issues of relative value/convertible arbitrage during periods of market stress.

A drawdown is the difference between a portfolios' highest value (i.e., high-water mark) for a period and any subsequent low point until a new high-water mark is reached. Maximum drawdown is the *largest* difference between a high-water mark and a subsequent low point. The results for maximum drawdown for the 48/32/20 portfolios are shown in Exhibit 22.

EXHIBIT 22   Maximum Drawdowns for 48/32/20 Portfolios, Where 20% Allocation Is to an Equal-Weighted Portfolio for Each Hedge Fund Strategy Category

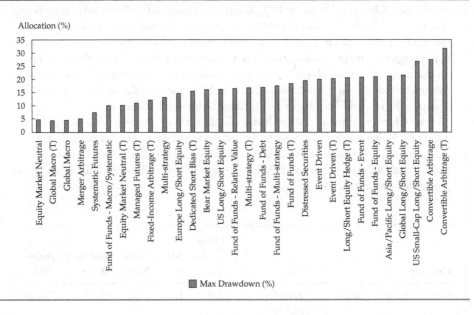

The graphic shows that when combined with the traditional stock and bond portfolio (with a maximum drawdown of 14.42%), the hedge fund strategy portfolios that generate the smallest maximum drawdowns are the opportunistic strategies—specifically, global macro and systematic futures as well as merger arbitrage and equity market-neutral strategies. Notably, the conditional risk model showed that these strategies did not have much exposure to high equity or credit risk during crisis periods. In addition, they also tend to be the strategies with the lowest serial autocorrelation, signaling good liquidity. This suggests that these types of strategies provide risk mitigation for traditional assets because they are not exposed to the same risks, are relatively opportunistic, and are liquid even during periods of market stress. On the other side of the spectrum, L/S equity strategies, event-driven/distressed securities strategies, and relative value/convertible arbitrage strategies show high maximum drawdowns when combined with the traditional portfolio. This is unsurprising because the conditional risk model showed that these event-driven and relative value strategies tended to hold equity risk and that their credit risk also became significant during crisis periods.

EXAMPLE 15   Combining a Hedge Fund Strategy with a Traditional Portfolio

DIY Investment Advisors is a "CIO in a box." Its clients are mainly small institutions and local college endowments. Evergreen Tech, a private 4-year college, is a client with a $150 million endowment and an enrollment of 3,000 students. The endowment's portfolio, which supports 5% of Evergreen's current annual spending needs, has a traditional asset allocation of 60% stocks/40% bonds. Evergreen plans to dramatically increase enrollment to 4,000 students over the next 5 years.

Patricia Chong, principal of DIY, wants to recommend to Evergreen's investment committee (IC) that it add alternative investments to the endowment's portfolio, specifically a 20% allocation to a hedge fund strategy. The IC has indicated to Chong that Evergreen's main considerations for the combined portfolio are that any hedge fund strategy allocation should a) maximize risk-adjusted returns; b) limit downside risk; and c) not impair portfolio liquidity. The IC is also sensitive to fees and considers it important to avoid layering of fees for any hedge fund allocation.

At Chong's request, DIY's hedge fund analysts perform due diligence on numerous hedge funds and assemble the following information on several short-listed funds, showing their past performance contribution to a 48% stocks/32% bonds/20% hedge fund strategy portfolio. Finally, Chong believes historical returns are good proxies for future returns.

Category	Type	Mean Return (%)	SD (%)	Sharpe Ratio	Sortino Ratio	Maximum Drawdown (%)
60% Stocks/40% Bonds	Traditional Portfolio	6.96	8.66	0.62	1.13	14.42
US small-cap long/short equity	Equity	7.53	8.75	0.68	1.23	27.02
Event driven	Event driven	7.19	7.83	0.71	1.31	20.57
Sovereign debt fixed-income arbitrage	Relative value	7.50	7.82	0.75	1.39	12.68
Fund-of-funds – equity	Multi-manager	6.39	7.76	0.62	1.11	21.63

Use the information provided to answer the following questions.

1. Discuss which hedge fund strategy Chong should view as *least* suitable for meeting the considerations expressed by Evergreen's IC.
2. Discuss which hedge fund strategy Chong should view as *most* suitable for meeting the considerations expressed by Evergreen's IC.

Solution to 1: Based on the IC's considerations, Chong should view a 20% allocation to the fund-of-funds equity hedge fund strategy as least suitable for Evergreen's endowment portfolio. Such an allocation offers no improvements in the combined portfolio's Sharpe and Sortino ratios (to 0.62 and 1.11, respectively). The substantially higher maximum drawdown (50% higher at 21.63%) indicates much more downside risk would be in the combined portfolio. Portfolio liquidity may also be impaired due to two levels of redemption lock-ups and liquidity gates. Finally, given the FoF structure for this strategy allocation, Evergreen would need to pay two layers of fees and would also likely face fee netting risk.

Solution to 2: Based on the IC's considerations, Chong should view a 20% allocation to the sovereign debt fixed-income arbitrage hedge fund strategy as most suitable for Evergreen's endowment portfolio. Such an allocation would result in significant increases in the combined portfolio's Sharpe and Sortino ratios (to 0.75 and 1.39, respectively), the highest such ratios among the strategies presented. Besides the improvement in Sortino ratio, the lower maximum drawdown (12.68%) indicates less downside risk in the combined portfolio than with any of the other strategy choices. Portfolio liquidity would also likely not be impaired as this strategy focuses on sovereign debt, which typically has good liquidity for most developed market issuers. Finally, similar to the other non-FoF strategies shown, Evergreen would pay only one layer of fees and would also not face any fee netting risk.

11. SUMMARY

- Hedge funds are an important subset of the alternative investments space. Key characteristics distinguishing hedge funds and their strategies from traditional investments include the following: 1) lower legal and regulatory constraints; 2) flexible mandates permitting use of shorting and derivatives; 3) a larger investment universe on which to focus; 4) aggressive investment styles that allow concentrated positions in securities offering exposure to credit, volatility, and liquidity risk premiums; 5) relatively liberal use of leverage; 6) liquidity constraints that include lock-ups and liquidity gates; and 7) relatively high fee structures involving management and incentive fees.
- Hedge fund strategies are classified by a combination of the instruments in which they are invested, the trading philosophy followed, and the types of risks assumed. Some leading hedge fund strategy index providers are Hedge Fund Research; Lipper TASS; Morningstar Hedge/CISDM; Eurekahedge; and Credit Suisse. There is much heterogeneity in the classification and indexes they provide, so no one index group is all-encompassing.
- This chapter classifies hedge fund strategies by the following categories: equity-related strategies; event-driven strategies; relative value strategies; opportunistic strategies; specialist strategies; and multi-manager strategies.
- Equity L/S strategies take advantage of diverse opportunities globally to create alpha via managers' skillful stock picking. Diverse investment styles include value/growth, large cap/ small cap, discretionary/quantitative, and industry specialization. Some equity L/S strategies may use index-based short hedges to reduce market risk, but most involve single name shorts for portfolio alpha and added absolute return.
- Equity L/S strategies are typically liquid and generally net long, with gross exposures at 70%–90% long vs. 20%–50% short (but they can vary).
- Equity L/S return profiles are typically aimed to achieve average annual returns roughly equivalent to a long-only approach but with standard deviations that are 50% lower. The more market-neutral or quantitative the strategy approach, the more levered the strategy application to achieve a meaningful return profile.
- Dedicated short sellers only trade with short-side exposure, but they may moderate short beta by also holding cash. Short-biased managers are focused on short-side stock picking, but they typically moderate short beta with some value-oriented long exposure and cash.

- Dedicated short strategies tend to be 60%–120% short at all times, while short-biased strategies are typically around 30%–60% net short. The focus in both cases is usually on single equity stock picking, as opposed to index shorting, and using little if any leverage.
- Dedicated short-selling and short-biased strategies have return goals that are typically less than most other hedge fund strategies but with a negative correlation benefit. Returns are more volatile than a typical L/S equity hedge fund given short beta exposure.
- Equity market-neutral (EMN) strategies take advantage of idiosyncratic short-term mispricing between securities. Their sources of return and alpha do not require accepting beta risk, so EMN strategies are especially attractive in periods of market vulnerability/ weakness. There are many types of EMN managers, but most are purely quantitative managers (vs. discretionary managers).
- As many beta risks (e.g., market, sector) are hedged away, EMN strategies generally apply relatively high levels of leverage in striving for meaningful return targets.
- Equity market-neutral strategies exhibit relatively modest return profiles. Portfolios are aimed at market neutrality and with differing constraints to other factor/sector exposures. Generally high levels of diversification and liquidity with lower standard deviation of returns are typical due to an orientation toward mean reversion.
- Merger arbitrage is a relatively liquid strategy. Defined gains come from idiosyncratic, single security takeover situations, but occasional downside shocks can occur when merger deals unexpectedly fail.
- Cross-border M&A usually involves two sets of governmental approvals. M&A deals involving vertical integration often face antitrust scrutiny and thus carry higher risks and offer wider merger spread returns.
- Merger arbitrage strategies have return profiles that are insurance-like, plus a short put option, with relatively high Sharpe ratios; however, left-tail risk is associated with otherwise steady returns. Merger arbitrage managers typically apply moderate to high leverage to generate meaningful target return levels.
- Distressed securities strategies focus on firms in bankruptcy, facing potential bankruptcy, or under financial stress. Hedge fund managers seek inefficiently priced securities before, during, or after the bankruptcy process, which results in either liquidation or reorganization.
- In liquidation, the firm's assets are sold off and securities holders are paid sequentially based on priority of their claims—from senior secured debt, junior secured debt, unsecured debt, convertible debt, preferred stock, and finally common stock.
- In re-organization, a firm's capital structure is re-organized and terms for current claims are negotiated and revised. Debtholders either may agree to maturity extensions or to exchanging their debt for new equity shares (existing shares are canceled) that are sold to new investors to improve the firm's financial condition.
- Outright shorts or hedged positions are possible, but distressed securities investing is usually long-biased, entails relatively high levels of illiquidity, and has moderate to low leverage. The return profile is typically at the higher end of event-driven strategies, but it is more discrete and cyclical.
- For fixed-income arbitrage, the attractiveness of returns is a function of the correlations between different securities, the yield spread pick-up available, and the high number and wide diversity of debt securities across different markets, each having different credit quality and convexity aspects in their pricing.

- Yield curve and carry trades within the US government space are very liquid but have the fewest mispricing opportunities. Liquidity for relative value positions generally decreases in other sovereign markets, mortgage-related markets, and across corporate debt markets.
- Fixed-income arbitrage involves high leverage usage, but leverage availability diminishes with trade and underlying instrument complexity.
- Convertible arbitrage strategies strive to extract "underpriced" implied volatility from long convertible bond holdings. To do this, managers will delta hedge and gamma trade short equity positions against their convertible positions. Convertible arbitrage works best in periods of high convertible issuance, moderate volatility, and reasonable market liquidity.
- Liquidity issues may arise from convertible bonds being naturally less-liquid securities due to their relatively small issue sizes and inherent complexities as well as the availability and cost to borrow underlying equity for short selling.
- Convertible arbitrage managers typically run convertible portfolios at 300% long vs. 200% short. The lower short exposure is a function of the delta-adjusted exposure needed from short sales to balance the long convertibles.
- Global macro strategies focus on correctly discerning and capitalizing on trends in global financial markets using a wide range of instruments. Managed futures strategies have a similar aim but focus on investments using mainly futures and options on futures, on stock and fixed-income indexes, as well as on commodities and currencies.
- Managed futures strategies typically are implemented via more systematic approaches, while global macro strategies tend to use more discretionary approaches. Both strategies are highly liquid and use high leverage.
- Returns of managed futures strategies typically exhibit positive right-tail skewness during market stress. Global macro strategies generally deliver similar diversification in stress periods but with more heterogeneous outcomes.
- Specialist hedge fund strategies require highly specialized skill sets for trading in niche markets. Two such typical specialist strategies—which are aimed at generating uncorrelated, attractive risk-adjusted returns—are volatility trading and reinsurance/life settlements.
- Volatility traders strive to capture relative timing and strike pricing opportunities due to changes in the term structure of volatility. They try to capture volatility smile and skew by using various types of option spreads, such as bull and bear spreads, straddles, and calendar spreads. In addition to using exchange-listed and OTC options, VIX futures, volatility swaps, and variance swaps can be used to implement volatility trading strategies.
- Life settlements strategies involve analyzing pools of life insurance contracts offered by third-party brokers, where the hedge fund purchases the pool and effectively becomes the beneficiary. The hedge fund manager looks for policies with the following traits: 1) The surrender value being offered to the insured individual is relatively low; 2) the ongoing premium payments are also relatively low; and 3) the probability is relatively high that the insured person will die sooner than predicted by standard actuarial methods.
- Funds-of-funds and multi-strategy funds typically offer steady, low-volatility returns via their strategy diversification. Multi-strategy funds have generally outperformed FoFs, but they have more variance due to using relatively high leverage.
- Multi-strategy funds offer potentially faster tactical asset allocation and generally improved fee structure (netting risk between strategies is often at least partially absorbed by the

general partner), but they have higher manager-specific operational risks. FoFs offer a potentially more diverse strategy mix, but they have less transparency, slower tactical reaction time, and contribute netting risk to the FoF investor.

- Conditional linear factor models can be useful for uncovering and analyzing hedge fund strategy risk exposures. This chapter uses such a model that incorporates four factors for assessing risk exposures in both normal periods and market stress/crisis periods: equity risk, credit risk, currency risk, and volatility risk.

- Adding a 20% allocation of a hedge fund strategy group to a traditional 60%/40% portfolio (for a 48% stocks/32% bonds/20% hedge funds portfolio) typically decreases total portfolio standard deviation while it increases Sharpe and Sortino ratios (and also often decreases maximum drawdown) in the combined portfolios. This demonstrates that hedge funds act as both risk-adjusted return enhancers and diversifiers for the traditional stock/bond portfolio.

REFERENCES

Hasanhodzic, Jasmina, and Andrew Lo. 2007. "Can Hedge-Fund Returns Be Replicated?: The Linear Case." *Journal of Investment Management* 5 (2): 5–45.

Lintner, John. 1983. "The Potential Role of Managed Commodity-Financial Futures Accounts (and/or Funds) in Portfolios of Stocks and Bonds." Working paper, Division of Research, Graduate School of Business Administration, Harvard University.

PRACTICE PROBLEMS

1. Bern Zang is the chief investment officer of the Janson University Endowment Investment Office. The Janson University Endowment Fund (the "Fund") is based in the United States and has current assets under management of $10 billion, with minimal exposure to alternative investments. Zang currently seeks to increase the Fund's allocation to hedge funds and considers four strategies: dedicated short bias, merger arbitrage, convertible bond arbitrage, and global macro.

   At a meeting with the Fund's board of directors, the board mandates Zang to invest only in event-driven and relative value hedge fund strategies.

   Determine, among the four strategies under consideration by Zang, the two that are permitted given the board's mandate. **Justify** your response.

   i. Dedicated short bias
   ii. Merger arbitrage
   iii. Convertible bond arbitrage
   iv. Global macro

Determine, among the four strategies under consideration by Zang, the two that are permitted given the board's mandate. (circle two)   **Justify** your response.

Dedicated short bias

Merger arbitrage

Convertible bond arbitrage

Global macro strategies

The following information relates to Questions 2 and 3

Jane Shaindy is the chief investment officer of a large pension fund. The pension fund is based in the United States and currently has minimal exposure to hedge funds. The pension fund's board has recently approved an additional investment in a long/short equity strategy. As part of Shaindy's due diligence on a hedge fund that implements a long/short equity strategy, she uses a conditional linear factor model to uncover and analyze the hedge fund's risk exposures. She is interested in analyzing several risk factors, but she is specifically concerned about whether the hedge fund's long (positive) exposure to equities increases during turbulent market periods.

2. **Describe** how the conditional linear factor model can be used to address Shaindy's concern.

   During a monthly board meeting, Shaindy discusses her updated market forecast for equity markets. Due to a recent large increase in interest rates and geopolitical tensions, her forecast has changed from one of modestly rising equities to several periods of non-trending markets. Given this new market view, Shaindy concludes that a long/short strategy will not be optimal at this time and seeks another equity-related strategy. The Fund has the capacity to use a substantial amount of leverage.

3. **Determine** the *most appropriate* equity-related hedge fund strategy that Shaindy should employ. **Justify** your response.

4. Gunnar Patel is an event-driven hedge fund manager for Senson Fund, which focuses on merger arbitrage strategies. Patel has been monitoring the potential acquisition of Meura Inc. by Sellshom, Inc. Sellshom is currently trading at $60 per share and has offered to buy Meura in a stock-for-stock deal. Meura was trading at $18 per share just prior to the announcement of the acquisition.

   The offer ratio is 1 share of Sellshom in exchange for 2 shares of Meura. Soon after the announcement, Meura's share price jumps to $22 while Sellshom's falls to $55 in anticipation of the merger receiving required approvals and the deal closing successfully.

   At the current share prices of $55 for Sellshom and $22 for Meura, Patel attempts to profit from the merger announcement. He buys 40,000 shares of Meura and sells short 20,000 shares of Sellshom.

Calculate the payoffs of the merger arbitrage under the following two scenarios:
   i. The merger is successfully completed.
   ii. The merger fails.

5. John Puten is the chief investment officer of the Markus University Endowment Investment Office. Puten seeks to increase the diversification of the endowment by investing in hedge funds. He recently met with several hedge fund managers that employ different investment strategies. In selecting a hedge fund manager, Puten prefers to hire a manager that uses the following:
   • Fundamental and technical analysis to value markets
   • Discretionary and systematic modes of implementation
   • Top-down strategies
   • A range of macroeconomic and fundamental models to express a view regarding the direction or relative value of a particular asset
   Puten's staff prepares a brief summary of two potential hedge fund investments:
   Hedge Fund 1: A relative value strategy fund focusing only on convertible arbitrage.
   Hedge Fund 2: An opportunistic strategy fund focusing only on global macro strategies.

   Determine which hedge fund would be *most appropriate* for Puten. **Justify** your response.

6. Yankel Stein is the chief investment officer of a large charitable foundation based in the United States. Although the foundation has significant exposure to alternative investments and hedge funds, Stein proposes to increase the foundation's exposure to relative value hedge fund strategies. As part of Stein's due diligence on a hedge fund engaging in convertible bond arbitrage, Stein asks his investment analyst to summarize different risks associated with the strategy.
   Describe how each of the following circumstances can create concerns for Stein's proposed hedge fund strategy:
   i. Short selling
   ii. Credit issues
   iii. Time decay of call option
   iv. Extreme market volatility

	Describe how each of the following circumstances can create concerns for Stein's proposed hedge fund strategy:
Short selling	
Credit issues	
Time decay of call option	
Extreme market volatility	

The following information relates to Questions 7 and 8

Sushil Wallace is the chief investment officer of a large pension fund. Wallace wants to increase the pension fund's allocation to hedge funds and recently met with three hedge fund managers. These hedge funds focus on the following strategies:

Hedge Fund A: Specialist—Follows relative value volatility arbitrage
Hedge Fund B: Multi-Manager—Multi-strategy fund
Hedge Fund C: Multi-Manager—Fund-of-funds

7. **Describe** three paths for implementing the strategy of Hedge Fund A.

After a significant amount of internal discussion, Wallace concludes that the pension fund should invest in either Hedge Fund B or C for the diversification benefits from the different strategies employed. However, after final due diligence is completed, Wallace recommends investing only in Hedge Fund B, noting its many advantages over Hedge Fund C.

8. **Discuss** *two* advantages of Hedge Fund B relative to Hedge Fund C with respect to investment characteristics.

---

9. Kloss Investments is an investment adviser whose clients are small institutional investors. Muskogh Charitable Foundation (the "Foundation") is a client with $70 million of assets under management. The Foundation has a traditional asset allocation of 65% stocks/35% bonds. Risk and return characteristics for the Foundation's current portfolio are presented in Panel A of Exhibit 1.

   Kloss' CIO, Christine Singh, recommends to Muskogh's investment committee that it should add a 10% allocation to hedge funds. The investment committee indicates to Singh that Muskogh's primary considerations for the Foundation's portfolio are that any hedge fund strategy allocation should: a) limit volatility, b) maximize risk-adjusted returns, and c) limit downside risk.

   Singh's associate prepares expected risk and return characteristics for three portfolios that have allocations of 60% stocks, 30% bonds, and 10% hedge funds, where the 10% hedge fund allocation follows either an equity market-neutral, global macro, or convertible arbitrage strategy. The risk and return characteristics of the three portfolios are presented in Panel B of Exhibit 1.

EXHIBIT 1

Hedge Fund Strategy	SD (%)	Sharpe Ratio	Sortino Ratio	Maximum Drawdown (%)
Panel A: Current Portfolio				
N/A	8.75	0.82	1.25	16.2
Panel B: Three Potential Portfolios with a 10% Hedge Fund Allocation				
Equity market neutral	8.72	0.80	1.21	15.1
Global macro	8.55	0.95	1.35	15.0
Convertible arbitrage	8.98	0.83	1.27	20.2

Discuss which hedge fund strategy Singh should view as most suitable for meeting the considerations expressed by Muskogh's investment committee.

The following information relates to Questions 10–17

Snohomish Mukilteo is a portfolio analyst for the Puyallup-Wenatchee Pension Fund (PWPF). PWPF's investment committee (IC) asks Mukilteo to research adding hedge funds to the PWPF portfolio.

A member of the IC meets with Mukilteo to discuss hedge fund strategies. During the meeting, the IC member admits that her knowledge of hedge fund strategies is fairly limited but tells Mukilteo she believes the following:

Statement 1: Equity market-neutral strategies use a relative value approach.
Statement 2: Event-driven strategies are not exposed to equity market beta risk.
Statement 3: Opportunistic strategies have risk exposure to market directionality.

The IC member also informs Mukilteo that for equity-related strategies, the IC considers low volatility to be more important than negative correlation.

Mukilteo researches various hedge fund strategies. First, Mukilteo analyzes an event-driven strategy involving two companies, Algona Applications (AA) and Tukwila Technologies (TT). AA's management, believing that its own shares are overvalued, uses its shares to acquire TT. The IC has expressed concern about this type of strategy because of the potential for loss if the acquisition unexpectedly fails. Mukilteo's research reveals a way to use derivatives to protect against this loss, and he believes that such protection will satisfy the IC's concern.

Next, while researching relative value strategies, Mukilteo considers a government bond strategy that involves buying lower-liquidity, off-the-run bonds and selling higher-liquidity, duration-matched, on-the-run bonds.

Mukilteo examines an opportunistic strategy implemented by one of the hedge funds under consideration. The hedge fund manager selects 12 AAA rated corporate bonds with actively traded futures contracts and approximately equal durations. For each corporate bond, the manager calculates the 30-day change in the yield spread over a constant risk-free rate. He then ranks the bonds according to this spread change. For the bonds that show the greatest spread narrowing (widening), the hedge fund will take long (short) positions in their futures contracts. The net holding for this strategy is market neutral.

Mukilteo also plans to recommend a specialist hedge fund strategy that would allow PWPF to maintain a high Sharpe ratio even during a financial crisis when equity markets fall.

The IC has been considering the benefits of allocating to a fund of funds (FoF) or to a multi-strategy fund (MSF). Mukilteo receives the following email from a member of the IC: "From my perspective, an FoF is superior even though it entails higher manager-specific operational risk and will require us to pay a double layer of fees without being able to net performance fees on individual managers. I especially like the tactical allocation advantage of FoFs—that they are more likely to be well informed about when to tactically reallocate to a particular strategy and more capable of shifting capital between strategies quickly."

Finally, Mukilteo creates a model to simulate adding selected individual hedge fund strategies to the current portfolio with a 20% allocation. The IC's primary considerations for a combined portfolio are (1) that the variance of the combined portfolio must be less than 90% of that of the current portfolio and (2) that the combined portfolio maximize the risk-adjusted return with the expectation of large negative events. Exhibit 1 provides historical performance and risk metrics for three simulated portfolios.

EXHIBIT 1   Performance of Various Combined Portfolios

Hedge Fund Strategy	Standard Deviation (%)	Sharpe Ratio	Sortino Ratio	Maximum Drawdown (%)
Current Portfolio				
NA	7.95	0.58	1.24	14.18
Three Potential Portfolios with a 20% Hedge Fund Allocation				
Merger arbitrage	7.22	0.73	1.35	5.60
Systematic futures	6.94	0.83	1.68	8.04
Equity market neutral	7.17	0.73	1.80	10.72

10. Which of the IC member's statements regarding hedge fund strategies is *incorrect*?
    A. Statement 1
    B. Statement 2
    C. Statement 3

11. Based on what the IC considers important for equity-related strategies, which strategy should Mukilteo *most likely* avoid?
    A. Long/short equity
    B. Equity market neutral
    C. Dedicated short selling and short biased

12. Which of the following set of derivative positions will *most likely* satisfy the IC's concern about the event-driven strategy involving AA and TT?
    A. Long out-of-the-money puts on AA shares and long out-of-the-money calls on TT shares
    B. Long out-of-the-money calls on AA shares and long out-of-the-money puts on TT shares
    C. Long risk-free bonds, short out-of-the-money puts on AA shares, and long out-of-the-money calls on TT shares

13. The government bond strategy that Mukilteo considers is *best* described as a:
    A. carry trade.
    B. yield curve trade.
    C. long/short credit trade.

14. The opportunistic strategy that Mukilteo considers is *most likely* to be described as a:
    A. global macro strategy.
    B. time-series momentum strategy.
    C. cross-sectional momentum strategy.

15. The specialist hedge fund strategy that Mukilteo plans to recommend is *most likely*:
    A. cross-asset volatility trading between the US and Japanese markets.
    B. selling equity volatility and collecting the volatility risk premium.
    C. buying longer-dated out-of-the-money options on VIX index futures.

16. Based on the email that Mukilteo received, the IC member's perspective is correct with regard to:
    A. layering and netting of fees.
    B. tactical allocation capabilities.
    C. manager-specific operational risks.

17. Based on the IC's primary considerations for a combined portfolio, which simulated hedge fund strategy portfolio in Exhibit 1 creates the *most suitable* combined portfolio?
    A. Merger arbitrage
    B. Systematic futures
    C. Equity market neutral

CHAPTER 15

OVERVIEW OF PRIVATE WEALTH MANAGEMENT

Christopher J. Sidoni, CFP, CFA
Vineet Vohra, CFA

LEARNING OUTCOMES

The candidate should be able to:

- contrast private client and institutional client investment concerns;
- discuss information needed in advising private clients;
- identify tax considerations affecting a private client's investments;
- identify and formulate client goals based on client information;
- evaluate a private client's risk tolerance;
- describe technical and soft skills needed in advising private clients;
- evaluate capital sufficiency in relation to client goals;
- discuss the principles of retirement planning;
- discuss the parts of an investment policy statement (IPS) for a private client;
- prepare the investment objectives section of an IPS for a private client;
- evaluate and recommend improvements to an IPS for a private client;
- recommend and justify portfolio allocations and investments for a private client;
- describe effective practices in portfolio reporting and review;
- evaluate the success of an investment program for a private client;
- discuss ethical and compliance considerations in advising private clients;
- discuss how levels of service and range of solutions are related to different private clients.

1. INTRODUCTION

Private wealth management refers to investment management and financial planning for individual investors. The private wealth sector has grown considerably as global wealth has

Portfolio Management, Second Edition, by Christopher J. Sidoni, CFP, CFA, and Vineet Vohra, CFA.
Copyright © 2019 by CFA Institute.

increased and as individuals have taken on more of the responsibility for managing their own financial resources. Private wealth managers can help individual investors seek the benefits as well as navigate the complexities of financial markets.

This chapter introduces candidates to the process of designing and executing an investment plan or strategy for the individual investor. We discuss the tools and techniques used by private wealth managers and how the wealth manager interacts with the client to serve the client's needs. Section 2 examines the key differences between private clients and institutional clients. In Section 3, we discuss how the wealth manager gains an understanding of the client and identifies key attributes of the client's financial situation that are relevant to the wealth management process. Section 4 covers investment planning, including capital sufficiency and retirement planning. Section 5 discusses the investment policy statement, including its various underlying parts. Section 6 analyzes portfolio construction, portfolio reporting, and portfolio review. Finally, in Section 7, we discuss the practice of private wealth management, including ethical considerations for private wealth managers, compliance considerations, and the various client segments that private wealth managers encounter.

Reflecting the variation in industry terms, we use the terms "private wealth managers," "wealth managers," and "advisors" interchangeably.[1] We also refer to "individual investors" as "private clients" or, simply, "clients." In practice, private wealth managers typically operate either independently or as representatives of organizations, such as wealth management firms, banks, and broker/dealers.

2. PRIVATE CLIENTS VERSUS INSTITUTIONAL CLIENTS

Private clients include individuals and families seeking to invest their personal wealth. These clients are asset owners but typically retain private wealth managers to undertake investment responsibilities on their behalf. Private clients and institutional clients have different concerns, including the following:

- *Investment objectives.*[2] Private clients have diverse investment objectives, some of which may be broadly defined. By contrast, institutional investors tend to have specific, clearly defined investment objectives.
- *Constraints.* Private clients face constraints that differ from those of institutional clients, such as generally shorter time horizons, smaller portfolio sizes (less scale), and more significant tax considerations.
- *Other distinctions.* Institutional investors operate under a formal governance structure and often have a greater level of investment sophistication than many private clients. Behavioral issues may also be more prominent for private clients. In addition, while regulation is common to both private clients and institutional clients, the regulatory bodies and frameworks may differ.

2.1. Investment Objectives

Private clients have several potential investment objectives. Some common objectives include financial security during the client's retirement years, the ability to provide financial support to family members, and the funding of philanthropic goals. These objectives, however, may

---

[1] It should also be noted that among client segments with high levels of wealth, the roles of wealth managers may vary.

[2] In practice, the terms "objectives" and "goals" are often used interchangeably. We also use them interchangeably in this chapter.

not be clearly defined or quantified. For example, a private client's goal may be to fund her retirement lifestyle, but she may not be able to quantify the annual cash flow requirement. She may be able to estimate what is required at the beginning of retirement but uncertain about how the required amount may fluctuate throughout retirement. A different client may wish to fund higher education expenses for his young children. However, he may not know how many of his children will attend a college or university, or what tuition and expenses will be.

Private client investment objectives often compete with one another and may change over time. Consider a business owner who wishes to fund a comfortable retirement for himself and also give generously to certain charities. An unexpected change in his business may shift his priorities considerably. For example, a business downturn may cause him to reduce his charitable goals or eliminate them completely. Conversely, a significant liquidity event, such as the sale of his business, may make a comfortable retirement virtually certain, causing the client to increase his charitable aspirations.

In contrast to private clients, institutional clients tend to have more clearly defined objectives, which are typically related to a specific liability stream. For example, the investment program of a pension plan is designed to meet its benefit obligation, while a university endowment allocates investments to achieve its spending policy. Unlike the objectives of private clients, the primary objectives of these institutional investors are unlikely to change materially over time.

2.2. Constraints

Private clients have unique constraints, resulting in investment strategies and approaches that are different from those of institutional clients. Such constraints include time horizon, scale, and taxes.

2.2.1. Time Horizon
In general, individual investors have a shorter time horizon than institutional investors, whose horizon is often theoretically infinite. With shorter time horizons, individual investors are typically more constrained than institutions with respect to risk taking and liquidity. Time horizons also depend on an investor's objectives. For example, individual investors may have different time horizons for different objectives, while institutional investors tend to have a single time horizon and a single investment objective.

2.2.2. Scale
In general, individual investor portfolios tend to be smaller in size (or scale) than those of institutional investors. Because of this smaller portfolio size, many individual investors face limitations relating to certain asset classes, such as private equity and private real estate, which require a significant investment and would result in an imbalanced portfolio. As with time horizon, the size of private client portfolios can vary widely.

2.2.3. Taxes
Taxes are a significant and complex consideration for many individual investors, and they vary by jurisdiction. The presence of taxes on investment income or on realized capital gains can impact such investment decisions as asset allocation and manager selection. Investment strategies that result in considerable taxable income may be more favored by a tax-exempt institution than by a taxable private client. Similarly, tax-efficient investments may be more

attractive to taxable private clients. An example of a tax-efficient investment is a low-turnover common stock portfolio.

2.3. Other Distinctions

In addition to investment objectives and constraints, there are other key distinctions between private clients and institutional clients. Private clients have a less formal governance structure, are typically less sophisticated at investing, may operate under a different regulatory regime, and are more individually unique and complex. Because of these aspects, the personality profile, time allocation, and resource needs/constraints of a private wealth manager differ significantly from those of an institutional manager.

2.3.1. Investment Governance

The investment governance model and the decision-making process for individual investors differ considerably from those of institutional investors. Institutional investors typically operate under a formal governance structure. This governance structure generally includes a board of directors and an investment committee, sometimes augmented by independent directors with investment expertise. The investment committee may consist of a subset of the board of directors, or the board may delegate this responsibility to an internal committee of staff members. The board and the investment committee play a key role in setting the investment strategy and monitoring investment performance.

By contrast, investment governance for individual investors tends to be less formal. The individual investor works with a private wealth manager to determine an appropriate investment policy. The investment policy is often described in an investment policy statement (which is discussed later in this chapter) and typically grants implementation and reporting responsibilities to the wealth manager.

2.3.2. Investment Sophistication

Institutional investors tend to have a higher degree of investment sophistication than the typical private investor as well as access to more investment resources. Unlike institutional clients, private clients do not normally benefit from the "checks and balances" of a formal investment governance framework. As a result, private clients can be more vulnerable to making "emotional" investment decisions.

2.3.3. Regulation

In most countries, the regulatory environment is different for individual and institutional investors. In some cases, separate regulators focus on these two investor segments. For example, in the United States, the Securities and Exchange Commission (SEC) and state regulators oversee independent registered investment advisors (RIAs), while the Financial Industry Regulatory Authority (FINRA) covers those advisors who work for broker/dealer organizations. In other cases, the individual and institutional investor groups share a common regulator but are subject to different regulations. An example of this structure occurs in Singapore, where the Monetary Authority of Singapore (MAS) is the primary regulator of financial institutions, yet the MAS also regulates individual investors through its Financial Advisors Act (FAA). This shared regulatory structure also exists in several other countries, such as Australia, China, India, Indonesia, and Malaysia.

2.3.4. Uniqueness and Complexity

One final difference between private and institutional clients relates to the uniqueness and complexity of individuals. Private clients with similar sets of financial considerations and objectives may nevertheless pursue different investment strategies. Multiple factors may influence each individual's preferences, needs, and concerns—notably, family background and upbringing, work history, sources of wealth, investment experience, groups of friends, and geographic location. Institutional clients with similar considerations and objectives may also follow different investment strategies, but this outcome is less likely with institutional clients than with private clients.

EXAMPLE 1 Private versus Institutional Clients

Garrett Jones, age 74, is a member of the investment committee for a local non-profit endowment. The endowment portfolio includes sizable allocations to less liquid and more volatile asset classes, such as hedge funds and private equity. Jones's personal portfolio, which is modest in size, contains no exposure to hedge funds or private equity. Jones asks his wealth manager about the lack of exposure to these asset classes.

Discuss why the wealth manager has likely not recommended investments in hedge funds and private equity to Jones.

Solution: Jones's wealth manager has likely not recommended these investments because of certain private client constraints. First, as an individual investor, Jones likely has a shorter time horizon and/or greater liquidity needs than an institutional investor (such as the endowment for which Jones is a committee member). Second, the relatively small size of Jones's personal portfolio will most likely preclude investing in certain asset classes, such as hedge funds and private equity, which require a significant investment and would result in an imbalanced portfolio. Finally, Jones's personal tax considerations may make these investments relatively unattractive.

---

3. UNDERSTANDING PRIVATE CLIENTS

Every new private client engagement begins with developing an understanding of the client. In this section, we begin with a discussion of the information needed in advising private clients and how wealth managers obtain this information. In addition, we discuss a process for formulating client goals, the evaluation of a private client's risk tolerance, and both the technical and "soft" skills needed to advise private clients.

3.1. Information Needed in Advising Private Clients

Wealth managers gather client information predominantly through conversations with clients and by reviewing various financial documents. In this section, we cover the relevant personal, financial, and other information needed in advising private clients.

3.1.1. Personal Information

The process of gathering personal information begins when the wealth manager first communicates with the individual investor. In introductory meetings or telephone calls, individuals typically learn about how wealth managers work with clients, the types of clients that they advise, their areas of expertise, and their fees for service. At the same time, wealth managers ask questions to learn more about prospective clients and what is important to them. While the main purpose of this first interaction is to determine mutual "fit," the introductory conversation often also provides valuable portfolio management information to both sides.

Once an individual becomes a private client, the wealth manager starts by learning about the client's family situation, including marital status, the number of children and grandchildren, and the ages of family members. In most jurisdictions, obtaining proof of client identification is required. For example, a copy of a passport may need to be obtained. The client's employment and career information is also important, as is a discussion about the client's future career, business, or retirement aspirations. In addition, wealth managers should assess the sources of a client's wealth. This information is not always evident from investment statements or reports. For example, a client who has gradually built her wealth through regular portfolio contributions over many years likely has significant experience with market volatility. She also may be able to articulate her emotional reactions (or lack thereof) to various market events. A different client who has relatively new wealth due to the sale of a business may not have this same experience or ability.

As part of the investment background conversation, the wealth manager should determine whether the client has an explicit return objective. Some clients have clear expectations for minimum absolute or relative return targets. Other clients are more concerned with meeting specific goals and may not have a particular return objective. Information about a client's investment preferences may also be generated through conversation with the wealth manager. For instance, liquidity preferences or a desire to consider environmental, social, and governance (ESG) issues in investments may surface in early conversations.

Finally, a detailed discussion of the client's financial objectives (often also referred to as "goals") and risk tolerance is part of the personal information gathering process. We discuss goals, objectives, and risk tolerance in more detail later in this chapter.

3.1.2. Financial Information

It is important for wealth managers to understand the financial information of a private client. In many cases, private clients do not maintain and regularly update personal financial statements, such as a *personal balance sheet* (also known as a net worth statement) or a statement of cash flows. Therefore, one responsibility of the wealth manager is to piece together these financial statements for the client.

On a private client's personal balance sheet, assets typically include the following:

- Cash and deposit accounts
- Brokerage accounts
- Retirement accounts (e.g., employer-sponsored defined contribution plan accounts or the present value of defined benefit pensions)
- Other employee benefits, such as restricted stock or stock options
- Ownership interests (stock) in private businesses

- Cash-value life insurance[3]
- Real property, including residences, rental property, and land
- Other personal assets (e.g., automobiles, art, or jewelry)

Liabilities on a private client's balance sheet typically include the following:

- Consumer debt, such as credit card balances and loans outstanding
- Automobile loans
- Student loans
- Property-related loans, such as mortgages and home equity loans (or lines of credit)
- Margin debt in brokerage accounts

Clients provide information about their assets and liabilities to wealth managers through copies of statements and reports. A key challenge for wealth managers is that the information provided by clients may not be comprehensive. To fully understand a client's financial profile, a wealth manager needs to analyze and synthesize these statements and reports. Exhibit 1 shows a sample personal balance sheet for a fictitious married couple, Steven and Jenny MacAuley.

EXHIBIT 1   Sample Personal Balance Sheet

ASSETS		LIABILITIES	
Cash and Deposit Accounts		**Consumer Debt**	
Bank deposit account	EUR 40,000	Credit cards	EUR 30,000
Brokerage and Retirements Accounts		**Property-Related Loans**	
Individual account for Steven	EUR 850,000	Mortgage for personal residence	EUR 320,000
Individual account for Jenny	EUR 1,200,000	Mortgage for rental property 1	EUR 110,000
Retirement account for Steven	EUR 1,400,000	Mortgage for rental property 2	EUR 180,000
Private Investment			
Private stock for Jenny	EUR 2,000,000		
Real Property			
Personal residence	EUR 900,000		
Rental property 1	EUR 250,000		
Rental property 2	EUR 350,000		
Automobiles	EUR 75,000		
Other personal property	EUR 50,000		
Total Assets	**EUR 7,115,000**	**Total Liabilities**	**EUR 640,000**
		Total Net Worth	**EUR 6,475,000**

---

[3]A cash-value life insurance policy involves a cash reserve in addition to protection for the death of an individual. This form of insurance usually combines life insurance with some type of cash accumulation vehicle.

Beyond assets and liabilities, cash flows are also highly relevant to a private client's financial situation. Sources of cash flows may include employment income, business profit distributions, government income benefits, pensions, annuity income, and portfolio income/distributions. A projection of the client's annual expenses is valuable even if clients do not maintain detailed expense information. In addition, the relevance of expense information varies by client. For example, consider a young, modestly affluent couple versus an older couple who possess wealth that is well beyond their needs. For the young couple, expense information is vital for the wealth manager in determining how much the couple can save toward their goals through improved budgeting. By contrast, obtaining detailed expense information is likely less important in the case of the older, wealthier couple, who are not as budget constrained.

3.1.3. Private Client Tax Considerations

A client's specific tax circumstances can be assessed from the client's tax returns. Tax returns, in particular, provide information that may not otherwise surface in conversations between the wealth manager and the client. In this section, we provide a basic overview of common types of taxes, discuss the global applicability of various tax types, and introduce basic tax strategies for private clients.

3.1.3.1. Common Tax Categories

Taxes for individuals vary by jurisdiction, although some categories are reasonably consistent globally:

- *Taxes on income.* These include taxes on salaries, interest, dividends, capital gains, and rental income.
- *Wealth-based taxes.* These include taxes on the holding of certain types of property (e.g., real estate) and taxes on the transfer of wealth (e.g., taxes on inheritance).
- *Taxes on consumption/spending.* These include sales taxes (i.e., taxes assessed on the final consumer of goods or services) and value-added taxes (i.e., taxes assessed in the intermediate steps of producing a good or service but ultimately paid by the final consumer).

Capital gains taxes are a good illustration of the variability and complexity of global taxes. For example, in Canada, only half of an individual's "net" capital gains (i.e., total capital gains minus total capital losses) are included in taxable income and are taxed at the client's top marginal rate (that is, the rate to be paid on additional income). In the United States and several other jurisdictions, gains on securities over short-term holding periods are taxed at the client's highest marginal income tax rate, while gains on securities over long-term holding periods are taxed at a "long-term" capital gains rate that is generally lower than the marginal income tax rate. India also distinguishes between long-term and short-term capital gains and has several additional considerations that relate to taxes on securities transactions.

3.1.3.2. Basic Tax Strategies

Taxes are normally reflected in a private client's financial plan and asset allocation decisions. While an in-depth discussion of tax strategies is beyond the scope of this chapter, the following considerations are common to many clients:

- *Tax avoidance.* Individuals clearly prefer to avoid paying taxes, if possible. Tax avoidance should not be confused with illegal tax evasion. Some countries allow investors to contribute limited amounts to certain accounts that permit tax-free earnings and future withdrawals. Another example of tax avoidance involves various wealth transfer techniques. In a jurisdiction that permits limited amounts of gifts to be transferred without incurring gift taxes, the client can reduce the effects of an estate or inheritance tax both on the amount of the gift and on future capital appreciation.

- *Tax reduction.* Wealth managers typically seek opportunities to reduce the effect of taxes for private clients. For example, a wealth manager may recommend tax-exempt bonds that can produce a higher tax-adjusted return than taxable bonds. Or a wealth manager may recommend limiting exposure to asset classes with less favorable tax characteristics while increasing exposure to more tax-efficient asset classes.

- *Tax deferral.* By deferring the recognition of certain taxes until a later date, clients can benefit from compounding portfolio returns that are not diminished by periodic tax payments. Some investors in a progressive tax system (i.e., a system in which the tax rate increases as income increases) may also seek to defer taxes because they anticipate lower future tax rates. For example, a client with a high level of compensation (and a high marginal tax rate) during her working years may seek to defer taxes on investment income or gains until after retirement (assuming her marginal income tax rate will then be lower). Another example of a tax deferral strategy is limiting portfolio turnover and thus the realization of capital gains.

EXAMPLE 2   Basic Tax Strategies

Roseanna Rodriguez meets with her wealth manager, Raj Gupta, CFA, to discuss her investment strategy and financial plan. Gupta mentions the importance of tax strategies in Rodriguez's financial plan and makes three recommendations:

1. Invest in two different account types: (1) an account that permits both earnings and future withdrawals to be tax-free and (2) an account that permits earnings to accumulate tax-free but requires that taxes be paid when assets are withdrawn from the account.
2. Reduce exposure to an asset class with undesirable tax characteristics in favor of an asset class that is more tax-efficient.
3. Delay the sale of shares of a stock position until the year following retirement.

Identify the basic tax strategy (or strategies)—tax avoidance, tax reduction, or tax deferral—represented in each of the three recommendations.

Solution: The first recommendation represents both tax avoidance and tax deferral. With the account that permits tax-free accumulation and distributions, Rodriguez would be avoiding taxes. With the account that permits tax-free accumulation but results in income taxes upon distribution, Rodriguez would be deferring taxes.

The second recommendation is an example of tax reduction because the recommended asset class would incur lower taxes. The third recommendation is an example of tax deferral and may also be an example of tax reduction if Rodriguez's tax rate declines after retirement.

3.1.4. Other Relevant Information

Private wealth managers typically gather other information from clients that is related to financial planning. For a client's estate plan (in applicable jurisdictions), the wealth manager obtains copies of relevant legal and governing documents, such as wills and trust documents. Wealth managers also obtain detailed information about the client's life insurance, disability insurance, excess liability coverage, and any other relevant insurance coverage.

We stated previously that private clients tend to have less formal governance models than institutional investors. As part of the information-gathering phase, wealth managers and clients typically establish decision-making parameters as part of investment governance. In fact, wealth managers have an opportunity to help *create* a governance model for clients. Wealth managers and clients normally agree on who can approve and/or change investment policies, who can authorize trading activity, and who can authorize money transfers. When advising couples, it is important to establish whether one individual will be the primary contact with the wealth manager and whether each individual is authorized to make decisions on behalf of the other. Clear guidelines on these issues can minimize the possibility of future misunderstandings or conflicts.

Wealth managers seek information regarding clients' service needs and expectations. For example, it is helpful for the wealth manager to describe her standard practices for portfolio reporting (i.e., frequency, format, information content, and delivery method) and discuss whether the client has reporting needs that differ from the wealth manager's standard practices. When clients expect to have regular cash flow activity, such as periodic withdrawals from their portfolio, the wealth manager should assist in creating an efficient and secure process for executing these transactions. Finally, some clients prefer that their wealth manager interact directly with their other service professionals, such as accountants and legal representatives. The wealth manager and the client should have a clear understanding of what information should and should not be shared with these parties.

3.2. Client Goals

As part of the information-gathering process, wealth managers help private clients formulate and prioritize their goals. These goals may relate to education, property, discretionary spending, gifts to loved ones, health care, or other significant financial considerations. Financial goals are not always apparent, defined, or measurable: they may be expressed by clients as wishes, desires, or aspirations. When goals are uncertain or ambiguous, wealth managers have an opportunity to help clients understand their true objectives, to assess trade-offs and issues with respect to goal prioritization, and to align the client's investment strategy accordingly. This section focuses on the two types of financial goals that are typical of private clients—planned goals and unplanned goals.

3.2.1. Planned Goals

Planned goals are those that can be reasonably estimated or quantified within an expected time horizon. The following are some examples of planned goals:

- *Retirement.* Maintaining a comfortable lifestyle beyond their working years is a goal for most clients.
- *Specific purchases.* Client goals may focus on specific purchases, which tend to be a function of the level of wealth and/or stage of life. For instance, younger clients or those with

relatively low levels of wealth may wish to save for a primary residence. In contrast, older clients or those with more significant levels of wealth may plan for a second residence, a vacation property, or other luxury items (e.g., art or rare collectibles).

■ *Education.* Clients often wish to fund their children's education. The amount of expenditure needed for education varies widely. In some locations, such as the United States, the increase in education costs has significantly exceeded the general rate of inflation. Foreign exchange risk may be a factor for clients whose children study abroad.

■ *Family events.* Family events, such as weddings, can be significant expenditures for clients.

■ *Wealth transfer.* Clients typically plan for their wealth to outlast their own lifetime. An inheritance for beneficiaries may be transferred when the client dies or, in some cases, during the client's lifetime. When clients have a definite amount that they wish to transfer, this goal may need to be prioritized over other goals.

■ *Philanthropy.* Clients often wish to make charitable donations during or after their lifetime. This objective may depend on a client's wealth level and country/region.

3.2.2. Unplanned Goals

Unplanned goals are those related to unforeseen financial needs. These goals are typically more challenging than planned goals because of the difficulty of estimating the timing and the amount of funding needed. The following are some examples of unplanned goals:

■ *Property repairs.* Although households may be insured against losses or catastrophes, clients may face additional spending needs if insurance does not fully cover such events. The timing of these potential obligations is often uncertain.

■ *Medical expenses.* Private client households normally have medical insurance for illness or hospitalization, but health insurance may not cover all medical expenses. The potential for unexpected medical expenses varies significantly by country/region. As with education costs, increases in health care costs in some countries/regions have far exceeded the general rate of inflation. A related issue in some locations is the potential cost of elder care for oneself or one's family members.

■ *Other unforeseen spending.* Beyond property repairs and medical expenses, various other unexpected events commonly occur in the lives of private clients that may require significant financial outlays.

3.2.3. The Wealth Manager's Role

Goals are among the more complex aspects of a client's financial profile. Because goals are often not clearly defined, wealth managers play a direct role in helping clients articulate these objectives. The following are some relevant considerations in client goal creation:

• *Goal quantification.* Sometimes clients do not have specific, quantifiable goals that wealth managers can analyze. For example, a young client may be unable to estimate her future retirement lifestyle needs, while another client's well-articulated retirement needs may not be realistic in the private manager's assessment. In both cases, the wealth manager has an opportunity to formulate specific client goals. The wealth manager can help the client quantify each goal and plan accordingly.

• *Goal prioritization.* Private clients tend to have multiple, sometimes competing, goals. For example, ensuring a more secure retirement may mean less funding for the education of a client's grandchildren. When clients have competing priorities, wealth managers have an opportunity to help them decide what matters most. Goal prioritization depends on what is most important to the client, not necessarily which needs occur sooner in the client's investment horizon.

- *Goal changes.* Individual investors' circumstances may change for a variety of reasons. When these changes occur, wealth managers sometimes must help clients re-prioritize their financial goals and reassess their investment strategy. Identifying client goals is not a one-time task but rather a part of an ongoing dialogue between wealth manager and client.

Example 3 provides an illustration of client goals for a fictitious individual, C.Y. Lee.

EXAMPLE 3 Client Goals

Mr. C.Y. Lee is a managing director for the investment firm Acme & Bass, which is located in the Asia-Pacific region. Lee is 43 years old, is married, and has two children, ages 12 and 10. He and his family reside in a home that they own in Singapore. In a conversation with his wealth manager, Lee states that he wishes to fund the undergraduate tuition for his children to study abroad. Lee expects the tuition cost to be approximately £40,000 per year. Lee also wishes to fund his children's weddings at some point in the future. Because the education costs will occur in the next 5–10 years, Mr. Lee states that they are his top priority.

Lee anticipates working until age 65 and does not know how much he and his wife will need to fund their retirement lifestyle. He mentions his desire to purchase a flat in London and let (rent) it as part of their retirement plan. The flat would cost approximately £1.5 million. Lee is also concerned about the future health care expenses of his wife's parents and to what degree he and his wife may need to support them financially.

1. Identify Lee's planned goals.
2. Identify Lee's unplanned goals.
3. Discuss the issue of goal quantification for Lee.
4. Discuss the issue of goal prioritization for Lee.

Solution to 1: Lee's planned goals are (a) funding his children's education; (b) funding his children's weddings; (c) funding his and his wife's retirement; and (d) purchasing and subsequently letting (renting) a flat in London.

Solution to 2: Lee's unplanned goals relate to the future health care expenses of his wife's parents, as well as possible uninsured property repairs for the Lee's Singapore residence and, if purchased, their London flat.

Solution to 3: Lee has quantified the education funding goal and the flat purchase. He and his wealth manager should work to estimate the cost of the weddings for Lee's children and the anticipated retirement lifestyle needs for Lee and his wife.

Solution to 4: Lee states that his first priority is education funding for his children. However, the timing of a need should not be the sole determinant of goal priority. If funding their children's education costs will leave Lee and his wife unprepared for retirement, for example, they may wish to reevaluate their priorities.

3.3. Private Client Risk Tolerance

Evaluating a private client's risk tolerance is a key step in the information-gathering process. In practice, the term *risk tolerance* sometimes is used to describe a set of risk-related concepts. The following are some key terms used in this context:

- **Risk tolerance** refers to the level of risk an individual is willing and able to bear. Put another way, risk tolerance is the willingness to engage in a risky behavior in which possible outcomes can be negative. Risk tolerance is the inverse of **risk aversion**, which is the degree of an investor's *unwillingness* to take risk.
- **Risk capacity** is the ability to accept financial risk. The key difference between risk capacity and risk tolerance is that risk capacity is more objective in nature, while risk tolerance relates to an attitude. Risk capacity is determined by the client's wealth, income, investment time horizon, liquidity needs, and other relevant factors. Clients with greater risk capacity can tolerate greater financial losses without compromising current or future consumption goals.
- **Risk perception** is the subjective assessment of the risk involved in the outcome of an investment decision. Unlike risk tolerance, risk perception—how a client perceives the riskiness of an investment decision or the investment climate—depends on the circumstances involved. Consequently, a wealth manager can help shape a client's risk perception. Generally speaking, risk perception varies considerably among individuals.

3.3.1. Risk Tolerance Questionnaire

In practice, wealth managers often utilize questionnaires to assess clients' risk tolerance. The result of a risk tolerance questionnaire, typically a numerical score, is often used as an input in the investment planning process. Exhibit 2 provides some common types of questions that may be found on a risk tolerance questionnaire.

EXHIBIT 2   Sample Questions from a Risk Tolerance Questionnaire

1. When you make investment decisions, on which of the following do you tend to focus?
   a. Always on the potential for gain
   b. Usually on the potential for gain
   c. Always on the potential for loss
   d. Usually on the potential for loss

2. Compared to your friends and family, are you:
   a. less willing to take risk?
   b. equally willing to take risk?
   c. more willing to take risk?

3. What potential percentage decline in your investment portfolio value over a one-year period are you willing to experience?
   a. 5%
   b. 10%
   c. 20%
   d. 30%
   e. More than 30%

4. Which of the following statements best describes your attitude about the performance of your investment portfolio over the next year?
   a. I can tolerate a substantial loss.
   b. I can tolerate a loss.
   c. I can tolerate a small loss.
   d. I would have a hard time tolerating a loss of any magnitude.

5. Suppose that you have made an investment that, due to a sudden broad market decline, has declined in price by 25%. Which of the following actions would you take?
   a. Sell all of the investment.
   b. Sell a portion of the investment.
   c. Hold the investment (take no action).
   d. Buy more of the investment.

6. Suppose that you have access to two types of investments: one investment with low risk and low expected return and one with high risk and high expected return. Which of the following portfolio mixes would you select?
   a. 100% low risk/low return
   b. 75% low risk/low return and 25% high risk/high return
   c. 50% low risk/low return and 50% high risk/high return
   d. 25% low risk/low return and 75% high risk/high return
   e. 100% high risk/high return

7. Suppose that you are offered employment that involves the choice of a fixed salary, variable compensation that could be higher or lower than the fixed salary, or some mix of the two. Which of the following would you choose?
   a. Entirely fixed salary
   b. Mostly fixed salary
   c. Entirely variable compensation
   d. Mostly variable compensation
   e. An equal mix of the two

Risk tolerance questionnaires are not perfect and it is unclear whether they are predictive of investor behavior. Recommending an investment or an asset allocation for a client based upon the questionnaire requires significant judgment on the part of a wealth manager. In fact, academic studies indicate a high degree of subjectivity in the client questionnaire approach. This subjectivity increases the potential for the wealth manager's own views on risk to become an influential factor in making investment decisions for a client. Other studies demonstrate how the structuring of questions affects investor responses. For example, presenting a loss in either percentage or dollar terms can lead to different responses from the same individual. Similarly, a question that involves a small dollar loss on a small portfolio may generate a different response than a question involving a large dollar loss on a large portfolio, even if the percentage losses are the same.

3.3.2. Risk Tolerance Conversation

As in the information-gathering process described earlier, conversations with the client can produce valuable insights into that individual's risk tolerance that may not be evident from a risk tolerance questionnaire or an assessment of personality type. These insights may include the following:

- The degree to which the client's financial decisions are influenced by friends or family members.
- The financial experiences that have shaped the client's perspective: For example, individuals who lived through deep recessions, even in childhood, may bring that perspective to present-day investment decisions.
- The client's past investment mistakes and successes.
- The client's accumulation of investment wealth—for example, whether the client achieved wealth through saving, inheritance, a liquidity event, or some combination thereof.
- The client's evaluation of investment risk—that is, whether the client thinks of investment losses in absolute or percentage terms.

Conversations about risk tolerance enable the wealth manager to educate a client about investment risk. For example, a wealth manager may demonstrate how certain risk factors (e.g., interest rate risk, credit risk, and equity risk) can produce incremental returns as well as incremental losses. As another example, a wealth manager may ask a client to select from a "menu" of portfolio options with a range of expected returns and degrees of volatility. The client's choice from this menu provides some information about the individual's risk tolerance.

3.3.3. Risk Tolerance with Multiple Goals

To this point, we have discussed a client's overall risk tolerance. Because clients often have multiple goals or objectives, their risk tolerance may vary for different goals. For example, a client may have a low risk tolerance with respect to near-term goals (such as education costs) but a higher risk tolerance when it comes to longer-term goals (such as retirement needs). A challenge for wealth managers in managing client relationships is to satisfactorily address potentially conflicting risk tolerance levels.

3.4. Technical and Soft Skills for Wealth Managers

Private wealth management resembles both an art and a science. That is, a wealth manager needs to have the professional aptitude to understand the client's financial goals, objectives, and constraints, as well as the financial acumen to recommend appropriate investments and portfolio management solutions. In short, wealth managers need both technical skills and non-technical ("soft") skills to succeed in their advisory roles.

3.4.1. Technical Skills

Technical skills represent the specialized knowledge and expertise necessary to provide investment advice to private clients. In some jurisdictions, regulators require minimum qualifications for technical skills among wealth managers. Examples of technical skills include the following:

- *Capital markets proficiency.* Private wealth management requires an understanding of capital market dynamics as part of helping clients achieve their financial goals. In most cases, wealth managers must have a broad understanding of capital markets and asset classes, as opposed to a specialist viewpoint. For example, a wealth manager will likely not have the same sector- or security-level expertise as an equity analyst who focuses on a specific industry.
- *Portfolio construction ability.* In conjunction with capital markets proficiency, private wealth managers need the ability to construct portfolios that are appropriate for each client's financial situation. This ability requires a deep understanding of asset class risks and returns; an awareness of the correlations among asset classes; and knowledge of investment vehicles, managers, products, and strategies for implementing a client's investment program.
- *Financial planning knowledge.* Wealth managers are typically not experts in specialized financial planning fields such as estate law, taxation, and insurance. However, these fields are highly relevant to the practice of wealth management. As a result, wealth managers who have a working knowledge of these related fields can add meaningful value for a client and can more effectively interact with the other professionals who serve that client.
- *Quantitative skills.* Given the need for investment analysis and portfolio construction, quantitative skills are critical for private wealth managers.
- *Technology skills.* Wealth managers use technology to manage client portfolios as well as improve efficiency in delivering advice and services. Examples of technology used by wealth managers include portfolio optimization software, simulation modeling tools, portfolio management software, portfolio accounting and performance reporting packages, and customer relationship management (CRM) software.
- *Language fluency.* In some situations, the ability to communicate in more than one language is a critical technical skill—for example, when a wealth manager has a multinational client base, manages cross-border transactions, or works in markets where more than one language is commonly spoken.

3.4.2. Soft Skills

Soft skills typically involve interpersonal relationships—that is, the ability to effectively interact with others. While soft skills are more qualitative and subjective than technical skills, they are critical nonetheless in the practice of private wealth management. Soft skills include the following:

- *Communication skills.* Because wealth managers interact extensively with clients, strong communication skills are essential. Communication skills begin with active listening when gathering client information. Effective verbal communication requires being able to ask the right questions as well as knowing *how* to ask questions. Meanwhile, effective written communication has become even more relevant with the increased use of email for communicating with clients. Presentation skills are commonly needed by wealth managers for engaging in group meetings and understanding the sophistication of the audience.
- *Social skills.* The ability to understand and relate to others and demonstrate empathy is a critical skill for wealth managers, particularly when "bad news" (e.g., poor investment performance) needs to be delivered to clients. Social skills also include the ability to read and interpret various non-verbal cues, such as body language.

- *Education and coaching skills.* An important role for a wealth manager is to educate and coach clients about investing and the wealth management process. Effective wealth managers are able to tailor this education and coaching to a client's level of sophistication.
- *Business development and sales skills.* Wealth managers often participate in or lead new business development for their firms or practices. Business development involves initiating contact with prospective clients (often called "prospects"), while the sales aspect involves successfully converting prospects into actual clients. Business development and sales entail several of the technical and soft skills previously mentioned. For example, wealth managers need to demonstrate capital markets and investment expertise while using effective communication and social skills.

EXAMPLE 4　Technical and Soft Skills

John Müller, CFA, a private wealth manager, recently received feedback from clients and colleagues as part of his performance review. Clients commented favorably on how Müller coordinates with external tax and legal professionals and on how well he listens to and understands his clients' needs. Colleagues remarked on Müller's broad knowledge of traditional and alternative asset classes and his ability to obtain new client engagements.

　　Describe which technical and soft skills Müller demonstrated as part of his performance review.

Solution: In his performance review, Müller demonstrated the technical skills of capital markets proficiency and financial planning knowledge. Müller's capital markets proficiency was shown through his broad knowledge of traditional and alternative asset classes, while his financial planning knowledge was shown by his successful coordination with tax and legal professionals. In addition to technical skills, Müller demonstrated the soft skills of communication and business development and sales. Communication skills were shown by his ability to listen well and understand client needs, while business development and sales skills were shown by his record of obtaining new client engagements.

---

4. INVESTMENT PLANNING

After developing an understanding of their clients, wealth managers begin the process of helping clients meet their objectives. In this section, we discuss key investment planning concepts, such as capital sufficiency analysis, retirement planning, and the client's investment policy statement.

4.1. Capital Sufficiency Analysis

To meet their financial goals and objectives, clients must have sufficient capital or follow a plan that will likely result in sufficient capital. **Capital sufficiency analysis**, also known as

capital needs analysis, is the process by which a wealth manager determines whether a client has, or is likely to accumulate, sufficient financial resources to meet his or her objectives.

4.1.1. Methods for Evaluating Capital Sufficiency

Two methods for evaluating capital sufficiency are deterministic forecasting and Monte Carlo simulation. Portfolio growth in a deterministic model occurs in a "straight-line" manner. For example, suppose a client's investment horizon is 15 years and the wealth manager has determined that the portfolio's likely compound annual return is 6%. In deterministic forecasting, the client is expected to achieve a 6% return in each of the 15 years in the analysis. While simple to understand, the deterministic method is typically unrealistic with respect to the variability in potential future outcomes.

By contrast, Monte Carlo simulation allows a wealth manager to model the uncertainty of several key variables and, therefore, the uncertainty or variability in the future outcome. Monte Carlo simulation generates random outcomes according to assumed probability distributions for these key variables. Instead of assuming, for instance, linear portfolio growth of 6% per year, Monte Carlo simulation would assume a simple average (arithmetic mean) return and a standard deviation of year-to-year returns for the portfolio. The portfolio's expected rate of return in a given year is determined randomly from this predefined distribution of possible returns. Monte Carlo simulation generates a large number of independent "trials," each of which represents one potential outcome for the client's investment horizon. By aggregating the outcomes of these various trials, the wealth manager is able to draw conclusions about the probability that the client will reach his or her objectives. It should be noted that such conclusions are sensitive to underlying assumptions, which may be subjective in nature.

4.1.2. Inputs to Capital Sufficiency Analysis

When using deterministic forecasting, the wealth manager must specify the following inputs: a portfolio return assumption, the current value of the portfolio, anticipated future contributions to the portfolio, and cash flows from the portfolio that represent client needs (according to the client's goals). As mentioned earlier, with Monte Carlo simulation, the wealth manager assumes a simple average return and a standard deviation of returns for the portfolio, rather than determining an annual portfolio growth rate. Wealth managers should be cautious about using historical rates of return as inputs to either a deterministic forecast or a Monte Carlo simulation. Instead, forward-looking capital market assumptions should be the foundation for the analysis.

In some cases, the inputs to Monte Carlo simulation are more complex. Portfolio return is not the only input that can be made variable. Some Monte Carlo simulation software requires separate asset class assumptions—such as simple average return, standard deviation, and correlation with other portfolio asset classes—rather than assumptions at the overall portfolio level. Some software packages enable variability in the client's investment horizon, such as their life expectancy. Other common inputs to capital sufficiency analysis for private clients include taxes, inflation, and investment management fees.

4.1.3. Interpreting Monte Carlo Simulation Results

When performing a capital sufficiency analysis, one role of a wealth manager is to interpret the results for the client. Suppose a wealth manager has run a Monte Carlo simulation for a client portfolio that generates a thousand trials. The output for this fictitious portfolio is shown in Exhibit 3.

The table in Exhibit 3 illustrates portfolio values (adjusted for inflation) at specific time intervals and at certain percentiles of the thousand trials. The table also shows the percentage of trials at a given horizon in which the client successfully achieved her objective. For instance, after 10 years, a portfolio value of $765,821 at the 75th percentile indicates that in 75% of the trials, the portfolio value after 10 years *exceeded* $765,821. Similarly, over this same 10-year period, only 5% of trials resulted in a portfolio value that exceeded $3,519,828. "Successful Trials" at the bottom of the table indicates, for example, that after 20 years, 69% of the trials were successful; that is, the client failed to meet her objective in 31% of trials. The percentage of successful trials is also known as the "probability of success." Wealth managers tend to guide clients toward a 75%–90% probability of success, although no industry standard range exists.

EXHIBIT 3   Monte Carlo Simulation Results

Percentile	Year 10 Portfolio Value	Year 15 Portfolio Value	Year 20 Portfolio Value
5th	$3,519,828	$3,651,264	$3,647,328
25th	$1,981,861	$1,698,449	$1,530,372
50th	$1,239,837	$843,820	$569,974
75th	$765,821	$305,126	($249,205)
95th	$197,179	($264,048)	($1,402,608)
Successful Trials	98%	88%	69%

When the probability of success falls below an acceptable range, potential solutions include the following:

- Increasing the amount of contributions toward a goal
- Reducing the goal amount
- Delaying the timing of a goal (e.g., retiring a few years later than originally planned)
- Adopting an investment strategy with higher *expected* returns, albeit within the client's acceptable risk tolerance and risk capacity

In light of these solutions, wealth managers should be careful about allowing capital sufficiency analysis to completely drive portfolio construction. For example, if a client's risk tolerance does not allow for an asset allocation with a higher expected return, adopting a higher-risk strategy may cause the client to abandon the strategy at a market extreme, thus undermining the portfolio's ability to meet the investor's objectives.

EXAMPLE 5   Monte Carlo Simulation

Reyansh and Pari Patel are saving to send their sons Rohan (age 4) and Vihaan (age 6) to college in the United States. Thus far, they have saved approximately $170,000. They will be able to save an additional $20,000 toward this goal in the next year and to increase the amount each year by 3% to address inflation. Current annual tuition costs are $40,000, and the Patels expect tuition to increase 6% annually.

The Patels' wealth manager, Sai Chhabra, CFA, uses a Monte Carlo simulation to calculate the probability of meeting the college tuition objective. The Monte Carlo simulation results are shown in Exhibit 4.

EXHIBIT 4   Monte Carlo Simulation Results

Percentile	Year 10 Portfolio Value	Year 15 Portfolio Value	Year 20 Portfolio Value
5th	$618,860	$608,445	$429,512
25th	$499,552	$409,753	$212,123
50th	$433,375	$309,823	$71,849
75th	$213,121	$219,852	($22,578)
95th	$301,502	$121,849	($79,845)
Successful Trials	100%	100%	67%

Discuss how the Patels might increase the probability of success in meeting their college tuition goal.

Solution: To increase the probability of success in meeting their tuition goal, the Patels should consider three possible solutions:

1. Increase their annual contributions toward this goal.
2. Reduce the goal amount, perhaps by funding a portion of the tuition costs or by identifying schools with lower tuition costs.
3. Adopt an investment strategy with higher expected returns that is still within the Patels' acceptable risk tolerance and risk capacity.

A fourth possibility—delaying the timing of the goal—is not a practical solution, given the ages of the sons and when they intend to enter college.

4.2. Retirement Planning

For many investors, funding their retirement lifestyle represents the largest and most important financial objective. Retirement planning has grown in significance as life expectancies have increased globally. In 1960, 65-year-old men in developed countries had a life expectancy of approximately 11 to 14 years, while 65-year-old women had a life expectancy of 14 to 16 years.[4] Since that time, the life expectancy of 65-year-old individuals (both men and women) has increased considerably. The increased emphasis on retirement planning has also been driven by a shift in the primary responsibility for funding retirement from employers and governments to individuals.

In this section, we discuss various principles of retirement planning, including the retirement stage of an individual's life, the analysis of retirement goals, and behavioral considerations for retired clients.

4.2.1. Retirement Stage of Life

A wealth manager's role in retirement planning includes assessing how much clients must save toward their retirement goals and helping clients determine at what age they will be financially prepared for retirement. Unlike institutional investors, which often have quantifiable liabilities, private clients may have difficulty estimating their future financial needs. Therefore, wealth managers have an opportunity to help shape clients' expectations about their future retirement lifestyle.

An overview of the following financial stages of life provides some context for our discussion of retirement planning:

- Education
- Early career
- Career development
- Peak accumulation
- Pre-retirement
- Early retirement
- Late retirement

During the education stage, an individual is typically developing human capital rather than financial capital. In this context, **human capital** is an implied asset that represents the net present value of an investor's future expected labor income, while **financial capital** represents the tangible and intangible assets (excluding human capital) owned by an individual or household. Individuals normally begin to accumulate assets for retirement in the early career stage. During this stage, individuals often have competing financial priorities, such as family needs, housing costs, and education. Retirement planning tends to take on greater importance as individuals move into the career development stage and, later, into the peak accumulation and pre-retirement stages. As individuals work and save money for retirement, they convert their human capital into financial capital. They also accumulate other financial benefits, such as pensions and government-provided retirement income, and they reduce non-retirement liabilities, such as mortgage loans and consumer debt.

In the early retirement stage, clients begin to draw from both financial resources and income sources for their retirement spending. Cash flows come from the client's investment

---

[4]These data were obtained from the Organisation for Economic Co-operation and Development (OECD).

portfolio as well as from pension income, government-provided retirement benefits, and if applicable, part-time or full-time employment.

In the late retirement stage, clients generally reduce expenditures on travel and leisure activities. Also during this stage, some individuals experience health issues that, in some countries, result in an increased burden on financial resources.

One of the wealth manager's roles in the early retirement and late retirement stages is determining a sustainable rate of distribution from the client's investment portfolio. This analysis is done on an ongoing basis to ensure that clients' financial resources will cover their remaining lifetime needs. That is, retirement planning does not begin or end with the client's retirement.

4.2.2. Analyzing Retirement Goals

Wealth managers may use several different methods to analyze a client's retirement goals. Three common methods—mortality tables, annuities, and Monte Carlo simulation—are discussed below.

4.2.2.1. Mortality Tables

A **mortality table** indicates individual life expectancies at specified ages. Wealth managers can use mortality tables to determine the probability that a client will live to a certain age; they can then estimate the client's anticipated retirement spending over his or her remaining lifespan.

Example 6 shows a sample mortality table. In the table, the plan year, client age, remaining life expectancy in years, and probability of surviving to a certain year are provided. This client is currently 72 years old and has a life expectancy of 12 years. The probability that he will survive to age 87 (i.e., 15 years from now) is 34%. The probability that he will survive to age 92 (i.e., 20 years from now) is 14%.

In practice, a wealth manager can use a mortality table to estimate the present value of a client's retirement spending needs by assigning associated probabilities to annual expected cash outflows.

EXAMPLE 6   Sample Mortality Table

Plan Year	Client Age	Life Expectancy	Survival Probability
0	72	12.0	100%
1	73	11.4	97%
2	74	10.8	93%
3	75	10.2	90%
4	76	9.7	86%
5	77	9.1	82%
6	78	8.6	77%
7	79	8.1	73%
8	80	7.6	68%

Plan Year	Client Age	Life Expectancy	Survival Probability
9	81	7.2	64%
10	82	6.7	59%
11	83	6.3	54%
12	84	5.8	49%
13	85	5.5	44%
14	86	5.1	39%
15	87	4.7	34%
16	88	4.4	29%
17	89	4.1	25%
18	90	3.8	21%
19	91	3.5	17%
20	92	3.3	14%

Source: Kitces and Hultstrom, "Joint Life Expectancy and Mortality Calculator." https://www.kitces.com/joint-life-expectancy-and-mortality-calculator/ (accessed September 14, 2018).

One potential drawback to using mortality tables is that an individual client's probability of living to a certain age may exceed that of the general population. Factors such as education level and access to quality health care tend to correlate with increased longevity. Therefore, the survival probabilities from an actuarial perspective may understate the true probability of a given client's living to a given age.

4.2.2.2. Annuities

Annuities can be used to analyze a client's retirement goals. A relatively simple way of calculating the present value of a client's desired retirement spending is by pricing an annuity. Annuities provide a series of fixed payments, either for life or for a specified period, in exchange for a lump sum payment. Many types of annuities exist, some of which are quite complex. Two basic forms are the immediate annuity and the deferred annuity. With an **immediate annuity**, an individual (called the "annuitant") pays an initial lump sum, typically to an insurance company, in return for a guarantee of specified future monthly payments—beginning immediately—over a specified period of time. With a **deferred annuity**, the specified future monthly payments begin at a later date. Suppose a husband and wife, both age 65, wish to retire with $100,000 per year in inflation-adjusted income. An immediate fixed annuity with "100% survivor income" might cost the couple approximately $2,500,000. The percent of survivor determines how much of the original annual income amount will go to the surviving spouse after the death of the first spouse. In this example, in exchange for $2,500,000 today (i.e., present value), the insurance company promises to pay $100,000 per year, adjusted for inflation, through the lifetime of the surviving spouse.

Life annuities are those in which the income stream continues as long as the annuitant lives. Using mortality tables, a wealth manager calculates the client's retirement liability based upon the individual's life expectancy. If the client lives longer than the actuarial statistics assume, the client's actual retirement spending needs will exceed the amount that the wealth manager and client planned for. This scenario introduces **longevity risk**, which is the risk of outliving one's financial resources. Life annuities help to mitigate longevity risk.

4.2.2.3. *Monte Carlo Simulation Revisited*

Earlier, we discussed Monte Carlo simulation in the context of determining a client's capital sufficiency. Monte Carlo simulation can also be used to analyze a client's retirement goals. One advantage of Monte Carlo simulation is its applicability to the client's actual asset allocation. For instance, if a client does not intend to use annuities for retirement needs, then annuity pricing will not be useful in estimating the client's lifestyle needs. Instead, Monte Carlo simulation can be used to analyze the likelihood that the client's actual portfolio will meet anticipated retirement needs.

Another advantage of Monte Carlo simulation for retirement planning is its flexibility in modeling different scenarios and exploring issues that are important to clients. Typically, retirement goals are more complex than a fixed annual cash flow requirement. For instance, if a client wishes to determine the effect of a significant purchase/gift or large unforeseen expense, the wealth manager can model these scenarios with Monte Carlo simulation.

Wealth managers should be careful about the degree of precision that Monte Carlo simulation provides. Simulation modeling is only a method of estimation; it cannot predict the future. Moreover, the output from Monte Carlo simulation can be highly sensitive to small changes in input assumptions. This is especially true for the portfolio rate of return assumption. Finally, a typical Monte Carlo output includes the probability of reaching a goal (or goals) but not necessarily the "shortfall magnitude." Shortfall magnitude matters because if clients are at risk of not meeting their objectives, they can make adjustments. If the shortfall is severe, the necessary adjustment may be significant.

EXAMPLE 7   Retirement Planning

Emily Whitfield, CFA, is meeting with two different clients today, Sam and Rebecca, regarding their retirement plans. Sam is retiring soon. He wants to be certain to have €100,000 per year in income throughout retirement. Rebecca is interested in exploring several possible scenarios for her retirement, using assumptions that are specific to her actual portfolio.

Recommend the method of analyzing retirement goals that is most appropriate for each of these two clients.

Solution: For Sam, annuities are most appropriate. The price of an annuity that produces €100,000 per year for life will determine how much Sam must have saved for retirement. For Rebecca, Monte Carlo simulation is most appropriate because she is interested in analyzing how different portfolio scenarios will affect her retirement plans.

4.2.3. Behavioral Considerations in Retirement Planning

Several behavioral considerations are relevant to retired clients and/or retirement planning. The following are some examples:

- *Heightened loss aversion.* Some studies suggest that retirees are much more loss-averse than younger investors. This observation has implications for clients' asset allocation through retirement and, therefore, for the return assumptions used in retirement planning.
- *Consumption gaps.* Due to loss aversion and uncertainty about future financial needs, many retirees spend less than economists would predict, resulting in a gap between actual and potential consumption.
- *The "annuity puzzle."* While annuities can help to mitigate longevity risk and, in some cases, may improve the probability of retirees meeting their spending objectives, individuals tend not to prefer to invest in annuities. This phenomenon is known as the "annuity puzzle." Explanations for the puzzle include investors' reluctance to give up hope of substantial lifestyle improvement, their dislike of losing control over the assets, and, in many cases, the high cost of annuities.
- *Preference for investment income over capital appreciation.* Behavioral economists have noted that individuals distinguish between income and capital when making spending choices. Evidence for this behavior includes the tendency of investors to spend dividend income rather than selling shares of securities and spending the proceeds. One possible explanation is that investors lack self-control with respect to spending. This theory suggests that spending only the income and not the principal is a self-control mechanism.

5. INVESTMENT POLICY STATEMENT

The **investment policy statement** (IPS) is a written planning document that describes a client's investment objectives and risk tolerance over a relevant time horizon, along with the constraints that apply to the client's portfolio. A wealth manager typically produces this document prior to constructing and implementing the client's investment portfolio. The IPS creates a link between the client's unique considerations and their strategic asset allocation. The IPS is also an operating manual, listing key ongoing management responsibilities. The client and wealth manager should review the IPS regularly and update it whenever changes occur either in the client's circumstances or in the capital markets environment that impact the client's investment strategy.

A well-constructed IPS has certain advantages for private clients. One advantage is that the IPS encourages investment discipline and reinforces the client's commitment to follow the strategy. This advantage is particularly important during adverse market conditions. A second advantage is that the IPS focuses on long-term goals rather than short-term performance. For the wealth manager, the IPS provides evidence of a professional, client-focused investment management process and the fulfillment of fiduciary responsibilities.

5.1. Parts of the Investment Policy Statement

The IPS includes the client's background and investment objectives, the key parameters of the investment program, the portfolio asset allocation, and some discussion of the duties and responsibilities of relevant parties. Topics addressed in most IPSs for private clients are discussed below.

5.1.1. Background and Investment Objectives

The client's background and investment objectives are critical parts of the IPS. Background items commonly include the client's name and age, as well as relevant personal and financial information. The wealth manager gains an understanding of the client's investment objectives during the information-gathering process. Common objectives include funding lifestyle needs during retirement, supporting family members, funding philanthropic activities, and meeting bequest goals. These examples typically represent ongoing objectives. By contrast, one-time objectives may include the purchase of a second home or a significant future travel expense. It is common for private clients to have multiple, competing objectives that they seek to achieve with the same portfolio.

Investment objectives should be detailed and quantified whenever possible. For instance, a client who is about to retire may seek to withdraw a specific amount each year that increases with the annual rate of inflation. A client also may have specific amounts in mind for future bequests or for charitable gifts. By comparison, oversimplified investment objectives such as "growth" or "growth and income" would not be sufficiently detailed.

Sometimes, clients have difficulty assigning specific amounts to future objectives. When this is the case, the wealth manager can create a more general objective, with the understanding that he will continue to work with the client to determine an achievable specific objective.

The wealth manager should also include in this section of the IPS other cash flows that are linked to investment objectives and that will therefore affect the capital sufficiency analysis. For instance, if a client intends to contribute additional amounts to her investment portfolio each year before subsequently beginning periodic withdrawals, the objective should reflect the expected contributions. Likewise, if the client anticipates that a significant liquidity event, such as the sale of a business, will be integral to meeting the investment objective, that information should be included in this section.

In a situation involving multiple objectives, the wealth manager should note which of the objectives is primary. For example, clients may wish to support their lifestyle needs through retirement while preserving an inheritance for their children. In this common example, the primary objective is the client's retirement security and the secondary objective is the inheritance for the children.

The investment objective, when linked to the client's asset allocation and the wealth manager's capital market assumptions, should provide the basic inputs to a capital sufficiency analysis. Whenever the capital sufficiency analysis does not support the investment objective, the wealth manager must work with the client to establish a revised objective that the manager judges to be achievable.

As part of the overall client background, the IPS should include the market value of the portfolio and of the accounts that make up the portfolio. The wealth manager should indicate the tax status of the account—that is, whether it is taxable, as in the case of an individual or joint account, or tax-deferred, as in the case of certain retirement plan accounts. When accounts are tax-deferred, the client pays tax on the distributions from the account rather than on the income generated by the investments. The background and investment objectives section should describe any other investment assets the client may have outside of the portfolio (e.g., accounts managed by another wealth manager) and any cash flows from external sources (e.g., pension income).

EXAMPLE 8   Background and Investment Objectives

Huang Zhuo Wei, age 51, is a private investor in Singapore. Wei is an engineer by trade but has also been successful in real estate development. His portfolio consists of CNY 16.5 million in a liquid securities portfolio, including some common stock positions in which he has large embedded capital gains, and several real estate investments valued at approximately CNY 9 million (combined). He expects to make additional real estate investments in the coming years. He estimates that he can invest approximately CNY 330,000 per year, inflation-adjusted, in real estate until retirement. He has a much higher than average tolerance for volatility, and historically, his liquid portfolio has consisted mostly of large-cap stocks of technology companies. He has stated that his time horizon is 10 years, since he anticipates retiring in approximately 10 years. He estimates that he will need approximately CNY 1 million per year, inflation-adjusted, to support his lifestyle in retirement. He wishes to grow his investment resources and create a significant inheritance for his children.

Discuss how Wei's wealth manager should create the investment objectives section of Wei's IPS.

Solution: The purpose of this portfolio is to support Wei's lifestyle in retirement and to provide an inheritance for his children. Aside from the investment assets in his portfolio, Wei has private real estate investments valued at approximately CNY 9 million and is likely to add to this segment of his net worth over the next several years. Wei does not anticipate needing distributions from this portfolio for at least 10 years.

Wei estimates an annual, inflation-adjusted lifestyle need of approximately CNY 1 million per year beginning at his retirement in 10 years. His cash needs will be satisfied in part through portfolio distributions and in part from his real estate portfolio. The wealth manager will continue to work with Wei to quantify his bequest objective and ensure that his portfolio distribution rate is sustainable throughout his retirement.

5.1.2. Investment Parameters

The investment parameters section of the IPS outlines important preferences that influence the client's investment program. Wealth managers may need to refine or customize these preferences to suit the particular client. Relevant components of investment parameters are discussed below.

5.1.2.1. Risk Tolerance

In this part of the investment parameters section, the wealth manager indicates that she has considered the client's ability and willingness to withstand portfolio volatility. The process by which the wealth manager has assessed the client's risk tolerance is included here.

For instance, if a risk tolerance questionnaire is used in the data-gathering process, the wealth manager may choose to include conclusions from the questionnaire.

5.1.2.2. Investment Time Horizon

A client's investment horizon is indicated in this section, but often as a range rather than a specific number of years. If the wealth manager determines that the client has a long horizon, the IPS may state, for instance, that it "exceeds 15 years." By contrast, a short horizon may be described as "less than 10 years." Clients do not often indicate their own investment time horizons because they may misjudge the appropriate length. For example, married couples might underestimate their joint life expectancy. In general, the wealth manager should determine the investment time horizon in collaboration with the client. Because each goal may have a different time horizon, a client may have multiple time horizons (some of which may exceed the client's lifetime).

EXAMPLE 9   Investment Time Horizon

In Example 8, Huang Zhuo Wei stated that his investment horizon is 10 years because he expects to retire at that point.

Discuss how his wealth manager should reflect Wei's investment horizon in the IPS.

Solution: Wei's true investment horizon is *through* retirement, a period that likely will be much longer than 10 years. His wealth manager should describe his time horizon as exceeding 10 years.

5.1.2.3. Asset Class Preferences

The IPS should indicate the asset classes that will comprise a client's portfolio. Alternatively, the wealth manager may list the asset classes that the client has not approved. Some wealth managers include a short narrative about the importance of asset allocation and the process that the wealth manager used to educate the client about asset class risk and return characteristics. The narrative captures in written form the risk–return trade-off that the client explored with the wealth manager during the information-gathering process.

5.1.2.4. Other Investment Preferences

Some clients have additional important investment preferences. One example relates to ESG investing, whereby a client may desire to invest in companies or sectors that are environmentally or socially focused. This section may contain a general comment about or specific criteria for these ESG preferences.

Other investment preferences described in this section might be a "legacy" holding that the client wishes to retain or a non-recommended investment that the client wishes to make. For example, a client may choose to retain a common stock investment received via inheritance or maintain a position in company stock due to the nature of the client's employment.

5.1.2.5. Liquidity Preferences

If the client has liquidity needs that are not established in the background and investment objectives section, those needs should be noted here. Some investors maintain a cash reserve in their portfolio, whereas other investors must initiate a portfolio distribution when they encounter an unanticipated cash need. Clients who require additional liquidity in their portfolios may instruct the wealth manager to maintain a specific cash balance in the portfolio.

If the client's liquidity preference constrains asset class selection decisions or implementation decisions, that constraint should be listed here. For example, if a client's liquidity needs dictate that the entire portfolio can be sold relatively quickly and easily, illiquid asset classes such as private equity would likely not be part of the client's portfolio.

5.1.2.6. Constraints

Some clients have constraints that restrict the wealth manager from implementing certain investments or strategies. For example, a client may be constrained by investment options in certain accounts, such as an employer-sponsored defined contribution retirement plan account. Another significant constraint can involve investments that have large unrealized capital gains and would create significant tax liabilities upon disposition. If a client has ESG-related constraints, such as prohibiting investment in certain sectors or individual securities, those constraints should appear in this section.

5.1.3. Portfolio Asset Allocation

This section contains the target allocation for each asset class in the client's portfolio. Wealth managers who use a strategic asset allocation approach typically define a target allocation for each asset class as well as upper and lower bounds. Wealth managers who use a tactical asset allocation approach may list asset class target "ranges" rather than specific target allocation percentages.

5.1.4. Portfolio Management

In this section of the IPS, the wealth manager discusses various issues involved in the ongoing management of the client portfolio. These issues may include the level of discretionary authority, how and when rebalancing activity will take place, and if relevant, tactical asset allocation changes within the client's portfolio.

5.1.4.1. Discretionary Authority

The IPS indicates the degree of discretionary authority that the client has granted to the wealth manager. Discretionary authority refers to the ability of the wealth manager to act without having to obtain the client's approval. Full discretion means that the wealth manager is free to implement rebalancing trades and replace fund managers without prior client approval. If the client has given the wealth manager discretion over certain changes (e.g., rebalancing), this section of the IPS should reflect that arrangement. The wealth manager operating in a non-discretionary capacity makes recommendations to the client but is not able to implement a recommendation without client consent.

5.1.4.2. Rebalancing

This section explains the wealth manager's rebalancing methodology. Some wealth managers use a "time-based" rebalancing policy, whereby client portfolios are rebalanced at a certain time interval (e.g., quarterly or annually) regardless of the difference between current asset class weights and target asset class weights. It is more common for wealth managers to use a "threshold-based" rebalancing policy, whereby the manager initiates rebalancing trades when asset class weights deviate from their target weights by a pre-specified percentage. The rebalancing section also sets expectations for how frequently the wealth manager reviews a client's portfolio for possible rebalancing opportunities.

5.1.4.3. Tactical Changes

A wealth manager who periodically makes tactical changes (adjustments) to the client's asset allocation establishes the parameters for implementing such changes in this section of the IPS. If target allocation ranges have been established in the portfolio asset allocation section, this section indicates whether—as well as under what circumstances and to what degree—the wealth manager is permitted to go outside those ranges when executing a tactical change. Note that a wealth manager who uses only a strategic asset allocation approach would likely not include this section in the IPS.

5.1.4.4. Implementation

This section includes information about the investment vehicles the wealth manager recommends to clients. Among the issues discussed here is whether the wealth manager recommends the exclusive use of third-party money managers, the exclusive use of proprietary investment offerings (those managed within the wealth manager's firm), or some combination of the two approaches. Also, this section indicates whether the wealth manager prefers to invest in mutual funds, exchange-traded funds (ETFs), or individual securities. A general discussion of the incremental cost of using third-party money managers is relevant here.

With respect to third-party managers, this section should include basic information about the wealth manager's due diligence process and how frequently it is performed. A more detailed option involves listing the quantitative screens used in the due diligence process and the qualitative criteria that influence the manager selection and retention decisions.

5.1.5. Duties and Responsibilities

This section discusses the wealth manager's overall responsibilities, including expectations about the ongoing review of a client's IPS.

5.1.5.1. Wealth Manager Responsibilities

A list of responsibilities helps the client understand how the wealth manager operates in helping the client reach his investment objectives. The wealth manager typically addresses the following issues (where applicable):

- Developing an appropriate asset allocation
- Recommending or selecting investment options, such as pooled investment vehicles or individual securities
- Monitoring the asset allocation and rebalancing
- Using derivatives, leverage, short sales, and repurchase agreements (repos)

- Monitoring the costs associated with implementing the investment strategy
- Monitoring the activities of third-party service providers (e.g., asset managers and/or custodians)
- Drafting and maintaining the IPS
- Reporting of performance, including an indication of the base currency
- Reporting of taxes and financial statements
- Voting proxies
- Assisting with the preparation of agreements associated with private fund offerings

The wealth manager might also consider listing the responsibilities of third-party service providers. A custodian, for example, maintains segregated client accounts, values the investment assets, collects income, and settles transactions. Listing the custodian's responsibilities separately creates an opportunity to educate the client about this provider's distinct and important role.

5.1.5.2. *IPS Review*
The wealth manager sets expectations for how frequently the client and wealth manager will review the IPS. As part of this review, it is important for the client to affirm that the investment objectives remain accurate. Likewise, it is important for the wealth manager to confirm that the strategy remains likely to meet those objectives.

5.1.6. IPS Appendix
The appendix includes additional details that typically change more frequently than the main portion of the IPS. Below are two examples of items that may be included in the appendix.

5.1.6.1. *Modeled Portfolio Behavior*
Modeled portfolio behavior describes a range of possible performance outcomes over various holding periods and can provide more value to the client than merely stating the return objective or the "expected compound return." As part of this section, the wealth manager may provide a modeled distribution of returns at various percentile ranges. The median of the modeled return distribution may be termed the "modeled compound return." This approach also enables the wealth manager to present modeled portfolio downside risk (volatility), particularly for short periods, and to confirm that the client can withstand such an outcome.

5.1.6.2. *Capital Market Expectations*
Capital market expectations include the wealth manager's modeled portfolio statistics—that is, the expected returns and standard deviations of asset classes, as well as modeled correlations between asset classes. Because clients sometimes confuse expected return (i.e., simple average return) with compound annual return, the wealth manager may consider including the modeled compound annual return for each asset class.

5.2. Sample Investment Policy Statement for a Private Client

Exhibit 5 demonstrates a sample IPS for a fictitious private client couple, David and Amelia King. The Kings' wealth manager does not use a tactical asset allocation approach for the couple, so the section on tactical changes is not relevant in this case.

EXHIBIT 5   Sample Investment Policy Statement

Investment Policy Statement Prepared for David and Amelia King

Background and Investment Objectives

This Investment Policy Statement (IPS) is designed to assist David and Amelia in meeting their financial objectives. It contains a summation of their objectives and expectations, sets forth an investment structure for attaining these objectives, and outlines ongoing responsibilities.

The purpose of this portfolio is to support the continuation of David and Amelia's current lifestyle, provide for their family's needs, and fund their philanthropic objectives. Maintenance of their current lifestyle is their primary objective, followed by support for family members and charitable aspirations, in that order. To meet these objectives, they anticipate needing approximately $350,000 per year in inflation-adjusted portfolio distributions. In addition, they intend to purchase a second residence within the next two years. They expect the purchase price for the second residence to be approximately $1.5 million. David and Amelia have not articulated a specific dollar amount that they intend to leave to their children, nor a specific dollar amount that they wish to leave to charity at their death. The wealth manager will continue to work with them to quantify these objectives.

In establishing their asset allocation, David and Amelia have considered their current assets and expected cash needs. They are seeking to achieve a higher long-term rate of return and are willing to assume the associated portfolio volatility.

Portfolio Accounts
Taxable joint account for David and Amelia
Tax-deferred account for David
Tax-deferred account for Amelia

Current Combined Market Value
$12,250,000

Investment Parameters
Risk Tolerance
The wealth manager has determined that David and Amelia are able and willing to withstand short- and intermediate-term portfolio volatility. They recognize and acknowledge the anticipated level of portfolio volatility associated with their asset allocation (as illustrated in the Modeled Portfolio Behavior section of the Appendix).

Investment Time Horizon
David and Amelia have an investment time horizon that exceeds 15 years.

Asset Class Preferences

The Kings and their wealth manager have selected the following asset classes:

- Short-term debt investments
- Intermediate-term bonds
- US stocks
- Non-US stocks
- Global real estate securities

Other Investment Preferences

The Kings wish to maintain their positions in Acme Manufacturing, Inc., which Amelia received through inheritance, and Artful Publishing, Ltd., which is her former employer. Neither position represents significant concentration risk in the context of their broader portfolio.

David has an interest in a private real estate limited partnership that invests primarily in office buildings throughout Asia. The wealth manager has taken this exposure into consideration in designing the broader asset allocation.

Liquidity Preferences

David and Amelia wish to maintain within their portfolio a minimum cash balance of $50,000. They typically maintain a more sizable cash balance at their primary bank.

Constraints

Amelia's position in Artful Publishing, Ltd., has significant embedded capital gains.

Portfolio Asset Allocation

Portfolio Asset Allocation

	Lower Rebalancing Limit	Strategic Allocation	Upper Rebalancing Limit
Short-term debt investments	8%	10%	12%
Intermediate-term bonds	16%	20%	24%
US stocks	30%	35%	40%
Non-US stocks	20%	25%	30%
Global real estate securities	8%	10%	12%

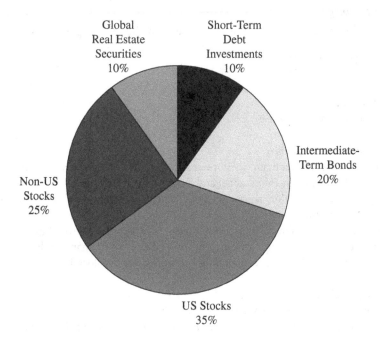

Portfolio Management

Discretionary Authority

The wealth manager will implement discretionary portfolio changes related to rebalancing the portfolio, investing new deposits, and generating liquidity to meet withdrawal requests.

The wealth manager will review with the client, prior to implementation, the addition of new positions or the elimination of existing positions.

Rebalancing

The wealth manager will review the portfolio on at least a monthly basis. Rebalancing will be determined by the lower and upper asset class limits set forth in the Portfolio Asset Allocation section of the IPS.

Implementation

To implement the investment strategy, the wealth manager will utilize third-party money managers via mutual funds, exchange-traded funds (ETFs), and separate accounts of individual securities. The wealth manager conducts a quarterly due diligence process to evaluate recommended managers as well as the universe of other available managers. This process involves quantitative risk and return comparisons to appropriate indexes and peer groups, as well as qualitative assessments of other factors that may impact a manager's ability to perform in the future. More information about this process is available at the client's request.

Duties and Responsibilities
Wealth Manager Responsibilities
The wealth manager is responsible for the following:

- Developing an appropriate asset allocation
- Selecting investment options
- Implementing the agreed-upon strategy
- Monitoring the asset allocation and rebalancing when necessary
- Monitoring the costs associated with implementing the investment strategy
- Monitoring the activities of other service vendors (e.g., custodians)
- Drafting and maintaining the IPS
- Performance reporting
- Tax and financial accounting reporting
- Proxy voting

IPS Review
The client will review this IPS at least annually to determine whether the investment objectives are still accurate. The wealth manager will review this IPS at least annually to evaluate the continued feasibility of achieving the client's investment objectives.

IPS Appendix
Modeled Portfolio Behavior[5]
Modeled Compound Return: 6.23%

Modeled Distribution of Returns

Year	10th Percentile	25th Percentile	50th Percentile	75th Percentile	90th Percentile
1	−10.45	−2.89	6.23	16.21	26.01
3	−3.75	0.86	6.23	11.88	17.24
5	−1.58	2.05	6.23	10.58	14.66
10	0.64	3.25	6.23	9.29	12.12
15	1.65	3.79	6.23	8.72	11.02
25	2.66	4.34	6.23	8.15	9.92

Portfolio downside risk, 1-year horizon:

- 25% likelihood of a return less than −2.89%
- 10% likelihood of a return less than −10.45%

Portfolio downside risk, 15-year horizon:

- 25% likelihood of a compound annual return less than 3.79%
- 10% likelihood of a compound annual return less than 1.65%

---

[5]The modeled returns and risk projections are based on forward-looking estimates and not on the past performance of specific funds or indexes. Modeled returns are before taxes and do not reflect investment management fees.

Modeled Portfolio Statistics

	Expected Return (%)	Standard Deviation (%)	Modeled Compound Return (%)
Short-term debt investments	2.5	2.0	2.5
Intermediate-term bonds	3.5	8.0	3.2
US stocks	8.5	22.0	6.1
Non-US stocks	10.0	26.0	6.6
Global real estate securities	7.5	23.0	4.9

Modeled Correlations

		(1)	(2)	(3)	(4)	(5)
1	Short-term debt investments	1.00				
2	Intermediate-term bonds	0.79	1.00			
3	US stocks	−0.08	−0.03	1.00		
4	Non-US stocks	−0.29	−0.27	0.76	1.00	
5	Global real estate securities	−0.15	0.08	0.42	0.39	1.00

6. PORTFOLIO CONSTRUCTION AND MONITORING

The practice of private wealth management involves aligning the unique attributes of the individual investor with the most appropriate investment plan and strategy. In prior sections, we discussed how wealth managers gather, synthesize, and analyze client information and goals/objectives. We now discuss the next phases of constructing the client's portfolio, monitoring the client's investment program, and reporting the portfolio to the client.

6.1. Portfolio Allocation and Investments for Private Wealth Clients

Once the client's IPS is developed, the next step is to implement the IPS through actionable investment advice. Portfolio construction, including asset and investment allocation, is a key aspect of this process. We first discuss two approaches to constructing a private client's portfolio—a traditional approach and a goals-based investing approach.

6.1.1. Portfolio Construction—Traditional Approach
Constructing portfolios for private clients involves several key steps:

- *Identify asset classes.* The wealth manager identifies the asset classes that may be appropriate for the client's portfolio. The identification of asset classes may vary by wealth manager.

For instance, one wealth manager may designate "UK Equities" as an asset class, whereas another wealth manager may designate "UK Large-Capitalization Equities" and "UK Small-Capitalization Equities" as separate asset classes.

- *Develop capital market expectations.* The wealth manager considers the expected returns, standard deviations, and correlations of asset classes in relation to the client's investment horizon. Wealth managers typically update their capital market expectations according to changes in the financial market environment.
- *Determine portfolio allocations.* Wealth managers sometimes use mean–variance optimization to identify possible portfolio allocations that meet the client's return requirement and risk tolerance. Mean–variance optimization provides a framework for determining how much to allocate to each asset to maximize the expected return for an expected level of risk. The "optimal" portfolio for a given client is the portfolio that maximizes expected return given the client's degree of risk tolerance. Note that a client's optimal portfolio may contain allocations to certain asset classes that may be impractical or difficult for the client to maintain. Therefore, wealth managers generally apply asset class constraints in the optimization process. For example, the minimum and maximum thresholds for a given asset class might be 0% and 20%, respectively.
- *Assess constraints.* As we noted earlier in the chapter, private clients often face certain constraints. For instance, suppose a client has a €5 million investment portfolio, with €2 million of the total portfolio invested in 14 individual stocks in Germany that have appreciated in value considerably. Selling these securities may be prohibitive due to potential taxes on any capital gains in the client's country of domicile. In this situation, the client's wealth manager may specify a minimum threshold for German equities to reflect the embedded capital gains. Another example of a constraint applies when a client owns a considerable amount of residential real estate. In this case, the client's wealth manager may limit the allocation to real estate investment trusts (REITs) in the client's investment portfolio.
- *Implement the portfolio.* At this stage, the wealth manager faces several decisions. One decision is the choice of active management or passive management (e.g., indexing) for each asset class. Once that decision is made, manager selection becomes an important consideration. Another decision for the wealth manager is which factors to recommend within a given asset class. Such factors may include "value" (value stocks over growth stocks) and "size" (small-capitalization stocks over large-capitalization stocks). Implementation also involves a decision to utilize individual securities or pooled vehicles, such as mutual funds and ETFs. Finally, the decision to apply currency hedging can be another important implementation decision.
- *Determine asset location.* When a client's portfolio comprises multiple accounts, the wealth manager must determine where to allocate the various asset classes and securities. This allocation decision is called **asset location**. Generally, tax considerations are a critical factor for asset location. If certain accounts offer unique tax benefits (e.g., tax deferral), the wealth manager will generally allocate to these accounts those investments that will likely produce a meaningful level of taxable income.

Example 10 demonstrates the portfolio construction process for a fictitious wealth manager and private client, ultimately resulting in a recommended allocation of the client's portfolio and underlying investments.

EXAMPLE 10   Portfolio Construction—Traditional Approach

Jonas Wilhelm, CFA, has just added a new private client. In Exhibit 6, Wilhelm identifies appropriate asset classes and develops capital market expectations for the new client's portfolio.

EXHIBIT 6   Asset Classes and Capital Market Expectations

Asset Class	Expected Return (%)	Standard Deviation (%)
Investment-grade bonds	3.0	3.0
High-yield bonds	4.5	8.0
European equities	9.0	18.0
Global (ex-European) equities	10.0	20.0
Real estate securities	8.5	18.0
Commodities	6.0	20.0

In determining portfolio allocations, Wilhelm developed a correlation matrix of these asset classes, as shown in Exhibit 7.

EXHIBIT 7   Asset Class Correlation Matrix

	IGB	HYB	EE	GEE	RE	COM
Investment-grade bonds (IGB)	1.00	0.84	−0.04	−0.01	0.14	0.02
High-yield bonds (HYB)	0.84	1.00	0.30	0.35	0.20	−0.04
European equities (EE)	−0.04	0.30	1.00	0.82	0.60	0.17
Global (ex-European) equities (GEE)	−0.01	0.35	0.82	1.00	0.52	0.36
Real estate securities (RE)	0.14	0.20	0.60	0.52	1.00	0.44
Commodities (COM)	0.02	−0.04	0.17	0.36	0.44	1.00

Based on a risk tolerance assessment, Wilhelm determines that the client can accept a portfolio standard deviation of return of approximately 10%. The client has a preference for European equities due to his familiarity with companies in Europe.

Wilhelm performs a mean–variance optimization that produces an optimal asset allocation. As shown in Exhibit 8, he modifies the portfolio allocation according to the client's preferences to arrive at a recommended allocation.

EXHIBIT 8   Portfolio Allocation

	Portfolio Allocation from Mean–Variance Optimization (%)	Portfolio Allocation Recommendation (%)
Investment-grade bonds (IGB)	30.92	34.00
High-yield bonds (HYB)	10.00	7.00
European equities (EE)	15.74	31.00
Global (ex-European) equities (GEE)	25.00	17.00
Real estate securities (RE)	15.00	8.00
Commodities (COM)	3.34	3.00
	100.00	100.00
Expected Return	6.77	6.69
Standard Deviation	10.00	10.00

6.1.2. Portfolio Construction—Goals-Based Investing Approach

With a **goals-based investing** approach, the wealth manager focuses on aligning investments with goals. That is, the manager identifies the client's goals and assigns the required funds to each goal. The manager then performs mean–variance optimization for each goal "portfolio" rather than at the overall portfolio level. Goal portfolios are optimized either to a stated maximum level of volatility or to a specified probability of success. Therefore, with goals-based investing, the allocation of the overall portfolio is a function of the respective allocations of the individual goal portfolios.

An advantage of the goals-based investing approach is that it may be easier for clients to express their risk tolerance on a goal-specific basis rather than at the overall portfolio level. A disadvantage is that the combination of goal portfolio allocations may not lead to optimal mean–variance efficiency for the entire portfolio. In other words, the aggregation of each goals-based portfolio allocation may not produce a total portfolio allocation that lies along the client's efficient frontier. Example 11 demonstrates how a wealth manager might allocate a client's portfolio using a goals-based investing approach.

It should be noted that the remaining steps of the portfolio construction process discussed previously—identifying asset classes, implementing the portfolio, and determining asset location—are the same for both the goals-based investing approach and the traditional approach.

EXAMPLE 11   Portfolio Allocation—Goals-Based Investing Approach

Using the information from Example 10, suppose that Jonas Wilhelm's client has two primary goals: (1) purchasing a ski cottage within the next 7 years and (2) supplementing his retirement income over the next 30 years. His total portfolio is valued at €3.1 million. The client will need approximately €500,000 for the ski cottage and desires low volatility for this goal.

If Wilhelm used a goals-based investing approach, his client's portfolio allocation might look like the example shown in Exhibit 9.

EXHIBIT 9   Portfolio Allocation—Goals-Based Investing

	Allocation in Ski Cottage Portfolio (%)	Allocation in Retirement Portfolio (%)	Aggregate Portfolio Allocation (%)
Investment-grade bonds (IGB)	70.00	27.00	34.00
High-yield bonds (HYB)	8.00	7.00	7.00
European equities (EE)	12.00	35.00	31.00
Global (ex-European) equities (GEE)	5.00	19.00	17.00
Real estate securities (RE)	3.00	9.00	8.00
Commodities (COM)	2.00	3.00	3.00
	100.00	100.00	100.00
Expected Return	4.42	7.12	6.69
Standard Deviation	4.56	11.15	10.00

The advantage of a goals-based approach in this case is that the client can express his expected return and risk tolerance with respect to the ski cottage goal.

6.2. Portfolio Reporting and Review

Portfolio reporting and portfolio review enable wealth managers to share information with clients, shape clients' expectations, and provide ongoing education. *Portfolio reporting* involves delivering information about their investment portfolio and performance in periodic physical or electronic mailings. *Portfolio review* refers to meetings or phone conversations between a wealth manager and a client to discuss the client's investment strategy. The key difference between portfolio reporting and portfolio review is that the wealth manager is more actively engaged with a review.

6.2.1. Portfolio Reporting

Typically, a portfolio report answers several questions, including, What is the portfolio asset allocation? How has the portfolio performed? and What transactions have occurred in the portfolio, such as contributions, withdrawals, interest/dividends, and capital appreciation? Accordingly, a portfolio report usually includes the following:

- A portfolio asset allocation report, which may reflect strategic asset allocation targets
- A performance summary report for the current (often year-to-date) period
- A detailed performance report, which may include asset class and/or individual security performance
- A historical performance report covering the period since the inception of the client's investment strategy

- A contribution and withdrawal report for the current period
- A purchase and sale report for the current period
- A currency exposure report detailing the effects of exchange rate fluctuations

A sample portfolio asset allocation report, performance summary report, and asset class performance report for the fictitious private client Hong Soo Wan are shown in Exhibit 10, Exhibit 11, and Exhibit 12, respectively.

EXHIBIT 10   Sample Portfolio Asset Allocation Report

Hong Soo Wan
Portfolio Asset Allocation Report
31 December 20XX

Asset Class	Market Value	Allocation	Target Allocation
Public fixed income	CNY 26,918,882	18.95%	20.00%
Private fixed income	CNY 4,109,563	2.89%	5.00%
Public equities	CNY 61,850,957	43.55%	41.00%
Private equities	CNY 18,233,357	12.84%	12.00%
Private real estate	CNY 21,008,677	14.79%	12.00%
Private natural resources	CNY 4,688,032	3.30%	5.00%
Hedge funds	CNY 5,222,597	3.68%	5.00%
Total Portfolio	CNY 142,032,065	100.00%	100.00%

EXHIBIT 11   Sample Performance Summary Report

Hong Soo Wan
Portfolio Summary Report
31 December 20XX

Beginning Portfolio Value	CNY 136,928,682
Contributions	CNY 0
Withdrawals	(CNY 2,130,481)
Interest and Dividends	CNY 2,840,641
Capital Appreciation	CNY 4,393,223
Ending Portfolio Value	CNY 142,032,065
Total Investment Gain	CNY 7,233,864
Time-Weighted Rate of Return	5.31%

EXHIBIT 12   Sample Asset Class Performance Report

Hong Soo Wan
Asset Class Performance Report
31 December 20XX

Asset Class	Allocation	Return for Period
Public fixed income	18.95%	2.71%
Private fixed income	2.89%	5.24%
Public equities	43.55%	5.72%
Private equities	12.84%	9.81%
Private real estate	14.79%	5.60%
Private natural resources	3.30%	(1.42%)
Hedge funds	3.68%	2.79%
Total Portfolio	100.00%	5.31%

For private clients, portfolio reports may lack some necessary context, such as commentary on recent economic and financial events or on the overall performance of asset classes. As a result, wealth managers often send an accompanying letter (or email) to clients with the portfolio report. This letter supplies some of the missing investment context and represents an opportunity for the wealth manager to provide education and advice.

Wealth managers often face an inherent conflict between the client's investment horizon, which may be decades in length, and the typical performance evaluation horizon, which may be one calendar quarter or one year. This horizon mismatch can potentially undermine long-term investment decision-making. For instance, short-term volatility can be mistaken for signs that a client's long-term strategy is not effective. With the expanded use of technology by clients (e.g., electronic report delivery and instant access to portfolio information), it is increasingly critical for wealth managers to appropriately communicate performance information to clients and manage their expectations.

When goals-based investing is used, portfolio reporting may focus on the client's progress toward a goal (or goals) rather than on the (often short-term) performance of asset classes or individual securities. For example, if a client has two different portfolios dedicated to two separate goals, a wealth manager's report may include the progress toward each of the goals based upon a capital sufficiency analysis.

Benchmark reports are another component of portfolio reporting. In a typical benchmark report, a wealth manager states a client's performance by asset class relative to an appropriate asset class benchmark, as well as the client's overall portfolio performance relative to a blended benchmark (according to asset class weighting). An advantage of benchmark reporting is the additional context that it provides to clients.

EXAMPLE 12   Portfolio Reporting

Simon Crosby provides investment advice for clients in Canada. Each quarter, he sends his clients only a detailed list of all the investments in their portfolio. The list includes the acquisition cost, the acquisition date, and the current market value for each investment, as well as the percentage gain or loss on each investment relative to its cost.

Discuss how Crosby's reporting practice can be more effective.

Solution: Crosby's reports do not enable his clients to determine their asset allocation or the performance of their overall portfolios. Crosby could address this issue by including a portfolio asset allocation report and a performance report. The current reporting structure also does not provide transaction details, such as portfolio contributions, withdrawals, interest/dividends, and capital appreciation, all of which could be provided by a portfolio summary report. Finally, Crosby's portfolio reporting can be improved by including market commentary, typically in a letter or email.

6.2.2. Portfolio Review

In comparison to portfolio reporting, portfolio reviews represent a higher level of engagement between the wealth manager and the client. Portfolio reviews provide an opportunity for the wealth manager to revisit the client's investment plan and reinforce the appropriateness of the strategy. The wealth manager can use these reviews to deepen the client's knowledge of the portfolio as well as to set and update expectations for the wealth manager's own responsibilities.

As part of the portfolio review, the wealth manager typically inquires about any changes in the client's objectives, risk tolerance, or time horizon. Changes in the client's employment, liquidity needs, family needs, external sources of cash flow, and estate planning can also result in changes to the client's investment strategy.

Another common aspect of a portfolio review is a comparison of the client's asset allocation to the target allocation. The following are some questions a wealth manager may consider: Should the portfolio be rebalanced? Are the client's asset class weights within the prescribed range for each asset class? Should there be any asset class adjustments? and What factors should influence tactical asset class positioning? Investment manager performance, relative to both applicable benchmarks and peers, is often discussed during portfolio reviews.

Wealth managers typically document the key points (or takeaways) from their portfolio reviews with clients. To maintain these notes, managers often use CRM software. Providing written communication to the client that reaffirms points from the meeting is also common practice. This communication can help avoid future misunderstandings and client disappointment.

6.3. Evaluating the Success of an Investment Program

Evaluating the success of an investment program in private wealth management is distinct from— and often more complex than—evaluating an investment program in the context of traditional asset (i.e., fund) management. For example, assume an asset management firm manages an emerging market stock fund. Evaluating the success of this fund would likely include comparing the fund's performance to that of an emerging market stock index over a representative holding period. The success or failure of this fund may be straightforward. In contrast, for private clients, portfolio performance, though important, is only part of the evaluation process.

6.3.1. Goal Achievement

A successful investment program for a private client is one that achieves the client's goals/objectives with an acceptable amount of risk. A private client's investment program is typically ongoing rather than short-term in nature. Therefore, the relevant question is not whether the investment strategy has succeeded for the client during a particular period, but whether the investment strategy remains likely to succeed in the future by achieving the client's longer-term goals. Capital sufficiency analysis, which we discussed earlier in the chapter, is often used to determine whether the client remains likely to meet his or her objectives.

Another aspect of a successful investment program is that the client should remain likely to meet his or her objectives without meaningful adjustments to the plan. For instance, if clients must work for many years beyond their original intended retirement date or must drastically reduce their retirement lifestyle, the existing investment program has not achieved its original objective.

6.3.2. Process Consistency

Following a consistent process is crucial to ensuring the overall success of the client's investment program. The following are some points that wealth managers may consider in evaluating success:

- If the wealth manager selects third-party fund managers to implement the client's portfolio, how have the managers performed relative to their own benchmarks? When the wealth manager has recommended fund manager changes, have those changes improved or detracted from subsequent portfolio performance?
- Has the wealth manager followed the prescribed process for rebalancing the client's portfolio?
- Has the wealth manager taken steps to reduce costs in the client's portfolio? Is the wealth manager overlooking any opportunities to reduce fees and expenses?
- Has the wealth manager considered taxation issues in the client's portfolio?
- For clients with ESG preferences, has the wealth manager implemented the client's portfolio strategy accordingly?
- If the wealth manager uses tactical asset allocation, how has tactical positioning impacted the portfolio's performance?
- Is the wealth manager maintaining an ongoing dialogue with the client to assess potential changes in the client's goals, time horizon, risk tolerance, and other relevant factors?
- Where applicable, has the wealth manager coordinated the investment strategy with the client's estate plan and philanthropic objectives?

6.3.3. Portfolio Performance

Performance evaluation of a private client's portfolio can be expressed in either absolute or relative terms. An absolute performance benchmark might be inflation plus a fixed percentage or simply a fixed percentage return that relates to a client's capital sufficiency analysis. Generally, these absolute performance benchmarks apply to relatively long holding periods, such as five or more years.

To measure relative returns, a wealth manager compares the client's investment portfolio results to those of an appropriately weighted benchmark. Typically, the benchmark weights include both return and risk metrics. A more useful comparison for a private client's portfolio is the relative risk-adjusted return. It is also important to evaluate whether the portfolio's actual downside risk is consistent with the client's risk tolerance. Many private clients tend to compare their own portfolio's performance to the performance of the investments with which they are most familiar, such as their home country's stock index. This tendency is an important consideration for wealth managers in the portfolio construction process and when communicating performance to clients.

6.3.4. Definitions of Success

When the wealth manager and the client have different definitions of success for the client's investment program, the potential for client disappointment can increase. For example, the client's definition of success may be achieving superior relative returns or attaining a particular absolute return. However, the wealth manager's definition of success for the client may be achieving certain financial goals. It is good practice for both parties to agree on the definition of success in the early stages of the relationship. Generally speaking, it is the wealth manager's responsibility to initiate a conversation with a client about how the success of the investment program will be evaluated.

EXAMPLE 13   Evaluating the Success of an Investment Program

Oliver Wellesley, CFA, a wealth manager, is preparing to meet with a longtime client, Eva Smith, age 83. Wellesley and Smith began working together when Smith was 64 and preparing for her retirement. She has earned a 6.5% compound annual return with Wellesley as her wealth manager. This return is close to the annual return that Wellesley modeled in his capital sufficiency analysis of Smith's portfolio many years ago. Distributions from Smith's portfolio have adequately met her need for retirement income, which has always been her highest-priority goal. According to Wellesley's most recent capital sufficiency analysis, Smith's portfolio is very likely to meet her retirement income and estate bequest objectives in the future. However, Smith's investment return has trailed the weighted benchmark return by 0.40% since the portfolio's inception and has exhibited slightly more volatility than the benchmark. Smith recently reviewed her IPS and concluded that Wellesley has consistently followed the process outlined in the IPS.

Discuss how successful Smith's investment program has been under Wellesley's management.

Solution: From the perspective of meeting goals/objectives, Smith's investment program has been successful. The strategy has met her retirement income needs, and Wellesley's capital sufficiency analysis suggests that she has a high probability of achieving future objectives (including ongoing retirement lifestyle goals and an estate bequest goal). Also, Wellesley has followed a consistent process, which is an indication of a successful investment program. However, if Smith and Wellesley agreed that outperforming a weighted benchmark was an important goal for her investment strategy, then the investment program has failed.

7. ETHICAL AND COMPLIANCE CONSIDERATIONS IN PRIVATE WEALTH MANAGEMENT

Like other investment practitioners, private wealth managers face many ethical and compliance issues. Some issues, however, are unique to the practice of private wealth management. In this section, we provide a brief overview of ethical and compliance considerations for private wealth managers. We then discuss the different client segments and service offerings within private wealth management.

7.1. Ethical Considerations

A starting point for ethical considerations in private wealth management is the CFA Institute Code of Ethics and Standards of Professional Conduct (Code and Standards). In this section, we discuss ethical considerations that are particularly relevant to private wealth management.

7.1.1. Fiduciary Duty and Suitability
In private wealth management, two primary ethical concepts are *fiduciary duty* and *suitability*. Fiduciary duty is the obligation to deliver a high standard of care when acting for the benefit of another party. Accordingly, private wealth managers are often said to be operating under a "fiduciary standard." Suitability is a key element of a wealth manager's fiduciary duty. According to the Code and Standards, when judging the suitability of a potential investment, the wealth manager should review many aspects of the client's knowledge, investing experience, and financial situation. The concepts of fiduciary duty and suitability are relevant to several components of the Code and Standards, including *Standard I(B): Independence and Objectivity*; *Standard III(A): Loyalty, Prudence, and Care*; *Standard III(C): Suitability*; and *Standard V(A): Diligence and Reasonable Basis.*

7.1.2. Know Your Customer (KYC)
The concept of "Know Your Customer" (KYC) applies globally in private wealth management. KYC requires wealth managers and their firms to obtain essential facts about every client for whom they open and maintain an account. These facts include the client's risk and return objectives and the origin of the client's wealth, which may help in identifying problems such as money laundering. KYC guidelines continue to evolve and can vary depending upon the country/region. The concept of KYC is relevant to *Standard III(C): Suitability* in the Code and Standards.

7.1.3. Confidentiality
Preserving client confidentiality is critical to maintaining trust in the relationship. Wealth managers typically possess highly personal and sensitive client information. This issue can be a particular challenge when a wealth manager advises multiple family members or advises clients who may know one or more of the wealth manager's other clients. Changes in electronic communication standards require wealth managers to have a thorough understanding of the confidentiality policies of their employers. Overall, the concept of confidentiality is relevant to *Standard III(E): Preservation of Confidentiality.*

7.1.4. Conflicts of Interest

The structure of wealth managers' revenue creates the potential for conflicts of interest. For example, when wealth managers earn commissions for recommending certain investment products, there may be an incentive to recommend only products that generate commissions (and perhaps those with the highest commissions). Conflicts of interest may also occur when wealth managers are subject to fee-based revenue models. For example, wealth managers who earn a percentage of the client's assets under management may have an incentive to recommend that the client not withdraw assets from the portfolio. The concept of conflicts of interest is relevant to *Standard I(B): Independence and Objectivity* and *Standard VI: Conflicts of Interest.*

EXAMPLE 14   Ethical Considerations in Private Wealth Management

Shirley Marshall wants to purchase a new home. She asks her wealth manager whether she should (1) obtain a mortgage loan to acquire the home or (2) withdraw money from her portfolio to purchase the home with cash.

Discuss potential ethical considerations for Marshall's wealth manager.

Solution: A conflict of interest could exist if the wealth manager earns revenues based on a percentage of Marshall's assets under management. If Marshall elects to withdraw money from her portfolio to purchase the home, her assets under management with the wealth manager will decline (all other things being equal), resulting in a lower fee for the wealth manager. In this case, the wealth manager should analyze the decision objectively and disclose this potential conflict of interest to the client.

7.2. Compliance Considerations

Changes in the regulatory environment have relevance to private wealth management. Exhibit 13 summarizes some globally enacted regulations relating to compliance.

In the United States, two additional proposed regulations are relevant for wealth managers. Both the US Department of Labor Fiduciary Rule (Fiduciary Rule) and the Securities and Exchange Commission Best Interest Rule (Best Interest Rule) seek to enhance investor protection. The Fiduciary Rule would expand the definition of fiduciary to all professionals providing advice for retirement plans and IRAs (Individual Retirement Accounts). The Best Interest Rule would require a broker/dealer to act in the best interest of the investor and would restrict certain broker/dealers and their employees from using the term "advisor" or "adviser" as part of their title. As of the publication of this chapter, neither of these rules has been enacted.

EXHIBIT 13   Key Compliance Regulations

Regulation	Summary
Markets in Financial Instruments Directive (MiFID II, European Union, 2018)	Designed to improve investor protection, market structure and transparency, firm governance, and external controls. Several of the investor protection provisions are of particular relevance to advisors. Investment advisors must demonstrate the suitability of their advice, including how it will meet client objectives, and must meet minimum levels of professional competence. Also, independent advisors and discretionary portfolio managers will no longer be permitted to receive commissions.
Common Reporting Standard (OECD Council/G20, 2014)	Requests that jurisdictions obtain information from their financial institutions and automatically exchange such information with other jurisdictions on an annual basis.
The Foreign Account Tax Compliance Act (FATCA, United States, 2010)	Enacted to prevent tax evasion by US individuals who hold "offshore" accounts and other financial assets. The rule requires non-US financial institutions to report information about financial accounts held by US taxpayers or by non-US entities in which US taxpayers hold a substantial ownership interest.

8. PRIVATE CLIENT SEGMENTS

The level of wealth varies considerably among private clients. Exhibit 14 provides a global breakdown of the number of adults within specific wealth ranges. Perhaps not surprisingly, the vast majority of individuals are in lower wealth ranges.

EXHIBIT 14   Private Wealth Composition

Wealth Range ($ millions)	Number of Adults Globally (millions)
0.1–1.0	391.0
1.0–5.0	31.4
5.0–10.0	3.0
10.0–50.0	1.5
>50.0	0.1

Source: Credit Suisse (2017).

On a geographic basis, the majority of adults with wealth in the $100,000 to $1 million range are in Europe (37% of the total wealth range) and the Asia-Pacific region (36%). In higher ranges, notably among those with wealth exceeding $1 million, the number of adults is more concentrated in the United States. While the United States has the highest proportion in this wealth segment, growth in the number of millionaire investors has been faster in emerging market economies.

The variation in global wealth ranges has implications for the issues private clients face and the services they require. Accordingly, private wealth management firms typically organize their services depending on the private client segment(s) they serve. In this section, we discuss key client segments and the services and solutions that clients within these segments may desire.

8.1. Mass Affluent Segment

The mass affluent segment is generally focused on building their investment portfolio and may have financial planning needs (e.g., education funding, cash flow or budget management, and risk management). Risk management needs may relate to future sources of income and may result in the need for various forms of insurance. Older clients in this segment tend to have a focus on retirement planning and investing for a secure retirement.

In servicing the mass affluent segment, wealth managers do not typically customize their investment management approach for each client. This segment tends to have a higher number of clients per wealth manager and involves a greater use of technology in service delivery (i.e., information gathering, account establishment, and reporting). Revenue models in this segment range from a traditional brokerage model (whereby the client is charged a commission on investment transactions) to a fee-only model (whereby the client is charged a percentage of assets under management for discretionary portfolio management). **Discretionary portfolio management** refers to an arrangement in which the wealth manager has a client's pre-approval to execute investment decisions. This arrangement is similar to the concept of discretionary authority discussed earlier in the chapter. By contrast, non-discretionary portfolio management refers to an arrangement in which the wealth manager makes recommendations to the client and seeks the client's approval prior to implementation.

8.2. High-Net-Worth Segment

Wealth managers that focus on the high-net-worth segment typically have a lower client-to-manager ratio than those that focus on the mass affluent segment. Also, wealth managers of high-net-worth clients tend to focus on customized investment management, tax planning, and wealth transfer issues (i.e., estate planning). Wealth transfer issues may lead to a longer investment time horizon and greater risk capacity (though not necessarily greater risk tolerance). The higher wealth levels of this segment may also lead to investment in less liquid asset classes and more sophisticated portfolios that require stronger product knowledge on the part of the wealth manager.

8.3. Ultra-High-Net-Worth Segment

The ultra-high-net-worth segment tends to have multi-generational time horizons, highly complex tax and estate-planning considerations, and a wider range of service needs. As a result, firms that represent this segment have relatively few clients per wealth manager.

Additional services may be provided to this segment, such as bill payment services, concierge services, travel planning, and advice on acquiring assets such as artwork or aircraft. Wealth managers focused on this segment often manage accounts for multiple family members and therefore also deal with family governance issues, such as preparing the client's heirs for the inheritance of substantial wealth. Wealth managers in this segment may assemble teams of service providers with specialized and complementary skills. For instance, firms may include specialized tax advisors, legal advisors, investment specialists, and a relationship manager (RM) as members of a client relationship team. Some ultra-high-net-worth individuals choose to hire these specialized experts to work exclusively for themselves and their family members. This arrangement is referred to as a "family office."

EXAMPLE 15   Client Segments

Olivia and her husband, Charles, recently hired a new wealth manager because (1) their financial needs have changed and (2) they felt that their former wealth manager had far too many clients to provide them with customized service. Olivia and Charles are interested in more sophisticated tax planning and more exposure to alternative investments. They are still concerned about having sufficient assets for their lifetime, but they are much more confident than they were several years ago.

Describe how Olivia and Charles shifted client segments upon the hiring of the new wealth manager.

Solution: Prior to hiring the new wealth manager, Olivia and Charles were likely in the mass affluent segment, given their previous wealth manager's high number of clients and lack of customized service. As their financial needs changed and they desired more customized service, Olivia and Charles likely moved to the high-net-worth segment. Their new focus on tax planning and alternative investments is also evidence of a shift to the high-net-worth segment. Because the couple are still concerned about having sufficient assets for their lifetime, they likely are not in the ultra-high-net-worth category.

8.4. Robo-Advisors

Amid the rapid growth of financial technology, a trend in private wealth management is the robo-advisor. The term *robo-advisor* applies to wealth management service providers that have a primarily digital client interface and experience. Robo-advisors gather information—such as risk tolerance, time horizon, goals/objectives, assets, and liabilities—directly from the client via web-based questionnaires. Using mean–variance optimization or other techniques, the robo-advisor recommends a suitable asset allocation for the client and typically implements the investment strategy using exchange-traded funds or mutual funds. The processes that robo-advisors use in information gathering and portfolio optimization can be quite similar to those utilized by human advisors. However, the primary distinction is in the digital interface.

Robo-advisors monitor and manage client portfolios on an ongoing basis and periodically rebalance portfolios as needed. Robo-advisors also provide regular reporting to clients through online applications and may make human wealth managers available to handle certain client inquiries. Cost is a key factor that differentiates robo-advisors from human wealth managers. Robo-advisor services are generally available at a cost that is lower than the fees charged by traditional wealth management firms. Scalability of technology has enabled robo-advisors to service investors with relatively small portfolios.

Robo-advisors have expanded their services to various areas of private wealth management—for example, constructing ESG-related portfolios. Other robo-advisors have focused on investor behavior (e.g., encouraging saving or discouraging a reaction to declining securities prices), on factor investing, and on more sophisticated techniques to improve tax efficiency. While many robo-advisors compete directly with traditional wealth management firms, others have partnered with these firms. Such partnerships can enable firms to lower fees or to offer services to clients they might not otherwise have been able to serve.

SUMMARY

- Private clients and institutional clients have different concerns, primarily relating to investment objectives and constraints, investment governance, investment sophistication, regulation, and the uniqueness of individuals.
- Information needed in advising private clients includes personal information, financial information, and tax considerations.
- Basic tax strategies for private clients include tax avoidance, tax reduction, and tax deferral.
- A client's planned goals are those that can be reasonably estimated or quantified within an expected time horizon, such as retirement, specific purchases, education, family events, wealth transfer, and philanthropy.
- Unplanned goals are those related to unforeseen financial needs, such as property repairs and medical expenses.
- When establishing client goals, private wealth managers consider goal quantification, goal prioritization, and goal changes.
- Risk tolerance refers to the level of risk an individual is willing and able to bear. Risk tolerance is the inverse of risk aversion. Risk capacity is the ability to accept financial risk. Risk perception is an individual's subjective assessment of the risk involved in an investment decision's outcome.
- Wealth managers often utilize questionnaires to assess clients' risk tolerance. The result of a risk tolerance questionnaire, typically a numerical score, is often used as an input in the investment planning process.
- Wealth managers need both technical skills and non-technical ("soft") skills in their advisory roles. Technical skills include capital markets proficiency, portfolio construction ability, financial planning knowledge, quantitative skills, technology skills, and in some situations, foreign language fluency. Soft skills include communication skills, social skills, education/coaching skills, and business development and sales skills.
- Capital sufficiency analysis, also known as capital needs analysis, is the process by which a wealth manager determines whether a client has, or is likely to accumulate, sufficient financial resources to meet his or her objectives.
- Two methods for evaluating capital sufficiency are deterministic forecasting and Monte Carlo simulation.
- Wealth managers use several different methods to analyze a client's retirement goals, including mortality tables, annuities, and Monte Carlo simulation.
- An investment policy statement (IPS) for an individual includes the following parts: background and investment objective(s); investment parameters (risk tolerance and

investment time horizon); asset class preferences; other investment preferences (liquidity and constraints); portfolio asset allocation; portfolio management (discretionary authority, rebalancing, tactical changes, implementation); duties and responsibilities; and an appendix for additional details.

- Two primary approaches to constructing a client portfolio are a traditional approach and a goals-based investing approach.
- Portfolio reporting involves periodically providing clients with information about their investment portfolio and performance. Portfolio review refers to meetings or phone conversations between a wealth manager and a client to discuss the client's investment strategy. The key difference between portfolio reporting and portfolio review is that the wealth manager is more actively engaged in a review.
- The success of an investment program involves achieving client goals, following a consistent process, and realizing favorable portfolio performance.
- Ethical considerations for private wealth managers include "know your customer" (KYC), fiduciary duty and suitability, confidentiality, and conflicts of interest.
- Several global regulations have relevance for private wealth managers.
- Key private wealth segments include mass affluent, high net worth, and ultra high net worth.
- Robo-advisors have emerged in the mass affluent client segment. These advisors have a primarily digital client interface. Robo-advisor service providers generally charge lower fees than traditional wealth management firms. Scalability of technology has enabled robo-advisors to service investors with relatively small portfolios.

REFERENCES

Browning, Chris, Tuo Guo, Yanshan Cheng, and Michael Finke. 2016. "Spending in Retirement: Determining the Consumption Gap." *Journal of Financial Planning* 29 (2): 42–53.

Deloitte. "Tax Guides and Highlights." https://dits.deloitte.com/#TaxGuides (accessed as of September 2018).

Grable, John E. 2017. *Financial Risk Tolerance: A Psychometric Review*. Research Foundation Briefs. Charlottesville, VA: Research Foundation of CFA Institute.

Kitces, Michael, and David Hultstrom. "Joint Life Expectancy and Mortality Calculator." https://www.kitces.com/joint-life-expectancy-and-mortality-calculator (accessed as of September 2018).

Klement, Joachim. 2015. *Investor Risk Profiling: An Overview*. Research Foundation Briefs. Charlottesville, VA: Research Foundation of CFA Institute.

KPMG. "Individual Income Tax Rates Table." https://home.kpmg.com/xx/en/home/services/tax/tax-tools-and-resources/tax-rates-online/individual-income-tax-rates-table.html (accessed as of September 2018).

OECD. "Information on Common Reporting Standard." Organisation for Economic Co-operation and Development. www.oecd.org/tax/automatic-exchange/common-reporting-standard (accessed as of September 2018).

OECD. "Life Expectancy at 65." Organisation for Economic Co-operation and Development. https://data.oecd.org/healthstat/life-expectancy-at-65.htm (accessed as of September 2018).

Suisse, Credit. 2017. *Global Wealth Report 2017*. Credit Suisse Research Institute.

PRACTICE PROBLEMS

The following information relates to Questions 1–3

Henlopen McZhao is a private wealth manager. After a successful introductory meeting with Nescopeck Cree, she is meeting again with this new client to plan a wealth management strategy. McZhao seeks additional personal information from Cree.

McZhao learns that Cree is 45 years old and is currently employed as an attorney. Cree has a number of specific financial goals that he wishes to achieve in the future but has no particular return objective for his portfolio. Because he has been investing for 20 years, Cree is comfortable with moderate levels of market volatility. His employment provides for his current expenses, so Cree's liquidity requirements are minimal. Cree prefers to have his environmental and social concerns reflected in his investment choices.

1. **Discuss** additional personal information that McZhao should gather from Cree in order to properly advise this new client.

   McZhao then focuses on Cree's financial goals:

- Cree wants to fund university expenses for his three children, with the first payment starting in 10 years. Cree does not know what to expect in terms of college costs.
- Cree plans to retire at age 62 and expects to need $80,000 per year to fund his retirement lifestyle. He is concerned that an increasing level of medical expenses for himself and his wife may reduce his financial assets.
- Cree expects to purchase an apartment building in three years and plans to use the rental income from this investment property to help fund his retirement needs.
- Cree's wife enjoys donating to philanthropic causes. She currently donates $10,000 per year, but by the time Cree retires, she hopes to increase this amount to $30,000 per year.
- Cree collects antique furniture and budgets $15,000 per year for additions to his collection. He mentions that this year's antique purchase will be his next large expense and currently has the highest priority of all his goals.

2. **Discuss** the issues relating to Cree's:
   i. goal quantification.
   ii. goal prioritization.

   McZhao continues the discussion with Cree in order to evaluate his degree of risk tolerance associated with each of the following individual goals:

Retirement:	Cree considers retirement a long-term goal and is willing to endure a 10% drop in expected retirement spending. However, he is very concerned with having sufficient funds to cover medical expenses.
Investment property:	Cree sees the investment property as a source of stable income, so it is very important to him to purchase the building. He realizes that maintenance and repair expenses will be necessary, and he also considers those very important.
Philanthropy:	Cree's wife strongly influences him to fund her philanthropic causes, and he wants to maintain some level of annual contribution. Cree believes that his wife would be willing to maintain her $10,000 per year contributions and not increase that amount.
Antique furniture:	Cree is willing to reduce or eliminate his spending on antique furniture.

3. **Determine** Cree's degree of risk tolerance associated with each of the following individual goals. **Justify** each response.

Determine Cree's degree of risk tolerance associated with each of the following individual goals. **Justify** each response.

Goal	Degree of Risk Tolerance	Justification
Retirement	Lower	
	Higher	
Investment Property	Lower	
	Higher	
Philanthropy	Lower	
	Higher	
Antique Furniture	Lower	
	Higher	

The following information relates to Questions 4–6

Sharfepto Zik, a private wealth manager, is meeting with a client, Garbanzo Patel, in order to create an investment policy statement (IPS) for Patel's upcoming retirement. Patel estimates that he will require €200,000 per year, with annual increases for inflation, during retirement. Patel's primary spending goals during retirement are to provide for his family's needs and maintain his retirement lifestyle. His secondary goals are to fund his philanthropic activities and leave a significant inheritance to his children.

During his retirement, Patel will receive union pension payments of €50,000 per year with annual increases for inflation. In his spare time, Patel runs a small business that provides him with an annual income of €120,000 and is valued at €1 million. He will continue running his business during retirement.

Patel holds a portfolio of securities valued at approximately €4 million. The portfolio primarily contains dividend-paying stocks and interest-bearing bonds. Patel has reinvested all these distributions back into his portfolio but anticipates that after retirement he may need to use some of the distributions to fund his expenses.

Patel plans to buy a vacation home in three years. His budget for the vacation home is approximately €1.4 million. Patel has not decided yet how he will fund this purchase.

4. **Prepare** the Investment Objectives section of Patel's IPS.

Patel has been working with Zik for 10 years. At the beginning of the 10-year period, Zik forecasted that the equities in Patel's portfolio would outperform their benchmark and that the bonds would match their benchmark. Now, at the end of the 10-year period, equities have outperformed the benchmark, but with higher volatility than the benchmark. In addition, the bonds in the portfolio matched their benchmark performance, but with lower volatility than the benchmark. However, returns and volatility are within IPS specifications for both equities and bonds.

Patel stated his goals to Zik at the beginning of the 10-year period and has not changed them. Patel's plan is to retire this year, and he wants to be able to support a specified annual spending level.

Zik's original capital sufficiency analysis modeled a 6% rate of return, and Patel's portfolio has earned slightly more than that over the 10-year period. Zik's most recent capital sufficiency analysis shows that the portfolio and strategy are very likely to meet Patel's needs as he transitions into retirement.

Zik has followed the guidelines stated in the original IPS in terms of rebalancing the portfolio, maintaining an ongoing dialog with Patel, and coordinating the strategy with Patel's retirement and philanthropic goals. Although fees have remained unchanged at 1%, Zik has been able to reduce expenses for equities by 20 bps and for bonds by 12 bps.

5. **Evaluate** the success of Zik's investment program for Patel in terms of:
    i. goal achievement.
    ii. process consistency.
    iii. portfolio performance.

After every regular monthly rebalancing, Zik sends an email to Patel with a portfolio report. Zik's portfolio report contains the following:

- An asset allocation report that reflects strategic asset allocation targets
- A detailed performance report that includes individual asset class and security performance
- A year-to-date performance summary report and a historical performance report starting from the inception of Patel's investment strategy

6. **Recommend** additional information that Zik could provide to enhance his portfolio reports for Patel.

The following information relates to Questions 7 and 8

Val Sili, age 22, has just graduated from college and begins making ambitious future financial plans. The four stages of his plan are summarized below. Sili would like to have outside financial advice at each of these stages.

Stage 1—Age 22–26: Sili plans to work as a software developer in a startup company, where he will earn both a salary and stock options. He will save as much as he can to invest, but his portfolio will be relatively small, and he will be willing to pay only low management fees. Sili would like to use a sophisticated mean–variance optimization technique for asset allocation, although he will limit his investments to exchange-traded funds and mutual funds.

Stage 2—Age 26–30: Sili will have reached a more senior position in the company. He plans to have accumulated assets of $350,000, and his investment focus will be on building his portfolio. Sili will want help with his increasing financial planning needs and will be able to afford the fees of a professional wealth manager.

Stage 3—Age 30–36:   Sili plans to exercise his stock options to buy a large quantity of the company's stock at a price significantly below its market value. The proceeds should increase his portfolio value to $8 million. Sili will quit his job to start his own software company. Sili will be interested in more sophisticated investments with longer time horizons, greater risk, and less liquidity. He will also want specialized advisers for taxes, legal issues, and investment strategies.

Stage 4—After Age 36:   Sili will sell his software company for $200 million and retire. He will spend his retirement traveling on his private jet and collecting artwork for his collection; therefore, he will need advice on acquiring high-end assets. The substantial increase in the value of his investment portfolio will allow him to have a multi-generational time horizon. He will require a wider range of investment advisory services, including complex tax planning, estate planning, and bill payment services.

7. **Determine** the client segment or adviser type that is *most appropriate* for each stage of Sili's plan. **Justify** each response.

Determine the client segment or adviser type that is *most appropriate* for each stage of Sili's plan. **Justify** each response.

Stage 1—Age 22–26	**Client Segment/Adviser Type:**
	Justification:
Stage 2—Age 26–30	**Client Segment/Adviser Type:**
	Justification:
Stage 3—Age 30–36	**Client Segment/Adviser Type:**
	Justification:
Stage 4—After Age 36	**Client Segment/Adviser Type:**
	Justification:

Sili next uses three approaches to analyze his retirement goals:

Approach 1.   Sili considers the probability that he will live to a certain age and then predicts his inflation-adjusted retirement spending according to the probability that he will still be living in a given year. This approach allows him to estimate the present value of his retirement spending needs by assigning associated probabilities to annual expected cash outflows.

Approach 2.   Sili determines that he can specify his level of annual spending during retirement and that he can model that spending as a series of fixed payments. He calculates the present value of that series of payments as of the day of his retirement, resulting in the amount of money that he will need to fund his retirement goals.

Approach 3.   Sili models the uncertainty of each key variable individually by assigning each one its own probability distribution and then generates a large number of random outcomes for each variable. He aggregates the outcomes to determine an overall probability of reaching his objectives. Sili sees this as a flexible approach that allows him to explore various scenarios, including unforeseen expenses.

8. **Identify** each approach that Sili uses to analyze his retirement goals. **Explain** each response.

Identify each approach that Sili uses to analyze his retirement goals. **Explain** each response.	
Approach 1	Identification:
	Explanation:
Approach 2	Identification:
	Explanation:
Approach 3	Identification:
	Explanation:

The following information relates to Questions 9–16

Noèmie Açor works for an international bank as a private wealth adviser. Açor speaks several regional languages in addition to her native language. She prepares for two client meetings next week. First, Açor will meet with Winifred Njau, who has recently retired. Njau has made a charitable pledge to a non-profit university endowment, the Udhamini Fund. Açor prepares a draft of the investment objectives section of an investment policy statement (IPS) for Njau using selected client information, which is presented in Exhibit 1.

EXHIBIT 1   Selected Client Information Items for Njau

Liquidity needs	$500,000 charitable pledge to Udhamini payable in 15 years
Risk tolerance	Moderate
Asset allocation	40% equities and 60% fixed income

Açor's notes from her previous meeting with Njau indicate the following behavioral considerations related to Njau's retirement planning:

- Njau would like to increase her level of spending if supported by investment projections.
- Although Njau could pay a lump sum and receive a series of fixed payments, she prefers not to lose control over her assets.
- Njau understands the risk–return relationship and is willing to accept some short-term losses to achieve long-term growth.

Next, Açor reviews a recent risk tolerance questionnaire completed by Njau, which relates to overall portfolio risk. Açor focuses on the type of capital sufficiency analysis to perform for Njau. To determine the optimal allocation, Açor seeks to ensure that Njau's charitable pledge can be met and implements a goal-based investing approach. Açor runs a Monte Carlo simulation to determine the probability of success, which is the likelihood that Njau can meet her charitable pledge objective. The simulation results are presented in Exhibit 2.

EXHIBIT 2   Monte Carlo Simulation Results for Charitable Pledge (adjusted for inflation)

	Year 10 Portfolio Value ($)	Year 15 Portfolio Value ($)	Year 20 Portfolio Value ($)
25th %	501,288	729,230	1,035,373
50th %	405,927	553,803	767,448
75th %	331,056	422,746	563,039

One week after this meeting, the bank sends a client satisfaction survey to Njau. In response to questions about Açor's soft skills and technical skills, Njau responds with the following comments:

Comment 1:   Açor constructed a portfolio that is appropriate for my unique situation.
Comment 2:   Açor spoke to me in my own regional language throughout the meeting.
Comment 3:   Açor educated me about how my investments perform and affect my portfolio.

Açor's second meeting will be with Thanh Bañuq. Bañuq is Njau's nephew and serves on the board of directors of Udhamini. Açor obtained the essential facts about Bañuq when she opened his account, including his risk and return objectives and the origin of his wealth. In preparation for the meeting, Açor considers the high level of taxes that Bañuq pays. Açor will recommend changing the asset location of high-dividend-paying equities that Bañuq owns from a taxable account to a retirement account with tax-free earnings and withdrawals.

During their meeting, Açor and Bañuq discuss charitable pledges that Udhamini has recently received and the likelihood that Njau will meet her charitable pledge. Bañuq then asks Açor the following question:

"How might my investment objectives and constraints differ from those of a typical university endowment, such as Udhamini?"

The day after Açor's meeting with Bañuq, Açor realizes that her actions in the meeting may have raised an ethical concern.

9. Based on Exhibit 1, which of the following items is Açor *most likely* to include in the section of the IPS she is drafting for Njau?
    A. Moderate risk tolerance
    B. 40% allocation to equities
    C. $500,000 charitable pledge in 15 years

10. Based on Açor's notes from her previous meeting with Njau, the behavioral consideration exhibited by Njau is *most likely*:
    A. a consumption gap.
    B. the "annuity puzzle."
    C. heightened loss aversion.

11. Açor's portfolio allocation for Njau is *most likely* optimized on the basis of:
    A. a stated maximum level of volatility.
    B. total portfolio mean–variance efficiency.
    C. the results of the risk tolerance questionnaire.

12. Based on Exhibits 1 and 2, the probability that Njau will be able to meet her charitable goal is *closest* to:
    A. 25%.
    B. 50%.
    C. 75%.

13. Which comment in Njau's response to the client satisfaction survey *best* describes a soft skill exhibited by Açor?
    A. Comment 1
    B. Comment 2
    C. Comment 3

14. Açor's recommendation regarding asset location in Bañuq's portfolio is *most likely* an example of tax:
    A. deferral.
    B. reduction.
    C. avoidance.

15. The *most appropriate* response to Bañuq's question is that he has:
    A. a shorter time horizon.
    B. less significant tax considerations.
    C. less diverse investment objectives.

16. The ethical concern that Açor *most likely* raised is:
    A. KYC.
    B. suitability.
    C. confidentiality.

CHAPTER 16

TOPICS IN PRIVATE WEALTH MANAGEMENT

Paul Bouchey, CFA
Helena Eaton, PhD, CFA
Philip Marcovici

Helena Eaton is a contributing author. Her contributions solely represent her views and should in no way be taken to reflect the views of JPMorgan Chase & Co.

Section 6 of this chapter draws from *Concentrated Single-Asset Positions* by Thomas J. Boczar, CFA, and Nischal Pai, CFA (©2013 CFA Institute). Section 7 draws on *Estate Planning in a Global Context* by Stephen Horan, CFA, and Thomas Robinson, CFA (©2009 CFA Institute). While both have been extensively rewritten, we wish to acknowledge the previous authors' contributions.

LEARNING OUTCOMES

The candidate should be able to:

- compare taxation of income, wealth, and wealth transfers;
- describe global considerations of jurisdiction that are relevant to taxation;
- discuss and analyze the tax efficiency of investments;
- analyze the impact of taxes on capital accumulation and decumulation in taxable, tax-exempt, and tax-deferred accounts;
- explain portfolio tax management strategies and their application;
- discuss risk and tax objectives in managing concentrated single-asset positions;
- describe strategies for managing concentrated positions in public equities;
- describe strategies for managing concentrated positions in privately owned businesses and real estate;
- discuss objectives—tax and non-tax—in planning the transfer of wealth;

- discuss strategies for achieving estate, bequest, and lifetime gift objectives in common law and civil law regimes;
- describe considerations related to managing wealth across multiple generations.

1. INTRODUCTION

This chapter focuses on three important areas of technical competency in the management of private client assets: the impact of taxes on wealth accumulation, the management of concentrated positions in public or private assets, and basic tools and techniques for preserving wealth through generations.

We begin with a discussion of taxes. Taxes are an important determinant of the taxable investor's final returns. While fees and trading costs have received a lot of attention in the press and academic spheres, the erosion of returns due to taxes can be much more significant.

Consider this scenario: After significant development and testing, your firm has just launched a new strategy that tactically shifts between different equity indexes. The backtests show significant alpha over most time horizons and especially strong performance during market downturns—a risk/return profile that should be highly attractive to your clients. You launch the strategy 1 January, and everyone is pleased with the performance in the first year. On 15 February of the following year, the founder of the firm receives a telephone call from the accountant for Charles and Ivy Lee, an important private client relationship. The accountant has been compiling the Lees' tax documents in preparation for filing the annual tax return. It seems that the trading activity inherent in your new strategy has generated a lot of capital gains, and the resulting tax bill is larger than the excess returns generated by your strategy!

This scenario is not uncommon. Because a significant proportion of actively managed assets is managed on behalf of tax-exempt institutions, such as retirement plans and sovereign wealth funds, strategies are often developed either without regard to taxes or with taxes as an afterthought and then applied—unsuccessfully—to taxable investors.

To illustrate the effect of taxes on wealth accumulation, let's examine a longer time horizon. The S&P 500 Index from 1 January 1990 through 30 June 2019 appreciated 7.5% per year, on average. With dividends reinvested and ignoring fees and transaction costs, the compound annual growth rate would have been 9.8%. If the Lees had invested $1 million on 1 January 1990, we would expect their portfolio to have grown to $16 million by the end of the nearly 30-year period. However, this is only true if the assets are not subject to taxation during the accumulation phase, as would be the case if they are held in a retirement account or a private family foundation. Exhibit 1 shows the growth of this hypothetical portfolio under several different tax assumptions.

If we assume the worst case, that both dividends and capital gains are taxed fully at a marginal tax rate of 50%, then the 9.8% compound annual growth rate would be cut roughly in half—to 5.0%. In other words, their $1 million would have only grown to $4 million after almost 30 years—only one-fourth of what the tax-exempt account realized. Clearly, taxes are an important investment consideration.

Fortunately, as a tax-aware practitioner, you may be able to use various tax-management techniques to reduce the tax drag. If capital gains and dividends are taxed at 25%, the final wealth of the taxable portfolio would have grown to $8 million. If capital gains taxes can be eliminated or deferred and only dividends are taxed at the 25% rate, then the $1 million would have grown to $13 million at the end of our horizon. It is still not as good as the tax-exempt case, but it is significantly better than our worst case.

EXHIBIT 1   Growth of $1 million in the S&P 500 Index

Notes: Growth of $1 million from January 1990 through June 2019 for the S&P 500 Index with dividends reinvested, ignoring fees and transaction costs. After-tax returns are computed in three ways: 1) Only dividends are taxed at 25%; 2) Dividends and capital gains are taxed at 25%; 3) Dividends and capital gains are taxed at 50%. In each month, we multiply the component of return by 1 minus the tax rate. For example, pre-tax returns of 10% and −10% would become 5% and −5% under a 50% tax rate. This calculation assumes that all capital gains and losses are realized each month and that when capital losses occur, there are sufficient capital gains from other investments so that the investor may deduct the losses in full. Essentially, the tax liability is deducted and the tax benefit added to the account as if it were a cash flow, thus reducing the magnitude and volatility of returns.

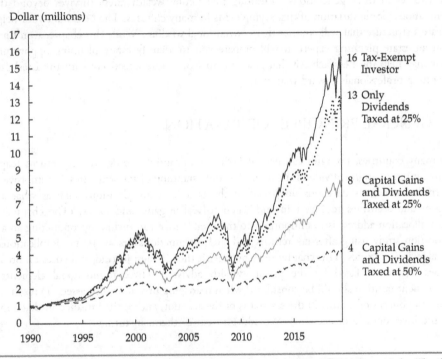

Sources: Authors' calculations using the S&P 500 Total Return Index and the S&P 500 Price Return Index. The after-tax return methodology follows Lucas and Sanz (2016).

Broadly speaking, a portfolio manager managing assets for a private client looks to maximize after-tax returns for a given level of risk. This chapter lays the groundwork for understanding how different types of taxes impact wealth accumulation. We review the general principles of taxation, how to measure tax efficiency, and how to reduce the impact of taxes on a portfolio.

Hopefully we've convinced you why it is important to manage your client's portfolio with taxes in mind. Tax considerations, however, are just one element of managing assets for private wealth clients. Suppose that only 50% of your private client's assets are invested in your tax-aware investment strategy. The other 50% of assets are tied up in a company that was the primary source of wealth creation for your client: Ivy Lee started a business in her early 20s that succeeded far beyond her initial expectations. While she has accumulated liquid assets outside of that business, a substantial portion of her net worth is held in company stock. From your earlier chapters in the course of the CFA Program, you realize that this is a very risky position. Taken in the aggregate, her portfolio is undiversified; however, to sell the position outright would create an enormous tax liability or lead to a loss of control over the business she created. How, then, do you help the client achieve her goals? This chapter discusses some practical tools that you can employ to manage the risk of this concentrated position.

Finally, Ivy and Charles want to maximize the likelihood that the strong financial foundation they have created will survive to provide support for their children's and grandchildren's future endeavors. Ivy has frequently heard the phrase "shirtsleeves to shirtsleeves in three generations," meaning that family wealth rarely survives beyond three generations. Some variation of that saying exists in many cultures. The Lees want your help to create a structure that will counter that conventional wisdom. While this chapter won't make you an estate planning expert, it will prepare you to identify estate planning opportunities that may help the Lees achieve that goal and to work more effectively with the Lees' estate planning professionals toward that end.

2. GENERAL PRINCIPLES OF TAXATION

In many countries, tax rates can exceed 50%, significantly eroding realized returns (capital gains, interest, and/or dividend income). An understanding of tax structures will improve the portfolio manager's decisions on behalf of the taxable client, decisions such as what asset classes and securities to invest in and when to realize gains and losses. (The chapters on asset allocation address issues important to the taxable investor, including conducting an asset allocation study using after-tax returns and such pragmatic issues as the tax implications of rebalancing strategies. This chapter does not revisit those issues; instead, it focuses on broader issues frequently faced by the private wealth adviser.) Three foundational elements of investment taxation should be considered when managing private wealth assets: 1) taxation of the components of return, 2) the tax status of the account, and 3) the jurisdiction that applies to the investor (and/or account). We address each of them, in turn.

2.1. Taxation of the Components of Return

Although the specifics of tax codes are country- and jurisdiction-specific, the following general categories of taxes are widely recognized:

- *Income Tax.* Income tax is calculated as a percentage of taxable income, often with different rates applied to various levels of income. Wages, rents, dividends, and interest earned are commonly treated as taxable income. Cross-border investments, common in the portfolios of many wealthy families, may also create taxable income in the investor's home country as well as in the country in which the investment is located.
- *Gains Tax.* Capital gains are the profits based on price appreciation that result from the sale of an asset, including financial assets. Gains are often distinguished from income and taxed at different rates.
- *Wealth or Property Tax.* A wealth or property tax most often refers to the taxation of real property (real estate) but may also apply to financial and other assets. Such taxes are

generally assessed annually. Comprehensive wealth taxes apply in a limited number of countries but are increasingly being considered by other countries as a mechanism to raise revenue.

- *Stamp Duties.* A number of countries impose a tax on the purchase price of shares or real estate. Foreign investors may be subject to higher rates than domestic investors.
- *Wealth Transfer Tax.* A wealth transfer tax is assessed as assets are transferred from one owner to another using some mechanism other than an outright sale/purchase transaction. Examples of wealth transfer taxes include "estate" or "inheritance" taxes paid at the investor's death and "gift" taxes paid on transfers made during the investor's lifetime. In some cases, these taxes are the responsibility of the person transferring the asset; in other cases, these taxes are imposed on the recipient.

Therefore, investors pay taxes on what they *earn* (income and gains tax), what they *own* (wealth or property tax), what they *buy* (stamp duty tax), and what they *transfer* (gift and estate tax). The income and capital gains taxes are the ones that most directly affect the day-to-day portfolio management of private client assets. These taxes are briefly described next, along with some tax preferences frequently accorded to real estate investments.

2.1.1. Interest, Dividends, and Withholding Taxes

Most bonds, debt instruments, and interest-bearing accounts produce income in the form of interest payments. Many countries' tax codes create preferential treatment for some types of interest income. For example, in Italy interest income on government bonds is taxed at a lower rate. In the United States, income from state and local government bonds (municipal bonds) is often exempt from both federal and state income taxes; unless special provisions exist, interest is taxed at the ordinary income tax rate.

Double taxation is a term used to describe situations in which income is taxed twice. For example, corporate earnings are taxed at the company level and then that portion of earnings paid as dividends is taxed again at the investor level. Some countries mitigate the burden of double taxation of dividend income with specific exemptions or provisions in the tax code. Here are some examples:

- In Australia, if your personal tax rate is higher than the corporate tax rate, you will earn "franking" credits such that you only pay the difference between your personal tax rate and the corporate tax rate.
- In the United States, dividends from most domestic companies and qualifying foreign companies are taxed at a lower tax rate if you hold the stock for at least 60 days. (**Qualified dividends** are generally dividends from shares in domestic corporations and certain qualified foreign corporations that have been held for at least a specified minimum period of time—in the United States, 61 days for common stock, 91 days for preferred stock. The position must be unhedged.)

Portfolio managers investing on behalf of private clients must also consider the tax ramifications of cross-border investments. **Withholding taxes** are often imposed in the country in which the investment is made, most frequently on payments of interest, dividends, and royalties. The income will be taxed in the country in which it was earned and may be taxed again in the home country of the investor. The taxing jurisdiction will withhold taxes on the *gross* income earned within the jurisdiction—without regard for offsetting investment expenses or losses that may be available from the taxpayer's other investment activities.

2.1.2. Capital Gains Taxes

To estimate the tax liability associated with a particular trade, we need to know the asset's **tax basis** and holding period. In many cases, the tax basis is the amount that was paid to acquire an asset, or its "cost" basis. In the case of equities, this would be the share price multiplied by the number of shares plus commissions and other trading costs. Other assets, such as discount or premium bonds or REITs, may be subject to annual accounting adjustments to the tax basis.

The tax basis serves as the foundation for calculating a **capital gain or loss**, which equals the selling price (net of commissions and other trading costs) less the tax basis. Capital gains may be realized or unrealized capital gains. A realized capital gain is the profit "booked" when the asset is sold. An unrealized capital gain is the appreciation on an asset currently held in the portfolio. If an asset is sold at a loss, the loss may often be used to offset a realized capital gain.

There are circumstances where the tax basis may be other than the investor's actual cost basis. For example, in some countries, such as the United States, there is a basis "step-up" on death, meaning that someone who inherits an asset would have a tax basis equal to the fair market value of the asset on the date of death. No capital gains taxes are due as a result of this step-up in basis. Other countries have laws that lead to a step-up in tax basis upon death or upon a change in citizenship or residency, but the unrealized, embedded gains would be subject to tax.

Capital gains may also be short-term or long-term capital gains. The *holding period* is the length of time between the purchase and sale of an asset. Capital gains are generally taxed as income unless the asset is held longer than some minimum period specified by the tax laws of the relevant jurisdiction. Where such provisions exist, gains realized from assets held for the minimum period are taxed at a lower rate, called the *long-term capital gains* rate. Governments that apply lower tax rates to long-term gains create a tax incentive for long-term investors and a disincentive to speculative short-term trading. In these jurisdictions, stocks are generally more tax-efficient investments than taxable bonds since a significant portion of equity returns comes from tax-advantaged appreciation.

In some jurisdictions, there is a distinction between investment gains and trading gains. For example, in a jurisdiction where capital gains are tax-free or taxed at lower rates, the tax benefits may be lost if the investor is considered to be in the *business* of stock or real estate trading.

2.1.3. Real Estate Taxes

While many countries provide favorable tax treatment for an individual's principal residence—exempting capital gains arising from the sale of the residence—real estate *investments* are subject to a broader range of tax preferences. How the real estate is owned and financed will have a significant bearing on the after-tax returns generated by the investment.

Generally, jurisdictions tax the net income from a real estate investment, allowing such expenses as maintenance, interest, and depreciation to be deducted from gross income prior to calculating the tax liability. Where interest expenses are deductible, it may be attractive to finance a real estate purchase even if the investor has the funds necessary to pay the purchase price in full.

Depreciation expenses may also be deductible. For example, an investor buys a property in a jurisdiction that allows the investor to depreciate the property over 10 years. A portion of the purchase price of the building may be recorded as an expense during each year of ownership, reducing the investor's income tax liability. The depreciation expense is deducted from the investor's cost basis. These deductions are usually recaptured on a sale of the investment if the sales price exceeds the depreciated cost base of the asset involved.

In some countries, one real estate investment can be exchanged for another in a qualifying exchange, enabling the investor to defer capital gains taxes until the second property is sold.

2.2. The Tax Status of the Account

The tax status of the account will also factor into investment decisions for private clients. There are three principal types of accounts: taxable, tax-deferred, and tax-exempt. In a **taxable account**, the normal tax rules of the jurisdiction apply. For a **tax-deferred account**, investment and contributions may be made on a pre-tax basis and investment returns accumulate on a tax-deferred basis until funds are withdrawn, at which time they are taxed at ordinary income tax rates. In a **tax-exempt account**, no taxes are assessed during the investment, contribution, or withdrawal phase, nor are they assessed on investment returns. The tax status of an account is an important factor in understanding the tax implications of investment and wealth management decisions.

Pension funds, endowment funds, and foundations are generally *tax-exempt*. The retirement accounts of individuals are usually *tax-deferred*. In Australia, retirement superannuation plans are taxed but at a discounted rate relative to the individual investor rate. Exhibit 2 shows the tax status for different accounts by investor type.

EXHIBIT 2   Tax Status by Type of Investor and Account

Type of Investment Account	Typical Tax Status
Individual Investor	
Individual Brokerage Account	Taxable
Individual Retirement Account	Tax-deferred
Roth IRA (US)	Tax-exempt
Personal Trust	Taxable
Charitable Trust	Tax-exempt
Institutional Investor	
Foundation	Tax-exempt
Corporation	Taxable
Corporation – Nonprofit	Tax-exempt
Insurance Company	Taxable
Pension Fund	Tax-exempt
Superannuation Fund (Australia)	Taxable at a discounted rate
Endowment	Tax-exempt
Sovereign Wealth Fund	Tax-exempt

EXAMPLE 1   Tax Considerations for the Private Client

You are managing a portfolio for Hugh Jackson, a private wealth client. Just a few weeks remain in the tax year.

	Market Value	Unrealized Short-Term Gain	Realized Short-Term Gain	Unrealized Long-Term Gain	Realized Long-Term Gain	Year-to-Date Income (Dividends / Interest)
Domestic Equities	€8,000,000	−€500,000	€250,000	€2,500,000	€500,000	€120,000
Domestic Fixed Income	€5,000,000	0	0	€1,000,000	0	€150,000
Income-Producing Real Estate	€1,000,000	0	0	€500,000	0	€60,000
Total	€14,000,000	−€500,000	€250,000	€4,000,000	€500,000	€330,000

1. Assuming this is a taxable account, what tax considerations are likely to influence your portfolio decisions?
2. If this were a tax-deferred retirement account and the client plans to take a €450,000 pre-tax withdrawal by year-end, how might the portfolio decisions be different?

Solution to 1:

- The client is subject to tax on the realized capital gains and income received year-to-date. (€250,000 + €500,000 + €330,000 = €1,080,000.)
- The dividend and interest income may be eligible for preferential tax treatment depending on the composition of the portfolio.
- The taxable component of the real estate income may be reduced through deductions of maintenance, interest, and depreciation.
- The €500,000 in short-term losses should be evaluated for possible sale prior to year-end. The losses could be used to offset the €250,000 in realized short-term gains and half of the realized long-term gains while raising the cash needed to fund the planned withdrawal.
- Any remaining long-term gain is subject to tax, typically at a rate lower than the investor's marginal income tax rate.

Solution to 2: The client would be taxed only on the €450,000 withdrawal. The applicable tax rate is the client's marginal income tax rate. The distinctions between realized and unrealized capital gains and losses are irrelevant in a tax-deferred retirement portfolio.

2.3. The Jurisdiction That Applies to the Investor

Tax systems are used by governments to encourage or discourage certain activities (e.g., investing in domestic companies or saving for retirement). These incentives vary globally and can change as the needs and objectives of the government change. Rather than listing the specific rules for each country and jurisdiction, this chapter provides a general framework to understand how different tax environments may affect clients. Private wealth advisers must become familiar with the tax provisions of each jurisdiction that affects their clients.

In general, the main types of tax systems we find internationally fall into three broad categories:

- Tax havens
- Territorial tax systems
- Worldwide tax systems, which may be based on either citizenship or residency

A **tax haven** is a country or independent area with no or very low tax rates for foreign investors. The Cayman Islands are a well-known tax haven—with no tax on income or capital gains, no tax on property holdings (other than on the transfer of a property to another individual or entity), and no corporate taxes. Similarly, the British Virgin Islands or The Bahamas do not tax income or capital gains. Russia and Saudi Arabia also have very low tax rates but aren't considered tax havens since the favorable tax treatment is reserved for residents.

Other jurisdictions operate **territorial tax systems**, where only locally-sourced income is taxed. For example, Hong Kong, a special administrative region of China, has much lower tax rates than the mainland and does not tax capital gains, dividends, or income earned outside of Hong Kong SAR. Examples of other territorial tax systems include the Philippines and Singapore.

Jurisdictions operating under a **worldwide tax system** tax all income regardless of its source. Examples are Switzerland, France, Germany, India, Canada, and Japan, among many other countries. Worldwide tax systems can give rise to double taxation as the country in which investments are made may impose taxes on this same income. This type of double taxation is often addressed through tax credits provided by the home country or through other forms of relief, such as tax treaties (i.e., bilateral agreements between countries).

Because countries operating under a worldwide tax system generally impose those taxes only on individuals considered to be residents of that country, residence rules become very important. Residence rules specify how much time a person can spend in a country without becoming a taxable resident. If an individual spends time in more than one country, tax treaties can play an important role in determining tax residence. Most tax treaties contain *tie-breaker* rules that prevent an individual from being considered a resident of more than one country at the same time.

The United States is one of the few countries that taxes citizens on a worldwide basis *regardless of residence*. As a result, US citizens living in Hong Kong SAR will be subject to US tax on their worldwide income, whereas Canadian citizens also living in Hong Kong SAR will not be taxed by Canada on income earned outside of Canada.

When working with wealthy families, it is essential to develop a full understanding of the tax jurisdictions that will affect investment and estate planning. It is not uncommon to have a client who is a citizen of one country, a resident of another, and who has investments (and heirs) in several others. A good rule of thumb is to start with the tax rules of the investor's home country. The home country rules may influence decisions on how to own assets in another country. The following example illustrates the various issues that must be addressed when considering cross-border investments for clients.

Considerations in Cross-Border Investing

Josie Boyd is a Hong Kong citizen living in Hong Kong SAR. She wants to invest in income-producing residential real estate in the United States. The ownership structure of an investment will have a material impact on its after-tax return. Consider the following:

- Hong Kong SAR operates under a territorial tax system; thus, it would not tax any income or gains arising from the US-located investment.
- The United States taxes investments in the United States regardless of the investor's citizenship or residence, taxing both income from the investment and any capital gain on a sale of an investment in which real estate is involved. The investment may also be subject to US estate and gift taxes. Depending on the location of the US investment, state taxation may come into play in addition to any federal tax obligation.
- Hong Kong SAR also has no inheritance or estate tax, so the only tax considerations to be addressed are those arising from the United States.
- If Josie owns the property directly in her name,
  - she may be subject to tax withholding on the gross rental income, with no opportunity to offset that income with investment expenses; and
  - there would be an estate tax payable upon her death, although the value of the estate would be reduced by any outstanding mortgage on the property.

- If Josie owns the property through a US corporation,
  - the US corporation could be owned by a non-US entity, either Josie herself or a non-US corporation, and investment expenses could be used to offset the rental income. Only the net income would be subject to withholding when it is paid to the non-US owner; and
  - at Josie's death,
    - the shares of the company either pass to Josie's heirs, or
    - if the company is liquidated, any gains on the property would be taxed at the corporate capital gains tax rate, which is higher than the capital gains tax rate for individuals. In addition, any retained earnings would be subject to withholding.

- If Josie owns the property through a non-US corporation,
  - the value of the asset would not be subject to US estate taxes at Josie's death: The shares of the company pass to Josie's beneficiaries, not the property itself, on her death. As a non-US company, it is not subject to US taxation. (This is not true in all countries, however.)

Clearly, the jurisdictional tax considerations are an integral part of any cross-border investment decision. While we used a corporation to illustrate some of the issues that might arise, corporations are not the only alternative, and for certain investments, they may be a poor choice. Trusts, private insurance companies, and private foundations are other alternative structures that can be used to maximize the after-tax return for private clients. The best solution is one tailored to the client's investment *and* estate planning objectives. An international tax specialist is needed to ensure that all relevant issues are considered in cross-border investment.

Exhibit 3 summarizes some relevant tax rates for the largest 25 jurisdictions by GDP as of 2018.

EXHIBIT 3   Top Marginal Tax Rates for Selected Jurisdictions, Largest 25 Jurisdictions by GDP

Income Tax Rate %

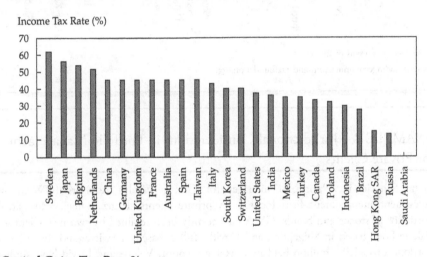

Capital Gains Tax Rate %

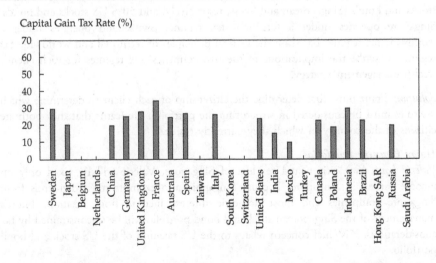

Estate Tax Rate %

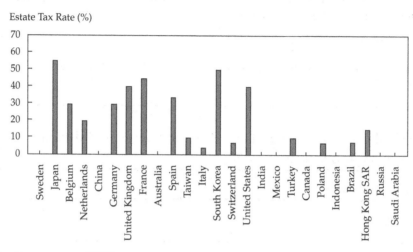

Estate Tax Rate (%)

Note: Tax rates are as of 2018.

Sources: tradingeconomics.com and taxfoundation.org.

EXAMPLE 2 Jurisdictional Considerations in Portfolio Management for Private Clients

Franz Schmid is a portfolio manager for Global Wealth Advisors (GWA), an investment management firm focused on private clients. Franz manages diversified portfolios of stocks and bonds. GWA has recently been retained by two new clients—Valerie Low, based in Singapore, and David Muller, based in Switzerland. Each has a portfolio of CHF10 million held in a taxable account. Valerie and David have similar risk and return objectives, and each has agreed to an asset allocation of 50% domestic stocks and bonds (Singaporean and Swiss, respectively) and 50% US stocks and bonds. Singapore operates under a territorial tax regime. Switzerland operates under a worldwide tax regime. Based on the general principles of territorial and worldwide tax regimes, describe the implications of the two countries' tax regimes for each client's wealth management strategy.

Solution: Franz must first determine the citizenship of each client to determine which tax rules must be considered in structuring the portfolio. He learns that they both are citizens of the country in which they currently reside.

Home Country Portfolios
Valerie Low. As a citizen and resident of Singapore, Valerie will be taxed only on income earned in Singapore. Because Singapore also exempts most dividends from Singapore companies and most domestic interest income from taxation, Franz's management of the Singaporean stock and bond portfolio will be unconstrained by tax considerations. His chief concern relates to the US taxation of the US stock and bond portfolio.

David Muller. As a citizen and resident of Switzerland, David will be subject to Swiss tax on all of his investments and US tax on his US investments. In broad terms, Switzerland taxes dividend and interest income but exempts individual investors' capital gains from taxation. Between local and federal taxes, David's dividend and interest income is likely to be taxed at a rate well over 40%. The portfolio Franz constructs for David will emphasize high-growth equities, where a large portion of the total return is derived from capital gains.

US Portfolios

Valerie Low. No tax treaty exists between Singapore and the United States, so the United States will impose a 30% withholding tax on gross dividends. Most interest income on government and corporate bonds is exempt from withholding, provided the investor supplies the issuer or corporate trustee proof of beneficial ownership. Because they are held by a non-US investor, any capital gains on the stocks and bonds in the US portfolio will not be taxed by the United States. The portfolio Franz develops for Valerie will emphasize fixed-income securities and high-growth, low-dividend equities.

David Muller. There is a tax treaty between Switzerland and the United States that will reduce the withholding rate on David's US dividends from 30% to 15%, a substantial savings. Thus, David's US equity portfolio may have a higher allocation to dividend-paying stocks than would Valerie's portfolio. Any capital gains on the stocks and bonds in the portfolio will not be taxed by the United States, and most interest income will be exempt from US taxation under the same rules applied in Valerie's circumstances.

Wealth and Estate Taxes

Valerie Low. Singapore has no estate tax, and there is no estate tax treaty between Singapore and the United States. The US estate tax applies to US stock holdings but not to holdings of qualifying corporate and government bonds. Therefore, Valerie's estate will be required to pay US estate taxes on her US stock investments. Franz may look to create a non-US company to hold Valerie's US stock investments.

David Muller. Switzerland's estate tax is relatively modest compared to the US estate tax rate. While there is an estate tax treaty between Switzerland and the United States, to obtain the estate tax exemption, David would have to disclose his entire net worth to the United States, something he is reluctant to do. Thus, David would like to consider the creation of a non-US company to hold his US investments. This is not a clear-cut solution for David, however. If the country in which this company is created does not have an income tax treaty with the United States, David's dividend income would be subject to the 30% withholding tax rate and capital gains realized within the company would be distributed to David as dividends, which are taxable in Switzerland. Short of pursuing other, more complex, options (e.g., a partnership or trust), David's best option appears to be direct ownership and full disclosure of his net worth.

International Transparency, the Common Reporting Standard, and FATCA

In the past, it was not uncommon for people investing on a cross-border basis to assume that their home country would not know about income generated outside that country. While not reporting the foreign income and assets to a home country with a worldwide tax system would have constituted illegal tax evasion, the existence of bank secrecy in such countries as Switzerland facilitated such wrongful activity. Today, substantial information exchange regimes are in operation, including the *automatic* information exchange under what is known as the Common Reporting Standard. Tax authorities have also increased their focus on the activities of those who enable tax evasion, such as banks and investment managers. Wealthy international families, with a growing awareness of these rules and of the significant penalties associated with tax evasion, are increasingly understanding the need for tax compliance. Thus, they are highly appreciative of investment management strategies that properly analyze tax exposures and make use of legal tax minimization opportunities.

Taxpaying obligations are also accompanied by reporting requirements internationally, and two major regulations are now in place to promote tax transparency and disclosure of beneficial ownership.

The Common Reporting Standard (CRS), also known as the Standard for Automatic Exchange of Financial Account Information, was developed by the OECD with G20 countries and is a reciprocal requirement for the automatic exchange of financial account information. As of April 2019, more than 100 jurisdictions have committed to implementing the Standard, including Switzerland and other financial centers.

FATCA, the Foreign Account Tax Compliance Act, is a US program designed to ensure that US taxpayers pay the appropriate taxes on wealth held outside the country. Financial institutions are required to report this information on US account holders. Failure to do so triggers a 30% withholding on all US income.

EXAMPLE 3 Making Use of Tax Treaties to Enhance the After-Tax Return

Your client is a resident of Hong Kong SAR and is interested in adding "safe haven" assets to a portfolio. The client asked that you consider adding Swiss equites and bonds to the portfolio. (Switzerland has long been considered a "safe haven" for investors; it is at the center of Europe, has a stable political climate, and is economically integrated with most of the world.) After research, you have identified Swiss equities and bonds that you believe will fit with the client's investment profile.

You contemplate adding to the portfolio the following equities and bonds, with the following estimated returns:

Swiss equities: CHF200,000, producing annual dividends of CHF5,000 and projected annual appreciation of 5% (CHF10,000)

Swiss bonds: CHF200,000, producing annual interest payments of 3% (CHF6,000)

In your projections, you assume that the appreciation in the equities will be realized through a sale of the shares at year end. So, for your client the total return on the CHF400,000 portfolio will be:

Dividends: CHF5,000
Capital gains: CHF10,000
Interest income: CHF6,000
Total gross income, pre-tax: CHF21,000
Projected return: 5.25%

1.   What questions do you need to ask your client in relation to tax matters, and what information regarding Hong Kong SAR and Swiss taxation do you need in order to determine the after-tax return?
2.   How can returns on the portfolio be enhanced by focusing on tax treaties?

Solution to 1: You need to confirm that the client is not a citizen or permanent resident of a jurisdiction that operates under a worldwide tax regime. (For example, US citizens and permanent residents are taxable in the United States even if not currently residing there.) You also need to confirm the Hong Kong SAR tax treatment of the Swiss portfolio. Here, your client confirms that under Hong Kong SAR tax law there is no Hong Kong SAR taxation on interest, dividends, or capital gains earned in relation to the contemplated Swiss investments.

You also need to understand the Swiss tax position. On review, you confirm with Swiss advisers that Swiss inheritance taxes would not apply to a non-Swiss investor (except on real estate) and that capital gains are tax-free. However, you also learn that Switzerland applies a 35% withholding tax on interest and dividends to foreign investors.

Thus, the after-tax return for your client is estimated as follows:
Total gross income, pre-tax: CHF21,000
35% Swiss withholding tax on CHF11,000 (dividends and interest): CHF3,850
After-tax income: CHF17,150
Projected after-tax return: 4.29% (CHF17,150/CHF400,000).

Solution to 2: You check on whether a tax treaty exists between Hong Kong SAR, the place of residence of your client, and Switzerland, and you find that there is one. Under the treaty, a qualifying resident of Hong Kong SAR is entitled to a reduction in Swiss withholding taxes on both dividends and interest. In the case of dividends, the withholding rate is reduced from 35% to 10%; in the case of interest, the withholding rate is reduced from 35% to 0%.

Your calculation of the after-tax return is revised as follows:
Total gross income pre-tax: CHF21,000
10% Swiss withholding tax on CHF5,000 (dividends): CHF500
0% Swiss withholding tax on CHF6,000 (interest): CHF0
After-tax income: CHF20,500
Projected after-tax return: 5.13%

In order to recover the Swiss withholding tax, your client, with your help, would apply online to the Hong Kong SAR Inland Revenue Department for a Certificate of Resident Status and then submit it online to the Swiss Federal Tax Administration with details on the withholding tax imposed for the processing of the refund.

3. MEASURING TAX EFFICIENCY WITH AFTER-TAX RETURNS

We've shown how taxes can materially affect an investor's net returns. Not only do they reduce the investor's return in the year they were paid, they also affect longer-term returns through the lost opportunity to compound gross returns over time. When managing portfolios for taxable investors, it is important to measure the tax efficiency of investments. We do this by quantifying the effects of taxation on returns. Calculating after-tax returns allows us to do a better job of selecting securities, managing trades, and evaluating the performance of portfolios. In this section, we discuss the "tax efficiency" of various asset classes and the calculation of after-tax returns.

3.1. Tax Efficiency of Various Asset Classes and Investment Strategies

A **tax-efficient strategy** is one that gives up very little of its return to the friction of taxes. Generally speaking, equity portfolios are often more tax efficient than strategies that rely on derivatives, real assets, or taxable fixed income. 1) Dividends on stocks often receive preferential tax treatment. 2) Capital gains are taxed less heavily than ordinary income in many jurisdictions. 3) The flexibility to manage the timing of the sell decisions gives asset managers an additional measure of control over the tax burden.

Alternative asset classes are favored by investors for their uncorrelated returns, but the tax considerations associated with these investments can be considerably more complicated than those associated with stocks and bonds. Real estate, timberland, and oil and gas partnerships often have their own tax rules. Market-neutral strategies typically employ leverage, short sales, convertible debt, options, futures contracts, and straddles. The tax rules around these instruments can be difficult to understand even for a tax expert. It is important to model these asset classes' contributions to portfolio risk and return on an after-tax, after-fee basis.

Within an asset class, the portfolio management process and style of investing can affect the tax efficiency of the portfolio. Generally speaking, higher-yield and higher-turnover strategies tend to be less tax efficient. However, the timing of the trading patterns is also an important factor. For example, momentum strategies, which tend to be high turnover strategies, are relatively tax efficient. They hold their winners and sell their losers—letting gains run and accelerating the realization of losses (which create a tax benefit, despite the tendency to have a higher turnover). On the other hand, value and small-cap strategies tend to be less tax efficient as they are likely to sell a security when it reaches a pre-determined target price and thus realize gains more frequently.

Using a "style box" approach to selecting managers can also create tax inefficiencies. A style box approach selects specialist managers to fill targeted large-cap, small-cap, value, growth, and alternative allocations within the equity portfolio. At the manager level, these style constraints force managers to realize gains if a security moves out of their style (or risk losing the account due to "style drift"). At the total fund level, rebalancing to the targeted style allocation can create additional taxable gains.

3.2. Calculating After-Tax Returns

To measure tax efficiency, we address the various return measures of interest to the private wealth manager:

- *After-tax holding period return*: Returns are adjusted for the tax liability generated in the period. There is an implicit, simplifying assumption that taxes are withdrawn from (or tax benefits deposited to) the account at the time the asset is sold. This measure allows an investor to judge the tax efficiency of an investment strategy, including how returns are affected by taxes on interest, dividends, and realized capital gains. After-tax holding period returns can be geometrically linked and annualized in the normal way.
- *After-tax post-liquidation return*: Post-liquidation returns assume that the portfolio is liquidated at the end of a hypothetical investment horizon—usually 1, 3, 5, and 10 years— and the taxes are paid on those gains. The post-liquidation measure allows an investor to consider the impact of the embedded tax liabilities (i.e., the unrealized capital gains) on ending wealth. This is especially useful in the evaluation of commingled funds, such as mutual funds.
- *After-tax excess returns*: Similar to regular returns, after-tax returns can be compared against a benchmark, helping an investor understand whether the tax drag is eroding the return benefits of a strategy.
- *Tax-efficiency ratio*: This ratio is the after-tax annualized total return divided by the pre-tax annualized total return. It helps to quickly sort managers by the efficiency of the product offering. When used in combination with the other measures, it is a useful tool to identify managers who can effectively manage taxable portfolios.

Each of these is discussed next.

3.2.1. After-Tax Holding Period Returns

The pre-tax holding period return, R, is calculated as the change in value (value − $value_0$) plus the income divided by the initial portfolio value:

$$R = \frac{(\text{value} - \text{value}_0) + \text{income}}{\text{value}_0} \tag{1}$$

The after-tax holding period return, R', modifies this formula to account for the tax liability created by the income received and capital gains realized in the period.

$$R' = \frac{(\text{value} - \text{value}_0) + \text{income} - \text{tax}}{\text{value}_0} \tag{2}$$

This is mathematically equivalent to:

$$R' = R - \frac{\text{tax}}{\text{value}_0}$$

The tax due in the period can be calculated by multiplying each component of realized return by the appropriate marginal tax rate. If we assume that there are a number of transactions (realized capital gains or losses, dividends, interest payments, etc.) that each produce a tax consequence and that the tax rate for a particular transaction i is denoted as t_i, then we can calculate the total tax for a portfolio in a given period as:

$$\text{tax} = \sum_{i=1}^{n} \text{transaction}_i \times t_i$$

If after-tax returns are calculated monthly, the cumulative after-tax return, R'_G, can be calculated by geometrically linking the monthly returns:

$$R'_G = [(1 + R'_1)(1 + R'_2)\ldots(1 + R'_n)]^{1/n} - 1$$

This equation is merely an *estimate* of how taxes can be expected to affect the compounding of the portfolio. It assumes that when capital losses are realized, sufficient capital gains from other investments exist so that the investor may deduct the losses in full. If there are no gains, the deductibility of investment losses can result in an after-tax return that is higher than the pre-tax return. The tax liability is deducted and the tax benefit is added to the account each period as if it were a cash flow, thus reducing the magnitude and volatility of returns. In practice, however, the intricacies of local laws and regulations mean that not all investors will receive full credit for the tax losses realized. Also, taxes are usually paid on an annual or quarterly basis rather than at the time of the taxable event and from an account other than the investment account (i.e., the investor's checking account). Thus, the taxable investment account is unlikely to compound at precisely the after-tax return rate.

Approximating Monthly After-Tax Returns

In many organizations, pre-tax holding period returns are automatically calculated by the firm's accounting systems on a daily basis, while after-tax returns are only calculated monthly. If you want an intra-month after-tax return that accounts for any cash flows during the period, this can be done using the modified Dietz method. We show the calculation of after-tax returns using the modified Dietz method:

$$R' = R - \frac{\text{tax}}{\text{value}_0 + \sum_{j=1}^{N} C_j(N - j)/N}$$

where:

       tax = cumulative tax liability for all transactions during the month

       $value_0$ = initial value at the beginning of the month

       C_j = cash flow on day j

       N = number of calendar days in a month

       $N - j$ = number of days from flow to end of month

       If, for example,

- the initial value of the portfolio on 1 January is $500,000,
- a $3,500 dividend is received on 10 January,
- the dividend tax rate is 20%, and
- the monthly pre-tax total return for the portfolio is 2.50%,

then the after-tax return can be approximated as

$$2.50\% - \frac{0.20(3,500)}{500,000 + \frac{3,500(31-10)}{31}} = 2.36\%$$

3.2.2. After-Tax Post-Liquidation Returns

When evaluating a mutual fund or other commingled vehicle as a potential investment, the taxable investor may need to consider the effect of unrealized capital gains embedded in the fund. One measure that can assist in the analysis is the **post-liquidation return**. The post-liquidation return assumes that all portfolio holdings are sold as of the end date of the analysis and that the resulting capital gains tax that would be due is deducted from the ending portfolio value. The US Securities and Exchange Commission requires that mutual funds report the post-liquidation return as well as an after-tax return calculated under an assumption that all income and capital gain distributions are taxed at the maximum federal rate at the time of distribution and that the after-tax portion of the dividend and interest income return is reinvested in the fund.

To calculate the post-liquidation return, R_{PL}, we must subtract the embedded tax liability at the end of the final period assuming that all remaining capital gains taxes are paid as they would be if the portfolio were liquidated.

$$R_{PL} = \left[(1 + R_1')(1 + R_2') \ldots (1 + R_n') - \frac{\text{liquidation tax}}{\text{final value}} \right]^{1/n} - 1$$

where the liquidation tax is given by:

    liquidation tax = (final value − tax basis) * capital gains tax rate.

These standardized calculations make comparing the tax efficiency of portfolios very straightforward.

EXAMPLE 4 Calculating the Post-Liquidation Return

A portfolio posts the following pre-tax and after-tax annual returns:

	Pre-Tax Return	After-Tax Return
Year 1	3.0%	2.5%
Year 2	10.0%	9.0%
Year 3	5.0%	4.2%
Year 4	−2.0%	−1.5%
Year 5	5.0%	4.4%
Cumulative Return	22.41%	19.72%
Annualized Return	4.13%	3.66%

Assume the portfolio has embedded gains equal to 10% of the ending value and must pay capital gains taxes at a 20% rate.

What is the annualized post-liquidation return over the 5-year period?

Solution: To calculate the post-liquidation return, we must first calculate the ending portfolio value. Given the five annualized after-tax returns shown, the final after-tax portfolio value is calculated as follows:

$$(1 + 0.025)(1 + 0.09)(1 + 0.042)(1 - 0.015)(1 + 0.044) = 1.197$$

The after-tax returns compounded in this way account for the tax on distributions and realized capital gains but do not account for any unrealized gains. The assumed tax liability from unrealized capital gains at liquidation is 2% of the final value (10% embedded gain times a 20% tax rate).

Therefore, the portfolio value net of the tax liability is 1.177:

$$1.197 - 0.02 = 1.177$$

and the annualized post-liquidation return is 3.32%:

$$1.177^{(1/5)} - 1 = 3.32\%$$

This compares to an annualized return for the non-taxable investor of 4.13%.

3.2.3. After-Tax Excess Returns

In an important article on tax management—"Is Your Alpha Big Enough to Cover Its Taxes?"—Jeffrey and Arnott (1993) showed that more than 85% of the active managers in their study underperformed the capitalization-weighted index fund on an after-tax basis. More recently, Sialm and Zhang (Forthcoming) found that, on average, high-tax bracket shareholders invested in equity mutual funds would have lost 108 basis points (bps) per year as a result of taxes due on investment income. This erosion of returns is similar in size to that created by fund expenses, a topic which has received much attention. Both papers confirm the widely-held belief that most mutual fund managers do not generate sufficient alpha to cover fees and taxes.

So, how do we measure the risk and return consequences of the tax management decisions? We use the **after-tax excess return**—the after-tax return of the portfolio, R', minus the after-tax return of the benchmark, B'. If the mandate is passive, the benchmark portfolio is an index. If the mandate is active, we might select an index as the benchmark *or* we could use a strategy benchmark—a model portfolio that represents the manager's stated investment approach. If we use an index as the benchmark, we are measuring whether the portfolio's excess return was sufficient to offset its tax burden. If we set the benchmark to be the model portfolio, we are measuring the implementation effects of tax management. In either case, the excess returns are calculated as follows:

$$x = \text{pre-tax excess return} = R - B, \text{ and}$$

$$x' = \text{after-tax excess return} = R' - B'$$

We use the following notation to measure the performance of a strategy on an after-tax basis:

$R = $ portfolio pre-tax return
$B = $ benchmark pre-tax return
R' and $B' = $ after-tax returns for the portfolio and benchmark, respectively
$x = $ pre-tax excess return
$x' = $ after-tax excess return

The **tax alpha** isolates the benefit of tax management by subtracting the pre-tax excess return from the after-tax excess return:

$$\alpha_{\text{tax}} = \text{tax alpha} = x' - x$$

3.2.4. Tax-Efficiency Ratio

The **tax-efficiency ratio (TER)** is simply the after-tax return divided by the pre-tax return:

$$\text{TER} = \frac{R'}{R}$$

For example, if the total annualized return for a portfolio is 10% and the after-tax return is 8%, the tax-efficiency ratio would be 80% (= 0.08/0.10).

Exhibit 4 illustrates the extent to which the tax efficiency of even top-performing funds can vary. It plots the five-year pre-tax return of top-decile, no-load, small-cap mutual funds against their tax-efficiency ratios. The funds in this chart are all top-decile funds, having outperformed a majority of their peers over the five-year period. But this top-decile ranking is based on pre-tax returns. An important question for the private wealth investor is how much of that return do I get to keep? Ideally, you would want to focus on funds in the upper right-hand quadrant of the graph—the higher-returning, more-efficient funds. Most of the funds have a TER in the range of 70% to 75%, with annual returns of 10% to 10.5%. There are a few outliers, however. Fund A has a much higher pre-tax return than all of its peers. Its TER, though, is below the median TER of the group. Managers B and C have high TERs but returns that place them at the bottom of the group. Manager D is a negative outlier, with both returns and TER at the bottom of the group.

EXHIBIT 4   Comparing Managers Using Tax-Efficiency Ratios

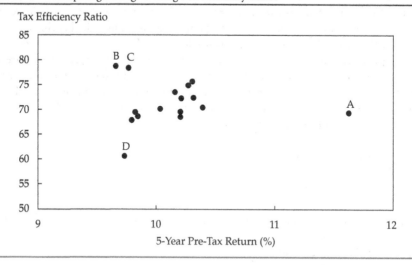

The tax-efficiency ratio can help an analyst or portfolio manager understand which funds may be more appropriate for the taxable account of a private client. If the client's other investments generate tax losses, perhaps Manager A would be a good fit. While it is difficult to predict what the performance of these managers will be over the next five years, it is likely that their investment process will produce levels of tax efficiency similar to those that each has produced in the past.

Note that the tax-efficiency ratio is not as useful when returns are negative. For example, if a portfolio had a −10% pre-tax return and −12% after-tax return, the ratio would be 120% (−0.12/−0.10). We know, however, that this cannot be right; taxes are making the returns worse. Rather than relying on the TER, the analyst could choose to simply plot the after-tax returns versus pre-tax returns directly or look at other metrics, such as tax alpha, instead.

EXAMPLE 5   Tax and the City

Cary Broadshawl lives in New York City and holds a portfolio of stocks, bonds, and funds in a taxable brokerage account. The following table lists the federal and state tax rates that apply to her various investments. The marginal tax rate is the combined income tax rate—federal, state, and local—that applies to an incremental dollar of investment income that the investor earns. In this case, the highest marginal rate adds up to well over 50%, which is a difficult environment for an investor attempting to compound wealth over time.

Some asset classes qualify for preferential income tax rates.

Income Tax Rates by Jurisdiction	
US Federal income tax rate	37.00%
NY State income tax rate	8.82%
NY City income tax rate	3.88%
Federal net investment income (NII) tax rate	3.80%
Total tax rate on ordinary investment income	53.50%

Cary's adviser, Mr. Bigg, has constructed a diversified portfolio using mutual funds and exchange-traded funds. The following table highlights some characteristics of those funds, obtained from Mr. Bigg's data service provider.

Income Tax Rates by Asset	Tax Rate	Requirement
NY State municipal bond interest income	0.00%	For NY state residents
Out-of-state municipal bond interest income	12.70%	
Capital gains	36.50%	If held longer than 1 year
Qualified dividend income from stocks	36.50%	If held longer than 61 days
US Treasury interest income	40.80%	
Dividend income from REITs	43.50%	
Other fixed-income instruments	53.50%	
Non-qualified dividend income from stocks	53.50%	

Questions:

	Annualized 5-Year Pre-Tax Return	5-Year Return after Taxes on Distributions	5-Year Post-Liquidation Return
Passive Equity ETF	10.85%	10.19%	8.71%
Active Equity Mutual Fund	12.05%	10.21%	9.05%
High-Yield Bond ETF	4.28%	1.72%	1.36%

Note: These returns are net of fund expenses and management fees.

1. Calculate the tax-efficiency ratio for each of the funds in the table. Which of the funds is most tax efficient? Why are the other funds less tax efficient?

2. Mr. Bigg's data provider assumes the highest federal tax rates. How will the after-tax returns on the funds be affected by Cary's actual tax rates?

3. Cary bought 1,000 shares of Microsoft (MSFT) in her brokerage account for $130 per share at the beginning of the month and sold all 1,000 shares at the end of the month for $155 per share. She also received a dividend on MSFT of $0.50 per share during the month. Ignoring any transaction costs, what taxes are due?

4. Discuss the tax efficiency of Cary's MSFT investment. How could the tax efficiency have been improved?

5. Discuss the tax efficiency of this same trade assuming a sale price of $120 per share.

6. Cary's portfolio also holds several NY State tax-exempt municipal bonds. She plans to hold the bonds to maturity. During the month, interest rates declined and the value of the bonds increased by 1%. While Cary didn't buy or sell during the month, she did receive 0.5% of the value of the bonds in interest payments. What are the pre-tax and after-tax returns of her NY state municipal bond portfolio?

Solution to 1:

- The tax-efficiency ratios for each of the funds are as follows:
  - Passive Equity ETF: 10.19/10.85 = 94%
  - Active Equity Mutual Fund: 10.21/12.05 = 85%
  - High-Yield Bond ETF: 1.72/4.28 = 40%

- The Passive Equity ETF is very tax efficient, as evidenced by its 94% tax-efficiency ratio. The after-tax return is only 0.66% lower than the pre-tax return over five years. The very low turnover in the passive portfolio produces little in the way of capital gains distributions. The tax drag from the ETF is largely due to the tax on dividend income. The post-liquidation returns are quite a bit lower but still tax efficient; in a passively managed portfolio, most shares are likely held long enough that the dividends qualify for preferential tax treatment. The capital gains are deferred (and the returns compounded) until Cary sells the ETF, and the gains on the sale of the ETF will qualify for the long-term capital gains tax rate.

- The Active Equity Mutual Fund has a higher pre-tax and after-tax return than the Passive Equity ETF but is less tax efficient as evidenced by its 85% tax-efficiency ratio. The after-tax return is 1.84% lower than the pre-tax return over five years. Ongoing capital gains, including the likelihood of some short-term gains, and dividend income on shares held for less than 61 days contribute to the lower tax-efficiency ratio. Still, on a post-liquidation basis, the active fund outperforms the passive fund by 34 basis points (9.05 − 8.71).

- The High-Yield Bond ETF is the least tax efficient. The after-tax return is 2.56% lower than the pre-tax returns. The tax-efficiency ratio is 40%, meaning that more than half of the compounded returns to this fund are paid in taxes. Interest income from high-yield bond investments receives no tax preferences. The after-tax return and post-liquidation returns are very low in this case, making the High-Yield Bond ETF quite unattractive to a taxable investor, especially given that the fund is likely to have significantly higher risks than other investments.

Solution to 2:

- Because Cary lives in New York City, she is subject to state and local taxes as well as federal tax. Therefore, her actual after-tax returns are likely to be lower than the after-tax returns shown in the table.

Solution to 3:

- Cary will realize a $25,000 capital gain on her sale of MSFT (1,000 shares × $25 gain per share). She will owe $13,375 in capital gains tax ($25,000 × 53.50% tax rate). Cary does not qualify for the long-term capital gains tax rate because she did not hold the stock for longer than a year.
- The $500 MSFT dividend received (1,000 shares × $0.50 per share) creates a $267.50 tax liability ($500 × 53.50% tax rate). Cary must pay the full tax rate because she did not hold the position for longer than 61 days to qualify for the preferential dividend tax rate.
- Her pre-tax return is 19.62%: (25,000 + 500) /130,000.
- Her after-tax return is 9.21%: [(25,000 + 500) − (500 × 0.535) − (25,000 × 0.535)]/130,000.

Solution to 4:

- This transaction was not very tax efficient, with a tax-efficiency ratio of 46% (9.12/ 19.62).
- The trading horizon of one month meant that Cary did not qualify for the lower tax rate on dividends and long-term capital gains.
- If Cary had held the stock for a year, then her transaction would have been much more tax efficient. Assuming she was still able to sell the stock for the same $155 per share after one year (and that she did not receive any further dividends), then her after-tax return would be 12.46%: [(25,000 + 500) − (500 × 0.365) − (25,000 × 0.365)]/130,000. The tax-efficiency ratio would be improved to 64% (12.46/19.62).

Solution to 5:

- If MSFT had fallen to $120 per share, then Cary's pre-tax return would be −7.31%: (−10,000 + 500)/130,000. She would realize a short-term capital loss of $10,000. This loss can be used to offset short-term gains that Cary realized at other times during the same tax year. The potential tax savings is $5,350 ($10,000 × 53.50%). Her after-tax return is −2.99% [(−10,000 + 500 − 500 × 0.535 + 10,000 × 0.535)/130,000]. Yes, the after-tax return is higher than her pre-tax return. In estimating after-tax returns, we are most concerned with the portfolio impact. In this example, the transaction creates an economic benefit; the loss becomes smaller due to the potential tax savings, increasing the after-tax return.

Solution to 6:

- The pre-tax return of the municipal bond portfolio is 1.5% (1.0% gain + 0.5% interest).
- The after-tax return of the portfolio is 1.5%, the same as the pre-tax return. The capital gains are unrealized gains, and the interest income on New York municipal bonds is exempt from federal and state taxes.

- This is a very tax-efficient portfolio, with a tax-efficiency ratio of 100%. Cary plans to hold the bonds to maturity, so there are unlikely to be any capital gains realized from a sale prior to maturity. If she does sell the bonds prior to maturity, capital gains will likely qualify for the long-term capital gains tax rate. Also, the interest income is exempt from federal and state taxes.

4. ANALYZING THE IMPACT OF TAXES IN TAXABLE, TAX-EXEMPT, AND TAX-DEFERRED ACCOUNTS

We have shown how tax efficiency can be measured at the security and fund level, but tax considerations will also affect the client's financial plan, asset allocation strategy, and wealth transfer plan. Often clients will have a mixture of taxable, tax-deferred, and tax-exempt accounts. On the front end of the investment planning process, effective management must consider the interaction of the underlying investment strategy and the accounts in which it might be deployed. At the back end of the investment planning process (as the client approaches retirement and begins to spend down—decumulate—assets), there are additional opportunities to maximize the after-tax value of the client's assets.

Exhibit 5 shows various phases of developing and executing a financial plan and provides an example of tax-aware and tax-indifferent planning for each. While each investor faces unique circumstances that may affect strategy, the following table gives an idea of how taxes might change the planning process.

EXHIBIT 5   Examples of Tax-Aware Approaches to Planning

Strategic Decisions	Common Tax-Indifferent Approach	Tax-Aware Approach
Financial planning	Use pre-tax growth assumptions	Use after-tax growth assumptions for taxable accounts
Asset allocation	Use pre-tax return and volatility expectations	Use after-tax return and volatility expectations
Asset location	A single allocation across taxable and tax-deferred accounts	Tax-advantaged assets favored in the taxable account
Retirement income planning	Withdraw from retirement accounts first	Optimize withdrawals from taxable and tax-advantaged accounts
Charitable giving	Gift cash	Gift highly appreciated stock

In this section, we assess the effect of account type on capital accumulation, consider some of the issues related to the allocation of asset classes across a client's various accounts, and discuss tax-efficient decumulation and charitable giving strategies.

4.1. Capital Accumulation in Taxable, Tax-Deferred, and Tax-Exempt Accounts

The value of a tax-exempt account compounds in the usual way. For an annual return R over n years, the future value multiplier is given by:

$$FV = (1 + R)^n$$

where n is the number of years.

The value of a taxable account compounds using the after-tax returns, R'. Compounding returns on an after-tax basis implicitly assumes that taxes on realized returns are paid (and tax credits received) each period. The tax payment is treated as a cash flow:

$$FV = (1 + R')^n$$

The value of a tax-deferred account compounds using the pre-tax returns and pays tax only when assets are withdrawn from the account. (Withdrawals are taxed at the applicable income tax rates.) If we assume all the assets are withdrawn in a lump sum at the horizon and have a tax rate t, then

$$FV = (1 + R)^n(1 - t)$$

EXAMPLE 6   Comparing Accumulations in Different Account Types

Chen Li lives in a tax jurisdiction with a flat tax rate of 20%, which applies to all types of income and capital gains. Assume that Li has the following account types:

Account 1: ¥1,000,000 invested in a taxable account earning 10%, taxed annually.
Account 2: ¥1,000,000 invested in a tax-deferred account earning 10%.
Account 3: ¥1,000,000 invested in a tax-exempt account earning 10%.

Compute the after-tax wealth for each account at the end of 20 years assuming the accounts are liquidated at the end of the horizon.

Solution:

Future value of taxable, tax-deferred, and tax-exempt accounts

Account 1	Account 2	Account 3
¥4,660,957	¥5,382,000	¥6,727,500
FV =¥1,000,000 $[1 + 0.10(1 - 0.20)]^{20}$	FV =¥1,000,000 $[(1 + 0.10)^{20}(1 - 0.20)]$	FV =¥1,000,000 $(1 + 0.10)^{20}$

4.2. Asset Location

A private wealth client typically has assets spread across taxable, tax-deferred, and tax-exempt portfolios. For these clients, asset allocation must not only consider the appropriate overall asset class mix but must also consider which asset classes are best suited to be held in which accounts. This is called **asset location**—the process for determining whether the assets will be held in a taxable, tax-deferred, or tax-exempt account. A general rule of thumb is to put tax-efficient assets in the taxable account and tax-inefficient assets in the tax-exempt or tax-deferred account. This is only a rule of thumb, however. While it suggests that taxable bonds should be held in a tax-exempt account and that equities (given the preferential tax rate applied to capital gains) should be held in the taxable account, investors with a long investment horizon or that have higher turnover equity strategies may find that putting equities in the tax-exempt account results in better after-tax returns.

Consider the following example. If the expected return for equities is 10% and for fixed income 6%, and if the asset allocation is 50% equity/50% fixed income, then we would expect a pre-tax 8% return. But for a taxable client, there are additional considerations. First, we should consider two additional asset classes: tax-exempt bonds and tax-managed equities. Tax-managed equities are more tax efficient than high-turnover equity strategies that do not consider taxes. Similarly, tax-exempt bonds are more tax efficient than regular bonds, although they typically have lower pre-tax return expectations. Exhibit 6 shows how the return expectations might change by asset class and account, assuming a 50% marginal tax rate on fixed income, 25% tax rate on equities, and 10% effective tax rate on tax-managed equities.

EXHIBIT 6   After-Tax Return Expectations by Asset Location

	Asset Location	
	Taxable Account	**Tax-Exempt Account**
Equity	7.5%	10%
Tax-Managed Equity	9%	10%
Fixed Income	3%	6%
Tax-Exempt Fixed Income	4%	4%

Exhibit 7 shows three potential asset location strategies. We assume the taxable and tax-exempt accounts each represent 50% of the client's total investment assets.

EXHIBIT 7   Maximizing the After-Tax Return of a Given Asset Allocation

Asset Class	Tax-Indifferent Allocation			Tax-Aware Allocation			Asset Location-Sensitive Allocation		
	Taxable Account	Tax-Exempt Account	Return Contrib.	Taxable Account	Tax-Exempt Account	Return Contrib.	Taxable Account	Tax-Exempt Account	Return Contrib.
Equity	25	25	4.38%	—	25	2.50%	—	—	—
Tax-Managed Equity	—	—	—	25	—	2.25%	50	—	4.50%
Fixed Income	25	25	2.25%	—	25	1.50%	—	50	3.00%
Tax-Exempt Bonds	—	—	—	25	—	1.00%	—	—	—
Total	50	50	**6.63%**	50	50	**7.25%**	50	50	**7.50%**

- The Tax-Indifferent strategy implements the same 50/50 strategy in each account.
- The Tax-Aware strategy replaces nominal equity and fixed-income assets in the taxable account with tax-managed equities and tax-exempt bonds.
- The Asset Location-sensitive strategy follows the rule "put tax-efficient assets (tax-managed equities) in the taxable account and tax-inefficient assets (fixed income) in the tax-exempt account."

The expected total after-tax returns for each strategy are 6.63%, 7.25%, and 7.50%, respectively. While the improvement in the annual return is small (87 basis points), that improvement compounds over time and can have a material impact on the client's wealth as the decumulation phase approaches.

An asset location strategy cannot be rigidly employed. The client may have a different goal and time horizon for each account type and may have multiple goals for the assets held within a single account. For example, a tax-efficient asset location strategy might suggest that the retirement savings account be allocated 100% to bonds while the taxable investment account is allocated 100% to tax-managed equities. If, however, a portion of the taxable account will be used in the next three years for the purchase of a vacation home, exposing these funds to the volatility of a 100% equity allocation may be unwise. Several quantitative tools are available to assist with after-tax portfolio optimization and rebalancing across account types.

EXAMPLE 7   Asset Location Strategy for Charles and Ivy Lee

- Charles Lee, 55 years old, has recently inherited $2,500,000 from his parents.
- Ivy Lee, 54 years old, will soon receive a $2,500,000 rollover from her company-sponsored retirement plan; this will be deposited in her tax-deferred retirement account.

- The Lees have agreed that they want to establish a $2,500,000 "angel" fund to make investments in small start-up companies, as they already have sufficient assets to fund their lifestyle needs. This angel investment, although technically equities, will be over and above the 60% allocated to equities in their core portfolio.
- The remaining $2,500,000 will be invested to maintain the 60/40 asset allocation using the same strategies employed for their other liquid assets.
- Their other investment assets are summarized as follows.

	Taxable Brokerage Account (tax basis)	Tax-Deferred Retirement Account	Other (tax basis)	Pre-Tax/ After-Tax Return Expectation*
Passive Global Equity Fund		$3,000,000		7.0% / 7.0%
Passive Fixed Income (taxable)		2,000,000		3.0% / 3.0%
Active Global Equity Fund	$3,000,000 (2,500,000)			9.0% / 6.5%
Tax-Exempt Fixed Income	2,000,000 (1,800,000)			1.5% / 1.5%
Residential Real Estate			$3,000,000 (2,750,000)	n/a
Concentrated Equity Position			15,000,000 (4,000,000)	n/a
Total	$5,000,000	$5,000,000	$18,000,000	

*Assumed tax rates: 50% marginal income tax rate and 20% capital gains tax rate.

The Lees' adviser has warned them that while the average angel investor realizes 2.5x per dollar invested, more than half of all angel investments lead to a loss.

1. Which account would you recommend that the Lees use to fund their angel investments? Justify your response.
2. Of the four strategies currently employed in the Lees' accounts, which should the adviser recommend for the balance of the new money? Justify your response.

Solution to 1: Charles' inheritance, which would be invested via the taxable brokerage account, should be used to make the angel investments. Held in the taxable account, the Lees can use any losses generated to offset gains elsewhere in the account. Over the long term, the Lees expect to realize significant capital gains on these investments. Held in the taxable account, these gains will be taxed at the 20% capital gains rate. If held in the tax-deferred retirement, the gains would be taxed at the 50% income tax rate as they are withdrawn.

Solution to 2: Because Charles' inheritance is being used to make the angel investments, the $2,500,000 rollover from Ivy's company-sponsored retirement plan will need to be allocated among the existing investment strategies in a manner to maintain the 60/40 asset allocation. The rollover is in Ivy's tax-deferred retirement account. The most tax-efficient asset location strategy would place the equity investments in the brokerage account and the fixed-income allocation in the retirement account. This would allow the Lees to take full advantage of the more favorable tax rate on capital gains. With the new cash in Ivy's retirement account, the Lees will be able to rebalance their portfolio to achieve a more tax-efficient allocation.

- With $12,500,000 in financial assets (aside from the angel fund), the 60% equity allocation ($7,500,000) would be allotted first to the brokerage account. The brokerage account balance is $5,000,000; it should be invested completely in equities to achieve the desired 60/40 asset allocation. However, the tax-exempt fixed-income position has an embedded gain of $200,000 that would need to be realized to accomplish the rebalancing. The Lees' adviser will need to assess the merits of incurring the capital gains tax liability in order to reinvest in the higher-returning strategy. If losses can be realized elsewhere in the portfolio, they may be used to offset this gain.
- The choice between equity strategies in the brokerage account is less clear-cut. While the passive equity strategy is likely more tax efficient (capital gains are realized less frequently), the return expectation for the active strategy is 200 basis points higher. Other considerations, such as the desire to maintain a given tracking error relative to the benchmark, are likely to play a role in the selection of the most appropriate equity strategy. Also, the ability of the investment manager to employ tax management trading strategies is an important consideration.
- The remainder of the equity allocation ($2,500,000) would be achieved through the tax-deferred retirement account. The appropriate strategy is the Active Global Equity strategy, where its higher return (9% vs. the 7% expected return for the passive strategy) will compound tax-free over the Lees' long investment horizon.
- The 40% fixed-income allocation ($5,000,000) is achieved through the tax-deferred retirement account. The appropriate strategy is the Passive Fixed-Income (taxable) strategy.

The final asset allocation is shown in the following table:

	Taxable Brokerage Account	Tax-Deferred Retirement Account
Passive Global Equity Fund	$5,000,000	0
Active Global Equity Fund		$2,500,000
Total Equity		
Tax-Exempt Fixed Income		0
Passive Fixed Income (taxable)	0	5,000,000
Total Fixed Income	**$5,000,000**	**$7,500,000**

4.3. Decumulation Strategies

Investment advisers should work closely with the client's financial planner, estate planner, and tax attorney to make sure the investment program is aligned with the larger financial plan. Our discussion so far has focused on capital accumulation. In this section, we assume that clients have reached retirement age and will soon be using their retirement assets to support spending needs over their expected remaining lifetime. We examine a **tax-efficient decumulation strategy** for a retirement account.

Since retirement accounts are tax-exempt or tax-deferred, they compound at a higher rate than taxable accounts. A common rule of thumb suggests that it is better to make withdrawals from the taxable account first and allow the retirement account to continue to compound. Designing the most effective decumulation strategy may require a significant level of financial planning expertise.

In Exhibit 8, we show a simplified example of a tax-aware decumulation strategy using a taxable and a tax-exempt account. (Practically speaking, the tax-advantaged account is most likely a tax-deferred account, such as a retirement savings account. For this illustration, however, we assume that it is tax exempt.) Each account has a beginning balance of $1,000,000. We assume a pre-tax rate of return of 10% for both accounts and a 25% effective tax rate on earnings in the taxable account, which equates to an after-tax rate of return of 7.5%. At the end of each year, the investor withdraws $200,000. The withdrawals are taken from the taxable account first, allowing the tax-exempt account to continue to compound at the higher effective rate. Once the taxable account is depleted, withdrawals are taken from the tax-exempt account. At the end of 10 years, the client has $1.80 million remaining. If the withdrawals are taken from the tax-exempt account first, as shown in Exhibit 9, the client will have only $1.48 million remaining at the end of 10 years.

EXHIBIT 8   Withdraw from Taxable Account First (Tax Aware)

Year	Withdrawal from Taxable Account	Withdrawal from Tax-Exempt Account	Year-End Taxable Account Balance	Year-End Tax-Exempt Account Balance
0			$1,000,000	$1,000,000
1	$200,000		875,000	1,100,000
2	200,000		740,625	1,210,000
3	200,000		596,172	1,331,000
4	200,000		440,885	1,464,100
5	200,000		273,951	1,610,510
6	200,000		94,497	1,771,561
7	101,585	$98,415		1,850,302
8		200,000		1,835,332
9		200,000		1,818,866
10		200,000		**$1,800,752**

EXHIBIT 9   Withdraw from Tax-Exempt Account First (Tax-Indifferent)

Year	Withdrawal from Taxable Account	Withdrawal from Tax-Exempt Account	Year-End Taxable Account Balance	Year-End Tax-Exempt Account Balance
0			$1,000,000	$1,000,000
1		$200,000	1,075,000	900,000
2		200,000	1,155,625	790,000
3		200,000	1,242,297	669,000
4		200,000	1,335,469	535,900
5		200,000	1,435,629	389,490
6		200,000	1,543,302	228,439
7		200,000	1,659,049	51,283
8	$143,589	56,411	1,639,889	
9	200,000		1,562,880	
10	200,000		**$ 1,480,097**	

Under progressive tax regimes (jurisdictions where tax rates rise as the level of income rises), a more tax-efficient strategy may be to withdraw from the retirement account until the lowest tax brackets have been fully utilized. Any additional withdrawals would then be taken from the taxable account.

4.4. Tax Considerations in Charitable Giving

When the client's overall financial plan includes charitable giving, the source of the assets to be gifted should be approached strategically. In some jurisdictions, appreciated securities can be gifted to a qualified charity without triggering the capital gain. In these jurisdictions, gifting low-cost-basis assets from taxable accounts is preferred. The investor may receive a tax *benefit* (a tax deduction, reducing the overall tax liability) from the gift while simultaneously removing a future tax liability on the unrealized gain from the portfolio. Advisers and portfolio managers can help investors identify highly appreciated securities for gifting, thereby reducing the tax liability embedded in the portfolio.

EXAMPLE 8   Identifying Assets for Charitable Giving

Charles and Ivy Lee wish to give $750,000 to a local art museum. Ivy Lee has a concentrated holding of $15 million in appreciated company stock (with a tax basis of $4 million and $11 million in unrealized capital gains) that they would like to diversify over time. They also have a diversified portfolio of securities and a retirement account, as shown in Example 7. Their tax rate is 50% on income and 20% on realized capital gains. How should the Lees fund this charitable gift?

Solution: The Lees should gift shares of the concentrated asset position. The museum, as a tax-exempt entity, can sell the shares without incurring a tax liability, and the Lees will reduce their exposure to the concentrated position. In many jurisdictions, the Lees will receive an income tax deduction, reducing their income tax liability by up to $375,000. Alternatively, the Lees might consider gifting appreciated assets from their brokerage account. However, the unrealized gains on the assets in this account are comparatively small and a larger financial advantage can be achieved by gifting part of the concentrated stock position.

5. TAX MANAGEMENT STRATEGIES

As the vast majority of professionally managed assets have historically been tax-exempt institutional portfolios, most investment theory and practice presume a pre-tax framework. The goal of this section is to give you an overview of tax management techniques so that when working with a taxable client you have the tools needed to understand and implement investment strategies efficiently.

Tax Avoidance vs. Tax Evasion—Ethical and Legal Obligations

As fiduciaries, portfolio managers and advisers are obligated to invest efficiently and avoid unnecessary frictions. Taxes are one of the frictions to be managed, but there is a risk in being too clever when attempting to reduce that particular friction. Denis Healey, a former UK Chancellor of the Exchequer, is often quoted: "The difference between tax avoidance and tax evasion is the thickness of a prison wall."

In 2010, the CEO of a hedge fund and private wealth management firm in Seattle ended up on the wrong side of that wall, setting up an offshore company to create tax losses its clients could then use to offset gains. However, the losing stocks didn't exist, and the offshore company had no employees and no earnings. The CEO of the firm and the tax attorney involved were both sentenced to six years in prison for the illegal tax scheme.

Because usage of the terms likely differs from jurisdiction to jurisdiction, we will start by defining what we mean by "tax avoidance" and "tax evasion." The general principle is that **tax avoidance** is the legal activity of understanding the tax laws and finding approaches that avoid or minimize taxation. **Tax evasion** is the illegal concealment and non-payment of taxes that are otherwise due. If the primary purpose of the activity is to avoid paying tax and the activities are misleading or do not have merit in their own right, then the activity is likely unethical and may be illegal.

The CFA Institute Code of Ethics and Standards of Professional Conduct require that CFA charterholders and candidates act with integrity, competence, diligence, respect, and in an ethical manner. Focusing on after-tax returns, minimizing unnecessary tax burdens, and being thoughtful about how taxation interacts with a portfolio are all elements of being a good steward of a client's assets. However, it is important to *never* be involved in helping a client disguise true ownership of assets or otherwise be involved in tax evasion. Charterholders and candidates must not engage in any professional conduct involving dishonesty, fraud, or deceit or commit any act that reflects adversely on their professional reputation, integrity, or competence.

5.1. Basic Portfolio Tax Management Strategies

Basic portfolio tax management strategies fall into two categories:

- Structuring a client's investments in a legitimate manner to reduce the amount of tax owed. Examples include:
  - holding assets in a tax-exempt account versus a taxable account;
  - investing in tax-exempt bonds instead of taxable bonds;
  - holding assets long enough to qualify for long-term capital gains treatment; and
  - holding dividend-paying stocks long enough to pay the more favorable tax rate.

- Deferring the recognition of certain taxable income until some future date, allowing investors to benefit from the compounding of pre-tax rather than after-tax portfolio returns. In a progressive tax system, investors may also benefit from deferring taxes to a future date if they anticipate their tax rate will be lower in retirement. Other examples of tax deferral strategies include:
  - limiting portfolio turnover and the consequent realization of capital gains and
  - selling securities at a loss to offset a realized capital gain (i.e., **tax loss harvesting**).

A frequent theme among these basic strategies is the holding period of an investment. Portfolio managers should be mindful of portfolio turnover and the timing of trades. Turnover is sometimes used as a proxy for tax efficiency. While low-turnover passive index funds tend to be more tax efficient than higher turnover active strategies, the relationship between turnover and tax efficiency is by no means straightforward. While it is true that turnover incurs transaction costs and can create a capital gains tax liability, turnover might also create tax benefits. Selling an asset at a loss can create a tax offset that can be applied to reduce capital gains taxes incurred in the current or even future tax periods (although, in some jurisdictions this type of trade is considered a wash sale and the tax offset is not allowed).

5.2. Application of Tax Management Strategies

A portfolio manager has to consider many things when implementing an investment strategy. Risks, returns, and costs are common concerns of all portfolio managers irrespective of whether the client is an institution or an individual. The manager of a private wealth portfolio is tasked with the additional complexity of minimizing the tax drag on returns. Here we take a closer look at several important topics for tax-aware portfolio management:

- selection of the investment vehicle (i.e., whether the assets are held in a partnership, fund, or separate account),
- tax lot accounting,
- tax loss harvesting,
- tax deferral, and
- quantitative tax management.

5.2.1. Investment Vehicles

As a private wealth manager, you may have the option of using commingled funds (e.g., mutual funds, UCITS, and partnerships), or the client portfolio may be a separately managed account in which the individual securities are owned directly. The structure of the investment vehicle in which the assets are held may affect the client's tax liability and the adviser's ability to manage the client portfolio in a tax-aware manner. When a portfolio has multiple owners, as in a partnership or fund, the tax consequences of the investment and trading activities are shared.

In a partnership, whether a hedge fund or private equity fund, the taxes are typically passed through to the underlying partners. Partnerships are an appealing tax structure since the fund itself operates free of taxation and distributions are typically classified as capital gains, not as ordinary income.

In a mutual fund, dividend and interest income is passed through to the underlying investors; thus, the investor is required to pay income taxes on that income in the year in which it was received. If the investor sells her mutual fund shares, she will be liable for any capital gains arising from the difference between the sale price and her tax basis. In addition, the investor may also be liable for capital gains taxes on transactions that take place *within* the fund. At the end of the year, the fund will issue a statement detailing the long- and short-term gains realized during the year. Investors must pay their proportionate share of the tax liability. The net asset value of the fund will be reduced by the amount of the capital gains distribution. This is true in the United States but is not true in all jurisdictions. In the United Kingdom, for example, investors are only liable for capital gains taxes at the time they sell their shares of the fund.

When new shareholders buy into the fund, they are also buying a share of the unrealized capital gains accrued in prior periods. These gains may become realized gains through the trading activity of the portfolio manager and through the redemption activity of other shareholders, creating a tax liability for investors who did not participate in the returns that created the gains. Let's illustrate this with a simple example.

> The JEMStone fund was launched in 20X0 with five investors and $5,000,000 in assets. Since that time, the assets in the fund have appreciated to $5,500,000. The embedded capital gain is $500,000. There has been no trading in the fund, and all the original investors hold their original shares. Each investor's tax basis is $1,000,000, and each investor's proportionate share of the fund is worth $1,100,000. The fund is open to new investors, and Mateo invests $1,100,000. The aggregate tax basis of the fund is now $6,100,000, and the net asset value of the fund is $6,600,000. Mateo owns one-sixth of the fund. His tax basis is $1,016,667. If the fund manager were to sell the underlying holdings, Mateo would receive a capital gains distribution of $83,333 on which he would be required to pay taxes, even though his investment has not appreciated. He effectively bought into some of the tax liability of the previous investors.

Mutual fund data providers calculate metrics like **Potential Capital Gain Exposure (PCGE)** to help investors determine whether a significant tax liability is embedded in a mutual fund. PCGE is an estimate of the percentage of a fund's assets that represents gains and measures how much the fund's assets have appreciated. It can be an indicator of possible future capital gain distributions.

$$PCGE = \text{net gains (losses) / total net assets}$$

Some commingled structures are more tax efficient than others. Exchange-traded funds (ETFs), for example, can reduce any embedded capital gain tax liability by delivering low cost-basis holdings to trading partners as part of the share creation and redemption process for the fund. ETFs aren't sold directly to investors like mutual funds. Instead, ETF managers use banks and brokerage firms as intermediaries. These intermediaries deliver or receive baskets of portfolio stocks as part of the share creation and redemption process. Independent of inflows to and outflows from the fund, they will also deliver or receive these baskets of stock whenever the price of the fund deviates from its underlying value to generate an arbitrage profit. This arbitrage keeps the price of the fund in line with the net asset value of the fund while reducing any unrealized gain in the portfolio. In addition, ETF managers can choose which shares to include in the basket of stock delivered to the intermediary; to reduce any unrealized gain, they are likely to include the low-basis shares in that basket of stock.

Separately-managed accounts (SMAs) offer the most flexibility for tax management. The assets have only one owner, so portfolio decisions can be tailored to the tax situation of that specific investor. Losses that are realized within the SMA portfolio can be used to offset gains on assets held outside the SMA. In contrast, any losses within a mutual fund can only be used to offset gains realized within the fund and cannot be distributed to the shareholders. This makes the losses within a fund considerably less valuable to the taxable investor.

Exhibit 10 summarizes the tax characteristics of partnerships, mutual funds, ETFs, and separately-managed accounts.

EXHIBIT 10   Tax Characteristics of Investment Vehicles

Vehicle	Tax Characteristics
Partnership	Tax liabilities are passed through to partners.
Mutual fund	Tax liabilities are influenced by co-investors. For example, a redemption by one shareholder can trigger a capital gains tax liability for all shareholders.
Exchange-traded fund (ETF)	Tax liabilities can be reduced or eliminated through the creation and redemption process.
Separate account	Realized losses and gains can be aggregated across all of the client's accounts.

EXAMPLE 9   Estimating the Future Tax Efficiency of Mutual Funds

Consider two mutual funds:

- Fund A started with $2 million in assets, experienced capital appreciation of $500,000, and distributed $100,000 of realized capital gains to shareholders.
- Fund B started with $2 million in assets, experienced capital appreciation of $100,000, and subsequently suffered a capital loss of $500,000.

What is the PCGE for each fund? What are the implications for a taxable investor?

Solution:

- Fund A has a PCGE of 16.7% (= the $400,000 gain remaining in the fund divided by total net assets of $2,400,000).
- Fund B has a PCGE of −25% (= the net −$400,000 loss divided by total net assets of $1,600,000).
- Fund B is more likely to be tax efficient going forward since it can use the losses in the portfolio to offset future realized gains.
- Fund A has net gains embedded in the portfolio. Managers can continue to hold the appreciated securities or sell them. If they sell a security at a gain, the fund must distribute the gains to shareholders that year. A high PCGE indicates the potential for capital gain distributions in the future.

5.2.2. Tax Loss Harvesting

The premise of **tax loss harvesting** is simple: Sell securities that are below their acquisition price in order to realize a loss that can be used to offset gains or other income. The rules vary by jurisdiction. Here is a sampling of rules around tax loss harvesting in a few jurisdictions:

- *Australia*—Trading for the sole purpose of realizing a tax benefit is not allowed. Each trade needs a non-tax motivation as its primary purpose. Tax management in the context of the overall investment strategy is allowed, but tax loss harvesting by itself is not.
- *Germany*—No limitations on tax loss harvesting trades.
- *United States*—A tax loss credit will be disallowed if you purchase the same, or a substantially identical, security within 30 days before or after the sale of the asset. This is the *wash sale rule*, and it applies across the taxpayer's accounts—including retirement accounts and in some cases even a spouse's account.

Effectively trading a portfolio to avoid short-term gains and harvest short-term losses is an important element of managing private client assets. All losses, whether long- or short-term, can be used to reduce current-year taxes. Most advisers and investors focus on these immediate and concrete dollar savings—for example, by making opportunistic loss harvesting trades during market corrections or at year end.

Central to tax loss harvesting is the concept of tax lot accounting. Typically, portfolio positions are built over time, with each purchase having its own tax basis. For example, a holding of 400 shares of Vodafone Group may be comprised of several tax lots, each with its own purchase date and tax basis. **Tax lot accounting**—keeping track of how much you paid for an investment and when you bought it—is crucial for understanding how much tax you might owe. An effective tax management program requires the portfolio accounting platform to keep track of this information.

The tax lot method is the rule for prioritizing the realization of losses and gains. The most common methods of tax lot accounting are first in, first out (*FIFO*); last in, first out (*LIFO*); and highest in, first out (*HIFO*). The *specified-lot method* (in which the portfolio manager identifies specifically which tax lot is to be traded) provides the most flexibility for ensuring a trade is tax efficient. If the investor does not specify which tax lot is to be sold at the time of the trade, the custodian will use its default rule for selecting tax lots for the calculation of gains. The default is typically FIFO. Given that equity markets generally appreciate through time, however, using FIFO means that the lowest tax basis shares are sold first—often making it the least tax-efficient option.

Tax lot accounting is not permitted in all jurisdictions. In Canada, for example, the cost basis used to determine gain or loss on any sale is the average acquisition cost of all lots in that security.

EXAMPLE 10   Tax Lot Selection

Consider the shares of Vodafone stock depicted in Exhibit 11. The investor owns 400 shares, which have been acquired over time. There are four tax lots of 100 shares each. The investor wants to sell 100 shares.

1. What would be the tax liability associated with each of the tax lot accounting rules: FIFO, LIFO, and HIFO?
2. Which tax lot is the most tax efficient to sell?

EXHIBIT 11   Tax Lots for Stock with Price of $40, Assuming Current Date is 1 July 20X9

Tax Lot Purchase Date	Shares	Acquisition Price	Gain (Loss)	Holding Period	Tax if Sold
A) 1 January 20X8	100	$30.00	$1,000	Long-term	$250
B) 1 June 20X8	100	$50.00	($1,000)	Long-term	($250)
C) 1 January 20X9	100	$48.00	($800)	Short-term	($400)
D) 1 June 20X9	100	$45.00	($500)	Short-term	($250)

Note: Assumes that the tax rate on long-term capital gains is 25% and short-term gains 50%.

Solution to 1:

- FIFO would select tax lot A, the earliest acquisition date. This results in a capital gain of $1,000 and a capital gains tax of $250.
- LIFO would choose tax lot D, the most recent acquisition date. This results in a capital loss of $500 and a $250 tax benefit, which could be used to offset short-term gain tax liabilities (or long-term gains) elsewhere in the client's portfolio.
- HIFO would choose tax lot B, the highest acquisition price. This results in a long-term loss of $1,000 and a $250 tax benefit, which could be used to offset short-term gain tax liabilities.

Solution to 2:

- In our example, the selection of tax lot C creates the most tax benefit—the largest short-term loss. HIFO is usually the most tax-efficient accounting methodology since selecting the tax lot with the highest acquisition price will usually produce the least capital gain or the deepest loss. In this case, however, tax lot B is a long-term lot and the tax benefit of a long-term loss is generally less than that of a short-term loss. None of the standard accounting methods would select tax lot C; the portfolio manager would need to specify the tax lot to be sold at the time of trading.

When managing a portfolio on behalf of a taxable client, it is important to ensure that the custodian is using the appropriate tax lot methodology. If the account is set up incorrectly, the tax-aware trades executed by the manager could be nullified by the custodian's accounting system.

Loss harvesting trades can create some difficulties in maintaining the desired portfolio exposures. To avoid the wash sale rule in the United States, you must hold cash or some other security for 31 days. Holding cash clearly leaves the portfolio underinvested and can create a drag on returns if the cash return is lower than the security. Managers will typically identify a replacement security to be held during the wash sale period to maintain a comparable portfolio exposure (e.g., buy Pepsi stock in lieu of Coca-Cola stock). Or, they will purchase an index or sector ETF. Another difficulty is that selling the placeholder and switching back to the original security after 31 days can create its own tax burden if a short-term capital gain is realized when the placeholder is sold.

Although a tax loss harvesting trade generates a loss to be used in the current tax year, recall that tax loss harvesting is a *tax-deferral* strategy. When you re-purchase the security after 31 days, you have re-established the position presumably with a lower tax basis, increasing the future capital gains tax liability.

5.2.3. Quantitative Tax Management

A core element of tax management is the ability to quantify and manage risk that is introduced as a result of the implementation of the portfolio. One common metric of risk versus a benchmark is tracking error. Quantitative methods can help the portfolio manager to optimize the portfolio for tax efficiency, and tracking error can be used to evaluate how much risk we are introducing by being tax aware.

Quantitative tax management uses a quantitative risk model to estimate the risks and correlations of each of the securities in the portfolio. The approach then uses the risk estimates from the model as an input to a portfolio optimization algorithm that:

- minimizes tracking error risk versus the index or model portfolio;
- maximizes realized losses;
- minimizes realized gains;
- minimizes trading costs; and
- satisfies any constraints, such as limits on security, industry, sector, and country weights as well as wash sale restrictions, turnover, and cash limits.

A quantitative approach to tax management can be used to minimize tax-drag and investment risk when onboarding a new client, in executing a loss harvesting strategy, and when delaying the realization of gains. Each of these is briefly discussed next.

Transitions: For an account funded with securities rather than cash, the portfolio manager must find a good trade-off between the tax cost of transitioning to the new portfolio and the risk of underperforming the new mandate if some of the appreciated securities continue to be held at an overweight in the portfolio. The goal of the quantitative model is to avoid realizing taxes at the time of inception by holding some of the existing securities but doing so in a risk-controlled way.

Tax-optimized loss harvesting: Instead of tax loss harvesting once a year, a portfolio manager can look for losses throughout the year, whenever they occur. Any investment management process, active or passive, can benefit from systematically monitoring the portfolio for tax opportunities. Where a country's rules nullify any tax benefits from trades undertaken for the sole purpose of realizing a tax benefit, losses arising from strategy-driven investment decisions can still be realized opportunistically. As securities are sold to realize a loss, replacement securities can be identified using a risk model and optimization algorithms to ensure that the desired portfolio exposures are maintained.

Gain-loss matching optimization: While you can avoid capital gains tax liabilities by never selling appreciated securities, this is likely to lead to a portfolio whose risk exposures are significantly out of balance. Portfolio managers can use a gain-loss matching optimization algorithm to balance the desire to avoid the realization of capital gains tax against the need to manage portfolio risk relative to the investor's benchmark or model portfolio.

EXAMPLE 11   Tax Loss Harvesting

Consider the following tax loss harvesting example. A $2 million portfolio has $365,000 in unrealized gains; $120,000 are short-term and $245,000 are long-term. There are also $48,000 of unrealized short-term losses. To determine the optimal trading strategy (i.e., how much gains and losses to realize), the portfolio manager will use the firm's algorithm and provide the inputs required by the framework just presented. Exhibit 12 shows the tax benefit generated for this portfolio trade.

EXHIBIT 12   Example of a Loss Harvesting Trade

	Pre-Trade Unrealized Gains and Losses	Post-Trade Unrealized Gains and Losses	Realized Gains and Losses
Short-Term Gains	$120,000	$120,000	$0
Long-Term Gains	$245,000	$242,000	$3,000
Short-Term Losses	($48,000)	($6,000)	($42,000)
Long-Term Losses	$0	$0	$0
Net Gain (Loss)			($39,000)
Tax Benefit			**$19,500**

Note: Assumes a 50% tax on short-term gains and a 25% tax on long-term gains.

The portfolio manager realized $42,000 of the $48,000 of short-term losses; there are $6,000 of unrealized short-term losses remaining. The portfolio manager also realized $3,000 of the $242,000 in long-term gains. The net realized loss from these trades is $39,000. This is a short-term loss (any loss remaining after netting retains its short-term or long-term character). The loss can be used to offset $39,000 in gains elsewhere in the portfolio. Of course, it would be most advantageous to use the short-term loss to offset short-term gains, as these are taxed at a higher rate. The resulting tax savings would be $19,500 ($39,000 × 50% short-term gains tax rate). In a $2 million portfolio, this is equivalent to a nearly 100-basis point improvement in after-tax returns (19,500/2,000,000 = 0.975%).

In addition to the tax savings, the trade also resulted in risk-related improvements, such as reducing predicted tracking error and keeping country, sector, and other risk factor weights within bounds.

6. MANAGING CONCENTRATED POSITIONS

Frequently, individuals' and families' wealth is concentrated in an asset or group of assets that has played a pivotal role in the creation of their wealth. Three major types of *concentrated positions* commonly encountered in managing private client assets are: (1) publicly traded stocks, (2) a privately-owned business, and (3) commercial or investment real estate.

Concentrated positions in public equity may derive from an initial public offering or the sale of a privately-owned business to a public company. Or, individuals may have worked at a publicly traded company, perhaps for many years, and received company stock as part of their compensation.

There is no universal agreement as to what constitutes a concentrated position; it frequently depends on the nature of the position. A 10% position in a small-cap stock might be considered a concentrated position. A 10% position in a liquid large-cap stock might be considered risky, but it likely doesn't meet the threshold of a "concentrated position" for the purposes of this discussion. In this chapter, the term "concentrated position" is used to describe a holding that, due to its low tax basis or personal association with the client, inhibits the development of an efficient, diversified portfolio.

Advisers must be able to assist clients with decisions concerning such positions, including the risk and tax consequences associated with managing them. This section will discuss approaches to managing those concentrated positions.

6.1. Risk and Tax Considerations in Managing Concentrated Single-Asset Positions

We have identified four risk and tax-related considerations relevant to concentrated single-asset positions:

1. The company-specific risk inherent in the concentrated position
2. The reduction in portfolio efficiency resulting from the lack of diversification
3. The liquidity risk inherent in a privately-held or outsized publicly-held security
4. The risk of incurring an outsized tax bill that diminishes return if one were to sell part of the concentrated position in an attempt to reduce the other risks

Private companies tend to be smaller than public companies with all of the attendant risks of being a small company. They may have a more limited operating history or an undiversified business mix. They may have difficulty attracting high-quality management personnel due to the family ownership. Or, their access to financing may be more constrained than that of a public company. These risks, alone or in combination, typically make a concentrated position in a family-owned company much riskier than a similar-sized position in a publicly-traded company.

Whether the position is publicly-traded or privately-held, however, a concentrated position subjects the portfolio to a higher level of risk. A significant proportion of the client's wealth is exposed to the risk of adverse events affecting this company—either a company-specific event, such as an earnings shortfall, or an industry-specific event, such as changes in tariffs on imported materials. In the course of *building* wealth, adverse events pose unavoidable risk. However, once a certain level of wealth has been attained, the wealth owner's focus tends to shift toward maintaining that status. Private wealth managers must be able to counsel clients through this changing view of risk.

A portfolio with a concentrated position may also be subject to liquidity risk. Shares in a private company cannot be readily sold to meet unexpected expenses. If not subject to regulatory restrictions, a large position in a public company can be sold, although the sale is likely to incur higher transaction costs than a position of more moderate size. This lack of liquidity complicates the management of the remaining portfolio.

Lastly, concentrated positions frequently have a very low tax basis, having been held by the investor for a long time. Sale of all or a part of the position can trigger a significant tax liability.

While these and other considerations (notably, a client's emotional attachment to an asset that has been the foundation for financial success) make a simple sale problematic, the risk inherent in the position may outweigh the tax and liquidity issues.

6.1.1. Approaches to Managing the Risk of Concentrated Positions

Given the risks associated with holding a concentrated position, well-informed investors will seek to diversify these risks. Several different strategies might be considered depending on the facts and circumstance of the client's situation. The key factors to consider when selecting a strategy include the following:

- *Degree of concentration*—The larger the concentrated position is relative to the total portfolio, the more concerned an investor should be about the risks and the more urgent the need to address those risks.
- *Volatility and downside risk of the position*—The higher the risk associated with the position, the greater the benefit of diversification.
- *Tax basis* —The lower the tax basis, the higher the tax liability.
- *Liquidity* —The lower the liquidity, the more costly it will be to achieve the risk-reduction goal.
- *Tax rate of the investor*—The higher the tax rate, the higher the tax liability.
- *Time horizon of the investor*—A longer investment horizon gives the portfolio a better chance to offset any tax impact of a sale.
- *Restrictions on the investor*—If the investor is restricted from selling the asset through an employment or acquisition agreement, then a strategy other than an outright sale must be developed.
- *Emotional attachment and other non-financial considerations*—Often the concentrated position is the original source of wealth for the individual and/or family, so there is an emotional attachment that makes them reluctant to sell. Alternatively, an owner might wish to maintain voting control of the company or retain shares to signal a continued association with the company.

Several approaches can be used to mitigate the risks of a concentrated position. Each has different tax consequences:

1. *Sell and diversify*—The simplest (and often best) approach is to sell the concentrated position, pay the capital gains taxes, and re-invest the proceeds into a diversified portfolio.
2. *Staged diversification*—In some cases, timing risk is a concern. Selling in multiple tranches can at least partially mitigate the risk of inconvenient timing.
3. *Hedging and monetization strategies*—Several strategies using derivatives can be used to hedge the risk of a concentrated position. Once the position is hedged, monetization—such as a loan against the value of the concentrated position—provides owners with funds to spend or re-invest without triggering a taxable event.
4. *Tax-free exchanges*—In some jurisdictions, an investor may be able to exchange assets, replacing an illiquid private company position with publicly traded stock, without creating a taxable event. In the United States, a 1031 exchange allows you to sell a real estate asset and transfer the tax basis to another property purchased within a few months of the sale. Some exchange funds allow investors to pool their public stock positions with others to achieve diversification without triggering a tax event.
5. *Charitable giving strategies*—Charitable trusts, private foundations, and donor-advised funds (an investment account established for the sole purpose of supporting the donor's charitable giving) allow the asset to be transferred to a tax-exempt account in which it can be sold without incurring capital gains taxes. While the assets of private foundations and donor-advised funds can be used to fund only the client's philanthropic goals, the charitable trust can be structured to provide income to the client in the present with the assets fulfilling the philanthropic purpose in the future.
6. *Tax-avoidance and tax-deferral strategies*—In some jurisdictions, holding the position until death allows heirs to receive a step-up in basis (a new tax basis based on the value at the date of death) that will allow them to diversify the position and avoid capital gains taxes. Tax loss harvesting strategies that invest in a diversified equity portfolio and generate extra capital losses can be paired with a staged diversification strategy that matches gains with losses. This allows the client to spread out the tax burden over time, creating flexibility to defer some portion of the tax.

A variety of financial tools can be used to implement these approaches. For example, an investor can synthetically sell a stock by shorting the stock or using options, swaps, forwards, or futures. Although these actions produce a similar economic result, they may not be taxed similarly.

In the next sections, we review some of the more common strategies for managing concentrated positions. There are many variations on these, with different benefits depending on the jurisdiction and the investor. The range of alternatives is continuously changing as advisers innovate to capitalize on opportunities in new and existing regulations and as tax authorities seek to close unintended loopholes.

6.2. Strategies for Managing Concentrated Positions in Public Equities

For the examples in this section, we will consider a client, Michael Stark, a US-based client who has $1,000,000 worth of Exxon stock that he received when he sold his company to Exxon. The restrictions on the sale of his stock recently have been lifted, so he is interested in exploring ways to reduce the risk of his concentrated position. The tax basis of his stock is approximately $100,000, or 10%, of the current market value, and Michael is concerned about the tax implications of an outright sale. His tax rate on long-term capital gains is 25%. We will explore several strategies that could be used to help Michael achieve his risk-reduction goal. Managers will typically use more than one approach to managing a concentrated position. Strategy selection is dependent not only on the objective facts and circumstances of the concentrated position but also on clients' sophistication. Putting clients into a strategy that they don't understand often leads to unhappy clients.

6.2.1. Staged Diversification and Completion Portfolios

The simplest approach to managing the risk of a concentrated position is to sell it, pay the tax, and reinvest the proceeds in a diversified portfolio. Often the client wishes to sell the stock over the course of several years. This type of **staged diversification strategy** has the advantage of spreading the tax liability across multiple tax years, but it also extends the time that Michael will be overly exposed to Exxon. The proceeds from the stock sales can be used to fund a diversified portfolio. For example, an adviser might recommend selling part of the stock position and buying an ETF that tracks the broad market.

A more sophisticated approach is to construct a **completion portfolio**. A completion portfolio is an index-based portfolio that, when added to the concentrated position, creates an overall portfolio with exposures similar to the investor's benchmark. This technique uses a quantitative portfolio optimization process to select individual stocks or sector ETFs to form a portfolio that considers the remaining stock when evaluating the risk of the portfolio.

The completion portfolio can also be tax optimized on an ongoing basis as discussed in the section on "Quantitative Tax Management." The index-tracking completion portfolio is funded with the partial sale of the concentrated position. On an ongoing basis, the portfolio is rebalanced using a quantitative model. The model minimizes active risk versus the benchmark and maximizes the after-tax return of the portfolio—primarily by realizing more capital losses than gains. The losses realized in the diversified portfolio can be used to offset some of the gains realized by the sale of the concentrated stock. The process is designed to track a broad-based index on a pre-tax basis and outperform it on an after-tax basis.

Let's explore how this might work using Michael Stark's situation.

Michael owns $1 million in Exxon stock. While Exxon stock volatility has typically been less than many other US stocks, a major oil spill or other company scandal could easily put his wealth unnecessarily at risk.

An outright sale would trigger a realized gain of $900,000. Given his 25% tax rate, the tax liability would be $225,000. Michael wants to understand the trade-off between incurring the tax liability and his goal to create a more diversified equity portfolio that tracks the S&P 100. We can use an optimizer to evaluate the trade-offs between the tax liability and the tracking error relative to the benchmark. Our optimization objectives are to minimize the tax liability from selling Exxon and to minimize the tracking error to the S&P 100. These are competing objectives; fewer shares sold minimizes the tax liability but increases the tracking error. We use a fundamental risk model to estimate our risk versus the benchmark, in this case the S&P 100 Index. The predicted tracking error for Exxon relative to this benchmark is 19.8%. (We are using tracking error to represent the risk of being undiversified relative to the benchmark.) Exhibit 13 shows the trade-off as we sell different proportions of Michael's Exxon stock and reinvest the proceeds into the S&P 100 Index.

EXHIBIT 13   Tax Liability vs. Tracking Error with Varying Levels of ExxonMobil (XOM) Exposure

Note: Tracking error estimated using the MSCI Barra US risk model as of June 2019.

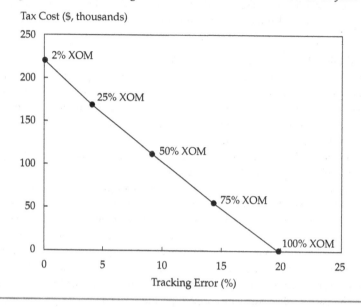

The final 2% of Michael's Exxon stock could be retained without negatively impacting tracking error because Exxon has a 2% weight in the index.

Michael will need to assess the expected trade-off between tax and risk to determine how much Exxon to sell. He might also stage the diversification over multiple tax years.

Using individual stocks to build out a completion portfolio has an advantage in that we can optimize the total portfolio to achieve desired factor exposures and tracking error targets. Whereas a broad-market ETF or mutual fund mirrors the entirety of the index (and likely includes Exxon), our completion portfolio can exclude Exxon or other stocks with a high correlation to the energy sector. The risk model considers Exxon to be 88% in the oil and gas industry and 12% in the chemicals industry. Thus, the completion portfolio should underweight oil, gas, and chemical companies relative to the index.

6.2.2. Tax-Optimized Equity Strategies—Equity Monetization, Collars, and Call Writing

Equity monetization refers to a group of strategies that allows investors to receive cash for their stock positions without an outright sale. These transactions are structured to avoid triggering the capital gains tax. In addition to avoiding the near-term tax liability, other factors might make this monetization strategy appealing. Investors may

- be subject to restrictions from the sale of the stock,
- not want to cede control of the voting rights, or
- want to keep the position but create short-term liquidity.

Monetization is a two-step process:

1. The first step is for the investor to hedge a large portion of the risk inherent in the concentrated position using a short sale, a total return swap, options, futures, or a forward

sale contract. This may be straightforward for a large public company with a liquid derivatives market that trades around the stock. It is likely to be more difficult or expensive for a smaller company with a thin derivatives market.

2. The second step is for the investor to borrow against the hedged position. In most instances, a high loan-to-value ratio can be achieved because the position is hedged. The loan proceeds are then invested in a diversified portfolio of other investments, thus reducing stock-specific risk of the portfolio significantly without triggering a capital gains tax.

A position can be hedged in a number of ways. You could sell the security short, sell a forward contract, or enter into a total return equity swap. In the chapter "Risk Management Applications of Option Strategies," the concept of a *zero-cost collar* was introduced as a commonly used hedging strategy. When structuring a zero-cost (cashless) collar, the investor buys a put with a strike price at or slightly below the current price of the stock. The investor must pay the put premium to acquire the protection. The put will fully protect the investor from a loss should the stock price fall below the strike price (subject to the credit risk of the counterparty). Simultaneously, the investor sells a call with the same maturity with a strike price above the current price. The strike price is set at the level that brings in the amount required to pay for the put. The sale of the call finances the purchase of the put. Risk is reduced but not eliminated.

Historically, the concept of capital gain realization has been tied to the "sale or disposition" of appreciated securities. In the case of monetization transactions, no actual transaction has occurred in the appreciated securities themselves. The investor still owns the securities, and if the securities are viewed in isolation, the investor remains fully exposed to the risk of loss and opportunity for profit in the associated securities.

The critical question is whether an equity monetization strategy will be treated as a taxable event in a particular country. If the tax authorities of a country respect legal form over economic substance, equity monetization strategies should not trigger an immediate taxable event. However, in some jurisdictions the process of hedging the stock is likely to trigger a taxable event if the economic risks of holding the stock are completely eliminated. (In the United States, this is known as a *constructive sale*.) Hedges can be structured to retain some economic risk in the position and thus avoid triggering a taxable event.

Other tax considerations include the following:

- How are the gains and losses from unwinding the position treated? In jurisdictions that favor long-term gains with a lower tax rate, structures that result in long-term gains and short-term losses are preferred.
- Does the hedge affect the taxation of dividends received on the shares? In some jurisdictions, the call options could affect the taxation of the stock dividends. For example, in the United States, if call options sold on the stock are in-the-money or have expiration periods less than 30 days, dividends earned on the stock are taxed at the regular income tax rate instead of at the more favorable qualified dividend rate.

In some cases, a client may want to implement only the call selling program without any hedging or monetization. *Covered call writing* is often viewed as attractive if the owner believes the stock will trade in a range for the foreseeable future. For example, assume that Exxon is trading at $70 per share and that Stark is unwilling to sell any portion of his position at less than $80 per share. We could sell call options with a strike price of $80. If the shares appreciate to that level, the call will be exercised and we will deliver the shares at that price.

But if the shares do not reach that level, Stark keeps the call premiums. Call writing can be a good substitute for a staged selling program. Perhaps the most significant benefit of implementing a covered call writing program, even if only on a portion of the position, is that it can psychologically prepare the owner to dispose of those shares.

EXAMPLE 12   Hedging a Concentrated Equity Position in Exxon

Michael Stark is holding 15,000 shares of Exxon stock, which is currently trading at $70 per share. Assume that Michael is unwilling to sell any portion of his position at less than $80 per share but wants to protect his shares over the next year should the stock price crash. With the help of his adviser, Michael looks at two strategies: a covered call and a zero-cost collar:

- *Covered call:* Sell one-year call options with a strike price of $80 for a $5 per share premium.
- *Zero-cost collar:* Sell the same calls as in the covered call and use the proceeds to buy one-year put options with a $70 strike price.

Exhibit 14 shows the profit and loss for the collar and for a covered call (holding the stock and selling the call without buying the put protection).

EXHIBIT 14   Payoff Diagram for a Zero-Cost Collar and a Covered Call

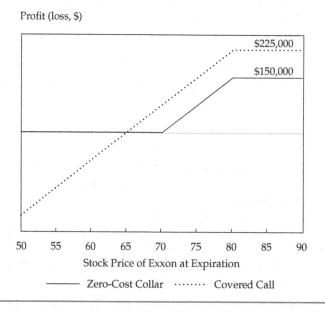

1. What is the maximum profit for the zero-cost collar? How much can Michael lose over the next year?
2. What are the pros and cons of a collar versus a covered call? What is the maximum profit for a covered call?

3. What are the tax consequences of opening the option positions?
4. What are the tax consequences at expiration?

Solution to 1: Michael's maximum profit is capped at $150,000, and his losses are limited to zero. For example, if the stock price rallies to $90 per share at the expiration date, he is obliged to sell his shares at $80. With 15,000 shares, his profit is only $150,000 instead of the $300,000 profit from just holding the stock. On the other hand, if the stock plunged to $50 his loss is zero since the protective put allows him to sell his shares at $70. If the stock price ends the year back where it started, at $70, his loss is still zero.

Solution to 2: Both strategies forfeit any profits above the $80 price. The collar protects against downside risk and allows for monetization of the position through borrowing. The covered call has a maximum profit of $225,000. If Michael sells only a covered call, he would keep the $75,000 in call premiums.

Solution to 3:

*   The premiums received on the short call are classified as a capital gain. The gain is not realized until the option expires or is bought back with an offset order. The holding period for the position is always considered to be short term since you "sell to open" and "buy to close" the position; thus, technically the purchase date and the closing date are the same day, even though the position may be open for a year or longer. If the call is sold deep in the money, the premiums would be very high, locking in the profit on the position. However, this is a very tax inefficient trade since an outright sell of the stock would qualify for the long-term tax rate of 25% but the call premium would be taxed at the much higher short-term gain rate.
*   It is possible to bundle the collar into a single transaction to avoid tax on the call premiums. In this case, the tax would be zero because the net premium is zero.
*   The call options could affect the taxation of the stock dividends.
*   Perhaps most importantly, hedging the risk of the position could trigger a taxable event. If you no longer bear the risk of the investment, you have essentially sold the position. If the collar is constructed so that there is still some risk of loss, then the taxable event can be avoided.

Solution to 4: Profits from the sale of the Exxon stock, including those shares called away by exercise of the call options, are treated as capital gains. If the stock was held for longer than a year, it qualifies for Michael's 25% long-term capital gain rate.

6.2.3. Tax-Free Exchanges

In some tax jurisdictions, a mechanism exists for accomplishing a tax-free exchange of a concentrated position. One mechanism in the United States is an **exchange fund**—a partnership in which each of the partners have each contributed low cost-basis stock to the fund. The partners then own a pro rata interest in the fund that holds a diversified pool of low-basis securities. Participating in the exchange fund is not considered a taxable event; the partners' tax basis in the partnership units remains the same as the tax basis of the stock each contributed. For tax purposes, each partner must remain in the fund for a minimum of seven years. When redeemed, the partner receives a basket of securities equal in value to the pro rata ownership in the fund.

Exchange funds have some limitations. First, the portfolio manager has discretion on whether to accept the shares and on the composition of the basket of shares distributed to partners when they withdraw. In addition, 20% of the portfolio must be "qualified assets," usually real estate investment trusts. The portfolio is often less diversified than a typical portfolio, and redemption fees may be required for early withdrawal.

Exhibit 15 assumes Michael invests in an exchange fund for seven years and then liquidates his portfolio. If the exchange fund provides the same return as the sell and diversify strategy (a big assumption), then the final liquidation value is higher for the exchange fund. This is another example of the benefit of tax deferral. Of course, the fund will charge management fees, which will reduce the benefit.

EXHIBIT 15   Exchange Fund Example

	Sell / Diversify	Exchange Fund
Market value	$1,000,000	$1,000,000
Tax basis	$100,000	$100,000
Capital gain	$900,000	
Tax on sale (at 25% rate)	$225,000	
Amount to invest	$775,000	$1,000,000
Market value in 7 years (10% return)	$1,510,256	$1,948,717
Tax basis	$775,000	$100,000
Capital gain	$735,256	$1,848,717
Tax on sale (at 25% rate)	$183,814	$462,179
Final Value	$1,326,442	$1,486,538

Note: Assumes a 25% tax rate and a 10% annual return for the exchange fund and the reinvestment portfolio of the diversification strategy.

6.2.4. Charitable Remainder Trust

Many estate planning techniques can be deployed to defray the risk associated with a concentrated position, especially if the investor has philanthropic goals. Exhibit 16 shows an example of a **charitable remainder trust**. In this structure, Michael would make an irrevocable donation of Exxon shares to a trust and receive a tax deduction for the gift. He would no longer have ownership of the assets. Within the trust, the shares could be sold and reinvested in a diversified portfolio without incurring a capital gain tax—since the charitable trust is exempt from taxes. The trust would provide income for the life of the named beneficiaries. (The beneficiaries would owe income tax on this income.) When the last-named beneficiary dies, any assets remaining in the trust would be distributed to the charity named in the trust.

EXHIBIT 16   Dynamics of a Charitable Remainder Trust

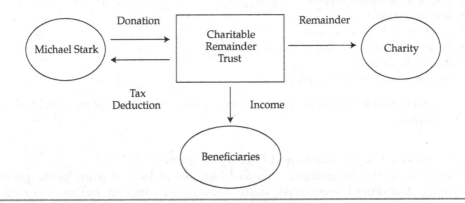

EXAMPLE 13   Exploring Alternatives to Selling

Michael Stark is reluctant to sell his shares of Exxon, primarily due to the large tax bill associated with a sale. What approaches to diversification would you discuss with Michael that do not involve the taxes from an outright sale of his stock?

Solution:

- *Covered Call Writing:* Out-of-the-money call options could be sold that would generate option premiums. While not an explicit diversification strategy, the cash generated by the options would somewhat reduce Michael's risk over time. If one of the options was exercised, Michael could buy shares on the open market to cover the option instead of delivering his company shares.
- *Equity Monetization:* Michael could construct a zero-cost collar or similar hedging strategy to reduce risk. A loan could then provide liquidity without realizing a taxable gain and without selling shares.
- *Exchange Fund:* Michael could deliver shares of stock to an exchange fund to get diversification without an outright sale.
- *Charitable Remainder Trust:* Michael could consult an estate planning attorney and devise a strategy for gifting shares to a charitable remainder trust.

6.3. Strategies for Managing Concentrated Positions in Privately Owned Businesses

Business owners are often asset rich but cash poor, with most of their personal net worth tied up in their businesses. Generating liquidity can be difficult, can trigger a taxable event, and may result in the loss of control or dilution of the ownership stake. Strategies for business owners to generate full or partial liquidity include the following:

- Initial public offering (IPO)
- Sale to a third-party investor
- Sale to an insider
- Divestiture of non-core assets
- Personal line of credit against company shares
- Recapitalization
- Employee stock ownership plan

We next discuss some of the key strategies to free up capital short of an outright sale of the company.

6.3.1. Personal Line of Credit Secured by Company Shares

Owners might consider arranging a personal loan secured by their shares in the private company. If structured properly, this should not cause an immediate taxable event to the company or the owner. The transaction usually contains a "put" arrangement whereby the borrower can "put" the loan to the company as a source of repayment. This would likely be considered a taxable event to the business owner. The company can support this put obligation either through its existing credit arrangement or with a standby letter of credit issued for this specific purpose. While this effectively leverages the client's portfolio and the debt will eventually need to be repaid, until then owners have access to cash to diversify their concentration risk, avoid triggering a taxable event, and maintain ownership and control of the company. In most jurisdictions, the interest expense paid on the loan proceeds should be currently deductible for tax purposes.

6.3.2. Leveraged Recapitalization

A leveraged recapitalization is a strategy that is especially attractive to middle-market business owners who would like to reduce the risk of their wealth concentration and generate liquidity to diversify but who are not yet ready to exit entirely and have the desire to continue to grow their businesses. Typically, a private equity firm will invest equity and take partial ownership of the business. The private equity firm then provides or arranges debt with senior and mezzanine (subordinated) lenders. The owner receives cash for a portion of her stock and retains a minority ownership interest in the freshly capitalized entity. The owner is typically taxed currently on the cash received. If structured properly, a tax deferral is achieved on the stock rolled over into the newly capitalized company. The after-tax cash proceeds the investor receives could be deployed into other asset classes to help build a diversified portfolio.

6.3.3. Employee Stock Ownership Plan

In some countries, legislation allows business owners to sell some or all of their company shares to certain types of pension plans. For instance, in the United States an employee stock ownership plan (ESOP) is a type of pension plan that can be created by the company and is allowed to buy some or all of the owner's shares of company stock. In a version known as a leveraged ESOP, if the company has borrowing capacity the ESOP borrows funds (typically from a bank) to finance the purchase of the owner's shares.

Depending on the legal form of company structure, it may be possible to defer any capital gains tax on the shares sold to the ESOP. Using an ESOP, owners can partially diversify their holdings and overall portfolios while retaining control of the company and maintaining upside potential in the retained shares.

6.4. Strategies for Managing Concentrated Positions in Real Estate

Real estate often constitutes a significant portion of a client's net worth, and consequently, some real estate owners may be exposed to a significant degree of concentration risk and illiquidity. Property-specific risk is the non-systematic risk associated with owning a particular piece of real estate. It is the possibility that the value of the property might fall because of an event—perhaps an environmental liability or the bankruptcy of a major tenant—that affects that property but not the broader real estate market. Clients often underestimate those risks and thus overestimate the value of their properties. Like concentrated positions in public or private equity, real estate positions may have a very low tax basis and selling may trigger the recognition of a tax liability.

Owners of concentrated real estate positions seeking to monetize their real estate will frequently use various forms of debt and equity financing instead of an outright sale. Similar to private businesses, the primary strategies that real estate owners can use to monetize their properties include mortgage financing (recourse and non-recourse, fixed rate, or floating rate) and a charitable trust or donor-advised fund.

Many other real estate monetization techniques are unique to each tax jurisdiction. For example, many of today's public real estate investment trusts in the United States were created by property developers who gathered a number of their investments into a portfolio and then sold shares in that portfolio to the public.

6.4.1. Mortgage Financing

Besides an outright sale, which is the most common strategy, the use of mortgage financing is the next most common technique investors use to lower concentration in a particular property and generate liquidity to diversify asset portfolios without triggering a taxable event.

Consider an investor who owns a high-quality, income-producing property with a fair market value of $10 million. Suppose that the property has a tax cost basis close to zero. An outright sale of the property, given a capital gains tax rate of 25%, would result in the investor receiving $7.5 million in after-tax proceeds from the sale. The investor would not participate in any future appreciation.

As an alternative to an outright sale, the owner might obtain a loan against the property. He might choose a fixed-rate mortgage, setting the loan-to-value (LTV) ratio at the point where the net rental income generated from the property equaled the fixed mortgage payment (composed of interest expense and amortization of the loan principal). Assuming this cash flow–neutral LTV ratio is 75%, the investor could monetize $7.5 million of the real estate's value with no limitations on the use of the loan proceeds. The proceeds could be invested in a liquid, diversified portfolio of securities. The loan proceeds will not be taxed because they are not "income" for tax purposes. In addition, the net rental income derived from the property exactly covers the cost of servicing the debt and other expenses of the property, so the net income from the real estate is zero. Therefore, there are no income tax consequences from the transaction. While the investor maintains economic exposure to the asset, participating in any future appreciation, the overall portfolio is now leveraged 1.75:1 ($17,500,000/$10,000,000).

The investor might also choose an interest-only loan with a balloon payment, using the property as collateral. The loan proceeds *and* the rental income could be used to fund other investment activities.

Borrowing against appreciated, income-producing real estate, especially on a non-recourse basis (meaning that the lender's only recourse upon an event of default is to look to the property that was mortgaged to the lender), can be an attractive technique to effectively "realize" unrealized real estate gains. In lieu of selling the asset outright to realize the gain and trigger an immediate taxable event, the owner can often borrow against the property to access the same or a similar amount of proceeds that a sale would have generated but without paying any tax—and often with a net cost of carry close to zero—while capturing 100% of any increase in the property's value.

6.4.2. Real Estate Monetization for the Charitably Inclined—An Asset Location Strategy

A donor-advised fund (DAF) can also be used to monetize a concentrated position in real estate. We'll illustrate with an example. Jules Menendez wants to endow a named professorship at the university from which he graduated several years ago. The amount needed to fund the professorship is $3 million. He owns a rental property that is worth $2 million. The growth prospects for the property are less compelling than those of some other asset classes (e.g., publicly traded securities). He can contribute the property directly to a DAF and receive an immediate $2 million charitable contribution deduction. The property is then sold by the DAF and the proceeds invested in those more promising investments. No capital gains tax is due when the property is sold. (Nor are the accumulated depreciation deductions taken by the investor ever "recaptured.") The full $2 million is available to invest and manage. The assets grow tax free until grants are made. When the target of $3 million is reached, the DAF could then fund the professorship at Menendez's alma mater.

EXAMPLE 14   Strategies for Managing Concentrated Positions in Privately Held Business and Real Estate

Emma Gagnon has built a successful chain of grocery stores of which she is majority owner. While she has accumulated some retirement assets via the company's various retirement and savings plans, 90% of her C$25,000,000 net worth is tied up in shares of the company she owns and unleveraged real estate that she leases to the stores. While she is only 50 years old and plans to continue growing the business, she is concerned that her eventual retirement is completely dependent upon the continued success of the business. Recommend two strategies that Emma might use to address this problem. Justify your response.

Solution: Emma might consider a personal line of credit against a portion of her shares in the company. She can use the proceeds to build a diversified portfolio of assets that complements her exposure to the grocery business while maintaining her ownership position.

To free up capital tied up in the real estate she has leased to the stores, she could mortgage the properties. If the loans were non-recourse, they would effectively provide Emma with downside protection. The capital could be invested in a diversified portfolio unrelated to the grocery business.

7. DIRECTING AND TRANSFERRING WEALTH

The previous section dealt with the day-to-day practicalities of managing investment portfolios for private clients. To be an effective private wealth manager, however, you must have a basic understanding of the tools and techniques available to your clients seeking to preserve their wealth for future generations. While you will not be expected to structure these entities, you must have enough knowledge to identify when your client might want to engage with an estate planning specialist and will be managing assets located within the entity. This section covers the basics of estate planning, common estate planning strategies, and the "human" side of intergenerational wealth transfer. We also discuss typical approaches to asset protection, including reference to the minimization of political, litigation, and other risks.

7.1. Objectives of Gift and Estate Planning

At some stage, most wealthy individuals face the task of planning for the management of their assets beyond their own lifetimes. They may seek an effective way of transferring their assets to the next generation or donating assets to achieve charitable goals, either during their life or after death. We refer to this process as "gift and estate planning." An **estate** is all of the property a person owns or controls, which may consist of financial assets (e.g., bank accounts, stocks, bonds, business interests), tangible personal assets (e.g., artwork, collectibles, vehicles), immovable property (e.g., residential real estate, timber rights), and intellectual property (e.g., royalties). **Estate planning** is the process of preparing for the disposition of one's estate upon death and during one's lifetime. It usually requires the counsel of a variety of professionals, including financial, legal, and tax professionals.

Effective gift and estate planning should consider several objectives; the most important are described here:

- *Maintaining sufficient income and liquidity* to achieve desired lifestyle of the donors and beneficiaries as well as to pay any estate taxes due.
- *Deciding on control over the assets.* For example, clients may desire to pass the beneficial ownership to the next generation without giving them control over the investment and distribution of the assets. Or, when creating a charitable giving strategy, clients may desire to maintain some control over the specific charitable activities their money supports as opposed to simply giving money to charities.
- *Asset protection.* Certain estate planning vehicles, such as trusts, may protect assets from creditors by separating the settlor (the creator of the trust) and beneficiaries from the legal ownership of the assets. In some jurisdictions, trusts may be used for taking the assets outside of the forced heirship regime under which wealth owners have limited decision power over the disposition of their assets. **Forced heirship** is a requirement that a certain

proportion of assets must pass to specified family members, such as a spouse and children. Those passing on wealth are therefore restricted in what they can pass on to non-family members. A forced heirship regime can be found mainly in the civil law countries, for example, Spain, France, and Switzerland. It does not apply in many common law countries, such as Canada, the United Kingdom, and the United States. Not all forced heirship jurisdictions are the same. In some cases, lifetime gifts are not covered; in others, they are. Some jurisdictions even allow the family to opt out of the forced heirship rules. Forced heirship also applies under Shari'a law, which is a religious law applicable to Muslim families. A number of countries in the Middle East, Africa, and Southeast Asia have Shari'a law as part of civil law.

Civil and Common Law Regimes

Civil law, which is derived from Roman law, is the world's predominant legal system. It is based on fixed codes and statutes. In civil law states, judges apply general, abstract rules or concepts to particular cases. Common law systems, which usually trace their heritage to Britain, draw abstract rules from specific cases. In civil law systems, law is developed primarily through legislative statutes or executive action. In common law systems, law is developed primarily through decisions of the courts.

- *Transferring assets in a tax-aware manner.* The two main forms of taxes on wealth transfers correspond to the primary ways of transferring assets. Gifting assets during one's lifetime may, depending on the tax laws of the relevant country, be subject to a **gift tax**, and bequeathing assets upon one's death may be subject to an estate tax or an inheritance tax. In some jurisdictions, a **generation-skipping tax** may be levied if one generation is skipped when transferring the assets (e.g., the grandparents make gifts directly to their grandchildren, bypassing the parents). A generation-skipping transfer tax (GST tax) exists in the United States; the grandparent pays a 40% tax on assets transferred to the grandchildren in excess of the lifetime GST exclusion amount of $11.4 million (as of 2019).
- *Preservation of family wealth.* Setting up a family governance system alongside the estate planning process mitigates potential disputes among the family members, ensuring that they work together toward achieving jointly agreed upon investment and charitable goals. Family governance is a process for a family's collective communication and decision-making. A good governance framework will serve current and future generations and should help to preserve and grow wealth across generations. Families often develop family constitutions designed to set out how governance will work for that family. While the family constitution is usually a non-binding document, the governance approach is made binding through the vehicles used in the succession plan, which might include trusts, foundations, life insurance, and companies.
- *Business succession.* Gift and estate planning helps the founder (or current generation of ownership) to pass control and beneficial ownership of the family business to the next generation. Additionally, the founder may face a choice between assigning managerial responsibilities to the outsider managers, keeping control of the business within the family, or even selling the business outright.

- *Achieving charitable goals.* Charitable giving to qualified charities or private foundations in most jurisdictions qualifies for gift tax or estate tax deduction or exemption, which leaves more capital to be deployed on charitable causes. If charitable giving is made during the donor's lifetime, it may also qualify for an income tax deduction. The creation of a private foundation may also serve to create a long-lasting family legacy around which subsequent generations can come to understand the family values.

Estate and Inheritance Tax Regimes

In general, the main difference between an **estate tax** and **inheritance tax** relates to who is responsible for paying it. An estate tax is levied on the total value of a deceased person's assets and paid out of the estate before any distributions to beneficiaries. An inheritance tax is paid by each individual beneficiary. Most jurisdictions only have one of these types of taxes. In the United Kingdom, for example, all taxes are paid at the donor/estate level. In the United States, there is an estate tax on the federal level, but the individual states may also levy estate and/or inheritance taxes.

Many jurisdictions have tax-free allowances that can be used for transferring assets under a certain threshold without paying an estate or inheritance tax.

Exhibit 17 shows some of the gift and estate tax regimes around the world. Be advised that the presentation of tax rates, exclusions, and payee are simplified for illustrative purposes. The actual tax laws are quite complex and cover many combinations of relationship and residency that are virtually impossible to summarize in any comprehensive fashion.

EXHIBIT 17   Estate and Inheritance Tax Rates for Selected Jurisdictions

Jurisdiction	Maximum Estate Tax Rate (%)	Allowances	Taxes Paid by:
Japan	55.0	Spousal exemption and up to ¥10 million per statutory heir	Beneficiary
Belgium	30.0[1]	Minor exemptions	Beneficiary
Netherlands	20.0[2]	Partner exemption of up to €650,913	Beneficiary
United Kingdom	40.0	Unlimited spousal or partner exemption	Estate
South Korea	50.0[3]	Spousal exemption of up to ₩3 billion; ₩50 million for a child of the deceased	Beneficiary
United States	40.0	First $11 million is exempt from taxation for citizens and domiciliaries. Unlimited spousal exemption for citizens and domiciliaries.	Estate

Note: Tax rates are as of 2018.
[1]For direct descendants. The maximum tax rate for other than direct descendants is 80%.
[2]For partner and children. Up to 40% for other persons.
[3]Higher for persons other than a son or daughter.
Source: EY 2019 Worldwide Estate and Inheritance Tax Guide

Sound gift and estate planning will seek to fully utilize all tax-free gift allowances. In certain circumstances, it is financially advantageous to transfer an asset prior to death so the capital appreciation (and associated capital gains tax liability) accrues outside of the estate where it is likely to be less-heavily taxed. Many wealthy families often manage these tax considerations across multiple tax regimes. Often, wealthy individuals use for investment and estate planning purposes solutions (e.g., trusts, personal holding companies) registered in tax-light jurisdictions, such as Cayman Islands, The Bahamas, Bermuda, British Virgin Islands, Guernsey, Jersey, and Isle of Man. Each country has its own legislation in relation to personal holding companies (PHCs), which typically hold income-generating investment assets and are also known as controlled foreign corporations (CFCs). Shares of a PHC are often owned by individual family members or a family trust. Most countries are tightening their legislation related to moving assets to tax light jurisdictions with the aim to combat tax avoidance.

EXAMPLE 15   Forced Heirship Regime

Philippe and Helena Berelli and their two children live in a country with forced heirship laws that entitle a spouse to one-third of the total estate and the children to split one-third of the total estate. Suppose Philippe passes away today with a total estate of €800,000 and wishes to leave €300,000 to his surviving mother.

1. What is the minimum that Helena should receive?
2. What is the minimum amount the children should receive under forced heirship rules?
3. May Philippe bequeath €300,000 to his mother?

Solution to 1: Under forced heirship rules, Helena is entitled to one-third of the total estate, or $(1/3)(€800,000) = €266,667$.

Solution to 2: The children are collectively entitled to receive one-third of the total estate equal to €266,667, or €133,333 for each child.

Solution to 3: Philippe is able to freely dispose of the remainder, which is €800,000 − €266,667 − €266,667 = €266,666. Therefore, Philippe is unable to bequeath €300,000 to his mother, but he may bequeath the remainder of €266,666.

The following vignette takes our private clients Ivy and Charles Lee and considers a set of estate planning objectives that would likely be relevant.

Investor Case Facts: The Lee Family

Client: Ivy and Charles Lee. Ivy is a 54-year-old life sciences entrepreneur; she is the CEO of one privately-held life science enterprise and has significant ownership interests in two others. Charles is 55 years old and employed as an orthopedic surgeon. They have two children, aged 25 (Deborah) and 18 (David). Deborah is divorced and has a daughter with physical limitations. The Lees' total portfolio is $25 million, with $1 million in margin debt, plus residential real estate of $3 million, with $1 million in mortgage debt. David will soon begin studying at a four-year private university; the present value of the expected parental contribution is $250,000. The Lees desire to give a gift to a local art museum in five years. In present value terms, the gift is valued at $750,000.

From this brief description of the family circumstances, we can identify several possible estate planning objectives:

- *Business succession*—As the CEO of one privately held firm and with significant ownership interests in two others, Ivy's estate planning objectives should encompass a solution for the transfer of ownership, either to her heirs or to a third party. Similarly, Charles' orthopedic practice likely has embedded value beyond his role as a surgeon, and a plan should be devised to extract and transfer that value.
- *Asset protection*—Given Charles' profession as an orthopedic surgeon and Ivy's involvement with the evolving field of life sciences, it is likely that their assets may be vulnerable to claims from creditors (e.g., a medical malpractice award or a shareholder settlement in the event of firm failure).
- *Control*—Charles and Ivy would likely want to consider placing some controls on the management of their assets if they were both to die in the near term. Neither David nor Deborah appear likely to have sufficient experience or expertise to oversee a $25 million estate. In addition, Ivy and Charles may want to ensure that their granddaughter's medical, education, and other needs are taken care of irrespective of their daughter's future choices. Thus, they may seek a mechanism to segregate a portion of their assets to ensure the granddaughter's needs are looked after.
- *Charitable gift*—The planned gift to the museum offers an opportunity for tax and estate planning.
- *Tax awareness*—To maximize the value of assets that will be available to heirs and other beneficiaries at their death, the Lees will want to ensure that any estate plan considers the taxes due during their lifetime and at their death.

7.2. Gift and Estate Planning Strategies

Having the right estate planning strategy is important to ensure smooth transition of wealth. The choice of gift and estate planning tools depends on the legal system as well as goals of each individual family. This section introduces the main concepts of estate planning, such as wills, probate (the legal process for administering the will), and the difference in approaches to wealth transfer in various legal systems. It also explains the main principles of using lifetime gifts and testamentary bequests (e.g., a transfer that is set out in an individual's last will) in wealth transfer. The most widely used estate planning tools, such as trusts, foundations, life insurance, and companies, are also discussed.

7.2.1. Introduction to Estate Planning: Wills, Probate, and Legal Systems

As discussed, an estate is all of the property a person owns or controls. **Estate planning** is the process of preparing for the disposition of one's estate upon death and during one's lifetime.

The core document most closely associated with an estate plan is a will or testament.

A **will** (or **testament**) outlines the rights others will have over one's property after death. A **testator** is the person who authored the will and whose property is disposed of according to the will. **Probate** is the legal process to confirm the validity of the will so that executors, heirs, and other interested parties can rely on its authenticity. Decedents without a valid will or with a will that does not dispose of their property are considered to have died **intestate**. In that case, a court will often decide on the disposition of assets under the intestacy laws of the applicable jurisdiction(s).

A country's legal system may constrain the ability of testators to freely dispose of their assets. The common law jurisdictions, such as the United Kingdom and the United States, generally allow testators freedom of disposition by will; that is, the right to use their own judgment regarding the rights others will have over their property after death.

Most civil law countries, however, place restrictions on testamentary disposition. Under forced heirship rules, for example, children have the right to a fixed share of a parent's estate. Wealthy individuals may attempt to move assets into an offshore trust governed by a different domicile to circumvent forced heirship rules. Or, they may attempt to reduce a forced heirship claim by gifting or donating assets to others during their lifetime to reduce the value of the final estate upon death.

Countries following **Shari'a**, the law of Islam, have substantial variation but are more like civil law systems, especially in regard to estate planning. Because Shari'a is not the law of the land in most countries, including some countries where a majority of the population is Muslim, those who wish to follow Islamic guidance on inheritance will want to do so through the making of a will as long as the contents of the will are not in conflict with the law of the specific jurisdiction.

A country's legal system defines which estate planning tools are available for the transfer of wealth. The legal concept of a trust, for example, is relatively unique to common law countries. A **trust** is a vehicle through which an individual (called a settlor) entrusts certain assets to a trustee (or trustees), who manages the assets for the benefit of assigned beneficiaries. A trust may be either a testamentary trust—a trust created through the testator's will—or a living or inter-vivos trust—a trust created during the settlor's lifetime. A trust is a legal relationship and not a legal person. A legal person is a person or organization that has legal rights and duties related to contracts, agreements, payments, transactions, obligations, and penalties (including the right to take legal action to enforce any related claims). The trust itself cannot hold assets, enter into contracts, or undertake other legal formalities. While assets may be placed "in trust," the legal owner of the assets is typically a trustee or a grantor depending on the type of trust. Some civil law countries may not recognize foreign trusts, and many civil law jurisdictions, including France and Germany, do not recognize trusts at all (though their tax laws do address the treatment of trusts). A *foundation*, unlike trusts, can hold assets in its own name. Foundations originated in civil law regimes as estate planning vehicles, and they are also available in some common law jurisdictions, predominantly used for similar purposes as charitable trusts.

7.2.2. Lifetime Gifts and Testamentary Bequests

Wealthy individuals can transfer their wealth by gifting it either during their lifetime or after death. In an estate planning context, lifetime gifts are sometimes referred to as lifetime gratuitous transfers, and they are made during the lifetime of the donor. The term "gratuitous" refers to a transfer made with purely donative intent—that is, without expectation of anything in exchange.[1] Gifts may or may not be taxed depending on the jurisdiction. In some civil law jurisdictions (e.g., France), tax-free allowances for lifetime gifts depend on the relationship between a beneficiary and a donor.

Bequeathing assets or transferring assets in some other way upon one's death is referred to as a **testamentary bequest** or a **testamentary gratuitous transfer**. From a recipient's perspective, it is called an inheritance. As discussed, taxes on wealth transfer may be applied to the transferor or the recipient. These taxes may be applied at a flat rate or based on a **progressive tax rate schedule**, where the tax rate increases as the amount of wealth transferred increases. Often the tax is applied after the deduction of a statutory allowance, described more fully later. The tax rate may also depend on the relationship between transferor and recipient. Transfers to spouses, for instance, are often tax exempt (e.g., in the United Kingdom, United States, and France).

Many jurisdictions establish periodic or lifetime allowances within which the gifts can be made without transfer tax. For example, UK taxpayers may make lifetime gifts up to £325,000 before inheritance tax is applied. In the United States, a donor's annual gift exclusions are limited to $15,000 per year, per donee (e.g., a parent may annually transfer $15,000 to each child or $30,000 from both parents). These amounts do not count toward the lifetime gift and estate tax exemption for citizens and domiciliaries ($22 million per couple as of 2019). There is no limit on the number of gift recipients. (These allowances are as of 2019 and are subject to change.) Other exclusions or relief may apply as well. It is common to be able to transfer some assets by gift in a tax-efficient manner.

EXAMPLE 16   UK Inheritance Tax Example

Paul Dasani, a widower, passed away in May 2019. Dasani was a resident and domiciliary of the United Kingdom at the time of his death and had a total estate valued at £700,000. His children are the beneficiaries of the estate. The United Kingdom imposes an inheritance tax threshold on estates valued above £325,000 in 2019. The tax is payable by the trustee of the estate out of estate assets at a rate of 40% on the amount over the statutory allowance of £325,000.

What is the amount of inheritance tax payable?

Solution: The inheritance tax is computed as:

Estate value	£700,000
Less threshold	(£325,000)
Excess	£375,000
Rate on excess	40%
Inheritance tax	£150,000

---

[1]"Gratuitous" means given freely and without obligation. It is a descendant of the Latin word "gratus," which means "pleasing" or "grateful."

EXAMPLE 17 Progressive Estate Tax Example

Ya-wen Chao passed away in a jurisdiction with progressive estate tax rates as provided in the following table.

Taxable Estate (€)	Tax Rate (%)
Up to 600,000	2
600,001–1,500,000	4
1,500,001–3,000,000	7
3,000,001–4,500,000	11
4,500,001–6,000,000	15
6,000,001–10,000,000	20
10,000,001–15,000,000	26
15,000,001–40,000,000	33
40,000,001–100,000,000	41
Over 100,000,000	50

After all applicable exemptions, Chao had a taxable estate of €2,000,000. What is Chao's estate tax?

Solution: The estate tax is computed as:

Tax on first 600,000 (2%) =	€12,000
Tax on next 900,000 (4%) =	36,000
Tax on remaining 500,000 (7%) =	35,000
Total estate tax =	€83,000

The choice between gifting assets during one's lifetime or after death depends on various considerations, including taxation system and expected return on the asset. Transferring assets during life using the tax-free allowances allows appreciation on gifted assets to be effectively transferred to the donee without gift or estate tax. Appreciation on the gifted asset is still subject to tax on investment returns (e.g., dividends and capital gains) whether it remains in the donor's estate or is transferred to a donee. But if the tax-free gift had not been made and had remained in the estate, the appreciation on it would have been subject to estate or inheritance tax. It is commonly believed that gifting assets that are expected to appreciate prior to death rather than transferring them after death is more tax efficient because the future estate tax liability will be greater. Depending on jurisdiction, there may be an economic difference between gifting during lifetime and testamentary transfer. In the United Kingdom, for example, a gift is not taxed but will be subject to inheritance tax if the donor passes away within seven years of the gift being made. In the United States, if a gift is made during the donor's lifetime, only the amount transferred is subject to gift tax; the taxes paid are independent of the gift (and effectively reduce the value of the donor's estate). If the transfer occurs at death, however, the entire estate is subject to estate tax and the amount available to transfer to the heirs is reduced. Here's a simple example to illustrate:

> Maria has an estate valued at $2,000,000. She lives in a jurisdiction with a unified gift and estate tax exemption of $1,000,000. The applicable estate tax rate is 40%. If, during her lifetime, she gifts $1,500,000 to her children, $500,000 is subject to tax. She pays the tax from her remaining assets and has $300,000 left after the payment of taxes. When she dies, she will owe an additional $120,000 in estate taxes and her children will receive an additional $180,000. In total, they will have received $1,680,000. If she waits until her death to transfer her assets to her children, her taxable estate will be $1,000,000 and the taxes due will be $400,000. The net assets available to her children will be $1,600,000.

Charitable gratuitous transfers. Most jurisdictions provide two forms of tax relief for wealth transfers to not-for-profit or charitable organizations. First, most charitable donations are not subject to a gift tax. Second, most jurisdictions permit income tax deductions for charitable donations. Therefore, families with philanthropic aspirations can transfer wealth very tax efficiently. Furthermore, if the family establishes its own charitable organization for the purpose of furthering its philanthropic objectives, investment returns on the assets transferred to the charity may compound tax free, increasing the amount of assets available to support the philanthropic objectives over the long term.

7.2.3. Efficiency of Lifetime Gifts versus Testamentary Bequests

In general, the relative after-tax value of a tax-free gift made during one's lifetime compared to a **bequest** that is transferred as part of a taxable estate can be expressed as the ratio of the future value of the gift to the future value of the bequest. The numerator is the future after-tax value of the tax-free gift. The denominator is the future after-tax value of a taxable transfer by bequest. The ratio is the relative value of making the tax-free gift compared to the bequest:

$$RV_{\text{Tax Free Gift}} = \frac{FV_{\text{Gift}}}{FV_{\text{Bequest}}}$$

The future value of the gift is a function of the expected pre-tax returns to the beneficiary, r_g, the effective tax rate on those returns, t_g, and the expected time until the donor's death, n:

$$FV_{\text{Gift}} = [1 + r_g(1 - t_g)]^n$$

The future value of the bequest is a function of the expected pre-tax returns to the estate, r_e, the effective tax rate on those returns, t_e, the expected time until the donor's death, and the estate tax rate, T_e:

$$FV_{\text{Bequest}} = [1 + r_e(1 - t_e)]^n(1 - T_e)$$

Putting it all together, the relative value of the gift made during the donor's lifetime is:

$$RV_{\text{Tax Free Gift}} = \frac{FV_{\text{Gift}}}{FV_{\text{Bequest}}} = \frac{[1 + r_g(1 - t_g)]^n}{[1 + r_e(1 - t_e)]^n(1 - T_e)} \tag{3}$$

If the pre-tax return and effective tax rates are equal for both the recipient and donor, the relative value of the tax-free gift in Equation 3 reduces to $1/(1 - T_e)$. For example, consider the value of a €10,000 bequest in today's value subject to a 40% inheritance tax, netting €6,000 after tax. If the wealth is instead transferred as a tax-free gift without having to pay the 40% inheritance tax, the relative value of the tax-free gift is 1.67 times, or $1/(1 - 0.40)$, as great as the taxable bequest, or €10,000 versus €6,000.

In practice, the respective tax rates on returns will vary with each situation based on the tax status of the recipient and the tax status of the donor. In many cases, the tax rate of the recipient is likely to be lower than the tax rate of the donor; thus, a greater proportion of the return will compound over the investment horizon.

In jurisdictions that allow for tax-free gifts to be made during the grantor's lifetime without reducing the aggregate gift and estate tax exemption, individuals have the opportunity to transfer wealth without taxes each year. If these allowances or exclusions expire at the end of a tax year and do not accumulate over time, tax-free gifts not made in a particular tax year are lost opportunities to capture the benefits of tax management and greater compounding of returns. It is, therefore, often beneficial for a family with wealth transfer goals to commence an early gifting program, taking advantage of annual exclusions, where applicable.

Opportunities to add value may even exist when a lifetime gift is taxable. In general, the value of making taxable gifts, rather than leaving them in the estate to be taxed as a bequest, can be expressed as a ratio of the *after-tax* future value of the gift and the bequest. Equation 3 can be modified to reflect the taxes payable on the gift, $(1 - T_g)$:

$$RV_{\text{Taxable Gift}} = \frac{FV_{\text{Gift}}}{FV_{\text{Bequest}}} = \frac{[1 + r_g(1 - t_g)]^n(1 - T_g)}{[1 + r_e(1 - t_e)]^n(1 - T_e)}$$

It is important to note that this model assumes that the gift tax is paid by the recipient rather than the donor.

For example, consider a family residing in Country A is contemplating a 30 million lifetime gratuitous transfer. In Country A, 18 million can be transferred free of tax, but the remaining 12 million transfer is subject to a 50% tax rate. The same 50% rate applies if the gift is delayed and transferred as a bequest, so no tax advantage related to differences between gift and estate tax rates exists. However, if the recipient of the 12 million gift had a lower marginal tax rate on investment returns (perhaps due to a progressive income tax schedule) of, say, 20% compared to the estate's marginal tax rate of, say, 50%, the gift can still create a tax advantage. Over a 10-year horizon, the advantage for locating an asset with an 8% pre-tax return with the donee rather than the donor would be equal to:

$$RV_{\text{Taxable Gift}} = \frac{[1 + 0.08(1 - 0.20)]^{10}(1 - 0.50)}{[1 + 0.08(1 - 0.50)]^{10}(1 - 0.50)} = \frac{0.9298}{0.7401} = 1.256$$

That is, the lower 20% tax rate associated with the gift recipient will create 25.6% more wealth in 10 years than if the asset had remained in the estate and been taxed at 50% annually for 10 years.

EXAMPLE 18   Gift and Estate Taxes

Philippe Zachary is 50 years old and resides in one of the EU countries. He is working with his wealth manager to develop an estate planning strategy to transfer wealth to his second cousin, Étienne. Annual exclusions allow Philippe to make tax-free gifts of €20,000 per year, and gratuitous transfer tax liabilities are the responsibility of the recipient. Philippe notes that the relevant tax rate for bequests from the estate is likely to be 60%. He notes further, however, that gifts (in excess of the €20,000 exception mentioned) made prior to age 70 enjoy 50% relief of the normal estate tax of 60%, for an effective tax rate of 30%. In addition, Étienne enjoys a low tax rate of 20% on investment income because he has relatively low income. Philippe, on the other hand, is subject to a 48% tax rate on investment income. Philippe is considering gifting assets that are expected to earn a 6% return annually over the next 20 years.

1. Considering the first year's tax-free gift associated with the annual exclusion, how much of his estate will Philippe have transferred on an inflation-adjusted basis in 20 years without paying estate tax?
2. What is the relative value of the tax-free gift compared to the value of a bequest in 20 years?
3. Suppose Philippe wishes to make an additional gift that would be subject to gift tax. What would be the relative after-tax value of that taxable gift compared to a bequest 20 years later?

Solution to 1: In 20 years, the future value (measured in real terms) equals €20,000 × $[1 + 0.06(1 - 0.20)]^{20}$ = €51,080.56. Note that although the gift was not subject to a wealth transfer tax, its subsequent investment returns are nonetheless taxable at 20%.

Solution to 2: The relative value of the tax-free gift compared to the bequest is:

$$RV_{\text{Tax Free Gift}} = \frac{[1 + 0.06(1 - 0.20)]^{20}}{[1 + 0.06(1 - 0.48)]^{20}(1 - 0.60)} = \frac{2.5540}{0.7395} = 3.45$$

The gift is substantially more tax efficient in this case for three reasons. First, the gift is tax free and the bequest is heavily taxed. Second, if Étienne receives the gift, subsequent investment returns will be taxed at a much lower rate than if it is kept inside the estate. Third, the difference has time to compound over a relatively long period of time since the time horizon is 20 years.

Solution to 3: In this case, the recipient is responsible for paying the gift tax at 30%, or half of the 60% estate tax. The relative value of the tax-free gift compared to a bequest subject to inheritance tax is:

$$RV_{\text{Taxable Gift}} = \frac{[1 + 0.06(1 - 0.20)]^{20}(1 - 0.30)}{[1 + 0.06(1 - 0.48)]^{20}(1 - 0.60)} = \frac{1.7878}{0.7395} = 2.42$$

Although the gift is taxed, the after-tax value of the gift relative to the bequest is still quite large because the gift tax rate is low and because the gift is located in a lightly taxed place (i.e., with Étienne) for a long period of time.

7.2.4. Estate Planning Tools: Trusts, Foundations, Life Insurance, Companies

The gratuitous transfers described are often implemented through structures that allow planning for taxes and produce a non-tax benefit. Common estate planning tools include, among others, trusts (a common law concept), foundations (a civil law concept), life insurance, and companies. The structure of each has implications for how assets are controlled, whether assets are protected from potential claims of future creditors, and how assets are taxed.

Trusts. A trust is an arrangement created by a *settlor* (sometimes called a grantor). The grantor transfers assets to the trust, naming a trustee. Depending on the type of trust and jurisdiction, the grantor can name as a trustee him/herself, another individual, or an institution (trust company). The trustee holds and manages the assets for the benefit of the beneficiaries. As a result, the beneficiaries are considered to be the beneficial, not legal, owners of the trust assets. (*Beneficial ownership* is a legal term that means that certain rights, such as the right to the income from the securities or the right to live in the house, belong to the beneficiary but that the title to the securities or the property are held by another person or entity.) The terms of the trust relationship and the principles used by the trustee to manage the assets and distributions to the beneficiaries are outlined in the trust document.

Trusts can be categorized in many ways, but two dimensions are particularly important in understanding their character. First, a trust can be either revocable or irrevocable. In a **revocable trust** arrangement, the settlor (the person whose assets are used to create the trust) retains the right to rescind the trust relationship and regain title to the trust assets. Under these circumstances, the settlor is generally considered to be the owner of the assets for tax purposes in most jurisdictions. As a result, the settlor is responsible for tax payments and reporting on the trust's investment returns. Additionally, the settlor's revocation power makes the trust assets vulnerable to the reach of creditors having claims against the settlor. Alternatively, where the settlor has no ability to revoke the trust relationship, the trust is characterized as an **irrevocable trust**. In an irrevocable trust structure, trustees may be responsible for tax payments and reporting in their capacity as owners of the trust assets for tax purposes. An irrevocable trust structure generally provides greater asset protection from claims against a settlor than a revocable trust.

Second, trusts can be structured to be either fixed or discretionary. Distributions to beneficiaries of a **fixed trust** are specified in the trust document to occur at certain times or in certain amounts. In contrast, if the trust document enables the trustee to determine whether and how much to distribute based on a beneficiary's general welfare, the trust would be called a **discretionary trust**. Under a discretionary trust, the beneficiaries have no legal right to income generated by the trust or to the assets in the trust itself. Therefore, the creditors of the beneficiaries cannot as easily reach the trust assets.

There are several main objectives for using a trust structure:

- *Control.* A common motivation for using a trust structure is to make resources available to beneficiaries without yielding complete control of those resources to them. For example, trusts can be used to provide resources to beneficiaries who may be unable or unwilling to manage the assets themselves—perhaps because they are young, immature, or disabled. Or, perhaps the settlor desires that the assets be used for particular purposes.
- *Asset protection.* In general, creditors are unable to reach assets that an individual does not own. As discussed, an irrevocable trust can protect assets from claims against the settlor and discretionary trusts can protect assets from claims against the beneficiaries. In community property jurisdictions (a marital property regime under which most property acquired by a spouse during a marriage is owned jointly by both spouses and is divided upon divorce, annulment, or the death of a spouse), trusts may also be used to ensure that ownership of a family business does not get diluted as a result of community property laws. Trusts can also be used to avoid probate.
- *Tax-related considerations.* Trusts can also be used for tax management purposes. For example, under a progressive tax rate regime, a wealthy individual's income may be taxed at relatively high rates. That individual might transfer assets to a trust where the income may be taxed at lower rates or where the income is paid to a beneficiary who is taxed at lower rates. Moreover, if an irrevocable trust is structured as discretionary, the trustee can manage distributions to a beneficiary in accordance with the beneficiary's tax situation. Alternatively, a settlor may create a trust in a jurisdiction with a low tax rate.

Foundations. A **foundation** is a legal entity available in certain jurisdictions. Foundations are typically set up to hold assets for a specific charitable purpose, such as to promote education or for philanthropy. When set up and funded by an individual or family and managed by its own directors, it is called a private foundation. The term family foundation usually refers to a private foundation where donors or members of the donors' family are actively involved.

Whereas a trust arrangement typically transfers decision-making authority to a trustee, a foundation allows the donor to retain control over the administration and decision-making of the foundation. Depending on the jurisdiction, private foundations may be required to make certain minimum annual distributions; for example, in the United States, 5% of the foundation's prior year average net investment assets must be distributed each year. Among the benefits of foundations are a current income tax deduction for the value of assets transferred to the foundation, favorable tax treatment of investment returns, and protection of assets from estate tax. Like trusts, foundations survive the settlor and allow the settlor's wishes to be followed after the settlor's death. There is a growing trend of foundations being set up to employ charitable capital during a pre-defined number of years rather than in perpetuity.

Life insurance. Life insurance is another planning tool in which the policyholder transfers assets (called a premium) to an insurer who, in turn, has a contractual obligation to pay death benefit proceeds to the beneficiary named in the policy. As is the case with trusts, insurance can produce tax and estate planning benefits. Death benefit proceeds paid to life insurance beneficiaries are tax exempt in many jurisdictions, and in some cases, no tax-reporting consequences arise. In addition, premiums paid by the policyholder typically are neither part of the policyholder's taxable estate at the time of death nor subject to a gratuitous transfer tax. Life insurance can also be paired with trust structures to transfer assets to the beneficiaries outside of the probate process. For example, in the United Kingdom, if a trust that holds family assets buys a life insurance policy on the life of the settlor, the life insurance proceeds are not included in the estate of the settlor and proceeds will be paid directly to the beneficiaries without going through probate. This may provide a more favorable tax outcome—such as in India, which treats insurance proceeds more favorably than trust distributions.

Other forms of insurance can also be part of the "wealth planning toolbox." For example, some retirement insurance products, such as deferred variable annuities, can be part of the development of a tax-efficient asset protection and succession plan for a family.

Companies. Companies may also be a useful tool in which to place assets. For example, a **controlled foreign corporation (CFC)** is a company located outside a taxpayer's home country in which the taxpayer has a controlling interest as defined under the home country law. Depending on the jurisdiction, the taxes on income from assets in a CFC can be deferred until the earnings are distributed to shareholders or until the company is sold or shares otherwise disposed. Many countries have CFC rules designed to ensure that tax is ultimately paid in the home country of the beneficial owner.

EXAMPLE 19   Estate Planning for the Harper Family

John Harper (56 years old) is a founder and CEO of a privately-owned supermarket chain recently valued by a financial consultant at $300 million. His wife, Breda Harper, is a 54-year-old housewife who took care of the family while John was building the business. The Harper family is based in a country with the common law regime. In addition to the business, John and Breda own commercial property, with an estimated value of $10,000,000, and a house. Most of the family wealth is concentrated in the family business and real estate. John and Breda have 3 children:

- James (35 years old) has been helping his father run the family business. At this stage, James intends to launch an online retail business of his own, which he would like to finance partially with a loan. James is married and has a 10-year-old daughter and a 12–year-old son.
- Nick (30 years old) is a young artist and currently relies on the family income to cover his living expenses. Nick has no financial knowledge and is not interested in investments. His father, John, would like to continue supporting Nick's lifestyle but would not be comfortable to let Nick manage his own funds. Nick is single.
- Ann (27 years old) is a pharmacist. She is married and has a 6-year-old daughter who requires medical care, care that is financed from the income generated by the family business. Ann's husband works in corporate finance.

John intends to retire from running the family business and is thinking about passing the wealth to the next generations and creating a family legacy. After retirement, John and Breda would like to travel and support several philanthropic causes. They want to be actively involved in philanthropic activity and believe that their children and grandchildren should be involved in making philanthropic decisions as well.

1. Identify possible estate planning objectives of the Harper family.
2. Discuss estate planning strategies that can be employed to achieve each of the estate planning objectives you identified in response to question 1.

Solution to 1: At least seven possible estate planning objectives are evident in the case facts presented:

- *Income and liquidity*—An estate planning solution should provide sufficient income to support the desired lifestyle of John and Breda, to cover medical care costs for Ann's daughter, to cover living expenses of other family members who rely on family income (Nick), and to cover any tax obligations related to wealth transfer.
- *Business succession*—John plans to retire, and the family needs to decide if the company will be run by a family member or an outsider. The family also needs to decide if the company remains in the family ownership or is sold to a third party.
- *Control over assets*—As John is not comfortable with Nick managing his own money, John needs an estate planning solution that will separate investment and income distribution decisions from the beneficial ownership. John would like to be actively involved in philanthropic decisions, thus he needs to maintain a certain degree of control over assets dedicated to philanthropy.
- *Transferring assets in a tax-aware manner*—An estate planning solution should be designed in a way that takes into account the jurisdiction-specific tax legislation.
- *Asset protection*—As James is planning to use a loan to set up his online retail business, protection of family assets from potential creditors may be one of the estate planning objectives.
- *Preservation of family wealth*—The Harper family consists of several generations (parents, children, grandchildren) who may have different goals and interests in relation to the family business. An estate planning solution should be developed in order to align interests of all family members while preserving family wealth.
- *Achieving charitable goals*—An estate planning solution should provide sufficient resources and instruments for achieving charitable goals of the family.

Solution to 2:

- *Income and liquidity*—The Harper family has several members who rely on the family income; thus, investment solutions should provide sufficient ongoing income in the long term. The following investment products should be considered: dividend paying equities, fixed income, or a combination of the two. Investment goals should be documented in the investment policy statement of the family alongside the risk and return objectives.
- *Business succession*—John is looking to retire. The main business succession options he has are as follows:
  - Keep both management and ownership of the business within the family. This might not be a plausible option, however, as the only person with the working knowledge of the business is James, who is planning to leave the family business and start his own firm.
  - Hire an external manager and keep the business in family ownership.
  - Sell the business fully or partially to a third party, or list its shares via an IPO.

- *Control over assets*—As John would like to provide for living expenses of his children and grandchildren but is not comfortable with giving some of them control over the investment and distribution decisions, a discretionary trust may be used, which gives trustees the power to decide on investments and distributions based on the circumstances of beneficiaries. It is important that John select a current and successor trustee in a way that avoids creating any tensions within the family. For example, John could name himself a trustee and select an institutional trustee as a successor to make sure that there is no conflict of interest among the family members.

- *Wealth transfer in a tax-aware manner*—John and Breda should take into account available tax-free allowances prescribed by law, such as spousal allowances or gifts to relatives. They should also consider if it makes sense to pass some assets to their grandchildren directly and what the tax implications would be, such as a generation-skipping tax. Founders should also consider if it makes sense to sell the business outright or put it into the trust for capital appreciation to occur outside of the estate.
- *Asset protection*—A trust structure can be used to protect the assets from creditors. An irrevocable trust can protect assets from claims against the settlor, and discretionary trusts can protect assets from claims against the beneficiaries.
- *Preservation of family wealth*—Creating a family governance system will help identify and align goals of various family members as well as smooth the process of wealth transfer to the next generation.
- *Charitable goals*—As John would like to be actively involved in decision-making-related charitable activities and expressed desire to involve the next generations of his family, a private foundation is more suitable than gifting to charities. A private foundation allows the donor to make decisions on the causes to support and run various charitable projects. It also allows the family members to be involved. (In the United States, a donor-advised fund may also be an option.)

Cross-Border Estate Planning

Cross-border families and cross-border investments require special care and coordination of advisers in more than one country. A trust established by a resident of one country may have beneficiaries not only in that country but also in other countries where children may be living. Sound estate planning must consider the rules of each jurisdiction. Similarly, cross-border asset ownership must be carefully considered. Consider investors located in Singapore and investing in US equities. While they may not be subject to worldwide estate and gift taxation (as they would be if they were citizens or residents of the United States), they *are* subject to US estate tax on assets located in the United States. And, unlike US citizens or residents who enjoy a significant estate tax exemption, non-US deceased receive minimal exemptions.

Occasionally, wealth or business owners will consider moving from one country to another, possibly even changing their citizenship. The change may be motivated by safety and political risk concerns, by tax considerations, or perhaps by estate planning considerations. An increasing number of countries (e.g., Japan, Canada, the United States, and many others) impose exit taxes on those giving up taxable residence. An exit tax often takes the form of a capital gains tax on unrealized capital gains accrued during the period in which the taxpayer was a tax resident of the country in question.

7.3. Managing Wealth across Generations

Modern wealthy families are often very large. In addition to the main wealth creator(s) or business founder(s), they may include numerous siblings, children with their families, grandchildren, etc. Families may face behavioral and emotional challenges, such as generational conflict, sibling rivalry, or other tensions, which may adversely impact decision-making regarding the family business and transfer of wealth. When many stakeholders are involved, families may establish a system of family governance to ensure the effective generation, transition, preservation, and growth of wealth through time. According to Stalk and Foley (2012), the family-owned enterprise tends to decline by the third generation. The founder *creates wealth*, the second generation *maintains wealth*, and the third generation *depletes wealth*.

This is such a common phenomenon that many countries have a saying to capture the reality:

- "Shirtsleeves-to-shirtsleeves in three generations"
- "The father buys, the son builds, the grandchild sells, and his son begs"
- "Wealth never survives three generations"
- "From stables to stars to stables"

While 70% of family businesses fail or are sold before the second generation can take over their management, the decline in wealth across generations can generally be attributed to

- the dilution of wealth among a larger number of descendants,
- a lack of interest in the family business by younger generations, and/or
- a lack of education and planning by family members.

A strong family governance framework can mitigate some of these issues. The next section explains the concept of family governance, its purposes, and the associated governing bodies. We also address specific issues related to wealth transfer across generations in the families with wealth concentrated in a family business.

7.3.1. General Principles of Family Governance

Family governance is defined as a process for a family's collective communication and decision-making designed to serve current and future generations. Family governance is based on the common values of the family, which are defined collectively by all members of the family, and is aimed at preserving and growing a family's wealth over a long period of time.

Family governance serves several purposes, such as:

- establishing principles for collaboration among family members,
- preserving and growing a family's wealth, and
- increasing human and financial capital across the generations.

The family governance framework consists of formal legal documents, non-binding family agreements, and the list of goals and values defined collectively and agreed upon by the members of the family during the meetings.

Charles Collier, who served as the senior philanthropic adviser at Harvard University for 25 years, highlights several factors essential to effective family governance (see Collier 2012). These include the following:

- Focusing on the human, intellectual, and social capital of the family:
  - *Human capital*—the unique gifts and experiences of individual family members

- *Intellectual capital*—the knowledge of family members outside of the family business
- *Social capital*—the role of family members as philanthropists and leaders in their local communities
- Recognizing the importance of individual goals of each family member
- Improving communication within the family
- Defining a family's mission and vision
- Educating younger generations to master the competences and responsibilities that come with financial wealth

---

Common Governance Entities for High-Net-Worth Families

Families use a number of governing bodies for business decision-making, investments administration, and philanthropy. These are the most common structures:

- *The board of directors* is established when the family business reaches a mature stage and a larger decision-making body with addition of experienced outside experts is required. Adding external experts to the board of directors also helps mitigate an overconfidence bias, which may affect decisions of the founder in relation to expanding the business areas in which the founder has limited or no expertise. The board of directors consists of both family members (typically active in the business) and outside experts. The board of directors is responsible for establishing the direction and goals of the business and protects the interests of shareholders. Often, founders of family businesses establish an *advisory board* as a precursor to a full-fledged board of directors. This allows the founder to do a "trial run" to determine such considerations as board structure, composition, and governing policies as well as to become more acclimated to the idea of reporting to a board.
- *The family council* consists of selected family members. The family council represents the family in dealing with the board of directors. The family constitution—which defines the operating principles of the family council, its composition, and responsibilities—is created in consultation with the entire family.
- *The family assembly* is a forum gathering all family members. The assembly typically meets at least annually to discuss the business direction of the family-owned company. It serves the purpose of increasing transparency and preventing conflict among family members. It also creates a platform for using the human and intellectual capital of individual family members for the overall benefit of the family.
- *The family office* fulfills the role of an investment and administrative center for the family; it is responsible for investment management, accounting, payroll, legal, concierge services, and financial matters.
- *The family foundation* is a platform for focused philanthropy. It unites family members toward achieving common charitable goals.

A sound family governance system also serves to mitigate many of the behavioral biases that impede effective decision-making. If established at an early stage and with all family members recognizing the importance of regular communication and collective decision-making, it can be an effective value-added tool.

7.3.2. Family Conflict Resolution

Conflict resolution mechanisms are necessary in virtually all legal relationships and are commonly found in shareholder agreements and other documentation associated with shared ownership and investment. In the case of family businesses and wealth, addressing how conflicts will be resolved is also important. Conflict resolution can be particularly challenging in a family context.

For many wealth- and business-owning families, the starting point of conflict resolution procedures is the **family constitution**, typically a non-binding document that sets forth an agreed-upon set of rights, values, and responsibilities of the family members and other stakeholders. The approach to conflict resolution provided for in the family constitution can then become legally binding by being included in shareholder agreements, trust documentation, and in relation to family assets. While it is true that family constitutions and the governance approaches they provide are used only by families at the higher end of the wealth spectrum, the principles involved are relevant to all families. Merely thinking about possible conflicts and how they can be addressed is an important step in asset protection and succession planning.

7.3.3. Family Dynamics in the Context of Business Exit

Having a family business as the core of the family's wealth adds an additional layer of complexity. At some point, the founder must face the question of business succession planning: Will the management and ownership of the business be transitioned to a new generation within the family, or will the business be sold?

- *Transition of the business to the new generation.* Founders may allocate shares in the business to the new generation during their lifetime or after their death. The shares may be transferred directly or via trust. Control is an important decision the founders must make: Who will control the business after transition? A founder may choose to keep voting shares in order to retain power and operating control—transferring only non-voting shares to children in trust by gift or other methods. Alternatively, a founder may decide to pass voting shares to family members who are actively involved in the business and non-voting shares to family members who are not actively involved in the business.

As discussed earlier, the creation of governing bodies plays a crucial role in the smooth transition of the business across generations and its longevity. A board of directors with external members provides an independent perspective during the business transition and increases the chances of the business succeeding across generations. A family council with representation from each generation of the family helps to maintain communication between family members during the business transition. The family council also focuses on balancing liquidity needs of the family and capital needs of the business to ensure that the business remains competitive in the long run.

Both a board of directors and a family council may be prone to a *social proof bias*—the tendency for individuals to follow the judgment or endorsement of other members of the group without being fully aware of all the relevant facts.[2] One of the ways to

---

[2] "Social proof," a term coined by Robert Cialdini in his 1984 book *Influence: The Psychology of Persuasion*, is also known as "informational social influence." It describes a psychological and social phenomenon wherein people who do not know what the proper behavior for a certain situation is will look to other people to imitate what they are doing and to provide guidance for their actions.

mitigate the risk of a social proof bias is to ensure that the board of directors and family council include members with diverse skills and experience. The members should also actively contribute to the discussion by sharing information and knowledge on the topic.

- *Sale of the business.* Family businesses frequently have an emotional value to the founder(s) and family. Thus, when selling the business, the founder(s) may exhibit an *endowment bias*, overestimating the value of the business and refusing to accept the fact that it has weaknesses. This is likely to complicate sale negotiations. Private wealth advisers must manage the expectations of the founder to ensure smooth execution of the business sale.

  Exiting a family business involves far more than determining a fair value of the business. Other business, personal, family, and charitable goals are likely impacted by this significant transition. Capital gains and income taxes will be due upon sale. Cash flow needs post-sale may be affected, as will estate and charitable gifting strategies.

- *Considerations related to timing of business sale.* Many business owners will transfer actual ownership of the business to a trust or other vehicle well in advance of a potential business sale to remove any future appreciation from the estate of the business owner. A discount may be applied to the transfer value due to lack of control or lack of marketability, which may reduce the gift and estate tax liability.

- *Selection of trustees.* When using a trust as a wealth transfer vehicle, the founder must choose between an individual or corporate trustee unless co-trustees are used. Individual trustees who are close to the family may have good knowledge of the grantor and beneficiaries, including their values and aspirations. Institutional trustees may be better suited to ensure continuity for a multigenerational family and tend to have lower administration costs and broader skills and resources. The grantors may choose to divide responsibility, giving a non-trustee (e.g., a family member, adviser, or committee) some degree of control over the business strategy, investments, or distributions. The beneficiaries usually do not have direct access to trust assets; however, depending on the governing law and trust provisions, they may be able to participate in decision-making in relation to trust administration or trustee succession. A good practice is to establish regular meetings that include trustees *and* beneficiaries to improve decision-making in relation to assets held in the trust.

  The ability to replace a corporate trustee is important for multigenerational trusts. In some jurisdictions, a family council can directly control family trusts; in other jurisdictions, family councils may serve only as informal governing bodies.

  Private trust companies (PTCs) are becoming increasingly common. These are trust companies established specifically for the use of a single family.

- *Post-sale considerations.* The sale of the family business creates liquidity that can be used to establish a new business or a philanthropic entity. However, without advance planning, it may also result in the assets being dispersed among numerous family members, causing the business activity that brought family members together to disappear. With suitable structures put in place in advance (such as a family foundation or a donor-advised fund), the family may be united following the business exit by pursuing philanthropic goals. In this way, the family can increase its social capital, train the younger generations, and promote the family's values via impact investing. Founders who prefer to maintain control over distribution of the funds may specify the charitable causes that should be funded by the foundation or even provide a list of specific charities and funding amounts.

Irrespective of the chosen method for transferring wealth across generations, a robust system of family governance must be established to facilitate communication among the family members and a transparent decision-making process. Family governance helps to unite the family members around common business- or philanthropy-related goals and facilitates the preservation and growth of family wealth across generations.

EXAMPLE 20   Estate Planning for the Harper Family (continued)

John Harper (from Example 19) has decided to continue managing the family business and keep it under family ownership for the next several years until a decision on business succession is made. He created $10,000,000 of liquidity by selling some commercial property. He plans to use this cash to build a portfolio of financial assets and start working toward achieving the family's charitable goals. John would like to set up a family governance structure to help transfer wealth to the next generations.

Discuss the family governance bodies that would be appropriate for the Harper family.

Solution: The Harper family should consider creating a corporate governance system, which includes the following governance bodies:

- *Board of directors*—A board of directors with independent external members will help John to prepare for business succession and possible transition to an advisory role after retiring. The board of directors will also provide an external perspective on the future development of the business, potentially increasing the business value for a possible sale.
- *Family council*—A family council should include members of the family who are best suited to represent the family in discussions with the board of directors. The council members should be elected by all family members. In the case of the Harper family, the family council may include James after he starts his own business, as he has a good knowledge of the family business. It might also include Ann's husband, who has knowledge of corporate finance.
- *Family assembly*—A family assembly should consist of all family members and serve as a platform for defining family goals and values.
- *Family office*—As John is looking to create an investment portfolio and start working on charitable goals, a family office will serve administrative, accounting, and other purposes.
- *Family foundation*—John plans to be actively involved in charitable projects and would like to involve the members of his family; a private foundation is suitable for this purpose. The family foundation will help to unite family members around a common goal and develop the social capital of the family.

7.3.4. Planning for the Unexpected

Many other needs of wealth- and business-owning families come in to the tax minimization, asset protection, and estate planning picture. It is important to identify these needs and discuss them with the family.

It is usually possible to address a variety of needs within the same asset protection and estate planning structure. Interestingly, the greater number of needs that are addressed within the same trust, foundation, or other structure, the stronger the structure becomes. Many jurisdictions have general anti-avoidance rules that allow a tax authority to deny tax benefits if there is no commercial purpose to an arrangement other than to achieve tax benefits. For example, although a trust may be established in a manner that provides tax benefits, if it can be demonstrated that the main motive of the trust was to address succession issues or to protect against possible political risk, then the tax authorities will have a difficult time proving that tax avoidance was a primary objective.

7.3.4.1. Divorce

Marital laws vary from jurisdiction to jurisdiction, and a variety of rights are accorded to spouses. In some jurisdictions, rights arise only in relation to formal marriages. In other jurisdictions, long-term domestic arrangements may provide their own rights or rights equivalent to those that arise in a formal marriage.

On the dissolution of a marriage, financial arrangements between former spouses need to be agreed upon; if they are not, procedures are available to allow for the courts to intervene and make financial determinations. In the United Kingdom, for example, the general principle is that family assets are divided on a 50/50 basis on the dissolution of the marriage. While a court can deviate from this where it is considered to be fair and reasonable to do so, the even division of assets has made the United Kingdom an important location for divorces, particularly where a spouse is seeking to enforce claims against a former partner. (For example, a Saudi or Russian family may have a second home in the United Kingdom, which helps a spouse seeking to benefit from the UK approach to the division of family assets establish grounds for the application of UK law.)

An important consideration for wealth- and business-owning families is that matrimonial assets are not necessarily restricted to assets that may have been earned during the marriage. Inherited assets that are available to a spouse may be considered a part of family assets and are thus subject to a 50/50 division in the event of a divorce. While there are clearly good reasons why the United Kingdom and a number of other countries take similar approaches to the division of assets, this can have a significant impact on a family's objective to keep a family business within the family for multiple generations. Taking the risk of divorce into account is therefore critical, particularly given that in some countries as many as half of marriages end up in divorce. Trusts and other arrangements can provide protection for a family business depending on how they are structured and implemented.

In many countries, it is possible to have an agreement between a couple in relation to the financial arrangements governing their relationship, including the issue of divorce. Where such an arrangement is entered into before the marriage, this is usually known as a *pre-nuptial agreement*; where the arrangement is entered into after the marriage, this is usually known as a *post-nuptial* agreement. Even in countries where such agreements are not binding, they are often taken into account as guidance in the event of disputes on a divorce. And pre-nuptial agreements can be a good way to encourage open discussion about financial matters relevant to a marriage, which is often a good thing.

How and when pre-nuptial (and post-nuptial) agreements are discussed can be a very personal and sensitive issue. Many advisers recommend that the younger generation be guided from an early age on the benefits of pre-nuptial agreements. Some families, through the trust and other structures that are in place, require a pre-nuptial agreement as a condition of the benefit.

7.3.4.2. Incapacity

While it is very good news that people around the world are living longer given improvements in nutrition and medical care, living to 100 (as opposed to 75) has a major impact on thinking in relation to succession and related planning. For example, if a wealthy or business-owning individual dies at the age of 75, the children might be in their late 40s or early 50s, perhaps a sensible time to be inheriting from a parent. But what if the parent lives to 100? The children will likely be in their 60s, with limited opportunity to positively influence the family legacy.

Linked to this issue of increasing longevity is the sad reality that a variety of disabilities can arise when people live well into their 90s and over 100. Dementia is not uncommon in various forms, and good planning requires careful consideration early on of how the family and their assets can be well protected. Asking the many *what-ifs?* is an important step. What happens if the wealth owner becomes disabled? Who will make decisions? What if the wealth owner lives to 100? At what age should children have power over assets they inherit?

In the event of disability, decision-making on both personal health-related issues and business issues may be accorded to a guardian. The procedures involved for appointing the guardian will vary from country to country. An unplanned transfer of decision-making authority carries with it two primary risks: 1) the process may take an extended period of time, during which the affairs of the wealth owner are left in limbo; 2) the person given decision-making authority may not be fully aware of the business and family situation. Disputes in relation to guardianship are very common, creating both bad feelings and delays that can be harmful to the family wealth and businesses.

Living wills and durable powers of attorney are among the tools available to wealth and business owners to address what can happen in the event of incapacity. A living will is a document that is used to convey people's wishes regarding medical care in the event they become incapacitated. The living will is generally legally binding. A durable power of attorney provides a third party with decision-making powers in areas specifically addressed by the power of attorney, which may include both financial and medical issues. The power of attorney is "durable" in that it continues to be effective even if the grantor becomes incapacitated. Trusts and other vehicles can also play a role if well thought through.

EXAMPLE 21   Incapacity Planning

Astrid is a widow and has been taking care of herself for many years. Retired, Astrid has a modest financial asset portfolio that she keeps an eye on, but she also relies on the input of her private wealth manager. Astrid is also the beneficiary of a life annuity that was set up by her now-deceased husband.

Astrid has two adult children, Frank and Edith. Edith has strong financial skills and is well-trusted by Astrid. Frank suffers from alcoholism and has been in and out of recovery. Astrid loves both her children and has supported Frank financially and emotionally. Frank is more than happy to have Edith handle financial matters.

Astrid holds a strong view that she does not want to be kept alive if she is permanently incapable of taking care of herself without dependence on life support. She has shared this view with her children, but Edith has always laughed and hugged Astrid—saying that if it was up to Edith, she would keep Astrid alive forever.

As Astrid turns 98, she develops dementia. Issues compound, Astrid's memory fades, and she requires constant care. Eventually she requires mechanical ventilation in order to remain alive.

1. What tools might Astrid have used to ensure that her medical and financial affairs are conducted smoothly?
2. What other eventualities are not covered by these tools?

Solution to 1: A living will would allow Astrid to specify what types of medical treatment she would want in the event of incapacity. Because her daughter would "keep Astrid alive forever," a living will would allow health care providers to ensure Astrid's wishes are respected. It also relieves Edith of the psychological burden of terminating the medical measures that are keeping her mother alive. A durable power of attorney giving Edith authority to act on behalf of Astrid with respect to her financial affairs would ensure that Edith could assume those responsibilities without any delays and would also avoid any potential disagreements between Frank and Edith.

Solution to 2: Astrid has not addressed what kind of financial support should be provided to Frank after her death. In the absence of a will, the rules of probate in her country of residence will determine how her assets are divided among her children. Given Frank's alcoholism, his share of the assets might quickly dwindle to nothing, leaving him with no source of financial support. Astrid might have created a trust to receive Frank's share of the inheritance, providing some reassurance that the assets would be spent wisely. She should carefully consider whether Edith is the appropriate trustee for this trust, as Edith may be conflicted about continuing to support Frank and his alcoholism.

8. SUMMARY

Even the best private wealth manager will never have all the answers. An effective private wealth manager will, however, be in a position to ask the right questions and consult the right experts to help clients navigate an increasingly complex world. This chapter covers important points for managing assets on a tax-aware basis and managing concentrated positions in real estate and private and public equities. It also provides an overview of estate planning.

- Three foundational elements of investment taxation include: 1) taxation of the components of return, 2) the tax status of the account, and 3) the jurisdiction that applies to the investor (and/or account).

- Many countries' tax codes create preferential treatment for some types of dividend and interest income. Long-term capital gains are typically taxed at a lower rate than other forms of income.
- Income from real estate investments may be reduced by maintenance, interest, and depreciation expenses.
- Private clients often have a mix of taxable, tax-deferred, and tax-exempt investment accounts. Returns in tax-deferred and tax-exempt accounts compound using the pre-tax rate of return. Tax-deferred accounts pay tax only when assets are withdrawn from the account. Taxable accounts compound using the after-tax rate of return.
- Broadly speaking, countries may operate under one of three tax regimes: tax havens, territorial tax systems, and worldwide tax systems. A tax haven has no or very low tax rates for foreign investors. A territorial regime taxes only locally-sourced income. A worldwide tax regime taxes all income, regardless of its source.
- The Common Reporting Standard exists to ensure exchange of financial account information to combat tax evasion. The United States uses FATCA, the Foreign Account Tax Compliance Act, for the same purpose.
- Equity portfolios are often more tax efficient than strategies that rely on derivatives, real assets, or taxable fixed income. Higher-yield and higher-turnover strategies tend to be less tax efficient.
- The tax considerations associated with alternative asset classes are more complicated than those associated with stocks and bonds.
- Measures of tax efficiency include after-tax holding period return, annualized after-tax return, after-tax post-liquidation return, after-tax excess return, and the tax-efficiency ratio.
- Asset location is the process for determining which assets should be held in each type of account. A general rule of thumb is to put tax-efficient assets in the taxable account and tax-inefficient assets in the tax-exempt or tax-deferred account. The actual solution may differ depending on the strategy and the investor's horizon.
- It is typically better to make withdrawals from the taxable account first and then from the tax-deferred accounts. Under progressive tax regimes, it may be more tax efficient to withdraw from the retirement account first until the lowest tax brackets have been fully utilized.
- Tax avoidance is the legal activity of understanding the tax laws and finding approaches that avoid or minimize taxation. Tax evasion is the illegal concealment and non-payment of taxes that are otherwise due.
- Tax avoidance strategies include holding assets in a tax-exempt account versus a taxable account, investing in tax-exempt bonds instead of taxable bonds, holding assets long enough to qualify for long-term capital gains treatment, and holding dividend-paying stocks long enough to pay the more favorable tax rate. Tax-deferral strategies include limiting portfolio turnover and the consequent realization of capital gains and tax loss harvesting.
- The structure of the investment vehicle in which a client's assets are held may affect the tax liability and the adviser's ability to manage the client portfolio in a tax-aware manner. In a partnership, the income, realized capital gains, and realized capital losses are passed through to the investors, who are then responsible for any tax liability. In a mutual fund, the income and realized capital gains (but not losses) are passed through to the investors. The taxation of capital gains varies by jurisdiction.

- Potential capital gain exposure (PCGE) can be used to gauge the amount of tax liability embedded in a mutual fund.
- Exchange-traded funds are very tax efficient. Separately-managed accounts offer the most flexibility for tax management.
- Tax loss harvesting is a technique whereby the manager realizes a loss that can be used to offset gains or other income. Tax loss harvesting requires diligent tax lot accounting.
- Common methods of tax lot accounting are first in, first out (FIFO); last in, first out (LIFO); and highest in, first out (HIFO).
- A concentrated position subjects the portfolio to a higher level of risk, including unsystematic risk and liquidity risk. Approaches that can be used to mitigate the risks of a concentrated position include sell and diversify; staged diversification; hedging and monetization strategies; tax-free exchanges; tax-deferral strategies; and estate and tax planning strategies, such as charitable trusts, private foundations, and donor-advised funds.
- A completion portfolio is an index-based portfolio that when added to the concentrated position, creates an overall portfolio with exposures similar to the investor's benchmark.
- Equity monetization refers to a group of strategies that allows an investor to receive cash for a stock position without an outright sale. The investor can hedge a part of the position using a short sale, a total return swap, options, futures, or a forward sale contract and then borrow against the hedged position. The loan proceeds are then invested in a diversified portfolio of other investments.
- Donating the appreciated asset to a charitable remainder trust allows the shares to be sold without incurring a capital gains tax. The trust can then build a diversified portfolio to provide income for the life of the beneficiaries.
- Strategies to free up capital concentrated in a privately-owned business or real estate include a personal line of credit secured by company shares, leveraged recapitalization, an employee stock ownership plan, mortgage financing, and a charitable trust or donor-advised fund.
- Estate planning is the process of preparing for the disposition of one's estate upon death and during one's lifetime. Objectives of gift and estate planning include maintaining sufficient income and liquidity, achieving the clients' goals with respect to control over the assets, protection of the assets from creditors, minimization of tax liability, preservation of family wealth, business succession, and achieving charitable goals.
- An estate tax is the tax on the aggregate value of a deceased person's assets. It is paid out of the estate. An inheritance tax is paid by each individual beneficiary. A gift tax is paid on a transfer of money or property to another person without receiving at least equal value in return. Many jurisdictions have tax-free allowances that can be used for transferring assets under a certain threshold without paying an estate or inheritance tax.
- A will outlines the rights others will have over one's property after death. Probate is the legal process to confirm the validity of the will.
- Common law jurisdictions give owners the right to use their own judgment regarding the rights others will have over their property after death. Many civil law countries place restrictions on the disposition of an estate, typically giving certain relatives some minimum share of the assets.
- Common estate planning tools include trusts, foundations, life insurance, and companies. A trust is a legal relationship in which the trustee holds and manages the assets for the benefit of the beneficiaries. A trust can be either revocable or irrevocable. An irrevocable trust generally provides greater asset protection from creditors. A foundation is typically

established to hold assets for a specific charitable purpose. The founder can exercise some control in the administration and decision-making of the foundation.

- Life insurance and other forms of insurance can be used to accomplish estate planning objectives.
- Companies—specifically, a controlled foreign corporation—may allow the owner to defer taxes on income until the earnings are distributed to shareholders or until the company is sold or shares otherwise disposed.
- Family governance is a process for a family's collective communication and decision-making designed to serve current and future generations. Good family governance establishes principles for collaboration among family members, preserving and growing the family's wealth, and increasing human and financial capital across the generations. A sound family governance system may mitigate many of the behavioral biases that impede effective decision-making.
- Conflict resolution can be particularly challenging in a family context. A family constitution can help wealthy families anticipate possible conflicts and agree on a common set of rights, values, and responsibilities.
- Managing a concentrated position arising from a family business is more than just an investment issue. The private wealth adviser should be prepared to work with the client in succession planning and post-sale considerations, such as the loss of a key activity that united family members.
- Effective estate planning requires planning for the unexpected, including divorce and incapacity.

REFERENCES

Collier, Charles W. 2012. *Wealth in Families.* 3rd ed. Cambridge, MA: Harvard University Press.

Jeffrey, Robert H., and Robert D. Arnott. 1993. "Is Your Alpha Big Enough to Cover Its Taxes?" *Journal of Portfolio Management* 19 (3): 15–25.

Jennings, William W., Stephen M. Horan, and William Reichenstein. 2010. "Private Wealth Management: A Review." *Research Foundation Literature Reviews* 5 (1).

Lucas, Stuart, and Alejandro Sanz. 2016. "Pick Your Battles: The Intersection of Investment Strategy, Tax, and Compounding Returns." *Journal of Wealth Management* 19 (2): 9–16.

Marcovici, Philip. 2016. *The Destructive Power of Family Wealth: A Guide to Succession Planning, Asset Protection, Taxation and Wealth Management.* Hoboken, NJ: John Wiley & Sons.

Sialm, Clemens, and Hanjiang Zhang. (Forthcoming). "Tax-Efficient Asset Management: Evidence from Equity Mutual Funds." *Journal of Finance.*

Stalk, George, Jr., and Henry Foley. 2012. "Avoid the Traps That Can Destroy Family Businesses." *Harvard Business Review* 2012 (January–February). https://hbr.org/2012/01/avoid-the-traps-that-can-destroy-family-businesses.

PRACTICE PROBLEMS

The following information relates to Questions 1–7

Jevan Chen is a tax adviser who provides tax-aware advice to various private clients. Two of Chen's clients are Sameeha Payne and Chaow Yoonim, who are US citizens and reside in the

United States. A third client, LaShawna Kaminski, lives in a tax jurisdiction with a flat tax rate of 20%, which applies to all types of income and capital gains.

Payne is the founder and sole owner of Solar Falls Power, a privately held renewable energy company located in the United States. In addition to owning Solar Falls Power, Payne is also the sole owner of the property that the company uses as its headquarters. The vast majority of Payne's wealth is represented by these two assets. Payne's tax cost basis in each asset is close to zero.

Payne consults with Chen to develop a strategy to mitigate the risk associated with the two concentrated ownership positions. Payne's primary objective is to mitigate the concentration risk of both positions without triggering a taxable event while maintaining sole ownership. Payne's secondary objective is to monetize the property.

Payne is considering becoming a resident of Singapore, which operates under a territorial tax system, while maintaining her US citizenship. She contacts Chen to discuss tax implications related to the potential change in residency. She asks Chen the following tax-related question:

As a US citizen, if I become a resident of Singapore, would I be taxed (1) only on income earned where I am a resident, (2) only on income earned where I am a citizen, or (3) on all income earned worldwide?

Chen next advises Yoonim, who recently inherited shares of Steelworq from a relative who passed away. Yoonim's deceased relative was a resident of the United States, which is a country that uses a "step-up" in basis at death. The deceased relative purchased the Steelworq shares 20 years ago for $14,900 (including commissions and other costs). At the time of the relative's death, the Steelworq shares had a market value of $200,000, and Yoonim recently sold the shares for $180,000. Yoonim's capital gains tax rate is 20%.

Yoonim seeks to diversify his portfolio by using the proceeds from the sale of Steelworq shares to invest in mutual funds. Yoonim's investment adviser identifies three mutual funds, and Yoonim asks Chen to determine which fund will be the most tax efficient going forward. Selected data for the three mutual funds is presented in Exhibit 1.

EXHIBIT 1   Selected Data on Mutual Funds A, B, and C

	Starting Assets	Gains	Capital Gains Distributions	Losses
Fund A	$3,000,000	$300,000	$400,000	—
Fund B	$4,000,000	$500,000	$300,000	$200,000
Fund C	$5,000,000	$700,000	—	$500,000

Yoonim next asks Chen to evaluate Mutual Fund D, which has an embedded gain of 5% of the ending portfolio value. Yoonim asks Chen to calculate a post-liquidation return over the most recent three-year period. Mutual Fund D exhibited after-tax returns of 7.0% in Year 1, 3.3% in Year 2, and 7.5% in Year 3, and capital gains are taxed at a 20% rate.

Finally, Chen turns his attention to Kaminski, who currently has $1 million invested in a tax-deferred account earning 7% per year. Kaminski will sell this investment at the end of five years, withdraw the proceeds from the sale in a lump sum, and use those proceeds to fund the purchase of a vacation home. Kaminski asks Chen to calculate the after-tax wealth that will be available in five years.

1. The risk mitigation strategy that would *most likely* allow Payne to achieve her primary objective with respect to the Solar Falls Power ownership position is to:
   A. have Solar Falls Power conduct a leveraged recapitalization.
   B. obtain a personal line of credit secured by Solar Falls Power shares.
   C. establish a charitable remainder trust using Solar Falls Power shares.

2. A strategy that would *most likely* allow Payne to achieve both her primary and secondary objectives would be to:
   A. contribute the property to a donor-advised fund.
   B. obtain a fixed-rate mortgage against the property.
   C. engage in a sale and leaseback transaction involving the property.

3. The *most appropriate* response to Payne's tax-related question is:
   A. on all income earned worldwide.
   B. only on income earned where Payne is a citizen.
   C. only on income earned where Payne is a resident.

4. The tax liability on the sale of the Steelworq shares is:
   A. −$4,000.
   B. $0.
   C. $33,020.

5. Based on Exhibit 1, the mutual fund *most likely* to be the most tax efficient going forward is:
   A. Fund A.
   B. Fund B.
   C. Fund C.

6. The annualized after-tax post-liquidation return calculated by Chen is *closest* to:
   A. 4.41%.
   B. 5.62%.
   C. 5.92%.

7. The after-tax wealth in Kaminski's tax-deferred account at the end of the five years will be *closest* to:
   A. $1,122,041.
   B. $1,313,166.
   C. $1,402,552.

The following information relates to Questions 8–9

Private wealth manager Udaga Wacho is discussing a decumulation strategy with client Dogenza Ka. The strategy involves two of Ka's accounts, a taxable account and a tax-exempt account, and will allow Ka to withdraw $200,000 each year. Both accounts have a current balance of $1 million.

Ka asks Wacho if he should withdraw funds from the taxable account first until it is depleted prior to withdrawing from the tax-exempt account, or vice versa. Wacho reviews the accounts to make a recommendation; he assumes a fixed, pre-tax rate of return of 10% for both accounts and that earnings in the taxable account are taxed at a fixed effective rate of

25%. Wacho recommends that Ka withdraw funds from the taxable account first until it is depleted prior to withdrawing from the tax-exempt account.

8. **Discuss** why Wacho's recommended decumulation strategy is the more tax-efficient strategy.

Wacho and Ka next discuss tax loss harvesting and tax lot accounting for one of Ka's other accounts. Ka has recently built a position in shares of Hachiko Corporation; Ka's purchase history is presented in Exhibit 1.

EXHIBIT 1   Tax Lot Purchase History of Hachiko Corporation

Tax Lot	Shares	Purchase Date	Acquisition Price ($)
A	200	July 19, 20×2	122.00
B	200	Nov. 17, 20×2	135.00
C	200	May 9, 20×3	129.00

Today is 23 August 20X3, and Ka sells 200 shares. The current share price is $124.00. The tax rate for long-term holdings is 25%, and the tax rate for short-term holdings is 40%. A holding period of less than six months is considered short-term for tax purposes. Ka has chosen HIFO (highest in, first out) as his tax lot accounting method.

9. **Determine** the tax lot that would be *most* tax efficient to sell given Ka's chosen tax lot accounting method. **Calculate** the tax liability/benefit from the sale.

Determine the tax lot that would be *most* tax efficient to sell given Ka's chosen tax lot accounting method. (Circle one.)	**Calculate** the tax liability/benefit from the sale.
Tax Lot A	
Tax Lot B	
Tax Lot C	

The following information relates to Questions 10–13

Tesando Omo is a highly successful entrepreneur. The software company that he started five years ago is now worth $200 million. It is a private company, and he is the controlling owner, with a 60% equity share. His only other investment is a position in the publicly traded shares of his previous employer, which he acquired by exercising stock options six years ago. This publicly traded share position has substantially increased in value and is now worth $36 million.

Omo recently sought financial advice from Umae Jing. After discussing Omo's personal situation and financial goals, Jing expresses concern about Omo's current portfolio and points out several important risk and tax-related considerations that are relevant to Omo's portfolio.

10. **Discuss** four important risk and tax-related considerations that are relevant to Omo's portfolio.

With most of Omo's personal net worth tied up in his software company, he is asset rich but cash poor. Jing suggests three possible strategies that Omo could use to generate liquidity from the software company:

Strategy 1: Personal loan secured by Omo's company's shares without a put arrangement
Strategy 2: Leveraged recapitalization
Strategy 3: Leveraged ESOP (employee stock ownership plan)

Omo tells Jing that his goals are to avoid an immediate taxable event for him or his company and to maintain his ownership and control of his company.

11. **Determine** the *most appropriate* strategy that can generate liquidity and accomplish Omo's goals. **Justify** your response.

Determine the *most appropriate* strategy that can generate liquidity and accomplish Omo's goals. (Circle one.)	**Justify** your response.
Strategy 1	
Strategy 2	
Strategy 3	

Jing asks Omo about his plans for the shares of his previous employer's company. Omo tells Jing that he would like to use the shares to fund charitable donations and to provide income for his children; however, he is concerned about adverse personal tax implications relating to those goals. Omo indicates that he is willing to cede control of the shares to meet these goals.

12. **Recommend** a strategy, alternative to an outright sale of the shares, that will satisfy Omo's goals and alleviate his concern.

The following information relates to Questions 13–14

Enlow Surgical is a medical practice specializing in plastic surgery. Dr. Tuscarora Enlow, a surgeon and sole owner of the business, meets with wealth manager Horphey Hinkle to discuss estate planning strategies.

Hinkle asks questions to learn about the medical practice. Enlow indicates that he founded the company 30 years ago and has built up a large customer base while investing in modern surgical equipment and surgery centers. In recent years, however, Enlow has had to frequently defend against malpractice lawsuits that target both the company's assets and his own personal assets.

Enlow's medical practice also employs Enlow's son, who is also a surgeon. Enlow tells Hinkle that he wants his son to benefit financially from the company's success, but he is reluctant to give his son control of the practice because of a lack of business acumen.

13. **Discuss** two estate planning objectives revealed in Hinkle's discussion with Enlow.

Enlow wants to transfer some of his wealth to his niece and nephew but isn't sure whether he should use lifetime gifts or testamentary bequests. The present value of the amount that he wants to transfer to each of them is $50,000.

Enlow's niece has a high income and is an aggressive and successful investor. Enlow's nephew, in contrast, has a low income and minimal interest in investing. Selected data for Enlow and his niece and nephew are presented in Exhibit 1.

EXHIBIT 1   Selected Data for Enlow and His Niece and Nephew

	Enlow	Enlow's Niece	Enlow's Nephew
Effective tax rate on investment returns	37%	52%	12%
Expected pre-tax returns	6%	9%	1%
Tax on gifts/inheritances	—	47%/47%	33%/39%
Statutory allowances on gifts/inheritances	—	$100,000 (gifts only)	None

Enlow asks Hinkle to advise him of the most tax-efficient way to make each wealth transfer. For the analysis, Hinkle assumes that the bequests, if chosen, would happen in 10 years.

14. **Recommend**, for both Enlow's niece and nephew, the *most* tax-efficient wealth transfer option (lifetime gift or testamentary bequest). **Show** your calculations.

Recommend, for both Enlow's niece and nephew, the *most* tax-efficient wealth transfer option. (Circle one.)   **Show** your calculations.

Enlow's Niece	Lifetime gift
	Testamentary bequest
Enlow's Nephew	Lifetime gift
	Testamentary bequest

CHAPTER 17

PORTFOLIO MANAGEMENT FOR INSTITUTIONAL INVESTORS

Arjan Berkelaar, PhD, CFA

Kate Misic, CFA

Peter C. Stimes, CFA

CFA Institute would like to thank Karl Mergenthaler, CFA, for his contributions to earlier drafts of this chapter.

LEARNING OUTCOMES

The candidate should be able to:

- discuss common characteristics of institutional investors as a group;
- discuss investment policy of institutional investors;
- discuss the stakeholders in the portfolio, the liabilities, the investment time horizons, and the liquidity needs of different types of institutional investors;
- describe the focus of legal, regulatory, and tax constraints affecting different types of institutional investors;
- evaluate risk considerations of private defined benefit (DB) pension plans in relation to 1) plan funded status, 2) sponsor financial strength, 3) interactions between the sponsor's business and the fund's investments, 4) plan design, and 5) workforce characteristics;
- prepare the investment objectives section of an institutional investor's investment policy statement;
- evaluate the investment policy statement of an institutional investor;
- evaluate the investment portfolio of a private DB plan, sovereign wealth fund, university endowment, and private foundation;
- describe considerations affecting the balance sheet management of banks and insurers.

1. INTRODUCTION

Institutional investors are corporations, trusts, or other legal entities that invest in financial markets on behalf of groups or individuals, including both current and future generations. On a global basis, institutional investors represent more than US$70 trillion in investable assets, and, as such, wield significant influence over capital markets.

The universe of institutional investors includes, but is not limited to, defined benefit and defined contribution pension plans, sovereign wealth funds, endowments, foundations, banks, and insurance companies. Pension plans, which account for approximately US$35 trillion in investable assets or roughly half of global institutional assets under management, include both defined benefit plans, in which the sponsor (employer) assumes investment risk, and defined contribution plans, in which the individual makes investment decisions and assumes the investment risk. Sovereign wealth funds, which account for about US$7 trillion in assets as of the end of 2016, are government-owned investment funds that invest in financial and/or real assets. Endowments and foundations, which account for approximately US$1.6 trillion in assets, manage assets on behalf of educational institutions, hospitals, churches, museums, and other charitable organizations. Banks and insurance companies, comprising net financial assets on the order of US$9 trillion, are financial intermediaries that balance portfolios of securities, loans, and derivatives for the purposes of (i) meeting the claims of depositors, counterparties, policyholders, and creditors and (ii) providing adequate returns to their contractual capital holders. The universe of institutional investors is comprised of large, complex, and sophisticated investors that must contend with a multitude of investment challenges and constraints.

There has been an important shift in the asset allocation of institutional investors over the last half century. In the 1970s, most pensions and endowments invested almost exclusively in domestic, fixed-income instruments. In the 1980s, many institutional investors began to invest in equity markets and often pursued a long-term strategic allocation of 60% equities/40% fixed income. In the 1990s, investors recognized the benefits of diversification and many made their first forays into international equity markets. At the turn of the 21st century, many of the world's largest pension funds and endowments further diversified their portfolios and increased investments in alternative asset classes, including private equity, hedge funds, real estate, and other alternative or illiquid assets.

Meanwhile, institutional investors have seen broad shifts in their strategic investment behavior. The trend toward Liability Driven Investing (LDI), long a mainstay of banks and insurance companies, has taken hold among many defined benefit pension plans, particularly US corporate and public pension funds. Sovereign wealth funds have amassed significant assets over the past several decades, and many have implemented innovative investment approaches characterized by active management. Many endowments have adopted the "Endowment Model" of investing that involves significant exposure to alternative investments. Meanwhile, banks and insurers must navigate a complex and ever-changing economic and regulatory environment.

In this chapter, we endeavor to put the numerous factors that affect investment by institutional investors into context. Section 2 discusses common characteristics of institutional investors as a group. Section 3 provides an overview of investment policies for institutional investors. Detailed coverage by institutional investor type begins with Section 4, pension funds, where we discuss various factors that influence investments, including: stakeholders, liability streams, investment horizons, and liquidity needs; major legal, regulatory, accounting, and tax constraints; investment objectives and key components of Investment Policy Statements; and, finally, asset allocation and investment portfolios that emanate from the foregoing factors and constraints. Section 5 follows the same approach for sovereign wealth funds, and Section 6 does the same for university endowments and private foundations. Section 7 covers banks and insurers and includes balance sheet management considerations. A summary of key points concludes the chapter.

2. INSTITUTIONAL INVESTORS: COMMON CHARACTERISTICS

For the purposes of this chapter, institutional investors include pension plans, sovereign wealth funds, endowments, foundations, banks, and insurance companies. As we will see in upcoming sections where we cover each of these six institutional types in detail, their objectives and constraints can vary widely. First, in this section we discuss important defining characteristics of institutional investors as a group, characteristics that set them apart from individual (retail and high-net-worth) investors. The common defining characteristics of institutional investors include the following:

1. **Scale (i.e., asset size):** The issue of scale is relevant for institutional investors because it may impact investment capabilities, access to investment strategies, liquidity, trading costs, and other key aspects of the investment process.
2. **Long-term investment horizon:** Institutional investors generally have a long-term investment horizon that is often determined by a specific liability stream, such as the benefit obligation of a pension plan, the spending policy of an endowment, or other obligations.
3. **Regulatory frameworks:** Institutional investors must contend with multiple regulatory frameworks that frequently vary by jurisdiction and complexity and are often evolving.
4. **Governance framework:** Institutional investors typically implement their investment programs through an investment office that often has a clearly defined governance model.
5. **Principal–Agent issues:** As institutional investors manage assets on behalf of others, principal–agent issues must be recognized and managed appropriately.

We discuss these five common characteristics in more detail next.

2.1. Scale

Institutional investors' assets under management can range from relatively small (e.g., less than US$25 million) to relatively large (e.g., more than US$10 billion). Smaller institutions may face challenges in building a diversified portfolio spanning public and private asset classes because they may be unable to access certain investments that have a high minimum investment size. For example, smaller institutions are less likely to be able to invest in private equity or real estate assets (i.e., property). Small institutional investors may also face challenges in hiring skilled investment professionals. As a result, they are more likely to outsource investments to external asset managers and rely on investment consultants. Larger institutional investors experience scale benefits that allow them access to a wider investment universe, and they can readily hire investment professionals. They may potentially manage part of their portfolios in-house if benefits outweigh costs. The largest institutional investors, however, may experience dis-economies of scale. For example, they might be unable to invest in certain niche investments like venture capital ("VC"). Given the huge asset size of investments under management, a small allocation to VC may not generate sufficient returns to justify the position (including due diligence costs). The largest institutional investors may also be unable to deploy as much capital as desired with some external managers as certain investment strategies are capacity constrained. External managers who want to avoid jeopardizing their ability to generate superior returns will close the strategy to new investors. To overcome these constraints, some of the largest institutions buy private companies, property, and infrastructure assets directly and manage their traditional asset-class portfolios in-house. Large institutional investors also face the costs of market impact given their sizable trading orders.

Rapidly growing institutional investors may experience high cash inflow relative to the size of their portfolios, which requires them to continuously invest inflows and to maintain the appropriate asset mix (strategic asset allocation). Ensuring access to investments capable of absorbing their growth in assets under management may be challenging when investing in capacity-constrained strategies, such as small-cap equity or venture capital.

2.2. Long-Term Investment Horizon

Pension funds, sovereign wealth funds, endowments, and foundations all typically have long investment horizons and relatively low liquidity needs. Cash outlays are relatively modest as a percent of assets under management, with net payouts typically around 5% or less. However, there are exceptions: For example, frozen defined benefit plans might be in a de-risking mode that increases their liquidity needs. Relatively low liquidity needs allow these institutions to invest in a broad range of alternative asset classes, including private equity, private real estate, natural resources, infrastructure, and hedge funds. Banks and insurance companies, however, tend to be much more asset/liability focused while operating within tight regulations designed to ensure adequacy of capital.

2.3. Regulatory Frameworks

Institutional Investors are typically subject to different legal, regulatory, tax, and accounting frameworks than individual investors. These frameworks define the set of rules an institutional investor must follow to qualify for reduced tax rates or tax-exempt status. Importantly, these frameworks and rules typically differ by national jurisdiction in which the institutional investor operates. Some examples of important relevant legal, regulatory, taxation, and accounting frameworks and organizations include the following:

- United States:
  - o Employee Retirement Income Security Act (ERISA)
  - o Pension Protection Act (PPA)
  - o Uniform Prudent Management of Institutional Funds Act (UPMIFA)
  - o Uniform Prudent Investor Act (UPIA)
  - o Freedom of Information Act (FOIA)
  - o Governmental Accounting Standards Board (GASB)
  - o Generally Accepted Accounting Principles (GAAP) set by the Financial Accounting Standards Board (FASB)
  - o Statutory Accounting Principles (SAP) set by the National Association of Insurance Commissioners (NAIC)

- United Kingdom:
  - o Pensions Act
  - o Finance Acts (various)

- European Union:
  - o Institutions for Occupational Retirement Provision (IORP) II

- South Korea:
  - o Employee Retirement Benefit Security Act

- Australia:
  - o Superannuation Industry (Supervision) Act (SIS Act)

- International:
  - o International Financial Reporting Standards (IFRS) set by the International Accounting Standards Board (IASB)
  - o International Organization of Securities Commissions (IOSCO)

Many relevant regulatory bodies govern and supervise institutional investors and their portfolios globally. The International Organization of Securities Commissions (IOSCO) is the international body that brings together the world's securities regulators, and it has 217 members. Ordinary members (127) include the national securities commissions or similar governmental bodies. Associate members (24) are supranational governmental regulators, subnational governmental regulators, intergovernmental international organizations, and other international standard-setting bodies. Affiliate members (66) include self-regulatory organizations, securities exchanges, and other financial market infrastructure and international regulatory bodies.

The key drivers of the legal and regulatory frameworks faced by institutional investors are investor protection, safety and soundness of financial institutions, and integrity of financial markets. Changes to these frameworks following the 2007–2009 global financial crisis focused on leverage limits, enhanced collateral requirements, increased liquidity requirements, central clearing, proprietary trading limits, private equity limits, trading tax implementation, brokerage fee limits, compensation limits, and requirements for more transparent reporting. Examples of regulations focusing on such reforms include the following:

- United States:
  - o Dodd-Frank Wall Street Reform and Consumer Protection Act (Dodd-Frank)
  - o Section 619 (12 U.S.C. Section 1851) of the Dodd-Frank Act (Volcker Rule)
  - o Foreign Account Tax Compliance Act (FATCA), which has international implications

- United Kingdom:
  - o Retail Distribution Review (RDR)

- European Union (with most adopted by the United Kingdom):
  - o Undertakings for the Collective Investment of Transferable Securities V (UCITS V)
  - o Alternative Investment Fund Managers Directive (AIFMD)
  - o Solvency II Directive (Solvency II)
  - o Markets in Financial Instruments Directive II (MIFID II)
  - o European Market Infrastructure Regulation (EMIR)
  - o Financial Transaction Tax (FTT)
  - o Packaged Retail Investment and Insurance Products (PRIIPs)

- International:
  - o Third Basel Accord / Capital Requirements Directive (Basel III / CRD IV)
  - o Santiago Principles (Generally Accepted Principles and Practices for Sovereign Wealth Funds)
  - o Principles of the Linaburg-Maduell Transparency Index (Sovereign Wealth Funds)

2.4. Governance Framework

Institutional investors typically operate under a formal governance structure. The governance structure generally includes a board of directors and an investment committee. The board may comprise company representative directors, employee representative directors, and independent directors. Independent directors are usually selected to increase the board's overall investment expertise. Investment committees can be sub-committees of the board with delegated authority to oversee investment policy. Alternatively, investment committees can be internal and consist of investment staff tasked with implementing the investment policy set by the board. The board and/or investment committee provide a key role in establishing the organization's investment policy, defining the risk appetite, setting the investment strategy, and monitoring the investment performance.

The board often sets the long-term strategic asset allocation and can delegate the setting of medium-term tactical asset allocation to its investment staff. It may also delegate manager selection to investment staff. Notably though, many institutional investor boards will seek to retain control through overseeing hiring and firing of managers. Best practice suggests, however, that it is better to delegate the hiring and firing of external managers to investment staff to ensure that the board focuses on such broader issues as governance, investment policy, and strategic asset allocation.

Institutional investors typically implement their investment strategy through an investment office. The investment office can be structured in different ways, but the most common model involves a Chief Investment Officer, who is supported by a team of asset-class specialists or a team of generalists working across asset classes. Institutional investors may manage investments in-house (e.g., some large Canadian pension plans and Australian superannuation funds) or outsource investment management partially or entirely to external asset managers. The factors affecting the decision to manage assets internally include the size of assets under management, capability of internal resources, or a desire to pursue custom strategies not readily offered by external managers. It can be costly to build the capability to manage assets internally, so in most cases asset owners need to achieve a certain threshold of assets under management before the benefits outweigh the costs of internalization.

For pension funds, sovereign wealth funds, endowments, and foundations, outsourcing elements of the investment function to external asset managers—or even outsourcing the entire investment operation to an outsourced chief investment officer (CIO) firm—is much more common than managing investments in-house. Such asset owners typically rely on specialized consultants to assist with asset allocation decisions and investment manager selection. These consultants often provide macro-economic forecasts and capital market assumptions for asset classes that are integral to determining the investor's optimal asset allocation. In addition, the consultant assists in monitoring the large universe of external asset managers. Finally, the consultant may provide independent performance attribution and reporting and may monitor any internally managed investments and benchmark them against the external asset manager universe.

In contrast, banks and insurance companies undertake most of their investing, risk budgeting, compliance, and balance sheet management activities internally.

2.5. Principal–Agent Issues

Institutional investors frequently experience conflicts of interest that stem from principal–agent issues. The principal–agent issue arises if one person, the agent, makes decisions on behalf of another person or institution, the principal, and their interests are not aligned. A dilemma exists for the agent when he/she may be motivated to act in his/her own best interests and not in the best interests of the principal. Because of operational and investment complexity, institutional investors generally rely on various parties (i.e., agents) to act on their behalf. Agents may be internal or external. Internal agents include investment committee members and investment staff. External agents include third-party asset managers, broker/dealers, consultants, and board members. A typical example of the principal–agent problem is where performance fee structures are designed by external fund managers to provide attractive compensation to them via a high base fee, which is due regardless of fund performance. This fee structure gives little incentive for the fund manager to produce superior performance. Such fee arrangements are common among hedge funds and have led to greater demand for fee transparency and alignment of interest between hedge fund managers and their clients. To manage principal–agent issues, institutional investors will typically have highly developed governance models and high levels of accountability with a board and/or investment committee typically overseeing the investment office. Such models should be designed to explicitly acknowledge and manage conflicts of interest and align the interests of all agents with those of the principals.

3. OVERVIEW OF INVESTMENT POLICY

Institutional investors codify their mission, investment objectives, and guidelines in an Investment Policy Statement (IPS). The IPS establishes policies and procedures for the effective administration and management of the institutional assets. A well-crafted IPS can help minimize principal–agent challenges by providing clear guidance on day-to-day management of the assets. Besides mission and investment objectives (i.e., return and risk tolerance), the IPS should cover any constraints that affect the asset allocation, asset allocation policy with ranges and asset class benchmarks, rebalancing policy, guidelines affecting the implementation of the asset allocation policy, and reporting requirements. The IPS should be reviewed annually; however, revisions should be infrequent, such as when material changes occur in investor circumstances and/or the market environment, as the IPS serves as the foundation for the investment program. The asset allocation policy and investment guidelines are typically included in an appendix that can be modified more easily.

Investment objectives flow from the organization's overall mission. For banks and insurance companies, the investment objective is to maximize net present value by balancing (i) the expected returns on assets, (ii) the expected cost of liabilities, (iii) the overall risks of assets and liabilities, and (iv) the economic relationships between and among assets and liabilities.

The investment objectives are more straightforward for the other types of institutions covered in this chapter. For example, the overall objective of a DB pension fund might be to maintain a funded ratio in excess of 100%; for an endowment, it may be to maintain long-term purchasing power while providing needed financial support to its university. Investment objectives are typically expressed as a desired return target over the medium-to-long term (which should be clearly specified) with an acceptable level of risk. This return target should be evaluated in the context of the organization's overall mission and should be tied to the evaluation of liabilities (e.g., discount rate used to value DB pension plan liabilities or spending rate for an endowment). When expressing the return target in real terms, the relevant inflation metric must be defined. For example, GIC—Singapore's sovereign wealth fund—uses global inflation defined as G3 (the US, Japan, and Eurozone) inflation, while some US endowments use the Higher Education Price Index (HEPI) published by Commonfund (an independent asset management firm serving non-profit organizations and promoting best practices among institutional investors).

Investment objectives and return targets must be consistent with an organization's risk tolerance and other constraints. Risk tolerance can be expressed in different ways, such as for:

- DB pension funds: surplus volatility (standard deviation of asset returns in excess of liability returns);
- Sovereign wealth funds (SWFs): probability of investment losses (or probability of not maintaining purchasing power) over a certain time period;
- Endowments and foundations: volatility of total returns (standard deviation of total returns); and
- Banks and insurance companies: value at risk (VaR) or conditional VaR (CVaR) and comprehensive, scenario-based stress tests.

Finally, constraints (legal, regulatory, tax, and accounting) have a bearing on investment objectives and should be incorporated into the design of an investment policy. For example, constraints might limit the scope of acceptable risk and available asset classes.

Once the investment objectives—the desired risk and return characteristics—have been established, a strategic asset allocation or policy portfolio is designed. The investment portfolio of an institutional investor is designed to meet its objectives and should reflect the appropriate risk and liquidity considerations addressed in the IPS. For example, a large allocation to private equity is probably not appropriate for institutions with a relatively short investment horizon and high liquidity requirements. Similarly, a large fixed-income allocation might not be appropriate for an institution with a long investment horizon and low liquidity requirements. While institutional investors each have unique liability characteristics, several investment approaches have emerged over the past couple of years. Broadly speaking, these can be grouped into four different approaches:

1. **Norway Model** popularized by Norway's global pension fund, Government Pension Fund Global (GPFG). The Norway model is characterized by an almost exclusive reliance on public equities and fixed income (the traditional 60/40 equity/bond model falls under the Norway model), with largely passively managed assets and with very little to no allocation to alternative investments. Investments are usually managed with tight tracking error limits. The advantages of this approach are that investment costs/fees are low, investments are transparent, the risk of poor manager selection is low, and there is little complexity for a governing board. The disadvantage is that there is limited potential for value-added (i.e., alpha from security selection skills) above market returns. However, Norway's GPFG has begun to seek additional value over market-capitalization benchmarks by attempting to capture systematic risk factors.

2. **Endowment Model** popularized by the Yale Endowment. The endowment model is characterized by a high allocation to alternative investments (private investments and hedge funds), significant active management, and externally managed assets. This investment approach stands in almost direct contrast to the Norway model. Although labeled 'endowment model,' this investment approach is not only followed by many university endowments and foundations but also by several sovereign wealth funds and defined benefit pension funds. The endowment model is appropriate for institutional investors that have a long-term investment horizon, high risk tolerance, relatively small liquidity needs, and skill in sourcing alternative investments (the nature of alternative investments is such that there is large variation between the worst and best performing asset managers, and selecting the right manager is therefore critically important). The endowment model is difficult to implement for small institutional investors as they might not be able to access high quality managers. It might also be difficult to implement for very large institutional investors because of their very large footprint. The endowment model is more expensive in terms of costs/fees compared to the Norway model.

3. **Canada Model** popularized by the Canada Pension Plan Investment Board (CPPIB). The Canada model, just like the endowment model, is characterized by a high allocation to alternatives. Unlike the endowment model, however, the Canada model relies more on internally managed assets. The innovative features of the Canada model are the: a) reference portfolio, b) total portfolio approach, and c) active management. The reference portfolio is a passive mix of public equities, fixed income, and cash that represents a cheap and easily implementable portfolio that is expected to achieve the long-term expected return consistent with the institution's investment objectives and risk appetite. The reference portfolio effectively defines a transparent, risk-equivalent benchmark for the investment portfolio, and serves as a low-cost alternative to the fund's actual portfolio. The reference portfolio might be different from the institution's strategic asset allocation or policy portfolio. Importantly, the reference portfolio is typically made up of only publicly traded securities (in the form of common public market indices in equities and fixed income) that can be more easily understood by the governing board, while the strategic asset allocation may include target allocations to private markets and hedge funds. The total portfolio approach is the method of constructing the portfolio to ensure that planned risk exposures at the total portfolio level are maintained as individual investments enter, leave, or change in value. It is an approach that is aimed at minimizing the unintended exposures and uncompensated risks that may arise as added value is sought by extending investments beyond the reference portfolio. For example, if private equity is added, management considers that it is leveraged equity and as a result the exposure to public equities needs to be reduced by more than the proposed allocation to private equity and the allocation to fixed-income needs to be increased to offset the leverage. Although the Canada model starts with a passive reference portfolio, it is important to note that the Canada model employs active management from tilting asset allocation through to stock selection. A good example of a sovereign wealth fund that has embraced the concept of the reference portfolio is the New Zealand Superannuation Fund.

4. **Liability Driven Investing (LDI) Model** has gained significant importance, particularly among corporate defined benefit pension plans in the United States, although some of the European pension funds—particularly in Denmark and in the Netherlands—adopted the LDI concept even prior to the 2007–2009 global financial crisis. In the LDI model,

the primary investment objective is to generate returns sufficient to cover liabilities. As such, the investor's focus shifts away from operating in an asset-only context, to a focus on maximizing expected surplus return (excess return of assets over liabilities) and managing surplus volatility. Although the implementation and resultant asset allocation may vary significantly, LDI portfolios—other than for banks and insurance institutions—typically have a significant exposure to long duration fixed-income securities. In some LDI implementations, institutional investors separate their portfolios into a hedging portfolio (this portfolio usually hedges the main risk factor in the liabilities, which is interest rate risk) and a return-generating portfolio (this portfolio needs to generate sufficient returns to offset the growth rate of liabilities, other than changes in the discount rate). The hedging portfolio for defined benefit pension funds, sovereign wealth funds, and endowments/ foundations usually consists of long duration fixed-income securities and may entail the use of derivatives, such as interest rate swaps, to extend the duration of the portfolio. The return-generating portfolio usually includes public equities and alternative investments.

Exhibit 1 summarizes these four investment approaches.

EXHIBIT 1   Common Investment Approaches Used by Institutional Investors

Investment Approach	Description
Norway Model	Traditional style characterized by 60%/40% equity/fixed-income allocation, few alternatives, largely passive investments, tight tracking error limits, and benchmark as a starting position. *Pros*: Low cost, transparent, suitable for large scale, easy for board to understand. *Cons*: Limited value-added potential.
Endowment Model	Characterized by high alternatives exposure, active management, and outsourcing. *Pros*: High value-added potential. *Cons*: Expensive and difficult to implement for most sovereign wealth funds because of their large asset sizes.
Canada Model	Characterized by high alternatives exposure, active management, and insourcing. *Pros*: High value-added potential and development of internal capabilities. *Cons*: Potentially expensive and difficult to manage.
LDI Model	Characterized by focus on hedging liabilities and interest rate risk including via duration-matched, fixed-income exposure. A growth component in the return-generating portfolio is also typical (exceptions being bank and insurance company portfolios). *Pros*: Explicit recognition of liabilities as part of the investment process. *Cons*: Certain risks (e.g., longevity risk, inflation risk) may not be hedged.

4. PENSION FUNDS

Pension funds are long-term saving and investment plans designed to accumulate sufficient assets to provide for the financial needs of retirees. There are two main types of pension plans:

defined benefit, in which a plan sponsor commits to paying a specified retirement benefit, and **defined contribution**, in which contributions are defined but the ultimate retirement benefit is not specified or guaranteed by the plan sponsor. Globally, there are many variations and nuances of these two broad categories of pension plans. Exhibit 2 compares the key features of defined benefit and defined contribution pension plans.

Pension funds are significant players in the global investment landscape. Over the past 20 years, there has been a move away from defined benefit (DB) plans (especially non-government DB plans) to defined contribution (DC) plans. Among drivers of this shift are DC plans' lower financial risk for plan sponsors, absence of risk of becoming underfunded, and ease of portability (simplifies job mobility). Willis Towers Watson reports in its "Global Pension Assets Study 2018" covering the seven largest pension markets, the "P7" (Australia, Canada, Japan, the Netherlands, Switzerland, the United Kingdom, and the United States)

EXHIBIT 2   Comparison of Defined Benefit and Defined Contribution Pension Plan Features

Characteristics/ Features	Defined Benefit Pension Plan	Defined Contribution Pension Plan
Benefit payments	Benefit payouts are defined by a contract between the employee and the pension plan (payouts are often calculated as a percentage of salary).	Benefit payouts are determined by the performance of investments selected by the participant.
Contributions	The employer is the primary contributor, though the employee may contribute as well. The size of contributions is driven by several key factors, including performance of investments selected by the pension fund.	The employee is typically the primary contributor—although the employer may contribute as well or may have a legal obligation to contribute a percentage of the employee's salary.
Investment decision making	The pension fund determines how much to save and what to invest in to meet the plan objectives.	The employee determines how much to save and what to invest in to meet his/her objectives (from the available menu of investment vehicles selected by the plan sponsor).
Investment risk	The employer bears the risk that the liabilities are not met and may be required to make additional contributions to meet any shortfall.	The employee bears the risk of not meeting his/her objectives for this account in terms of funding retirement.
Mortality/Longevity risk	Mortality risk is pooled. If a beneficiary passes away early, he/she typically leaves a portion of unpaid benefits in the pool offsetting additional benefit payments required by beneficiaries that live longer than expected. As a result, the individual does not bear any of the risk of outliving his/her retirement benefits.	The employee bears the risk of not meeting his/her objectives for this account in terms of funding retirement. The employee bears longevity risk.

Source: World Economic Forum, "Alternative Investments 2020: The Future of Alternative Investments" (2015).

EXHIBIT 3   Split Between DB or Hybrid Plans and DC Plans in Select Countries (2017)

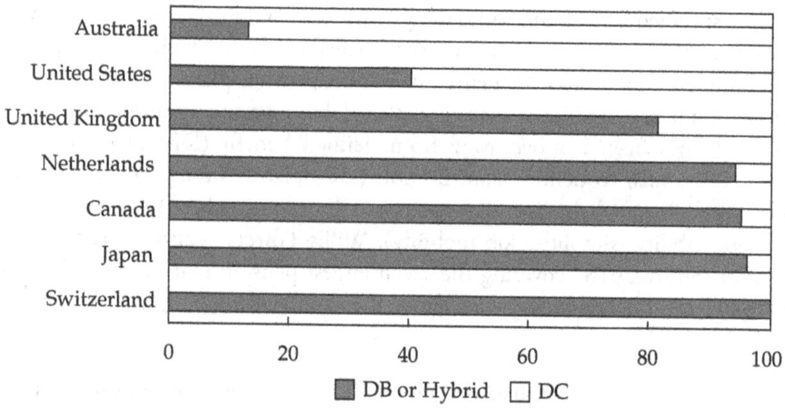

Source: Willis Towers Watson Thinking Ahead Institute (2018).

that during the past 20 years DC pension plans have risen from 33% to 49% of total plan assets.

The split between DB and DC plans can vary significantly from country to country. One of the challenges of classifying countries by this split is that many countries offer hybrid pension plans, such as that in Switzerland where defined contribution connotes a cash balance plan in which all assets are pooled and the plan sponsor shares the investment risk. There are basically no pure DC plans in Switzerland. Exhibit 3 presents the split between DB and DC plans for the P7 countries. Together these countries comprise more than 80% of worldwide pension assets. In these data, DB plans and hybrid plans are combined (as for Switzerland). Note that a substantial difference exists between countries. Some countries rely almost exclusively on DC plans (like Australia), while others predominantly use DB plans (like Canada).

4.1. Stakeholders

Many entities are involved with institutional retirement plans. These include the employer, employees, retirees, unions, management, the investment committee and/or board, and shareholders. Governments have generally encouraged pension plans as a tool to assist individuals to build sufficient financial resources to fund their retirement needs. Government support typically comes in the form of favorable tax treatment for both companies and individuals who contribute to or manage pension plans, provided they operate according to local pension plan regulations. The government and taxpayers will bear some of the shortfall risks (in terms of added welfare or Social Security payments) in instances of employers failing to pay agreed on defined benefit payments and where individuals fail to accumulate sufficient wealth for retirement.

4.1.1 Defined Benefit Pension Plans
The stakeholders of a defined benefit pension plan are the employer [typically referred to as the plan sponsor and usually represented by management and the Chief Financial

Officer (CFO)]; plan beneficiaries (employees and retirees); the Chief Investment Officer (CIO) and investment staff; the investment committee and/or board; and the government, unions, and shareholders in the case of corporate DB plans. Defined benefits promised to beneficiaries create liabilities for the plan sponsor. In operating the pension plan, the sponsor and investment staff must make investment decisions in the interest of the ultimate beneficiaries (employees and retirees). Defined benefit pension liabilities are typically funded from two sources: 1) employer and employee contributions and 2) investment returns on funded assets. Employee contributions can be fixed or variable, but employer contributions usually vary depending on the plan's funded status. Although each of the stakeholders has a strong interest in plan assets being invested appropriately, opinions might differ over the acceptable level of investment risk and the magnitude of employer contributions to the plan.

The plan sponsor may have an interest in 1) minimizing employer contributions due to budget constraints and/or 2) managing the volatility of employer contributions (by aiming for less volatility in investment returns). This allows management to plan future contributions with less uncertainty. Management and the CFO may also want to manage the impact of pension assets and liabilities on the sponsor's balance sheet. Employees and retirees, however, want to maximize the probability that plan liabilities are met and thus want the sponsor to make timely and sufficient plan contributions. Finally, the CIO and investment staff should be interested in meeting the investment objectives and constraints of the investment policy statement.

In a defined benefit pension plan, the sponsor bears the ultimate risk of the portfolio falling short of meeting liabilities. This risk manifests itself in the form of higher contributions from the plan sponsor when the plan becomes underfunded. In the extreme case of default, however—when the plan sponsor can no longer meet its legal obligations and cannot contribute further to the plan—the employee bears the ultimate risk and may need to find alternative means to meet financial needs in retirement. Some of this risk may be shared by taxpayers via additional Social Security or welfare payments, making the government a stakeholder in a defined benefit pension plan.[1]

The investment office of the DB pension plan is tasked with investing assets appropriately and may have variable compensation (bonuses) tied to investment performance. The investment committee or board will consider recommendations from investment staff, such as setting strategy and investment manager selection. In setting and executing strategy, all stakeholders' positions must be considered, including the sponsor's ability to make plan contributions. Ultimately, however, the board has a fiduciary duty to employees and retirees.

Finally, for corporate DB plans the company's shareholders are stakeholders. They are interested in the sustainability of the pension plan because if it is underfunded, any shortfall becomes a liability on the balance sheet, reducing the value of the company. Contributions to an underfunded plan also reduce net income. Underfunded status also increases financial risk, which may cause higher volatility in the stock price.

4.1.2 Defined Contribution Pension Plans

The main stakeholders of a defined contribution pension plan are the plan beneficiaries, the employer, the board, and the government.

---

[1]Some risk is also shared by other plan sponsors through agencies like the Pension Benefit Guaranty Corporation (PBGC) in the US. It is not funded by the government; rather, PBGC's funding comes primarily from insurance premiums paid by DB plan sponsors, assets of failed pension plans it takes over, and investment income.

A key stakeholder in a DC plan is the participant. Each participant has an individual account into which contributions are made on a regular basis—either by the employee, the employer, or both. Plan participants must ensure that 1) adequate contributions are made and 2) appropriate investment options are selected to generate sufficient investment returns. For a DC pension plan, the individual participant bears the investment risk of the portfolio failing to meet future liabilities (i.e., retirement needs). If plan participants outlive their savings, they will need to find other ways to meet their financial needs in retirement. In that case, the government (via taxpayers) may need to provide additional social welfare benefits, making the government another stakeholder in a DC plan.

Although DC plan participants control the investment decisions for their individual accounts, perhaps acting upon the advice of their financial adviser, the plan sponsor still has important fiduciary responsibilities, including overseeing the appropriate investment of plan assets (either by internal staff or by third-party asset managers or a combination thereof), offering suitable investment options, and selecting administrative providers. The plan sponsor, therefore, is an important stakeholder in a DC plan. The plan sponsor typically has an obligation to contribute to the DC plan on behalf of the employee as specified by the employment contract or through a government-mandated system. In some countries, a plan sponsor may also have an obligation to provide employees with a choice of different investment options within the employer-sponsored DC plan or even the choice of different DC plans. The sponsor typically must ensure that the investment options provide appropriate levels of diversification. It may also need to provide investment education and communications so that employees can make well informed investment choices. Running DC plans can be more expensive than DB plans given their increased complexity of administration and meeting regulatory compliance, all of which may result in higher fees for DC plan participants.

The board of a DC plan sponsor must consider the differing levels of sophistication among participants and provide adequate disclosure in communications to ensure participants are well informed. The board may be required to select a default investment option when participants do not explicitly make an investment choice. In such cases, the board has a higher obligation because by entering the default option, the participant is indicating that he/she either does not have sufficient understanding to make an informed choice or that he/she trusts the board of the pension plan to make the best choice.

4.2. Liabilities and Investment Horizon

4.2.1 Defined Benefit Pension Plans

The liabilities of a DB pension plan are the present value of the future payments it will make to beneficiaries upon retirement, disability, or death. Calculating DB liabilities is complex and typically undertaken by actuaries employed by the plan sponsor or by external actuaries. Here we will highlight some key elements and focus on the discount rate used in calculating the present value of future benefit payments.

The first step in determining DB liabilities is to calculate the expected future cash flows (i.e., retirement benefits). These depend on the design and specifics of the pension plan. Some of the key elements common among DB plans in the calculation of expected cash flows are:

1. **Service/tenure:** The number of years the employee has been with the company or organization (or service years) determines the defined benefit the employee is expected to receive upon retirement. The higher the service years, the higher the retirement benefit. Sometimes a minimum number of service years is required before retirement benefits become vested (i.e., the employee becomes eligible to receive a pension).
2. **Salary/earnings:** The salary or earnings level of the employee affects the calculation of the defined benefit the employee is expected to receive upon retirement. The defined benefit may be a function of the average earnings over the entire career or the average earnings over the last several years prior to retirement (e.g., last three years).
3. **Mortality/longevity:** The length of time that retirement benefits are expected to be paid to plan participants is important in calculating expected cash flows. This requires assumptions about employees' and retirees' life expectancies. Importantly, ever-increasing life expectancies is a key factor in making DB pension plans less affordable from the sponsor's perspective. Longevity risk is the risk to the plan sponsor that participants will live longer than assumed in the pension liabilities calculations.

In estimating future benefits, the plan sponsor must make several key assumptions, such as the growth rate of salaries, expected vesting, and mortality and disability assumptions. **Vesting** means that employees only become eligible to receive a pension after meeting certain criteria, typically a minimum number of years of service. In measuring defined benefit obligations, the plan sponsor must consider the likelihood that some employees may not satisfy the vesting requirements. Under both International Financial Reporting Standards (IFRS) and US generally accepted accounting principles (GAAP), pension obligations are determined as the present value of future benefits earned by employees for service provided to date. Assumptions about future salary increases, expected vesting, and life expectancy change over time and will change the estimated pension obligation. Given the importance of these factors, pension plans require periodic actuarial reviews to determine the value of the liabilities and the sponsor's annual required contribution rate.

Once expected future benefits are calculated, they must be discounted to determine their present value. Practices of marking-to-market liabilities using market discount rates can vary considerably based on country, or even within a country, between private and public pension plans. Typical discount rates include government bond yields or swap rates, corporate bond yields, and constant actuarial discount rates (long-term expected rate of return). Plan sponsors might be inclined to use a higher discount rate that will, all else equal, result in lower pension liabilities, a better funded status, and potentially lower contributions. Beneficiaries prefer to see a lower discount rate being used that will, all else equal, result in higher pension liabilities, a worse funded status, and potentially higher contributions. There is a delicate balance, however, because if contributions become unsustainable, the plan sponsor might decide to shut down its DB plan and substitute it with a less risky DC plan.

Over the past 15 years, a shift has occurred in many countries toward tying the discount rate to market rates. As a result, many pension plans have adopted a more liability-driven investment approach to partially or fully hedge the interest rate risk in their liabilities. Given the low interest rate environment since the 2007–2009 financial crisis, this has posed tremendous challenges for pension funds globally.

Discount Rates for Defined Benefit Plans in the US

In the United States, private and corporate DB pension plans may discount liabilities at rates based on high-grade bond yields averaged over 25 years. This was allowed under the 2012 update to the Pension Protection Act (PPA), part of broader legislation known as MAP-21. The change effectively raised the applicable discount rates (and reduced DB pension liabilities), providing some relief to defined benefit plans given what were perceived to be 'artificially' low interest rates. Prior to the PPA, corporate DB plans had to discount liabilities using current investment-grade corporate bond yields, not a historical average.

US public DB pension plans use actuarial discount rates which, as required by the US Governmental Accounting Standards Board (GASB), are based on the expected return of the pension plan asset portfolio. These are typically far higher than bond rates. The higher discount rates lower their liabilities and raise their funded status. However, this may cause such pension plans to potentially make inadequate plan contributions and take on excessive risk by investing heavily in equities and alternatives in hope of generating an expected rate of return that supports the high discount rate.

Exhibit 4 summarizes the key elements in the calculation of defined benefit pension plan liabilities.

EXHIBIT 4   Factors Affecting Calculation of Defined Benefit Liabilities

Factor	Impact on Liabilities
Service/tenure	Depending on plan design, often the longer the period of service or tenure, the larger the benefit payments.
Salary/earnings	The faster salaries or earnings grow, the larger the benefit payments.
Additional or matching contributions	Additional or matching contributions are often rewarded by a step change increase in benefit payments.
Mortality/Longevity assumptions	If life expectancy increases, the obligations or liabilities will increase.
Expected Vesting	If employee turnover decreases, expected vesting will increase.
Expected Investment Returns	In some cases, increases in expected returns will result in a higher discount rate being used—hence, lower obligations or liabilities.
Discount Rate	A higher (lower) discount rate results in lower (higher) liabilities.

The main objective of a DB plan is to have sufficient assets to cover future benefit payments. A common pension industry metric used to gauge asset sufficiency is the funded ratio, also known as the vested benefit index (VBI) in some countries. The funded ratio is defined as:

$$\text{Funded ratio} = \text{Fair value of plan assets/PV of Defined benefit obligations}$$

In some countries, if the funded ratio is less than 100%, the sponsor must increase contributions until it exceeds 100%. Improving the plan's funded ratio can transform the pension obligation from a liability to an asset on the plan sponsor's balance sheet. It is important to note that in some cases, underfunded pension plans may take more investment risk in the hope of achieving higher returns and growing assets sufficiently to return to fully funded status. In other cases, underfunded pension plans reduce investment risk and rely on other actions to improve their funded status, such as increasing contributions or reducing benefits.

Additional considerations in DB pension design are:

1. the size of the pension plan relative to the size of the sponsor's balance sheet; and
2. the cyclicality of the plan sponsor's core business.

If plan assets and liabilities are small relative to the sponsor's balance sheet, then there may be more flexibility in taking investment risk and more tolerance for volatility in employer contributions. If, on the other hand, plan asset and liabilities are large in relation to the sponsor's balance sheet, then there may be less appetite for volatility of employer contributions and hence a reduced desire for taking investment risk.

Another important factor is the core business of the plan sponsor. If the plan sponsor's revenues are highly cyclical, it will not want plan funded status to deteriorate when the core business suffers from a cyclical downturn. In such cases, the DB plan's asset allocation would be modified to ensure adequate diversification so as not to have significant exposure to assets highly correlated with the sponsor's core business or industry. In sum, it is desirable for plan assets to have low (high) correlations with the sponsor's operating assets (liabilities).

The plan sponsor's ability to tolerate volatility of contribution rates may impact the investment horizon, and hence the pension plan's appetite for such illiquid investments as private equity and venture capital. Another important factor determining the investment horizon is the mix of active plan participants (i.e., current employees) versus retirees. The higher the proportion of retirees (so the higher the liability associated with retirees only) relative to the proportion of active participants (or the liability associated with active participants), the more mature the plan—hence, the lower its risk tolerance. Some mature DB pension plans have been frozen (closed to new participants) as they typically experience negative cash flow where benefit payments exceed contributions. Generally, the more mature a pension fund, the shorter its investment horizon, which directly affects risk tolerance and the allocation between fixed-income assets and riskier assets.

4.2.2 Defined Contribution Pension Plans

In a DC plan, participants' pension benefits are based on amounts credited to their individual accounts in the form of contributions (from the employee and possibly the employer) and investment returns. Consequently, the liabilities of a DC pension plan sponsor are equal only to its required contributions. DC plan assets are typically pooled, and the sponsor invests according to the investment choices selected by plan participants. Often the DC plan may invest in a broadly diversified portfolio that may include investments not generally offered to retail investors, such as private equity and hedge funds. This is possible since pooling of assets gives rise to scale and the long-term horizon of the aggregate beneficiaries. In such a case, the plan sponsor takes on the residual investment risk of its asset allocation. Once invested in such alternative asset types, the DC plan sponsor bears liquidity risk if any event occurs that causes a significant proportion of its participants to exit the plan. The asset allocation may be impacted to such an extent that the plan sponsor is unable to provide the asset allocation promised to its participants. Such a circumstance will have regulatory and reputational consequences for the DC plan sponsor.

Individuals in a DC plan are at different stages of their careers, so each has a different investment time horizon (the time period from his/her current age until expected death or expected death of a spouse, whichever is longer) as well as different risk tolerances. Therefore, key considerations for most DC plans are participants' ages and invested balances. If the plan has a larger proportion of older (younger) participants with large (small) invested balances, the investment options might reflect a shorter (longer) investment horizon. Many DC plans offer investment options that allow participants to select the investment horizon that best aligns with their own investment horizon. Examples are life-cycle options or target date options, which feature a glide path that manages the asset mix based on a desired retirement date. In the United States, most DC plans offer target-date options as default options; in Hong Kong SAR it is mandated that every default option plan have a life-cycle option.

There are two main types of life-cycle options. **Participant-switching life-cycle options** automatically switch members into a more conservative asset mix as their age increases. There may be several automatic de-risking switches at different age targets. A **participant/cohort option** pools the participant with a cohort that has a similar target retirement date. For example, if a participant is 40 years old in 2020 and plans to retire at the age of 65, he/she could invest in an option with a target date of 2045 and the fund would manage the appropriate asset mix over the next 25 years. In 2020, the assets might be 90% invested in equities and 10% in bonds. As time passes, however, the fund would gradually change the asset mix (less equities and more bonds) to reflect an appropriate allocation given the time to retirement.

4.3. Liquidity Needs

Although pension plans typically have long investment time horizons, they still must maintain sufficient liquidity relative to their projected liabilities. Liquidity needs are driven by:

- Proportion of active employees relative to retirees—The former contribute to the plan, while the latter receive benefit payments. More mature pension funds have higher liquidity needs. Frozen DB pension plans, often facing negative cash flow, must hold even more cash and other liquid investments compared to open mature plans.
- Age of workforce—Liquidity needs rise as the age of the workforce increases, since the closer participants are, on average, to retirement, the sooner they will switch from the contribution phase to benefit payment stage. This is true for both DB and DC plans.
- DB plan funded status—If the plan is well funded, the plan sponsor may reduce contributions, generating a need to hold higher balances of liquid assets to pay benefits.
- Ability of participants to switch/withdraw from plan—If pension plan participants can switch to another plan or withdraw on short notice, then higher balances of liquid assets must be held to facilitate these actions. This applies to DB and some DC plans.

A pension plan with lower liquidity needs can hold larger balances in private investments—such as real estate, infrastructure, private equity, and hedge funds—and can invest a higher proportion in equities and credit. A pension plan with higher liquidity needs, however, must invest a higher proportion of its assets in cash, government bonds, and highly liquid, investment-grade corporate bonds.

It is important for pension plans to regularly perform liquidity stress tests, which may include stressing the value of their assets and modelling reduced liquidity of certain asset classes in a market downturn. Such stress-testing may also help DC plans anticipate whether participants might switch out of more volatile investment options during market downturns.

EXAMPLE 1   Comparing Defined Benefit (DB) and Defined Contribution (DC) Pension Plans

Geoff Albright is 35 years old and has been working at Henley Consulting in Melbourne, Australia, for 10 years. Henley Consulting offers a defined benefit (DB) pension plan for its employees. The defined benefit plan is fully funded. Geoff Albright's benefit formula for monthly payments upon retirement is: final monthly salary × benefit percentage (=1.5%) × number of years of service, where final monthly salary equals his average monthly earnings for the last three financial years immediately prior to retirement date. Having been at Henley Consulting for 10 years, his benefits have vested and can be transferred to another pension plan.

Geoff has been offered a job at rival Australian firm, Horizon Ventures Consulting, which is offering a similar salary; however, Horizon Ventures Consulting offers a defined contribution (DC) pension plan for its employees. Horizon Ventures Consulting will pay 15% of annual salary into the plan each year. Employees can choose to invest in one of three diversified portfolios offered by the plan sponsor— Horizon Growth, Horizon Balanced, and Horizon Conservative—based upon their risk appetite, and employees can elect to make additional contributions to the plan. The monthly pension payments will depend on what has accumulated in Geoff's account when he retires.

Discuss the features that Geoff should consider in evaluating the two plans. Please address benefit payments, contributions, shortfall risk, and mortality/longevity risks.

Solution:

- Geoff notes his benefits at Henley Consulting have vested and can be transferred to Horizon Ventures Consulting's DC plan.
- Henley Consulting's plan provides a defined benefit payment linked to years of service and final salary, whereas Horizon Ventures Consulting's plan provides an uncertain benefit payment linked to the company's and Geoff's contribution rates and investment performance of plan assets. The benefits he can achieve in Henley Consulting's DB plan increase both by time employed as well as by growth in his wages. Geoff considers his capacity to achieve wage growth and compares this to the return objectives of his chosen option in Horizon Ventures Consulting's DC plan. Geoff notes his risk appetite and time horizon are suited to the Horizon Growth option.
- Although Henley Consulting's contribution rate is not known, Geoff is aware that the plan is currently fully funded and that it is Henley Consulting's obligation to maintain a fully funded status. Horizon Ventures Consulting's contribution rate is known (15% of annual salary), and Geoff can also make additional contributions himself.

- Geoff notes that the shortfall risk of plan assets being insufficient to meet his retirement benefit payments falls to his employer in the case of Henley Consulting's DB plan. But, for Horizon Ventures Consulting's DC plan, the shortfall risk falls to Geoff and depends on the contribution rate (15% from the company plus any additional contributions he chooses to make) and the performance of his chosen investments.
- Henley's DB plan pools mortality risk such that those in the pool who die prematurely leave assets that help fund benefit payments for those who live longer than expected. Horizon Venture Consulting's DC plan pays out the amount accumulated in Geoff's account, and he bears the risk of outliving his savings.

4.4. External Constraints Affecting Investment

In this section, we take a high-level view of some of the legal and regulatory constraints faced by pension funds. In the next section, we consider tax and accounting constraints that may affect investing by pension funds.

4.4.1. Legal and Regulatory Constraints

Regulatory bodies supervising pension funds typically cover financial services licensing and regulation, prudential supervision, capital adequacy, market integrity, and consumer protection. Breeching key regulations may result in loss of operating licenses and/or loss of tax benefits, where applicable, which provides a strong incentive to comply. Regulations do vary from country to country; for example, some countries specify minimum and maximum percentage allocations to certain asset classes, while other countries require a minimum contribution rate by employers, particularly if the plan's funded ratio falls below 100%. However, despite national differences, there are similar themes in regulation globally.

Reporting and transparency are heavily influenced by regulatory requirements, as some regulators now require extensive reporting, not only on direct investment fees and costs incurred by pension plans but also on indirect fees and costs of external commingled vehicles. Drivers of more detailed reporting and transparency are avoidance of corruption by government officials involved with public pension plans and increased consumer protection for private pension plans so participants and stakeholders make appropriate investment choices. Many countries have increased personal liability for pension trustees to ensure they act in the best interests of ultimate beneficiaries. For example, DC plan participants must choose their contribution rates and the investment risk they are willing to bear. However, regulators are aware that many DC plan participants have little understanding of how to invest for retirement. Although regulators may require the plan sponsor to provide investor education to their employees, DC plan trustees, as fiduciaries, are still required to operate with prudence and as if they were the asset owners.

In Australia, for example, most employees are covered by the DC Superannuation Guarantee, under which employers must contribute 9.5% of an employee's salary. Since many participants do not actively make investment decisions, the government applies strict licensing and other obligations for trustees when offering the default option (MySuper), including: providing a single diversified investment strategy as a default option suitable for the majority of participants; avoiding unnecessary or excessive fees; and delivering value for money (measured by long-term net returns). A similar default DC plan account exists in the United States (known as the Qualified Default Investment Alternative), which must also be diversified.

In Europe the updated Institutions for Occupational Retirement Provision (IORP II) will lead to regulatory changes for pension plans. Although each country will interpret the provisions slightly differently, the changes relate to governance, risk management, and disclosure. A number of key functions are defined, such as an internal audit, and standards are applied to those executing these key functions, including a requirement that such a person does not carry out a similar function for the plan sponsor. Many pension plans will need to document their risk management policies and procedures. For example, each fund must document its "own risk assessment" covering items such as the risk of not meeting benefit obligations and operational risk, including administrative error or fraud. For disclosure, there will also be greater harmonization of pension benefit statements with certain items required to be included.

US corporate pension plans are subject to significant regulatory oversight. The Employee Retirement Income Security Act of 1974 (ERISA) regulates vesting, funding requirements, and payouts. ERISA includes a fiduciary code of conduct and required disclosures. ERISA established the Pension Benefit Guaranty Corporation, a US government agency that collects premiums from pension plan sponsors and pays benefits to participants (approximately 630,000) in terminated plans. Although ERISA protects benefits that workers have earned, an employer may still terminate a plan, essentially freezing a worker's ability to earn additional benefits. Moreover, the US Pension Protection Act of 2006 established minimum funding standards for DB plans, while later revisions raised the rates corporations could use to discount their liabilities (high-grade bond yields averaged over 25 years). Importantly, a potential consequence of using higher discount rates is these DB plans must generate higher returns for their funding status to remain sustainable, which typically requires taking on greater investment risk.

4.4.2. Tax and Accounting Constraints

Governments around the world encourage citizens to save for retirement by typically providing favorable tax treatment to retirement savings. Favorable tax treatment may come in different forms: reduced taxes on retirement plan contributions, favorable tax rates on investment income and/or capital gains, and lower tax rates on benefit payments drawn throughout retirement (versus higher taxes on lump sum payments). Foregone tax revenues from such favorable tax treatment are costly, so to ensure pension plans actually reduce tax burdens for retirement savers, governments typically place restrictions on plan design, governance, and investment activities in order for plans to qualify for the favorable tax treatment.

In the United States, 401(k) plans are tax deferred as participants make pre-tax contributions and do not pay tax on investment earnings; benefit payments, however, are taxed as ordinary income. To encourage savings retention within the pension plan, early withdrawals before age 59½ are taxed an additional 10%. In the United Kingdom, private pension plans are also tax deferred, with no tax on contributions or on investment earnings. The first 25% of benefit payments are tax free, and the remaining 75% is taxed as ordinary income after a tax-free personal allowance. In China, companies providing occupational pensions (known as Enterprise Annuities) are given tax relief amounting to 4% of wages; however, there are taxation differences between regions.

Pension plans taxed on investment earnings must be aware of tax implications of their investment activities. For example, there may be favorable capital gains tax treatment for investments held over 1 year, which should incentivize investing in lower turnover strategies. Also, pension plans must consider tax implications when returns from investing via futures and other derivatives are treated as income and taxed at higher rates than returns from investing in the underlying securities, which are typically taxed at lower capital gains and dividend rates. When investing internationally, double taxation may occur when the same income or capital gain is taxed both by the jurisdiction in which it is earned *and* in the jurisdiction where the pension fund resides. To achieve tax efficiency, pension plans should invest via legal structures that provide access to double taxation treaties, whereby taxes paid in the country of residence are exempt in the country where they arise (alternatively, the plan receives a foreign tax credit in its country of residence to reflect taxes withheld in the country where the income/gain arose).

Accounting treatment is another important external factor that drives investment decision making by pension funds. These treatments may differ across countries, so it is important to be fully aware of them. Here we focus on the United States to illustrate how accounting treatment may influence investment choices. Corporate DB pension plans must follow generally accepted accounting principles—notably, Accounting Standards Codification (ASC) 715, Compensation—Retirement Benefits, which requires that an overfunded (underfunded) plan must appear as an asset (liability) on the balance sheet of the corporate sponsor. Such plan sponsor must also report gains, losses, and service costs as part of net income. This accounting treatment significantly increased the transparency of US plans' funded status, and it prompted many corporate plans to implement liability-driven investing techniques to reduce the effect of funded ratio volatility on their financial statements.

Public pension plans in the US must follow Governmental Accounting Standards Board (GASB) rules. Under GASB rules, public plan sponsors must report fair market values of plan assets and can use a blended approach to valuing plan liabilities. The latter involves discounting the funded portion of pension liabilities using the (higher) expected return on plan assets as well as discounting the unfunded portion of liabilities based on the (lower) yield on tax-exempt municipal bonds. Using a higher discount rate for the funded portion of liabilities skews the risk tolerance of public pension plans and incentivizes them to allocate relatively large proportions of assets to equities and alternative investments.

4.5. Risk Considerations of Private Defined Benefit Pension Plans

Despite the long-term trend in the shift away from DB plans toward DC plans, as previously demonstrated, DB plans (and their hybrids) are still a key part of the pension landscape in several P7 countries, such as Canada, Japan, the Netherlands, and Switzerland. As such, it is important to review risk management considerations of private defined benefit pension plans—a topic that has intensified following the global financial crisis of 2007-2009. Key risk considerations of such plans must be measured and managed.

1. Plan funded status

   When a defined benefit pension plan is fully funded, the value of assets is greater than or equal to the present value of the liabilities. If the value of the assets falls below the present value of the liabilities, the pension plan is considered to be underfunded and the plan sponsor is left with a financial liability. The plan sponsor can take several approaches in order to minimize the risk of generating a financial liability:

   a. Seek to match assets to liabilities in terms of quantity, timing, and risk using a Liability Driven Investing (LDI) approach. Duration gap management or cash flow–matching suits plans that are close to fully funded and seek to maintain that status.

   b. Seek to grow assets at a higher rate of return than the expected growth in liabilities—which typically involves taking on more investment risk. This form of investment suits plans that are underfunded and wishing to return to a fully funded status. It may also suit fully funded plans that are seeking to lower their contribution rate over time and are willing to endure the increased volatility in funded status that this approach entails.

   c. Seek to invest in more defensive assets expected to deliver less volatile returns. This may suit defined benefit pension plans where the plan sponsor is willing to make higher contributions over time in exchange for less variability in the plan funded status.

   In cases where a plan is adequately funded, the sponsoring corporation may seek to remove pension-driven balance sheet volatility by engaging pension risk transfer through such mechanisms as:

   • offering lump sum payments to beneficiaries in exchange for voluntarily leaving the plan; or

   • negotiating a transfer of the risk to an insurance provider.

2. Sponsor financial strength

   When a defined benefit pension plan sponsor is not financially strong, there is a considerable risk that it may fail to make the necessary contributions to the plan. The plan sponsor may not be able to meet its defined benefit pension plan liabilities if there is a funding shortfall. If the plan sponsor files for bankruptcy protection, an underfunded pension plan is in the same difficult position as other creditors, having to join the queue claiming the firm's remaining assets.

   The relative size of the plan also influences the sponsor's ability to assume risk. If the pension plan is small (large) relative to the size of the sponsor, then volatility in pension assets, liabilities, and/or contributions will have a smaller (larger) effect on the sponsoring company's balance sheet.

3. Interactions between the sponsor's business and the fund's investments

   In the past, many private defined benefit pension plans have held significant stakes in the equity of the sponsor company. However, due to the risk involved, many regulators have restricted how much a plan may invest in the stock of the sponsor company. This risk materializes in circumstances in which the company performs poorly and its share price falls, thereby increasing the risk that pension plan assets fall below liabilities. This may coincide with a point in time when the sponsor's financial strength is poor, constraining its ability to make additional contributions necessary to address the developing funding shortfall. For this reason, it is advisable for the plan to diversify out of the sponsor company's stock. It is also prudent to diversify away from companies operating in the same industry, because their risk and return are expected to be highly correlated with those of the sponsor company's stock.

4. Plan design

   Poor plan design can contribute many risks for the private defined benefit pension plan sponsor. When setting out the formula for calculation of defined benefit payments, the plan sponsor must balance adequacy (will the benefit payment be sufficient to meet income needs in retirement) and sustainability (what contribution rate is sustainable, and what investment return can realistically be achieved) within the context of its risk tolerance. There is a significant risk that a company will be overly optimistic in predicting its ability to make contributions to its pension plan decades into the future. The plan design is informed by its purpose as an employee retention tool to mitigate the risk of losing employees to a competitor. The company/sponsor may also wish to increase future defined benefit payments to address worker unrest, which may otherwise lead to strike action or lengthy negotiations with unions. If a company does not have immediate excess cash flow, it may prefer to increase future defined benefit payments instead of granting immediate pay raises.

5. Workforce characteristics

   The nature of the workforce is an important risk consideration for companies because it impacts what the duration of the assets should be. The younger the workforce, the longer the duration of assets and the greater risk tolerance the plan will have. If a company's workforce has high turnover, it may have few employees whose entitlements to defined benefit payments will vest. On the other hand, if the average tenure of the workforce increases, then more liabilities will vest, thereby reducing the plan's funded status. If the workforce is older and nearer to retirement age, an important risk consideration is keeping sufficient liquidity so the plan can meet liabilities when they become due. Conversely, in a plan where the workforce is younger, on average, the sponsor may take on more liquidity risk. A workforce with a high level of vested benefits may constrain the company in terms of flexibility in managing its workforce. For example, a company may prefer to downsize its workforce, but doing so might require it to pay out excessive vested benefits.

   Retired workers also influence the longevity risk of DB plans. Longevity risk is the risk that an individual will live longer than expected and draw more in benefit payments than the amount determined in the calculation of plan liabilities. In private DB pension plans, longevity risk is pooled such that if a participant dies earlier than expected, he/she leaves more assets in the pool that can then cover additional payments for those who live longer than expected. However, this pooling of longevity risk does not mitigate the effect of rising life expectancies, which implies, all else equal, an increase in total DB plan liabilities.

In setting a risk objective, plan sponsors must consider plan status, sponsor financial status and profitability, sponsor and pension fund common risk exposures, plan features, and workforce characteristics, as shown in Exhibit 5.

EXHIBIT 5   Factors Affecting Risk Tolerance and Risk Objectives of Defined Benefit Plans

Category	Variable	Explanation
Plan status	• Plan funded status (surplus or deficit)	• Higher pension surplus or higher funded status implies potentially greater risk tolerance.
Sponsor financial status and profitability	• Debt to total assets • Current and expected profitability • Size of plan compared to market capitalization of sponsor company	• Lower debt ratios and higher current and expected profitability imply greater risk tolerance. • Large sponsor company size relative to pension plan size implies greater risk tolerance.
Sponsor and pension fund common risk exposures	• Correlation of sponsor operating results with pension asset returns	• The lower the correlation, the greater the risk tolerance, all else equal.
Plan features	• Provision for early retirement • Provision for lump-sum distributions	• Such options tend to reduce the duration of plan liabilities, implying lower risk tolerance, all else equal.
Workforce characteristics	• Age of workforce • Active lives relative to retired lives	• The younger the workforce and the greater the proportion of active lives, the greater the duration of plan liabilities and the greater the risk tolerance.

EXAMPLE 2   Andes Sports Equipment Corporation—Defined Benefit Plan

1. Frank Smit, CFA, is chief financial officer of Andes Sports Equipment Company (ADSE), a leading Dutch producer of winter and water sports gear. ADSE is a small company based in Amsterdam, and all of its revenues come from Europe. Product demand has been strong in the past few years, although it is highly cyclical. The company has rising earnings and a strong (low debt) balance sheet. ADSE is a relatively young company, and as such, its defined benefit pension plan has no retired employees. This essentially active-lives plan has €100 million in assets and an €8 million surplus in relation to the projected benefit obligation (PBO). Several facts concerning the plan follow:
   • The duration of the plan's liabilities (which are all Europe-based) is 20 years.
   • The discount rate applied to these liabilities is 6 percent.
   • The average age of ADSE's workforce is 39 years.
   Based on the information provided, discuss ADSE's risk tolerance.
2. Smit must set risk objectives for the ADSE pension plan. Because of excellent recent investment results, ADSE has not needed to make a contribution to the

pension fund in the two most recent years. Smit considers it very important to maintain a plan surplus in relation to PBO. Because an €8 million surplus will be an increasingly small buffer as plan liabilities increase, Smit decides that maintaining plan funded status, stated as a ratio of plan assets to PBO at 100 percent or greater, is his top priority.

Based on the information provided, state an appropriate risk objective for ADSE.

Solution to 1: ADSE appears to have above average risk tolerance for the following reasons:

a. The plan has a small surplus (8 percent of plan assets); that is, the plan is overfunded by €8 million.
b. The company's balance sheet is strong (low use of debt).
c. The company is profitable despite operating in a cyclical industry.
d. The average age of its workforce is low.

Solution to 2: Given Smit considered it very important to maintain a plan surplus in relation to PBO, an appropriate risk objective for ADSE relates to shortfall risk with respect to the plan's funded status falling below 100 percent. For example, ADSE may want to minimize the probability that funded status falls below 100 percent, or it may want the probability that funded status falls below 100 percent to be less than or equal to 10 percent. If a plan surplus is maintained, ADSE may experience more years in which it does not need to make a contribution. Indeed, a major motivation for maintaining a plan surplus is to reduce the contributions ADSE needs to make in the future. As such, another relevant type of risk objective would be to minimize the present value of expected cash contributions.

4.6. Investment Objectives

4.6.1 Defined Benefit Pension Plans

Defined benefit pension plans ultimately need to meet pension liabilities through a combination of investment returns and contributions. In practice, the investment objective of a DB pension plan is often to achieve a long-term rate of return on plan assets that exceeds the assumed rate of return used by the pension plan actuaries, typically the discount rate used in valuing pension liabilities. Importantly, targeting a long-term return based on the discount rate may be inappropriate in some cases. For example, when the discount rate is set using yields on government bonds, the target return is likely too low. In such a case, it may be preferable to fully hedge interest rate risk by adopting a liability-driven investing approach.

In determining an appropriate target return, it is worth noting that, ideally, the asset base should grow—through investment returns and contributions—in line with the growth of liabilities. If a plan is underfunded, the asset base must grow faster than liabilities. Because the growth of liabilities is met through investment returns and contributions (from the plan sponsor and/or employees), the DB plan's board and investment committee must consider the appropriate level of portfolio risk relative to the plan sponsor's willingness and ability to raise contribution rates should investment returns fall short of expectations.

In summary, the primary objective for DB pension plans is to achieve a long-term target return (usually defined in nominal terms) over a specified investment horizon (3–5 years or even as long as 10 or 25 years) with an appropriate level of risk that allows the plan to meet its contractual liabilities. The secondary objective could be to minimize the present value of expected cash contributions.

In setting overall investment strategy, many DB pension plans engage in detailed Asset Liability Management studies every 3–5 years. These studies include Monte Carlo simulations of thousands of scenarios for asset returns and factors driving pension liabilities (importantly, the discount rate) aimed at producing probability distributions for funded ratios and contribution rates at different horizons. These distributions are useful for determining key metrics, such as the expected funded ratio in 10 or 15 years, surplus volatility, surplus-at-risk, and volatility of contribution rates. Additionally, many pension funds engage in detailed liquidity modeling and stress testing that involve modeling contributions, benefit payments, capital calls for funding private equity investments, stressed asset values, and reduced liquidity of certain asset classes in market downturns. Besides providing an assessment of the appropriateness of the pension fund's liquidity profile, such stress testing provides insights into meeting liquidity needs during a financial crisis.

4.6.2 Defined Contribution Pension Plans

The main objective of defined contribution pension plans is to prudently grow assets that will support spending needs in retirement. Defined contribution plans usually offer a variety of investment options with differing investment objectives to suit participants of different ages, asset balances, and risk appetites. The investment options offered by the DC plan sponsor can be managed either in-house or externally as well as passively or actively. Most DC pension plans also provide a default option for disengaged participants. Plan trustees/boards must set an appropriate investment objective of the default option after reviewing the characteristics of existing default participants. Unsurprisingly, many DC plans end up with a balanced asset allocation mix as the default option—frequently in the form of a life-cycle fund. In cases where a DC plan provides participants a balanced asset allocation option with active management, a secondary objective may be to outperform the long-term policy benchmark consisting of the weighted average of individual asset class benchmarks and the policy weights defined by the strategic asset allocation. Finally, for some DC plans it is important their investment options outperform those of other DC pension plans, which is particularly relevant in countries where participants can voluntarily switch between DC plan providers.

Sample Investment Objectives of Different Pension Plans

Public DB Pension Plan:

1. The assets of Public Plan will be invested with the objective of achieving a long-term rate of return that meets or exceeds the Public Plan actuarial expected rate of return.
2. Public Plan will seek to maximize returns for the level of risk taken.
3. Public Plan will also seek to achieve a return that exceeds the Policy Index.
4. Public Plan will seek to achieve its objectives on an after fees basis.

Corporate DB Pension Plan:

The Trustee wishes to ensure that the Corporate Plan can meet its obligations to the beneficiaries while recognizing the cost implications to the Company of pursuing excessively conservative investment strategies. The objectives of the Plan are defined as: wishing to maximize the long-term return on investments subject to, in its opinion, an acceptably low likelihood of failing to achieve an ongoing 105% funding level.

Corporate DC Pension Plan:

The Fund currently offers a range of investment options to its participants and has adopted an age-based default strategy for participants who do not choose an investment option.

The investment strategy of the Fund is to put in place portfolios to achieve the objectives of its stakeholders over a reasonable period of time with a reasonable probability of success.

In establishing each option's investment objectives, the Trustee takes into account the average participant's age, account balance, and risk appetite. The participant's choice of investment option indicates his/her risk appetite.

For example, a participant selecting the growth option indicates a higher risk tolerance over a longer investment time horizon. The investment objective for the growth option is to build an investment portfolio to outperform inflation + 4% per annum over 7-year periods while accepting a high level of risk that is expected to generate 4–6 negative annual returns over any 20-year period.

4.7. Asset Allocation by Pension Plans

An examination of pension fund asset allocations shows very large differences in average asset allocations by country. Moreover, examining pension fund asset allocations within a country also typically shows large differences despite these plans seeking to achieve similar goals. Such inter- and intra-national differences are driven by many factors discussed earlier in this chapter, including the differences in legal, regulatory, accounting, and tax constraints; the investment objectives, risk appetites, and investment beliefs of the stakeholders; the liabilities to and demographics of the ultimate beneficiaries; the availability of investment opportunities; and the expected cost of living in retirement.

Exhibit 6 presents the average asset allocation of pension funds in the world's largest pension fund markets. The data are an aggregation of both DB and DC plans as presented (the split between DB and DC plans for each of the P7 countries is shown in Exhibit 3).

Note the category Other includes hedge funds, private equity funds, loans, structured products, other mutual funds (i.e., not invested in equities, bonds, or cash), land, buildings, and other miscellaneous investments.

The key observations regarding the data presented in Exhibit 6 are as follows:

- *Equities*: Equities provide a long-term risk premium over bonds and cash and are typically viewed as the asset class of choice for long-term investors, like pension plans because of the higher expected returns they offer. Traditionally, equities are also viewed as an inflation hedge, as opposed to bonds that do not perform well in an inflationary environment.

EXHIBIT 6   Pension Asset Allocation for P7 Countries (2017)

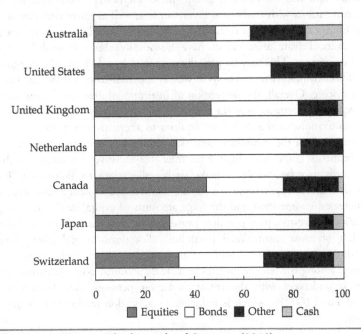

Source: Willis Towers Watson Thinking Ahead Institute (2018).

However, over the past decade, there has been a decrease in the equity allocation in several countries, particularly in Japan, the United Kingdom, and the United States. In aggregate, the resulting reallocation has been to the category Other, which includes such alternatives as private equity and debt, real assets, and hedge funds, as well as to bonds (and fixed income, generally) as DB pension funds have reduced their risk appetite to lower the volatility of their funded ratios. Australia and the US have the largest proportions of DC pension assets and also the largest allocations to equities. Although not shown in Exhibit 6, it is worth noting that the United States, Australia, and the Netherlands have the highest proportions of their equities allocations invested in their local markets. Given the size of the domestic equities markets in Australia and the Netherlands, this implies significant home bias.

- *Fixed Income*: Fixed income plays a defensive role in pension fund portfolios, because during times of financial market stress, equity markets and interest rates tend to fall. Fixed-income investments also help DB pension plans hedge the interest rate risk relative to their pension liabilities. Many regulators, in fact, require DB pension plans to hold a minimum allocation in fixed-income investments. Over the last decade, US corporate pension plans have increased their allocations to fixed-income investments, despite low expected returns, driven by the desire to reduce their funded ratio volatility. Conversely, US public pension plans have reduced their fixed-income allocations overall while increasing their allocations in the fixed-income space to high yield (riskier) bonds. The reallocation and repositioning are driven by the large gap that has opened between their expected rate of return and the yield available on long-term government securities.

- *Alternatives (Other)*: This category includes private equity and debt markets, real estate, hedge funds, and real assets. As a group, these alternative assets tend to have low, or negative, correlations with traditional investments as well as lower drawdowns. In the case of hedge funds, this may be explained by the lower volatility of these strategies versus equity markets. Private asset classes have historically also exhibited lower drawdowns compared to equities. This may be partially explained by a lack of fully marking-to-market because of limited market transactions as well as appraisal-based valuations that lag changes in market pricing. Overall, the perception of institutional investors is that alternatives can produce equity-like returns over the long run with relatively low drawdowns, which has been the motivation for the shift from equities to alternatives over the past decade and a half. However, given the complexity and skill required to manage alternative investments, these investments come with high fees; thus, fee-sensitive institutions with significant liquidity needs may be unable to make sizable allocations to alternatives. Furthermore, attractive investment opportunities in private markets and in hedge fund strategies may be scarce. Increased competition and the huge amounts of capital deployed on a global scale by institutional investors may put downward pressure on future returns. Although still a smaller part of most institutional portfolios, allocations to real assets have increased significantly because they are considered an attractive way to hedge inflation. Japan has been slowest among the select countries to increase allocations to alternatives; however, the transition is underway with the country's largest pension plan, Government Pension Investment Fund (GPIF), which is reducing its allocation to domestic bonds in favor of alternatives.

EXAMPLE 3   Asset Allocation by a Public Defined Benefit Plan

Susan Liew, CFA, is the chief investment officer of the Lorenza State Pension Plan (LSPP), a public DB plan. The plan maintains an asset allocation of 30% US equities, 30% international equities, 30% US fixed income, and 10% international fixed income. Liew's investment team developed the following long-term expected real returns for the asset classes in which the LSPP has traditionally invested. The outlook for US and international equities is slightly below long-term averages, while the outlook for US and international fixed income is well below long-term averages.

Asset Class	Expected Long-Term (10-Year) Annual Return
US equities	4.0%
International equities	5.0%
US fixed income	1.0%
International fixed income	−0.5%

Given the poor prospects for fixed income and the mediocre expectations for equities, Liew is exploring making allocations to various alternatives and has asked LSPP's asset consultant to provide comments on considerations for each alternative asset class, as shown here:

Asset Class	Comments
Alternative debt	Represents a diverse range of high yielding and floating-rate debt expected to return 300 bps annually over traditional fixed income (default-adjusted basis). The additional returns are compensation for increased liquidity risk in private debt, added credit risk in high yield and EM debt, and non-performing loans.
Infrastructure funds	Strong income-like characteristics given contracted cash flows for most underlying infrastructure projects. This asset class entails increased liquidity risk but offers some inflation protection (many contracted cash flows are linked to inflation).
Hedge funds	Provide access to various diversifying strategies, including those with potential to generate gains in both rising and falling markets. Expected to return 250 bps annually over traditional long-only equities. Careful manager selection and underlying strategy selection (especially exposure to equity market beta) are important factors.

Liew recommends to LSPP's Board of Trustees the following change in asset allocation:

Asset Class	Current Asset Allocation	Recommended Asset Allocation
US equities	30%	25%
International equities	30%	25%
US fixed income	30%	15%
International fixed income	10%	5%
Alternative debt	—	10%
Infrastructure funds	—	10%
Hedge funds	—	10%

How would the recommended change in asset allocation be expected to affect LSPP's funded status?

Solution: The recommended changes in asset allocation would likely affect LSPP's funded status as follows:

- The changes would increase expected returns, implying higher expected asset values for LSPP over time.
- Given that both alternative debt and hedge funds have higher projected long-term returns than traditional debt and equities, respectively, the discount rate applied to LSPP's liabilities can be increased, thereby reducing their present value.
- On balance, LSPP's funded status would be expected to improve because of the recommended changes in asset allocation. In addition to generating higher asset values and lower present value of liabilities, the volatility of assets (and therefore the risk to funded status) should be reduced because of the lower correlation among asset returns.

Note that although these alternative investments entail reduced liquidity, this does not impact funded status; in fact, funded status improves because of the factors mentioned previously. However, the reduced liquidity must be considered to ensure sufficient coverage of prospective liabilities. Alternative investments entail greater manager selection risk and larger dispersion of returns around the policy benchmark relative to a passive allocation to public markets. Careful manager selection would likely require resources that would increase internal costs, and also require paying higher fees to access skilled alternative asset managers.

Exhibit 7 shows the evolution of pension fund asset allocation trends from 1997–2017 for the P7 countries. It is apparent that the allocation to equities has decreased from about 57% in 1997 to about 46% in 2017, while allocations to the Other category of alternatives has increased from about 4% to 25% over the same time period. This is consistent with the general trend among institutional investors of diversifying out of equities and into alternative investments, including private equity, natural resources, real estate, and hedge funds.

EXHIBIT 7   Evolution of Pension Asset Allocation from 1997 to 2017

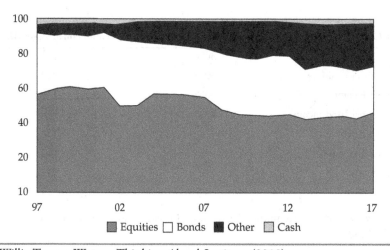

Source: Willis Towers Watson Thinking Ahead Institute (2018).

5. SOVEREIGN WEALTH FUNDS

Sovereign wealth funds (SWFs) are state-owned investment funds or entities that invest in financial or real assets. Sovereign wealth funds have increased significantly in number and size over the past two decades. Governments have established SWFs from budget surpluses to meet different objectives. The International Monetary Fund (IMF) has defined five broad types of sovereign wealth funds, and each pursues different investment objectives. Exhibit 8 summarizes these five types with their main objectives and some notable examples.

EXHIBIT 8   Major Types of Sovereign Wealth Funds

Type	Objective	Examples
Budget stabilization funds	Set up to insulate the budget and economy from commodity price volatility and external shocks.	Economic and Social Stabilization Fund of Chile; Timor-Leste Petroleum Fund; Russia's Oil Stabilization Fund
Development funds	Established to allocate resources to priority socio-economic projects, usually infrastructure.	Mubadala (UAE); Iran's National Development Fund; Ireland Strategic Investment Fund
Savings funds	Intended to share wealth across generations by transforming non-renewable assets into diversified financial assets.	Abu Dhabi Investment Authority; Kuwait Investment Authority; Qatar Investment Authority; Russia's National Wealth Fund
Reserve funds	Intended to reduce the negative carry costs of holding reserves or to earn higher return on ample reserves.	China Investment Corporation; Korea Investment Corporation; GIC Private Ltd. (Singapore)
Pension reserve funds	Set up to meet identified future outflows with respect to pension-related contingent-type liabilities on governments' balance sheets.	National Social Security Fund (China); New Zealand Superannuation Fund; Future Fund of Australia

Source: International Monetary Fund, "Sovereign Wealth Funds—A Work Agenda" (29 February 2008).

Exhibit 9 shows some of the largest sovereign wealth funds, which manage a total of about US$3.6 trillion in assets—close to 50% of all SWF assets (more than US$7.3 trillion).

EXHIBIT 9   Select Large Sovereign Wealth Funds

Fund	Inception Date	Country	Type
Saudi Arabian Monetary Authority (SAMA) foreign holdings	1952	Saudi Arabia	Reserve Fund
Kuwait Investment Authority	1953	Kuwait	Savings Fund
Abu Dhabi Investment Authority	1976	Abu Dhabi, United Arab Emirates	Savings Fund
Norway's Government Pension Fund—Global	1990	Norway	Budget Stabilization/ Savings/Pension Reserve
China Investment Corporation	2007	China	Reserve Fund

Source: SWF Institute (www.swfinstitute.org).

5.1. Stakeholders

SWF stakeholders include the citizens, the government, and external asset managers as well as the SWF management, investment committees, and boards.

The ultimate SWF stakeholders are the current and future citizens (or residents) of the country. Depending on the objectives of the SWF, these stakeholders either benefit directly in the form of payments (e.g., for pension reserve funds) or indirectly through stabilization of government budgets, lower taxes, or investments by the SWF in the domestic economy. If the SWF fails to meet its objectives, citizens/residents might be impacted through higher future taxes. Several SWFs are explicitly set up to benefit not only the current generation but also future generations. When such intergenerational wealth transfer is part of the objective, significant transparency and communication are required by the SWF and government to gain support from all stakeholders. This also requires long-term thinking by the government, which can be challenging when some governments have tenures of only a few years and when fiscal budgets vary significantly over the economic cycle.

The management or investment office of an SWF is tasked with investing its assets according to the investment policy and objectives of the fund. They monitor assets, make recommendations on investment strategy, and either select external asset managers or manage assets in-house. Appointment to an SWF's board, which oversees the management or investment office, is typically executed through a formal process that may include appointment by the current ruling government. In any case, the board has a fiduciary duty to the ultimate beneficiaries, the nation's current and future generations.

5.2. Liabilities and Investment Horizons

There is a wide variety in investment objectives, liabilities, investment horizons, and liquidity needs among the five types of SWFs, so we will discuss each type separately. As a group, however, SWFs are different from the other institutional investors covered in this chapter when it comes to liabilities. The liabilities of DB pension funds, endowments and foundations, insurance companies, and banks are clearly defined, which facilitates asset/liability management (ALM) processes. SWFs, however, do not generally have clearly defined liabilities given their mission of intergenerational wealth transfer. It is also worth noting that SWFs do not necessarily fit neatly into one of the five different types discussed in this section. For example, Norway's Government Pension Fund Global (formerly known as Norway's Petroleum Fund) undertakes elements of stabilization and sterilization, accumulating pension reserves, and saving for future generations.

5.2.1 Budget Stabilization Funds

Budget stabilization funds are established to insulate the fiscal budget from commodity price volatility and other external shocks, particularly if a nation's revenue is tied to natural resource production or other cyclical industries. These funds have uncertain liabilities and relatively short investment horizons. Their main purpose is risk management because such funds may be needed on a short-term basis to help support the government budget. The investment objective is usually to deliver returns in excess of inflation with a low probability of a negative return in any year. Budget stabilization funds typically avoid assets that are highly correlated with the main sources of government revenue, and they may engage in hedging against declines in prices of commodities that are important revenue generators for the local economy. These funds mainly invest in government bonds and other debt securities. Examples of budget stabilization funds include the Economic and Social Stabilization Fund of Chile and Russia's Oil Stabilization Fund.

5.2.2 Development Funds

Development funds are established to support a nation's economic development through investing in essential infrastructure, innovation, or by supporting key industries. Liabilities are not clearly defined and typically uncertain for development funds, but their overall objective is to raise a country's economic growth or to diversify the economy. As such, these funds have an implicit real return target: to increase real domestic GDP growth and productivity. Some initiatives, such as infrastructure/industrial development, may be ongoing and long-term, while others may have a fixed, medium-term horizon, such as a medical research fund. Examples of development funds include Mubadala Development Corp. (UAE) and the National Development Fund of Iran.

5.2.3 Savings Funds

Savings funds are typically established to transform proceeds from the sale of non-renewable natural resources into long-term wealth and a diversified portfolio of financial assets. The mission of a savings fund is wealth transfer to future generations after the sources of natural wealth have been depleted. As such, their liabilities are long-term. Some savings funds have a real return objective or an explicit spending policy (like endowments). Norway's Government Pension Fund Global (GPFG) uses a fiscal spending rule whereby it intends to withdraw 3% of the fund's value annually with the goal of gradually phasing oil revenue into the Norwegian economy. This spending rate is linked to the expected real return earned by the GPFG. A special case of savings funds involves government investment holding companies, which are funded from the privatization proceeds of national companies (e.g., Singapore's Temasek Holdings). Because of their long-term horizons, savings funds invest in risky and illiquid assets, including equities and a wide range of alternative investments. Of course, savings funds should avoid investing in assets highly correlated with the non-renewable resources from which the government is trying to diversify.

5.2.4 Reserve Funds

Reserve investment funds are established from central bank excess foreign currency reserves. The objective is to achieve a return higher than that on FX reserves (usually invested in low-duration, high-grade debt instruments) and to reduce the negative cost-of-carry of holding FX reserves. Reserve funds are common in export-intensive economies that have built up large FX reserves. Central banks accumulate such reserves as they print local currency to buy FX (like US dollars or euros) from local firms selling export goods. The central banks then issue monetary stabilization bonds to absorb the excess local currency. So, the central banks typically end up with FX reserves invested in low-yielding US Treasury or other high-quality sovereign debt instruments, while their liabilities (monetary stabilization bonds) pay much higher yields that create the negative cost-of-carry. Countries mitigate this cost by creating sovereign wealth reserve funds, placing excess FX reserves in these funds, and investing them globally in higher yielding, risky assets. Although their true liabilities are the central bank's monetary stabilization bonds, in practice, reserve funds operate somewhat similarly to endowments and foundations by having either a nominal or real return target. Also, their investment horizons are very long, with typically no immediate or interim payout expectation. Consequently, reserve funds generally invest in diversified portfolios with significant exposure to equities and other high-yielding alternative investments. Examples of reserve funds include China Investment Corporation (CIC), Korea Investment Corporation (KIC), and GIC Private Limited (GIC), formerly known as Government of Singapore Investment Corporation.

5.2.5 Pension Reserve Funds

Pension reserve funds are established to help prefund contingent pension-related liabilities on the government's balance sheet. Pension reserve funds are usually funded from fiscal surpluses during economic booms. The goal is to help reduce the burden on future taxpayers by prefunding Social Security and health care costs arising from aging populations, so these funds generally have long-term investment horizons. There is usually an **accumulation phase** (**decumulation phase**) where the government predominantly contributes to (withdraws from) the fund. However, additional uncertainty also exists around expected cash flows, particularly in the case of funding health care because those costs are quite volatile. The investment objective of pension reserve funds is to earn returns sufficient to maximize the likelihood of meeting future pension, Social Security, and/or health care costs as they arise. Therefore, such funds will typically invest in a diversified portfolio with the majority in such equities and alternative investments as property, infrastructure, hedge funds, and private markets. An example of a pension reserve fund is Future Fund of Australia (FFA). Its goal is to meet unfunded pension liabilities (retirement payments or superannuation payments in Australia) that will be owed to former public employees starting in 2020. FFA was funded from budget surpluses and privatization proceeds of Telstra, an Australian telecommunications company that was formerly a state-owned enterprise. The investment mandate for FFA is to achieve an average annual return of at least the Consumer Price Index (CPI) + 4% to 5% per year over the long term with an acceptable level of risk.

5.3. Liquidity Needs

5.3.1 Budget Stabilization Funds

Stabilization funds must maintain a high level of liquidity and invest in assets that have a low risk of significant losses over short time periods. For example, in the event of a negative commodity price shock, the government might experience a significant budget deficit caused by lower commodity-based revenues. To stabilize the budget and meet spending needs, the stabilization fund's assets must be readily accessible. As a result, budget stabilization funds invest a significant portion of their portfolios in cash and high-grade, fixed-income instruments that are very liquid and carry little risk of significant drawdown.

5.3.2 Development Funds

A development fund supports national economic development. Liquidity needs depend on the particular strategic economic development initiatives the fund was created to support. For example, infrastructure investments are very long-term, so funds established to develop infrastructure would have low liquidity needs. Development funds designed to promote research and innovation may also require long time periods to see the fruits of investments in innovation and research and are likely to have low liquidity needs as well.

5.3.3 Savings Funds

Savings funds have a very long-term investment horizon and low liquidity needs. Their main objective is to grow wealth for future generations, so their liquidity needs, being long-term in nature, are comparable to those of endowments and foundations. In instances where the savings fund was established to transform the proceeds from the sale of non-renewable commodities into long-term wealth, the fund's liquidity needs may change once the nation's natural resources have been depleted because the government is more likely to begin withdrawing money from the fund to support its budgetary needs.

5.3.4 Reserve Funds

Reserve funds operate to offset negative carry effects of holding FX reserves, and consequently, excess reserves are invested in higher growth investments. The liquidity needs of reserve funds are lower than those of stabilization funds but higher than those of savings funds. Reserve funds typically hold 50%–70% in equity or equity-equivalent investments to achieve their return targets. The remainder, however, is likely to be invested in liquid fixed-income securities that could be readily sold should a dramatic change in the balance of trade require additional central bank reserves.

5.3.5 Pension Reserve Funds

Pension reserve funds need to meet future pension or health care liabilities when they come due. Depending on when significant fund withdrawals are expected, liquidity needs change over time. During the accumulation phase, reserve funds can hold a significant part of their portfolios in equities and relatively illiquid investments. Once the decumulation phase begins, the asset allocation will gradually shift toward more liquid, high-quality, fixed-income investments.

5.4. External Constraints Affecting Investment

In this section and the next, we briefly highlight some legal/regulatory and tax constraints, respectively, that sovereign wealth funds must consider when investing.

5.4.1. Legal and Regulatory Constraints

Sovereign wealth funds are typically established by national legislation that contains details on: the fund's mission; contributions to the fund; circumstances allowing withdrawals from the fund; and governance structure, including selection of board members, their roles, and the level of board independence. Some SWFs are set up with clear rules on asset allocation. For example, a technology development fund may be required to be 100% invested in offshore technology assets to provide diversification (versus local economic drivers) and eventual technology transfer. Alternatively, an industrial development fund may be required to invest 100% locally to support the development of key industries in the domestic economy. In any case, SWFs should operate in a transparent and accountable manner as they are ultimately established for the benefit of a nation's people and future generations. Sound governance, independence, transparency, and accountability are all essential to ensure that SWFs are protected from political influence.

The International Forum of SWFs (IFSWF) is a self-governing body established to promote best practices among SWFs. All IFSWF members have endorsed a set of generally accepted principles and practices (GAPP). Known as the "Santiago Principles" for the city where they were drafted, the GAPP provide a best practices framework by which SWFs should operate that addresses such key elements as sound legal framework, well-defined mission, independence, accountability, transparency, disclosure, ethics and professionalism, effective risk management, and regular review for compliance with the Santiago Principles.

5.4.2. Tax and Accounting Constraints

Typically, sovereign wealth funds are given tax-free status by the legislation that governs them. However, SWFs may be ineligible to claim withholding taxes or tax credits that are ordinarily available to taxable investors. As SWFs invest in offshore markets, they also need to consider any tax treaties that may exist between the countries in which they are investing and their own country. Some regulators allow SWFs to be exempt from domestic tax rules that have been put in place to deter tax avoidance by corporations and individuals. To prevent any international diplomatic issues, SWFs should be sensitive to ensuring they are not perceived as trying to avoid paying taxes in any offshore jurisdictions where they operate or invest.

5.5. Investment Objectives

5.5.1 Budget Stabilization Funds

The investment objective of budget stabilization funds is capital preservation. This is achieved by endeavoring to deliver returns in excess of inflation with a low probability of a negative return in any given year. In addition, budget stabilization funds should avoid cyclical assets whose returns are highly correlated to the main sources of government revenue (such as natural resources industries). According to the stated investment objectives of Chile's Economic and Social Stabilization Fund, *"the main aim of its investment policy is to maximize the fund's accumulated value in order to partially cover cyclical reductions in fiscal revenues while maintaining a low level of risk. Its risk aversion is reflected by the choice of an investment portfolio with a high level of liquidity and low credit risk and volatility, thereby ensuring the availability of the resources to cover fiscal deficits and preventing significant losses in the fund's value."*

5.5.2 Development Funds

Development funds are established to support a nation's economic development with the ultimate goal of raising a country's long-term economic growth. The implicit investment objective of development funds is therefore to achieve a real rate of return in excess of real domestic GDP or productivity growth. Accordingly, Khazanah Nasional Berhard, the strategic investment fund of the government of Malaysia, *"strives to create sustainable value and cultivate a high-performance culture that helps contribute to Malaysia's economic competitiveness. Utilizing a proactive investment approach, we aim to build true value through management of our core investments, leveraging on our global footprint for new growth, as well as undertaking catalytic investments that strategically boost the country's economy. We also actively develop human, social and knowledge capital for the country."*

5.5.3 Savings Funds

The mission of savings funds is to ensure wealth transfer to future generations. Therefore, their primary objective is to maintain purchasing power of the assets in perpetuity while achieving investment returns sufficient to sustain the spending necessary to support ongoing governmental activities. According to Alaska Statutes 37.13.020, the Alaska Permanent Fund, *"should provide a means of conserving a portion of the state's revenue from mineral resources to benefit all generations of Alaskans; the fund's goal should be to maintain safety of principal while maximizing total return; the fund should be used as a savings device managed to allow the maximum use of disposable income from the fund for purposes designated by law."*

5.5.4 Reserve Funds

The investment objective of reserve funds is usually to achieve a rate of return above the return the government must pay on its monetary stabilization bonds, thereby eliminating the negative cost-of-carry of holding excess FX reserves (that are typically invested in low duration, high-grade, fixed-income instruments). For example, Singapore's Government Investment Corporation (GIC) has a clearly defined purpose: *"We aim to achieve good long-term returns for the Government—a reasonable risk-adjusted rate above global inflation over a 20-year investment horizon. By achieving these returns, we meet our responsibility to preserve and enhance the international purchasing power of Singapore's foreign reserves. The reserves provide a stream of income that can be spent or invested for the benefit of present and future generations."*

5.5.5 Pension Reserve Funds

The investment objective of pension reserve funds is to earn sufficient returns to maximize the likelihood of being able to meet future unfunded pension, Social Security, and/or health care liabilities of plan participants as they arise. Accordingly, among its mandates, the Australian government states that its Future Fund should *"maximise the return earned on the Fund over the long term; ... adopt an average return of at least the Consumer Price Index (CPI) +4 to +5 per cent per annum over the long term as the benchmark return on the Fund; [and] in targeting the benchmark return, the Board must determine an acceptable but not excessive level of risk for the Fund...."*

EXAMPLE 4 The People's Fund of Wigitania—A Pension Reserve Fund

The People's Fund is a pension reserve fund established by the government of Wigitania by setting aside current government surpluses. Its objective is to meet future unfunded Social Security payments caused by an aging population. The following is an extract from the People's Fund IPS.

> Effective from 2030, the government will have the ability to withdraw assets to meet pension and Social Security liabilities falling due each year. Actuarial projections estimate annual payouts to be about 5% of the total fund value at that time. Given this level of cash flow, the Fund is expected to maintain most of its asset base for the foreseeable future. As such, 2030 does not represent an 'end date' for measurement purposes. A long-term investment horizon remains appropriate at present. However, the appropriate timeframe, risk tolerance, portfolio construction, and liquidity profile may change.

1. What are the liquidity needs of the People's Fund?
2. What factors does the Board need to consider when reviewing the Fund's investment horizon?

Solution to 1: From the extract, we see that the unfunded pension and Social Security liabilities that the Fund is meant to cover are expected to be about 5% of total fund value per year, starting in 2030. Management of the fund will need to ensure that they have sufficient liquidity at that time to meet those ongoing liabilities. Until that time, liquidity needs are very low, which should allow the People's Fund to invest a significant part of its portfolio in less-liquid alternative asset classes.

Solution to 2: The Board should consider two separate phases when reviewing the Fund's investment horizon and investment policy: an accumulation phase and a decumulation phase. The accumulation phase lasts until 2030 and allows the Fund to invest with little to no liquidity needs and little concern for interim volatility. The decumulation phase starts after 2030, when the government expects to withdraw about 5% of the assets on an annual basis. The investment horizon, liquidity needs, and risk tolerance will need to be modified during the decumulation phase, which will affect the investment policy.

5.6. Asset Allocation by Sovereign Wealth Funds

Each of the five types of sovereign wealth funds have very different objectives and purposes. Not surprisingly then, these funds have very different asset allocations. Development funds usually have little flexibility with their asset allocations as they operate within a limited investment universe as part of their mandate (e.g., they are required to invest in local infrastructure development projects). Given that national development projects can be different in nature and purpose between countries, it would be difficult to envision a 'typical' asset allocation for a development fund. The other four types of sovereign wealth funds are more homogeneous within their respective groups, for which Exhibit 10 provides illustrative asset allocations.

EXHIBIT 10   Illustrative Asset Allocations for Different Types of Sovereign Wealth Funds

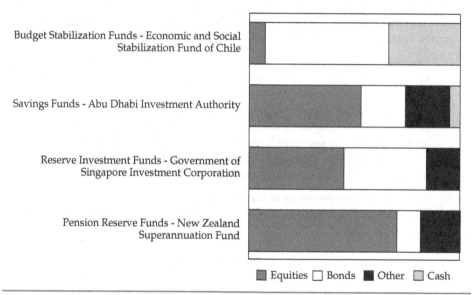

■ Equities □ Bonds ■ Other ▨ Cash

Sources: 1. Economic and Social Stabilization Fund of Chile website; 2. Abu Dhabi Investment Authority (ADIA), *2015 Review*; 3. Government Investment Corporation (GIC), *Report on the Management of the Government's Portfolio for the Year 2016/17*; 4. NZSUPERFUND, *New Zealand Superannuation Fund Annual Report 2017*.

Several key points stand out from the data in Exhibit 10:

- The portfolios of budget stabilization funds are dominated by fixed-income investments because of their defensive nature, relatively stable investment returns, and diversification against cyclically-sensitive factors (such as commodity prices) that drive government budget revenues in some countries. The conservative asset allocation may be partly explained by the fact that several major stabilization funds are managed by their countries' central bank or Ministry of Finance; these entities tend to be relatively risk averse.
- The portfolios of savings funds are shown to be tilted toward growth assets, equities, and alternatives (the "Other" category). Due to their very long investment horizons, these funds can take on more equity-related risks, and they consequently hold relatively high

allocations to such alternative investments as real assets, private equity and debt (loans), and hedge funds.

- Reserve investment funds have a similar allocation to savings funds but they tend to allocate less to alternatives. This may be partially explained by reserve funds having potentially higher liquidity needs compared to savings funds because of central bank activities. Public equities are typically the most liquid growth asset available and help counter the negative carry generated by foreign exchange reserves, while bonds and other fixed-income investments help to reduce reserve funds' portfolio volatility.
- The portfolios of pension reserve funds are relatively heavily tilted toward equities with a significant allocation to alternative assets, such as real assets and infrastructure, private equity and debt markets, and hedge funds. Pension reserve funds generally have long-term investment horizons (but not necessarily inter-generational as with savings funds) and low liquidity needs during their accumulation phases, which can explain their high allocation to alternatives compared with other SWFs.

Sovereign wealth funds with savings or pension reserve objectives typically follow the endowment investment model. Some also adopt the Canada reference portfolio model. An example of the latter is the New Zealand Superannuation Fund (NZSF). As noted previously, this model makes use of a reference portfolio comprising passive investment in stocks and bonds that are expected to meet the fund's investment objectives. The total portfolio is then invested to replicate the risk factors of the reference portfolio, while individual investments are benchmarked against a combined stock and bond benchmark representing the risk factors driving the individual investments. Both models result in higher allocations to alternative investments, as observed in Exhibit 10.

In the Asia Pacific region, sovereign wealth funds are the largest institutional investors. Some examples include China Investment Corporation (CIC), State Administration of Foreign Exchange (SAFE) Investment Company (China), Hong Kong Monetary Authority Investment Portfolio (HKMAIP), and Government Investment Corporation of Singapore (GIC). Given the huge size of their assets, these SWFs tend to dominate the regional investment landscape. They typically have fewer investment constraints than other Asia Pacific institutional investors. These SWFs also have broader investment mandates, minimal investment management fee constraints, and longer time horizons as compared to (for example) pension funds. Such flexibility allows these SWFs to implement higher allocations to alternative assets.

6. UNIVERSITY ENDOWMENTS AND PRIVATE FOUNDATIONS

This section introduces university endowments and private foundations. As will be seen shortly, these two types of institutional investors have some similarities but also important differences that affect their investing activities.

University Endowments

Many institutions have endowments, including universities, churches, museums, and hospitals. These endowments are typically funded through gifts and donations and are intended to help the institutions provide for some of their main services. Endowment funds invest in capital markets to provide a savings and growth mechanism that allows the institution to meet its mission in perpetuity. The main objective is to provide intergenerational equity. As James Tobin wrote in 1974: "The trustees of an endowed institution are the guardians of the future against the claims of the present. Their task is to preserve equity among generations."

Throughout this chapter, for simplicity we will focus on university endowments. The investment objectives and philosophies of the endowments of other institutions are typically not very different from those of university endowments. Exhibit 11 shows some large (by assets) university endowments.

EXHIBIT 11   Select US University Endowments

University	Assets (US$ bn)
Harvard University	34.5
Yale University	25.4
University of Texas System	24.2
Stanford University	22.4
Princeton University	22.2

Source: Commonfund and the National Association of College and University Business Officers (NACUBO), *2016 NACUBO–Commonfund Study of Endowments (NCSE)*.

Private Foundations

Foundations are nonprofit organizations that typically make grants to outside organizations and persons who carry out social, educational, and other charitable activities. Many foundations are located in the United States, but some large foundations are outside the United States, such as the Wellcome Trust in the United Kingdom. Foundations are more common in the United States because of favorable tax treatment. Outside the United States, charitable giving is typically undertaken by family offices.

There are four different types of foundations:

1. *Community foundations*: These are charitable organizations that make social or educational grants for the benefit of a local community (e.g., the New York Community Trust). These foundations are usually funded by public donations.
2. *Operating foundations*: Organizations that exist to operate a not-for-profit business for charitable purposes. They are typically funded by individual donors or donor families.
3. *Corporate foundations*: These are established by businesses and funded from profits.
4. *Private grant-making foundations*: These are established by individual donors or donor families to support specific types of charities. Most of the largest foundations in the US fall into this category.

Community foundations are a type of public charity associated with such community organizations as hospitals, schools, and churches. They are funded by many relatively small donors, and they typically provide charitable support in the region or community where they are located. Private operating foundations are established to provide funding and support for related programs and activities (e.g., operating a museum) rather than giving grants to outside organizations or activities.

Private grant-making foundations (also called private non-operating foundations) are by far the largest group (in number of foundations and in total assets), so they are our primary focus. Private grant-making foundations support different types of charities and usually run a large grant-making operation in addition to an investment office. The main objective of most private grant-making foundations is to maintain purchasing power into perpetuity, so that the organization can continue making grants. In recent years, however, there has been a trend toward limited-life foundations as original donors seek to maintain control over foundation spending during their lives.

The focus of grants varies widely and includes issues such as health, education, environment, arts, and culture. Some foundations make large and targeted grants to very specific causes while others make many smaller grants to a wide variety of causes. Exhibit 12 shows some large US foundations and their missions.

EXHIBIT 12   Select US Foundations

Foundation	Mission
Bill & Melinda Gates Foundation	Focus on global health and poverty. In US focus on education.
Ford Foundation	Focus on inequality.
Robert Wood Johnson Foundation	Improve health and health care of all Americans.
Lilly Endowment Inc.	Support religion, education, community development.
William and Flora Hewlett Foundation	Help people build measurably better lives by focusing on education, the environment, global development, performing arts, philanthropy, and population. Also supports disadvantaged communities in San Francisco.

Source: Foundation Center (www.foundationcenter.org).

6.1. University Endowments—Stakeholders

Stakeholders of a university endowment include current and future students, alumni, current and future university faculty and administrators, and the larger university community. Each of these stakeholders has a strong interest in seeing the endowment invested prudently. There is potential, however, for tension between increasing spending to meet current needs versus preserving sufficient funds to serve future generations. Endowment boards or investment committees, therefore, need to determine an appropriate balance.

University endowments are generally funded by gifts and donations from alumni. It is common that donors specify the handling and use of their gifts—for example, that only the income portion be spent or that only specific scholarships, programs, or departments benefit. Other gifts may be unrestricted and can be spent for general purposes. Alumni are concerned about current students and faculty and also future generations, so they expect endowment assets to be invested for the long-run. Endowment payouts support the university's operating budget and provide an important source of income. Endowments provide stability and continuity when other revenue sources, such as tuition and government funding, fluctuate. Endowments also allow universities to more readily undertake long-term capital projects, knowing required resources are available to meet those future commitments.

Stakeholders of a university endowment often have representation on the endowment's board or investment committee, including alumni who are investment professionals running or working for financial services organizations.

6.2. University Endowments—Liabilities and Investment Horizon

Although most endowments operate on an asset-only basis, their main purpose is to support the university's operating budget based on the principle of intergenerational equity. The investment horizon for endowments is thus perpetuity, and their main objective is to maintain long-term purchasing power. An endowment's liabilities are the future stream of payouts to the university, which are typically codified in an official spending policy. The spending policy serves two important purposes: 1) to ensure intergenerational equity; and 2) to smooth endowment payouts to partially insulate contributions to the university from capital market volatility.

Although the spending policy defines how much of the endowment's assets are paid out annually, several other liability characteristics should be considered when designing an appropriate investment policy, including:

a. What is the university's capacity for fund-raising: How much in gifts and donations are contributed (on average) each year?
b. What percentage of the university's operating budget is supported by the endowment?
c. Balance sheet health: Does the endowment or university have the ability to issue debt?

We first discuss different types of spending policies and then discuss other important liability-related characteristics. Broadly speaking, there are three different types of endowment spending policies:

1. *Constant Growth Rule*: The endowment provides a fixed amount annually to the university, typically adjusted for inflation (the growth rate). The inflation rate is usually based on the Higher Education Price Index (HEPI)[2] in the United States or a more general consumer price index elsewhere, possibly with an additional spread. A shortcoming of constant growth spending rules is that spending does not adjust based on the endowment's value. If the endowment experiences weak (strong) average returns, the spending amount expressed as a percentage of assets may become very high (low). This spending rule is therefore commonly complemented with caps and floors, typically between 4% and 6% of average assets under management (AUM) over one or three years.
2. *Market Value Rule*: The endowment pays a pre-specified percentage (the spending rate) of the moving average of asset values, typically between 4% and 6%. Asset values are usually smoothed using a 3- to 5-year moving average. A disadvantage of this spending rule is that it tends to be pro-cyclical; when markets have performed well (poorly), the overall payout increases (decreases).
3. *Hybrid Rule*: Spending is calculated as a weighted average of the constant growth and market value rules. Commonly referred to as the Yale spending rule, weights can range from 30% to 70%. This spending rule was designed to strike a balance between the shortcomings of the respective spending rules.

All three spending rules can be summarized by the following formula:

$$\text{Spending Amount in Year } t + 1 = w \times [\text{Spending Amount in Year } t \times (1 + \text{Inflation Rate})] \\ + (1 - w) \times \text{Spending Rate} \times \text{Average AUM},$$

---

[2]The Higher Education Price Index is calculated annually by Commonfund and tracks the most important components in the cost of higher education. More information can be found at https://www.commonfund.org/commonfund-institute/higher-education-price-index-hepi/.

where w denotes the weight put on the prior year's spending amount. When $w = 1$, the formula simplifies to a constant growth rule; when $w = 0$, it simplifies to a market value rule. For any other choice of w ($0 < w < 1$), the formula represents a hybrid spending rule. Most US endowments use a market value spending rule, but some of the larger ones use a hybrid rule. As noted, a market value spending rule is pro-cyclical: This may not be an issue for universities that receive only a small percentage of their operating budgets from their endowment, but this may be more problematic otherwise. The goal of providing intergenerational equity means university endowments aim to maintain their purchasing power. Therefore, endowments target a real rate of return (after inflation) equal to or greater than their spending rates. Given that endowments pay out (on average) between 4% and 6% of assets annually, they typically target a 5% to 5.5% real, long-term rate of return.

Other liability-related factors must be considered when managing an endowment. Universities regularly raise money from donors. Depending on the wealth of their alumni base, such fund-raising activity may be more or less successful. Because of gifts and donations, endowments' net spending rate tends to be lower than the headline spending of 4% to 6% of assets previously discussed. On average, net spending is closer to 2% to 4% of assets. Another important distinction between endowments is how much the university relies on its endowment to support the operating budget. Such support may be less than 5% for some universities, while in other cases, 40% to 50% of the university's operating budget is provided by its endowment. All else equal, endowments that support a smaller percentage of the overall budget should be able to tolerate more market, credit, and liquidity risk. In practice, however, this important distinguishing factor is typically insufficiently incorporated in the design of investment policies. It is common for university endowments to be benchmarked against each other, which creates herding behavior even though the organizations might have very different liability characteristics. A final consideration is the debt issuance capability of the endowment (or university). Some endowments access the public and private debt markets on a regular basis. The capability to access debt markets, especially during periods of market stress, affects the levels of risk and illiquidity endowments can accept in their investments.

6.3. University Endowments—Liquidity Needs

The liquidity needs of university endowments are relatively low (compared to foundations). On average, endowments' annual net spending is 2% to 4% of assets, after factoring in gifts and donations. Low liquidity needs combined with long investment horizons allow endowments to accept relatively high short-term volatility in pursuit of superior long-term returns. Consequently, many university endowments have relatively high allocations to equity markets and illiquid private asset classes and small allocations to fixed income. Having significant allocations to illiquid asset classes, such as private equity and private real estate, creates additional liquidity needs to meet annual net capital calls from general partners managing these assets. Finally, to the extent that endowments use derivatives for rebalancing or portable alpha strategies, there may be further liquidity needs—particularly during times of financial market stress—to meet margin calls or to cover higher collateral demands.

6.4. Private Foundations—Stakeholders

Stakeholders of a foundation include the founding family, donors, grant recipients, and the broader community that may benefit indirectly from the foundation's activities. Each has a strong interest in seeing the foundation's assets invested appropriately. As with university endowments, a tension may exist between increasing current grant spending versus preserving sufficient funds to serve future generations of grant recipients. The founding family and donors typically want their donations to support grant recipients in perpetuity. There is a trend, however, toward limited-life foundations as donors seek to maintain control over foundation spending during their lives. Finally, the government (Internal Revenue Service in the United States) may also be a stakeholder because of the favorable tax treatment that foundations enjoy. The government's main concern is that foundations remain engaged strictly in charitable work.

The boards of foundations tend to be different in terms of skill sets than the boards of endowments. University endowments typically have alumni sitting on their boards—people with a special relationship to the university and who may have significant financial market skills (for example, in private equity or hedge funds). Board members for foundations, however, are typically individuals involved with grant making and not necessarily investment professionals. This difference in skill sets may affect the quality of board oversight, the level of delegation of decision making to investment staff, and the quality of investment decisions.

Mission-related investing (also known as "**impact investing**"), which aims to direct a significant portion of assets in excess of annual grants into projects promoting the foundation's mission, is becoming increasingly important. For example, the Ford Foundation has allocated up to US$1.0 billion (more than 8% of assets) over 10 years to investments related to its mission of addressing global inequality. The challenge for foundations is to ensure that mission-related investments generate financial returns commensurate with risks assumed. As typically lower yielding mission-related investments are undertaken at the expense of higher return investment opportunities, portfolio returns (expected and realized) may decline, which could result in foundation assets being spent down sooner and annual grant-making activities being reduced.

6.5. Private Foundations—Liabilities and Investment Horizon

In practice, the investment philosophy of private foundations is typically similar to that of university endowments, despite important differences between them in terms of liabilities and liquidity needs. Foundations and endowments both typically have perpetual investment horizons (although, as noted shortly, some foundations may have finite lives) and both invest to maintain purchasing power; however, foundations generally have higher liquidity needs. In the United States, private grant-making foundations are legally required to pay out 5% of assets (on a trailing 12-month basis) plus investment expenses, while university endowments have more-flexible spending rules. In addition, foundations must spend any donations in the year received, known as flow-through (but this is not necessarily the case outside the United States). Foundations typically use a smoothing formula similar to that of university endowments to ensure payouts do not fluctuate with the market volatility of assets. The constant growth spending rule and the hybrid spending rule, discussed previously for university endowments, are rarely used by foundations.

Foundations sometimes issue bonds. The capability to access debt markets, especially during periods of market stress, is positively associated with the levels of investment risk and liquidity risk that foundations can accept in their investments. The Wellcome Foundation (United Kingdom), with a credit rating of AAA, has occasionally issued bonds. For example, in early 2018, it issued £750 million of century bonds (i.e., 100-year maturity) with a coupon of 2.517%.[3] Proceeds from such bonds have been used to support charitable work, and bondholders are repaid by the returns generated on the investment portfolio.

Spending Rate and Investment Expenses of Foundations

Costs of running a foundation are included in the 5% required payout, excluding investment expenses, which means the investment office is considered a cost center. Consequently, the investment office of a foundation will typically be much smaller compared to that of a similar-sized (by AUM) endowment, leading to potentially different investment behavior. For example, many small foundations have limited investment staff and therefore rely on an outsourced CIO model, whereby assets are managed by an external organization that assumes fiduciary duty and takes responsibility for the strategic asset allocation and investments across various asset classes. Although many outsourced CIOs do offer allocations to alternative asset classes, the result of such outsourcing may typically be a heavier allocation to public markets, more-intensive use of passive strategies, and a heavier reliance on beta as a driver of returns.

Many foundations typically receive a one-time gift from the founding family. Some foundations are allowed to raise money on an ongoing basis, but in the US, any such donations must be spent on a flow-through basis. Unlike universities that derive revenues from other sources besides their endowments, such as tuition and research grants, foundations rely almost exclusively on their investment portfolios to support operating budgets. This high dependency has important implications for risk tolerance, and as a result, foundations (on average) have more conservative, more-liquid investment portfolios compared to endowments.

Typically, the original gift must be maintained in perpetuity (principal protection). There is, however, a trend toward **limited-life foundations**, as some founders seek to maintain control of spending while they (or their immediate heirs) are still alive. For example, the Bill and Melinda Gates Foundation is mandated to spend down assets to zero within 30 years of the Gates' death. There is risk—and concern by some founding donors—that as the foundation's leadership changes over time, the mission may move away from the founder's vision. Thus, to minimize this risk, more limited-life foundations are being established. Importantly, a limited-life foundation faces a different investment problem than a perpetual foundation: As the investment horizon of a limited-life foundation shortens, its liquidity needs increase and risk tolerance decreases.

Real-Life Example of a Limited-Life Foundation

The Atlantic Philanthropies, set up by Chuck Feeney in 1982, is among the largest limited-life foundations to complete its grant-making activities. After giving a total of US$8 billion over 35 years to human rights, health care, and education causes, the last grant was made in 2016 and the Atlantic Philanthropies expects to close in 2020. All stakeholders have been informed of the spend-down process and critical challenges are

---

[3]In late 2017, Oxford University issued a century bond with the same size and similar coupon.

being addressed, including: 1) choosing who will oversee the portfolio wind-down process with staff departing for other employment opportunities; and 2) deciding how best to liquidate private investments. As a limited-life foundation gives away its assets, liquidity needs increase and risk tolerance decreases, resulting in lower financial returns and thus limiting the size of the grants that can be made. The de-risking process requires a very "hands-on" investment approach and includes liquidating private portfolios by reducing/stopping commitments, selling private portfolios in the secondary markets, and reinvesting distributions. This becomes increasingly challenging as talented investment staff depart the organization. Actions taken and lessons learned by The Atlantic Philanthropies provide a great case study for other limited-life foundations.

6.6. Private Foundations—Liquidity Needs

The liquidity needs of foundations are relatively low but still higher than those of university endowments. US foundations are legally required to spend 5% of assets or face a tax penalty. They must set aside monies to pay one-year grants and to meet annual installments for longer-term (typically two- to five-year) grants. Having a significant allocation to such relatively illiquid asset classes as private equity and private real estate creates additional liquidity needs to meet general partners' annual net capital calls. Also, derivatives used for such activities as portfolio rebalancing or implementing portable alpha strategies may result in added liquidity demands to meet increased margin calls or to cover higher collateral demands (especially during times of financial market stress).

Exhibit 13 presents a summary comparison of foundations and endowments.

EXHIBIT 13   Comparison Between Private US Foundations and US University Endowments

	US FOUNDATION	US UNIVERSITY ENDOWMENT
Purpose	Grant-making for social, educational, and charitable purposes; principal preservation focus.	General support of institution or restricted support; principal preservation focus.
Stakeholders	Founding family, donors, grant recipients, and broader community that may benefit from foundation's activities.	Current/future students, alumni, university faculty and administration, and the larger university community.
Liabilities/ Spending	Legally mandated to spend 5% of assets + investment expenses + 100% of donations (flow-through).	Flexible spending rules (headline spending rate between 4% and 6% of assets) with smoothing.
Other liability considerations	Future gifts and donations, or just one-time gift?	Gifts and donations, percentage of operating budget supported by endowment, and ability to issue debt.
Investment time horizon	Very long-term/perpetual (except limited-life foundations).	Perpetual.
Risk	High risk tolerance with some short-term liquidity needs.	High risk tolerance with low liquidity needs.
Liquidity needs	Annual net spending is at least 5% of assets.	Annual net spending is typically 2% to 4% of assets, after alumni gifts and donations.

6.7. External Constraints Affecting Investment

In this section and the next we briefly touch on some legal/regulatory and tax constraints, respectively, that affect investing by university endowments and private foundations.

6.7.1. Legal and Regulatory Constraints

Charitable organizations, including endowments and foundations, are typically subject to rules and regulations in their country of domicile that: 1) require investment committees/officers/boards to invest on a total return basis and consider portfolio diversification when managing assets (i.e., follow the principles of modern portfolio theory, MPT); and 2) require investment committees/officers/boards to exercise a duty of care and prudence in overseeing the assets and making investment decisions (i.e., fiduciary duty).

In the United States, endowments and foundations are governed by the Uniform Prudent Management of Institutional Funds Act of 2006 (UPMIFA). Two important features of UPMIFA include:

1. Allowing charitable organizations flexibility in spending decisions, which could be adjusted for fluctuations in the market value of assets. Endowments, particularly, could meet the fiduciary standard of prudence by maintaining purchasing power of the fund.
2. Modernizing the standard of prudence for the management of charitable funds by adopting the principles of MPT established by the Uniform Prudent Investor Act (1994).

UK endowments and foundations are typically organized as trusts. Until 2000, UK trusts were limited to spending only income earned from investments (not capital gains). The Trustee Act (2000) changed that and, like UPMIFA in the United States, required trustees to manage trust assets based on MPT principles. The act also imposed a duty of care upon trustees. The shift toward managing portfolios using MPT principles has enabled endowments and foundations to embrace a broader range of asset classes compared to the traditional 60/40 equity/bond mix. It has also allowed them to focus on total return rather than solely on income return (high coupon bond and/or high-dividend-yield stocks).

6.7.2. Tax and Accounting Constraints

Endowments and foundations typically enjoy tax-exempt status. Tax-exempt status has three elements:

1. *Taxation of gifts and donations to endowments and foundations*: Gifts and donations to endowments and foundations are usually tax-deductible (up to a certain percentage of adjusted gross income) for the person or entity making the gift or donation.
2. *Taxation of income and capital gains on assets*: Income and capital gains on assets are usually tax-exempt in countries that have endowments and charitable organizations, which are tied to such non-profit, tax-exempt organizations as universities, religious organizations, or museums.
3. *Taxation on payouts from endowments and foundations*: Payouts are tax exempt if the receiving institution is exempt from income tax. If payouts are made to support the operating budget of a for-profit business, then that business is required to treat the payout as taxable income.

In the United States, private grant-making foundations enjoy the same tax-exempt status as endowments. But unlike endowments, such private foundations are subject to minimum payout (spending) requirements, whereby they must distribute a minimum of 5% of their asset value on an annual basis in grants that support their mission. Failing to meet this spending requirement subjects such foundations to 30% tax on undistributed income. Most tax-exempt private foundations also have an excise tax of 2% on their net investment income. In the United Kingdom, charitable organizations do not pay taxes on most of their income and gains if these are used for charitable purposes; however, taxes must be paid on funds that are not used for charitable purposes.

6.8. Investment Objectives

We now consider the investment objectives and investment policy statements for university endowments and the investment objectives of private foundations.

6.8.1. University Endowments

A university endowment's mission is to maintain the purchasing power of the assets into perpetuity while achieving investment returns sufficient to sustain the level of spending necessary to support the university budget. For a university endowment, investment policy and spending policy are intertwined, so the IPS should cover spending policy. As discussed previously, endowments use different spending rules. In general, endowments target a spending rate of about 5% of (average) assets. The effective spending rate will, however, be reduced after accounting for gifts and donations. An endowment's primary investment objective is typically to achieve a total real rate of return (after inflation) of $X\%$ with an expected volatility of $Y\%$ over the long term (K years). A common target for $X\%$ is 5%, with inflation being measured using the Higher Education Price Index (HEPI), to be achieved over 3 to 5 years (i.e., $K = 3$ or 5). The expected volatility of returns, $Y\%$, is typically in the range of 10% to 15% annually. Note that the target rate of return may also be expressed as a nominal (as opposed to real) return.

Endowments sometimes have secondary and tertiary investment objectives. A secondary objective might be to outperform the long-term policy benchmark. A third objective might be to outperform a set of pre-defined peers (e.g., outperform the average of the 20 largest university endowments). Peer comparison can lead to herding behavior and be detrimental to long-term success if the focus moves away from managing investments based on each organization's unique liability characteristics to exploit their own comparative advantages. To achieve their objectives, endowments invest in a broad range of asset classes, including fixed income, public equities, hedge fund strategies, private equity, private real estate, and natural resources (e.g. energy and timber). Given that endowments aim to maintain the purchasing power of their assets, they tend to have significant allocations to real assets that are expected to generate returns commensurate with inflation.

The following box provides two examples of investment objectives found in IPSs for real-life endowments.

Investment Objectives of University Endowments

Oxford University Endowment: *"The Oxford Endowment Fund aims to preserve and grow the value of perpetuity capital across the collegiate University of Oxford, while providing a sustainable income stream. ... The Oxford Endowment Fund's investment objective is to produce an average (often referred to as annualised) real return of 5% in excess of the Consumer Price Index (CPI) over the long term."*

> *Source*: http://www.ouem.co.uk/wp-ontent/uploads/2017/10/OUem_Fund_Report_17.
> pdf.
>
> *Note*: Oxford Endowment Fund defines its investors as the University of Oxford, including 23 of its colleges and five associated foundations and trusts.
>
> **Massachusetts Institute of Technology Endowment:** *"Our primary long-term goal is to generate sufficient investment returns to maintain the purchasing power of the endowment after inflation and after MIT's annual spending. Assuming inflation will average around 3% over the long-term and MIT's spending rate will average around 5%, we need to earn approximately 8% to meet this goal. As a secondary check on the quality of our performance, we compare our returns to other endowments and to passive benchmark alternatives."*
>
> *Source*: http://www.mitimco.org/wp-content/uploads/2017/03/MITIMCo-Alumni-Letter.pdf.

One of the lessons from the 2007–2009 global financial crisis is that liquidity risk must be managed carefully, particularly for institutions that invest heavily in illiquid assets. Most endowments now engage in detailed cash flow modeling for the illiquid portions of their portfolios, and some use a liquidity risk band as part of their overall risk profile. The liquidity risk band is defined as total NAV allocated to illiquid investments plus uncalled commitments to total fund AUM. If the liquidity band is violated (i.e., when the total allocation to illiquid investments exceeds a pre-specified upper bound), this may trigger a reduction (or even a stoppage) of commitments or possibly a sale of some illiquid investments in secondary markets to bring the overall illiquid allocation back to within the liquidity risk band.

EXAMPLE 5   Investment Objectives of the Ivy University Endowment

The hypothetical Ivy University Endowment was established in 1901 by Ivy University and supports up to 40% of the university's operating budget. Historically, the endowment has invested in a traditional 20% public US equities and 80% US Treasury portfolio, entirely implemented through passive investment vehicles. The investment staff at the endowment is relatively small. With the appointment of a new chief investment officer, the investment policy is being reviewed. Endowment assets are US$250 million, and the endowment has an annual spending policy of paying out 5% of the 3-year rolling asset value to the university.

An investment consultant hired by the new CIO to assist with the investment policy review has provided the following 10-year (nominal) expected return assumptions for various asset classes: US equities: 7%, Non-US equities: 8%, US Treasuries: 2%, hedge funds: 5%, and private equity: 10%. Additionally, the investment consultant believes the endowment could generate an extra 50 bps per year in alpha from active management in equities. Expected inflation for the next ten years is 2% annually.

1. Draft the investment objectives section of the IPS of the Ivy University Endowment.

2. Discuss whether the current investment policy is appropriate given the investment objectives of Ivy University Endowment.

3. What decisions could the CIO and board of the Ivy University Endowment take to align the investment policy and the spending policy?

Solution to 1: The mission of the Ivy University Endowment is to maintain purchasing power of its assets while financing up to 40% of Ivy University's operating budget in perpetuity. The investment objective, consistent with this mission, is to achieve a total real rate of return over the Higher Education Price Index (HEPI) of at least 5% with a reasonable level of risk; the volatility of returns should not exceed 15% annually.

Solution to 2: Given the expected returns provided by the consultant, a portfolio of 80% fixed income and 20% public equities, invested passively, is expected to provide a nominal expected return of 3% per year ($= 0.8 \times 2\% + 0.2 \times 7\%$). Given, expected inflation of 2%, this implies a 1% real rate of return, which falls well short of the 5% spending rate and the stated objective of a 5% real rate of return. The endowment will see its purchasing power deteriorate over time if it continues with its current asset mix and spending rate.

Solution to 3: The CIO and board could either change the investment policy by adopting an asset mix that has a more reasonable probability of achieving a 5% real rate of return (an asset allocation including non-US equities and private equity); they could change the spending rate to more accurately reflect the expected real rate of return of the current investment policy; or the new CIO may want to recommend a combination of both.

Below is an example of a university endowment Investment Policy Statement. In this case the university endowment has clearly articulated primary and secondary investment objectives.

University Endowment Investment Policy Statement

A. Introduction

The hypothetical Ivy University Endowment Fund (the "Endowment") has been established to fund scholarships, fellowships, faculty salaries, programs, activities, and facilities designed to promote and advance the mission of Ivy University (the "University"). This investment policy statement (IPS) is established by the Investment Committee of the Board of Trustees (the "IC") for the guidance of the IC, the Investment Office, the Endowment's investment managers, and other fiduciaries in the course of investing the monies of the Endowment. This IPS establishes policies and procedures for the administration and investment of the Endowment's assets. This document formally defines the goals, objectives, and guidelines of the Endowment's investment program.

B.   Mission and Investment Objectives

The Endowment provides financial support for the operations of the University. Investment and spending policies are designed to balance the current goals of the University with its future needs, in order to achieve parity in supporting both current and future generations of Ivy students. The goal for the Endowment is to provide a real total return that preserves the purchasing power of the Endowment's assets while generating an income stream to support the academic activities of the University.

The primary investment objective of the Endowment is to earn an average annual real total return (net of portfolio management fees) of at least 5% per year over the long term (rolling five-year periods), within prudent levels of risk. Attainment of this objective will be sufficient to maintain, in real terms, the purchasing power of the Endowment's assets and support the defined spending policy.

A secondary investment objective is to outperform, over the long term, a blended custom benchmark based on a current asset allocation policy of: 30% MSCI World Index, 20% Cambridge Associates LLC US Private Equity Index, 10% NCREIF Property Index, 10% Consumer Price Index for All Urban Consumers (annualized CPI-U) + 5%, 20% HFRI Fund of Funds Index, and 10% Citigroup US Treasury Index.

C.   Spending Policy

The Endowment's spending policy was developed to meet several objectives, namely to: (a) provide a sustainable level of income to support current operations, (b) provide year-to-year budget stability, and (c) meet intergenerational needs by protecting the future purchasing power of the Endowment against the impact of inflation. Under this policy, spending for a given year equals 80% of spending in the previous year, adjusted for inflation (CPI within a range of 0% and 6%), plus 20% of the long-term spending rate (5.0%) applied to the 12-quarter rolling average of market values. This spending policy has two implications. First, by incorporating the previous year's spending, the policy eliminates large fluctuations and so enables the University to plan for operating budget needs. Second, by adjusting spending toward a long-term rate of 5.0%, the policy ensures that spending levels will be sensitive to fluctuating market value levels, thereby providing stability in long-term purchasing power.

D.   Asset Allocation Policy, Allowable Ranges, and Benchmarks

The single most important investment decision is the allocation of the Endowment to various asset classes. The primary objective of the Endowment's asset allocation policy is to provide a strategic mix of asset classes that produces the highest expected investment return within a prudent risk framework. To achieve this, the Endowment will allocate among several asset classes with a bias toward equity and equity-like investments caused by their higher long-term return expectations. Other asset classes may be added to the Endowment to enhance returns, reduce volatility through diversification, and/or offer a broader investment opportunity set.

To ensure broad diversification among the major categories of investments, the Endowment has adopted the following capital allocation policy ranges for each asset class within the overall portfolio set forth in the Annex. This asset allocation framework is reviewed annually by the IC, but because of the long-term nature of the Endowment, changes to the framework are expected to be infrequent:

Asset Class	Policy Range	Benchmark
Global equity	20%–40%	MSCI World Index
Private equity & venture capital	15%–25%	Cambridge Associates LLC US Private Equity Index
Private real estate	5%–15%	NCREIF Property Index
Real assets	5%–15%	Consumer Price Index for All Urban Consumers (annualized CPI-U) + 5%
Absolute return strategies	15%–25%	HFRI Fund of Funds Index
Fixed income & cash	5%–15%	Citigroup US Treasury Index

The following core investment principles provide the foundation for the asset allocation policy:

- Equity dominance: Equities are expected to be the highest-performing asset class over the long term and thus will dominate the portfolio.
- Illiquid assets: In general, private illiquid investments are expected to outperform more-liquid public investments by exploiting market inefficiencies.
- Global orientation: The Endowment will consider the broadest possible set of investment opportunities in its search for attractive risk/return profiles.
- Diversification: Thoughtful diversification within and between asset classes by region, sector, and economic source of return can lower volatility and raise compound returns over the long term.

E. Rebalancing

The IPS establishes the long-term asset allocation targets for the endowment and policy ranges for the various asset classes approved by the IC. The role of the capital allocation ranges is to allow for short-term fluctuations caused by market volatility or near-term cash flows, to recognize the flexibility required in managing private investments, and to provide limits for tactical investing. The IC will rely on investment staff to determine allocations within the stated ranges and to regularly manage actual asset class allocations to be within the ranges where possible. In addition, the IC will review actual asset allocations relative to this asset allocation framework at each quarterly meeting.

F. Reporting

The Investment Team, with the oversight of management, must provide adequate reporting to the Board of Trustees, the IC, and other stakeholders. The reporting structure should include the following:

- Performance measurement and attribution for the quarter and trailing periods for the portfolio both in absolute terms and relative to the established benchmarks
- Asset allocation of the total portfolio
- Market value of the total portfolio

6.8.2. Private Foundations

As discussed previously, private foundations in the United States are legally required to pay out a minimum of 5% of assets annually to be eligible for tax-exempt status. Foundations strive to be capable of making grants that support their overall missions in perpetuity while meeting the minimum 5% payout requirement. The primary investment objective for foundations is typically to generate a total real return over consumer price inflation of 5%, plus investment expenses, with a reasonable expected volatility (approximately 10%–15% annual standard deviation) over a 3- to 5-year period. A secondary investment objective may include outperforming the policy benchmark with a specified tracking error budget. Monte Carlo-based modeling for generating expected returns and risk distributions as well as liquidity modeling and asset stress testing mentioned earlier for DB pension plans are also used by management and consultants to develop cogent investment objectives and policies for foundations and endowments. Foundations, like endowments, invest in a broad range of asset classes, including fixed income, public equities, hedge fund strategies, and private equity.

The following box provides two real-life examples of investment objectives for foundations.

Investment Objectives for Private Foundations

Wellcome Trust (UK):

"Our overall investment objective is to generate 4.5% real return over the long term. This is to provide for real increases in annual expenditure while preserving the Trust's capital base to balance the needs of current and future beneficiaries. We use this absolute return strategy because it aligns asset allocation with funding requirements and provides a competitive framework in which to judge individual investments."

Note: Wellcome Trust's IPS mentions that the real return is based on an average of US and UK consumer price inflation.

Source: https://wellcome.ac.uk/about-us/investments.

Robert Wood Johnson Foundation:

"The Robert Wood Johnson Foundation's mission is to help Americans lead healthier lives and get the care they need. Reflecting that mission and our Guiding Principles, we recognize that as a private foundation, 'We are stewards of private resources that must be used in the public's interest.' ... Achieving comprehensive and meaningful change in health and health care will require sustained attention over many years to come. The Foundation therefore seeks to earn an investment return that, over time, equals or exceeds the sum of its annual spending, as a percentage of the Foundation's assets plus the rate of inflation. This balance of investment return and spending is designed to spread risk and promote a steady, stable flow of support for our grantees."

Source: http://www.rwjf.org/en/about-rwjf/financials.html.

The IPS of a private foundation is not very different from that of a university endowment and follows a similar format as outlined in the previous section. The mission statement would be framed slightly differently, but the IPS would cover the same elements.

6.9. Asset Allocation

We now consider asset allocation, investment portfolios, and investment performance of university endowments. We follow with a similar discussion focusing on private foundations.

6.9.1. University Endowments

Most large endowments follow the endowment investment model and rely heavily on alternative investments to achieve their long-term investment objectives. This approach is not without risks. During the global financial crisis, several large endowments faced significant liquidity challenges and were forced to either sell portions of their private investment portfolios in the secondary markets, reduce payouts to their universities, or issue bonds to bridge their liquidity needs. The rapid post-crisis recovery arguably bailed out many endowments, but had the crisis lasted longer, the pain would have been substantially worse. David Swensen, the longtime CIO of the Yale Endowment, and his colleagues have regularly warned against a blanket application of the endowment model. Yale and some of the other large endowments have enjoyed a first-mover advantage in their private investments, and their alumni networks have provided access to investment opportunities that may not be as easily accessible to other institutions.

Exhibit 14 shows the average asset allocation for US endowments by size at the end of June 2017 using data from a study in which more than 800 colleges and universities participated. Here alternatives include private equity and venture capital, hedge funds and other marketable alternative strategies, private real estate, energy and natural resources (e.g., oil, gas, timber, commodities, and managed futures), and distressed debt.

These data reveal several important points. First, the larger endowments have a significantly higher allocation to alternatives. Larger endowments have achieved better returns over the past 10 years, and their larger allocation to alternatives has played an important role.

EXHIBIT 14   Average Asset Allocation for US University Endowments, as of June 2017 [note: x-axis is in US$ and y-axis is Allocation (%)]

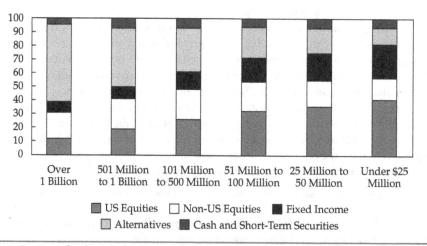

Source: Commonfund and the National Association of College and University Business Officers (NACUBO), *2017 NACUBO–Commonfund Study of Endowments*.

Second, the larger endowments do not face the "home bias" issue that smaller endowments seem to suffer. The allocation of smaller endowments to US equities is significantly larger than their allocation to non-US equities. Finally, the larger endowments hold a significantly smaller amount of their assets in fixed-income securities. This might pose a challenge during liquidity crises—such as in the 2007–2009 global financial crisis when some larger endowments struggling to meet their liquidity needs pressured managers of private investment funds to delay any calls (i.e., demands) for additional capital. Some universities also issued bonds during the crisis to help relieve the liquidity pressures faced by their endowments.

Exhibit 15 shows the average asset allocation at the end of FY 2002 and at the end of FY 2017 for university endowments of more than US$1 billion in size. During this period, the largest endowments significantly increased their allocation to alternatives from 32% to 57%. Although not shown here, most of the increase has been in the allocations to private equity, venture capital, and private real estate—with the allocation to hedge funds remaining roughly the same. This increased allocation to alternatives has come at the expense of public equities (reduced from 45% to 32%) and fixed income (reduced from 21% to 7%).

EXHIBIT 15   Average Asset Allocation for the Largest (> US$1 billion) US Endowments: FY2002 versus FY2017 [note: y-axis is Allocation (%)]

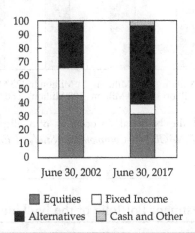

June 30, 2002   June 30, 2017

■ Equities ☐ Fixed Income
■ Alternatives ▨ Cash and Other

Sources: Commonfund and the National Association of College and University Business Officers (NACUBO), *2002 NACUBO–Commonfund Study of Endowments* and *2017 NACUBO–Commonfund Study of Endowments.*

Given asset allocations that are tilted toward alternative investments, how have endowments fared over the past 10 years? Exhibit 16 shows the average annual 10-year return (net of fees) for US endowments by size as of end-June 2017. The US Consumer Price Index averaged 1.6% over the same period, while the Higher Education Price Index (HEPI) averaged 2.4%. It is apparent, overall, that US endowments have fallen well short of generating an annualized real return of 5% over the past 10 years. Moreover, larger endowments have generally been able to generate higher returns during this period. Endowments of more than US$1 billion have generated anywhere between 50 bps to 60 bps higher returns (annually) compared to the smaller endowments (with less than US$500 million). This difference compounds to a significant gap over a 10-year period. These higher returns have allowed the larger endowments to pay out a larger part of their assets to support their universities. Interestingly, the smallest endowments (less than US$25 million) have produced a 10-year return identical to those of the largest endowments. This can be attributed to their large allocation to US equities, which outperformed other international markets by a significant margin over the last 10 years.[4] It is worth noting that the 10-year period ending 30 June 2017 is time-period specific. A different 10-year period might lead to a different conclusion. However, this 10-year period is reasonably representative of long-term asset class returns because capital markets have generally rewarded growth assets over the period.

EXHIBIT 16   Average Annual 10-Year Nominal Returns for US University Endowments as of June 2017 [note: x-axis is in US$ and y-axis is Nominal Return (%)]

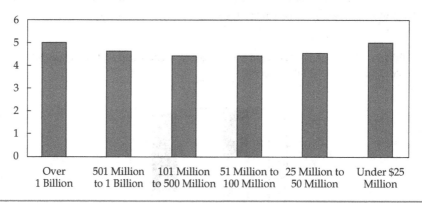

Source: Commonfund and the National Association of College and University Business Officers (NACUBO), *2017 NACUBO–Commonfund Study of Endowments*.

EXAMPLE 6   Investment Portfolio of the Ivy University Endowment

The hypothetical Ivy University Endowment was established in 1901 and supports Ivy University. The endowment supports about 40% of the university's operating budget. Historically, the endowment has invested in a traditional 20% public US equities, 80% US Treasury portfolio, and it is entirely implemented through passive investment vehicles. The investment staff at the endowment is relatively small. With the appointment of a new chief investment officer, the investment policy is being reviewed. Endowment assets are US$250 million, and the endowment has a spending policy of paying out 5% of the 3-year rolling asset value to the university.

The new CIO has engaged an investment consultant to assist her with the investment policy review. The investment consultant has provided the following

---

[4]The S&P 500 Index experienced a 100% cumulative total return over the 10-year period to 1 July 2017, while the MSCI World ex-US Index (developed markets) and the MSCI Emerging Market Index increased by 10% and 20%, respectively, over the same period.

10-year (nominal) expected return assumptions for various asset classes: US equities: 7%, Non-US equities: 8%, US Treasuries: 2%, hedge funds: 5%, private equity: 10%. In addition, the investment consultant believes that the endowment could generate an additional 50 bps in alpha from active management in equities. Expected inflation for the next 10 years is 2%.

The new CIO was at a previous endowment that invested heavily in private investments and hedge funds and recommends a change in the investment policy to the board of Ivy University Endowment. She recommends investing 30% in private equity, 30% in hedge funds, 30% in public equities (15% US and 15% non-US with *active* management), and 10% in fixed income. This mix would have an expected real return of 5.1% based on the expected return assumptions provided by the investment consultant.

1. Given the expected return assumptions from the investment consultant, provide an asset mix that would be more appropriate for Ivy University's Endowment?
2. Should the board approve the new CIO's recommendation? Provide your reasoning.

Solution to 1: To achieve a 5% real rate of return, the endowment will need to accept significantly more equity risk, diversify its assets internationally, allocate some of its assets to hedge funds and private equity, and engage in active management. There are several possible combinations that could result in a portfolio with a 5% expected real rate of return. Here are two possible asset mixes:

I: 40% in US equities with active management (7.5% expected return), 40% in non-US equities with active management (8.5% expected return), 10% in US Treasuries (2% expected return), 10% in hedge funds (5% expected return). This asset mix would result in an expected nominal return of 7.1% or an expected real return of 5.1%.

II: 50% in US equities with passive management (7% expected return), 30% in non-US equities with active management (8.5% expected return), 10% in US Treasuries (2% expected return), 10% in private equity (10% expected return). This asset mix would result in an expected nominal return of 7.25% or an expected real return of 5.25%.

Solution to 2: The board should reject the CIO's recommendation. This is a very significant departure from the current practice. The size of the investment team is small, and they have no prior experience in managing hedge fund and private equity portfolios (except for the new CIO). Additionally, given the size of the endowment, it is unlikely to have access to top quartile managers in the hedge fund and private equity spaces. The CIO should explain why the recommended asset mix with 60% in alternatives is preferable over asset mixes that deliver the same or higher expected real return (such as I and II in Solution 1).

6.9.2. Private Foundations

Foundations tend to follow a similar investment approach compared to endowments, despite important differences in their liability structures. Two of the most notable differences between foundations and endowments that should have a bearing on their asset allocation are that:

1. foundations support the entire budget of their organization, while universities have significant other sources of financing available besides the endowment; and
2. foundations (in the United States) are mandated to pay out at least 5% of their assets to maintain tax-exempt status and typically receive no additional inflows in the form of gifts and donations (or, if there are gifts/donations, these need to be spent in the same year that they are received and do not count against the 5% mandated payout), whereas university endowments typically have a net payout of less than 5%.

Exhibit 17 shows the average asset allocations for US foundations by size and type at year-end 2016. The underlying data cover 203 institutions (123 private foundations and 80 community foundations). Here, alternative investments include private equity and venture capital, hedge funds and other marketable alternative strategies, private real estate, energy and natural resources, and distressed debt.

EXHIBIT 17   Average Asset Allocation for US Foundations as of Year-End 2016 [note: x-axis is in US$ and y-axis is Allocation (%)]

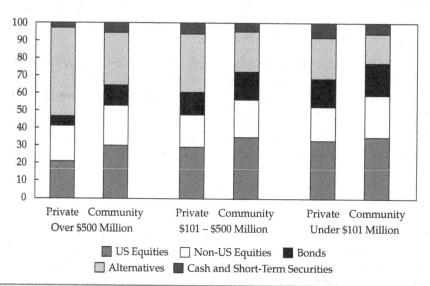

Source: Council on Foundations–Commonfund, *2016 Council on Foundations–Commonfund Study of Investment of Endowments for Private and Community Foundations (CCSF)*: https://www.cof.org/content/2016-council-foundations-commonfund-study-investment-endowments-private-and-community.

These data highlight several key points. The larger foundations have a significantly higher allocation to alternatives, and private foundations have higher allocations to alternatives compared to community foundations. The largest private foundations (more than US$500 million) have about half of their assets invested in alternatives. Although not shown, the largest private and community foundations have similar allocations to marketable alternatives (hedge funds), but the private foundations have significantly higher allocations to the higher-return-generating, illiquid alternatives—such as private equity, venture capital, private real estate, and distressed debt. Smaller foundations seem generally to have a higher allocation to US equities compared to the larger foundations. Finally, the larger private foundations hold a smaller amount of their assets in fixed-income securities.

Foundations must generate real (net of fee) returns above 5% to maintain their purchasing power. Exhibit 18 shows that over the 10-year period to year-end 2016 (when US CPI averaged 1.8%), US foundations have fallen well short of this minimum target. As a result, their purchasing power has deteriorated. However, during this period larger private foundations (more than US$500 million) have been able to generate higher returns—anywhere between 10 bps to 60 bps higher returns (annually)—compared to medium/small private foundations. Their larger allocation to alternatives likely played a key role in this outperformance. Note that the effective spending rate in 2016 was 5.8% for private foundations.

EXHIBIT 18   Average Annual 10-Year Nominal Return for US Foundations as of Year-End 2016 [note: x-axis is in US$ and y-axis is Nominal Return (%)]

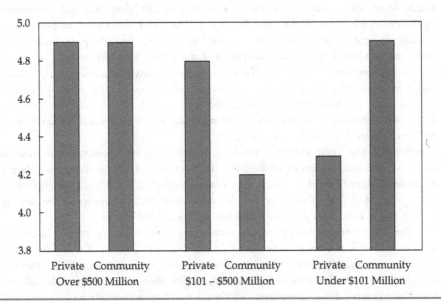

Source: Council on Foundations–Commonfund, *2016 Council on Foundations–Commonfund Study of Investment of Endowments for Private and Community Foundations (CCSF)*: https://www.cof.org/content/2016-council-foundations-commonfund-study-investment-endowments-private-and-community.

Real-Life Case Study: Wellcome Trust (UK)

Wellcome Trust ("the Trust") provides an interesting study of how a foundation transformed its investment approach and asset allocation and, in the process, significantly improved its investment performance. The Wellcome Trust was founded in 1936 and manages about £23 billion in its investment portfolio (as of end-September 2017).

The investment portfolio supports all of the charitable work of the Trust, which provides funding for scientific and medical research to improve health worldwide. During FY2016–17, charitable grants were more than £1 billion.

Between 1936 and 1986, the Trust was the sole owner of Burroughs Wellcome, the pharmaceutical company founded by Henry Wellcome. In 1986, the Trust began selling shares in the company and used the proceeds to diversify its assets. Over the past two decades, the portfolio has generated an average annual (nominal) return of 14%. The overall investment objective is to generate a 4.5% real return over the long term. The Trust used to target a payout rate of 4.7% of the weighted average value of the portfolio over the previous three years. Historically, this resulted in an average annual payout of 4.3%.

Daniel Truell joined the Trust as CIO in 2005 and initiated radical changes to its investment approach and asset mix, shifting from short-term, liquid, and low-risk assets to longer-term, less-liquid, and higher risk assets. The most notable changes were an increase in the allocation to private equity (including buyout and venture capital funds) and hedge funds as well as reduced allocations to public equities and cash. In addition to radically changing its allocations, the decision was made to concentrate assets with fewer managers and in fewer, higher quality investments, such that by 2017 less than 100 investments represented nearly 85% of the portfolio's value. The Trust also shifted to more direct investments, and active management in public equities was brought predominantly in-house and conducted by an investment team of more than 30 professionals.

At end-September 2017, the Trust's investment portfolio consisted of 53% in public equities, 9% in hedge funds, 24% in private equity, 9% in property and infrastructure, 1% in commodity futures and options, and 4% in cash. The Trust has issued bonds totaling £2 billion—representing about 8% of total assets. Proceeds from the bond issuance are used for investments.

In 2017, the Trust adopted a new approach to determine how much to fund its charitable activities. According to the latest IPS (October 2017), the Trust now "*targets an annual real cash spend in the Primary Fund (based on UK CPI) of £900 million in 2017 prices. This level of spending will be reviewed in 2022, or earlier in the event of declines in the investment portfolio below £20 billion in 2017 prices.*"

The Trust manages risk by ongoing monitoring of the following key risk factors: 1) 95% value-at-risk at a one-year horizon (if more than 20%, then this is highlighted to the Investment Committee), 2) foreign currency exposure (if more than 85%, then this is highlighted to the Investment Committee), 3) forecast of cash levels (unencumbered cash should exceed 2% of gross assets within a 5-year forecast period), and 4) estimated equity beta for the portfolio should be in the range of 0.4 to 0.8.

Sources: 1. Wellcome Trust, "Investment Policy" (October 2017): https://wellcome. ac.uk/sites/default/files/investment-policy-october-2017.pdf. 2. Wellcome Trust, *Annual Report and Financial Statements 2016* (https://wellcome.ac.uk/sites/default/files/WellcomeTrustAnnualReportFinancialStatements_160930.pdf). 3. Wellcome Trust, Annual Report and Financial Statements 2017 (https://wellcome.ac.uk/sites/default/files/wellcome-trust-annual-report-and-financial-statements-2017.pdf). 4. World Economic Forum, "Alternative Investments 2020: The Future of Alternative Investments" (2015). 5. Steve Johnson, "Uncovering Little Investment Gems among the Shrunken Heads," *Financial Times* (12 April 2014): https://www.ft.com/content/c49bb40c-be63-11e3-b44a-00144feabdc0.

7. BANKS AND INSURERS

This section focuses on institutional investors that are also financial intermediaries, namely banks and insurance companies.

Banks

Banks are financial intermediaries that take deposits, lend money, safeguard assets, execute transactions in securities and cash, act as counterparties in derivatives transactions, provide advisory services, and invest in securities. The universe of banks is quite large and diverse, ranging from small community banks to global diversified financial services institutions. A precise estimate of total worldwide banking assets is difficult to obtain; nevertheless, using publicly available data from such sources as the Bank for International Settlements (BIS), Reuters, and individual balance sheets for the largest public banks, an estimate of more than US$100 trillion seems reasonable.[5] An order-of-magnitude estimate for bank equity capitalization works out to US$7 trillion. Our focus here is on the largest, most globally important banks—the two to three dozen banks that account for the great majority of international commercial bank assets and liabilities. Exhibit 19 shows some of these banks, all of which are designated as global systemically important banks by the Financial Stability Board, an international body that monitors the global financial system.

EXHIBIT 19   Select Large Global Banks

Bank	Country/Region
Industrial & Commercial Bank of China	China
China Construction Bank Corp.	China
Agricultural Bank of China	China
Bank of China	China
HSBC Holdings Plc	Hong Kong SAR/ United Kingdom
JPMorgan Chase & Co.	United States
BNP Paribas	France
Mitsubishi UFJ Financial Group	Japan
Bank of America	United States
Credit Agricole Group	France

Source: Kevin P. Johnston, "The World's Top 10 Banks." Investopedia (25 April 2017).

Insurers

The universe of insurance companies can be divided into two broad categories:

- Life insurers
- Property and Casualty (P&C) insurers

---

[5]Inter-company and cross-border transactions, non-contemporaneous reporting dates, differing accounting treatment (IFRS vs. GAAP, for example), and currency exchange rate conversions are inescapable complications.

According to the OECD (Organization for Economic Co-Operation and Development) data on 35 large countries (ex-China and India), aggregate direct-insurance assets for both types of insurers had combined totals of more than US$22 trillion, with equity capitalization of more than US$2.2 trillion.[6]

The life insurance product set includes traditional whole and term insurance, variable life insurance and annuity products, as well as health insurance. The P&C product suite encompasses insurance against a wide range of perils—covering commercial property and liability, homeowner's property and liability, and automotive as well as such multiple specialty coverage lines as marine, surety, and workers' compensation. Exhibit 20 lists some of the largest global insurance companies.

EXHIBIT 20   Select Large Global Insurance Companies

Entity	Country/Region
AXA	France
Zurich Insurance Group	Switzerland
China Life Insurance	China
Berkshire Hathaway	United States
Prudential plc	United Kingdom
United Health Group	United States
Munich Re Group	Germany
Assicurazioni Generali S.p.A.	Italy
Japan Post Holding Co., Ltd.	Japan
Allianz SE	Germany

Source: Prableen Bajpai, "World's Top 10 Insurance Companies," Investopedia (23 March 2016).

7.1. Banks—Stakeholders

Bank stakeholders include external parties (such as shareholders, creditors, customers, credit rating agencies, regulators, and even the communities where they operate) as well as internal parties (such as employees, management, and boards of directors). A bank's investment program must meet the needs and expectations of multiple parties. Most large, international banks are typically companies with publicly issued securities, which are expected to maximize the net present value of shareholders' capital. As will be seen shortly in greater detail, this hinges importantly on the ability of banks to manage the volatility of the value of shareholders' capital.

On the liability side, bank customers are comprised of a variety of depositors, including individuals, corporations, and municipalities. Individuals deposit cash and depend on banks to safeguard their assets over time. Legal entities, ranging from small privately held companies to large publicly listed corporations, often have multiple banking relationships and depend on banks to provide financing throughout economic cycles. Similarly, municipalities and other public entities deposit funds and rely on banks' safekeeping and transaction services. In addition, both for their own account and for the benefit of customers, banks are important

---

[6]OECD (2016).

counterparties to both publicly traded and over-the-counter derivatives transactions. Finally, most global banking institutions are significant issuers of fixed-income securities, either directly or via such other means as asset-backed trusts.

On the asset side, bank customers include both retail and commercial borrowers. Individuals borrow money from banks to finance large purchases, such as houses that are often financed with mortgages. On the corporate side, real estate developers often require bank financing through commercial real estate loans. Additionally, large companies require commercial and industrial loans from banks in order to finance working capital, ongoing operations, or capital improvements.

Internal stakeholders include a bank's employees, management, and board of directors. Notably, the largest banks may each have more than 200,000 employees around the globe. At banks with a national or global presence, management teams are often highly visible in regulatory and economic affairs. At the regional and local level, bank management teams are often integrated within the local business community.

7.2. Banks—Liabilities and Investment Horizon

Banks are unique in that they originate assets (loans), liabilities (deposits, derivatives, fixed-income securities), and capital (preferred and common stock) in the normal course of business. The ability to originate and manage both assets and liabilities has implications for the management of a bank's interest rate risk exposure (i.e., asset/liability gap management) and the volatility of equity capitalization.

The largest component of bank assets is loans, typically comprising up to 50% or more of the assets of the large, international banks that dominate the sector. The next largest component of assets is debt securities, typically accounting for 25% or more of total assets. The largest remaining portion of assets consists of currency, deposits with central banks (e.g., Federal Reserve or Bank of London), receivables, and bullion.

Banks' liabilities are comprised of deposits and also include short-term funding, such as commercial paper, as well as longer term debt. Deposits are the largest component of liabilities, usually more than half of total liabilities. Bank deposits include the following:

- **Time deposits or term deposits** – These interest-bearing accounts have a specified maturity date. This category includes savings accounts and certificates of deposit (CDs). Banks have visibility on the duration of these deposits because they require advance notice prior to withdrawal.
- **Demand deposits** – These accounts can be drawn upon regularly and without notice. This category includes checking accounts and certain savings accounts that are often accessible through online banks or automated teller machines (ATMs). Consequently, banks have limited visibility on the expected lives of these accounts and tend to assume they are short-term in duration.

In addition to deposits, banks can access wholesale funding, sources of which include Federal Funds, public funds, and other government-supported, short-term vehicles. Banks must actively monitor the expected cash outlays and timing of their liabilities. For time deposits, the amount and timing of the cash outlay are known, while for demand deposits, the amount is known but the timing is uncertain. Other liabilities comprise (1) long-term debt, 10%–15% of total balance sheet; and (2) such items as trading/securities payables and repurchase finance payables, also on the order of 10%–20% of balance sheet liabilities.

The tactical investment horizon for a bank's investment portfolio is directly impacted by the nature and maturities of its asset base and liability structure.[7] Although commercial banks, as corporations, have a perpetual time horizon (possibly longer than the other institutions in this chapter), the instruments held in a bank portfolio tend to have far shorter maturities than those held by other financial institutions.

The difference between the long time horizon of the institution and the much shorter maturity of most of its assets and liabilities may seem counterintuitive. Suppose that in the current market, the credit spreads on loans are narrow and the economy is nearing recession. The long-term horizon of the bank is evidenced by it: (1) cutting back new lending, (2) selling part of its existing loan portfolio, (3) increasing allocations to short-maturity, liquid securities, and (4) decreasing leverage through fewer large wholesale time deposits. The bank is sacrificing current earnings while looking forward to an uncertain time horizon when it can aggressively expand in the more favorable future environment. The long-term time horizon means that it expects to apply similar tactics—with medium to short-term maturity assets and liabilities—many more times over the indefinite future.

7.3. Banks—Liquidity Needs

Liquidity management is a core consideration in the management of bank portfolios. Given the short duration of deposits, as well as the potential need for increased liquidity in adverse market conditions, management and regulators have developed a robust framework around liquidity management for bank portfolios. Apart from asset or cash flow securitization, banks must have the ability to liquidate their investment portfolios within a certain period to generate adequate cash in the event of a crisis.

Bank liquidity needs have evolved since the global financial crisis of 2007–2009. Prior to that period, deficiencies in liquidity from deposits were made up with wholesale funding; banks would use their portfolios as a source of return so were invested in lower quality, less liquid securities. In the post-crisis environment, however, bank portfolios are increasingly comprised of higher quality, more liquid securities. This trend to more conservative management of investment portfolios has largely been driven by increased regulatory scrutiny on a global basis, most noticeably through the introduction of mandated liquidity coverage ratios (LCRs) and net stable funding ratios (NSFRs).[8]

In general, contrasting commercial banks and retail-oriented banks, commercial banks have a higher cost of funds and lower liquidity because of wholesale funding of loan commitments and other contingent commitments. Conversely, retail banks have a lower cost of funds and better liquidity because their retail deposits are relatively low cost and tend to be more stable.

7.4. Insurers—Stakeholders

The stakeholders of insurers include such external parties as shareholders, derivatives counterparties, policyholders, creditors, regulators, and rating agencies as well as such internal

---

[7]Its strategic horizon is perpetuity because of its corporate structure, which makes it as long, or longer, than many defined benefit plans, endowments, foundations, and sovereign wealth funds.

[8]LCRs require that highly liquid assets must constitute more than 100% of highly probable near-term expected cash outflows. NSFRs set minimum requirements for stable funding sources relative to assets; such stable sources include capital, long-term debt, and non-volatile deposits.

parties as employees, management, and boards of directors. Insurance companies are organized as either companies with publicly listed securities or mutual companies.

In North America and Europe, most large insurers are companies with publicly issued securities, with the inherent shareholder concerns and pressures. As such, there is significant interest and scrutiny on quarterly investment performance, corporate earnings, and balance sheet strength. Within this context, as with banks, optimal management must focus on the long-term maximization of net present value of shareholders' capital. Concretely, this requires balancing expected returns on investments and policy writing in such a way that all insurance liabilities will be met. This requires a very strong focus by management and regulators on maintaining tight control over the volatility of the value of shareholder capital. Capital must be maintained at all investment horizons and under all scenarios so that the company will be able to honor its obligations, especially to policyholders.

Mutual companies are owned by policyholders. Mutual companies either retain profits as surplus or rebate excess cash to policyholders in the form of dividends or premium reductions.[9] Although mutual companies are free from the shareholder pressure for earnings performance, they have less access to capital markets than peers with publicly issued securities. Mutual companies remain quite prevalent in the United States, Canada, Japan, and many European countries. To provide certainty that policyholders are paid under all economic conditions, the need to control and maintain capital surplus is fundamentally the same as in the case of for-profit insurers.

Customers are primarily policyholders who have a need to protect themselves against specific risks. The main objective of any insurance company investment program is to fund policyholder benefits and claims.

Given the nature and requirements of their product suite, life insurers maintain both a **general account** and **separate accounts**. For traditional life insurance products and fixed annuities, insurers bear all the risks—particularly mortality risk and longevity risk, respectively—so they maintain a general account of assets to fund future liabilities from these products. However, in the case of variable life and variable annuity products, customers make investment decisions from a menu of options and themselves bear investment risk. Consequently, insurers invest the assets arising from these products within separate accounts. Exhibit 21 summarizes the main bearers of investment risk and the account structure for the major categories of insurance and annuity products.

EXHIBIT 21   Main Investment Risk Bearers for Different Insurance Products

Products	Bearer of Investment Risk	Account
Whole and term life insurance	Company	General
Universal life insurance	Company	General
Fixed annuities	Company	General
Variable life insurance	Policyholder	Separate
Variable annuities	Policyholder	Separate

---

[9]Mutual companies can also increase the amount of "paid up insurance" for whole-life policies.

The insurance industry is tightly regulated in most countries, usually by state or national authorities. The regulatory environment, including constraints impacting insurance asset management, will be discussed shortly. The rating agencies—including A.M. Best, Standard & Poor's, Moody's, and Fitch—are stakeholders in the management of insurance investment portfolios because they monitor the financial stability of insurance companies and provide credit ratings and data on the industry to the investment community globally.

An insurance company's management team and employees are also direct stakeholders. The large global insurance companies may have thousands of employees spread over many countries. Their management teams are often highly visible in terms of regulatory and economic affairs. Clearly, the employees are impacted by the amount of risks taken on an insurance company's balance sheet.

7.5. Insurers—Liabilities and Investment Horizon

Insurance companies manage their investment portfolios with an intense focus on asset/liability management (ALM). Within the insurance industry, the business line is critical because it determines the nature and structure of the liabilities. Further, effective management of liabilities is crucial to the long-term viability of any insurance company.

7.5.1 Life Insurers

Broadly speaking, life insurers face a liability stream and time horizon with a long duration. Life insurance involves a range of products, including Individual Life, Group Life and Disability, Individual Annuity, and Retirement Plan products. Life insurance portfolios are comprised of asset accumulation products, with some nuances in the associated liability stream. The liability stream is driven by the predictability of claims, which can vary based on the specific product line. For example, Term Life products have a one-time payout and the predictability is relatively high using statistical and actuarial analyses on large portfolios with many policies. Meanwhile, annuity products involve an ongoing payout with shorter duration that is subject to longevity risk. The nature of the liability stream has important implications for the amount of investment risk that can be tolerated.

Within life insurance, product features and resulting liabilities as well as policyholder behavior are key determinants of the associated portfolios' investment horizons. Historically, life insurance companies set portfolio return objectives with long time horizons of 20 to 40 years.

7.5.2 Property & Casualty Insurers

In general, P&C insurers face a shorter duration liability stream and investment horizon than life insurers. Further, P&C insurance involves events with lower probability of occurrence and potentially higher cost (especially in the case of natural disasters), leading to highly volatile business claims. This results in a liability stream with short duration and high uncertainty.

For example, a P&C insurance company may initiate policies against catastrophic events, such as hurricanes or other natural disasters. By definition, this insurance involves unpredictable and infrequent events that are difficult to hedge against. Insurance companies utilize statistical and actuarial analyses to forecast liability cash flows on a probabilistic (scenario) basis. P&C insurers may benefit from developing global, diversified portfolios that are more applicable to statistical analysis because of the law of large numbers. In any case, P&C insurers face a liability stream with a shorter duration and more potential volatility than life insurers.

With both life and P&C insurers, as with banks, the nature and timing of expected policy claims strongly influence the time horizon and nature of investments held. Even so, the ultimate management time horizon is perpetuity. A natural and frequently occurring example for both types of insurers is the case of underwriting cycles. Such cycles relate to the pricing of newly issued policies relative both to then-existing expected security returns and to the actuarial outlook for life and casualty loss claims. Long-term strategic investment and balance-sheet management policies result in modifications to portfolios and overall company leverage at different points in time to adjust to the varying relative attractiveness of bearing investment risk versus bearing underwriting risk and/or financial (leverage) risk.

7.6. Insurers—Liquidity Needs

Insurance companies must actively manage and monitor the liquidity of their portfolios. The level of liquidity required has important implications across the portfolio management process, including the insurer's ability to utilize leverage. Further, liquidity needs can vary greatly based on the business line.

Both life and P&C insurers need a sound, two-part liquidity plan that includes internal and external components. An insurer's internal liquidity includes cash and cash equivalents maintained on the balance sheet. Insurers must actively manage cash from operations (including investment income) that involves steady inflows and outflows. Further, insurers manage and project the cash flows from investment portfolio income and principal repayments. An insurer's external liquidity includes the ability to issue bonds in the capital markets and to access credit lines through syndicated commercial bank credit lines or other lines of credit. Finally, insurers manage short-term liquidity by actively buying and selling repurchase agreements. In this way, insurers consistently manage both internal and external sources of liquidity.

The liquidity needs of life insurance companies must also be considered in the context of the interest rate environment. In periods of rising/high interest rates, insurance companies may face the risk of significant net cash outflow as policies are surrendered by customers searching for higher yields in other investments. P&C insurers face uncertainty regarding both the value and timing of the payment of benefits. This significant cash flow uncertainty necessitates maintaining ample liquidity and results in P&C portfolios comprised of high proportions of cash and cash substitutes as well as short-term fixed-income instruments.

Insurers segment general account investment portfolios into two major components: **reserve portfolio** and **surplus portfolio**. Insurance companies are typically subject to specific regulatory requirements to maintain a reserve portfolio that is intended to ensure the company's ability to meet its policy liabilities. The surplus portfolio is intended to realize higher expected returns. Insurance companies manage reserve assets relatively conservatively. The size of the reserve portfolio is typically dictated by statute, and assets must be highly liquid and low risk. Meanwhile, insurance companies have more of an ability to assume liquidity risk in the surplus portfolio. Insurance companies are often willing to manage these assets aggressively with exposure to alternative assets, including private equity, hedge funds, and non-security assets.

7.7. External Constraints Affecting Investment

The legal and regulatory environments, as well as tax and accounting constraints, faced by banks and insurers are complex and may vary according to the national and local jurisdictions in which these institutional investors do business. In this section, we take a high-level view of some of the major legal and regulatory constraints within which banks and insurers must operate. In the following section, we consider tax and accounting constraints that affect investing by banks and insurers.

7.7.1. Legal and Regulatory Constraints

For banks and insurance companies, the liabilities to depositors, the claims of policyholders, and the amounts due to creditors are clearly and contractually defined. This is different from the other types of institutions discussed previously where there typically can be a great deal of discretion in the timing and amounts due and paid to stakeholders. Furthermore, banks and insurance companies carry out important functions with respect to the underlying economies in which they operate. These include facilitation of individual and commercial payments, extensions of credit, safeguarding of assets, and transfers of risk—to name the more important. The activities of companies in the financial industry not only are deeply intertwined with the non-financial, or *real,* economy, but their activities also are deeply intertwined with each other. Thus, a disturbance in the operation of individual banks and insurance companies can spread through the entire financial industry with great speed and with compounding damage; significant adverse effects can easily overflow into the real economy. Such negatives can include depositor runs on a banking system, credit crunches whereby companies or governments cannot obtain funding for maintaining operations, or the failure of insurance companies that undermine the viability of large sectors of the economy, such as residential housing or the health care markets. Consequently, banking and insurance regulators in most jurisdictions are intensely focused on capital adequacy, liquidity, and leverage to mitigate systemic or contagion risk.

Banks and insurance companies are primarily regulated at national and state levels and are increasingly overseen by supranational regulatory and advisory bodies. The need to regulate banks and insurance companies at high, rather than local, levels stems from the fact that financial institutions are mainly large and spread across many local and national jurisdictions. At its most essential, the regulation of financial institutions centers on making sure banks and insurance companies have adequate capitalization to absorb losses rather than allowing losses to be borne by the rest of the financial system or the real economy—including depositors, insurance policyholders, creditors, or taxpayers.

Lowering the risk of assets through regulation is the first way to lower the potential strains on bank and insurance company capitalization. This can be through requirements for diversification, asset quality (including adequate reserve provisioning for credit, market, and operational risk losses) and liquidity maintenance. Likewise, setting requirements on liabilities can lower potential stress on bank and insurance capital resources. Such regulation of liabilities may include requirements for funding sources to be diversified over time and among different groups of depositors and debtholders. In the case of insurance companies, potential losses from liabilities can be regulated through rules limiting the size and concentration of potential policy claims. In addition to limiting potential losses from assets and liabilities—or from other operational risks—regulators may mandate certain minimum required capitalization.

Turning to insurers, the US insurance industry is regulated by individual states, each having its own administrative agency; the federal government does not play a major role in oversight. The National Association of Insurance Commissioners (NAIC), of which every state is a member, provides a forum for industry issues and sets accounting policies and financial reporting standards for the industry. In Europe, regulators have developed the Solvency II framework to standardize insurance regulation across member states.

The size and diversity of financial institutions result from powerful economies of scale. These economies of scale arise because most activities of banks and insurance companies (such as extension of credit, underwriting health or property risks, or taking of deposits) are made in large numbers, where the successes and failures of individual transactions are not normally highly correlated among each other. By the law of large numbers, the volatility of the weighted sum of independent risks decreases as a function of the square root of the number of independent risks assumed. This diversification effect would be a benefit to a financial firm that grows larger than its competitors. In fact, it would represent increasing returns to scale because the largest institution could hold a portfolio of assets with less capital than its competitors, because asset and liability volatility would be much less and would result in a higher and less volatile return on capital for the largest institution. Of course, offsetting factors keep this effect from dominating. Other marginal costs of operation, communications, and management keep the industry from eventually evolving into one giant financial firm. Nevertheless, the powerful impacts of diversification in terms of credit defaults, deposit funding, casualty insurance claims, and life-and-health mortality/morbidity claims are very strong factors in contributing to the existence of a small number of large national and international financial firms that comprise most of the financial industry's assets and earnings.

These few large firms are regarded as systemically important financial institutions (SIFIs). Since the worldwide financial system meltdown of 2008–2009, legislators and regulators worldwide have moved in the direction of bolstering the financial system by raising capital requirements—directly, by requiring higher absolute amounts of primary capital, and indirectly, by (1) effectively increasing the amount of capital needed to support the holding of certain investments, (2) limiting the payout of dividends and repurchases of common equity, and (3) making subordinated debt and preferred shareholders less able to assert their claims in the event of bankruptcy or regulator-mandated restructuring. Furthermore, regulators' actions have resulted in tightening regulations on the use of derivatives, proprietary trading, and off-balance-sheet liabilities/guarantees. These actions require institutions through stress testing to show how they can survive severe economic and financial market turbulence, and they impose more stringent accounting/disclosure rules and reserving requirements. The consequences of a relatively small number of SIFIs dominating the financial industry and the existence of regulatory cycles mean that the management of a financial institution must take into account the actions of its SIFI competitors and must integrate its asset and liability portfolio decisions with a view to where the rules are today *and* where they are likely heading.

7.7.2. Accounting and Tax Considerations

Three different types of accounting systems apply for every financial institution. For the enterprise and its subsidiaries, the first is standard financial accounting, whether in the form of GAAP or IFRS, and which is used for communicating results to shareholders (or members), deposit or policyholders, and suppliers of debt capital. Regulators of banks and insurance companies, in addition, impose a second type of accounting in various forms and is known as *statutory* accounting. Statutory accounting rules can be very different across different national and local regulatory jurisdictions. Although statutory results are normally available to the public, they mostly are utilized by regulators. Finally, the third type, true economic accounting, marks all assets and liabilities (net of imputed income taxes) to current market values.

Each accounting system is designed with a particular objective in mind, and it is incumbent upon financial institution managers and investment analysts to understand the purposes of all three. Economic or mark-to-market (MTM) accounting provides the best picture of an entity's assets, liabilities, and changes in economic well-being. MTM earnings are the most volatile of all because they reflect all value changes contemporaneously rather than being smoothed over time. The results of MTM reporting are likely to differ from those from financial reporting, where the reporting rules are consistently and conservatively applied over time (but where asset and liability values may depart from reported balance sheet amounts). Financial reporting has moved increasingly in the direction of MTM accounting over the past several decades, although changes in asset and liability values often are reported by way of balance sheet comprehensive income accounts rather than directly through an income statement. On balance, financial reporting will provide the smoothest reporting of income and asset/liability valuations.

Statutory accounting represents essentially a system of adjustments to standard financial accounting. For both bank and insurance regulators, this means most significantly the subtracting of intangible assets from asset and common equity accounts and/or the acceleration of certain expenses, such as policy underwriting and sales costs. In other cases, it is the recognition and assignment of additional reserves against losses on assets or unexpectedly large losses on guarantees or insurance claims. Statutory accounting usually results in lower earnings and lower common equity capital than in financial accounting. Capital requirements for both banks and insurance companies are predicated on one or another version of statutory reporting.

In terms of taxation, banks and insurance companies typically are taxable entities, and the industry-specific tax rules can be quite complicated. As taxable entities, banks and insurance companies must manage their investment programs with consideration of after-tax returns.

7.8. Investment Objectives

We now consider the investment objectives of banks followed by a discussion of investment objectives and an investment policy statement for insurers.

7.8.1. Banks
The investment securities portfolio of a bank is an integral component of the overall banking enterprise. The primary objective of a bank's securities investment portfolio is to manage the bank's liquidity and risk position relative to its non-securities assets, derivatives positions, liabilities, and shareholders' capitalization. Given the highly regulated nature of the industry, banks typically have formally documented investment policies as well as multiple levels of oversight in the form of internal committees and external regulators.

What follows provides a real-life example of how investment objectives are framed at banks.

Bank Investment Objective

JPMorgan Chase & Co., Treasury and Chief Investment Officer Overview
"Treasury and CIO are predominantly responsible for measuring, monitoring, reporting and managing the Firm's liquidity, funding and structural interest rate and foreign exchange risks, as well as executing the Firm's capital plan. ... The risks managed by Treasury and CIO arise from the activities undertaken by the Firm's four major reportable business segments to serve their respective client bases, which generate both on- and off-balance sheet assets and liabilities.

Treasury and CIO achieve the Firm's asset-liability management objectives generally by investing in high-quality securities that are managed for the longer-term as part of the Firm's investment securities portfolio. Treasury and CIO also use derivatives to meet the Firm's asset- liability management objectives."
Source: JPMorgan Chase & Co., *Annual Report 2016*, https://www.jpmorganchase.com/corporate/investor-relations/document/2016-annualreport.pdf.

Banks establish an asset/liability management committee ("ALMCo") that provides direction and oversight of the investment portfolio. The ALMCo has significant visibility with the bank's management and board of directors, as well as with external regulators. This ALMCo sets the investment policy statement (IPS), monitors performance on an ongoing basis, and has the ability to mandate adjustments on the asset and liability sides of the balance sheet. The ALMCo also ensures that market (interest rate and FX), credit, liquidity, and solvency (capital adequacy) risk positions are within the limits of the bank's specified risk tolerances. Once the overall investment objectives and risk levels are set, the investment team establishes policy benchmarks. The investment team monitors performance and such portfolio characteristics as duration and convexity relative to the benchmark for each asset class. Further, the investment team may monitor performance relative to a set of peers with comparable business models and investment objectives. Finally, the investment team makes periodic presentations to senior management and the board of directors regarding performance and characteristics of the investment portfolio.

7.8.2. Insurers
Given the highly regulated nature of the insurance industry, a detailed and well-documented Investment Policy Statement is of paramount importance. It is a best practice for an IPS to take a holistic approach and include the parent company's strategic enterprise risk management framework. Similar to banks, insurers manage their investment portfolios with a focus on liquidity as well as interest rate, foreign exchange, credit, and other risk factors.

The investment oversight function is a critical part of an insurer's overall governance. Insurers typically have a committee on the board of directors that maintains oversight of all investment policies, procedures, strategies, and performance evaluation. Insurers provide significant transparency to their underlying portfolios—including showing the inherent duration, credit, and other risks to regulators and other external stakeholders.

The IPS should encompass the insurer's appetite for market risk, credit risk, and interest rate risk. An insurer's risk tolerance may vary relative to the competitive environment for various product lines, regulatory and tax changes, market conditions, and other factors. Moreover, the IPS should be a "living document" that evolves as market, regulatory, and business conditions change.

Hypothetical Life Insurance Company—Investment Policy Statement

I. Introduction

XYZ Life Insurance Company ("the Company") underwrites and markets life insurance and annuity products. The Company is licensed to provide insurance products in all 50 US states, as well as several foreign countries. This investment policy statement ("IPS") documents the policies and procedures that govern the Company's general account securities portfolio. There are detailed policy statements for each asset segment within the portfolio that provide a more granular breakdown of investment guidelines.

II. Governance and Stakeholders

The Company's investment policies, including investment objectives and constraints, are the responsibility of the Investment and Finance Committee ("IFC") of the board of directors ("BoD"). The insurer's senior management team ("Mgmt") is responsible for implementation of the investment program consistent with this policy. In turn, the investment team ("InvTeam") manages the investment portfolio on a day-to-day basis.

The IFC will review the investment policy on an annual basis. The IFC must consider changes to the Company's strategic direction, regulatory changes, tax changes, financial market conditions, and any other relevant factors that may arise. The IFC proposes adjustments to the IPS to the BoD, and all material changes must be approved by the BoD in their entirety.

The IFC has responsibility to employ appropriate resources for the management of the investment portfolio. The IFC may retain or dismiss InvTeam personnel at its discretion. Further, the IFC may retain investment consultants or other advisers to manage specific asset classes or other sub-components of the portfolio. All consultant, external investment managers, and other advisers are required to comply with this IPS.

III. Mission and Investment Objective

The core mission of the general account is twofold:

1. Provide liquidity for the payment of policyholder claims in the normal course of insurance operations.

2. Grow the Company's surplus over the long-term.

The investment objective must follow prudent investing practices and achieve an appropriate balance between maintaining short-term liquidity and contributing to long-term asset growth.

IV. Risk Tolerance and Constraints

The Company is subject to significant scrutiny from internal and external stakeholders, including shareholders, regulators, and others. The general account investment program must take into account the following key factors:

- **Liquidity.** The investment portfolio must maintain sufficient liquidity to meet all policyholder claims that may arise on a short-term and long-term basis. The InvTeam monitors investment cash flow to ensure the Company's ability to meet all obligations in a timely manner. Further, the InvTeam may liquidate publicly traded securities as a secondary source of liquidity.

- **Interest Rate Risk.** The InvTeam monitors the portfolio's exposure to changes in interest rates, including the relative exposure of both assets and liabilities.
- **Credit Risk.** The InvTeam monitors the credit (default) risk inherent in the portfolio and must continually monitor the financial health of key counterparties.
- **Foreign Exchange Risk.** The Company is subject to foreign exchange risk in the normal course of business. The InvTeam monitors the aggregate foreign exchange risk of the portfolio.
- **Regulatory Requirements.** All investments must adhere to the insurance code of the Company's state of domicile as well as all other applicable domestic and foreign guidelines. Further, the investment program must comply with risk-based capital considerations and rating agency requirements.
- **Tax Considerations.** Further, the securities portfolio must account for tax considerations, and all investment decisions should be evaluated on an after-tax basis. The income tax planning of the Company may impact the timing of realization of capital gains and losses.

V. Asset Allocation Policy, Allowable Ranges, and Benchmarks

The primary investment vehicles within the Company's investment portfolio will consist of highly liquid instruments, including US and foreign government obligations, corporate debt, and other fixed-income instruments. Further, the Company may invest in private placement bonds, commercial mortgage loans, and other less liquid instruments within the parameters specified. Further, the Company may invest in real estate and private equity in order to enhance long-term returns and contribute to the surplus growth of the company. However, strict guidelines apply for less liquid asset classes.

The IFC establishes the strategic asset allocation that is consistent with the long-term constraints of the Company. The IFC will review the strategic asset allocation annually and may make adjustments as appropriate. Further, the IFC sets out allowable ranges of allocation for each asset class. Further, the IFC approves appropriate benchmarks for each asset class upon consultation with the InvTeam.

VI. Investment Guidelines

The InvTeam should seek to diversify holdings in terms of economic exposure, counterparty, and other applicable attributes to the extent possible. Securities that are guaranteed by the US government or its agencies must constitute at least 25% of the portfolio.

VII. Reporting

The InvTeam, with the oversight of Mgmt, must provide adequate reporting to the BoD and other stakeholders. The reporting structure should include the following:

- Daily Flash Report: Summary of market values, yield, and interest rate position of entire portfolio
- Monthly Investment Performance Detail: Detailed investment performance by asset class, including market values, yields, and interest rate position
- Quarterly Investment Summary: Detailed analysis of market values, yield, and interest rate exposure, including long-term performance metrics and attribution.

7.9. Banks and Insurers—Balance Sheet Management and Investment Considerations

We turn now to the portfolio investment strategy for banks and insurance companies. The objectives and constraints are very different from what we have seen with respect to pensions, sovereign wealth funds, endowments, and foundations. In the case of banks and insurance companies, the need is to fund deposits, policy claims, derivatives payoffs, and debtholders. A financial institution's fundamental purpose is to assure such contractual parties the full and timely payment of claims when they come due. A firm can only hope to earn a profit if it can provide counterparties assurance it will be able to meet all claims with extremely high probability.

The financial claims against banks and insurers may not always be known with certainty, but they are, at any point in time, measurable. Such measurement may require the use of probabilistic methods to account for such outcomes as: (1) the liquidation of bank deposits; (2) insurance policy claims and surrenders; (3) losses on derivatives, guarantees, or forward purchase commitments; and (4) returns on variable annuities, among other outcomes. Thus, in the case of banks and insurers, the well-defined, contractual nature of the financial claims, along with their measurability, imply that—unlike with defined benefit and defined contribution pension plans, sovereign wealth funds, endowments, and foundations—the underlying investment strategy is mainly liability driven investing (LDI as earlier defined).

We can obtain insight about both investment strategy and regulation of financial institutions by applying a fairly simple but intuitive economic model. The model's first two equations define the relationship between an institution's assets A, liabilities (claims) L, and residual equity of the institution's shareholders or members E:

$$A = L + E \qquad (1)$$

$$\Delta A = \Delta L + \Delta E \qquad (2)$$

Assets are equal to the sum of contractual claims and residual ownership. Likewise, all changes in assets must equal the sum of changes in the value of contractual claims and ownership interest (equity capitalization). These equations are set forth in terms of current market—or economic—values, which will not necessarily coincide with GAAP, IFRS, or regulatory/statutory values. However, using current market values will facilitate the subsequent application of these other accounting valuations.

These equations can be used to understand not just market value changes but also the impact of earnings, the consequences of adding or selling off assets in total, and changes in an institution's capital structure. All of these are relevant to investment strategy and are additional layers of complexity as compared with the other portfolio strategies in this chapter.

By multiplying the various terms by 1 (i.e., $A \div A$ or $L \div L$), dividing both sides by E, and doing a little regrouping, we obtain a useful expression, namely:

$$\frac{\Delta A}{A}\left(\frac{A}{E}\right) = \frac{\Delta L}{L}\left(\frac{L}{E}\right) + \frac{\Delta E}{E} \qquad (3)$$

Using Equation 1 and moving liabilities and assets to the same side of the equation, we rewrite this as:

$$\frac{\Delta E}{E} = \frac{\Delta A}{A}\left(\frac{A}{E}\right) - \frac{\Delta L}{L}\left(\frac{A-E}{E}\right) = \frac{\Delta A}{A}\left(\frac{A}{E}\right) - \frac{\Delta L}{L}\left(\frac{A}{E}-1\right) \tag{4}$$

Equation 4 provides an easy way to see how percentage changes in market value of both assets and liabilities are magnified by the leverage factors.

To demonstrate this point, Exhibit 22 presents the effects on the market value of the institution's equity capital as a function of (i) declines in underlying asset value,[10] and (ii) beginning degree of leverage. Asset values can decline for several reasons, such as deterioration in credit quality and/or liquidity of loans or securities held. The value of assets can also be hurt by rising interest rates in the case of fixed-rate loans or securities.

EXHIBIT 22   Effects on Market Value of Equity Due to Change in Market Value of Assets (Given Beginning Degree of Leverage)

Beg. Equity to Assets Ratio	Leverage (x)	Percentage Change in Institution's Equity Value Due to Change in Asset Value of:			
(E÷A)	(A÷E)	−0.5%	−1.0%	−1.5%	−2.0%
20%	5.0	−2.5%	−5.0%	−7.5%	−10.0%
15%	6.7	−3.3%	−6.7%	−10.0%	−13.3%
10%	10.0	−5.0%	−10.0%	−15.0%	−20.0%
5%	20.0	−10.0%	−20.0%	−30.0%	−40.0%

This analysis reveals that even small losses in the market value of assets can have a pronounced negative effect on the institution's equity capital account because of the leverage factor. Naturally, it works in reverse; Small gains in assets can have a very positive impact for equity capital holders. These relationships give rise to a conflict of interest: Because equity capital holders can only lose the value of their investment but also can make extremely large gains if assets perform well, liability holders require some form of protection against the potential inclination of the institution to take excessive risks. Contractual, regulatory, and reputational methods all come into play to provide such protection. In one form or another, they relate to limiting the volatility of assets and providing for a capital cushion so that equity capital holders, rather than liability holders, are expected to absorb unforeseen losses on assets.

Similarly, financial institutions face the possibility of loss from adverse changes in the market value of liabilities. In the case of insurance companies, unexpectedly high policy loss claims are the most notable cause of expanding liabilities. For banks, it could be having to make a forward-funding commitment to a struggling company, the exercise of a guarantee, or a loss on forward currency purchase contracts. Exhibit 23 uses Equation 4 to illustrate the effect on the market value of the institution's equity capital as a function of (i) increases in its liabilities and (ii) beginning degree of leverage.

---

[10]Which, for our analysis, focuses on the investment portfolio assets. The net equity described here is net financial equity. The portion of an institution's equity associated with financing other assets, such as buildings and equipment, are not a focus of this chapter.

EXHIBIT 23   Effects on Market Value of Equity Due to Change in Market Value of Liabilities (Given Beginning Degree of Leverage)

Beg. Equity to Assets Ratio	Leverage (x)	Percentage Change in Institution's Equity Value Due to Change in Liability Value of:			
(E÷A)	[(A÷E) − 1]	+0.5%	+1.0%	+1.5%	+2.0%
20%	4.0	−2.0%	−4.0%	−6.0%	−8.0%
15%	5.7	−2.8%	−5.7%	−8.5%	−11.3%
10%	9.0	−4.5%	−9.0%	−13.5%	−18.0%
5%	19.0	−9.5%	−19.0%	−28.5%	−38.0%

Exhibit 23 bolsters the conclusions reached in Exhibit 22. Mainly, liability holders, regulators, and owners (equity shareholders) of a financial institution all are motivated to limit the volatility and magnitude, relative to the base capital level, of market value changes in the institution's liabilities.

Now we must integrate the analysis of both sides of the balance sheet with the capital management strategy of the financial institution. To do this, we would like to have a framework for understanding various interactions in a more rigorous manner. A customary starting point is with an analysis of interest rate risk. Our framework comfortably accommodates the standard duration-based model of value changes with respect to interest rate changes. In order to find the percentage change in the value of the institution's equity capital associated with a change in the reference yield, y, on the asset holdings, we divide Equation 4 by the change in such yield, thereby obtaining:

$$\frac{\Delta E}{E\Delta y} = \frac{\Delta A}{A\Delta y}\left(\frac{A}{E}\right) - \frac{\Delta L}{L\Delta y}\left(\frac{A}{E}-1\right) \tag{5}$$

Likewise, we want to understand how this relates to the change in the effective yield on the liabilities, i. Multiplying by $1 = \Delta i \div \Delta i$ in the appropriate location, we restate Equation 5 as:

$$\frac{\Delta E}{E\Delta y} = \frac{\Delta A}{A\Delta y}\left(\frac{A}{E}\right) - \frac{\Delta L}{L\Delta i}\left(\frac{\Delta i}{\Delta y}\right)\left(\frac{A}{E}-1\right) \tag{6}$$

Recall that the modified duration of asset W with respect to its yield-to-maturity, r, (D_W^*) is defined as:

$$D_W^* = -\frac{\Delta W}{W\Delta r} \tag{7}$$

This allows us to revise Equation 6 to a practical and intuitive analytical tool, namely,

$$D_E^* = \left(\frac{A}{E}\right)D_A^* - \left(\frac{A}{E}-1\right)D_L^*\left(\frac{\Delta i}{\Delta y}\right) \tag{8}$$

Over reasonably modest yield changes, Equation 8 provides a useful way to break down the volatility of a financial institution's equity capital as a function of degree of leverage, comparative (modified) duration of assets and liabilities, and correlation (or sensitivity) of changes in yields of assets and liabilities.

Exhibits 24 and 25 show how sensitive the valuation of equity is to changes in the security portfolio yield for differing degrees of mismatching of asset and liability durations. In both these exhibits, the x-axis shows the duration of the financial institution's liabilities, the y-axis shows the duration of its security portfolio assets, and the z-axis (vertical axis) shows the resulting duration of the institution's shareholders' equity. The yields on liabilities are assumed to move only 90% as much as the yields on portfolio assets. That is,

$$\frac{di}{dy} = \frac{\Delta i}{\Delta y} = 0.90$$

Exhibits 24 and 25 show results for differing initial degrees of leverage, as measured by the equity-to-assets ratio, which is 20% and 10%, respectively.

EXHIBIT 24   Duration of Shareholders' Equity as a Function of Asset and Liability Durations (Given Equity/Assets = 20% and Sensitivity of Yield Changes = 0.90)

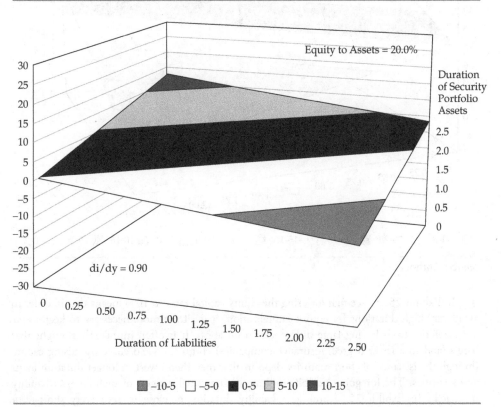

Source: Authors

Exhibit 24 indicates that, even at relatively high capital ratios of 20%, moderate differences between asset and liability durations can imply durations for equity that can be sizable in either a positive or negative direction. Remember that, by definition, the modified duration of a zero-coupon bond is its final maturity divided by one plus its yield. Thus, by comparison, a 10-year zero coupon bond would have a modified duration around 9.75. Utilizing Equation 7, a +/− 100 basis point change in interest rates when multiplied by a modified duration of 9.75 implies an approximate +/− 10% change in value. It is highly unlikely that regulators would like to see large asset/liability duration mismatches, since regulators want equity capital to remain stable in periods of large adverse interest rate changes.

EXHIBIT 25   Duration of Shareholders' Equity as a Function of Asset and Liability Durations (Given Equity/Assets = 10% and Sensitivity of Yield Changes = 0.90)

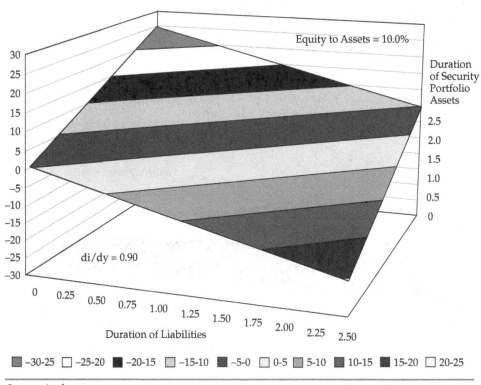

Source: Authors

In Exhibit 25, we see that lowering the equity capital ratio to 10% means that in order to avoid very high durations for equity capitalization, it is all the more necessary to keep assets and liabilities from having large differences in duration. It is often mistakenly thought that banks (and to a lesser degree, insurance companies) climb the yield curve by raising capital through the issuance of short maturity deposits that they then invest in longer duration loans and securities. The foregoing exhibits indicate the potential dangers of such an asset/liability mismatch. In Exhibit 25, assuming a liability duration of close to zero (very short-term deposits and overnight borrowing), even if the security portfolio duration is only 2.5 years, the duration of shareholder's equity reaches 25 years (about the equivalent of a 26-year zero coupon bond). In such a case, a +/– 100 basis point change in asset yields would produce a +/– 25% change in shareholder equity value. The loss potential is a danger that neither deposit holders, creditors, stockholders, nor regulators would be keen to embrace.

In actuality, in order to lower asset duration, financial institutions hold cash, deposits at central banks, foreign currency reserves, and other highly liquid (zero duration) assets. Also, as a means of lowering effective asset durations, banks typically make business loans that float according to market reference rates, which are expected to move in line with the variable cost of deposits. Likewise, credit card and many real estate loans are tied to variable rate indexes in order to minimize the sensitivity of values to interest rates. Moreover, many fixed-rate mortgage loans are securitized and sold off to private investors. All these foregoing techniques are ways of limiting the duration of asset portfolios.

On the liability side, there are many ways in which the duration of liabilities can be extended far beyond the implicit zero duration of demand deposits. These include issuance of intermediate and longer-term debt instruments, deeply subordinated capital securities, and perpetual preferred stock. Finally, banks can and do utilize financial futures and interest rate swaps to alleviate asset/liability mismatches.

In the light of persistent low interest rates since the global financial crisis of 2007–2009, many large international banks have an asset/liability structure where earnings are poised to benefit from a rise in interest rates. In such cases, the duration of assets is actually shorter than the duration of liabilities. This is clearly not the naïve "borrow short and lend long" strategy.

EXAMPLE 7

MegaWorld Bancorp has an equity capital ratio for financial assets of 9%. The modified duration of its assets is 2.0 and of its liabilities is 1.5. Over small changes, the yield on liabilities is expected to move by 85 bps for every 100 bps of yield change in its asset portfolio.

1. Compute the modified duration of the bank's equity capital.
2. What would be the impact on the value of shareholder capital of a 50 basis point rise in the level of yields on its asset portfolio?
3. Management is considering issuing common stock, selling investment portfolio assets, and paying off some liabilities in order to achieve an equity capitalization ratio of 10%. Assuming no change in the durations of assets and liabilities and assuming no change in the sensitivity of liability yields to asset yields, what is the resulting modified duration of the bank's equity capital?
4. Using the facts in question 3 but assuming the bank rebalances its investment portfolio to achieve a modified duration of assets of 1.75, what happens to the duration of the bank's equity capital?

Solution 1:
Using Equation 8, $A \div E = 1/0.09 = 11.11$; $(A \div E) - 1 = 10.11$; $D_A^* = 2.0$; $D_L^* = 1.5$; and $\Delta i \div \Delta y = 0.85$.

Therefore, the modified duration of shareholders' capital is:

$$D_E^* = (11.11 \times 2) - (10.11 \times 1.50) \times 0.85 = 9.33$$

Solution 2:
Using the implications of Equation 7, the change in equity capitalization value is computed as:

$$0.5\% \times -9.33 = -4.67\%.$$

Solution 3:
With this less leveraged balance sheet, $A \div E = 1/0.1 = 10$; $(A \div E) - 1 = 9$; and the duration of shareholders' equity is:

$$D_E^* = (10 \times 2) - (9 \times 1.50) \times 0.85 = 8.53$$

Solution 4:
The duration of shareholders' capital now declines to:

$$D_E^* = (10 \times 1.75) - (9 \times 1.50) \times 0.85 = 6.03$$

Our previous discussion has given us some insight into the effects of leverage and the volatility of underlying assets and liabilities on the value of a financial institution's equity. The degree of leverage was given; the sensitivity of changes in liability to asset yields (di/dy) was constant; and the durations of assets and liabilities varied. Although quite useful in many circumstances, such duration analysis captures the effects of only small changes in overall levels of interest rates and only over short time intervals.[11] Although of great significance, changes in the overall levels of interest rates are only one source of volatility. An expansion of Equation 4 is therefore necessary. A natural step is to extend it in a probabilistic way. We can thereby capture the volatility of the market value change in the financial institution's equity capital as shown in Equation 9. Volatility is defined here as standard deviation, where $\sigma_{\frac{\Delta E}{E}}$, $\sigma_{\frac{\Delta A}{A}}$, and $\sigma_{\frac{\Delta L}{L}}$ represent the standard deviations of the percentage changes in market value of equity capital, asset holdings, and liability claims, respectively.[12] Furthermore, $-1 \leq \rho \leq 1$ denotes the correlation between percentage value changes of assets and liability claims.[13]

$$\sigma_{\frac{\Delta E}{E}}^2 = \left(\frac{A}{E}\right)^2 \sigma_{\frac{\Delta A}{A}}^2 + \left(\frac{A}{E}-1\right)^2 \sigma_{\frac{\Delta L}{L}}^2 - 2\left(\frac{A}{E}\right)\left(\frac{A}{E}-1\right)\rho\sigma_{\frac{\Delta A}{A}}\sigma_{\frac{\Delta L}{L}} \qquad (9)$$

Equation 9 states the relationship in precise mathematical terms. It also incorporates the concept of correlation, which is an essential element of liability-driven investing. Exhibit 26 is a graphical representation of Equation 9 and illustrates the magnitude of the asset/liability

---

[11]Most notably, the duration model does not reflect well on non-linear factors, such as convexity and embedded options in many fixed-income securities and derivatives.

[12]The variance of any random variable is equal to the square of the standard deviation of the variable.

[13]Transforming Equation 4 into Equation 9 follows the basic statistical property that, for any random variable Z, which is a linear sum of two other random variables X and Y (specifically, $Z = AX + BY$), the variance of Z is $\sigma_Z^2 = A^2\sigma_X^2 + B^2\sigma_Y^2 + 2AB\rho\sigma_X\sigma_Y$. This expression does not depend on the nature and shape of the underlying probability distributions of either X or Y.

correlation effect (ρ is measured on the x-axis) on the volatility of the financial institution's equity capital ($\sigma_{\Delta E}$ is measured on the y-axis) for various levels of leverage (the downward-sloping dotted lines). For purposes of this exhibit, the volatilities of asset and liability percentage value changes ($\sigma_{\Delta A}$, $\sigma_{\Delta L}$) are both assumed to be constant at 1.5%.

Exhibit 26 demonstrates that over the range of leverage shown (equity/assets ratios from 5% to 20%), the volatility of the financial institution's equity capital decreases as the correlation between asset and liability *value changes* (ρ) increases toward +1.0. This beneficial effect is most pronounced when the financial institution is highly leveraged.

For example, assuming leverage of 20% (assets/equity = 5x) and correlations (ρ) of 0.5 and then 0.9, the volatility of equity declines from 6.9% to 3.5%. However, if higher leverage is assumed, at 5% equity/assets, and ρ takes the same two values, then the decrease in volatility of equity from 29.3% to 13.2% is more dramatic.

If the correlation between assets and liabilities is 1.0, the volatility of shareholders' equity capital shrinks to minimal amounts, even for high leverage (equity to assets = 5.0%). However, the flip side is that any divergence in correlations—such as can often occur in turbulent markets—causes equity volatility to increase and especially dramatically when leverage is high.

EXHIBIT 26   Volatility of Value of Shareholders' Equity as a Function of Correlation of Asset and Liability Value Changes and Beginning Leverage

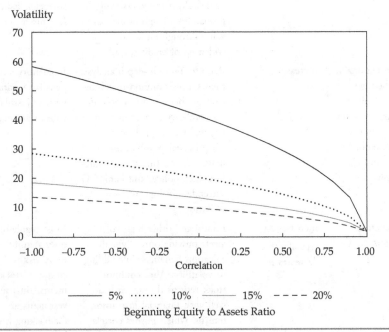

Source: Authors

With the comprehensive framework provided by Equation 9, we next turn to a brief catalogue, shown in Exhibit 27, of how differing portfolio strategies and actions affect the inputs and thus the results of the volatility paradigm in Equation 9. Before doing so, however, it is important to note that hedging with derivatives, duration-based portfolio management and funding, and other techniques for raising the correlation between asset and liability values are not a cure-all. High correlations between assets and liabilities are not easy to achieve in practice, and often break down during periods of financial industry stress or stress in an individual institution. In the final analysis, techniques for raising correlations are not a pure substitute for maintaining adequate capitalization buffers.

EXHIBIT 27   Investment Strategies and Effects on Bank/Insurer Asset & Liability Volatility

Portfolio Strategy Considerations	Main Factors Affected	Explanation/Rationale	Additional Regulatory Concerns
Diversified fixed-income investments	Decreases $\sigma_{\underset{A}{\Delta A}}$	Debt securities are less volatile than common equities, real estate, and other securities.	Effective diversification involves a multiplicity of issuers and industries, both domestic and foreign.
High-quality bond/debt investments	Decreases $\sigma_{\underset{A}{\Delta A}}$	Overall, higher quality securities are less likely to be downgraded or default, thereby lessening the probability of significant loss of value through either losses or widening of credit spreads.	Regulatory structures and central banks favor sovereign issuers most for this reason.
Maintain reasonable balance between asset and liability durations, key rates durations, and sensitivity to embedded borrower and claimant options	Increases ρ	Requires more in-depth analysis than simple duration-matching strategy, because must account for convexity and asymmetric payoffs due to (i) defaults, (ii) principal payoffs prior to maturity, and (iii) annuity, life-insurance policy, and bank CD surrenders in high interest rate scenarios.	Regulatory structures penalize institutions with unjustifiable asset/liability mismatches.
Common stock investments	Increases $\sigma_{\underset{A}{\Delta A}}$, typically decreases ρ	Equity and other high-volatility assets provide only slight diversification benefits while adding to volatility. Also, common stock returns do not correlate well with financial institution returns, which pushes correlation, ρ, away from 1.0 toward 0.0.	Most regulatory structures require 100% or more risk weighting for common stock investments, thus such investments are ineligible for backing financial liability issuance.

Portfolio Strategy Considerations	Main Factors Affected	Explanation/Rationale	Additional Regulatory Concerns
Derivatives transparency, collateralization	Decreases both σ_{AA} and σ_{LL}, and increases ρ	Whether derivatives are used to hedge or synthesize (i) assets or (ii) liabilities, the more "plain vanilla" (and protected against counterparty default) they are, the less likely they will revalue in unexpected directions.	Transparency fosters regulatory "financial stress test" confidence. It also allows regulators and claimants to ascertain whether derivatives are being used in a justifiable manner.
Liquidity of portfolio investments	Decreases σ_{AA}	Includes short-maturity debt securities of highly rated issuers, currency reserves, access to credit lines, and access for banks to emergency central bank borrowing.	Problems occur for regulators when financial contagion extends beyond just a few institutions.
Surrender penalties	Decreases σ_{LL}	For typical life insurance, annuities, and bank deposits, such penalties cushion losses to financial institutions for having to pay back liabilities "at par" when rising interest rates would otherwise have reduced the discounted present value of the obligations.	Properly computed surrender penalties must account for interest rate volatility and slope of the yield curve. Typically, regulators/customers do not tolerate economically justified surrender penalties (they are usually priced too low to offset the institution's risk).
Prepayment penalties on debt investments	Increases ρ	When interest rates are declining, borrowers must incur a penalty to repay loans at par to refinance. Also, prepayment penalties help institutions offset rising values of their fixed-rate liabilities in falling rate environments.	None.
Catastrophic insurance risks	Increases σ_{LL}	By definition, these losses faced by insurance companies are less predictable and possibly very large.	Regulators and insurance customers usually expect (i) higher capital ratios, (ii) higher quality and liquid investment portfolios, and (iii) strong reinsurance agreements compared with typical home, health, auto, and fire insurance.

Portfolio Strategy Considerations	Main Factors Affected	Explanation/Rationale	Additional Regulatory Concerns
Predictability of underwriting losses	Decreases $\sigma_{\frac{\Delta L}{L}}$	High frequency, low cost loss events caused by law of large numbers make total insurance liabilities less uncertain.	Adverse changes in legal or regulatory systems cannot be offset by actions on the asset side of the financial institution. These are risks borne by owners of the institution's equity capital.
Diversifying insurance business	Decreases $\sigma_{\frac{\Delta L}{L}}$	Diversifying across several business lines increases aggregate risk-reduction potential (due to law of large numbers).	None.
Variable annuities	Increases ρ, and $\sigma_{\frac{\Delta A}{A}}$, $\sigma_{\frac{\Delta L}{L}}$ diminish in relevance	Where equity/bond market risks are fully borne by policyholders, the correlation between asset and liability returns approaches 1.0, independent of investment performance of the underlying, segregated account assets.	Assuming adequate risk disclosure to policyholders, and sufficient asset custody protections, regulators permit greater investment flexibility than in insurer's standard business lines.

The last key implication of the aggregate risk framework in Equation 9 relates to the importance of raising equity capitalization externally. The ability to raise capital is not just the key to expanding operations; more importantly, it is a way of buffering financial uncertainty. It diminishes both the probability of default to liability holders and the total volatility of equity capitalization values.[14] Over the past several decades, the financial industry has moved increasingly to publicly traded, for-profit, corporations, rather than mutual or membership co-ops. This is primarily because publicly traded companies can issue new common stock capital in cases of either opportunity or emergency. Mutual and membership co-ops (for example, credit unions) are restricted by the growth of their membership, which usually cannot change much over short periods of time.

EXAMPLE 8

Foresight International Assurance is an international multiline insurance conglomerate. Under its overall strategic financial plan, it computes the annualized standard deviation of returns on investment assets as 5.0% and on liabilities as 2.5%. The bulk of its liabilities are constituted by the net present value of expected claims payouts.

---

[14]Although raising equity ratios negatively impacts return on common equity (ROCE) and earnings per share of financial companies, the diminished volatility of earnings and economic value acts toward raising price-earnings and market-to-book ratios. Perhaps somewhat counterintuitively, the issuing of common stock by financial companies can be neutral or even a net benefit to pre-existing shareholders.

The correlation between asset and liability returns is therefore a very low 0.25. Foresight's common equity to financial assets ratio is 20.0%.

1. What is the standard deviation of changes in the value of Foresight's shareholder capitalization?
2. Management believes the overall risk profile of the company is too high and desires to increase the common equity ratio by issuing additional shares of common equity and listing such shares on several international stock market exchanges. The new target equity ratio will be 25.0%. All other things being equal, how does this impact the volatility of value changes in shareholder capitalization?
3. Management believes it also needs to lower the volatility of its assets. It shifts out of low-quality bonds into higher quality, more liquid government securities and, by doing so, expects to lower the standard deviation of asset returns to 4.0% per year without having any impact on the correlation ratio between assets and liabilities. Along with the stronger capital ratios premised in question 2, what does this do to the volatility of shareholder equity value?
4. What is the impact of the various portfolio and capitalization changes on the value of Foresight's common shares outstanding? Explain your answer.

Solution to 1: We use Equation 9 recognizing that $A \div E = 1/0.20 = 5$; $(A \div E) - 1 = 4$; the standard deviation of asset returns $(\sigma_{\frac{\Delta A}{A}}) = 0.05$; the standard deviation of changes in liability values $(\sigma_{\frac{\Delta L}{L}}) = 0.025$; and the correlation between asset and liability value changes $(\rho) = 0.25$.

First, we compute the variance of shareholders' capital value changes:

$$\sigma^2_{\frac{\Delta E}{E}} = 5^2 \times 0.05^2 + 4^2 \times 0.025^2 - 2 \times 5 \times 4 \times 0.25 \times 0.05 \times 0.025 = 0.06.$$

The standard deviation of shareholder capital valuation change is the square root of the variance. Thus,

$$\sigma_{\frac{\Delta E}{E}} = \sqrt{\sigma^2_{\frac{\Delta E}{E}}} = \sqrt{0.06} = 0.245 = 24.5\% \text{ per year.}$$

Solution to 2: The new asset to equity ratio is $A \div E = 1/0.25 = 4$, and so $(A \div E) - 1 = 3$. Using the existing values of the other variables in Equation 9, we obtain

$$\sigma^2_{\frac{\Delta E}{E}} = 4^2 \times 0.05^2 + 3^2 \times 0.025^2 - 2 \times 4 \times 3 \times 0.25 \times 0.05 \times 0.025 = 0.038125.$$

from which we see $\sigma_{\frac{\Delta E}{E}} = \sqrt{\sigma_{\frac{\Delta E}{E}}^2} = \sqrt{0.038125} \approx 0.195 = 19.5\%$ per year.

Solution to 3: Equation 9 now produces the following results:

$$\sigma^2_{\frac{\Delta E}{E}} = 4^2 \times 0.04^2 + 3^2 \times 0.025^2 - 2 \times 4 \times 3 \times 0.25 \times 0.04 \times 0.025 = 0.025225$$

from which we obtain $\sigma_{\frac{\Delta E}{E}} = \sqrt{\sigma_{\frac{\Delta E}{E}}^2} = \sqrt{0.025225} \approx 0.159 = 15.9\%$.

Solution to 4: We note that the proposed changes are likely to reduce earnings per share, first by having a greater number of shares outstanding and second by lowering the expected returns on assets (because there will now be a greater percentage of safer, lower yielding assets). All other things being equal, this would pressure the common stock price. However, Foresight is also lowering its overall equity risk exposure while strengthening its reputation as a more soundly operated and capitalized insurance company. The lower risk profile might well result in a higher credit rating and a lower discount rate at which the lower earnings per share trajectory is valued. Also, the improved long-term survivability and underwriting strength could result in a higher *long-term* growth outlook. In sum, the impact on common equity prices cannot be predicted merely by a change in capital structure and near-term reduction in earnings and portfolio expected returns.

Implementation of Portfolio Decisions for Banks and Insurance Companies

With sovereign wealth funds, endowments, foundations, and employee benefit plans (DB and DC), the investment adviser must primarily focus on the investment of assets. In the case of financial institutions, optimal management must simultaneously focus on liabilities, particularly the volatility and convexity of asset and liability payouts. Consequently, the investment strategy of financial institutions must also consider the appropriate degree of leverage and total amount of common equity capital. Returning to the basic framework of Equations 2 and 4, the proper way to maximize long-term economic earnings thus might be to raise (lower) leverage through: (a) the acquisition (disposal) of portfolio assets; (b) the underwriting (retirement) of liabilities; or (c) the repurchase (issuance) of capital stock.

The financial management of a bank or insurer has not only to deal with the level and direction of interest rates, credit spreads, derivatives markets, economic cycles, and stock markets as they impact the investment portfolio, but we also now see it needs to have a keen understanding of the valuation of its own common equity and debt capital securities. Financial management also requires a view on the actions of competitors. For example, will they create a housing bubble through excessive lending to low-quality borrowers? Will they drive down insurance policy premiums through overly aggressive underwriting? Finally, financial management must satisfy all existing regulations as well as the ones that may evolve with changes in global economic circumstances and other political pressures.

In sum, financial and portfolio management of banks and insurance companies is an attempt to create positive net present value for capital holders by solving simultaneously several different conditions with several different variables. Consequently, key decisions are typically made at the highest levels of the institution's management. Specific analysts and investment managers are typically assigned only to specialized subsets of the institution's varied assets and liabilities.

In such dynamically changing economic and regulatory environments, it is difficult to specify particular portfolio investment rules and policies. Therefore, the following mini-case studies are offered to provide illustrations of the types of high-level portfolio decisions that are required.

EXAMPLE 9 Mini-Case A:

A bank considers reducing its ownership of commercial loans in smaller businesses. These loans pay interest quarterly at various contractually pre-specified spreads above the floating market reference rate (MRR). The runoff of the loan portfolio through repayments, together with proceeds of outright sales and securitizations of other loans, are to be reinvested in a portfolio of fixed-rate government securities of comparable maturities. The securities will be hedged fully against general interest rate risk through the use of publicly traded options and futures on government securities. Additionally, hedging interest rate risk completely would create a synthetic variable rate asset. If interest rates rise, gains on hedges can be reinvested to raise overall portfolio income; if interest rates fall, losses on hedges will require some assets to pay counterparties, thereby lowering overall portfolio income.

1. How would this portfolio restructuring affect the asset/liability profile of the bank?
2. What is the expected impact on the volatility of bank shareholder equity valuation?
3. What is the likely impact on bank earnings?
4. What are reasons that argue in favor of this portfolio redeployment?

Solution to 1: Switching from variable rate to fixed-rate assets of similar maturities increases the duration of the bank's overall portfolio. However, entering into hedging positions with futures and options on fixed-rate assets has the effect of shortening overall duration. As described, the net effect of the portfolio alteration likely should have little effect on the bank's existing asset/liability duration profile, because floating-rate corporate loans also have little price exposure in the event of rising or falling interest rates.

Solution to 2: The overall volatility of assets and bank capitalization should decrease, because a hedged portfolio of government securities is more liquid than a portfolio of individual small business loans and also less subject to volatility arising from changes in credit default spreads on corporate loans.

Solution to 3: Bank earnings would be expected to decline, independent of subsequent changes in the overall level of interest rates. This is because the yields on business loans, adjusting for expected default rates, are higher than on government securities, adjusting for the costs of hedging the government securities. Furthermore, if overall interest rates subsequently rise, the business loan portfolio would generate higher income to the bank. However, hedges on the government securities generate gains when interest rates rise—offsetting losses on the underlying securities and thus permitting more money to be reinvested in now higher yielding government securities. Similarly, a decline in interest rates would lead to a loss on the hedges and a sale of appreciated underlying government securities to cover these hedge losses. The portfolio value is approximately unchanged, but the (reduced) ability to generate income has tracked interest rates downward. In sum, *changes* in overall interest rates impact income-generating ability similarly for both the loan portfolio and the hedged securities portfolio. This is the flip side of the coin; in other words, the two portfolios have similar modified durations. In any environment, the net yields on the hedged government securities are lower than on the business loans. Thus, bank net income is unambiguously lower because of the portfolio rebalancing.

Solution to 4: Although the proposed redeployment is expected to lower bank earnings, there are at least three good reasons for this action, any of which would justify the decision: (a) the bank believes it needs to have a more liquid investment portfolio because of the risk of unexpected claims against assets; (b) the bank needs to raise its regulatory "equity to risky assets" ratio (by substituting low credit-risk for high credit-risk assets); and (c), the bank believes it will be able to reverse the trade in the future after a recession has driven up the effective default-adjusted spreads (i.e., driven down the prices) on small business loans. In all three rationales, overall volatility is expected to decline and the reduction in volatility is expected to provide a benefit that more than offsets the anticipated reduction in earnings. That is, the risk-adjusted return is projected to rise.

Mini-Case B:

A medium size insurance company plans to sell a large portion of its diversified, fixed-rate, investment-grade-rated securities in order to redeploy proceeds into a special purpose trust holding a diversified portfolio of automobile loans with original loan lives of 5 years. The loans are collateralized by direct liens on the vehicles, and the underlying borrowers meet minimum consumer credit scores set by a national credit rating agency. The underlying loans were randomly selected for the trust, and the collateral constitutes a nationwide sample of automobiles of different foreign and domestic manufacturers.

1. What does this transaction reveal about the regulatory capital of this insurer?
2. What key information must the insurer know about the automobile loans held by the trust in order to manage its asset/liability duration profile?
3. What external factors might the insurer need to consider with respect to the duration of trust assets?
4. What is the expected impact from the proposed investment transaction on (a) the insurer's earnings, and (b), the overall volatility of the insurer's common equity capitalization?

Solution to 1: The portfolio redeployment reduces the insurer's liquidity. Given that the insurer is able to undertake this action, the company has excess regulatory capital, because the underlying illiquid loans require more regulatory capital than high-quality/investment-grade, marketable, fixed-income securities.

Solution to 2: The insurer must make actuarial projections of contractual cash flows from the auto loans, which must take into account full and partial pre-payments because of accidents, auto trade-ins, and loan defaults. The acceptable credit quality of the borrowers and the geographical and brand diversity contribute to the accuracy of such predictions. The overall asset/liability profile for the insurer might well change depending on how the projected modified duration of the auto loan receivables compares with the investment-grade marketable securities to be sold. A material difference might require management to undertake (a) changes in the modified duration of the insurance company's liabilities, such as by altering the maturities of future debt issuances; or (b), implementation of interest rate-hedging transactions.

Solution to 3: The insurer must be concerned about an adverse change in the economic cycle, changes in technology, and/or energy prices—all of which could adversely impact the value of the auto loan receivables (as compared with the marketable securities portfolio to be sold) and which could undermine the cash flow assumptions made with respect to setting the company's overall asset/liability profile.

Solution to 4: The portfolio redeployment is likely to raise the insurer's earnings, because the expected yield on the auto loans, net of credit losses, is higher than for investment-grade, liquid securities. However, the company is taking on more credit risk, which should translate into higher volatility of the value of assets and, thus, higher volatility of equity capitalization.

Mini-Case C:
Floating-rate securities, paying a fixed spread over the floating MRR, are trading at historically narrow yield spreads over MRR. In addition, issuers of these securities tend to be concentrated disproportionately in a small number of industries—notably in banks, insurers, and other financial services companies. A bank's investment manager considers selling the bank's portfolio holdings of these floating-rate securities, which have a 5-year maturity and trade at 0.1% over MRR. The proceeds will be used to buy more-diversified (by issuer type), investment-grade, fixed-rate securities that are selling at more normal spreads versus government bond yields of comparable duration (which trade at 1.0% over 5-year US Treasury bond yields). The fixed-rate securities portfolio is to be combined with pay-fixed/receive-floating interest rate swaps under standard mark-to-market collateralization terms. The 5-year interest rate swap terms permit one to receive MRR while paying 0.4% over Treasury yields.

1. What does the portfolio alteration do to required regulatory risk-based capital?
2. What might indicate that the bank's senior managers are more concerned about risks to equity capitalization than are regulators?
3. What is the expected effect on the bank's asset/liability profile?
4. What is the expected effect on expected earnings?
5. Summarize the rationale for the portfolio alteration.

Solution to 1: To a first approximation, substituting one kind of marketable security for another should have little effect on regulatory risk-based capital requirements, because there is little apparent change in average credit quality. The new portfolio will have more issuer and industry diversification than the securities being sold. Thus, under robust scenario simulation testing, the new portfolio should be somewhat more resistant to loss than the more-concentrated portfolio assets being sold.

Solution to 2: The bank's senior managers appear to be concerned about systemic risk in the financial sector, especially since the securities the bank plans to sell are concentrated in the financial sector and are trading at unusually high prices (narrow spreads to MRR). Apart from interest rate risk, the probability of underperformance for financial company securities is higher than for a diversified portfolio of fixed-rate securities. In the bank's view, the prospective volatility of floating-rate bank assets—and thus, the company's own equity capital—is higher than what is reflected in the regulatory risk-weight framework, because the latter does not take into account relative price risk. Thus, from the bank's perspective, the proposed trade lowers asset and equity volatility.

Solution to 3: Substituting fixed-rate securities in place of variable-rate securities tends to increase the modified duration of the bank's assets. However, entering into a pay-fixed/receive-floating swap is equivalent to creating a synthetic liability, which becomes (i) smaller as interest rates rise and (ii) greater as interest rates fall. The interest rate swap can be tailored to offset the tendency of the newly acquired fixed-rate securities to lose value as interest rates rise and gain value as interest rates fall. Said differently, the synthetic liability increases the duration of the bank's liabilities to counterbalance the rise in asset duration from replacing variable-rate with fixed-rate debt securities.

Solution to 4: Earnings are expected to rise. The securities sold pay a low spread over MRR. The new package (fixed-rate securities plus pay-fixed/receive-floating interest rate swap) pays a higher expected spread over MRR. The high yield received on the fixed-rate securities, net of the fixed-rate leg of the interest rate swap paid, represents the new built-in spread that is then added to the MRR received in the floating-leg of the interest rate swap. Specifically, the new portfolio will (i) receive 5-year Treasury yield plus 1.0% on the fixed-rate securities, (ii) pay 5-year Treasury yield plus 0.4% on the fixed leg of the interest rate swap, and (iii) receive MRR on the floating side of the interest rate swap. The net result is that the hedged, fixed-rate holdings will pay the bank the 5-year Treasury yield (T) + 1.0% – (T + 0.4%) + MRR = MRR + 0.6%. This synthetic floating-rate portfolio compares with the original floating-rate portfolio that paid just MRR + 0.1%.

Solution to 5: A pay-fixed/receive-floating interest rate swap is "plain vanilla; it is easy to value and unwind. The trade would thus not have any major adverse impact on the institution's liquidity. The bank, by selling securities in the banking and financial services industry, can lower its own exposure to systemic financial risk. In essence, the trade achieves better diversification while creating cheap (i.e., higher yielding) synthetic MRR floaters in place of true MRR floaters. The regulatory system in which the bank operates likely has a statistical system that penalizes excessive use of derivatives by deeming worst-case liabilities in a stress test. This should not be an issue assuming the proposed trade is small enough, relative to the institution's size, to have no significant impact on stress test results. Overall, the trade would be a duration-neutral trade, achieving higher net earnings and lower asset and equity risk without significantly impacting the bank's regulatory capital ratios.

Mini-Case D:
In the aftermath of prolonged financial turmoil and a recession, a large pan-European life insurance company believes that corporate debt securities and asset-based securities are now very attractive relative to more-liquid government securities. The yield spreads more than compensate for default and credit downgrade risk. Interest rates for government securities are near cyclical lows. The insurance company is concerned that rates may rise and that, as a result, many outstanding annuities might be surrendered.

The insurer believes the probability of a large, adverse move in interest rates is much higher than is currently reflected by the implied volatility of traded options on government securities in the eurozone. The insurer's regulatory capital and reserves are deemed to be healthy.

1. What are the consequences of lowering allocations to government securities and raising allocations to corporate and asset-backed securities?
2. Are there steps that the insurer should take on the liability side?

Solution to 1: These proposed asset reallocations have several implications. First, corporate debt securities have higher yields and thus shorter durations than government securities of similar maturity. Asset-backed securities tend to have lower effective durations than corporate and government bonds. Thus, the proposed rebalancing would likely lower the overall duration of the investment portfolio, which is consistent with the insurer's concerns about rising interest rates and the expected consequences. Second, the change in portfolio allocation would likely lower the company's overall liquidity and lower regulatory risk-based capital measures, because the new securities are treated less favorably for regulatory purposes (less liquid, higher credit risk corporate debt and asset-backed securities require a higher equity charge than liquid, low credit risk government securities, so regulatory "equity to risky assets" is reduced). Thus, the proposed portfolio moves make sense only if the regulatory capital position of the insurer is already ample and if the existing liquidity elsewhere in the portfolio is enough to fund an uptick of annuity surrenders in the case of rising interest rates. Finally, the reallocation would increase expected earnings (from higher interest income) and set the stage for price gains if credit spreads versus government securities contract to more normal levels.

Solution to 2: Because overall interest rates are low, the company must also deal with an asymmetric risk separate and apart from the reallocation of its investment portfolio. In other words, the insurer must alter its liability profile in order to minimize potential adverse changes in its common equity capitalization. A spike up in interest rates could result in a rise in surrenders of annuities during a time when asset values are coming under pressure. Because the company is more concerned about higher interest rate volatility than is reflected in current option prices, the insurer might consider purchasing out-of-the-money puts on government securities and/or purchasing swaptions with the right to be a fixed-payer/floating-receiver. Sharp rises in rates would make both positions profitable[15] and offset some of the burden of premature annuity surrenders. If time passes without any substantial rise in interest rates, the cost of purchasing option protection would detract from the incremental benefits from the proposed switch into higher yielding securities.

---

[15]A put option becomes valuable to the holder if prices of the underlying asset fall. A swaption with the right to enter a swap paying fixed and receiving floating is economically analogous to a put option on a bond. If rates rise, the swaption owner has the right to receive a rising stream of floating payments in exchange for what will have then become a stream of reasonably low fixed payments. The swaption contract will have gained in value.

8. SUMMARY

This chapter has introduced the subject of managing institutional investor portfolios. The key points made in this chapter are as follows:

- The main institutional investor types are pension plans, sovereign wealth funds, endowments, foundations, banks, and insurance companies. Common characteristics among these investors include a large scale (i.e., asset size), a long-term investment horizon, regulatory constraints, a clearly defined governance framework, and principal–agent issues.
- Institutional investors typically codify their mission, investment objectives, and guidelines in an Investment Policy Statement (IPS).
- Four common investment approaches to managing portfolios used by institutional investors are the Norway model, the Endowment model, the Canada model, and the Liability Driven Investing (LDI) model.
- There are two main types of pension plans: defined benefit (DB), in which a plan sponsor commits to paying a specified retirement benefit; and defined contribution (DC), in which contributions are defined but the ultimate retirement benefit is not specified or guaranteed by the plan sponsor.
- Pension plan stakeholders include the employer, employees, retirees, unions, management, the investment committee and/or board of directors, and shareholders.
- The key elements in the calculation of DB plan liabilities are as follows:
  - Service/tenure: The higher the service years, the higher the retirement benefit.
  - Salary/earnings: The higher the salary over the measurement period, the higher the retirement benefit.
  - Mortality/longevity: The longer the participant's expected life span, the higher the plan sponsor's liability.
  - Vesting: Lower turnover results in higher vesting, increasing the plan sponsor's liabilities.
  - Discount rate: A higher discount rate reduces the present value of the plan sponsor's liabilities.

- DB plan liquidity needs are driven by the following:
  - Proportion of active employees relative to retirees: More mature pension funds have higher liquidity needs.
  - Age of workforce: Liquidity needs rise as the age of the workforce increases.
  - Plan funded status: If the plan is well funded, the sponsor may reduce contributions, generating a need to hold higher balances of liquid assets to pay benefits.
  - Flexibility: Ability of participants to switch among the sponsor's plans or to withdraw from the plan.

- Pension plans are subject to significant and evolving regulatory constraints designed to ensure the integrity, adequacy, and sustainability of the pension system. Some incentives, such as tax exemption, are only granted to plans that meet these regulatory requirements. Notable differences in legal, regulatory, and tax considerations can lead to differences in plan design from one country to another or from one group to another (e.g., public plans vs. corporate plans).
- The following risk considerations affect the way DB plans are managed:
  - Plan funded status
  - Sponsor financial strength

o Interactions between the sponsor's business and the fund's investments
o Plan design
o Workforce characteristics

- An examination of pension fund asset allocations shows very large differences in average asset allocations by country and within a country despite these plans seeking to achieve similar goals. Such inter- and intra-national differences are driven by many factors, including the differences in legal, regulatory, accounting, and tax constraints; the investment objectives, risk appetites, and investment views of the stakeholders; the liabilities to and demographics of the ultimate beneficiaries; the availability of suitable investment opportunities; and the expected cost of living in retirement.
- The major types of sovereign wealth funds (SWFs) follow:
  o Budget Stabilization funds: Set up to insulate the budget and economy from commodity price volatility and external shocks.
  o Development funds: Established to allocate resources to priority socioeconomic projects, usually infrastructure.
  o Savings funds: Intended to share wealth across generations by transforming non-renewable assets into diversified financial assets.
  o Reserve funds: Intended to reduce the negative carry costs of holding foreign currency reserves or to earn higher return on ample reserves.
  o Pension reserve funds: Set up to meet identified future outflows with respect to pension-related, contingent-type liabilities on governments' balance sheets.
- Stakeholders of SWFs include the country's citizens, the government, external asset managers, and the SWF's management, investment committee, and board of directors.
- Given their mission of intergenerational wealth transfer, SWFs do not generally have clearly defined liabilities, so do not typically pursue asset/liability matching strategies used by other institutional investor types.
- Sovereign wealth funds have differing liquidity needs. Budget stabilization funds require the most liquidity, followed by reserve funds. At the other end of the spectrum are savings funds with low liquidity needs, followed by pension reserve funds.
- The investment objectives of SWFs are often clearly articulated in the legislative instruments that create them. They are often tax free in their home country, although they must take foreign taxation into consideration. Given their significant asset sizes and the nature of their stakeholders, SWFs have aimed to increase transparency regarding their investment activities. In this regard, the Santiago Principles are a form of self-regulation.
- The typical asset allocation by SWF type shows budget stabilization funds are invested mainly in bonds and cash given their liquidity needs. Reserve funds invest in equities and alternatives but maintain a significant allocation of bonds for liquidity. Savings funds and pension reserve funds hold relatively higher allocations of equities and alternatives because of their longer-term liabilities.
- Endowments and foundations typically invest to maintain purchasing power while financing their supporting university (endowments) or making grants (foundations) in perpetuity—based on the notion of intergenerational equity. Endowments and foundations usually have a formal spending policy that determines how much is paid out annually to support their mission. This future stream of payouts represents their liabilities. For endowments, other liability-related factors to be considered when setting investment policy

are: 1) the ability to raise additional funds from donors/alumni, 2) the percentage of the university's operating budget provided by the endowment, and 3) the ability to issue debt.

- Foundations and endowments typically enjoy tax-exempt status and face relatively little regulation compared to other types of institutional investors.
- Foundations face less flexible spending rules compared to endowments; foundations in the US are legally mandated to pay out 5% of their assets annually to maintain tax-exempt status. Endowments and foundations have relatively low liquidity needs. However, foundations have somewhat higher liquidity needs (vs. endowments), because they 1) typically pay out slightly more as a percentage of assets, and 2) finance the entire operating budget of the organization they support.
- Endowments and foundations typically have a long-term real return objective of about 5% consistent with their spending policies. This real return objective, and a desire to maintain purchasing power, results in endowments and foundations making significant allocations to real assets. In general, endowments and foundations invest heavily in private asset classes and hedge funds and have relatively small allocations to fixed income.
- Banking and insurance companies manage both portfolio assets and institutional liabilities to achieve an extremely high probability that obligations on deposits, guarantees, derivatives, policyholder claims, and other liabilities will be paid in full and on time.
- Banking and insurance companies have perpetual time horizons. Strategically, their goal is to maximize net present value to capital holders; tactically, this may be achieved by liability driven investing (LDI) over intermediate and shorter horizons.
- Financial institutions are highly regulated because of their importance to the non-financial, or real, sectors of the economy. Such institutions are also regulated in order to minimize contagion risk rippling throughout the financial and real sectors.
- The underlying premise of regulation is that an institution's capital must be adequate to absorb shocks to both asset and liability values. This implies limiting the volatility of value of the institution's shareholder capital.
- The volatility of shareholder capital can be managed by (a) reducing the price volatility of portfolio investments, loans, and derivatives; (b) lowering the volatility from unexpected shocks to claims, deposits, guarantees, and other liabilities; (c) limiting leverage; and (d) attempting to achieve positive correlation between changes in the value of assets and liabilities.
- Ample liquidity, diversification of portfolio and other assets, high investment quality, transparency, stable funding, duration management, diversification of insurance underwriting risks, and monetary limits on guarantees, funding commitments, and insurance claims are some of the ways management and regulators attempt to achieve low volatility of shareholder capital value.

REFERENCES

OECD. 2016. *OECD Insurance Statistics 2008–2016*. https://read.oecd-ilibrary.org/finance-and-invest-ment/oecd-insurance-statistics-2016_ins_stats-2016-en#page1.

Tobin, James. 1974. "What Is Permanent Endowment Income?" *American Economic Review* 64 (2), Papers and Proceedings of the Eighty-Sixth Annual Meeting of the American Economic Association (May): 427–432.

Willis Towers Watson Thinking Ahead Institute. 2018. *"Global Pension Assets Study 2018"* (February). https://www.willistowerswatson.com/-/media/WTW/Images/Press/2018/01/Global-Pension-Asset-Study-2018-Japan.pdf.

PRACTICE PROBLEMS

The following information relates to Questions 1–7.

William Azarov is a portfolio manager for Westcome Investments, an asset management firm. Azarov is preparing for meetings with two of Westcome's clients and obtains the help of Jason Boulder, a junior analyst. The first meeting is with Maglav Inc., a rapidly growing US-based technology firm with a young workforce and high employee turnover. Azarov directs Boulder to review the details of Maglav's defined benefit (DB) pension plan. The plan is overfunded and has assets under management of $25 million. Boulder makes the following two observations:

Observation 1:   Maglav's shareholders benefit from the plan's overfunded status.
Observation 2:   The funded ratio of Maglav's plan will decrease if employee turnover decreases.

Maglav outsources the management of the pension plan entirely to Westcome Investments. The fee structure requires Maglav to compensate Westcome with a high base fee regardless of performance. Boulder tells Azarov that outsourcing offers small institutional investors, such as Maglav's pension plan, the following three benefits:

Benefit 1: Regulatory requirements are reduced.
Benefit 2: Conflicts of interest are eliminated from principal–agent issues.
Benefit 3: Investors have access to a wider range of investment strategies through scale benefits.

In the meeting with Maglav, Azarov describes the investment approach used by Westcome in managing the pension plan. The approach is characterized by a high allocation to alternative investments, significant active management, and a reliance on outsourcing assets to other external asset managers. Azarov also explains that Maglav's operating results have a low correlation with pension asset returns and that the investment strategy is affected by the fact that the pension fund assets are a small portion of Maglav's market capitalization. Azarov states that the plan is subject to the Employee Retirement Income Security Act of 1974 (ERISA) and follows generally accepted accounting principles, including Accounting Standards Codification (ASC) 715, *Compensation—Retirement Benefits*.

Azarov's second meeting is with John Spintop, chief investment officer of the Wolf University Endowment Fund (the Fund). Spintop hired Westcome to assist in developing a new investment policy to present to the Fund's board of directors. The Fund, which has assets under management of $200 million, has an overall objective of maintaining long-term purchasing power while providing needed financial support to Wolf University. During the meeting, Spintop states that the Fund has an annual spending policy of paying out 4% of the Fund's three-year rolling asset value to Wolf University, and the Fund's risk tolerance should consider the following three liability characteristics:

Characteristic 1:   The Fund has easy access to debt markets.
Characteristic 2:   The Fund supports 10% of Wolf University's annual budget.
Characteristic 3:   The Fund receives significant annual inflows from gifts and donations.

The Fund has a small investment staff with limited experience in managing alternative assets and currently uses the Norway model for its investment approach. Azarov suggests a change in investment approach by making an allocation to externally managed alternative assets—namely, hedge funds and private equity. Ten-year nominal expected return assumptions for various asset classes, as well as three proposed allocations that include some allocation to alternative assets, are presented in Exhibit 1.

EXHIBIT 1   10-Year Nominal Expected Return Assumptions and Proposed Allocations

Asset Class	Expected Return	Allocation 1	Allocation 2	Allocation 3
US Treasuries	4.1%	45%	10%	13%
US Equities	6.3%	40%	15%	32%
Non-US Equities	7.5%	10%	15%	40%
Hedge Funds	5.0%	0%	30%	5%
Private Equity	9.1%	5%	30%	10%

Expected inflation for the next 10 years is 2.5% annually.

1. Which of Boulder's observations regarding Maglav's pension plan is correct?
   A. Only Observation 1
   B. Only Observation 2
   C. Both Observation 1 and Observation 2

2. Which of the benefits of outsourcing the management of the pension plan suggested by Boulder is correct?
   A. Benefit 1
   B. Benefit 2
   C. Benefit 3

3. Westcome's investment approach for Maglav's pension plan can be *best* characterized as the:
   A. Norway model.
   B. Canadian model.
   C. endowment model.

4. The risk tolerance of Maglav's pension plan can be *best* characterized as being:
   A. below average.
   B. average.
   C. above average.

5. Based on Azarov's statement concerning ERISA and ASC 715, which of the following statements is correct?
   A. Maglav is not allowed to terminate the plan.
   B. Maglav can exclude the plan's service costs from net income.
   C. Maglav's plan must appear as an asset on Maglav's balance sheet.

6. The risk tolerance of the Wolf University Endowment Fund can be *best* characterized as:
   A. below average.
   B. average.
   C. above average.

7. Which proposed allocation in Exhibit 1 would be *most appropriate* for the Fund given its characteristics?
   A. Allocation 1
   B. Allocation 2
   C. Allocation 3

The following information relates to Questions 8–12.

Bern Zang is the recently hired chief investment officer of the Janson University Endowment Investment Office. The Janson University Endowment Fund (the Fund) is based in the United States and has current assets under management of $12 billion. It has a long-term investment horizon and relatively low liquidity needs. The Fund is overseen by an Investment Committee consisting of board members for the Fund. The Investment Office is responsible for implementing the investment policy set by the Fund's Investment Committee.

The Fund's current investment approach includes an internally managed fund that holds mostly equities and fixed-income securities. It is largely passively managed with tight tracking error limits. The target asset allocation is 55% equities, 40% fixed income, and 5% alternatives. The Fund currently holds private real estate investments to meet its alternative investment allocation.

8. **Identify** the investment approach currently being used by the Investment Committee for managing the Fund. **Justify** your response.

Identify the investment approach currently being used by the Investment Committee for managing the Fund.
(circle one)

Norway Model	Endowment Model	Canadian Model	LDI Model

Justify your response.

---

9. **Discuss** the advantages and the disadvantages of the investment approach currently being used by the Investment Committee.

Discuss the advantages and the disadvantages of the investment approach currently being used by the Investment Committee.

Advantages

Disadvantages

---

10. **Describe** how *each* of the following common characteristics of institutional investors supports the Fund's allocation to private real estate:
    i.   Scale
    ii. Investment horizon
    iii. Governance framework

	Describe how *each* of the following common characteristics of institutional investors supports the Fund's allocation to private real estate.
Scale	
Investment Horizon	
Governance Framework	

After a thorough internal review, Zang concludes that the current investment approach will result in a deterioration of the purchasing power of the Fund over time. He proposes a new, active management approach that will substantially decrease the allocation to publicly traded equities and fixed income in order to pursue a higher allocation to private investments. The management of the new investments will be outsourced.

11. **Identify** the new investment approach proposed by Zang for managing the Fund. **Justify** your response.

Identify the new investment approach proposed by Zang for managing the Fund. (circle one)

Norway Model	Endowment Model	Canadian Model	LDI Model

Justify your response.

---

12. **Discuss** the advantages and the disadvantages of the new investment approach proposed by Zang.

Discuss the advantages and the disadvantages of the new investment approach proposed by Zang.

Advantages
Disadvantages

13. Fiona Heselwith is a 40-year-old US citizen who has accepted a job with Lyricul, LLC, a UK-based company. Her benefits package includes a retirement savings plan. The company offers both a defined benefit (DB) plan and a defined contribution (DC) plan but stipulates that employees must choose one plan and remain with that plan throughout their term of employment.

The DB plan is fully funded and provides full vesting after five years. The benefit formula for monthly payments upon retirement is calculated as follows:
- Final monthly salary × Benefit percentage of 2% × Number of years of service
- The final monthly salary is equal to average monthly earnings for the last five financial years immediately prior to the retirement date.

The DC plan contributes 12% of annual salary into the plan each year and is also fully vested after five years. Lyricul offers its DC plan participants a series of life-cycle funds as investment choices. Heselwith could choose a fund with a target date matching her planned retirement date. She would be able to make additional contributions from her salary if she chooses.

Discuss the features that Heselwith should consider in evaluating the two plans with respect to the following:
  i. Benefit payments
  ii. Contributions
  iii. Shortfall risk
  iv. Mortality/longevity risks

Discuss the features that Heselwith should consider in evaluating the two plans with respect to the following:

Benefit Payments
Contributions
Shortfall Risk
Mortality/ Longevity Risks

14. Dianna Mark is the chief financial officer of Antiliaro, a relatively mature textile production company headquartered in Italy. All of its revenues come from Europe, but the company is losing sales to its Asian competitors. Earnings have been steady but not growing, and the balance sheet has taken on more debt in the past few years in order to maintain liquidity. Mark reviews the following facts concerning the company's defined benefit (DB) pension plan:

- The DB plan currently has €1 billion in assets and is underfunded by €100 million in relation to the projected benefit obligation (PBO) because of investment losses.
- The company to date has made regular contributions.
- The average employee age is 50 years, and the company has many retirees owing to its longevity.
- The duration of the plan's liabilities (which are all Europe based) is 10 years.
- The discount rate applied to these liabilities is 6%.
- There is a high correlation between the operating results of Antiliaro and pension asset returns.

Determine whether the risk tolerance of the DB plan is below average or above average. **Justify** your response with *two* reasons.

Determine whether the risk tolerance of the DB plan is below average or above average. (circle one)	**Justify** your response with *two* reasons.
Below Average	1.
Above Average	2.

The following information relates to Questions 15–17.

The Prometheo University Scholarship Endowment (the Endowment) was established in 1950 and supports scholarships for students attending Prometheo University. The Endowment's assets under management are relatively small, and it has an annual spending policy of 6% of the five-year rolling asset value.

15. **Formulate** the investment objectives section of the investment policy statement for the Endowment.

Prometheo University recently hired a new chief investment officer (CIO). The CIO directs her small staff of four people to implement an investment policy review. Historically, the endowment has invested 60% of the portfolio in US equities and 40% in US Treasuries. The CIO's expectation of annual inflation for the next 10 years is 2.5%.

The CIO develops nominal 10-year return assumptions for US Treasuries and US equities, which are presented in Exhibit 1.

EXHIBIT 1   Asset Class Return Assumptions

Asset Class	10-Year Return Assumptions (Nominal)
US Treasuries	4.0%
US Equities	7.4%

16. **Discuss** whether the current investment policy is appropriate given the Endowment's annual spending policy.

Upon completion of the investment policy review by her four-person staff, the CIO makes some recommendations to the Endowment's board regarding the investment objectives and asset allocation. One of her recommendations is to adopt the endowment model as an investment approach. She recommends investing 20% in private equity, 40% in hedge funds, 25% in public equities, and 15% in fixed income.

17. **Determine** whether the board should accept the CIO's recommendation. **Justify** your response.

Determine whether the board should accept the CIO's recommendation. (circle one)	**Justify** your response.
Accept Reject	

18. Meura Bancorp, a US bank, has an equity capital ratio for financial assets of 12%. Meura's strategic plans include the incorporation of additional debt in order to leverage earnings since the current capital structure is relatively conservative. The bank plans to restructure the balance sheet so that the equity capitalization ratio drops to 10% and the modified duration of liabilities is 1.90. The bank also plans to rebalance its investment portfolio to achieve a modified duration of assets of 2.10. Given small changes in interest rates, the yield on liabilities is expected to move by 65 bps for every 100 bps of yield change in the asset portfolio.

Calculate the modified duration of the bank's equity capital after restructuring. **Show** your calculations.

CHAPTER 18

TRADE STRATEGY AND EXECUTION

Bernd Hanke, PhD, CFA
Robert Kissell, PhD
Connie Li
Roberto Malamut

LEARNING OUTCOMES

The candidate should be able to:

- discuss motivations to trade and how they relate to trading strategy;
- discuss inputs to the selection of a trading strategy;
- compare benchmarks for trade execution;
- select and justify a trading strategy (given relevant facts);
- describe factors that typically determine the selection of a trading algorithm class;
- contrast key characteristics of the following markets in relation to trade implementation: equity, fixed income, options and futures, OTC derivatives, and spot currency;
- explain how trade costs are measured and determine the cost of a trade;
- evaluate the execution of a trade;
- evaluate a firm's trading procedures, including processes, disclosures, and record keeping with respect to good governance.

1. INTRODUCTION

This chapter discusses trading and execution from a portfolio manager's perspective. The chapter covers a broad range of topics related to trade strategy selection and implementation and trade cost measurement and evaluation. Growth in electronic trading has led to increased automation in trading, including the use of algorithmic trading and machine learning to

Portfolio Management, Second Edition, by Bernd Hanke, PhD, CFA, Robert Kissell, PhD, Connie Li, and Roberto Malamut. Copyright © 2019 by CFA Institute.

optimize trade strategy and execution. Various markets, including equities, fixed income, derivatives, and foreign exchange, are examined. Adequate trading processes and procedures are also discussed from a regulatory and governance perspective.

Portfolio managers need to work closely with traders to determine the most appropriate trading strategy given their motivation for trading, risk aversion, trade urgency, and other factors, such as order characteristics and market conditions. Trade execution should be well integrated with the portfolio management process, and although trading strategies will vary on the basis of market and security type, all trade activity should be evaluated for execution quality and to assess broker and trade venue performance consistent with the fund's objectives. Additionally, firms should have proper documentation of trade procedures in place to meet regulatory and governance standards.

This chapter is organized as follows: Section 2 discusses portfolio manager motivations to trade. Section 3 discusses inputs to trade strategy selection and the trade strategy selection process. Section 4 covers the range of trade implementation choices and trading algorithms and provides a comparison of various markets. Section 5 explains how trade costs are measured and how to evaluate trade execution. Section 6 provides guidance on evaluating a firm's trading procedures for good governance practices. Section 7 concludes and summarizes the chapter.

2. MOTIVATIONS TO TRADE

Portfolio managers need to trade their portfolio holdings to ensure alignment with the fund's underlying investment strategy and objectives. The reasons for trading, or motivations to trade, and the extent of trading vary by investment strategy and circumstance. Even a passive buy-and-hold index portfolio requires some trading because of corporate actions, fund flows, or changes in the benchmark index. Portfolio managers for actively managed funds have additional reasons for trading based on their changing views for individual assets and market conditions. A portfolio manager's motivation to trade in addition to the fund's investment objectives play an important role in determining an overall trading approach.

Broadly speaking, a portfolio manager's motivation to trade falls into one of the following categories:

- Profit seeking
- Risk management/hedging needs
- Cash flow needs
- Corporate actions/index reconstitutions/margin calls

2.1. Profit Seeking

The primary added value that most active managers seek to provide is risk-adjusted outperformance relative to their benchmark. Superior returns originate from a manager having a unique insight that can be capitalized on ahead of the market. Trading in these cases is based on information portfolio managers have uncovered that they believe is not fully recognized by the market and, therefore, offers the potential to earn an excess return from the trade. Active managers will seek to transact in securities believed to be mispriced (under- or overvalued) at more favorable prices before the rest of the market recognizes the mispricing.

To prevent information leakage, or the disclosure of information about their trades, which might alert the market to the mispricing, active managers take steps to hide their trades from other market participants by executing in multiple or less transparent trade venues. *"Lit" markets* (a term referring to illumination), such as exchanges and other displayed venues, provide pre- and post-trade transparency regarding prices, volumes, market spreads, and depth. In contrast, alternative trading systems, such as dark pool trading venues, are available only to select clients and provide far less transparency, reporting only post-trade transactions and quantities. Because of these characteristics, orders in dark pool venues have a higher likelihood of going unfilled since clients receive executions only if an offsetting order arrives while their order is pending. For example, to prevent information about their trading activity from leaking to the market, a manager executing a large, directional trade may choose to execute the order in a less transparent venue.

As their investment views change with changing market and macroeconomic environments, portfolio managers will trade their holdings to align the portfolio with their views. Portfolio managers seeking longer-term profits may have relatively stable views from one period to the next whereas, in contrast, managers seeking shorter-term profits may have more rapidly changing views based on short-term movements in the market or individual securities that require higher turnover and trading.

To capitalize on investment views ahead of the market, trading the order faster, at an accelerated pace, may be needed. Portfolio managers may execute their orders at prices nearer to the market if they believe the information they have uncovered is likely to be realized by the rest of the market in the near term. **Trade urgency** refers to how quickly (aggressively) or slowly (patiently) the order is executed over the trading time horizon. Greater trade urgency is associated with executing over shorter execution horizons, whereas lower trade urgency is associated with executing over longer execution horizons.

A portfolio manager with a short-term event-driven strategy will trade with greater urgency if the expected alpha, or return payoff associated with the investment view over the trading horizon, is likely to be rapidly acted on by other market participants. In this case, the rate or level of expected alpha decay is high. In a trading context, **alpha decay** refers to the erosion or deterioration in short-term alpha once an investment decision is made. Portfolio managers following a longer-term strategy based on company fundamentals will trade more patiently, with less urgency, if the rate or level of expected alpha decay is lower.

Following are examples of short-term and long-term profit-motivated trading with differing levels of trade urgency.

Michigan Index of Consumer Sentiment (short-term profit seeking)

The University of Michigan Index of Consumer Sentiment (ICS) is one of the primary indicators of US consumer confidence. It is based on a nationwide survey of households. The ICS is closely watched by market participants, and changes in the index can prompt significant moves in the US equity market. Since 2007, Thomson Reuters, a financial data vendor, has held the exclusive right to disseminate the ICS. Until mid-2013, the firm had a two-tiered process for disseminating the ICS. A small number of trading clients received the ICS at 9:54:58, or two seconds earlier than the broader market release at 9:55:00. The two-tiered process was abolished in July 2013 after receiving negative public attention. Hu, Pan, and Wang (2017) examined how quickly the information contained in the ICS was incorporated into S&P 500 Index prices during the period of the two-tiered process.[1] They

---

[1]Hu, G., J. Pan and J. Wang. 2017. "Early peek advantage? Efficient price discovery with tiered information disclosure." *Journal of Financial Economics* 126 (2): 399–421.

found that most of the price adjustment happened within the first 200 milliseconds. This is an example of profit-driven trading with high associated trade urgency and an extremely short-term execution horizon.

Value manager (long-term profit seeking)

An investment manager following a value strategy might attempt to identify undervalued companies on the basis of such metrics as earnings yields and price-to-book ratios. The manager might favor companies that score well according to these metrics. To capitalize on their views, individual positions may be held for months or years by value managers. Minimal trading is required, and any necessary trading can often be carried out in a more patient manner. Trading in this case has no trade urgency, given the managers' much longer trade execution horizons.

As more news and market information become available on a close-to-real-time basis, combined with the increase in electronic trading, markets have become more competitive. Information is being incorporated into security prices at even faster rates. Surprises in companies' earnings announcements, interest rate changes by central banks, and other macroeconomic announcements are being incorporated into security prices on a nearly instantaneous basis. Portfolio managers trying to act on this information must trade quickly and ahead of others to capitalize on the perceived opportunity. If more immediate execution cannot be achieved at a reasonable trading cost and risk, the trade may not be worthwhile given high rates of alpha decay. Therefore, these trades may be possible only in more liquid markets, such as equities, exchange-traded derivatives, foreign exchange, and fixed-income Treasury. In less liquid markets, such as non-Treasury fixed income or over-the-counter (OTC) markets where more immediate executions cannot be achieved, trades may not be worthwhile. For active managers seeking to maximize net returns to the portfolio, the expected rate of alpha decay of the security being traded is an important trading consideration.

2.2. Risk Management/Hedging Needs

As the market and the risk environment change, portfolios need to be traded or rebalanced to remain at targeted risk levels or risk exposures. Risk horizons and risk forecasts used by portfolio managers vary by investment strategy type and by investment time horizon. Fixed-income portfolio managers, for example, may have investment objectives to adhere to target portfolio durations. For these managers, portfolio rebalancing is usually required to match a benchmark duration target over time. Trading may be required because of a changing interest rate environment, a change in the benchmark index, or the passage of time. Equity portfolio managers may wish to manage their portfolio's beta or remain market neutral by hedging market risk and targeting a beta of zero relative to the equity market. To do this, the manager could trade to adjust holdings in the underlying portfolio or trade futures or exchange-traded funds (ETFs) to adjust the fund's equity beta to zero. Similarly, hedge fund managers may wish to maintain exposure to higher market volatility without having a view on directional price movement.

In general, the risks being managed, or hedged, in addition to such factors as security liquidity considerations and the fund's investment mandate, determine whether derivatives can be used or whether trades in the underlying portfolio (cash) securities are necessary. For example, an equity portfolio's beta to a broad equity market may be managed to the portfolio's target beta by trading equity index futures (e.g., S&P 500 futures, FTSE 100

Index futures, or Nikkei 225 futures). Using futures for hedging is often a simpler, more cost-effective approach because many futures contracts are liquid and can be traded at minimal cost. In addition, the standardization of futures contracts makes them attractive to investors. They can also be traded on margin, requiring relatively small amounts of capital. Similarly, for fixed-income strategies in the United States, interest rate risk can often be (at least partially) hedged using futures on Treasury securities, such as T-bond futures. Using liquid derivatives for risk management can provide an inexpensive and straightforward means of hedging versus trading in the underlying cash securities. In addition, the ability to trade derivatives or underlying securities may depend on the fund's investment mandate. In some cases, the fund's investment mandate may not allow the use of derivatives, and the portfolio manager must instead trade ETFs or the underlying to achieve the desired exposures.

For quantitative funds, targeted volatility is usually explicitly stated in the fund's offering documents whereas for fundamental funds, it may be an implicit assumption within the investment process. Regardless of fund type, portfolio managers should understand target risk levels and when changes in the market environment might require trading to adjust portfolio risk back to targeted volatility.

Portfolio managers may also trade to hedge risks when they do not have a view on the specific risk in question. For example, a global fixed-income long/short manager without strong currency views may choose to minimize currency exposure through a currency hedging trade. A fixed-income manager who wants to trade expected changes in the shape of the yield curve may not have a view on the level of the yield curve. In this case, the manager's yield curve trade would incorporate a hedge for duration risk. A manager of a high-yield bond portfolio may need to manage portfolio sector risk as well as geographical risk. Although credit default swaps (CDSs) might be used to manage this type of risk, finding a counterparty for a more specialized CDS can be difficult and costly. Because few derivatives to manage these risks exist, the underlying cash securities are generally traded. Using more illiquid securities for these risk trades generally increases the difficulty and cost of implementation.

A portfolio manager using option strategies may want to hedge the portfolio against certain risk factors: for example, the buyer of a long straddle position (a long position in a call and a put option on the same underlying security, both with the same strike price) who is implementing a view on higher expected volatility, irrespective of whether higher volatility will lead to higher or lower security prices. This is inherently an investment view on volatility that requires hedging directional price movement in the security.

The amount and nature of trading required for risk management generally depend on the risk profile of the portfolio as well as the amount of leverage used in the fund. Although various types of funds permit the use of leverage, leverage is typically used more by hedge funds that hold both long and short positions. For highly levered funds, risk must be monitored closely because the portfolios can quickly accumulate large losses with sudden increases in market risk. This strong risk sensitivity makes trading for risk management crucial.

2.3. Cash Flow Needs

A considerable amount of trading for portfolios is neither return seeking nor for risk management purposes but instead is driven by cash flow needs. Cash flow needs may involve high or low trade urgency depending on their nature. For example, collateral/margin calls could require close-to-immediate liquidation, whereas a fund redemption due to longer-term client asset allocation changes might not require immediate liquidation.

This type of trading is often client driven, arising from fund inflows (orders, mandates) and outflows (redemptions, liquidations). Fund inflows and outflows require capital to be invested or positions to be liquidated. To minimize cash drag on a portfolio, or fund underperformance from holding uninvested cash in a rising market, fund inflows may be equitized using futures or ETFs until the next portfolio rebalance or positions in the underlying can be traded. Equitization in this case refers to a strategy of temporarily investing cash using futures or ETFs to gain the desired equity exposure before investing in the underlying securities longer term. Equitization may be required if large inflows into a portfolio are hindered by lack of liquidity in the underlying securities. For example, a large inflow into a small-capitalization equity portfolio often cannot be invested immediately in the underlying stocks owing to limited market liquidity. Instead, the manager may equitize the cash using equity futures or ETFs and then gradually trade into the underlying positions and trade out of the futures/ETF position. For client redemptions, fund holdings may need to be liquidated if redemptions are larger than expected and cannot be funded by portfolio cash or offsetting fund inflows. Currency trades in which one currency needs to be exchanged (traded) into another may be required if fund inflows or outflows are not in the desired currency for receipt or payment. Many funds offer daily liquidity, which means investors can invest or redeem on a daily basis, often without limitation. Cash positions for these funds must be carefully managed in order to satisfy all fund flows and, at the same time, minimize the fund's cash drag. Trading is often required to manage the fund's cash position appropriately.

Hedge funds often have lockup periods in which fund redemptions are made according to a regular schedule, such as calendar quarter-ends. The stated objective is to protect remaining investors from incurring transaction charges resulting from other investors' redemption activity. These types of fund liquidations generally must be requested in advance to allow fund managers time to trade out of potentially illiquid positions and thereby minimize trading costs.

In most cases, client redemptions are based on the fund's net asset value (NAV), where NAV is calculated using the closing price of the listing market for listed securities. Clients receive proceeds based on the fund's NAV calculation. In these cases, trading at the closing price eliminates the risk (to the fund and the trader) associated with executing at prices different from those used to calculate the fund's NAV and resulting redemption proceeds.

Trading to raise or invest cash proceeds may not require specific securities to be traded to meet cash flow needs. Instead, these trades may involve strategically choosing from those securities considered optimal to trade from a risk–return or cost perspective. Trade size and security liquidity considerations play a determining role, and understanding trade-offs between costs, liquidity, and other factors is key. For example, selling a liquid security that generates a substantial tax liability is preferred over selling an illiquid security that has a smaller associated tax liability with substantially higher trading costs that overwhelm any savings in tax liability. Similar considerations apply to risk–return and liquidity trade-offs.

2.4. Corporate Actions/Index Reconstitutions/Margin Calls

Trading may also be necessitated by such activity as corporate actions and operational needs (e.g., dividend/coupon reinvestment, distributions, margin calls, and expiration of derivative contracts). The companies held in a manager's portfolio might be undergoing corporate actions, such as mergers, acquisitions, or spinoffs, that require trading. Cash equity dividends or bond coupons may need to be reinvested. For funds that make regular distributions, the timing of distributions may not align with the timing of dividends or coupons received on the individual securities. Therefore, raising proceeds for fund distributions may require individual holdings to be sold to meet distribution needs.

Cash needs can also arise from margin calls on leveraged positions as portfolio managers are asked to increase cash collateral on trades that have moved against them. Margin or collateral calls may drive high levels of trade urgency, given a need for the immediate sale of portfolio holdings. For example, the use of derivatives within a portfolio often requires collateral posting, which can necessitate a move to more liquid government bonds or cash in order to meet or fund collateral requirements.

Long-only managers may manage funds using a market-weighted index as a benchmark (e.g., the S&P 500, the MSCI World Index). If the benchmark constituents change, it could affect the manager's desired portfolio composition. If the manager runs an active portfolio, in the case of a change in index constituents, the manager might choose to sell holdings in a security that has been removed from the benchmark index.

For index tracking portfolios, such index changes as additions, deletions, and constituent weight changes are generally traded in the manager's portfolio to reflect benchmark exposure. Since the fund's NAV is calculated using the official market close for each security, trading index changes at the closing price ensures that the same price is used for fund and benchmark valuation (which also uses the closing price in its calculation) and thus minimizes the fund's tracking error to the benchmark index.

In-Text Question

The trading desk of a large firm receives three orders from the senior portfolio manager. Based on his research, the portfolio manager has identified two investment opportunities: a short-term stock buy and a longer-term stock sell. The third order is to raise proceeds to accommodate an end-of-day client withdrawal from the fund.

Discuss the motivation to trade and the associated trade urgency for each order:

a. Short-term buy
b. Longer-term sell
c. Client withdrawal

Solution:

a. This is a profit-seeking trade because the portfolio manager has identified the short-term buy as an investment opportunity. Short-term profit-seeking trades typically involve higher levels of trade urgency as managers attempt to realize short-term alpha before it dissipates (decays). These managers seek to transact before the rest of the market recognizes the mispricing and as a result are less price sensitive and more aggressive (seek to transact at accelerated rates) in their trading.
b. This is a profit-seeking trade because the portfolio manager has identified the longer-term sell as an investment opportunity. Managers seeking long-term profits are typically more patient in trading and willing to wait for favorable prices by

spreading executions over a longer time horizon, which may be days or weeks. Managers trading for long-term profits generally have much lower trade urgency for these orders.

c. This is a cash flow–driven trade arising from the need to raise proceeds for the client withdrawal. For funds that offer daily liquidity, clients can invest and redeem at the end of each trading day. In this case, managers raising proceeds for client withdrawals will generally target end-of-day closing prices to match trade prices to those used to calculate the fund's valuation and redemption proceeds to the client. Hedge funds that hold less liquid positions may allow redemptions only at quarter-end and with a relatively long notice period (e.g., one month), allowing them more time to sell illiquid positions. Client-driven redemptions usually involve much lower levels of trade urgency.

3. TRADING STRATEGIES AND STRATEGY SELECTION

Once a portfolio manager has made an investment decision, the portfolio manager and the trader must work together to identify the most appropriate trading strategy to meet the portfolio manager's trade objective given cost, risk, and other considerations. Selecting the appropriate trading strategy involves a number of important trade input considerations to ensure the strategy is transacted in the most efficient manner possible.

3.1. Trade Strategy Inputs

In addition to a portfolio manager's motivation to trade, other factors play a role in the selection of a trading strategy by affecting trade urgency, expected costs, and risks for the desired trade. Portfolio managers can manage the trading costs and execution risks they incur through their selection of an appropriate trading strategy.

Key inputs for trade strategy selection include

- order characteristics,
- security characteristics,
- market conditions, and
- individual risk aversion.

3.1.1. Order Characteristics
Order-related considerations include the following:

- **Side:** the side or trade direction of the order—for example, buy, sell, cover, or short
- **Size:** the total amount or quantity of the security being transacted
- **Relative size (% of ADV):** order size as a percentage of the security's average daily volume (ADV)

The side of the order, such as buy or sell, may be important when there is expected price momentum associated with trading the security or when trading a basket of securities where managing the risk of the entire trade list is required. If prices are rising, executing a buy order may take longer than executing a sell order, given the presence of more buyers (liquidity demanders) than sellers (liquidity suppliers) in the market. Trading a list that consists of only buys or only sells will have greater market risk exposure than a list of buys and sells in which the securities have offsetting market risk exposures.

Order size is the amount or quantity of the security being traded. Larger order sizes create greater market impact in trading. Market impact is the adverse price movement in a security caused by trading an order and is one of the most significant costs in trading. Larger orders usually take longer to trade than smaller orders do, and portfolio managers will often trade larger orders in a more patient manner (lower trade urgency) to reduce market impact. All else equal, trading larger order sizes more quickly will increase market impact cost whereas trading smaller order sizes more slowly will decrease market impact cost.

To have a consistent order size measure across securities, portfolio managers often divide the order size by the security's ADV. For example, a 1 million share order in Stock ABC may be much different than a 1 million share order in Stock XYZ. If Stock ABC has an average daily volume of 50 million shares, the 1 million share order represents 2% (1 million/50 million) of ADV. If Stock XYZ has an average daily volume of 4 million shares, its order represents 25% (1 million/4 million) of ADV. The larger the size of the trade expressed as a percentage of ADV, the larger the expected market impact cost.

3.1.2. Security Characteristics
Security-related considerations include the following:

- **Security type:** the type of security being traded (underlying, ETF, American depositary receipt, global depositary receipt)
- **Short-term alpha:** the expected price movement in the security over the trading horizon
- **Price volatility:** the annualized price volatility of the security
- **Security liquidity:** the liquidity profile of the security (e.g., ADV, bid–ask spread, average trade size)

The security type distinguishes the instrument being traded and can include underlying securities, ETFs, American depositary receipts (ADRs), global depositary receipts (GDRs), derivative contracts, and foreign exchange currencies. Identifying the best means of exposure—for example, whether to trade a foreign security in its local market or trade its associated ADR (if US listed) or GDR (if non-US listed)—requires an evaluation of the trade-offs. Trading costs and liquidity will vary by local exchange. Gaining emerging market exposure, in particular, may be less expensive and operationally easier when trading available ADRs and GDRs than when trading the security in the local market. In addition, compliance, regulatory, and custody costs can be lower with ADRs and GDRs.

Short-term alpha in a trading context is the expected movement in security price over the trading horizon (independent of the trade's impact). Short-term alpha (also called *trading alpha* or *trade alpha*) may arise from an appreciation, a depreciation, or a reversion (i.e., reversal) in security price.

Alpha decay is the erosion in short-term alpha that takes place after the investment decision has been made. Alpha decay results from price movement in the direction of the investment forecast and occurs regardless of whether the trade takes place. Alpha decay is a function of the time required for a relevant piece of information (used by a portfolio manager to form her investment view) to be incorporated into a security's price. If this information is rapidly incorporated into the security's price, then its alpha is considered to decay quickly. High rates of alpha decay, or alpha loss, require faster, or more accelerated, trading to realize alpha before it is traded on by other market participants.

Depending on the expected rate of alpha decay, portfolio managers may be better off trading the order faster (higher trade urgency) or slower (lower trade urgency). In an adversely trending market—for example, buying in a rising market or selling in a falling market—portfolio managers may trade at an accelerated rate if less favorable prices are expected later in the trading horizon. In a favorably trending market—for example, buying in a falling market or selling in a rising market—portfolio managers are better off trading more slowly to execute at more favorable prices expected later in the trading horizon. Adverse price movements increase trading costs, whereas favorable price movements decrease trading costs.

The price volatility of a security primarily affects the execution risk of the trade. *Execution risk* is the risk of an adverse price movement occurring over the trading horizon owing to a change in the fundamental value of the security or because of trading-induced volatility. Execution risk is often proxied by price volatility. Securities with higher levels of price volatility have greater exposure to execution risk than securities with lower price volatility.

A security's liquidity profile affects how quickly the trade can be executed, in addition to expected trading cost, and is a significant consideration in determining trade strategy. All else being equal, greater liquidity reduces execution risk and trading costs, such as market impact. Bid–ask spreads indicate round-trip trading costs for trades of a given maximum size (as they are associated with a maximum quantity). As a result, bid–ask spreads indicate both trading costs and the amount of a security that can be traded at a given point in time (market depth), which affects how larger trades might need to be broken down into smaller orders for trading. Average trade sizes observed in past data provide additional information on quantities that can be traded at reasonable trading costs for a given security.

3.1.3. Market Conditions
Inputs relating to market conditions include the following:

- **Liquidity crises:** deviations from expected liquidity patterns due to periods of crisis

Market liquidity refers to the liquidity conditions in the market at the time the order is traded. At the time of trading, current or realized market conditions, such as traded volumes, price volatility, and bid–ask spreads, are additional factors that affect trade strategy selection, given that real-time market conditions are likely to be different from those anticipated and the conditions at the time the investment decision was made.

During market events or crises, the volatility and liquidity of the market and the security will be critical to consider as conditions result in sudden and significant deviations from normal trade patterns. Such seasonal considerations as local market holidays and quarter-end or year-end dates may have more predictability in their liquidity variations and are also important to consider.

Security liquidity will also change over time, often because of changes in market-wide liquidity. For example, in August 2007, stocks with high exposure to widely used quantitative factors became very hard to liquidate as many quantitative asset managers tried to reduce their exposures to certain factors around the same time. In the fall of 2008, during the credit crisis, short selling in certain stocks, mostly financials, was banned. During this time, many structured credit securities became "toxic assets" and became extremely difficult to liquidate.

Even during "normal" market environments, liquidity will vary. For example, over time certain companies reach market values that may result in them being added to or removed from widely used equity indexes. When this happens, their stocks' liquidity often improves or deteriorates as their shares become more widely or more narrowly held. Government bonds are generally liquid as long as they are the most recently issued (so-called on the run) among a particular bond type. However, once they become off-the-run bonds, their liquidity generally decreases.

Moreover, market volatility and liquidity are dynamic. They are also generally negatively related, which becomes apparent especially during periods of crisis, when volatility increases and liquidity decreases. For example, during the 1987 stock market crash, the Long-Term Capital Management crisis in 1998, and the global financial crisis in 2008, market volatility increased sharply and market liquidity collapsed. Portfolio managers can be hurt in such environments: Lower liquidity might suggest a longer trading horizon for order completion, but higher volatility might lead people to speed up their trades and incur higher costs. However, as trading horizon lengthens, market risk increases, particularly during periods of high volatility.

3.1.4. User-Based Considerations: Trading Cost Risk Aversion

In addition to order, security, and market considerations, the risk aversion of the individual(s) trading affects trade strategy selection.

Risk aversion is specific to each individual, and in a trading context, it refers to how much risk the portfolio manager or trader is willing to accept during trading. A portfolio manager or trader with a high level of risk aversion is likely to be more concerned about market risk and will tend to trade with greater trade urgency to avoid the greater market exposure associated with trading more patiently. A portfolio manager with a low level of risk aversion might be less concerned about market risk and may tend to trade more patiently (more passively), with lower levels of trade urgency.

3.1.5. Market Impact and Execution Risk

The temporary market impact cost of trading an order is the often short-lived impact on security price from trading to meet the need to buy or sell. For example, in situations where a portfolio manager is looking to buy shares but there are not enough sellers in the market to complete the order, the portfolio manager will need to increase his buying price to attract sellers to complete the order. In situations where a portfolio manager is looking to sell shares but there are not enough buyers in the market to complete the order, the portfolio manager will need to decrease his selling price to attract buyers to complete the order. In these situations, there is usually price reversion after the trade has been completed since the price change was driven by short-term buying or selling pressure rather than a fundamental change in security value. Therefore, post-trade prices should revert, with prices decreasing after buy order completion and increasing after sell order completion.

The permanent component of price change associated with trading an order is the market price impact caused by the information content of the trade. Trading in the market often conveys information to other market participants that the asset may be under- or overvalued. If market participants discover there are more buyers demanding liquidity than sellers supplying liquidity, the market interprets this situation as the pricing being relatively too low and prices will move in the direction of the trade imbalance on average. In this case, market participants will increase their selling price.

If market participants find out that there are more sellers than buyers, the market interprets this situation as the pricing being relatively too high and market participants will decrease their buying price. In other words, market participants may believe there is some information component of the trade that is causing the counterparty to buy or sell shares in the market that they have not yet discovered or incorporated into their own asset valuations. Therefore, market participants will adjust the price at which they are willing to buy or sell to reflect this potential new information.

To minimize information leakage, which may result in market participants adjusting the prices at which they are willing to buy or sell, portfolio managers may attempt to hide their trading activity by executing orders across different venues and using a mix of order types, such as market and limit orders. Market (marketable) orders instruct execution at the best available price at the time of trading, whereas limit orders instruct execution at the best available price as long as the price is equal to or better than the specified limit price—that is, a price equal to or lower than the limit price in the case of buys and equal to or higher in the case of sells. To hide their activity, portfolio managers will also trade less on displayed venues (e.g., exchanges with greater trade transparency regarding the intentions of market participants) and make greater use of dark pool venues.

Execution risk—the risk of adverse price movement during the trading horizon due to a change in the fundamental value of the security—arises as time passes and occurs even if the order is not traded. Trading faster (greater trade urgency) results in lower execution risk because the order is executed over a shorter period of time, which decreases the time the trade is exposed to price volatility and changing market conditions. Trading slower (lower trade urgency) results in higher execution risk because the order is executed over a longer period of time, which increases the time the trade is exposed to price volatility and changing market conditions.

Trader's dilemma.

To alleviate the market impact effect of entering a large order into the market, traders will "slice" the order into smaller pieces to trade over time. This results in a lower market price impact on the value of the asset, but in trading in smaller pieces over time, the fund is exposed to market risk, which could result in an even higher trading cost than if the order was entered into the market in its entirety. This phenomenon is known as the trader's dilemma and is stated as follows:

Trading too fast results in too much market impact, but trading too slow results in too much market risk.

The goal in selecting a trading strategy is to choose the best price–time trade-off given current market conditions and the unique characteristics of the order.

In-Text Question

Discuss how order size and security liquidity considerations affect market impact and execution risk for an order.

Solution: Trading a large order creates greater market impact than trading a smaller order, all else being equal. To minimize market impact, large orders are often traded over longer trade time horizons, which increases the corresponding execution risk of the order. Smaller orders have less market impact and can be traded more quickly over shorter time horizons, with lower associated execution risk. The liquidity profile of a security has important implications for trading strategy. More liquid securities (higher traded volumes, tighter bid–ask spreads, etc.) have lower levels of market impact and execution risk given that they can be transacted over shorter time horizons with greater certainty of execution. Finally, higher rates of alpha decay would speed up order execution time horizons and increase market impact costs given greater trade order urgency, whereas lower rates of alpha decay would increase trade time horizons and associated execution risk.

3.2. Reference Prices

Reference prices, also referred to as *price benchmarks*, are specified prices, price-based calculations, or price targets used to select and execute a trade strategy. Reference prices are used in determining trade prices for execution strategy and in calculating actual trade costs for post-trade evaluation purposes. Following is a discussion of reference prices used in the selection and execution of a trade strategy.

Reference prices are categorized as follows:

- pre-trade benchmarks, where the reference price for the benchmark is known before trading begins;
- intraday benchmarks, where the reference price for the benchmark is computed on the basis of market prices that occur during the trading period;
- post-trade benchmarks, where the reference price for the benchmark is established after trading is completed; and
- price target benchmarks, where the reference price for the benchmark is specified as a price to meet or beat (transact more favorably).

3.2.1. Pre-Trade Benchmarks

A pre-trade benchmark is a reference price that is known before the start of trading. For example, pre-trade benchmarks include decision price, previous close, opening price, and arrival price. A pre-trade benchmark is often specified by portfolio managers who are buying or selling securities on the basis of decision prices (the price at the time the investment decision was made) or seeking short-term alpha by buying undervalued or selling overvalued securities in the market. Portfolio managers making trading decisions based on quantitative models or portfolio optimizers that use historical trading prices, such as the previous close, as model inputs may also specify a pre-trade benchmark.

Decision price.

The **decision price** benchmark represents the security price at the time the portfolio manager made the decision to buy or sell the security. In many situations, portfolio managers have exact records of the price when they decided to buy or sell the security. Quantitative portfolio managers will often have records of their decision price because these prices may be inputs into their quantitative models.

There are times, however, when portfolio managers do not have a record of their decision price. In these situations, portfolio managers may decide to buy or sell securities on the basis of long-term growth prospects or higher-than-expected return potential and will specify the previous close or opening price as their reference price benchmark.

Previous close.
The previous close benchmark refers to the security's closing price on the previous trading day. A previous close benchmark is often specified by quantitative portfolio managers who incorporate the previous close in a quantitative model, portfolio optimizer, or screening model. The previous close is often used as a proxy for the decision price by quantitative portfolio managers.

Opening price.
An opening price benchmark references the security's opening price for the day. This benchmark price is most often specified by portfolio managers who begin trading at the market open and wish to minimize trading costs. The opening price is often used as a proxy for the decision price by fundamental portfolio managers who are investing in a security for long-term alpha or growth potential. Portfolio managers may choose an opening price instead of the decision price or previous close because, unlike a reference price from the prior day or earlier, the opening price does not have associated overnight risk, or the risk that prices will adjust at market open to incorporate information released after the close of the previous business day.

If the trade is to be executed in the opening auction, then using the opening price as a reference benchmark is not appropriate because the trade itself can influence the reference benchmark. An auction in this case is a market where buyers compete for order execution and orders are aggregated for execution at a single price and point in time. An auction taking place at market open is referred to as an opening auction, and one taking place at market close is a closing auction. The impact of trading any amount of the order in the opening (or closing) auction would be incorporated in the opening (or closing) price auction calculation, thus inappropriately influencing the reference benchmark level.

Arrival price.
The **arrival price** is the price of the security at the time the order is entered into the market for execution. Portfolio managers who are buying or selling on the basis of alpha expectations or a current market mispricing will often specify an arrival price benchmark. In these cases, the portfolio manager's goal is to transact at or close to current market prices in order to complete trade execution and realize as much potential alpha as possible. Portfolio managers looking to minimize trading cost will also in many cases specify the arrival price as their benchmark.

3.2.2. Intraday Benchmarks
An intraday price benchmark is based on a price that occurs during the trading period. The most common intraday benchmarks used in trading are volume-weighted average price (VWAP) and time-weighted average price (TWAP).

Portfolio managers often specify an intraday benchmark for funds that are trading passively over the day, seeking liquidity, and for funds that may be rebalancing, executing a buy/sell trade list, and minimizing risk. Portfolio managers who do not expect the security to exhibit any short-term price momentum commonly select an intraday benchmark.

VWAP.

The VWAP benchmark price is the volume-weighted average price of all trades executed over the day or the trading horizon. Portfolio managers may specify the VWAP benchmark when they wish to participate with volume patterns over the day.

Portfolio managers who are rebalancing their portfolios over the day and have both buy and sell orders may select the VWAP as a price benchmark. In these situations, the preference is to participate with market volume. Exposure to market risk is reduced in this case by having a two-sided trade list of buys and sells, as opposed to a trade list containing all buys or all sells. Portfolio managers who are rebalancing and using cash from sell orders to purchase buy orders will also often select an intraday benchmark, such as VWAP. Doing so allows the portfolio managers to structure their executions over time to ensure cash received from sell orders is sufficient to fund remaining buy orders. If trades are not executed properly, portfolio managers could be short cash for buy orders and need to raise additional money for order completion.

TWAP.

The TWAP benchmark price is defined as an equal-weighted average price of all trades executed over the day or trading horizon. Unlike VWAP, TWAP price does not consider volume traded and is simply the average price of trades executed over the specified time horizon. Portfolio managers may choose TWAP when they wish to exclude potential trade outliers. Trade outliers may be caused by trading a large buy order at the day's low or a large sell order at the day's high. If market participants are not able to fully participate in these trades, then TWAP may be a more appropriate choice. The TWAP benchmark is used by portfolio managers and traders to evaluate fair and reasonable trading prices in market environments with high volume uncertainty and for securities that are subject to spikes in trading volume throughout the day.

3.2.3. Post-Trade Benchmarks

A post-trade benchmark is a reference price that is determined at the end of trading or sometime after trading has completed. The most common post-trade benchmark is closing price. Portfolio managers for funds valued at the closing price on the day or who wish to minimize tracking error to an underlying benchmark price, such as index funds, often select a post-trade reference price, such as the official closing price. In this case, the objective is to target consistency between the trade execution price and the price used in fund valuation and benchmark calculation.

Closing price.

The closing price is typically used by index managers and mutual funds that wish to execute transactions at the closing price for the day. For managers with index mandates, where the fund's securities are typically valued using the official market close for each security, it is important to know how close their executions are to the benchmark price, which also uses the official market close in its calculation. A portfolio manager who is managing tracking error to a benchmark will generally select a closing price benchmark since the closing price is the price used to compute the fund's valuation and resulting tracking error to the benchmark.

An advantage of the closing price benchmark is that it provides portfolio managers with the price used for fund valuation and thus minimizes potential tracking error. A disadvantage is that the benchmark price is not known until after trading is completed. Thus, portfolio managers have no way of knowing whether they are performing more or less favorably relative to the benchmark until after trading is completed.

3.2.4. Price Target Benchmarks

Portfolio managers seeking short-term alpha may select an alternative benchmark known as a price target benchmark. In this case, a portfolio manager would like to transact in a security—believed to be undervalued or overvalued—at a more favorable price. For example, if a stock currently trading in the market at $20.00 is believed to be undervalued by $0.50, the portfolio manager will seek to purchase shares by specifying a price target of $20.50 or better (better being lower than $20.50 in the case of a buy). In this example, the benchmark price is specified as the perceived fair value price of $20.50. In this setting, the portfolio manager wishes to purchase as many order shares as possible at a price equal to or better (lower) than the specified price target.

3.3. Trade Strategies

The primary goal of any trading strategy is to balance the expected costs and risks associated with trading the order in the market consistent with the portfolio manager's trading objectives, risk aversion, and other known constraints. A portfolio manager's motivation to trade, risk aversion, trade urgency for the order, and other factors, such as order size and market conditions at the time of trading, are thus key in determining an appropriate trade strategy.

Will the value in completing the trade dissipate if the trade is not completed in a timely enough manner? Trade urgency, the importance of execution certainty, is critical in determining trade strategy. For alpha-driven trades, trading with greater urgency to maximize short-term alpha capture must be weighed against the costs of trading faster and expected alpha decay. For trades with low or no trade urgency, trading over a longer trade horizon or at the market close may be optimal.

Portfolio managers also have expectations or insights regarding short-term market conditions, such as price trends and market liquidity, particularly if these factors are used in the security selection process. For example, does the stock exhibit momentum, where any observed trend will continue through the end of the day, or does the stock exhibit reversion, where the observed trend is more likely to reverse during the day? Portfolio managers may also have insights into expected trading volumes for assets and whether trading volumes may be expected to continue or may reverse in direction. Traders will also have insights regarding volume patterns and potential information leakage during execution. These expectations combined with actual market conditions at the time of trading help inform an appropriate trade strategy.

The selection of a trade strategy is best illustrated through a discussion of common trade types. Trading strategies for the following types of trades involving equities, fixed income, currency, and derivatives are explained in this section:

- **Short-term alpha:** short-term alpha-driven equity trade (high trade urgency)
- **Long-term alpha:** long-term alpha-driven fixed-income trade (low trade urgency)
- **Risk rebalance:** buy/sell basket trade to rebalance a fund's risk exposure
- **Cash flow driven:** client redemption trade to raise proceeds
- **Cash flow driven:** cash equitization (derivatives) trade to invest a new client mandate

3.3.1. Short-Term Alpha Trade

A portfolio manager has determined that the market has overreacted to weak earnings announced in the pre-market trading session for Stock XYZ. The stock price is trading at a significant discount in the pre-market relative to the portfolio manager's valuation and now represents a significant buying opportunity based on the portfolio manager's analysis. The portfolio manager would like to buy 50,000 shares, which represents 10% of the stock's average daily volume. Based on the heavy pre-market trading, however, the trader believes that this order will only constitute 2% of the day's volume.

The pre-market price is currently $50, down $15 relative to the previous night's close. The portfolio manager believes that the stock's fair value is in the low $60 range and sets her limit price at $60.

In this situation, the portfolio manager believes that the market has overreacted to the weak earnings announced by the company. If she is correct and the market eventually adopts her view going forward, Stock XYZ's price should increase closer to her estimated fair value in the low $60 range. In setting her limit price of $60, the portfolio manager is also specifying the reference price for the trade, which, in this case, represents a price target benchmark.

Given the possibility of short-term price increases in XYZ, this order has associated trade urgency and the trader does not have the benefit of trading the order passively (such as using a VWAP or TWAP participation strategy) during the day, since XYZ's price could increase to fair value at any time. To trade this order, the trader would not likely attempt to use dark pool venues, given their greater risk of unfilled executions if offsetting orders do not arrive. The trader will likely want to trade a portion of the order in the opening auction and then continue trading any residual in the open market. Doing so provides greater execution certainty, which is important in this situation given the trade urgency of the order.

Since the order represents approximately 2% of expected volume, the trader would not likely place the full order into the opening auction. Research shows the US opening auction typically makes up between 1% and 4% of a day's volume,[2] so sending the entire order into the opening auction would result in the ordering being roughly 50%–200% of the expected opening auction volume, on average. Because this is an unusual trading day, the trader could use volume information from pre-market trading and any auction-related data made available by the exchanges to determine the optimal amount to place into the opening auction.

Given the trade urgency of the order, the very liquid market for XYZ, and the order size not being large relative to XYZ's expected volume, the trader could trade any remaining shares using an arrival price trade strategy that would attempt to execute the remaining shares close to market prices at the time the order was received. This strategy could be executed using a programmed strategy to electronically execute, also known as an algorithm, such as an arrival price algorithm. Most importantly, the trader will want to make sure that the orders sent to the auction and traded in the open market use limit prices consistent with the portfolio manager's price view, reflected in her limit price of $60.

3.3.2. Long-Term Alpha Trade

A portfolio manager believes that a company whose bonds he holds is likely to experience a deteriorating credit position over the next year. The deterioration in credit is expected to be

---

[2]See J. Bacidore, K. Berkow, and J. Wong, "Inside the Opening Auction," *Journal of Trading* 7 (Winter 2012): 7–14.

gradual as information becomes available over the next several quarters, confirming the company's deteriorating financial position. The portfolio manager's position is not large in aggregate, but the market for these bonds is not very active, with infrequent transactions and low volumes. The portfolio manager approaches the trader to determine how best to liquidate his holdings in the bond so that he can exploit his view while still getting a favorable execution.

Because the market for these bonds is not very liquid, it is likely the trader will need to approach various dealers to get quotes for these bonds. Given the portfolio manager's view that the deterioration in credit will occur gradually over the coming year, there is no order urgency from a trading perspective. Because the position is not large, the trader believes he could execute it over the next day or two if needed.

The trader, however, may not want to execute this quickly for two reasons. First, the sudden trading in an illiquid security may inadvertently leak information, leading the dealer involved to think the order is an information-based trade and consequently to price the trade less favorably for the trader. Second, requiring dealers to take on substantial illiquid inventory exposes them to risk, for which they will demand compensation in the form of inferior (unfavorable) pricing.

Therefore, a reasonable trade approach would be to sell these bonds off gradually over the course of a few days or even weeks, depending on the relative size of the bond holdings and their liquidity. By selling off smaller portions, varying the amounts sold, and trading over a longer execution horizon, the trader can reduce information leakage regarding the order and avoid placing pressure on dealer inventories, which would result in inferior pricing. Using this approach, the dealers will likely provide better (more favorable) initial quotes, and subsequent quotes may also be more favorable if the dealers have enough time between trades to reduce their inventory.

The use of reference prices for fixed-income trades executed over multiple days is not widespread and can be difficult in practice. A decision price, for example, would not only capture market impact and alpha loss but would also reflect unrelated market moves, which can be much larger than the former when a trade is spread out over days or weeks. Impact costs, for example, would decrease as the trade horizon lengthens, whereas price volatility impact would increase with time.

3.3.3. Risk Rebalance Trade

A macro fund manager is concerned that potential trade tariffs and a deteriorating financial situation in a number of key emerging markets may lead to a significant increase in currency volatility. The manager is holding long and short developed market currency positions and has, so far, not seen a significant impact on his fund's valuation because the fund's long and short positions have been constructed to offset one another, immunizing the fund from sudden price moves. The fund's mandate, however, specifies a target risk level of 10%. With the increase in volatility, the fund's risk level is currently closer to 14%. Although the increase has not caused the portfolio to breach any guidelines, the portfolio manager believes that volatility will remain at current levels for the next several months and wishes to reduce risk in a controlled and gradual manner by liquidating positions to bring the fund's volatility back to its target risk level. The portfolio manager approaches a trader to discuss an appropriate strategy.

In this situation, the macro fund manager is holding long and short positions and has no view as to whether the fund's value will rise or fall in the near term owing to the sudden increase in volatility. Consequently, the hedge fund manager simply wishes to reduce current positions (as opposed to rebalancing the fund's relative positions). The holdings in developed market currencies are actively traded, and it is unlikely the positions are large enough that they would dislocate (substantially move) the currency markets, as long as trading is done in an appropriate manner.

Although volatility has significantly increased, the risk exposure of the trade is more limited if the list of buys and sells is balanced in market risk exposure, such as a buy/sell trade list with a net beta of approximately zero (i.e., the trade-weighted average beta of the securities traded is zero). Therefore, the trader does not have the same trade urgency as a trade with a positive or negative net beta, such as one containing all buys or all sells, which might involve significantly more risk arising from exposure to potential market movement. Risk-averse market participants will typically have greater trade urgency for trades that have directional market exposure than for trades that are balanced, or hedged, in market exposure.

Since the portfolio is not in breach of its guidelines and the portfolio manager wishes to reduce risk on a controlled and gradual basis, the trader can trade this order in a passive manner to lower the fund's risk level. In this situation, using a TWAP reference price for the trade and a TWAP algorithm to execute over the next day or two (or longer, depending on the size of the position) would be an appropriate trading strategy. By trading all the orders over the same trading horizon using a TWAP strategy, the trader is maintaining the hedge that exists between the buys and sells, which helps reduce execution risk. And because currency markets in developed economies are very liquid and deep, trading algorithmically will not likely dislocate prices.

3.3.4. Client Redemption Trade

A client has decided to redeem its position in a small-cap/mid-cap value fund managed by ABC Investment Advisers. The fund holdings are US small- and mid-cap stocks, with the only constraints being that the stocks satisfy the criteria of the fund (e.g., stocks meet the definition of a small- or mid-cap stock, stocks are listed on a major exchange). Client redemptions from the fund are done at the fund's net asset value at the close of trading, where the NAV is calculated using the closing price of the stock's listing market. To raise the necessary cash to meet the client redemption request, the portfolio manager asks the trader to sell 0.1% of every position held in the fund.

In this scenario, the client will receive the NAV of the fund *regardless of how well or poorly the trader executes the trade*. Therefore, the trader bears risk (for executing at any price other than the closing price) unless she can guarantee that each position is executed at the closing price. A closing price reference price is, therefore, most appropriate for this trade. Because these stocks are traded on either the NASDAQ or the NYSE, the trader can send the order to the closing auction for these exchanges and receive the auction-guaranteed closing price on all orders submitted to the auction. Such a strategy eliminates all potential risk of executing at prices that are different from those used to calculate the fund's NAV.

However, the trader should make sure that the size of the orders does not have an undue impact on the closing price. Executing a relatively large sell order in the closing auction (e.g., 50% of the closing volume) may lead to a significant price decline at the close, lowering calculated NAV and resulting in less cash being returned to the client.

Following a strategy to receive a guaranteed closing price on all orders submitted eliminates risk to the fund (and trader) since the client is receiving proceeds at NAV. From a fiduciary standpoint, however, trading in a manner that will lead to a poorer (less favorable) execution for a client is inappropriate. An alternative approach that portfolio managers follow when their trades are large relative to expected liquidity in the closing auction is to execute in the market and in the closing auction. For example, they would identify a reasonable amount to send to the closing auction (e.g., 90% of the order to be sent to the closing auction), trade the order remainder in the market prior to the close of trading (e.g., 10% of the order to be traded VWAP in the market up to the close of trading),[3] and then send the identified amount (90% of the order) to the closing auction.

3.3.5. New Mandate Trade

An investment manager has just been awarded a $150 million mandate to track the Russell 2000 Index benchmark with a 3% tracking error. The investment manager and the client have agreed that performance measurement of the mandate will begin at the current day's close. The appropriate reference price for the trade is, therefore, also the closing price. Given the large size of the investment mandate, the trader is concerned that trading into the positions at the close of trading will cause significant price impact. The trader would instead prefer to trade into the positions over multiple days. The client, however, requests that the mandate be fully invested as quickly as possible. The portfolio manager for the fund also prefers not to have the fund holding cash, given that the performance evaluation for the mandate begins as of the close of trading. Holding a cash position in the fund exposes the portfolio manager to significant performance risk relative to the fund's Russell 2000 benchmark. For example, if the Russell 2000 increases while the fund is holding cash, the fund's uninvested cash amounts would result in underperformance (arising from cash drag) relative to the Russell 2000.

The trader can get more immediate exposure to the Russell 2000 by buying $150 million worth of futures near the end of the trading day. After establishing this initial exposure, the trader can begin building the underlying stock positions over time and unwinding (selling) the equivalent futures exposure. This approach allows the client mandate to achieve full $150 million exposure to the Russell 2000, eliminating the opportunity cost of holding cash balances in the fund. This approach also gives the trader additional time to establish the underlying positions, thereby receiving (hopefully) better execution prices. For smaller mandates in more liquid securities, the trader could possibly skip the equitization-via-futures step and instead invest directly in the underlying securities. For larger mandates, however, investing in the index via liquid futures contracts initially is often an effective means to equitize cash and reduce tracking error for the client mandate and fund.

---

[3]Some brokers provide special "close algorithms" that will size the closing auction trade appropriately, route the order into the closing auction, and trade any residuals in the open market, effectively automating the strategy discussed in this example.

Two considerations should be noted in this situation. First, futures markets may not have closing auctions, as is the case with the Russell 2000 futures contract. If no closing auction exists, the trader will likely want to time the trade as close to the benchmark close as possible; for example, in the United States, this equates to a 4:00 p.m. cash close. For a small trade that is less than the quoted size, the trader could send a market order at 4:00 p.m. For larger trades or less liquid futures, the trader may trade using a VWAP or TWAP algorithm into the market close. Second, this futures-based strategy assumes the fund's investment mandate allows the use of derivatives. If the fund's mandate does not allow the use of derivatives, such as futures, but does permit ETF usage, the trader could equitize cash using a liquid Russell 2000 ETF.

In-Text Question

A portfolio manager for a global fixed-income index fund is required to trade for quarterly index changes taking place at the end of the trading day. To keep the fund in line with the anticipated index constituent changes, the portfolio manager generates a fund rebalance list consisting of buys and sells. He approaches the senior trader to discuss the best trade strategy for the list.

1. Identify the most appropriate reference price benchmark for his trade.
2. Select and justify the most appropriate trading strategy to execute his trade.

Solution:

1. A closing price is the most appropriate reference price benchmark for an index fund. The portfolio manager needs to trade to maintain the same security holdings and weights as the benchmark index. Since the index fund will be valued using official closing prices, he should select the closing price as the reference price benchmark for trading the rebalance names. By executing the buys and sells at the close, he will be minimizing the fund's potential tracking error to the benchmark index.

   The previous close would not be an appropriate reference price benchmark since it would be the security's closing price on the previous trading day. A previous close benchmark is often used by quantitative portfolio managers whose models or optimizers incorporate the previous close as an input or who wish to use this price as a proxy for the decision price. The opening price benchmark would not be an appropriate benchmark because it references the security's opening price on the day and is often selected by portfolio managers and traders who wish to begin trading at the market open. The opening price may also be used as a proxy for the decision price.

2. A market-on-close (MOC) trade strategy would be the most appropriate strategy for his rebalance list. Trading the rebalance list at the market's closing prices best aligns the trade execution prices with the same closing prices used for the fund's NAV and benchmark calculation, thus minimizing tracking error of the fund to the benchmark index.

4. TRADE EXECUTION (STRATEGY IMPLEMENTATION)

Once the appropriate trade strategy is determined by the portfolio manager and the trader, the trade must be executed in a market and in a manner consistent with the trade strategy chosen. A variety of implementation choices are available based on the specific order, market, and trade strategy involved. Trade implementation choices range from higher-touch approaches, which involve greater degrees of human interaction for order completion, to fully automated trade execution through electronic trading venues with varying levels of trade transparency. Higher-touch orders include principal and agency trades, the main difference being who assumes the risk of trading the order. In **principal trades**, the executing broker assumes all or part of the risk related to trading the order, pricing it into her quoted spread. In **agency trades**, the broker is engaged to find the other side of the trade but acts as an agent only, and risk for trading the order remains with the buy-side portfolio manager or trader. Electronic trading includes alternative or multilateral trading venues (ATS or MTF), direct market access (DMA), and dark pools.

4.1. Trade Implementation Choices

In general, trading in large blocks of securities requires a higher-touch approach involving greater human engagement and the need for a dealer or market maker to act as counterparty and principal to trade transactions.[4] For these transactions, also called *principal trades* or *broker risk trades*, market makers and dealers become a disclosed counterparty to their clients' orders and buy securities into or sell securities from their own inventory or book, assuming risk for the trade and absorbing temporary supply–demand imbalances. In the case of a less active security, the expected time to offset the trade for the dealer is longer. For taking on this additional risk, the dealer will demand greater compensation, generally by quoting a wider bid–ask spread.

Markets characterized by dealer-provided quotes may be referred to as *quote-driven, over-the-counter*, or *off-exchange markets*. In such bilateral dealer markets, customers trade at prices quoted by dealers. Depending on the instrument traded, dealers may work for commercial banks, investment banks, broker/dealers, or proprietary trading firms. Worldwide, most trading besides that in stocks, ETFs, and exchange-traded derivatives takes place in quote-driven markets, where the matching of buyers and sellers takes longer because of less frequent trading and greater market illiquidity.

---

[4]Large trades that exceed the normal trade size in a given security are often referred to as "block trades." Brokers offer dedicated services for block trades where human facilitation is higher than for regular trades, particularly for less liquid securities.

In some cases, dealers may be unable or unwilling to hold the securities in their inventories and take on position (principal) risk. In agency trades, dealers try to arrange trades by acting as agents, or brokers, on behalf of the client. Brokers are often used for transactions in securities or markets in which finding a buyer or a seller is difficult.

High-touch approaches involve human sell-side traders as intermediaries. These traders, employed by sell-side brokerage firms, may first attempt to fill a customer order by matching it with offsetting orders from other customers before trying to fill it from their own position book. Crossing an order with a broker's own book is known as a broker risk trade or principal trade. If this does not occur, the broker would then route the order to the open market and "slice," or divide, the order into smaller pieces to trade in the market. This approach involves human judgment unique to each trade and is suited to trading illiquid securities in which the execution process is difficult to automate.

A variation of quote-driven markets often used to trade less liquid securities is a **request for quote** (RFQ). In RFQ markets, dealers or market makers do not provide quotes continuously but do so only upon request by a potential buyer or seller. These quotes are nonbinding and are valid only at the time they are provided.

For relatively liquid, standardized securities where continuous two-way trading may exist, buyers and sellers display prices and quantities at which they are willing to transact (limit orders) on an exchange or other multilateral trading venue. In order-driven markets, order-matching systems run by exchanges, brokers, and other alternative trading systems use rules to arrange trades. Trading is done electronically with multiple venues, often through a consolidated limit order book that presents a view of the limit buy (bid)/sell (ask) prices and order sizes for all venues with orders for a security. Centralized clearing for trades exists on those venues. Equities, futures, and exchange-traded options are generally traded using this approach.

Exhibit 1 shows the proportion of trading that was conducted electronically in 2012 and 2015. In most asset classes, electronic trading increased over the period to more than 50% of total trading volume. Markets with higher trading activity have seen strong growth in electronic trading. For example, cash equities and futures are now predominantly traded electronically, whereas some other (generally less liquid) markets, such as high-yield bonds, still feature trading with a high-touch, manual approach.

EXHIBIT 1   Electronic Trading in Various Asset Classes (in %)

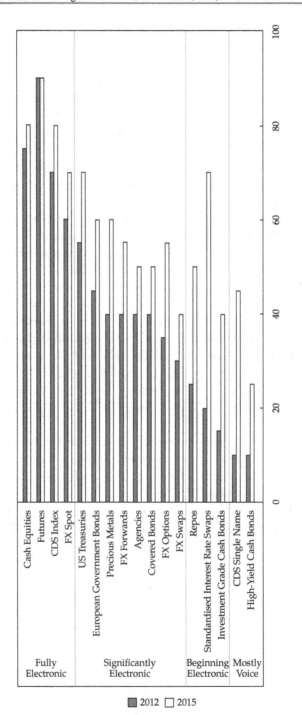

Source: Bank for International Settlements, "Electronic Trading in Fixed-Income Markets," Markets Committee Study Group (2016).

Automated execution approaches work well for liquid securities and most trade sizes other than extremely large orders (relative to the total volume traded of a particular security), which might require a more customized, high-touch approach. *Algorithmic trading*, or the use of programmed strategies to electronically trade orders, is well established in most equity, foreign exchange, and exchange-traded derivative markets. In fixed income, algorithmic execution is mostly limited to trading highly liquid government securities, such as US Treasury securities.

For liquid securities that trade in high volumes, high-touch execution approaches are generally inefficient, opaque, slow, and susceptible to front running. Front running occurs when speculative traders try to profit by buying ahead of other traders' anticipated activity. Front running is illegal in many jurisdictions if the information acted on is improperly obtained. Moreover, given that they require human involvement for each execution, they tend to be costly. Hence, for straightforward trades in liquid securities' low-touch automated execution strategies are often preferred whenever available. These generally involve direct market access (DMA) and/or execution algorithms.

Direct market access (DMA) gives all market participants a way to interact directly with the order book of an exchange, usually through a broker's exchange connectivity. This activity is normally restricted to broker/dealers and market-making firms. With DMA, buy-side firms use a broker's technology infrastructure and market access to execute orders themselves rather than handing orders over to the broker. DMA often involves the use of algorithms.

Alternatively, a broker can be instructed to execute client orders using certain execution algorithms. The desired urgency of an order is a key input for the choice and nature of the execution algorithm.

4.2. Algorithmic Trading

Algorithmic trading is the computerized execution of the investment decision following a specified set of trading instructions. An algorithm's programmed strategies used to electronically execute orders will slice larger orders into smaller pieces and trade over the day and across venues to reduce the price impact of the order. The primary goal of algorithmic trading is to ensure that the implementation of the investment decision is consistent with the investment objective of the fund. In this section, we describe factors that help determine the selection of a trading algorithm class.

Trading algorithms are primarily used for two purposes—trade execution and profit generation.

Execution algorithms.
An execution algorithm is tasked with transacting an investment decision made by the portfolio manager. The manager determines what to buy or sell on the basis of his investment style and investment objective and then enters the order into the algorithm. The algorithm will then execute the order by following a set of rules specified by the portfolio manager.

Profit-seeking algorithms.
A profit-seeking algorithm will determine what to buy and sell and then implement those decisions in the market as efficiently as possible. For example, these algorithms will use real-time

price information and market data, such as volume and volatility, to determine what to buy or sell and will then implement the decision consistent with the investment objective. Profit-seeking algorithms are used by electronic market makers, quantitative funds, and high-frequency traders.

This section describes the common classification of execution algorithms and their use.

4.2.1. Execution Algorithm Classifications

Although there are many different types of execution algorithms, they can generally be classified into the following categories.

4.2.1.1. Scheduled (POV, VWAP, TWAP)

Scheduled algorithms send orders to the market following a schedule that is determined by historical volumes or specified time periods. Scheduled algorithms include *percentage of volume (POV)* algorithms, *volume-weighted average price* algorithms, and *time-weighted average price* algorithms.

POV algorithms (also known as participation algorithms) send orders following a volume participation schedule. As trading volume increases in the market, these algorithms will trade more shares, and as volume decreases, these algorithms will trade fewer shares. Investors specify the POV algorithm through the participation rate, which determines the volume participation strategy. For example, a participation rate of 10% indicates that the algorithm will participate with 10% of the market volume until the order is completed. In this case, for every 10,000 shares that trade in the market, the algorithm will execute 1,000 shares. An advantage of volume participation algorithms is that they will automatically take advantage of increased liquidity conditions by trading more shares when there is ample market liquidity and will not trade in times of illiquidity. While POV algorithms incorporate real-time volume, by following (or chasing) volumes, they may incur higher trading costs by continuing to buy as prices move higher and to sell as prices move lower. An additional disadvantage of these algorithms is that they may not complete the order within the time period specified.

VWAP and TWAP algorithms release orders to the market following a time-specified schedule, trading a predetermined number of shares within the specified time interval; for example, trade 5,000 shares between 10:00 a.m. and 1:00 p.m. An advantage of a time slicing strategy is that it ensures the specified number of shares are executed within the specified time period. A disadvantage of a time slicing strategy is that it will force the trades even in times of insufficient liquidity and will not take advantage of increased liquidity conditions when available.

VWAP algorithms slice the order into smaller amounts to send to the market following a time slicing schedule based on historical intraday volume profiles. These algorithms typically trade a higher percentage of the order at the open and close and a smaller percentage of the order during midday. Because of this, the VWAP curve is said to resemble a U-shaped curve. Following a fixed schedule as VWAP algorithms do may not be optimal for illiquid stocks because such algorithms may not complete the order in cases where volumes are low.

TWAP algorithms slice the order into smaller amounts to send to the market following an equal-weighted time schedule. TWAP algorithms will send the same number of shares and the same percentage of the order to be traded in each time period.

Scheduled algorithms are appropriate for orders in which portfolio managers or traders do not have expectations of adverse price movement during the trade horizon. These algorithms are also used by portfolio managers and traders who have greater risk tolerance for longer execution time periods and are more concerned with minimizing market impact. Scheduled algorithms are often appropriate when the order size is relatively small (e.g., no more than 5%–10% of expected volume), the security is relatively liquid, or the orders are part of a risk-balanced basket and trading all orders at a similar pace will maintain the risk balance.

4.2.1.2.   Liquidity seeking

Liquidity-seeking algorithms, also referred to as *opportunistic algorithms*, take advantage of market liquidity across multiple venues by trading faster when liquidity exists at a favorable price. These algorithms may trade aggressively with offsetting orders when sufficient liquidity is posted on exchanges and alternative trading systems at prices the algorithms deem favorable (a practice called "liquidity sweeping" or "sweeping the book"). These algorithms may also use dark pools and trade large quantities of shares in dark venues when sufficient liquidity is present. If liquidity is not present in the market at favorable prices, these algorithms may trade only a small number of shares. These algorithms will often make greater use of market order types than limit order types.

Liquidity-seeking algorithms are appropriate for large orders that the portfolio manager or trader would like to execute quickly without having a substantial impact on the security price. Liquidity-seeking algorithms are also used when displaying sizable liquidity via limit orders could lead to unwanted information leakage and adverse security price movement. In these cases, the priority is to minimize information leakage associated with order execution and avoid signaling to the market the trading intentions of the portfolio manager or trader. These algorithms are also appropriate for trading securities that are relatively less liquid and thinly traded or when liquidity is episodic (e.g., the order book is typically thin with wide spreads but occasionally experiences tight spreads or thick books).

4.2.1.3.   Arrival price

Arrival price algorithms seek to trade close to current market prices at the time the order is received for execution. Arrival price algorithms will trade more aggressively at the beginning of trading to execute more shares nearer to the arrival price, known as a front-loaded strategy. Arrival price algorithms tend to be time schedule based but can also be volume participation based.

Arrival price algorithms are used for orders in which the portfolio manager or trader believes prices are likely to move unfavorably during the trade horizon. In these cases, the portfolio manager wishes to trade more aggressively to capture alpha ahead of the unfavorable prices expected later in the trade horizon. These algorithms are also used by portfolio managers and traders who are risk averse and wish to trade more quickly to reduce the execution risk associated with trading more passively over longer time horizons. These algorithms are used when the security is relatively liquid or the order is not outsized (e.g., the order is less than 15% of expected volume) such that a participatory strategy is not expected to result in significant market impact from order execution.

4.2.1.4.   Dark strategies/liquidity aggregators

Dark aggregator algorithms execute shares away from "lit" markets, such as exchanges and other displayed venues that provide pre- and post-trade transparency regarding prices, volumes, market spreads, and depth. Instead, these algorithms execute in opaque, or less transparent, trade venues, such as dark pools.

Dark aggregator algorithms are used in trading when portfolio managers and traders are concerned with information leakage that may occur from posting limit orders in lit venues with pre- and post-trade transparency. These algorithms are used when order size is large relative to the market (i.e., a large percentage of expected volume) and when trading in the open market using arrival price or VWAP strategies would lead to significant market impact. These algorithms are appropriate for trading securities that are relatively illiquid or have relatively wide bid–ask spreads. Since trading in dark pools offers less certainty of execution (offsetting orders may never arrive), these algorithms are appropriate for trades in which the trader or portfolio manager does not need to execute the order in its entirety.

4.2.1.5. Smart order routers

Smart order routers (SORs) determine how best to route an order given prevailing market conditions. The SOR will determine the destination with the highest probability of executing the limit order and the venue with the best market price—known in the United States as the National Best Bid and Offer (NBBO)—for market orders. The SOR continuously monitors real-time data from exchanges and venues and also assesses ongoing activity in dark pools.

SORs are used when a portfolio manager or trader wishes to execute a small order by routing the order into the market as either a market(able) or non-marketable (limit) order.

Market orders.

SORs are used for orders that are sufficiently small that they will not have a large market impact if sent as marketable orders—for example, when the order size is less than the quantity posted at the best bid or offer. SORs are also best used for orders that require immediate execution because of imminent price movement, high portfolio manager or trader risk aversion, or abnormally high risk levels. Using SORs for marketable orders is also appropriate in cases where the market moves quickly, such that having the trader choose the venue(s) could lead to inferior executions (e.g., the trader chooses the venue but the venue with the best price changes before she can send the order).

Limit orders.

SORs are also used for orders that are small enough that posting the order as a limit order will not leak information to the market and move prices (e.g., orders that are similar to those currently posted in the market). In addition, SORs are appropriate for stocks that have multiple markets actively trading the stock and for which it is not obvious to which venues the order should be routed (e.g., there are multiple venues currently posting orders at the trader's limit price).

In-Text Question

A portfolio manager has identified a stock with attractive long-term growth potential and would like to place an order of moderate size, relative to the stock's average traded volume. The stock is very liquid and has attractive short-term alpha potential. The portfolio manager expects short-term buying pressure by other market participants into the market close, ahead of the company's earnings call scheduled later in the day.

1. Explain when the following algorithms are used: (a) arrival price, (b) dark aggregator, and (c) SOR.
2. Discuss which of the three algorithms is most suited to trading this order.

Solution:

1.
   a. Arrival price algorithms are used for relatively liquid securities and when the order is not expected to have a significant market impact. Arrival price algorithms are also used when portfolio managers and traders have higher levels of risk aversion and wish to trade more aggressively at an accelerated pace to reduce the execution risk associated with trading over longer time horizons.

   b. Dark aggregator algorithms are appropriate for trading securities that are relatively illiquid or that have relatively wide bid–ask spreads or for relatively large order sizes in which trading in the open market is expected to have a significant price impact. Additionally, they are used by portfolio managers and traders who are concerned with information leakage that may occur when posting limit orders in lit venues. Given their higher risk of unfilled executions, these algorithms are also used when the order does not need to be filled in its entirety.

   c. Smart order routing systems are used to electronically send small orders into the market. Based on prevailing market conditions, SORs will determine which trade destinations have the highest probability of executing for limit orders and which trading venues have the best market prices for market orders and will route orders accordingly. SORs continuously monitor market conditions in real time in both lit and dark markets.

2. An arrival price algorithm would be most appropriate for trading this order because the portfolio manager has adverse price expectations. In this case, the portfolio manager wants to trade more aggressively to capture alpha ahead of less favorable prices expected later in the day. By trading the order more quickly, the portfolio manager can execute at more favorable prices ahead of the adverse price movement and the less favorable prices expected from other participants' buying pressure into the close, in line with his trade urgency.

Algorithmic Selection

Choosing the best algorithm to execute a given trade can be a difficult and complex decision. There has been a proliferation of choices for the buy-side trader, with multiple broker offerings and multiple algorithm types per broker, such as VWAP, POV, and implementation shortfall. For a given stock, what is the best algorithm to choose? Intuitively, it seems that selecting an algorithm by considering specific characteristics about the stock and its liquidity profile should be superior to selecting an algorithm without regard for these attributes. Additionally, it seems intuitive that stocks with similar characteristics might best be executed in a similar manner. This rationale has motivated firms that provide execution services to apply a machine learning technique called "clustering" to the problem of algorithmic strategy selection.

Clustering, generally used in unsupervised machine learning, groups data objects solely on the basis of information found in the data. The use of clustering for algorithmic strategy selection for stocks will generally include microstructure factors, such as bid–ask spread, trade size, price volatility, tick size, depth of the order book queue, and trading volume. Stocks are characterized from the results of the data analysis (i.e., placed into groups, or clusters, based on similarities informed by the data). For each cluster, the historical executions for each stock are examined for comparative performance. From this analysis, the optimal algorithmic strategy can be selected.

To illustrate a simple intuitive example, stocks with wider bid–ask spreads may be more effectively traded using an algorithm that executes more in off-exchange venues (such as dark pools) since on those venues trading can occur at mid-market if an offsetting order arrives and the cost of crossing the bid–ask spread (buying at the offer or selling at the bid) is high. In contrast, for a cluster of stocks with tight bid–ask spreads, the benefit of trading at mid-market is smaller and the optimal algorithm is likely to trade less on off-exchange/dark venues.

In some cases, the optimal decision may be clear from the data because the performance of one algorithm dominates all other choices. In other cases, even if the optimal choice is unclear, the historical execution data of the given cluster help narrow the research space and form the basis for further optimization using either traditional regression-based or machine learning techniques. Although our example is quite simple and the rationale intuitive, one might ask, if the answer is that obvious, why bother with machine learning at all? In practice, the answers are usually much less obvious and the conditions far more complicated.

High-Frequency Market Forecasting

One of the primary challenges in trading (and investing) is forecasting asset prices. Even for a long-term investor, the ability to forecast short-term market direction can help make execution more efficient.

Building a model to forecast short-term market movements involves two steps: The first is to identify key factors, or predictors (independent variables in a regression context), and the second is to estimate the model. One might identify many (hundreds, if not more) potential predictors; for example, for a period of time, one stock—perhaps for which there has been a significant news release—may "lead" the rest of the market and be a good predictor of short-term movement in other stocks.

LASSO (least absolute shrinkage and selection operator) is a machine learning technique used to help with this identification problem. LASSO is a penalized regression technique that relies on the underlying assumption of sparsity, meaning that at any point in time, even in the presence of many potential predictors, only a handful of variables are significant. LASSO minimizes the residual sum of squares, which has the effect of reducing many of the coefficients to zero, leaving only the most significant variables.

For example, consider a trader building a forecast model to predict the near-term value of the S&P 500 ETF (SPY). There are a multitude of variables that she might want to consider, including the order book imbalance (excess of buys or sells for a given price) on each exchange, SPY trade executions, SPY returns over a number of recent time horizons, and similar attributes for correlated instruments, such as other ETFs, equity index futures contracts, and stocks making up the underlying portfolio of the

ETF. It is clear that there are hundreds of potential variables. Working with a regression model to identify the most important variables would likely be unwieldy and challenging, given potential collinearity. Using LASSO, the trader can reduce the problem to a more manageable number of variables.

4.3. Comparison of Markets

Although algorithmic trading is common in highly liquid, technologically developed markets, such as equities, trades in other markets require different implementation treatment, with greater human involvement. In this section, we compare and contrast key characteristics relating to trade implementation for the following markets:

- Equities
- Fixed income
- Exchange-traded derivatives (options and futures)
- Off-exchange (OTC) derivatives
- Spot currencies

4.3.1. Equities

Equities are generally traded on exchanges and dark pools. Exchanges are known as lit markets (as opposed to dark markets) because they provide pre-trade transparency—namely, limit orders that reflect trader intentions for trade side (buy or sell), price, and size. Dark pools provide anonymity because no pre-trade transparency exists. However, regardless of the trading venue, transactions and quantities are always reported. On exchanges, trade price, size, quote, and depth of book data are publicly available. However, detailed book data can be costly and may be available only to some market participants.

Most countries with open economies have at least one stock exchange. The United States has a total of 13 stock exchanges. There are more than 40 **alternative trading systems** (ATS)/dark pools globally. In Europe, these alternative trading venues are called **multilateral trading facilities** (MTF) and *systematic internalisers (SI)*. MTFs are operated by investment firms or market operators that bring together multiple third-party buying and selling interests in financial instruments. SIs are single-dealer liquidity pools. In the United States and Canada, these venues are called alternative trading systems (ATS). They are non-exchange trading venues that match buyers and sellers to find counterparties for transactions. They are typically regulated as broker/dealers rather than as exchanges (although an ATS can apply to be regulated as a securities exchange). In the United States, ATS must be approved by the Securities and Exchange Commission (SEC).

In Asia, although trading volume on alternative trading venues has grown rapidly over the last few years, such activity remains less common than in North America and Europe. Even in markets with the highest share of dark pool trading, most equity trading still takes place on traditional exchanges. In emerging markets, dark pool trading volume is minimal compared with trading volume on traditional exchanges.

Equities are the most technologically advanced market. Algorithmic trading is common, and most trades are electronic. Equity exchanges may use different trading systems for stocks depending on their level of liquidity. Large, urgent trades, particularly in less liquid small-cap stocks, are generally executed as high-touch broker risk trades, where the broker acts as dealer and counterparty. Large, non-urgent trades may be executed using trading algorithms (particularly for more liquid large-cap stocks) or, for less liquid securities, a high-touch agency approach. For small trades in liquid securities, most buy-side traders use electronic trading.

In recent years, average trade sizes have generally decreased for most asset classes; market participants break down their trades into smaller pieces that they trade either sequentially on the same trading venue or simultaneously across different venues. In equities, growth in the number of trading venues has resulted in fragmentation of trading and increased competition among trading venues.

4.3.2. Fixed Income

Fixed-income markets are quite different from equity markets. Market transparency and price discovery for fixed-income markets are generally much lower; information available and how quickly it is made available vary by market. Individual bond issuers can have a large number of bonds outstanding with very different features—for example, different maturities, coupons, and optionality. As a result, fixed income is a very heterogeneous asset class that encompasses a large number of individual securities. Institutional investors will often hold bonds until maturity or may trade large quantities infrequently. Trade imbalances often occur in corporate bonds owing to illiquidity. As a result, sourcing market liquidity relies heavily on dealers acting as counterparties (i.e., principal trades), and matching buyers and sellers is generally difficult in the corporate bond market.

Fixed-income securities are generally traded in a bilateral, dealer-centric market structure.[5] Investors will generally get quotes from dealers, often banks, which make markets in the securities. Historically, these quotes were accessed via phone, but they increasingly are disseminated using electronic chat (e.g., Symphony, Bloomberg) or electronic RFQ platforms. Just as it was before the onset of these electronic platforms, dealers do not provide quotes continuously; they provide them only on request by a potential buyer or seller.

There is limited algorithmic trading in bond markets, except for on-the-run (most recently issued) US Treasuries in benchmark maturities and bond and interest rate futures contracts. Although algorithmic/electronic trading in corporate bonds is growing, it remains a relatively low proportion of overall corporate bond trading.[6] The combination of market illiquidity and the large size and low frequency of potential trades creates challenges for algorithmic trading and electronic trading generally. For other fixed-income instruments, high-touch trading persists, particularly for larger trades and less liquid securities. Small trades and large, urgent trades are usually implemented through broker risk trades (via RFQs), where the broker acts as the counterparty, because securities are hard to source otherwise. Large, non-urgent trades are generally implemented using a high-touch approach, with brokers acting as agents to source liquidity (agency trades instead of principal trades).

4.3.3. Exchange-Traded Derivatives

As of 2018, there were fewer than 1,000 liquid and highly standardized exchange-traded derivatives outstanding. The market is very large, and trading volume exceeds several trillion

---

[5]Some fixed-income securities trade on exchanges (e.g., the NYSE, the London Stock Exchange, and some Italian exchanges list corporate bonds). However, the volume traded on centralized exchanges is small.
[6]As of 2018, Greenwich Associates has estimated that as of 2018, a fifth of all investment-grade US corporate bond trades are now traded electronically—almost double the volume of a decade ago.

dollars per day. Most of the trading volume is concentrated in futures, although the number of futures is considerably smaller than the number of options outstanding. Similar to exchange-traded equities, market transparency is high and trade price, size, quote, and depth of book data are publicly available.

Electronic trading is widespread for exchange-traded derivatives; however, algorithmic trading is not as evolved as in equity markets and is currently used more for trading in futures than in options. Large, urgent trades "sweep the book" where market depth is relatively good. In these cases, trades are executed against the most aggressive limit orders on the other trade side first and then against decreasingly aggressive limit orders until the entire order has been filled. Large, non-urgent trades are generally implemented electronically through trading algorithms. Buy-side traders generally use direct market access, particularly for small trades.

4.3.4. Over-the-Counter Derivatives

In recent years, regulators have been placing pressure on OTC markets to introduce central clearing facilities and to display trades publicly. Although liquidity has increased for more standardized OTC trades that are centrally cleared, liquidity has decreased for OTC instruments not suited to central clearing or trade reporting.

OTC derivative markets have historically been opaque, with little public data about prices, trade sizes, and structure details. Regulatory efforts have focused on increasing transparency and reducing counterparty risk in these markets. In the United States, the Dodd–Frank Wall Street Reform and Consumer Protection Act, enacted in 2010, significantly increased post-trade transparency in the OTC derivative markets with the establishment of swap data repositories (SDRs) to which trade details must be submitted. Under the Dodd–Frank regulation, swaps entered into by parties exempt from mandatory clearing and exchange trading (and where at least one counterparty to the swap is a US person) are still subject to data reporting rules. Dodd–Frank forms part of a broader 2009 agreement by the G–20 countries whose primary long-term focus includes the trading of all OTC derivatives on exchanges or other electronic platforms with centralized clearing for all more standardized derivatives.

Trading OTC derivatives takes place through dealers. Because this type of security is typically traded by institutions, trade sizes are relatively large. Large, urgent trades are generally implemented as broker risk trades, where risk is transferred to a broker who takes the contract into his inventory. Large, non-urgent trades are generally implemented using a high-touch agency trade, where the broker attempts to match buyers and sellers directly. Doing so can be difficult, however, since OTC derivatives are often highly customized. Hence, at times, a strong price concession is required to find a buyer or seller.

4.3.5. Spot Foreign Exchange (Currency)

There is no exchange or centralized clearing place for the majority of spot foreign exchange (currency) trades. Spot currency markets consist of a number of electronic venues and broker markets. The currency market is an entirely OTC market. Despite being a global market, there is almost no cross-border regulation.

The spot currency market consists of multiple levels. The top level is called the interbank market, where participants are mostly large international banks and other financial firms that act as dealers. Trades between these foreign exchange dealers can be extremely large. The next market level is generally made up of small and medium-sized banks and other financial institutions that turn to the dealers in the interbank market for their currency trading needs and that, therefore, pay slightly higher bid–ask spreads. The level below that one consists of commercial companies and retail traders that turn to the second-level institutions for their currency trading. Once again, a higher bid–ask spread applies to these market participants.

The spot currency market is sizable in terms of daily trading volume, with often more than $1 trillion traded per day. Although large, the spot currency market is relatively opaque; there are usually only quotes available and only from some venues.

Electronic trading in currencies has grown substantially over the years in parallel with algorithmic trading strategies of equities. For large, urgent trades, RFQs are generally submitted to multiple dealers competing for a trade. Large, non-urgent trades are mostly executed using algorithms (such as TWAP) or a high-touch agency approach. Small trades are usually implemented using DMA.

In-Text Question

A hedge fund manager has three trades that she would like to execute for her fund. The orders are for:

1. a large, non-urgent sell of OTC options,
2. a large, urgent sell of corporate bonds, and
3. a small, non-urgent buy of six liquid emerging market currencies.

Describe factors affecting trade implementation for each trade.

Solution:

1. A large, non-urgent sell of OTC options would generally involve a broker agency trade in which the broker would act on behalf of the manager to find a matching buyer for the options. Depending on the level of contract customization, however, a significant price concession may be required by the manager to complete order execution.
2. A large, urgent sell of corporate bonds would usually involve a broker risk trade via the RFQ process. Because of corporate bond illiquidity, the likelihood of finding a matching buyer is low. For more immediate (urgent) order execution, a broker would be needed to act as counterparty to the trade, taking the bonds and their associated risk into his inventory.
3. Small, non-urgent trades in foreign exchange are generally executed using direct market access. DMA allows the buy-side trader to electronically route orders using the broker's technology infrastructure and market access and typically involves algorithmic trading.

5. TRADE EVALUATION

5.1. Trade Cost Measurement

After trade implementation is complete, it is important for portfolio managers and traders to assess the trading that has taken place. Was the trade implemented in a manner consistent with the trade strategy chosen? What costs were incurred from trading the order, where did costs arise, and were these reasonable given market conditions? How well did the trader, broker, or algorithm selected for trade execution perform?

Unfortunately for the portfolio manager, trade implementation is not a frictionless transaction. In economic terms, trade costs are value paid by buyers but not received by sellers and value paid by sellers but not received by buyers. In finance, trade costs represent the amount paid above the investment decision price for buy orders and the discount below the decision price for sell orders. An important aspect of trade cost measurement is to identify where costs arise during implementation of the investment decision. Understanding where these costs arise will help portfolio managers carry out proper trade cost management, more efficient implementation, and better portfolio construction. This ultimately leads to lower trading costs and higher portfolio returns.

Proper trade cost management begins with an understanding of the implementation shortfall formulation.

5.1.1. Implementation Shortfall
The **implementation shortfall** (IS) metric[7] is the most important *ex post* trade cost measurement used in finance. The IS metric provides portfolio managers with the total cost associated with implementing the investment decision. This spans the time the investment decision is made by the portfolio manager up to the completion of the trade by the trader. IS also allows portfolio managers to identify where costs arise during the implementation of the trade.

IS is calculated as the difference between the return for a notional or paper portfolio, where all transactions are assumed to take place at the manager's decision price, and the portfolio's actual return, which reflects realized transactions, including all fees and costs.

Mathematically, IS is calculated as follows:

$$IS = \text{Paper return} - \text{Actual return}$$

The paper return shows the hypothetical return that the fund would have received if the manager were able to transact all shares at the desired decision price and without any associated costs or fees (i.e., with no friction):

$$\text{Paper return} = (P_n - P_d)(S) = (S)(P_n) - (S)(P_d)$$

Here, S represents the total order shares, $S > 0$ indicates a buy order, $S < 0$ indicates a sell order, P_d represents the price at the time of the investment decision, and P_n represents the current price.

The actual portfolio return is calculated as the difference between the current market price and actual transaction prices minus all fees (e.g., commissions):

---

[7]A.F. Perold, "The Implementation Shortfall: Paper versus Reality," *Journal of Portfolio Management* 14 (Spring 1988): 4–9.

$$\text{Actual return} = \left(\sum s_j\right)(P_n) - \sum s_j p_j - \text{Fees}$$

Here, s_j and p_j represent the number of shares executed and the transaction price of the jth trade, respectively, $\left(\sum s_j\right)$ represents the total number of shares of the order that were executed in the market, and "Fees" includes all costs paid by the fund to complete the order.

This IS formulation decomposes the total cost of the trade into three categories: execution cost, opportunity cost, and fixed fees. **Execution cost** corresponds to the shares that were transacted in the market. Execution cost occurs from the buying and/or selling pressure of the order, which often causes buy orders to become more expensive and sell orders to decrease in value, thus causing the fund to incur higher costs and lower realized returns. Execution cost will also occur owing to price drift over the trading period. For example, buying stocks that are increasing in value over the trading period and selling stocks that are decreasing in value over the trading period.

It is important to note that since there is no guarantee that the portfolio manager will be able to execute the entire order, the number of shares transacted in the market may be less than the original order size—that is, $\sum s_j \leq S$ for a buy order and $\sum s_j \geq S$ for a sell order. **Opportunity cost** corresponds to the unexecuted shares of the order. It is the cost associated with not being able to transact the entire order at the manager's decision price and is due to adverse price movement over the trading period. Opportunity cost may also arise in times of insufficient market liquidity, when the fund is not able to find counterparties to complete the trade. The opportunity cost component provides managers with insight into missed profit opportunity for their investment idea.

The *fixed fees* component includes all explicit fees, such as commissions, exchange fees, and taxes.

The IS formulation decomposing costs into these categories is calculated as follows:

$$IS = \underbrace{\sum s_j p_j - \sum s_j p_d}_{\text{Execution cost}} + \underbrace{\frac{(S - \sum s_j)(P_n - P_d)}{}}_{\text{Opportunity cost}} + \text{Fees}$$

Consider the following facts:

On Monday, the shares of Impulse Robotics close at £10.00 per share.

On Tuesday, before trading begins, a portfolio manager decides to buy Impulse Robotics. An order goes to the trading desk to buy 1,000 shares of Impulse Robotics at £9.98 per share or better, good for one day. The benchmark price is Monday's close at £10.00 per share. No part of the limit order is filled on Tuesday, and the order expires. The closing price on Tuesday rises to £10.05.

On Wednesday, the trading desk again tries to buy Impulse Robotics by entering a new limit order to buy 1,000 shares at £10.07 per share or better, good for one day. During the day, 700 shares are bought at £10.07 per share. Commissions and fees for this trade are £14. Shares for Impulse Robotics close at £10.08 per share on Wednesday.

No further attempt to buy Impulse Robotics is made, and the remaining 300 shares of the 1,000 shares the portfolio manager initially specified are canceled.

The paper portfolio traded 1,000 shares on Tuesday at £10.00 per share. The return on this portfolio when the order is canceled after the close on Wednesday is the value of the 1,000 shares, now worth £10,080, less the cost of £10,000, for a net gain of £80.

The real portfolio contains 700 shares (now worth 700 × £10.08 = £7,056), and the cost of this portfolio is 700 × £10.07 = £7,049, plus £14 in commissions and fees, for a total cost of £7,063. Thus, the total net gain on this portfolio is –£7. The implementation shortfall is the return on the paper portfolio minus the return on the actual portfolio, or £80 – (–£7) = £87.

We can break this IS down further, as follows:

- Execution cost, which is calculated as the difference between the cost of the real portfolio and of the paper portfolio and reflects the execution price paid for the amount of shares in the order actually filled: (700 × £10.07) – (700 × £10.00) = £7,049 – £7,000 = £49.
- Opportunity cost, which is based on the amount of shares left unexecuted and reflects the cost associated with not being able to execute all shares at the decision price: (1,000 shares – 700 shares) × (£10.08 – £10.00) = £24.
- Fixed fees, which are equal to total explicit fees paid: £14.

IS (£) is equal to the sum of execution cost, opportunity cost, and fixed fees: £49 + £24 + £14 = £87. More commonly, the shortfall is expressed as a fraction of the total cost of the paper portfolio trade: £87/£10,000 = 87 bps.

5.1.2. Expanded Implementation Shortfall

Wagner (1991) further expanded the IS measure to decompose the execution cost component into a delay-related cost component and a trading-related cost component.[8] These two decomposed execution components allow portfolio managers to more precisely isolate where their execution costs arise during the implementation cycle and help traders better manage overall execution quality and reduce trading costs.

The expanded implementation shortfall can be broken down as follows:

Expanded IS =

$$\underbrace{\underbrace{\left(\sum s_j\right)p_0 - \left(\sum s_j\right)p_d}_{\text{Delay cost}} + \underbrace{\sum s_j p_j - \left(\sum s_j\right)p_0}_{\text{Trading cost}}}_{\text{Execution cost}} + \underbrace{\left(S - \sum s_j\right)\left(P_n - P_d\right)}_{\text{Opportunity cost}} + \text{Fees}$$

In this representation, the additional notation p_0 represents the arrival price, and it is defined as the asset price at the time the order was released to the market for execution.

This expanded IS formulation decomposes execution cost further into two categories: delay cost and trading cost. **Delay cost** arises when the order is not submitted to the market in a timely manner and the asset experiences adverse price movement, making it more expensive to transact. Delay cost is often caused by a delay in selecting the most appropriate broker or trading algorithm to execute the order and by adverse price movement (also known as price drift) over the trading period.

Delay cost, however, can be minimized by having proper trading practices in place to provide traders with all the information they need to make an immediate decision, such as pre-trade analysis and post-trade analysis.

For example, consider the same Impulse Robotics example from before but with the following additional fact: *The buy-side trading desk releases the order to the market 30 minutes*

---

[8]Wagner, W. (Ed.), 1991. *The Complete Guide to Security Transactions.* John Wiley.

after receiving it, when the price is £10.03. We now have additional information that helps identify where costs arise during the implementation of the trade.

The execution cost component in the expanded implementation shortfall can be decomposed into the following:

- Delay cost, which reflects the adverse price movement associated with not submitting the order to the market in a timely manner and is based on the amount of shares executed in the order: $(700 \times £10.03) - (700 \times £10.00) = £7,021 - £7,000 = £21$.
- Trading cost, which reflects the execution price paid on shares executed: $(700 \times £10.07) - (700 \times £10.03) = £7,049 - £7,021 = £28$.

While,

- Opportunity cost (£24) and fixed fees (£14) remain unchanged.

Therefore, expanded implementation shortfall (£) = $£21 + £28 + £24 + £14 = £87$.

The expanded IS provides further insight into the causes of trade costs. The delay cost is £21, which accounts for 24.1% (£21/£87) of the total IS cost, whereas the opportunity cost of £24 accounts for 27.6% (£24/£87) of the total IS cost. Quite often, delay cost and opportunity cost account for the greatest quantity of cost during implementation. These costs can often be eliminated with proper transaction cost management techniques.

Improving Execution Performance

In many situations, delay cost arises from a lag in time between when the buy-side trader receives the order from the portfolio manager and when the trader determines which broker or algorithm is most appropriate for the specific order. Delay costs can be reduced by having a process in place that provides traders with broker performance metrics. Traders can then immediately release the order to the broker without any delay or corresponding adverse price movement. In theory, the delay cost component should have an expected value of zero. In practice, however, the delay cost component is often due to the simultaneous buying and selling pressure from multiple funds buying and selling the same stocks on the same side and over similar trading horizons, resulting in adverse price movement over the trading period. Stock alpha may also contribute to the delay cost component.

Portfolio managers can use IS to help determine appropriate order size for the market within the portfolio manager's price range and to minimize the opportunity cost of the order. For example, IS analysis will help portfolio managers determine the number of shares that can be transacted within the manager's price range or better, and if the manager has incremental cash on hand from specifying a smaller order size, she can invest this amount into her next most attractive investment opportunity at presumably better market prices. If the portfolio manager does not perform IS analysis, she may try to transact a position size that is too large to execute in the market within the desired price range and may not realize this until it is too late to change the investment decision. If the manager knew beforehand that her position size was too large to execute within her price range, she could have reduced the order size for the stock and invested the remaining capital into the next most attractive investment opportunity.

Similar to the delay cost, opportunity cost is not mean zero and often represents a cost to the fund. This is due to two reasons: adverse price movement and illiquidity. First, portfolio managers will often buy shares at a specified price or better. If prices decrease over the trading period, the order will likely be filled. If prices increase by too much, the manager may feel that the asset is no longer an attractive investment opportunity, will cancel the order, and invest in a different asset, thus realizing an opportunity cost. Second, traders may not be able to complete the order if there is insufficient market liquidity. In times of favorable prices, fund managers may be willing to incur additional market impact to attract additional counterparties into the market. But during times of adverse market prices, fund managers may not be as willing to increase their purchase price to attract additional sellers into the market because doing so might increase the stock price to a level where it is no longer deemed an attractive investment opportunity. Thus, the order is less likely to be completed in times of adverse price movement and insufficient market liquidity. Both of these situations result in an opportunity cost to the fund.

Delay Cost

A portfolio manager decides to buy 100,000 shares of RLK at 9:30 a.m., when its price is $30.00. The manager gives the order to his buy-side trader and requests the order be executed in the market at a price no higher than $30.50. The trader is then tasked with determining the best broker and/or the best algorithm to execute the trade. We next discuss two different scenarios to illustrate how a trader's actions can affect the delay cost component.

Scenario 1:

The trader receives the order for 100,000 shares at 9:30 a.m., when its price is $30. The trader is not familiar with RLK and needs to review the stock's liquidity, volatility, and intraday trading patterns and current market conditions. The trader next needs to review the historical performance of brokers trading similar order sizes and trading characteristics. After a thorough review, the trader determines the best broker to execute the order is Broker KRG. The trader then submits the order to Broker KRG at 10:30 a.m. but the market price increases to $30.10. The buy-side trader's delay in submitting the order to the broker is caused by the trader's need to evaluate and determine the best broker to execute the order given the order characteristics and market conditions. This delay costs the fund $0.10 per share. Note that if the price had decreased to $29.90, the delay would have benefited the fund by $0.10 per share.

Scenario 2:

The trader receives the order for 100,000 shares at 9:30 a.m., when the price is $30.00. Because the buy-side trader exercises proper transaction cost management practices, the trader has analyses on hand indicating who is the best broker and what is the best algorithm to execute the order. The trader is able to immediately submit the order to Broker KRG for execution when the market price is $30.00 per share.

Opportunity Cost

The research department of an asset management firm identifies two stocks currently undervalued in the market. Stock ABC is currently trading at $30.00 and is undervalued by $0.50/share. Stock XYZ is also currently trading at $30.00 and is undervalued by $0.40/share.

The portfolio manager has $3 million and is looking to invest in the stock(s) that will provide the highest return for the fund. What stock(s) should she buy?

On the surface, it may appear most appropriate to invest the entire $3 million in Stock ABC because it is the most undervalued ($0.50/share) and represents the highest short-term alpha. However, if the portfolio manager does not incorporate opportunity cost into her analysis, she is unlikely to achieve the highest return for the fund.

The effect of opportunity cost on fund performance is explained in the following two scenarios.

Scenario 1:
The portfolio manager decides to purchase 100,000 shares of ABC because it represents the highest short-term alpha potential. The portfolio manager does not want to purchase shares at a price higher than $30.50, which the research department has determined to be fair value for ABC. The trader tries to execute 100,000 shares of ABC but finds that only 80,000 shares can be executed at an average price of $30.25 before the price increases above $30.50. After ABC reaches a price of $30.50, it remains at this price through the end of the day. Additionally, Stock XYZ closes at its fair value of $30.40.

In this situation, the portfolio manager incurred an opportunity cost of $10,000 (20,000 shares multiplied by $0.50 = $10,000) and realized a profit of $20,000 (80,000 shares multiplied by $0.25 = $20,000).

Since Stock XYZ (which was the second most attractive investment opportunity at the beginning of the day) also increased to its fair value over the day, the portfolio manager is no longer able to invest the residual dollar value in XYZ and capture alpha. Thus, the portfolio manager has missed out on an opportunity to achieve maximum returns.

Scenario 2:
The portfolio manager of the fund exercises proper transaction cost management practices. Based on pre-trade analysis, the manager determines that she can purchase only 80,000 shares of ABC before its price will recover to its fair value of $30.50. Because the manager will not be able to invest all funds into Stock ABC, she decides to invest the residual dollar value into Stock XYZ (the second most attractive asset) and buy 20,000 shares.

In this scenario, the portfolio manager transacts all shares from both orders at prices below the fair value. The manager purchases 80,000 shares of ABC at an average price of $30.25 and purchases 20,000 shares of XYZ at an average price of $30.20. Stock ABC closes at its fair value of $30.50, and Stock XYZ closes at its fair value of $30.40. Since the manager executed all shares, she does not incur any opportunity cost.

The manager realizes an overall profit of $24,000. Stock ABC realized a profit of $20,000 (80,000 shares multiplied by $0.25/share). Stock XYZ realized a profit of $4,000 (20,000 shares multiplied by $0.20/share).

In this scenario, where the portfolio manager practiced proper trading cost management and evaluated opportunity cost prior to submitting the order, she was able to increase portfolio returns by $4,000.

Knowledge of where costs arise during execution allows portfolio managers and traders to take necessary steps to reduce and manage these costs appropriately. For example, the delay cost component can be reduced by knowing beforehand which broker is best suited to execute the trade and/or which algorithm is the most appropriate given the order, price benchmark, and investment objectives. Opportunity cost can be reduced by knowing the order size and share quantity that is most likely to be executed in the market within a specified price range. The trading cost component can also be effectively managed so that it is consistent with the underlying investment objectives of the fund by selecting the proper price benchmarks and trading urgency.

In-Text Question

Implementation Shortfall

A portfolio manager decides to buy 100,000 shares of RLK at 9:00 a.m., when the price is $30.00. He sets a limit price of $30.50 for the order. The buy-side trader does not release the order to the market for execution until 10:30 a.m., when the price is $30.10. The fund is charged a commission of $0.02/share and no other fees. At the end of the day, 80,000 shares are executed and RLK closes at $30.65. Order and execution details are summarized as follows:

Order	
Stock Ticker	RLK
Side	Buy
Shares	100,000
Limit Price	$30.50

Trades	Execution Price	Shares Executed
Trade 1	$30.20	30,000
Trade 2	$30.30	20,000
Trade 3	$30.40	20,000
Trade 4	$30.50	10,000
Total		80,000

a. Calculate execution cost.
b. Calculate opportunity cost.
c. Calculate fixed fees.
d. Calculate implementation shortfall in basis points.
e. Discuss how opportunity cost could be minimized for the trade.
f. Calculate delay cost.
g. Calculate trading cost.
h. Show expanded implementation shortfall in basis points.
i. Discuss how delay cost could be minimized for the trade.

Solution:

a. **Execution cost** is calculated as the difference between the costs of the real portfolio and the paper portfolio. It reflects the execution price(s) paid for the amount of shares in the order that were actually filled, or executed. Execution cost can be calculated as follows:

Execution cost $= \sum s_j p_j - \sum s_j p_d$

$= (30{,}000 \text{ shares} \times \$30.20 + 20{,}000 \text{ shares} \times \$30.30 + 20{,}000 \text{ shares} \times$

$\quad \$30.40 + 10{,}000 \text{ shares} \times \$30.50) - 80{,}000 \times \$30.00$

$= \$2{,}425{,}000 - \$2{,}400{,}000$

$= \$25{,}000$

b. **Opportunity cost** is based on the amount of shares left unexecuted in the order and reflects the cost of not being able to execute all shares at the decision price. Opportunity cost can be calculated as follows:

Opportunity cost $= (S - \sum s_j)(p_n - p_d)$

$= (100{,}000 - 80{,}000)(\$30.65 - \$30.00)$

$= \$13{,}000$

c. **Fixed fees** are equal to total explicit fees paid and can be calculated as follows:

$$\text{Fees} = 80{,}000 \times \$0.02 = \$1{,}600$$

d. **Implementation shortfall** can be calculated as follows:

$$\text{Implementation shortfall (\$)} = \underbrace{\$25{,}000}_{\text{Execution cost}} + \underbrace{\$13{,}000}_{\text{Opportunity cost}} + \underbrace{\$1{,}600}_{\text{Fees}}$$

$$= \$39{,}600$$

The implementation shortfall is expressed in basis points as follows:

$$\text{Implementation shortfall (bps)} = \frac{\text{Implementation shortfall (\$)}}{(\text{Total shares})(p_d)} \times 10{,}000 \text{ bps}$$

$$= \frac{\$39{,}600}{(100{,}000 \times \$30.00)} \times 10{,}000 \text{ bps}$$

$$= 132 \text{ bps}$$

e. **Minimizing opportunity cost:** Based on the decomposition of IS, the portfolio manager incurred an opportunity cost of \$13,000 on 20,000 shares. The opportunity cost could be lowered by reducing order quantity to a size that can be absorbed into the market at the portfolio manager's price target or better. In this example, opportunity cost represented 32.8% (\$13,000/\$39,600) of the total IS cost. If the portfolio manager had known this in advance, he could have reduced the size of the order to 80,000 shares and invested the extra \$600,000 (20,000 shares × \$30.00/share = \$600,000) in his second most attractive investment opportunity.

f. **Delay cost** can be calculated as follows:

$$\text{Delay cost} = \left(\sum s_j\right) p_0 - \left(\sum s_j\right) p_d$$

$$= 80{,}000 \times \$30.10 - 80{,}000 \times \$30.00 = \$8{,}000$$

g. **Trading cost** can be calculated as follows:

Trading cost $= \sum s_j p_j - (\sum s_j) p_0$
$= (30{,}000 \text{ shares} \times \$30.20 + 20{,}000 \text{ shares} \times \$30.30 + 20{,}000 \text{ shares} \times$
$\$30.40 + 10{,}000 \text{ shares} \times \$30.50) - 80{,}000 \times \$30.10$
$= \$2{,}425{,}000 - \$2{,}408{,}000$
$= \$17{,}000$

h. **Expanded implementation shortfall** can be calculated as follows:

Expanded IS $= \underbrace{\$8{,}000}_{\text{Delay cost}} + \underbrace{\$17{,}000}_{\text{Trading cost}} + \underbrace{\$13{,}000}_{\text{Opportunity cost}} + \underbrace{\$1{,}600}_{\text{Fees}} = \$39{,}600$

The delay cost is $8,000, which accounts for 20.2% ($8,000/$39,600) of the total IS cost, whereas the opportunity cost of $13,000 accounts for 32.8% ($13,000/$39,600) of the total IS cost.

i. **Minimizing delay cost:** The delay cost of $8,000 accounts for a sizable portion (20.2%) of the total IS cost and could be minimized by having a process in place that provides the buy-side trader with broker performance metrics. This would allow the trader to quickly identify the best broker and/or algorithm to execute the order given its characteristics and current market conditions, thereby minimizing the time between order receipt and market execution.

5.2. EVALUATING TRADE EXECUTION

The evaluation of trade execution is also referred to as trade cost evaluation, trade cost analysis (TCA), and post-trade analysis. Its goal is to evaluate and measure the execution quality of the trade and the overall performance of the trader, broker, and/or algorithm. Here, we discuss different methodologies to evaluate the execution of a trade.

Proper trade cost evaluation enables portfolio managers to better manage costs throughout the investment cycle and helps facilitate communication between the portfolio manager, traders, and brokers to better understand how and why costs occur during the implementation of investment decisions. Trade cost analysis also provides the basis for peer group comparisons, allowing a firm's portfolio managers to compare trading performance and costs with a universe of similar funds trading similar securities.

Trade evaluation helps buy-side traders quantify a broker's performance and rank brokers and/or algorithms most appropriate for implementation of different investment decisions. This helps minimize delay costs associated with trading.

Trade cost evaluation calculates trading costs and performance relative to a specified trading cost or trading performance benchmark. Costs are determined by the transaction amount paid above the reference price benchmark for a buy order and the discount below the reference price benchmark for a sell order. It is important that portfolio managers select the reference price for use on the basis of their selected trading price benchmark. For example, if the portfolio manager selected an arrival price benchmark, it is important to perform trade execution evaluation using the arrival price. If the fund manager selected the VWAP price as the price benchmark, then the reference price used in the post-trade analysis should include the VWAP price. If the fund selected a post-trade benchmark, such as the market on close, it is essential that the fund evaluate trading performance using the closing price benchmark.

Although one benchmark is used in execution, to represent the tradable strategy, multiple reference price benchmarks may be used to measure trading cost and to evaluate performance, typically on an intraday basis. For example, to measure trading costs, a pre-trade benchmark, such as the arrival price benchmark, may be used to provide the portfolio manager or trader with the estimated money required to complete the transaction. The trader may also compare the execution price of the order with an intraday benchmark such as the VWAP of the asset over the trading horizon to determine whether she achieved prices consistent with those of other market participants. Additionally, the trader may compare the last trade price of the order with a post-trade benchmark to understand whether there was price reversion after order completion. The use of multiple price benchmarks may provide valuable insights into different aspects of trading execution.

Trade cost calculations are expressed such that a positive value indicates underperformance and represents underperformance compared with the benchmark. A negative value indicates a savings and is a better performance compared with the benchmark. These calculations are as follows:

Cost in total dollars ($):

$$\text{Cost (\$)} = \text{Side} \times (\bar{P} - P^*) \times \text{Shares}$$

Cost in dollars per share ($/share):

$$\text{Cost (\$/share)} = \text{Side} \times (\bar{P} - P^*)$$

Cost in basis points (bps):

$$\text{Cost (bps)} = \text{Side} \times \frac{(\bar{P} - P^*)}{P^*} \times 10,000 \text{ bps}$$

$$\text{Side} = \begin{cases} +1 & \text{Buy order} \\ -1 & \text{Sell order} \end{cases}$$

$\bar{P}$ = Average execution price of order
P^* = Reference price
Shares = Shares executed

In most situations, investment professionals express costs in basis points because they represent a standardized measure across order sizes, market prices, and currencies. Portfolio managers will multiply the formulas listed by -1 to represent cost as a negative value and savings as a positive value.

5.2.1. Arrival Price

The arrival price benchmark measures the difference between the market price at the time the order was released to the market and the actual transaction price for the fund. This benchmark is used to measure the trade cost of the order incurred while the order was being executed in the market. This calculation follows the trading cost component from the expanded implementation shortfall formula.

Consider the following facts. A portfolio manager executes a buy order at an average price of $\bar{P} = \$30.05$. The arrival price at the time the order was submitted to the market was $P_0 = \$30.00$. The arrival cost expressed in basis points is as follows:

$$\text{Arrival cost (bps)} = \text{Side} \times \frac{(\bar{P} - P_0)}{P_0} \times 10^4 \text{ bps}$$

$$= +1 \times \frac{(\$30.05 - \$30.00)}{\$30.00} \times 10^4 \text{ bps}$$

$$= 16.7 \text{ bps}$$

Therefore, the fund incurred an arrival cost of 16.7 bps, underperforming the arrival price benchmark by this amount.

5.2.2. VWAP

Portfolio managers use the VWAP benchmark as a measure of whether they received fair and reasonable prices over the trading period. Since the VWAP comprises all market activity over the day, all buying and selling pressure of all other market participants, and market noise, it provides managers with a reasonable indication of the fair cost for market participants over the day. In this situation, the VWAP reference price serves as a performance metric.

Consider the following facts. A portfolio manager executes a buy order at an average price of $\bar{P} = \$30.05$. The VWAP over the trading horizon is $\$30.04$. The VWAP cost benchmark is computed as follows:

$$\text{VWAP cost (bps)} = \text{Side} \times \frac{(\bar{P} - \text{VWAP})}{\text{VWAP}} \times 10^4 \text{ bps}$$

$$= +1 \times \frac{(\$30.05 - \$30.04)}{\$30.04} \times 10^4 \text{ bps}$$

$$= 3.3 \text{ bps}$$

Therefore, the fund underperformed the VWAP by 3.3 bps. In most cases, the order will underperform the VWAP generally because of the bid–ask spread and the buying or selling pressure associated with the order.

5.2.3. TWAP

The TWAP benchmark is an alternative measure to determine whether the fund achieved fair and reasonable prices over the trading period and is used when managers wish to exclude potential trade price outliers.

Consider the following facts. A portfolio manager executes a buy order at an average price of $\bar{P} = \$30.05$. The TWAP over the trading horizon is $\$30.06$. The VWAP cost benchmark is computed as follows:

$$\text{TWAP cost (bps)} = \text{Side} \times \frac{(\bar{P} - \text{TWAP})}{\text{TWAP}} \times 10^4 \text{ bps}$$

$$= +1 \times \frac{(\$30.05 - \$30.06)}{\$30.06} \times 10^4 \text{ bps}$$

$$= -3.3 \text{ bps}$$

Therefore, the fund outperformed the TWAP benchmark by 3.3 bps.

5.2.4. Market on Close

The closing benchmark, also referred to as an MOC benchmark, is used primarily by index managers and mutual funds that wish to achieve the closing price on the day and compare their actual transaction prices with the closing price. These funds will typically be valued using the closing price, and it is important that the portfolio manager perform benchmark analysis using the execution price of the order and the closing price on the day. Doing so ensures that the benchmark cost measure will be consistent with the valuation of the fund. The closing price benchmark is also the benchmark that is consistent with the tracking error calculation. MOC benchmarks are often used in fixed-income trading.

Consider the following facts. A portfolio manager executing a buy order using an MOC strategy transacts the order at an average price of $30.40. The stock's official closing price is $30.50. The closing benchmark cost is calculated as follows:

$$\text{Close (bps)} = \text{Side} \times \frac{(\bar{P} - \text{Close})}{\text{Close}} \times 10^4 \text{ bps}$$

$$= +1 \times \frac{(\$30.40 - \$30.50)}{\$30.50} \times 10^4 \text{ bps}$$

$$= -32.8 \text{ bps}$$

Thus, a closing benchmark cost of −32.8 bps indicates that the order was executed 32.8 bps more favorably than the closing price of the order. In the case of an index fund, the outperformance would contribute positive tracking error for the fund.

5.2.5. Market-Adjusted Cost

The market-adjusted cost is a performance metric used by managers and traders to help separate the trading cost due to trading the order from the general market movement in the security price (i.e., the price movement that would have occurred in the security even if the order was not executed in the market). For example, buying stock in a rising market and selling stock in a falling market will cause the fund to incur higher costs than expected, and selling stock in a rising market and buying stock in a falling market will cause the fund to incur lower costs than expected. A market-adjusted cost benchmark will help isolate the price movement due to the general market from the cost due to the impact of the order.

The market-adjusted cost is calculated by subtracting the market cost due to market movement adjusted for order side from the total arrival cost of the trade. The market cost is computed on the basis of the movement in an index and the stock's beta to that index, as follows:

$$\text{Index cost (bps)} = \text{Side} \times \frac{(\text{Index VWAP} - \text{Index arrival price})}{\text{Index arrival price}} \times 10^4$$

The index VWAP is the volume-weighted price of the index computed over the trading horizon. The index VWAP is often computed using an overall market index or a related ETF to compute a volume-weighted price. Alternatively, portfolio managers and traders may use a sector or industry index instead of the overall market index.

The market-adjusted cost is calculated as follows:

$$\text{Market-adjusted cost (bps)} = \text{Arrival cost (bps)} - \beta \times \text{Index cost (bps)}$$

In this case, β represents the stock's beta to the underlying index. The expectation in this formulation is that the stock would have exhibited price movement based on the market movement and the stock's sensitivity to the index measured via its beta to the index. This formulation thus helps remove the movement in the stock that would have occurred even if the order was not entered into the market.

Buying in a Rising Market
Consider a portfolio manager who executes a buy order at an average price of $30.50. The arrival price at the time the order was entered into the market was $30.00. The selected index price at the time of order entry was $500, and market index VWAP over the trade horizon was $505. If the stock has a beta to the index of $\beta = 1.25$, the market-adjusted cost can be calculated as follows:

Step 1.   Calculate arrival cost.

$$\text{Arrival cost (bps)} = \text{Side} \times \frac{(\bar{P} - P_0)}{P_0} \times 10^4 \text{ bps}$$

$$= +1 \times \frac{(\$30.50 - \$30.00)}{\$30.00} \times 10^4 \text{ bps}$$

$$= 166.7 \text{ bps}$$

Step 2.   Calculate index cost.

$$\text{Index cost (bps)} = \text{Side} \times \frac{(\text{Index VWAP} - \text{Index arrival price})}{\text{Index arrival price}} \times 10^4$$

$$= +1 \times \frac{\$505 - \$500}{\$500} \times 10^4$$

$$= 100 \text{ bps}$$

Step 3.   Calculate market-adjusted cost.

Market-adjusted cost (bps) = Arrival cost (bps) $- \beta \times$ Index cost (bps)
$= 166.7 \text{ bps} - 1.25 \times 100 \text{ bps}$
$= 166.7 \text{ bps} - 125 \text{ bps}$
$= 41.7 \text{ bps}$

The portfolio manager bought stock in a rising market, and prices were generally increasing over the trading horizon because of market movement and the buying pressure of the order. The manager's arrival cost was 166.7 bps, and the market index cost over the period was 100 bps. The stock price would be expected to increase 125 bps over the period on the basis of the movement in the market index and the stock's beta to the index. In this situation, we subtract 125 bps in cost from the arrival cost of 166.7 bps because this amount represents expected market movement not due to the order. The market-adjusted cost due to the order is 41.7 bps, much lower than the total arrival cost.

In-Text Question

Selling in a Falling Market

A portfolio manager executes a sell order at an average price of $29.50. The arrival price at the time the order was entered into the market was $30.00. The selected index price at the time of order entry was $500, and market index VWAP over the trade horizon was $495. The stock has a beta to the index of 1.25.

1. Calculate arrival cost.
2. Calculate index cost.
3. Calculate market-adjusted cost.

Solution:

1. Calculate arrival cost.

$$\text{Arrival cost (bps)} = \text{Side} \times \frac{(\bar{P} - P_0)}{P_0} \times 10^4 \text{ bps}$$
$$= -1 \times \frac{(\$29.50 - \$30.00)}{\$30.00} \times 10^4 \text{ bps}$$
$$= 166.7 \text{ bps}$$

   A positive arrival cost in this case indicates that the fund underperformed the arrival price benchmark.

2. Calculate index cost.

$$\text{Index cost (bps)} = \text{Side} \times \frac{(\text{Index VWAP} - \text{Index arrival price})}{\text{Index arrival price}} \times 10^4$$
$$= -1 \times \frac{\$495 - \$500}{\$500} \times 10^4$$
$$= 100 \text{ bps}$$

3. Calculate market-adjusted cost.

$$\text{Market-adjusted cost (bps)} = \text{Arrival cost (bps)} - \beta \times \text{Index cost (bps)}$$
$$= 166.7 \text{ bps} - 1.25 \times 100 \text{ bps}$$
$$= 166.7 \text{ bps} - 125 \text{ bps}$$
$$= 41.7 \text{ bps}$$

> In this example, the arrival cost is calculated to be +166.7 bps, indicating that the order underperformed the arrival price. Although this is true, much of the adverse prices were likely due to market movement rather than inferior performance from the broker or algorithm. This sell order was executed in a falling market, which resulted in an arrival cost of 166.7 bps for the investor. However, an estimated 125 bps of this cost was due to market movement, which would have occurred even if the order had not traded in the market. Thus, the market-adjusted cost for this order is 41.7 bps.

5.2.6. Added Value

Another methodology used by investors to evaluate trading performance is to compare the arrival cost of the order with the estimated pre-trade cost. The expected trading cost is calculated using a pre-trade model and incorporates such factors as order size, volatility, market liquidity, investor risk aversion, level of urgency (i.e., how fast or slow the trade is to be executed in the market), and the underlying market conditions at the time of the trade. If a fund executes at a cost lower than the pre-trade estimate, it is typically considered superior trade performance. If the order is executed at a cost higher than the pre-trade cost benchmark, then the trade is considered to have underperformed expectations. This metric helps fund managers understand the value added by their broker and/or execution algorithms during the execution of the order. The added value metric is computed as follows:

$$\text{Added value (bps)} = \text{Arrival cost (bps)} - \text{Est. pre-trade cost (bps)}$$

Consider the following facts. A portfolio manager executes a buy order at an average price of $\bar{P} = \$50.35$. The arrival price at the time the order was entered into the market was $P_0 = \$50.00$. Prior to trading, the buy-side trader performs pre-trade analysis of the order and finds that the expected cost of the trade is 60 bps, based on information available prior to trading. The pre-trade adjustment is calculated as follows:

$$\text{Pre-trade adjustment} = \text{Arrival cost} - \text{Est. pre-trade cost}$$

We have,

$$
\begin{aligned}
\text{Arrival cost (bps)} &= \text{Side} \times \frac{(\bar{P} - P_0)}{P_0} \times 10^4 \text{ bps} \\
&= +1 \times \frac{(\$50.35 - \$50.00)}{\$50.00} \times 10^4 \text{ bps} \\
&= 70 \text{ bps}
\end{aligned}
$$

$$\text{Added value} = \text{Arrival cost} - \text{Est. pre-trade cost} = 70 \text{ bps} - 60 \text{ bps} = 10 \text{ bps}$$

The pre-trade adjusted cost in this example is 10 bps, indicating that the fund underperformed pre-trade expectations by 10 bps.

Proper trade cost measurement and evaluation are critical to understanding the costs and risks arising from trading. These help inform where a firm's trading activities may be improved through better internal trade management practices, such as the use of appropriate trading partners and venues. Trade governance involves the policies and processes used by firms to manage their trading-related activities.

6. TRADE GOVERNANCE

All asset managers should have a trade policy document that clearly and comprehensively articulates the firm's trading policies and escalation procedures (i.e., calling on higher levels of leadership or management in an organization to resolve issues when they cannot be resolved by standard procedures). Such a document is mandated by major market regulators and regulations, including the SEC in the United States, the updated Markets in Financial Instruments Directive (MiFID II) in the European Union, the Financial Services Agency in Japan, and the Securities and Futures Commission in Hong Kong SAR.

The objective of a trade policy is to ensure the asset manager's execution and order-handling procedures are in line with the duty of best execution that is owed to clients. Any trade policy needs to include several key aspects. These include the following:

- **Meaning of best execution:** A trade policy document should outline the meaning of best execution as defined by the relevant regulatory framework. This meaning may be supplemented by additional details. For example, generally best execution does not just mean achieving the best execution price at the lowest possible cost but also involves achieving the right trade-off between different objectives.
- **Factors determining the optimal order execution approach:** A trade policy document should describe the factors used in determining how an order can be executed in an optimal manner for a given scenario. For example, the optimal execution approach may differ by asset class, level of security liquidity, and security trading mechanism (order-driven markets, quote-driven markets, and brokered markets). The optimal execution approach can also depend on the nature of a manager's investment process.
- **Listing of eligible brokers and execution venues:** A trade policy should allow the investment manager flexibility to use different brokers and trading venues to achieve best execution in a particular scenario. To reduce operational risk, checks should be in place to ensure only reputable brokers and execution venues that meet requirements for reliable and efficient order execution are used.
- **Process to monitor execution arrangements:** Optimal order execution arrangements may change over time as markets and securities evolve. Therefore, continual monitoring of current arrangements is needed. The details of the monitoring process should be outlined in a trade policy document.

Asset managers that aggregate trades for client accounts and funds should have a "trade aggregation and allocation" policy in place. These policies seek to ensure executed orders are allocated fairly to individual clients on a pre-trade and post-trade basis, there are remedies for misallocations, and an escalation policy is in place. For example, if several accounts (e.g., pooled funds or separate accounts) follow the same or a similar investment strategy and have similar trading needs, then pooling the trades for trade execution may make sense in some situations. If a pooled trade is not fully executed, the order amount that is executed generally needs to be allocated to accounts on a pro-rata basis so that no account is disadvantaged relative to the others. In all cases, the aggregation and allocation process should be transparent and provide an audit trail in case questions are raised after the fact.

Firms should have a policy in place for the treatment of trade errors. Errors from trading and any resulting gains/losses need to be disclosed to a firm's compliance department and documented in a trade error log. The trade error log should include any related documentation and evidence that trade errors are resolved in a way that prevents adverse impact for the client.

6.1. Meaning of Best Order Execution within the Relevant Regulatory Framework

A trade policy document should outline the meaning of best execution within the relevant regulatory framework. Although there may be slight differences in how best execution is defined by different regulators and in different financial market regulations, the underlying concept requires orders to be executed on terms most favorable to the client, where firms consider the following:

- execution price,
- trading costs,
- speed of execution,
- likelihood of execution and settlement,
- order size, and
- nature of the trade.

Rather than simply trying to obtain the best price at the lowest possible trading cost, best execution involves identifying the most appropriate trade-off between these aspects. For example, although market impact costs can generally be lowered by trading more patiently, patient trading may be suboptimal for an asset manager that uses extremely short-horizon expected return forecasts, which decay quickly.

6.2. Factors Used to Determine the Optimal Order Execution Approach

Firms need to have a list of criteria or factors used in determining the optimal order execution approach to achieve the best possible results for clients on a consistent basis.

Best execution requires investment managers to seek the most advantageous order executions for their customers given market conditions. Best execution includes several key factors that brokers examine, track, and document when choosing how to execute an order. An asset manager needs to ensure that after examining these factors, the broker achieved the best possible execution for the client.

At a firm level, execution policy and procedures need to specify the factors or criteria considered in determining the optimal order execution approach in each scenario. These criteria include the following:

- **Urgency of an order:** Does the order need to be executed aggressively at an accelerated pace, or can it be traded over a longer period of time? What is the size of the order relative to the security's normal liquidity?
- **Characteristics of the securities traded:** How liquid are the securities to be traded (e.g., the average daily volume)? Are the securities standardized or highly customized?

EXHIBIT 2   Key Considerations for Best Execution

Asset Class	Considerations
Equities and Exchange-Traded Options and Futures	An investment manager needs to choose the type of market or venue used for execution. In many cases, there are lit (on-exchange) markets and dark markets available for more liquid securities. Lit markets provide pre-trade and post-trade transparency, whereas dark markets provide post-trade transparency. The liquidity of a security and the percentage of average daily volume traded are critical in the choice of optimal execution algorithm. Historical transaction data—including liquidity characteristics and price volatility—are widely available and can be readily assessed.
Fixed Income	There are two main issues: market transparency and price discovery. Only some of the trading, particularly in corporate bonds, takes place on venues that provide market transparency as well as simultaneous, competitive quotes enabling price discovery, which is a necessary condition to ensure best execution. Generally, trade policy should dictate that, if at all possible, bids/offers should be requested from multiple independent third parties before a trade is executed. This process fosters competition and provides a more precise estimate of the likely market price at a particular time in an effort to achieve the best price possible.
	If there is no market transparency and if multiple competing quotes cannot or should not be obtained, then a trade policy should outline alternative means to achieve price discovery. These may include data sources (such as TRACE data)* for historical transaction prices or quotes for a given security or comparable securities. In the absence of any relevant transaction prices or quotes, an internal or external pricing model could be used to establish a market price estimate.
OTC Derivatives	Broker selection may depend on the exact terms of the proposed OTC derivative instruments, counterparty risk, and a broker's settlement capabilities.
Spot Currencies	Quotes should be requested from multiple independent dealers before a trade is executed. This process fosters competition in an effort to achieve the best price possible.

* In 2002, the National Association of Securities Dealers introduced TRACE (Trade Reporting and Compliance Engine) in an effort to increase price transparency in the US corporate debt market.

- **Characteristics of the execution venues used:** Which type of trading mechanism or venue is used? Are both lit (on-exchange) markets and dark markets available to trade a security?
- **Investment strategy objectives:** Is the investment strategy short term or long term in nature?
- **Rationale for a trade:** Is a trade intended to capture an investment manager's expected return views? Or is it a risk trade or a liquidity trade? Underlying trade objectives may have important implications for the optimal trade approach.

MiFID II, which came into effect in January 2018 and covers the European Economic Area, provides additional regulations on best execution. MiFID II requires firms to take all sufficient steps to obtain the best possible result in executing client orders. The best possible result is not limited to execution price but also includes consideration of cost, speed, likelihood of execution, likelihood of settlement, and any other factors deemed relevant. MiFID II's "all sufficient steps" test sets a higher standard than the previous "all reasonable steps" standard of MiFID I.

MiFID II prohibits the bundling, or combining, of trading commissions with research provided by brokers, known as a soft dollar arrangement. Under MiFID II, investment managers need the firm to pay for broker research costs or establish a research payment account funded by a special charge to clients. Other jurisdictions place limitations on soft dollar arrangements and are expected to follow MiFID II requirements in making execution and research payments explicit and transparent for clients.

Ensuring best execution often requires different criteria for each asset class that should be incorporated into trade policy and procedures. In terms of execution factors, the relative importance of individual factors often differs by asset class. Exhibit 2 shows key considerations by asset class.

6.3. List of Eligible Brokers and Execution Venues

Asset managers should have a list of approved brokers and execution venues for trading and the criteria used to create this list. In determining the list, there should not be discrimination against brokers or execution venues. Any decisions should be made according to the policy and procedures put in place. Creating and maintaining the list should be a collaborative effort shared by portfolio execution, compliance, and risk management. A best practices approach is to create a Best Execution Monitoring Committee within an investment management firm that is responsible for maintaining and updating the list regularly, or as circumstances require, and distributing the list to all parties involved in trade execution.

Although the criteria used to approve an execution venue or broker differ by asset class, the principles behind the decision and the process followed should be consistent across asset classes, broker firms, regions, and jurisdictions. A number of qualitative and quantitative factors are relevant to this decision, such as the following:

- **Quality of service:** Does a broker provide competitive execution compared with an execution benchmark, such as submission price or VWAP?
- **Financial stability:** Will the broker or execution venue be able to fulfill obligations in all market environments? When such brokers as Lehman Brothers and MF Global went bankrupt, it caused substantial disruption to their clients' activities.
- **Reputation:** Does the broker or execution venue uphold high ethical standards and treat clients fairly?
- **Settlement capabilities:** Are the operations supporting the broker/execution venue robust? Can trades be settled in a reliable and efficient manner?
- **Speed of execution:** Can urgent trades be implemented with minimal delay and at the best price possible? What is the maximum volume that can be traded with minimal delay?
- **Cost competitiveness:** Are the explicit costs (such as commissions or exchange fees) competitive?

- **Willingness to commit capital:** Is the broker willing to act as a dealer to facilitate trading for a client? This can be particularly important for less liquid securities that need to be traded in a timely manner.[9]

A sensible trade policy is particularly important in trade venue selection for transactions that are executed off exchange in so-called over-the-counter markets. Best execution is generally harder to measure for these trades, and there are unique risks associated with OTC trading. For example, OTC trades are not subject to any trading venue rules designed to ensure fair and orderly treatment of orders or minimum levels of price transparency. In addition, there may be counterparty and settlement risk for OTC trades.

6.4. Process Used to Monitor Execution Arrangements

All brokers and execution venues used by the asset manager should be subject to ongoing monitoring for reputational risk, irregularities (such as trading errors), criminal actions, and financial stability. Brokers and execution venues that no longer meet minimum requirements should be promptly removed from the approved list.

Execution quality on realized transactions through different brokers or execution venues should also be monitored continuously. Systems that allow ongoing monitoring of order execution quality should be in place. Although the specific process may vary by asset class and security type, the underlying principles remain the same. Summary reports of execution quality should be produced, examined, and evaluated on a regular basis.

Checkpoints for trade execution monitoring include the following:

- Trade submission: Has the trading/execution strategy been implemented consistent with the investment process (alpha and risk forecasting horizon, rebalancing frequency, etc.), and is it optimal for the asset type traded?
- What was the execution quality of a trade relative to its benchmark (e.g., arrival price, VWAP, TWAP, market close)?
- Is there an appropriate balance between trading costs and opportunity costs (for non-executed trades)?
- Could better execution have been achieved using a different trading strategy, different intermediaries, or different trading venues?

Asset managers are well advised to have in place the equivalent of a Best Execution Monitoring Committee (BEMC) that has firm-wide responsibility for trade execution monitoring. The BEMC should collaborate with portfolio managers and risk management and legal/compliance departments to ensure potential issues with execution quality are identified, discussed, and acted on in a timely manner.

Trading records and the evaluation of those records should generally be stored and kept accessible by firms for several years (e.g., in the United Kingdom, the requirement is five years). Trading records may be used to do the following:

- **Address client concerns:** For example, trading records can be used as evidence by an investment manager to show clients that their accounts have been treated fairly. This is particularly relevant if an investment manager runs similar strategies that might frequently

---

[9]In this case, the broker, acting as principal rather than agent, is the counterparty to client transactions. Although this can be useful for clients, potential conflicts of interest may arise, and principal trades should be monitored closely by managers for potential conflicts of interest the broker may have.

trade in the same direction. For instance, there may be a need to demonstrate fair trade allocation or that particular strategies are not being favored at the expense of others.

- **Address regulator concerns:** A regulator may be interested in assessing how the investment manager has met best execution standards. In addition, regulators need to monitor market integrity and detect criminal behavior, such as "fake volumes," "quote stuffing," and "spoofing," which are illegal activities in most markets.[10]
- **Assist in improving execution quality:** A database of past transactions may be used to analyze and refine the execution process to control and improve trading costs.
- **Monitor the parties involved in trading/order execution:** Trading records can be used to evaluate how performance by brokers and execution venues may compare in execution quality. This helps inform which services should be retained in the future.

These policies and procedures should be outlined in a comprehensive document and reviewed regularly (for example, quarterly) and when the need arises. Updates should be made when circumstances change. This document could be created by a BEMC and should involve portfolio management, risk management, and legal/compliance departments. If no formal committee is tasked with owning this document, then the legal/compliance department might take responsibility, with collaboration from portfolio management and risk management functions.

In-Text Question

Choice of Broker

ABC Asset Management (ABCAM) is one of the world's largest asset managers. ABCAM has been using AAA Brokerage (AAAB) as its exclusive broker for a number of its funds for many years. Other brokers are used only for market segments in which AAAB does not have business operations. The leadership of ABCAM explains its choice of broker by stating, "Because of its long-standing business relationship with AAAB, ABCAM has a uniquely informed insight into the operations of AAAB, which provides greater comfort and assurance that AAAB will fulfill its duties when compared with other brokers."

Discuss whether this practice is permissible and can be justified.

Solution: ABCAM needs to show that it takes all sufficient steps to ensure best execution for its clients' trades. This includes choosing brokers that provide the best service for potential best execution. In order to justify that AAAB is the right broker to use, ABCAM must demonstrate that it has done comparisons of different brokers, that this analysis is regularly conducted with updates, and that each time AAAB is found to

---

[10]*Fake volumes* refer to the practice whereby a trading venue or exchange executes transactions with itself (i.e., it is on both sides of a trade) to artificially inflate reported trading volume to attract client business. *Quote stuffing* is a practice that has been used by high-frequency traders that involves entering and withdrawing a large number of orders within an extremely short period of time in an attempt to confuse the market and create trading opportunities for the high-frequency trader. *Spoofing* is a manipulative practice defined as bidding or offering with the intent to cancel before execution. All these practices are attempts to gain an unfair advantage over other market participants by engaging in manipulative behavior.

be the best choice for order implementation. A thorough and unbiased analysis is required for this. Stating a subjective opinion, such as the explanation provided by ABCAM leadership, is not sufficient justification.

In-Text Question

Trade Policy Document

For several decades, XYZ Capital has been running enhanced index funds. These funds have low levels of target tracking error compared with their market-weighted benchmarks. The firm's trade policy document has a focus on minimizing trading costs and defines best execution as follows:

"The firm takes all sufficient steps to obtain the best possible result in executing orders; that is, the firm makes its best attempt to achieve the best execution price and lowest trading cost possible for every transaction. In this way, the firm achieves best execution for its client portfolios."

Discuss whether the trade policy statement is in line with regulatory requirements and client best interests.

Solution: Achieving the best execution price at the lowest trading cost possible is only part of the best execution effort. To ensure that clients and their portfolios are served in the best manner possible, other factors require consideration. These considerations include the speed of execution, the alignment of execution approach and execution horizon with the investment process, the likelihood of execution to be optimal, and so on. An exclusive focus on best execution price and lowest trading cost is too narrow a definition to achieve best client execution. For example, doing so could leave many trades unexecuted, which would result in increased opportunity costs from lost opportunities that could not be implemented.

---

7. SUMMARY

- Portfolio manager motivations to trade include profit seeking, risk management (hedging), liquidity driven (fund flows), and corporate actions and index reconstitutions.
- Managers following a short-term alpha-driven strategy will trade with greater urgency to realize alpha before it dissipates (decays). Managers following a longer-term strategy will trade with less urgency if alpha decay is expected to be slower.
- Trading is required to keep portfolios at targeted risk levels or risk exposures, to hedge risks that may be outside a portfolio manager's investment objectives or that the portfolio manager does not have an investment view on.

- Trading may be liquidity driven, resulting from client activity or index reconstitutions. In these cases, managers typically trade using end-of-day closing prices because these prices are used for fund and benchmark valuation.
- Inputs affecting trade strategy selection include the following types: order related, security related, market related, and user based.
- Order characteristics include the side (or trade direction) and size of an order. Percentage of average daily volume is a standardized measure used in trading that indicates what order size can realistically be traded. Large trades are generally traded over longer time horizons to minimize market impact.
- Security characteristics include security type, short-term (trade) alpha, security price volatility, and a security's liquidity profile.
- Market conditions at the time of trading (intraday trading volumes, bid–ask spreads, and security and market volatility) should be incorporated into trade strategy since they can differ from anticipated conditions.
- Market volatility and liquidity vary over time, and liquidity considerations may differ substantially during periods of crisis.
- Individuals with higher levels of risk aversion are more concerned with market risk and tend to trade with greater urgency.
- Market impact is the adverse price impact in a security caused from trading an order and can represent one of the largest costs in trading.
- Execution risk is the adverse price impact resulting from a change in the fundamental value of the security and is often proxied by price volatility.
- Reference price benchmarks inform order trading prices and include pre-trade, intraday, post-trade, and price target benchmarks.
- Managers seeking short-term alpha will use pre-trade benchmarks, such as the arrival price, when they wish to transact close to current market prices (greater trade urgency).
- Managers without views on short-term price movements who wish to participate in volumes over the execution horizon typically use an intraday benchmark, such as VWAP or TWAP.
- Managers of index funds or funds whose valuation is calculated using closing prices typically select the closing price post-trade benchmark to minimize fund risk and tracking error.
- The primary goal of a trading strategy is to balance the expected costs, risks, and alpha associated with trading the order in a manner consistent with the portfolio manager's trading objectives, risk aversion, and other known constraints.
- Execution algorithms can be classified into the following types: scheduled, liquidity seeking, arrival price, dark aggregators, and smart order routers.
- Equities are traded on exchanges and other multilateral trading venues. Algorithmic trading is common, and most trades are electronic, except for very large trades and trades in illiquid securities.
- Fixed-income securities are generally traded not on exchanges but in a bilateral, dealer-centric market structure where dealers make markets in the securities. The majority of fixed-income securities are relatively illiquid, especially if they have been issued in prior periods, so-called off-the-run bonds.
- Most of the trading volume in exchange-traded derivatives is concentrated in futures. Electronic trading is pervasive, and algorithmic trading is growing.
- OTC derivative markets have historically been opaque, with little public data about prices, trade sizes, and structure details. In recent years, regulators have been placing pressure on

OTC markets to introduce central clearing facilities and to display trades publicly in an attempt to increase contract standardization and price discovery and reduce counterparty risk.

- There is no exchange or centralized clearing place for the majority of spot currency trades. Spot currency markets consist of a number of electronic venues and broker markets. The currency market is entirely an OTC market.
- The implementation shortfall measure is the standard for measuring the total cost of the trade. IS compares a portfolio's actual return with its paper return (where transactions are based on decision price).
- The IS attribution decomposes total trade cost into its delay, execution, and opportunity cost components.
- Delay cost is the cost associated with not submitting the order to the market at the time of the portfolio manager's investment decision.
- Execution cost is the cost due to the buying and/or selling pressure of the portfolio manager and corresponding market risk.
- Opportunity cost is the cost due to not being able to execute all shares of the order because of adverse price movement or insufficient liquidity.
- Trade evaluation measures the execution quality of the trade and the performance of the trader, broker, and/or algorithm used.
- Various techniques measure trade cost execution using different benchmarks (pre-trade, intraday, and post-trade).
- Trade cost analysis enables investors to better manage trading costs and understand where trading activities can be improved through the use of appropriate trading partners and venues.
- Major regulators mandate that asset managers have in place a trade policy document that clearly and comprehensively articulates a firm's trading policies and escalation procedures.
- The objective of a trade policy is to ensure the asset manager's execution and order-handling procedures are in line with their fiduciary duty owed to clients for best execution.
- A trade policy document needs to incorporate the following key aspects: meaning of best execution, factors determining the optimal order execution approach, handling trading errors, listing of eligible brokers and execution venues, and a process to monitor execution arrangements.

PRACTICE PROBLEMS

The following information relates to Questions 1–9

Robert Harding is a portfolio manager at ValleyRise, a hedge fund based in the United States. Harding monitors the portfolio alongside Andrea Yellow, a junior analyst. ValleyRise only invests in equities, but Harding is considering other asset classes to add to the portfolio, namely derivatives, fixed income, and currencies. Harding and Yellow meet to discuss their trading strategies and price benchmarks.

Harding begins the meeting by asking Yellow about factors that affect the selection of an appropriate trading strategy. Yellow tells Harding:

Statement 1. Trading with greater urgency results in lower execution risk.
Statement 2. Trading larger size orders with higher trade urgency reduces market impact.
Statement 3. Securities with high rates of alpha decay require less aggressive trading to realize alpha.

After further discussion about Yellow's statements, Harding provides Yellow a list of trades that he wants to execute. He asks Yellow to recommend a price benchmark. Harding wants to use a benchmark where the reference price for the benchmark is computed based on market prices that occur during the trading period, excluding trade outliers.

Earlier that day before the meeting, Yellow believed that the market had underreacted during the pre-market trading session to a strong earnings announcement from ABC Corp., a company that Yellow and Harding have been thoroughly researching for several months. Their research suggested the stock's fair value was $90 per share, and the strong earnings announcement reinforced their belief in their fair value estimate.

Right after the earnings announcement, the pre-market price of ABC was $75. Concerned that the underreaction would be short-lived, Harding directed Yellow to buy 30,000 shares of ABC stock. Yellow and Harding discussed a trading strategy, knowing that ABC shares are very liquid and the order would represent only about 1% of the expected daily volume. They agreed on trading a portion of the order at the opening auction and then filling the remainder of the order after the opening auction. The strategy for filling the remaining portion of the order was to execute trades at prices close to the market price at the time the order was received.

Harding and Yellow then shift their conversation to XYZ Corp. Harding tells Yellow that, after extensive research, he would like to utilize an algorithm to purchase some shares that are relatively liquid. When building the portfolio's position in XYZ, Harding's priority is to minimize the trade's market impact to avoid conveying information to market participants. Additionally, Harding does not expect adverse price movements during the trade horizon.

Harding and Yellow conclude their meeting by comparing trade implementation for equities with the trade implementation for the new fixed-income, exchange-traded derivatives, and currency investments under consideration. Yellow tells Harding:

Statement 4.   Small currency trades and small exchange-traded derivatives trades are typically implemented using the direct market access (DMA) approach.

Statement 5.   The high-touch agency approach is typically used to execute large, non-urgent trades in fixed-income and exchange-traded derivatives markets.

The next day, Harding instructs Yellow to revisit their research on BYYP, Inc. Yellow's research leads her to believe that its shares are undervalued. She shares her research with Harding, and at 10 a.m. he instructs her to buy 120,000 shares when the price is $40.00 using a limit order of $42.00.

The buy-side trader releases the order for market execution when the price is $40.50. The only fee is a commission of $0.02 per share. By the end of the trading day, 90,000 shares of the order had been purchased, and BYYP closes at $42.50. The trade was executed at an average price of $41.42. Details about the executed trades are presented in Exhibit 1.

EXHIBIT 1   BYYP Trade Execution Details

Trades	Execution Price	Shares Executed
Trade 1	$40.75	10,000
Trade 2	$41.25	30,000
Trade 3	$41.50	20,000
Trade 4	$41.75	30,000
Total		90,000

While the buy-side trader executes the BYYP trade, Harding and Yellow review ValleyRise's trade policy document. After reviewing the document, Yellow recommends several changes: 1) add a policy for the treatment of trade errors; 2) add a policy that ensures over-the-counter derivatives are traded on venues with rules that ensure minimum price transparency; and 3) alter the list of eligible brokers to include only those that provide execution at the lowest possible trading cost.

1. Which of Yellow's statements regarding the factors affecting the selection of a trading strategy is correct?
   A. Statement 1
   B. Statement 2
   C. Statement 3

2. Given the parameters for the benchmark given by Harding, Yellow should recommend a benchmark that is based on the:
   A. arrival price.
   B. time-weighted average price.
   C. volume-weighted average price.

3. To fill the remaining portion of the ABC order, Yellow is using:
   A. an arrival price trading strategy.
   B. a TWAP participation strategy.
   C. a VWAP participation strategy.

4. What type of algorithm should be used to purchase the XYZ shares given Harding's priority in building the XYZ position and his belief about potential price movements?
   A. Scheduled algorithm
   B. Arrival price algorithm
   C. Opportunistic algorithm

5. Which of Yellow's statements regarding the trade implementation of non-equity investments is correct?
   A. Only Statement 4
   B. Only Statement 5
   C. Both Statement 4 and Statement 5

6. Based on Exhibit 1, the execution cost for purchasing the 90,000 shares of BYYP is:
   A. $60,000.
   B. $82,500.
   C. $127,500.

7. Based on Exhibit 1, the opportunity cost for purchasing the 90,000 shares of BYYP is:
   A. $22,500.
   B. $60,000.
   C. $75,000.

8. The arrival cost for purchasing the 90,000 shares of BYYP is:
   A. 164.4 bp.
   B. 227.2 bp.
   C. 355.0 bp.

9. As it relates to the trade policy document, ValleyRise should implement Yellow's recommendation related to:
   A. the list of eligible brokers.
   B. a policy for the treatment of trade errors.
   C. a policy for over-the-counter derivatives trades.

The following information relates to Questions 10–16

Michelle Wong is a portfolio manager at Star Wealth Management (SWM), an investment management company whose clients are high-net-worth individuals. Her expertise is in identifying temporarily mispriced equity securities. Wong's typical day includes meeting with clients, conducting industry and company investment analysis, and preparing trade recommendations.

Music Plus

Wong follows the music industry and, specifically, Music Plus. After highly anticipated data about the music industry is released shortly after the market opens for trading, the share price of Music Plus quickly increases to $15.25. Wong evaluates the new data as it relates to Music Plus and concludes that the share price increase is an overreaction. She expects the price to quickly revert back to her revised fair value estimate of $14.20 within the same day. When the price is $15.22, she decides to prepare a large sell order equal to approximately 20% of the expected daily volume. She is concerned about information leakage from a public limit order. Wong's supervisor suggests using algorithmic trading for the sell order of the Music Plus shares.

West Commerce

Later the same day, West Commerce announces exciting new initiatives resulting in a substantial increase in its share price to $27.10. Based on this price, Wong concludes that the stock is overvalued and sets a limit price of $26.20 for a sell order of 10,000 shares. By the time the order is released to the market, the share price is $26.90. The share price closes the day at $26.00. SWM is charged a commission of $0.03 per share and no other fees. Selected data about the trade execution are presented in Exhibit 1.

EXHIBIT 1   Selected Trade Data: West Commerce Sell Order

Trades	Execution price	Shares executed
Trade 1	$26.80	6,000
Trade 2	$26.30	3,000
Total		9,000

The value of the market index appropriate to West Commerce was 600 when the West Commerce sell order was released to the market, and its volume-weighted average price (VWAP) was 590 during the trade horizon. West Commerce has a beta of 0.9 with the index.

Trading Policies

At the end of the day, Wong meets with a long-term client of SWM to discuss SWM's trade policies. The client identifies two of SWM's trade policies and asks Wong whether these are consistent with good trade governance:

Policy 1.   SWM works only with pre-approved brokers and execution venues, and the list is reviewed and updated regularly.

Policy 2.   SWM is allowed to pool funds when appropriate, and executed orders are allocated to the accounts on a pro-rata basis.

10.   The *most appropriate* price benchmark for the sell order of Music Plus shares is the:
   A.   closing price.
   B.   decision price.
   C.   time-weighted average price (TWAP).

11.   The *most* appropriate trading strategy for the sell order of Music Plus shares is:
   A.   trading in the open market.
   B.   selling at the closing auction for the day.
   C.   passive trading over the course of the trading day.

12.   The trade algorithm that Wong should consider for the sell order of Music Plus shares is:
   A.   a POV algorithm.
   B.   an arrival price algorithm.
   C.   a liquidity-seeking algorithm.

13.   The implementation shortfall, in basis points (bps), for the sell order of West Commerce shares is *closest* to:
   A.   139.
   B.   198.
   C.   206.

14.   The delay cost in dollars for the sell order of West Commerce shares is:
   A. $1,800.
   B. $2,000.
   C. $2,700.

15.   The market-adjusted cost in basis points for the sell order of West Commerce shares is *closest* to a:
   A.   cost of 249 bps.
   B.   savings of 50 bps.
   C.   savings of 68 bps.

16.   Which of SWM's trading policies identified by the client are consistent with good trade governance?
   A.   Only Policy 1
   B.   Only Policy 2
   C.   Both Policy 1 and Policy 2

The following information relates to Questions 17–18

Lindsey Morris is a trader at North Circle Advisors, an investment management firm and adviser to a suite of value-oriented equity mutual funds. Will Beamon, portfolio manager for the firm's flagship large-cap value fund, the Ogive Fund, is explaining its investment strategy and objectives to Morris. Morris wishes to know how the Ogive Fund's underlying trading motivations may impact trade urgency and alpha decay. Beamon notes the following relevant characteristics of the Ogive Fund:

- Seeks long-term outperformance vs. S&P 500 by investing in undervalued companies
- Evaluates company fundamentals to identify persistent mispricing opportunities
- Has a three-year average holding period

17. **Determine**, based on Beamon's description of the Ogive Fund's characteristics, his likely inclination to aggressively implement the fund's strategy. **Justify** your response.

Morris next meets Robin Barker, portfolio manager for North Circle Advisors' small-cap value fund, the Pengwyn Fund, which just received a very large cash inflow. Barker expects equity markets will drift higher in the near-term and asks Morris about the best ways to minimize cash drag for the Pengwyn Fund after the inflow.

18. **Describe** an appropriate cash management strategy for Barker.

The following information relates to Questions 19–20

Last year, Larry Sailors left his trading position at Valley Ranch Partners, a multi-strategy hedge fund, to join North Circle Advisors. Discussing his job experiences with a colleague, Sailors remarks that, prior to starting at North Circle, he didn't fully appreciate the significant differences in trading motivations between the two firms and how such motivations feed into trade strategy. In particular, he notes the following trade characteristics:

EXHIBIT 1   Features of Trades by Sailors' Employers

Feature	Valley Ranch Partners	North Circle Advisors
Investment Philosophy	Short-term long and short alpha trades across equity and non-equity securities	Long equity value investing
Trade Size	Small	Large
Risk Appetite	Low	Moderate to high
Trading Venue	Listed securities only	Listed and non-listed securities
Bid–Ask Spreads Experienced in Downturn	Moderate-to-wide	Very wide

19. **Identify** one difference between the trading features of Valley Ranch and North Circle, as noted by Sailors, for each trade strategy selection criterion.

Selection Criterion for Trade Strategy	**Identify** one difference between the trading features of Valley Ranch and North Circle, as noted by Sailors, for each trade strategy selection criterion.
Order Characteristics	
Security Characteristics	
Market Conditions	
Individual Risk Aversion	

The next day, Sailors is asked to implement the following buy orders, with target execution price set at Last Trade. He is concerned about minimizing execution risk and market impact.

EXHIBIT 2   Descriptions of Prospective Buy Orders

Stock	Order Size (#)	Last Trade ($)	Avg. Daily Volume (#)	Price Volatility	Bid–Ask Spread ($)
ABC	45,000	$310.10	195,000	Low	$309.75–$310.35
DEF	55,000	$40.45	4,125,260	Low	$40.39–$40.56
XYZ	8,000	$101.94	750,850	High	$100.82–$102.00

20. **Determine** which trades are *most likely* to exhibit the greatest execution risk and market impact. **Justify** each selection.

Determine which trades are *most likely* to exhibit the greatest execution risk and market impact. (Circle one in each column)

Execution Risk	Market Impact
ABC	ABC
DEF	DEF
XYZ	XYZ

Justify each selection.

The following information relates to Questions 21–23

Although focused on long-term value, North Circle Advisors will exploit temporary mispricings to open positions. For example, portfolio manager Bill Bradley pegged LIM Corporation's fair value per share at $28 yesterday; however, LIM's stock price seems to have overreacted to a competitor announcement prior to market open today. The follow events unfold over the course of the morning:

- PRIOR CLOSE: LIM closed at $30.05
- PRE-MARKET: LIM priced at $20.34
- MARKET OPEN: LIM opens at $22.15
- 10:00 AM: LIM trading at $23.01
- 10:00 AM: Bradley confirms the overreaction with target price of $28
- 10:05 AM: Bradley instructs trader to buy 25,000 shares, with a limit price of $28 when LIM is trading at $23.09
- 10:22 AM: Trader finishes the buy with an average purchase price of $23.45

Bradley and the trader conduct a post-trade evaluation. In picking an appropriate reference price, the trader asks Bradley if that would be a pre-trade, intraday, post-trade, or price target benchmark.

21. **Identify** the likely appropriate price benchmark for the LIM trade. **Justify** your response.

Identify the likely appropriate price benchmark for the LIM trade. (Circle one)

Pre-Trade	Intraday	Post-Trade	Price Target
	Justify your response.		

Bradley also performs a cost analysis on the LIM trade. Noting the time gap between his trade instructions and the order's submission to the market, Bradley quantifies the cost of the delay.

22. **Calculate** the delay cost incurred in trading the LIM order.

Bradley also sees that following a 10 a.m. Federal Reserve press conference, the market rose significantly throughout that day. He wants to separate out the pricing effect of this general market movement from the cost of trading LIM. Bradley and the trader agree to use an arrival price benchmark for this analysis and gather the following data related to a broad market index:

- Index price at time of order entry: $2,150
- Index volume-weighted average price over trade horizon: $2,184
- LIM beta to index: 0.95

23. **Calculate** the market-adjusted cost of the trade. **Discuss** the finding.

The following information relates to Questions 24–25

Beatrice Minchow designs and implements algorithmic trading strategies for Enlightenment Era Partners LLC (EEP). Minchow is working with Portfolio Manager James Bean on an algorithm to implement a sell order for Bean's small position in the lightly-traded shares of public company Dynopax Inc. In a conversation with Minchow, Bean states the following:

- I have no expectations of adverse price movements during the trade horizon and would like to use a scheduled algorithm.

- I want to minimize market impact, but I'm more concerned about getting the sell order completely executed in one day.

Based on Bean's comments, Minchow considers three algorithms: POV, VWAP, and TWAP.

24. **Determine** which algorithm Minchow is likely to use for the Dynopax sell order. **Justify** your response.

Determine which algorithm Minchow is likely to use for the Dynopax sell order. (Circle one)

POV	VWAP	TWAP

Justify your response.

Minchow is also tasked to help EEP exit from a large position in a widely-traded blue chip stock. While the trade is non-urgent, given the position's size, Bean is worried about telegraphing intentions to the market. Minchow discusses alternative trading systems with Bean, highlighting dark pools, and makes the following comments:

- Comment 1: A feature of a dark pool is that transactions and quantities won't be reported.
- Comment 2: While a dark pool does provide anonymity, there is less certainty of execution.

25. **Determine** the veracity of each comment. **Justify** each response.

Determine the veracity of each comment. **Justify** each response.

Comment	Veracity (Circle one for each row)	Justification
1	Correct	
	Incorrect	
2	Correct	
	Incorrect	

The following information relates to Question 26.

Karen Swanson and Gabriel Russell recently co-founded Green Savanah Securities, an asset management firm conducting various equity and fixed-income strategies. Swanson and Russell are formulating Green Savannah's trade policy. During a meeting, they agree on an initial set of themes regarding trade policy formation:

- Theme 1: We should determine an optimal execution approach and apply that approach to each asset class managed.
- Theme 2: In aggregating trades for pooled accounts, any partially executed orders need to be allocated on a pro-rata basis.

- Theme 3: The principles behind our process to find a broker should be consistent across each asset class managed.
- Theme 4: To act in our clients' best interests, we need to disclose all trade errors to them.

26. **Identify** two inappropriate themes in the partners' set. **Justify** your response.

CHAPTER 19

PORTFOLIO PERFORMANCE EVALUATION

Marc A. Wright, CFA

LEARNING OUTCOMES

The candidate should be able to:

- explain the following components of portfolio evaluation and their interrelationships: performance measurement, performance attribution, and performance appraisal;
- describe attributes of an effective attribution process;
- distinguish between return attribution and risk attribution and between macro and micro return attribution;
- describe returns-based, holdings-based, and transactions-based performance attribution, including advantages and disadvantages of each;
- interpret the sources of portfolio returns using a specified attribution approach;
- interpret the output from fixed-income attribution analyses;
- discuss considerations in selecting a risk attribution approach;
- distinguish between investment results attributable to the asset owner versus those attributable to the investment manager;
- discuss uses of liability-based benchmarks;
- describe types of asset-based benchmarks;
- discuss tests of benchmark quality;
- describe problems that arise in benchmarking alternative investments;
- describe the impact of benchmark misspecification on attribution and appraisal analysis;
- calculate and interpret the Sortino ratio, the appraisal ratio, upside/downside capture ratios, maximum drawdown, and drawdown duration;
- describe limitations of appraisal measures and related metrics;
- evaluate the skill of an investment manager.

Portfolio Management, Second Edition, by Marc A. Wright, CFA. Copyright © 2019 by CFA Institute.

1. INTRODUCTION

Performance evaluation is one of the most critical areas of investment analysis. Performance results can be used to assess the quality of the investment approach and suggest changes that might improve it. They are also used to communicate the results of the investment process to other stakeholders and may even be used to compensate the investment managers. Therefore, it is of vital importance that practitioners who use these analyses understand how the results are generated. By gaining an understanding of the details of how these analyses work, practitioners will develop a greater understanding of the insights that might be gathered from the analysis and will also be cognizant of the limitations of those approaches, careful not to infer more than what is explicit or logically implicit in the results.

We will first consider the broad categories of performance measurement, attribution, and appraisal, differentiating between the three and explaining their interrelationships. Next, we will provide practitioners with tools to evaluate the effectiveness of those analyses as we summarize various approaches to performance evaluation. We will cover returns-based, holdings-based, and transactions-based attribution, addressing the merits and shortcomings of each approach and providing guidance on how to properly interpret attribution results. Again, by reviewing how each approach generates its results, we reveal strengths and weaknesses of the individual attribution approaches.

Next, we will turn to the subject of benchmarks and performance appraisal ratios. We will review the long-standing tests of benchmark quality and differentiate market indexes from benchmarks. We will also review different ratios used in performance appraisal, considering the benefits and limitations of each approach.

Lastly, we will provide advice on using these tools to collectively evaluate the skill of investment managers. This advice relies heavily on understanding the analysis tools, the limitations of the approaches, the importance of data to the quality of the analysis, and the pitfalls to avoid when making recommendations.

2. THE COMPONENTS OF PERFORMANCE EVALUATION

Performance evaluation includes three primary components, each corresponding to a specific question we need to answer to evaluate a portfolio's performance:

- Performance measurement—what was the portfolio's performance?
- Performance attribution—how was the performance achieved?
- Performance appraisal—was the performance achieved through manager skill or luck?

We will consider each of these components on their own and the interrelationships between them.

Performance measurement provides an overall indication of the portfolio's performance, typically relative to a benchmark. In its simplest form, performance measurement is the calculation of investment returns for both the portfolio and its benchmark. This return calculation is a critical first step in the performance evaluation process, building the foundation on which performance evaluation is based. The investment return tells us what the portfolio achieved over a specific period, irrespective of peer or benchmark performance. For purposes of this chapter, we will call this the *absolute return*. But it also provides the basis to understand the difference between the portfolio return and its benchmark return, the **excess return**.

In addition to return, performance measurement must consider the risk incurred to achieve that return. We measure risk using a variety of *ex post* (looking back in time) and *ex ante* (looking forward in time) techniques. For *ex post*, we might consider the volatility or standard deviation of the past returns, along with many other performance appraisal ratios considered later in this chapter. The calculation of a portfolio's value at risk (VaR) at a point in time is an example of an *ex ante* measure. These measures of risk allow us to quantify the risk in a portfolio and better assess the performance.

Performance attribution then builds on the foundation of the investment returns and risk, helping us explain *how* that performance was achieved or that risk was incurred. Performance attribution can be used to explain either absolute returns or relative returns. It can be used to understand what portion of returns was driven by active manager decisions and what portion was a result of exposures not specifically targeted by the portfolio manager. Performance attribution can also be used to decompose the excess return into its component sources, where it is used to help explain why a manager over- or underperformed the target benchmark. Similarly, risk attribution can be used to decompose the risk incurred in the portfolio.

The third component of performance evaluation, performance appraisal, makes use of risk, return, and attribution analyses to draw conclusions regarding the *quality* of a portfolio's performance. Performance appraisal attempts to distinguish manager skill from luck. Did the portfolio manager's decisions help achieve a better outcome, or was the outcome due to market changes outside of the manager's control? If superior results can be attributed to skill, there is a higher likelihood that the manager will generate superior performance in the future. The analysis may affirm the management process or may contain insights for improving the process. This is a key feedback loop in the investment management process.

EXAMPLE 1   Performance Evaluation

1. Performance attribution:
   A. measures the excess performance of a portfolio.
   B. explains the proportion of returns due to manager skill.
   C. explains how the excess performance or risk was achieved.

2. Performance appraisal:
   A. identifies the sources of under- or outperformance.
   B. decomposes a portfolio's risk and return into their constituent parts.
   C. uses the results of risk, return, and attribution analyses to assess the quality of a portfolio's performance.

Solution to 1: C is correct. Performance attribution identifies the drivers of investment returns. A is not correct because measuring the excess performance of a portfolio is the subject of performance measurement. B is not correct because it is performance appraisal that distinguishes skill from luck.

Solution to 2: C is correct. Performance appraisal combines all the techniques of performance measurement and attribution to assess the quality of performance. Both A and B describe performance attribution.

3. PERFORMANCE ATTRIBUTION

As previously described, performance attribution is a critical component of the portfolio evaluation process. Used by senior management, client relationship specialists, risk controllers, operations staff, portfolio managers, and sales and marketing professionals, attribution analysis provides important insights to the investment decision-making process. Clients and prospects also use attribution analysis as part of their evaluation of that process. Effective performance attribution analysis requires a thorough understanding of the investment decision-making process and should reflect the active decisions of the portfolio manager.

An effective performance attribution process must

- account for *all* of the portfolio's return or risk exposure,
- reflect the investment decision-making process,
- quantify the active decisions of the portfolio manager, and
- provide a complete understanding of the excess return/risk of the portfolio.

If the return or risk quantified by the attribution analysis does not account for all the return or risk presented to the client, then at best the attribution is incomplete and at worst the quality of the attribution analysis is brought into doubt. If the attribution does not reflect the investment decision-making process, then the analysis will be of little value to either the portfolio manager or the client. For example, if the portfolio manager is a genuine bottom-up stock picker who ignores sector benchmark weights, then measuring the impact of sector allocation against these weights is not measuring decisions made as part of the investment process; sector effects are merely a byproduct of the manager's investment decisions.

Performance attribution includes return attribution and risk attribution (although in practice, "performance attribution" is often used to mean "return attribution"). **Return attribution** analyzes the impact of active investment decisions on *returns*; **risk attribution** analyzes the *risk* consequences of those decisions. Depending on the purpose of the analysis, risk may be viewed in absolute or benchmark-relative terms. For example, when risk relative to a benchmark is the focus, a risk attribution analysis might identify and evaluate a portfolio's deviations from a benchmark's exposures to risk factors.

Performance attribution provides a good starting point for a conversation with clients, explaining both positive and negative aspects of recent performance. Return attribution analysis is particularly important when performance is weak; portfolio managers must demonstrate an understanding of their performance, provide a rationale for their decisions, and generate confidence in their ability to add value in the future. When it accurately reflects the investment decision-making process, return attribution provides quality control for the investment process and provides senior management with a tool to manage a complex business with multiple investment strategies.

The attribution process described earlier—understanding the drivers of a manager's returns and whether those drivers are consistent with the stated investment process—is a common application of attribution analysis. But attribution can also be conducted to evaluate the asset owner's tactical asset allocation and manager selection decisions (called **macro attribution**) or to evaluate the impact of the portfolio manager's decisions on the performance of the asset owner's total fund (called **micro attribution**). A defined-benefit pension plan makes the decision to allocate a given percentage of the fund to each asset class and decides which manager(s) to hire for each asset class. Macro attribution measures the effect of the sponsor's choice to deviate from the strategic asset allocation, including the effect of "gaps" between the strategic asset allocation and its implementation (e.g., where the sum of the managers' benchmarks is equal to something other than the benchmark index).

Micro attribution measures the impact of portfolio managers' allocation and selection decisions on total fund performance.

Performance attribution may be either returns based, holdings based, or transactions based. The decision to use one set of inputs rather than another depends on the availability of data as well as the investment process being measured.

Returns-based attribution uses only the total portfolio returns over a period to identify the components of the investment process that have generated the returns. Returns-based attribution is most appropriate when the underlying portfolio holding information is not available with sufficient frequency at the required level of detail. For example, one might use returns-based attribution to evaluate hedge funds, because it can be difficult to obtain the underlying holdings of hedge funds. Returns-based attribution is the easiest method to implement, but because it does not use the underlying holdings, it is the least accurate of the three approaches and the most vulnerable to data manipulation.

Unlike returns-based attribution, **holdings-based attribution** references the beginning-of-period holdings of the portfolio. Calculated with monthly, weekly, or daily data, the accuracy of holdings-based attribution improves when using data with shorter time intervals. For longer evaluation periods, we link together the attribution results for the shorter measurement periods. Because holdings-based attribution fails to capture the impact of any transactions made during the measurement period, it may not reconcile to the actual portfolio return. For example, in a daily holdings-based attribution, securities are included at the end of the day they are purchased and excluded at the end of the day they are sold. If the transaction price is significantly different from the closing price, the attribution analysis can differ significantly from the actual performance.

The residual caused by ignoring transactions might be described as a timing or trading effect. Holdings-based analysis is most appropriate for investment strategies with little turnover (e.g., passive strategies). Holdings-based analysis may be improved by valuing the portfolio with the same prices used to calculate the underlying benchmark index, removing one potential difference between the portfolio and benchmark returns that is not a management effect.

The third approach, **transactions-based attribution**, uses both the holdings of the portfolio and the transactions (purchases and sales) that occurred during the evaluation period. For transaction-based attribution, both the weights and returns reflect *all transactions* during the period, including transaction costs. Transaction-based attribution is the most accurate type of attribution analysis but also the most difficult and time-consuming to implement. To obtain meaningful results, the underlying data must be complete, accurate, and reconciled from period to period. Because all the data are available, the entire excess return can be quantified and explained. The return used in the attribution analysis will reconcile with the return presented to the client, and attribution analysis can be used as a diagnostic tool to identify errors.

The choice of attribution approach depends on the availability and quality of the underlying data, the reporting requirements for the client, and the complexity of the investment decision-making process.

EXAMPLE 2 Performance Attribution

1. Effective attribution analysis must:
   A. use intraday transaction data.
   B. reconcile to the total portfolio return or risk exposure.
   C. measure the contribution of security and sector selection decisions.

2. Which of the following most accurately describes macro attribution?
   A. Attribution analysis at the portfolio level
   B. Attribution analysis of the fund sponsor decisions
   C. Attribution analysis of asset allocation decisions

3. Risk attribution differs from return attribution in that it:
   A. is not conducted relative to a benchmark.
   B. quantifies the risk consequences of the investment decisions.
   C. quantifies the investment decisions of the investment manager.

4. An analyst is *most likely* to use returns-based attribution when:
   A. the portfolio has a low turnover.
   B. the holdings for the portfolio are not available.
   C. she wants the analysis to be as accurate as possible.

Solution to 1: B is correct. An effective attribution process accounts for all of the portfolio's return or risk exposure. A is not correct; an attribution analysis is improved with intraday transaction data, but an effective attribution analysis can be produced with a returns- or holdings-based approach. C is not correct because an attribution process that measures the sector selection effects of a bottom-up stock-picker does not measure the effectiveness of the investment decision-making process.

Solution to 2: B is correct. Macro attribution measures the effect of the sponsor's choice to deviate from the strategic asset allocation and the sponsor's manager selection decisions. A is not correct because attribution analysis at the portfolio level may be either macro attribution or micro attribution. C is not correct because macro attribution measures both asset allocation and manager selection decisions of the asset owner.

Solution to 3: B is correct. Risk attribution, unlike return attribution, attempts to quantify the risk consequences of the investment decisions. A is not correct because risk attribution may be conducted on either an absolute or a relative basis. C is not correct because risk attribution does not capture the return impact of a manager's investment decisions.

Solution to 4: B is correct. Returns-based attribution is typically used when the holdings data are not available. Neither A nor C is correct because returns-based attribution is the least accurate of the three approaches.

3.1. Approaches to Return Attribution

Return attribution allows us to look across a specific time horizon and identify which investment decisions have either added value to or detracted value from the portfolio, relative to its benchmark. As feedback to the portfolio management process, return attribution quantifies the active decisions of portfolio managers and informs management and clients. In this way, return attribution can be thought of as "backward looking" or *ex post*, meaning that it is used to evaluate the investment decisions for some historical time horizon.

Return attribution is a set of techniques used to identify the sources of excess return of a portfolio against its benchmark, quantifying the consequences of active investment decisions.

Specific return attribution approaches have been designed to evaluate particular types of assets. In this section, we will consider two common approaches for equity attribution: Brinson–Fachler and factor-based attribution. We will also review the output and findings from a typical fixed-income attribution approach.

Practitioners may also encounter the concept of geometric attribution and arithmetic attribution, two approaches to measuring attribution effects over longer periods. **Arithmetic attribution** approaches are designed to explain the **excess return**, the arithmetic difference between the portfolio return, R, and its benchmark return, B.

When using an arithmetic attribution approach, the attribution effects will sum to the excess return. Arithmetic approaches are straightforward for a single period, for which there is no difference between the sum of the attribution effects and the excess return. However, when combining multiple periods, the sub-period attribution effects will *not* sum to the excess return. Because the excess return is calculated by *geometrically* linking the sub-period returns, adjustments must be made to "smooth" the *arithmetic* sub-period attribution effects over time. Multiple smoothing approaches exist in the industry, including algorithms suggested by David Cariño (1999) and Jose Menchero (2000).

Geometric attribution approaches extend the arithmetic approaches by attributing the geometric excess return (G), as defined below:

$$G = \frac{1 + R}{1 + B} - 1 = \frac{R - B}{1 + B}$$

Note that the geometric excess return is simply the arithmetic excess return divided by the wealth ratio of the benchmark (1 plus the return on the benchmark during the period).

In a geometric attribution approach, the attribution effects will compound (multiply) together to total the geometric excess return. Because the attribution effects compound together to exactly equal the geometric excess return, the compounding works across multiple periods. Therefore, no smoothing is required to adjust the geometric attribution effects across multiple periods.

Practitioners typically choose arithmetic attribution approaches when they want to use the attribution analysis with non-practitioner clients or in marketing reports. With results that add up to the total excess return for all periods, arithmetic approaches are more intuitively understood. Geometric approaches tend to be limited to practitioners who understand the approach and who appreciate that they do not have to adjust the attribution effects over time.

A Simple Return Attribution Example
Suppose a portfolio's return for the past year was 5.24% and the portfolio's benchmark return for that same period was 3.24%. In this case, the portfolio achieved a positive arithmetic excess return of 2.00% (5.24% − 3.24% = 2.00%) over the past year.

To understand how the 2.00% was achieved, we apply return attribution. In this example, return attribution will quantify two typical sources of excess return: *security selection* and *asset allocation*. Security selection answers the question, Was the return achieved by selecting securities that performed well relative to the benchmark or by avoiding benchmark securities that performed relatively poorly? Asset allocation answers the question, Was the return achieved by choosing to overweight an asset category (e.g., economic sector or currency) that outperformed the total benchmark or to underweight an asset category that underperformed the total benchmark? (The term "allocation" is used somewhat differently here. It is not measuring the plan sponsor's asset allocation decision but, rather, the *manager's* decision to allocate among countries, sectors, or, in cases where the manager has a broad mandate, asset classes.)

Models of equity return attribution often attempt to separate the investment process into those two key decisions—selection and allocation—assigning each a magnitude and direction (plus or minus) for both decisions. For instance, for the portfolio referenced previously, we might calculate the return attribution results shown in Exhibit 1:

EXHIBIT 1   Total Portfolio Return Attribution Analysis (Time Period: Past 12 Months)

Portfolio Return	Benchmark Return	Excess Return	Allocation Effect	Selection Effect
5.24%	3.24%	2.00%	−0.50%	2.50%

As we noted, the investment decisions generated a positive excess return of 200 basis points (bps) relative to the benchmark. We use the "return attribution analysis" to see how this 200 bps was generated. First, note that the *negative* allocation effect indicates that the allocation decisions over the past 12 months, whatever they were, had a negative impact on the total portfolio performance. They *subtracted* 50 bps from the excess return. In contrast, the *positive* selection effect indicates that the security selection decisions—decisions to overweight or underweight securities relative to their benchmark weights—*added* 250 bps to the excess return. Our return attribution analysis implies that the portfolio manager's security selection decision was far superior to his or her asset allocation decision for the past 12 months.

3.1.1. Equity Return Attribution—The Brinson–Hood–Beebower Model

The foundations of return attribution were established in two articles, one written by Brinson and Fachler (1985) and the other by Brinson, Hood, and Beebower (1986). The Brinson–Fachler model is more widely used in performance attribution today, but we introduce the Brinson–Hood–Beebower (BHB) model first to lay an important foundation.

BHB is built on the assumption that the total portfolio and benchmark returns are calculated by summing the weights and returns of the sectors within the portfolio (Equation 1) and the benchmark (Equation 2):

$$\text{Portfolio return} \qquad R = \sum_{i=1}^{i=n} w_i R_i \qquad\qquad (1)$$

$$\text{Benchmark return} \quad B = \sum_{i=1}^{i=n} W_i B_i \qquad\qquad (2)$$

where

   w_i = weight of the *i*th sector in the portfolio
   R_i = return of the portfolio assets in the *i*th sector
   W_i = weight of the *i*th sector in the benchmark
   B_i = return of the benchmark in the *i*th sector
   n = number of sectors or securities

The sum of the weights in both the portfolio and the benchmark must equal 100%. The presence of leverage would require a position with a negative weight (borrowings or short positions) to balance to 100%.

Attribution analysis quantifies each of the portfolio manager's active decisions that explain the difference between the portfolio return, *R*, and the benchmark return, *B*. Note that for this example, we are concerned with only single-period, single-currency return attribution models.

Exhibit 2 provides data for a three-sector domestic equity portfolio, used to illustrate the BHB model.

EXHIBIT 2   BHB Model Illustration—Portfolio and Benchmark Data

Sector	Portfolio Weight	Benchmark Weight	Portfolio Return	Benchmark Return
Energy	50%	50%	18%	10%
Health care	30%	20%	–3%	–2%
Financials	20%	30%	10%	12%
Total	**100%**	**100%**	**10.1%**	**8.2%**

Total portfolio return $R = (50\% \times 18\%) + (30\% \times -3\%) + (20\% \times 10\%) = 10.1\%$

Total benchmark return $B = (50\% \times 10\%) + (20\% \times -2\%) + (30\% \times 12\%) = 8.2\%$

Thus, the excess return is 1.9% (10.1% − 8.2% = 1.9%), or 190 bps.

We will use the weights and returns data shown in Exhibit 2 to calculate the basic attribution effects using the BHB model, including the allocation effect, the security selection effect, and the interaction effect. The allocation effect refers to the value the portfolio manager adds (or subtracts) by having portfolio sector weights that are different from the benchmark sector weights. A sector weight in the portfolio greater than the benchmark sector weight would be described as *overweight*, and a sector weight less than the benchmark sector weight would be described as *underweight*.

To calculate allocation, we first calculate the contribution to allocation (A_i) for each sector. The contribution to allocation in the *i*th sector is equal to the portfolio's sector weight minus the benchmark's sector weight, times the benchmark sector return:

$$A_i = (w_i - W_i)B_i \tag{3}$$

Using the data from Exhibit 2, we calculate individual sector allocation effects as follows:

• Energy: (50% − 50%) × 10% = 0.0%

- Health care: $(30\% - 20\%) \times -2.0\% = -0.2\%$
- Financials: $(20\% - 30\%) \times 12\% = -1.2\%$

To find the total portfolio allocation effect, A, we sum the individual sector contributions to allocation:

$$A = \sum_{i=1}^{i=n} A_i \qquad\qquad (4)$$

Total allocation effect $= 0.0\% - 0.2\% - 1.2\% = -1.4\%$

We can then use the results to state the following conclusions:

- The portfolio weight in the energy sector is equal to the benchmark weight; therefore, there is no contribution to allocation in energy.
- In health care, the portfolio manager held a higher weight than the benchmark (30% versus 20%), but the sector underperformed the aggregate benchmark (–2.0% versus 8.2%). Therefore, the decision to overweight health care lowered the overall excess return; the contribution to allocation is –0.2%.
- In financials, the portfolio manager chose to underweight versus the benchmark (20% versus 30%). But because financials outperformed the aggregate benchmark (12% versus 8.2%), the decision to underweight financials also lowered the overall excess return; the contribution to allocation is –1.2%.
- Overall, the combined allocation effect for this portfolio was –1.4%, demonstrating that the weighting decisions negatively contributed to the performance of the portfolio.

The other attribution effect in the BHB model is security selection—the value the portfolio manager adds by holding individual securities or instruments within the sector in different-from-benchmark weights.

To calculate selection, we first calculate the contribution to selection (S_i) for each sector. The contribution to selection in the ith sector is equal to the benchmark sector weight times the portfolio's sector return minus the benchmark's sector return.

$$S_i = W_i(R_i - B_i) \qquad\qquad (5)$$

Using the data from Exhibit 2, we calculate individual sector selection effects as follows:

- Energy: $50\% \times (18\% - 10\%) = 4.0\%$
- Health care: $20\% \times (-3\% - -2.0\%) = -0.2\%$
- Financials: $30\% \times (10\% - 12\%) = -0.6\%$

To find the total portfolio selection effect, S, we sum the individual sector contributions to selection:

$$S = \sum_{i=1}^{i=n} S_i \qquad\qquad (6)$$

Total selection effect $= 4.0\% + -0.2\% + -0.6\% = 3.2\%$

We can use the results to state the following conclusions:

- The portfolio's energy sector outperformed the benchmark's energy sector by 800 bps (18% – 10%); 800 bps times the benchmark weight of 50% for this sector results in a 4.0% contribution to selection.
- The portfolio's health care sector underperformed the benchmark's health care sector by 100 bps [(–3%) – (–2%)]; 100 bps times the benchmark weight of 20% for this sector results in a contribution of –0.2%.
- The portfolio's financials sector underperformed the benchmark's financials sector by 200 bps (10% – 12%); 200 bps times the benchmark weight of 30% to this sector results in a contribution of –0.6%.
- Overall, the combined selection effect for this portfolio was 3.2%.

In the BHB model, selection and allocation do not completely explain the arithmetic difference. For example, in the attribution analysis based on Exhibit 2, allocation (–1.4%) and selection (3.2%) together represent just 1.8% of the arithmetic difference between the portfolio return of 10.1% and the benchmark return of 8.2%; 0.1% is missing. To explain this remaining difference in the excess return, the BHB model uses a third attribution effect, called "interaction." The **interaction effect** is the effect resulting from the interaction of the allocation and selection decisions combined.

To calculate interaction, we first calculate the contribution to interaction for each sector. The contribution to interaction in the *i*th sector is equal to the portfolio sector weight minus the benchmark sector weight, times the portfolio sector return minus the benchmark sector return:

$$I_i = (w_i - W_i)(R_i - B_i) \tag{7}$$

Using the data from Exhibit 2, we calculate individual sector selection effects as follows:

- Energy: (50% – 50%) × (18% – 10%) = 0.0%
- Health care: (30% – 20%) × (–3% – –2.0%) = –0.1%
- Financials: (20% – 30%) × (10% – 12%) = 0.2%

To find the total portfolio interaction effect, we sum the individual sector contributions to interaction:

$$I = \sum_{i=1}^{i=n} I_i \tag{8}$$

Total interaction effect = 0.0% + –0.1% + 0.2% = 0.1%

We can use the results to state the following conclusions:

- For the energy sector, the portfolio weight equals the benchmark weight and thus there is no contribution to interaction.
- Because the manager had an overweight to a sector in which selection was negative, the contribution from interaction in health care was also negative, –0.1%.
- In the financials sector, the manager was underweight by 10% and selection was negative. The effect of being underweight in a sector in which the manager underperforms leads to a contribution from interaction of +0.2%.
- Total contribution from interaction is +0.1%, representing the combined effect of the interaction of the selection and allocation effects.

EXAMPLE 3   Interpreting the Results of a BHB Attribution

BHB Attribution Analysis Results Table

Region	Portfolio Return	Benchmark Return	Portfolio Weight	Benchmark Weight	Allocation	Selection	Interaction	Total
Americas	2.80%	1.20%	30%	30%	0.00%	0.48%	0.00%	0.48%
APAC	−1.50%	−0.50%	20%	30%	0.05%	−0.30%	0.10%	−0.15%
EMEA	0.70%	1.50%	50%	40%	0.15%	−0.32%	−0.08%	−0.25%
Total	**0.89%**	**0.81%**	**100%**	**100%**	**0.20%**	**−0.14%**	**0.02%**	**0.08%**

Use the table above to answer the following questions.

1. Why is the contribution to selection for Europe, the Middle East, and Africa (EMEA) negative?
   A. The total benchmark return is less than the total portfolio return.
   B. The manager selected securities in EMEA that underperformed the benchmark.
   C. The manager underweighted an outperforming sector.

2. Why is the contribution to allocation for Asia Pacific (APAC) equal to +5 bps?
   A. The benchmark weight and the portfolio weight are equal.
   B. The manager has an overweight position in an overperforming region.
   C. The manager has an underweight position in an underperforming region.

3. Which of the following conclusions from the above attribution analysis is *most* correct?
   A. The manager's security selection decisions were better in the Americas than in APAC.
   B. The manager's security selection decisions were better in EMEA than in APAC.
   C. The manager's allocation decisions were better in APAC than in EMEA.

4. Which of the following conclusions from the above attribution analysis is *most* correct?
   A. Overall, the manager made better allocation decisions than selection decisions.
   B. Overall, the manager made better selection decisions than allocation decisions.
   C. Contribution from interaction was most noticeable in the Americas.

Solution to 1: B is correct. The manager selected securities that underperformed the benchmark, with a portfolio return for EMEA of 0.7% versus a benchmark return for EMEA of 1.5%.

Solution to 2: C is correct. The manager is underweight in APAC, 20% versus a benchmark weight of 30%. The APAC portion of the portfolio underperformed, with a −0.50% benchmark return versus the total benchmark return of 0.81%.

Solution to 3: A is correct. As reflected in the contribution to selection, the manager's security selection decisions were better in the Americas (0.48%) than in APAC (−0.30%).

Solution to 4: A is correct. Overall, the manager made better allocation decisions (0.20%) than selection decisions (−0.14%).

3.1.2. Brinson–Fachler Model

The Brinson–Fachler (BF) model differs from the BHB model only in how individual sector allocation effects are calculated.

In the BHB model, all overweight positions in sectors with positive returns will generate positive allocation effects irrespective of the overall benchmark return, whereas all overweight positions in negative markets will generate negative allocation effects. Thus, overweighting a sector i that earns a positive return, $B_i > 0$, results in a positive allocation effect, $A_i = (w_i - W_i)B_i > 0$, even when the sector return is less than the overall benchmark return (i.e., $B_i < B$). When the sector return is negative, $0 > B_i$, overweighting produces a negative allocation effect, $A_i = (w_i - W_i)B_i < 0$.

Clearly, if the portfolio manager is overweight in a negative market that has outperformed the overall benchmark, the effect should be positive.

The BF model solves this problem by modifying the asset allocation factor to compare returns with the overall benchmark as follows:

$$B_S - B = \sum_{i=1}^{i=n}(w_i - W_i)B_i = \sum_{i=1}^{i=n}(w_i - W_i)(B_i - B) \tag{9}$$

Because $\sum_{i=1}^{i=n} w_i = \sum_{i=1}^{i=n} W_i = 1$, the constant B can be introduced. The contribution to asset allocation in the ith sector is now:

$$A_i = (w_i - W_i)(B_i - B) \tag{10}$$

Note that in Equation 10, the allocation effect at the portfolio level, $B_S - B$, is unchanged from the BHB model.

The contribution to arithmetic excess return from sector allocation for the portfolio data shown in Exhibit 2 is $B_S - B = 6.8\% - 8.2\% = -1.4\%$. Revised BF sector allocation effects are calculated for the portfolio data in Exhibit 2 as follows, using $A_i = (w_i - W_i)(B_i - B)$:

Energy	(50% − 50%) × (10% − 8.2%) = 0.0%
Health care	(30% − 20%) × (−2.0% − 8.2%) = −1.02%
Financials	(20% − 30%) × (12% − 8.2%) = −0.38%
Total	0.0% − 1.02% − 0.38% = −1.4%

The impact in health care is much greater. In addition to being overweight in a negative market, which costs −0.2%, the portfolio manager is correctly penalized the opportunity cost of not being invested in the overall market return of 8.2%, generating a further cost of 10% × −8.2% = −0.82% and resulting in a total impact of −1.02%. To describe it another way, the portfolio is 10% overweight in a market that is underperforming the overall market by −10.2% (i.e., −2.0% − 8.2%) and generating a loss of −1.02%

The impact in financials is much smaller. Although being underweight in a positive market cost −1.2%, we must add back the opportunity cost of being invested in the overall market return of 8.2%, generating a contribution of −10% × −8.2% = 0.82% and resulting in a total impact of −0.38%. To describe it another way, the portfolio is 10% underweight in an industry that is outperforming the overall market by 3.8% (i.e., 12.0% − 8.2%), generating a loss of −0.38%. As expected, at the portfolio level, the allocation effect of −1.4% remains the same as that calculated with the BHB model.

The revised attribution effects are summarized in Exhibit 3.

EXHIBIT 3   BF Return Attribution Results

	Portfolio Weight	Benchmark Weight	Portfolio Return	Benchmark Return	Allocation	Selection	Interaction
Energy	50%	50%	18%	10%	0.0%	4.0%	0.0%
Health care	30%	20%	−3%	−2%	−1.02%	−0.2%	−0.1%
Financials	20%	30%	10%	12%	−0.38%	−0.6%	0.2%
Total	**100%**	**100%**	**10.1%**	**8.2%**	**−1.4%**	**3.2%**	**0.1%**

EXAMPLE 4   Allocation Using the BF Model

EXHIBIT 4   Sample Portfolio Data

	Portfolio Weight	Benchmark Weight	Portfolio Return	Benchmark Return
Technology	20%	30%	−11.0%	−10.0%
Telecommunications	30%	40%	−5.0%	−8.0%
Utilities	50%	30%	−8.0%	−5.0%
Total	**100%**	**100%**	**−7.7%**	**−7.7%**

Using the BF method, the allocation effect of utilities based on the portfolio data in Exhibit 4 is:

A.   −1.50%.

B.   0.54%.

C.   1.35%.

Solution:

B is correct: $(w_i - W_i)(B_i - B) = (50\% - 30\%)(-5.0\% + 7.7\%) = 0.54\%$. The portfolio is 20% overweight in a sector outperforming the overall benchmark by 2.7%, therefore contributing 0.54% to the overall allocation effect.

A is incorrect: $W_i B_i = 30\% \times -5.0\% = -1.5\%$ is the contribution to the benchmark return from utilities.

C is incorrect: $w_i(B_i - B) = 50\% \times (-5.0\% + 7.7\%) = +1.35\%$. Only the portfolio weight of 50% has been used, not the overweight position of 20%.

3.1.3. Equity Return Attribution—Factor-Based Return Attribution

As we have seen, return attribution allows us to analyze a portfolio's excess return by comparing the accounting information (weights and returns) in the portfolio with the information in the benchmark. The Brinson–Fachler model focuses on security selection, asset allocation, and the interaction of selection and allocation. But what if we want to assess other decisions within the investment process?

Another type of return attribution uses fundamental factor models to decompose the contributions to excess return from *factors*. Fundamental factor analysis allows us to quantify the impact of specific active investment decisions within the portfolio, showing how they add or remove value relative to the benchmark. We want to remove the effects of the market to identify the excess return generated by the active investment decisions. To do that, we return to our definition of excess return: Excess return $= R - B$.

Many different factor models can be used to decompose excess returns. The choice of factor model is driven by which aspects of the investment process you want to measure. One of the factor models commonly used in equity attribution analyses is the Carhart four-factor model, or simply the **Carhart model**, given in Equation 11 (Carhart 1997). The Carhart model explains the excess return on the portfolio in terms of the portfolio's sensitivity to a market index (RMRF), a market-capitalization factor (SMB), a book-value-to-price factor (HML), and a momentum factor (WML).

$$R_p - R_f = a_p + b_{p1}\text{RMRF} + b_{p2}\text{SMB} + b_{p3}\text{HML} + b_{p4}\text{WML} + E_p \tag{11}$$

where

R_p and $R_f =$ the return on the portfolio and the risk-free rate of return, respectively

$a_p =$ "alpha" or return in excess of that expected given the portfolio's level of systematic risk (assuming the four factors capture all systematic risk)

$b_p =$ the sensitivity of the portfolio to the given factor

RMRF = the return on a value-weighted equity index in excess of the one-month T-bill rate

SMB = small minus big, a size (market-capitalization) factor (SMB is the average return on three small-cap portfolios minus the average return on three large-cap portfolios)

HML = high minus low, a value factor (HML is the average return on two high-book-to-market portfolios minus the average return on two low-book-to-market portfolios)

WML = winners minus losers, a momentum factor (WML is the return on a portfolio of the past year's winners minus the return on a portfolio of the past year's losers)

$E_p =$ an error term that represents the portion of the return to the portfolio, p, not explained by the model

By analyzing the results of a factor return attribution analysis, we can identify the investment approach and infer the relative strengths and/or weaknesses of the investment decisions. For example, using the Carhart factor model, we calculate the following results for a hypothetical manager.

EXHIBIT 5　　Sample Carhart Factor Model Attribution

	Factor Sensitivity				Contribution to Active Return	
Factor	Portfolio (1)	Benchmark (2)	Difference (3)	Factor Return (4)	Absolute (3) × (4)	Proportion of Total Active
RMRF	0.95	1.00	−0.05	5.52%	−0.28%	−13.30%
SMB	−1.05	−1.00	−0.05	−3.35%	0.17%	8.10%
HML	0.40	0.00	0.40	5.10%	2.04%	98.40%
WML	0.05	0.03	0.02	9.63%	0.19%	9.30%
			A. Factor tilts return =		2.12%	102.40%
			B. Security selection =		−0.05%	−2.40%
			C. Active return (A + B) =		2.07%	100.00%

This attribution analysis yields information about this portfolio's investment approach, how the manager generated excess return, and his or her ability to consistently add value relative to the benchmark.

Let's first look at the analysis of the benchmark (column 2). The sensitivity to RMRF of 1 indicates that the assigned benchmark has average market risk, consistent with it being a broad-based index. The benchmark's negative sensitivity to SMB indicates a large-cap orientation. Assuming, of course, that the benchmark is a good fit for the manager's stated strategy, we can describe the approach as large cap without a value/growth bias (HML is zero) or a momentum bias (WML is close to zero).

Let's now look at where the portfolio manager's approach differed from that of the benchmark. Based on the factor sensitivities shown in column 1 (positive sensitivity to HML of 0.40) and the differences relative to the benchmark shown in column 3, we can see that the manager likely had a value tilt but was otherwise relatively neutral to the benchmark. We would expect the portfolio to hold more value-oriented stocks than the benchmark, and we would want to evaluate the contribution of this tilt.

We can examine the effects of this decision by looking at the balance of the table. Positive active exposure to the HML factor—the bet on value stocks—contributed 204 bps to the realized active return, about 98% of the 207 bps of total realized active return. The manager's minor active exposures to small stocks and momentum also contributed positively to return, whereas the active exposure to RMRF was a drag on performance. However, because the magnitudes of the exposures to RMRF, SMB, and WML were relatively small, the effects of those bets were minor compared with the value tilt (HML).

What about the manager's ability to contribute return through stock selection? Again, assuming that the benchmark is a good fit for the manager's investment process, the overall active return from security selection is the portion of return not explained by factor sensitivities. In this period, the contribution from selection was slightly negative (−0.05%).

In the aggregate, the manager's positive active return was largely the result of the large active bet on HML (+0.40) and a high return to that factor during the period (+5.10%). Is this type of tilt consistent with the manager's stated investment process? If yes, the manager can be credited with an active decision that contributed positively to return. If no, then the excess return in the period is unlikely to result from manager skill but, rather, is a byproduct of luck. What does the manager's investment process say about the role of security selection? If the manager does not profess skill in security selection but instead focuses on sector or factor allocation, then the minimal contribution of security selection should not be perceived as a negative reflection on manager skill.

EXAMPLE 5   Factor-Based Attribution

Use the data from Exhibit 5 to answer the following questions.

1. Which of the following statements is *not* correct?
   A. The manager's slight small-cap tilt contributed positively to return.
   B. The manager's slight momentum tilt contributed positively to return.
   C. The manager's below-benchmark beta contributed negatively to return.

2. What investment approach, not taken by the portfolio manager, could have delivered more value to the portfolio during the investment period?
   A. A momentum-based approach
   B. A growth-oriented approach
   C. A small-cap-based approach

Solution to 1: A is the correct answer. The negative coefficient on SMB indicates that the manager had a slight large-cap bias relative to the benchmark. The slight tilt on WML (+0.02) combined with a positive return to the factor resulted in a positive contribution to return. The below-benchmark beta of RMRF (–0.05) combined with a positive return to the factor resulted in a negative contribution to return.

Solution to 2: A is correct. Had the manager overweighted momentum stocks during the period, the momentum factor (WML) return of 9.63% would have contributed significant positive performance to the portfolio.

3.1.4. Fixed-Income Return Attribution

Fixed-income portfolios are driven by very different sources of risk, requiring attribution approaches that attribute returns to decisions made with respect to credit risk and positioning along the yield curve. Building on work by Groupe de Reflexion en Attribution de Performance, or GRAP, outlined in Giguère (2005) and Murira and Sierra (2006), we will discuss three typical approaches to fixed-income attribution:

- Exposure decomposition—duration based
- Yield curve decomposition—duration based
- Yield curve decomposition—full repricing based

Candidates are not responsible for *calculating* fixed-income attribution but should be able to interpret the results of a fixed-income attribution analysis.

3.1.4.1. Exposure Decomposition—Duration Based

Exposure decomposition is a top-down attribution approach that seeks to explain the active management of a portfolio relative to its benchmark, typically working through a hierarchy of decisions from the top to the bottom. These decisions might include portfolio duration bets, yield curve positioning, or sector bets, each relative to the benchmark. The term "exposure decomposition" relates to the decomposition of portfolio risk exposures by means of grouping a portfolio's component bonds by specified characteristics (e.g., duration, bond sector). The term "duration based" relates to the typical use of duration to represent interest rate exposure decisions.

Models that take an exposure decomposition approach are similar to Brinson-type equity attribution models, where we might group the portfolio by its market value weights in different economic sectors. In this case, however, we group the portfolio by its market value weights in duration buckets (i.e., exposure to different ranges of duration). This approach simplifies the data requirements and allows straightforward presentation of results relative to other fixed-income approaches. For these reasons, the exposure decomposition approach is used primarily for marketing and client reports, where an important benefit is that users can easily understand and articulate the results of active portfolio management.

3.1.4.2. Yield Curve Decomposition—Duration Based

The duration-based yield curve decomposition approach to fixed-income attribution can be either executed as a top-down approach or built bottom-up from the security level. This approach estimates the return of securities, sector buckets, or years-to-maturity buckets using the known relationship between duration and changes in yield to maturity (YTM), as follows:

$$\% \text{ Total return} = \% \text{ Income return} + \% \text{ Price return},$$

where % Price return $\approx$ –Duration $\times$ Change in YTM.

Duration measures the sensitivity of bond price to a change in the bond's yield to maturity. So, the percentage price return of a bond will be approximately equal to the negative of its duration for each 100 bp change in yields. The change in yield to maturity of the portfolio or instrument can be broken down into yield curve factors and spread factors to provide additional insights. These factors represent the changes in the risk-free government curve (e.g., changes in level, slope, and curvature) and in the premium required to hold riskier sectors and bonds. When they are combined and applied to the duration, we can determine a percentage price change for each factor.

For example, a manager may have a view as to how the yield curve factors will change over time. We can use the attribution analysis to determine the value of the yield curve views as they unfold over time.

This approach is applied to both the portfolio and the benchmark to identify contributions to total return from changes in the yield to maturity. Comparing the differences between the benchmark's return drivers and the portfolio's return drivers gives us the *effect of active portfolio management decisions.*

In this regard, this group of models is quite different from the exposure decomposition. One consequence of this difference is that we require more data points to calculate the separate absolute attribution analyses for the portfolio and the benchmark. Thus, the yield decomposition approach exchanges better transparency for more operational complexity. These models are typically used when preparing reports for analysts and portfolio managers, rather than in marketing or client reports.

3.1.4.3.   Yield Curve Decomposition—Full Repricing

Instead of estimating price changes from changes in duration and yields to maturity, bonds can be repriced from zero-coupon curves (spot rates). Recall that a bond's price is the sum of its cash flows discounted at the appropriate spot rate for each cash flow's maturity. The discount rate to compute the present value depends on the yields offered on the market for comparable securities and represents the required yield an investor expects for holding that investment. Typically, we discount each cash flow at a rate from the spot curve that corresponds to the time the cash flow will be received.

As with the duration-based approaches, instruments can be repriced following incremental changes in spot rates, whether resulting from changes in overall interest rates, spreads, or bond-specific factors. This bottom-up security-level repricing can then be translated into a contribution to a security's return and aggregated for portfolios, benchmarks, and active management.

This full repricing attribution approach provides more precise pricing and allows for a broader range of instrument types and yield changes. It also supports a greater variety of quantitative modeling beyond fixed-income attribution (e.g., *ex ante* risk). This approach is better aligned with how portfolio managers typically view the instruments. However, it requires the full capability to reprice all financial instruments in the portfolio and the benchmark, including the rates and the characteristics of the instrument. Its complex nature can make it more difficult and costly to administer operationally and can make the results more difficult to understand, particularly for non-fixed-income professionals.

All three approaches can be applied to single-currency and multi-currency portfolios. We can most clearly demonstrate the principles of fixed-income attribution by using a single-currency domestic portfolio, without digressing into the relative merits of the various multi-currency approaches. Therefore, this example is a single-currency example.

3.1.4.4.   Fixed-Income Attribution—Worked Example

Let's begin with an example of exposure decomposition analysis.

Exhibit 6 shows a breakdown of the portfolio and the benchmark by weights, duration, and each bucket's contribution to duration, aggregated by sector and duration buckets. For this example, the short-, mid-, and long-duration buckets are defined as follows:[1]

Bucket	Duration
Short	Less than or equal to 5
Mid	Greater than 5 and less than or equal to 10
Long	Greater than 10

---

[1]Note that the practitioner should take care when selecting the upper and lower bands of each duration bucket. By grouping bonds of different durations in the same bucket, one is measuring the combined impact of those bonds relative to the combined impact of similar bonds in the benchmark. In this example (Exhibit 6 and the related discussion), for instance, a bond with a duration of 5.5 is treated the same as a bond with a duration of 9.5 in terms of its relative impact on the portfolio versus its benchmark.

EXHIBIT 6   Sample Exposure Decomposition: Relative Positions of Portfolio and Benchmark

Portfolio Weights	Short	Mid	Long	Total
Government	10.00%	10.00%	20.00%	40.00%
Corporate	10.00%	20.00%	30.00%	60.00%
Total	20.00%	30.00%	50.00%	100.00%

Benchmark Weights	Short	Mid	Long	Total
Government	20.00%	20.00%	15.00%	55.00%
Corporate	15.00%	15.00%	15.00%	45.00%
Total	35.00%	35.00%	30.00%	100.00%

Portfolio Weights	Short	Mid	Long	Total
Government	10.00%	10.00%	20.00%	40.00%
Corporate	10.00%	20.00%	30.00%	60.00%
Total	20.00%	30.00%	50.00%	100.00%

Benchmark Weights	Short	Mid	Long	Total
Government	20.00%	20.00%	15.00%	55.00%
Corporate	15.00%	15.00%	15.00%	45.00%
Total	35.00%	35.00%	30.00%	100.00%

Portfolio Duration	Short	Mid	Long	Total
Government	4.42	7.47	10.21	8.08
Corporate	4.40	7.40	10.06	8.23
Total	4.41	7.42	10.12	8.17

Benchmark Duration	Short	Mid	Long	Total
Government	4.42	7.47	10.21	7.11
Corporate	4.40	7.40	10.06	7.29
Total	4.41	7.44	10.14	7.19

Portfolio Returns	Short	Mid	Long	Total
Government	-3.48%	-5.16%	-4.38%	-4.35%
Corporate	-4.33%	-6.14%	-5.42%	-5.48%
Total	-3.91%	-5.81%	-5.00%	-5.03%

Benchmark Returns	Short	Mid	Long	Total
Government	-3.48%	-5.16%	-4.38%	-4.34%
Corporate	-4.33%	-6.14%	-5.86%	-5.44%
Total	-3.84%	-5.58%	-5.12%	-4.83%

Portfolio Contribution to Duration	Short	Mid	Long	Total
Government	0.44	0.75	2.04	3.23
Corporate	0.44	1.48	3.02	4.94
Total	0.88	2.23	5.06	8.17

Benchmark Contribution to Duration	Short	Mid	Long	Total
Government	0.88	1.49	1.53	3.91
Corporate	0.66	1.11	1.51	3.28
Total	1.54	2.60	3.04	7.19

Portfolio Contribution to Return	Short	Mid	Long	Total
Government	-0.35%	-0.52%	-0.88%	-1.74%
Corporate	-0.43%	-1.23%	-1.63%	-3.29%
Total	-0.78%	-1.74%	-2.50%	-5.03%

Benchmark Contribution to Return	Short	Mid	Long	Total
Government	-0.70%	-1.03%	-0.66%	-2.39%
Corporate	-0.65%	-0.92%	-0.88%	-2.45%
Total	-1.35%	-1.95%	-1.54%	-4.83%

From Exhibit 6, we can make the following inferences regarding the manager's investment decisions:

- With a higher duration than the benchmark (8.17 compared with 7.19 for the benchmark), the manager likely expected the rates to fall and took a bullish position on long-term bonds (interest rates) by increasing exposure to the long end of the interest rate curve (e.g., investing 50% of the portfolio in the longest-duration bucket versus 30% for the benchmark).
- Based on the overweight in the corporate sector (60% versus the 45% benchmark weight), the manager likely expected credit spreads to narrow.[2] Notice that this bet increases the 4.94 contribution to duration of the corporate sector in the portfolio compared with the 3.28 contribution to duration for the benchmark. This allocation makes the portfolio more exposed to market yield fluctuations in the corporate sector.
- The total portfolio return is –5.03%, relative to a total benchmark return of –4.83%, showing an underperformance of –0.20% over the period.

We can then use the portfolio and benchmark information from Exhibit 6 to calculate the portfolio's attribution results. These results are summarized in Exhibit 7. (Note that candidates are expected to be able to interpret, but not calculate, these results.)

Total interest rate allocation is the contribution from active management resulting from the manager's active exposures to changes in the level and shape of the yield curve. This can be decomposed into the duration effect (the contribution to active management from taking a different-from-benchmark aggregate duration position) and the curve effect (the specific points along the yield curve at which the manager made his benchmark-relative duration bets).

Sector allocation measures the effect of the manager's decision to overweight corporate bonds, whereas the selection effect measures the impact of the manager's decision to hold non-benchmark bonds in the portfolio. The hypothetical portfolio underlying this example contains only one bond that is not in the benchmark—a long-duration corporate bond, Corp. (P). Accordingly, there is no selection effect in the other duration buckets.

EXHIBIT 7   Sample Exposure Decomposition: Attribution Results

Duration Bucket	Sector	Duration Effect	Curve Effect	Total Interest Rate Allocation	Sector Allocation	Bond Selection	Total
Short	Government					0.00%	0.00%
	Corporate				0.04%	0.00%	0.04%
	Total	*0.40%*	*0.12%*	*0.52%*	*0.04%*	*0.00%*	***0.56%***
Mid	Government					0.00%	0.00%
	Corporate				–0.05%	0.00%	–0.05%
	Total	*0.23%*	*0.03%*	*0.26%*	*–0.05%*	*0.00%*	***0.21%***
Long	Government					0.00%	0.00%
	Corporate				–0.22%	0.13%	–0.09%
	Total	*–1.25%*	*0.37%*	*–0.88%*	*–0.22%*	*0.13%*	***–0.97%***
Total		**–0.62%**	**0.52%**	**–0.10%**	**–0.23%**	**0.13%**	**–0.20%**

---

[2]If corporate yields were at a historically large spread with respect to governments, the overweight to corporates might also have been a yield bet. Even if spreads do not narrow, the higher-yielding corporates are likely to outperform the government bonds in the portfolio.

Using the results from Exhibit 7, we can draw the following conclusions about the investment decisions made by this manager:

- The portfolio underperformed its benchmark by 20 bps.
- 62 bps were lost by taking a long-duration position during a period when yields increased (benchmark returns were negative in each duration bucket).
- 52 bps were gained as a result of changes in the shape of the yield curve. Given the manager's overweighting in the long-duration bucket, we can infer that the yield curve flattened.
- 23 bps were lost because the manager overweighted the corporate sector during a period when credit spreads widened (the benchmark corporate returns in each duration bucket were less than the government returns in those same duration buckets).
- 13 bps were added through bond selection.

Exhibit 8 provides an example of a sample duration-based yield curve decomposition attribution analysis. Again, we do not include the calculations for this analysis but instead present the results and suggested interpretations.

EXHIBIT 8   Yield Curve Decomposition—Duration Based: Active Return Contribution

Bond	Yield	Roll	Shift	Slope	Curvature	Spread	Specific	Residual	Total
Gov't. 5% 30 June 21	−0.19%	−0.04%	0.43%	0.01%	0.15%	0.00%	0.00%	−0.01%	0.35%
Gov't. 7% 30 June 26	−0.22%	−0.03%	0.71%	0.04%	0.04%	0.00%	0.00%	−0.03%	0.52%
Gov't. 6% 30 June 31	0.12%	0.01%	−0.48%	0.05%	0.09%	0.00%	0.00%	−0.01%	−0.22%
Corp. 5% 30 June 21	−0.11%	−0.02%	0.21%	0.05%	0.05%	0.04%	0.02%	−0.02%	0.22%
Corp. 7% 30 June 26	0.12%	0.01%	−0.35%	−0.02%	−0.02%	−0.07%	0.00%	0.02%	−0.31%
Corp. (B) 6% 30 June 31	−0.39%	−0.03%	1.41%	−0.26%	−0.11%	0.30%	0.00%	−0.04%	0.88%
Corp. (P) 6% 30 June 31	0.78%	0.06%	−2.82%	0.52%	0.33%	−0.60%	0.15%	−0.05%	−1.63%
Total	0.11%	−0.04%	−0.89%	0.39%	0.53%	−0.33%	0.17%	−0.14%	−0.20%
	Time:	0.08%	Curve Movement:	0.03%					

Note: There may be minor differences due to rounding in this table.

Using the data from Exhibits 6 and 8, we can infer the following about the portfolio investment process over this period:

- *Yield*: The portfolio overweighted corporate bonds and longer-term maturities relative to the benchmark (from Exhibit 6), which generally offer higher yield than government bonds and short-term maturities. This decision contributed 11 bps to the excess return (from Exhibit 8).
- *Roll*: The portfolio overweighted longer maturities (from Exhibit 6). Because of the shape of the yield curve, bonds with longer maturities generally sit on a flatter part of the yield curve, where the roll return is limited. The overweighting of the longer maturities reduced the portfolio roll return by 4 bps.
- *Shift*: The portfolio overall duration of 8.17 is greater than the benchmark duration of 7.19 (from Exhibit 6), which reduced the portfolio return by 89 bps.

- *Slope*: The slope flattening caused the long-term yields to increase less than yields on shorter terms to maturity. The overweight at the long end of the curve contributed 39 bps to the excess return.
- *Curvature*: The reshaping of the yield curve resulted in a larger yield increase at the five-year maturity point. The manager underweighted that part of the yield curve. This decision contributed 53 bps to the excess return.
- *Spread*: The manager overweighted the corporate sector, which resulted in a 33 bp reduction in return because corporate spreads widened.
- *Specific spread*: Looking at the bond-specific spreads in Exhibit 8, the corporate 5% 30 June 2021 bond added 2 bps of selection return and the corporate (P) 6% 30 June 2031 bond added 15 bps of selection return. These decisions added a total of 17 bps to active return.
- *Residual*: A residual of −0.14% is unaccounted for because duration and convexity can only *estimate* the percentage price variation. It is not an accurate measure of the true price variation. The residual becomes more important during large yield moves, which is the case here, with a +1% yield shift.

EXAMPLE 6   Fixed-Income Return Attribution

Use the data in Exhibits 7 and 8 to answer the following questions.

1. Which decision had the most positive effect on the overall performance of the portfolio?
   A. Taking a long-duration position
   B. Security selection of bond issues
   C. Overweighting the long end of the yield curve

2. Explain the contribution of the long-duration bucket to overall portfolio performance.

Solution to 1: C is correct: 52 bps were gained by overweighting the long end of the yield curve during a period when the slope of the yield curve flattened.

Solution to 2: The long-duration bucket cost the portfolio 97 bps of relative return. From Exhibit 7, the curve and selection effects were positive (37 bps and 13 bps, respectively) whereas the duration and sector allocation effects were negative (−125 bps and −22 bps, respectively). The negative duration effect indicates that the manager took a longer-than-benchmark-duration position in the long-duration bucket, a decision that hurt performance because interest rates rose. The positive curve effect implies that the manager's specific positioning along the long end of the yield curve benefited from changes in the shape of the yield curve. This implication is further supported by the positive slope effect shown in Exhibit 8. Taken together, the duration and curve effects accounted for the majority of the manager's underperformance relative to the benchmark. In the long-duration bucket, the manager overweighted corporate bonds relative to the benchmark. This decision penalized returns because credit spreads widened, which can be inferred from the weaker performance of the long-duration corporate segment of the benchmark (–5.42%) relative to the long-duration government segment (–4.38%). The positive selection effect of 13 bps implies that the manager's specific bond selections added to return. This implication is supported by the specific spread contribution reflected in Exhibit 8.

3.2. Risk Attribution

Performance attribution, on its own, is typically insufficient to evaluate the investment process. In addition to performance, we need to understand the impact of exposure to risk by including risk attribution.

Risk attribution identifies the sources of risk in the investment process. For absolute mandates, it identifies the sources of portfolio volatility. For benchmark-relative mandates, it identifies the sources of tracking risk. Managers seek opportunities for profit by taking specific exposures to risk (e.g., portfolio volatility or tracking risk). Risk attribution identifies these risks taken and, together with return attribution, quantifies the contributions to both the return and risk of the investment manager's active decisions.

Risk attribution should reflect the investment decision-making process. Exhibit 9 classifies investment decision-making processes and suggests appropriate risk attribution approaches. The columns indicate whether the focus is absolute risk or benchmark-relative risk. The rows categorize investment decision-making processes as bottom up, top down, or factor based. A bottom-up approach focuses on individual security selection. Top-down approaches focus first on macro decisions, such as allocations to economic sectors, and then on security selection within sectors. A factor-based approach looks for profits by taking different-from-benchmark exposures to the risk factors believed to drive asset returns.

EXHIBIT 9   Selecting the Appropriate Risk Attribution Approach

| Investment Decision- | Type of Attribution Analysis | |
Making Process	Relative (vs. Benchmark)	Absolute
Bottom up	Position's marginal contribution to tracking risk	Position's marginal contribution to total risk
Top down	Attribute tracking risk to relative allocation and selection decisions	Factor's marginal contribution to total risk and specific risk
Factor based	Factor's marginal contribution to tracking risk and active specific risk	

For portfolios that are managed against benchmarks, a common measure of risk is tracking risk (TR), also often called tracking error. The objective of an attribution model for a benchmark-relative portfolio is to quantify the contribution of active decisions to TR. For bottom-up benchmark-relative investment processes, each position's marginal contribution to TR multiplied by its active weight gives the position's contribution to TR. For benchmark-relative top-down investment processes, the active return is explained first by the allocation decisions. Risk attribution, accordingly, will identify the total contribution of allocation and selection to TR.

For absolute mandates, the risk of the portfolio is explained by exposures to the market, size and style factors, and the specific risk due to stock selections. The attribution model quantifies the contribution of each exposure and of specific risk. Suppose that the manager follows an absolute bottom-up process where the measure of risk is the volatility (standard deviation) of returns. In this case, we want to measure the contribution of selection decisions to overall portfolio risk. To do this, we need to know the marginal contribution of each asset to the portfolio risk—the increase or decrease in the portfolio standard deviation due to a slight increase in the holding of that asset. If we know the marginal contribution of a security to absolute portfolio risk, we can then calculate the overall risk contribution of the portfolio manager's selection decisions.

In all cases, risk attribution explains only where risk was introduced into the portfolio. It needs to be combined with return attribution to understand the full impact of those decisions. For example, if a manager has added to excess return through asset allocation (e.g., positive return attribution allocation effect), we use risk attribution to understand whether those allocation decisions introduced additional risk. As such, risk attribution complements the return attribution by evaluating the risk consequences of the investment decisions.

EXAMPLE 7   Risk Attribution

Manager A is a market-neutral manager following a systematic investment approach, scoring each security on a proprietary set of risk factors. He seeks to maximize the portfolio score on the basis of the factor characteristics of individual securities. He has a hurdle rate of T-bills plus 5%.

Manager B has a strong fundamental process based on a comprehensive understanding of the business model and competitive advantages of each firm. He also uses sophisticated models to make explicit three-year forecasts of the growth of free cash flow to determine the attractiveness of each security's current valuation. His objective is to outperform the MSCI World ex-US Index by 200 bps.

Manager C specializes in timing sector exposure and generally avoids idiosyncratic risks within sectors. Using technical analyses and econometric methodologies, she produces several types of forecasts. The manager uses this information to determine appropriate sector weights. The risk contribution from any single sector is limited to 30% of total portfolio risk. She hedges aggregate market risk and seeks to earn T-bills plus 300 bps.

1. Which risk attribution approach is most appropriate to evaluate Manager A?
   A. Marginal contribution to total risk
   B. Marginal contribution to tracking risk
   C. Factor's marginal contributions to total risk and specific risk

2. Which risk attribution approach is most appropriate to evaluate Manager B?
   A. Marginal contribution to total risk
   B. Marginal contribution to tracking risk
   C. Factor's marginal contributions to total risk and specific risk

3. Which risk attribution approach is most appropriate to evaluate Manager C?
   A. Marginal contribution to total risk
   B. Marginal contribution to tracking risk
   C. Factor's marginal contributions to total risk and specific risk

Solution to 1: A is correct. Manager A is a bottom-up manager with an absolute return target. B is incorrect because tracking risk is not relevant to an absolute return mandate. C is incorrect because, as a market-neutral manager, Manager A is not seeking to take different-from-market exposures.

Solution to 2: B is correct. Manager B is a bottom-up manager with a relative return target. A and C are incorrect because they are best suited to absolute return mandates.

Solution to 3: C is correct. Manager C is a top-down manager with an absolute return target. A factor-based attribution is best suited to evaluate the effectiveness of the manager's sector decisions and hedging of market risk.

3.3. Return Attribution Analysis at Multiple Levels

To this point, the return attribution presented in the Brinson examples focused on the bottom-up approach, where we calculated attribution effects at security and sector levels and summed those effects to determine their impact at the total portfolio and fund levels. We can use a similar return attribution approach at multiple levels of the decision process to evaluate the impact of different decisions.

3.3.1. Macro Attribution—An Example

Consider an example in which the top level is the fund sponsor (e.g., a university endowment or a defined-benefit pension plan sponsor). At the fund sponsor level, the first decision might be to allocate a certain weight to asset classes—the strategic asset allocation. If the fund sponsor does not manage funds internally, it would delegate a second investment decision to the investment managers to decide on any tactical deviations from the strategic asset allocation. The sponsor might also select multiple portfolio managers to manage against specific mandates within a given asset class.

The attribution analysis that we use to determine the impact of these fund sponsor decisions is sometimes called macro attribution. The attribution of the individual portfolio manager decisions is sometimes called micro attribution.

Assume our hypothetical fund sponsor has the following total equity benchmark:

- 50% large-cap value equities
- 25% small-cap value equities
- 25% large-cap growth equities

The fund sponsor hires two investment managers to manage the equity portion of the fund. The Value Portfolio Manager manages the large-cap and small-cap value allocations, and the Growth Portfolio Manager manages the growth equity allocation. The investment returns are shown in Exhibit 10.

EXHIBIT 10   Performance of Value and Growth Equity Managers

	Fund Weight	Fund Return	Benchmark Weight	Benchmark Return
Total	**100%**	**0.95**	**100%**	**–0.03**
Value Portfolio Manager	78%	0.99	75%	0.32
Small-cap value equities	20%	2.39	25%	1.52
Large-cap value equities	58%	0.51	50%	–0.28
Growth Portfolio Manager	22%	0.82	25%	–1.08
Large-cap growth equities	22%	0.82	25%	–1.08

To evaluate the decisions of the fund sponsor, we perform a return Brinson–Fachler attribution analysis using the set of weight and return data in Exhibit 10. "Allocation" measures the tactical asset allocation decision of the sponsor against its own strategic benchmark. In this example, the fund sponsor overweighted value equities and underweighted growth equities. "Selection" measures the fund sponsor's manager selection decision: Did the selected managers add value relative to their assigned benchmarks?

For the decision to hire the Value Portfolio Manager, we would calculate the effects as follows:

$$\text{Allocation} = (78\% - 75\%)[0.32 - (-0.03)] = 0.01$$

- The fund sponsor overweighted value equities (78% − 75%).
- Value equities outperformed the fund's aggregate benchmark [0.32 − (−0.03)].
- The decision to overweight value equities added to portfolio return.

$$\text{Selection} + \text{Interaction} = [(75\%)(0.99 - 0.32)] + [(78\% - 75\%)(0.99 - 0.32)] = 0.52$$

- The value manager outperformed the value benchmark (0.99 − 0.32). Thus, the fund sponsor's manager selection decision, independent of the decision to overweight value equities, added value.
- The fund sponsor overweighted a manager who outperformed his benchmark [(78% − 75%)(0.99 − 0.32)]. This is the interaction effect. (For simplicity, we combine interaction with selection, rather than showing interaction separately. By combining with selection, we assume that the selection decisions include the interaction and leave the allocation decision separate.) The interaction effect was positive.

For the decision to hire the Growth Portfolio Manager, we would calculate the effects as follows:

$$\text{Allocation} = (22\% - 25\%)[-1.08 - (-0.03)] = 0.03$$

- The fund sponsor underweighted growth equities (22% − 25%)
- Growth equities underperformed the fund's aggregate benchmark (−1.08 versus −0.03)
- The decision to underweight growth equities added to portfolio return

Selection + Interaction = [(25%)(0.82 − (−1.08)] + [(22% − 25%)(0.82 − (−1.08)] = 0.42

- The growth manager outperformed the growth benchmark (+0.82 versus −1.08). Thus, the fund sponsor's manager selection decision, independent of the decision to underweight growth equities, added value.
- The fund sponsor underweighted a manager who outperformed his benchmark [(− 3%) (0.82 − (− 1.08)]. The interaction effect was negative.

The results are summarized in Exhibit 11.

EXHIBIT 11   Macro Attribution

Return Attribution (Plan Sponsor Level)	Selection + Interaction	Allocation	Total
Total	0.94	0.04	0.98
Value Portfolio Manager	**0.52**	**0.01**	**0.53**
Growth Portfolio Manager	**0.42**	**0.03**	**0.45**

Return attribution analysis is most often calculated with reference to the portfolio's agreed-upon benchmark. But it is entirely possible to attribute one portfolio against another when both are using the same or a similar investment strategy. The purpose of such analysis might be to explain an unexpected difference in return between two portfolios managed by the same portfolio manager using the same investment decision-making process.

3.3.2. Micro Attribution—An Example

Using the same return data, we now move to the next level of the investment decision-making process and will evaluate the impact of the portfolio managers' decisions on total fund performance. We calculate the return attribution effects using the Brinson–Fachler approach at the segment level (i.e., small-cap value, large-cap value, and large-cap growth):

$$\text{Allocation} = (w_i - W_i)(B_i - B)$$

$$\text{Selection} + \text{Interaction} = W_i(R_i - B_i) + (w_i - W_i)(R_i - B_i)$$

We calculate the attribution effects for the small-cap value equities:

$$\text{Allocation} = (20\% - 25\%)[1.52 - (-0.03)] = -0.08$$

$$\text{Selection} + \text{Interaction} = [(25\%)(2.39 - 1.52)] + [(20\% - 25\%)(2.39 - 1.52)] = 0.17$$

Using the same approach for large-cap value equities and large-cap growth equities yields the results shown in Exhibit 12. (Note that the numbers are rounded to two decimal places and may not sum because of this rounding.)

EXHIBIT 12   Segment-Level Return Attribution

Return Attribution (Segment Level)	Fund Weight	Selection + Interaction	Allocation	Total
Total	**100%**	**1.05**	**−0.07**	**0.98**
Value Portfolio Manager	78%	0.63	−0.10	0.53
Small-cap value equities	*20%*	*0.17*	*−0.08*	*0.10*
Large-cap value equities	*58%*	*0.46*	*−0.02*	*0.44*
Growth Portfolio Manager	22%	0.42	0.03	0.45
Large-cap growth equities	*22%*	*0.42*	*0.03*	*0.45*

In Exhibit 12, the attribution results in italics are calculated at the segment level. The attribution results at the next level above, the Value Portfolio Manager and Growth Portfolio Manager, are sums of the segment-level results. For example, the allocation effect for the Value Portfolio Manager is equal to the sum of the small-cap and large-cap segments: −0.08 + −0.02 = −0.10.

Summing up the segment-level results for each manager, we reach the following conclusions:

- The total outperformance at the overall fund level of 98 bps is almost entirely the result of positive security selection decisions (105 bps in total).
- The decision of the Value Portfolio Manager to underweight small cap in favor of large cap detracted from total fund performance because the small-cap value benchmark outperformed the total benchmark (1.52% versus −0.03%), leading to an allocation effect of −0.10.
- The large-cap value benchmark underperformed the total benchmark (−0.28% versus − 0.03%). Because the portfolio was underweight large-cap value, this led to a positive allocation effect of 0.03.
- In total, allocation decisions contributed −7 bps.

Note that in using the total fund benchmark in this analysis, we are evaluating the *impact* of the Value Portfolio Manager's decision on the performance of the total fund.

We can extend the attribution analysis down another level and examine the investment manager's results relative to the investment process. The manager may have an investment process that specifically targets country allocations.[3] At this level of analysis, the same allocation formula will calculate the impact of country allocation decisions within the manager's portfolio and the selection formula will calculate the impact of selection decisions within each country.

If the portfolio manager has an investment process that specifically targets sector allocations within each country, the allocation formula can be used to calculate the impact of sector selection decisions within countries and the selection decisions within sectors.

Whatever the level of analysis, the return attribution must reflect the decision-making process of the portfolio manager. For example, a eurozone investment strategy might use a country allocation process with security selection within each country or a sector allocation

---

[3]For some portfolios, the next level may be asset classes (as an example).

process with security selection within each industrial sector. Exhibits 13 and 14 illustrate the different results that might be reached from an analysis based on the investment process. In each case, an arithmetic Brinson approach has been used.

EXHIBIT 13   Country Allocation

	Portfolio Weight	Benchmark Weight	Portfolio Return	Benchmark Return	Allocation	Selection
France	20%	30%	8.0%	6.0%	0.15%	0.40%
Germany	20%	35%	8.0%	7.0%	0.07%	0.20%
Holland	20%	10%	9.0%	15.0%	0.76%	−1.20%
Italy	30%	15%	10.0%	9.0%	0.23%	0.30%
Spain	10%	10%	3.0%	3.5%	0.00%	−0.05%
Total	100%	100%	8.3%	7.45%	1.20%	−0.35%

EXHIBIT 14   Industry Sector Allocation

	Portfolio Weight	Benchmark Weight	Portfolio Return	Benchmark Return	Allocation	Selection
Energy	25%	30%	18.0%	12.0%	−0.23%	1.50%
Health care	30%	20%	−3.0%	−6.0%	−1.35%	0.90%
Financial	20%	30%	10.0%	12.0%	−0.46%	−0.40%
Transportation	10%	15%	12.0%	8.0%	−0.03%	0.40%
Metals and mining	15%	5%	10.0%	5.0%	−0.25%	0.75%
Total	100%	100%	8.3%	7.45%	−2.30%	3.15%

Exhibit 13 suggests that the manager demonstrated good country allocation but negative security selection within countries, whereas Exhibit 14 suggests that the manager demonstrated poor sector allocation but strongly positive security selection within industrial sectors. This apparent "contradiction" illustrates the importance of designing an attribution approach around the investment decision-making process used by the manager.

Drilling down to the lowest level, the same allocation and selection formulas can be used to calculate the contribution of individual security decisions within sectors. For example, the allocation formula can be used to determine the impact of over- or underweighting individual securities, whereas the selection formula can be used to determine the contribution arising from a difference in the return of a security in the portfolio and the return of the same security in the benchmark. If the pricing sources used in the portfolio and the benchmark are identical, then any difference in return will be caused by transaction activity. Transaction activity because of trading expenses and bid–offer spreads will negatively affect returns, but occasionally because of timing, the portfolio manager may be able to trade at advantageous prices during the day and recover all the transaction costs by the end of the day, resulting in a positive effect.

Exhibit 15 shows the security-level return attribution effects for a small portfolio of oil stocks against a customized benchmark consisting of the same oil stocks. This approach would be used by a pure stock picker, the only decisions in the portfolio being individual stock weighting and timing decisions.

EXHIBIT 15   Security-Level Return Attribution Effects of Pure Stock Picker

	Portfolio Weight	Benchmark Weight	Portfolio Return	Benchmark Return	Allocation	Transaction Costs and Timing Effects
Chevron	24%	30%	10%	10%	–0.18%	0.00%
ConocoPhillips	21%	25%	8%	8%	–0.04%	0.00%
ExxonMobil	41%	35%	5%	6%	–0.06%	–0.41%
Marathon Oil	6%	5%	4%	4%	–0.03%	0.00%
Newfield Expl.	8%	5%	–5%	–5%	–0.36%	0.00%
Total	**100%**	**100%**	**5.97%**	**7.05%**	**–0.67%**	**–0.41%**

The arithmetic allocation effects of each security using the Brinson approach are as follows:

Chevron	(24% – 30%) × (10% – 7.05%) = –0.18%
ConocoPhillips	(21% – 25%) × (8.0% – 7.05%) = –0.04%
ExxonMobil	(41% – 35%) × (6.0% – 7.05%) = –0.06%
Marathon Oil	(6% – 5%) × (4.0% – 7.05%) = –0.03%
Newfield Exploration	(8% – 5%) × (–5.0% – 7.05%) = –0.36%

Allocation in this context measures the value added from individual security selection. Transactions occur for only one security during the period—ExxonMobil. Therefore, the only selection effects (transaction costs and timing) occur for this security. The calculation is as follows:

ExxonMobil   41% × (5.0% – 6.0%) = –0.41%

EXAMPLE 8   Macro Attribution

AAA Asset Management runs a fixed-income fund of funds. The fund's benchmark is a blended benchmark comprising 80% Bloomberg Barclays Global Aggregate Index and 20% Bloomberg Barclays Global Treasury Index (both in US dollars, unhedged). Two internal investment teams have been selected to manage the fund's assets. The allocations to the two products are determined by the firm's chief fixed-income strategist. The fund has underperformed its benchmark in each of the last three years. You are a member of the board of directors, which is meeting to determine what action should be taken. Based solely on the data in the table below, which of the following courses of action would you recommend? Justify your response.

A. Terminate the manager of Product A.
B. Terminate the manager of Product B.
C. Remove the chief fixed-income strategist as manager of the fund of funds.

	Fund-of-Funds Return			
	Year 1	Year 2	Year 3	Cumulative Return (Annualized)
Total Fund	3.72%	−3.00%	−0.13%	0.47%
Benchmark:	3.84%	−2.94%	0.07%	0.86%

	Product Returns					
	Year 1		Year 2		Year 3	
	Weight	**Return**	**Weight**	**Return**	**Weight**	**Return**
Product A	0.7	4.45%	0.75	−2.50%	0.8	−0.10%	1.74%
Benchmark: Bloomberg Barclays Global Aggregate		4.32%		−2.60%		0.29%	1.90%
Product B	0.3	2.00%	0.25	−4.50%	0.2	−0.25%	−2.83%
Benchmark: Bloomberg Barclays Global Treasury		1.93%		−4.30%		−0.79%	−3.22%

Solution: C is correct. Based solely on the information provided, the chief fixed-income strategist's allocation decision was the main driver of the fund's underperformance. Product A modestly underperformed its benchmark over the three-year period (−16 bps). Product B outperformed its benchmark (+39 bps). The strategist's allocation decisions were strongly negative in Years 1 and 2, when he overweighted the Treasury allocation and the Treasury index underperformed the aggregate fund benchmark. The results of the attribution analysis are shown below:

AAA Asset Management Fixed-Income Fund-of-Funds Attribution Analysis

	Year 1		Year 2		Year 3	
	Allocation	**Selection**	**Allocation**	**Selection**	**Allocation**	**Selection**
Product A	−0.05%	0.09%	−0.02%	0.07%	0.00%	−0.31%
Product B	−0.19%	0.02%	−0.07%	−0.05%	0.00%	0.11%
Total	−0.24%	0.11%	−0.09%	0.02%	0.00%	−0.20%

4. BENCHMARKING INVESTMENTS AND MANAGERS

An investment benchmark is typically a collection of securities that represents the pool of assets available to the portfolio manager. For example, an investor in Japanese small-cap stocks might have a benchmark consisting of a broad portfolio of small-cap Japanese equities. A benchmark should reflect the investment process and the constraints that govern the construction of the portfolio. If the benchmark does not reflect the investment process, then the evaluation and analysis that flow from the comparison with the benchmark are flawed.

Benchmarks communicate information about the set of assets that may be considered for investment and the investment discipline. They provide investment managers with a guidepost for acceptable levels of risk and return and can be a powerful influence on investment decision making.

In investment practice, we use benchmarks as

- reference points for segments of the sponsor's portfolio,
- communication of instructions to the manager,
- communication with consultants and oversight groups (e.g., a board of directors),
- identification and evaluation of the current portfolio's risk exposures,
- interpretations of past performance and performance attribution,
- manager selection and appraisal,
- marketing of investment products, and
- demonstrations of compliance with regulations, laws, or standards.

Benchmarks help analysts measure the effectiveness of a manager's decisions to depart from benchmark weights.

When considering benchmarks, we need to understand the differences between a "benchmark" and a "market index." A market index represents the performance of a specific security market, market segment, or asset class. For example, the FTSE 100 Index is constructed to represent the broad performance of large-cap UK equities. The S&P US Aggregate Bond Index is designed to measure the performance of publicly issued US dollar-denominated investment-grade debt. The constituents of these indexes are selected for their appropriateness in representing the target market, market segment, or asset class.

A market index may be considered for use as a benchmark or a comparison point for an investment manager. Consider the case of passive managers, who typically invest in portfolios designed to closely track the performance of market indexes. For example, the iShares Core S&P 500 ETF seeks investment results, before fees and expenses, that correspond to the price and yield performance of US large-cap stocks as represented by the S&P 500 Index. Because the investment objective of the iShares Core S&P 500 ETF is to track the performance of the S&P 500, the S&P 500 is the appropriate benchmark for the iShares Core S&P 500 ETF.

However, the most appropriate benchmark for an investment manager is not necessarily a market index. Many active managers follow specific investment disciplines that cannot be adequately described by a security market index. For example, market-neutral long–short managers typically have absolute return benchmarks—a specific minimum rate of return or a specified spread over a risk-free rate. Benchmarks must be suitable to the specific needs of the asset owner and any investment manager hired to manage money; market indexes are typically meant to serve the general public's purposes and to have broad appeal. Nonetheless, indexes can sometimes serve as valid benchmarks.

Another category of benchmarks is liability-based benchmarks, which focus on the cash flows that the asset must generate. Liability-based benchmarks are most often used when the assets are required to pay a specific future liability (e.g., as in a defined benefit pension plan). They allow the asset owner to track the fund's progress toward fully funded status (assets greater than or equal to liabilities) or, if fully funded, to track the performance of assets relative to the changes in liabilities. The performance relative to liabilities is important because it would be possible for the portfolio to outperform a market index but still not meet its liabilities. Furthermore, a market-value-weighted index would likely be an inappropriate benchmark because the liability often has a targeted asset allocation and risk exposures that are different from those of the index.

As an example, consider the fixed-income portion of a pension fund. A cap-weighted index is typically not a suitable benchmark because the duration of the index is usually shorter than the duration of most pension plans' liabilities. Furthermore, many fixed-income indexes are heavily weighted toward corporate bonds in the short maturities, which may represent a greater degree of credit risk than the plan desires. As an alternative, a well-diversified portfolio of individual bonds that minimizes idiosyncratic risk could be used as the benchmark. A more recent innovation is liability-driven investment (LDI) indexes. The Bloomberg Barclays LDI Index Series is a series of six investible indexes designed specifically for portfolios intended to hedge pension liabilities. However, they may not describe a plan's liability structure as accurately as a benchmark constructed specifically for the plan.

To best determine how a liability-based benchmark should be constructed, the manager first needs to understand the nature of the plan's liabilities and the plan's projected future cash flows. Although each plan will have its own unique characteristics, the following plan features will influence the structure of the liability:

- the average number of years to retirement in the workforce,
- the percentage of the workforce that is retired,
- the average participant life expectancy,
- whether the benefits are indexed to inflation,
- whether the plan offers an early retirement option,
- whether the sponsor could increase its plan contributions (e.g., whether the sponsor is profitable and diversified),
- the correlation between plan assets and the sponsoring company's operating assets (a lower correlation is desired so that the sponsor can make contributions when the plan requires funds), and
- whether the plan is a going concern (e.g., plans will eventually terminate if the sponsor has exited its business).

These characteristics influence the composition of the pension plan portfolio and hence its liability-based benchmark. Nominal bonds, real return bonds, and common shares are the assets most commonly found in liability-driven portfolios. The allocation to each asset class is driven by the proportion of accrued versus future obligations, whether the benefits are inflation indexed, and whether the plan is growing. A younger workforce means that more is allocated to equities. Greater inflation indexing of the benefits would imply more inflation-indexed bonds. If the fund's managers outperform the benchmark constructed according to these principles, the pension obligations should be met. Risk and noise that cannot be modeled in the benchmark may require additional future contributions.

EXAMPLE 9   Liability-Based Benchmarks

1. Which of the following portfolios is most likely to use a liability-based benchmark?
   A. A portfolio managed for a private client with a goal of capital appreciation
   B. An intermediate-duration fixed-income portfolio managed for a defined benefit pension fund
   C. The total portfolio for a defined benefit pension fund with an asset allocation of 80% fixed income/20% equity

2. Which of the following most accurately describes a liability-based benchmark?
   A. It focuses on the cash flows that the benchmarked asset must generate.
   B. It represents the performance of a specific security market, market segment, or asset class.
   C. It is a collection of securities that represents the pool of assets available to the portfolio manager.

Solution to 1: C is correct. A liability-based benchmark is most likely to be used for the total pension fund portfolio as the plan sponsor tracks its funded status.

Solution to 2: A is correct. A liability-based benchmark is constructed according to the cash flows that the benchmarked asset must generate.

4.1. Asset-Based Benchmarks

Benchmarks are an important part of the investment process for both institutional and private wealth clients. In the following discussion, we introduce the types of benchmarks based on the discussion in Bailey, Richards, and Tierney (2007). The seven types of benchmarks introduced in this section are

- absolute (including target) return benchmarks,
- broad market indexes,
- style indexes,
- factor-model-based benchmarks,
- returns-based (Sharpe style analysis) benchmarks,
- manager universes (peer groups), and
- custom security-based (strategy) benchmarks.

An **absolute return benchmark** is a minimum target return that the manager is expected to beat. The return may be a stated minimum (e.g., 9%), stated as a spread above a market index (e.g., the Euro Interbank Offered Rate + 4%), or determined from actuarial assumptions. An example of an absolute return benchmark is 20% per annum return for a private equity investment. Market-neutral long–short equity funds often have absolute return benchmarks. Such funds consist of long and short positions in perceived undervalued and overvalued equities. Overall, the portfolio is expected to be insensitive to broad equity market movements (i.e., market neutral with a market beta of zero). Therefore, market-neutral fund benchmarks may be specified as a three-month Treasury bill return; the investment objective is often to outperform the benchmark consistently by a given number of basis points.

Broad market indexes are measures of broad asset class performance, such as the JP Morgan Emerging Market Bond Index (EMBI) for emerging market bonds or the MSCI World Index for global developed market equities. Broad market indexes are well known, readily available, and easily understood. The performance of broad market indexes is widely reported in the popular media.

Market indexes have also been more narrowly defined to represent investment styles within asset classes, resulting in style indexes. An **investment style** is a natural grouping of investment disciplines that has some predictive power in explaining the future dispersion of returns across portfolios.[4] In the late 1970s, researchers found that stock valuation (e.g., the price-to-earnings ratio) and market capitalization explained much of stock return variation. In response, many index providers created various style versions of their broad market indexes (e.g., the Russell 2000 Value and Russell 1000 Growth Indexes).

Factor-model-based benchmarks can be constructed to more closely capture the investment decision-making process. Building a factor model identifies the relative explanatory powers of each factor in the portfolio return. Examples of factors include broad market index returns, industry exposure, and financial leverage. To determine the factor sensitivities, the portfolio's return is regressed against the factors believed to influence returns. The general form of a factor model is:

$$R_p = a_p + b_1F_1 + b_2F_2 \ldots b_kF_k + \varepsilon_p \tag{12}$$

where

R_p = the portfolio's periodic return

a_p = the "zero-factor" term, which is the expected portfolio return if all factor sensitivities are zero

b_k = the sensitivity of portfolio returns to the factor return

F_k = systematic factors responsible for asset returns

ε_p = residual return due to nonsystematic factors

The sensitivities (b_k) are then used to predict the return the portfolio should provide for given values of the systematic-risk factors. Earlier, we discussed the four-factor Carhart model, but any key element of the investment process can be considered for inclusion in a factor model. As an example, if the investment manager believes that interest rates are inversely related to security prices, then the model can incorporate an interest rate factor. If interest rates unexpectedly rise, then security returns can be expected to fall by an amount determined by the security's sensitivity (b_k) to interest rate changes.

Returns-based benchmarks (Sharpe style analysis) are like factor-model-based benchmarks in that portfolio returns are related to a set of factors that explain portfolio returns. With returns-based benchmarks, however, the factors are the returns for various style indexes (e.g., small-cap value, small-cap growth, large-cap value, and large-cap growth). The style analysis produces a benchmark of the weighted average of these asset class indexes that best explains or tracks the portfolio's returns. Unlike the investment-style indexes previously discussed, returns-based benchmarks *view style on a continuum*. For example, a portfolio may be characterized as 60% small-cap value and 40% small-cap growth. To create a returns-based benchmark using Sharpe style analysis, we use an optimization procedure to force the

---

[4]Brown and Goetzmann (1997).

portfolio's sensitivities (analogous to the b_k's in factor-model-based benchmarks) to be non-negative and sum to 1.

A **manager universe**, or **manager peer group**, is a broad group of managers with similar investment disciplines. Although not a benchmark, per se, a manager universe allows investors to make comparisons with the performance of other managers following similar investment disciplines. Managers are typically expected to beat the universe's median return. Manager universes are typically formed by asset class and the investment approach within that class.

Peer groups as benchmarks suffer from some significant weaknesses. Although managers within a peer group may all nominally be classified as "large-cap value" or "small-cap growth," for example, they may not truly be substitutable for one another. Some may have tilts or constraints that create an investment product very different from that of the median manager. A manager's ranking within the peer group might change considerably with very small changes in performance, often in response to factors outside of the manager's control: A change in the ranking may be driven not by something he did but by the actions of others in the peer group (e.g., other managers in the peer group may have chosen to overweight a "hot" sector, whereas the target manager's investment discipline constrains him from making a similar bet).

Lastly, **custom security-based benchmarks** are built to more precisely reflect the investment discipline of an investment manager. Such benchmarks are developed through discussions with the manager and an analysis of past portfolio exposures. After identifying the manager's investment process, the benchmark is constructed by selecting securities and weightings consistent with that process and client restrictions. If an allocation to cash is a key component of the investment process, an appropriate cash weight will be incorporated into the benchmark. The benchmark is rebalanced on a periodic basis to ensure that it stays consistent with the manager's investment practice. Custom security-based benchmarks are also referred to as *strategy benchmarks* because they should reflect the manager's strategy. Custom security-based benchmarks are particularly appropriate when the manager's strategy cannot be closely matched to a broad market index or style index. These benchmarks are costly to calculate and maintain.

4.2. Properties of a Valid Benchmark

The choice of benchmark often has a significant effect on the assessment of manager performance. Investment managers should be compared only with benchmarks that reflect the universe of securities available to them. A valid benchmark must satisfy certain criteria. We examine the characteristics of a valid benchmark by using the definitive list from Bailey and Tierney (1998).

- *Unambiguous*—The individual securities and their weights in a benchmark should be clearly identifiable. For example, we should be able to identify whether Nestlé is included in a global equity benchmark and its weight.
- *Investable*—It must be possible to replicate and hold the benchmark to earn its return (at least gross of expenses). The sponsor should have the option of moving assets from active management to a passive benchmark. If the benchmark is not investable, it is not a viable investment alternative.
- *Measurable*—It must be possible to measure the benchmark's return on a reasonably frequent and timely basis.

- *Appropriate*—The benchmark must be consistent with the manager's investment style or area of expertise.
- *Reflective of current investment opinions*—The manager should be familiar with the securities that constitute the benchmark and their factor exposures. Managers should be able to develop an opinion regarding their attractiveness as investments; they should not be given a mandate of obscure securities.
- *Specified in advance*—The benchmark must be constructed prior to the evaluation period so that the manager is not judged against benchmarks created after the fact.
- *Accountable*—The manager should accept ownership of the benchmark and its securities and be willing to be held accountable to the benchmark. The benchmark should be fully consistent with the manager's investment process, and the manager should be able to demonstrate the validity of his or her benchmark. Through acceptance of the benchmark, the sponsor assumes responsibility for any discrepancies between the targeted portfolio for the fund and the benchmark. The manager becomes responsible for differences between the benchmark and her performance.

The properties outlined by Bailey and Tierney help ensure that a benchmark will serve as a valid instrument for the purposes of evaluating the manager's performance. Although these qualities for a desirable benchmark may seem straightforward, we will show later that many commonly used benchmarks do not incorporate them.

EXAMPLE 10 Benchmarks

1. You have hired a bond manager to run an intermediate-duration government fixed-income portfolio. Which type of benchmark is most suitable for this portfolio?
   A. A broad market index
   B. A liability-based benchmark
   C. A factor-model-based benchmark

2. You have hired a top-down quantitative equity manager who has built a proprietary process based on timing the fund's exposures to systematic risks. Which type of benchmark is most suitable for this portfolio?
   A. A broad market index
   B. A liability-based benchmark
   C. A factor-model-based benchmark

3. You are on the board of a pension fund that is seeking to close the gap between its assets and its liabilities. What is the most appropriate benchmark against which to measure the performance of the plan's outsourced chief investment officer?
   A. A broad market index
   B. A liability-based benchmark
   C. A factor-model-based benchmark

4. You are a portfolio manager at JEMstone Capital. Your firm has been hired to run a global small-cap developed market equity portfolio. The agreement with the client sets a minimum market cap of US$500 million and a liquidity constraint that states that a portfolio holding is capped at 5 times its average daily liquidity over the past 12 months. Most portfolios managed by the firm are managed

without constraint against the MSCI ACWI Small Cap Index, which has an average market cap of approximately $1.2 billion and a median market cap of approximately $650 million. A stock is eligible for inclusion in the index if the shares traded over the prior three months are equal to at least 20% of the security's free-float-adjusted market capitalization.[5] Your team is discussing the suitability of the MSCI ACWI Small Cap Index for this portfolio. Discuss the validity of this benchmark using the Richards and Tierney framework.

Solution to 1: A is correct. A broad market index is a suitable benchmark for a government bond portfolio provided the maturity and duration characteristics of the benchmark align with those of the investment mandate.

Solution to 2: C is correct. Factors represent systematic risks. The manager's approach attempts to create alpha by timing the portfolio's exposure to factors. A factor-model-based benchmark can be constructed to represent the manager's investment approach.

Solution to 3: B is correct. The primary investment objective of the pension portfolio is to close the gap between assets and liabilities. The performance of the pension fund's manager should be evaluated relative to this objective.

Solution to 4:

- The benchmark meets the criteria of *unambiguous*. The individual securities and their weights are clearly identifiable.
- The benchmark most likely meets the criteria of *investable*. The shares in the index are freely tradeable.
- The benchmark meets the criteria of *measurable*. Index returns are published daily.
- The benchmark *does not* meet the criteria of *appropriate*. The liquidity and capitalization constraints imposed by the client are not consistent with the manner in which the manager runs other portfolios managed by the firm.
- The benchmark meets the criteria of *reflective of current investment opinions*. The benchmark was selected by the manager and is presumed to be representative of the manager's investment process.
- The benchmark meets the criteria of *specified in advance*. The benchmark is not created after the fact.
- The manager may choose to be *accountable* to this index if the liquidity and capitalization constraints are not expected to interfere with the ability to execute the investment strategy. The client should be made aware of the discrepancies between the portfolio constraints and the benchmark.

---

[5]This is a very abbreviated representation of the liquidity constraint used in the construction of the MSCI indexes. For a more complete description of the liquidity requirements, refer to "MSCI Global Investable Market Indexes Methodology": www.msci.com/eqb/methodology/meth_docs/MSCI_GIMIMethodology_Nov2018.pdf (accessed 5 December 2019).

4.3. Evaluating Benchmark Quality: Analysis Based on a Decomposition of Portfolio Holdings and Returns

Once a benchmark is constructed, we can evaluate its quality using tests. To understand these tests, it helps to first decompose the benchmark's returns. Using the decomposition from Bailey et al. (2007), we can first state the identity where a portfolio's return (P) is equal to itself:

$$P = P \qquad\qquad (13)$$

Then, add an appropriate benchmark (B) to, and subtract this benchmark from, the right-hand side of the equation:

$$P = B + (P - B) \qquad\qquad (14)$$

The term P – B is the result of the manager's active management decisions, which we denote as A. Thus, we have

$$P = B + A \qquad\qquad (15)$$

From Equations 13–15, we see that the portfolio return is a function of the benchmark and the manager's active decisions.

Next, add the market index return (M) to and subtract it from the right-hand side of the equation:

$$P = M + (B - M) + A \qquad\qquad (16)$$

The difference between the benchmark return and the market index (B – M) is the manager's style return, which we denote as S:

$$P = M + S + A \qquad\qquad (17)$$

Equation 17 states that the portfolio return (P) is a result of the market index return (M), a style return (S), and the active management return (A).

If the manager's portfolio is a broad market index where S = 0 and A = 0, then the portfolio earns the broad market return: P = M.

If the benchmark is a broad market index, then S is assumed to be zero and the prediction is that the manager earns the market return and a return to active management: P = M + A. However, if the benchmark is a broad market index and the manager *does* have style differences from the benchmark, the analysis using the broad market benchmark is incorrect. In this case, any style return (S) will be lumped together with the measured active management component (A), such that an analysis of a manager's true added value will be obscured.

We can use these benchmark building blocks to further search for systematic biases between the active management return and the style return, identified through correlation. For instance, if we measure the correlation between active management return, A = (P – B), and style return, S = (B – M), we can identify whether the manager's active selection decisions align with the style currently favored by the market. A good benchmark should not reflect these systematic biases, where the correlation between A and S should not be statistically different from zero. Likewise, we define the difference between the portfolio and the broad market index as E = (P − M). When a manager's style (S) is in (out of) favor relative to the market, we expect both the benchmark and the account to outperform (underperform) the market. Therefore, a good benchmark will have a statistically significant positive correlation coefficient between S and E.

EXAMPLE 11   Decomposition of Portfolio Return

1. Assume that the Courtland account has a return of −5.3% in a given month, during which the portfolio benchmark has a return of −5.5% and the market index has a return of −2.8%.
   A. Calculate the Courtland account's return due to the manager's style.
   B. Calculate the Courtland account's return due to active management.

2. Assume that Mr. Kuti's account has a return of 5.6% in a given month, during which the portfolio benchmark has a return of 5.1% and a market index has a return of 3.2%.
   A. Calculate the return due to the manager's style for Mr. Kuti's account.
   B. Calculate the return due to active management for Mr. Kuti's account.

3. An actively managed mid-cap value equity portfolio has a return of 9.24%. The portfolio is benchmarked to a mid-cap value index that has a return of 7.85%. A broad equity market index has a return of 8.92%. Calculate the return due to the portfolio manager's style.

4. A US large-cap value portfolio run by Anderson Investment Management returned 18.9% during the first three quarters of 2019. During the same time period, a US large-cap value index had a return of 21.7% and a broad US equity index returned 25.2%.
   A. Calculate the return due to style.
   B. Calculate the return due to active management.
   C. Using your answers to A and B, discuss Anderson's performance relative to the benchmark and relative to the market.

Solution to 1:

A. The return due to style is S = B − M = −5.5% − (−2.8%) = −2.7%.
B. The return due to active management is A = P − B = −5.3% − (−5.5%) = 0.2%.

Solution to 2:

A. The return due to style is S = B − M = 5.1% − 3.2% = 1.9%.
B. The return due to active management is A = P − B = 5.6% − 5.1% = 0.5%.

Solution to 3: The return due to style is the style-specific benchmark return of 7.85% minus the broad market return of 8.92%: −1.07%.

Solution to 4:

A. The return due to style is the difference between the benchmark and the market index, or S = (B − M) = (21.7% − 25.2%) = −3.5%.

B. The return due to active management is the difference between the portfolio and the benchmark, or A = (P − B) = (18.9% − 21.7%) = −2.8%.

C. Anderson's underperformance relative to the broad US equity index is partly a function of style and partly a function of the manager's weak performance within the style. Given that the US large-cap value index underperformed the US market index by 3.5%, we can infer that large-cap value was out of favor during the period measured. Provided the US large-cap value index is an appropriate benchmark for Anderson, the manager's underperformance bears further investigation. The client would want to understand the specific drivers of the underperformance and relate those decisions to the manager's stated investment process.

4.4. Benchmarking Alternative Investments

Performance evaluation for alternative asset classes presents many challenges. The selection of an appropriate benchmark is stymied by the lack of high-quality, investible market indexes, the frequent use of leverage in many strategies, the limited liquidity and lack of readily available market values for many underlying assets, and the use of internal rates of return rather than time-weighted rates of return.

In the following sections addressing each of the major alternative asset classes, we will consider how these challenges affect performance evaluation.

4.4.1. Benchmarking Hedge Fund Investments

Hedge funds do not represent an asset class, such as equities or fixed income. Rather, hedge funds encompass a broad range of possible strategies designed to exploit market inefficiencies. Hedge funds may have an unlimited investment universe, vary substantially from one to another, and can vary their asset allocations over time. Hedge funds also use leverage, sell assets short, take positions in derivatives, and may be opportunistic in their choice of strategy. These characteristics make it difficult to create a single standard against which hedge funds should be judged.

Some hedge funds lever many times their capital base, which increases their expected return and risk. Short positions and derivatives used in long–short strategies can increase return or reduce risk. A manager's use of style, leverage, short positions, and derivatives may change over time. Hedge funds also typically lack transparency, are difficult to monitor, and are often illiquid.

These characteristics of hedge funds make it clear that broad market indexes are unsuitable as hedge fund benchmarks.

The risk-free rate (e.g., Libor) plus a spread (e.g., 3%–6%) is sometimes advocated as a hedge fund benchmark for arbitrage-based hedge fund strategies. The argument for using the risk-free rate is that investors desire a positive return and that arbitrage strategies are risk free, with the spread reflecting the active management return and management costs.

However, most funds, even those that target market-neutral strategies, are not completely free of systematic risk, and the use of leverage could magnify that systematic risk. In this case, the spread relative to the risk-free rate should be adjusted upward.

Both broad market indexes and the risk-free rate will be weakly correlated or uncorrelated with hedge fund returns, thus failing the benchmark quality test of Bailey et al. (2007) that states that portfolio and benchmark factor sensitivities should be similar.

Because of the shortcomings of broad market indexes and the risk-free rate, hedge fund manager universes from such providers as CSFB/Tremont are often used as hedge fund benchmarks. Hedge fund peer universes are subject to a number of limitations:

1. The risk and return characteristics of a strategy peer group is unlikely to be representative of the approach taken by a single fund.
2. Hedge fund peer groups suffer from survivorship and backfill bias. Backfill bias occurs when the index provider adds a manager to the index and imports the manager's entire return history.
3. Hedge fund performance data are often self-reported and typically not confirmed by the index provider. A fund's reported net asset value may be a managed value. Even if the manager has no intention to misreport the data, hedge funds hold illiquid assets that require some subjectivity in pricing. If the previous period's price is used as the current price or an appraisal is used, then the data will be smoothed. The presence of stale pricing will result in downward-biased standard deviations and temporal instability in correlations, with hedge funds potentially given larger portfolio allocations as a result.

4.4.2. Benchmarking Real Estate Investments

There are numerous private real estate indexes offered by industry associations, large and small index providers, investment consultants, and others who collect real estate data. There are indexes and sub-indexes for nearly all the major developed countries, major sectors, investment styles, and structures (open-end and closed-end funds). Choosing the appropriate real estate benchmark requires careful consideration and an understanding of the limitations of such benchmarks—and their relevance to the investment strategy under evaluation. The following are some limitations of the available real estate benchmarks:

1. The benchmarks are based on a subset of the real estate opportunity set and, therefore, are not fully representative of the asset class.
2. Index performance is likely to be highly correlated with the returns of the largest fund data contributors.
3. Benchmark returns are based on manager-reported performance and may be inherently biased.
4. Benchmarks weighted by fund or asset value may place a disproportionate emphasis on the most expensive cities and asset types.
5. Valuations of the underlying properties are typically based on appraisals because there are few transactions to measure. Appraisals are infrequent, they smooth changes in property values, and they can lag underlying property performance. Transaction-based indexes are becoming more readily available.
6. Some benchmark returns are unlevered, whereas others contain varying degrees of leverage based on the structure used by the investor that contributed the data.

7. Real estate indexes do not reflect the high transaction costs, limited transparency, and lack of liquidity that drive performance for actual real estate investments.

Further complicating the performance evaluation of real estate funds is the selection of the appropriate return measure. Open-end funds, for which the contributions and withdrawals are at the discretion of the investor, generally use time-weighted rates of return. Closed-end funds, however, for which the timing of the contributions and withdrawals is at the discretion of the fund manager, generally report using internal rates of return.

4.4.3. Benchmarking Private Equity

When measuring the performance of a private equity investment, investors typically calculate an internal rate of return (IRR) based on cash flows since inception of the investment and the ending valuation of the investment (the net asset value or residual value). Similarly, major venture capital benchmarks, such as those of Cambridge Associates, provide IRR estimates for private equity funds that are based on fund cash flows and valuations. Major indexes serving as benchmarks for US and European private equity include those provided by Cambridge Associates, Preqin, and LPX.

These benchmarks can be used to compare the managers' individual funds with an appropriate peer group, normally defined by subclass, geography, and vintage year of the underlying fund. Benchmarks commonly used for this purpose include ones prepared by Burgiss, Cambridge Associates, and the Institutional Limited Partners Association.

Although relative performance measures help an investor understand how a fund performs relative to peers or a relevant public index, there are several limitations to be aware of when comparing returns among managers:

1. The valuation methodology used by the managers may differ.
2. A fund's IRR can be meaningfully influenced by an early loss or an early win in the portfolio.
3. The data are from a specific point in time, and the companies in a fund can be at different stages of development.

The public market equivalent (PME) methodology has been developed to allow comparisons of private equity IRRs with returns of publicly traded equity indexes. The methodology uses cash flow data to replicate the general partner's capital calls and distributions, assuming these same cash flows were invested in the chosen equity index. Comparing the performance of the PME index with the net IRR of the fund reveals the extent of over- or underperformance of the PME index relative to the public index. Several PME methodologies exist, the most common being Long–Nickels PME, PME+, Kaplan and Schoar PME, and Direct Alpha PME. It is important to choose the appropriate PME for each private equity fund; a poorly chosen PME raises the risk of leading the investor to an incorrect conclusion.

4.4.4. Benchmarking Commodity Investments

Commodity benchmarks tend to use indexes based on the performance of futures-based commodity investments. These include the Reuters/Jefferies Commodity Research Bureau (RJ/CRB) Index, the S&P Goldman Sachs Commodity Index (GSCI), and the Bloomberg Commodity Index (BCOM). However, because the indexes use futures, rather than actual assets, they attempt to replicate the returns available to holding long positions in commodities. The S&P GSCI, the BCOM, and the RJ/CRB Index provide returns comparable to those of passive long positions in listed futures contracts. Because the cost-of-carry model ensures that the return on a fully margined position in a futures contract mimics the return on an underlying spot deliverable, futures contract returns are often used as a surrogate for cash market performance.

These indexes are considered investable. The major indexes contain some common groups of underlying assets. For example, the RJ/CRB Index, the BCOM, and the S&P GSCI all include energy (oil and gas), metals (industrial and precious), grains (corn, soybeans, and wheat), and soft commodities (cocoa, coffee, cotton, and sugar). However, beyond these basic groupings, they and other commodity indexes vary greatly in their composition and weighting schemes. A market-cap-weighting scheme, so common for equity and bond market indexes, cannot be carried over to indexes of commodity futures. Because every long futures position has a corresponding short futures position, the market capitalization of a futures contract is always zero.

Benchmarking of commodity investments presents similar challenges to other alternatives, including

1. the use of derivatives to represent actual commodity assets,
2. varying degrees of leverage among funds, and
3. the discretionary weighting of exposures within the index.

4.4.5. Benchmarking Managed Derivatives

Because market indexes do not exist for managed derivatives, the benchmarks are typically specific to a single investment strategy. For example, the Mount Lucas Management Index takes both long and short positions in many futures markets based on a technical (moving-average) trading rule that is, in effect, specific to an active momentum strategy.

Other derivative benchmarks are based on peer groups. For example, the BarclayHedge and CISDM CTA trading strategy benchmarks are based on peer groups of commodity trading advisers (CTAs). The CISDM CTA Equal Weighted Index reflects manager returns for all reporting managers in the CISDM CTA database. These indexes suffer from the known limitations of peer group–based benchmarks, including survivorship bias.

4.4.6. Benchmarking Distressed Securities

Distressed securities are illiquid and almost non-marketable at the time of purchase, making it very difficult to find suitable benchmarks. If the companies' prospects improve, the values of the distressed securities may go up gradually and liquidity may improve. Typically, it takes a relatively long time for this strategy to play out; thus, valuing the holdings may be a challenge. It is difficult to estimate the true market values of distressed securities, and stale pricing is almost inevitable.

One possible strategy is to use market indexes, such as the Barclay Distressed Securities Index. This index is constructed from fund managers who invest in distressed securities. Because this index is constructed from multiple strategies, however, it is difficult to discern whether the index is suitable for a given investment approach. In addition, because the valuations for the member funds are calculated at random intervals, it doesn't necessarily correct for the valuation issues noted previously.

4.5. Importance of Choosing the Correct Benchmark

As we have described, performance evaluation and attribution require appropriate benchmarks. When benchmarks are misspecified, subsequent performance measurement will be incorrect; both the attribution and the appraisal analyses will be useless.

For example, consider a manager who invests in Japanese stocks. The sponsor uses the MSCI Pacific Index to evaluate the manager. Japanese stocks constitute most of the MSCI Pacific, but the index also includes four other developed markets (Australia, New Zealand, Hong Kong SAR, and Singapore). Thus, the MSCI Japan Index more closely represents the manager's normal portfolio. The 2018 returns are as follows:

- Manager return: 24.5%
- MSCI Pacific (investor's benchmark) return: 25.0%
- MSCI Japan (normal portfolio) return: 24.0%

Although the manager *underperformed* the investor's benchmark (24.5% for the manager versus 25.0% for the MSCI Pacific), the manager *outperformed* when correctly benchmarked against the normal portfolio (24.5% for the manager versus 24% for the normal portfolio). In summary,

- the manager's "true" active return is 24.5% − 24.0% = 0.5%, and
- the manager's "misfit" active return is 24% − 25% = –0.5%.

Measuring the manager's results against the normal portfolio instead of the investor's benchmark more accurately evaluates the manager's performance. The manager's negative "true" active return indicates that the manager outperformed the normal portfolio. Fundamentally, any further performance attribution against the investor's benchmark will also be useless. By using the incorrect benchmark, the attribution would attempt to explain an underperformance, rather than the true active return, which contributed positively to the investor's return.

Peer group benchmarking is particularly susceptible to selection problems. For example, practitioners must select the appropriate peers without suggesting to the portfolio managers that median peer group performance is the target. Peer group benchmarks provide an incentive not to underperform the peer group median, often leading to herding around the median return. As a result, the investment decisions of the fund manager can be biased by the structure of the benchmarks chosen.

Sometimes, benchmarks are chosen for the wrong reasons. Underperforming managers have been known to change benchmarks to improve their measured excess return, which is both inappropriate and unethical.

Benchmark misspecification can lead to mismeasurement of the value added by the portfolio managers. A "normal portfolio" or "normal benchmark" is the portfolio that most closely represents the manager's typical positions in his investment universe. The manager's "true" active return is equal to his return minus his normal portfolio return.

Most investors, however, tend to use a broad market benchmark for manager evaluation. The manager's active return is thus measured as the manager's return minus the investor's benchmark return. There is a mismatch between the broad market benchmark and the manager's "normal" portfolio or benchmark; this is not the manager's "true" active return but is more appropriately termed the "misfit active return" (see, e.g., Gastineau, Olma, and Zielinski 2007). Using a broad market index typically misses the manager's style (i.e., creates style bias). This decomposition is useful for understanding the impact of a misspecified benchmark on performance appraisal.

For example, consider a manager who invests in US value stocks. The sponsor uses the broad Russell 3000 equity index (the "investor's benchmark") to evaluate the manager. However, the manager's normal portfolio is better represented by his or her universe of value stocks. In this example, the manager returns 15%, the Russell 3000 (the investor's benchmark) return is 10%, and the manager's normal portfolio return is 18%. Although the manager has outperformed the investor's benchmark (15% versus 10%), the manager has underperformed when correctly benchmarked against the normal portfolio (15% versus 18%).

5. PERFORMANCE APPRAISAL

Investment performance appraisal identifies and measures investment skill, providing the information to assess how effectively money has been invested given the risks that were taken. (Risk-adjusted past performance is just one of many considerations when choosing investment managers. Qualitative considerations, although not within the scope of this chapter, are also very important.)

Performance appraisal is most often concerned with ranking investment managers who follow similar investment disciplines. Return attribution provides information that can complement a performance appraisal analysis by providing more details about the consequences of managerial decisions. Performance attribution identifies and quantifies the sources of added value, whereas performance appraisal seeks to ascertain whether added value was a result of managerial skill.

Skill in any profession can be thought of as the ability to influence outcomes in desired directions. We define active investment management skill as the ability of a portfolio manager to add value on a risk-adjusted basis through investment analysis and insights. In everyday language, active investment skill is typically viewed as the ability to "beat the market" or an assigned benchmark with some consistency. The evaluation of active management skill is the focus of performance appraisal and this chapter.

5.1. Distinguishing Investment Skill from Luck

An investment manager's record for any specific period will reflect good luck (unanticipated good developments) and bad luck (unanticipated bad developments). One reason that luck should be considered important when appraising investment performance is the paradox of skill. As people become more knowledgeable about an activity, the difference between the worst and the best performers becomes narrower. Thus, the ever-increasing aggregate skill level of investment managers, supplemented by massive computing power and access to "big data," may lead to narrower investment performance differentials and a greater likelihood that these differentials can be explained by luck.

Deciding whether a portfolio manager has or lacks active investment skill on the basis of past returns is difficult and always subject to error. Financial market returns have a large element of randomness. Some of this randomness reflects the impact of news and information that relate directly or indirectly to asset values. Trading motivated by liquidity needs and by the emotions of investors adds to return volatility.

When we observe the historical performance of an investment portfolio, we see only one out of a potentially unlimited number of outcomes for a manager applying the same investment discipline but with different luck. Perhaps we gain additional insight into skill by examining the consistency of performance over time. But the hypothesis that the manager's underlying mean return exceeds the benchmark's mean return may require many years of observations to confirm with a reasonably high degree of confidence.[6]

5.2. Appraisal Measures

The academic and the professional investment literatures have developed several returns-based measures to assess the value of active management. Important measures include the following:

- Sharpe ratio
- Treynor ratio
- Information ratio
- Appraisal ratio
- Sortino ratio
- Capture ratios

The selection of an appropriate appraisal measure requires an understanding of which aspect of risk is most important given the role of the investment in the client's total portfolio. It is also important to understand the assumptions a measure makes about the probability distribution of possible returns and any assumptions regarding the underlying theoretical pricing model. The Sharpe, information, and Treynor ratios are covered elsewhere in the curriculum and are not covered in depth here. This section will focus primarily on the remaining measures.

5.2.1. The Sharpe Ratio

The **Sharpe ratio** measures the additional return for bearing risk above the risk-free rate, stated per unit of return volatility. In performance appraisal, this additional return is often referred to as **excess return**. This use contrasts with how "excess return" is used in return performance attribution—that is, as a return in excess of a benchmark's return.

The Sharpe ratio is commonly used on an *ex post* basis to evaluate historical risk-adjusted returns, as in

$$S_A = \frac{\overline{R}_A - \overline{r}_f}{\widehat{\sigma}_A} \tag{18}$$

One weakness of the Sharpe ratio is that the use of standard deviation as a measure of risk assumes investors are indifferent between upside and downside volatility. For example, for an investor looking for a potentially high-rewarding investment, volatility on the upside is

---

[6]Can you be lucky once and correctly pick the flip of a fair coin? Of course! How about four times in a row? Yes, although this outcome is much less likely. Can a portfolio manager be lucky enough to generate 15 continuous years of superior investment performance? This outcome is very unlikely, but with hundreds or even thousands of portfolio managers, a few might succeed solely because of luck. One problem faced in investment performance appraisal is that many investment management performance records are only a few years long, making it difficult to distinguish between luck and skill.

not necessarily a negative. Similarly, risk-averse investors concerned about the preservation of capital are clearly most concerned with downside risk.

5.2.2. The Treynor Ratio

The Treynor ratio (Treynor 1965) measures the excess return per unit of systematic risk. With the Treynor ratio, as well as the systematic-risk-based appraisal measures that follow, we must carefully choose an efficient market benchmark against which to measure the systematic risk of the manager's fund. In contrast, the Sharpe ratio can be compared among different funds without the explicit choice of a market benchmark.

$$T_A = \frac{\overline{R}_A - \overline{r}_f}{\hat{\beta}_A} \tag{19}$$

The usefulness of the Treynor ratio depends on whether systematic risk or total risk is most appropriate in evaluating performance. Because of its reliance on beta, the Treynor ratio shows how a fund has performed in relation not to its own volatility but to the volatility it would bring to a well-diversified portfolio. Thus, a ranking of portfolios based on the Treynor ratio is most useful if the portfolios whose performance is being evaluated are being combined in a broader, fully diversified portfolio. The ratio is most informative when the portfolios being evaluated are compared with the same benchmark index.

5.2.3. The Information Ratio

The information ratio (IR) is a simple measure that allows the evaluator to assess performance relative to the benchmark, scaled by risk. The implicit assumption is that the chosen benchmark is well matched to the risk of the investment strategy. The IR is calculated by dividing the portfolio's mean excess return relative to its benchmark by the variability of that excess return, as shown in Equation 18. The denominator of the information ratio, $\sigma(r_p - r_B)$, is the portfolio's tracking risk, a measure of how closely a portfolio follows the index to which it is benchmarked. (Many writers use "tracking error" in the sense of "tracking risk," although, confusingly, tracking error is also used to refer to simply the return difference between a passive portfolio and its benchmark.)

$$IR = \frac{E(r_p) - E(r_B)}{\sigma(r_p - r_B)} \tag{20}$$

5.2.4. The Appraisal Ratio

The appraisal ratio (AR) is a returns-based measure, like the IR. It is the annualized alpha divided by the annualized residual risk. In the appraisal ratio, both the alpha and the residual risk are computed from a factor regression. Although the AR can be computed using any factor model appropriate for the portfolio, the measure was first introduced by Treynor and Black (1973) using Jensen's alpha and the standard deviation of the portfolio's residual or non-systematic risk. Treynor and Black argued that security selection ability implies that deviations from benchmark portfolio weights can be profitable and showed that the optimal deviations from the benchmark holdings for securities depend on what they called an "appraisal ratio." The appraisal ratio is also referred to as the *Treynor–Black ratio* or the *Treynor–Black appraisal ratio*.

The appraisal ratio measures the reward of active management relative to the risk of active management (alpha from a factor model):

$$AR = \frac{\alpha}{\sigma_\varepsilon} \tag{21}$$

where σ_ε equals the standard deviation of ε_t, commonly denoted as the "standard error of regression," which is readily available from the output of commonly used statistical software.

5.2.5. The Sortino Ratio

The Sortino ratio is a modification of the Sharpe ratio that penalizes only those returns that are lower than a user-specified return. The Sharpe ratio penalizes both upside and downside volatility equally.

Equation 22 presents the *ex ante* Sortino ratio, where r_T is the minimum acceptable return (MAR), which is sometimes referred to as a *target rate of return*.[7] Instead of using standard deviation in the denominator, the Sortino ratio uses a measure of downside risk known as target semi-standard deviation or target semideviation, σ_D, as shown in Equation 23. By using this value, the Sortino ratio penalizes managers only for "harmful" volatility and is a measure of return per unit of downside risk.

$$SR_D = \frac{E(r_p) - r_T}{\sigma_D} \tag{22}$$

$$\widehat{SR}_D = \frac{\bar{r}_p - \bar{r}_T}{\widehat{\sigma}_D} \tag{23}$$

$$\sigma_D = \left[\frac{\sum_{t=1}^{N} \min(r_t - r_T, 0)^2}{N} \right]^{1/2} \tag{24}$$

Assume a portfolio has an MAR of 4.0%. The portfolio's returns over a 10-year period are given in Exhibit 16. The numerator of the Sortino ratio is the average portfolio return minus the target return: $\bar{r}_p - \bar{r}_T = 6.0\% - 4.0\% = 2.0\%$. The calculation of target semi-standard deviation is reported in Exhibit 16. Based on the information in the table, the Sortino ratio is approximately 0.65.

---

[7]The MAR is the lowest rate of return at which an investor will consider investing. For example, an MAR set equal to the expected rate of inflation would be associated with capital preservation in real terms. It is possible to use the benchmark return as the MAR. The MAR does not determine intrinsic value. Rather, it is a constraint or decision criterion that applies to all investment considerations.

EXHIBIT 16 Sortino Ratio Using Target Semi-Standard Deviation

Year	Rate of Return: r_t	Target Return: $r_T = 4\%$ $\min(r_t - r_T, 0)^2$
1	6.0%	0
2	8.0%	0
3	−1.0%	0.0025
4	18.0%	0
5	12.0%	0
6	3.0%	0.0001
7	−4.0%	0.0064
8	5.0%	0
9	2.0%	0.0004
10	11.0%	0

$$\sum_{t=1}^{N} \min(r_t - r_T, 0)^2 = 0.0094$$

$$\sigma_D = \left[\frac{\sum_{t=1}^{N} \min(r_t - r_T, 0)^2}{N} \right]^{1/2} \qquad = \left(\tfrac{0.0094}{10} \right)^{1/2} = 3.07\%$$

More so than traditional performance measures, the Sortino ratio offers the ability to accurately assess performance when return distributions are not symmetrical. For example, because of its underlying assumption of normally distributed returns, the Sharpe ratio would not effectively distinguish between strategies with greater-than-normal upside volatility (positively skewed strategies, such as trend following) and strategies with greater-than-normal downside volatility (negatively skewed strategies, such as option writing). Both types of volatility are penalized equally in the Sharpe ratio. The Sortino ratio is arguably a better performance metric for such assets as hedge funds or commodity trading funds, whose return distributions are purposefully skewed away from the normal.

The Sortino ratio formula is not a risk premium. It is the return a portfolio manager generates that is greater than what is minimally acceptable to the investor. Essentially, the Sortino ratio penalizes a manager when portfolio return is lower than the MAR; it is most relevant when one of the investor's primary objectives is capital preservation.

Although there are arguments in favor of both the Sharpe ratio and the Sortino ratio, the Sharpe ratio has been much more widely used. In some cases, this preference may reflect a certain comfort level associated with the use of standard deviation, which is a more traditional measure of volatility. Also, cross-sectional comparisons of Sortino ratios are difficult to make applicable to every investor, because the MAR is investor-specific.

EXAMPLE 12   Performance Appraisal Measures

1. Portfolio B delivered 10.0% annual returns on average over the past 60 months. Its average annual volatility as measured by standard deviation was 14.0%, and its downside volatility as measured by target semi-standard deviation was 8.0%. Assuming the target rate of return is 3.0% per year, the Sortino ratio of portfolio B is closest to:
   A. 0.66.
   B. 0.77.
   C. 0.88.

2. Why might a practitioner use the Sortino ratio, rather than the Sharpe ratio, to indicate performance?
   A. He is measuring option writing.
   B. The return distributions are not symmetrical.
   C. The investor's primary objective is capital preservation.
   D. All of the above

3. Portfolio Y delivered an average annualized return of 9.0% over the past 60 months. The annualized standard deviation over this same time period was 20.0%. The market index returned 8.0% per year on average over the same time period, with an annualized standard deviation of 12.0%. Portfolio Y has an estimated beta of 1.40 versus the market index. Assuming the risk-free rate is 3.0% per year, the appraisal ratio is *closest* to:
   A. −0.8492.
   B. −0.0922.
   C. −0.0481.

4. The appraisal ratio is the ratio of the portfolio's alpha to the standard deviation of its:
   A. total risk.
   B. systematic risk.
   C. non-systematic risk.

5. Portfolio C delivered an average annualized return of 11.0%, with an annualized standard deviation of 14.0% based on the past 60 months of data. The market index returned 12.0% per year over the same time period, with an annualized standard deviation of 16.0%. A market model regression estimates beta of 0.90 for Portfolio C, with an R^2 of 0.64. Assuming the risk-free rate is 3.0% per year, the appraisal ratio is *closest* to:
   A. −0.1701.
   B. −0.1304.
   C. −0.0119.

6. Assume a target return of 3.0%. Annual returns over the past four years have been 6.0%, −3.0%, 7.0%, and 1.0%. The target semi-standard deviation is *closest* to:
   A. 1.33%.
   B. 3.16%.
   C. 4.65%.

Solution to 1: C is correct.

$$\widehat{SR}_D = \frac{\bar{r}_p - \bar{r}_T}{\hat{\sigma}_D} = \frac{0.10 - 0.03}{0.08} = 0.88$$

Solution to 2: D is correct, because the Sortino ratio is more relevant when return distributions are not symmetrical, as with option writing. The Sortino ratio is also preferable when one of the primary objectives is capital preservation.

Solution to 3: B is correct. Jensen's alpha is –1.0%: $\alpha_p = 9.0\% - [3.0\% + 1.40(8.0\% - 3.0\%)] = -1.0\% = -0.01$. Non-systematic risk is 0.011776: $\sigma_{\varepsilon_p}^2 = 0.20^2 - 1.40^2(0.12^2) = 0.011776$. The appraisal ratio is approximately –0.0922: $\widehat{AR} = \frac{-0.01}{\sqrt{0.011776}} = -0.0922$.

Solution to 4: C is correct. The appraisal ratio is the ratio of the portfolio's alpha to the standard deviation of the portfolio's non-systematic risk. Essentially, this ratio allows an investor to evaluate whether excess returns warrant the additional non-systematic risk in actively managed portfolios.

Solution to 5: C is correct. Jensen's alpha is –0.10%: $\alpha_p = 11.0\% - [3.0\% + 0.90(12.0\% - 3.0\%)] = -0.10\% = -0.001$. Non-systematic risk is 0.007056: $\sigma_{\varepsilon_p}^2 = (1 - 0.64)0.14^2 = 0.007056$. The appraisal ratio is approximately –0.0119: $\widehat{AR} = \frac{-0.001}{\sqrt{0.007056}} = -0.0119$.

Solution to 6: B is correct.

Year	Rate of Return: r_t	Target Return: $r_T = 3\%$ $\min(r_t - r_T, 0)^2$
1	6.0%	0
2	–3.0%	0.0036
3	7.0%	0
4	1.0%	0.0004
$\sum_{t=1}^{N} \min(r_t - r_T, 0)^2 =$		0.004
$\sigma_D = \left[\dfrac{\sum_{t=1}^{N} \min(r_t - r_T, 0)^2}{N} \right]^{1/2} =$		$\left(\frac{0.004}{4}\right)^{1/2} \approx 0.0316 = 3.16\%$

5.2.6. Capture Ratios and Drawdowns

In investing, we understand that large losses require proportionally greater gains to reverse or offset. Performance measures used to monitor this aspect of manager performance include capture ratios and drawdowns. Capture ratios have several variations that reflect various aspects of the manager's gain or loss relative to the gain or loss of the benchmark. Capture ratios also help assess manager suitability relative to the investor, especially in relation to the investor's time horizon and risk tolerance. **Drawdown** is the loss in value incurred in any continuous period of negative returns. A manager who experiences larger drawdowns may be less suitable for an investor with a shorter time horizon. This section reviews capture ratios and drawdowns, their implications for performance, and their use in evaluating manager performance and suitability.

5.2.6.1. Capture Ratios

Capture ratios measure the manager's participation in up and down markets—that is, the manager's percentage return relative to that of the benchmark. The upside capture ratio, or upside capture (UC), measures capture when the benchmark return is positive. The downside capture ratio, or downside capture (DC), measures capture when the benchmark return is negative. Upside capture greater (less) than 100% generally suggests outperformance (underperformance) relative to the benchmark, and downside capture less (greater) than 100% generally suggests outperformance (underperformance) relative to the benchmark. Practitioners should note that when the manager and benchmark returns are of the opposite sign, the ratio will be negative—for example, a manager with a 1% return when the market is down 1% will have a downside capture ratio of –100%.

The expressions for upside capture and downside capture are

$$UC(m,B,t) = R(m,t)/R(B,t) \text{ if } R(B,t) \geq 0$$

$$DC(m,B,t) = R(m,t)/R(B,t) \text{ if } R(B,t) < 0$$

where

$UC(m,B,t)$ = upside capture for manager m relative to benchmark B for time t
$DC(m,B,t)$ = downside capture for manager m relative to benchmark B for time t
$R(m,t)$ = return of manager m for time t
$R(B,t)$ = return of benchmark B for time t

The upside/downside capture, or simply the capture ratio (CR), is the upside capture divided by the downside capture. It measures the asymmetry of return and, as such, is like bond convexity and option gamma. A capture ratio greater than 1 indicates positive asymmetry, or a convex return profile, whereas a capture ratio less than 1 indicates negative asymmetry, or a concave return profile. Exhibit 17 illustrates what is meant by concave and convex return profiles. The dotted-line curve for a concave return profile resembles a downward-facing bowl, and the solid-line curve for a convex return profile resembles an upward-facing bowl. The horizontal and vertical axes are, respectively, benchmark returns [$R(B)$] and portfolio returns [$R(m)$]. As benchmark returns increase (i.e., moving to the right on the horizontal axis), portfolio returns increase—but at a *decreasing* rate for a concave return profile and at an *increasing* rate for a convex return profile. The expression for the capture ratio is

$$CR(m,B,t) = UC(m,B,t)/DC(m,B,t)$$

where

$CR(m,B,t)$ = capture ratio for manager m relative to benchmark B for time t

EXHIBIT 17   Convex and Concave Return Profiles

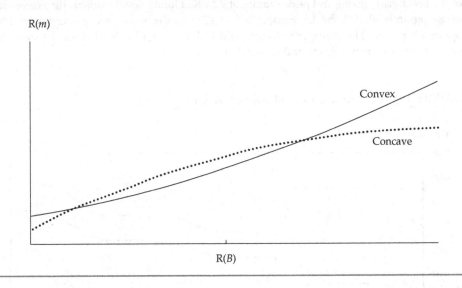

Consider the following return series for the manager, R(*m*), and the benchmark, R(*B*), shown in Exhibit 18. The upside columns calculate the cumulative return for the manager, Cum R(*m*), and the benchmark, Cum R(*B*), for those periods when the benchmark return is positive. The downside columns calculate the cumulative returns when the benchmark return is negative.

EXHIBIT 18   Capture Ratio

					Upside Return				Downside Return	
t	R(*m*)	R(*B*)	R(*m*)	R(*B*)	Cum R(*m*)	Cum R(*B*)	R(*m*)	R(*B*)	Cum R(*m*)	Cum R(*B*)
1	0.6%	1.0%	0.6%	1.0%	0.60%	1.00%			0.00%	0.00%
2	−0.3%	−0.5%			0.60%	1.00%	−0.3%	−0.5%	−0.30%	−0.50%
3	1.0%	1.5%	1.0%	1.5%	1.61%	2.52%			−0.30%	−0.50%
4	0.1%	0.2%	0.1%	0.2%	1.71%	2.72%			−0.30%	−0.50%
5	−1.0%	−2.0%			1.71%	2.72%	−1.0%	−2.0%	−1.30%	−2.49%
6	0.5%	0.6%	0.5%	0.6%	2.22%	3.34%			−1.30%	−2.49%
7	0.2%	0.1%	0.2%	0.1%	2.42%	3.44%			−1.30%	−2.49%
8	−0.8%	−1.0%			2.42%	3.44%	−0.8%	−1.0%	−2.09%	−3.47%
9	0.8%	1.0%	0.8%	1.0%	3.24%	4.47%			−2.09%	−3.47%
10	0.4%	0.5%	0.4%	0.5%	3.65%	5.00%			−2.09%	−3.47%
Geometric average		0.51%	0.70%				−0.70%	−1.17%		
Upside capture			0.51%/0.70% = 72.8%			Downside capture		−0.70%/−1.17% = 59.8%		
Capture ratio			72.8%/59.8% = 121.7%							

During up markets, the geometric average return is 0.51% for the manager and 0.70% for the benchmark, giving an upside capture of 72.8%. During down markets, the geometric average return is –0.70% for the manager and –1.17% for the benchmark, giving a downside capture of 59.8%. The manager's capture ratio is 1.217, or 121.7%. Exhibit 19 shows a graph of the cumulative upside and downside returns.

EXHIBIT 19　　　Cumulative Upside and Downside Returns

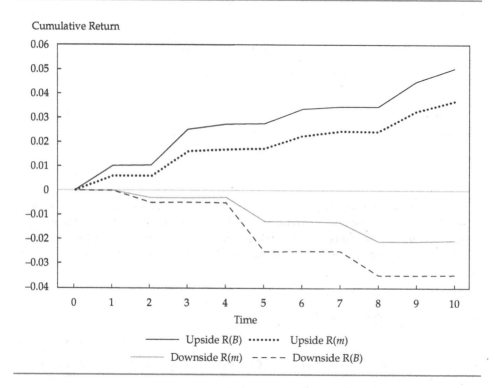

5.2.6.2. Drawdown

Drawdown is measured as the cumulative peak-to-trough loss during a continuous period. Drawdown duration is the total time from the start of the drawdown until the cumulative drawdown recovers to zero, which can be segmented into the drawdown phase (start to trough) and the recovery phase (trough-to-zero cumulative return).

$$\text{Maximum DD}(m,t) = \min([V(m,t) - V(m,t^*)]/V(m,t^*), 0)$$

where

$V(m,t)$ = portfolio value of manager m at time t

$V(m,t^*)$ = peak portfolio value of manager m

$t > t^*$

Consider the return on the S&P 500 Index from January 2011 to February 2012, shown in Exhibits 20 and 21. The drawdown is 0% until May 2011, when the return is −1.13% and the drawdown continues to grow, reaching a maximum of −16.26% in September 2011. The strong returns from October 2011 to February 2012 reverse the drawdown. The total duration of the drawdown was 10 months, with a 5-month recovery period.

EXHIBIT 20   Drawdown

Month	R(*m*)	Cumulative R (*m*)	Drawdown	Cumulative Drawdown	
January 2011	2.37%	2.37%		0.00%	
February 2011	3.43%	5.88%		0.00%	
March 2011	0.04%	5.92%		0.00%	
April 2011	2.96%	9.06%		0.00%	
May 2011	−1.13%	7.83%	−1.13%	−1.13%	Drawdown begins
June 2011	−1.67%	6.03%	−1.67%	−2.78%	
July 2011	−2.03%	3.87%	−2.03%	−4.75%	
August 2011	−5.43%	−1.77%	−5.43%	−9.93%	
September 2011	−7.03%	−8.67%	−7.03%	−16.26%	Maximum drawdown
October 2011	10.93%	1.31%		−7.11%	Recovery begins
November 2011	−0.22%	1.09%	−0.22%	−7.31%	
December 2011	1.02%	2.12%		−6.36%	
January 2012	4.48%	6.69%		−2.17%	
February 2012	4.32%	11.30%		0.00%	Drawdown recovered

EXHIBIT 21   Drawdown

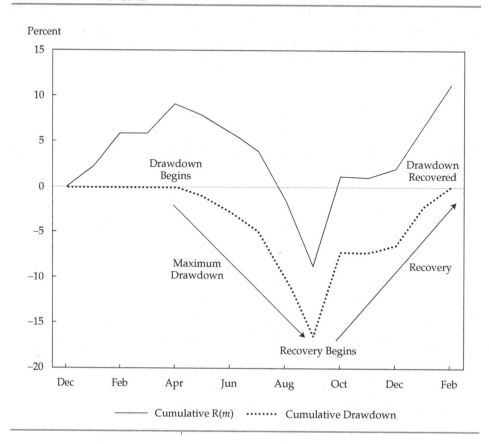

An asymmetrical return profile or avoiding large drawdowns, particularly during periods when the market is not trending strongly upward, can result in higher risk-adjusted returns. The reason is the all-too-familiar reality for investors that it takes proportionally larger gains to recover from increasingly large losses. This asymmetry arises from basis drift, from the change in the denominator when calculating returns, or from the practical problem of recovering from a smaller asset base after a large loss. For example, a portfolio decline of 50% must be followed by a gain of 100% to return to its previous value. Exhibit 22 illustrates this relationship.

EXHIBIT 22   Percentage Gain Necessary to Offset a Given Loss

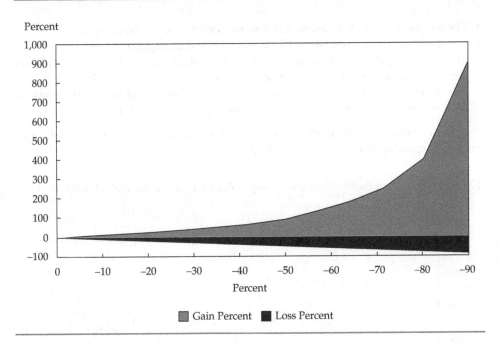

To further illustrate, consider the four return profiles with different upside and downside capture ratios shown in Exhibit 23.

EXHIBIT 23   Return Profile Summary

Profile	Upside Capture	Downside Capture	Ratio
Long only	100%	100%	1.0
Positive asymmetry	75%	25%	3.0
Low beta	50%	50%	1.0
Negative asymmetry	25%	75%	0.3

We designed these four trading strategies to illustrate the potential effects of the capture ratio and drawdown on return performance and to highlight why understanding the capture ratio and drawdown is important for manager selection.[8] Each strategy's allocation to the S&P 500 Total Return (TR) Index and to 90-day T-bills (assuming monthly rebalancing to simplify the calculations) is based on the realized monthly return from January 2000 to December 2013. (We chose this time period to illustrate the need to examine the asymmetry

---

[8]If the market return is known beforehand, the correct strategy is to allocate 100% to the S&P 500 Total Return (TR) Index in up months and 100% to 90-day T-bills in down months (or −100% S&P 500 TR Index if shorting is allowed).

in a strategy's returns specifically because it encompasses the extreme drawdown of 2008–2009.)

- The long-only profile is 100% allocated to the S&P 500 throughout the period.
- The low-beta profile is allocated 50% to the S&P 500 throughout the period.
- The positive asymmetry profile is allocated 75% to the S&P 500 for months when the S&P 500 return is positive and 25% when the S&P 500 return is negative.
- The negative asymmetry profile is allocated 25% to the S&P 500 for months when the S&P 500 return is positive and 75% when the S&P 500 return is negative.

The remainder for all profiles is allocated to 90-day T-bills. Exhibit 24 shows each profile's cumulative monthly return for the period.

EXHIBIT 24   Each Profile's Cumulative Monthly Return, January 2000–December 2013

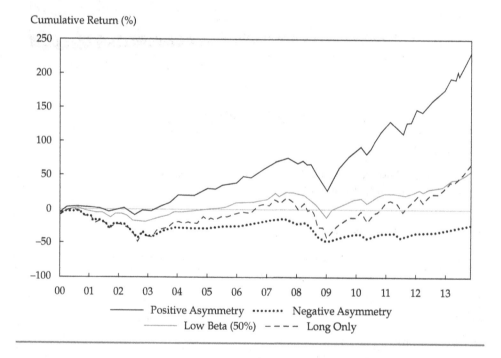

Exhibit 25 provides summary statistics for each profile based on monthly returns from January 2000 to December 2013. Although the long-only profile outperformed the low-beta profile, this outperformance resulted from the strong up market of 2013. The low-beta profile outperformed the long-only profile for most of the period, with lower realized volatility and higher risk-adjusted returns during the entire period. The low-beta profile declined only 18.8%, compared with the long-only decline of 42.5%, from January 2000 to September 2002. As a result, the low-beta profile had higher cumulative performance from January 2000 to October 2007 despite markedly lagging the long-only profile (56.0% to 108.4%) from October 2002 to October 2007.

Although a low-beta approach may sacrifice performance, it shows that limiting drawdowns can result in better absolute and risk-adjusted returns in certain markets. Not surprisingly, positive asymmetry results in better performance relative to long only, low beta, and negative asymmetry. Although the positive asymmetry profile lags in up markets, this lag is more than offset by the lower participation in down markets. Not surprisingly, the negative asymmetry profile lags, with lower participation in up markets insufficient to offset the greater participation in down markets.

EXHIBIT 25   Summary Statistics for Each Profile, January 2000–December 2013

Strategy	Long Only	Low Beta	Positive Asymmetry	Negative Asymmetry
Cumulative return	64.0%	54.2%	228.1%	–24.4%
Annualized return	3.60%	3.14%	8.86%	–1.98%
Annualized standard deviation	15.64%	7.79%	9.61%	10.01%
Sharpe ratio	0.10	0.14	0.71	–0.40
Beta	1.00	0.50	0.61	0.64
Drawdown (maximum)	–50.9%	–28.3%	–26.9%	–48.9%

Although positive asymmetry is a desirable trait, only some strategies are convex. We need to understand the strategy and how the return profile is created, particularly whether the strategy is inherently convex or whether convexity relies on manager skill. For example, a hedging strategy implemented by rolling forward out-of-the-money put options will typically return many small losses because more options expire worthless than are compensated for by the occasional large gain during a large market downturn. This strategy will likely exhibit consistent positive asymmetry because it depends more on the nature of the strategy than on investment skill.

We should also evaluate the consistency between the stated investment process and reported investment performance. An inconsistency could indicate issues with the strategy's repeatability and implementation or more serious reporting and compliance concerns. Capture ratios can be useful in evaluating consistency issues. We also need to understand the strategy's robustness and potential risks. For example, the expected benefits of diversification—in particular, mitigating downside capture—might not be realized in a crisis if correlations converge toward 1.

Manager responses to a large drawdown provide evidence of the robustness and repeatability of the investment, portfolio construction, and risk management processes, as well as insight into the people implementing the processes. This information requires an understanding of the source of the drawdown and the potential principal–agent risk, operational risk, and business risk that it entails. Drawdowns are stress tests of the investment process and provide a natural point to evaluate and improve processes, which is particularly true of firm-specific drawdowns.

As noted, practitioners should also consider investment horizon and its relationship with risk capacity. An investor closer to retirement, with less time to recover from losses, places more emphasis on absolute measures of risk. In addition, even if the manager maintains her discipline during a large drawdown, the investor may not. This dynamic arises if the investor's perception of risk is path dependent or the drawdown changes risk tolerance. If there has been no change to investment policy and no change in the view that the manager remains suitable, the temptation to exit should be resisted to avoid exiting at an inauspicious time. Investors with shorter horizons, with lower risk capacity, or who are prone to overreact to losses may bias selection toward managers with shallower and shorter expected drawdowns.

EXAMPLE 13   Capture Ratios and Drawdown

1. Do losses require proportionally greater gains to reverse or offset? Choose the best response.
   A. Yes, because in investing, it is easier to lose than to gain.
   B. No, gains should reflect losses.
   C. Yes, because we calculate percentage gains/losses on the basis of the starting amount of portfolio holdings.

2.

t	$R(m)$ (%)	$R(B)$ (%)
1	−3.06	−3.60
2	6.32	3.10
3	6.00	6.03
4	3.21	1.58
5	−9.05	−7.99
6	−4.09	−5.23
7	4.34	7.01
8	−5.72	−4.51
9	12.76	8.92
10	5.38	3.81
11	0.33	0.01
12	5.68	6.68

Using the return information in the table above, what is the manager's downside capture ratio?
   A. 103%
   B. 108%
   C. 115%

Solution to 1: C is the correct response. If the denominator of the gain calculation is lower, a higher percentage gain is required to offset the loss. For example, if you lose 10% of $100, your new holding is $90. To earn back the $10 loss, you must earn 10/90, or 11%. A is not correct because the "ease" of gaining or losing is not relevant. B is not correct because proportionally higher gains are required.

Solution to 2: A is the correct answer. See the table below.

t	R(m)	R(B)	Upside Return				Downside Return			
			R(m)	R(B)	Cum R(m)	Cum R(B)	R(m)	R(B)	Cum R(m)	Cum R(B)
1	−3.06%	−3.60%			0.00%	0.00%	−3.06%	−3.60%	−3.06%	−3.60%
2	6.32%	3.10%	6.32%	3.10%	6.32%	3.10%			−3.06%	−3.60%
3	6.00%	6.03%	6.00%	6.03%	12.70%	9.32%			−3.06%	−3.60%
4	3.21%	1.58%	3.21%	1.58%	16.32%	11.04%			−3.06%	−3.60%
5	−9.05%	−7.99%			16.32%	11.04%	−9.05%	−7.99%	−11.83%	−11.30%
6	−4.09%	−5.23%			16.32%	11.04%	−4.09%	−5.23%	−15.44%	−15.94%
7	4.34%	7.01%	4.34%	7.01%	21.36%	18.83%			−15.44%	−15.94%
8	−5.72%	−4.51%			21.36%	18.83%	−5.72%	−4.51%	−20.28%	−19.73%
9	12.76%	8.92%	12.76%	8.92%	36.85%	29.43%			−20.28%	−19.73%
10	5.38%	3.81%	5.38%	3.81%	44.21%	34.36%			−20.28%	−19.73%
11	0.33%	0.01%	0.33%	0.01%	44.69%	34.37%			−20.28%	−19.73%
12	5.68%	6.68%	5.68%	6.68%	52.91%	43.35%			−20.28%	−19.73%
Geometric average			5.45%	4.60%			−5.51%	−5.35%		
Upside capture			5.45%/4.60% = 118%			**Downside capture**	−5.51%/−5.35% = 103%			
Capture ratio			118%/103% = 115%							

5.3. Evaluation of Investment Manager Skill

Using the tools and principles of performance evaluation presented in this chapter, this section presents a specific case to use those tools in an evaluation of manager skill.

For this section, we will consider the case of Manager A, benchmarked against the MSCI Pacific Index. Drawing from the previous sections in this chapter, we compiled sample data to evaluate the skill of Manager A. For simplicity of analysis and presentation, we exclude the impact from currency.

Over a five-year period, Manager A's performance is 9.42%, versus the benchmark performance of 9.25%. So, we know that the manager added 17 bps (9.42 − 9.25) of outperformance. But did the manager earn the 17 bps through skill, or was she the beneficiary of luck?

To further evaluate the outperformance, we turn to the tools presented throughout this chapter. We include a sample attribution analysis to tell us how the outperformance was achieved. We then use appraisal ratio analysis to compare Manager A's performance to other managers during the same period. Combining the analyses helps present a more balanced assessment of the manager's skill.

5.3.1. Performance Attribution Analysis

Attribution analysis, as we have shown, is one of the most important tools for evaluating manager skill. Attribution will tell us how the outperformance was achieved, distinguishing the stock selection from country allocation. In Exhibit 26, we present the sample attribution analysis (for simplicity, we have combined the interaction effect with stock selection).

EXHIBIT 26   Sample Attribution Analysis

| Market | Manager A | | MSCI Pacific | | Attribution Effects | | |
	Weight	5-Year Return	Weight	5-Year Return	Allocation	Selection + Interaction	Total
Japan	51.0%	12.40%	60.5%	11.48%	−0.21%	0.47%	0.26%
Australia	30.0%	5.12%	25.4%	4.10%	−0.24%	0.31%	0.07%
Hong Kong SAR	15.0%	8.90%	10.0%	10.08%	0.04%	−0.18%	−0.14%
Singapore	3.5%	5.10%	3.0%	5.38%	−0.02%	−0.01%	−0.03%
New Zealand	0.5%	8.75%	1.0%	9.08%	0.00%	0.00%	0.00%
Total	100%	9.42%	100%	9.25%	−0.43%	0.59%	0.17%

Using this analysis, let us consider the impacts of country allocation weights versus the benchmark weights. Overall, the portfolio manager lost 43 bps of performance as a result of allocation decisions. Specifically, the manager's decision to overweight Australia (30% to 25%) lost 24 bps, because Australia underperformed the total MSCI Pacific benchmark (4.10% versus 9.25%). In addition, the decision to underweight Japan (51% to 60%) lost 21 bps, because Japan outperformed the total benchmark (12.4% versus 9.25%). With this attribution analysis, we can say the manager did not make good weighting decisions over the five-year period.

Now, let us consider the impact from the manager's stock selection decisions. Overall, the portfolio manager gained 59 bps of performance from stock selection decisions. Specifically, the manager added 47 bps through selecting Japanese stocks and 31 bps from selecting Australian stocks. Stock selection in Hong Kong SAR was not as successful, where the manager lost 18 bps.

Overall, we can conclude from the attribution analysis that the manager is a good stock picker, especially for Japanese and Australian stocks. But the manager has not been as successful in choosing the markets to allocate assets. We infer these conclusions on the basis of an analysis of the manager's performance attribution over a five-year period. To better evaluate the manager's performance, we need to understand the risk incurred to achieve that performance. For that risk assessment, we will consider Manager A relative to other managers, using a sample appraisal ratio analysis over the same five-year period.

5.3.2. Appraisal Measures
As described previously, appraisal analysis uses techniques to review past periods of performance and risk. Consider the sample results presented in Exhibit 27. For the same five-year period, we have calculated a set of performance appraisal measures for Manager A, presented previously, as well as two other managers with the same benchmark over the same period, Managers B and C.

EXHIBIT 27   Sample Analysis Using Various Appraisal Measures

	Appraisal Measures			
	Manager A	Manager B	Manager C	Benchmark
Annualized return	9.42	8.23	10.21	9.25
Annualized std. dev.	10.83	8.10	12.34	9.76
Sharpe ratio	0.68	0.76	0.66	0.73
Treynor ratio	0.35	0.32	0.19	0.57
Information ratio	0.43	0.41	0.30	0.00
Sortino ratio (MAR = 3%)	0.82	0.51	1.03	0.97

In considering this historical analysis, note that Manager A has a higher volatility of returns than the benchmark (manager standard deviation of 10.83 versus benchmark standard deviation of 9.76). This volatility is greater than that for Manager B (8.10) but is less than that for Manager C (12.34). In general, Manager A's return is slightly more volatile—riskier—than the benchmark's and slightly more and less volatile than that of Managers B and C, respectively.

This consistency is demonstrated in the Sharpe ratio measurement as well. Recall that the Sharpe ratio indicates the amount of performance earned over a risk-free proxy per unit of risk. In this assessment, Manager A's Sharpe ratio is less than the benchmark's Sharpe ratio (0.68 versus 0.73) and less than Manager B's Sharpe ratio (0.76). Thus, for this period, we know Manager A certainly incurred more risk than the benchmark and Manager B did for the same amount of return generated. Is the manager incurring too much risk for the return generated? To answer this question, we should consider some of the other appraisal measures as well.

Unlike the Sharpe ratio, the Treynor ratio measures the return earned per unit of *systematic* risk. The information ratio indicates how well the manager has performed relative to the benchmark, *after accounting for the differences in the volatility of the portfolio and the benchmark.* Given that Manager A has the highest Treynor and information ratios for this period, she has been able to produce a higher return relative to systematic risk. In addition, consider her Sortino ratio of 0.82, not significantly higher than the Sharpe ratio, but again indicative of an ability to generate higher returns relative to downside risk (where the target is 3%).

5.3.3. Sample Evaluation of Skill

In summary, the analysis based on these appraisal measures supports the conclusion generated by the performance attribution analysis that Manager A has been able to generate excess return over the benchmark through stock selection. She has done so without incurring significant excess risk relative to the benchmark and two similar managers. Therefore, within the limits of these analyses, Manager A has exhibited some level of skill worthy of further analysis.

The analysis does not, however, help us evaluate the country allocation conclusions of our attribution analysis. We know that the manager made incorrect bets in Japan and Australia. What beliefs about country selection are embedded in her investment philosophy?

Are country allocations an integral part of her investment approach, or are they a by-product of her stock selection? Answers to these questions will help us determine whether our assessment of skill should be penalized by the poor outcomes of the country selection decisions in this period.

It is important to recognize that our analysis encompasses only a small sample of the possible outcomes that are not necessarily indicative of future outcomes. A long track record is necessary to have any statistical certainty in a conclusion of skill or no skill. Practitioners will want to conduct additional analyses to increase their confidence in their conclusions. These additional studies could include some of the other tools presented in this chapter, such as risk attribution or *ex ante* analyses. In addition, practitioners will want to include qualitative analyses of the manager (e.g., direct interviews with management to assess abilities), assessment of investment goals and management fees, and so on. In the end, we must understand and acknowledge the limits of all tools, being careful to qualify any conclusions regarding investment skill with the appropriate level of prudence.

EXAMPLE 14   Investment Manager Skill

Use the examples in Exhibits 26 and 27 to help answer the following questions.

1. Which statement *best* describes Manager A's performance during this five-year period?
   A. On an absolute basis, Manager A performed better than either Manager B or Manager C.
   B. Relative to systematic risk, Manager A performed better than either Manager B or Manager C.
   C. Manager C incurred the least risk.

2. Which of the following *best* provides evidence of manager skill?
   A. Security selection attribution effect of 47 bps
   B. Annualized performance equal to 9.42%
   C. Annualized standard deviation equal to 12.34%

3. How can a practitioner *best* distinguish manager skill from luck?
   A. Run thousands of analyses of the same manager over an extended period.
   B. Avoid making broad-based judgments without statistical evidence.
   C. Use multiple analysis tools to jointly infer conclusions, sensitive to the limits of those tools.

Solution to 1: B is correct. The Treynor ratio measures performance relative to systematic risk. Manager A's Treynor ratio was better than that of both Manager B and Manager C for the period. A is not correct because Manager A's return for the period was less than Manager C's return. C is not correct because Manager C's annualized standard deviation (volatility) was highest.

Solution to 2: A is correct. Performance attribution can be indicative of manager skill, especially over longer historical time periods. Neither B nor C is correct because neither performance nor standard deviation, on their own, is necessarily indicative of manager skill.

> *Solution to 3:* C is correct. Practitioners should use multiple analyses with different tools to find multiple sources that agree on evidence of skill. A is not correct, because thousands of analyses, especially the same types of analyses, may not necessarily lead to more conclusive results. B is not correct because it states best practice but not necessarily techniques to distinguish skill from luck.

SUMMARY

Performance evaluation is an essential tool for understanding the quality of the investment process. Practitioners must take care, however, to understand how performance results are generated. They need a good understanding of the performance methods used, the data inputs, and the limitations of those methods. They particularly need to be careful not to infer results beyond the capabilities of the methods or the accuracy of the data. In this chapter, we have discussed the following:

- Performance measurement provides an overall indication of the portfolio's performance.
- Performance attribution builds on performance measurement to explain how the performance was achieved.
- Performance appraisal leverages both returns and attribution to infer the quality of the investment process.
- An effective attribution process must reconcile to the total portfolio return/risk, reflect the investment decision-making process, quantify the active portfolio management decisions, and provide a complete understanding of the excess return/risk of the portfolio.
- Return attribution analyzes the impact of investment decisions on the returns, whereas risk attribution analyzes the risk consequences of the investment decisions.
- Macro attribution considers the decisions of the fund sponsor, whereas micro attribution considers the decisions of the individual portfolio manager.
- Returns-based attribution uses returns to identify the factors that have generated those returns.
- Holdings-based attribution uses the holdings over time to evaluate the decisions that contributed to the returns.
- Transactions-based attribution uses both holdings and transactions to fully explain the performance over the evaluation period.
- There are various techniques for interpreting the sources of portfolio returns using a specified attribution approach.
- Fixed-income attribution considers the unique factors that drive bond returns, including interest rate risk and default risk.
- When selecting a risk attribution approach, practitioners should consider the investment decision-making process and the type of attribution analysis.
- Attribution is used to calculate and interpret the contribution to portfolio return and volatility from the asset allocation and within-asset-class active/passive decisions.
- Liability-based benchmarks focus on the cash flows that the assets are required to generate.
- Asset-based benchmarks contain a collection of assets to compare against the portfolio's assets.

- Valid benchmarks should be unambiguous, investable, measurable, appropriate, reflective of current investment opinions, specified in advance, and accountable.
- Benchmark misspecification creates subsequent incorrect performance measurement and invalidates the attribution and appraisal analyses.
- Alternative investments are difficult to benchmark because they are typically less liquid, have fewer available market benchmarks, and often lack transparency.
- Investment performance appraisal ratios—including the Sortino ratio, upside/downside capture ratios, maximum drawdown, and drawdown duration—measure investment skill.
- Appraisal ratios must be used with care, noting the assumptions of each ratio and affording the appropriateness to the measured investment process, risk tolerance, and investor time horizon.
- Although appraisal ratios help identify manager skill (as opposed to luck), they often are based on investment return data, which are often limited and subject to error.
- Evaluation of investment manager skill requires the use of a broad range of analysis tools, with fundamental understanding of how the tools work, how they complement each other, and their specific limitations.

REFERENCES

Bailey, Jeffery V. and David E. Tierney. 1998. *Controlling Misfit Risk in Multiple-Manager Investment Programs*. Charlottesville, VA: Research Foundation of CFA Institute.

Bailey, Jeffery V., Thomas M. Richards, and David Tierney. 2007. "Evaluating Portfolio Performance." In *Managing Investment Portfolios: A Dynamic Process*. 3rd ed., ed. Maginn, John, Donald Tuttle, Dennis McLeavey, and Jerald Pinto. Hoboken, NJ: John Wiley & Sons.

Brinson, Gary and Nimrod Fachler. 1985. "Measuring Non-US Equity Portfolio Performance." *Journal of Portfolio Management* 11 (5): 73–76.

Brinson, Gary, Randolph Hood, and Gilbert Beebower. 1986. "Determinants of Portfolio Performance." *Financial Analysts Journal* 42 (4): 39–44.

Brown, Stephen and William Goetzmann. 1997. "Mutual Fund Styles." *Journal of Financial Economics* 43 (3): 373–99.

Carhart, M. M. 1997. "On Persistence in Mutual Fund Performance." *Journal of Finance* 52 (1): 57–82.

Cariño, David. 1999. "Combining Attribution Effects over Time." Summer*Journal of Performance Measurement*.

Gastineau, Gary L., Andrew L. Olma, and Robert G. Zielienski. 2007. "Equity Portfolio Management." In *Managing Investment Portfolios: A Dynamic Process*. 3rd ed., ed. Maginn, John, Donald Tuttle, Dennis McLeavey, and Jerald Pinto. Hoboken, NJ: John Wiley & Sons.

Giguère, C. 2005. "Thinking through Fixed Income Attribution—Reflections from a Group of French Practitioners." *Journal of Performance Measurement* (Summer): 46–65.

Khandani, Amir E. and Andrew W. Lo. 2011. "What Happened to the Quants in August 2007? Evidence from Factors and Transactions Data." *Journal of Financial Markets*, 14 (1): 1–46.

Menchero, Jose. 2000. "An Optimized Approach to Linking Attribution Effects over Time." Fall *Journal of Performance Measurement*.

Murira, Bernard and Hector Sierra. 2006. "Fixed Income Attribution: A United Framework—Part 1." *Journal of Performance Measurement* 11 (1): 23–35.

Treynor, J. 1965. "How to Rate Management of Investment Funds." *Harvard Business Review* 43 (1): 63–75.

Treynor, J. and F. Black. 1973. "How to Use Security Analysis to Improve Portfolio Selection." *Journal of Business* 46 (1): 66–86.

PRACTICE PROBLEMS

The following information relates to Questions 1–5

Alexandra Jones, a senior adviser at Federalist Investors (FI), meets with Erin Bragg, a junior analyst. Bragg just completed a monthly performance evaluation for an FI fixed-income manager. Bragg's report addresses the three primary components of performance evaluation: measurement, attribution, and appraisal. Jones asks Bragg to describe an effective attribution process. Bragg responds as follows:

Response 1: Performance attribution draws conclusions regarding the quality of a portfolio manager's investment decisions.

Response 2: Performance attribution should help explain how performance was achieved by breaking apart the return or risk into different explanatory components.

Bragg notes that the fixed-income portfolio manager has strong views about the effects of macroeconomic factors on credit markets and follows a top-down investment process.

Jones reviews the monthly performance attribution and asks Bragg whether any risk-adjusted historical performance indicators are available. Bragg produces the following data:

EXHIBIT 1   10-Year Trailing Risk-Adjusted Performance

Average annual return	8.20%
Minimum acceptable return (MAR)	5.00%
Sharpe ratio	0.95
Sortino ratio	0.87
Upside capture	0.66
Downside capture	0.50
Maximum drawdown	−24.00%
Drawdown duration	4 months

1. Which of Bragg's responses regarding effective performance attribution is correct?
   A. Only Response 1
   B. Only Response 2
   C. Both Response 1 and Response 2

2. The *most appropriate* risk attribution approach for the fixed-income manager is to:
   A. decompose historical returns into a top-down factor framework.
   B. evaluate the marginal contribution to total risk for each position.
   C. attribute tracking risk to relative allocation and selection decisions.

3. Based on Exhibit 1, the target semideviation for the portfolio is *closest to:*
   A. 2.78%.
   B. 3.68%.
   C. 4.35%.

4. Based on Exhibit 1, the capture ratios of the portfolio indicate:
   A. a concave return profile.
   B. positive asymmetry of returns.
   C. that the portfolio generates higher returns than the benchmark during all market conditions.

5. The maximum drawdown and drawdown duration in Exhibit 1 indicate that:
   A. the portfolio recovered quickly from its maximum loss.
   B. over the 10-year period, the average maximum loss was –24.00%.
   C. a significant loss once persisted for four months before the portfolio began to recover.

The following information relates to Questions 6–14

Stephanie Tolmach is a consultant hired to create a performance attribution report on three funds held by a defined benefit pension plan (the Plan). Fund 1 is a domestic equity strategy, Fund 2 is a global equity strategy, and Fund 3 is a domestic fixed-income strategy.

Tolmach uses three approaches to attribution analysis: the return-based, holdings-based, and transaction-based approaches. The Plan's investment committee asks Tolmach to (1) apply the attribution method that uses only each fund's total portfolio returns over the last 12 months to identify return-generating components of the investment process and (2) include the impact of specific active investment decisions and the attribution effects of allocation and security selection in the report.

Tolmach first evaluates the performance of Fund 1 by constructing a Carhart factor model; the results are presented in Exhibit 1.

EXHIBIT 1   Fund 1 Factor Model Attribution

	Factor Sensitivity				Contribution to Active Return	
Factor*	Portfolio (1)	Benchmark (2)	Difference (3)	Factor Return (4)	Absolute (3) × (4)	Proportion of Active Return
RMRF	1.22	0.91	0.31	16.32%	5.06%	126.80%
SMB	0.59	0.68	–0.09	–3.25%	0.29%	7.33%
HML	–0.17	0.04	–0.21	–9.60%	2.02%	50.53%
WML	–0.05	0.07	–0.12	3.38%	–0.41%	–10.17%
			A. Factor Tilt Return:		6.96%	174.49%
			B. Security Selection:		–10.95%	–274.49%
			C. Active Return (A + B):		–3.99%	100.00%

*RMRF is the return on a value-weighted equity index in excess of the one-month T-bill rate, SMB is the small minus big market capitalization factor, HML is the high minus low factor, and WML is the winners minus losers factor.

Tolmach turns her attention to Fund 2, constructing a region-based, Brinson–Fachler micro attribution analysis to evaluate the active decisions of the portfolio manager. The results are presented in Exhibit 2.

EXHIBIT 2   Fund 2 Performance—Allocation by Region

Return Attribution (Region Level)	Portfolio Weight	Benchmark Weight	Portfolio Return	Benchmark Return
North America	10.84%	7.67%	16.50%	16.47%
Greater Europe	38.92%	42.35%	23.16%	25.43%
Developed Asia and Australasia	29.86%	31.16%	11.33%	12.85%
South America	20.38%	18.82%	20.00%	35.26%
Total	**100.00%**	**100.00%**	**18.26%**	**22.67%**

Next, Tolmach evaluates Fund 3 and the appropriateness of its benchmark. The benchmark is a cap-weighted bond index with daily reported performance; the index is rebalanced frequently, making it difficult to replicate. The benchmark has a meaningful investment in foreign bonds, whereas Fund 3 invests only in domestic bonds.

In the final section of the report, Tolmach reviews the entire Plan's characteristics, asset allocation, and benchmark. Tolmach observes that the Plan's benefits are no longer indexed to inflation and that the workforce is, on average, younger than it was when the current fund allocations were approved. Tolmach recommends a change in the Plan's asset allocation policy.

6. Of the three attribution approaches referenced by Tolmach, the method requested by the committee:
   A. is the least accurate.
   B. uses the underlying holdings of the actual portfolio.
   C. is the most difficult and time consuming to implement.

7. Based on Exhibit 1 and relative to the benchmark, the manager of Fund 1 *most likely* used a:
   A. growth tilt.
   B. greater tilt toward small cap.
   C. momentum-based investing approach.

8. Based on Exhibit 1, which of the following factors contributed the *least* to active return?
   A. HML
   B. SMB
   C. RMRF

9. Based on Exhibit 1, the manager could have delivered more value to the portfolio during the investment period by weighting more toward:
   A. value stocks.
   B. small-cap stocks.
   C. momentum stocks.

10. Based on Exhibit 2, the allocation effect for South America is *closest* to:
    A. −0.04%.
    B. 0.03%.
    C. 0.20%.

11. Based on Exhibit 2, the decision to overweight or underweight which of the following regions contributed positively to performance at the overall fund level?
    A. North America
    B. Greater Europe
    C. Developed Asia and Australasia

12. Based on Exhibit 2, the underperformance at the overall fund level is predominantly the result of poor security selection decisions in:
    A. South America.
    B. greater Europe.
    C. developed Asia and Australasia.

13. The benchmark for Fund 3 has which of the following characteristics of a valid benchmark?
    A. Investable
    B. Measurable
    C. Appropriate

14. Based on the final section of Tolmach's report, the Plan should use:
    A. a liability-based benchmark.
    B. an absolute return benchmark.
    C. a manager universe benchmark.

CHAPTER 20

INVESTMENT MANAGER SELECTION

Jeffrey C. Heisler, PhD, CFA

Donald W. Lindsey, CFA

LEARNING OUTCOMES

The candidate should be able to:

- describe the components of a manager selection process, including due diligence;
- contrast Type I and Type II errors in manager hiring and continuation decisions;
- describe uses of returns-based and holdings-based style analysis in investment manager selection;
- describe uses of the upside capture ratio, downside capture ratio, maximum drawdown, drawdown duration, and up/down capture in evaluating managers;
- evaluate a manager's investment philosophy and investment decision-making process;
- evaluate the costs and benefits of pooled investment vehicles and separate accounts;
- compare types of investment manager contracts, including their major provisions and advantages and disadvantages;
- describe the three basic forms of performance-based fees;
- analyze and interpret a sample performance-based fee schedule.

1. INTRODUCTION

Most investors do not hold securities directly but rather invest using intermediaries. Whether the intermediary is a separately managed account or a pooled investment vehicle, such as mutual funds in the United States, unit trusts in the United Kingdom, Undertakings for the Collective Investment of Transferable Securities (UCITS) in the European Union, hedge

Portfolio Management, Second Edition, by Jeffrey C. Heisler, PhD, CFA, and Donald W. Lindsey, CFA.
Copyright © 2020 by CFA Institute.

funds, private equity funds, or exchange-traded funds (ETFs), a professional investment manager is being entrusted with helping investors achieve their investment objectives. In all of these cases, the selection of appropriate investment managers is a challenge with important financial consequences.

Evaluating an investment manager is a complex and detailed process that encompasses a great deal more than analyzing investment returns. The investigation and analysis in support of an investment action, decision, or recommendation is called **due diligence**. In conducting investment manager due diligence, the focus is on understanding how the investment results were achieved and on assessing the likelihood that the investment process that generated these returns will produce superior or at least satisfactory investment results going forward. Due diligence also entails an evaluation of a firm's integrity, operations, and personnel. As such, due diligence involves both quantitative and qualitative analysis.

This chapter provides a framework that introduces and describes the important elements of the manager selection process. Although it is important to have a well-defined methodology, this chapter is not intended to be a rigid checklist, a step-by-step guide, or an in-depth analysis but rather to present a structure from which the reader can develop their own approach.

We assume that the investment policy statement (IPS) has been drafted, the asset allocation determined, and the decision to use an outside adviser has been made. As a result, the focus is on determining which manager offers the "best" means to implement or express those decisions. The discussion has three broad topics:

- Outlining a framework for identifying, evaluating, and ultimately selecting investment managers (Section 2).
- Quantitative considerations in manager selection (Section 3).
- Qualitative considerations in manager selection (Section 4).

The chapter concludes with a summary of selected important points.

2. A FRAMEWORK FOR INVESTMENT MANAGER SEARCH AND SELECTION

An underlying assumption of investment manager due diligence is that a consistent, robust investment process will generate a similar return distribution relative to risk factors through time, assuming the underlying dynamics of the market have not dramatically changed. One important goal of manager due diligence is to understand whether the manager's investment process, people, and portfolio construction satisfy this assumption—that is, will the investment process generate the expected return from the expected sources? The manager search and selection process has three broad components: the universe, a quantitative analysis of the manager's performance track record, and a qualitative analysis of the manager's investment process. The qualitative analysis consists of investment due diligence, which evaluates the manager's investment process, and operational due diligence, which evaluates the manager's infrastructure and firm. Exhibit 1 details these components.

EXHIBIT 1   Manager Selection Process Overview

Key Aspects	Key Question
Universe	
Defining the universe	What is the feasible set of managers that fit the portfolio need?
• Suitability	Which managers are suitable for the IPS?
• Style	Which have the appropriate style?
• Active vs. passive	Which fit the active versus passive decision?
Quantitative Analysis	
Investment due diligence	Which manager "best" fits the portfolio need?
Quantitative	What has been the manager's return distribution?
• Attribution and appraisal	Has the manager displayed skill?
• Capture ratio	How does the manager perform in "up" markets versus "down" markets?
• Drawdown	Does the return distribution exhibit large drawdowns?
Qualitative Analysis	
Investment due diligence	Which manager "best" fits the portfolio need?
Qualitative	Is the manager expected to continue to generate this return distribution?
• Philosophy	What market inefficiency does the manager seek to exploit?
• Process	Is the investment process capable of exploiting this inefficiency?
• People	Do the investment personnel possess the expertise and experience necessary to effectively implement the investment process?
• Portfolio	Is portfolio construction consistent with the stated investment philosophy and process?
Operational due diligence	Is the manager's track record accurate, and does it fully reflect risks?
• Process and procedure	Is the back office strong, safeguarding assets and able to issue accurate reports in a timely manner?
• Firm	Is the firm profitable, with a healthy culture, and likely to remain in business? Is the firm committed to delivering performance over gathering assets?
• Investment vehicle	Is the vehicle suitable for the portfolio need?
• Terms	Are the terms acceptable and appropriate for the strategy and vehicle?
• Monitoring	Does the manager continue to be the "best" fit for the portfolio need?

EXAMPLE 1   Components of the Manager Selection Process

1. Qualitative analysis of the manager selection process includes:
   A. attribution.
   B. defining the universe.
   C. investment and operational due diligence.

2. Which of the following is considered a key aspect of operational due diligence?
   A. People
   B. Philosophy
   C. Procedures

Solution to 1: C is correct. Qualitative analysis consists of investment due diligence, which evaluates the manager's investment process, and operational due diligence, which evaluates the manager's infrastructure and firm.

Solution to 2: C is correct. Process and procedures are key aspects of operational due diligence, whereas people and philosophy are key aspects of investment due diligence.

2.1. Defining the Manager Universe

The manager selection process begins by defining the universe of feasible managers, those managers who potentially satisfy the identified portfolio need. The objective is to reduce the manager universe to a manageable size relative to the resources and time available to evaluate it. This process also involves balancing the risks of too narrow a search, which potentially excludes interesting managers, and too broad a search, which leads to little gain in reducing the list of potential managers. Like many inexact problems, this step is a combination of art and science. In the initial screening process, the search parameters can be narrowed and widened to determine which managers enter and exit and to evaluate whether these additions or deletions improve the universe.

The IPS and the reason for the manager search largely determine the universe of managers considered and the benchmark against which they are compared. A new search based on a strategic or tactical view, such as adding a new strategy or risk exposure, will examine a broad universe of comparable managers and look to select the best within the universe. Adding a manager to increase capacity or diversification within a strategy already held will look for a complement to current holdings. Replacing a single manager in a particular strategy will look for the best manager within the strategy universe. The IPS in part determines what the relative terms "best," "complement," and "cost/benefit" mean.

Typically, a search starts with a benchmark that represents the manager's role within the portfolio. The benchmark also provides a reference for performance attribution and appraisal. There are several approaches to assigning a manager to a benchmark:

- **Third-party categorization:** Database or software providers and consultants typically assign managers to a strategy sector. This categorization provides an easy and efficient way to define the universe. The risk is that the provider's definition may differ from the desired portfolio role. As such, it is important to understand the criteria used by the provider.

- **Returns-based style analysis:** The risk exposures derived from the manager's actual return series has the advantage of being objective. The disadvantage is additional computational effort and the limitations of returns-based analysis.
- **Holdings-based style analysis:** This approach allows for the estimation of current factor exposures but adds to computational effort and depends on timing and amount of transparency.
- **Manager experience:** The assignment can be based on an evaluation of the manager and observations of portfolios and returns over time.

Not surprisingly, a hybrid strategy that combines elements of each approach is recommended. Using third-party categorizations is an efficient way to build an initial universe that can then be complemented and refined with quantitative methods and experience. The screening should avoid using performance at this point. The focus should be on understanding the manager's risk profile and identifying candidates to fill the desired role in the portfolio. Lastly, the universe of potential managers is not static—it will evolve through time not only as manager strategies evolve but also as a result of the entry and exit of managers.

2.2. Type I and Type II Errors in Manager Selection

Certain concepts from the area of inferential statistics known as hypothesis testing can be relevant to the decision to hire an investment manager or to retain or dismiss a manager previously hired.

The determination of whether a manager is skillful typically starts with the null hypothesis (the hypothesis assumed to be true until demonstrated otherwise) that the manager is not skillful. As a result, there are two types of potential error:

- Type I: Hiring or retaining a manager who subsequently underperforms expectations. Rejecting the null hypothesis of no skill when it is correct.
- Type II: Not hiring or firing a manager who subsequently outperforms, or performs in line with, expectations. Not rejecting the null hypothesis when it is incorrect.

EXHIBIT 2   Type I and Type II Errors

		Realization	
		Below Expectations (no skill)	**At or above Expectations (skill)**
Decision	Hire/Retain	Type I	Correct
	Not Hire/Fire	Correct	Type II

Type I and Type II errors can occur anytime a decision is made regarding the hiring or firing of a manager. The decision maker must determine which error is preferred based on the expected benefits and costs of changing managers.

2.2.1. Qualitative Considerations in Type I and Type II Errors

Decision makers appear predisposed to worry more about Type I errors than Type II errors. Potential reasons for this focus on Type I errors are as follows:

- Psychologically, people seek to avoid feelings of regret. Type I errors are errors of commission, an active decision that turned out to be incorrect, whereas Type II errors are errors of omission, or inaction. As a result, Type I errors create explicit costs, whereas Type II errors create opportunity costs. Because individuals appear to put less weight on opportunity costs, Type I errors are psychologically more painful than Type II errors.
- Type I errors are relatively straightforward to measure and are often directly linked to the decision maker's compensation. Portfolio holdings are regularly monitored, and managers' out- and underperformance expectations are clearly identified. Type II errors are less likely to be measured—what is the performance impact of not having selected a particular manager? As such, the link between compensation and Type II errors is less clear.
- Similarly, Type I errors are more transparent to investors, so they entail not only the regret of an incorrect decision but the pain of having to explain this decision to the investor. Type II errors, firing (or not hiring) a manager with skill, are less transparent to investors, unless the investor tracks fired managers or evaluates the universe themselves.

Although Type I errors are likely more familiar and more of a concern to most decision makers, a consistent pattern of Type II errors can highlight weaknesses in the manager selection process. One approach to examine this issue is to monitor not only managers currently held but also managers that were evaluated and not hired as well as managers that were fired. The goal of monitoring is to determine the following:

- Are there identifiable factors that differentiate managers hired and managers not hired?
- Are these factors consistent with the investment philosophy and process of the decision maker?
- Are there identifiable factors driving the decision to retain or fire managers?
- Are these factors consistent with the investment philosophy and process of the decision maker?
- What is the added value of the decision to retain or fire managers?

The objective is to avoid making decisions based on short-term performance (trend following) and to identify any evidence of behavioral biases (regret, loss aversion) in the evaluation of managers during the selection process.

2.2.2. Performance Implications of Type I and Type II Errors

The cost of Type I errors is holding a manager without skill, as opposed to the cost of Type II errors, which is not holding managers with skill. The cost is driven by the size, shape, mean, and dispersion of the return distributions of the skilled and unskilled managers within the universe. The smaller the difference in sample size and distribution mean and the wider the dispersion of the distributions, the smaller the expected cost of the Type I or Type II error. More-efficient markets are likely to exhibit smaller differences in the distributions of skilled and unskilled managers, indicating a lower opportunity cost of retaining and the lower the cost of hiring an unskilled manager.

The extent to which a strategy is mean-reverting also has a bearing on the cost of Type I and Type II errors. If a strategy's performance is mean reverting, firing a poor performer (or hiring a strong performer) only to see a reversion in performance results is a Type I error. A

Type II error would be not trimming strong performers and avoiding hiring managers with weaker short-term track records, which can be costly. There is evidence that individual investors significantly underperform the average mutual fund because of poor timing and fund selection decisions. A study of institutional plan sponsor allocation decisions found that investment products receiving contributions subsequently underperformed products experiencing withdrawals. The study estimated that more than $170 billion was lost during the period examined (Stewart, Neumann, Knittel, and Heisler 2009).

EXAMPLE 2   Type I and Type II Errors

1. A Type I error is:
   A. hiring or retaining a manager that subsequently underperforms expectations.
   B. hiring or retaining a manager that subsequently outperforms, or performs in line with, expectations.
   C. not hiring or firing a manager who subsequently outperforms, or performs in line with, expectations.

2. A Type II error is:
   A. hiring or retaining a manager that subsequently underperforms expectations.
   B. hiring or retaining a manager that subsequently outperforms, or performs in line with, expectations.
   C. not hiring or firing a manager who subsequently outperforms, or performs in line with, expectations.

3. The difference in expected cost between Type I and Type II errors is *most likely*:
   A. higher the smaller the perceived difference between the distribution of skilled and unskilled managers.
   B. lower the smaller the perceived difference between the distribution of skilled and unskilled managers.
   C. zero.

Solution to 1: A is correct. The error consists of rejecting the null hypothesis (no skill) when it is correct.

Solution to 2: C is correct. The error consists of not rejecting the null hypothesis (no skill) when it is incorrect.

Solution to 3: B is correct. The less distinct the distribution of skilled managers from unskilled managers, the lower the opportunity cost of retaining and cost of hiring an unskilled manager. That is, the smaller the perceived difference between the distribution of skilled and unskilled managers, the lower the cost and incentive to fire a manager.

3. QUANTITATIVE ELEMENTS OF MANAGER SEARCH AND SELECTION

Performance appraisal captures most aspects of quantitative analysis, evaluating a manager's strengths and weaknesses as measured by that manager's ability to add value to a stated benchmark. Although the determination of whether the manager possesses skill is important, it is equally important to understand the manager's risk profile. The manager has likely been selected to fill a particular role in the portfolio. As such, although it is important to select a skillful manager, the "best" manager may be one that delivers the desired exposures and is suitable for the investor's assumptions, expectations, and biases.

3.1. Style Analysis

An important component of performance appraisal and manager selection is understanding the manager's risk exposures relative to the benchmark and how they evolve over time. This understanding helps define the universe of potential managers and the monitoring of selected managers. The process is referred to as style analysis.

A manager's self-reported risk exposures, such as portfolio concentration, industry exposure, capitalization exposure, and other quantitative measures, are the starting point in style analysis. They provide a means to classify managers by style for defining the selection process, a point of reference for evaluating the returns-based and holdings-based style analysis, and an interesting operational check on the manager.

The results of the returns-based style analysis (RBSA) and the holdings-based style analysis (HBSA) should be consistent with the manager's philosophy and the investment process. If not, the process might not be repeatable or might be implemented inconsistently. It is essential to look at all portfolio construction and risk management issues.

The results of the returns-based style analysis and the holdings-based style analysis should be tracked over time in order to ascertain if the risk trends or exposures are out of line with expectations or the manager's stated style. Deviations may signal that issues, such as style drift, are developing.

Returns-based and holdings-based style analyses provide a means to determine the risks and sources of return for a particular strategy. To be useful, style analysis must be:

- *Meaningful:* The risks reported must represent the important sources of performance return and risk.
- *Accurate:* The reported values must reflect the manager's actual risk exposures.
- *Consistent:* The methodology must allow for comparison over time and across multiple managers.
- *Timely:* The report must be available in a timely manner so that it is useful for making informed investment decisions.

Style analysis is most useful with strategies that hold publicly traded securities where pricing is frequent. It can be applied to other strategies (hedge funds and private equity, for example), but the insights drawn from a style analysis of such strategies are more likely to be used for designing additional lines of inquiry in the course of due diligence rather than for confirmation of the investment process.

Returns-based style analysis (RBSA) is a top-down approach that involves estimating a portfolio's sensitivities to security market indexes representing a range of distinct factors. Although RBSA adds the additional analytical step of estimating the risk factors, as opposed to using a third-party or self-reported style categorization, the analysis is straightforward and typically does not require a large amount of additional, or difficult to acquire, data. RBSA should identify the important drivers of return and risk factors for the period analyzed and can be estimated even for complicated strategies. In addition, the process is comparable across managers and through time, and the use of returns data provides an objective style check that is not subject to window dressing. The analysis can be run immediately after the data is available, particularly in the case of publicly traded securities. As such, RBSA has many of the attributes of effective risk reporting.

The disadvantage is that RBSA is an imprecise tool. Although the additional computational effort required is not onerous, accuracy may be compromised, because RBSA effectively attributes performance to an unchanging average portfolio during the period. This attribution limits the ability to identify the impact of dynamic investment decisions and may distort the decomposition across sources of added value. Furthermore, the portfolio being analyzed might not reflect the current or future portfolio exposures. If the portfolio contains illiquid securities, stale prices may understate the risk exposure of the strategy. This is a particular problem for private equity (PE) and venture capital (VC) managers that hold illiquid or non-traded securities. VC and PE firms report performance based on the internal rate of return of cash distributions and appraisals of ongoing projects. As a result, reported performance can understate the volatility of return for shorter horizons or time periods with limited liquidity events. Longer periods generally provide more-accurate estimates of the manager's underlying standard deviation of return. The timeliness of any analysis depends on the securities that take the longest to price, which can be challenging for illiquid or non-traded securities.

Holdings-based style analysis (HBSA) is a bottom-up approach that estimates the risk exposures from the actual securities held in the portfolio at a point in time. This approach allows for estimation of current risk factors and offers several advantages. Similar to RBSA, HBSA should identify all important drivers of return and risk factors; be comparable across managers and through time; provide an accurate view of the manager's risk exposures, although potentially subject to window dressing; and be estimated immediately after the data become available.

Exhibit 3 presents a typical holdings-based style map. The manager being evaluated, along with the other managers in the universe, is placed along the size (*y*-axis) and style (*x*-axis) dimensions. The portfolio holdings of the manager being evaluated exhibit a large-cap value bias in what is otherwise a rather diverse universe.

EXHIBIT 3   Example of Holdings-Based Style Analysis

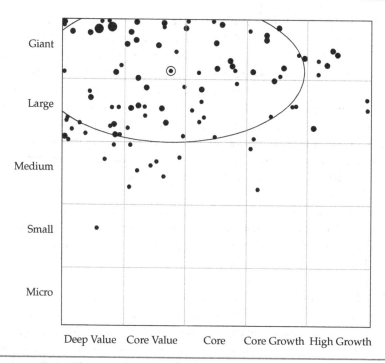

Deep Value   Core Value   Core   Core Growth High Growth

Source: Morningstar Direct, The Mutual Fund Research Center.

As with RBSA, HBSA has some disadvantages. The computational effort increases with the complexity of the strategy and depends on the timing and degree of the transparency provided by the manager. This extra effort can be challenging for hedge fund, private equity, and venture capital managers that may be averse to or unable to provide position-level pricing. Even with mutual funds, the necessary transparency may come with a time lag. The usefulness of the analysis may be compromised, because the portfolio reflects a snapshot in time and might not reflect the portfolio going forward, particularly for high-turnover strategies. Some factors may be difficult to estimate if the strategy is complex because HBSA requires an understanding of the underlying strategy. In general, HBSA is typically easier with equity strategies. If the portfolio has illiquid securities, stale pricing may underestimate the risk exposure of the strategy. The report's timeliness depends on the securities that take the longest to price, which can be challenging for illiquid or non-traded securities.

EXAMPLE 3   Style Analysis

1. Which of the following is an advantage of RBSA?
    A. It is a more precise tool than HBSA.
    B. It does not require potentially difficult to acquire data.
    C. It is more accurate than HBSA when the portfolio contains illiquid securities.

2. Which of the following is an advantage of HBSA?
    A. It works well for high-turnover strategies.
    B. It can identify important drivers of return and risk factors and is comparable across managers and through time.
    C. It effectively attributes performance to a snapshot of the portfolio at a particular time and thus is not subject to window dressing.

Solution to 1: B is correct. The data needed for RBSA are usually easier to obtain than the data required for HBSA. RBSA is not a precise tool, and it is not more accurate than HBSA when the portfolio holds illiquid securities.

Solution to 2: B is correct. Although HBSA allows for estimation of current risk factors and is comparable across managers and through time, the necessary computational effort increases with the strategy's complexity and depends on the timing and degree of the transparency provided by the manager. Some factors may be difficult to estimate if the strategy is complex because this approach requires an understanding of the underlying strategy. In general, HBSA is typically easier for equity strategies. If the portfolio has illiquid securities, stale pricing may underestimate the risk exposure of the strategy. Window dressing and high turnover can compromise the results because the results are attributed to a snapshot of the portfolio.

3.2. Capture Ratios and Drawdowns in Manager Evaluation

Because large losses require proportionally greater gains to reverse or offset, drawdowns and capture ratios can be important factors in investment manager evaluation. A manager that experiences larger drawdowns may be less suitable for an investor closer to the end of their investment horizon. Capture ratios help assess manager suitability relative to the investor's IPS, especially in relation to the investor's time horizon and risk tolerance.

Recall that: 1) Upside capture (UC) measures capture when the benchmark return is positive. UC greater than 100% suggests out-performance relative to the benchmark. 2) Downside capture (DC) measures capture when the benchmark return is negative. DC less than 100% generally suggests out-performance relative to the benchmark. 3) The **capture ratio** (CR)—upside capture divided by downside capture—measures the asymmetry of return. 4) **Drawdown** is the cumulative peak-to-trough loss during a particular continuous period and **drawdown duration** is the total time from the start of the drawdown until the cumulative drawdown recovers to zero.

Let's illustrate the use of capture ratios in the analysis of manager returns. Consider the four stylized return profiles in Exhibit 4.

EXHIBIT 4   Return Profile Summary

Profile	Upside Capture	Downside Capture	Ratio
Long only	100%	100%	1.0
Positive asymmetry	75%	25%	3.0
Low beta	50%	50%	1.0
Negative asymmetry	25%	75%	0.3

Each strategy's allocation to the S&P 500 Total Return (TR) Index and to 90-day T-bills (assuming monthly rebalancing to simplify the calculations) is based on the realized monthly return from January 2000 to December 2013. (This time period encompasses two significant drawdowns: the "tech bubble burst" of the early 2000s and the extreme drawdown of the Global Financial Crisis in 2008–2009.)

- The long-only profile is 100% allocated to the S&P 500 throughout the period.
- The low-beta profile is allocated 50% to the S&P 500 throughout the period.
- The positive asymmetry profile is allocated 75% to the S&P 500 for months when the S&P 500 return is positive and 25% when the S&P 500 return is negative.
- The negative asymmetry profile is allocated 25% to the S&P 500 for months when the S&P 500 return is positive and 75% when the S&P 500 return is negative.

The remainder for all profiles is allocated to 90-day T-bills. Exhibit 5 shows each profile's cumulative monthly return for the period.

EXHIBIT 5   Each Profile's Cumulative Monthly Return, January 2000–December 2013

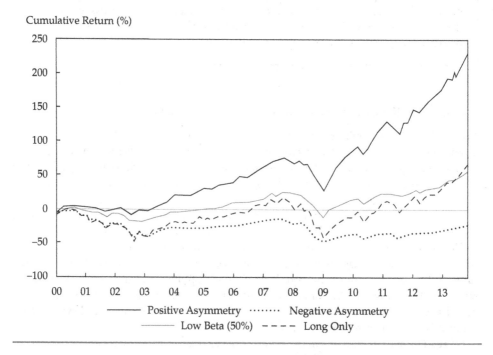

Exhibit 6 provides summary statistics for each profile based on monthly returns from January 2000 to December 2013. Although the long-only profile outperformed the low-beta profile over the full period, this outperformance resulted from the strong up market of 2013—the long-only profile lagged the low-beta profile for most of the period. The low beta profile achieved higher risk-adjusted returns and only half the volatility for the full period. The low-beta profile declined only 18.8% from January 2000 to September 2002, compared with the long-only decline of 42.5%. As a result, the low-beta profile had higher cumulative performance from January 2000 to October 2007, despite markedly lagging the long-only profile (56.0% to 108.4%) from October 2002 to October 2007.

Although a low-beta approach may sacrifice performance, it shows that limiting drawdowns can result in better absolute and risk-adjusted returns in certain markets.

Not surprisingly, positive asymmetry results in better performance relative to long only, low beta, and negative asymmetry. Although the positive asymmetry profile lags in up markets, this lag is more than offset by the lower participation in down markets. Not surprisingly, the negative asymmetry profile lags.

EXHIBIT 6   Summary Statistics for Each Profile, January 2000–December 2013

Strategy	Long Only	Low Beta	Positive Asymmetry	Negative Asymmetry
Cumulative return	64.0%	54.2%	228.1%	−24.4%
Annualized return	3.60%	3.14%	8.86%	−1.98%
Annualized standard deviation	15.64%	7.79%	9.61%	10.01%
Sharpe ratio	0.10	0.14	0.71	−0.40
Beta	1.00	0.50	0.61	0.64
Drawdown (maximum)	−50.9%	−28.3%	−26.9%	−48.9%

We've shown that positive asymmetry is a desirable trait. When evaluating a manager that exhibits positive asymmetry in their returns, we need to understand whether the strategy is inherently convex or whether the profile is a result of manager skill. For example, a hedging strategy implemented by rolling forward out-of-the-money put options will typically return many small losses because more options expire worthless than are compensated for by the occasional large gain during a large market downturn. A manager employing this strategy will likely exhibit consistent positive asymmetry in his returns, but the positive asymmetry is likely due to the nature of the strategy rather than on investment skill.

Let's consider now the use of drawdowns in the analysis of manager returns. Drawdowns are stress-tests of the investment process and can expose potentially flawed or inconsistently implemented investment processes, inadequate risk controls, or operational issues. Did the manager implement the stated investment process consistently? If yes, what lessons were learned and how might the investment process have been adapted as a result? If the drawdown resulted from a deviation from the stated investment process, why? During a large or long drawdown, a manager could start to worry more about business risk than investment risk and act in their own best interest rather than that of their investors. How a manager responds to a large drawdown as it occurs, and what lessons are learned, provides evidence of the robustness and repeatability of the investment, portfolio construction, and risk management processes, as well as insight into the people implementing the processes.

Events of August 2007

Starting on 7 August 2007, many quantitative equity long–short strategies began to experience large drawdowns. Many managers had never experienced such losses or market conditions and started to sell positions as stop-loss and risk management policies were triggered (Khandani and Lo 2011). This activity added to additional selling pressure, and the S&P 500 declined 13.4% by 8 August. Those managers who sold ended up locking in large losses because the underperforming stocks and market subsequently recovered, with the S&P 500 down only 5.7% for the month. In many cases, those funds that sold experienced redemptions or ended up closing.

As August 2007 demonstrated, distinguishing prudent risk management from a misalignment of interests is not always straightforward. Should a manager continue to actively trade a portfolio if the market environment no longer reflects their investment philosophy? In addition, traders will claim that it is better to cut losses because losses can signal that something has changed or that the timing of the trade is not right. Conversely, selling into a down market raises the risk of crystallizing losses and missing any subsequent reversal. The decision maker must assess whether the manager's behavior was a disciplined application of the investment process, reflected a misalignment of interests, or simply resulted from panic or overreaction by the manager.

One aspect of suitability for the IPS is the investment horizon and its relationship to risk capacity. An investor closer to retirement, with less time to recover from losses, places more emphasis on absolute measures of risk. If there has been no change to investment policy and no change in the view that the manager remains suitable, the temptation to exit should be resisted to avoid exiting at an inauspicious time. Investors with shorter horizons, with lower risk capacity, or who are prone to overreact to losses may be better served by allocating to managers with shallower and shorter expected drawdowns.

The Concept of Active Share

Active share measures the difference in portfolio holdings relative to the benchmark. A manager that precisely replicates the benchmark will have an active share of zero; a manager with no holdings in common with the benchmark will have an active share of one.

Given a strategy with N securities ($i = 1, 2, ..., N$), active share is calculated as

$$\text{Active Share} = \frac{1}{2} \sum_{i=1}^{N} |\text{Strategy Weight}_i - \text{Benchmark Weight}_i|$$

Typically, managers are somewhere along the spectrum. The categorization of active share and tracking risk in Exhibit 7 has been suggested for active managers. It is clear that full replication will appear as a closet indexer. A manager that uses sampling techniques to build the portfolio may, however, appear as a diversified stock picker depending on the universe under consideration and the dispersion of active share of the constituents. Tracking risk will be low, but active share might not be because only a subset of constituents is held. One reason is that high and low are relative to the universe being examined and the category definitions used. As such, it is important to examine risk factors and portfolio construction techniques of both active and passive managers.

EXHIBIT 7   Active Share vs. Tracking Risk

| | | **Active Share** | |
		Low	High
Tracking risk	High	Sector rotation	Concentrated stock pickers
	Low	Closet indexer	Diversified stock pickers

4. QUALITATIVE ELEMENTS OF MANAGER DUE DILIGENCE

The goal of manager due diligence is to weigh the potential risks that may arise from entering into an investment management relationship and entrusting assets to a firm. Although it is impossible to eliminate all potential risks, the allocator must assess how the firm will manage the broad range of risks it is likely to face in the future. This section outlines the general aspects of manager due diligence and the particular questions the investor needs to answer.

Investment due diligence examines and evaluates the qualitative considerations that illustrate that the manager's investment process is repeatable and consistently implemented. The objective is to understand whether the investment philosophy, process, people, and portfolio construction satisfy the assumption that past performance provides some guidance for expected future performance. In other words, are the conclusions drawn from performance measurement, attribution, and appraisal reliable selection criteria? In addition, it is important to remember that investment managers are businesses. Regardless of the strength of the investment process or historical performance, investment management firms must be operated as successful businesses to ensure sustainability. Operational due diligence examines and evaluates the firm's policies and procedures, to identify potential risks that might not be captured in historical performance and to assess the firm's sustainability.

4.1. Investment Philosophy

The investment philosophy is the foundation of the investment process. Every investment strategy is based on a set of assumptions about the factors that drive performance and the manager's beliefs about their ability to successfully exploit these sources of return. The investment manager should have a clear and concise investment philosophy.

First, every manager makes assumptions about market efficiency, including the degree and the time frame. Passive strategies assume markets are sufficiently efficient and that active management cannot add value after transaction costs and fees. As a result, passive strategies seek to earn risk premiums. A **risk premium** is the expected return in excess of a minimal-risk ("risk-free") rate of return that accrues to bearing a risk that is not easily diversified away—so-called systematic risk.

Passive strategies seek to capture return through exposure to systematic risk premiums, such as equity risk, duration risk, or credit risk. These strategies can also look to capture alternative risk premiums, such as liquidity risk, natural disaster risk (e.g., insurance-linked securities, such as catastrophe bonds and quota shares), volatility risk, or some combination of these premiums (e.g., distressed strategies seek to capture credit and liquidity risk premiums).

In contrast, active strategies assume markets are sufficiently inefficient that security mispricings can be identified and exploited. These opportunities typically arise when market behavior deviates from the manager's fundamental assumptions. Generally speaking, inefficiencies can be categorized as behavioral or structural.

- *Behavioral inefficiencies* are perceived mispricings created by the actions of other market participants, usually associated with biases, such as trend following or loss aversion. These inefficiencies are temporary, lasting long enough for the manager to identify and exploit them before the market price and perceived intrinsic value converge.
- *Structural inefficiencies* are perceived mispricings created by external or internal rules and regulations. These inefficiencies can be long lived and assume a continuation of the rules and regulations rather than a convergence.

Active strategies also typically make assumptions about the dynamics and structures of the market, such as the following: The correlation structure of the market is sufficiently stable over the investment horizon to make diversification useful for risk management; prices eventually converge to intrinsic value, which can be estimated by using a discounted cash flow model; or market prices are driven by predictable macroeconomic trends.

It is important to evaluate these assumptions and the role they play in the investment process to understand how the strategy will behave through time and across market environments.

- Can the manager clearly and consistently articulate their investment philosophy? It is hard to have confidence in the repeatability and efficacy of an investment process if the manager, and investment personnel, cannot explain the assumptions that underpin the process. This clarity also provides a consistency check that the investment process and personnel are appropriate for the stated philosophy.
- Are the assumptions credible and consistent? That is, does the decision maker agree with the assumptions underlying the strategy, and are these assumptions consistent with the investment process? A decision maker who believes a market is efficient would likely not find the assumptions of an active manager in that market credible. In the decision maker's judgment, the assumptions must support a repeatable and robust investment process.
- How has the philosophy developed over time? Ideally, the philosophy is unchanged through time, suggesting a repeatable process. If philosophy has evolved, it is preferred that changes are judged to be reasonable responses to changing market conditions rather than a series of ad hoc reactions to performance or investor flows. Such changes suggest a lack of repeatability and robustness.
- Are the return sources linked to credible and consistent inefficiencies? The decision maker must judge whether the investment philosophy is based on an inefficiency that is based on an informational advantage, likely a behavioral inefficiency by interpreting information better than other market participants, or a structural inefficiency that suggests the investment process is repeatable.

If the source of return is linked to a credible inefficiency, there is the additional issue of capacity. Capacity has several related aspects, such as the level of assets the strategy or opportunity can absorb without a dilution of returns, the number of opportunities or securities available, and the ability to transact in a timely manner at or near the market price—that is, liquidity. Overall, capacity is the level, repeatability, and sustainability of returns that the inefficiency is expected to support in the future.

- Does the inefficiency provide a sufficient frequency of opportunity and level of return to cover transaction costs and fees? If so, does this require leverage?
- Does the inefficiency provide a repeatable source of return? That is, can the opportunity be captured by a repeatable process, or is each opportunity unique, requiring a different process or skill set to exploit?
- Is the inefficiency sustainable? That is, at what asset level would the realized return from the inefficiency be unacceptably low? Sustainability will be a function of the market's depth and liquidity, as well as how much capital is allocated, either by the manager or competitors, to the inefficiency.

Uncommon Ways of Passing the Investment Philosophy Test

1. Managers that measure the success of the steps of the process and not just the ultimate outcome.
For example, consider a bond manager that makes the claim that his or her credit research not only predicts upgrades and downgrades, but makes those predictions before the expectation of a rating change is reflected in the market price. This manager tracks every prediction to see if the market consensus (as reflected by price) and rating agencies come around to his or her view. I get comfort from the facts that (1) such managers know their views only have value if they are not only correct but different than consensus, and (2) they track how prices eventually come to reflect, or not reflect, their views. Similarly, managers that evaluate their own performance with strategy benchmarks designed to replicate their selection universe demonstrate they understand the importance of attempting to differentiate alpha from noise (see Kuenzi [2003]).

2. Managers that recognize that every strategy they come up with is potentially subject to being arbitraged away.
For example, consider a quantitative equity manager that plays many themes at once. Each theme is viewed as having a finite life, and the performance of each theme is isolated and monitored so as to observe the decay in the value of the theme. The manager considers his or her competitive advantage to be in the identification of new themes, and in the technology for measuring the contribution of each theme to performance. A similar idea is presented in the adaptive market hypothesis of Lo [2004], where the market is always tending toward efficiency, but the types of trades needed to move it towards efficiency rotate and evolve over time.

3. Managers that claim they exploit inefficiencies, and identify the specific inefficiency they are exploiting with every position they take.
Most managers that say they exploit inefficiencies use this claim as a broad justification for their investment process, but are unable to identify the specific inefficiency they are exploiting in any given decision they make. Those that routinely specify how their information or point of point differs from that reflected in price are much more credible.

4. Managers that know their companies so well that they are quicker to interpret change, even though they have no explicit alpha thesis.

There is always an exception to the rule. Sometimes a manager is simply talented and cannot articulate an alpha thesis.

Despite examples such as these, it remains frustratingly difficult to distinguish between true alpha-generators and alpha-pretenders. I believe there is more that alpha-generators can do to distinguish themselves, and that consultants should be more insistent that they do it.

Excerpted from: John R. Minahan. 2006. CFA, "The Role of Investment Philosophy in Evaluating Investment Managers: A Consultant's Perspective on Distinguishing Alpha from Noise," *Journal of Investing* 15. Copyright © 2006 by Institutional Investor Journals. Reprinted with permission.

EXAMPLE 4   Investment Philosophy

1. Which of the following is **not** an important consideration when evaluating a manager's investment philosophy?
   A. What are the compensation arrangements of key employees?
   B. Are the investment philosophy assumptions credible and consistent?
   C. Can the manager clearly and consistently articulate their investment philosophy?

2. Generally speaking, inefficiencies can be categorized as:
   A. large and small.
   B. internal and external.
   C. structural and behavioral.

3. Which of the following is **not** an important consideration when evaluating the capacity of an inefficiency?
   A. Does the strategy rely on unique information?
   B. Does the inefficiency provide a repeatable source of return?
   C. Does the inefficiency provide a sufficient frequency of opportunity and level of return to cover transaction costs and fees?

Solution to 1: A is correct. Employee compensation is a legal and compliance issue considered as part of operational due diligence.

Solution to 2: C is correct. Behavioral inefficiencies are created by the actions of other participants in the market. These inefficiencies are temporary, lasting long enough for the manager to identify and exploit them before the market price and perceived intrinsic value converge. Structural inefficiencies are created by external or internal rules and regulations. These inefficiencies can be long lived and assume a continuation of the rules and regulations rather than a convergence.

Solution to 3: A is correct. The uniqueness of information used by the manager is a consideration when evaluating the assumptions of the investment process.

4.2. Investment Personnel

An investment process can only be as good as the people who create and implement it, and even the best process can be compromised by poor execution by the people involved. This view is not a question of liking the manager or team but of trusting that they possess the expertise and experience to effectively implement the strategy.

- Does the investment team have sufficient expertise and experience to effectively execute the investment process? The need for expertise is self-evident. The greater the experience, particularly managing the current strategy across market environments, the greater the confidence in the manager's ability to effectively execute the investment process. As noted with drawdowns, it is especially instructive to see how the manager responded to stressed markets and poor performance.
- Does the investment team have sufficient depth to effectively execute the investment process? A strategy that focuses on a small universe of publicly traded stocks might not require a large investment team. A global macro or multi-strategy fund, which holds positions across numerous global markets, likely requires a large team with expertise and experience supporting the manager.
- What is the level of key person risk? A strategy that is overly dependent on the judgment or particular skills of an individual or small team of people faces **key person risk**, an overreliance on an individual or individuals whose departure would negatively affect the strategy's performance.
- What kinds of agreements (e.g., non-compete) and incentives (ownership, bonus, pay) exist to retain and attract key employees to join and stay at the firm?
- What has been the turnover of firm personnel? High personnel turnover risks the loss of institutional knowledge and experience within the team.

4.3. Investment Decision-Making Process

The investment decision-making process has four elements: signal creation, signal capture, portfolio construction, and portfolio monitoring.

4.3.1. Signal Creation (Idea Generation)

An investment signal is a data point or fact that can be observed early enough to implement as an investment position. The basic question is, how are investment ideas generated? The efficient market hypothesis posits that the key to exploiting inefficiencies is to have information that is all of the following:

- **Unique:** Does the strategy rely on unique information? If so, how is this information collected, and how is the manager able to retain an informational edge, particularly in a regulatory environment that seeks to reduce informational asymmetries?
- **Timely:** Does the strategy possess an information timing advantage? If so, how is this information collected, and how is the manager able to retain a timing edge, particularly in a regulatory environment that seeks to reduce informational asymmetries?
- **Interpreted differently:** Interpretation is typically how managers seek to differentiate themselves. Does the manager possess a unique way of interpreting information? Or does the manager claim their strategy possesses a "secret sauce" component or that its team is simply smarter than other managers?

4.3.2. Signal Capture (Idea Implementation)

The second step is signal capture, translating the generated investment idea into an investment position.

- What is the process for translating investment ideas into investment positions?
- Is this process repeatable and consistent with the strategy assumptions?
- What is the process, and who is ultimately responsible for approving an investment position?

4.3.3. Portfolio Construction

The third element is portfolio construction; how investment positions are implemented within the portfolio. This element begins to capture the manager's risk management methodology. Good investment ideas need to be implemented properly to exploit opportunities and capture desired risk premiums. It is also important that portfolio construction is consistent with the investment philosophy and process as well as the expertise of investment personnel.

- How are portfolio allocations set and adjusted? The allocation process should be consistent with investment philosophy and process. For example, if the portfolio is actively managed, its turnover should agree with the frequency of signals generated and the securities' liquidity. The allocation process should be well-defined and consistently applied, supporting the repeatability of the investment process. For example, are allocations made quantitatively or qualitatively?
- Are portfolio allocations based on the manager's conviction? In other words, do the positions the manager believes will most likely outperform or exhibit the greatest outperformance receive the largest active overweighting, and the securities the manager believes will underperform receive the largest active underweighting?
- How have the portfolio characteristics changed with asset growth? Has the number and/or characteristics of the positions held changed to accommodate a larger amount of AUM?
- Does the portfolio use **stop-losses** to manage risk? If so, are they hard (positions are automatically sold when the loss threshold is reached) or soft (positions are evaluated when the loss threshold is reached)? Although stop-losses represent a clear risk management approach, the goal of protecting against large losses must be balanced with the risk of closing positions too frequently.
- What types of securities are used? Does the manager use derivatives to express investment ideas? What experience does the manager have investing in these securities? The manager should be sufficiently well-versed and experienced with the securities used to understand how they will behave in different market environments.
- How are hedges implemented? What security types are used? How are hedge ratios set? Consider a manager that focuses on stock selection to generate alpha and hedges to reduce or remove market risk. The hedges must be sized correctly, or they can be ineffective (underhedged) or they can overwhelm stock selection (overhedged), with performance driven more by beta than by alpha.
- How are long and short ideas expressed? Are they paired—that is, each long position has a corresponding short position—or are long and short positions established independently? How long and short positions are allocated is important for understanding the portfolio's overall exposure. If long and short positions are paired, with the idea of capturing alpha as

prices converge while offsetting market risk, the positions must be well-matched and sized correctly.

An important risk is liquidity. Strategies that are not intending to capture a liquidity risk premium must be aware of portfolio liquidity in terms of adapting to changing information, changing market conditions, and changing investor liquidity demands. An existing portfolio consisting of illiquid securities will be more costly to change, not only to take advantage of new opportunities but also to trade, because of higher transaction costs. There is the additional cost of having to sell positions at inopportune times as a result of market events or investor liquidity demands. When assessing security liquidity, it is important to consider all of the assets under management for that particular manager and investment process.

• What percentage of the portfolio can be liquidated in five business days or less? What percentage requires more than 10 business days to liquidate? The less liquid the portfolio, the higher the transaction costs if the manager is forced to sell one or more positions. A more liquid portfolio offers flexibility if the manager faces unexpected investor liquidity demands or rapidly changing market conditions.
• What is the average daily volume weighted by portfolio position size?
• Have any of the portfolio holdings been suspended from trading? If so, what is the name of the company, and what are the circumstances pertaining to the suspension?
• Are there any holdings in which ownership by the firm across all portfolios collectively accounts for more than 5% of the market capitalization or float of the security?
• What is the firm's trading strategy? Does the investment manager tend to provide liquidity or demand it? Has the trading strategy changed in response to asset growth?

4.3.4. Monitoring the Portfolio

The investment decision-making process is a feedback loop that consists of ongoing monitoring of the portfolio in light of new information and analysis. This monitoring includes an assessment of both external and internal considerations. External considerations include the economic and financial market environments. Has anything meaningful occurred that might affect the manager's ability to exploit the market inefficiency that is the strategy's focus? Internal considerations include the portfolio's performance, risk profile, and construction. Has anything changed that might signal potential style drift or other deviations from the investment process? Ongoing monitoring and performance attribution help to ensure that the manager remains appropriate for the clients' mandates.

4.4. Operational Due Diligence

Performance appraisal assumes that reported returns are accurate and fully reflect the manager's risk profile. Unfortunately, as we have seen, this assumption is not always true. Although investment due diligence is one step toward understanding these risks, one must remember that investment management firms are *businesses*, and in many cases they are small businesses with a high degree of business risk. Regardless of the strength of the investment process or historical investment results, investment management firms must be operated as successful businesses in order to ensure their sustainability. This requirement creates the potential for a misalignment of interests between the manager and the investor. Operational due diligence analyzes the integrity of the business and seeks to understand and evaluate these risks by examining and evaluating the firm's policies and procedures.

Weaknesses in the firm's infrastructure represent latent risks to the investor. A strong back office (support staff) is critical for safeguarding assets and ensuring that accurate reports are issued in a timely manner. The manager should have a robust trading process that seeks to avoid human error. A repeatable process requires consistent implementation. The allocator needs to understand the following:

- What is the firm's trading policy?
- Does the firm use soft dollar commissions? If so, is there a rigorous process for ensuring compliance?
- What is the process for protecting against unauthorized trading?
- How are fees calculated and collected?
- How are securities allocated across investor accounts, including both pooled and separately managed accounts? The allocation method should be objective (e.g., based on invested capital) to avoid the potential to benefit some investors at the expense of others.
- How many different strategies does the firm manage, and are any new strategies being contemplated? Is the firm's infrastructure capable of efficiently and accurately implementing the different strategies?
- What information technology offsite backup facilities are in place?
- Does the firm have processes, software, and hardware in place to handle cybersecurity issues?

An important constituent of the infrastructure is third-party service providers, including the firm's prime broker, administrator, auditor, and legal counsel. They provide an important independent verification of the firm's performance and reporting.

- Are the firm's third-party service providers known and respected?
- Has there been any change in third-party providers? If so, when and why? This information is particularly important with regard to the firm's auditor. Frequent changes of the auditor is a red flag and may mean the manager is trying to hide something.

The risk management function should be viewed as an integral part of the investment firm and not considered a peripheral function. The extent to which integration exists provides insight into the firm's culture and the alignment of interests between the manager and the investor. The manager should have a risk manual that is readily available for review:

- Does the portfolio have any hard/soft investment guidelines?
- How are these guidelines monitored?
- What is the procedure for curing breaches?
- Who is responsible for risk management?
- Is there an independent risk officer?

4.4.1. Firm

An investment management firm must operate as a successful business to ensure sustainability. A manager that goes out of business does not have a repeatable investment process. An important aspect of manager selection is assessing the level of business risk.

- What is the ownership structure of the firm?
- What are the total firm AUM and AUM by investment strategy?
- What is the firm's breakeven AUM (the asset base needed to generate enough fee revenue to cover total firm expenses)?
- Are any of the firm's strategies closed to new capital?
- How much capital would the firm like to raise?

A firm that is independently owned may have greater autonomy and flexibility than a firm owned by a larger organization, but it may have a higher cost structure and lack financial support during market events, raising potential business risks. Outside ownership could create a situation in which the outside owner has objectives that conflict with the investment strategy. For instance, the outside owner might want to increase the asset base to generate higher fee revenue, but this action could prevent the portfolio from holding lower-capitalization stocks. Ideally, ownership should be spread across as many employees as is feasible and practical. A firm managing a smaller asset base may be more nimble and less prone to dilution of returns but will likely have lower revenues to support infrastructure and compensate employees. At a minimum, the asset base needs to be sufficient to support the firm's current expenditures.

Last, and by no means least important, are legal and compliance issues. It is critical that the firm's interests are aligned with those of the investor.

- What are the compensation arrangements for key employees? For example, are any people compensated with stock in the firm, and if so, what happens to this stock when they leave the firm?
- Do employees invest personal assets in the firm's strategies? Investing their own money in the same products in which the firm's clients invest creates an alignment of interests, but too large a proportion of their own assets invested in this one product may create personal/business risk for the manager that overrides the alignment of interests.
- Does the firm foster a culture of compliance?
- What is covered in the compliance manual?
- Has the firm or any of its employees been involved with an investigation by any financial market regulator or self-regulatory organization?
- Has the firm been involved in any lawsuits?
- Are any of the firm's employees involved in legal actions or personal litigation that might affect their ability to continue to fulfill their fiduciary responsibilities?

Hiring a manager requires trust. A firm's culture as expressed by its compliance policies and procedures should provide a level of confidence that the manager's and investor's interests are aligned.

The Investment Process

Bernard "Bernie" L. Madoff ran one of the biggest frauds in Wall Street history. One of the first indications that something was amiss at Bernard L. Madoff Investment Securities arose when Harry Markopolos was unable to reconcile the return track record with the investment process. In addition to observing the unrealistically consistent nature of the claimed returns, Markopolos concluded that there was no way to generate the returns using the claimed investment process. Further analysis convinced him that

Madoff's returns resulted not from front running—that is, taking positions to exploit knowledge of investor trade flows—but rather from fraud.

In hindsight, there were many red flags over the years that indicated there was something wrong with Madoff's investment management process. The firm claimed to generate steady returns in every market environment. Mr. Madoff was known to dismiss questions about his strategy, arguing that his business was too complicated for outsiders to understand. He also operated as a broker/dealer with an asset management division, profiting from trading commissions rather than the investment management fees that hedge funds charged. The structure seemed odd to other investment professionals, raising concerns about the firm's legitimacy. Another red flag was raised when it became known that the firm used a small, unknown auditor with only three employees. If, as Mr. Madoff claimed, the strategy was so complex that no one could understand it, a small, three-person audit firm would be unlikely to be able to effectively audit the financial statements (Zuckerman 2008).

Self-Reported Risk Factors

Requesting and obtaining self-reported risk factors not only is important for understanding the manager's investment process but also provides an interesting operational check. A manager should readily comply with all requests for risk reporting. If not, it suggests a lack of transparency that may become challenging for monitoring the manager and strategy in the future. Additionally, it might indicate an inability to generate essential reports, which raises questions about the firm's policies and procedures.

All risk reporting should be meaningful, consistent, accurate, and timely. A lack of meaningful reporting indicates that the reports are not useful in monitoring the manager and that there is a lack of transparency. In the worst case, the manager does not understand the risk exposures or does not want to disclose them.

A lack of consistent reporting also reduces the usefulness of the reporting. Inconsistent reports preclude the ability to track levels and trends of important risk factors. The manager may be choosing to selectively report particular risks that they deem important or interesting. In the worst case, it may mean that the manager is selectively reporting in order to hide risks created by deviations from the stated investment process.

A lack of accuracy suggests that the manager cannot properly measure portfolio risks or is intentionally misreporting results. A lack of timeliness reduces the reports' usefulness and suggests either inefficient procedures or attempts to manipulate the flow of information. In all of these cases, poor risk reporting, at a minimum, suggests a reevaluation of the manager and, if issues are identified, potential termination.

4.4.2. Investment Vehicle

There are two broad options for implementing investment strategies: individual separate accounts and pooled (or commingled) vehicles. An additional operational consideration is the evaluation of the investment vehicle—its appropriateness to the investment strategy and its suitability for the investor. Separate accounts offer additional control, customization, tax efficiency, reporting, and transparency advantages, but these come at a higher cost.

In a pooled or commingled vehicle, the money from multiple investors is held as a single portfolio and managed without potential customization for any investor. Such vehicles include open-end funds, closed-end funds, exchange-traded funds, exchange-traded notes, and hedge funds. As the name infers, a separately managed account (SMA) vehicle holds the money in a segregated account in the investor's name. The funds are managed to a particular mandate with the potential to customize the strategy for each investor. The advantages of SMA vehicles include the following:

- **Ownership:** In an SMA, the investor owns the individual securities directly. This approach provides additional safety should a liquidity event occur. Although the manager continues to make investment decisions, these decisions will not be influenced by the redemption or liquidity demand of other investors in the strategy. An SMA also provides clear legal ownership for the recovery of assets resulting from unforeseen events, such as bankruptcy or mismanagement.
- **Customization:** SMAs allow the investor to potentially express individual constraints or preferences within the portfolio. SMAs can thus more closely address the investor's particular investment objectives.
- **Tax efficiency:** SMAs offer potentially improved tax efficiency because the investor pays taxes only on the capital gains realized and allows the implementation of tax-efficient investing and trading strategies.
- **Transparency:** SMAs offer real-time, position-level detail to the investor, providing complete transparency and accurate attribution to the investor. Even if a pooled vehicle provides position-level detail, such information will likely be presented with a delay.

If the SMA is customized, additional investment due diligence may be required to account for differences in security selection or portfolio construction. In addition, there are operational due diligence considerations.

- **Cost:** Separate accounts represent an additional operational burden on the manager, which translates into potentially higher costs for the investor. SMAs do not scale as easily as pooled vehicles. Once a pooled investment is established and the fixed costs paid, the cost of each new investor is largely the incremental costs of custody, trading larger positions, and generating an additional report. With an SMA, a new account must be established for each investor. In addition, SMAs are likely to face higher transaction costs to the degree that trades cannot be aggregated to reduce trade volumes. These costs are a function of the extent to which the strategy is customized or traded differently to accommodate different investor needs.
- **Tracking risk:** Customization of the strategy creates tracking risk relative to the benchmark, which can confuse attribution because performance will reflect investor constraints rather than manager decisions.
- **Investor behavior:** Transparency, combined with control and customization, allows for potential micromanagement by the investor—that is, the investor attempting to manage the portfolio. Such an effort not only negates the benefit of hiring a manager but is

particularly problematic if these changes decrease the portfolio's value. Potential investor behaviors include performance chasing, familiarity bias (being overly averse to unfamiliar holdings), and loss aversion (a tendency to disaggregate the portfolio and not appreciate the value of hedging).

The allocator's goal is to evaluate the costs and benefits of the vehicle used and judge its suitability for the IPS:

- Is the vehicle structure consistent with the investment process?
- Does the manager have the operational infrastructure necessary to manage the SMA?
- Is there a benefit to holding the securities in a separate account? If so, are these benefits sufficient to compensate for additional costs?
- Is tax efficiency an important objective of the IPS?
- Are there concerns that the available transparency and ability to customize will result in decisions by the investor that do not add value?

EXAMPLE 5 Pooled Investments and Separate Accounts

Which of the following are advantages of separately managed accounts compared with pooled investments?

A. Typically lower cost
B. Potential management of the portfolio by the investor
C. Ability to take close account of individual client constraints or preferences

Solution: C is correct. With SMAs, the investor owns the individual securities directly and can potentially express individual constraints or preferences within the portfolio. In particular, SMAs offer potentially improved tax efficiency because the investor pays taxes only on the capital gains realized and allows the implementation of tax-efficient investing and trading strategies.

4.4.3. Evaluation of the Investment's Terms

An additional and important aspect of manager selection is understanding the terms of the investment as presented in the prospectus, private placement memorandum, and/or limited partnership agreement. These documents are, in essence, the contract between the investor and the manager, outlining each party's rights and responsibilities. Although these documents cover numerous topics, this section focuses on liquidity and fees. The objective of the decision maker is to determine whether the liquidity and fee structure make the manager suitable for the investor's needs and the "best" manager for expressing a particular portfolio need.

4.4.3.1. Liquidity

Different vehicles provide different degrees of liquidity. Liquidity is defined as the timeliness with which a security or asset can be sold at or near the current price. The same criteria can be applied to managers.

The most liquid vehicles are closed-end funds and ETFs. As listed securities, they can be bought and sold intra-day, and the price received will depend on the trading volume and depth of the fund. The obvious advantage of these funds is ease of trading, although there can be some price uncertainty for less liquid funds, particularly when trying to buy or sell a large number of shares. Open-end funds are slightly less liquid, providing daily liquidity but also price certainty; shares are bought and sold at the end-of-day NAV.

Unlike open-end funds, ETFs, or closed-end funds, limited partnerships, such as hedge funds, venture capital funds, and private equity funds, typically require investors to invest their money for longer periods. Hedge fund liquidity has four basic features: redemption frequency, notification period, lockup, and gates. Redemption frequency indicates how often an investor can withdraw capital from the fund, and the notification period indicates how far in advance of the redemption investors must tell the fund of their intention to redeem. A lockup is the initial period, after making an investment, during which investors cannot redeem their holding. Lockups have two types: a hard lock, which allows for no redemptions, and a soft lock, which charges a fee, paid into the fund, for redemptions. A mutual fund redemption fee is equivalent to a hedge fund soft lock. Gates limit the amount of fund assets or investor assets that can be redeemed at one redemption date.

Private equity and venture capital funds provide the least liquidity. Investors are contractually obligated to contribute specific amounts (capital calls) during the investment phase and then receive distributions and capital as investments are harvested during the remaining term of the fund. A typical investment phase is 5 years. The typical life of a fund is 10 years, with the option to extend the term for two 1-year periods.

The obvious disadvantage of partnership liquidity terms is the reduced flexibility to adjust portfolio allocations in light of changing market conditions or investor circumstances, as well as the reduced ability to meet unexpected liquidity needs. The advantage of such terms is that they do lock up capital for longer horizons, allowing funds to take long-term views and hold less liquid securities—such as start-up companies, buyouts, turnarounds, real estate, or natural resources—with reduced risk of having to sell portfolio holdings at inopportune times in response to redemption requests. An additional advantage, which was apparent during the 2008 financial crisis, is that limited liquidity imposes this long horizon view on investors, reducing or removing their ability to overreact.

Because SMA assets are held in the investor's name, the securities in the portfolio can be sold at any time. As a result, an SMA's liquidity will depend on the liquidity of the securities held. An SMA holding listed large-cap stocks will likely be highly liquid, whereas an investor in an SMA that holds unlisted or illiquid securities will have to accept a discount when selling.

4.4.3.2. Management Fees[1]
Investors seek strong performance net of fees. Managers charge fees to cover operating costs and earn a return on their capital—primarily human capital. A manager's fixed costs are relatively small and primarily cover the costs of technology and the long-term lease of office space. Variable costs, which consist largely of payroll and marketing costs, dominate the income statements of asset management companies. Because a considerable portion of

---

[1]This section based on Chapter 6 in *Essays on Manager Selection*, by Scott D. Stewart, PhD, CFA, Research Foundation of CFA Institute. © 2013 CFA Institute. All rights reserved.

employee compensation comes in the form of bonuses, senior management can reduce bonus payouts as fee revenue declines in order to smooth a company's profitability.

Investors are increasingly sensitive to management fees. Average asset-weighted expense ratios (management fees and fund expenses) incurred by mutual fund investors have fallen substantially. In 2000, equity mutual fund investors incurred expense ratios of 0.99 percent, on average, or 99 cents for every $100 invested. By 2016, that average had fallen to 0.63 percent, a decline of 36 percent. Hybrid and bond mutual fund expense ratios also have declined. The average hybrid mutual fund expense ratio fell from 0.89 percent in 2000 to 0.74 percent in 2016, a reduction of 17 percent. The average bond mutual fund expense ratio fell from 0.76 percent in 2000 to 0.51 percent in 2016, a decline of 33 percent. The decline is a function of several factors: the allocation of the fixed portion of expenses over a larger asset base, increasing investor preference for no-load share classes, and the increasing allocations to lower-cost index funds. Aside from these structural factors lowering average expense ratios, there has been more generalized downward pressure on fees—the average expense ratio of actively managed equity mututal funds has declined from 1.06% in 2000 to 0.82% in 2016. Likewise, the average expense ratio of actively managed bond mutual funds has declined from 0.78% in 2000 to 0.58% in 2016.[2]

Investment firms charge fees in several different ways. In general, mutual funds charge fees based on assets under management in a fund.[3] Some classes of mutual funds, including those with reduced fees, require minimum balances. In contrast, institutional managers frequently offer declining percentage fees on increasing account sizes for separate or commingled pool accounts. Institutional accounts frequently specify minimum account sizes or minimum dollar fees. Fixed-percentage fees facilitate managers' and investors' planning for future cash flows, whereas dollar fees are subject to the variability of asset values.

Fee structures can influence which managers will be willing to accept a particular investment mandate. They can also strongly affect manager behavior. Economic theory suggests that the principal–agent problem is complicated by the fact that an agent's skills and actions are not fully visible to the principal. Although principals control asset availability, agents control both their expenditure of effort and portfolio risk. Moreover, the agent and principal may have different preferences; each might care about different time horizons and agents might not view losses the same way that principals do.[4] Finally, total performance is, to some extent, beyond the control of either party. As a result of these factors, the principal's and agent's interests may not be fully aligned. In reality, managers are motivated to work hard even without incentive fees because they want to retain current clients and expand their client base and pricing power. Incentives are useful, however, to help *ensure* that managers routinely act in their clients' best interest.

Assets under Management Fees

Assets under management fees, also called *ad valorem* fees (from the Latin for "according to value"), result from applying stated percentage rates to assets under management. These fees reward managers who attract and retain assets, generate added value, and experience benefits from rising markets. Managers primarily grow their assets through skillful investing, hard

---

[2]ICI *Investment Company Fact Book*, 2017.

[3]Although mutual funds may offer a declining management fee as fund assets increase, the individual investor does not benefit from investing more money unless the extra money qualifies the investor for a lower-fee fund class.

[4]For a summary of theoretical research on investment compensation, see Stracca (2006).

work, and effective marketing. A manager's success, however, also results partly from luck, especially in the short term. Managers benefit from rising portfolio values, which are attributable to the combination of alpha and beta decisions, but are also, at least for long-only managers, greatly affected by market cycles beyond the manager's control. A decline in *ad valorem* percentages as assets grow helps reduce the fee impact on investors from rising markets, but does not eliminate it.

Once a manager's assets are large, he might not want to risk losing them. Assets are typically "sticky"—that is, once investors allocate their assets to a manager, the manager often does not need to generate the same level of returns to retain the assets as he did to attract them. Empirical evidence suggests this stickiness is the case, to some extent, for mutual fund assets. To motivate such managers to work harder or discourage them from closet indexing, an incentive fee determined by future performance may be useful.

Performance-Based Fees

Performance-based fees are determined by portfolio returns and are designed to reward managers with a share of return for their skill in creating value. Performance can be calculated by using either total or relative return, and the return shared can be a percentage of total performance or performance net of a base or fixed fee. Performance-based fees are structured in one of three basic ways:

1. A symmetrical structure in which the manager is fully exposed to both the downside and upside (Computed fee = Base + Sharing of performance);
2. A bonus structure in which the manager is not fully exposed to the downside but is fully exposed to the upside [Computed fee = Higher of either (1) Base or (2) Base plus sharing of positive performance]; or
3. A bonus structure in which the manager is not fully exposed to either the downside or the upside [Computed fee = Higher of (1) Base or (2) Base plus sharing of performance, to a limit].

Performance fees are paid annually or, in some cases, less frequently. These fees may include maximum and high-water mark (or clawback) features that protect investors from situations such as paying for current positive performance before the negative effects of prior underperformance have been offset. Private equity, hedge fund, and real estate partnerships commonly earn performance fees on total returns and typically do not limit the amount of the performance fee. Hedge funds commonly include high-water mark features.

Consider the example of private equity partnerships, in which base fees are commonly applied to committed (not just invested) capital. Performance fees are earned as profits are realized, and invested capital is returned to investors. A common provision that helps protect private equity limited partners (the investors) is a requirement that the limited partners receive their principal and share of profits before performance fees are distributed to the general partner (the manager).

Specific performance-based fee structures are designed by both clients and managers. A formula is agreed upon based on the anticipated distribution of returns and the perceived attractiveness of the investment strategy. Managers who can command attractive terms, such as real estate managers that are in high demand and have limited capacity, have the power to stipulate the highest base fees and profit sharing in their fee agreements. Fee schedules are typically designed by fund managers, included in marketing materials, and set forth in partnership agreements. Large investors may influence the terms of fee schedules or negotiate side letters for special treatment.

EXHIBIT 8   Sample Performance-Based Fee Schedule

Panel A. Sample Fee Structure

Standard fee	0.50%
Base fee	0.25%
Sharing*	20%
Breakeven active return	1.50%
Maximum annual fee	0.75%

Panel B. Numerical Examples for Annual Periods

	Active Return				
	≤0.25%	**1.00%**	**1.50%**	**2.00%**	**≥2.75%**
Billed fee	0.25%	0.40%	0.50%	0.60%	0.75%
Net active return	≤0.00%	0.60%	1.00%	1.40%	≥2.00%

* On active return, beyond base fee.

A simple performance-based fee, as illustrated in Exhibit 8, specifies a base fee below which the computed fee can never fall. In this case, the manager is protected against sharing for performance below 25 bps. To make the result symmetrical around the commonplace 50 bps fee, the manager does not share in active performance beyond 2.75%.

If investment outcomes result from a mix of skill and luck (i.e., a probability distribution around a positive mean alpha), then performance fees constitute risk sharing. Fee structures must be designed carefully to avoid favoring one party over the other. Performance-based fees work to align the interests of managers and investors because both parties share in investment results. Investors benefit by paying performance-based fees, rather than standard fees, when active returns are low. Managers may work harder to earn performance-based fees, inspiring the term "incentive based." Empirical evidence suggests a correlation between performance-based fees and higher alphas (also, lower fees) for mutual funds and higher risk-adjusted returns for hedge funds.[5] Asset managers may consider performance-based fees attractive because such fees provide an opportunity to enhance profits on the upside and ensure guaranteed, although perhaps minimal, streams of revenue from base fees when performance is poor.

Performance-based fees can also create tensions between investors and managers. Investors must pay base fees even when managers underperform. Management firm revenues decline when cash is needed to invest in operations or retain talent. In fact, the failure rate for poor-performing and even zero-alpha managers may tend to be higher when performance-based rather than standard fees are used.[6]

Performance-based fee structures may also lead to misestimates of portfolio risk. Such fee structures convert symmetrical gross active return distributions into asymmetrical net active return distributions, reducing variability on the upside but not the downside. As a result, a

---

[5]See Elton, Gruber, and Blake (2003) and Ackermann, McEnally, and Ravenscraft (1999).
[6]See Grinold and Rudd (1987).

single standard deviation calculated on a return series that incorporates active returns, above and below the base fee, can lead to the underestimation of downside risk.[7]

Investors and managers may have different incentives when performance-based fees are used. For example, according to a utility maximization model, fully symmetric fees, in which the manager is fully exposed to the downside, tend to yield closer alignment in risk and effort than bonus-style fees.[8] Understandably, symmetrical fee structures are unpopular with managers because of their impact on bankruptcy risk.

Bonus-style fees are the close equivalent of a manager's call option on a share of active return, for which the base fee is the strike price. Consider Exhibit 9, which shows a familiar-

EXHIBIT 9   Payoff Line of Sample Performance-Based Fee Schedule

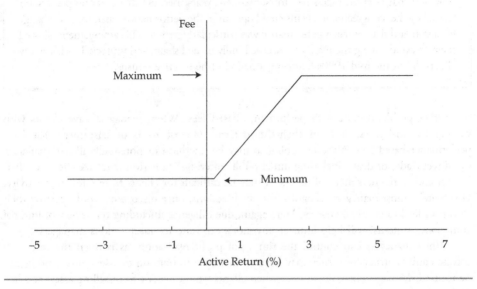

looking option payoff pattern using the fee parameters defined in Exhibit 8. In this case, the option payoff is modified by a maximum fee feature. The graph illustrates three fee components: a 25 bps base fee, plus a long call option on active return with a strike price equal to the minimum (base) fee, minus another (less valuable) call option with a strike price equal to the maximum fee.

Managers must retain clients year to year, avoid poor performance, and not violate management guidelines. But managers also tend to have an interest in increasing risk, which may conflict with these goals. Based on option pricing theory,[9] higher volatility leads to higher option value, which encourages managers to assume higher portfolio risk. This behavior has been observed in the marketplace.[10] As a result, investors, when possible, should

---

[7]See Kritzman (2012).
[8]See Starks (1987).
[9]Margrabe (1978) notes that an incentive fee (without a maximum) consists of a call option on the portfolio and a put on the benchmark. As a result, the value depends on the volatility of the portfolio and the benchmark and the correlation between the two—in other words, the active risk.
[10]See Elton et al. (2003).

carefully select benchmarks and monitor risk in their portfolios.[11] Senior management at investment firms should also ensure that their compensation systems penalize portfolio managers for assuming excessive risk as well as reward them for earning superior returns.[12]

Real Story: The Client's Free Option in a Performance Fee Agreement

Consider the case of an equity manager in the early 1990s offering a performance-based fee that consisted of a 10 bps base fee and a 20% share of active return in excess of the benchmark index (net of the 10 bps). The fee structure also included a maximum annual fee provision that reserved excess fees for subsequent years. Because there was no penalty for cancelling the fee agreement, clients could opt out of the performance-based fee in exchange for a standard flat fee when performance was particularly strong. This arrangement allowed them to avoid paying the manager's accrued, fully earned share, and is precisely what many clients did in the mid-1990s following a period of high active returns.

Other problems exist with performance-based fees. When managers have clients with varying fee structures, it is in their (short-term) interest to favor customers that have performance-based fees. Although doing so may be unethical or potentially illegal, managers can direct trades or deals (including initial public offerings) to performance-fee clients to their benefit and to the detriment of others. It may be difficult for clients to monitor this activity. Fortunately, most managers recognize that such actions, once discovered, could destroy their careers or lead to criminal charges. Here again, due diligence, including the review of internal compliance systems, will help limit an investor's exposure to unscrupulous managers.

When managers can control the timing of profit realization, as is often the case with private equity partnerships, they may have an incentive to hold on to assets until a profit can be realized. Managers may do so even when clients would benefit from selling assets at a loss and investing the proceeds outside of the partnership. In contrast, hedge fund managers have an incentive to return assets in poor-performing partnerships when the high-water mark is substantially above current value (i.e., the performance-fee option is considerably out of the money). This action results in the investor missing the opportunity to recoup previously paid fees based on future strong performance.

Funds of funds (FoFs) commonly charge fees in addition to the fees charged by the underlying funds.[13] These fees pay for the investor's access to the underlying funds and for the FoFs' due diligence, portfolio construction, and monitoring. In addition to these two sets of fees, investors are required to share the profits from well-performing underlying funds but incur the full loss from poorly performing funds.[14] To protect investors from paying overly high fees, hedge fund consortiums have recently begun to offer fee structures based on the

---

[11]Starks (1987) notes that an investor can simply set a fee schedule incorporating penalties for observed risk to align interests regarding risk levels.

[12]Although it adds a layer of complexity to the evaluation process, an active-risk-adjusted bonus formula can be specified.

[13]When funds of funds were popular in the 2000s, it was common for them to charge a performance-based fee.

[14]Kritzman (2012) calls this result an "asymmetry penalty."

total portfolio value of underlying funds, rather than the sum of fees computed at the individual fund level.

The Impact of Fee Structure on Net Returns

Consider four fee structures applied to the same 12-month return series gross of fees:

- 0.50% management fee, 0% performance fee
- 0.50% management fee, 15% performance fee
- 1.50% management fee, 0% performance fee
- 1.50% management fee, 15% performance fee

The fees are accrued at the end of each month. This example is a simplification but illustrates the important effects of fee level and structure on net performance. As Exhibit 10 shows, the average monthly gross return is 0.72% with a 1.37% monthly

EXHIBIT 10   Effects of Expense on Portfolio Performance

| | | Monthly Gross Return | | | | | | | | | | | | Avg. | |
MF	PF	1	2	3	4	5	6	7	8	9	10	11	12	Ret.	S.D.
0.0%	0.0%	2.00%	3.00%	−0.20%	−0.50%	0.50%	0.90%	1.00%	−2.00%	1.50%	2.00%	−0.50%	1.00%	0.72%	1.37%
0.5%	0.0%	1.96%	2.96%	−0.24%	−0.54%	0.46%	0.86%	0.96%	−2.04%	1.46%	1.96%	−0.54%	0.96%	0.67%	1.37%
0.5%	15.0%	1.66%	2.51%	−0.21%	−0.46%	0.39%	0.73%	0.81%	−1.74%	1.24%	1.66%	−0.46%	0.81%	0.57%	1.16%
1.5%	0.0%	1.88%	2.88%	−0.32%	−0.62%	0.37%	0.77%	0.88%	−2.12%	1.37%	1.88%	−0.62%	0.88%	0.59%	1.37%
1.5%	15.0%	1.59%	2.44%	−0.28%	−0.53%	0.32%	0.66%	0.74%	−1.81%	1.17%	1.59%	−0.53%	0.74%	0.50%	1.16%

EXHIBIT 11   Cumulative Return

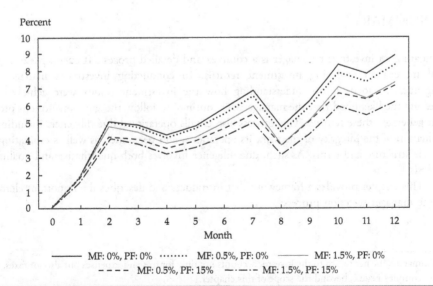

MF: 0%, PF: 0%   MF: 0.5%, PF: 0%   MF: 1.5%, PF: 0%
MF: 0.5%, PF: 15%   MF: 1.5%, PF: 15%

standard deviation. Not surprisingly, charging a management fee (MF) lowers the level of realized return without affecting the standard deviation of the series. The management fee is a constant shift in the level and thus does not affect volatility. The addition of a performance fee (PF) also lowers the level of realized returns but has the added effect of lowering the realized standard deviation. This dynamic occurs because in up months, the performance fee is accrued, and in down months, it is subtracted from the accrual balance to reflect the appropriate fee for the cumulative performance. This accounting has the effect of adjusting the monthly returns toward zero and lowering the measured volatility. The larger the performance fee, the more pronounced this effect. Exhibit 11 shows a graph of the cumulative returns for each fee structure.

Given the potentially significant effect of expenses, a clear distinction must be drawn between performance analysis based on gross returns and net of expenses returns.

An additional consideration is the different degree of uncertainty between expenses and the potential added value of the active portfolio manager. Expenses are paid for certain, whereas the added value of the active strategy compared with the passive strategy is uncertain. For example, suppose an active strategy is expected to generate a gross return that is 2% greater than the passive strategy, but the cost of the active strategy is 2% greater than the passive strategy. A risk-averse investor would likely prefer the passive strategy; although the expected net return of the strategies is the same, the uncertainty of the outperformance would be unappealing. The riskier the active strategy, the greater the return volatility and the greater the volatility of the added value relative to the passive strategy. The significance is, the added value of the active strategy has to be sufficiently large and certain to justify the higher cost of the strategy.

In sum, the presence of positive significant average excess return is evidence for manager skill. This excess return, however, must be net of fees and expenses for the benefit of this skill to accrue to the investor.[15] The preference is for more linear compensation to the manager to reduce the incentives to change the portfolio's risk profile at inflection points.

5. SUMMARY

Evaluating an investment manager is a complex and detailed process. It encompasses a great deal more than analyzing investment returns. In conducting investment manager due diligence, the focus is on understanding how the investment results were achieved and assessing the likelihood that the manager will continue to follow the same investment process that generated these returns. This process also entails operational due diligence, including an evaluation of the integrity of the firm, its operations, and personnel, as well as evaluating the vehicle structure and terms. As such, due diligence involves both quantitative and qualitative analysis.

This chapter provides a framework that introduces and describes the important elements of the manager selection process:

---

[15]Ultimately, the net return to the investor accounts not only for fees and expenses but also for taxes. This more complex issue is beyond the scope of this chapter.

- Investment manager selection involves a broad set of qualitative and quantitative considerations to determine whether a manager displays skill and the likelihood that the manager will continue to display skill in the future.
- The qualitative analysis consists of investment due diligence, which evaluates the manager's investment process, investment personnel, and portfolio construction; and operational due diligence, which evaluates the manager's infrastructure.
- A Type I error is hiring or retaining a manager who subsequently underperforms expectations—that is, rejecting the null hypothesis of no skill when it is correct. A Type II error is not hiring or firing a manager who subsequently outperforms, or performs in line with, expectations—that is, not rejecting the null hypothesis when it is incorrect.
- The manager search and selection process has three broad components: the universe, a quantitative analysis of the manager's performance track record, and a qualitative analysis of the manager's investment process. The qualitative analysis includes both investment due diligence and operational due diligence.
- Capture ratio measures the asymmetry of returns, and a ratio greater than 1 indicates greater participation in rising versus falling markets. Drawdown is the loss incurred in any continuous period of negative returns.
- The investment philosophy is the foundation of the investment process. The philosophy outlines the set of assumptions about the factors that drive performance and the manager's beliefs about their ability to successfully exploit these sources of return. The investment manager should have a clear and concise investment philosophy. It is important to evaluate these assumptions and the role they play in the investment process to understand how the strategy will behave over time and across market environments. The investment process has to be consistent and appropriate for the philosophy, and the investment personnel need to possess sufficient expertise and experience to effectively execute the investment process.
- Style analysis, understanding the manager's risk exposures relative to the benchmark, is an important component of performance appraisal and manager selection, helping to define the universe of suitable managers.
- Returns-based style analysis is a top-down approach that involves estimating the risk exposures from an actual return series for a given period. Although RBSA adds an additional analytical step, the analysis is straightforward and should identify the important drivers of return and risk factors for the period analyzed. It can be estimated even for complicated strategies and is comparable across managers and through time. The disadvantage is that RBSA is an imprecise tool, attributing performance to an unchanging average portfolio during the period that might not reflect the current or future portfolio exposures.
- Holdings-based style analysis is a bottom-up approach that estimates the risk exposures from the actual securities held in the portfolio at a point in time. HBSA allows for the estimation of current risk factors and should identify all important drivers of return and risk factors, be comparable across managers and through time, and provide an accurate view of the manager's risk exposures. The disadvantages are the additional computational effort, dependence on the degree of transparency provided by the manager, and the possibility that accuracy may be compromised by stale pricing and window dressing.
- The prospectus, private placement memorandum, and/or limited partnership agreement are, in essence, the contract between the investor and the manager, outlining each party's rights and responsibilities. The provisions are liquidity terms and fees. Limited liquidity reduces the investor's flexibility to adjust portfolio allocations in light of changing market

conditions or investor circumstances. However, limited liquidity allows the funds to take long-term views and hold less liquid securities with reduced risk of having to divest assets at inopportune times in response to redemption requests. A management fee lowers the level of realized return without affecting the standard deviation, whereas a performance fee has the added effect of lowering the realized standard deviation. The preference is for more-linear compensation to reduce the incentives to change the portfolio's risk profile at inflection points.

- The choice between individual separate accounts and pooled (or commingled) vehicles is dependent upon the consistency with the investment process, the suitability for the investor IPS, and whether the benefits outweigh the additional costs.

- Investment management fees take one of two forms: a fixed percentage fee based on assets under management or a performance-based fee which charges a percentage of the portfolio's total return or excess return over a benchmark or hurdle rate. Performance-based fees work to align the interests of managers and investors because both parties share in investment results. Most managers that charge a performance fee also charge some level of fixed percentage fee to aid business continuity efforts. Fee structures must be designed carefully to avoid favoring one party over the other.

REFERENCES

Ackermann, Carl, Richard McEnally, and David Ravenscraft. 1999. "The Performance of Hedge Funds: Risk, Return and Incentives." *Journal of Finance* 54 (3): 833–74.

Elton, Edwin, Martin Gruber, and Christopher Blake. 2003. "Incentive Fees and Mutual Funds." *Journal of Finance* 58 (2): 779–804.

Grinold, Richard, and Andrew Rudd. 1987. "Incentive Fees: Who Wins? Who Loses?" *Financial Analysts Journal* 43 (1): 27–38.

Khandani, Amir E., and Andrew W. Lo. 2011. "What Happened to the Quants in August 2007? Evidence from Factors and Transactions Data." *Journal of Financial Markets*, vol. 14, no. 1 (February):1–46.

Kritzman, Mark. 2012. "Two Things about Performance Fees." *Journal of Portfolio Management* 38 (2): 4–5.

Kuenzi, David E. 2003. "Strategy Benchmarks." *Journal of Portfolio Management* 29 (2): 46–56.

Lo, Andrew W. 2004. "*The Adaptive Markets Hypothesis: Market Efficiency from an Evolutionary Perspective.*" *Journal of Portfolio Management*, vol. 30, no. 5 (30th Anniversary):15–20.

Margrabe, William. 1978. "The Value of an Option to Exchange One Asset for Another." *Journal of Finance* 33 (1): 177–86.

Starks, Laura. 1987. "Performance Incentive Fees: An Agency Theoretic Approach." *Journal of Financial and Quantitative Analysis* 22 (1): 17–32.

Stewart, Scott D., John J. Neumann, Christopher R. Knittel, and Jeffrey Heisler. 2009. "Absence of Value: An Analysis of Investment Allocation Decisions by Institutional Plan Sponsors." *Financial Analysts Journal*, vol. 65, no. 6 (November/December):34–51.

Stracca, Livio. 2006. "Delegated Portfolio Management: A Survey of the Theoretical Literature." *Journal of Economic Surveys* 20 (5): 823–48.

Zuckerman, Gregory. 2008. "Fees, Even Returns and Auditor All Raised Red Flags." *Wall Street Journal* (13 December 2008).

PRACTICE PROBLEMS

1. Which of the following qualitative considerations is *most* associated with determining whether investment manager selection will result in superior repeatable performance?
   A. Transparency
   B. Investment process
   C. Operational process

2. Which of the following is *most likely* a key consideration in investment due diligence?
   A. Suitability of the investment vehicle
   B. Back office processes and procedures
   C. Depth of expertise and experience of investment personnel

3. A decision-making investor is *most likely* to worry more about making a Type I error than a Type II error because:
   A. Type II errors are errors of commission.
   B. Type I errors are more easily measured.
   C. Type II errors are more likely to have to be explained as to why a skilled manager was fired.

4. An investor is considering hiring three managers who have the following skill levels:

Manager	Large-Cap Skill Level	Small-Cap Skill Level
1	Skilled	Unskilled
2	Skilled	Skilled
3	Unskilled	Unskilled

   Type I and Type II errors both occur when the investor is:
   A. hiring Manager 1 for large-cap stocks and not hiring Manager 3 for small-cap stocks.
   B. hiring Manager 3 for large-cap stocks and not hiring Manager 2 for small-cap stocks.
   C. hiring Manager 3 for large-cap stocks and not hiring Manager 1 for small-cap stocks.

5. Suppose that the results of a style analysis for an investment manager are not consistent with the stated philosophy of the manager and the manager's stated investment process. These facts suggest the:
   A. absence of style drift.
   B. investment process may not be repeatable.
   C. manager should be included in the universe of potential managers.

6. Compared with holdings-based style analysis (HBSA), a returns-based style analysis (RBSA):
   A. is subject to window dressing.
   B. requires less effort to acquire data.
   C. is more accurate when illiquid securities are present.

7. A manager whose relative performance is worse during market downturns *most likely* has a capture ratio that is:
   A. less than one.
   B. equal to one.
   C. greater than one.

8. Which of the following is consistent with the expectation that exploiting a structural inefficiency is repeatable?
   A. The inefficiency is a unique event that occurs infrequently.
   B. The level of gross return is equal to the amount of transaction costs and expenses.
   C. The aggregate value of all assets affected by the inefficiency is larger than the AUM of the manager and its competitors.

9. Which of the following is **not** a reason that an investor might favor a separately managed account rather than a pooled vehicle? The investor:
   A. is tax exempt.
   B. requires real-time details on investment positions.
   C. has expressed certain constraints and preferences for the portfolio.

10. Which of the following investment vehicles provide investors with the highest degree of liquidity?
    A. Open-end funds
    B. Private equity funds
    C. Limited partnerships

11. Which of the following statements is consistent with the manager adhering to a stated investment philosophy and investment decision-making process?
    A. Senior investment team members have left to form their own firm.
    B. A senior employee has been cited by the SEC for violating insider trading regulations.
    C. A large drawdown occurs because of an unforeseen political event in a foreign country.

12. A manager has a mandate to be fully invested with a benchmark that is a blend of large-cap stocks and investment-grade bonds. Which of the following is **not** an indication that style drift has occurred? The manager:
    A. initiates an allocation to small-cap stocks.
    B. decreases investments in investment-grade corporate bonds.
    C. increases allocation to cash in anticipation of a market decline.

13. The manager selection process begins by defining the universe of feasible managers. When defining this manager universe, the selection process should avoid:
    A. excluding managers based on historical risk-adjusted returns.
    B. identifying the benchmark against which managers will be evaluated.
    C. using third-party categorizations of managers to find those that might fill the desired role in the portfolio.

14. A return distribution of skilled managers that is highly distinct from the return distribution of unskilled managers, *most likely* implies a:
    A. highly efficient market.
    B. low opportunity cost of not hiring a skilled manager.
    C. high opportunity cost of not hiring a skilled manager.

15. An advantage of a returns-based style analysis is that such analysis:
    A. is comparable across managers.
    B. is suitable for portfolios that contain illiquid securities.
    C. can effectively profile a manager's risk exposures using a short return series.

16. Which of the following types of style analysis use(s) a bottom-up approach to estimate the risk exposures in a portfolio?
    A. Returns-based style analysis only
    B. Holdings-based style analysis only
    C. Both return-based and holdings-based style analysis

17. In a quarter, an investment manager's upside capture is 75% and downside capture is 125%. We can conclude that the manager underperforms the benchmark:
    A. only when the benchmark return is positive.
    B. only when the benchmark return is negative.
    C. when the benchmark return is either positive or negative.

18. Which of the following fee structures *most likely* decreases the volatility of a portfolio's net returns?
    A. Incentive fees only
    B. Management fees only
    C. Neither incentive fees nor management fees

19. An investor should prefer a pooled investment vehicle to a separately managed account when she:
    A. is cost sensitive.
    B. focuses on tax efficiency.
    C. requires clear legal ownership of assets.

20. Which of the following investment types is the most liquid?
    A. ETFs
    B. Hedge funds
    C. Private equity funds

The following information relates to Questions 21–26

The Tree Fallers Endowment plans to allocate part of its portfolio to alternative investment funds. The endowment has hired Kurt Summer, a consultant at Summer Brothers Consultants, to identify suitable alternative investment funds for its portfolio.

Summer has identified three funds for potential investment and will present the performance of these investments to the endowment's board of directors at their next quarterly meeting.

Summer is reviewing each of the fund's fee schedules and is concerned about the manager's incentive to take on excess risk in an attempt to generate a higher fee. Exhibit 1 presents the fee schedules of the three funds.

EXHIBIT 1   Fee Schedules

Fund	Computed Fee	Base Fee	Sharing	Maximum Annual Fee
Red Grass Fund	Higher of either (1) base or (2) base plus sharing of positive performance; sharing is based on return net of the base fee.	1.00%	20%	na
Blue Water Fund	Higher of either (1) base or (2) base plus sharing of positive performance, up to a maximum annual fee of 2.50%; sharing is based on active return.	0.50%	20%	2.50%
Yellow Wood Fund	Base plus sharing of both positive and negative performance; sharing is based on return net of the base fee.	1.50%	20%	na

Exhibit 2 presents the annual gross returns for each fund and its respective benchmark for the period of 2016–2018. All funds have an inception date of 1 January 2016. Summer intends to include in his report an explanation of the impact of the fee structures of the three funds on returns.

EXHIBIT 2   Fund and Benchmark Returns

	2016		2017		2018	
Fund	Gross Return (%)	Benchmark Return (%)	Gross Return (%)	Benchmark Return (%)	Gross Return (%)	Benchmark Return (%)
Red Grass Fund	8.00	8.00	−2.00	−10.00	5.00	4.50
Blue Water Fund	10.00	9.00	−4.00	−1.50	14.00	2.00
Yellow Wood Fund	15.00	14.00	−5.00	−6.50	7.00	9.50

The board of directors of the Tree Fallers Endowment asks Summer to recalculate the fees of the Red Grass Fund assuming a high-water mark feature whereby a sharing percentage could only be charged to the extent any losses had been recouped.

21. Based on Exhibit 1, which fund has a symmetrical fee structure?
    A. Red Grass
    B. Blue Water
    C. Yellow Wood

22. Based on the fee schedules in Exhibit 1, the portfolio manager of which fund has the greatest incentive to assume additional risk to earn a higher investment management fee?
    A. Red Grass
    B. Blue Water
    C. Yellow Wood

23. Based on Exhibit 1 and Exhibit 2, the Yellow Wood Fund's 2016 investment management fee is:
    A. 3.00%.
    B. 4.20%.
    C. 4.50%.

24. Based on Exhibit 1 and Exhibit 2, the Red Grass Fund's 2017 investment management fee is:
    A. 0.40%.
    B. 1.00%.
    C. 2.60%.

25. Based on Exhibit 1 and Exhibit 2, the Blue Water Fund's 2018 investment management fee is:
    A. 2.40%
    B. 2.50%.
    C. 2.90%

26. In which year would the Red Grass Fund's investment management fee be affected by Summer's recalculation using the high-water mark?
    A. 2016
    B. 2017
    C. 2018

The following information relates to Questions 27–29

John Connell inherited $700,000 at the beginning of the year and has been developing related investment goals and policies with a financial adviser. The adviser has identified three

EXHIBIT 1   Fund Characteristics

Characteristic	Zeta	Eta	Theta
Organization	Independent investment fund	Part of a medium-sized investment firm with multiple funds	Part of a large investment firm that rotates investment professionals among funds
Team Size	Small	Small	Small
Staff Turnover	High	Medium	Low
Incentive Compensation	Salary adjustment when returns exceed benchmark	Annual salary adjustment	Annual salary adjustment and performance-based bonus
Key People	Founder directs all trades and investment decisions	Fund manager and assistant fund manager make investment decisions	Fund manager and assistant fund manager lead team in selecting investments
Longevity/ Experience	Founder in the investment business for >25 years	Fund manager in the investment business for >15 years; assistant fund manager for >12 years	Fund manager in the investment business for >20 years; assistant fund manager for >10 years. Fund family is more than 50 years old.

potential investment funds for consideration. All three have earned similar returns over the last five years and are expected to earn similar returns going forward. Publishing their investment results on a timely and routine basis, they include the following asset classes:

- US equities
- Global equities
- Venture capital
- Corporate bonds
- Government bonds
- Cash reserves

Exhibit 1 presents information about the funds.

Select the fund, based on the Exhibit 1 data, that is *most appropriate* for Connell's needs. (Circle one)	**Justify** your selection with *two* reasons.
Zeta	
Eta	
Theta	

27. **Select** the fund, based on the Exhibit 1 data, that is *most appropriate* for Connell's needs. **Justify** your selection with *two* reasons.

Connell elects to defer fund selection and places his inheritance in a short-term money market account. A year later, Connell reviews the one-year performance results of the three funds compared to the benchmark, as shown in Exhibit 2.

EXHIBIT 2   Fund Performance Compared to Benchmark*

Fund	Underperforms	In Line	Outperforms
Zeta		X	
Eta	X		
Theta			X

*Assume performance is mean reverting within this period.

Connell believes he now has two main alternatives for fund investment:

- Alternative 1: Keep his inheritance in the money market account to avoid the Eta fund.
- Alternative 2: Place his inheritance in the Theta fund.

28. **Identify** the type of error Connell is at risk of committing and its associated cost for *each* alternative. **Justify** your selection.

Connell asks the adviser about the conditions under which any form of style analysis would be useful for understanding the funds he is considering.

29. **Identify** the conditions under which the adviser would find style analysis *most* useful.

The following information relates to Questions 30–31

Cassandra Yang, age 59, is a manager at a large US manufacturing firm. Yang is single, owns a home, is debt free, and saves 20% of her pre-tax income in a company retirement plan and 15% of her after-tax income in a short-term money market account. Her accounts are self-directed; Yang makes all related decisions independently.

While Yang hates to suffer investment losses, she now seeks higher returns on 80% of the funds in her money market account. To help achieve her goal of retiring within three years, she is considering the actively managed investment funds listed in Exhibit 1.

EXHIBIT 1   Return Profile Summary

Fund	Upside Capture	Downside Capture	Most Recent Drawdown Loss	Most Recent Drawdown Duration
Alpha	80	20	57%	21 months
Beta	55	45	38%	15 months
Gamma	50	50	28%	12 months

30. **Select** the *best* fund for Yang, using only the information provided. **Justify** your selection.

Yang is also considering Aspen Investments (Aspen) for a portion of her money market funds. Aspen's investment philosophy states: "We pursue a passive investment strategy, which seeks to identify and exploit structural inefficiencies through identifying mispricings created by loss aversion. Our strategy and philosophy have evolved over time in response to fund and market performance."

Select the *best* fund for Yang, using only the information provided. (Circle one)	**Justify** your selection.
Alpha	
Beta	
Gamma	

31. **Determine** whether Yang is likely to judge that Aspen follows a consistent investment philosophy, using only the information provided. **Justify** your response with *two* reasons.

Determine whether Yang is likely to judge that Aspen follows a consistent investment philosophy, using only the information provided. (Circle one)	**Justify** your response with *two* reasons.
Yes	
No	

The following information relates to Questions 32–33

Donna Grimmett is working with a financial adviser to establish her investment goals for $850,000, which she recently earned as a bonus. She asks the adviser about how to best select a manager for her funds.

The adviser responds that both qualitative and quantitative components are involved in outlining a framework for identifying, evaluating, and ultimately selecting a manager.

32. **Describe** *two* considerations for *each* type of component recommended to Grimmett for her manager selection process.

Manager Selection Components	**Describe** *two* considerations for *each* type of component recommended to Grimmett for her manager selection process.
Qualitative	
Quantitative	

Grimmett asks the adviser if any other preparatory steps should be taken before choosing the best investment manager(s). The adviser produces a checklist related to manager selection in response to Grimmett's question.

33. **Describe** the content of the adviser's checklist related to manager selection.

Describe the content of the adviser's checklist related to manager selection.

The following information relates to Question 34

Boinic Corporation introduced an employee pension plan and set aside $20 million to fund the plan. Assessing five investment management firms, A through E, and expecting all to perform in line with their benchmarks, Boinic selected three firms (A, D, and E) to manage part of the pension plan assets. Exhibit 1 shows the managers' performance compared to their benchmark in the one year after being selected.

EXHIBIT 1   Year 1 Investment Firm Performance versus Benchmark

	Firm A	Firm B	Firm C	Firm D	Firm E
Year 1 performance versus benchmark	Above	Above	Below	Below	Above

On analyzing these results, Boinic determines that it has made both a Type I and Type II error.

34. **Identify** the firm associated with Boinic's Type I and Type II error. **Justify** your selection for *each* error type, discussing the psychological effects of its Year 1 performance on Boinic.

Identify the firm associated with Boinic's Type I and Type II error. (Circle one for each error type)	**Justify** your selection for *each* error type, discussing the psychological effects of its Year 1 performance on Boinic.
Type I Error	
Firm A	
Firm B	
Firm C	
Firm D	
Firm E	
Type II Error	
Firm A	
Firm B	
Firm C	
Firm D	
Firm E	

The following information relates to Question 35

Susan Patnode, age 66, was recently widowed and received £2,000,000 from a spousal life insurance policy. Patnode would like to invest the proceeds to generate predictable income to cover her ongoing living expenses.

Patnode is considering three investment managers, Laurbær Partners, Alcanfor Limited, and Mylesten Management, to manage the insurance policy proceeds. All three take an active investment approach. Further information regarding each of the investment manager's investment philosophy and approach is provided in Exhibit 1.

EXHIBIT 1   Information on Investment Manager Philosophy/Approach

Investment Manager	Investment Philosophy / Approach
Laurbær Partners	Seeks to produce returns through investing in new investment themes and emphasizes measuring the contribution of each to performance.
Alcanfor Limited	Seeks to produce returns through investing in securities that appear to be mispriced in their industry sectors and tracks their ultimate performance against market benchmarks.
Mylesten Management	Seeks to produce returns through investing with maximum flexibility to the most popular investor sentiments worldwide.

35. **Identify** which investment manager is *most* suitable for Patnode. **Justify** your response based solely on *each* manager's investment philosophy and approach

Identify which investment manager is *most* suitable for Patnode. (Circle one)	**Justify** your response based solely on *each* manager's investment philosophy and approach.
Laurbær Partners	
Alcanfor Limited	
Mylesten Management	

The following information relates to Questions 36–37

Frances Lute is an investment manager for a large institutional investment management firm in London. His client, Parade University (Parade), has an endowment worth approximately GBP1.6 billion. Lute is considering three active investment managers in order to add one new style. Parade's investment policy statement (IPS) highlights the endowment's preference for low turnover and trading costs.

Lute is particularly concerned about portfolio construction and the prospective implementation of investments within the portfolio. All else equal, Lute has identified these distinguishing characteristics for the processes affecting portfolio construction by the three managers.

- Manager A uses hard-stop losses to manage risk.
- Manager B's portfolio can be liquidated within five business days or less.
- Manager C's portfolio turnover is greater than the frequency of signals generated.

36. **Identify** which manager is *most* appropriate for Parade. **Justify** your response.

Identify which manager is *most* appropriate for Parade. (Circle one)		
Manager A	Manager B	Manager C
	Justify your response.	

Upon choosing a manager, Lute must allocate the funds either to a separately managed account (SMA) customized for Parade or a pooled vehicle called Diversified. In addition to low turnover and trading costs, Parade's IPS also prioritizes the following characteristics for its investment: transparency, investor behavior, cost, liquidity, and tracking risk. While each type of investment vehicle offers distinct advantages, Parade is unclear as to which advantage is applicable by type.

37. **Identify** which investment vehicle *best* addresses *each* characteristic highlighted in Parade's IPS by placing a check mark where appropriate. **Justify** your response.

Identify which investment vehicle *best* addresses *each* characteristic highlighted in Parade's IPS by placing an x where appropriate.			**Justify** your response.
Characteristic	**SMA**	**Diversified**	**Justification**
Transparency			
Investor Behavior			
Cost			
Liquidity			
Tracking Risk			

The following information relates to Questions 38–40

Jack Porter and Melissa Smith are co-managers for the Circue Library Foundation (Circue) in Canada. Within the next six months, Porter and Smith will be replacing one of Circue's underperforming active managers. This choice will rely on the terms of investment management contracts—specifically, liquidity and management fee structure. Circue's IPS indicates some tolerance for lower liquidity, a moderate sensitivity to management fees, and a heightened sensitivity to closet indexing.

Circue is considering the following three investment vehicles with distinct fee structures:

- Hedge funds with a soft lock
- Open-end funds with an incentive fee
- Closed-end funds with no incentive fee

38. **Determine** which of the three investment vehicles is *most* appropriate for Circue's IPS. **Justify** your response.

Determine which of the three investment vehicles is *most* appropriate for Circue's IPS. (Circle one)

Hedge funds with a soft lock	Open-end funds with an incentive fee	Closed-end funds with no incentive fee

Justify your response.

Porter and Smith next consider how the performance-based fee structures of the prospective managers may affect portfolio risk.

Porter states: "I've noticed more managers are applying a bonus structure in which the manager is not fully exposed to the downside but is fully exposed to the upside."

Smith states: "Circue's current market view is that there are increasing risks to the downside."

39. **Discuss** how Smith's stated expectation would be reflected in estimated portfolio risk under the fee structure identified by Porter.

After narrowing their choice to three managers with different fee structures, Porter and Smith analyze the effect of the performance-based fee structure for each manager. Exhibit A provides applicable data for one of the managers.

EXHIBIT 1   Selected Performance-Based Fee Data for a Prospective Manager

Fee Structure	Fee (%)
Standard Fee	0.35
Base Fee	0.20
Sharing*	0.25
Breakeven Active Return	1.25
Maximum Annual Fee	0.90

*On active return, beyond base fee.

To understand the effect each fee structure has on its respective portfolio, Porter and Smith must estimate the net active return for several possible gross active returns, including less than or equal to 0.20%, 0.75%, 1.25%, and 1.75%.

40. **Calculate** the net active return based on each possible gross active return provided using the selected data in Exhibit 1. **Show** your calculations.

Calculate the net active return based on each possible gross active return provided using the selected data in Exhibit 1.

Gross Active Return	≤0.20%	0.75%	1.25%	1.75%
Net Active Return				

Show your calculations.

The following information relates to Question 41

Brickridge Investment Consultants meets weekly to review the positives and negatives of investment managers being considered for client portfolios. In the latest meeting, analyst Brad Moore discusses investment manager Lyon Management (Lyon). His in-depth analysis of one of Lyon's investment strategies includes the following summary details:

Detail 1: Long and short positions are paired.
Detail 2: Investment strategy relies on unique information.
Detail 3: AUM connected with the strategy have grown substantially, while the number and characteristics of positions have stayed the same.

Asked about Lyon's regulatory context, Moore states, "The regulatory environment is strong and seeks to decrease information symmetries."

41. **Identify** whether each detail from Moore's summary is *most likely* a benefit or a drawback of the strategy. **Justify** your selection.

Identify whether each detail from Moore's summary is *most likely* a benefit or a drawback of the strategy. (Place an x in the preferred box.)   **Justify** your selection.

Detail	Benefit	Drawback	Justification
1			
2			
3			

The following information relates to Question 42

Institutional investment consultant Wilsot Consultants (Wilsot) is reviewing multiple investment managers within a prospective client's portfolio. Two of the managers, Vaudreuil Capital Management (Vaudreuil) and Pourtir Investments (Pourtir), have similar strategies that show comparable performance on a net-of-fees basis. Assessing the portfolio effects of management fees, a Wilsot analyst reviews both manager contracts to determine their advantages and disadvantages to the client. Checking client fee structures, the analyst notes Vaudreuil's fees are AUM-based while Pourtir's are performance-based.

42. **Discuss** *one* advantage and *one* disadvantage to the client of *each* manager's contracted fee structure.

Discuss *one* advantage and *one* disadvantage to the client of *each* manager's contracted fee structure.

Manager	Advantage	Disadvantage
Vaudreuil		
Pourtir		

The following information relates to Question 43

At a meeting for the local municipal pension fund, a group of beneficiaries expressed concern about current investment management fees. The beneficiaries asked the Investment Committee for a fee summary of each manager in the portfolio.

The next day, a pension fund staff member briefed the Committee on the managers' full contracted fee schedules. The Committee was surprised to hear that the managers work under numerous different fee structures and rates. A sample of these fee schedules for two managers is provided in Exhibit 1:

EXHIBIT 1   Fee Schedules for Selected Managers: Hidden Lake and Carpenter Management

Fee Type	Hidden Lake	Carpenter Management
Base Fee	0.30%	0.18%*
Sharing**	15%	20%
Maximum Annual Fee	N/A	0.80%

*Minimum fee.
**On active return, beyond base fee.

In explaining the differences, the staff member said that fee structures may lead to misestimates of portfolio risk. She also noted that performance-based fees sometimes are a close equivalent to a manager's call option on active return.

43. **Identify** which manager's fee structure is *most* similar to a call option on a share of active return. **Justify** your selection.

Identify which manager's fee structure is *most* similar to a call option on a share of active return. (Circle one)

Hidden Lake	Carpenter Management

Justify your selection.

GLOSSARY

Absolute return benchmark A minimum target return that an investment manager is expected to beat.

Accounting defeasance Also called in-substance defeasance, accounting defeasance is a way of extinguishing a debt obligation by setting aside sufficient high-quality securities to repay the liability.

Accumulation phase Phase where the government predominantly contributes to a sovereign wealth pension reserve fund.

Active management An approach to investing in which the portfolio manager seeks to outperform a given benchmark portfolio.

Active return The portfolio's return in excess of the return on the portfolio's benchmark.

Active risk budgeting Risk budgeting that concerns active risk (risk relative to a portfolio's benchmark).

Active risk The annualized standard deviation of active returns, also referred to as *tracking error* (also sometimes called *tracking risk*).

Active share A measure, ranging from 0% to 100%, of how similar a portfolio is to its benchmark. The measure is based on the differences in a portfolio's holdings and weights relative to its benchmark's holdings and their weights. A manager who precisely replicates the benchmark will have an active share of zero; a manager with no holdings in common with the benchmark will have an active share of one.

Activist short selling A hedge fund strategy in which the manager takes a short position in a given security and then publicly presents his/her research backing the short thesis.

After-Tax Excess Return Calculated as the after-tax return of the portfolio minus the after-tax return of the associated benchmark portfolio.

Agency trade A trade in which the broker is engaged to find the other side of the trade, acting as an agent. In doing so, the broker does not assume any risk for the trade.

Alpha decay In a trading context, alpha decay is the erosion or deterioration in short term alpha after the investment decision has been made.

Alternative data Non-traditional data types generated by the use of electronic devices, social media, satellite and sensor networks, and company exhaust.

Alternative trading systems (ATS) Non-exchange trading venues that bring together buyers and sellers to find transaction counterparties. Also called *multilateral trading facilities (MTF)*.

Arithmetic attribution An attribution approach which explains the arithmetic difference between the portfolio return and its benchmark return. The single-period attribution effects sum to the excess return, however, when combining multiple periods, the sub-period attribution effects will not sum to the excess return.

Arrival price In a trading context, the arrival price is the security price at the time the order was released to the market for execution.

Artificial intelligence Computer systems that exhibit cognitive and decision-making ability comparable (or superior) to that of humans.

Asset Location The process for determining whether the assets will be held in a taxable, tax-deferred, or tax-exempt account.

Asset location The type of account an asset is held within, e.g., taxable or tax deferred.

Asset-only With respect to asset allocation, an approach that focuses directly on the characteristics of the assets without explicitly modeling the liabilities.

Authorized participants Broker/dealers who enter into an agreement with the distributor of the fund.

Base With respect to a foreign exchange quotation of the price of one unit of a currency, the currency referred to in "one unit of a currency."

Basis risk The risk resulting from using a hedging instrument that is imperfectly matched to the investment being hedged; in general, the risk that the basis will change in an unpredictable way.

Behavioral biases A tendency to behave in a way that is not strictly rational.

Bequest The transferring, or bequeathing, of assets in some other way upon a person's death. Also referred to as a testamentary bequest or testamentary gratuitous transfer.

Best-in-class An ESG implementation approach that seeks to identify the most favorable companies and sectors based on ESG considerations. Also called *positive screening*.

Bid price In a price quotation, the price at which the party making the quotation is willing to buy a specified quantity of an asset or security.

Big Data The vast amount of data being generated by industry, governments, individuals, and electronic devices that arises from both traditional and non-traditional data sources.

Bitcoin A cryptocurrency using blockchain technology that was created in 2009.

Blockchain A type of digital ledger in which information is recorded sequentially and then linked together and secured using cryptographic methods.

Buffering Establishing ranges around breakpoints that define whether a stock belongs in one index or another.

Business cycle Fluctuations in GDP in relation to long-term trend growth, usually lasting 9-11 years.

Calendar rebalancing Rebalancing a portfolio to target weights on a periodic basis; for example, monthly, quarterly, semiannually, or annually.

Canada model Characterized by a high allocation to alternatives. Unlike the endowment model, however, the Canada model relies more on internally managed assets. The innovative features of the Canada model are the: a) reference portfolio, b) total portfolio approach, and c) active management.

Capital Gain or Loss For tax purposes equals the selling price (net of commissions and other trading costs) of the asset less its tax basis.

Capital market expectations (CME) Expectations concerning the risk and return prospects of asset classes.

Capital needs analysis See *capital sufficiency analysis*.

Capital sufficiency analysis The process by which a wealth manager determines whether a client has, or is likely to accumulate, sufficient financial resources to meet his or her objectives; also known as *capital needs analysis*.

Capture ratio A measure of the manager's gain or loss relative to the gain or loss of the benchmark.

Carhart model A four factor model used in performance attribution. The four factors are: market (RMRF), size (SMB), value (HML), and momentum (WML).

Carry trade A trading strategy that involves buying a security and financing it at a rate that is lower than the yield on that security.

Cash drag Tracking error caused by temporarily uninvested cash.

Cash flow matching Immunization approach that attempts to ensure that all future liability payouts are matched precisely by cash flows from bonds or fixed-income derivatives, such as interest rate futures, options, or swaps.

Cell approach See *stratified sampling*.

Charitable Gratuitous Transfers Asset transfers to not-for-profit or charitable organizations. In most jurisdictions charitable donations are not subject to a gift tax and most jurisdictions permit income tax deductions for charitable donations.

Charitable Remainder Trust A trust setup to provide income for the life of named-beneficiaries. When the last named-beneficiary dies any remaining assets in this trust are distributed to the charity named in the trust, hence the term *charitable remainder* trust.

Code of ethics An established guide that communicates an organization's values and overall expectations regarding member behavior. A code of ethics serves as a general guide for how community members should act.

Completion overlay A type of overlay that addresses an indexed portfolio that has diverged from its proper exposure.

Completion Portfolio Is an index-based portfolio that when added to a given concentrated asset position creates an overall portfolio with exposures similar to the investor's benchmark.

Contingent immunization Hybrid approach that combines immunization with an active management approach when the asset portfolio's value exceeds the present value of the liability portfolio.

Contingent immunization Hybrid approach that combines immunization with an active management approach when the asset portfolio's value exceeds the present value of the liability portfolio.

Controlled Foreign Corporation (CFC) A company located outside a taxpayer's home country in which the taxpayer has a controlling interest as defined under the home country law.

Creation units Large blocks of ETF shares often traded against a basket of underlying securities.

Cross hedge A hedge involving a hedging instrument that is imperfectly correlated with the asset being hedged; an example is hedging a bond investment with futures on a non-identical bond.

Cross-sectional consistency A feature of expectations setting which means that estimates for all classes reflect the same underlying assumptions and are generated with methodologies that reflect or preserve important relationships among the asset classes, such as strong correlations. It is the internal consistency across asset classes.

Cross-sectional momentum A managed futures trend following strategy implemented with a cross-section of assets (within an asset class) by going long those that are rising in price the most and by shorting those that are falling the most. This approach generally results in holding a net zero (market-neutral) position and works well when a market's out- or underperformance is a reliable predictor of its future performance.

Cryptocurrency An electronic medium of exchange that lacks physical form.

Cryptography An algorithmic process to encrypt data, making the data unusable if received by unauthorized parties.

Currency overlay programs A currency overlay program is a program to manage a portfolio's currency exposures for the case in which those exposures are managed separately from the management of the portfolio itself.

Currency overlay A type of overlay that helps hedge the returns of securities held in foreign currency back to the home country's currency.

Custom security-based benchmark Benchmark that is custom built to accurately reflect the investment discipline of a particular investment manager. Also called a *strategy benchmark* because it reflects a manager's particular strategy.

Data science An interdisciplinary field that brings computer science, statistics, and other disciplines together to analyze and produce insights from Big Data.

Decision price In a trading context, the decision price is the security price at the time the investment decision was made.

Decision-reversal risk The risk of reversing a chosen course of action at the point of maximum loss.

Decumulation phase Phase where the government predominantly withdraws from a sovereign wealth pension reserve fund.

Dedicated short-selling A hedge fund strategy in which the manager takes short-only positions in equities deemed to be expensively priced versus their deteriorating fundamental situations. Short exposures may vary only in terms of portfolio sizing by, at times, holding higher levels of cash.

Deep learning nets Machine learning using neural networks with many hidden layers.

Deep learning Machine learning using neural networks with many hidden layers.

Deferred annuity An annuity that enables an individual to purchase an income stream that will begin at a later date.

Defined benefit A retirement plan in which a plan sponsor commits to paying a specified retirement benefit.

Defined contribution A retirement plan in which contributions are defined but the ultimate retirement benefit is not specified or guaranteed by the plan sponsor.

Delay cost The (trading related) cost associated with not submitting the order to the market in a timely manner.

Delta hedging Hedging that involves matching the price response of the position being hedged over a narrow range of prices.

Demand deposits Accounts that can be drawn upon regularly and without notice. This category includes checking accounts and certain savings accounts that are often accessible through online banks or automated teller machines (ATMs).

Diffusion index An index that measures how many indicators are pointing up and how many are pointing down.

Direct market access (DMA) Access in which market participants can transact orders directly with the order book of an exchange using a broker's exchange connectivity.

Discretionary portfolio management An arrangement in which a wealth manager has a client's preapproval to execute investment decisions.

Discretionary Trust A trust that enables the trustee to determine whether and how much to distribute based on a beneficiary's general welfare.

Dispersion The weighted *variance* of the times to receipt of cash flow; it measures the extent to which the payments are spread out around the duration.

Distributed ledger technology Technology based on a distributed ledger.

Distributed ledger A type of database that may be shared among entities in a network.

Dividend capture A trading strategy whereby an equity portfolio manager purchases stocks just before their ex-dividend dates, holds these stocks through the ex-dividend date to earn the right to receive the dividend, and subsequently sells the shares.

Domestic asset An asset that trades in the investor's domestic currency (or home currency).

Domestic currency The currency of the investor, i.e., the currency in which he or she typically makes consumption purchases, e.g., the Swiss franc for an investor domiciled in Switzerland.

Domestic-currency return A rate of return stated in domestic currency terms from the perspective of the investor; reflects both the foreign-currency return on an asset as well as percentage movement in the spot exchange rate between the domestic and foreign currencies.

Double Taxation A term used to describe situations in which income is taxed twice. For example, when corporate earnings are taxed at the company level and then that portion of earnings paid as dividends is taxed again at the investor level.

Drawdown A decline in value (represented by a series of negative returns only) following a peak fund valuation.

Due diligence Investigation and analysis in support of an investment action, decision, or recommendation.

Duration matching Immunization approach based on the duration of assets and liabilities. Ideally, the liabilities being matched (the liability portfolio) and the portfolio of assets (the bond portfolio) should be affected similarly by a change in interest rates.

Dynamic asset allocation A strategy incorporating deviations from the strategic asset allocation that are motivated by longer-term valuation signals or economic views than usually associated with tactical asset allocation.

Dynamic hedge A hedge requiring adjustment as the price of the hedged asset changes.

Econometrics The application of quantitative modeling and analysis grounded in economic theory to the analysis of economic data.

Economic balance sheet A balance sheet that provides an individual's total wealth portfolio, supplementing traditional balance sheet assets with human capital and pension wealth, and expanding liabilities to include consumption and bequest goals. Also known as *holistic balance sheet*.

Economic indicators Economic statistics provided by government and established private organizations that contain information on an economy's recent past activity or its current or future position in the business cycle.

Endowment model Characterized by a high allocation to alternative investments (private investments and hedge funds), significant active management, and externally managed assets.

Enhanced indexing strategy Method investors use to match an underlying market index in which the investor purchases fewer securities than the full set of index constituents but matches primary risk factors reflected in the index.

Environmental, social, and corporate governance (ESG) Also called socially responsible investing, refers to the explicit inclusion of ethical, environmental, or social criteria when selecting a portfolio.

Equity Monetization A group of strategies that allow investors to receive cash for their concentrated stock positions without an outright sale. These transactions are structured to avoid triggering the capital gains tax.

Estate Planning The process of preparing for the disposition of one's estate upon death and during one's lifetime.

Estate Tax Levied on the total value of a deceased person's assets and paid out of the estate before any distributions to beneficiaries.

Estate Consists of all of the property a person owns or controls, which may consist of financial assets (e.g., bank accounts, stocks, bonds, business interests), tangible personal assets (e.g., artwork, collectibles, vehicles), immovable property (e.g., residential real estate, timber rights), and intellectual property (e.g., royalties).

Ethical principles Beliefs regarding what is good, acceptable, or obligatory behavior and what is bad, unacceptable, or forbidden behavior.

Evaluated pricing See *matrix pricing*.

Excess return Used in various senses appropriate to context: 1) The difference between the portfolio return and the benchmark return; 2) The return in excess of the risk-free rate.

Exchange Fund A partnership in which each of the partners have each contributed low cost-basis stock to the fund. Used in the United Sates as a mechanism to achieve a tax-free exchange of a concentrated asset position.

Exchange-traded fund Exchange-traded Funds or ETFs are hybrid investment products with many features of mutual funds combined with the trading features of common stocks or bonds. Essentially, ETFs are typically portfolios of stocks or bonds or commodities that trade throughout the day like common stocks.

Execution cost The difference between the (trading related) cost of the real portfolio and the paper portfolio, based on shares and prices transacted.

Exhaustive An index construction strategy that selects every constituent of a universe.

Extended portfolio assets and liabilities Assets and liabilities beyond those shown on a conventional balance sheet that are relevant in making asset allocation decisions; an example of an extended asset is human capital.

Factor-model-based benchmarks Benchmarks constructed by examining a portfolio's sensitivity to a set of factors, such as the return for a broad market index, company earnings growth, industry, or financial leverage.

Family Constitution Typically a non-binding document that sets forth an agreed-upon set of rights, values, and responsibilities of the family members and other stakeholders. Used by many wealth- and business-owning families as the starting point of conflict resolution procedures.

Family Governance The process for a family's collective communication and decision making designed to serve current and future generations based on the common values of the family.

Fiduciary duty The obligation to act in the best interest of the client, exercising a reasonable level of care, skill, and diligence.

Financial capital The tangible and intangible assets (excluding human capital) owned by an individual or household.

Fintech Technological innovation in the design and delivery of financial services and products in the financial industry.

Fixed Trust Distributions to beneficiaries of a fixed trust are specified in the trust document to occur at certain times or in certain amounts.

Forced Heirship   Is the requirement that a certain proportion of assets must pass to specified family members, such as a spouse and children.

Foreign assets   Assets denominated in currencies other than the investor's home currency.

Foreign currency   Currency that is not the currency in which an investor makes consumption purchases, e.g., the US dollar from the perspective of a Swiss investor.

Foreign-currency return   The return of the foreign asset measured in foreign-currency terms.

Forward rate bias   Persistent violation of uncovered interest rate parity that is exploited by the carry trade.

Foundation   A legal entity available in certain jurisdictions. Foundations are typically set up to hold assets for a specific charitable purpose, such as to promote education or for philanthropy. When set up and funded by an individual or family and managed by its own directors, it is called a *private foundation*. The term *family foundation* usually refers to a private foundation where donors or members of the donors' family are actively involved.

Fulcrum securities   Partially-in-the-money claims (not expected to be repaid in full) whose holders end up owning the reorganized company in a corporate reorganization situation.

Full replication approach   When every issue in an index is represented in the portfolio, and each portfolio position has approximately the same weight in the fund as in the index.

Funding currencies   The low-yield currencies in which borrowing occurs in a carry trade.

Fund-of-funds   A fund of hedge funds in which the fund-of-funds manager allocates capital to separate, underlying hedge funds (e.g., single manager and/or multi-manager funds) that themselves run a range of different strategies.

General account   Account holding assets to fund future liabilities from traditional life insurance and fixed annuities, the products in which the insurer bears all the risks—particularly mortality risk and longevity risk.

Generation-Skipping Tax   Taxes levied in some jurisdictions on asset transfers (gifts) that skip one generation such as when a grandparent transfers asset s to their grandchildren. (see related Gift Tax).

Gift Tax   Depending on the tax laws of the country, assets gifted by one person to another during the giftor's lifetime may be subject to a gift tax.

Goals-based investing   An investment industry term for approaches to investing for individuals and families focused on aligning investments with goals (parallel to liability-driven investing for institutional investors).

Goals-based   With respect to asset allocation or investing, an approach that focuses on achieving an investor's goals (for example, related to supporting lifestyle needs or aspirations) based typically on constructing sub-portfolios aligned with those goals.

Grinold–Kroner model   An expression for the expected return on a share as the sum of an expected income return, an expected nominal earnings growth return, and an expected repricing return.

Hard-catalyst event-driven approach   An event-driven approach in which investments are made in reaction to an already announced corporate event (mergers and acquisitions, bankruptcies, share issuances, buybacks, capital restructurings, re-organizations, accounting changes) in which security prices related to the event have yet to fully converge.

Hedge ratio   The relationship of the quantity of an asset being hedged to the quantity of the derivative used for hedging.

High-frequency trading   A form of algorithmic trading that makes use of vast quantities of data to execute trades on ultra-high-speed networks in fractions of a second.

High-water mark   A specified net asset value level that a fund must exceed before performance fees are paid to the hedge fund manager.

Holdings-based attribution   A "buy and hold" attribution approach which calculates the return of portfolio and benchmark components based upon the price and foreign exchange rate changes applied to daily snapshots of portfolio holdings.

Holdings-based style analysis   A bottom-up style analysis that estimates the risk exposures from the actual securities held in the portfolio at a point in time.

Home bias   A preference for securities listed on the exchanges of one's home country.

Home currency See *domestic currency*.

Home-country bias The favoring of domestic over non-domestic investments relative to global market value weights.

Horizon matching Hybrid approach that combines cash flow and duration matching approaches. Under this approach, liabilities are categorized as short-and long-term liabilities.

Human capital An implied asset; the net present value of an investor's future expected labor income weighted by the probability of surviving to each future age. Also called *net employment capital*.

Immediate annuity An annuity that provides a guarantee of specified future monthly payments over a specified period of time.

Immunization An asset/liability management approach that structures investments in bonds to match (offset) liabilities' weighted-average duration; a type of dedication strategy.

Impact investing Investment approach that seeks to achieve targeted social or environmental objectives along with measurable financial returns through engagement with a company or by direct investment in projects or companies.

Implementation shortfall (IS) The difference between the return for a notional or paper portfolio, where all transactions are assumed to take place at the manager's decision price, and the portfolio's actual return, which reflects realized transactions, including all fees and costs.

Inheritance Tax Paid by each individual beneficiary of a deceased person's estate on the value of the benefit the individual received from the estate.

Initial coin offering An unregulated process whereby companies raise capital by selling crypto tokens to investors in exchange for fiat money or another agreed-upon cryptocurrency.

Input uncertainty Uncertainty concerning whether the inputs are correct.

Interaction effect The attribution effect resulting from the interaction of the allocation and selection decisions.

Internet of Things A network arrangement of structures and devices whereby the objects on the network are able to interact and share information.

Intertemporal consistency A feature of expectations setting which means that estimates for an asset class over different horizons reflect the same assumptions with respect to the potential paths of returns over time. It is the internal consistency over various time horizons.

Intestate A person who dies without a valid will or with a will that does not dispose of their property are considered to have died intestate.

Intrinsic value The difference between the spot exchange rate and the strike price of a currency option.

Investment currencies The high-yielding currencies in a carry trade.

Investment policy statement A written planning document that describes a client's investment objectives and risk tolerance over a relevant time horizon, along with the constraints that apply to the client's portfolio.

Investment style A natural grouping of investment disciplines that has some predictive power in explaining the future dispersion of returns across portfolios.

Irrevocable Trust The person whose assets are used to create the trust gives up the right to rescind the trust relationship and regain title to the trust assets.

Key person risk The risk that results from over-reliance on an individual or individuals whose departure would negatively affect an investment manager.

Key rate duration A method of measuring the interest rate sensitivities of a fixed-income instrument or portfolio to shifts in key points along the yield curve.

Knock-in/knock-out Features of a vanilla option that is created (or ceases to exist) when the spot exchange rate touches a pre-specified level.

Leading economic indicators A set of economic variables whose values vary with the business cycle but at a fairly consistent time interval before a turn in the business cycle.

Liability driven investing (LDI) model In the LDI model, the primary investment objective is to generate returns sufficient to cover liabilities, with a focus on maximizing expected surplus return (excess return of assets over liabilities) and managing surplus volatility.

Liability glide path A specification of desired proportions of liability-hedging assets and return-seeking assets and the duration of the liability hedge as funded status changes and contributions are made.

Liability-driven investing An investment industry term that generally encompasses asset allocation that is focused on funding an investor's liabilities in institutional contexts.

Liability-relative With respect to asset allocation, an approach that focuses directly only on funding liabilities as an investment objective.

Life settlement The sale of a life insurance contract to a third party. The valuation of a life settlement typically requires detailed biometric analysis of the individual policyholder and an understanding of actuarial analysis.

Limited-life foundations A type of foundation where founders seek to maintain control of spending while they (or their immediate heirs) are still alive.

Longevity risk The risk of outliving one's financial resources.

Machine learning Computer based techniques that seek to extract knowledge from large amounts of data by "learning" from known examples and then generating structure or predictions. ML algorithms aim to "find the pattern, apply the pattern."

Macro attribution Attribution at the sponsor level.

Manager peer group See *manager universe*.

Manager universe A broad group of managers with similar investment disciplines. Also called *manager peer group*.

Matrix pricing An approach for estimating the prices of thinly traded securities based on the prices of securities with similar attributions, such as similar credit rating, maturity, or economic sector. Also called *evaluated pricing*.

Micro attribution Attribution at the portfolio manager level.

Minimum-variance hedge ratio A mathematical approach to determining the optimal cross hedging ratio.

Mission-related investing Aims to direct a significant portion of assets in excess of annual grants into projects promoting a foundation's mission.

Model uncertainty Uncertainty as to whether a selected model is correct.

Mortality table A table that indicates individual life expectancies at specified ages.

Multi-class trading An equity market-neutral strategy that capitalizes on misalignment in prices and involves buying and selling different classes of shares of the same company, such as voting and non-voting shares.

Multilateral trading facilities (MTF) See *Alternative trading systems (ATS)*.

Multi-manager fund Can be of two types—one is a multi-strategy fund in which teams of portfolio managers trade and invest in multiple different strategies within the same fund; the second type is a fund of hedge funds (or fund-of-funds) in which the manager allocates capital to separate, underlying hedge funds that themselves run a range of different strategies.

Multi-strategy fund A fund in which teams of portfolio managers trade and invest in multiple different strategies within the same fund.

Mutual funds A professionally managed investment pool in which investors in the fund typically each have a pro-rata claim on the income and value of the fund.

Natural language processing Computer programs developed to analyze and interpret human language.

Negative screening An ESG implementation approach that excludes certain sectors or companies that deviate from an investor's accepted standards.

Net asset value Value established at the end of each trading day based on the fund's valuation of all existing assets minus liabilities, divided by the total number of shares outstanding.

Neural networks Computer programs based on how our own brains learn and process information.

Non-deliverable forwards Forward contracts that are cash settled (in the non-controlled currency of the currency pair) rather than physically settled (the controlled currency is neither delivered nor received).

Nonstationarity A characteristic of series of data whose properties, such as mean and variance, are not constant through time. When analyzing historical data it means that different parts of a data series reflect different underlying statistical properties.

Norway model Characterized by an almost exclusive reliance on public equities and fixed income (the traditional 60/40 equity/bond model falls under the Norway model), with largely passively managed assets and with very little to no allocation to alternative investments.

Offer price The price at which a counterparty is willing to sell one unit of the base currency.

Opportunity cost The (trading related) cost associated with not being able to transact the entire order at the decision price.

Optional stock dividends A type of dividend in which shareholders may elect to receive either cash or new shares.

Overbought When a market has trended too far in one direction and is vulnerable to a trend reversal, or correction.

Overfitting An undesirable result from fitting a model so closely to a dataset that it does not perform well on new data.

Overlay A derivative position (or positions) used to adjust a pre-existing portfolio closer to its objectives.

Oversold The opposite of overbought; see *overbought*.

Packeting Splitting stock positions into multiple parts.

Pairs trading An equity market-neutral strategy that capitalizes on the misalignment in prices of pairs of similar under- and overvalued equities. The expectation is the differential valuations or trading relationships will revert to their long-term mean values or their fundamentally-correct trading relationships, with the long position rising and the short position declining in value.

Parameter uncertainty Uncertainty arising because a quantitative model's parameters are estimated with error.

Participant/cohort option Pools the DC plan member with a cohort that has a similar target retirement date.

Participant-switching life-cycle options Automatically switch DC plan members into a more conservative asset mix as their age increases. There may be several automatic de-risking switches at different age targets.

Passive investment Investment that seeks to mimic the prevailing characteristics of the overall investments available in terms of credit quality, type of borrower, maturity, and duration rather than express a specific market view.

Passive management A buy-and-hold approach to investing in which an investor does not make portfolio changes based upon short-term expectations of changing market or security performance.

Percent-range rebalancing An approach to rebalancing that involves setting rebalancing thresholds or trigger points, stated as a percentage of the portfolio's value, around target values.

Performance attribution Attribution, including return attribution and risk attribution; often used as a synonym for return attribution.

Permissioned networks Networks that are fully open only to select participants on a DLT network.

Permissionless networks Networks that are fully open to any user on a DLT network.

Portfolio overlay An array of derivative positions managed separately from the securities portfolio to achieve overall intended portfolio characteristics.

Positive screening An ESG implementation approach that seeks to identify the most favorable companies and sectors based on ESG considerations. Also called *best-in-class*.

Post-Liquidation Return Calculates the return assuming that all portfolio holdings are sold as of the end date of the analysis and that the resulting capital gains tax that would be due is deducted from the ending portfolio value.

Potential Capital Gain Exposure (PCGE) Is an estimate of the percentage of a fund's assets that represents gains and measures how much the fund's assets have appreciated. It can be an indicator of possible future capital gain distributions.

Present value of distribution of cash flows methodology Method used to address a portfolio's sensitivity to rate changes along the yield curve, this approach seeks to approximate and match the yield curve risk of an index over discrete time periods.

Principal trade A trade in which the market maker or dealer becomes a disclosed counterparty and assumes risk for the trade by transacting the security for their own account. Also called *broker risk trades*.

Probate The legal process to confirm the validity of the will so that executors, heirs, and other interested parties can rely on its authenticity.

Profession An occupational group that has specific education, expert knowledge, and a framework of practice and behavior that underpins community trust, respect, and recognition.

Program trading A strategy of buying or selling many stocks simultaneously.

Progressive Tax Rate Schedule A tax regime in which the tax rate increases as the amount of income or wealth being taxed increases.

Protective put An option strategy in which a long position in an asset is combined with a long position in a put on that asset.

Pure indexing Method investors use to match an underlying market index in which the investor aims to replicate an existing market index by purchasing all of the constituent securities in the index to minimize tracking risk.

Put spread A strategy used to reduce the upfront cost of buying a protective put, it involves buying a put option and writing another put option.

Qualified Dividends Generally dividends from shares in domestic corporations and certain qualified foreign corporations which have been held for at least a specified minimum period of time.

Quantitative market-neutral An approach to building market-neutral portfolios in which large numbers of securities are traded and positions are adjusted on a daily or even an hourly basis using algorithm-based models.

Rebalancing overlay A type of overlay that addresses a portfolio's need to sell certain constituent securities and buy others.

Rebalancing range A range of values for asset class weights defined by trigger points above and below target weights, such that if the portfolio value passes through a trigger point, rebalancing occurs. Also known as a corridor.

Rebalancing In the context of asset allocation, a discipline for adjusting the portfolio to align with the strategic asset allocation.

Re-base With reference to index construction, to change the time period used as the base of the index.

Rebate rate The portion of the collateral earnings rate that is repaid to the security borrower by the security lender.

Reduced-form models Models that use economic theory and other factors such as prior research output to describe hypothesized relationships. Can be described as more compact representations of underlying structural models. Evaluate endogenous variables in terms of observable exogenous variables.

Regime The governing set of relationships (between variables) that stem from technological, political, legal, and regulatory environments. Changes in such environments or policy stances can be described as changes in regime.

Relative value volatility arbitrage A volatility trading strategy that aims to source and buy cheap volatility and sell more expensive volatility while netting out the time decay aspects normally associated with options portfolios.

Repo rate The interest rate on a repurchase agreement.

Repurchase agreements (repos) In a repurchase agreement, a security owner agrees to sell a security for a specific cash amount, while simultaneously agreeing to repurchase the security at a specified future date (typically one day later) and price.

Request for quote (RFQ) A non-binding quote provided by a market maker or dealer to a potential buyer or seller upon request. Commonly used in fixed income markets these quotes are only valid at the time they are provided.

Reserve portfolio The component of an insurer's general account that is subject to specific regulatory requirements and is intended to ensure the company's ability to meet its policy liabilities. The assets in the reserve portfolio are managed conservatively and must be highly liquid and low risk.

Resistance levels Price points on dealers' order boards where one would expect to see a clustering of offers.

Return attribution A set of techniques used to identify the sources of the excess return of a portfolio against its benchmark.

Returns-based attribution An attribution approach that uses only the total portfolio returns over a period to identify the components of the investment process that have generated the returns. The Brinson–Hood–Beebower approach is a returns-based attribution approach.

Returns-based benchmarks Benchmarks constructed by examining a portfolio's sensitivity to a set of factors, such as the returns for various style indexes (e.g., small-cap value, small-cap growth, large-cap value, and large-cap growth).

Returns-based style analysis A top-down style analysis that involves estimating the sensitivities of a portfolio to security market indexes.

Reverse repos Repurchase agreement from the standpoint of the lender.

Revocable Trust The person whose assets are used to create the trust retains the right to rescind the trust relationship and regain title to the trust assets.

Risk attribution The analysis of the sources of risk.

Risk aversion The degree of an investor's unwillingness to take risk; the inverse of risk tolerance.

Risk budgeting The establishment of objectives for individuals, groups, or divisions of an organization that takes into account the allocation of an acceptable level of risk.

Risk capacity The ability to accept financial risk.

Risk perception The subjective assessment of the risk involved in the outcome of an investment decision.

Risk premium An extra return expected by investors for bearing some specified risk.

Risk reversal A strategy used to profit from the existence of an implied volatility skew and from changes in its shape over time. A combination of long (short) calls and short (long) puts on the same underlying with the same expiration is a long (short) risk reversal.

Risk tolerance The capacity to accept risk; the level of risk an investor (or organization) is willing and able to bear.

Robo-adviser A machine-based analytical tool or service that provides technology-driven investment solutions through online platforms.

Seagull spread An extension of the risk reversal foreign exchange option strategy that limits downside risk.

Securities lending A form of collateralized lending that may be used to generate income for portfolios.

Selective An index construction methodology that targets only those securities with certain characteristics.

Separate accounts Accounts holding assets to fund future liabilities from variable life insurance and variable annuities, the products in which customers make investment decisions from a menu of options and themselves bear investment risk.

Sharpe ratio The average return in excess of the risk-free rate divided by the standard deviation of return; a measure of the average excess return earned per unit of standard deviation of return. Also known as the *reward-to-variability ratio*.

Short-biased A hedge fund strategy in which the manager uses a less extreme version of dedicated short-selling. It involves searching for opportunities to sell expensively priced equities, but short exposure may be balanced with some modest value-oriented, or index-oriented, long exposure.

Shortfall probability The probability of failing to meet a specific liability or goal.

Shrinkage estimation   Estimation that involves taking a weighted average of a historical estimate of a parameter and some other parameter estimate, where the weights reflect the analyst's relative belief in the estimates.

Single-manager fund   A fund in which one portfolio manager or team of portfolio managers invests in one strategy or style.

Situational influences   External factors, such as environmental or cultural elements, that shape our behavior.

Smart beta   Involves the use of simple, transparent, rules-based strategies as a basis for investment decisions.

Smart contract   A computer program that is designed to self-execute on the basis of pre-specified terms and conditions agreed to by parties to a contract.

Smart order routers   (SOR) Smart systems used to electronically route small orders to the best markets for execution based on order type and prevailing market conditions.

Soft-catalyst event-driven approach   An event-driven approach in which investments are made pro-actively in anticipation of a corporate event (mergers and acquisitions, bankruptcies, share issuances, buybacks, capital restructurings, re-organizations, accounting changes) that has yet to occur.

Special dividends   A dividend paid by a company that does not pay dividends on a regular schedule, or a dividend that supplements regular cash dividends with an extra payment.

Spread duration   A measure used in determining a portfolio's sensitivity to changes in credit spreads.

Staged Diversification Strategy   The simplest approach to managing the risk of a concentrated position involves selling the concentrated position over some period of time, paying associated tax, and reinvesting the proceeds in a diversified portfolio.

Standards of conduct   Behaviors required by a group; established benchmarks that clarify or enhance a group's code of ethics.

Static hedge   A hedge that is not sensitive to changes in the price of the asset hedged.

Stock lending   Securities lending involving the transfer of equities.

Stop-losses   A trading order that sets a selling price below the current market price with a goal of protecting profits or preventing further losses.

Stops   Stop-loss orders involve leaving bids or offers away from the current market price to be filled if the market reaches those levels.

Straddle   An option combination in which one buys *both* puts and calls, with the same exercise price and same expiration date, on the same underlying asset. In contrast to this long straddle, if someone *writes* both options, it is a short straddle.

Strangle   A variation on a straddle in which the put and call have different exercise prices; if the put and call are held long, it is a long strangle; if they are held short, it is a short strangle.

Strategic asset allocation   1) The process of allocating money to IPS-permissible asset classes that integrates the investor's return objectives, risk tolerance, and investment constraints with long-run capital market expectations. 2) The result of the above process, also known as the policy portfolio.

Stratified sampling   A sampling method that guarantees that subpopulations of interest are represented in the sample. Also called *representative sampling* or *cell approach*.

Structural models   Models that specify functional relationships among variables based on economic theory. The functional form and parameters of these models are derived from the underlying theory. They may include unobservable parameters.

Structural risk   Risk that arises from portfolio design, particularly the choice of the portfolio allocations.

Stub trading   An equity market-neutral strategy that capitalizes on misalignment in prices and entails buying and selling stock of a parent company and its subsidiaries, typically weighted by the percentage ownership of the parent company in the subsidiaries.

Supervised learning   A machine learning approach that makes use of labeled training data.

Support levels   Price points on dealers' order boards where one would expect to see a clustering of bids.

Surplus portfolio The component of an insurer's general account that is intended to realize higher expected returns than the reserve portfolio and so can assume some liquidity risk. Surplus portfolio assets are often managed aggressively with exposure to alternative assets.

Surplus The difference between the value of assets and the present value of liabilities. With respect to an insurance company, the net difference between the total assets and total liabilities (equivalent to policyholders' surplus for a mutual insurance company and stockholders' equity for a stock company).

Tactical asset allocation Asset allocation that involves making short-term adjustments to asset class weights based on short-term predictions of relative performance among asset classes.

Tax Alpha Calculated by subtracting the pre-tax excess return from the after-tax excess return, the tax alpha isolates the benefit of tax management of the portfolio.

Tax Avoidance The legal activity of understanding the tax laws and finding approaches that avoid or minimize taxation.

Tax Basis In many cases, the tax basis is the amount that was paid to acquire an asset, or its 'cost' basis, and serves as the foundation for calculating a capital gain or loss.

Tax Evasion The illegal concealment and non-payment of taxes that are otherwise due.

Tax Haven A country or independent area with no or very low tax rates for foreign investors.

Tax Loss Harvesting Selling securities at a loss to offset a realized capital gain or other income. The rules for what can be done vary by jurisdiction.

Tax Lot Accounting Important in tax loss harvesting strategies to identify the cost of securities sold from a portfolio that has been built up over time with purchases and sales over time. Tax lot accounting keeps track of how much was paid for an investment and when it was purchased for the portfolio. Not allowed in all jurisdictions.

Taxable Account An account on which the normal tax rules of the jurisdiction apply to investments and contributions.

Tax-Deferred Account An account where investments and contributions may be made on a pre-tax basis and investment returns accumulate on a tax-deferred basis until funds are withdrawn, at which time they are taxed at ordinary income tax rates.

Tax-Efficiency Ratio (TER) Is calculated as the after-tax return divided by the pre-tax return. It is used to understand if a fund is appropriate for the taxable account of a client.

Tax-Efficient Decumulation Strategy Is the process of taking into account the tax considerations involved in deploying retirement assets to support spending needs over a client's remaining lifetime during retirement.

Tax-Efficient Strategy An investment strategy that is designed to give up very little of its return to taxes.

Tax-Exempt Account An account on which no taxes are assessed during the investment, contribution, or withdrawal phase, nor are they assessed on investment returns.

Taylor rule A rule linking a central bank's target short-term interest rate to the rate of growth of the economy and inflation.

Term deposits Interest-bearing accounts that have a specified maturity date. This category includes savings accounts and certificates of deposit (CDs).

Territorial Tax Systems Jurisdictions operate where only locally-sourced income is taxed.

Testamentary Bequest See Bequest.

Testamentary Gratuitous Transfer See Bequest.

Testator The person who authored the will and whose property is disposed of according to the will.

Text analytics The use of computer programs to analyze and derive meaning from typically large, unstructured text- or voice-based datasets.

Thematic investing An investment approach that focuses on companies within a specific sector or following a specific theme, such as energy efficiency or climate change.

Time deposits Interest-bearing accounts that have a specified maturity date. This category includes savings accounts and certificates of deposit (CDs).

Time value   The difference between the market price of an option and its intrinsic value, determined by the uncertainty of the underlying over the remaining life of the option.

Time-series estimation   Estimators that are based on lagged values of the variable being forecast; often consist of lagged values of other selected variables.

Time-series momentum   A managed futures trend following strategy in which managers go long assets that are rising in price and go short assets that are falling in price. The manager trades on an absolute basis, so be net long or net short depending on the current price trend of an asset. This approach works best when an asset's own past returns are a good predictor of its future returns.

Tokenization   The process of representing ownership rights to physical assets on a blockchain or distributed ledger.

Total factor productivity   A variable which accounts for that part of Y not directly accounted for by the levels of the production factors (K and L).

Total return payer   Party responsible for paying the reference obligation cash flows and return to the receiver, but will also be compensated by the receiver for any depreciation in the index or default losses incurred on the portfolio.

Total return receiver   Party receives both the cash flows from the underlying index as well as any appreciation in the index over the period in exchange for paying Libor plus a pre-determined spread.

Total return swap   A swap in which one party agrees to pay the total return on a security. Often used as a credit derivative, in which the underlying is a bond.

Tracking error   The standard deviation of the differences between a portfolio's returns and its benchmark's returns; a synonym of active risk. Also called *tracking risk*.

Tracking risk   The standard deviation of the differences between a portfolio's returns and its benchmark's returns; a synonym of active risk. Also called *tracking error*.

Trade urgency   A reference to how quickly or slowly an order is executed over the trading time horizon.

Transactions-based attribution   An attribution approach that captures the impact of intra-day trades and exogenous events such as a significant class action settlement.

Trigger points   In the context of portfolio rebalancing, the endpoints of a rebalancing range (corridor).

Trust   A legal is a vehicle through which an individual (called a settlor) entrusts certain assets to a trustee (or trustees) who manages the assets for the benefit of assigned beneficiaries. A trust may be either a testamentary trust—a trust created through the testator's will—or a living or inter-vivos trust—a trust created during the settlor's lifetime.

Unsupervised learning   A machine learning approach that does not make use of labeled training data.

Vesting   A term indicating that employees only become eligible to receive a pension after meeting certain criteria, typically a minimum number of years of service.

Volatility clustering   The tendency for large (small) swings in prices to be followed by large (small) swings of random direction.

Will (or Testament)   A document that outlines the rights others will have over one's property after death.

Withholding Taxes   Taxes imposed on income in the country in which an investment is made without regard for offsetting investment expenses or losses that may be available from the tax-payer's other investment activities.

Worldwide Tax System   Jurisdictions that tax all income regardless of its source.

ABOUT THE AUTHORS

Bidhan L. Parmar, PhD, is at the University of Virginia (USA).

Dorothy C. Kelly, CFA, is at McIntire School of Commerce, University of Virginia (USA).

Colin McLean, MBA, FIA, FSIP, is at SVM Asset Management (United Kingdom).

Nitin M. Mehta, CFA (United Kingdom).

David B. Stevens, CIMC, CFA, is at Wells Fargo Private Bank (USA).

Robert Kissell, PhD, is at Molloy College and Kissell Research Group (USA).

Barbara J. Mack is at Pingry Hill Enterprises, Inc. (USA).

Christopher D. Piros, PhD, CFA (USA).

William W. Jennings, PhD, CFA, is at the US Air Force Academy (USA).

Eugene L. Podkaminer, CFA, is at Franklin Templeton Investments (USA).

Jean L.P. Brunel, CFA, is at Brunel Associates LLC (USA).

Thomas M. Idzorek, CFA, is at Morningstar (USA).

John M. Mulvey, PhD, is at the Bendheim Center for Finance at Princeton University (USA).

Peter Mladina is at Northern Trust and UCLA (USA).

Brian J. Murphy, CFA, is at Willis Towers Watson (USA).

Mark Ruloff, FSA, EA, CERA, is at Aon (USA).

William A. Barker, PhD, CFA (Canada).

Bernd Hanke, PhD, CFA, is at Global Systematic Investors LLP (United Kingdom).

Brian J. Henderson, PhD, CFA, is at The George Washington University (USA).

James Adams, Ph.D, CFA is at New York University (USA).

Donald J. Smith, PhD, is at Boston University Questrom School of Business (USA).

James Clunie, PhD, CFA, is at Jupiter Asset Management (United Kingdom).

James Alan Finnegan, CAIA, RMA, CFA (USA).

David M. Smith, PhD, CFA, is at the University at Albany, New York (USA).

Kevin K. Yousif, CFA, is at LSIA Wealth & Institutional (USA).

Bing Li, PhD, CFA, is at Yuanyin Asset Management (Hong Kong SAR).

Yin Luo, CPA, PStat, CFAx, is at Wolfe Research LLC (USA).

Pranay Gupta, CFA, is at Allocationmetrics Limited (USA).

Barclay T. Leib, CFE, CAIA, is at Sand Spring Advisors LLC (USA).

Kathryn M. Kaminski, PhD, CAIA, is at Alpha Simplex Group, LLC (USA).

Mila Getmansky Sherman, PhD, is at Isenberg School of Management, UMASS Amherst (USA).

Christopher J. Sidoni, CFP, CFA, is at Gibson Capital, LLC (USA).

Vineet Vohra, CFA, is at Cognasia Talent (Singapore and Hong Kong SAR).

Paul Bouchey, CFA, is at Parametric Portfolio Associates, Seattle, WA, (USA).

Helena Eaton, PhD, CFA, is at J.P. Morgan, London, (UK).

Philip Marcovici is at Offices of Philip Marcovici, Hong Kong SAR, (China).

Arjan Berkelaar, PhD, CFA, is at KAUST Investment Management Company (USA).

Kate Misic, CFA, is at Telstra Super Pty Ltd (Australia).

Peter C. Stimes, CFA, is a private investor in Fallbrook, California (USA).

Connie Li (USA).

Roberto Malamut (USA).

Marc A. Wright, CFA, is at Russell Investments (USA).

Jeffrey C. Heisler,, PhD, CFA is at TwinFocus Capital Partners (USA).

Donald W. Lindsey, CFA (USA).

CFA Institute

ABOUT THE
CFA PROGRAM

If the subject matter of this book interests you, and you are not already a CFA Charterholder, we hope you will consider registering for the CFA Program and starting progress toward earning the Chartered Financial Analyst designation. The CFA designation is a globally recognized standard of excellence for measuring the competence and integrity of investment professionals. To earn the CFA charter, candidates must successfully complete the CFA Program, a global graduate-level self-study program that combines a broad curriculum with professional conduct requirements as preparation for a career as an investment professional.

Anchored in a practice-based curriculum, the CFA Program body of knowledge reflects the knowledge, skills, and abilities identified by professionals as essential to the investment decision-making process. This body of knowledge maintains its relevance through a regular, extensive survey of practicing CFA charterholders across the globe. The curriculum covers 10 general topic areas, ranging from equity and fixed-income analysis to portfolio management to corporate finance—all with a heavy emphasis on the application of ethics in professional practice. Known for its rigor and breadth, the CFA Program curriculum highlights principles common to every market so that professionals who earn the CFA designation have a thoroughly global investment perspective and a profound understanding of the global marketplace.

www.cfainstitute.org

INDEX